THE NEW ILLUSTRATED
GARDENING ENCYCLOPÆDIA

[*Photo : Sutton & Sons.*]

A bowl of annual flowers can be raised from seed in a single

THE
NEW ILLUSTRATED GARDENING ENCYCLOPÆDIA

Edited by

RICHARD SUDELL, F.I.L.A., A.R.H.S.

*With Coloured Frontispiece,
48 pages of Half-tone Illustrations and 400 Black and White
Sketches.*

ODHAMS PRESS LIMITED
LONG ACRE - LONDON, W.C.2

All places are to a wise man
Ports and happy havens, so in
All gardens and in all gardeners
We find a home and brothers.

DEAN HOLE.

*

PREFACE

THERE is no need, in these days, to explain the need for new gardening books; no need to reiterate the statement that we are all gardeners in Britain. The achievements of amateur gardeners in food production are common knowledge. The inevitable buttonhole in the coat of the city worker is known too—travellers on the morning trains use it as an introduction, for no real gardener ever fights shy of a chat about his hobby. Yes, we are all gardeners, but we cannot all of us indulge our hobby with as much disregard of the time spent on it as was once the case. We are all busy people, and life becomes more crowded and more complex as the years pass.

It is this complexity in life that justifies, if any excuse is needed, the preparation of an up-to-date Encyclopædia of Gardening. Gardening is a very wide subject. Even the most experienced horticulturist is always learning, and no one would dare to profess to be expert in any but a small part of practical or theoretical horticulture. At the same time there are occasions when each amateur gardener comes up against a problem that can only be solved by the expert: he wants the help and advice of the research worker, and he wants that help to be given quickly, and to be up to date. Only in an Encyclopædia, compiled by a number of experts, and presented in the alphabetical form that makes for easy and rapid reference, can the many problems of the amateur gardener be solved satisfactorily.

Both in the preparation and revision of these pages I have tried, not to *avoid* technicalities, but to simplify them where I can, without descending to useless generalisations. I have tried to cater for the absolute beginner in gardening, and at the same time for the real amateur, the man who has developed such a love for his pet flower—carnation, rose or whatever it may be—that he is interested in every detail of history, legend, practice and laboratory knowledge that has the slightest bearing on his chosen subject. I have tried to cater for the man who wants a pleasant, well-groomed garden with well-chosen shrubs and flowers and good effects obtained with a minimum of time and trouble, and I have tried to cater also for the man who is prepared to give his whole garden over to a single flower, and who is out to carry off the highest awards at local or national flower shows.

This is aiming high, but I have laid down certain rules to help. First, every common plant known to our gardens, and most uncommon ones too, can be found under its best-known name. The popular subjects are dealt with fully, as for a novice, and they will be found under the name that the beginner would know and look for first. For instance, such a flower as a " pink " will be found under that heading. But common names are not always common to all parts of the country, and often the only way to be clear to everyone is to use the Latin names, which are *international* names, known to gardeners of all countries. So, if you look up " Flag ", you will be referred to *"Iris"*, the name which is more common among gardeners than " flag ". You will also be referred to *Acorus*, for this plant is also known to some as " flag ". Cross references in such cases should help to make the items easy of reference to all concerned.

Everything is arranged in alphabetical order. Even the calendar of gardening operations, which has been included for the benefit of the novice, is given a month at a time and each month appears under its appropriate letter—April and August among the " A's ", January among the " J's " and so on.

Certain sections are dealt with very fully—Allotments, Paths, Roses, Town Gardens, for instance. As already stated, the reason is that these things concern thousands of amateur gardeners, whereas other items may concern only a few hundreds. I have made a special study of gardens cultivated under difficult conditions, such as town gardens, where fumes, shade, and acid soils make cultivation difficult. As a landscape architect I have been called on to make gardens from the fringe of the sea to the roof-tops of London, and I have tried to put the cream of this experience into these pages.

Colleagues who have assisted me in this work are specialists in a variety of subjects, and I am glad and proud to acknowledge their help. We need the specialist, the research worker, the experimenter. They, as we, are constantly learning and constantly discovering; they are almost constantly crossing swords over important new ideas, while we benefit from their arguments. As an example, controversy is now raging concerning the use of artificial fertilisers prepared in laboratories, or the alternative " humus " treatment of the soil. Soilless culture advocates consider that humus is quite unnecessary for cultural success. (N.B.—This does not mean that they consider humus unnecessary in soil, but they consider the same quality of crop can be produced without humus, in water tanks.) An opposing camp hold the theory that diseases and pests are encouraged where artificial fertilisers are used, that crops so produced do not give any powers of disease-resistance to the animals who feed on them, and that for proper nutrition, for proper retention of fertility over the earth's surface, etc., a complete cycle of organic matter must be arranged. (This complete cycle means the feeding of vegetable crops to animals, animals to humans, human waste to the soil, and into the vegetables again.)

Theories and experiments such as these are referred to in this Encyclopædia only briefly, as space permits, but it can be seen that changes are still occurring in the world of practical gardening, changes that make revision of such reference books as this Encyclopædia desirable.

It remains only for me to thank the very large army of helpers who contributed to the production of this new edition. I want to thank specially the compositors, printers, typists, binders—all the important crowd of workers whose efforts are often overlooked in book production. I thank too the various writers who have contributed special sections, and friends and readers who have read previous editions and offered their helpful suggestions for the present production. And lastly a word of appreciation for the information I have drawn from commercial horticulturists, and for the really fine work which horticultural firms in general have done and are always doing to encourage the amateur gardener.

RICHARD SUDELL.

LIST OF CONTRIBUTORS

D. W. Simmonds . . . . . Annuals.

Blackmore & Langdon . . . . Begonia.

R. W. Hale (from material supplied by
Dr. W. E. Collinge, M.Sc., F.S.A.,
F.L.S.) . . . . . . Birds in the garden.

Keith Luxford & Co. . . . . Chrysanthemum.

Joseph Cheal, V.M.H. . . . . Dahlia.

Technical Staff of Imperial Chemical
Industries . . . . . . Fertilisers.

N. Catchpole, N.D.H., F.R.H.S. . . Fruit culture.

Cecil H. Hooper . . . . . Fruit pollination.

H. A. Brown, F.R.H.S. . . . . Fuchsia.

W. H. Cotton, B.E.N.A. . . . Garden ponds and aquatics.

William Platt, M.R.S.T. . . . Geology of soils.

Donald Blaxill . . . . . Greenhouse annuals.

R. C. Ellis (Head Gardener, Selfridge &
Co.) . . . . Greenhouse plants.

Kelway & Son . . . . . Hardy border flowers.

H. J. Jones . . . . . . Hydrangea.

Dr. L. E. Robinson, A.R.C.S., and
C. A. W. Duffield, N.D.H. . . Insect pests and diseases.

S. Kusumoto . . . . . . Japanese garden.

Ernest Ballard . . . . . Michaelmas daisy.

E. H. Hereford, M.S.I.E. . . . Mushroom.

Sutton & Sons . . . . . Photographs.

Clarence Elliott, F.R.H.S. . . . Rock garden construction and
sink gardens.

Benjamin Cant . . . . . Rose.

John Scott & Co. . . . . . Seaside plants.

Dobbie & Co. . . . . . Sweet peas.

Bowell & Skarratt . . . . Terrestrial orchids.

Gerald Dyas (of Thos. Gunn, Ltd.) . Tools.

R. Keene, N.D.H. . . . . . Vegetables and herbs.

Ministry of Agriculture . . . Allotment notes.

A. & W. Allen-Brown . . . . Violet.

THE NEW GARDENING ENCYCLOPÆDIA

AARON'S BEARD. *See* HYPERICUM.

AARON'S ROD. *See* VERBASCUM.

ABELE, the White Poplar. *See* POPULUS ALBA.

ABELIA (a-bē-lia. Caprifoliaceæ). Evergreen and deciduous flowering shrubs, 2–10 ft., from China, Japan, India, and Mexico. Tubular, funnel-shaped, white to rosy-purple flowers.

Greenhouse Culture.—Compost: equal parts loam, peat and sand. Well-drained pots, sunny, cold house. Water moderately during winter, increasing with growth. Prune lightly after flowering. Stand outside during summer months.

Propagation.—By layers in March, or by cuttings in cold frame. July or August.

SPECIES.

Rupestris, white, fragrant; *floribunda*, purple; *grandiflora*, pink (this is the hardiest and may be grown in warm, sheltered borders outdoors).

Outdoors.—Plant in spring in open loamy soil, with peat or leaf-mould and sand added to start them off. Hardy in warm, sheltered gardens. Fine wall or trellis plants, and in pots in cold house. Cuttings of half-ripened wood in July, planted in pots of sandy soil, and placed in frame or hand-light root readily. Cut back old wood after flowering.

The following are in cultivation:

A. chinensis (syn. *rupestris*). China, 1816. Deciduous, 3–4 ft., bush or climber. Flowers fragrant pink passing to white, free flowering during summer and autumn. Rather tender, best in cold house, or warm wall. The true plant uncommon in cultivation. *A. grandiflora*, a hybrid, *A. chinensis uniflora* often being substituted.

A. floribunda (Mexico), 1841. Evergreen; the most beautiful Abelia that can be grown out of doors in Britain; needs protection of wall. Thrives at Kew against wall of greenhouse. Will reach a height of 3 ft. The rosy-red pendulous flowers are freely produced in June and July.

A. grandiflora, *hybrid* (see *Chinensis*). Evergreen, 3–5 ft. The flowers are fragrant, white tinged pink. July to October. Of graceful habit, and brilliant green foliage. Hardy in Surrey.

A. spathulata (Japan), 1880. Deciduous, 3–4 ft., flower, white, yellow throat. Hardy in Sussex.

A. triflora (Himalayas), 1847. Deciduous. Flowers rosy-white and deliciously fragrant, produced in June. Hardy, even in open, in Surrey and Sussex. Sometimes known as *Linnea triflora*.

A. uniflora (syn. *serrata*). China, 1845. Evergreen, 5–6 ft. (see *Chinensis*). Flowers creamy white blush-tinted with orange markings in throat, suggesting a small foxglove.

A. Schumannii (syn. *longituba*). China. Will grow to 8 ft. on sunny wall. Flowers rosy-lilac in July and August.

A. Græbneriania (China). Flowers pink and white. A new species, and one of the hardiest.

The genus Abelia is named after Dr. Clarke Abel, who visited China as physician to Lord Amherst's Embassy, 1816-17. The doctor first discovered *A. chinensis*. He wrote an account of his travels in 1818. The plant was not introduced to cultivation until some years after his death in 1826.

ABIES (ā'-bī-ēs. Coniferæ). "Silver Firs." A group of evergreen conifers mostly of a symmetrical habit of growth, attaining to noble dimensions; in some species, growing up to 300 ft. The Abies (firs) are readily distinguished from the spruces (Picea) by pulling off a leaf. With the spruce a little of the bark always comes away with the leaf. In the Abies the leaf comes away clean. Female cones always erect, leaves flattened; in spruces they are needle-shaped.

Culture.—Abies thrive most successfully in a moist climate. In dry districts the soil should be deep. Propagation is best by seed. Cuttings will root, and they should be taken from the leading branches, in preference to lateral or side shoots. The trees intended to be increased in this way are headed back, and the resultant shoots will supply the cuttings. They should be removed with a small piece of the old wood attached, and placed singly in small pots of sandy soil, and placed in gentle bottom heat; but seedlings make the most satisfactory plants.

A. cephalonica (*Reginæ-Amaliæ*), the "Greek Fir," 100 ft. A very distinct silver fir, and does well in most soils, including those of a chalky nature.

A. cilicica, the "Cicilian Fir," growing wild with the Cedar of Lebanon in Asia Minor, 100 ft.

A. concolor, the "Colorado White Fir," 80–100 ft. One of the finest of conifers, with glorious foliage and purple cones.

A. c. candicans. A variety of exquisite silvery whiteness.

A. nobilis (West U.S.A.), well named the "Noble Fir," up to 200 ft. Foliage glaucous, cones 6–10 in. long. Resembling *A. magnifica*, but of a more spreading habit. Not for chalky soils.

A. n. glauca. Foliage most beautiful glaucous blue.

A. n. g. prostrata. Suitable for rock gardens.

A. Normanniana, the "Caucasian Fir," 200 ft. A beautiful and vigorous-growing species.

A. numidica, the "Algerian Fir," 70 ft. A fine dark glossy-leaved species, thriving on chalky soils.

A. pectinata (*alba*), the "Common Silver Fir" (Europe), 120 ft. Does best in those parts of the country where there is an abundant rainfall. Sensitive to spring frosts.

ABRONIA (abrō'-nia). Sand Verbena. Low trailing fleshy-leaved plants. The flat verbena-like flower heads emit a most delicious perfume. They are usually treated as annuals, being doubtfully hardy, but in a sheltered, sunny, dry position in light soil will often survive the winter. Easily raised from seed.

A. arenaria (*latifolia*). Lemon-yellow. California.

A. fragrans. A night-blooming white-flowered variety. Columbia River to New Mexico.

A. umbellata. Rose pink. California. There is a larger-flowered garden variety. It may be difficult to obtain seed of *A.*

fragrans, but the other two are offered by those seedsmen whose stock extends beyond bedding plants and vegetables.

ABRUS (a-brus. Leguminosæ). *A. precatorius* is an ornamental stove climber with purple flowers and is of interest on account of the bright scarlet, white or black seeds that are used chiefly by the Buddhists to make rosaries.

Propagate by seeds sown in heat, or by cuttings placed under a hand-light in heat. Use light sandy loam with some leaf-mould. 10 ft.

ABUTILON (a-bū-tilon. Malvaceæ). Although abutilons are generally regarded as greenhouse plants, one or two may be grown out of doors in warm sheltered gardens. The height of modern hybrids grown as pot plants is from 2–6 ft. and the plants often have beautifully mottled foliage with shades of yellow and green.

A. vitifolium. The vine-leaved abutilon, a native of Chile, is the least tender, but not really hardy except in favoured gardens; it is a soft-wooded, fast-growing shrub, with silvery foliage, and exquisite lavender or porcelain-blue flowers, each 2–3 in. across, in form like the flower of a single hollyhock; blooming in May and June, in great profusion.

Like most Chilean shrubs, it enjoys partial shade, and succeeds on an east wall, but sheltered from cold biting winds. In full sun this plant is apt to drop its flower-buds unexpanded. Not long-lived in some gardens, dying off suddenly without any apparent cause, but possibly owing to exhaustion following its very profuse flowering and free setting of seed. It is, however, easily raised from seed, and a small stock of young plants should be kept in pots in case of need. Cuttings also strike freely. An excellent seaside shrub if not exposed to rough winds. In Devon and Cornwall there are some very fine specimens growing in the open. *A. vitifolium* should be planted in the spring in ordinary garden soil, well drained. The only pruning necessary is to shorten the youngest shoots each year, during the winter months, to prevent the plants becoming "leggy."

A. megapotamicum (*vexillarium*). The "big-river" abutilon from Brazil. A very desirable and unique wall shrub reaching a height of 10 ft. on a south or west wall. Quite hardy within 10 miles of the south and west coast. The flowers, produced for quite 8 months, are cup-shaped, yellow, with a red calyx. Well-drained soil very important.

A. Milleri, a hybrid between *A megpotamicum* and *A. pictum*, 6-9 ft. Flowers bell-shaped yellow, with bronze anthers. Suitable for a south wall.

Greenhouse Culture.—Compost: 2 parts loam, 1 part peat, ½ part sharp sand. Sunny position. Prune March. May be used for bedding in summer. The species *vitifolium* is hardy outdoors in the South of England. Temperature, winter, 50°; summer, 65°.

Propagation.—By cuttings in pots of light sandy soil in propagator. Temperature 70°, spring, or by seed (*see* POT PLANTS FROM SEED).

SPECIES OR VARIETIES.

Aurantiacum, orange; *esculentum*, yellow; *pulchellum*, white; *Thomsonii*, mottled leaves; *venosum*, flame; *vitifolium* (this is a lovely porcelain blue).

ACACALLIS (ak-a-kal'-is. Orchidaceæ). Stove epiphytal orchids.

For cultivation of these orchids, a compost of fibrous peat and charcoal should be prepared. The pots in which they are to be planted should have ample drainage. They should be stood on blocks of wood, where they can be exposed to the sun. During their resting period, which is in the winter, little water should be given, but while they are growing they will need to be watered freely. During the winter a temperature of 65°-70° should be maintained, and in the summer from 75°-85°.

Propagate by division of the pseudo-bulbs.

SPECIES.

A. cyanea, which has light blue flowers in the summer. This plant reaches a height of 1 ft. and originated from Brazil.

ACACIA (ā-cā-cia. Leguminosæ). Mimosa. Evergreen flowering shrubs or small trees, mostly from Australia (New South Wales) and Tasmania. Flowers usually some shade of yellow, occasionally white, rarely red, produced in globular heads or cylindrical spikes, containing many small flowers. Leaves very variable, and in some species, such as *A.*

Drummondii, very handsome. Economically valuable for timber, and the drug catechu is produced from *A. catechu.*

Culture.—Acacias are grown and sent out in pots by nurserymen and may be planted at any time. Turfy loam and leaf-mould in equal parts, well mixed, and a fair amount of coarse sand is their favourite soil; charcoal may be added. Propagation is by cuttings of tips of half-ripened wood in summer, in very sandy soil under a hand-light, or bell-glass in cold frame, and by seeds, also in sandy soil, sown in pots or pans in greenhouse. Temperature 55°-60°. Pruning should be done after flowering, when any straggling bushes may be cut back well into the old wood. Syringing will help to produce young growth. Occasional doses of weak soot water are beneficial.

Propagation.—By cutting of half-ripened shoots in sandy peat. June or July.

VARIETIES.

Although the Acacias are all more or less beautiful, yet only a few may be now seen in greenhouses, the most popular being *Armata*, 6-10 ft., yellow globular heads; *Baileyana*, silvery-blue foliage, yellow *Dealbata* (*Mimosa*), yellow, height 10-25 ft.; *Podalyriæfolia*, silvery foliage, yellow (great value for cutting); *Verticilliata*, asparagus-like foliage, bright yellow, 6-20 ft.

Some species are well-known greenhouse plants, but many are nearly hardy and are successfully grown on sheltered walls, and in the warmer parts of the country on a warm sunny border protected by other plants from cold winds which are very harmful.

The following are the principal species and hybrids generally grown out of doors, and they comprise some of the most beautiful in cultivation.

A. armata (Australia), 6-10 ft. Handsome plant, yellow, free flowering in young state.

A. Baileyana (Cootamundra Wattle). One of the most beautiful; small fern-like silvery leaves and small deep yellow flowers, very free flowering in quite a young state. Much in demand for cutting. One of the hardiest, and worthy a place in every garden where these lovely plants are grown. The most successful Acacia in Cornwall.

A. dealbata, 10–25 ft. Probably the best known of the whole family, being the Mimosa of the Riviera, and the silver wattle of Australia and Tasmania. The leaves are bluish-green and the flowers yellow, freely produced.

A. floribunda (syn. Retinoides). Handsome small green leaves, very continuous flowering over a considerable period, and the earliest to bloom. Flowers pale yellow.

B. elata (Cedar Wattle). Young foliage very attractive, dark and shining. Pale yellow flowers.

A. falcata. Succeeds in poor sandy soil. Flowers cream colour.

A. juniperiana, 6–8 ft. Foliage resembles the Juniper. Small yellow flowers. A rare species, but cultivated in Cornwall.

A. longifolia (Long-leaved Golden Wattle), 10 ft. A bushy species of rapid growth, leaves long and narrow, sweet-scented flowers, very free blooming. Succeeds in coastal districts and in sandy soil. The variety *angustifolia* has longer leaves.

A. Drummondii, 10 ft. A very handsome foliage species, in demand for subtropical bedding. Flowers lemon-yellow.

A. mollisima (syn. *decurrens*). Soft-leaved, resembling *Dealbata*, foliage larger, yellow flowers. Requires a warm sheltered spot.

A. melanoxylon (Blackwood), 6-10 ft. One of the most attractive, very hardy, and does not object to wind.

A. podalyriæfolia (Queensland Silver Wattle). One of the earliest to flower and continues in beauty for about three months. Even when not in flower this beautiful species is of most attractive appearance, its blue or silvery-coloured leaves imparting to it considerable distinction. Flowers bright yellow.

A. riceana, 20 ft. A very graceful weeping species, handsome and distinct. Flowers greenish yellow.

A. verticillata. One of the best. Handsome dark green wiry foliage and abundance of yellow flowers.

ACÆNA (*akaina*, a thorn. Rosaceæ). New Zealand Burr. Hardy trailing perennials. Evergreen. The New Zealand Burr is suitable for growing on the rockery in moist sandy loam. It will grow either in the shade or in the open. The flowers are inconspicuous but carried in spiny burr-like heads. Foliage bluish-green.

Plant any time from October to April, and increase by seeds sown $\frac{1}{16}$ in. deep in March in a temperature of 65°, or by cuttings in a cold frame in August. Also by division of roots in April. All in sandy soil.

SPECIES.

A. adscendens, purple flowers in summer.

A. argentea, metallic bronze foliage and red burrs.

A. Buchananii, silvery green foliage with red burrs, 6 in.

A. lævigata, strong distinct, almost shrubby. Glaucous.

A. microphylla, crimson burrs.

A. myriophylla, green feathery foliage, densely tufted, 6–12 in.

A. Novæ Zealandiæ, trailing bronze foliage, purple burrs, 9 in.

A. ovina, erect, green foliage, purple burrs on spikes, 9 in.

A. pulchella, bronzy foliage.

A. sanguisorbæ, large silky leaves, rounded burrs, purple.

A. splendens, hairy foliage.

ACANTHOLIMON (a-can-tho-li-mon. Plumbagineæ, Plantaginaceæ). See Lavender. Prickly Thrift. Dwarf hardy evergreen perennials remarkable for their stiff sharp-pointed leaves. They are of tufted habit and do well in sandy loam in a sunny corner of the rockery. They like a nook to themselves where they will not be overrun by other plants, and are not successful in smoky districts.

Propagate by seeds sown in a warm sheltered spot in March, by cuttings placed in pots of sandy soil in August or by division. Plant in spring.

SPECIES.

The best is *glumaceum* (syn. *Statice Ararati*, which has charming rosy flowers in summer and spiny leaves which form dense spiny cushions. 6 in.

ACANTHOPANAX (a-can-thō-pā-nax Araliaceæ). Deciduous shrubs and trees allied to Aralia and Fatsia, from China and Japan. Flowers inconspicuous.

Culture.—Plant in autumn or spring in

rich, light, warm, loamy soil in sunny positions. *Propagation* is by root cuttings, division, and offshoots and by seed.

PRINCIPAL SPECIES.

A. ricinifolium (*Aralia Maximowiczii*), Japan 1865, 18-20 ft. An elegant tree of striking tropical appearance reaching a height of 80 ft. in its wild state.

A. Henryi (*Eleutherococcus Henryi*), China, 1901, 6 ft.

A. Leucorrhizum (Eleutherococcus), China, 1901, 6–8 ft. One of the finest species.

A. pentaphyllum (*A. spinosum*), China and Japan, 1874, 8–10 ft. At one time treated as a cool greenhouse plant, but is quite hardy if protected from north and east. A very elegant and handsome foliage plant. Even more striking is the var. *variegatum* with creamy white-edged leaves, making one of the most pleasing of shrubs. Needs a sheltered position.

A. senticosum (*Eleuterococcus senticosus*), China, 1893, 4–6 ft.

ACANTHOPHŒNIX (a-kanth-o-feenix. Palmaceæ). Prickly Date Palm. Stove palms that thrive in a compost of three parts of loam to one each of peat and leaf-mould with a little sand.

Propagate by seeds. Repot in February.

SPECIES.

Crinita with thorny stems.

ACANTHORHIZA (a-kanth-o-rhi-za. Palmaceæ). A genus of stove palms allied to *Trithrinax*, but differing from them in having the aerial roots hardening into spines and a divided leaf.

Propagate by seeds sown in heat in spring, and grow on good fibrous loamy soil with a little sand. Repot in February.

SPECIES.

A. aculeata of which the trunk is covered with spines (syn. *Chamærops stauracantha*).

ACANTHUS (a-can'-thus. Acanthaceæ). Bear's Breech or Bear's Foot. Herbaceous plants useful for beds, borders and cold greenhouse. Height 3–4 ft. Lilac pink or white blooms in August, but chiefly valued for their foliage. Should be grown in warm, deep soil in sheltered sunny spots for the best results, although they will succeed almost anywhere. Plant from October to April. *Propagate* by seed

sown ½ in. deep in light soil in the green house and by division of roots in October or March.

SPECIES CULTIVATED.

A. mollis, ornamental foliage.

A. mollis latifolius, finer, with rose-coloured blooms in August.

A. montanus, etc.

A. mollis is the plant whose leaves are said to have inspired the Corinthian style of architecture.

ACER (ā-ser. Aceraceæ). Maple. An extensive genus of shrubs and trees, principally deciduous, from the Old and New World. They are valuable for shrubberies, plantations, and ornamental planting generally. Flowers yellow or of a greenish colour and very ornamental. The trees are highly prized for their foliage, which is generally very handsome, and in some varieties quite superb. For garden purposes the Japanese species and varieties are most useful, and are exceedingly decorative as specimens on lawns. They also make attractive pot plants. Sugar is produced from some of the North American Maples, including the Maple Sugar so much appreciated in America.

Culture.—Plant in autumn in good well-drained loam. They appreciate a mulch of stable manure in autumn. Propagation by layering, budding in August, and in some species by cuttings. Seeds may be sown out of doors or in the case of rare species under glass. The *japonicum* and *palmatum* varieties when grown in the open like to be protected from cold winds. Those grown in pots may be repotted every few years. They should also be placed out of doors to ripen their wood, if used for forcing.

PRINCIPAL SPECIES.

A. argutum (Japan), 1881, 15–20 ft. An elegant pale-green-leaved maple.

A. campestre, Common Maple of South England, 20–35 ft., occasionally reaching 70 ft. On the Continent much used as a hedge. The wood is valuable, being hard with a fine grain. There are several varieties in cultivation.

A. japonicum (Japan). A handsome bushy Japanese Maple, leaves deep green, richly coloured in autumn. There is a variety known as *ficifolium* (*laciniatum*), and var. *aureum*, with pale golden-yellow foliage throughout the summer.

A. macrophyllum, Oregon Maple (W.N. America). The largest-leaved Acer, and perhaps the noblest of the genus. Grows to a great height up to, and sometimes exceeding, 100 ft. with a trunk 4 ft. in diameter. Timber valuable for furniture and indoor work.

A. negundo, Box Elder of the U.S.A. A fast-growing tree up to 70 ft. high. One of the sugar-yielding maples. There are several varieties.

A. nikoënse, Niko Maple (Japan and China), 1881, 20–25 ft. A slow-growing maple of interesting and distinctive appearance at all times of the year, with richly red-coloured foliage in autumn.

A. opalus, Italian Maple, 1752, 30–50 ft. Most ornamental with its bold foliage and clear yellow blossoms in March and April. Specimens up to 50 ft. high and with trunks 5 ft. in diameter can be seen at Kew. The var. *neapolitanum* is much used in the vineyards about Naples as a support to train the vines.

A. palmatum, Japanese Maple (Japan and Central China). This maple has been cultivated in Japanese gardens for a very long time and is the type from which has been produced the wonderful Japanese Maples. It is a strong - growing and healthy maple in good loamy soil and fairly sheltered position, one facing west being very suitable: height up to 18 ft. The bright green leaves fade to bronzy purple in autumn. There are numerous varieties and sub-varieties: the following can be recommended:

A. p. atropurpureum, the finest dark-leaved form.

A. p. dissectum atropurpureum. Leaves finely cut; leaves deep crimson throughout the season.

A. p. septemlobum. Larger leaves than type, dazzling red in autumn.

A. p. Osakazuki. Perhaps the most beautiful of all. The large green leaves change in autumn to shades of orange, crimson, and scarlet. The true plant is rare.

A. pennsylvanicum, Snake-bark Maple (east N. America), 1755. 30 ft. A very conspicuous and handsome maple, with white striped stems, covered with blue bloom. The large leaves of a pinkish tinge on opening, turn to golden yellow in autumn. Sometimes known in America as "Moose-wood."

A. platanoides, Norway Maple (Central Europe). Long cultivated in England. A very handsome, vigorous and hardy tree, reaching a height of from 60–90 ft. It thrives in most soils, even in poor sandy ones. Most useful for forming a screen quickly, dotting in woods, or against tall evergreen backgrounds. The green leaves turn to clear yellow in autumn.

A. pseudoplatanus, Common Sycamore Plane in Scotland (Europe). Although existing in England for many centuries, it is doubtful if it is a true native. A very hardy tree, useful for exposed and windy positions. There is a magnificent specimen at Studley Park, 106 ft. high and 18 ft. in girth, which is regarded as the finest in this country. The foliage lacks autumn beauty, turning a dingy brown. Valuable as a timber tree, the wood being easily worked. There are many varieties and forms.

ACERAS (Green-man Orchis). Orchidaceæ. Hardy terrestrial tuberous-rooted orchid, and a native of Britain. This plant should be grown in good loam with limestone or chalk added, in an open, dry, sunny position. It can be planted at any time from October to March, and can be increased by division of the tubers in October or March. The species cultivated, *A. anthropophora*, is known as the Man Orchis. The flower is of dull yellow, and has a curious resemblance to a man.

ACHILLEA (ak-il'lea. Compositæ). Yarrow or Milfoil. Hardy herbaceous perennials, mostly from E. Europe, mainly used for borders or rockeries. Height 1–2 ft. with white rose or yellow flowers. Will grow in practically any soil. Plant from October to April.

Propagate by division of roots in autumn, or by seeds in spring. Do not lift too frequently.

SPECIES.

A. rupestris, white, May, 3 in.

A. Griesbachii, suitable for rockeries.

A. argentea, suitable for rockeries.

A. millefolium, summer, 1–3 ft.

A. ptarmica (The Pearl Flower), white, double, summer, 2 ft.

The Pearl Flower is very useful for cutting. Only one of the Achilleas is tender—*Achillea Tournefortii*. This requires the protection of a greenhouse.

ACHIMENES (achime'-nes. Gesneraceæ). Greenhouse tuberous-rooted perennials. Deciduous. (South America, 1778).

Culture.—1 part fibrous loam, 1 part leaf-mould, ½ part sand. Pot tubers early spring, well-drained pots, 2 in. deep. Four in a 4½ in. pot. Water freely when in full growth. After flowering, allow plants to dry off gradually. Store under staging until following spring.

Propagation.—By division of tubers in February. (*See also* POT PLANTS FROM SEED).

SPECIES AND VARIETIES.

See Catalogues for numerous beautiful hybrids of this genus, such as Pink Pearl, Lilac Queen, Old Ivory, Delicacy (coral red), Brightness (salmon-rose).

ACHRAS (ak-ras. Sapotaceæ). A tree which is cultivated for the edible fruit which it produces. A native of Central America, and first introduced in 1731. The tree bears russet-brown fruits and attains a height of 65 ft.

This tree needs a rich loamy soil, and should be grown in the borders of the warm greenhouse in a temperature of 75°–90° from March to September, and 65°–70° from September to March.

Propagation takes place by cuttings in spring or early summer, in a temperature of 75°–85°. The only species which is cultivated is known as *A. sapota* (Marmalade Plum, Sapodilly Plum), its fruits measuring from 3–6 in. long.

ACIDANTHERA (as-id-an-ther-a. Iridaceæ). Tender bulbous plants, first introduced in 1893. As implied by the name Acidanthera, the flowers have anthers. The pointed flowers, which bloom in November, are of various colours, and the plant attains a height of 1½ ft.

These plants should be grown in pots in a compost of equal parts sandy loam and leaf-mould, in the warm greenhouse, with the exception of *A. bicolor*, which should be grown in the cool greenhouse.

During the growing period they will need plenty of water, but very little at other times.

SPECIES.

A. æquinoctialis, white and crimson flowers.

A. bicolor, white and purple flowers.

A. candida, white flowers.

ACID SOILS. Soils either deficient or lacking in lime. Nearly all waterlogged land is acid, as are matted lawns and shallow soils.

ACINETA (Orchidaceæ). *Akineta*, immovable, referring to the lip being jointless. Sub-terrestrial orchids, allied to Peristeria, that are best grown in baskets in a compost of sphagnum moss and fibrous peat in the cool or Odontoglossum house. The flowers grow through the bottom of the basket.

Propagate by division of the pseudobulbs or by seeds. Water well during the growing period and syringe but keep fairly dry during the resting time.

SPECIES.

Barkeri with yellow or crimson fragrant flowers in May, 2 ft., and *Humboldtii* (syn. *Peristeria Humboldtii* and *Anguloa superba*) with dark crimson flowers in May. 2 ft.

ACIPHYLLA (a-si-phy'lla. Umbelliferæ). Spear Grass. Hardy perennials that are of little value, except that the rosettes of spiny foliage are somewhat decorative. They succeed in light, moist sandy soil, and are suitable for the rockery or wild garden.

Propagate by seeds or division in spring when they should be planted.

SPECIES.

Colensoi, white, 6 ft., and *squarrosa*, the Bayonet Plant, white, 6 ft., summer blooming.

ACMENA (ak-mē-no. Myrtaceæ). A genus of greenhouse evergreen shrubs with small flowers and pretty berries. Use a compost of equal parts of peat loam and sand. Pot in March.

Propagate by cuttings of half-ripened wood struck in sand in spring in the cool greenhouse.

SPECIES.

A. floribunda, numerous white flowers from May to September, and purple berries. 4 ft. Keep in a winter temperature of 40°–45°.

ACOKANTHERA (a-kok-an-the-ra). Poisonous greenhouse shrubs that succeed in loamy soil and are propagated by cuttings.

SPECIES.

A. spectabilis (syn. *Toxicophlœa spectabilis*), white flowers in spring, 10 ft.

A. venenata (syn. *Toxicophlœa Thunbergii*), white, spring, 6 ft.

ACONITE (Winter). *See* ERANTHIS.

ACONITUM (Monkshood) Ranunculaceæ. Hardy herbaceous perennial. Height 5 ft. with blue, white and yellow blooms during the summer. It prefers shady ground but will grow anywhere. Forms a good background for a flower border. Best known is the blue-hooded variety, but as this is one of the most poisonous plants care should be taken when dividing the roots in the spring or autumn to avoid leaving any about. Also the hands should be washed immediately after the division of the roots. Used in medicine for cases of fever and for inflammatory diseases.

SPECIES.

Among a large number of varieties of Aconitum, the following are specially valuable in the garden:

A. napellus, blue.

A. napellus album, white.

A. japonicum, flesh.

A. japonicum cœruleum, blue.

A. lycocontum, creamy-yellow.

A. aureum, greenish-yellow.

ACORUS (ak-or-us. Aroideæ). Sweet Flag. A hardy perennial which grows in marsh or water gardens. *Acorus Calamus* or Sweet Flag has yellow flowers, sword-shaped leaves and fragrant roots. It flowers in July and August. Acorus requires to be planted in sunny marshy spots or in shallow water.

Propagate by division in March.

Acorus gramineus and its variegated form are often seen in the little bronze trays of water plants in Japanese gardens.

The roots of Acorus are used for tonic medicines.

ACRADENIA (akra-dēnia. Rutaceæ). Tasmania, 4–7 ft. An interesting and rare shrub for mild districts, with aromatic green leaves, trifoliate and dotted with glands. Flowers white, freely produced from March to May, of compact pyramidal habit. Generally cultivated as an evergreen shrub for the cool greenhouse.

Propagate by cuttings of side shoots in spring in a close propagating frame. Pot-up in good loam.

PRINCIPAL SPECIES.

A. Frankliniæ.

ACRE. An area of land containing 4,840 square yards.

ACROCLINIUM. *See* HELIPTERUM.

ACROLITH. A bust, usually of some Greek or Roman deity or hero, mounted in the classical style on a column or pedestal. It may be in stone, lead, bronze or wood as desired. Suitable only for the formal garden with clipped hedges, and most appropriate as an ornament for the entrance to a drive, or at the end of an " alley."

ACROPHYLLUM (ak-ro-fil-lum. Saxifragaceæ, Cunoniaceæ). *Akros*, a top, and *phyllon*, a leaf, referring to the fact that the leaves grow at the top of the branches above the flowers. Dwarf greenhouse evergreen shrubs that thrive in fibrous peat with sandy loam.

Propagate by cuttings of the half-ripened shoots taken in July, struck in the cool house and covered with a bell-glass. Good drainage is essential. Repot and prune in February.

SPECIES.

The only species is *venosum* (syn. *verticillatum*), with pink or white flowers in May. 6 ft.

ACROSTICHUM (a - kros - ti - kum. Filices). A genus composed almost entirely of stove ferns showing great variation in the shape of the fronds and the size of the plants.

They are propagated by spores, or division of the rhizomes and thrive in a compost of two-thirds of peat to one of loam with sphagnum, sand and charcoal. All require plenty of water.

SPECIES.

A. acuminatum, fronds 1–2 ft. long (syn. *Polybotrya acuminata*).

A. apodum, 12 in. fronds (syn. *Elaphoglossom apodum*).

A. aureum (syn. *Chrysodium aureum*), 2–6 ft. fronds, sub-aquatic species.

A. auritum (*Stenosemia aurita*), 1½–2 in. fronds.

A. canaliculatum (syn. *Polybotrya canaliculata*), 2–3 ft. fronds.

A. cervinum (syn. *Olfersia cervina*), 2–4 ft. fronds.

A. crinitum (syn. *Chrysodium crinitum*), 4–18 in.

A. fœniculaceum (syn. *Rhipidopteris fœniculaceum*).

A. latifolium, 12 in.

A. peltatum (syn. *Rhipidopteris peltata*). 2–6 in.

A. scandens (syn. *Stenochlaena scandens*), 1–3 ft.

A. simplex (syn. *Elaphoglossum simplex*), 6–12 in.

A. tomentosum.

A. viscosum, 6–12 in.

There are numerous other species as several other genera of the Fern family are included with Acrostichum.

ACTÆA (akte-e-a. Ranunculaceæ). Baneberry. Herb Christopher. Herbaceous perennials with white flowers in racemes that are rarely grown on account of the poisonous nature of the berries.

They are quite useful for shady places and grow in any soil.

Propagate by division of the roots or by seed sown in spring.

SPECIES.

A. alba, white, April and May, 12–18 in.

A. spicata. Baneberry, bears black berries and its variety *rubra* has red. 1–2 ft.

ACTINELLA (ac-tin-ell-a. Compositæ). Pigmy Sunflower. Hardy herbaceous perennials that are not in general cultivation. They are, however, useful for the rock garden and do well in light friable loam.

Propagate by division.

The best of the species are *A. grandiflora* with yellow flower heads 3 in. across in summer, 1 ft., and *scaposa*, which has narrow downy leaves, otherwise similar to the former.

ACTINIDIA (ac-tin-id-ia. Ternstrœmiaceæ). Hardy deciduous climbing shrubs from India, China and Japan with fruits in form of a fleshy berry, edible. Suitable for walls, pergolas, pillars and tree stumps. In autumn the colouring of the leaves in some species is very beautiful.

Culture.—They like loamy soil and good feeding. *Propagation* by seeds, layers and cuttings. Any necessary pruning may be done in February by thinning out and shortening the branches.

SPECIES.

A. arguta (China and Japan). Strong grower: one of the hardiest. Leaves large, lustrous; flowers white, fragrant; followed by greenish-yellow berries of poor flavour.

A. chinensis (China). Vigorous. Flowers creamy-white to buff-yellow in clusters. Fruit about size of a walnut, of pleasant flavour. Diœcious or hermaphrodite.

A. Henryi (China). White flowers. Needs protection.

A. kolomikta (China, Japan, Manchuria). Flowers white, fragrant. Leaves beautifully variegated.

A. polygama (Japan). Flowers white, fragrant. Fruit, yellow. This plant has a great attraction for cats.

A. purpurea (China). Resembling *A. aguta*, but with purple fruit.

ACTINIOPTERIS (ak-tin'-i-op-ter'-is. Filices). A small genus of stove ferns that thrive in a compost of sandy loam and peat with charcoal, and plentiful crocks to ensure good drainage. They require a winter temperature of 60°.

Repot in February or March.

SPECIES.

A. radiata, a pretty plant like a tiny Fan Palm.

A. r. australis, a more robust variety.

ACTINOMERIS (ak-tin-o-mer-is. Compositæ). North American Sunflower. Coarse-growing herbaceous perennials allied to the sunflowers.

Propagate by seeds and root division. Common garden soil suits them. May be planted at any time during the winter until the end of March.

SPECIES.

A. squarrosa (syn. *Verbesina coreopsis*) and *A. helianthoides*, both yellow-flowered and July to September blooming. 3 ft.

ACTINOTUS (ak-tin-o-tus. Umbelliferæ). Flannel Flower. Greenhouse herbaceous perennials propagated by root division and seeds and grown in a mixture of loam and peat. Winter temperature, 40°-45°. A sunny shelf in the greenhouse and plenty of water during the summer are needed.

SPECIES.

A. helianthi (sunflower), white, June, 2 ft

A. leucocephalus (white headed), similar to *A. helianthi.*

ADA (ad-a. Orchidaceæ). The only species of any value in this small genus of Orchids is *A. aurantiaca*, a neat plant that bears erect spikes of orange-coloured flowers in late winter and spring. For several years after importation it does well in the cool house, but is more successful in the warm greenhouse. It requires well-drained peat and sphagnum. Repot and divide when new growth begins. Owing to its season of flowering it is highly valued.

ADAM'S NEEDLE. *See* YUCCA GLORIOSA.

ADELIA (Oleaceæ). A group of shrubs from the New World of botanical interest only. Grown in peat and loam in the warm greenhouse.

Propagate by cuttings inserted, after the cut end has dried, in sandy loam.

ADENANDRA (adenan'-dra. Rutaceæ). Greenhouse flowering shrubs. Evergreen. Cape of Good Hope, 1720.

Culture.—Compost: equal parts loam, peat and sand. Pot spring. Winter temperature, 45°; summer, 60°.

Propagation.—By cuttings of young shoots in sandy soil in the spring. Temperature, 60°.

SPECIES.

Amœna, red; *fragrans*, pink; *marginata*, pink; *uniflora*, white, pink. Height 1½–2 ft.

ADENANTHERA (adenanthe'-ra. Leguminosæ). Stove flowering shrubs. Evergreen. East Indies, 1759.

Culture.—Compost: 1 part loam, 1 part peat, ½ part silver sand and charcoal. Position: light part of stove. Pot spring. Winter temperature, 60°; summer, 75°.

Propagation.—By cuttings of young shoots taken with a heel of the old wood, and inserted in sand in propagator in spring. Temperature, 65°.

Species.—*Bicolor*, yellow; *pavonina*, yellow and white. 5 ft.

ADENOCARPUS (adenō-karpus. Leguminosæ). Deciduous flowering shrub from Spain. Yellow, broom-like flowers, May to July.

Culture.—Plant in sandy loam in hot sunny position or south wall. Not very long lived; keep a stock of seedlings which are easily raised from seed sown in March.

Cuttings can also be taken in spring or summer. No pruning necessary.

A. angyrus. An interesting and uncommon species with deep yellow flower in summer, resembling a Genista. Prefers soil containing a little peat.

A. decorticans (Spain). Prefers a soil containing a little peat. Flowers golden yellow in great profusion, resembling the Spanish Broom, *Spartium juncium.*

A. frankenioides (Tenerife). Similar to *angyrus.*

ADENOPHORA (ad-en-oph-ora. Campanulaceæ). Gland Bellflower. Herbaceous perennial with fleshy roots. Height 1–4 ft., with blue flowers in August. Suitable for sunny borders in well-drained soil and is said to do well in Scotland. *Propagate* by seeds in a frame in spring and plant out later fo. flowering the following year. Originally from Siberia and Manchuria, it is now well acclimatised.

VARIETIES.

A. latifolia, blue.

A. lilifolia, whitish-blue; fragrant.

A. stylosa, blue (May).

ADIANTUM (adian'-tum. Filices). Maidenhair Fern. Stove, greenhouse and hardy ferns. Evergreen and deciduous.

Culture.—Compost: 1 part loam, 1 part peat, sharp sand and charcoal. Position, shady at all times. Repot spring. Temperature, greenhouse species, winter, 45°; summer, 60°. Stove species, winter, 60°; summer, 75°.

Propagation.—By spores sown on fine sandy soil or peat in propagator. Temperature 60°. Spores must be kept moist and shaded.

STOVE SPECIES.

The species are far too numerous to give complete list, so only a few of the best are mentioned: *Birkenheadii; cristatum; curvatum; cuneatum; palmatum; Weigandii.*

GREENHOUSE SPECIES.

Æthiopicum seabrum (silver maidenhair); *Æthiopicum sulphureum* (golden maidenhair); *Capillus veneris* (common maidenhair).

ADLUMIA (ad-lu-mia. Papaveraceæ). Climbing Maidenhair Fern. Hardy climbing biennial. First introduced in 1788. This plant climbs to a height of 10–15 ft. The flowers are white and pink and usually 4 together. The plants bloom in August. It also has ornamental foliage, prefers a light, rich soil, and is particularly suitable for growing over rustic fences, or in a warm border against a south wall. Sow seeds in the border in April or in pots in the greenhouse in March. Plant out in May. The seeds in some districts germinate freely and quickly and give the impression that they are perennials. The only species cultivated is *A. cirrhosa* which originated from N. America.

ADONIS (ad-ō-nis. Ranunculaceæ). Pheasant's Eye, Ox-eye. Hardy annuals and perennials. The plants are 1–1½ ft. high, mostly summer flowering. They will grow almost anywhere, in ordinary rich soil. The annuals prefer to grow in an open border and the perennials will thrive well on the rockery. Seeds may be sown in autumn or spring in the position in which the plants are to flower. Perennials can be increased by division of roots in October or, like the annuals, by seeds sown in spring.

SPECIES.

A. æstivalis. Pheasant's Eye. Crimson flowering in June.

A. Aleppica, scarlet, summer flowering.

A. amurensis, yellow flowers in January, originated from China. Perennial.

A. autumnalis. Red Chamomile. Scarlet flowers from May to September. Annual.

A. distorta, yellow flowers in May. Annual. Alps.

A. pyrenaica, yellow flowers in July. Pyrenees. Perennial.

A. vernalis. Ox-eye. Yellow flowers from March to May. Perennial.

The most commonly grown species is the *Adonis Aleppica* which is a brilliant scarlet-flowered hardy annual, originally from Aleppo. This species is undoubtedly the best of the family. The flowers are tulip-shaped, 3 in. across, and last quite a long time. It flourishes in a moist sandy soil but the seed is erratic in germinating.

ADVENTITIOUS (*ad*, to; *venio*, I come). Adventitious roots are those which do not arise from the radicle, but from some other part of the plant.

ÆCHMEA (æch′-mea, Bromeliaceæ). Stove evergreen flowering plants. S. America, 1824.

Culture.—Compost, turfy loam, leaf mould and sand in equal parts. Pot spring, good drainage essential. Winter temperature, 60°; summer, 75°.

Propagation.—By off-sets in small pots at all times.

SPECIES.

Bracteata, yellow; *cœlestis*, blue; *fulgens*, scarlet; *Veitchii*, red.

AEGLE or **ÆGLE**, syn. *Citrus trifoliata, C. trifolia, Limonia trifoliata, Pseudœgle sepiaria, Triphasia trifoliata*, (Rutaceæ). Hardy Orange or Bengal Quince.

Culture.—Plant in March or October in well-drained fibrous loam and leaf-mould in warm position. Sow seed in spring in a frame, or take cuttings of half-ripened shoots. No regular pruning required. Cut out dead wood after pruning.

This is a plant every garden should contain for its hardiness, beauty and distinction and its being allied to the orange and lemon. In the public garden of Milan there is a hedge about 100 yards long. The fruit is too bitter to be eaten raw, but may be made into a conserve by boiling in sugar. There is a hybrid between this and the orange called Citrange.

Æ. marmelos. An Indian fruit with highly medicinal qualities. Stove evergreen shrub. Increase by cuttings rooted in sand, and peat in stove propagating pit.

Æ. sepiara. A deciduous spiny shrub from China and Japan allied to Citrus (orange, lemon, etc.). Fragrant pale lemon flowers in April or May followed by orange-like fruits about 1½ in. across, in warm districts.

ÆRIDES (æ′-rides. Orchidaceæ). From *aer*, air; in reference to the power these have of deriving their sustenance from the atmosphere. Stove flowering orchids. Evergreen. India, 1800.

Culture.—Compost, 3 parts sphagnum moss, 1 part finely-cut fibre. Repot early spring. Give good drainage.

Propagation.—By division or roots.

SPECIES.

Crassifolium, purple; *Crispum*, white and rose; *Odoratum*, white and lilac.

ÆSCHYNANTHUS (es-ki-nan-thus. Gesneraceæ). Brilliantly beautiful stove plants that may be grown successfully in hanging baskets like those used for

Orchids. A compost of loam, leaf-mould and sand with some charcoal suits them best. They require perfect drainage, and when grown in baskets chopped sphagnum should be added to the compost.

Propagate by cuttings of half-ripened shoots inserted in sandy soil under a bell-glass with a little bottom heat.

SPECIES.

Æ. atrosanguinea, dark red flowers in July, 12 in.

Æ. bracteata, scarlet or yellow flowers in August, 18 in.

Æ. grandiflorus, large scarlet flowers, August, 5 ft.

Æ. javanicus, bright red flowers with yellow throats, June to July, 12 in.

Æ. lobbianus, rich scarlet flowers and dark purple corolla.

Æ. longiflorus, scarlet flowers in bunches, June to August, 2 ft.

Æ. pulchrus, scarlet, July, 12 ft.

Æ. speciosus, flowers of rich orange, July, 2 ft. This, being of more sturdy growth than the other species, makes an excellent pot plant.

Æ. splendida, violet or orange flowers in July, 12 in.

Æ. tricolor has flowers of blood-red with bright orange throat and short black corolla tube, 12 in. Other species of these epiphytic flowers are numerous and equally attractive.

AESCULUS or ÆSCULUS (ĕs-cu-lus. Sapindaceæ). Horse chestnut, Buckeye. Deciduous flowering tree, most handsome in form and foliage, and strikingly beautiful when in flower, May to August.

Culture.—Plant in November in good, deep, well-drained moist soil. Seed is the best means of increase and it should be sown as soon as it falls and covered with its own depth of soil.

Æ. carnea, Red Horse Chestnut. Origin uncertain. Possibly a hybrid between the common horse chestnut *Æ. hippocastanum* and *pavia*. Flowers deep rose.

Æ. carnea Briotii, 1858. Of French origin. A fine, almost crimson-flowered variety.

Æ. hippocastanum, Common Horse Chestnut. The best known and most beautiful of large flowering trees, of most stately and noble proportions, and handsome and striking flower clusters. Native

of Northern Greece and Albania. Of no great economic value, the wood being soft and lacking in strength. Chiefly used for articles for which durability is unnecessary, such as toys and kitchen utensils. Deer are fond of the nuts, as well as boys for playing the game of "conkers." There are several forms in cultivation, the finest being var. *flore pleno*, with double flowers. Originated in a garden near Geneva about 1820. It has a longer flowering period than the type, and as it produces no nuts, it is strongly recommended for planting in streets and public places as it has no attraction for children.

Æ. parviflora, Shrubby Pavia or Dwarf Buckeye, U.S.A., 1785. 8–12 ft. A most valuable flowering shrub of graceful habit, producing its large erect panicles of white flowers in late July and August. Of great value as a lawn shrub, flowering as it does when but few shrubs are in flower.

ÆTHIONEMA (e-the-on-ema. Cruciferæ). *Aitho*, scorch; *nema*, filament, having reference to the burnt appearance of the stamens. Burnt Candytuft. Lebanon Candytuft. Neat little bushlings mainly from the limestone soils of Southern Europe.

Culture.—A light gritty soil in a sunny corner of the rock garden suits them. 6 in. May–June. *Propagate* by cuttings in sand under glass in spring and autumn.

SPECIES.

Æ. coridifolium. The true variety of this perennial plant has compact heads of rose-pink and comparatively stout unbranching stems densely set with narrow blue-grey leaves. From Lebanon.

Æ. grandiflorum. Often confused with *coridifolium*, but distinguishable by the seed pods, which are heart-shaped (instead of boat-shaped as in *coridifolium*). The branches are longer, about 12 in., and the pink flower-heads larger and laxer than the foregoing. Perennial. Persia.

Æ. iberideum. A white-flowered variety from the Levantine Alps having the usual grey foliage on rather flopping stems. A pretty enough thing, but outclassed by most of its relatives. (Syn. *brachystachium*).

Æ. pulchellum. Often confused with *Æ. coridifolium* and *grandiflorum*, but distinguishable from both by the stems, which are much branched. Bright rose-pink flowers in June and July. Armenia.

Warley Rose. A hybrid probably of *Æ. pulchellum.* The bright rose-pink flowers are very large, the habit neat and compact. Originated in Miss Willmott's garden at Warley. May, 9 in.

AFRICAN CORN FLAG. *See* ANTHO-LYZA.

AFRICAN LILY. *See* AGAPANTHUS.

AGALMYLA (a-gal-mi-la. Gesneraceæ). Fine stove plants suitable for growing on branches of trees, in baskets or in pots.

Propagate from cuttings placed under a bell-glass. Use a compost of fibrous peat, moss, with charcoal and sand. The only two species are *A. longistyla,* with crimson flowers, 12 in., and *A. staminea,* with scarlet flowers, 6 in. Both bloom in June and July.

AGANISIA (a-gan-is-i-a. Orchidaceæ). *Aganos,* desirable. Attractive, neat epiphytic orchids that make very pretty subjects for the warm house. Grown on a block in the stove house or in baskets. Use a compost of peat and sphagnum with sand.

Propagate by division of the rhizomes. Water frequently and syringe daily during the growing-period, but keep fairly dry when the plants are resting.

SPECIES.

A. graminea, red and yellow flowers in January, 6 in.

A. ionoptera, purplish-white flowers in July, 12 in.

A. pulchella, pretty white or creamy-yellow flowers, June, 9 in.

A. tricolor, blue and yellow flowers, May, 15 in.

AGAPANTHUS (ag-a-pan'-thus. Liliaceæ). African Lily. Greenhouse herbaceous plant. Height 18–40 in. Blue and white blooms in spring or summer with graceful foliage. They have light green sword-shaped leaves with flowers borne in umbels. Best suited for rich warm soil, and although not quite hardy will thrive outdoors in winter if roots are protected with leaves. Often grown in tubs for conservatories or greenhouses.

Culture.—Compost: 2 parts loam, 1 part leaf-mould, ½ part sand. Large pots or tubs. Sunny position. Repot only every

4 or 5 years. Water freely during the growing period, give frequent applications of liquid manure. Gradually withhold water after flowering. Winter temperature, 35°.

Propagation.—By division of plants in spring.

SPECIES.

A. umbellatus, blue; and its varieties, *alba,* white; *flore pleno,* double; and *variegatus* (leaves variegated).

A. umbellatus giganteus is the largest, with umbels bearing from 150–120 flowers.

A. umbellatus maximus has full heads of flowers which alternate in opening and thus provide continuous blossomings.

A. mooreanus is hardy, has narrow leaves and comes true from seed. This flowers in late summer.

AGATHÆA (agathæ'-a. Compositæ). Blue Marguerite. Greenhouse herbaceous perennial. Cape of Good Hope, 1753.

Culture.—Compost, *see* AGAPANTHUS. Sunny position, may be planted outdoors, May to September; pot early spring. Water freely during summer. Winter temperature 45°.

Propagation.—By cuttings of young shoots, March, in light sandy soil, in propagator. Temperature 65°.

SPECIES.

Amelloides, cœlestis, both blue.

AGATHIS (ag'-a-this. Coniferæ). Distinct tall-growing trees on the tender side, best in quite mild districts.

A. Australis. The Kauri Pine of New Zealand, with brownish leaves.

AGAVE (aga'-ve. Amaryllidaceæ). Aloe. From *agavos,* referring to the stately form in which some of them flower. Greenhouse, ornamental foliage and flowering plants. Perennial. The flowers are mostly yellowish-green or red, borne on tall stately spikes. Often these plants die after once flowering. Mexico, 1640.

Culture.—Compost: *see* AGAPANTHUS. Pots or tubs sunny position, greenhouse. Water freely during growing period, little after. Winter temperature 45°; summer 65°.

Propagation.—By offsets in small pots at any time.

SPECIES.

Americana variegata, dark green and yellow leaves; *attenuata, ingens picta,* leaves green, yellow edge; *poselgeri*, leaves striped; *Curacoa variegata*, leaves green, white margin.

AGERATUM (ager-a'-tum. Compositæ). Floss flower. Hardy and half-hardy annuals, first introduced in 1822.

They will grow in any ordinary soil in a sunny spot. Plant from 6–8 in. apart, June.

These plants may be propagated by seeds sown in light soil in a temperature of 65°–70° in March, or by cuttings of young shoots from plants grown in pots especially for stock. These should be pinched periodically to prevent flowering, and should be wintered in the greenhouse in a temperature of 50°. The species cultivated is *A. mexicanum*.

This plant grows to a height of 1–2 ft., and bears blue flowers during the summer. It makes a useful pot plant, or it can be grown in the mixed border or in beds. There are now dwarf varieties and these are very suitable as edging plants.

The plant is of compact habit and the foliage is almost hidden by the great profusion of lavender-blue flowers. "Imperial Dwarf Blue," and "Imperial Dwarf White," "Blue Ball," "Covent Garden," "Swanley Blue," are all good modern varieties of the species.

AGLAONEMA (aglaone'-ma. Aroideæ). Poison-dart. Stove perennials. Flowers arum-shaped. Leaves mottled green and grey.

Culture.—Compost: 2 parts fibrous loam, 1 part leaf-mould, and sand. Shady position in well-drained pots. Water freely while growing, syringe daily. Repot early spring.

Propagation.—By division of roots in March.

SPECIES.

Angustifolium, greenish-white; *costatum*, white; *Oblongifolium*, crimson; there are several others, but all very similar.

AGRIMONY. *Of old a cure for sore throat, ulcers and cancer.*

AGROSTEMMA (agros' - tem' - ma. Caryophyllaceæ). Rose Campion. A small genus of hardy perennials closely allied to Lychnis and of which *coronaria* (*Lychnis coronaria*), with grey woolly leaves above which rise 2 ft. stems bearing at the summit summer-blooming flowers of rich wine-red, is the only grown species. A native of Southern Europe, it has been cultivated in England since 1596. Dioscorides, the Greek physician and botanist who lived about the time of Nero (A.D. 37–68), in his "Materia Medica" prescribes the seed drunk in wine as a remedy for the sting of a scorpion. *See also* LYCHNIS.

Propagation.—Too easily grown from seed to make any other method worth while. There is a white variety.

AGROSTIS (ag-ros-tis. Gramineæ). Cloud Grass. Hardy annual flowering grasses attaining a height of 1½ ft. A pretty ornamental grass, useful for table decoration, with other flowers in summer, or to dry for winter decoration. It will grow in any ordinary soil in a sunny position. Seeds should be sown $\frac{1}{16}$ in. deep in April in their permanent position.

SPECIES CULTIVATED.

A. alba (Fine-top grass), in July.

A. nebulosa (Cloud grass), July, originated from Spain.

A. pulchella, July, originated from Sicily.

AILANTHUS (ail-an-thus. Simarubaceæ). Tree of Heaven, 1751. A very fine deciduous Chinese tree with long, almost palm-like leaves assuming a rich yellow hue in autumn. Flowers of no beauty and unpleasant smell, followed by very decorative fruits.

Culture.—Plant in November in ordinary soil in a sunny open position.

Propagate by root suckers in August placed in a frame. Quite hardy, but best planted in sheltered place as strong winds may impair the beauty of the leaves. Few trees thrive so well in towns. If used for this purpose, female trees alone should be used owing to the objectionable odour of the male when in flower. If young plants are cut close to the ground in spring, and reduced to one growth, magnificent leaves are produced giving quite a tropical effect. Rich deep moist soil is necessary for this.

SPECIES.

A. glandulosa is the principal species. There is a variety *pendulifolia*, with leaves even larger than the type drooping downwards in a most graceful manner.

A. Vilmoriniana (W. China), resembling above, with young growths spiny.

A. Giraldii (China). A new species, leaves enormous, of a vivid green.

A. flavescens. See CEDRELA SINENSIS.

AIRA (ai-ra. Gramineæ). Hair Grass. A genus of hardy perennial grasses with graceful spikelets of flowers and fine hair-like foliage. Useful for drying and keeping for indoor winter decoration or for mixing with cut flowers. They are easily grown in ordinary moist garden soil, and seed may be sown outdoors in April.

SPECIES.

Most of the species are now classed with other genera. *A. flexuosa*, 12–18 in., and *A. pulchella*, 6–8 in., are worth growing.

AJUGA (a'-juga. Labiatæ). Name meaning "without a yoke," in reference to the calyx being one-leaved. Bugle. The Bugles form, as a rule, spreading mats of relatively broad leaves above which rise 4 in. spikes of usually dark blue flowers in summer. They grow anywhere without trouble, but in nature have a preference for dampish spots in full sun.

Propagate by division or cuttings.

SPECIES.

Good species are *A. reptans*, which throws out runners in every direction, and *A. genevensis Brockbankii*, which does not. Garden forms of particular merit are *Metallica crispa*, with curled leaves of a metallic sheen; *multicolor*, whose leaves are splashed with white, yellow and wine-red; and best of all *A. reptans variegata*, whose light green and silver-white leaves so admirably set off the flowers of Cambridge blue.

Members of the genus are found in every continent except America. Writing of the English flowers (type *A. reptans*), Gerarde (1548-1612) says that the juice of the bruised leaves has strong curative properties when applied to wounds or sores.

A K E B I A (ă-kē-bia. Berberideæ). Vigorous, deciduous or partially evergreen climbers from China and Japan with purple flowers.

Plant in good loamy soil against shady walls or on trellis. They need but little training or tying. Layering best method of propagation; also by cuttings and division. Cuttings should be made from wood just getting firm, and placed in gentle heat.

SPECIES.

A. lobata (China and Japan). Hardy. Flowers in April, and these are often destroyed by frost; consequently its conspicuous and highly-coloured fruits are seldom seen.

A. quinata (China, Japan and Korea). 1845. Flowers pale purple and of spicy fragrance, which is perceptible some distance from the plants. Its fruit has been produced in Hampshire.

ALANGIUM (Alangiaceæ). A deciduous shrub or stove evergreen of no garden value.

ALBIZZIA (Leguminosæ). A deciduous-flowering, small acacia-like tree from the Orient; common in China and other countries, wild or cultivated. Flowers pink or yellow. Not hardy. Plant against wall, among some evergreen climber, as it grows quickly in young state and becomes leggy. Useful for tropical bedding. Seeds should be sown in heat in spring, and the plants gradually hardened off and planted out in May. They should be wintered in greenhouse, temperature not less than 55°.

A. julibrissin is the principal species. The Nemu Tree of the Orient. Pink siris. A specimen covered with its pink flowers is a wonderful sight.

A. lophantha. Flowers pale yellow. Tender until established.

A. odoratissima. Flowers pale yellow. Attains to 45 ft. in Cornwall.

A. procera. Flowers pale yellow.

ALBUCA (al-bu-ca. Liliaceæ). Greenhouse bulbs that may be planted out under conditions similar to those given to the Amaryllis (Belladonna Lily).

Propagate by seeds, suckers from the old bulbs or by leaves taken off with a scale. They like a light sandy loam with leaf-mould. The bulbs must be well protected in winter or they will be destroyed by frost.

SPECIES.

A. abyssinica, 2 ft.; *altissima*, 4 ft.; *coarctata*, 2 ft.; *fastigiata*, 2 ft.; *physodes*, 1 ft.; *spiralis*, 1 ft.; and *viscosa*, are all white-flowered and bloom from June to August. The prevalence of these white-flowered forms have given rise to the name of the genus, *albuca* (from *albus*, white). The popular form *aurea*, like *caudata*,

Cooperi fibrosa fragrans (fragrant), *minor*, *setosa* and *viridiflora*, has greenish-yellow flowers in summer and is about 2 ft. high.

ALCHEMILLA (al'-ke'-mil'-la. Rosaceæ). The Arabic name of a local species.

A. alpina. Alpine Ladies Mantle. The

ALLIUM NEAPOLITANUM

A close ally to the onion, Allium neapolitanum, likes a sandy soil. It grows 1½ ft. high, and has white flowers

light green and kidney-shaped leaves bear on the under side and on their stems a beautiful silvery sheen. They have the power of condensing moisture from the air. The yellow-green flowers are produced in dense corymbs and though individually inconspicuous are in the mass extremely decorative. It inhabits the mountain ranges of the N.W. hemisphere generally, and is found in mountainous localities in North England, Scotland, Kerry and Sligo. Height 6 in.

A. vulgaris. Is larger and coarser and fairly widely distributed in a wild state in Britain. It is not worth growing if *alpina* is available. Gerarde in his "Herbal" says that *A. vulgaris* is useful for stopping bleeding. Both are propagated by seeds or by division of the roots, and grow in any good well-drained soil.

ALDERS. *See* ALNUS.

ALEXANDRIAN LAUREL. *See* DANAE.

ALISMA (Water Plantain or *Plantago-aquatica*). Alismaceæ. Hardy aquatic perennial of tufted habit with lance-shaped leaves. It grows to about 2 ft., bearing pink flowers in summer. Sow in March in peat, and plant in a sunny position at edge of a lake or pool.

A. plantago bears pretty rosy blossoms in summer.

A. ranunculoides, purple flowers, summer.

ALKANET. *See* ANCHUSA.

ALLAMANDA (allaman'-da. Apocynaceæ). In honour of Dr. Allamand of Leyden. Stove evergreen climbing plants. America, 1785.

Culture. Compost: 2 parts loam, 1 part leaf-mould, ½ part sand and charcoal. Pots or prepared greenhouse border, so that shoots may be trained to roof. Repot or plant early spring. Winter temperature 60°; summer 75° to 80°.

Propagation.—By cuttings of previous year's growth inserted in sand in propagation January. Temperature 80°.

ALLIUM. (*See also* LEEK, ONION, SHALLOTS.) Liliaceæ. Hardy bulbs, many of which are grown for their ornamental flowers. These plants can be cultivated in any ordinary soil, preferably of a light sandy nature. They like a position in sunny borders and are particularly suited for cultivation in pockets in the rock garden. If liked, they can be grown in the greenhouse in pots filled with a mixture of loam, leaf-mould and silver sand. They can be forced to flower quite well in the cold house. For greenhouse decoration they are potted in October; and for outdoor cultivation the bulbs are planted also in October or November, generally about 3 in. deep and 4 in. apart, according to the size of the bulbs.

VARIETIES.

The varieties generally grown in the rockery are: *A. azureum*, with blue flowers; *neapolitanum*, with white and green flowers; *cyaneum*, a charming dwarf, blue species, 4–5 in. high; *glaucum*, heads of mauve-coloured flowers in June; *macranthum*, large round heads of pale pink blossoms; *sp. Tibet*, a delightful plant with showy lilac heads; *A. Moly-luteum*, heads of bright yellow flowers.

SPECIES.

Cathartica, yellow; *grandiflora,* yellow.

ALLOTMENTS. Almost every amateur gardener in the country (except in very congested districts) is now able, through the activities of the National Allotments Society Limited, and the legislation which they were able to get carried through Parliament, to obtain an allotment sufficient for the cultivation of vegetables for an average family. The size of the plot usually cultivated by the spare-time gardener is 10 rods, and a great deal of research work has been done by the officials of the Ministry of Agriculture in order to discover the best method of cropping a piece of ground of this size to obtain a vegetable supply all the year round.

After the allotment holder takes over a piece of virgin ground, that is, rough meadow land or waste ground, the first problem will be to bring the soil into good condition to receive the crops. In many cases during the war, exceedingly rough building land was taken over by amateurs, sometimes with rubbish, bricks, old timber, etc., strewn over it to a depth of 3 or 4 ft. Thus the first thing to do where such is the case is to clear away rough surface rubbish and to dispose of it according to its nature. Fertile soil is always the soil which has been recently in cultivation or left lying fallow to grow weeds or grass.

This portion of the soil is usually darker in colour and different in texture from the subsoil, which may be either chalk, heavy clay or infertile sand or gravel. In the case of a neglected piece of land where rubbish has accumulated, it may be necessary to excavate to a depth of 3 ft. before fertile soil is discovered, but unless this fertile soil is actually brought to the top it will be almost impossible to grow satisfactory crops for a year or two on the plot. The initial work, therefore, consists in a survey of the plot, and it will probably help if a deep hole is dug in one corner of the plot in order to ascertain the nature of the soil. Having decided how much work there is to do in the matter of excavation, the next business is to bring the actual

NO: OF ROWS	RHUBARB HORSERADISH HERBS	COMPOST PIT ·6'-0"
1.	PARSLEY	1'-0"
1.	AUTUMN CABBAGE	2'-6"
2.	BRUSSELS SPROUTS	5'-0"
1.	BROCCOLI (A)	2'-6"
1.	AUTUMN CAULIFLOWER	2'-6"
1.	DWARF KIDNEY BEANS	2'-6"
6.	PEAS – EARLY, MID. AND LATE	12'-0"
2.	BROAD BEANS	3'-0"
/////////	CELERY TRENCH///////////// LETTUCE ON RIDGE	3'-0"
1.	PARSNIPS	1'-6"
1.	TURNIPS	1'-6"
2.	BEET (B)	3'-0"
4.	CARROTS	4'-0"
5.	ONIONS	5'-0"
2.	SHALLOTS	3'-0"
1.	RADISH	1'-0"
/////////	LEEK TRENCH ///////////	3'-0"
6.	POTATOES– MAIN CROP (C)	15'-0"
2.	POTATOES – SECOND EARLY	4'-0"
3.	POTATOES - EARLY	6'-0"
2.	RUNNER BEANS	3'-0"

This chart shows the arrangement of vegetables on a ten rod allotment. The order of rotation is : 1st year, A—B—C; 2nd year, C—A—B; 3rd year, B—C—A.

soil into usable condition. With ordinary rough meadow land, double digging will probably be ample preparation. This operation provides for the breaking up and improvement of the subsoil without bringing it to the surface. The method is as follows:

A deep trench, fully 2 ft. in width and 10 in. deep, should be opened across one end of the plot. Keep the sides of this trench upright. The soil moved from it can be carried to the part of the plot where the digging will be finished. The subsoil exposed at the bottom of this trench must then be thoroughly broken up, and the deeper this is broken the better will be the condition of the soil. On to this broken subsoil turn the turf with the grass side down. From the second 2 ft. of the plot throw on to the subsoil any rough material such as weeds, vegetable refuse, torn-up rags, etc., from the house, anything in fact which will decay and form humus. If manure is available it is advisable to put a good layer over the subsoil in addition to the turf and other refuse. Then turn the second 2 ft. of topsoil over on to this turf or manure, which will leave a second trench similar to the first. Repeat this process until the whole of the plot has been dug.

It eases the work of digging in this way if the trench is carried only half across the plot. In this manner the soil moved from the first part of the trench need only be moved to the other side of the plot instead of right down to the far end.

If when the first hole is opened for the purpose of investigating the soil it is found that the darker, more fertile soil has been buried under heaps of clay, it will of course be necessary to vary the method of digging so that eventually the fertile soil remains at the top of the dug plot. The ground should, of course, be roughly levelled at the same time as the digging is done, though the surface should certainly be left rough for a time to weather, particularly if the digging can be done at the beginning of the winter, when the frosts will assist in breaking down the lumps. After digging, spread a dressing of lime over the surface of the soil, using from 2 to 8 oz., according to the condition of the soil. The value of LIME as an aid to successful culture of vegetables cannot be over-estimated, and if the allotment is in or near a town, lime will be specially desirable.

Lime makes the plant food locked up in the soil more readily available and increases the crop; it reduces "finger and toe" in Turnips and "club-root" in Cabbage; it improves a clay soil by making it friable and easier to work; it tends to reduce certain weeds and insects in the soil; in the form of chalk, it gives body to a loose sandy soil. Ground quicklime, air-slaked or water-slaked lime and powdered chalk can all be used to advantage. Lime may be used at the rate of 14 lb. per square rod once in three years, or (except for potatoes) 4 lb. per square rod annually.

Chalk may be used at double these rates. Dressings are best given when the ground is vacant; but chalk or air-slaked lime can be given at any time by raking it into the topsoil.

Although greatly increased crops almost always follow the use of lime on soils in which it was hitherto lacking, it should be remembered that it is not a substitute for manure, adequate dressings of which should not be omitted. Where crops have been exceptionally heavy, increased manure should be given to maintain the fertility of the soil. Lime should not be mixed with manures of any kind before application to the soil.

Seeds. It pays to buy good seed, and in the case of allotments it pays to obtain seed potatoes from a distance. Immune varieties should be used, even though Wart Disease may be unknown in the district. The digging of an allotment is always best done in the winter, and if possible at the beginning of the winter, so that the land can settle before seed-sowing time. For seed sowing the novice should provide himself with a line sufficient in length to stretch across the width of the plot and attached to a pointed stick at each end. This line can be rolled up when not in use so as to keep it from getting entangled. The method of sowing small seed is pretty much the same in every case: it is essential that the surface soil should be broken to a fine tilth. If the soil is heavy, it will only break down finely after it has been subjected to frosts. When the time for the actual sowing comes, tread over the large lumps to break them down or break them with a fork or a wooden rake. Then rake over with a fine-toothed iron rake so that there is about 1 in. deep of fine soil over the surface. Now take the line attached to the sticks and stretch it across the plot in the position where the first row of seeds is to be planted. With a pointed hoe or edge of the rake draw a shallow trench alongside this line about 1 in deep for fine seeds, and deeper if the seeds are large. Then sow the seeds as finely as possible all along the drill. In the case of expensive seeds it is sometimes advisable to sow just a tiny pinch every 6 in. instead of sowing seeds all along the drill. This means that less thinning will be done and there will be less wastage of seeds.

Then move the line along the plot to where the second row is to be. The distance between the rows will, of course, vary according to the crops. Cover the fine seed in the first row by using the back of the rake, pressing the soil fairly firm with this. Always put a label at the end of the row to indicate where the seeds are sown, and on this label mark clearly the name of the seed, the variety, and the date of sowing.

The Ministry of Agriculture gives the following particulars of the depth and quantity of the seeds to be sown on a 10 rod plot.

BROAD BEANS. Broad Beans should be planted $3\frac{1}{2}$–4 in. deep and 9 in. between the seeds. One pint will be required.

SHALLOTS. These should be planted singly about 4 in. to 6 in. apart, and should be pressed firmly into the soil, but not entirely covered. 1 lb. will be sufficient.

PARSNIPS. Drills should be $\frac{3}{4}$ in. to 1 in. deep and the seed sown at the rate of 1 oz. to 200 ft. of drill, evenly or in groups about 8 in. apart.

LEEKS. Seed should be sown in the seed bed, thinned and later transplanted in a trench 6–9 in. apart. $\frac{1}{4}$ oz. seed will be required.

PEAS. These are best sown in a flat drill 3 in. in depth in light soil, and 2 in. in heavy. Early Peas require 1 pt. to 70 ft. of drill and the late varieties 1 pt. to 85 ft. of drill.

ONIONS. The drills should be $\frac{3}{4}$ in. to 1 in. deep. Spring-sown Onions need to be thinned at least twice, leaving them 4 in. to 8 in. apart at the final thinning. 1 oz. of seed is sufficient for 200 ft. of drill. In the case of bunching Onions sown in autumn, double the quantity of seed should be used.

LETTUCE. Lettuce may be sown $\frac{1}{4}$ in. deep in small quantities at intervals of a fortnight, either in the seed bed or in drills planted 9 in. to 12 in. apart, according to variety. $\frac{1}{8}$ oz. seed is sufficient for 160 ft. of drill.

CABBAGE. Cabbage of all kinds should be sown in the seed bed in drills $\frac{3}{4}$ in. deep and 12 in. apart. September plantings may be 12 in. apart in rows, alternate cabbages being cut in the early spring to give room for the remainder to mature. April plantings should be 16 in. to 20 in. apart. $\frac{1}{4}$ oz. of each variety is quite sufficient.

BORECOLE. (Kale). Sow as for Cabbage and plant 18 in. apart.

BROCCOLI. Sow as for Cabbage and plant $1\frac{1}{2}$ ft. to $2\frac{1}{2}$ ft. apart.

SAVOYS. Sow as for Cabbage and plant $1\frac{1}{2}$ ft. apart.

BRUSSELS SPROUTS. Sow as for Cabbage and plant $2\frac{1}{2}$ ft to 3 ft. apart.

CAULIFLOWER. Sow as for Cabbage and plant little more seed and plant 2 ft. to $2\frac{1}{2}$ ft. apart.

POTATOES. It is usual to plant first-early varieties 12 in., second-early 15 in., and maincrop 18 in. apart between the sets, which should be 4 in. deep. The "seed" required is about 18 lb. of first-early, 12 lb. of second early, and 20 lb. of maincrop varieties.

CELERY. Celery may be raised in the seed bed, but it is preferable to purchase the 80 plants required. Plant about 9 in. apart alternately in a double-row trench. The first earthing should be given when the plants are 15 in. high; the second three weeks later, and the final before the frost sets in.

CARROTS. The drills should be ¾ in. to 1 in. in depth. Thin out gradually 6 in. to 8 in. apart, according to the season and variety. For 150 ft. of drill 1 oz. of seed is required.

TURNIPS. The drills should be ½ in. to ¾ in. deep and plants thinned out 5 in. to 9 in. apart, according to variety. For 200 ft. of drill 1 oz. of seed is required.

BEET. The drills should be ½ in. deep and plants thinned out to 8 in. apart. For 150 ft. of drill 1 oz. of seed is required.

DWARF BEANS. Plant about 2 in. deep and 6 in. apart in the drill. ¼ pt. will plant 40–50 ft.

RUNNER BEANS. Plant about 2 in. deep and 9 in. apart. 1–½ pt. of seed will be required for 30 ft. row.

PARSLEY. Sow in drills ¾ in. deep and thin out 6 in. to 12 in. apart. ¼ oz. seed is sufficient for 60 ft. of drill.

THYME AND SAGE. Six plants of each planted in February or March should be sufficient.

MINT. A mint bed may be made by planting roots in the early spring or cuttings in the early summer planted 6 in. apart.

MARROWS. Seeds should be planted singly in small pots in a greenhouse or frame in April. Transplant on the bed in May. The number of plants required varies with size of hotbed, but one packet of 10-12 seeds is sufficient.

Allotment holders would be well advised to make full use of the various advisory leaflets issued by the Ministry of Agriculture and Fisheries on the subject of Allotment Cultivation. These leaflets are prepared by experts who have been in charge of demonstration allotments all over the country for many years, and who have had ample opportunity to test in practice the application of the theories which are given in the leaflets. The leaflets cover such subjects as Manuring and Cultivation, Autumn treatment of the soil, Insect Pests, as well as a good many leaflets on particular crops, such as peas, beans, potatoes, etc.

For fuller details concerning garden vegetables, see under separate headings, PEAS, POTATOES, etc.

ALLOTMENTS ACT, 1922. Allotment holders are to some extent protected by the Allotments Act of 1922, which provides for compensation to be paid to them in certain cases on the termination of their tenancies. This provides for a six months' or longer notice to quit in the case of land let by private landlords except under certain conditions. It also lays down rules for the determination of tenancies of land owned by local authorities. The Act further lays down the rules for the compulsory acquisition of land for Allotments in certain cases. It compels Local Councils to establish local Allotment Committees, where necessary, in every borough or urban district with a population of 10,000 and upwards, unless exempted by the Ministry of Agriculture and Fisheries after consultation with the Ministry of Health.

One section of the Act provides that any person who by any act done without lawful authority or by negligence causes damage to any allotment garden or any crops or fences, or buildings thereon, shall be liable on summary conviction to a penalty not exceeding £5, but the provision shall not apply unless notice of the provision is conspicuously displayed on the allotment garden.

Notice to this effect is usually displayed by the local authority on any lands used for allotments. Copies of the Allotments Act can be purchased from the Ministry of Agriculture and Fisheries.

ALLOTMENT SOCIETY, THE NATIONAL. This Society is the Headquarters of the Allotment movement in England and Wales. Its object is the circulation of information on all matters appertaining to the Allotment movement, and the securing of improved legislation and better conditions for Allotments. Monthly bulletin is issued free to all Members, and The National Allotments Journal is published quarterly, price 8d. per dozen. *President*: Rt. Hon. Lord Trent, J.P., *Hon. Sec.*: G. W. Giles, M.B.E., The National Allotments Society, Drayton House, Gordon Street, London, W.C.1. *Subscriptions*: Individual Members, 5s. minimum per annum, in addition to taking

this country. Unfortunately it flowers so early that the blossoms are generally damaged by frosts.

Soil.—A warm, well-drained loam is best.

Planting.—Planting may be done any time during the dormant season between October and March. It makes a big tree, sometimes 30 ft. in height, and ample room must be allowed for development.

Pruning.—No pruning is required after

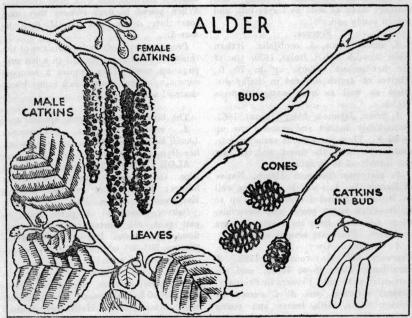

ALDER

FEMALE CATKINS

MALE CATKINS

BUDS

CONES

CATKINS IN BUD

LEAVES

The clogs of Lancashire are made from the wood of Alder. The Rialto Bridge, Venice, is built on Alder piles. It is easily recognised by its leaves, buds and catkins.

up one 2s. 6d. share upon admission. For Associates: One 2s. 6d. for a fully paid-up share when joining, and an annual affiliation contribution based upon 3d. per Member.

ALLSPICE. *See* CALYCANTHUS.

ALMOND, THE. *Prunus Amygdalus.* The Almond is not widely grown in this country for the production of its fruits, but more usually for its beauty of flower. A native of parts of Asia, and probably principally Algeria, it is perfectly hardy in

the main branches of the tree have been formed.

Propagation.—Almonds may be raised from seed, but when so grown are less hardy than those budded on to plum stock.

VARIETIES.

There are only two varieties worthy of consideration:

P. amara. Bitter Almond. Fruit used for confectionery and cooking.

P. dulcis. Produces dessert almonds. The fruit of the bitter almond should be used with caution, as it contains hydrocyanic acid, which is poisonous. *See also* PRUNUS.

ALNUS (al-nŭs. Betulaceæ). Alders. Deciduous flowering trees and shrubs allied to the birches (Betula). Valuable for growing in wet situations, where few other trees will succeed; also in ordinary deep loamy soils. Of rapid growth and easily cultivated. Flowers on catkins of pleasing appearance in spring, the male catkins being longer than the female. Plant in November.

Propagation by seed, grafting, and cuttings taken as soon as leaves fall, and put in sandy soil.

SPECIES.

A. cordata, syn. *A. cordifolia*. Italian Alder (Corsica and S. Italy), 1820. One of the handsomest Alders, up to 70 ft. Thrives on dryish soil and in chalky districts as well as near water. Flowers March.

A. firma, Japanese Alder (Japan), 1862. Remarkably distinct and graceful tree up to 30 ft. There are several varieties, var. *multinervis* being the finest, and the first one introduced to Britain.

A. glutinosa (Common Alder). Native of Europe, W. Asia and N. Africa as well as Britain. A useful timber tree—up to 90 ft.—from boggy places and waterside. Clogs are made from its wood. Flowers in March. There are several varieties.

A. ineana, Grey Alder (Europe, Caucasus and N. America), 1780. A very hardy alder up to 70 ft., and not particular as to soil. Flowers in February. Several varieties, one, *A. i. aurea*, the Golden Alder, with leaves and young shoots yellow.

A. japonica, Japanese Alder. A distinct species with narrow ovate leaves.

A. maritima, Seaside Alder, 1878. An American species up to 30 ft., flowering in autumn. Not very hardy in low, wet situations.

A. nitida, Himalayan Alder, 1882. A handsome, distinct tree flowering in September. Loves the waterside.

A. oregona, Oregon Alder. Native of western N. America to California. Up to 50 ft. Flowers in March.

A. sitchensis (sinuata), Sitka Alder (western N. America). Up to 40 ft. Very

free flowering. Catkins up to 5 in. long.

A. subcordata, Caucasian Alder (Caucasus and Persia), 1838. 50 ft. A very large-leaved alder retaining its foliage until November.

ALOCASIA (al-o-kas-i-a. Aroideæ). These stove perennials are highly valued for their handsome variegated foliage, which is developed at the expense of the flowers, which are small and inconspicuous. Although requiring the moist atmosphere of the stove to attain to their full beauty, they do well as room plants if carefully watered and provided with good drainage. When placed in dark corners they soon lose their colour, and should then be moved.

Propagate by seeds or by divisions of the rhizones rooted in sandy soil in a hot propagating case. They require a compost consisting of well-drained rich sandy loam, charcoal and a little peat.

SPECIES.

The best of the numerous species are : *A. argentea, argyrea, gandavensis, Lowii, macrorhiza*, Martin Cahuzac, *metallica* (syn. *cuprea*), *sanderiana* and *zebrina*.

ALOE (a′-loe. Liliaceæ). Medicinal Aloe. Greenhouse succulent. Ornamental foliage ; leaves more or less prickly. Evergreen. S. Africa, 1596.

Culture.—Compost : 2 parts loam, 1 part peat, old mortar and river sand. Sunny greenhouse. Pot in March. Temperature 50°–55° winter ; 55°–65° summer.

Propagate by seeds.

SPECIES.

Succotrina, vulgaris, spicata, etc.

ALONSOA (al-on-soa. Scrophulariaceæ). Mask Flower. Half-hardy shrubby perennials.

For their cultivation a compost of 2 parts loam, 1 part leaf-mould and sand should be prepared. They like warm sunny beds outdoors, or pots near the greenhouse windows.

They should be planted from May to September and should be watered moderately. Seeds sown in March will make good plants for bedding out in May, or they can be grown for greenhouse decoration only by seeds sown $\frac{1}{16}$ in. deep in March in a temperature of 60°, in sandy soil, or by cuttings in pots of sandy soil in August.

The plants are semi-trailing, and may also be grown in hanging baskets.

SPECIES.

A. albiflora, white and yellow flowers in the summer.

A. insicifolia, scarlet flowers in the summer.

A. linearis, scarlet flowers in summer.

A. linifolia, scarlet flowers in summer.

A. myrtifolia, scarlet flowers and its variety *alba*, white.

A. Warscewiczi, summer flowering. The most popular of all, with rosy scarlet flowers. Splendid as a dwarf bedding plant to carpet taller flowers.

ALOYSIA CITRIODORA. *See* LIPPIA CITRIODORA.

ALPINIA (al-pin'-e-a. Scitaminaceæ). Indian Shell Flower. Stove herbaceous perennials. Some varieties are valued for their beautiful variegated foliage. These plants will thrive well if planted in large pots, tubs or beds in a compost of equal parts loam, leaf-mould and peat. The best time to plant is in March. Water should be given freely in the summer, when a temperature of 70°–80° should be maintained. In the winter, however, not so much water is needed, and the plants should be grown in a temperature of 55°–65°.

Divide the roots of old plants in March, and insert in a compost similar to that used for the original plants, keeping the new plants in a moist atmosphere. They like plenty of pot room during their growing season.

SPECIES.

A. allughas, which bears red flowers in *February*. Height, 3–6 ft.

A. mutica, with white, red, and yellow flowers in July and August. Height, 1 ft.

A. rafflesiana (syn. *A. vitata*). Height, 2–3 ft.

A. Sanderæ. Height, 8 in.

A. speciosa (syn. *A. nutans*), white, purple and yellow, fragrant flowers. Height, 12 ft.

ALPINE GARDEN SOCIETY. *See* ROCK GARDEN.

ALSOPHILA (also'phila. Cyatheaceæ). Grove Fern. From *Alsos* a grove, in reference to the best situation for the plants. Stove and greenhouse tree ferns, 1833.

Culture.—Compost: *see* ADIANTUM. Re-

pot early spring. Large pots, shady position. Winter temperature: stove species 60°; greenhouse species 45°.

Propagation. See ADIANTUM.

STOVE SPECIES.

A. aspera, A. astrovirens.

GREENHOUSE SPECIES.

Australis, colensoi, Cooperi, pruinata, Rebeccæ.

ALSTROEMERIA (al-stro-me'-ria. Amaryllidaceæ). Peruvian Lily. Tuberous-rooted summer flowering plants that will continue to bloom until late in the season. appreciate sheltered position in well-drained sandy soil. For propagation, should be taken up in autumn when roots are less likely to be damaged.

BEST-KNOWN VARIETIES ARE:

A. aurantiaca, orange blooms with red streaks.

A. chilensis, pink, lined yellow.

A. pelegrina, red tipped, green, spotted red.

A. Peruviana, yellow, tipped green and spotted maroon.

Useful flowers for cutting.

ALTERATIONS TO GARDEN. *See* GARDEN DESIGN.

ALTHÆA. Hardy annuals, biennials and perennials. Sow annuals and biennials in spring, and herbaceous species as soon as the seed is ripe, or increased by cuttings.

SPECIES.

A. cannabina. Rose flowers in June, and its variety *narbonensis* with red flowers. Perennial.

A. ficifolia. Fig-leaved Hollyhock, with yellow flowers in June. Biennial.

A. officinalis. Marsh Mallow. Rose flowers from July to August. Perennial.

A. rosea. Hollyhock. Rose flowers during the summer. Perennial. *See also* HOLLYHOCK.

ALTHÆA FRUTEX. *See* HIBISCUS.

ALUM ROOT. *See* HEUCHERA.

ALYSSUM (al'-i-sum. Cruciferæ). Madwort. Pretty dwarf annual or perennial plants. Height 3–10 in. with yellow, white or lilac blossoms from May to June. Fit for sunny beds, edging and rock gardens: they prefer sandy soil in a sunny situation and perish in heavy rich clay in winter.

Propagation takes place by seeds or cuttings, also frequently by division.

SPECIES.

The perennial *Alyssum saxatile* or Gold Dust, a favourite rock plant, is generally propagated by seed.

A. saxatile citrinum, similar, but sulphur yellow.

A. tortuosum, prostrate, silvery leaves, a plant for the scree of the rock garden.

A. maritimum, white, fragrant.

A. compactum, white, dwarf.

A. "Primrose Queen," yellow, and *A. "Lilac Queen,"* coloured forms of the Sweet Alyssum.

AMARANTH GLOBE. *See* GOMPHRENA.

AMARANTHUS (am-ar-an-thus). Amarantaceæ). Love-lies-bleeding. Half-hardy annuals. First introduced 1596.

These plants grow to a height of from 2–3 ft. and the long "tails" are very striking in appearance. The flowers are borne on tail-like inflorescences which rise from the axils of the leaves, and they are of bright crimson, orange-red and green. They will grow in any ordinary soil in a sunny bed, and they should be planted out in June. They can be propagated by seeds sown $\frac{1}{16}$ in. below the surface in March, in a temperature of 65°–70°. The seedlings must be hardened-off gradually before being planted out.

SPECIES.

A. caudatus, Love-lies-bleeding. Syns. *A. paniculatus* and *A. sanguineus*, crimson-purple flowers in summer.

A. hypochondriacus, Prince's Feather. Crimson flowers.

A. tricolor splendens, fine crimson foliage. This species is not so hardy as most and is best suited for pot culture in the greenhouse.

AMARYLLIS (am-ar-il-lis. Amaryllideæ). Belladonna Lily. This name is commonly given to a large number of genera including Brunsvigias, Crinums, Hippeastrums, Nerines, Phycellas, Sprekelias, Sternbergias, Vallotas and Zephyranthes. The true Amaryllis is an indoor summer-flowering bulbous plant.

It is propagated by seeds or offsets. Seed should be sown as soon as ripe in shallow pans of loam and leaf-mould opened with sand. Keep the pans in a temperature of 60°–70° and provide plenty of light and moisture when the seedlings appear. When they have made a few leaves, they may be transferred singly to pots of well-drained soil similar to that in their previous home. They may be had in flower two to three years after sowing. To increase by offsets, these are taken off when potting and set in the same line as the established plants. They may be planted out in a warm sheltered position at the foot of a wall facing south in light, deep, fairly rich soil and must be protected with litter during the winter. Plant in September or October, and once planted leave the plants undisturbed for several years. If grown in pots they should be lifted early in the year and repotted. Syringe freely but water sparingly until growth is well established. When they are in full growth liquid manure and top dressings of fertiliser will be found beneficial. Keep the bulbs dry during the winter and rest them in the soil until it is time to repot them in spring. Use two parts of loam to one of decayed manure with a little sand for potting.

SPECIES.

The chief difference between Amaryllis and Hippeastrums lies in the fact that the bulbs of the former grow only during autumn and winter, while those of the latter may be induced to grow at any time in the year. *A. Belladonna* is the Belladonna Lily which is available in several colours, pink, rose, crimson, and white. It blooms from June to September. An objection to these plants is that leaves and flowers are not produced together, as the leaves are at their best in winter and very early spring. Many hybrids have been evolved that have been included in this genus but in reality they should be classified as Hippeastrums. Good varieties of *A. Belladonna* are *blanda*, summer, pale rose; and *pallida*, summer, flesh, 2 ft.

AMASONIA (am-a-son-ia. Verbenaceæ). Dwarf herbaceous perennials from the tropics. They are easily grown in a warm intermediate house in rich sandy loam and leaf-mould.

Propagate by division or preferably by suckers.

SPECIES.

A. calycina with red and yellow flowers in September.

A. erecta, white and pink flowers in July, 18 in.

1. Eschscholtzia—dainty yellow-orange flowers with pleasing grey-green foliage.
2. Larkspur—annual Delphiniums, varying blue and other delphinium shades.
3. Arctotis—white flowers with mauve centre. Whole plant covered with white down.

1. Erigeron—dainty flowers, chiefly blue or pink.
2. Rock Garden showing the placing of the rocks and use of shrubs as background.
3. Anemone pulsatilla—purple-violet flowers, hairy foliage stems.

4. Gentiana—the bluest of blue flowers.
5. Cistus—Rock Rose. Dwarf shrubby plants for full sun.

AMELANCHIER (am-ĕl-an-kĭ-ēr. Rosaceæ). The Snowy Mespilus, June Berry, Shad Flower, Grape Pear. Beautiful deciduous flowering small trees or shrubs from Mexico, China and W. N. America. Flowers white, in April and May.

Culture.—Plant in October or November in loamy soil. Cut out dead wood and thin when necessary after flowering.

Propagation is by seeds sown in March,

April. Autumn foliage very beautiful, changing to a rich soft red, or clear bright yellow in some forms. Fruit ripens in June, hence name of June Berry.

A. florida (N.W. America), 1826, 8–10 ft. Flowers early May. Autumn foliage rich yellow.

A. Laeris. See A. CANADENSIS.

A. oblongifolia (E. N. America), 6–8 ft. Beautiful autumn foliage.

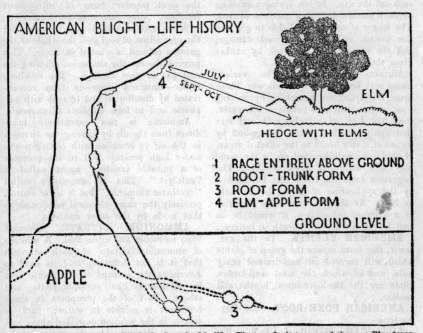

Woolly Aphis or American Blight leads a double life. First on fruit trees and then on Elm trees.

by cuttings in open in October, and by layering in spring.

SPECIES.

A. alnifolia, Western Shad Bush or June Berry (Western N. America); 10–20 ft., 1826. One of the most beautiful and ornamental species. Flowers in May, followed by fruits resembling black-currants.

A. asiatica, Service Berry (Japan). Near to *A. canadensis*, but flowers later. Foliage brilliant in autumn. Largely grown by Japanese in vicinity of their temples.

A. canadensis, Service Berry, June Berry, 1746 (N. America, etc.). Perhaps the best of the genus, a mass of flower about mid-

A. rotundifolia (vulgaris), Europe. Amelanchier or Snowy Mespilus, the largest flowered of the genus.

A. utahensis (N. America), 4 ft., compact growing. Flowers in May. Autumn foliage dark yellow.

AMERICAN BLIGHT (*Eriosoma lanigera*). This pest, also known as Woolly Aphis, may be found commonly on old apple trees, its presence being indicated by masses of white cottony excretion with which it covers itself. Its life history is complicated, for we find four distinct races. One lives upon the trunk or branches all the year; a second form lives wholly upon the roots; a third migrates from the roots to the trunk at the end of May; while a fourth appears upon apples in July, having migrated from hedge elms. In the majority of cases, the winter is passed in the egg stage, but females may also be found in crevices of bark. In the spring the eggs hatch out, and at the same time the viviparous females give rise to young. These bury their beaks into the bark and suck out the sap. In late spring a swelling appears round which they continue to feed. The spores of canker are liable to get into the wound, so causing indirect damage, and the cracking of the bark by canker gives shelter to the aphis.

METHOD OF CONTROL.—The various forms may be controlled as follows: Those upon the trunk or branches, by mixing 4 oz. of soft soap in a gallon of hot water, then add 1 oz. of carbolic acid and mix thoroughly. This should be applied by means of a stiff brush to the affected areas. Methylated spirit brushed on in the same way will also give good results. The migration from the roots may be checked by the application of grease bands early in May. As the elm form may give rise to a summer infestation, it would be as well to cut out all elm growth in hedges.

AMERICAN PLANTS. To the gardener, this term means the group of plants which will succeed on well-drained peaty soils, and of which the most well-known kinds are the rhododendrons, heaths and azaleas.

AMERICAN POKE ROOT. See PHYTOLACCA.

AMERICAN WOOD LILY. See TRILLIUM.

AMMOBIUM (amm-ō-bium. Compositæ). *Alatum grandiflorum* (half-hardy annual), 1½–2 ft., a native of New Holland, is an interesting "everlasting-flowered" plant, and a relative of the Swiss Edelweiss. The pearly-white flowers, nearly 2 in. across, are carried on the tips of each branch of a much-branched flowering stem, and the stems being peculiarly flanged, or winged, have a unique appearance. The flowers "dry" easily if cut when fully expanded and hung heads downwards in a dry, warm place, and are very much sought for winter decorations. Seeds may be sown in autumn, and the

plants wintered in a cool greenhouse, or in spring in a temperature of 50°–55°. Plant out into flowering quarters in April.

AMMONIA. A gas containing 82.25 per cent. nitrogen and 17.75 per cent. hydrogen. Ammonia is produced when coal is heated in ovens to break it up into its various constituents. If it is passed into sulphuric acid, a crystalline substance, sulphate of ammonia, is formed, which is the most popular form of nitrogenous fertiliser. (*See* SULPHATE OF AMMONIA).

When coke is being heated in retorts for the production of coal gas, the whole of the gaseous effluent is washed in water. This process absorbs the ammonia, allowing the coal gas to pass through. The resulting liquor—ammonia liquor—is then concentrated by distillation and treated with sulphuric acid to form sulphate of ammonia.

Ammonia is now extensively made direct from the air by causing the nitrogen in the air to combine with hydrogen gas under high pressure and in the presence of a suitable assisting agent called a "catalyst." This is sometimes called "synthetic ammonia," but it is, of course, precisely the same chemical compound as that made by the other methods.

AMMONIUM CITRATE. Formed from ammonia and citric acid. A solution of ammonium citrate of such strength that it is not definitely acid, is used to determine the amount of phosphoric acid in fertilisers like superphosphate and others. Part of the phosphate in these fertilisers is soluble in water: part is soluble in the solution described above and is termed citric soluble; the rest is known as insoluble phosphate. Citric soluble phosphate is likely also to be soluble in very weak acids found in all soils and, therefore, the water and citric solubility of a phosphatic fertiliser is a very fair guide to the availability of a phosphatic fertiliser when applied to the soil.

AMMONIUM SULPHATE. See SULPHATE OF AMMONIA.

AMORPHA (am-or-fa. Leguminosæ). Small deciduous flowering shrubs from U.S.A., with violet pea-shaped flowers June to September.

Culture.—Prefers dry sandy soil.

Propagate by seeds, layers in summer or cuttings in autumn, or suckers in winter.

SPECIES.

A. canescens, Lead Plant, 1812, 2–4 ft. (E.N. America). Flowers purple-blue in spikes, graceful acacia-like foliage. Suitable for front or sunny border. It owes its name of Lead Plant to the belief that its presence indicated the existence of lead ore beneath the ground.

A. fruticosa, False Indigo (U.S.A.), 1724. Taller growing than the preceding with purple-blue flowers in July. Suitable for rough shrubberies, where it can look after itself. Prune back shoots in spring.

AMORPHOPHALLUS (a-morf-o-fallus. Aroideæ). Stove or greenhouse tuberous-rooted perennials. The flowers appearing in spring are the first sign of recurring growth, the solitary branched leaf following the flowers.

They require rich loam and leaf-mould with a little sand. They should be rested during part of the year when they need only enough water to keep them from becoming dust dry. When growing give an abundance of water and keep them in a fairly shady place.

Propagate by seeds, but better by offsets or division of the tubers when growth is commencing in spring. Winter temperature 60°–65°; summer, 75°–90°.

SPECIES.

A. campanulatus, has a very bright purple spathe and fœtid flowers. Its roots should be allowed to dip in a tank of water during growth. 2 ft.

A. rivieri, with lurid purple spathe in spring is almost hardy and may be grown in the open border in summer.

A. grandis, spathe green, white inside, spadix purplish.

A. Lacourii, leaves spotted white.

A. nobilis, spathe livid purple, spotted white.

A. titanum is the most remarkable. The spathe and spadix are blackish purple, the former 3 ft. across, the latter 5 ft. high. The leaf stalk is 10 ft. high and the divided blade overshadows an area of 45 ft. The spring flowers are very fœtid. The roots like to dip in a tank while growing.

AMPELOPSIS. *See* VITIS.

AMPHICOME (am-fik-o-me. Bignoniaceæ). Half-hardy perennial herbs with lovely trumpet-shaped flowers that succeed in a cool greenhouse under conditions similar to those given to Cape Heaths.

Propagated by seeds sown in a hotbed in March or by cuttings of half-ripened shoots inserted in sandy soil in a warm pit or propagating case.

The genus is closely allied to Incarvilleas.

SPECIES.

A. arguta, red, orange-throated flowers in August, 12 in.

A. Emodi, flowers rose with orange throats, August to October, 18 in.

AMPHIRAPHIS. *See* MICROGLOSSA.

AMYGDALUS. *See* PRUNUS AMYGDALUS.

ANACAMPSEROS (ană-camp-sērŏs. Portulaceæ). *Anakampto*, I cause to return; *Eros*, love. Love-plant. Possesses the virtue of restoring the tender passion to those whose hearts have grown cold. Succulent herbs: about a dozen species from the Cape of Good Hope, and therefore tender.

A. Borderi, however, comes from the Pyrenees and is hardy. The fleshy leaves are grey (there is a bronze-leaved variety) and are topped by flat heads of dull crimson flowers. Butterflies, particularly Red Admirals and Peacocks, are much attracted by it. 2½ ft. July–September.

Propagates easily from cuttings in spring in sandy soil.

ANACARDIUM (an-a-kar-di-um. Anacardiaceæ). Stove evergreen American trees with entire oval leaves and sweet-smelling flowers produced in panicled corymbs. The kernal of the pear-shaped false fruit may be eaten when roasted and is used for flavouring wine. Moist stove culture is necessary.

Propagate by seeds or by cuttings of ripened shoots with leaves which root readily in pots of sand under a bell-glass or in a propagating case. A compost of loam and peat with sufficient sand to open the soil is suitable.

SPECIES.

A. occidentale, the Cashew Nut, green, red. *A. indicum*, green, red.

ANAGALLIS (ana-ga-lis. Primulaceæ). Pimpernel. There are a number of annual and perennial species of the family, and the latter are best treated as annuals as they are so easily raised from seeds, and young plants are more free flowering. The best for general garden purposes are:

A. grandiflorus, a true half-hardy annual, a charming little plant 4 in. high and remarkably floriferous. Flowers in varying shades of blue are produced from May to September.

A. Monelli Parksii, A. Monelli Phillipsii, are forms of *A linifolia* and have flowers of red and blue shades. *A. linifolia cærulea* is the best of the flax-leaved linifolia kinds and grows to 9–12 in. in height and produces flowers of an intense gentian-blue fully 1 in. across.

All the anagallis mentioned may be sown in gentle heat in spring or in the open ground during May and June.

ANAGYRIS (ana-gyris. Leguminosæ). "Like a spiral." A deciduous flowering bush or tree from S. Europe, with yellow pea-shaped flowers, inodorous. Tender. In France known as *bois puant* on account of the unpleasant odour of the leaves when crushed. Plant in ordinary soil with a little peat. *Propagation* by cuttings.

ANANAS (Pine-apple). Bromeliaceæ. From *Nanas,* the S. American name for the pine-apple. Stove plants, bearing the well-known fruit. Ornamental foliage. Evergreen. S. America, 1690.

Culture.—Compost, 2 parts loam, 1 part leaf-mould, ½ part well-rotted cow manure, liberal sprinkling of crushed bones. Position pots plunged in hotbed in stove facing south. Winter temperature, 60°; summer, 80°-90°. Water freely in summer, moderately during winter. When fruits begin to ripen gradually withhold water. A moist atmosphere, and full exposure to sun essential. Plants fruit in their second year.

Propagation.—By suckers, or crowns of fruits in small pots, early spring. Propagator, temperature 80°.

SPECIES.

Sativus, and its varieties *variegatus* (leaves striped), and *porteanus* (leaves with central yellow band).

ANAPHALIS (an-apha-lis. Compositæ). The ancient Greek name of a similar plant.

A. nukigena. Pearly Everlasting. Snow-white woolly leaves, corymbose heads of whitish flowers. 2½ ft., July onwards. (Himalayas).

Propagate by division. Every scrap will grow.

ANASTATICA (an-as-tat-i-ka. Cruciferæ). Resurrection Plant. Rose of Jericho. A dwarf annual with white flowers that is more curious than valuable. Known as the Resurrection Plant because in the sandy deserts of its native regions it grows up in the rainy season, flowers, seeds; and in the dry season contracts its rigid branches and is blown about by the wind until it alights in water or on damp ground, where it expands as if life was renewed. The ferny foliage always reacts to the condition of the soil; when dry it contracts and when wet it expands. Said to have first bloomed on Christmas Eve to welcome the birth of Christ and remained in bloom until Easter in homage to His resurrection. Full-grown plants will keep for any amount of time out of the ground.

Propagate by seeds sown in gentle heat and later pricked off prior to planting out. Plant in any common soil.

SPECIES.

A. Hierochuntica. Said to have curative properties. A mature plant will emit a pleasant odour when standing in a saucer of water and this helps to dissipate a cold.

ANATTO. *See* BIXA.

ANBURY. *See* CLUB ROOT.

ANCHUSA (an-shu'-sa. Boragineæ). Alkanet. *A. capensis,* Blue Bird or Blue Gown, is a charming hardy annual species from South Africa. It grows to a height of 1½ ft. and produces a wealth of flowers of a clear indigo-blue over a long period. Sow in patches or clumps in April in sunny position, and thin out to at least 1 ft. apart. Will succeed in almost any kind of soil that has been well dug.

VARIETIES.

The best varieties for the border are:

A. italica "Dropmore," the deepest gentian-blue.

A. italica "Opal," similar to Dropmore, but of a Cambridge blue.

The annual "Blue Bird" and the perennial "Dwarf Blue" are specially useful for beds and rockeries.

ANCISTROCHILUS (Orchidaceæ). Stove terrestrial orchids. Plant in pots or hanging baskets of peat, sphagnum moss and leaves. Water freely when growing.

Propagate by division at potting time.

SPECIES.

A. thomsoniana (syn. *Pachystoma thom-seniana*), white and purple, October, 6 in.

ANDRACHNE (Euphorbiaceæ). A group of shrubby plants of no interest to gardeners. If grown, need the protection of a greenhouse.

ANDROMEDA (an-drom'-e-da. Erica-ceæ). Moorwort, Wild Rosemary, Bog Rosemary. Dwarf, evergreen ornamental shrub with beautiful pink, pitcher-shaped, wax-like flowers in clusters, during May and onwards. Native of N. Europe, England and Ireland. Foliage beautifully tinted in autumn.

Culture.—Moist, peaty soil. *Propagation* by layers pegged down in autumn, cuttings, and by seed sown in pots of sandy, peaty soil. Partial shade and shelter from cold winds desirable. In gardens where these conditions are absent, the ground should be covered with an inch or two of sphagnum moss, which will help to ensure moisture.

A. polifolia, the only true species, including the forms *A. p. angustifolia* (narrow leaved) and *A. p. major* (broad leaved). The plant has no relation to the true Rosemary. A number of plants formerly known as Andromeda are now included in other genera, such as Cassandra, Cassiope, Leucothoë, Oxydendron, Lyonia, Zenobia, Pieris, Enkianthus, Dabœcia.

Andromeda. *So named by Linnæus because he found it solitary—blooming in a watery waste.*

ANDROPOGON (an-dro-po-gon. Gramineæ). Lemon Grass. Warm house grasses that are of the easiest culture.

Propagate by seeds or by division of the clumps or tufts. Grown in good fibrous loam with ample sand to keep it porous. With very heavy soil mix one-third of peat.

SPECIES.

A. Schœnanthus (syn. citratus). When bruised the leaves are very fragrant.

ANDROSACE (an-drŏs-a-cĕ. Primulaceæ). *Aner:* a man; *sakos:* a buckler. The anthers are supposed to resemble an ancient buckler. Rock Jasmine. The Androsaces are among the élite of rock-garden plants and are responsible for

more blighted hopes and cries of despair than any other family. Fortunately the least exacting are among the most beautiful, and we shall concern ourselves with these only. They can be propagated from seed (a doubtful business) or more certainly by division or cuttings, while many throw out runners which can be taken up

ANDROMEDA SPECIOSA

Andromeda Speciosa is a peat lover. The pretty bell-shaped flowers and stamens spring open on being touched.

and potted, using a well-drained, gritty soil. All flower in early summer.

SPECIES.

A. carnea. A valuable species. The type forms emerald-green mats studded with loose heads of pink flowers. There are many forms which differ in size or shape of leaf, degree of colour, and size of blossom. Some of these forms have been given specific names to which they really have no claim. *A. carnea* does best in a mixture of peat and gritty loam. Pyrenees and Alps. 2 in.

A. Chamæjasme. Small heads of relatively large pearl-white flowers, which change as the flower fades through cream-yellow to pale bluish-pink. It inhabits the mountain turf of a great part of the northern hemisphere, differing forms of it being found in Siberia, Tibet, the Kurile Islands, and the American Rocky Mountains. It should be put in the moraine, or in a similar compost to *A. carnea*.

A. lactea. Airy sprays of milk-white, golden-eyed little flowers above tufts of glossy, narrow-pointed leaves. It throws up runners and can be easily propagated from them. It inhabits the Austrian

The latest of the Anemones to bloom is the white or pink Anemone japonica which prefers a shady position in clay soil. It is very useful for cutting.

Alps to Transylvania. Light, gritty soil in sun.

A. languinosa. A downy, silver-leaved, prostrate plant from the Himalayas. Verbena-like heads of pale rosy-pink, produced continuously throughout spring and summer. Its variety *A. l. Leichtlinii* has white flowers with a crimson eye. Both grow without trouble in warm, sandy soil, and are easily propagated from cuttings.

A. sarmentosa. Foliage in silky, silver, rosetta-like tufts when young, turning later to pale green. Verbena heads of pale pink. A plant very prolific with its run-

ners, soon forming large mats. *A. s. Chumbyi* is a smaller, neater, silkier and brighter-flowered variety; 4 in. Himalayas.

Propagate by runners or division. Any light soil in sun.

A. sempervivioides. After the manner of *A. sarmentosa* except that the fleshy pale green leaves are smooth but for a single fringe of reddish hair. Flowers pink.

Propagate by runners or division. 4 in. N.W. Himalayas.

ANEMONE (a-ne-mon-e. Ranunculaceæ). Windflower. Hardy tuberous-rooted or herbaceous perennials. Height from 1-2 ft. Anemones like soil that is deep and rich, with plenty of well-decayed manure, so that it holds moisture. A sunny or partially shaded position will do.

Propagate tuberous-rooted anemones by seeds sown in prepared beds in January or in July. The best varieties should be taken up annually and offsets removed for propagation, but others are usually left undisturbed.

BEST TUBEROUS VARIETIES.

A. coronaria (poppy anemone), spring flowering, various colours.

A. hortensis fulgens (scarlet windflower), spring. (Best for naturalising).

(The St. Brigid, Empress, Aldenborough, and other commercial varieties are mostly selected or crossed varieties of these two).

A. nemerosa robinsoniana, a good subject for the rock garden; sky blue.

A. blanda, blue, winter flowering.

A. palmata, yellow, likes peaty soil. 6 in., May.

HERBACEOUS VARIETIES.

A. alpina, 6 in., white.

A. pulsatilla, purple, spring. This is the Pasque flower that is so common in S.E. England.

A. sylvestris, the snowdrop-flowered anemone. This dislikes cold soils.

A. hepatica, spring, flowering various colours.

A. japonica, September-flowering perennial 2 ft. in height, very useful for mixed borders. In addition to the white form, rose shades are now offered in catalogues.

EXHIBITION HINTS.

The stem of a single anemone should be erect and elastic and not less than 9 in. high. The cup should be broad and shallow. Colours clear and distinct. Petals should be large and well rounded. If the flower is double, the petals should graduate in size so that the open flower resembles a hemisphere. Double flowers should not show more than one colour.

To make up an ideal bed for cultivation of these flowers dig out 1½ ft. of soil. Put in a 6 in. layer of cow dung. Then refill the bed with good fresh loam.

On this can be sown the seed, which must first be separated carefully so that it is evenly distributed. Generally the plants will flower the same season, but only the best kinds should be retained for the following year. Never let the plants lack moisture, but do not let water become

ST BRIGID ANEMONE

The brilliant colours of St. Brigid Anemone are welcome in spring. They are best raised from seeds sown where they are to bloom.

stagnant in the soil or the leaves will become distorted and swollen.

When planting, put the tubers two or three inches deep in soil similar to that of the seed bed described above, i.e., soil containing good loam and rotted cow dung, with a quantity of sand.

Anemones will not respond to much forcing, but they may be potted in September and grown in a cold frame or pit until spring, when they may be removed to the greenhouse. In this way excellent pot blooms may be obtained.

ANEMONOPSIS (an-e-mo-nop-sis. Ranunculaceæ). Yerba Mansa. One species of this genus is worth growing, *A. macrophylla*, a hardy herbaceous perennial that resembles *Anemone japonica*. It bears lilac-blue flowers with twelve petals,

ANEMONE NEMOROSA ALLENII.

The dainty woodland Anemone thrives best in the shade of trees or shrubs.

in July, 3 ft. Very easily cultivated; it likes a sandy soil that is not too dry, in a partially shaded position.

Propagate by seeds or by division of the roots. The latter operation should be done to the individual plant every four or five years in March or November which are the seasons for planting.

ANGELICA (an-jel-i-ka. Umbelliferæ). The name refers to its mythical angelic virtues in medicine. A small genus of short-lived hardy biennial or perennial herbs that are only suited to the wild or herb garden. *A. officinalis* (syn. *Archangelica*) is the angelica of which the stalks are cut in May for candying. Formerly blanched and eaten like celery.

Propagate by seeds or by division of the stools and grown in any common soil.

ANGELICA-TREE. *See* ARALIA CHINENSIS.

ANGELONIA (an-gel-o-nia. Scrophularineæ). Pretty herbaceous perennials some of which require to be grown in a dry stove while others do well in a greenhouse or in a frame.

Propagate by seed sown in heat in February, resulting in flowering plants the same year. Also by cuttings of shoots taken when 3 in. long and inserted in sandy soil under a bell-glass; must not be kept too damp.

Two parts of loam to 1 of leaf-mould with some sand will make the best soil. Summer temperature, 60°-70°; winter, 55°-60°.

SPECIES.

A. angustifolia, greenhouse, dark violet flowers in June and July, 12 in.

A. conigera, stove, purple, August, 12 in.

A. floribunda, stove, numerous purple flowers in August, 12 in.

A. Gardneri, greenhouse, purple, white, May, 12 in.

A. grandiflora, greenhouse, purple, July to September.

A. miniata, greenhouse, purple, white, May.

ANGIOPTERIS (an-gi-op-ter-is. Filices). Strong-growing stove ferns which need plenty of room for their perfect development.

Propagate by spores or the plants may be imported. Moist stove temperature with plenty of water all the year is necessary. Use fibrous loam with peat and sand in thoroughly well-drained pots or tubs.

A. evecta throws up large fronds that are often as thick as giant Rhubarb. There are several varieties with slight differences in formation, 6–15 ft.

ANGRÆCUM (angr'-æcum. Orchidaceæ). From *Angrik*, a Malayan name for air plants. Stove epiphytal orchids. Tropical Africa, 1815.

Culture.—Compost: *See* AERIDES. Position suspended baskets or pots. Shade is

a very important factor in the successful growing of this genus. Winter temperature, 60°; summer, 75°.

Propagation.—By division of plants early spring.

SPECIES.

A. citratum, lemon yellow; *A. eburneum*, white; *A. Ellisii*, white; *A. Scottianum*, white.

ANGULOA (angulo'-a. Orchidaceæ). The Cradle Orchid. Greenhouse orchid. Flower fragrant. Columbia, 1842. The flowers are more showy than beautiful in this genus.

Culture.—Compost: equal parts fibre and sphagnum moss. Repot when making new growth, and give shade. If given plenty of water during growing season it grows vigorously and flowers freely. Winter temperature, 50°; summer, 65°.

Propagation.—By division of pseudobulbs when repotting.

SPECIES.

A. Clowesii, yellow; *A. Ruckerii*, yellow and crimson; *A. uniflora*, cream.

ANHALONIUM (an-ha-lo-ni-um. Cacteæ). *An*, without; *helos*, spike. Dwarf or tufted spineless succulents, rather like a globe artichoke, frequently confounded with the genus Mamillaria, from which they differ in having triangular sub-leafy tubercules. They require warm greenhouse treatment and to be kept very dry in winter. Increase by seeds or by offsets in the case of the tufted species. Grow in fibrous loam with plenty of sand and containing soft red brick very finely broken up.

SPECIES.

A. Engelmanni (syn. *fissuratum*), rather small flowers.

A. prismaticum (prism-shaped).

ANIGOZANTHOS (an-ig-o-san-thos. Hæmodoraceæ). *Anoigo*, to expand; *anthos*, a flower, referring to the branching expansion of the flower stalks. Greenhouse tufted herbaceous plants resembling sedge. Should be grown in a greenhouse that is just warm enough to exclude frost in a position where they will obtain plenty of light. The various coloured flowers are raised well above the tufts of leaves and are both curious and showy.

Propagate by division of the clumps when repotting in early spring. Use soil consisting of 2 parts of peat to 1 of loam, opened with sharp sand.

SPECIES.

A. bicolor presents a pleasing combination of scarlet and green flowers in May, 3 ft.

A. flavidus (syn. *coccinea, grandiflora*) greenish-yellow flowers in May, 3 in.

A. pulcherrima, beautiful yellow and white flowers in May, 2½ ft.

A. rufa, purplish-brown flowers in June, 2 in.

ANISE. *See* PIMPINELLA.

ANNATTO. *See* BIXA.

ANNUAL. Is the term applied to a plant which is raised from seed, flowers and dies the same year.

ANŒCTOCHILUS (an-ec-to-chi-lus. Orchidaceæ). *Anoikios*, open; *cheilos*, lip referring to the spreading apex of the lip.

These are greatly valued on account of their beautiful foliage, which is perhaps the most ornamental in the world. The background of the leaves is either olive or dark velvety-green, and they appear to be inlaid with the finest gold tracery which, if examined in the sun under a microscope, seems to be made of the richest rubies.

They are terrestrial orchids of creeping habit that require to be grown in the moist stove under bell-glass or cases. Increase by division of the fleshy rhizomes, keeping a bud, and, if present, a few roots to each piece. Keep close until fresh roots have formed. Soil should be composed of fibrous peat, chopped sphagnum, finely-broken soft red brick and sand. They are frequently grown in large pans that are kept covered and slightly tilted to encourage the circulation of air and prevent damping.

SPECIES.

In Ceylon these plants are so much admired as to be called by the Cingalese "The King of the Woods." The flowers should be taken off as soon as they are seen, as this helps the foliage to develop.

A. argyroneurus, olive background, silvery veins, 6 in.

A. Heriotii, mahogany, veined gold.

A. dawsonia, white.

A. discolor: A. setaceus, one of the most handsome and most cultivated. Velvety-green with gold veins (syn. *regalis*), has several varieties: *albo-marginatus*, edged white; *cordatus*, blotched gold; *inornatus*, velvety-green. There are many species and varieties, but they are rarely cultivated, as they require special conditions that are not always available.

ANONA (ano'-na. Anonaceæ). Custard Apple. Stove evergreen shrubs, leaves fragrant. Fruit of *reticulata* edible. Tropical America, 1690.

Culture.—2 parts loam, 1 part leaf-mould or peat, and sharp sand. Repot spring, sunny position, water freely, and syringe daily during summer months. Winter temperature 60°; summer 80°.

Propagation.—By cuttings of well-ripened shoots in sand, place in propagator. Temperature 60° summer.

SPECIES.

A. cherimolia, brown; *A. muricata*, yellow; *A. reticulata* (Custard Apple), yellow and brown; *A. squamosa*, white.

ANOPTERUS (an-op'-ter-us. Saxifrageæ). Tasmania. A superb evergreen shrub with shiny laurel-like leaves, and white waxy flowers as big as snowdrops, in April and May. A peaty soil and sheltered spot are advisable. Not quite hardy. Handsome as pot plants for cold house. Increased by cuttings of half-ripened wood in sandy, peaty soil.

A. glandulosus, a very fine thing indeed.

ANTENNARIA (an-ten-a-ria. Compositæ). Cat's Ear. A rock plant growing 2 ft. in height with white chaffy flowers and silvery leaves. Will grow in ordinary soil in a sunny position or rockeries. *Propagate* by division of roots in March.

SPECIES.

A. tomentosa.

A. margaritacea, a N. American plant.

The Mountain Cat's Ear is used as a carpet bedding plant. The white flowers of this plant can be dyed and preserved in a dry state for winter decoration.

ANTHEMIS (an-thē-mis. Compositæ). Rock Chamomile. Hardy perennials used for borders; 1–2 ft. high with white flowers in July. Will grow in ordinary soil. Sunny position in borders for tall kinds and rockeries for dwarf kinds.

Propagation by seeds sown outdoors in April, or by division of roots in March.

SPECIES.

A. tinctoria, from which a dye for the hairdresser is obtained.

A. Kitaibeli. Excellent for cutting.

A. aujoor, dwarf rock plant, 2–4 in. high.

A. nobilis, the common chamomile, has white flowers and is easily propagated by division in spring.

The last variety is the one of which the flowers have long been used for the making of Chamomile Tea.

ANTHER.—The tiny round "knob"

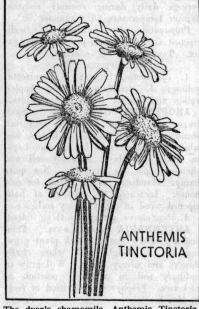

The dyer's chamomile, Anthemis Tinctoria, with bright yellow flowers, thrives in any soil.

containing pollen seen at the tops of the stamens.

ANTHERICUM (an-ther-i-cum. Liliaceæ). Hardy herbaceous perennials. Height 2 ft. Flowers white, summer. These require deep, rich, sandy soil, well drained. Increase by division of roots after flowering, or by seed sown in light soil in the cold frame in September or March.

VARIETIES.

A. liliago, or St. Bernard's Lily, and *A. liliago major*, a superior form, both

flowering in July and August. These flowers are specially valuable for cultivation in a partially shaded border.

ANTHOLYZA (an-tho-ly-za. Iridaceæ). African Corn Flag. Hardy bulbous-rooted perennial, which grows 2 ft. high. It has scarlet and yellow spikes of flowers in late spring. It will grow in almost any soil but is not quite hardy.

Propagate by dividing the corms in spring or autumn and plant about 5 in. deep and 6 in. apart.

The most commonly grown species is the *A. coccinea*, a plant somewhat resembling Montbretia.

ANTHOXANTHUM (an-thox-anthum. Gramineæ). A genus of grasses from the temperate zones. One species, *A. odoratum* (Sweet Vernal Grass), a hardy perennial, is a native of Britain and contains coumarin, the active principle in the sweet smell associated with newly-mown hay.

It is of no garden value but is used for pasture.

Propagated by seeds or division of the tufts and grown in any soil.

ANTHRISCUS (an-thris-kus. Umbelliferæ). Chervil, Sweet Cicely. Coarse growing biennial or perennial herbs that are of little garden value but are used for salads or for flavouring soups. To maintain a continuous supply, seed should be sown at intervals throughout the spring and summer. Either broadcast the seeds or sow in drills 10 in. apart, and $\frac{1}{2}$ in. deep. Thin out the seedlings to 6 in. apart when large enough to handle. They may be sown in winter in boxes under glass. Chervil may be grown in any soil, but the edible varieties are more tender when the plants are quickly raised, and for this reason they should be grown in light, well-drained, rich soil in a cool position.

SPECIES.

A. cerefoliata, curly-leaved Chervil.

A. aromaticum, Sweet Cicely.

A. bulbosum, parsnip-rooted Chervil.

ANTHURIUM (anthu'-rium. Aroideæ). Flamingo plant. Stove perennial. Ornamental foliage and flowering plants. S. America, 1828.

Culture.—Compost: equal parts loam, peat, and sphagnum moss. Well-drained

pots, shady position. Repot early spring.
Water freely during flowering period, i.e.,
March to August, moderately afterwards.
Winter temperature, 60°; summer, 75°.

Propagation.—By division of roots,
March; or by seed sown in light mixture
of sand, peat and charcoal dust. Place
pans in propagator. Temperature 75° to
80°. Early spring.

SPECIES.

A. Andreanum, scarlet and white; *A.
scherzercanum*, scarlet. Foliage only; *A.
magnificum*, green and white; *A. Veitchii*,
green. There are also numerous hybrid
varieties included in good trade lists.

ANTHYLLIS (an-thil'-lis. Leguminosæ). *Anthos*, a flower; *ioulos*, downy.
Kidney Vetch. Evergreen and deciduous
flowering shrub from South Europe to
Turkey, with yellow pea-shaped flowers,
in June and July. Rather tender.

Culture.—Warm, well-drained soil in
very sunny position.

Propagation by seeds and cuttings.

A. Barba-Jovis, Jupiter's Beard, Silver
Bush, 8–12 ft. A charming wall shrub
with its silvery grey leaves and yellow
flowers.

A. hermanniæ, 1½–2 ft. A much-
branched triggy bush of greyish aspect
flowering freely in June and July.
Flowers yellow. Suitable for sunny place
in rock garden.

A. montana. Largest heads of clustered
pea flowers; prostrate or grey foliage.
Washy pink. Southern Alps. The variety
m. rubra has deep red flowers and is
altogether superior to the type. Cuttings;
seeds.

A. vulneraria. Ladies' Fingers. A
native of Britain and locally common,
especially on chalk. Crowded heads of
sessile, bright yellow flowers. There is a
red variety, *A. v. rubriflora*, which is
found on the Cornish cliffs.

ANTIGONON (an-tig-on-on. Polygonaceæ). Lovely herbaceous stove climbers
from Central America. In their native
state they find support by clinging with
their twisted leaf stalks. Their flowers,
small at first, mature into showy conspicuous blooms comparable to Bougain-
villeas. Under cultivation they have been
difficult to flower and have been tried in
stoves, greenhouses and in the open. A

dry stove is now thought to be the best
means of inducing them to flower early.

Their roots should be restricted in a
narrow well-drained border and they
should be trained under glass, at the same
time giving all the air and light possible
to make them attain a good height.

Propagate by imported seeds or by
cuttings of half-ripened wood inserted in
sandy soil under a hand-light in April.
Light, well-drained, fibrous loam suits
them. Summer temperature, 60°–85°;
winter, 50°.

SPECIES.

A. amabile, rosy.

A. insigne, rose-pink.

A. leptopus, the best known; crimson
flowers from August to October.

ANTIRRHINUM (an-tir-i-num.
Scrophulariaceæ). All the antirrhinums
of the majus, maximum or nanum types,
although, strictly speaking, hardy perennials, are usually treated as half-hardy
annuals or biennials, the seed being sown
in autumn or spring. For most of the
modern kinds, spring. i.e., March, sowing
is best. Where it is desirable to increase
the stock of any particular plant, cuttings
are the only safe way as seeds will give
plants of variable characters, and cuttings
root readily if taken in August to September and put into sandy soil in a cold frame.

Antirrhinums (as pot plants). These
handsome perennial plants are usually
treated as annuals when used for pot
cultivation. There are four types in cultivation: (1) the tall or majus; (2) a robust
intermediate type known as Majestic, a
branch of the *nanum grandiflorum;* (3)
the true intermediate or *nanum grandiflorum*, and (4) the dwarf or Tom Thumb.
For pot plants either the Majestic or the
true *nanum grandiflorum* varieties are
usually used, unless particularly long disbudded spikes are required.

Cultivation.—Seeds should be sown in
the frame or cool greenhouse in July or
August and the plants pricked out, when
large enough, into boxes containing an
open compost of loam, leaf-mould and
sand. A similar compost may be used for
potting young plants into 60-size pots
when hey are about 2 in. high. When
large enough and well rooted they may
be potted in into 48- or 32-size pots using

good fibrous loam, old rotted manure which has passed through a ¼ in. sieve, leaf-mould, a little fertiliser and mortar rubble. The whole compost should pass freely through a ¾ in. sieve.

VARIETIES.
(Greenhouse.)

Majestic Sunset, Majestic Twilight, Majestic Orange King, Victory, Flame, Golden Monarch, His Excellency, Mauve Queen, Madonna, Empress, Nelrose Pink, Appleby Matthews.

Soil.—Antirrhinums prefer a well-drained loamy soil, and a dressing of garden lime—2 oz. per sq. yd.—applied in spring when preparing the land for planting, will be a great help in warding off "stem rot," a disease which attacks the plants at the ground level, in most soils which are rich in organic matter and deficient in lime.

The following is a list of the most out-standing of modern antirrhinums in their respective sections.

A. majus. The majus section is the most common of the older forms. Plants grow 2–2½ ft. in height and are very free flowering. Peachblow, Prince of Orange, and Vermilion Brilliant are well-known representatives.

A. maximum majus. This is a greatly improved *majus.* The plants grow to 3½–4 ft., the flowers are large, finely formed, and carried on immense spikes, making a most notable addition to the list of tall plants suitable for large beds or borders. Some of the chief varieties, all of remarkable vigour and purity of colour, are: the Cardinal (scarlet), Crimson Monarch, Golden Spire, Her Majesty (pure white), Rosy Emblem (rich rose), and Pink Princess (soft pink).

A. nanum grandiflorum. To this section regard must be given as it is the most important and the most popular. The plants grow to a convenient bedding height, 1¼–1½ ft., are much branched and very free flowering. If sown in gentle heat in February or March, transplanted in due course, and bedded out in April, will flower from June to November if the old stems are cut out as soon as the flowers have faded. There is a host of varieties, among the best of which are: Amber Queen, Carmine Queen, Defiance (scarlet),

Gloria (rose-pink), Golden Emblem, Majestic Orange, Red Chief, Peerless (pink), Pink Perfection (salmon-pink).

A. nanum, or Tom Thumb varieties, are remarkable for their dwarf habit, about 9 in., and are useful for edgings, or for very small beds. Album, Firefly and Wild Rose are good representatives of the type.

Antirrhinum Rock Hybrids are forms of the Tom Thumb section, grow to a height of 6–9 in. in compact bushes, very free flowering, and the flower spikes grow to a uniform height, giving a flat effect. They bloom about a fortnight earlier than the general antirrhinums and the best place for them seems to be on exposed rockeries. So far the range of colours is limited to rose-pink, white and purple.

Those suitable for the rock-garden are:

A. asarina. Trailing fleshy stems and leaves. In the axils of the leaves sit large pale lemon-yellow snapdragons. A dry, sunny situation with a poor soil is needed, for faring too well the leaves and stems develop unduly at the expense of the flowers. It makes a good wall plant. Italy. Cuttings in sandy soil or seed.

A. glutinosum. A neat little plant with pale yellow flowers and very sticky leaves. Spain. 6 in. Seeds and cuttings.

A. hispanicum roseum. A delightful miniature pink snapdragon from Spain. The flowers are a pretty rose pink. Cuttings or seeds. The latter do not always come true.

ANTS. These interesting and well-known insects need no description, for they are familiar to all. The three commonest are the Garden Ant (*Lasius niger*), the Yellow Ant (*Lasius flavus*), and the Red Ant (*Myrmica rubra*). Although these insects are of no great direct importance, they often cause annoyance and indirectly much damage by tunnelling into lawns and flower borders, loosening the soil and throwing up "casts." By working around the roots, they have been known to expose potatoes to the air. They may be found swarming up roses and plants attacked by greenfly. These they tend, feeding upon the honey dew excreted by the greenfly. On rare occasions they will eat away the developing buds of roses and peonies.

METHODS OF CONTROL.—If the greenfly

are kept down the ants will cease to crawl up roses; and if really bad in lawns, on paths, or in flower beds, an ounce of carbon bisulphide poured into the nest will eradicate them. Care must be taken when applying carbon bisuphide to flower beds. If the liquid actually touches the roots of plants it will cause damage, but in moderation the fumes appear to be harmless to plant life. In houses, powdered alum sprinkled around their haunts will drive them away. Powdered naphthalene also acts as a repellant.

AOTUS (a-ō-tus. Leguminosæ). Graceful, slender evergreen shrub of dwarf habit, bearing a profusion of yellow, blotched crimson pea-shaped flowers the whole length of its arched growth. 1790.

Culture.—Compost, equal parts sandy loam and peat, with a little charcoal. Repot early spring, well-drained pots, sunny position. Prune after flowering. Winter temperature, 45°; summer, 60°.

Propagation.—By cuttings of half-ripened shoots in light sandy soil, placed in propagator, temperature 60°. April.

PRINCIPAL SPECIES.

Gracillima, yellow and crimson.

APHANANTHE (af-an-an'-thē. Urticaceæ). A deciduous tree 60–70 ft. Japan. Only species *A. aspera*. Of no flower beauty, or value for gardens.

APHELANDRA (aphelan'-dra. Acanthaceæ). Stove evergreen shrubs. The flowers are surrounded by beautiful bracts. W. Indies, 1733.

Culture.—Compost (*see* ABELIA). Repot early spring. Prune shoots back in February to within 1 in. of base. Require moist atmosphere. Winter temperature, 60°; summer, 75°–80°.

Propagation.—By cutting of side shoots, April; insert in sandy peat with strong bottom heat.

SPECIES.

A. aurantiaca, flame; *A. aurantiaca Roezlii*, scarlet, twisted leaves; *A. Chamissoniana*, yellow; *A. Margaritæ*, orange, leaves green and rose; *A. squarrosa*, yellow and orange.

APHIDES. A few of the commonest aphis pests are dealt with elsewhere, but it will be as well to give a general life-history of those insects often termed "greenfly" and "blight." In nearly all cases, the winter is passed in the egg stage, these being placed upon twigs, branches and even trunks of trees. As soon as the buds begin to swell in the spring, these eggs hatch out and the little larvæ crawl up, waiting for the foliage to appear. As soon as this does so, they begin to suck the sap, at the same time growing rapidly. After three moults they develop wing buds and correspond to the pupal stage of the butterfly, only they are still active. After a short period the skin is again cast and a wingless, viviparous female appears. This first adult is often termed the "stem mother." She gives rise asexually to yet more young which in turn rapidly grow, giving rise to still more viviparous females. We find this going on for three generations, by which time the foliage is smothered. About the end of May or beginning of June, winged, viviparous females appear, which float off rather than fly to a second host plant which may be of quite another kind. After three or four generations are produced on this secondary host plant, they will return in the autumn to the original type of host. Oviparous females and males are now produced. The females, after fertilisation, lay eggs which remain upon the tree throughout the winter.

Besides the smothering of the young shoots and foliage and weakening of the plant generally by the incessant loss of sap sucked out of the plant by the aphides, we find indirect damage being done to the plant on which aphides abound by the constant evacuation of the digested sap. This falls on to the foliage in the form of a colourless, sticky and sweet liquid termed "honey dew." This honey dew itself chokes up the breathing pores of the plant and at the same time forms a medium on which certain fungi thrive. Again, owing to its sticky nature, particles of dust and dirt will adhere to the foliage, making them not only unsightly but weakly.

APHIS. *See* MEALY PLUM APHIS, LEAF-CURLING PLUM APHIS, AMERICAN BLIGHT.

APHYLLANTHES (ă-phill-an-thēs. Liliaceæ). *Aphyllos*, leafless; *anthos*, a flower. The delicate blue flowers are produced on rush-like stems, the plant appearing to be leafless. An interesting monotype occurring locally in North

Africa, Spain, and on the Riviera. A hot, sunny situation in deep light soil is what it requires in our cold climate. Once planted it should be left alone as it dislikes disturbance.

Propagate from seeds or, if you must, division.

APIOS (a-pi-os. Leguminosæ). Ground Nut. Of this genus of four twining perennials, only one is known.

A. tuberosa, a hardy tuberous-rooted plant, that is a native of Canada and the United States. It bears pretty purplish pea-shaped flowers and likes to climb over a trellis or shrub.

Propagate by root division and plant in a warm moist soil in a sunny position in spring. Mulch in winter.

APIUM. *See* CELERY.

APLOPAPPUS (Compositæ). Evergreen shrub 3–5 ft., from California, with dark green heath-like foliage and yellow flowers in August and September.

Culture.—Plant in sandy loam. West wall very suitable position. Hardy except in cold districts.

Propagate by seeds or cuttings in frame in July.

A. ericoides the only species.

APONOGETON (ap-o-no-ge-ton. Naiadaceæ). Cape Pond Flower. *Apon*, Celtic for water; *geiton*, neighbour, referring to natural habitat.

Beautiful hardy, stove and greenhouse aquatics that will all thrive in the stove. The tender species do well in small tanks under glass with a winter temperature of 60°–65°, rising in summer to 75°. The hardy species should be grown in ponds or small tanks in the open air. Increased by seeds or division. The hardy species increase so rapidly that division is necessary to prevent overcrowding.

SPECIES.

A. angustifolium, white flowers in July. A desirable greenhouse plant.

A. distachyon. The Cape Pond Weed or Water Hawthorn that beautifies so many ponds, lakes and rivers during the summer. The flowers are white and scented like Hawthorns. It must be kept in check near Water-lilies. Its several varieties include *roseum*, with rosy-pink flowers, and *Legrangei*, pink and white flowers.

APPLE (*Pyrus Malus*). The countless numbers of different varieties of apples now in general cultivation in all parts of the world, have been derived from the common crab, *Pyrus Malus*. This species is a native of Western Europe and North-West Asia, and is frequently to be seen in the hedgerows of this country. The production of varieties is the result of constant selection which dates back from the time of the Romans. Many of the older varieties were chance seedlings, whilst the novelties of the last generation are in many cases the results of definite crosses.

Apples are generally grown as trained specimens in one of the following forms: Cordon, Espalier, Bush, Half-standard and Standard.

Culture and Soil.—Apples are grown in every type of soil in this country. The ideal soil is a light, well-drained loam. Good drainage is an essential, and on the heaviest clays, pipe draining is almost always essential to produce the best results. The roots of apples penetrate to a greater depth than is generally anticipated, and waterlogged conditions in the subsoil frequently lead to canker, a disease which does a great deal of damage and which is difficult to eradicate. A similar state of affairs frequently results in chalky subsoils. One of the finest orchards in this country is on heavy clay in Sussex, where the plantation is drained throughout. On the other hand, thousands of acres in Essex are laid down to fruit where the soil is light with a gravel subsoil. Heavy soils tend to produce fruit with little colour but with excellent flavour and keeping qualities. Light soils produce highly-coloured fruit which matures early.

Aspect.—A southern aspect used always to be considered ideal. It has now been demonstrated that a northern slope is to be preferred. Damage to blossoms at flowering-time by frost is due not so much to the freezing, but to the thaw which follows. A rapid thaw ruptures the cells in the blossoms, whilst with a slow thaw the damage is not so great. The brilliant sunshine which so often follows frost therefore does less damage on a northern slope where its rays do not strike so directly. Altitude is a matter of importance. A high position which is not bleak and exposed is best, partly because of drainage and partly because frosts are less severe. Low-lying frost-holes must always be guarded against, and are more numerous than is generally thought.

Distances Apart.—Cordons, on walls, 2 ft. apart; in rows (rows 6 ft. apart), 2 ft. apart.

Bushes, 10–12 ft. apart.

Half-standards, 18 ft. apart.

Standards, 24 ft. apart.

Espaliers, 14 ft. apart.

Planting.—Planting may be carried out at any time between October and the beginning of March. There should be no frost, and the soil should preferably be dry and in a fit state for knocking down to a fine tilth. Holes should be taken out slightly larger than the full span of the roots, and sufficiently deep so that the union between stock and scion where the graft has been made on the tree can just be buried. Any damaged roots should be cut with a sharp knife. The tree should be planted very firmly. After it has been placed in position the soil should be filled layer by layer, each succeeding shovelful receiving a good treading. Insecure planting causes more deaths than is supposed. Where standards and half-standards are being planted, it is better to drive in the stakes in their proper places before planting. Damage to roots is thus obviated.

Pruning.—Pruning is a vast subject, and can occupy a whole volume. Essential details can therefore only be mentioned. It is better not to prune a young tree at all during the first season after planting. The first autumn after planting pruning should be done with a view to building up the foundation of a strong tree.

It should always be borne in mind that the harder pruning is done, the stronger will be the resultant growth. In the cases of bushes, half-standards and standards, each leading shoot should be cut back by about half its length, making the cut to be a bud facing outwards. In subsequent seasons the leading shoot should always be pruned to an outside bud. Cut back hard if the tree is making little growth, but only lightly, say about 6 in., if the

growth is strong. (A leading shoot, or leader, is represented by the youngest end of each branch, and consists of wood made during the previous growing-season only). Leaders must not be confused with other young growths. If there are twelve branches on a tree, there can only be twelve leaders, which are represented by the tips of each branch. All young growths growing from lower down on the main branches are referred to as lateral growths, or laterals. These laterals must not be permitted to grow into small branches. If they are, the centre of the tree will be thickened with weakly growths, which will not produce fruit. Laterals must be turned into fruit spurs set close on to the main branch from which they emanate. The procedure is as follows: Prune the lateral back to approximately within 1 in. of the old wood from which it has sprung. About four or five buds now remain on this lateral. The following spring, the topmost one or two will break into growth, but one of the basal ones is almost certain to commence turning into a fruit bud. If, when next pruning-time comes along, the bud has turned into a fruit bud, cut away everything above it. (A fruit bud is readily recognisable in that it is plump, and stands out square from its twig rather than lying flat.) If the fruit bud has not yet appeared, a further season must be given to its development, and this is done by cutting back the sub-laterals, which were produced from the tip of the original pruned lateral, to 1 in. As soon as the fruit bud appears, cut away all wood above it. It may here be mentioned that some varieties respond easily to this shortening of laterals, or "spur pruning," as it is called. They are: *Charles Ross, Cox's Orange, Ellison's Orange, James Grieve, King of the Pippins, Rival, Laxton's Superb, Emneth Early, Grenadier, Lane's Prince Albert, Lord Derby* and *Stirling Castle.* Others do not respond so readily. If difficulty is experienced in making them produce fruit buds, they must be pruned a trifle more lightly, the original laterals to about six buds, and the sub-laterals the year following about the same. The following are likely offenders: *Allington Pippin, Beauty of Bath, Lady Sudeley,*

Mr. Gladstone, Worcester Pearmain, Bismarck and *Newton Wonder.*

Such is the treatment for all young wood on apples. The exception is supplied only in cordons and espaliers, where it is wisest to leave the leaders unpruned. The subsequent treatment consists of cutting out all dead and diseased wood and also all weakly branches, or those which tend to cross in bush trees and standards. Always tend to keep the centre well open and fully exposed to sun and air, even if it means

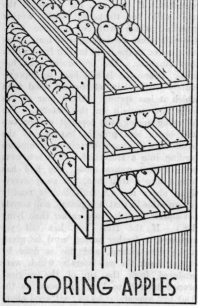

STORING APPLES

Cool, airy conditions are necessary to keep Apples in a sound condition.

the removal of an entire branch to serve this end. Pruning operations should be carried out between November and the middle of March, but not during frosty weather.

Pests.—Trees should be looked over at regular intervals for pests and diseases. At least two sprayings should be given regularly every year. Tar distillate or D.N.C. washes applied in Jan. or Feb. kill most eggs which would otherwise hatch into greenfly and caterpillars. Lime sulphur applied immediately before flowering, when the buds are showing pink,

should eradicate Apple Scab, one of the worst diseases known to apple growers. For further information *see* APPLE AND PEAR SCAB and CAPSID BUG.

VARIETIES—DESSERT.

The best ten for general purposes:

Beauty of Bath—August.
Lady Sudeley—August-September.
James Grieve—September
Worcester Pearmain—September.
Ellison's Orange—October.
Charles Ross—October-November.
Allington Pippin—November-December.
Rival—December.
Cox's Orange Pippin—December.
Laxton's Superb—January-February.

Old favourites such as *Blenheim Orange* and *Ribston Pippin* are not recommended as they take so long to come into bearing. Of the above, *Beauty of Bath* and *Allington Pippin* should be pruned more lightly than the rest.

CULINARY.

Early Victoria—July-August.
Grenadier—September.
Stirling Castle—October.
Rev. Wilks—October.
Warner's King—October-November.
Lord Derby—November.
Monarch—November-December.
Annie Elizabeth—November-December.
Lane's Prince Albert—November-March.
Edward VII—January-April.

APPLE APHIDES. Two species of aphides, commonly found upon apples, are the apple corn aphis (*Rhopalosiphum prunifolæ*) and the permanent green apple aphis (*Aphis pomi*, De Geer).

The apple corn aphides are delicate green with medium and lateral dark green lines. The cornicles are brown in colour. The black eggs are laid singly in crevices of the bark and at the base of buds : these hatch out early, the young living under the developing leaves. They then invade the blossom trusses on which they feed by sucking the sap, often causing considerable damage. Just when the fruit forms they fly away to grasses and corn and there breed for the rest of the summer, returning to the apples in the autumn. They may also be found on pear, quince and hawthorn. The eggs of the permanent apple aphis are also black in colour, but laid in dense masses on the shoots. In the spring these hatch out, and the young collect in masses on the tips of shoots and under the top leaves, but do not appear to touch the trusses, nor do they cause the leaves to curl In May, when they become winged, they migrate from tree to tree, but always remain on apple, if that was the tree the eggs were laid on. At the same time, they have been known to breed upon pear, quince and hawthorn, but they appear not to migrate from these to apple nor *vice versa*.

METHODS OF CONTROL.—The best control measures are spraying with a tar distillate wash in winter, or with a nicotine

ters in the spring, and as soon as the blossom trusses begin to show colour, they bite a small hole in the buds and therein place their eggs. Should the weather be warm and the buds develop and open rapidly the weevils will have time to lay only a small number of eggs. If, on the other hand, a cold spell sets in and the development of the buds is retarded, they have time to lay their full complement of eggs, in which case a bad attack of "capped" blossom will follow. On hatching out, the young larvæ feed in the interior of the buds, causing the petals to wilt and wither. These become stiff,

RETURN MIGRATION — SEPTEMBER

MAY-JUNE OUTWARD

APPLE

CORN OR GRASSES

LIFE HISTORY OF APPLE CORN APHIDES

The apple aphis or fly spends part of its life on corn or grasses and the remainder on the foliage of apple trees.

or derris preparation in the spring, before the foliage has had time to develop, and form a protection.

APPLE BLOSSOM WEEVIL (*Anthonomus pomorum*). The adult weevil is about ¼ in. in length, black in colour and, when freshly hatched, dusted with minute white scales. A transverse band of these scales crosses the wing cases, forming a white V-shaped mark. Like all weevils, the head is drawn out into a long proboscis. The larva is a yellowish-white grub about ⅛ in. in length with a black head and tapers posteriorly. The pupa is yellowish, with dark eyes. As it matures it darkens considerably in colour. The females issue from their winter quar-

forming a "cap," within which the larvæ live for about a fortnight, when they change to pupæ. After a week in the pupal stage, the adults hatch and, eating their way out of the "capped" buds, live a free life for a short period upon the trees before going into hibernation. The winter is spent under pieces of loose bark, lichen, moss, and around the foot of the tree.

METHODS OF CONTROL.—The "trap" method is the only satisfactory one to control the Apple Blossom Weevil. Pieces of old sacking should be loosely tied round the trees, in order to provide a suitable place for hibernation. In the winter these must be carefully taken off, placed in a bucket, and burnt. As the weevils are easily dislodged, every care must be taken in carrying out this operation.

APPLE BLOSSOM WILT (*Sclerotinia cinerea*). Cox's Orange Pippins, James Grieve, Lord Derby, Allington Pippin, Worcester Pearmain, Lane's Prince Albert, Bismarck, Newton Wonder and Beauty of Bath are apples very susceptible to the disease known as Apple Blossom Wilt. It reveals its presence in the spring by causing not only the blossom but also the foliage to wilt and die for some distance along the branches. It may then spread into the wood and by extending along the branch, cause the death of considerable areas. The spores gain an entrance in the first place through the blossoms which they kill. The mycelium then works down through the spur, so killing the whole branch.

METHODS OF CONTROL.—Very little can be done to prevent this disease, but it may be controlled by cutting away the dead wood in the spring, after the foliage has begun to wilt. If left till the winter it will be difficult to pick out the dead twigs and boughs, and some are sure to be left to set up a fresh infestation the following spring. All dead foliage should be cut well back into the healthy wood and then burnt.

APPLE BROWN ROT (*Monilia fructigena*). Fruit attacked one year usually remains on the tree in a withered and dried state till the following year, when it acts as a source of fresh infection. The spores are washed or blown off and these, settling upon the young fruit, will give rise to mycelium which soon causes the well-known brown patches surrounded by white pustules to appear. As these develop the flesh of the apple dries and finally only the skin with countless spores is left hanging on the tree. The disease not only affects fruit on the tree, but may also cause a loss after the fruit has been stored. Again, on soft-wooded trees the mycelium may work from the fruit down into the spur, making its presence known by the white pustules which form near the base of the bud.

METHODS OF CONTROL.—Collect and burn all mummified fruit both on the trees and on the ground. Again, watch for the first appearance of the disease amongst the fruit the following year and pick and destroy all apples showing any sign of fungus. Where it has worked its way into the spurs cut these out with a sharp knife, preferably in the summer, when it will be most conspicuous.

APPLE CANKER (*Nectria galligena*). Spores of apple canker gain access to the tree through small wounds in the bark. Here they develop, causing the bark to crack, usually in rings. As time goes on the wounds open out and the wood around becomes dead. If this should happen near the base of a branch the whole of the limb may die away. In the summer the fungus will be recognised by the greyish pustules forming on the cankered areas and in the winter by the reddish pustules which may be found during the dormant period on dead wood.

METHODS OF CONTROL.—As there is no doubt that the spores gain access through the wounds made by insects, and more especially by the woolly aphis, every effort must be made to keep these insects down. If trees have become so badly attacked that they cease to bear, they should be cut down and burnt. Where they are still bearing, however, much good may be done by cutting out the diseased areas and smearing the wound with pruning paint to prevent re-infestation. All dead wood beneath the trees should be collected and, with that already cut away, burnt. Too much stress cannot be laid on the need for burning all diseased wood.

APPLE AND PEAR SCAB. Though the same in appearance and controlled by similar methods, the scab of apple (*Venturia inæqualis*) is not the same species as scab of pears (*Venturia pirina*). Scab does damage in two direct ways: by causing blotching or scabbing of the fruit and by attacking the young wood. In both cases indirect damage may result by the entrance of other fungus spores into the diseased areas. For example, when scab appears on the wood an excellent "home" is formed for canker spores.

LIFE-HISTORY.—The disease first makes its appearance in the spring on the young leaves surrounding the blossom clutches. This gradually spreads until the attack is general. It may be known by the sooty areas on the foliage. As the fruit forms spores are spread and any alighting on the fruit germinate, the fungus attacking the skin. These spores fructify, giving rise to a fresh outbreak on other fruit. If the weather is suitable and a really bad attack occurs, the fruit will drop off. In the case of pears, however, the fruit may remain on the trees but cracking badly. The fungus may be recognised on the wood by rough blisters, caused by the formation of mycelium, but the appearance of the attack varies with the species of apple or pear. The fact that the fungus can remain in a dormant state on the wood, causes a fresh and early outbreak the next year. Another winter form may be found within the fallen leaves; these also give rise to a fresh attack the following year.

METHODS OF CONTROL.—All scabby fruit and as much of the fallen leaves as possible should be collected and destroyed by burning, also all diseased wood should be cut out during the winter and destroyed. By these methods scab can be controlled considerably. Spraying should also be resorted to, either Bordeaux or lime-sulphur being used, but the former, though a stronger fungicide, is liable to cause "russeting" of the fruit. The best times of application are firstly, when the trees are in the pink-bud stage and again soon after petal fall.

APPLE MAGGOT. See CODLING MOTH.

APPLE SAWFLY (*Hoplacampa testudinea*). DESCRIPTION. *Adult.*—A ¼ in. in length, black above, reddish-yellow beneath. *Larva.*—Head brown, abdomen white. May be distinguised by the number of legs, which are eighteen.

LIFE-HISTORY.—The adult sawflies may be seen flying about the blossom on any sunny day. The females lay their eggs within the blossoms, usually one to each flower. The young larvæ hatch out in from five to seven days, soon eating their way into the skin and then to the core of the apple which they hollow out. The interior becomes filled with coffee-coloured "frass" which drains out through the entrance hole. Massee has recently found that the larvæ leave the fruit at night and may then be found crawling about thereon. About dawn they will either re-enter the same apple or bore their way into a fresh one, so causing further damage. On becoming full-grown the larvæ leave the

apple, enter the soil and there spin a cocoon, within which they pass the winter, pupating the following spring. The perfect insect appears in May.

METHODS OF CONTROL.—The usual method of control is to spray with nicotine five to seven days after petal fall and before the young caterpillar has had time to enter the fruit. Massee's discovery, however, may lead to other methods, such as dusting with a powder of vegetable origin.

APPLE SUCKER (*Psylla mali*). The adult insect is about $\frac{1}{5}$ in. in length, green in colour when first hatched, but changing to yellow later. It resembles an aphis, but is more robust and has the power of hopping. The young immature stages (larva and nymph) are dark green, with red eyes and flattened bodies. The eggs of the apple sucker are orange in colour and elongate in form with a pointed process at one end by which the egg is fixed to the tree. The eggs are to be found in the winter months in leaf scars at the base of the buds, etc. As the buds begin to swell in the spring, the eggs hatch out and the little larvæ crawl up on to the buds. As soon as the buds have opened sufficiently, the larvæ push their way in. They then begin to suck the juices of the young leaves and so weaken their growth. After blossoming, the trusses often wither up on the tree. About the beginning of June, the apple suckers become mature and then skip from branch to branch, but easily take fright and disappear. In the early autumn the eggs are laid, and remain dormant on the tree throughout the winter.

METHODS OF CONTROL.—Apply tar oil winter washes during the dormant season. Spray with nicotine as the buds swell, and while the larvæ are waiting to enter. It is useless to spray after they have entered the buds.

APRICOT (*Prunus Armeniaca*). This small tree is a native of Armenia, Manchuria, and Northern China, in which countries it is supposed to have been cultivated for many hundreds of years B.C.

Soil.—The apricot prefers a soil which is on the light side, and in all cases the position must be well drained; heavy soils either being thoroughly lightened by adding mortar rubble, sand, wood-ash and turf parings, or, better still, dug out to a depth of two spits, and light loam replaced. In any case, on all soils the addition of lime in some form is recommended.

Position.—Out of doors the apricot likes a sunny situation and in the very warmest localities it succeeds as a standard. Such trees may be planted 20 ft. apart; but the most satisfactory method of culture is as a fan-trained specimen on a south wall. Here a thoroughly drained border at least 6 ft. wide must be prepared, the trees being planted 15 ft. apart.

Planting.—The middle to the end of October is the best time.

Pruning.—This is very similar to that recommended for peaches (*q.v.*); the only difference being that the apricot will form fruit spurs on older wood, whereas the peach does not. The finest fruit is. however, produced on one-year-old wood and it is better to disbud and prune, as suggested for the latter. Where deemed necessary, spurs may be formed on the older wood.

Root Pruning.—Apricots are liable to exhibit excessive vigour when young, and any such tendency should be checked by means of root pruning. If the tree has not been planted more than two years, it is safe to lift it, shorten strong roots and then replant. Older trees must be treated by taking out a semi-circular trench around the stem at a radius of 2 ft. or more according to age, cutting all roots with a sharp knife.

Watering and Feeding.—During the growing period the roots must never be allowed to dry out or failure will follow. During dry periods water thoroughly twice a week. If a heavy crop is set, give a mulch in June. Lime is very necessary, and light dressings of sulphate of potash and bonemeal may be given in alternate years during winter.

Propagation.—Some varieties, such as Moor Park, grow true from seed, and may be raised by budding during June or July on the Mussel or St. Julien plum stock.

Pests and Diseases.—The only troublesome pest likely to be a nuisance is Red Spider.

Forcing under Glass.—Apricots may be grown as bushes in pots or as fan-trained trees in a border under glass. They should

not be subjected to great heat until after the fruit is set. A mean temperature of 45° is ample. Allow plenty of ventilation as the fruit swells, and syringe frequently. Blossoms must be hand-pollinated, a rabbit's tail being useful for the purpose. Atmosphere should be dry during this operation.

VARIETIES.

Breda, hardy, and a good cropper; Moor Park, very hardy, generally requires root pruning.

Historical.—History has it that the apricot was introduced to our country by King Henry VIII's gardener.

APRIL WORK IN THE GARDEN.
Flowers.

All hardy annuals and biennials may now be sown in the open border to produce large patches of colour. Sow thinly.

Prick out seedlings of half-hardy annuals. After a week or so allow them all the air and sun possible, closing the frames before dusk in case of frosts.

Plant out rooted cuttings of antirrhinums, pentstemons, and violas.

Pinch out the tips of the antirrhinums. This makes them grow bushy and also makes it possible for plants of even height to be obtained.

Plant gladioli. These are easily used to form colour schemes. Grow them with dwarf, bushy or carpet plants, such as sweet alyssum or phlox *drummondii*.

Finish all lifting and division among herbaceous plants.

Give a good mulch of manure to the roses. Prune the last of the roses (the most tender) early in the month.

Plant hardy lilies (in variety).

Plant begonias and Cape hyacinths.

Start tubers of dahlias and salvia patens, ready for May planting.

It is not too late to sow seeds for summer fragrance. Sweet alyssum, balsam, sweet pea, night-scented stock and mignonette may all be sown to bloom during the coming summer.

Sweet peas, whether sown for garden decoration, for table flowers or for exhibition, need support. Blooms show well in the garden if plants are grown in groups, six or eight of a single colour in each group, supported on hazel branches or on tubes of wire netting. The flower stems will push through the wire netting in search of sunshine.

For cut flowers sweet peas are best grown in rows, for ease in cutting. Twiggy hazel stakes are the simplest supports.

Exhibition flowers can only be grown where plants are carefully trained. Single canes, one for each stem, or several wires stretched from end to end of the row are needed.

Tie each stem separately, removing tendrils which may cling to the leaves or stems and distort them. Pinch out unwanted side growths.

Lift and replant snowdrops where too crowded.

Divide kniphofias if necessary.

Stake hyacinths.

Preparation should be made for summer bedding, and bulbs should be lifted.

Lift and divide the large white border daisies—chrysanthemum maximum.

In the Shrubbery.

A top dressing of decayed manure among old rhododendrons, azaleas, and other shrubs, works wonders. Give at least a good forkful to each shrub.

Plant Evergreens.

Evergreens can be moved this month. The hardiest of our evergreens, and therefore the most precious, are the holly, ivy, and the yew, which appear to withstand the hardest frosts that ever visit us.

Cold damp soils are fatal to many shrubs in severe winters. To avoid future losses, thoroughly prepare each site, adding plenty of grit, leaves and strawy manure to clay soils. Dig deeply and improve the drainage where needed.

Prune shrubs as follows: Cut out old weak shoots of arundinaria, arundo, bamboo, lilac, rose species; trim back where needed arbutus, aucuba, choisya ternata, laurus, olearia, haastii, laurels; cut back salix for peeling rods, cornus grown for coloured bark; trim ivy, rhus, and magnolia on walls; thin out old shoots of ruscus.

The Rockery.

Attack weeds on the rockery at once or they will choke the plants.

Give a top dressing of good sandy soil where rains have washed roots bare.

Stir the soil and sow a few hardy annuals of the dwarf kinds where bare patches occur on a new rockery. Nemophila, antirrhinums, candytuft, alyssum, mimulus and mignonette are often despised by alpine specialists, but they serve to clothe the rockery in a very charming manner during the first year after construction.

Warm showery days invite slugs to the rockery, and tender plants are soon destroyed or damaged. Search for the marauders after dark or in the early morning and destroy them.

Half oranges, from which the juice has been squeezed, make an excellent trap for slugs. These inverted domes are not unsightly in the rock garden, and are a great attraction to these pests. Also, they discourage cats !

Fruit.

Hoe all the land that has been dug to keep down weeds.

Finish grafting. This is a job for the expert, but the amateur can be quite successful.

New strawberry beds can be made this month.

Pears growing on grass land are often affected by Pear Midge. This pest eats out the centre of tiny new fruits and makes them appear swelled or " bottled." Such infested fruits must be picked off and burned.

Spray with insecticides apples coming into bloom, to check apple-blossom weevil, codlin moth and March moth.

Never spray when the blossoms are open ; you may kill bees.

Prune wall figs.

Dust or spray black-currant bushes affected with Big Bud with lime-and-sulphur mixture every other week.

Peaches and nectarines may be summer pruned.

Prune figs grown on walls or railings outdoors.

Cut out weak or dead wood now and pinch out the points of the young shoots in July. New fig plants can be put in this month.

Vegetables.

Protect seeds from birds by stretching black cotton over the beds

Kale, Brussels sprouts, cabbage, savoys and perpetual spinach sown now will provide green vegetables for the winter months.

Grow Globe Artichokes. New plants can be purchased now, and should be planted immediately on arrival. Large stocks can be raised from suckers later, so that the initial outlay need not be repeated.

They like well-prepared soil containing gritty material, wood ashes and salt. Also they appreciate a dressing of sifted coal ashes, which helps to keep away slugs. Old plantations should be forked over during the present month between the rows, a dressing of manure being given at the same time.

Sow salads. Rapid growth is the secret of tender succulent salad crops. Sown now, while sun and showers are plentiful, salads grow quickly to maturity.

Successional sowing at intervals of two or three weeks should be made of lettuce, radishes, mustard and cress, and silver-skinned onions.

A part of the vegetable plot is nearly always the ideal place for the herb garden. Make this now. Herbs need full sunshine to develop a good flavour.

Herbs grown from seed should be sown this month. These include: Borage, sorrel, pot marjoram, thyme, angelica, sage, chervil, summer savoury.

Dress old asparagus beds with salt, and make new ones.

Make mushroom beds.

Mulch rows of early peas and strawberries.

Prepare ground for the reception of Brussels sprouts, cauliflowers, lettuces, etc., grown in frames.

The ground should also be ready for runner beans.

Celery trenches should be dug.

There is still a danger of frost and provision should be made for this. Mats, straw, newspaper, and dry litter all make useful protective material.

Young plants should also receive protection from birds. Black cotton is the best.

Thin out carrots, onions, parsnips, etc., as necessary, and use the hoe as soon as possible between the rows.

Under Glass.

Do not hurry to remove plants from the shelter of the greenhouse. There may be late frosts.

Keep the windows open whenever the days are warm, to prevent seedlings and cuttings from becoming drawn.

Pinch back the shoots of grape vines, and tie them to trellis. Syringe frequently until the blossom opens. Thoroughly wet the staging and floor each day to create a moist growing atmosphere.

Repot hard wood plants in the greenhouse, such as hydrangeas, where needed.

Take cuttings of geraniums, fuchsias, etc., for late flowering.

Sow seeds of balsam, celosia, gloxinia, petunia, lobelia, zinnia and dahlia.

Early strawberries are obtained by potting up plants now and forcing them. Keep the pots in cold frames for a time. Bring a fresh batch into greater heat every week or two, and from now onwards give a stimulant in the form of artificial manure. As soon as the fruits begin to colour, discontinue feeding.

Ridge cucumbers, marrows, pumpkins and gourds, which it is intended to grow in the open later, can be sown in pots under glass. Sow in sandy soil, with some leaf-mould mixed. Keep them close for a short time, but as soon as growth commences allow as much air as possible in the daytime. Cover always at night to prevent damage from frosts.

Prepare beds outdoors for these plants. A bed of leaves and long litter, covered with a depth of a foot of moderately rich soil is best. Choose an open sunny position.

Gourds are tender and like a warm situation, but can be usefully employed as a decoration of distinction on fences and archways in a sheltered garden.

Seedlings under glass must receive careful attention or they will damp off.

Give ventilation daily to all seedlings and cuttings. As the planting out season approaches, give more air to produce sturdy plants.

First raise the frames or open the greenhouse windows slightly in the middle of the day.

As the days become warmer, and the plants stronger, the frame lights can be removed entirely in the daytime and replaced at night in anticipation of late frosts.

Stand boxes of seedlings and cuttings on to the path for a few days before planting out, to accustom them to outside conditions.

Pinch out the tips of any plants that become straggly and drawn. This will make them send out side shoots, and recover some of their lost stamina.

Pests.

With the approach of the sun, warmth and showers, greenflies wake from their winter sleep. Watch plum and cherry trees. Greenflies may be seen climbing the trunks. Spray immediately with paraffin emulsion or insecticide and repeat as often as necessary.

Aphis spread rapidly to other plants and insecticide should be used as required.

A quarter pound of soft soap, half a pint of paraffin and a gallon of hot water makes a good emulsion, and, diluted with ten times the amount of water, is a suitable spray for most garden plants.

Where tender foliage is desired in perfect condition, a spray should always be followed the next day by clear water to cleanse the leaf surfaces.

Lawns.

Grass seed will germinate quickly if sown now in showery weather.

Sow 1–3 oz. per square yard. (*See* LAWNS).

Cut and roll the established lawn twice weekly, or more often if required.

Dress with weedkiller, fertiliser, etc., according to the condition of the turf.

Repair bare patches, and level hollows made by subsidence, moles, or other cause.

AQUARIUM. *See* WATER PLANTS.

AQUATIC OR WATER PLANTS. *See* WATER PLANTS.

AQUIFOLIUM. *See* ILEX *and* BERBERIS.

AQUILEGIA (aquil-e-gia. Ranunculaceæ). Columbine. A most graceful and popular hardy herbaceous plant which is 1 ft. high and which flowers in May and continues for a long period. It thrives in any soil but prefers cool well-drained

shady borders and deep loam and leaf-mould. For propagation sow outside in June, transplant in August for flowering the following year, or to obtain strong plants early, sow in frames in spring. If preferred the plants may be propagated by division in April or September. The best known are hybrids of which *A. alpina*, blue, *A. pyrenacia*, blue and lilac, *A. sibirica*, blue, are good for rockeries.

AQUILEGIA (COLUMBINE)

Columbines or Aquilegias are some of the daintiest garden flowers suitable for cutting or border decoration. Long-spurred hybrids are the best for general display.

The long-spurred cærulea hybrids give a variety of colour, including a crimson and cream flower that is excellent used for bedding. These plants are useful for cutting.

Hybrid columbines raised under glass and planted out in early summer require considerable attention and ample water. A few may bloom in the first summer, but the best results will be obtained in the following spring.

Of recent years a scented Columbine from the Himalayas has been crossed with the long-spurred hybrids, resulting in a variety that is long-spurred and to some extent scented. At present only a percentage of the seedlings are truly fragrant, but doubtless the scented type will be improved in the near future.

ARABIS (ără´-bis. Cruciferæ). Named from Arabia, probably from the dry situations in which they will grow. This derivation seems doubtful. Wall Cress.

SPECIES.

A. albida is chiefly known for its double form *A. a. flore pleno*, the single variety having little to recommend it. *A. a. flore pleno* is the familiar wall plant which forms huge grey masses covered with countless spikes thickly set with large, white, double flowers, the foliage almost disappearing under the closely-packed multitude. This occurs in May and early June, though a few flowers can be found during most of the year. It is useful where much ground is to be covered, or for walls and path edges. A small rock-garden is better without it. There is a single form with golden variegated leaves which does not ramp, and a good single pink *A. a. rosea*.

A. aubrietioides. As its name suggests, this pretty pink-flowered plant has somewhat the appearance of an Aubrietia. It flowers early and though quite hardy, makes a very pretty pot plant in a cold greenhouse. 4 in. Sicilian Alps.

A. sturii has glossy green leaves and large white flowers on 3 in. stems.

ARACHIS (ar-a-kis. Leguminosæ). Monkey Nut. Earth Nut. Dwarf plants that are chiefly interesting on account of their edible seeds known to everyone as Monkey Nuts. In tropical regions they are cultivated for these nuts, which are exported all over the world. After the flowers have died off, the fruit stalk lengthens and bends down, pushing the seed-pod into the ground, where it enlarges and becomes the familiar wrinkled yellow pod containing two seeds.

Only one species is grown in the stoves in this country, *A. hypogeæ*. This requires fibrous mellow loam with plenty of sand and a temperature of 55°-65° in winter and 60°-75° in summer.

ARALIA (ăr-ā-li-a. Araliaceæ). Handsome deciduous foliage plants, most useful for tropical bedding, and for pots and tubs. 1865. Hardy in all but coldest parts, but seen at best in mild districts.

Culture.—Plant in November in not too rich soil. In rich soil they make fine foliage, but are not so long lived.

Propagation by root cuttings in autumn or suckers in spring. Likes abundance of water; while not objecting to sun prefers partial shade.

PRINCIPAL SPECIES.

A. chinensis. Chinese Angelica Tree. China, Japan and Manchuria. 1865. Usually up to about 12 ft. In Cornwall up to 30 ft. Flowers creamy-white and fragrant black fruits.

A. albo marginata, immense leaves, variegated silver; up to 30 ft.

A. aureo-marginata with golden variegation.

A. Sieboldii, see FATSIA.

A. spinosa. Hercules Club. Rare. Similar to *A. chinensis*, but not quite so hardy.

ARAUCARIA (ăr-āu-kār´-i-a. Coniferæ). Chile. Evergreen trees up to 80 ft. *A. imbricata*, the Chile Pine, or Monkey Puzzle. 1780. Among the most remarkable trees ever introduced to this country. Looks best isolated.

Culture.—Compost, 2 parts loam, 1 part leaf-mould, 1 part sharp sand. Repot early spring. Position, sunny part of greenhouse. Winter temperature, 45°; summer, 60°. Not particular as to soil, but prefers deep loam, well drained. Best raised from seeds. In warm favoured districts will seed itself.

Propagation.—By cutting of young ripened wood in the autumn, or tall plants by stem rooting, early spring.

SPECIES.

Bidwillii, Cunninghamii, excelsia.

A. excelsa. Norfolk Island Pine. Tender, only suitable for mildest localities.

It is of interest to note that *A. imbricata* is the only tree from south of the Equator to attain to timber-producing dimensions in this country.

ARAUJIA (ār-āu´-jia. Asclepiadeæ). Twining evergreen shrubs or climbers.

Culture.—Soil, loam and peat in equal parts, and plenty of sand, perfectly drained.

Propagation by seeds and cuttings. Only suitable for mild districts, although in parts of Surrey grows and flowers well.

PRINCIPAL SPECIES.

A. sericifera, the White Bladder Flower of Brazil. An evergreen climber from South America with white, fragrant blooms in July and August.

ARBOR-VITÆ. *See* THUYA.

ARBOUR. An arbour or "herber" of romantic tradition and a bower were medieval names for garden shelters. They still conjure up visions of flower-covered seats, designed not so much for weather shelter as for screening the users from prying eyes.

An arbour is usually formed of light trellis, or may be only the branches of trees interwoven above a seat. It is altogether lighter in structure than the garden house (*see* GARDEN SHELTERS).

A better-finished chair is made from thin whole cane, woven to comfortable designs. These chairs are more comfortable than any other type of garden seat, are very lasting in wear, and so neat and artistic that they can be used both indoors and out.

The more permanent types of garden furniture should have a definite place in the garden design. They are generally heavy and unwieldy, and therefore should not have to be moved. The site for permanent seats will have been chosen when the plan of the garden is first made, and before the seat is actually placed, some attention should be given to the surround. For instance, if a seat of permanent type is placed direct on a lawn, the grass will soon wear away from the spot beneath the seat, and a muddy and unsightly patch will result.

Slabs of stone, crazy paving, or a patch of gravel would prevent this, but if the gravel patch is the choice, care must be given to its level. The surface should be slightly above the elevation of the grass, so that water never stands on it. A slight fall in gravel from front to back is the best way of preventing the collection of water.

The site for the seat will determine to some extent the size and design of the seat itself. For instance, at the terminal of a garden walk, a straight seat of solid appearance, painted or stained, would be appropriate.

A stone seat would be suitable if near a stone-edged pond, or on a stone terrace. Such a seat will be more ornamental than useful in this cold climate, unless the seat is sufficiently near the house for an ample supply of garden cushions to fill it.

Under a tree a circular seat might find a place, and under a group of trees on a lawn furniture of somewhat unconventional character could be grouped. Of this unconventional furniture several new kinds are now on the market.

There are other informal kinds of chairs —the old monk chairs, for instance, so designed that one could never go off to sleep in them without toppling over! A plain bench, such as one meets in well-designed wild gardens, has also a use in some other positions.

Solid, everlasting furniture is made in designs that are both elegant and restful from the weathered oak and teak of old battleships. In the same material are fashioned tea-wagons, garden tubs, rose trellises, and a number of other articles for garden use. These are quite the most lasting of all wooden types, and need no staining or preservative. Their appearance is improved if they are rubbed over occasionally with a little linseed oil, but otherwise no labour is required in their upkeep.

ARBUTUS (är'-būt-us. Ericaceæ). Strawberry Trees. Evergreen trees and shrubs with attractive, abundant dark green foliage, white pitcher-shaped flowers and ornamental fruit.

Culture.—Plant in loamy soil, with peat or leaf-mould. *Propagation* is best effected by seed, keeping the young plants in pots as they transplant badly, until ready to plant out, which should be done as soon as possible. The named varieties are grafted on seedlings of *A. Unedo*.

PRINCIPAL SPECIES.

A. Andrachne (S.E. Europe), 1724. A rare species up to 30–40 ft.

A. andrachnoides. Natural hybrid found in Greece. *A. Andrachne* + *A. Unedo.* Beautiful reddish stems.

A. canariensis. A long-leaved species for favoured districts.

A. furiens (*Gautheria furiens, Pernettya*

ciliaris). Tender. Does well in Ireland.

A. hybrida, *A. Andrachne* + *A. Unedo*. A natural hybrid found in Greece. The most useful of the genus. There are several forms.

A. Menziesii (syn. *A. procera*). The Madroña of California. 1827. 20–40 ft. The finest species. A most beautiful tree with large leaves, panicles of pitcher-shaped flowers, deliciously scented, freely produced in May, and peeling bark in spring, revealing a striking cinnamon-

ARBUTUS UNEDO
STRAWBERRY TREE

The handsome red bark and evergreen foliage gives the Strawberry Tree a distinguished appearance. The fruits are suitable for eating when quite ripe.

coloured inner bark. Fruit orange-yellow.

A. Unedo. Strawberry Tree. Native of Mediterranean region and S.W. Ireland. One of the few ericaceous plants that can be grown in limestone formations and chalky soils; succeeds also on peaty or loamy soil. The best known and perhaps most ornamental species. Very attractive in autumn and even winter when the pinkish-white flowers and the previous year's scarlet fruit resembling strawberries are borne at the same time. The fruit is edible when ripe, but its appearance is distinctly superior to the flavour.

A. U. var. *coccinea*. A very good form with deep pink flower.

A. U. var. *microphylla*. A narrow-leaved form and very free flowering.

ARCHES. *See* PERGOLA.

ARCHONTOPHŒNIX (ar-kon-to-fee-nix. Palmæ). Tall - growing handsome stove palms that require the usual treatment for palms. They are raised from imported seed and their only requirements are good drainage and abundant supplies of water. The seeds should be sown thickly in pans or boxes of loam and leaf-soil opened with sand, and the pans plunged in a hot bed or warm pit and kept fairly moist. When two leaves have formed they should be potted singly and given a fair amount of light. Later they should be firmly potted in larger pots in a compost of loam and leaf-soil with sand.

SPECIES.

A. Alexandræ (syn. *Seaforthia Alexandræ*).

A. elegans (syn. *Ptychosperma elegans*, *Seaforthia elegans*).

ARCTERICA (Ericaceæ). Japan. A rare, diminutive, shade-loving evergreen shrub with tiny leaves, and sprays of lily-of-the-valley flowers in May. Peaty soil.

ARCTOSTAPHYLOS (ark-toe-staphi'-löss. Ericaceæ). *Arktos*, a bear; *staphyle*, a berry. Bears eat its berries. A large family of small trailing shrubs, with glossy leaves and small white or pink flowers. The berries are red but neither flowers nor berries are conspicuous. The two best are *A. uva-ursi*, the Bearberry, which is small, and *A. nevadensis*, which is larger. Beyond the fact that the leaves of *A. uva-ursi* are used in medicine for their action on the kidneys, the genus is not particularly interesting. The most suitable soil is sandy peat. Cuttings from matured wood root easily under glass.

Propagate by seed, which should be soaked in water at boiling-point for at least 20 sec., or make a fire over them. They may also be increased by budding and by inarching and division.

SPECIES.

A. alpina. A low-growing deciduous shrub from the mountains of the North of Europe (including North of Scotland), N. Asia and N. America. Loves damp cool conditions; its roots may be surfaced with sphagnum moss, where these conditions are absent. Its leaves turn brilliant red in autumn. Flowers white.

A. Manzanita (California), 1897. A rare evergreen shrub or small tree of glaucous appearance, 4–6 ft. high, with spikes of pink or white campanulate flowers in March and April.

A. myrtifolia (California). Prostrate species, pink flowers and scarlet berries.

A. nevadensis. Resembling *A. uva-ursi*.

A. tomentosa (California), 1793. 3–5 ft. Rare. Resembling *A. Manzanita*.

A. uva-ursi (Red Bearberry). Native of Great Britain and other temperate regions of northern hemisphere. Trailing, evergreen, bearing rosy-pink wax-like pitcher-shaped flowers in April and May. A good carpeter for rockery.

ARCTOTIS (arc-to-tis. Compositæ). Half-hardy perennials and annuals. Best treated as annuals and raised yearly by seed. S. Africa, 1710.

A. grandis, the Blue-eyed South African Daisy, is undoubtedly the best of the family. It grows to 1½–2 ft. and makes bushy plants 2 ft. across, and flowers most profusely all through the summer in ordinary garden soil in a sunny position. Its delicate shades and the faultless symmetry of its flowers give it a most distinct character. Sow under glass in March, plant out in May, or may be sown out of doors in light soil in April. There are a number of other species as *A. breviscarpa*, *A. scapigera*, *A. acaulis*, but these are hardly worth growing and during recent years have been given far greater publicity than they deserve. All are easily raised from seed sown outside in April. Natives of S. Africa.

Culture.—Compost, 1 part loam, 1 part leaf-mould, ½ part sand and a little charcoal. Position, sunny part of greenhouse, but will do in shade, or sun in the open.

Propagation.—Seeds in temperature 55° to 65° March, and by cuttings in early summer.

SPECIES.

A. leptorhiza breviscarpa, orange, into summer, annual.

A. grandis, white marguerite flowers, lavender blue reverse, 2 ft. summer, etc.

The flowers are usually beautiful in colour and form.

ARDISIA (ardi'sia. Myrsinaceæ).

Spear Flower. Beautiful evergreen stove, flowering and berry-bearing shrubs, from E. Indies, China and Japan, 1809. 1 ft. or rather more in height. Useless for chalky soils.

Culture.—Compost (*See* ABELIA). Light sunny position. Repot early spring. Prune back hard in March. Winter temperature, 55°; summer, 80°.

Propagation.—By seed in spring, or by cuttings of side shoots in light sandy soil in propagator, temperature 70°.

SPECIES.

A. crenata (China). Reddish-violet flowers, bright coral-red berries.

A. japonica (China and Japan). About 1 ft. Dark glossy leaves, white flowers in August and September, bright red berries. There is a form with white berries. Suitable for rock garden. Not quite hardy.

ARECA (ar-e-ka. Palmæ). Betel Nut Palm. Cabbage Palm. A large number of the palms formerly included in this genus are now transferred for botanical classification to *Chrysalidocarpus*, *Oncosperma*, *Ptychosperma* and *Hyophorbe*. Increased by seeds and grown in a moist stove. Use a compost of peat or leaf-soil and loam for the younger plants, and sandy loam for the mature plants.

SPECIES.

A. catechu. The Betel Nut Palm has leaves 3–6 ft. long and is 30 ft. high; it yields a powerful astringent medicine.

A. lutescens (syn. *Chrysalidocarpus lutescens*) is one of the most popular of palms and produces long plume-like, bright green leaves with yellow petioles on its numerous branches. Madagascar. 20 ft.

AREGELIA (ar-e-je-lia. Bromeliaceæ). Stove flowering evergreens. Pot in February or March in a compost of equal parts fibrous loam, rough peat, leaf-mould and silver sand. Water moderately in winter, freely in summer.

Propagate by offshoots in sandy peat in a temperature of 80° from February to April.

SPECIES.

A. princeps (syn. *Karatas Meyendorfi*). Violet, 18 in.

A. spectabilis, red, white and blue. 1 ft.

A. tristis, purple, 1 ft.

ARENARIA (ä-ren-air-ia. Caryophyllaceæ). *Arena*, sand. Sandwort. Low growing plants, mostly forming mats studded with white flowers in early summer.

SPECIES.

A. balearica is perhaps the best known and most useful for the speed with which it progresses, covering rocks and ground (and smothering one's choicest treasures almost in the twinkling of an eye) with a flat, filmy, light-green carpet studded with innumerable white stars. It does best in a cool light soil, though not necessarily shaded. On rocks of porous stone it is indestructible, but on hard stone in sun, a hot day may wither it. Balearic Islands.

A. cœspitosa aurea (syn. *Sagina subulata*). A golden "moss." The flowers are not conspicuous.

A. graminifolia (syn. *Alsine Rosanii*). Grass-like foliage. Flowers clusters on wire stems, 6 in. Siberia. Seed or division.

A. Ledebouriana. Blue-grey rosettes in light clumps; flowers on branching 3 in. sprays. Levantine Alps. Seed or division.

A. montana. Produces cascades of shining white flowers, very much larger than the others of the genus. 6 in. Spain. It is best propagated by cuttings in sand or by seed.

A. purpurascens. The only coloured variety, having pretty lilac-pink flowers on a mat of shiny foliage. A cool position is essential. It flowers in July and August, 2 in. Aragon and Catalonia. Seed or division. It is definitely less easy to grow than the others, but worth a little trouble.

ARGEMONE (arg-e'm-onee. Papaveraceæ). Devil's Fig, Prickly Poppy. Hardy Annual. 2 ft. Mexico.

A. grandiflora is a good annual with pure white poppy-like flowers and ornamental silvery foliage. *A. mexicana* has yellow flowers and is similar in appearance. Both species will grow in ordinary garden soil. Should be sown in March-April where to bloom.

ARIA. *See* PYRUS ARIA.

A R I S Æ M A (ar-is-e-ma. Aroideæ). Tuberous-rooted stove, greenhouse and hardy perennials with peculiar flowers.

Propagate by division of the rootstock. Grow in peat with fibrous loam, a little sphagnum, charcoal and a little sand. Water copiously, except when the plants are at rest, and give doses of liquid manure during the flowering season.

SPECIES.

A. atrorubens (syn. *triphyllum, zebrinum*), bears purplish-brown flowers in June, and may be grown outdoors in sheltered districts, although it is normally grown in the greenhouse.

A. speciosum, has whitish-green flowers in March in the greenhouse, 2 ft.

A. ringens, white-greenish flowers in spring in the greenhouse.

ARISTEA (ari'-stea. Iridaceæ). Greenhouse flowering shrubs, evergreen, S. Africa, 1759.

Culture.—Compost, 1 part sandy loam, 1 part peat and sand. Repot early spring. Light airy position. Winter temperature, 45°; summer, 60°.

Propagation.—Chiefly by offsets in April, but seed may be sown in pans at the same time, temperature 50° to 55°.

SPECIES.

A. capitata, magnificent plant, blue.

ARISTOLOCHIA (ăr-is-tol-ō'-ki-a. Aristolochiaceæ). Although most of these remarkable plants are natives of tropical countries, some half-dozen may be cultivated out of doors in this country. Plant in March in good soil. *Propagation* by division, or cuttings, or seed.

PRINCIPAL SPECIES.

A. altissima. A distinct species from Sicily and Algeria, in appearance like a smilax. Flowers narrow, tubular, brownish-yellow in June and July. Not generally hardy.

A. moupinensis (China) 1886. Deciduous, vigorous. Hardy. Flowers yellow mottled purplish-red. Perhaps the best of genus.

A. sipho, Dutchman's Pipe (E. U.S.A.), 1783. Flowers yellowish, handsome foliage. The best known.

A. tomentosa. Similar to preceding species.

ARISTOTELIA (ăr-is-tō-tē'lĭ-a. Tiliaceæ). Half-hardy evergreen shrub with handsome foliage and berries.

Culture.—Ordinary garden soil.

Propagation by layers and by cuttings of half-ripened wood under a hand-glass.

PRINCIPAL SPECIES.

A. fruticosa. A rare and very variable shrub, from New Zealand. Flowers and berries small.

A. Macqui. An evergreen, spreading

shrub, 6–10 ft. higher in warm districts, from Chile, 1773. Flowers greenish-white followed by fruit about the size of a pea, at first purplish, turning to black. Wine is made from the fruit.

A. M. variegata. A handsome form with yellow variegated leaves.

A. racemosa. Deciduous tree up to 25 ft. From New Zealand. Only suitable for the mildest gardens.

ARITHMETIC OF GARDENING. *See* GARDEN DATA.

ARMENIÆA. *See* PRUNUS ARMENI-ACEA.

ARMERIA (ar-meer-ia. Plumbagina-ceæ). Thrift. The Thrifts or Sea Pinks form tufts and hummocks of grass-like foliage from which rise stems of greater or less length, bearing heads of crowded, chaffy flowers. The colours vary with the species from a washy pink to a virulent magenta. Gerard calls them "Our Lady's Cushions." They are suited by a light sandy loam in sun, but are accommodating in almost any soil. The flowers are produced in spring and early summer. All propagate by seeds or division.

A. alpina forms low-growing clumps set with pale pink flowers. 6 in. Alps and Pyrenees. *A. a. Bee's Ruby*, a rich ruby-red garden variety.

A. cæspitosa from the Sierra de Guadar-rama. Tight little clumps with large, almost stemless heads of pale pink. 1 in.

A. cephalotes (syn. *A. latifolia*). A tall-growing species with comparatively broad, bright green leaves. The flower heads are a fine rosy-pink on 18 in. stems. This is a good plant for a front position in the border, or in the rougher parts of a large rock garden. Valentia.

A. maritima is the British species found all round our coasts. It is a pale and un-exciting pink, but it atones by having given rise to two very striking varieties. *A. m. Laucheana*, deep clear rose, and *Vindictive*, a particularly brilliant, though not harsh magenta.

A. plantaginea is probably only a broad-leaved form of *A. maritima* with larger flowers on taller stems.

ARNEBIA (ar-ne′bia. Boragineæ). Prophet Flower. Hardy annual. 1 ft. Flowers yellow with five black spots one on each petal. Tradition says that the

prophet Mahomet touched the flower with the tips of his fingers. A native of the East, but will succeed in many places in Britain, sown out of doors in March-April where the plants are to flower.

ARNICA (ar-ni-ka. Compositæ). Lamb's Skin. Dwarf hardy herbaceous perennials that are closely related to Senecio. They are propagated by seeds and by division of the roots in spring. Grow in peat mixed with loam and sand.

SPECIES.

A. montana, 12 in., of which the flowers and roots are used for treating bruises and swellings. This is useful for the rockery.

A. Chamissonis, flowering from July to September.

A. foliosa, flowering in August, are use-ful plants.

All the species bear yellow flowers, but the rest are scarcely worth cultivating.

AROPOPHYLLUM (aropophy′llum). Orchidaceæ). Greenhouse terrestrial orchids, 1838.

Culture.—Compost, equal parts fibrous peat, sphagnum moss and charcoal. Repot spring. Sunny position. Good drainage essential. Winter temperature 45°; sum-mer, 60°.

SPECIES.

A. Cardinale, rose; *A. spicatum,* purple.

ARROW. An instrument used in con-nection with surveying. Ten arrows are supplied with each surveyor's chain. They are pointed at one end and have a ring at the other. They are placed in the ground to mark the end of each chain length.

ARSENATE OF LEAD. A stomach insecticide used for the destruction of caterpillars, beetles, sawfly larvæ and all kinds of leaf-eating insects. A heavy white powder, very slightly soluble in water. It is best to obtain it from a reputable firm of insecticide manufacturers, as the home-made article, unless prepared with great care, is liable to cause serious scorching of the foliage. Arsenate of lead is sold in three forms—powder, paste and cream. The two latter contain more or less water, and more is required to form a spraying mixture than if the powder is used. Fine-ness of division of the substance is very important, as the capacity for remaining suspended in water for a reasonably long time is dependent upon this quality. Coarse particles separate too rapidly. The strength of the spraying wash depends upon the arsenical strength of the preparation, which is usually stated and guaranteed by the manufacturer. In arsenate pastes the amount of arsenic, expressed as arsenic oxide, is usually about 15 per cent., and of such a paste from 4–8 oz. would be required to 10 gallons of water. Most makers issue instructions for the method of preparation of their particular products. Arsenate of lead should be applied as a fine, misty spray, the object being to cover the foliage without allowing the spray to drip from the leaves. Spraying should be carried out generally as soon as the pest is observed and while the leaves are still young. The small caterpillars are thus more quickly killed, before the foliage and buds have suffered serious damage.

ARTEMISIA (ăr-te-mis′-ĭ-a. Compositæ). Evergreen and deciduous shrubs and plants needing a sunny position, and well-drained, not rich, soil. *Propagation* by division in October, cuttings in July.

PRINCIPAL SPECIES.

A. Abrotanum (S. Europe). The old-fashioned Southernwood, or Old Man. In north of England known as "Lad's love," whose fragrant leaves are so well known. Cultivated in this country since 16th century.

A. cina, Wormwood. Pretty and distinct. Turkestan species from which the drug Santonica is obtained.

ARTHROPODIUM (arthropo′dium. Liliaceæ). Greenhouse perennial. New South Wales, 1800.

Culture.—Compost (*see* AGAPANTHUS). Repot spring in well-drained pots. Sunny position. Water freely during flowering period. Winter temperature, 45°; summer, 60°.

Propagation.—By seed sown in same mixture as for potting, in temperature 55°–60°, or by offsets when repotting.

SPECIES.

A. circatum, large white flowers; *A. paniculatum*, white.

ARTICHOKE, CHINESE (*Stachys tubifera*. Labiatæ). As the name implies, this plant is a native of the Orient, some authorities claiming that it originated in China, others that it is a native of Japan.

It is a perennial tuberous-rooted plant, and it is these somewhat spiral and knobbly roots that are used for edible purposes. Although not universally popular, it is frequently grown in those large establishments where a wide range of vegetables is demanded, and it is also being cultivated in increasing quantities by the market growers in the Evesham district.

Culture.—Plant tubers in March or April in deeply-dug, well-drained soil in a sunny position, spacing them 9 in. apart and 4 in. deep in rows 18 in. asunder. Keep the hoe going constantly during the growing period, and give occasional heavy waterings in dry weather. For winter use, lift the tubers in October, clean off soil, and store in sand; but if required for exhibition leave in the ground to preserve the colour until shortly before the show.

VARIETIES.

Common White and Old Red.

Uses.—It is generally used as a winter vegetable, but may also be used raw in salads, pickled or fried.

ARTICHOKE, GLOBE (*Cynara Scolymus*. Compositæ). This is an entirely different plant from the Chinese Artichoke, and is of European origin. It is grown for the flower heads, which form large fleshy scales or bracts. It is largely cultivated on the Continent, where it is relished by all classes, but in this country it is rarely used except in large establishments and leading hotels and restaurants.

It is of perennial habit and forms a large, imposing plant, so much so that it is frequently grown in a border for decorative purposes only. The well-formed, but not over-developed, flower heads, make a valuable addition to a summer collection of exhibition vegetables, six heads being classed as one dish.

Culture.—Globe Artichokes may be propagated by seeds sown in March in a temperature of 55°–60°, or by young off-shoots from older plants of a good variety. Deeply-dug, good rich soil is essential for the best results, as the plant is a gross feeder. The site should be worked in good time (autumn or winter for preference), to allow it to settle before planting in April. The most usual method of planting is in clumps of three, 1½ ft. apart with 4½ ft. between the clumps.

Liberal watering and frequent hoeing is all that are necessary during the summer. In the autumn old and dead leaves should be removed, the crowns covered with a little dried bracken kept in place with hazel sticks, and the bed then tidied over by forking in a light dressing of decayed manure. Young plants cannot be expected to bear usable heads until the second year, but from then on for five or six years they should prove very prolific.

VARIETIES.

Purple Globe; Green Globe.

Uses.—The heads should be cut with a few inches of stem when fully developed, but before the scales open. In this state they will keep for several days if placed with their stems in water in a cool place. The French method of cooking is to cleanse thoroughly, place in boiling water to which one tablespoonful of salt has been added to each quart of water. Boil quickly from 25 to 30 minutes, or until heads are tender, then drain and serve with sauce or melted butter. Globe Artichokes may also be fried in a savoury batter, made of milk, flour, egg, olive oil and parsley, but the heads need boiling first.

ARTICHOKE, JERUSALEM (*Helianthus tuberosus*. Compositæ). This species of Artichoke originated in North America, and is the one most commonly grown in this country. It belongs to the Sunflower family, but very rarely flowers in the British Isles.

It will grow almost anywhere, and in good soils the stems may attain a height of 8 ft. during the season. On account of its rapid growth, it is frequently used as a summer screen plant for odd corners and unsightly buildings, or even as a wind break for more delicate plants.

Culture.—Although amenable to almost any soil or position, the best culinary roots or tubers are obtained in a light soil in an open sunny position. This should be deeply dug and well manured as early as possible, to be ready for planting fair-sized tubers in February or March. Many gardeners make a practice of digging and planting at the same time. The tubers should be set 6 in. deep, 2 ft. apart and 3 ft. between the rows. Very little attention beyond weeding is required during the summer. In November the old stems may be cut down to within 9 in. or so of the ground and the crop lifted and stored, or the tubers may be left in the ground during the winter for digging as required for use.

VARIETIES.

New White; Old Red; or Purple-skinned.

Uses.—The Jerusalem Artichoke tubers contain no starch, so that the mealiness of potatoes cannot be obtained by cooking.

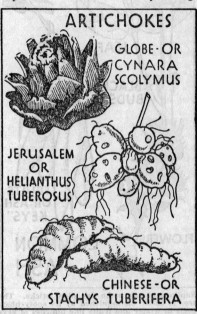

ARTICHOKES

GLOBE - OR CYNARA SCOLYMUS

JERUSALEM OR HELIANTHUS TUBEROSUS

CHINESE - OR STACHYS TUBERIFERA

The three types of Artichokes make a useful change of vegetables. They are in season: Globe—July, Jerusalem—winter, and Chinese —late autumn.

To prevent the tubers becoming discoloured during cooking, an acid (lemon juice) should be added to the rinsing and cooking water. They may be boiled, fried, served with sauce or used in soups.

ARTIFICIAL STONE. *See* ROCK GARDENS.

ARTILLERY PLANT. *See* PILEA.

ARTOCARPUS (ar-to-kar-pus. Urticaceæ). Bread Fruit. *Artos*, bread; *carpus*, fruit. Stove evergreen trees allied to the Upas Tree. The connection between this plant and the Upas Tree and the Cow Tree of Caraccas is interesting, as the fruits of the first-named are edible, and resemble bread when baked, while the Javan Upas Tree is virulently poisonous.

Propagate by cuttings of ripened side shoots inserted in sand under a hand-light with brisk bottom heat or by suckers. Grown in a soil consisting of two parts of good loam to one of leaf-mould with a little sand.

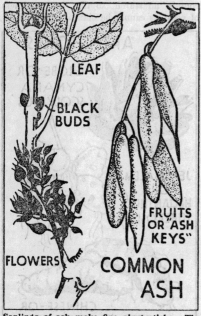

LEAF

BLACK BUDS

FLOWERS

FRUITS OR "ASH KEYS"

COMMON ASH

Saplings of ash make fine plant sticks. The tree is easily distinguished by its sooty-black buds in winter and fruits like bunches of keys in summer.

Summer temperature, 60°–70°; winter temperature, 60°–65°.

SPECIES.

All the species have greenish-white flowers.

A. incisa, the fruit produced in the axils of the leaves.

ARUM (arum. Aroideæ). Cuckoo-pint. Hardy and half-hardy tuberous-rooted perennials. Grown more as a curiosity than for its beauty.

Culture.—Compost: 2 parts loam, 1 part leaf-mould, 1 part sand. Plant or repot in the autumn. Water freely when growing, allow to dry off after flowering. Suitable for the cold house.

Propagation.—By offsets, when repotting.

SPECIES.

A. Italicum, creamy-white; *A. maculatum* (English Cuckoo-pint), light green, spotted purple. (Hardy, plant in autumn.)

ARUM LILY. *See* RICHARDIA.

ARUNDINARIA. *See* BAMBOO.

ARUNDO (a-run′-do. Gramineæ). Great Reed. Comparable to the Pampas Grass. Distinguishable by fine silky white panicles which are from 8–12 ft. high, and by the flowers which appear early in the summer. Thrives in semi-shade on slightly swampy banks in light rich loam. Only suitable for marsh or water gardens. Will perish in cold soil and needs plenty of water all the year round. Increased by seed or division of roots in May.

ASCLEPIAS (as-kle-pi-as. Asclepiadeæ). Swallow Wort. Milkweed. Ornamental perennials of considerable interest and value in the garden. The hardy species may be grown in a warm sunny position in the herbaceous border.

Propagate the hardy species by seeds sown when ripe, or under glass in sand, in spring, or by division at the same season; the tender plants by division in spring, or by cuttings struck in moderate heat under a bell-glass.

Grow the outdoor plants in light rich loam with leaf soil, and the greenhouse plants in fibrous loam with leaf-mould. Nearly all the plants require a little protection in winter.

SPECIES.

A. Cornutti, a pretty border plant with pale mauve fragrant blooms. 4 ft. July.

A. incarnata, red flowers in June, a useful plant for the bog garden, or for a very damp border. 2 ft.

A. tuberosa is the best of the border plants with orange flowers from July onwards. It is rather difficult to grow, and needs a dry place with protection in winter.

A. curassavica, with orange or scarlet flowers in July, is a beautiful stove plant.

A. c. alba, a white variety.

Some of the species like *lanceolata*, white, July; *rubra*, red, July; and *speciosa*, July, are true marsh plants, and need to be grown in moist soil, while the rest of the species like a fairly dry situation.

1. Formal bedding—Geraniums and Alyssum in a small garden.

2. A white weeping Rose above scarlet Geraniums in a circular bed.

3. Massed planting of mixed single Asters for separate beds on the lawn.

BERRIED SHRUBS FOR WINTER COLOUR

1. Snowberry—symphoricarpus, white berries, shade-loving.

2. Butcher's Broom—Ruscus, red berries, loves shade.

3. Clerodendron—blue berries, white fragrant flowers.
4. Vaccinium—bluish-black fruit, rosy-white flowers.
5. Pernettya—purple berries, compact, peat-loving evergreens.

ASH. The residue left from various burnt products is used in several ways in garden making.

Coal or coke ash is used for making pathways, coarse ashes forming a good foundation to assist drainage and the finer sifted ashes making a useful surfacing material for pathways through the less conspicuous parts of the garden.

Wood ashes can be used as a fertiliser.

May. Soil of peat and sand most suitable.

Propagation by seed and layers put down in autumn. The yellow bottle-shaped fruits are edible.

ASPARAGUS (*Asparagus officinalis.* Liliaceæ). This delectable vegetable is a native of the British Isles, and can be found growing wild at several points on the south and west coast. Its distribu-

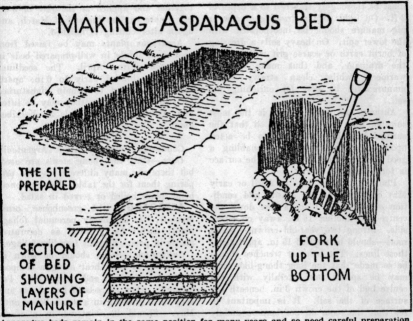

—MAKING ASPARAGUS BED—

THE SITE PREPARED

SECTION OF BED SHOWING LAYERS OF MANURE

FORK UP THE BOTTOM

Asparagus beds remain in the same position for many years and so need careful preparation before planting.

See also FRAXINUS, PLANT ASH, and WOOD ASH.

ASH, MANNA. *See* FRAXINUS ORNUS.

ASH, MOUNTAIN. *See* PYRUS AUCUPARIA.

ASIMINA (ă-sim-i-na. Anonaceæ). Hardy, usually deciduous. Shrub not much grown in English gardens.

PRINCIPAL SPECIES.

A. triloba (syn. *Anona triloba*). The Papau Tree or Custard Apple of south-eastern U.S.A. The only hardy species. Slow-growing up to 6–15 ft., according to locality. Large and striking foliage, pale purple and yellow flowers 2 in. across, in

tion also extends over a large part of Europe, but it is only found flourishing in the wild state where the soil and air are heavily charged with salt.

The general impression is that Asparagus is a costly and difficult crop to grow, but this is only half the truth. On the one hand there is a period of tending and waiting for 2 or 3 years whilst the bed matures, and on the other there is the fact that a good bed when once it starts will produce delicious and remunerative crops for a score or more years.

Asparagus has been known as a vegetable since the time of the ancients, and with certain classes it has never lost its popularity. At the present time considerable areas are cultivated commercially, principally in Essex and in the Evesham district of Worcestershire.

Culture.—The preparation of the beds is an all-important matter. A site in a sunny position should be thoroughly cleaned of all perennial weeds, and on this beds 4 ft. wide and any convenient length should be marked out. The soil must be thoroughly trenched to a depth of 3 ft. On light soils a dressing of cow or pig manure should be incorporated with the lower spit. On heavy soils a dressing of burnt earth or coarse grit will improve the drainage, and thus make the bed warmer; whilst clean strawy stable manure will be best for enriching the soil.

Autumn and early winter is the most suitable time for this work, so that the surface may be left rough to be acted upon by winter frosts, and enabling a good tilth to be obtained when the surface is forked over in April.

Planting may be done in April or early May according to the season and condition of the soil. Place a line down the centre and another 15 in. away on either side. Strong two year-old crowns—young roots—should be planted 15 in. apart along these lines. The holes or trenches should be so made that the long thong-like roots may be spread out laterally with the centre bud of the crown 3 in. beneath the surface of the soil. It is important to see that the roots do not become unduly dry whilst planting is in progress.

After planting, a light dressing of well-decayed manure should be spread over the bed. The paths on either side should then be forked up, and about 3 in. of the finer soil shovelled out and over the bed to finish off.

Strong crowns properly planted in a well-made bed should make abundant growth during the first year, but in no circumstances should any stalks be cut until the second year after planting.

When the beds commence to bear, no cutting should be done after June. The shoots will then grow and strengthen the crowns for the following season. It is also most important to cut down the tops

in autumn before the berries fall, otherwise the bed becomes a mass of useless seedlings.

After clearing off the top in autumn, hand weed and lightly fork the surface of the bed, and give a 3 in. dressing of well-decayed manure.

A very beneficial top-dressing can be made up with 6 lb. common salt, 2 lb. sulphate potash, 3 lb. nitrate of soda, and 3 lb. superphosphate of lime, well mixed together and applied at the rate of 3 oz. per square yard at the end of March, and again after cutting is finished.

Asparagus plants may be raised from seed sown thinly in well-prepared beds in the open during April. The seedlings should be thinned early to 6 in. apart, and then allowed to remain undisturbed for two seasons, when they may be lifted and planted in special beds as described above.

VARIETIES.

Connovers Colossal; Giant Argenteuil.

Uses.—Only the young stems are used, but there are many different ways of preparing them for the table, the commonest being plain boiled or served in salad.

ASPARAGUS (the greenhouse, ornamental). A half-hardy perennial foliage plant, useful for growing as decorative plants in pots. Elegant fern-like foliage.

Cultivation.—Seeds should be sown in the spring in good heat using a compost of loam, leaf-mould and sharp sand. Pot up singly when the second leaf shows and keep them growing in a warm house until May. Should be wintered in a warm house and given atmospheric moisture and, in the following season, will make handsome plants in 48- or 32-size pots. They respond readily to feeding with diluted manure water or with a complete fertiliser when well-rooted in their final pots.

SPECIES.

Those chiefly cultivated for greenhouse decoration are: *Asparagus plumosus* and *A. p. nanus*. Compact growing plants with wide, spreading foliage. Very useful for decorating.

A. sprengeri. Long and graceful drooping foliage of a very fresh green colour. The sprays are much used for bouquets, wreaths, or for mixing with cut flowers in vases. The plants are often used in conjunction with Ivy-leaved Geraniums for decorating window boxes or large retainers on buildings.

ASPARAGUS BEETLE (*Crioceris asparagi*). DESCRIPTION. *Adults.*—About ¼ in. in length, bluish-black in colour with yellow sides to the wing cases, just before and just after the middle this yellow is produced inwards forming two yellow spots on each wing case. *Eggs.*—Spindle-

damage by stripping the needles. In bad attacks they will also eat away the skin of the stalk. When full grown they again pupate in the soil, the resulting adults hibernating.

METHODS OF CONTROL.—Spraying with arsenate of lead will poison both beetles and larvæ, but this method can only be resorted to after cutting has ceased A derris dust will kill both beetles and larvæ by contact.

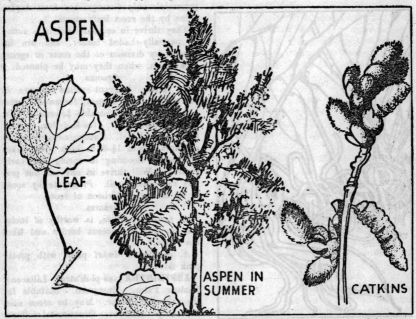

ASPEN

LEAF

ASPEN IN SUMMER

CATKINS

" To tremble like an Aspen leaf " is a metaphor derived from the fact that the leaves of the Aspen will tremble in the slightest breeze. This is because the leaf stalks are flattened laterally.

shaped, brownish in colour and usually laid in rows. *Larvæ.*—Fat, wrinkled and greyish in colour.

LIFE-HISTORY.—The beetles hibernate in the soil, hollow stems and other suitable places. They come out in the spring and lay their eggs on the developing shoots. The eggs hatch in a few days and the resulting larvæ gnaw off the skin of the young shoots. The larvæ become full grown in about twelve days and then pupate in the soil. A second generation of beetles appears in the summer. Eggs are again laid, this time on the fronds and the resulting larvæ may cause much

ASPECT. This term applied to gardening refers chiefly to the points of the compass. A site facing south is generally considered the best for a garden, but this is not always ideal, especially if the soil is of a nature which quickly dries out, and so does not need excessive sunshine. A garden facing east or west can be quite as pleasant as a southerly one, so long as sufficient protection is secured against strong, cold winds. Trellis, hedges or shrub and tree shelter belts will break the force of a wind and raise the temperature of the garden several degrees.

Marshy ground should be drained and

tall overhanging trees thinned, so that light and air can reach the plants. Thus an ideal aspect can be gradually formed.

ASPEN. *See* Populus Tremula.

ASPERULA (as-per-u´la. Rubiaceæ). Sweet Woodruff. Hardy dwarf perennials and annuals belonging to same family as Coffee plant. White, blue and red blooms in summer. These require light, rich soil under the shade of trees or rockeries or in open borders. A really good plant for

Overgrown Aspidistras are best divided in March when growth begins. Shake away old soil and repot in fresh soil.

mass-carpeting, or for the rockery, to flower during an otherwise dull period. *A. azureæ setosa* is its full name, and Royal Blue is the best variety. Native of California.

Propagate perennials by division of the roots in spring or summer and by seeds sown in the early autumn. Annuals by seed sown in April where they are to flower.

Species.

Perennial.—*A. odorata*, white flowers. The well-known sweet woodruff of the woods. *A. cynanchica* or *alpina* has rosy red bloom.

Annual.—*A. azurea*, blue flowered, fragrant, 6–10 in.

When dried the stems and leaves of this plant give off a very pleasant odour.

ASPHALT. A bituminous material used for surfacing pathways, *which see.*

ASPHODEL. *See* Asphodelus.

Asphodel. *One of the flowers dedicated to Juno.*

ASPHODELINE (as-fo-del-ine. Liliaceæ). King's Spear. Hardy herbaceous perennials only distinguished from Asphodelus by the erect leafy stems.

They thrive in ordinary soil in a sunny or partially-shaded border, and are increased by division of the roots in spring or autumn, when they may be planted.

Species.

A. luteus, fragrant yellow flowers in summer and awl-shaped, furrowed leaves.

A. l. flore pleno, double flowers, 3–4 ft.

ASPHODELUS (as-fo-de-lus. Liliaceæ). Asphodel. Tuberous-rooted hardy perennial about 1½–3 ft. high with spikes of flowers blooming in spring and early summer. Will thrive in any soil but prefers rich sandy soil. *Propagate* by seeds or by means of division of roots.

Species.

A. ramosus, white, is worthy of inclusion in any herbaceous border and likes the shade.

A. acaulis, a dwarf plant with pretty pink flowers.

ASPIDISTRA (as-pi-di´stra. Liliaceæ). Parlour Palm. Evergreen. Suitable for the cold greenhouse. May be often seen in cottage windows. Ornamental foliage, green, or green and white. China, 1822.

Culture.—Compost (*see* Greenhouse Asparagus). Repot in spring. Syringe freely during summer.

Propagation.—By division of plants when repotting.

Species.

A. elatior, green; *A. elatior variegata*, green and white; *A. lurida*, green; *A. lurida variegata*, green striped yellow and white.

ASPIDIUM (as-pid-ium. Filices). Shield Fern. An extensive genus of stove, greenhouse and hardy ferns. Increased by spores sown when ripe. Use a compost of three parts of sandy peat to one of loam. The hardy species do well under the shade of trees. A top dressing of leaf-soil is beneficial in autumn and the dead fronds, if left on, afford protection in winter. All require plenty of water all the year round. The greenhouse and stove species do well in the sun as these leathery fronds give protection.

Greenhouse minimum temperature, 45°; stove minimum, 60°.

The species are numerous, and now include plants formerly classified under the genera Cyclodium, Cyclopeltis and Polystichum.

A. acrostichoides (syn. *Polystichum acrostichoides*), fronds, 1–2 in. Many attractive varieties.

A. aristatum (syn. *Polystichum aristatum*), greenhouse, fronds, 1–2 ft. Many varieties, as *variegatum* and *A. a. atratum*.

A. angulare, Soft Shield Fern. There are many beautiful varieties of this hardy fern that make good pot plants for room decoration. Varieties: *Cruciato-polydactylum; foliosum; plumosum; alatum; grandiceps; proliferum* and *Woolastonii*.

A. falcatum (syn. *Polystichum falcinellum*), greenhouse. Varieties: *Fensoni; Fortunei*.

A. laserpitiifolium (syn. *Lastrea Standishii. Polystichum laserpitiifolium*). Fronds, 1–1½ ft.

A. aculeatum. Hard Shield Fern. *Proliferum* and *vestitum* are two good varieties.

ASPLENIUM (as-plē-ni-um. Filices). Spleenwort. Stove greenhouse and hardy ferns. Cultivation of hardy species. These should be grown in a soil containing equal parts of peat, loam, leaf-mould and sand, and old mortar rubble. Scale, Wallrue and Maidenhair Spleenwort can be grown on old walls. The Lady Fern likes moist, shady borders. The other species can be grown on ordinary rockeries. All can be propagated by spores sown in sandy peat, any time when they are available, and also by division of the roots in April.

Culture.—Compost: equal parts loam, peat, leaf-mould and sand. Repot, spring. Shady position.

Propagation.—By spores, sown in sandy peat.

SPECIES.

A. adiantum nigrum (hardy).

A. Filix fœmina (hardy).
A. Nidus (Bird's Nest, stove).
A. elegantissimum (stove), etc.

HARDY SPECIES.

A. adiantum nigrum, Black Maidenhair Spleenwort, "French Fern" of the markets.

A. Ceterach (syn. *Ceterach officinarum*), the Scale Fern.

A. fontanum, Rock Spleenwort.

A. Ruta-muraria, Wall-rue Fern.

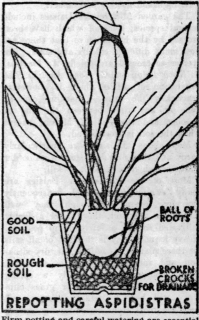

REPOTTING ASPIDISTRAS

Firm potting and careful watering are essential for success with Aspidistras.

A. trichomanes, Maidenhair Spleenwort.

A. thelypteroides (syn. *Athyrium thelypteroides*).

A. viride, Green Spleenwort.

ASSIMILATION AND PHOTO-SYNTHESIS are the involved processes by which plants take in carbon dioxide from the air through the leaves. The chlorophyll or green matter in the leaves then acts on the gas, separating it into carbon and oxygen. The oxygen is returned to the atmosphere, but the carbon —in conjunction with the water supplied by the roots—is formed into a soluble plant-food, sugar, and later on into a less soluble food, starch, which is used for storing.

ASTER (Compositæ). Starwort; Michaelmas Daisy; Perennial Aster. Hardy herbaceous perennials, suitable for borders or rock gardens, flowering chiefly in autumn. Splendid flowers for cutting.

Cultivation of Michaelmas Daisies.— The true Michaelmas Daisy is the *A. Tradescanti*, from N. America, which grows 4 ft. high and flowers in October.

The garden Michaelmas Daisies include several species, some of which have been crossed by the hybridist so that there are now many different colours and sizes. The species so crossed are chiefly *A. Amellus*, *A. Novæ Belgii* and *A. Novæ Angliæ*. The cultivation of all of them is, however, practically the same. Planting can be done at any time between the end of October and the end of March, except when the soil is frost-bound.

Michaelmas Daisies are particularly hardy and they may be regarded as border plants which it is difficult to kill.

Most of the Michaelmas Daisies are really swamp plants and consequently moisture lovers. Although they will succeed in any soil, they prefer a deeply cultivated soil in a fairly damp position. Heavy loam or clay is the best of all soils for these plants. If only a hot, dry situation and rather light soil is available, heavy manuring, particularly a spring mulch of leaves, manure, or grass clippings will help to retain moisture and keep the roots from becoming dry during the summer. At times they benefit by a thorough soaking of water, but this is not usually necessary. To get the best results, that is to produce sprays suitable for exhibition at shows, never allow more than two or three stems on each plant to flower. One stem is sufficient and will result in a plant of perfect symmetry and outstanding beauty. Cut out all the other stems while they are still young, that is, in the spring. Otherwise a score of thin stems may grow up from a single clump. One grown singly will always give finer flowers, and the quantity of bloom will actually be more than if a number of stems are allowed to grow. All the

stronger-growing varieties of Michaelmas Daisy should be lifted every autumn. They should not be left for three years as is the case with most perennial border plants. When the clump is lifted, only the strongest outside shoots should be selected for re-planting, as these produce better flowers than the centre part of the clump. This procedure also keeps the plants healthy and free from disease.

Staking.—It is a great mistake to tie a number of growing stems of Michaelmas Daisies to a single stake. When the young growths have been thinned, a cane should be put to each remaining stem. If this is done early in the summer, while the stems are only a foot or so high, the stakes will be invisible as the flowers develop.

The proper distance between the plants varies according to the type and size, but anything up to 3 ft. apart may be desirable for the production of good flowers. If the stems seem crowded they can sometimes be spread out in the process of staking. The only further cultivation necessary is the hoeing of the soil between the plants to prevent development of weeds, and in the case of young plants it is advisable to keep a look-out for slugs, particularly among rare and expensive varieties.

In cutting Asters for exhibition, it is best to cut them very early in the morning while the dew is still on them, and before the flowers are fully open. Stand them in water (right up to the base of the flowers) in a cool shady place and do not let them become dry before staging them, or the flowers will shrivel and be ineffective.

The following is a list of modern hybrids now in commerce which are useful for those who desire the best for their gardens or for exhibition.

USEFUL VARIETIES FOR THE AMATEUR.

Anita Ballard. A striking Aster of splendid habit, producing a profusion of flowers 2 in. in diameter most elegantly recurved. An exquisite shade of soft china-blue. The abundant broad ray florets are of great substance, their pale curved silvery undersides giving a charming effect.

Bab Ballard. Height under 9 in., flowering in October. A dwarf *Novæ*

Belgii, with neat foliage. The flowers are large and of lavender-blue colour. Suitable for Alpine rock garden.

Beauty of Colwall. 4-5ft. high, flowering in September. Inflorescence a fine rigidly branched pyramid, colour deep lavender-blue, very double on opening, and remaining so for many days.

Beechwood Challenger. Deep strawberry red, quilled petals, light branching habit.

Col. Durham. Clear mauve, dark green foliage, 3½ ft.

Cordibelgii " Pioneer." A cross between *Cordifolius* and *Novæ Belgii.* A branching bushy plant 2½ft. high with a profusion of single clear pink flowers. An early-flowering variety.

Countess. Rose colour. Some of the rays remain for some days over the eye giving a semi-double appearance. A moderate grower and very free flowering.

Elizabeth Bright. Flesh pink, semi-double, 3½ ft.

Empress of Colwall. Large double flowers of rosy-lilac or heliotrope. Excellent habit with fine small foliage.

Freedom. Large, single, lavender-blue flowers, with good eye and clean-cut rays. Free-growing and free-flowering plants.

Lavender. Large, semi-double, lavender-coloured flowers, good early border variety.

Little Boy Blue. Very dwarf. Neat upright little pyramids, smothered with semi-double, deep blue flowers. Suitable for pot culture if desired.

Little Pink Lady. Dwarf bushy variety with large semi-double deep pink flowers.

Mother of Pearl (late). Large single flowers of pale mauve colour with light silvery shades. The eye is green on opening. Vigorous branching grower.

Mount Everest. 6-7 ft., flowering in mid-season. A plant which forms very tall, well-shaped pointed pyramids with large white flowers down to the ground.

Mrs. George Monro. Fine white variety. 4 ft. high, flowering in October.

Mulberry. A late-flowering variety of graceful habit, standing 5 ft. high, with rich mulberry-colour blooms.

October Dawn. Dwarf, early October variety. The flowers are very large, lilac-mauve, single, with long rays, resembling the best *Amellus* varieties, but without their stiffness.

Peace. Soft rosy mauve, enormous, semi-double flowers 3-4 ft.

Petunia. Purple red, semi-double, good for cutting.

Pink Pearl. Early-flowering variety, standing 4½ ft. high. Grows very upright with large single, fringed flowers of pale pink shade. The rays are broad and incurved and the eye very small.

Plenty. Very large, soft pale blue flowers, 3-4 ft.

Royal Blue. Cup-shaped flowers of deep purple blue. Strong grower, 3 ft. high and flowering early.

Ruby Tips. Single rich rose-colour variety, with yellow eye, flowering in mid-season. 4 ft.

Silver Spray (*Cordifolius* section). This plant throws out long arching sprays smothered with small pale lilac-coloured flowers. Flowers in early October and is 5 ft. in height.

Snow Sprite. Dwarf, branching, mid-season. Of bushy growth with small leaves. Pure white, semi-double flowers which are produced in profusion down to the ground. Needs no stakes.

Sunset Glow. Early-flowering variety, 4 ft. high. Neat, with good habit. Flowers of deep rich pink, which are produced in September, of medium size, single and abundant.

Tousle. Very early flowering, 3 ft. in height. Double aster with twisted and crinkled rays of lavender-mauve shade, resembling the Ostrich Plume type of China Aster.

AMELLUS ASTERS.

King George, violet-blue.

Sonia, pink.

Ultramarine, violet-blue.

The tiny yellow daisy-like flower offered as Yellow Aster or *Aster luteus*, is really *Solidago missouriensis*.

In a long border of Michaelmas Daisies it is a decided acquisition, as it introduces the real yellow colour which is absent from the true Michaelmas Daisy.

See also CALLISTEPHUS (China Aster) and MICHAELMAS DAISY.

ASTILBE (as-til-be. Saxifrageæ). Vigorous hardy perennials with flowers from May until July. Suitable for water edge, or for forcing in pots. Plant in rich soil in permanent position, and leave for three or four years. Divide in spring or autumn.

SPECIES.

A. japonica, best for forcing.

A. rivularis, cream, 3–5 ft.

A. simplicifolia, Japanese species, white.

There are in the trade lists numerous varieties of hybrid Astilbes which provide rich colouring in pink, rose and salmon shades. These include:

Gloria, deep lilac-pink, dwarf; Gloria purpurea, deep pink tinged with violet, foliage bronze; Granat, dark crimson; Gruno, salmon-pink; Marguerite van Rechteren, bright red, tinged lilac; Moerheimi, creamy-white.

ASTRAGALUS (ăs-trăg-al-us. Leguminosæ). Herbs or sub-shrubs known as Milk Vetches. On the rockery only a few are worthy of the gardener's attention. They form in the main prostrate, often trailing stems carrying tufts of bright green pinnate foliage, the flowers being yellow, purple, pink or white, but lacking in brightness. A hot sunny position in light soil is the best situation for the few worth growing.

Propagate by seeds, or cuttings under a hand-light in sandy soil.

SPECIES.

A. tragacantha, the Goat's Thorn. A spiny, dwarf shrub, a foot or more high, from the Mediterranean region, with greyish leaves and purple-red pea-shaped flowers in June. Easily grown in rather light, dryish soil.

Propagate by seeds and cuttings.

A. monspessulanus. A purple-flowered trailer from the South of France. July.

A. serinicus. In bloom, the plant is covered with hundreds of little yellow pea-flowers. Mount Serinus.

ASTRANTIA (as-tran-tia. Umbelliferæ). Master-wort. Hardy herbaceous perennials, suitable for banks, borders or woodland walks. Height 1–2 ft. with pink and white blooms in May and July. Will grow anywhere, but prefer a shady position and cool moist loam.

Propagate by division of roots in winter or spring. Lift occasionally to prevent clumps from becoming too large and dress with fresh soil.

SPECIES.

A. Biebersteinii, white, May, 2 ft.

A. carniolica, white, May, 1 ft.

A. helleborifolia, pink, July, 2 ft.

ATAVISM. *Atavus*, an ancestor. Reversion to an older type.

ATHROTAXIS (ath'-ro-tax'-is. Coniferæ). Slow-growing evergreen trees or shrubs, with whipcord-like foliage; known as the "Tasmanian Cedars."

Culture.—Soil: loam, leaf soil and sand.

Propagate by cuttings under a bell-glass, in sandy soil.

SPECIES.

A. cupressoides. Green leaves and slender, cord-like branches.

A. laxifolia. Similar to above, leaves slightly larger, of densely pyramidal habit.

A. selaginoides. King William Pine. The most striking of genus, a beautiful rare tree larger in all its parts than the foregoing species. Leaves with conspicuous white stomata.

ATOMIZER. *See under* SPRAYING.

ATRAGENE. *See* CLEMATIS.

ATRIPLEX (at-ri-plex. Chenopodiaceæ). Orache. Hardy annual. 4 ft. An ornamental-foliaged plant belonging to the spinach family. Evergreen or semi-evergreen shrubs with bluish-green or silvery foliage, suitable for seaside planting. Flowers small and unattractive. Light, dry soil and sunny position.

Atriplex hortensis cupreata is the best of the genus for garden purposes. The foliage is of a rich coppery-bronze, and makes a conspicuous feature in the mixed border. A perfectly hardy annual and will flourish almost anywhere.

A. Halimus. Tree Purslane. Native of southern Europe. 4–6 ft. Silvery foliage.

A. canescens. The American Grey Sage Bush, with narrow, whitish-grey foliage.

ATROPA (Belladonna).—A poisonous perennial 2–3 ft. high which grows in waste places. *See* BELLADONNA.

AUBERGINE or EGG PLANT (*Solonum Melongena*). Solanaceæ. The exact habitat of this plant is not known, but it is certainly a native of the tropics, and in this country must be regarded as a half-hardy annual to be cultivated under glass except in the most favoured districts. It is excellent for culinary purposes, and is also well worth growing for its decorative effect. Other popular names by which this plant is known are Mad Apple, Jew's Apple and Bringall.

Culture.—Seeds should be sown in light soil in a temperature of about 75° from the end of January to March. When the seedlings have formed three leaves carefully prick off into small pots, and pot on as required until May, when they should be in 6 in. pots. When they have recovered from the first potting they may be kept in a lower temperature, but not below 50°. The final potting compost should consist of two parts fibrous loam and one part each of leaf-mould and well-decayed manure, with a good sprinkling of sharp sand.

Syringe the foliage with tepid water twice daily, and pinch out the growing point when the seedlings are 6 in. high. When the fruits set restrict them to three or four per plant. As the plants swell give one or two weak doses of a reliable soluble manure each week.

VARIETIES.

Long Purple; Round Purple ; Egg-shaped White; and Striped.

Uses.—The fruits are picked when ripe and are either baked with cheese, fried with onions, butter and condiments, or boiled and served with poached eggs.

AUBRETIA (o-bre-she-a. Cruciferæ). Rock Cress. Hardy evergreen trailing border or rock plants that are highly valued for spring bedding, or for edgings.

Propagate by division after flowering, by cuttings taken at the same time, and struck in light soil under a hand-light, or by seeds sown in spring. The plants flower in the first year after sowing, but are more productive of flowers in the second year. If the old plants are cut back, growth will be more compact and equally floriferous.

They love the sun, and do well in light sandy soil in chinks of old walls, or between paving stones, and are very effective grown as a carpeting for spring bulbs.

SPECIES.

A. deltoidea is the best known of the species, and has many beautiful varieties that excel the type for beauty.

The best of these are *A. d. Leichtlinii*, red flowers.

A. d. Campbellii, violet blue, 4 in.

A. d. Moerheimii, large rose flowers, 6in.

Other species are numerous. All bloom from April to July, and are from 4–6 in. high.

Modern-named hybrids, particularly the well-known rich purple, " Dr. Mules," should be grown by the amateur. The colours range through reds and purples, and some are very striking.

AUCUBA (ău-kū-ba. Cornaceæ). Japan 6–10 ft. Unisexual Japanese evergreens, with red berries and very beautiful laurel-like glossy leaves. Most accommodating in regard to culture, thriving in ordinary soil, chalky or otherwise, and under the shade and drip of overhead trees. They make good town plants and succeed in pots or tubs. They may be planted at mid-winter or midsummer, but March or October are the best months. Cut back any long weak shoots in May. To propagate, take cuttings or small branches and strike in open ground in autumn, or sow seeds in frames. One male plant at least should be planted with the female varieties, to ensure a plentiful crop of berries. If the pollen is ready before the female flowers are in a receptive condition for fertilisation, it may be kept some time in a dry place without losing its potency.

MALE VARIETIES.

A. japonica crassifolia, thick green leaves.

A. japonica latimaculata, variegated gold.

A. japonica maculata, the common variegated variety.

A. japonica viridis, large glossy green leaves.

FEMALE VARIETIES.

A. japonica erotonensis, green and gold.

A. japonica fructo albo, white berries yellow speckled foliage.

A. japonica grandis, broad green leaves.

A. japonica longifolia, narrow bright green leaves, very free berry-bearing variety.

A. japonica maculata, common variegated female form.

A japonica nana rotundifolia, dwarf, green, very free bearing.

A. japonica salicifolia, distinct, long narrow green leaves, imparting quite a sub-tropical appearance.

A. japonica sulphurea, broad bands of yellow.

A. japonica viridis Hillieri, new very large green lustrous leaves and large crimson berries. Quick growing.

AUGUST WORK IN THE GARDEN.

Flowers.

Carnations layered last month will need water if the weather is dry. There is still time to layer more, or to insert cuttings in sandy soil in the cold frame.

Keep them close for some time, only opening the lights morning and evening to refresh the air. They will root in a few weeks, and can then be left exposed to all weathers unless severe storms or night frosts occur.

Seedlings of many plants need attention now. The early sowings of biennials may be ready for transplanting to their permanent position.

Pansy and Viola seedlings can be transplanted to the borders as soon as they are large enough to handle. The June sowings will probably flower a little all through the winter if the weather is not too cold.

Polyanthus seedlings should be large enough to prick out in a half-shady border now.

Hollyhocks and other perennials raised from seed must be kept free from weeds. As soon as possible transplant them where they are to flower next year, but only do this in showery weather.

Spring bulbs should be potted from now onwards. Good varieties for forcing for Christmas are Tulips and Hyacinths (*which see*).

Madonna Lilies usually need no attention, but where a clump is overgrown, or where it is desirable to move the lilies from one position to another, this should be done now. Prepare the soil by deep digging, adding plenty of leaf-mould and lime.

Madonna Lilies are among the few lilies that do need lime in the soil if they are to succeed.

Clematis, honeysuckle and wistaria should be trained before the shoots become too long.

Show dahlias should be disbudded and staked. Earwig traps should be set.

Lavender hedges may now be trimmed.

Dead flower spikes should be cut down.

Roses may still be budded.

Sweet Peas require ample water and doses of liquid manure.

All flower-beds should be hoed whenever posisble.

Sow Hardy Annuals.

Certain of the hardiest annuals will stand the winter in the open garden. If these are sown now, they will make healthy seedlings before the frosts come, and will be ready to flower early next year, long before the spring-sown annuals come into bloom.

Annuals which will succeed in this way are:

Alyssum, "Carpet of Snow."

Blue Woodruff (Asperula).

Marigolds, "Orange King," "Lemon Queen," and "Radio."

Calliopsis, "Drummondii," yellow and chestnut.

Candytuft, all colours.

Blue Cornflowers (Centaurea cyanus).

Clarkia, "Salmon Queen."

Collinsia bicolor, "Salmon Beauty."

Eschscholtzia, "Orange King."

Gypsophila.

Godetia, all colours.

Larkspur, Giant Imperial, mixed.

Limnanthes douglassii (Eggs and Bacon).

Nigella, "Miss Jekyll."

Double Shirley Poppies.

Sweet Scabious.

Sweet Sultan, all colours.

Viscaria, "Fire King."

The Shrubbery.

Favourite trees and shrubs can be raised quite easily from cuttings. A new shrub of good variety makes an ideal gift for a gardening friend.

Choose half-ripened shoots. There are many in the right condition this month.

Strip off the two lower pairs of leaves and insert the cutting in gritty open soil under a hand-light or in a cold frame.

Keep it close for a few weeks or until it shows signs of growth.

The glass should be raised daily, and wiped free from surplus moisture.

Most cuttings are best cut immediately below a joint, but Clematis and one or two others root more readily if the cut is made midway between the joints. If in doubt, try some both ways to ensure success.

Another method of increasing shrubs is to notch a shoot and bend the notched portion down so that it can be laid under the soil. Roots form easily at the cut, and when they have formed, the new plant can be servered from the parent.

Hedges of plants such as Box can be clipped at the end of this month, for the last time this season. It is a mistake to clip too late in the year as this spoils the effect during the winter months.

No pruning need be done in the shrubbery this month except the trimming of topiary and hedges, and removal of broken branches.

Shrubs to Increase by Cuttings or Layers in August.

Roses.	Escallonia.
Artemisia abrotanum.	Garrya.
Aucuba.	Hibiscus syriacus.
Berberis stenophylla.	Hypericum.
Catalpa.	Ilex (holly).
Ceanothus.	Kalmia.
Colutea.	Lavender.
Cotoneaster.	Lonicera.
Olearia.	Ribes.
Osmanthus.	Rubus.
Pernettya.	Rhus.
Viburnum laurustinus.	

The Rockery.

If the rockery is to be re-made before next spring, the sooner it is done the better.

Wait for a showery day and lift out every plant carefully with as much soil as possible, replanting each one temporarily in a trench in one of the borders. You can then rebuild at your leisure.

Take out all large stones, thoroughly dig over the soil, and if needed, improve the drainage by adding large bricks and other rough material to the inside portion.

Begin to rebuild from the bottom upwards, sloping the rocks inwards and filling the pockets so formed with light soil, well mixed with sand. Add lime where you wish to grow lime-loving plants.

Replant as the stones are placed in position; you can usually get the deep roots in a better position while the stones are not too firmly set.

Fruit.

The earliest apples are ready for gathering. Soon the fruit harvest will be in full swing and those who store for winter use should see that sheds and trays are ready.

Strawberries should be looked over, and a few strong plants of early fruiting varieties selected for planting in a south border. Here they will stand a good chance of producing fine early berries.

New strawberry plantations can be made where potatoes have been lifted. Complete this work as early in the month as possible.

Wall fruits make abundant growth at this season. Tie in young wood wanted for next season and remove the rest. In very dry weather give an occasional good soaking.

Gather apples when they break easily from the tree on being lifted in the palm of the hand.

When gathering fruits from apples, pears and plums, keep and eye open for the eggs of the Lackey Moth. This moth deposits eggs in a "bracelet" round the stems. Each bracelet contains two or three hundred eggs, which if left will hatch out next spring and do considerable damage. They can be easily crushed and destroyed. The moth itself is light yellow or reddish-yellow, but as it flies at night it is rarely seen.

This is the time to take stock of your bush and standard trees. Note the amount of new leaf and stem on each. If a tree continually makes exceptionally strong growth, but never has much blossom or fruit, it is being overfed with nitrogenous manure. The remedy is sometimes to be found in root pruning, which will have to be done later in the year.

Wall fruit should be protected, as it ripens, from wasps and birds. Earwigs and snails should be trapped. The fruit should be exposed to the sun as much as possible.

Summer pruning may be continued and fruit trees may be budded.

Bands round fruit trees should be examined, the pests being destroyed.

Late apples, pears and plums require thinning out if the crop is too heavy.

Apricots, peaches and nectarines should be exposed to the sun as much as possible.

Loganberry and Raspberry canes that have borne fruit should be cut down.

Vegetables.

As the first crops are harvested, the ground should be filled again with seedlings of Broccoli, Savoys and Endive, or seeds of the following can be sown: Cabbage, including Red Cabbage, Stump-rooted carrots, such as Early Horn, Cauliflower (Autumn Giant), Lettuce, Onions, Spinach and Turnips.

Earth up Celery.

If the weather is dry, water peas and give a mulch of manure.

Continue to pinch outside shoots from outdoor tomatoes, thin the lower leaves, remove any that are turning yellow and when the plants have made four or five trusses of fruit, pinch out the tips.

Potato blight is a trouble which is pretty sure to arrive sooner or later if spraying is not done. In small gardens it is best to buy Bordeaux mixture ready prepared, and to use it in accordance with instructions. If the mixture is too strong it burns the foliage; if too weak, it is not effective.

All kinds of herbs can be gathered this month and stored for winter use. They are best gathered in bunches, washed and hung up to dry.

Paper bags can be used to keep dust and insects from the leaves.

Thyme, Marjoram, Sage, Parsley and Mint should be available in every garden.

Rose petals and other flowers should be dried in full sunshine for Pot Pourri.

Keep the plot clean. The best place for most soft green rubbish is *under* the soil, where it will decay and form plant food.

Hard woody refuse should be burned, together with any vegetable matter that is likely to spread disease.

Green manuring is a good way to add humus to light soil. It can only be done where land is plentiful. As the early crops are harvested, sow mustard seed thinly over the soil, after turning in all weeds and dead plant tops.

The mustard germinates and grows until you are ready to dig over the plot in winter, when it will be turned into the soil.

This is one of the best substitutes for stable manure and very easily applied, but it will need to be supplemented with artificials.

Bean stalks and the remains of other gathered crops should be burnt as soon as possible.

A row or two of French beans should be left for seed.

Artichokes must be cut down as the heads are gathered.

Globe artichokes must not be allowed to flower.

Asparagus beds must be kept clear of weeds. Unless seed is wanted, the bearing heads should be cut off.

Under Glass.

In the cool greenhouse now there should be pans of seedlings of bedding Primulas, Pansies, Antirrhinums, etc., for next season. As soon as possible they should be hardened-off and planted out in sheltered nursery beds, or pricked out into frames as the space in the greenhouse itself will be needed next month for Azaleas and other shrubs that have been recovering in the open air.

Sow Calceolaria seed in pans filled with sandy soil and leaf-mould. Cover with sand only and put a sheet of glass over. The soil should be wet before sowing is done and any further watering must be done with great care to avoid washing out the seedlings. Stand the pans in a cool part of the greenhouse until germination has taken place, but transfer them afterwards to a shelf near the glass.

Early bulbs should now be potted. Roman Hyacinths are the best for the amateur who wishes to have flowers at Christmas, as they come into bloom more rapidly than most indoor bulbs.

Sown now and grown under glass, dwarf French beans will mature rapidly, and late supplies will be available of the same delicacy as those of the summer crop. Use light soil over a bed of well-decayed manure in the cold frame. Sow and grow on without transplanting. Egg plants, or Aubergines, should be developing their white or purple fruits now. Not more than four sprays should be given at frequent intervals while the fruits are swelling.

Red Spider frequently attacks these plants and to keep it under control the plants should be well syringed with water.

A temperature of 50°–60° suits these plants.

Sow cauliflower seeds in a frame but uncover them as soon as the seed is up.

As Achimenes go out of bloom, they should be placed in a frame to ripen the tubers.

Late-flowering Azaleas must be repotted and so trained that the foliage is properly drawn out before winter.

Chrysanthemums should be disbudded.

Climbing plants should be cut back to keep the greenhouse in order.

Lilies that have flowered require less water.

Preparatory to cutting down, Pelargoniums which have gone out of flower should be stood outdoors to ripen the wood.

On Wet Days.

Sponge the foliage of all indoor plants. If the showers are warm and not too heavy, stand the pots in the open so that the rains can soak them.

Tidy up the potting shed. Soil for potting should be kept in heaps, the floor being swept clean. Sticks, tools and tying material should all have their proper place.

Wash greenhouse stages and glass. Warm soapy water is best for this job.

Take cuttings. There is always some plant or shrub in the garden or greenhouse in the right condition for this.

Prepare labels. Old labels can be rubbed with sandpaper, or shaved with a knife, so that they can be used again.

Wash empty or new pots. A good plan is to keep a tub handy in which to soak old dirty pots, so that they are easy to clean when opportunity occurs.

Re-surface soil in pots. It adds to the vigour of plants that have been in pots for some time if a thin layer of soil is removed from the surface and replaced with fresh compost.

AURICULA. *See* PRIMULA AURICULA.

AVAILABILITY. Applied to fertiliser materials, this word means water soluble potash and water and citric soluble phosphate. A definition of available nitrogen is rather more difficult. Very broadly speaking, available nitrogen is that part which readily breaks down into a nitrate form and thus becomes available to the plant. Recent research indicates that ammoniacal nitrogen may also be directly absorbed by the plant. All inorganic nitrogenous fertilisers do this very easily, but organic forms only become available much more slowly; some of them, like fur and wool waste, leather and shoddy, may take years to do so.

AVENA (a-ve′-na. Graminaceæ). *A. sterilis.* Animated Oat. 1½ ft. H.A. A curious member of the Oat family, the

The Auricula is excellent for a shady garden and is easy to cultivate.

seed awns being greatly extended, like the legs of the daddy-long-legs, and the seeds are sometimes glued on to a piece of stout cardboard with the awns, or legs, free to act as a weather indicator, the awns curling up when rain is imminent. A hardy annual which does well in poor dry soils and is only grown for its peculiar seeds—as an ornamental grass.

AVENUE. Formed by planting specimen shrubs or trees at regular intervals either side of a pathway. Flowering trees such as Cherries, Almonds and trees of small dimensions can be planted over a

4–6 ft. pathway. They should be spaced not less than 8 ft. apart.

Clipped specimens of box and standard rose trees can be used to give the same effect in very small gardens, while forest trees such as poplars, birches and ash, would be in proportion with large walks or drives.

AXIL (Latin, armpit). The angle formed between the axis and any organ which arises from it. This is generally used by gardeners in connection with the angle between the stem and a leaf.

AZALEA. *See* RHODODENDRONS.

AZALEODENDRON. *See* RHODODENDRONS.

AZARA (Bixaceæ). Fine hardy or half-hardy flowering shrub from Chile, with fragrant flowers.

Culture.—Plant in well-drained loam and leaf-mould.

Propagate by cuttings. Protection may be necessary in cold districts except for *A. microphylla.*

Recommended for walls (east or west) and trellis.

SPECIES.

A. Browneæ. Rare, resembling *A. integrifolia* with larger foliage and small bright yellow flowers from December to March.

A. dentata. 1830. 8–12 ft. Fragrant yellow flowers.

A. Gilliesii. The most ornamental flowered species. Regarded as tender generally, but has withstood 27° of frost in Hampshire, protected by other shrubs.

A. integrifolia. Orange-yellow fragrant flowers in winter and early spring.

A. integrifolia var. *variegata.* Leaves edged pink.

A. lanceolata. A new species requiring a south or west wall. Very showy yellow flower.

A. microphylla. 1861. An elegant shrub or small tree with frond-like branches clothed with glistening small box-like leaves. In the west will reach to 30 ft. The sweetly-scented flowers open in February and March in favourable weather, or later if inclement weather prevails, and their vanilla-like fragrance manifests itself some distance from the bush. Hardiest of genus, and one of the most beautiful of all evergreens. Most useful for table decorations. An ideal plant for north walls and very attractive as a standard.

A. serrata. Flowers creamy-white and fragrant.

AZOLLA (a-so-lla. Rhizocarpeæ). Small floating aquatics with tiny overlapping leaves with two kinds of fruit on the under side of the branches. There are both stove and greenhouse species, but the only one grown is *A. caroliniana,* an attractive hardy fern-like plant that may be cultivated in still water outside. The mature plant floats on the water, and has no true roots, but the small divided leaves on the under side of the stem are often mistaken for them. The spores are found amongst these so-called roots. The plants grow annually from these spores. Frequently these are lost through insufficient care. They may be preserved by placing the plants in a tank of water that is half filled with sandy loam. When the plants die in winter, the spores remain and germinate in the following year. It is thought by some, however, that having been set in the water with the root-like leaves downwards, they need no further care and they continue to appear each year.

They are very pretty plants, and hardly rise above the surface of the water which they cover with a carpet of green that becomes bronze in summer.

B

BABIANA (bab'-i-a'-na. Iridaceæ). Baboon Root. Half-hardy bulbous plants, with fragrant flowers, from May to June. Originally from S. Africa. First introduced in 1752.

Outdoor Culture.—Grow in a sunny, well-drained border in light, sandy soil. They can be planted at any time from September to January, placing the bulbs 4 in. deep and 2 in. apart.

When the plants have finished flowering, and the foliage has died down, they should be lifted and stored until planting time.

Indoor Culture.—For the cultivation of these bulbs, a compost of sandy soil and leaf-mould, or decayed cow manure, is necessary.

They should be planted 3 in. deep in 4½ in. pots, in which the drainage has been attended to by placing plenty of crocks in the bottom of the pots.

The bulbs may be planted in autumn or spring, allowing five bulbs in each pot. The pots should be covered with coco-nut fibre refuse until growth begins. Water should be given freely during growth, but as the flowers fade watering should be gradually ceased. While at rest the bulbs should be kept absolutely dry.

Bulbs potted in autumn must be kept in a cold pit or greenhouse during the winter.

The temperature in the greenhouse for these bulbs should be, September to February from 40°–50° and at other times from 50°–60°.

Propagation takes place by offsets, which should be treated as larger bulbs.

SPECIES.

B. disticha, blue, flowering in June.

B. plicata, blue, flowering in June.

B. ringens, scarlet, flowering in June.

B. stricta, white and blue, flowering in May.

BABOON ROOT. *See* BABIANA.

BACCHARIS (bak'-kăr-is. Compositæ). A large genus of shrubs, small trees and plants from the New World, of but little garden value. Useful for dry or windy positions.

SPECIES.

B. halimifolia, 1683. Tree Groundsel. Deciduous, small white flowers.

B. Patagonica. Patagonian Groundsel Tree. Dark green foliage, small white flowers.

BACTRIS (bak'-tris. Palmaceæ). Tobago Cane or Maharajah Palm. Stove palms. Valued for ornamental foliage. They reach a height of 20–80 ft.

A compost of equal parts loam, leaf-mould and sand is necessary, with a summer temperature of 65°–85°; while in the winter 60° is sufficient.

Propagate by removing the young plants, which grow from the base of the old one, in March. These should be put into small pots.

The Maharajah Palm can also be grown from seeds.

Walking-sticks made from this palm are much used in England and are known as "Penang lawyers."

SPECIES.

B. caryotæfolia.

B. Maraja.

B. pallidispina.

BADMINTON COURT. Double court, 44 ft. by 20 ft.; single court, 44 ft. by 17 ft.

BÆRIA (bē-ri-a. Compositæ). Hardy annual, first introduced in 1835.

These plants bear yellow flowers in May and attain a height of 8–12 in. Sown in a sunny border, they will thrive in any ordinary soil. Seeds may be sown in March or April, ⅛ in. deep. They should be sown where the plants are to flower.

SPECIES.

B. chrysostoma; B. gracilis (syn. *Burrielia gracilis*).

BAHIA (Woolly Bahia. Compositæ). Hardy, herbaceous perennial herb, of branching habit, with grey foliage and yellow flowers from May to August. It attains a height of from 12–18 in.

Planted in a sunny border, Bahia will thrive in any ordinary soil. It should be planted at any time from October to April. Seeds may be sown ⅛ in. deep in the open border in April, or the old plants can be divided in March.

SPECIES CULTIVATED.

B. lanata.

B. oppositifolia.

BAKING SOIL. *See* STERILISATION.

BALCONY GARDENS. *See* TOWN GARDENS.

BALL. The mass of soil which surrounds the roots of a plant or tree is known as a ball. When transplanting, either from the garden or pots, care should be taken not to damage this ball. The larger the unbroken ball surrounding a tree or plant the quicker will the plant recover from the shock of transplanting.

BALM OF GILEAD. *See* POPULUS CANDICANS.

BALSAM (*Impatiens balsamia*. Geraniaceæ). A half-hardy annual. Height 2 ft. A wide range of colours such as rose, pink, cerise, white, mauve and purple.

Cultivation.—Sow in spring in pans on slight bottom heat and, when large enough, prick out and pot on as required. They flower well in size 48 pots, using a good compost of fibrous loam, leaf-mould and sand to which a little old rotten manure has been added.

VARIETIES.

New Bush Mixed; Rose Queen; Superb Double Mixed and Camellia-flowered. *See also* IMPATIENS.

BALUSTRADE. This is the term applied to a series of balusters which are usually placed at the front of a terrace and are connected by a coping or rail. They give a degree of protection and also serve as a beautiful addition to the garden design.

Wood, iron, stone, brick and tile can all be used to form various designs, but the material chosen should be in harmony with that used for the house.

Where space and time permit, living balustrades are very beautiful. These are formed of some thick-growing subject such as box, yew or ivy. They can be trained to take the place of a temporary wooden or iron balustrade if desired.

BAMBOO. Arundinaria, Bambusa, etc. Gramineæ. A genus of extremely beautiful, quick - growing evergreen shrubby grasses, of unequalled grace and charm among hardy foliage plants. Of very diverse habit of growth—ranging from quite dwarf species 1½ ft. high, with stems no thicker than a knitting-needle, to noble species reaching to a height of 100 ft. with stems 9 in. in diameter—they all spread by means of rhizomes running just under the ground like couch-grass.

Bamboos are of great value for planting by woodlands, walks, in shrubberies, and especially by the sides of ponds and streams, imparting quite an oriental effect. Some species make very effective individual specimens for lawns.

BANANA. *See* MUSA.

BANE BERRY. *See* ACTÆA.

BANKS. Where a garden site is undulating or slopes steeply and level lawns and formal flower gardens are required, the excavated soil will have to be heaped up to form banks.

These may be turfed or sown with grass seed, but in this case there is always the difficulty of mowing to be considered. Dwarf trailing shrubs such as hypericum and periwinkle or brooms and small berberis, will clothe the bank with flower and foliage and need little after-care. A more expensive alternative is to build a retaining wall (*which see*).

For shifting banks, willow stakes driven in every 3 ft. will take root and hold the soil firm.

BANKSIA (bank'-sĭ-a. Proteaceæ). Handsome evergreen shrubs from Australia, only half-hardy and need every protection. They need a warm position, and a soil of loam, leaf-mould and sand, and perfect drainage. Abundance of water.

Propagate by cuttings of the ripened shoots, cut off at a joint and having none of the leaves removed.

SPECIES.

B. ericifolia. Thin, narrow, dark green leaves, silvery reverse.

B. marginata. Similar to above.

B. quercifolia. A noble and most striking evergreen. The foliage resembles, as the name suggests, the Oak (Quercus), with silvery under side and gives a most delightful effect when the long growths are swayed by a slight breeze.

B. attenuata; B. collina; B. speciosa.

BAPTISIA (bap-tis'-i-a. Leguminosæ). Hardy herbaceous perennials, bearing white, blue or yellow flowers during June and July, and attaining a height of 2-4 ft.

They thrive in any ordinary soil in a sunny, well-drained border. Plant from October to April. Increase by seeds sown in sandy soil ½ in. deep, in shallow boxes in the cold frame in April, or in open, sunny borders in May. Also by division of old plants in March.

Some species of this genus possess dyeing qualities, as is implied by the common name "False Indigo."

SPECIES.

B. *alba*, white, June.

B. *australis*, blue, June.

B. *australis minor*, blue, June.

B. *tinctoria*, yellow, July.

BARBERRY. *See* BERBERIS.

Barberry (*Berberis*). *From the yellowness of its bark, the herbalists of old used it to cure jaundice, but it is now only found useful as a dye. Rouen makes a famous "Barberry preserve." The plant has a curious blight, which in alternating generations produces the blight of wheat.*

BARBERTON DAISY. *See* GERBERA.

BARLERIA (bah-lēr-i-a. Acanthaceæ). Evergreen, stove flowering shrubs. Pot in March in well-drained pots containing a compost of two parts peat and loam, one part decayed manure and sand. A temperature of 70° at first should be gradually increased to 85° by September, but from September to March the temperature may be from 55°–65°. During the winter these shrubs should be watered moderately, but in the summer the amount may be gradually increased. They should also be syringed daily during the spring and summer. After flowering, all shoots should be pruned back.

To increase, take cuttings of young shoots and insert in sandy peat under a bell-glass in a temperature of 85° any time from March to July.

SPECIES.

B. *cristata*, 2 ft., purple and white, July.

B. *flava*, 18 in., yellow, winter.

B. *involucrata*, 18 in., blue, winter.

B. *lupulina*, 2 ft., yellow, August.

B. *strigosa* (*cærulea*), 2–3 ft., blue, July.

BAROSMA (Rutaceæ). Evergreen shrub from the Cape, with showy heath-like flowers. A warm position and good garden soil are suitable.

SPECIES.

B. *ericioides*. White flowers.

BARRENWORT. *See* EPIMEDIUM.

BARROWS. There are two materials used for the manufacture of these useful articles—wood and metal. In the former it is most important that it should be made of well-seasoned hard wood—usually Ash frame and Elm sides—this because it is exposed to all weathers and must not warp. The wheel should be fitted with an iron tread at least 2 in. wide to avoid sinking in soft ground. These barrows can be had, at slightly extra cost, with a detachable top to increase the capacity, and also with a movable handle board to facilitate emptying. The galvanised metal barrow

A USEFUL BARROW FOR GENERAL PURPOSES

GALVANIZED GARDEN BARROW

Types of wheelbarrows. The latest idea is a pneumatic tyre which can be fitted to any barrow. This is useful in negotiating steps.

is rapidly gaining in popularity as it is lighter in use, which is a most important point. The chief point to look for in comparison with other barrows, at the same or different prices, is the gauge or thickness of the metal used and whether it has been thoroughly galvanised. This is most important to the life of the barrow. These barrows can also be had with a ball-bearing wheel at a negligible extra cost, with a flat solid rubber tyre, a pneumatic tyre, or caterpillar wheel. These extras, especially the first, have the advantages of longer life and easier work.

BARTONIA (bar-to'-nia. Loasaceæ).
B. aurea is the best representative. Height
1½ ft., spreading flowers 2 in. across of
a rich golden yellow and most freely produced. It likes a deep soil and a sunny
position. Sown in March where to flower,
and thinned to 1 ft. apart at least, it will
give a full display of flowers all the season.
Native of California.

BASIC SLAG. A by-product of steel
manufacture. (*See* FERTILISERS). Slag
must conform to certain definite regula-

**BARTONIA: AUREA
A YELLOW HARDY ANNUAL**

One of the best annuals for a continuous supply
of golden flowers is Bartonia aurea. It grows
anywhere.

tions affecting its fineness of division
(grinding) and analysis. Very high-grade
slags are becoming rare with the decline
of the Bessemer process of steel manufacture. The open hearth process, now in
fairly general use, results in a slag of
low phosphoric acid content and low citric
solubility. Slags should always be purchased on a high citric solubility basis.

BASIL. *See* HERBS.

BASS or BAST. A dried vegetable
fibre used in gardens for tying-in shoots of
plants. It is creamy coloured and sold in
bundles. There are now on the market
green-coloured substitutes which are neatly
wound, ready for use. The green colouring is a great improvement as it is practically invisible amongst leaves and stems.

BASTARD OR FALSE INDIGO. *See*
AMORPHA.

BASTARD TRENCHING. *See*
DOUBLE DIGGING.

BATEMANNIA (bāt-man-i-a. Orchidaceæ). An evergreen stove orchid, allied
to Maxillaria, which flowers in August and
grows to a height of 6–8 in.

For the cultivation of these orchids, a
compost of equal parts fibrous peat and
sphagnum moss will be needed. They can
be planted in shallow baskets or on blocks
of wood. If in pots, the plants should be
raised considerably above the surface.

They should be repotted in March, and
watered on alternate days from April to
August. From August to April water is
only needed once a week. They need a
temperature of 55°–65° from September to
March; 75°–85° from March to September.

Propagation takes place by division of
old plants at potting time.

SPECIES.

B. Colleyi, purple and green, flowering
in August.

BATTER. *See* WALLS.

BAUHINIA (bō-hin-i-a. Leguminosæ).
Mountain Ebony. Evergreen flowering
shrub grown in the stove greenhouse. It
is a shy bloomer, and is of no great value.
It should be grown in a compost of equal
parts loam and peat and one-sixth sand.
Pot firmly in March, and place in a light,
sunny position with plenty of moisture in
the summer.

Give the plants plenty of water from
March to September, but less at other
times.

Propagate by cuttings inserted in well-
drained pots of sandy peat under bell-glass
in a temperature of 75° in July.

SPECIES.

B. galpini, white, 6 ft., July.

B. grandiflora, white, 6 ft., July.

B. natalensis, white, September.

B. tomentosa, yellow and white, 6 ft.

BAY. *See* LAURUS NOBILIS.

BAYONET PLANT. *See* ACIPHYLLA.

BEAN APHIS (*Aphis rumicis*) Commonly known as "Collier," "Dolphin,"
" Black Fly," or " Black Army."

DESCRIPTION. *Larvæ and Adults.*—Black in colour with yellow and black legs.

LIFE-HISTORY.—In the autumn eggs are laid on docks and thistles; the winter may also be passed on Euonymus. In the early summer the aphides migrate to the beans, and clustering round the tops of the plant soon give rise to thousands of individuals, which not only suck the sap of the beans but cover them with a sticky substance called "honey-dew." This honey-dew not only blocks up the breathing-pores of the plant, but it also acts as a breeding-ground for fungus. As the beans die away the aphides—which are now all winged—fly back not only to the original host plants, but also to mangolds.

METHOD OF CONTROL.—It is well known that autumn-sown beans are better able to withstand an attack than spring-sown beans. Spraying or dusting with any of the powders or washes of vegetable origin will also control an attack; but the operation should be carried out as soon as the aphis appears on the beans.

BEANS, BROAD (*Vicia Faba*). Leguminosæ. This is an annual plant which is supposed to have originated in Northern Africa.

Only the beans or "seeds" are used for culinary purposes, and if picked whilst still young and before they form a black scar or "eye" they are most deliciously flavoured, and have an exceptionally high food value.

Grows and crops best on a heavy soil, and is extremely hardy, so much so that autumn sowings are frequently practised for the production of early crops. For this purpose the Long-podded types are used, whilst the Broad-podded or Windsor type forms the basis of later supplies.

Culture.—Seeds should be sown early, especially in the South of England. If autumn sowings are to be made they should be put in in October or November. Spring sowings should commence in January or February according to the location and weather conditions.

The site should be dug thoroughly and well manured, for the Broad Bean is a rank feeder. A dressing of slaked lime at 4 oz. per sq. yd. applied to the surface after digging is of advantage to the subsequent crop.

The most usual method of sowing is in double lines 9 in. apart, 6 in. between the beans, and at least 4 ft. between each double row.

A flat-bottomed trench 3 in. deep may be taken out with a spade or hoe, and the seeds set along and then re-covered, or a blunt-ended dibber may be used to make the necessary holes at the requisite distances and depth. It is always advisable to sow a few extra seeds at the end of each row to provide plants for filling any gaps occasioned by birds or mice.

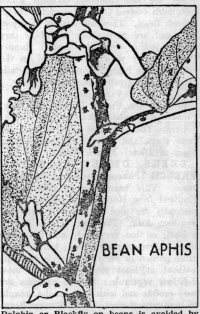

BEAN APHIS

Dolphin or Blackfly on beans is avoided by early sowing and timely spraying.

Still earlier crops may be obtained by sowing in boxes in a moderate temperature in early January, and by carefully hardening off for planting out in March.

Successional sowings may be made at intervals up to the end of May, but these later sowings must be afforded shade and ample moisture at the roots.

Late-sown Broad Beans usually become infested with Black Fly or Dolphin. If the pests appear early, the plants should be regularly sprayed with a good insecticide until sufficient pods have set to allow of the top of the plant being pinched off.

VARIETIES.

Long-podded: Bunyard's Exhibition; Masterpiece Green Seeded; Johnson's Wonderful. Broad-podded; Harlington Windsor; Green Windsor.

Uses.—The beans are used in many different ways, but principally boiled and served with sauce. If the tops are kept clean, and no fly has appeared, they can be boiled when removed. They make a delicious vegetable of fine flavour.

BEANS, CLIMBING FRENCH. These are tall climbing varieties which have been evolved from types of the Dwarf French Bean. They are usually very prolific, and are particularly useful as they mature earlier than the Scarlet Runner Beans. They may be cultivated in the same way as Scarlet Runners, full details of which are given under that heading.

VARIETIES.

First in the Field; Tender and True; Climbing Canadian Wonder.

Uses.—The pods are gathered at the same stage, and used in the same way as those of Dwarf French Beans.

BEANS, DWARF KIDNEY or FRENCH (*Phaseolus vulgaris*). Leguminosæ. This bean was introduced into England from Holland about 1509, but is generally regarded as being a native of Southern Asia. The plant is a half-hardy annual, so that very early and late crops must be grown under glass, but no vegetable garden in early summer is complete without at least one row of this most delicious vegetable. Several varieties are very prolific and with care can be brought to bear several weeks before Runner Beans are ready. With this bean both the pod and the seed are used for food, and it is stated to have a definite medicinal value. There are both green and golden podded varieties—the latter are delicious—and there is also a great variation in the colour of the seed; dark brown, black, white and red and white spotted, being the commonest.

Culture.—For the earliest outdoor crop the seeds should be sown in boxes in early April in a temperature of about 55°. As soon as the first leaves are fully formed, they should be moved to a cold frame to harden off. Some extra protection for the frames may be necessary at night, but on all fine days plenty of ventilation should be given, whilst care must be exercised not to over or under water, so as to check the plants. Under this treatment the plants should be ready for planting out by the middle of May unless the weather is unusually severe. A sunny, sheltered position should be chosen for this early crop, and they should be planted in four rows or shallow drills as an extra precaution. The young plants should be buried up to the first two leaves, and should be in single rows with 6 in. between each plant.

The first outdoor sowing should not be made before the first week in May, and not until the end of the month or early June if the position is at all exposed. In all cases it is wise to make small successional sowings rather than one large one as the beans mature quickly and lose their value when they become old.

Outdoor sowings should be made in drills 3 in. deep and 3 ft. apart, placing the beans in a double line along the bottom of the drill so that they are 6 in. apart each way, finally covering with 2 in. of soil.

As one degree of frost will kill or seriously check the plants, they should be covered with paper or hessian if frost appear imminent. The young plants are very succulent and may fall a prey to slugs and snails unless protected from these pests.

Hoe frequently and water freely during very dry weather, and once the pods have set, give a weak feed of soluble manure every 10 days.

VARIETIES.

Canadian Wonder Improved; King of the Dwarfs; Golden Wonder; Negro Longpod.

Uses.—The whole of the pod and seed is used, and these may be boiled and served in many ways with different sauces. They also make an excellent pickle, and on the Continent especially are largely used in salads.

BEANS, HARICOT. These are types of Dwarf French beans which are grown on to maturity for the production of seed alone. Their early cultivation is exactly the same as that of the ordinary Dwarf French, but instead of gathering the young pods they are allowed to ripen on the plant. In the autumn when the foliage loses colour, and before they can become blackened by frost, the plants are pulled up and hung in convenient bundles in a dry, airy structure. As soon as the pods show signs of cracking the seeds can be shelled out, when they should be sufficiently dry for storing in a cool dry place until required for use.

VARIETIES.

Everbearing; Dutch Brown.

Uses.—If required for boiling, the dried beans are placed in cold water and allowed to soak for several hours according to their age. Then place in cold salted water, boil and allow to simmer until tender. Drain, and add butter, salt and pepper.

BEANS, SCARLET RUNNER

(*Phaseolus multiflorus*). Leguminosæ. The home of this plant is in Mexico and northern South America, and there the original types may be found growing freely in the wild state. There is some doubt as to who first introduced it into this country, but it has certainly been known to English gardens for over 300 years. It is a tuberous rooted half-hardy perennial, usually grown in this country as an annual.

With the exception of the potato it is probably the most popular of all vegetables, and there are few vegetable plots either in town or country where room cannot be found for at least a few plants.

The runner bean may be fairly described as a general utility plant, for when necessary its rapid and abundant growth may be turned to advantage for screening off any objectionable feature in the garden, whilst at the same time it will provide a plentiful supply of most useful green vegetable produce at a time of the year when other types of green vegetables are difficult to obtain.

Culture.—Any ordinary good garden soil will grow runner beans, though a rich light loam is best. Heavy soil should be especially well prepared, making sure that it is well drained, and adding long strawy manure and a dressing of lime.

If possible a sunny position in the open should be chosen, though as previously stated they may be grown over fences, trellis, or permanent supports.

As the young shoots of the runner bean are extremely tender they should not be sown until all fear of sharp night frosts is over. In the south early May is usually soon enough, whilst in the north it is rarely safe to sow before the end of May. Early crops are obtainable by sowing in boxes for planting out in early June.

Assuming that the ground has previously been deeply dug and well manured, the seeds may be sown 3 in. deep either in single or double rows. For the former

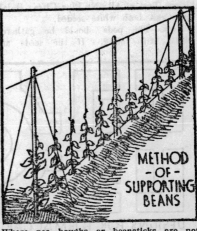

METHOD -OF- SUPPORTING BEANS

Where pea boughs or beansticks are not available wire and strong supports are the best alternatives.

they should be set 4 in. apart with 6 ft. between the rows, and for the latter 9 in. between the seeds with the double rows 8 ft. apart.

If the ground is not so well prepared beforehand, trenches 1 ft. deep should be excavated, placing a 3 in. layer of well-decayed manure in the bottom, and covering with 6 in. of good soil in which to plant the seeds.

Moisture.

The runner bean requires a plentiful supply of moisture at the roots, and once the pods have set they will improve by weak doses of a good soluble manure.

If the lower roots become dry, or on the other hand waterlogged, or too strong a fertiliser is applied, the plants are checked and the blossoms fall without setting. A check caused by a sudden fall in the night temperature may also bring about the same result. In such cases it is a good plan to give the plants a forcible spraying with clean tepid water each evening until the pods commence to set freely.

Almost any support will do for those intended to climb, but the best are long freshly cut poles of hazel, ash, or alder, which should be made firm in the ground, allowing one to each plant before they have a chance to trail on the ground.

VARIETIES.

Hackwood Park Success; Scarlet Exhibition; Best of All; Ne Plus Ultra; Rajah and Czar, both white seeded.

Uses.—The pods should be gathered whilst still young. If the seeds are

SPECIES.

B. decussata, scarlet; *B. purpurea*, purple.

BEAUMONTIA (bō-mont-i-a. Apocynaceæ). Nepal Trumpet Flower. Stove climbers from the East Indies, attaining a height of from 18–20 ft. They bear large white trumpet-shaped flowers in clusters at the end of the shoots, which bloom in June. They succeed best planted in the borders of the stove house, in a compost of equal parts lumpy loam and peat, and one-sixth sand. Pot or plant in March. Water abundantly from May to August, but after this water should be given moderately. The temperature in the house from Sep-

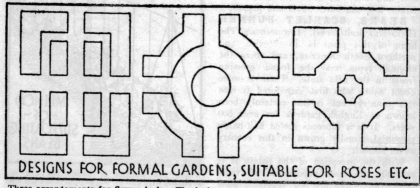

DESIGNS FOR FORMAL GARDENS, SUITABLE FOR ROSES ETC.

Three arrangements for flower-beds. The beds are narrow enough to make the flowers easily accessible from the pathways.

allowed to swell they become tough and stringy. It is usual to "top and tail," and remove the two outer ribs of the pods. They are then thinly sliced and cooked like French beans, or they may be pickled or salted down for winter use.

BEARD TONGUE. *See* PENTSTEMON.

BEAR'S BREECH. *See* ACANTHUS.

BEAUFORTIA (beaufor′tia. Myrtaceæ). Beaufort Myrtle. Greenhouse evergreen flowering shrubs. Named after Mary, Duchess of Beaufort. Australia, 1803.

Culture.—Compost: equal parts loam, leaf-mould, and peat with a little sand and charcoal. Repot and prune early spring. Good drainage essential. Winter temperature, 45°; summer, 60°.

Propagation.—By cuttings of well-ripened shoots, summer.

tember to March should be 60°–70° and from March to September, 70°–80°. Increase by cuttings inserted in sandy soil in a temperature of 75° in March.

SPECIES.

B. grandiflora; B. longifolia.

BEDS AND BEDDING-OUT. The practice of cutting out innumerable small flower-beds in grass is not to be recommended. A piece of lawn so treated is very difficult to mow, and odd corners to the beds are very difficult to fill with plants

A simple arrangement of formal beds is much more restful in appearance and easy of upkeep. Designs based on the square, circle or rectangle are much better than those based on the triangle. (*See* diagrams for shaping beds)

Where space permits, the beds should be

surrounded entirely by grass or entirely by path, either gravel or paving, etc. (*See also* FORMAL GARDENING).

Every spring sees florists and nurserymen's shops full of boxes of young seedlings—termed bedding-out plants. If a cold frame is available, these plants can be raised from seed by the amateur, but where space or time is limited, the nurserymen's seedlings have to be relied on. There are many plants other than geraniums and calceolarias, mostly biennials and annuals, which are raised for bedding-out purposes. The gardener with imagination will try such arrangements as :

Scarlet gladioli with yellow antirrhinums ;

Shell pink gladioli with pale blue violas ;

Orange marigolds with blue salvia ;

Double scarlet begonias with white alyssum ;

Scarlet Coltness Gem dahlias with white violas.

When selecting the plants choose those which have sturdy dark green foliage and do not look "leggy" and "drawn."

(*See also* SPRING BEDDING SCHEMES).

BEE'S BALM. *See* MONARDA.

BEETLE. *See* FLEA BEETLE, RASPBERRY BEETLE.

BEETROOT (*Beta vulgaris*). Chenopodiaceæ. This useful vegetable has been cultivated in England for nearly four hundred years, but records show that it was grown for food in other countries many years before that, and it is acknowledged that the ancient Greeks appreciated its dietetic value.

The plant is a true biennial, i.e., it makes a fleshy root from seed during the first year, in which it stores the necessary food to enable it to produce a strong flowering stem and abundant crop of seed the following year, after which the parent plant dies. When grown as a vegetable, beetroot is treated as an annual, or rather the roots are lifted for food at the end of the first season's growth.

In its native habitat, Southern Europe, the roots are safe in the ground during the resting period, but in our colder climate it is necessary to lift them before sharp frosts occur, and to store in sand or dry earth in a cool, dry, frost-proof place until required for use.

Culture.—Whilst it is possible with proper treatment to get a crop of beet on almost any soil, a deep light loam with good drainage is the ideal. A rich soil is necessary to produce the best roots, but on no account should manure be added when preparing the ground for this crop. Where it can be arranged it is an excellent plan to sow beetroot on ground vacated by other crops which were heavily manured ; for instance celery, potatoes or beans. The two former are best as their proper culture

TWIST THE TOPS OF BEETROOTS INSTEAD OF CUTTING

Beetroot can best be stored in moist sand or sifted coal ashes during the winter.

ensures a better and deeper working of the soil.

The effect of adding fresh manure to ground for beet is to induce the formation of many fangs or thong-like roots instead of one nicely thickened and symmetrical tap-root.

Early and deep digging is advisable, so that a good tilth is obtainable early in May for the first outdoor sowings. Drills 2 in. deep and 1–1½ ft. apart, according to the variety of beet, should be drawn out with a hoe and along these the seed should be thinly scattered. This is probably the better method though some gardeners prefer to sow groups of two or three seeds every 6 in.

The seeds usually germinate in 10 to 18 days. They should then be protected from birds or re-sowing may become necessary. As soon as the seedlings are 2 in. high thin them to groups 6 in. apart, and a week or so later thin these to single plants

Begonias, Streptocarpus, and some of the ferns are increased by pegging the leaves on to moist soil.

1 ft. apart. Always choose dull damp weather for this operation.

"Bolting" or premature running to seed is a common trouble with beet, and is usually caused by the plants receiving a sudden check to their growth. Such a check may be caused by too early sowing so that the seedlings encounter unfavourable weather; by a sudden period of drought, or by a severe attack of greenfly.

Thorough preparation of the soil beforehand, careful selection of time for sowing, and constant use of the hoe during the summer, will do much to overcome the trouble. Very rarely should it be neces-

sary to water the plants by artificial means.

Two or three successional sowings are advisable, and for early exhibition seeds of a globe- or turnip-rooted kind may be sown in frames or on a warm border in March. Weak doses of a good soluble manure may also be given to exhibition roots when they have commenced to swell, but only when the soil is already damp.

Roots may be pulled for use during the late summer, and the whole crop should be ready for lifting in October. This operation must be carried out carefully, for bruised and broken roots bleed and are of little culinary value.

After lifting, the leaves should be twisted (not cut) off 2 or 3 in. beyond the crown, and the roots stored in sand or dry earth or ashes until required for use.

For exhibition the roots should be soaked in water, and cleaned with a sponge, as brushing is liable to damage the skin.

VARIETIES.

GLOBE: Egyptian; Crimson Ball; July Globe.

LONG: Dells Crimson; Cheltenham Green Top; Covent Garden.

Uses.—The culinary uses of beetroot are many and varied. Boiling, for use in salads when cold, is the commonest, but they may also be baked, pickled, preserved in syrup, used as a flavouring for soup, or together with carrots made into an appetising Jam.

BEGONIA (Begoniaceæ). Tender fibrous- and tuberous-rooted perennials. Valuable for their ornamental leaves, and showy flowers, some of which are quaintly crested and frilled.

Begonias are useful both in the open garden, where they make a fine display of colour through the summer months, and in the greenhouse. Some of them are tuberous rooted and some fibrous rooted and the cultivation of each type varies slightly.

Cultivation of Fibrous-rooted species.— These succeed best in a soil composed of equal parts loam and leaf-mould with one part of dried cow manure and silver sand. Good results have been obtained lately by including peat moss in the soil to keep it light and open. They can be raised from seed sown in a temperature of 60° F., in January, or from basal cuttings potted up and kept in the warm greenhouse through the winter.

The large-leaved begonias are often increased by leaf cuttings which are pegged down in fibre in a temperature of 60° F. The veins of the leaves are scored through with a sharp knife in order to induce the formation of roots. When grown from seed the plants should be grown on very steadily without any check, in order to obtain good flowers the first season.

Cultivation of Tuberous-rooted species.— These also are used for bedding out as well as for greenhouse decoration. If raised from seed it should be sown in January or February in well-drained pots or seed pans. The pots will be filled with crocks to within 1½ in. of the top. Over this the coarser part of the prepared compost should be placed, and the fine soil should then be put over the surface, making it perfectly level. Water the pots before the seed is sown, allowing them to drain for a short time before the actual sowing is done. Begonia seed is remarkably fine and it is best to mix it with fine silver sand in order to distribute it over the surface of the pots. Stand the pots in a temperature of between 60° and 70°, covering each with a pane of glass and a sheet of paper over the whole. It is necessary to keep the seed and the surface of the soil moist and shaded until germination has taken place. The best way is to dip the pot in tepid water to within ½ in. of the top of the soil, as watering in the ordinary way would probably wash out the fine seed. Seedlings will probably take about a fortnight to appear and from then onwards they will gradually be exposed to more light and air.

Starting tubers.—Stored Begonia tubers may be started into growth in February or March. The easiest way is to put them into shallow boxes containing a mixture of loam, leaf-mould, and sand. Meanwhile prepare the potting soil. Good top soil mixed with one-sixth part of manure, and stacked for six months, should form the basis. To this prepared soil add leaf-mould in a proportion of one part leaf-mould to three of loam and enough sand to make a fairly porous compost.

The quantity of sand will vary according to the texture of the rest of the soil. Soot and bonemeal added to the compost will be appreciated. As soon as the shoots of the tubers are about ½ in. long, pot them up in 4 or 5 in. pots, and pot them into larger pots as the roots reach the sides of the pots.

It is advisable to use as little heat as possible so as to keep the plants slow and sturdy in growth, and it is also a good

DOUBLE BEGONIA

The rich velvet colours and waxlike flowers of Begonias make this plant useful in formal beds.

practice to pick off all the flower buds as they appear until the plants are well established in their final pots. This will encourage a finer display of flowers later. Weak liquid manure can be given twice a week at this stage. When the plants cease flowering, water should be given only very sparingly and as soon as the stems fall away from the tubers no more water should be given at all. The tubers will then be dried carefully and stored in pots of almost dry soil until the following season.

Begonias in the open.—Seedling begonias are particularly useful for bedding purposes, and if planted in beds which are enriched with well-rotted manure or leaf-

mould, the begonias will make a fine show.
Tuberous begonias started in rich light
soil, in shallow boxes, can also be used
for bedding out as soon as all danger of
frost is past. In addition to these uses
the begonia makes a fine plant for cultivation in wire baskets or in earthenware
bowls. If baskets are used they should
be lined with moss on the inside, level with
the top. Over the moss put a thick layer
of turfy loam, or coarse soil, and then fill
in with the same compost as already advised for pots. The begonias should be
planted so that the tubers are just covered
with soil, and after watering, the baskets
should be suspended in the greenhouse for
a time. Later they can if desired be
brought out into the open garden, or used as
a decoration on verandas and garden houses.

Tuberous rooted.—No plant has repaid
the attention of the hybridist better than
the tuberous-rooted begonia. The first
species all had single flowers, the largest
being about 2½ in. in diameter. The single
flowers of today may often be seen 6 or
7 in. in diameter, but the greatest achievement has been the raising of the wonderful double varieties. These have now
reached a standard of excellence and
beauty of form that must surpass the
wildest dreams of those who were the fore-
runners of hybridisation. There are now
many different classes or types of tuberous-
rooted begonias, each in their way desirable and useful in the scheme of gardening. The various types are generally
divided into the following sections. The
doubles (these are considered to be the
most valuable); the singles; the frilled
doubles; the frilled singles (these have
many beautiful shades not found in the
ordinary singles); the new variety *Crispa
marginata*, with its brilliant scarlet or
rose edging on a creamy-yellow or deep-
yellow ground. Lastly we have the basket
section, *Begonia pendula*. This is a very
beautiful variety, and should not be left out
in the decorating of the greenhouse or
conservatory. The chief charm of the
double begonias is in their great diversity
of form and colouring, as unlike so many
of our florists' flowers have, they have not
been made to conform to one type, until
they would appear to have been turned out
of the same mould.

For greenhouse or conservatory use during the summer-time, nothing can equal
the begonia, and they can be had in bloom
from May until October.

Fibrous-rooted species.—*Alba coccinea*,
scarlet and white; *fuchioides*, scarlet;
incana, white; *semperflorens*, and its many
hybrid varieties of scarlet, rose and white.
There are also numerous other hybrids
such as *Gloire de Lorraine*, etc.

Tuberous-rooted species. — *Boliviensis*,
cinnabar, red; *Pearcei*, yellow; *Veitchii*,
vermilion-red; *roscæflora*, red; *Davisii*,
scarlet; *Clarkei*, red.

It is chiefly from these species that the
hybridists have raised the beautiful
varieties of the present day.

Some of the best of the modern varieties
of begonias are as follows:

Albatross—double, pure white.
Caroline Coe—carmine red, double.
Corientia—old rose, double.
Dora Hay—double, yellow shaded.
Florence Bigland—apricot, deeper at
    edge, double.
H. Frankling—double, rich vermilion.
Ida Reeves—double, salmon-pink.
Lady Cory—salmon-pink, suspicion of
    orange, double.
Lady Rhondda—double, salmon-pink.
Lady Sidey—double, fiery orange.
May Marriott—double, blush pink,
    shading in centre to shell pink, with
    suspicion of yellow.
Millicent—double, flesh pink.
Mrs. J. S. Brunton—double, lilac-rose.
Mrs. W. Cuthbertson—double, lilac-rose.
Mrs. C. F. Langdon—double, deep
    orange.
Ruth Ward—deep rose-pink, double.
Snowdrift—double, fine white.

BEGONIAS FOR BEDDING.

Bath Bedder—multiflora type, single
    crimson flowers.
Bertini—single, vermilion.
Burgomaster Max—double, dwarf, crim-
    son-scarlet.
Flamboyant—semi-double, cherry-red.
Worthiana—single, vermilion.

TUBEROUS BEGONIAS FOR HANGING
    BASKETS AND BOWLS.

Betha—salmon-pink.
Eunice—light pink, flushed peach.
Golden Shower—resembles Wm. Allan
    Richardson rose.

Lena—bright rosy-crimson.

Stella—red.

Venus—greenish-white, pure white when open.

BELAMCANDA (bel'-am-can'-da. Iridaceæ). Leopard Flower. Half-hardy perennial, first introduced from China in 1759. This plant bears orange and red flowers in June, and it reaches to a height of from 2–4 ft.

Outdoor culture.—For cultivation of the leopard flowers in the open garden, light, rich, sandy soil is necessary. They will thrive best in a sunny, well-drained border, where they should be planted from September to January, placing the tubers 4 in. deep and 2 in. apart. Lift and replant annually. In March, mulch the surface with cow manure.

These plants can also be cultivated in pots, and for this purpose they should be placed in pots of 4½ in. diameter in a compost of two parts sandy loam, one part leaf-mould, or decayed cow manure. Good drainage is essential. Five tubers may be planted 3 in. deep in each pot in November. The pots should then be covered with coco-nut fibre refuse in the cold frame, or put under the cool greenhouse stage until growth commences. From the time of growth until the flowers fade the plants should be watered moderately, gradually ceasing when the flowers have faded. They should then be kept dry till January. The temperature of the greenhouse from September to March should be 40°–50°; at other times, 50°–60°.

The method of increase is by offsets treated as the larger tubers.

SPECIES.

B. chinensis (*B. punctata*), orange and red flowers in June.

BELLADONNA LILY. *See* AMARYLLIS.

BELLFLOWER. *See* CAMPANULA.

BELLIS (bell-is. Compositæ). Daisy. Spring-flowering hardy perennial that produces masses of bright flowers.

Culture.—Propagate by seed sown in the open in June or by division of the roots after flowering. The plants are improved by periodical division. Plant in ordinary soil in any sunny spot.

SPECIES.

Bellis perennis, of which there are

several named garden forms with either flat, quilled, or double petals and red, rose or white colouring.

BELLIUM (bell-ium. Compositæ). Dwarf daisy-like annuals and perennials which flower from May to September

Culture.—These hardy plants will grow anywhere, but prefer a sunny position in sandy loam with shelter from N.E. winds.

Propagate by division or seeds in spring. Height 2–6 in.

SPECIES.

B. rotundifolium, with violet-blue flowers, suitable for the rockery.

B. minutum, white, August, 3 in.

BELLOWS. For spraying powder on mildew or blight. Tobacco powder, Keating's sulphur, and other insecticides can be sprayed over a large surface, especially since the latest bellows are finished in a fan-shape at the end to distribute the powder. These bellows are very cheap and effective. The latest development is a powder-sprayer of the atomizer type.

BELOPERONE (bel-o-per-on-ē. Acanthaceæ). Stove flowering shrubs; evergreen. First introduced from Brazil in 1832.

Cultivation.—A compost of equal parts leaf-mould, loam and sand will be necessary, and also a shady, moist position. They should be potted in March, placed moderately firm in the soil. These shrubs need plenty of water from May to September, but after this not so much will be needed. They require a temperature of from 60°–70° from September to March, and 70°–80° from March to September.

To induce dwarf growth, the points of all shoots should be removed occasionally in summer.

They may be propagated by cuttings inserted singly in small pots of light sandy soil in a temperature of 75° in February, March or April.

SPECIES.

B. atropurpurea, purple flowers in September.

B. oblongata, rosy-purple in August.

B. violacæ, violet flowers in August.

All grow to a height of about 3 ft.

BENEFICIAL INSECTS. We have a number of insects in our gardens which are of decided benefit to us. These insects may be divided into two groups, those which are predaceous, i.e., hunting and killing their prey, and those which are parasitic, living on other insects, keeping them alive the while to supply food.

Of the first we find the Ladybird, the Lace Wing and the Hover Fly, and of the latter group, insects usually called *Ichneumon* and the *Tachinid* flies.

In the case of the Ladybirds, not only the adults feed upon the aphis but also their offspring, commonly called "niggers." Eggs are laid by the parents on aphis-

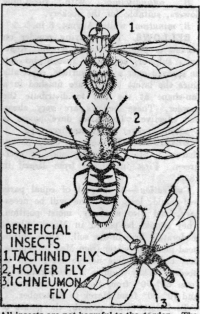

BENEFICIAL INSECTS
1. TACHINID FLY
2. HOVER FLY
3. ICHNEUMON FLY

All insects are not harmful to the garden. The Hover fly is sometimes mistaken for a wasp but its habit of hovering over flowers especially distinguishes it.

infected plants and the young, on hatching out, devour the green fly. Although the control is not complete, much good is done by these beetles and "niggers."

The Lace Wing, on the other hand, is only beneficial in the larval stage, the young and so-called aphis "lions" preying upon the colonies of aphis. These voracious little creatures suck the aphis dry and then cover themselves with the dried skins of their prey, so camouflaging themselves while they continue their attack upon the green fly.

The Hover Fly works in a similar way, but as the larvæ are legless, their range is more restricted. Whereas aphis "lions" and "niggers" may be found upon the foliage of the plants the larvæ of a Hover Fly confine themselves more to the stem, living usually where a leaf joins the stalk. There is no doubt all these do an immense amount of good, but they will never completely control an attack of aphis.

The parasitic insects such as the Ichneumon fly, Chalcid fly and Brachonid flies belong to the bee group and are not therefore true flies. They lay their eggs in their victims—which may be either caterpillars or aphides—by means of a long ovipositor. Young grubs on hatching out enter the victim and there live upon the food it has eaten for its own sustenance. They do not touch any vital organ of their host for this would bring about, not only its death, but their own. Their object is to keep the host alive. When they are full grown, which coincides with the maturity of their host, they pupate. The host now usually dies, but in some cases it will pupate enclosing the pupa of the parasite in its own pupal case. About the time the host would be hatching out the parasites hatch and are then ready to carry on fresh egg-laying.

Another example is the Tachinid flies, related to the blow fly, several species of which are parasitic on caterpillars. These flies are not unlike a large housefly, but they are somewhat greyer in colour and they lay their eggs upon caterpillars. On hatching out the young maggots enter the caterpillar and feed upon the contents of the stomach. Meantime, the caterpillar eats ravenously in order to take in sufficient food for itself and "lodgers." When full grown the caterpillars will die and the maggots then eat their way out, changing into brown barrel-shaped pupæ on the ground and from which fresh flies hatch in a couple of weeks. Whereas these so-called beneficial insects will never completely control any pest, they certainly keep them in check; and there is no doubt that without their aid our troubles would be greatly increased and more time, labour and expense would be incurred in keeping our fruit, flowers and vegetables clean.

BENTHAMIA. *See* Cornus.

BERBERIDOPSIS (ber-beri-dop'-sis.
Bixaceæ). The "Coral Plant" from Chile,
1862. An evergreen climbing shrub of
great beauty. One of the most beautiful
of all evergreen climbers. It likes a
partially shaded position on a warm wall,
and a little peat should be added to the
soil to give the plant a start. In Cornwall it will reach to 20 ft. May be grown
among Rhododendrons in mild districts.
The deep coral and crimson flowers appear
in July, and the plant continues to bloom
until September.

Propagation is by seeds, cuttings in
summer, and layers in October. Plant
in April or October.

B. corallina, the only species.

BERBERIS (běr-běr-is. Berberida-
eæ). Barberry. Highly ornamental evergreen and deciduous shrubs, of erect or
trailing habit, and useful for many purposes in the garden and shrubbery.

Culture.—Plant evergreens from March
to April or October and November;
deciduous, November to March, in ordinary soil. Thin out shoots after flowering
when overcrowded and trim to shape.
Those grown for autumn foliage should
not be trimmed until the spring.

Propagate by seeds sown in open in
October, by half-matured cuttings in a
frame in July or August, or by layering
in August.

SPECIES.

There are a great number of species,
all bearing showy yellow flowers, followed
by beautiful coral or glossy red berries,
occasionally purple or black. The following are some of the most useful and distinct species, evergreen unless otherwise
stated :

B. aquifolium (*Mahonia aquifolium*).
See MAHONIA SECTION.

B. brevipaniculata. Deciduous Chinese
species of great beauty in leaf and berry.
Berries, coral-pink, in clusters. 4–6 ft.

B. concinna. Deciduous species with
very beautiful leaves, silvery-white reverse, gorgeous autumn colour. Remarkable carmine-red fruits nearly as large
as cherries. 3 ft.

B. Darwinii. A great favourite and
one of the most beautiful of all flowering
shrubs during April and May. Will grow
in semi-shade. 4–8 ft. Flowers orange-

yellow, reddish exterior, very freely produced, followed by dark blue berries.

B. dictyophylla. Distinct Chinese
deciduous species. Stems are covered with
white bloom and contrast well with the
dark green leaves, with white reverse.
Berries bright coral-red. 8–10 ft.

B. Gagnepainii. Compact growing.
Flowers in June. Glaucous purplish-black
fruits. 3–4 ft.

B. Sargentiana. One of the most beautiful. Its handsome ornamental leaves turn-

BERBERIS

Berberis are economical shrubs to plant as
they need little after-attention.

ing in autumn to vivid bronze and scarlet
and ivory-white make a fine picture. The
berries are black, and persist throughout
the winter. 6–8 ft.

B. stenophylla (hybrid), *B. Darwinii* +
B. empetrifolia. One of the most beautiful, especially when massed. Its long,
graceful, arching sprays, clothed with
narrow leaves and masses of deep golden-
yellow flowers in April and May make a
wonderful display. An excellent plant as a
specimen, and for use on sloping banks
where there is room for the plant to

develop fully. Makes a very fine hedge 8-10 ft.

B. s. gracilis. Of the various forms of B. stenophylla, this is one of the most beautiful. Dwarf, with arching stems and small, neat foliage, suitable for the rock garden. It sometimes blooms again in autumn. 2-3 ft.

B. s. Irwinii. Another compact neat-growing form. Very charming when in flower. 2-3 ft.

B. Thunbergii. Compact deciduous Japanese and Chinese species, lovely in spring with its hanging yellow flowers, followed by brilliant red berries, and magnificent in autumn when the foliage turns brilliant scarlet. Up to 8 ft. and 15 ft. across.

B. T. atropurpurea. A striking variety with rich red foliage throughout spring and summer. A fine shrub to associate with Rhus Cotinus foliis purpureis.

B. vulgaris. The Common Barberry. Deciduous. Native species. Very pretty in autumn with its bright red berries and in spring when in flower. 6-10 ft. Prune back every second year.

B. v. foliis purpureis. The Purple Barberry. Retains its colour through the growing season.

B. Wilsonæ. The finest Chinese species. An exquisitely beautiful dwarf deciduous shrub, with neat leaves brilliantly tinted in autumn. The profusely-borne golden-yellow flowers are followed in autumn by abundance of berries in clusters, at first cream, gradually suffusing with pink until they become bright coral. This most charming of dwarf barberries, 2-4 ft., was discovered in China about 1904 by W. E. H. Wilson and named after his wife.

MAHONIA SECTION.

B. aquifolium. The well-known ever-green Mahonia with dark glossy green leaves turning to purple and bronze in winter. Golden-yellow flowers, violet-black berries. Native of western N. America, 1823. Does well in shade, 2-4 ft.

B. a. japonica. Evergreen Japanese Mahonia, up to 10 ft., with large hand-some leaves, composed of 7-13 leaflets. Flowers lemon-yellow, very fragrant, from February to March. Loves semi-shade.

B. j. Bealei (China), 1845. One of the most striking of all the Mahonias. Large

bold foliage and long racemes (18-24 in long), of lemon-yellow, lily-of-the-valley scented flowers during winter. The tru plant is rare, B. a. japonica often doing duty for it; likes half-shade in southern parts; at one time regarded as a distinct species. Does not come true from seed 8-10 ft.

B. j. hyemalis. An even finer form than the preceding, and quite the most beautifu of this section. Formerly accepted as B Bealei, but quite distinct. The leaves are longer and are formed of a greater num ber of leaflets, which are longer and not so broad as in B. j. Bealei; neither do the leaves overlap as in that variety. It also flowers earlier, beginning in October and continuing throughout the winter into early spring. The pale yellow fragrant flowers are borne in longer, almost horizon tal and drooping racemes, instead of being erect. 8-10 ft. Rare.

B. nepalensis. A rather tender species from Kashmir for mild districts, resembling B. japonica, with longer leaves but smaller inflorescences.

B. nervosa, 1822. Dwarf evergreen species from western N. America, rarely more than 12-18 in. in height. Foliage resembles B. nepalensis, turning red in autumn. Flowers yellow; berries, pur-plish-blue.

B. pinnata, 1819. A handsome and distinct Mahonia from California and New Mexico, and one of the most desirable. Foliage deep green. Flowers, rich yellow, very abundantly produced over the entire plant from February to April. 8-12 ft.

B. repens. A very dwarf evergreen species from western N. America, spread-ing by underground stems. Dull bluish foliage, flowers deep yellow in April and May. Berries black, covered with a blue bloom.

B. Swayseyi. A beautiful glaucous foliaged species from Texas.

BERCHEMIA (bĕr-kē'-mĭ-a. Rham-naceæ). Deciduous climbing shrubs. They like a moist loamy soil and can be in-creased by cuttings and layers.

SPECIES.

B. Giraldiana (China). 8-10 ft. Glau-cous green leaves. Flowers white, small, in clusters, followed by red and black berries.

B. racemosa (Japan). Forms a spreading tangled shrub with bright green leaves, turning yellow in autumn. Flowers white, small, followed by red and finally black, berries.

B. volubilis. Of but little beauty and less hardy than *B. racemosa.*

BERGAMOT. *See* MONARDA.

BERKHEYA (berk-hē-ya. Compositæ). South African Thistle. Biennials or perennials mostly cultivated in the greenhouse. Valued for their handsome foliage. Height 3 ft. Sown in a hot sunny situation in the open, in a porous, gritty soil, with some lime rubble added, these plants will thrive well. If it is intended to grow them in the greenhouse, they should be potted in a sandy loam. Seeds should be sown in spring, and when in a young state, the seedlings should be potted up and later planted in their permanent quarters as soon as they are well rooted. They should be treated as tender annuals.

Propagate also by dividing the roots in spring, and in the case of the evergreen species, propagate by cuttings placed under glass in a sandy soil in a temperature of 40°–50°.

SPECIES.

B. Adlami, yellow or lilac flowers.
B. purpurea, bluish-purple flowers.

BERTHOLLETIA (berth-ol-et′-i-a. Myrtaceæ). Brazil Nut, Para Nut.

B. excelsa is a tall evergreen species from which the Brazil nuts are obtained, but this tree is very seldom grown in this country as it is of no decorative value. If cultivated, it is grown in peat and loam in the stove greenhouse, and is increased by cuttings.

BERTOLONIA (ber-tol-ō-ni-a. Melastomaceæ). Stove trailing plants with ornamental foliage, the upper sides of the leaves being dark green, white and purple, while the under sides are of pink and purple.

These plants require a moist, moderate stove temperature, and should be planted in a compost of equal parts peat, leafmould and sandy loam, and covered with bell-glass in the shade. Pot in February or March. Water should be given daily from April to September, but at other times, water given once a week is quite sufficient.

These plants require careful attention, but when well grown, they are very attractive. Cuttings can be taken in the spring, and inserted in light soil in pots or pans, under bell-glass, in a temperature of 75°. They may also be increased by divisions, which should be placed in the close frame.

SPECIES.

B. Houtteana, leaves green and carmine.
B. maculata, leaves pink and purple.
B. marmorata, leaves silvery-white and purple.
B. pubescens, leaves light and dark green.
B. vittata (striped), pale rose.

BESSERA (Liliaceæ). Coral Drops. Half-hardy bulbous plants first introduced in 1850, originally from Mexico.

A compost of equal parts loam, leafmould, peat and coarse silver sand is the most suitable for the cultivation of this plant. Placed in well-drained pots in the cold greenhouse, where they can get the sun, "Coral Drops" will thrive well. They should be potted in October or November. During active growth the plants should be plentifully watered, but when the foliage dies down, watering should almost cease. This condition should be maintained until new growth commences.

These plants may also be grown outdoors at the foot of a south wall in a well-drained border.

When the bulbs are not growing, they should be kept dry and cool, but quite secure from frost.

Method of increase is by offsets, which grow from the old bulb. These should be removed and treated as the older bulbs at planting-time.

SPECIES.

B. elegans, with scarlet flowers in September.
B. e. fistulosa (hollow-stalked), purple flowers in September.
B. e. Herberti, purple and white flowers in September
B. e. miniata, scarlet and white flowers.

BETA. *See* BEETROOT and SPINACH.

BETONICA. Now united to STACHYS, *which see.*

BETEL NUT PALM. *See* ARECA.

BETULA (bet′-ū-la. Betulaceæ). Birch. Deciduous trees and shrubs of exceptional elegance and beauty. Most attractive in winter with their silvery-white stems. The exotic birches have the most richly-coloured trunks of all cultivated trees, from creamy-white and orange, to a polished red colour. Some are remarkable for their shaggy peeling bark.

Culture.—Plant in November. All species thrive in poor gravelly soil.

Propagate by seeds, layering or grafting.

SPECIES.

B. alaskana. The common birch of the Yukon valley in Alaska.

B. lenta. Black or Cherry Birch of N. America. Glossy, dark, almost black non-peeling bark.

B. lutea. Yellow Birch of N. America.

B. Maximowiczii. This fine Japanese species is distinguished by having the largest leaves of the genus, up to 7 in. long and 5 in. wide. Bark brownish becoming silvery. A quick grower and one of the best birches.

B. nana. A dwarf-growing species. 2–4 ft. Native of Britain, N. Europe and

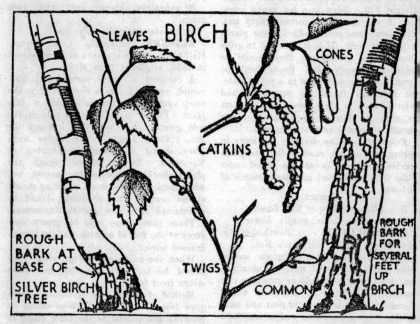

The Silver Birch and the Common Birch can be distinguished by these simple features.

B. Delarayi Forrestii (China). A handsome tree with beautiful creamy-white stems. Exact name doubtful.

B. Ermanii. Widely dispersed handsome Asiatic species with peeling coffee-cream trunk and branches orange-red.

B. E. nipponica. A Japanese form of the foregoing. Starts later into growth than the type, and is useful in districts where late frosts prevail. One of the handsomest and most striking of the white-stemmed group.

B. japonica. A Japanese species with trunk of silvery-white to orange.

N. America.

B. nigra. River Birch of N. America. One of the finest for planting in damp ground, but thrives in ordinary soil.

B. papyrifera. The Paper Birch of N. America, and one of the whitest-barked of all the birches. Canadian canoes are made from its bark.

B. pubescens. Common White Birch. Recommended for moist places.

B. verrucosa. Common Silver Birch, or Queen of the Forest. Thriving in moist as well as dry soils. Native of Britain, N. Europe and N. Asia. There are several forms, including "weeping" ones, the best being var. *pendula Youngi*, a very elegant tree suitable for even small gardens. Var. *dalecarlica*, the Swedish Birch, is one of the most graceful.

BIDENS (bi-dens. Compositæ). Burr Marigold. Annual and perennial herbs, mostly hardy. They will grow in ordinary soil in a sunny border. Perennial species should be planted out in October or April.

Propagation of the annuals takes place by sowing seed ⅛ in. deep in sandy soil under glass in a temperature of 70°. The seedlings should be planted out into the open in May. Perennials may be increased by division of old plants in April.

SPECIES.

(Annual).

B. *grandiflora*, yellow, 2 ft., July, useful for waterside planting.

(Perennial).

B. *humilis*, yellow, dwarf, July.

B. *heretophylla*, yellow, August (greenhouse).

B. *procera*, yellow, November.

B. *tripartita*, yellow, 18 in. Autumn.

BIENNIAL. *See* HARDY BIENNIAL.

BIG BUD IN BLACK CURRANT (*Eriophyes ribis*). DESCRIPTION OF MITE.— About $\frac{1}{100}$ in. in length, semi-transparent, but often greenish in colour. Cylindrical in shape, but tapering somewhat at the posterior end. It has two pairs of legs, and the last segment is provided with a "sucker" and two long upturned bristles.

LIFE-HISTORY.—The winter is passed in the swollen buds on the bushes. As the leaves begin to appear in the spring the mites begin to leave these buds and collect on the stalks and flower trusses. Here they remain for some little time, and at this period they get distributed over large areas by means of birds and bees. They may also spread from one bush to another, when these are close or over-lapping, by their own effort. After fixing themselves to a leaf by means of the anal sucker they can jerk themselves off by the aid of the two long hair-like bristles which act as springs. As soon as the new buds begin to form they crawl up and enter them. Egg-laying now takes place and the buds eventually become full of young mites. These set up an irritation which causes the buds to swell, and it is within this

"big bud" the mite develops and lives until the following spring.

METHODS OF CONTROL.—It is useless to attempt anything during the winter months, when the mites are protected inside the buds. It has recently been shown, however, that a lime-sulphur wash (1 in 20) applied first when the leaves are opening and again a week later, will be effective.

BIGELOWIA (big-e-lŏ-i-a. Compositæ). Rayless Golden Rod. Evergreen sub-

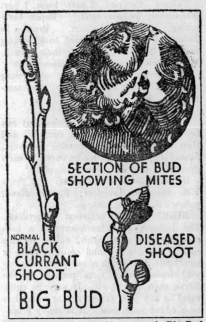

SECTION OF BUD SHOWING MITES

NORMAL BLACK CURRANT SHOOT

DISEASED SHOOT

BIG BUD

The worst pest of black currants is Big Bud.

shrubby plant suited for sheltered places and warm sunny walls. This plant needs well-drained soil and should be placed in the warmest position available, where it will grow well. It is not hardy in exposed situations. Plant out from pots in spring, and train the growths to a wall, spreading them out well.

Increase by cuttings of young growths, placed in gentle bottom heat. Pot them singly, and harden-off before planting out. During the first summer the rooted cuttings should be left in the open, but brought into the cool house for the first winter.

They may be planted out the following spring.

SPECIES.

B. *graveolens*, 6–8 ft., yellow, late summer.

BIGNONIA (bigno'-nia. Bignoniaceæ). Trumpet Flower. Greenhouse and hardy climbing plants. Deciduous. Tropics, 1710. Named after Abbé Bignon, librarian to Louis XIV. This order provides some of our most beautiful climbers. 30–40 ft.

Culture.—Compost, 2 parts loam, 1 part leaf-mould, ½ part sand. Repot early spring. Sunny position. Prune in February, weak shoots hard back, strong ones about one-third to half their growth. Winter temperature, 45°; summer, 60°.

Propagation.—By cuttings of young shoots in sandy soil in propagator, temperature, 60°.

SPECIES.

B. *capreolata*, the only species that can be grown outside in this country, and then only in mild districts. Flowers, funnel-shaped, orange-red on current year's growth, during June and onwards.

B. *grandiflora.* See TECOMA.

B. *speciosa*, lavender; B. *tweediana*, yellow; B. *venusta*, orange.

BILBERRY (*Vaccinium Myrtillus*). The Bilberry or Whortleberry is a low-growing deciduous shrub, native of this country, generally found on mountains or moorlands. It is one of our most delicious wild fruits, being more popular in the North than the South. It may be cultivated in any poor garden soil to which has been added some peat. It is easily propagated by means of layers. Bilberries make excellent tarts or preserves, or as Gerard suggests, "The people of Cheshire do eate the blacke Wortles in creame and milke, as in these South parts we eate Strawberries." See also VACCINIUM.

BILLARDIERA (bil-lard-ĭ-ē'-ra. Pittosporaceæ). Labillardere. Delightful evergreen, twining plant from Tasmania. Only hardy in mild districts.

Culture.—Fibrous loam and peat. Propagate by seeds and cuttings in sand under bell-glass.

SPECIES.

B. *longiflora.* Flowers greenish-yellow followed by beautiful, brilliant dark blue fruit, very attractive in October and November.

B. *fructu-albo.* A form with beautiful white berries.

BILLBERGIA (billber'-gia. Bromeliaceæ). Stove evergreen flowering plant. S. America, 1817.

Culture.—Compost, equal parts fibrous loam, peat and sand, with the addition of a little well-rotted cow manure. Repot spring. Give good drainage. Winter temperature, 55°; summer, 75°.

Propagation.—By suckers inserted singly into small pots of sandy peat, place in propagator, temperature, 80°. Spring.

SPECIES.

B. *iridifolia*, scarlet and yellow; B. *Lietzei*, rose-pink; B. *Morele*, blue and rose-pink.

BINDWEED. See CONVOLVULUS.

BIOTA. See THUYA.

BIRCH. See BETULA.

BIRD BATHS. To encourage birds to enter the garden is to rid the plants of many pests. Many of our beautiful birds are gardeners' friends, although, of course, there are some that are a nuisance. Birds can find their own food, but frequently suffer from lack of water, and if they are provided with drinking-water, they will in many instances leave the ripening fruit for its rightful owner. A receptacle for holding water, usually known as a bird bath, should be placed on the ground level. Bird baths on pedestals are pleasing placed just outside house windows, where they can be more easily seen, but as a general rule the birds are more at home when their water is near the ground. See that the bath is not placed near trees or bushes which could hide lurking cats, or you will never be able to admire the graceful antics of your feathered friends, for they are quick to sense danger.

Bird-bath designs vary considerably from the mass-production article in artificial stone or cement, to the hand-finished type in soft-coloured, weathered stone. The price, of course, increases with the type of stone used. The points to verify before buying are that the stone is frost-proof and hard-wearing; and if not already so, will weather quickly to a pleasing colour.

Also, take care to choose a type which

will be in harmony with the garden design. It is quite possible to construct a bird bath at home, using a wooden mould and cement. It is possible to obtain material for mixing with the cement to tone it to a buff, or grey shade, thus relieving the severity of the cement colouring. In construction, a bird bath should be wide in proportion to its depth, thus allowing ample room for bathing. Let the bath be shallow towards the edges to allow the birds ease of access to the water. The water itself should not be more than 3 in. deep. If the bath is always kept full of clean water, the birds will quickly make it a favourite spot; but if it is left empty for a day or two, or dirty water left in it, it will be purely an uninteresting garden feature, having no purpose or meaning in its introduction to the garden.

BIRDS. Birds are the natural enemies of our insect pests, and when—by killing and egg-collecting—we reduce their numbers, we are at the same time assisting in the increase of insects. However carefully one may spray one's roses with patent insecticides the result is only partially effective, but a pair of tits—working 16 hours a day—will prove an incalculable asset in the reduction of injurious insects such as greenfly. In connection with insecticides it should be remembered that if a preparation is used which is injurious to both insects *and birds*, the natural enemies of the insects will also be destroyed, with the result that an increase of insects is very likely to follow. Such vermin as rats and mice are in the same way kept down to a very great extent by birds such as the owl and kestrel.

When condemning a bird for fruit-eating, it is frequently forgotten that while certain birds may do damage for a short period of the year (during the cherry season, for instance), throughout the rest of the year they are doing immeasurable good by eating slugs, snails, wireworms, etc. If, therefore, for two months of the year birds show a partiality for fruit, the fruit should be protected as well as possible, but what fruit is taken should be regarded as payment of the birds' wages for the destruction of thousands of noxious insects *during other much longer periods*. It should be borne in mind that the harm

done by birds is always quickly noticed, whereas *the good is seldom observed.*

All food eaten by a bird may be divided into three categories, namely: (i) food by the eating of which man is benefited: for example, injurious insects such as greenfly; (ii) food by the eating of which man is harmed, such as fruit, and (iii) food by the eating of which man is unaffected, such as wild grasses. From the horticulturist's point of view the birds referred to in category (i) above are termed *beneficial*, in category (ii) *harmful*, in category (iii) *neutral*. For obvious reasons only some of the more common birds are in-

One of the hardest workers in the garden is the Blue Tit. It collects for its young enormous quantities of insects and grubs during the breeding-season.

cluded in this book, and it must not be assumed that birds omitted are harmful.

As will be seen from these brief notes on the subject, a great number of birds are well worth encouraging to the garden on account of the good they do; a few methods for attracting some of them are mentioned in the notes for individual species. It should be remembered that birds need water both in summer and winter, and a wide but shallow bird bath— preferably with some shelving pebbles in the centre—is always an attraction for them. A bird-table (well protected from cats) will prove very fascinating, as well as being a means of bringing many useful birds to the garden. Whilst they will appreciate the food provided for them, they will be only too ready to partake of their natural diet whenever it is sufficiently plentiful.

BIRD CHERRY. *See* PRUNUS PADUS.

BIRD'S FOOT TREFOIL. *See* LOTUS.

BITTER CRESS. *See* CARDAMINE.

BITTER SWEET. *See* CELASTRUS.

BIXA (bĭk'-sa. Bixaceæ). Annatto, Arnotto. Evergreen flowering tree which

One of the prettiest of the wild cherries is the Bird Cherry. It is a dwarf tree and should be more widely cultivated in our garden.

is cultivated in the stove greenhouse. Originally from the West Indies and first introduced to this country in 1690. It bears pink and purple flowers in the summer. In a compost of 2 parts loam, 1 part peat and silver sand it thrives well. Pot in March and water freely from March to September. After this, water should be given in moderation. Winter temperature, 60°–70°; summer, 75°–85°.

Cuttings should be taken of half-ripened shoots about six to twelve months old, and inserted in small pots of sandy soil in a temperature of 85° from June to August, or in a close propagating pit.

The reddish pulp which surrounds the seeds of the species *B. orellana* is the annatto of commerce.

SPECIES.

B. orellana, pink flowers in June.

B. purpurea, purple flowers in July.

BLACKBERRY (*Rubus fruticosus*). Not only are there numerous British species and varieties, but also many continental kinds are often grown. The Blackberry is best grown trained to horizontal wires, and should be pruned in autumn each year by cutting out the old wood and tying on the young for next year's fruiting.

Propagation is easily carried out by layering. Planting may be done at any time between November and March. Allow a distance of 10 ft. apart.

VARIETIES.

Probably the best variety in cultivation is the "Cut-leaved," or "Parsley-leaved," *Rubus laciniatus*. This variety bears well, has large shining black fruits, and is an excellent market variety, as it travels well.

"Himalayan Giant," which is actually a German species, is a very heavy cropper,

The Blackbird sings, gathers worms and grubs, and easily earns his wages of a few fruits in the summer time.

but the flavour is not so good as the former. Edward Langley is an early cropping variety of excellent flavour. Both "white" and yellow varieties of Blackberry are obtainable from nurserymen.

BLACK SPOT ON ROSES (*Actinonema rosæ*). A disease almost as important as mildew.

Fully-grown leaves become infected

about midsummer, and the fungus shows itself in causing dark green areas to appear on the upper surface of the leaves. Should the attack be really bad the leaves are shed, which prevents a proper ripening of the wood. Moreover, the loss of foliage causes a fresh crop of young leaves to appear which weakens the bush considerably for the following year. In some of the more delicate varieties the disease may extend down on to the wood, in which case there is a ready source of infection for the next year unless the branch is pruned away.

METHODS OF CONTROL.—Prune away all diseased portions of branches, collect all

light from plants—chiefly vegetables—at certain stages of growth. This is done with the object of making the vegetables more tasty by removing the green colouring matter, which in some cases is rather bitter. Also blanching, by forcing artificial growth, renders the plant more succulent and better suited for table use. (See CELERY, etc.)

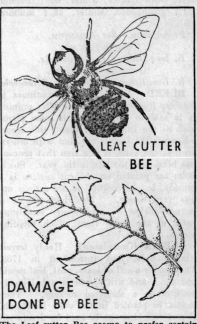

LEAF CUTTER BEE

DAMAGE DONE BY BEE

The Leaf-cutter Bee seems to prefer certain roses, and uses the circlets of leaf to make its nest. It is kept away by spraying with quassia extract (see Rose Leaf-Cutter Bee).

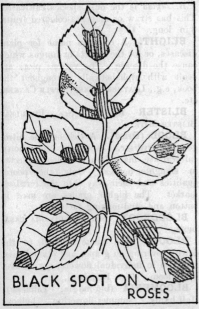

BLACK SPOT ON ROSES

Collect and burn all diseased flowers. Spray the young leaves with Bordeaux mixture or liver of sulphur.

fallen leaves showing the disease, and burn with the prunings. Spray in the spring with Bordeaux mixture or liver of sulphur.

BLACKTHORN. *See* PRUNUS SPINOSA.

BLADDERNUT. *See* STAPHYLEA.

BLADDER SENNA. *See* COLUTEA.

BLANCHING. A method of excluding

BLANDFORDIA (bland'-fordia. Liliaceæ). Named after George, Marquis of Blandford. Greenhouse fleshy - rooted plants. Evergreen. N.S. Wales, 1803.

Culture.—Compost, *see* AGAPANTHUS. Water freely during growing season, very little at other times. Repot in the autumn, giving good drainage. Winter temperature, 45°; summer, 65°.

Propagation by offsets when repotting.

SPECIES.

B. *Cunninghamii*, crimson; B. *flammia*, yellow; B. *nobilis*, orange.

BLANKET FLOWER. *See* GAILLARDIA.

BLAZING STAR. *See* LIATRIS.

BLECHNUM (ble'-chnum. Filices). Brazilian Tree Fern. Stove and greenhouse ferns. Evergreen. Name from *Blechnon*, a Greek name for a fern. 1691.

Culture.—Compost, *see* ADIANTUM. Repot early spring. Shady position. Water freely during summer months. Temperature, stove species, winter, 60°; summer, 80°; greenhouse, winter, 45°; summer, 65°.

Propagation.—See ADIANTUM.

STOVE SPECIES.

B. longifolium; B. occidentale.

GREENHOUSE SPECIES.

B. Braziliense; B.hastatum; B.lanceola.

BLEED. When a plant continues to lose sap from the cut surface after pruning it is said to "bleed." With some plants such as the Indiarubber plant, this occurs whenever the tree is cut, but with others, such as the Vine, it is a sign that pruning has been done too late in the year. Stockholm tar painted on the cut surface is a remedy, but "bleeding" is not serious unless very severe. The chief trouble it causes is that diseased spores sometimes enter at the point from which bleeding occurs.

BLETIA (Orchidaceæ). Hardy terrestrial orchids, first introduced in 1733. They prefer a soil of loam, peat, leaf-mould and sand, and will thrive in a half-shady position on a sheltered rockery. They should be planted in the open in March. If preferred they can be used for decoration in pots, planted at the same time. They should be watered freely during period of growth, but in the resting period they may be left dry.

Propagate by division of the pseudobulb after flowering.

Some of the species must be grown in the greenhouse. They should be planted in pots with 2 in. of drainage, and a compost of loam or leaf-mould. Keep a temperature of 65° to 75° from March to September and 60° to 65° from September to March. Water should be given freely from March to August, but less should be given from August to October, and after this only very occasionally.

HARDY SPECIES.

B. hyacinthina (*B. Gebina*), a Chinese species with attractive rose-pink flowers. Also *B. hyacinthina alba*, with creamy-white semi-pendent bells.

STOVE SPECIES.

B. Shepherdii, purple and yellow. *B. verecunda*, purple.

BLIGHIA (blī-e-a. Sapindaceæ). A tender tree cultivated in the tropics on account of its edible fruits. First introduced in 1793. This tree attains a height of 30-40 ft. It grows best in sandy loam and peat in the borders of the warm greenhouse, in a summer temperature of 75°-90° and 65°-75° in winter.

Increase by cuttings of half-ripened shoots inserted in sandy soil under a handglass in a temperature of 75°.

B. sapida is the only species cultivated. This has straw or magenta-coloured fruits, 3 in. long.

BLIGHT. A common name for plant diseases, or for the insects or fungus which cause the disease. The various pests are dealt with alphabetically throughout the book, e.g., LEATHER-JACKET, APPLE CANKER, etc.

BLISTER MITE. *See* PEAR-LEAF BLISTER MITE.

BLOOD (Dried). A rich organic nitrogenus fertiliser, especially for horticultural use, made from the blood collected in slaughter-houses. Only the poorer qualities find their way into the fertiliser market. The higher grades are used in button and stud-making factories.

BLOODROOT. *See* SANGUINARIA CANADENSIS.

BLOOM. The name applied to the downy covering on grapes and other fruits, and also to individual flowers, e.g., Sweet Pea bloom. (*See* BLOSSOM).

BLOOMERIA (blū-mē-ria. Liliaceæ). Half-hardy summer-flowering bulbous plant, first introduced in 1869. Bears yellow flowers in July. 1 ft. in height.

These bulbs thrive well in light sandy soil, and prefer a position in the warm border or on the rockery where they will succeed the spring-flowering bulbs. Good drainage is essential to the health of the plants. The bulbs should be planted 2-3 in. deep and 3 in. apart from September to November. Method of increase is offsets planted as directed for original by bulbs.

The bulbs Bloomeria are closely allied to Brodiæa.

SPECIES.

B. aurea and *Clevelandii*, both natives of California.

BLOSSOM. The term usually applied to an inflorescence or cluster of flowers which gives promise of fruit, e.g., apple blossom. (*See* BLOOM.)

BLUE APPLE APHIS (*Aphis malifoliæ*). A serious pest in the early summer, attacking the leaves and shoots. The leaves become tightly curled and crumpled and soiled by honey-dew which often causes them to turn brown and fall. The young fruits become distorted and the shoots are stunted in growth. About the middle of July the aphides begin to disappear and have usually disappeared entirely by the end of the month. Winged females migrate to some other plant, the identity of which is at present uncertain. Similar females return to the apple trees in the autumn and produce sexual females and males. After fertilisation, the sexual females lay their oval, black, shining eggs, either singly or in groups, on the shoots, in the angles of the buds and on the trunk and branches. The eggs hatch in April and from them develop the stem mothers which give birth to living young. These young larvæ gather upon the buds and enter them as they open. As these larvæ mature they also produce successive generations of their kind and cause the characteristic leaf and shoot injury.

Treatment.—Spray in the dormant season with a tar-oil winter wash to destroy the eggs. If this is not done, a nicotine and soap or a derris wash will destroy the infestation if applied to the young foliage and shoots *before leaf curling has occurred.*

BLUEBELL. *See* SCILLA.

BLUMENBACHIA (Loasaceæ). Half-hardy annual, biennial and perennial twining plants. Grow in any ordinary soil in a warm border, or bed, against a south wall. Sow seeds in March in shallow boxes of light soil in a temperature of 65°. Divide the roots of perennials in April.

SPECIES.

B. chuquitensis, red and yellow, September. Climbing perennial.

B. coronata. White, June. Height, 1½ ft.

B. insignis. White, July. Trailing annual, 9 in.

B. lateritia (syn. *Loasa lateritia*). Red, May. Perennial.

B. multifida. Red, July. Annual. 1 ft.

BOAT-HOUSE. When a garden contains an area of water sufficiently large to allow for boating, a boat-house is necessary to provide shelter for the boats while out of use. Such a shelter will of course vary in design according to the size and extent of its use. It may be constructed of wood, stone, brick, etc., with thatch or tiled roof, so long as it harmonises with the other architectural garden features. Suitable planting should be introduced to give the building a pleasing background.

BOBARTIA (bō-bar′-ti-a. Bobart's Iris). Iridaceæ. Half-hardy, summer-flowering, bulbous plants, originally from the Cape of Good Hope and first introduced into this country in 1810.

They thrive best in a warm bed or border or on the rockery. The soil must be well drained. The bulbs should be planted 3 in. deep and the same distance apart in October. When the flowers have faded and the foliage has died down the bulbs should be lifted, dried, and stored in a cool place till planting time.

Propagation takes place by offsets. These can be removed, planted and treated in the same manner as the old bulbs.

SPECIES.

B. aphylla, with white and purple flowers.

B. filiformis, with purple flowers.

B. gladiata, with yellow flower.

B. spathacea, with yellow flowers.

BOCCONIA (boc-co-nia. Papaveraceæ). Plume Poppy. Handsome, ornamental herbaceous plants for flower gardens, with large plumes of feathery-like flowers.

Culture.—Plant in rich heavy soil.

Propagate by suckers in July or by cuttings from June to August, inserted in sandy soil under a bell-glass.

SPECIES.

B. cordata, a very decorative plant for back of the border, creamy buff flowers, 9 ft. in height.

B. microcarpa, resembling *cordata* but of richer yellow colouring.

BOG ARUM. *See* CALLA.

BOG BEAN. *See* MENYANTHES.

BOG GARDEN. A naturally marshy or boggy site can be turned into a bog garden at little expense. By drainage it may be possible to form a pool which would greatly add to the interest of the design. Stepping-stones, either logs of wood or slabs of stone, are the best materials to use for forming pathways through the garden; of the two, stone of course is the more practical and lasting.

Artificial bog gardens can be formed by

particularly so in the case of biennials. The commonest examples of plants which bolt are lettuce, cabbage and celery.

BOLTONIA (bol-to′-ni-a. Compositæ). False Chamomile. Hardy, summer-flowering, herbaceous perennials. First introduced from N. America in 1758.

Species of this genus have various coloured flowers which bloom in July, and the plants vary in height from 2–8 ft. These plants will grow in any ordinary moist loam in sunny or shady borders. Plant in October or April.

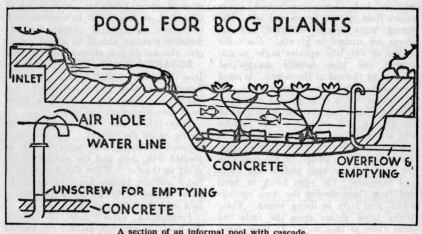

A section of an informal pool with cascade.

allowing water from an artificial pool to flow over the ground for a foot or so from the pool edge.

Trees of the willow and alder family are best for bog planting. Weeping varieties of trees are particularly pleasing, if planted so as to be reflected in the water.

There are many flowers which will thrive in a boggy soil, especially the primulas, kæmpferi irises, astilbe, bamboo, musk, etc. A suitable compost for bog plants is sand and loam with peat and leaf-mould. When planting, allow plenty of room for the plants to increase and develop. Lift and divide the clumps when they become too large for healthy growth. (*See also* WATER PLANTS).

BOG VIOLET. *See* PINGUICULA.

BOLTING. Several plants "bolt" or run to seed in dry weather, especially towards the autumn months. This is

Propagate by division of roots in April.

SPECIES.

B. asteroides, white flowers, 4–5 ft.

B. asteroides decurrens, blush-pink flowers, 4 ft.

B. latisquama, blue-violet flowers, 2–8 ft.

BOMAREA (bomar′ea. Amaryllidaceæ). Greenhouse climbing and flowering perennials. S. America, 1806.

Culture.—Compost, *see* AGAPANTHUS. Repot March, large pots or tubs, sunny position. Water freely during growing period, very little after. Winter temperature, 45°; summer, 60°.

Propagation.—By division when repotting, or by seed sown in light sandy soil in propagator. Temperature, 60°–65°.

SPECIES.

B. acutifolia, red and yellow; *B. Carderi*, rose; *B. edulis*, crimson.

BOND. The arrangement of bricks in

a wall so as to tie the courses together by overlapping is known as the bond. There are several types such as English, Flemish, etc.

BONE FLOUR (Steamed). This is made from bones that have been boiled or steamed before grinding to dissolve out the glue. This process removes much of the nitrogen but renders the fertiliser more readily available. Steamed bone flour is a popular dressing for lawns in many districts but like bonemeal is expensive per unit of plant food. Its beneficial action on lawns is problematical and modern research condemns it.

BONEMEAL (Raw). The availability of this fertiliser depends largely on its fineness of grinding. Like all organic fertilisers, it is expensive per unit of nitrogen and phosphates.

BONES (Dissolved). Raw bones or bone flour, treated with sulphuric acid to make a product somewhat similar to superphosphate.

BONFIRE. All burnable garden refuse should be stacked to be burnt on a favourable occasion. Add inflammable material to assist burning. The residue known as wood-ash contains a fair amount of potash. It should be stored immediately in a dry place so that its useful properties are not washed away. Sifted wood-ashes are very useful in the preparation of seed beds in spring. A garden "smother" is the name given to a bonfire which burns very slowly, possibly taking days or weeks before all the rubbish has been converted.

BONGARDIA (bon-gard'i-a. Berberidaceæ). Hardy tuberous-rooted flowering perennials from Persia and Syria.

These plants require a light sandy soil in a south bed or border which is well drained. Plant in October or April. The plants should be protected in severe weather by covering with hand-light or litter.

This plant is also suitable for the rockery, but as the dampness and winter weather is liable to perish the tubers a hand-light should be placed over the site from October to April.

Propagate by division of tubers in October or April, or by seeds sown in shallow boxes of light soil in a temperature of 55°–65° in March.

SPECIES.

B. Rauwolffi, yellow, 9 in.   Spring.

BORAGE. *See* BORAGO.

Borage. *The Cingalese say that borage will only thrive when near the dwellings of man.*

BORAGO (Bor'-ago. Boraginaceæ). Borage. Pretty hardy annuals and perennials with blue flowers. Best suited for dry, sunny places or banks. Sow in March in the open and raise fresh plants each year.

SPECIES.

B. laxiflora, blue, August.   1 ft. (perennial).

B. officinalis (common borage), blue, summer, 1–2 ft. (annual).

BORDEAUX MIXTURE. A copper fungicide, used as a spring and summer spray for most fungous diseases of plants. The mixture is prepared by the addition of milk of lime to a solution of sulphate of copper. The ingredients consist of sulphate of copper (bluestone), which should be purchased with a guarantee of 98 per cent. purity and freshly-burnt lime of high quality. Wooden, earthenware or copper vessels should be used for preparing the mixture—never iron or zinc vessels. To make up a quantity of the mixture in amount sufficient for ordinary garden use, take sulphate of copper, 1 lb.; lime (freshly burnt), in lumps, 1 lb.; water, 12½ gal. Put 2½ gal. of the water in a suitable vessel and dissolve in it the sulphate of copper. This is best done by wrapping the sulphate in a piece of sacking, suspending it just beneath the surface of the water and leaving it overnight. Place the lime in another vessel and slake it by adding water, a little at a time. If an earthenware vessel be used, care must be taken lest the heat generated by the slaking causes the vessel to crack. When the lime is slaked, make up the water to 10 gal. and stir thoroughly. Then pour the sulphate solution into the milk of lime and stir thoroughly. The mixture should be strained before it is poured into the sprayer to remove any coarse particles that might choke the sprayer nozzle. A piece of coarse sacking or the metal gauze strainer supplied with the sprayer will serve this purpose. The mixture should be applied as soon as possible after mixing. If there is any doubt about the quality of the lime, the mixture may be tested by immersing in it a *clean* steel knife blade. If after a few seconds' immersion the blade shows a red deposit of metallic copper, more milk of lime should be added, and the test repeated. The deposit of copper indicates that unchanged sulphate of copper remains in the mixture, and if the latter were used in

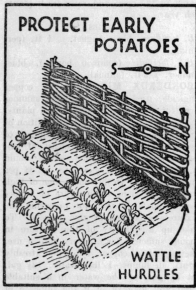

Wattle hurdles are easily erected and form an effective protection against frosty winds.

this condition, serious scorching of the foliage would follow.

BORDER. *See* HERBACEOUS AND SHRUB.

BORDER FORK. *See under* FORKS.

BORDER SPADE. *See under* SPADE.

BORECOLE or **KALE** (*Brassica oleracea acephala*). Cruciferæ. Like most of the Brassicas or Cabbage tribe this plant is a biennial usually grown as an annual. It is one of the hardiest of winter greens, and for this reason is most valuable as a food plant. There are a number of different types, some producing short leafy shoots or sprouts, and others large, crisp, curly leaves, but all of them have a valuable dietetic property, and some, at

least, should be grown in every vegetable garden.

Culture.—Under all normal conditions seeds should not be sown before April, as earlier sowings usually result in the plants "bolting" or running to seed. A seed bed should be thoroughly prepared early in the year, so that at the appropriate time the seed may be sown broadcast and covered with a fine tilth of soil. Protection from birds and slugs is essential or the seedlings may be damaged or irretrievably lost.

Borecole may follow early peas or beans, and in this case it is advisable to plant out the young greens between the rows of the earlier crop, so that they may receive some protection from sun and wind during the first week or two. If the soil between the peas has been kept well hoed there is no need to re-dig as firm ground suits most of the Brassicas better than freshly-turned soil. Set the plants out with a dibber, placing them 2 ft. apart and 2½–3 ft. asunder. When the peas or beans are removed lightly fork and clean the ground between, and no further work beyond occasional hoeing will be necessary.

VARIETIES.

Labrador; Crested Frost Proof; Victoria; Arctic Curled; Ragged Jack; Cottagers' Kale.

Uses.—The leaves or sprouts are gathered as required for use during the winter, and are boiled and served as greens.

BORONIA (bo-ro-n-ia. Rutaceæ). Greenhouse flowering shrubs. Evergreen (Australia, 1794).

Culture.—Compost: equal parts peat and sand with liberal supply of charcoal dust. Repot after flowering. The firming of compost when potting, and good drainage are essential. Place plants in semishade. Winter temperature, 50°; summer, 65°.

Propagation.—By cuttings of half-ripened wood inserted in sandy soil. Summer temperature, 55°.

SPECIES.

E. elatior, carmine; *B. heterophylla*, rose; *B. megastigma*, maroon and yellow.

BOTRYCHIUM (bot-rik'-i-um. Filices). Moon Fern, Moon Wort. Hardy and half-hardy deciduous ferns. Height about 18 in.

The hardy species will thrive well in a compost of equal parts sandy loam and peat on a moist shady rockery, or in grass. The half-hardy species, however, need to be grown in the cool greenhouse. Plant in April. Give them plenty of water in the dry weather during the summer.

Propagate by division of roots in April.

SPECIES.

B. lunaria (Common Moonwort).

B. ternatum (not hardy in Britain).

B. virginianum.

BOTTLE BRUSH. *See* CALLISTEMON.

BOTTLE SPRAYER. *See under* SPRAYING.

BOUGAINVILLEA (bou-gain-vi'-llea. Nyctaginaceæ). Stove climbing plants. Deciduous. Fine plants for pillars, or for trellis screen at the back of a lean-to house. Their chief attraction is the wonderful loose panicles of rich-coloured leaf-bracts, in the centre of which are small white blossoms. 1829.

Culture.—Compost: 2 parts loam, 1 part leaf-mould, ½ part sand. Repot, or plant direct into the border of the house, in February. Prune previous year's growth to within 1 in. of base annually, as the flowers are borne on the current year's wood. Completely cut away all weak growths. Water freely during growing period; after flowering, gradually withhold, and in October cease watering altogether. Winter temperature, 55°; summer, 75°–80°.

Propagation.—By cuttings of young shoots removed with heel of the old wood. Insert in 2 in. pots in sandy soil; place in propagator; temperature, 70°. Spring.

SPECIES.

B. glabra, rose; *B. speciosa;* rose shaded mauve.

BOUNDARY. A one- or two-strand wire fence with straining posts every 6 or 8 ft., is sufficient to mark the limits or boundaries of a new garden, unless the maintenance of a special type of fence is necessary by the terms of the title deeds.

An existing boundary fence is usually the property of the owner on whose land the posts stand.

Occupants are nearly always liable for the state of their boundaries and are responsible for any damage done on their land to straying cattle, etc., who have gained admittance through any obvious defect in their boundary. (*See also* FENCES, WALLS AND HEDGES).

BOUSSINGAULTIA (bous-sin-galt'-i-a. Chenopodiaceæ). Madeira Vine. Half-hardy tuberous-rooted climbers, with fragrant white or rose flowers in the autumn. First introduced in 1835.

These plants will flourish in light sandy soil, trained to the back wall of the greenhouse, or a south wall or fence outdoors during the summer.

The tubers should be planted in March in small pots in a temperature of 55°, and should be transplanted outdoors in June, or set in a bed in February for greenhouse culture. Tubers planted outdoors should be lifted in October and stored in sand during the winter. Those in the greenhouse bed may be left undisturbed. Water may be given freely in the summer, but the plants should be quite dry in the winter.

Summer temperature in the greenhouse should be 60°–70°, and the winter temperature, 45°–55°.

Propagate by inserting tubercles removed from the stems in sandy soil in a temperature of 55° in spring or autumn.

SPECIES.

B. baselloides, white flowers, autumn, 6–8 ft.

B. cordata, heart-shaped.

B. lachaumei, rose flowers.

BOUTELOUA (Graminaceæ). Hardy perennial flowering grass from Mexico that will grow almost anywhere to nearly 1 ft. in height. Sow in spring, or propagate by division in spring or autumn.

SPECIES.

B. racemosa.

BOUVARDIA (bou-var'-dia. Rubiaceæ). Greenhouse evergreen flowering shrubs (named after Dr. Bouvard, one time curator of the Botanic Gardens at Paris). For supplying a quantity of lasting, fragrant flowers for the decoration of the greenhouse, bouvardias can hardly be surpassed (Mexico, 1794).

Culture.—Compost: 1 part fibrous loam, 1 part peat, ½ part leaf-mould and silver sand. Prune previous year's growth hard back to within 1 in. of their base, place in brisk heat, and repot at end of March. Place in cold frame during summer months. Winter temperature, 50°.

Propagation.—By cuttings of young shoots in sandy soil; place in propagator (temperature, 60°–65°). March. Cuttings root quite easily.

SPECIES.

B. angustifolia. red; *B. Humboldtii*, white; *B. triphylla*, scarlet. There are numerous beautiful hybrids as: *Alfred Neuner, Dazzler, Hogarths, flore-pleno* (a lovely double scarlet), *President Garfield* (double pink), etc.

BOWKERIA (bo-kē′-ria. Scrophulariaceæ). Evergreen shrubs from Natal with trifoliate leaves and white calceolaria-like flowers in summer. A rare shrub only suitable for mild districts. Thrives in Isle of Wight.

SPECIES.

B. Gerrardiana, the only known species Erroneously known as *B. triphylla*. ·

BOWLING GREEN. A standard green is 126 ft. square.

BOX. *See* BUXUS.

BOX EDGING. *See* BUXUS SUFFRUTICOSA.

BOX-ELDER. *See* ACER NEGUNDO.

BRACHYCHITON (brak′i-kī′-ton. Sterculiaceæ). Australian shrubs and trees for mild districts.

SPECIES.

B. acerifolium. Bright glossy green maple-like foliage resembling Aralia. Beautiful bright-red bell-shaped flowers.

B. populneum, rare.

BRACHYCOME (brachy-come. Compositæ). Swan River Daisy. Half-hardy annual, 1 ft.

B. iberidifolium is the best of the genus for garden purposes, and can now be obtained in a good range of blue-mauve and rose shades. The plants are bushy, much branched, and flower most profusely all through the summer. Good for edgings or small beds: sow in greenhouse in March, plant out in May, or sow where to flower, in April, thin out to 6 in. apart. A sunny place suits them best.

BRACHYGLOTTIS (brak′-i-glot′-is. Compositæ). A noble foliaged plant from New Zealand, with silver bark and handsome green leaves, 12 in. long and 9 in. wide, silvery beneath, and mignonette-scented small creamy-white flowers in large panicles. Only suitable for mild districts. Splendid seaside shrub, unaffected by sea air or wind.

BRACHYPODIUM (brak-i-pō′-di-um. Gramineæ). False Brome Grass. Hardy annual flowering grass. Inflorescence can be dried and used for winter decorations. This grass will grow in any ordinary soil in sunny borders. Sow seeds outdoors in April. If the inflorescence is to be dried, it should be cut while in full flower.

SPECIES.

B. distachyon, flowers in the summer and attains a height of 9 in.

BRACHYSEMA (brak-is-e-ma. Leguminosæ). Greenhouse climbing plants from Australia. Flowering, evergreen.

Culture.—Compost of equal parts loam, peat, leaf-mould and silver sand is needed. Pot in February in well-drained pots or tubs, or in beds 3 ft. wide and 18 in. deep. The shoots should be trained round wire trellis, or up the roof and fully exposed to the sun.

From April to August the plants should be watered plentifully, but at other times watered in moderation. A winter temperature of 45°–50° should be maintained and 55°–65° in summer.

Propagate by seeds sown $\frac{1}{16}$ in. deep in sandy soil in March, in a temperature of 55°, or by cuttings of shoots inserted in similar soil and temperature, under a bell-glass in June, July or August. Also by layering shoots in September.

SPECIES.

B. latifolium, with crimson and scarlet flowers, 8–10 ft.

B. lanceolatum, with scarlet, yellow and white flowers, spring, 3 ft.

B. undulatum, with violet flowers, March, 3–6 ft.

BRACT. A modified leaf on the flower stalk. It is usually green, but in some cases the bracts are blue, purple, red, or white in colour.

BRAHEA (brā-hē-a. Palmaceæ). Greenhouse palm, of dwarf habit, with ornamental fan-shaped foliage. This plant only reaches a height of 3 ft. First introduced in 1865.

Cultivation.—Pot in February in a compost of equal parts loam, peat and sand. During the summer, water may be given freely, but moderately at other times. A winter temperature of 50°–60° should be maintained and 65°–75° in summer.

Increase by seeds sown ½ in. deep in light soil in a temperature of 85° in March.

SPECIES.

B. dulcis.

BRAMBLE. See RUBUS.

BRASENIA (bras-ēn-ia. Nymphæaceæ). Water Shield. Hardy aquatic, for pond or aquarium. This plant has purple flowers which bloom in the summer.

It will grow in any ordinary soil in shallow lakes or ponds, or aquariums. Plant in pots or baskets, sinking these 1–1½ ft. deep into the water during April or May. It can also be grown on the margin of ponds.

Increase by offsets in May.

SPECIES.

B. Schreberi (syn. peltata).

BRASSAVOLA (brassa-vola. Orchidaceæ). Stove epiphytal orchid (named in honour of A. M. Brassavol, a Venetian botanist). This genus has one outstanding species, viz.: Digbyana, from which the hybridist has given us the wonderful hybrids, Brassocattleya; Brassolæliocattleya, etc. (Honduras, 1844.)

Culture.—Compost, sphagnum moss. Best grown on blocks of wood suspended from the roof. Water abundantly during growing period, but little during the rest period in the winter. Summer temperature, 80°, moist; winter, 60°, dry.

Propagation.—By division when repotting.

SPECIES.

B. Digbyana, cream, white and purple; B. glauca, yellow; B. nodosa, yellowish-green.

BRASSIA (bra-ssia. Orchidaceæ). Stove, epiphytal orchids. The flowers of this genus are not brilliant in colour, but their spider-like formation makes them exceedingly interesting (Jamaica, 1806).

Culture.—Compost: mixture of sphagnum moss, fibre and charcoal. Repot early spring. Good drainage essential. Shady or part shady position. Flowers appear at base when growth is completed. Winter temperature, 60°; summer, 80°.

Propagation.—By division when repotting.

SPECIES.

B. antherotes, yellow and black flowers in May and June.

B. brachiata, yellow, white and orange flowers from July to September.

B. gireoudiana, yellow and red flowers in August.

B. lanceana, yellow-brown and red flowers from January to September.

B. lawrenceana, yellow cinnamon and green flowers in April.

B. maculata, yellow, red and brown flowers in May.

B. verrucosa, green and brown flowers in March.

BRASSICA. The generic name applied to green vegetables which have been raised from the wild cabbage, Brassica oleracea, which grows wild on the seashore. These plants include borecole, broccoli, Brussels sprouts, cabbage, cauliflower, etc., all of which are members of the Cruciferæ family. The crops are dealt with under their various names. See BORECOLE; BROCCOLI; BRUSSELS SPROUTS; CABBAGE; CAULIFLOWER; TRONCHUDA, COUVE; KOHL RABI; TURNIP.

BRASSOCATTLEYA (brasso'-cattle-ya). A very popular new race of orchids, obtained by crossing the species of Brassavola with those of Cattleya. The flowers are large, beautifully coloured, and magnificent for exhibition or decoration. The cultural requirements and temperature are similar to the Cattleyas (which see).

VARIETIES.

The varieties are numerous and only a few can be given here: B. Alfred Dean, sepals and petals orange-yellow with a rich bronze margin on the sepals, lips gold-lined, flushed with rose at base. Grande Monarque, sepals and petals mauve, with a fine fringe lip and orange-yellow throat; Ilene, sepals and petals mauve, mottled with rose; lip rosy-mauve lined yellow.

BRASSOLÆLIA (brasso'-lælia). Another new race of hybrid orchids, the result of crossing Brassavola species with those of Lælia. A very handsome group; brilliant in colouring, but not quite so good in shape as the Brassocattleyas. Excellent for exhibition bench. Require similar culture to the Cattleyas (which see).

VARIETIES.

The Mikado, sepals and petals, rosy-mauve, lip mottled rose-purple. The Queen, a beautiful variety, sepals and petals white, slightly flushed at tips, lip soft mauve.

BRASSOLÆLIOCATTLEYA (brasso'-lælio-catt-le-ya). A splendid new race of hybrid orchids. The result of crossing Brassavola, Lælia and Cattleya. These are very showy, and include a magnificent range of colours in mauve, rose, white, white with coloured lip, and yellow in several shades.

Culture.—Similar in every way to Cattleya (*which see*).

VARIETIES.

There are numerous varieties, only a few of which can be given. Ambrosia, large rich mauve flower, lip beautifully fringed, yellow throat; Aprica, sepals and petals rich apricot-yellow, lip open with rose-coloured flush, throat deep orange; Gordon Highlander, Rugh flower, sepals and petals rich mauve, lip deep purple; Ring Emperor, a flower of enormous-sized sepals and petals rich mauve, lip crimson-purple with yellow throat.

BRAVOA (bra-vo-a. Amaryllidaceæ). Scarlet Twin Flower. Half-hardy bulbous plants, deciduous. Originating from Mexico, they bear orange-red flowers in July and attain a height of 2 ft. Besides being grown in the open, the Scarlet Twin flowers can be grown in the greenhouse.

Outdoor Cultivation.— Plant the bulbs 4 in. deep in September in a well-drained sunny border of light sandy soil. In winter protect with a covering of cinder ashes.

For Greenhouse Culture.—Plant four bulbs in a 5 in. pot, with ample drainage, in October, set it into a cold frame and cover with ashes. Leave them till January, when they should be removed to the greenhouse. A moderate quantity of water should be allowed until the foliage turns yellow, then the soil should be kept quite dry.

SPECIES.

B. geminiflora is the most common species cultivated.

BRAZIL NUT. *See* BERTHOLLETIA.

BREAD FRUIT. *See* ARTOCARPUS.

BREAK. This term is applied to a plant when its shoots make fresh growth after being "pinched" or "stopped." When a break occurs which is not caused by stopping, it is termed a "natural-break."

The term "break" also describes the departure of tulips from the shade shown in the seedlings.

Seedling tulips are known as breeders or mother tulips. They retain this name so long as the flowers remain of one colour. At any time, however, they may "break" into feathered or flamed flowers, when they are said to be "rectified" or "broken."

BREASTWOOD. The term applied to the thin shoots which appear on the branches of bush and pyramid trees. The young twiggy summer growths which come out at right angles to the front of the main branches of espalier, cordon and wall-trained trees, are also called breast-wood; but a more correct term is "foreright" or forthright shoots. These shoots should be cut out, leaving only the side growths to train in as new wood.

BREVOORTIA (bre-voor-ti-a. Liliaceæ). Brodie's Lily. Hardy bulbous-rooted plant, with red and green flowers which bloom in June. Height 1 ft.

Cultivate in the same way as for BRODIÆAS (*which see*).

SPECIES.

B. Ida-Maia (syn. *Brodiæa coccinea*).

BRIAR. A stem of a wild rose on to which garden roses are grafted or budded.

BRICK. Bricks are used extensively in garden design for steps and walling, garden houses and similar buildings, also for paving (*see* PATHWAYS). The brick used chiefly in garden design is approximately 9 in. by 4½ in. by 3 in. One sq. yd. of paving requires 32 bricks laid flat, i.e., 9 in. by 4½ in.

One sq. yd. of paving requires 48 bricks laid on edge, i.e., 9 in. by 3 in.

Allow about 4 extra bricks per square yard for irregularities in sizes.

BRIDAL WREATH. *See* FRANCOA RAMOSA.

BRIDGE. Any structure, however slight, which gives access from one side of a piece of water to the other may be termed a bridge. Interest can be added to both natural and artificial water employed in the garden by this means.

Simple structures such as a slab of stone,

or stepping stones, are in harmony with the rock or bog garden pool design.

More elaborate designs in wood, stone or brick can be planned to suit individual sites. In bridge designing there is a degree of safety gained by noting the relation of the span to the rise:

Span	2½ ft.	5 ft.	10 ft.
Thickness of arches	1 ft.	1¼ ft.	1½ ft.
Rise	6 in.	9 in.	2 ft.

BRIZA (bri'-za. Gramineæ). "Quaking Grass." Very pretty, hardy, ornamental grasses. *B. maxima* grows 1½ ft. tall, and bears purple-coloured panicles of large tear-like seed heads, which shimmer in the slightest breeze.

B. media is the more common form, and is not so large or tall. Both are of value for drying as soon as fully developed. Put loosely into vases without water, and stand in an airy place. Sow in patches in spring, where to flower.

BROCCOLI (*Brassica oleracea botrytis asparagoides*). Cruciferæ. To the uninitiated broccoli and cauliflowers are one and the same thing, but the discerning gardener knows that they are now quite distinct, though one may have been derived from the other. The broccoli is usually thicker and coarser leaved, is more hardy and matures during autumn, winter and spring, whereas the normal season for cauliflowers is just the opposite.

During the last decade seedsmen have devoted much care and time to this plant, and many of them now offer a range of first-class varieties grouped together in their seasons for sowing and maturing.

Culture.—In general principles the cultivation previously recommended for borecole is quite suited for broccoli.

To obtain good heads or "curds" for cutting, September to December seeds should be sown in March or early April in gentle heat under glass, or in favoured districts in a warm border outside. If raised under glass harden-off as soon as possible, and in all cases transplant when a few inches high to prepared beds, spacing them about 6 in. apart. In this way good sturdy plants are obtained ready for setting in their permanent quarters at the end of May or early June.

Seeds of those intended for cutting from January to April should be sown from the middle of April to beginning of May in a prepared bed outside. Where it is at all possible it always pays to transplant the seedlings at an early date to a reserve bed, rather than to allow them to remain in the seed bed until planting-out time.

This section may follow peas, potatoes, and similar crops, and should be planted in firm ground as advised for borecole.

BRICK PATHWAYS

Brick makes an effective pathway, but enquire about the weathering quality of the brick before use.

The last sowing at the end of May is of those varieties intended for cutting in late spring, and the initial operations may be carried out in the same manner as the earlier ones.

In each case if the weather is at all dry when transplanting, the freshly set plants should be well watered in, or their roots dipped in a thick mud paste just prior to planting.

When the winter is very severe, and in exposed districts, it is advisable to protect the heads. Sometimes a few of the outer leaves snapped and folded over is sufficient, or a covering of dry straw or bracken may be used and removed as soon as mild weather ensues. Another method is to take out a forkful of soil close to the stem on the south side, and then by inserting the fork to its full depth on the opposite side to partly lift and lay the plant over on the ground facing north, afterwards covering the stem and roots with the soil previously taken out.

VARIETIES.

For use September to December: Veitch's Self Protecting; Penzance; Snow's Winter White; Michaelmas. For use January to April: Leamington; Adam's Early; Evesham Giant; Cooling's Matchless. For use April to July: Cattell's Eclipse; Veitch's Model; April Queen; May Giant.

Roscoff Broccoli. These are a special type of broccoli, raised by the French market gardeners. The seed was jealously guarded for many years, and only recently has it been possible to buy it in this country. Even now there are only one or two genuine and reliable strains; the others are hopelessly mixed. Its chief value lies in its extreme hardiness and abundant cropping qualities. It is now the leading variety of the Cornish and Devon growers.

Uses.—The heads should always be cut whilst quite white, and before they commence to split. The outer leaves should be stripped off and the broccoli placed in salt water head downwards for half an hour or so. This should bring out any grubs which are hidden inside. Afterwards the heads should be immersed in boiling salt water and kept boiling for 10 to 30 minutes according to size. Many attractive dishes may be prepared with broccoli.

Sprouting Broccoli. The cultivation of this useful vegetable is exactly the same as for ordinary broccoli, but instead of the whole head being cut the sprouting side shoots are gathered as required for use. It is extremely hardy, and in fact its flavour is enhanced by frost.

VARIETIES.

Xmas Purple Sprouting; White Sprouting.

BRODIÆA (bro-di-e-a. Liliaceæ). Missouri Hyacinths. Hardy, deciduous, bulbous plants, introduced to this country in 1806.

These plants will thrive well if planted in September or October in rich sandy loam in a warm, well-drained border. The bulbs should be planted 4 in. deep and 3 in. apart. They should be lifted and replanted annually.

They can also be cultivated indoors, and for this use a compost of 2 parts sandy loam and 1 part equal proportions of leaf-mould and sand. The bulbs should be grown in $4\frac{1}{2}$ in. pots, placing them 1 in. apart and just below the surface. This should be done in October. The pots should then be placed in the cold frame and covered with ashes until growth begins, when they should be removed to a temperature of 45°–55°. During the growing period the bulbs should be watered freely, but when the foliage dies they should be kept quite dry.

Increase by seeds sown $\frac{1}{8}$ in. deep in sandy soil in the cold frame in March.

They can also be increased by offsets, which should be treated as bulbs.

SPECIES.

B. Bridgesii, pale lilac, June, 18 in.

B. californica, rosy-purple, June, 18 in.

B. congesta, blue, July, 1 ft.

B. congesta alba, white, July.

B. capitata, violet-blue, May, 1 ft.

B. capitata alba, white.

B. grandiflora, blue and purple, June, 18 in.

B. Hendersoni, salmon-yellow with violet stripe, 6–8 in.

B. ixioides, yellow, June, 9 in.

B. Howelli, blue, July, 2 ft.

B. Howelli lilacina, pale lilac.

B. hyacintha, white, July, 2 ft.

B. laxa, blue, June, 1–2 ft.

B. stellaris, deep blue, 6 in.

BRODIE'S LILY. *See* BREVOORTIA.

BROMELIA (bro-me-li-a. Bromeliaceæ). Stove herbaceous perennials, flowering and with ornamental foliage. Bearing for the most part red and purple flowers in early spring and late summer.

Use a compost of equal parts fibrous loam, rough peat, leaf-mould and silver sand. Pot in March. Good drainage is essential to the health of the plants. They will always need plenty of water and should never be allowed to become dry.

Temperature of the greenhouse should be from 60°-70° in winter, and 70°-80° in summer.

Propagate by large-sized offshoots or suckers. These should be inserted singly in small pots in a compost of sandy peat in a temperature of 85° in April.

SPECIES.

B. fastuosa, purple, August, 4 ft.

B. Pinguin, red, March, 3 ft.

BROMUS (bro-mus. Gramineæ). "Greek Oat." A good ornamental grass of a biennial nature is *B. brizaeformis*, and as its name implies is of a form similar to that of the Briza or Quaking Grass. Seed should be sown in July where the plants are to bloom; a good place is in the mixed border, where during the following season the long drooping panicles will make a conspicuous feature. It grows 2 ft high, and likes a sandy loam soil.

BROOM. *See* CYTISUS, GENISTA *and* SPARTIUM.

BROUGHTONIA (brow-to-ni-a. Orchidaceæ). Stove orchid, evergreen. First introduced in 1793.

These plants may either be grown in crocks and fibrous peat, in which case the plant should be raised above the pot, or on blocks without moss, and placed near a roof. Cultivated by the latter method the plants will thrive particularly well. They need a high temperature in the summer from 60°-85°, with a moist atmosphere, but in the winter keep them cooler and drier.

The resting period of these flowers is in the winter, and after this period the flowers appear at the apex of new pseudobulbs.

Increase is by division of the pseudobulbs.

SPECIES.

B. sanguinea, crimson, August, 18 in.

B. nitida, red, June, 18 in.

BROUSSONETIA (brŭ-sŏn-et-ti-a Moraceæ). Chinese and Japanese unisexual trees and shrubs allied to the Mulberry. They thrive in ordinary soil and are increased by cuttings taken with a "heel" (i.e., a shoot with a "heel" or piece of older wood attached) in July or August.

PRINCIPAL SPECIES.

B. Kazinoki (syn. *B. Kæmpferi*). Jap-

anese Paper Mulberry. Deciduous; 10–15 ft.

B. papyrifera. Chinese species up to 30 ft. A paper is made from the bark and the fibre is made into a cloth. The male plants have drooping yellow catkins.

BROWALLIA (bro-al-ia. Solanaceæ). The half-hardy annual, *B. elata* (blue), 1½ ft., and its white form, *B. elata alba*, are quite useful bedding subjects in some districts as the plants flower over a long period; a light sandy soil in a sunny position suits them best, and they are most effective when planted with another subject of contrasting colour. Alone they are rather "lifeless." Amongst the most interesting of the biennials and perennials from Peru for greenhouse decoration is the perennial *B. speciosa major* with bright blue flowers. The habit is spreading and the height about 1 ft. It should be treated as a biennial.

Cultivation.—Sow the seeds in May for late winter and spring flowering. Use light sandy loam, which has been opened, with good leaf-mould. Sown in October, they will flower the following summer.

BROWNEA (brown'-e-a. Leguminosæ). Stove-flowering evergreens which bear red flowers in the summer.

A compost of equal parts peat and loam with a little sand is the best for these shrubs. They should be potted in February or March and watered moderately in the summer, but at other times only occasionally. From September to March a temperature of from 55°-60° should be maintained, and from March to September 70°-80°.

Propagate by cuttings of established shoots. These should be inserted in sandy peat in a temperature of 80° in spring, and placed under a bell-glass.

SPECIES.

B. ariza, with red flowers. 10–20 ft.

B. Birschellii, rose flowers. 10 ft.

B. Crawfordii, scarlet flowers. A hybrid between *B. grandiceps* and *B. macrophylla*.

B. grandiceps, red flowers. 6 ft.

B. macrophylla, orange-scarlet, with large leaves.

BROWN SCALE. A pest that attacks small fruits and shrubs. Best controlled by paraffin soda wash (caustic soda 2 lb., soft soap ½ lb., paraffin 5 pints, water 10 gallons).

BRUCKENTHALIA (bruk - en - ta - lia. Ericaceæ). Dwarf evergreen shrub 6 in. high, heath-like in appearance, from the mountains of E. Europe and Asia Minor, with erect racemes of bell-shaped rosy-red flowers in June and July. Requires a non-calcareous soil.

Increased by seed and young cuttings as advised for hardy heaths. The open-

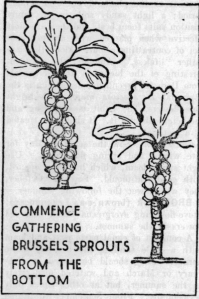

COMMENCE GATHERING BRUSSELS SPROUTS FROM THE BOTTOM

Brussels Sprouts need a long season of growth to get good results.

mouthed corolla differentiates it from hardy Ericas.

SPECIES.

B. spiculifolia. A miniature Heath from Bulgaria with rose-pink flowers. Peat soil.

Propagate by cuttings inserted in sandy peat under glass.

BRUNSFELSIA (bruns-felz-i-a. Solanaceæ). Evergreen flowering shrubs cultivated in the stove house. Pot firmly in four parts each of fibrous peat and leaf-mould, one part loam and sand, immediately after flowering, and prune moderately. The tips of young shoots should be pinched off when they are 6 in. long. Water moderately from October to March, then water freely. Syringe freely from March

to August. In the summer healthy plants should receive liquid manure. Temperature 50°-55° October to March, and 60°-65° March to October.

Propagate by cuttings 2–3 in. long, inserted in sand, and placed under a bell-glass in a temperature of 60°-70° any time from February to August.

SPECIES.

B. americana, pale yellow or white flowers in June. 4 ft.

B. calycina (syn. *Franciscea calycina*), purple flowers which are fragrant in summer. 2 ft.

B. gracilis, cream flowers in June. 2 ft.

B. latifolia, white, lavender, or purple flowers in winter or early spring. 3–4 ft.

BRUNSVIGIA (bruns-vi-gia. Amaryllidaceæ). Candelabra-flower. Greenhouse bulbous plants. Deciduous. Named after the house of Brunswick. Cape of Good Hope. 1752.

Culture.—Compost, equal parts fibrous loam, peat and sand. Repot autumn. Sunny position. Water moderately during growing period. After flowering, gradually withhold water. Winter temperature, 50°; summer, 70°.

Propagation.—By offsets inserted in small pots when repotting.

SPECIES.

B. gigantea, red; *B. Josephine,* scarlet.

BRUSSELS SPROUTS (*Brassica oleracea bullata gemmifera*). Cruciferæ. As the name implies, this vegetable originated in Belgium, where it is regarded as an essential crop in every vegetable garden. As compared with some other vegetables its introduction to this country is comparatively recent, but it is now grown extensively in all parts of the country, and hundreds of acres are devoted to it in the market-gardening districts.

Culture.—Providing the land is free from that disease known as "club root" or "finger and toe" Brussels sprouts may be grown successfully on almost any type of soil. The crop amply repays liberal treatment, so that deep digging and a good dressing of half-rotted manure, or decayed garden refuse and fertiliser, is advisable.

The earliest crops are obtained by sowing in gentle heat in March, pricking off as soon as the seedlings are large enough to handle, and growing on in a cool house or frame until they can be hardened-off for planting out in April. When raised under cover they must be kept near the glass and given ample ventilation to keep them sturdy.

A succession of outdoor sowings may commence in early April, and be continued at intervals up to the middle of June. As a rule they take 30 to 40 weeks from time of sowing to reach maturity.

Birds, mice and slugs often create great havoc amongst seedling Brussels sprouts, so precautions must be taken against these pests.

Broadcast sowing is usually preferred to sowing in drills, and if possible the seedlings should be transplanted 4 in. apart in a reserve bed until they can go into their final quarters. This ensures stocky little plants which will lift with a good mass of roots. In planting out it is essential to set them in to the first pair of leaves, and to make the soil around the roots quite firm.

The practice of planting Brussels sprouts between potatoes is not one to be encouraged; far better to keep them in a reserve bed until a sufficient area becomes vacant. On no account should the plants be crowded, and only the dwarf kinds should be set less than 3 ft. apart each way.

Little attention is required during the summer beyond occasional hoeing.

As the lower leaves turn yellow in the autumn they should be collected and placed on the refuse heap to decay, but the heads or tops of the stalks should not be cut until the very last, when the supply of sprouts has finished. Well - settled ground and firm planting does much to induce the formation of sound, solid sprouts, and loose soil and planting just the reverse.

VARIETIES.

Dwarf Gem; Aigburth; Darlington; Covent Garden.

Uses.—Brussels sprouts should not be picked before the first frosts occur. Afterwards they may be gathered as required for boiling.

BRYANTHUS. *See* PHYLLODOCE.

BRYOPHYLLUM (bryo - phyl - lum. Crassulaceæ). Greenhouse succulent-leaved plants, chiefly grown as a curiosity. South Africa. 1800.

Culture.—Compost: 2 parts loam, 1 part old brick and mortar rubble, and sand. Repot early spring. Good drainage essential. Fairly dry atmosphere. Sunny position. Winter temperature, 50°; summer, 65°.

Propagation.—Very simple; lay a single

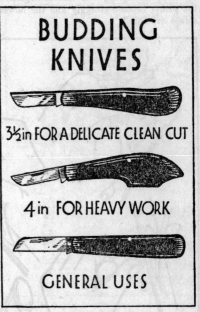

Various types of garden knives are obtainable from sundriesmen for special purposes. The budding knife has a blunt, flattened handle, useful for lifting the back of the stock ready for the insertion of the bud.

leaf on the surface of moist sand. Young plants will form all round its margin.

SPECIES.

B. calycinum, green and purple.

BUCKBEAN. *See* MENYANTHES.

BUCKEYE. *See* ÆSCULUS.

BUCKTHORN. *See* RHAMNUS.

BUDDING. *See* PROPAGATION.

BUDDING KNIVES. *See under* PRUNING.

BUDDLEIA (bŭd-lē-a. Loganiaceæ). Beautiful flowering deciduous and evergreen shrubs of great garden value, mostly hardy.

Culture.—Plant from October or March in ordinary soil, with manure added if possible, in open sunny positions.

Propagate by cuttings, about 4 in. long taken from just under a joint, in late summer. The cuttings may be struck in the open ground or may be placed round the edges of pots. Pruning of the *variabilis* section consists in cutting back to about 10 in. in the spring. If this is neglected the plants become straggly and the flower spikes are small.

Holds Award of Garden Merit of R.H.S.

B. Fallowiana (China). A handsome silvery-foliaged species with large panicles of sweetly-scented pale lavender-blue flowers. There is a form with white flowers.

B. Farrerii (China). Rather tender. Flowers fragrant, and of a deeper mauve than most Buddleias.

B. Forrestii. Rare, large-leaved species, white or pale lilac, cream-coloured flowers.

B. globosa. Orange Ball Tree. (Chile and Peru). A very old plant in gardens,

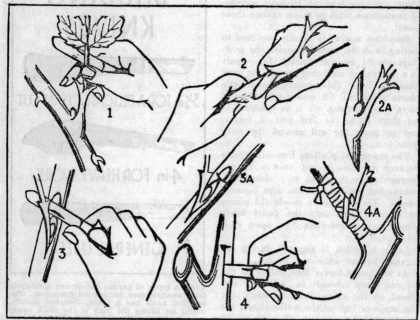

How to bud roses : (1) remove leaf from bud ; (2) cut bud from stem ; (2a) prepare bud ; (3) insert the bud ; (3a) the bud in position ; (4) how to open the bark of the briar ; (4a) bud bound with raffia.

B. globosa and *B. alternifolia* should have a little old wood removed after flowering only.

SPECIES.

B. albiflora (China), 20–30 ft. Flowers fragrant lilac, orange centre.

B. alternifolia (China). Resembling a fine-leaved, graceful weeping willow, with pendulous sprays of fragrant purple blossoms in late spring and early summer. A very charming and distinct species discovered by the late Reginald Farrer in 1914.

being introduced in 1774. Of handsome and striking appearance. The bright orange-coloured flowers, arranged in globular heads, are freely produced in May and June and are sweetly fragrant. This species is not generally pruned, but if straggly, may be cut back every second year after flowering.

B. variabilis (Davidii). This section contains a number of varieties, of which the following are the most distinct:

B. v. var. *amplissima.* Finest deep mauve variety.

B. v. var. *magnifica (superba)*. The finest. Flowers dark purplish.

B. v. var. *Pink Pearl*. Distinct. Flowers pale lavender-mauve with straw-coloured tube to each tiny flower.

To produce the fine flower-panicle, 2-2½ ft. long of *B. variabilis* and its forms, it is important to remember to prune hard back every spring. A rich loamy soil is also helpful.

BUDS. The two main types of buds are flower or fruit buds and leaf buds. It is important to understand the difference between the types before pruning is undertaken. As a rough guide it may be taken that leaf buds are usually thin and conical in shape, while flower buds are thick and globular. Underground buds are seen in the case of the potato where they are borne on the underground stems or tubers. In this case they are commonly called "eyes."

BUGBANE. *See* CIMICIFUGA.

BULB. An underground bud with fleshy scale leaves surrounding it. The roots die down annually. In a full-grown bulb the flower spike is present in perfect condition, but develops perfectly or otherwise, according to the care it receives from the grower. Some very good examples of bulbs are tulips and hyacinths (*see* CORMS).

BULB FLIES (*Meredon equestris*, the Large Bulb Fly; *Eumerus strigatus*, the Lesser Bulb Fly).

Meredon equestris.

DESCRIPTION.—Very like a small bumble-bee, but with two wings instead of four; variable in colour, ranging from tawny brown to black with orange tails. *Larva*.—Greyish in colour, fat and wrinkled and legless.

LIFE-HISTORY.—The flies appear after the flowering period and lay their eggs on the leaves near the base. On hatching out the young larvæ bore their way down into the bulb and feed on the interior, eating away the layers of which the bulb is made up. As they grow, the interior of the bulb is filled with a soft brown frass. When full grown they eat their way out, pupating in the soil.

Eumerus strigatus.

DESCRIPTION.—About ¼ in. long, black and shiny in colour. *Larva*.—Yellowish-white and with a horny process on the posterior end of the body.

LIFE-HISTORY.—The Lesser Bulb Fly appears a little later than *Meredon equestris* and lays its eggs in much the same position. Instead of only one, however, there are usually several larvæ in each bulb. While feeding they cause the bulb to turn black and become "squashy." On becoming full grown they change to small brownish pupa.

METHODS OF CONTROL.—In districts where the bulb flies are common, it is as well to lift and examine all bulbs after flowering. Before planting fresh bulbs examine them, and those appearing soft when pressed between the thumb and finger should be opened and destroyed. It is said if the bulbs are steeped in warm water for 48 hours before planting the larvæ will come out, but as the heart of the bulb will be destroyed it is of little use planting the bulb. Nothing will kill the larvæ when once they are in the bulb in the soil, but as a preventive the dusting with a strong-smelling soil fumigant will tend to repel the fly and prevent egg-laying. Dusting should be done some little time after flowering.

Of later years a poison bait has been applied to the foliage with good results. This bait is made up from:

Sodium arsenite	...	...	4 oz.
Crude glycerine	...	...	2 lb.
White sugar	...	...	2 lb.
Water	...	...	...	4 gal.

It should be applied in large drops in sunny corners, first at the end of May and again in mid-June. The flies are attracted, suck the liquid and are poisoned before they have laid their eggs.

BULB MITE (*Rhizoglyphus echinopus*). A small mite which often causes much damage to bulbs and more rarely to tubers.

A discoloration of the foliage which assumes a sickly pale yellow colour points to the bulbs being infected. The growth may also be dwarfed but not distorted, the latter pointing to eel-worm. At the same time both mite and eel-worm may be found in the same bulb. An examination of the actual bulb will reveal reddish areas and should the outer shell be peeled off little clusters of mite will be found.

METHODS OF CONTROL.—Badly infested bulbs should be burned. At the same time a great deal of good will result if all bulbs suspected of having mite are steeped before planting in either potassium sulphide, 1 oz. to 3 gal. of water, or a dilute lime-sulphur. After a thorough immersion of about one hour they should be drained and planted as soon as possible.

BULBOCODIUM CONSPICUUS

Closely allied to the Daffodil, Bulbocodium is easily recognised by its curious flowers.

BULBINELLA (bul-bi-nel-la. Liliaceæ). Hardy herbaceous perennials. First introduced from New Zealand in 1848.

They require a rich, well-drained soil containing plenty of leaf-mould. Plant in spring in a partially-shaded warm border or at the base of rockery. Increase by division in spring.

SPECIES.

B. Hookeri (syn. *Chrysobactron Hookeri*), white, summer. 2–3 ft.

B. latifolia, white, April. 1 ft.

BULBOCODIUM (Liliaceæ). Spring Meadow Saffron. Hardy bulbs first introduced in 1649. These can be cultivated in any ordinary soil and will grow either in sunshine or in shade. The bulbs should be planted 3 in. deep and 3 in. apart in autumn and every second year they should be lifted and replanted, offsets being removed at the same time and planted elsewhere.

SPECIES.

B. vernum, which has purple flowers in March, and *B. vernum versicolor*.

BULBOPHYLLUM (bulbo-phyl-lum. Orchidaceæ). From *bulbos*, a bulb, and *phyllon*, a leaf: referring to the leaves issuing from the apex of the pseudo-bulb. Stove epiphytal orchids. This genus includes some of the very smallest orchids grown, and many of the species produce flowers of a weird and uncanny nature. Chiefly of botanical interest.

Culture.—Compost. Rough peat and sphagnum moss. Position, baskets or pots suspended from the roof of the house. All are easily grown in a warm moist heat, and should never be allowed to become quite dry. Winter temperature, 55°; summer, 75°–80°.

SPECIES.

B. barbigerum, purple; *B. Dearei*, yellow and red; *B. grandiflorum*, yellow and white; *B. Lobbii*, yellow and purple.

Lay bulbs out on the beds or borders before planting.

Bulbs are easy to plant if you space them out on the bed before planting.

BULBS. Every kind of bulb has its individuality, and likes, perhaps, slightly different treatment from others; but there are general terms in which one can advise on bulb cultivation which will apply to practically every kind. Take first the simplest form of bulb growing, that of planting bulbs in the garden border. Bulbs, as we have already said, are storeouses of plant food. They do not, therefore, need an extraordinarily rich soil, hough if it is intended that they should grow on from year to year they will naturally need feeding to recuperate their strength after the flowers are over. Large supplies of manure are unnecessary for garden borders where bulbs will be lifted immediately after flowering. The soil

is done. This ensures that the planting is even.

The time to plant — which varies for each kind of bulb—is generally as early as convenient after the bulbs have been harvested and properly ripened. That is to say, plant your bulbs as soon as they are offered on the market. The long period of growth which you give them by

BULBS IN POTS MUST HAVE AMPLE DRAINAGE, AND PLACE BULBS AT RIGHT LEVELS SO THAT WHEN COVERED WITH SOIL THERE IS ROOM AT THE TOP FOR WATERING

LEAVE TOP

EXPOSED

PLUNGE POTS INTO ASHES AND COVER OVER WITH SHEETS OF WOOD OR ZINC

Bulbs are a great stand-by for the town gardener. All kinds can be grown in pots.

must, however, be deeply dug, so that the drainage is good. Bulbs allowed to stand in stagnant water will rapidly decay. When dealing with clay soil which holds moisture, it will be found beneficial to allow the base of each bulb to rest on a little sand. This prevents water from collecting round the bulb.

Planting of bulbs is best done with a trowel. If a dibber be used on heavy soils, there is a tendency for the soil under the bulb to cake hard and the roots are not able to penetrate freely. On light sandy soils a dibber is permissible. It is advisable to lay out the bulbs first on the surface of the border before any planting

early planting improves the quality of the blooms. Tulips are an exception, and late planting is best for these, otherwise they appear above the ground too soon, and may be damaged by frost.

Bulbs in Pots and Bowls. The spring-flowering bulbs can almost all of them be grown quite well indoors even where a greenhouse is not available. If ordinary pots are used care must be taken to see that the drainage holes are covered with broken crocks, concave side down, which will keep the holes open and prevent the soil becoming soured by stagnant water. A good potting mixture would be composed of loam, leaf-mould and sand in equal parts; but any ordinary garden soil will do if it is open and crumbly. Sticky clay soil should be burnt, or well mixed with sand before use. It is unnecessary to cover the bulbs deeply in pots and tubs. The tip of each may just reach the soil surface at potting time.

If bowls are used without drainage, then the bulbs must be planted in fibre. This is sold in a specially prepared form by all florists and nurserymen. At planting time the fibre should be moist, but not so wet that water can be squeezed from it. Line each bowl with fibre before putting in any bulbs. Place the bulbs on this, near together, but not actually touching each other, and then fill in with more fibre. The fibre should fill the bowl to within an inch of the top, and the bulb tips should just protrude a little above the fibre. After planting, the treatment of pots and bowls is the same. They must be kept in a cool, dark, airy place until the tops begin to grow. A cellar, a cold frame, a bed of ashes six or eight inches thick out of doors, but protected from excessive wet—these are all suitable places for the newly-planted bulbs to remain for about six weeks. As top growth begins they may be brought into the light, and by degrees, into more warmth. If a greenhouse is used, a succession of blooms can be obtained by bringing successive batches of bulbs into the warmth each fortnight, but in all cases they must be grown in the cool for some weeks. If the bulbs are to be grown in a living-room, be careful not to allow them to get too warm in the early stages. Water when necessary, using tepid water, but never let excess water stand in the bowls or the plants will be ruined. Plants are very much like human beings. They like even temperatures, and are upset by sudden shocks. On the whole, it suits them best to treat them as hardy, for if they are coddled they become tender and succumb to the first shock. Hardy plants resist diseases better than those which have been made tender by hot-house treatment.

It may be mentioned here that after spring bulbs have flowered, the bowls can be used again, if desired, for the cultivation of Begonias. These can be grown in fibre in exactly the same manner as Hyacinths or Tulips, but it is not necessary to keep them in the dark at first.

Bulbs all the year round. It is not impossible to have bulbs in flower outdoors at all times of the year, and the following are suggestions for each season:

SPRING.—Crocus, Narcissus, Fritillary, Tulips, Hyacinths, Leucojum, Bulbocodium, Muscari, Scillas, Anemones.

SUMMER.—Lilies, Gladiolus, Begonias, Iris.

AUTUMN.—Colchicum, Gladiolus, Montbretias.

WINTER.—Snowdrops, Winter Aconites, Iris stylosa, Iris reticulata.

BULLACE (*Prunus insititia*). The Bullace is a native of this country and of Europe. It is by some authorities considered to be a form only of the plum, *Prunus communis*, whilst others list it as a separate species.

Cultivation.—The Bullace is as a rule grown only as a standard. It makes a useful shelter tree, and as such is frequently planted in rows along the boundary of orchards. Trees should be put in twenty-five feet apart, and their cultivation is similar to that of the plum.

VARIETIES.

The best variety is Langley Black Bullace, which is a cross between a damson and Early Orleans plum.

Propagation.—Budding or grafting on Myrobalan stock.

BUMELIA (bū-me′-li-a. Sapotaceæ). A genus of deciduous small trees from U.S.A. but not ornamental enough for general cultivation.

BUPHANE (bū-fa-ne. Amaryllidaceæ). Half-hardy bulbous-rooted plants, mostly grown in the greenhouse. Said to be poisonous to cattle. Pot in September in a compost of equal parts peat, loam and sand. These plants should only be watered when the new growth begins and then moderately. Cease to water when the leaves turn yellow.

Temperature from September to November, 50°-55°; from November to March, 55°-65°; and from March to September, 65°-75°. The plants must be fully exposed to the sun.

Propagate by means of offsets inserted in small pots, in the same way as the larger bulbs, and moved on into larger pots as necessary. Repotting should be done in spring before growth commences.

SPECIES.

B. ciliaris, dull purple, 1 ft.

B. disticha (syn. *Brunsvigia*), red, 18 in.

BUPHTHALMUM (buph-thal-mum. Compositæ). Tall, hardy and greenhouse perennials with heads of bright yellow flowers in summer and autumn. Best suited for growing in masses or in the shrubbery. These will grow in any soil in a sunny position.

Propagate by division in spring.

SPECIES.

B. salicifolium, June, 18 in.

B. speciosum, June, 5 ft.

BUPLEURUM (bū-plūr'-um. Umbelliferæ). Hare's Ear. Evergreen or semi-evergreen shrub about 6 ft. high from the Mediterranean regions. Its yellow flowers and blue-green or glaucous foliage make a pleasing contrast. Not generally hardy. One of the best shrubs for exposed seaside gardens and cliffs. Likes a chalky soil.

B. fruticosum, yellow.

B. ranunculoides is as good a representative as any. A neat little plant, about 4 in. high with green-gold flowers in July, and short strap-shaped leaves. It is more quaint than conspicuous. Europe.

Propagate by division.

BURBIDGEA (Bur-bi-ge-a. Scitamineaceæ). Stove herbaceous flowering perennial. Originally introduced from Borneo in 1870.

These plants grow best in a compost of equal parts peat, leaf-mould and loam. They should be planted in large pots, tubs or beds in March. They need plenty of water from March to August, but a moderate amount at other times. Good drainage and a moist atmosphere are essential, and they should be placed in light shade. The method of increase is by division of roots in April. They are very easy to cultivate.

SPECIES.

B. nitida, orange-scarlet, summer, 2–4 ft.

B. schizocheila, orange-yellow, summer, 2–ft.

BURCHELLIA (bur-chel-li-a. Rubiaceæ). Bufflehorn-wood. Stove flowering evergreen shrubs attaining a height of 3 ft. A compost of equal parts peat, loam,

leaf-mould and sand should be used. Pot in March and water freely from April to September, but only a moderate amount should be given at other times. The temperature from September to March should be 55°–60°, and from March to September 65°–75°. Cuttings of young shoots that are firm at the base can be taken in spring, and inserted in sandy

BUDS & LEAVES

DISPERSING SEEDS

FLOWERS

BOX

Box grows wild in some parts of the country and its various varieties are most useful evergreen shrubs.

peat under a bell-glass in a temperature of 75°.

The main species cultivated is that of *B. capensis*, which bears scarlet flowers in spring.

BURGUNDY MIXTURE. A copper fungicide, easier to prepare than, and used as a substitute for, Bordeaux mixture. It differs from the latter in that soda crystals are used in place of the lime. Take sulphate of copper (98% purity) 1 lb.; washing-soda crystals 1¼ lb.; water 10 gal. Dissolve the sulphate of copper in about 7 gal. of the water, and the soda crystals in the remaining 3 gal. Add the soda solution to the sulphate solution and stir well.

BURNET. *See* POTERIUM.

BURNING-BUSH. *See* RHUS COTINUS and DICTAMNUS.

BURR MARIGOLD. *See* BIDENS.

BURSARIA (bur-sar'-i-a. Pittosporaceæ). Evergreen shrub from New South Wales, suitable for mild districts. 6 ft. The white flowers are very small but produced in such profusion as to make a pretty display during August and September when but few other shrubs are in flower.

Culture.—Sandy loam and peat in equal parts or well-manured garden soil.

Propagate by cuttings of half-ripened shoots placed in gentle heat.

BUTCHER'S-BROOM. *See* RUSCUS ACULEATUS.

BUTOMUS (bu'-tom-us. Alismaceæ). Flowering Rush. A hardy aquatic perennial that bears pink flowers from June to August. It likes a warm sunny position in a bog, or in shallow ponds with several inches of water above the crowns. Plant October or March.

Propagate by division in March or April.

SPECIES.

B. umbellatus, rose, summer, 2–3 ft.

BUTTERCUP. *See* RANUNCULUS.

BUTTERFLIES. *See* CABBAGE CATERPILLARS.

BUTTERFLY FLOWER. *See* SCHIZANTHUS.

BUTTERNUT. *See* JUGLANS CINEREA

BUTTERWORT. *See* PINGUICULA.

BUTTON-BRUSH. *See* CEPHALANTHUS

BUXUS (bŭx'-us. Euphorbiaceæ). Box Evergreen shrubs and trees, flourishing in almost any soil or aspect, in sun or shade and useful for planting under the drip of trees and in poor chalky soils.

Culture.—Plant in April or September Clip in May and August.

Propagate by cuttings in August or September under bell-glasses, or layers in August.

SPECIES.

B. sempervirens, Common Box. Europe N. Africa and West Asia. Shares the distinction with the holly and the yew of being the most useful of hardy evergreens. Much used for topiary work and for planting in formal arrangements, and for boxedging. There are a number of named varieties, of which the following are among the most distinct:

B. s. elegantissima. Dwarfer than type, with marginal silver variegation.

B. s. handsworthensis. Densely bushy, erect growing, leaves dark green, large and broad.

B. s. suffruticosa, Box Edging. By persistent clipping can be kept a few inches high. Left to itself will reach 4–5 ft. Easily increased by division and cuttings. The best-known site for naturally-grown box trees in this country is Box Hill, near Dorking, Surrey.

C

CABBAGE (*Brassica oleracea*). Cruciferæ. This is probably the most largely grown of all Brassicas, and for many hundreds of years it has been credited with great medicinal qualities. The old herbalists expounded its merits at great length, and some of their writings make most interesting reading.

The forerunner of our garden varieties, the wild cabbage is a native of the English and European coasts The wild type still grows in this country, and is to be found in several parts, especially along the eastern seaboard from the Wash to the Tyne.

The evolution of numerous garden varieties has resulted in the production of two main groups; those suitable for summer sowing to mature the following spring, and known as Spring cabbage; and those for sowing in spring to mature in summer and autumn, and known by this name.

In both groups are many different types, such as Conical, Drumhead, Dwarf, Large, and many variations in colour and texture.

VARIETIES.

Spring Cabbage (sow July to August): Ellams Early; Flower of Spring; Harbinger; Meins No. 1; Early Rainham; Greyhound.

Autumn Cabbage (sow March onwards): Primo; Winningstadt.

Uses.—Cabbage is almost invariably boiled, and its uses in this way are too well known to warrant description here. Young tender cabbages can, however, be used in the salad bowl, where the hearts, finely shredded, will be much appreciated.

CABBAGE, AUTUMN. The first sowing of this should be made in boxes under glass early in March, followed by small successional sowings at intervals to the beginning of June. Its general treatment is the same as for Spring cabbage, though as a quicker growth is required it may be planted in land more recently dug and manured. The actual distances for setting out must be governed by the varieties. The small compact Coleworts or "Collards" may be set 1 ft. apart each way, whilst some of the larger Drumhead types,

such as "Primo," require 18 in. by 2 ft.

CABBAGE, RED or PICKLING. These should be sown in August, and when a few inches high transplanted 6 in. apart in a reserve bed where they may remain through the winter. Early in spring they may be set out in a plot previously well dug and manured, and as most red varieties are large they should not be set closer than 18 in. each way.

CABBAGE, SAVOY (*Brassica oleracea bullata major*). Cruciferæ. This is another garden type derived from the wild cabbage, and one which is extremely useful on account of its hardiness, ease of culture, and quantity of foodstuff produced on a given area.

Culture.—Any good garden soil free from club root disease will produce a crop of Savoys. A site which was deeply dug and well manured for the previous crop suits them admirably, and as firm soil is an advantage, the surface need only be cleaned over and lightly forked when the earlier crop is cleared off.

The seed should be sown in prepared beds as advised for Borecole. The Savoy is essentially a winter green, and the flavour is much enhanced after frost. If it is necessary to obtain an early crop, seeds of a dwarf variety should be sown in boxes in a frame the last week in February, but the middle of March is early enough for all ordinary purposes, followed by further sowing for succession the first and last weeks of April.

The seedlings should either be drastically thinned at an early age, or moved to a reserve bed to keep short and sturdy until June or July, when they may be planted out.

Transplanting should be done in the evening, and if possible during dull, showery weather. If the weather is dry and settled the roots should be dipped in a thick solution of mud, water, and, if obtainable, cow manure. This practice is resorted to by gardeners when moving many classes of plants, and is known as "puddling."

Some of the modern dwarf varieties may be set out 15 in. apart in the rows, and

18 in. asunder, but the distances must naturally be increased with the larger types. Those of the drumhead type require not less than 2 ft. apart each way.

Unless the soil is in a very fertile condition a top dressing of a well-balanced fertiliser should be applied at the rate of about 4 oz. per square yard in September, and lightly hoed in around the plants.

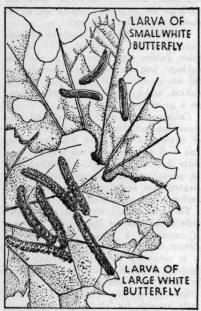

LARVA OF SMALL WHITE BUTTERFLY

LARVA OF LARGE WHITE BUTTERFLY

The caterpillars of the white butterfly are the worst enemy of green crops.

VARIETIES.

Dwarf Green Curled; Drumhead; Tom Thumb; Norwegian; Perfection; Sugar Loaf.

Uses.—The heads should be cut as required during the winter, and before the centre bursts open. The stump, if left in, will produce a later crop of useful "greens."

The savoy is rarely used other than as a boiled vegetable.

CABBAGE, SPRING. *Culture.*—The main essentials in the cultivation of good Spring cabbage are the selection of a guaranteed strain of seed of a proved variety, and an open yet sheltered site

which was deeply dug and well manured for the previous crop. At the time of planting this should only be lightly forked over, for in firm ground there is less likelihood of the plants prematurely running to seed—"bolting."

Too early sowing is another cause of "bolting." The end of July is usually early enough, followed by a second sowing at the end of August. As with most other Brassicas, sowing broadcast in a prepared bed of fine soil, burnt earth and wood ashes, is to be preferred to sowing in drills in the open garden.

In parts of Wales, where Spring cabbage is perhaps most popular, it is a common practice to burn off the top growth on some of the rough hill land, and to broadcast the seed direct on the burnt earth. This is known as "Beetling," and in this way very sturdy plants are obtained.

The plants should be finally set out as soon as possible, placing them 1 ft. apart and 18 in. asunder. Unless the variety is a very dwarf compact one, such as Harbinger, every alternate one should be pulled and used for greens during the winter and early spring, to allow the others to mature fully.

Before winter finally sets in a little soil should be drawn up around the plants. Other than this, little attention is required beyond occasional hoeing to keep down weeds.

If the plants appear at a standstill in the spring a teaspoonful of nitrate of soda or a good soluble manure hoed in around each plant during showery weather will improve their growth tremendously.

CABBAGE CATERPILLARS. The caterpillars of the large white (*Pierris brassicæ*) and small white butterflies (*Pierris rapæ*) often do considerable damage to cruciferæ, especially in the autumn. The large yellow and black caterpillars of the large white butterfly are first to be found in June and early July. When full grown they leave the plants, seeking out fences, walls and windowledges on which to pupate. In August a second generation of butterflies appears; and this, often augmented by swarms from Europe, gives rise to the numbers of caterpillars to be found in September. In bad years, all cabbages may be "skeletonised," and even flowering plants such as nasturtiums and mignonette may be stripped. Again, when full-fed, they leave the plants, seeking out a suitable place in which to change to a chrysalis for the winter. The green velvety caterpillars of the small white may be found a little earlier than the preceding, and not in colonies, for the yellow conical eggs are not laid in groups, as is the case with the former. In other respects the life-history is similar to the large white.

METHOD OF CONTROL.—A derris-containing wash will give excellent control if applied when the caterpillars are beginning to appear.

CABBAGE MOTH (*Mamestra brassicæ*). DESCRIPTION. Adult.—About 1½ in. in expanse. Upper wings dark grey to almost black with a lighter transverse mottling. Near the costa and about the centre of the wing is a whitish reniform mark. *Caterpillar.*—About 1½ in. in length and varying from pale green to dark mahogany-brown on the back. The underneath is pale green.

LIFE-HISTORY.—Eggs are laid on the leaves in late summer, and after about seven days these hatch into caterpillars which eat their way into the heart of the cabbage. Damage is done not only by the amount of food eaten but also by the moist and foul-smelling excrement which is deposited in the galleries. When full grown the caterpillars leave the plants for the ground, where they change into a brown chrysalis. The moth appears in the following summer.

METHODS OF CONTROL.—Much good may be done by hand picking; failing this a salt solution forced into the crown will kill many of the caterpillars. It is as well to carry out any such remedial measures before the caterpillar has had time to reach the heart of the plant.

CACALIA (kak-ā-lia. Compositæ). Tassel Flower. Hardy annual, 1 ft. Pretty, hardy annuals with scarlet or golden flowers. Suitable for sowing in poor soils, where the plants are to bloom. The flowers are carried in loose heads at the top of slender stems, but are not much good for cutting as only a few blooms are open at the same time.

SPECIES.

C. coccinea (syn. *Emilia flammea*), scarlet, summer, 1–2 ft.

CACTUS (*Cactaceæ*). The families are broadly classed in two parts:

Opuntieæ, of which the leaves, usually small or absent, are more or less awl-shaped. The flowers sit on the joints without flower-stalks, and the areoles bear glochids except in one genus.

Cerceæ have areoles without glochids, no leaves, and with the exception of Rhipsalis the flowers have definite tubes. This class contains all in the list except Opuntias.

These two classes are mentioned to give the broad botanical difference, but in actual practice there are many different varieties of each of these main classes.

In identifying the family or genus experience will soon tell in which genus a plant falls.

Cereus.—These cacti are columnar as well as trailing. The columnar kinds stand upright on their own, while trailing plants wander about in growth, and if not propped up will fall to the ground. The family contains the world-famous "Queen of the Night," whose flower does not open till after dusk and closes again for ever before dawn. Whether columnar or trailing, the plants have ridges in various forms and the bunches of spines, etc., grow from slight hollows on the top of the ridges.

Echinocactus are round in shape and are never seen in this country anything like the size they attain in their original homes. We never see the mighty Visnages that are so often seen in the American deserts where they are commonly called barrel cactus. The forms and shapes are bewildering in their variety and there is no regularity in design. Generally speaking, they are divided into ridges, but the ridges are often broken and not continuous, and in some cases the ridges degenerate into blobs or dumplings projecting from the plant.

Echinocereus are very similar to the columnar cereus, but the ridges are not long and connected but broken up into nodules, almost nipples, like Mamillarias. But the two plants could not be confused, the flowers being too large and distinctive.

This is the class so often seen with the protuberances and spines in spirals.

Echinopsis.—A class specially interesting for its flowers and their long tube-stems. The plants are distinctly and prominently ridged vertically, much more so than other plants, and are always round. They are common in our greenhouses and usually grow to good sizes.

Mamillaria.—Practically always round, but a few are slightly columnar. Do not attain large size. Very easily identified as their outside growths always take the form of nipples.

Opuntias.—The best known is the awl-shaped stemmed prickly pear, but there are many kinds. Some are balls like *O. diademata calva*, some elongated balls more like ovals, as *O. corrugata* and *O. andicola*; some are almost trailing, such as *O. salmiana*, and some are cylindrical as *O. cylindrica*. This family is so familiar that it is hardly necessary to make any further explanations.

Rhipsalis.—If you can imagine miniature *opuntias* you have a very good idea of *rhipsalis*, although some of the stems are flattened and some are distended. In most cases the joints are very short, not more than 2 in. long. The flowers are the smallest known among cacti.

Culture.—Before purchasing your plants you will want to know what accommodation is necessary.

If you have a greenhouse or a sunny window you have the requirements necessary to cultivate cacti. The main things to avoid are frost and excessive moisture. It is not necessary to have a heated greenhouse—that is, boiler and pipes—as a small oil-stove is sufficient to keep the plants free from frost. Of course if you have boiler-heat so much the better, as the nearer you can keep the temperature to 60° or 70°, the better are the results. Some cacti can even stand frost, but you would be wiser to consider frost the enemy, as most of the plants are killed by it.

When potting do not ram the soil. Put some over the crocks as it is not wise for the roots of the newly potted plants to come in contact with the crocks, or the slightest movement will fray and damage. Suspend the plant with the hand in the centre of the pot and trickle the soil in round it. Gently press the soil down but do not ram it. If you like to incorporate a little bone-meal with the soil, it will do the plant good, but as bone-meal has the nasty knack of floating in water, finish off the top of the pot with soil that has no bone-meal. Cacti are lime-loving plants, and if your soil is deficient in lime, it is best to mix in a little builder's rubble in small lumps, like peas.

CÆSALPINIA (sēz-al-pin′-ĭa. Leguminosæ). Deciduous shrubs or small trees with fern-like leaves and pea-shaped flowers, requiring wall protection and loamy soil.

Propagate by seeds and layers.

SPECIES.

C. Gilliesii (Argentine). Up to 25 ft. Flowers rich yellow with long scarlet stamens, very brilliant and effective.

C. japonica (China and Japan). 8 ft. Leaves acacia-like, soft green. Flowers canary-yellow with red stamens. This is a very beautiful shrub both in leaf and in flower and worthy of a snug corner.

CAFFRE BUTTER SHRUB. *See* COMBRETUM.

CAJOPHORA. *See* LOASA.

CAKILE (ka-ki-le. Cruciferæ). Sea Rocket. The only species of this genus is *C. maritima*, a hardy annual found growing by the seashore. Distinguishable by its fleshy leaves, lilac-coloured flowers and peculiarly-divided seed pods. It grows readily in sandy loam.

CALADIUM (ca′-ladium. Aroideæ). Stove deciduous perennials. Grown for the wonderful colouring of their leaves. Fine plants for decorating.

Culture.—Compost. Equal parts loam, leaf-mould and sharp sand, with a good portion of broken, dried cow manure. The loam should be chopped into a condition like rubble, not sifted. Pot firmly in small pots in early spring; transfer to larger size directly roots reach side of pots. Water freely during summer months.

Propagation.—By division of tubers when potting.

SPECIES.

Chiefly *C. bicolor; C. Humboldtii; C. rutescens; C. venosum;* and hybrids.

CALAMINT. *See* CALAMINTHA.

CALAMINTHA (Labiatæ). Calamint. Hardy sweet-scented annuals and perennials that form a carpet of foliage and bear violet-coloured flowers all through the summer. Best in a sunny position in sandy loam. Sow seeds in March, or divide in March or September. Plant October to April.

SPECIES.

C. alpina, purple, 6 in., June.

C. grandiflora, purple, 1 ft., June.

C. Acinos (annual), "Basil Thyme," purple, 6 in., July.

CALAMUS (Palmaceæ). Rattan Palm. Stove evergreen climbing plants with ornamental foliage. These plants should be potted in March in well-drained pots, in a compost of two parts turfy loam, one part leaf-mould and coarse sand, and should be placed in the shade.

During the winter they will need a moderate amount of water, but after that period they should be watered plentifully. A summer temperature of 70°–85° should be maintained, and during the winter from 60°–65°. The shoots can be trained up trellis or up the rafters of the greenhouse.

Seeds may be sown 1 in. deep in light soil in March when the temperature should be at 80°.

Increase by suckers growing from the roots. These should be inserted in pots of light soil under a bell-glass in a temperature of 80°.

SPECIES.

C. ciliaris. From Malaya.

C. rotang. Rotang Cane, from India.

CALANDRINIA (kalan-drin-ia. Portulaceæ). Half-hardy annuals. Natives of Peru. Distinguished by succulent stems and leaves and showy large flowers.

SPECIES.

C. grandiflora, 1 ft., rose.

C. Menziesii (*speciosus*), 1 ft., purple-crimson.

C. umbellata, 6 in., crimson, are the best, and thrive in a sunny position in sandy soil. Seed should be sown in a cool greenhouse early in the year, and the plants put into flowering quarters in May-June. In habit they are semi-prostrate, and show to best advantage in colonies of 5-10 plants.

CALANTHE (cala'nthe. Orchidaceæ). Stove terrestrial orchids Java, 1819. For table decoration during the winter these orchids are extremely useful, producing an abundance of flowers which last a long time in perfection.

Culture.—Compost. 2 parts rich loam, 1 part dried cow manure, and a quantity of small broken crocks to keep it open. After flowering give a short rest, but must be repotted directly they show signs of growing again. Water very little until good root progress can be seen, add more water gradually, and when the plant is well established, manure water may be liberally applied. Shade from strong sun, or leaves will lose their colour and fall off. A good growing temperature is 70° at night with 10° to 15° rise during the day.

Propagate by division when potting.

SPECIES AND HYBRID VARIETIES.

C. Reginieri, white and pink; *C. Turneri*, white and rose; *C. Veitchii*, rose; *C. Sedeni*, rose and purple; *C. veratifolia*, white.

CALCEOLARIA (cal-ce'-o-lar'-ia. Scrophulariaceæ). Slipper Flower. Half-hardy or greenhouse shrubs and herbaceous perennials. Peru, 1773. Some of the most valuable of herbaceous perennials for greenhouse decoration, chiefly the result of numerous selections from hybrids between *C. corymbosa* and *C. crenatiflora*. Flowering plants are from 15–18 in. high, and usually flower about May from seed sown the previous June. The plants have numerous flowers of varying shades of colour including yellow, white, cream, bronze, brown, red and carmine; many of them are handsomely overlaid with spots of a contrasting colour to the ground-work, while others are pure "self" colours.

Propagation.—The seeds, which are very small, should be sown in June in pans of soil composed of leaf-mould, loam and fine sand. Covering should be very light and on no account should the pans be exposed to hot sun. When the tiny seedlings have germinated, keep them shaded in a cold frame and, when large enough, prick them out. They will be ready for their first small pots about the middle or end of August, and subsequent pottings may be made as required, flowering them in size 48, 32 or 24 pots. The soil for the larger pots should be coarse in texture, being composed of good fibrous loam, well decayed (sifted) manure, a little leaf-mould, old mortar rubble and a little sharp sand all passed through an inch sieve. Calceolarias will not tolerate firm potting, and the soil should only be made finger-tight. They respond to feeding when well rooted.

An equally important group of cal-ceolarias consists of the shrubby kinds, generally used as summer bedding plants, because of their half hardy nature.

These are very easily propagated, even where a greenhouse or frame is not avail-able. In a propagating frame, cuttings three or four inches long are inserted in autumn when the first frosts threaten, and potted up singly when the roots have formed. Pinching back the central stem will make bushy plants develop for the next season's summer bedding.

Amateurs who have no ordinary con-veniences for taking soft wood cuttings can excavate a pit about ten inches deep in a border, making it of a size that can be covered by a sheet of glass. Work a little sandy soil into the pit bottom, and insert the cuttings in September, three inches apart. Keep them covered by the glass, and in very severe periods of frost cover the glass with straw or an old mat or thick paper. Otherwise leave them undis-turbed until spring, when they can be allowed a little more air, and plenty of light. In March pot them separately, pinch out the tips, and keep them in a light sunny window until the end of May, when they can be planted out.

SPECIES.

C. integrifolia (China), Flowers large, yellow, in late summer.

C. sinclairii (New Zealand), Flowers white, spotted purple.

C. violacea (China). Flowers pale violet or mauve, with darker marking during summer.

C. amplexicaulis, yellow; *C. Burbidgei*, yellow and white; *C. corymbosa*, yellow and purple; *C. crenatifolia*, yellow and brown. It is chiefly from these species that our present hydrids have reached us.

All up-to-date seedsmen stock good strains of large-flowered hybrids:

C. Clibrani, with small golden yellow flowers and spreading habit, and—

C. Albert Kent, with flowers of yellow and bronze, are among the best.

Calceolaria. From Latin *Calceolarius*, a shoemaker—the shape of the flower some-what resembling a shoe.

CALCIUM PHOSPHATE. *See* SUPER-PHOSPHATE.

CALCIUM SULPHATE. *See* GYPSUM.

CALENDULA (kal-end-ula). Composi-tæ). Marigold. Scotch or Pot Marigold. Hardy annual, 1½–2 ft. The present-day forms and varieties of Calendulas are among the very best of all annuals for general purposes, as they will succeed almost anywhere even in the poorest soils and most " unlikely " places. It does not seem to matter much when they are sown, the plants will grow along, and flower in due course, and if left to themselves, seed so very freely as to become practically naturalised. The best of the named kinds such as Orange King, Prince of Orange, Radio, Dania, Meteor, etc., are all varie-ties of the original *C. officinalis* and grow to 1½–2 ft. Market growers have paid particular attention to Calendulas during recent years and grow them in pots for spring flowering, the rich golden blooms being particularly welcome at that time. For this purpose seed is sown in boxes in July and the seedlings are potted. firmly, 3 to a 5 in. pot, and grown on in good light, in cold frames or greenhouses for the winter, just keeping frost away. With the turn of the year growth is fairly rapid, and there is no difficulty in having them in bloom for Easter.

CALICHE. *See* NITRATE OF SODA.

CALIFORNIAN FUCHSIA. *See* ZAUSCHNERIA.

CALLA (cal-la). Aroideæ). Bog Arum. A hardy aquatic with small white flowers in summer and autumn. Likes a sunny position at the margin of ponds in shallow water. Plant in March or April in about 12 in. of water.

Propagate by inserting portions of the stem in boggy soil where the plants are to grow.

SPECIES.

C. palustris, white, 6 in.

CALLICARPA (kal-li-kär'-pa. Ver-benaceæ). Deciduous shrubs up to 5 ft.,

thriving in ordinary garden soil. Need
winter protection. Foliage pale rose
madder, in autumn is an attractive
feature. Fruit, generally bluish or purple,
persists for some weeks after the fall of
the leaf.

SPECIES.

C. americana (U.S.A.), 3–5 ft. Grey-
lue flowers, violet berries. Only suitable
or mildest districts.

C. chinensis (China). Similar to preceding.

C. Giraldiana (China). Distinguished
by its large leaves, 8 in. long and 4 in.
wide, and rose-coloured flowers. Berries
violet-blue.

C. japonica (Japan), 3–4 ft. Flowers
pale pink. Berries violet-blue, about the
size of peppercorns.

C. j. angustata (*longifolia*), China. A
distinct form with large leaves up to 9 in.
long, turning a clear yellow in autumn.

C. koreana (Korea). New species with
serrated leaves.

C. purpurea (*rubella*), China and Korea,
5–6 ft. Leaves up to 8 in. long, narrow,
lance-shaped. Stems and leaves purple,
becoming darker in autumn. Berries
lilac-coloured.

CALLIOPSIS (kali-op-sis. Compositæ).
Sometimes called Coreopsis, but the first
name is usually now applied to the annual
members of the family—using the name
Coreopsis to designate those of perennial
duration. The annual species (Calliopsis)
are of great merit and invaluable for
borders or cutting. Of the taller kinds
C. tinctoria, 2 ft., yellow, with scarlet-
maroon centre, and *C. Drummondii*, 2 ft.,
rich yellow, are the best, and there are
also a number of *tinctoria* varieties with
various coloured flowers in shades of orange
and crimson. The dwarf or nana group
is of value for edgings. Beauty, Crimson
King and Star of Fire are the best. They
will thrive in almost any kind of soil,
even in town gardens—and the light,
daisy-like blooms are most lavishly produced. Sow where to bloom—March to
May.

CALLIPHRURIA (kal-li-fur-e-a.
Amaryllideæ). Pretty, half-hardy and
greenhouse bulbous plants that look like
the Guernsey Lily flower when not in leaf.
Propagate by seeds sown in heat when

ripe and by offsets. Grown in sandy loam
and a little peat.

SPECIES.

C. hartwegiana, with white flowers in
June and broad plaited leaves.

CALLIRHOE (cal-ir-ho-e. Malvaceæ).
Poppy Mallow. Pretty purplish-red or
blue-flowered annuals and perennials
suited to the rock garden or for a trellis.
They like a well-drained ordinary soil and

**CALLIOPSIS. A TALL GROWING
HARDY ANNUAL**

A good flower for poor soils is the Calliopsis.
Its gold and chocolate blooms are useful for
cutting.

a sunny position. Propagate perennials
after flowering by cuttings in September
or in spring, sow in heat in late winter and
put out in May to flower the same year.
Annuals from seed sown in pans of light
soil in March, or outdoors in April.

SPECIES.

C. pedata, cherry red, 2 ft. (annual),
summer.

C. pedata compacta, crimson and white.

C. involucrata, crimson, summer, 6 in.
(perennial).

CALLISTEMON (kal-lis-tē′-mon. Myrtaceæ). Bottle Brush Tree. Greenhouse
evergreen flowering shrubs. Australia,

E

1788. Name from *kalistos*, most beautiful, and *stemon*, a stamen; referring to the graceful, long, scarlet stamens. Leaves long and pointed. Flowers are in dense spikes, with long yellow or scarlet stamens, giving them the appearance of a bottle brush or globe-cleaner.

Culture.—Compost, turfy peat, loam, and sharp sand in equal parts. Repot early spring. Prune straggly shoots after flowering. Water freely during growing period. Winter temperature, 45°; summer, 60°. Good drainage desirable.

Propagation.—By seeds in greenhouse and cuttings of well-ripened shoots in the summer; insert in sandy peat, place in propagator; temperature, 60°. They need the protection of a wall except in very favoured gardens. In some of the Cornish gardens they are a feature, assuming tree-like dimensions and flowering freely.

SPECIES.

C. lanceolatus, crimson.

C. linearis. Grass-like leaves, scarlet inflorescence.

C. salignus. Similar to preceding, but with pale yellow flowers.

C. speciosus (florabunda). The well-known Scarlet or Crimson Bottle Brush, presenting a most beautiful and striking appearance when in bloom. The form known as *C. s. magnifica* is especially fine.

CALLISTEPHUS (kali'-ste-fus. Compositæ). Half-hardy annual. Aster; Chinese Aster; Japanese Aster. Perhaps the best known of all annuals, not excepting Stocks and Sweet Peas, which are of more recent development, while some of the types of Asters yet in cultivation, and still popular, were known, and extensively grown, very many years ago; as, for instance, the Chrysanthemum Flowered, the Pæony Flowered, the trim, neat Victoria Aster, and the Single Flowered, or Chinensis varieties. The Comet or Japanese—the Ostrich Plume, and American or Californian Branching types with their large, full flowers, like shaggy Japanese Chrysanthemums, are of more recent origin, and on account of their long stems are more suitable for growing for cut flowers than the older kinds first mentioned.

The cultivation of Asters is very simple, and best results are obtained if the plants are grown without any serious check at any stage. Do not sow too early, the end of March is soon enough, and sow in a cold frame for preference. Transplant as required, give free ventilation, and plant into their flowering-quarters during May. They like a well-dug soil, and any manure used should be old, and well decayed. A dressing of lime, 2 oz. per sq. yd., forked in during March, will help to ward off attacks of stem-rot, or Aster "wilt" disease, the spores of which are generally present in soils deficient in lime, and rich in organic matter. The following is a list of Aster types all worth growing. Named varieties can be ignored:

Dwarf types, 9 in. to 1 ft.: Chrysanthemum Flowered, all colours; Liliput and Dwarf Bouquet, in all colours.

Intermediate types, 1½–2 ft.: Comet; Ostrich Plume; Vicks Branching; Victoria; Pæony Flowered; Single or Chinensis, and the new "Sunshine" single, or "Anemone Quilled" centred varieties, in all colours.

Tall types, 2¼–3 ft.: Californian Giant Double Comet flowered; and Californian Giant, single-flowered, in all colours.

Special note. — The single-flowered varieties are easy to grow, and on light soils in sheltered places may be sown out of doors in April. *See also* CHINA ASTER.

CALLITRIS (kal'-i-tris. Coniferæ). "Tasmanian Cypress Pine," of elegant habit, only suitable for mild districts. Plant in sandy loam.

Propagate by cuttings of half-ripened shoots in sandy soil in frame.

SPECIES.

C. oblonga, the only species suitable for outdoor cultivation. Slender cypress-like shrub or small tree.

C. rhomboides. Resembling the Italian Cypress.

C. robusta. A stronger-growing form.

CALLUNA (căl-ū-na. Ericaceæ). The Heather of Scotland and the Ling of England. Almost too well known to need description. The large, coloured calyx with four minute bracts at its base, called the "outer calyx," differentiates it from Erica. A good "bee" flower, and the honey made therefrom is highly prized. In the North, besoms are made from branches of heather. For culture *see* ERICA.

SPECIES.

C. vulgaris. The only species, consisting of so many varieties that only the most distinct are enumerated. Although lime-hating, the type may be found thriving on the chalk downs in the neighbourhood of Salisbury, Wilts.

C. v. Alportii, distinct bright crimson.

C. v. argentea, silvery foliage in winter.

C. v. aurea, purple flowers, golden foliage, turning red in winter.

C. v. coccinea, crimson flowers, prostrate habit.

C. v. cuprea, compact-growing, striking yellow foliage, changing to copper-bronze and red.

C. v. darleyensis, deep pink flowers.

C. v. flore pleno, double pink flowers.

C. v. H. E. Beale, A small double-flowered silvery-pink form from the New Forest, blooming from early August to late October. Height, 1-2 ft. A distinct and notable addition. A.M., R.H.S.

C. v. pygmæa, low-growing (6 in.), purple flowers.

C. v. tenuis, reddish-purple, flowers early and late.

The following varieties have white flowers:

C. v. alba, the White Heather of Scotland.

C. v. a pumila dwarf habit, 6 in.

C. v. a. pyramidalis, tall, erect.

C. v. a. Hammondii, tall-growing.

C. v. a. auræfolia, young growths, golden.

C. v. a. Mairs (variety *elongata*), notable new introduction with flower spikes 9–12 in. long. 3 ft.

C. v. a. Serleii, later than *C. v. alba*. September to November.

CALLUS. A swelling of the skin, at the base of a cutting or where a wound has been made in the bark by a tree.

CALOCHORTUS (kal-o-kor-tus. Liliaceæ). Mariposa Lily, Star Tulip. These plants are amongst the most beautiful of summer-flowering bulbs and may be grown to advantage in a warm border. The soil should be light and well-drained peat, but it is as well to make up a bed for them. Take out the soil to a depth of 2 ft. and put in 6 in. of drainage. Fill up with a compost of sandy loam with leaf-mould and road grit. Raise the bed well above the surrounding ground so that it keeps dry in winter. Plant from September to November, 3 in. deep and 4 in. apart. Choose a sunny site and protect in winter with bracken, litter, ashes, or, better still, a cold frame. Lift the bulbs every fourth or fifth year and remake the bed.

In many gardens frame culture is best. Plant in the same way as for open-air culture and allow plenty of air when growth commences. If planted in pots, they should be kept in a cold frame until they flower.

Propagate by seeds sown in pans, the resulting seedlings being kept in the cool greenhouse until the third year, when they may be planted out. Also by offsets taken when the plants are resting or by the small bulbs formed by some of the species.

SPECIES.

By a careful selection of plants, the flowering may be prolonged from May to August.

C. albus (syn. *Cyclobothra alba*), charming plant with ten to twelve drooping flowers in July. 12 in.

C. clavatus, golden-yellow flowers in July. 12 in.

C. cæruleus, lilac, with dark blue spots and lines; several good varieties such as *major* and *roseus*. July. 6 in.

C. luteus, one of the prettiest, with yellow flowers fringed with purple hairs. August. 12 in.

C. nitidus, white blotched with dark lilac. June to August. 18 in.

C. pulchellus, hardier than most, with drooping yellow flowers. July. 12 in. (syn. *Cyclobothra pulchella*).

C. splendens, purple-lilac. August. 2 ft. Fine forms are *atroviolaceus* and *rubrum*.

C. venustus is perhaps the most useful of the genus with white, crimson-blotched flowers in July. Its varieties are particularly good and vigorous.

C. lilacinus, lilac; *C. Benthamii*, yellow with dark blotches, one of the first to flower, 8 in.; and *B. macrocarpus*, pale lavender, 15 in., are all good species.

The rest of the species are rather more rare, but are equally beautiful.

CALODENDRON (calo-den'-dron. Rutaceæ). Cape Chestnut. Greenhouse evergreen flowering shrubs. A beautiful genus from the Cape. Remarkable for its pretty pink flowers, and for their slightly offensive odour. S. Africa, 1789.

Culture.—Compost, *see* CALLISTEMON. Repot and prune early spring. Light sunny position.

Propagation.—By cuttings of half-ripened wood in sandy soil in propagator. Temperature, 60°. July.

SPECIES.

C. capensis, pink.

CALOPHACA (cal-of'-a-ka. Leguminosæ). Prostrate spreading shrub from S.E. Russia with yellow pea-shaped flowers, in June and July, followed by reddish seed pods. Dryish soil and very sunny position. Seedlings difficult to rear. Plants generally grafted on laburnum. Hardy in the South.

CALOPOGON (Orchidaceæ). Grass Pink Orchis. Hardy herbaceous orchid, first introduced in 1791.

These plants like a soil composed of equal parts peat and leaf-mould, on a sheltered rockery where the ground is moderately moist. Plant in March or April. They can be increased by offsets treated as old plants. In exposed places these should be grown in pots in the cold frame or greenhouse, in a compost of equal parts peat and loam.

SPECIES.

C. pulchellus, which has purple flowers in July, 18 in. in height.

CALOSTEMMA (kal-os-tēm'-ma. Amaryllideæ). Greenhouse bulbous plants with flowers that vary from white to yellow and purple. Australia, 1819.

Culture.—Compost, *see* AGAPANTHUS. Repot August. Light sunny position. Water freely during growing period, very little after. Winter temperature, 45°; summer, 65°.

Propagated by offsets and grown in the cool greenhouse in sandy fibrous loam.

SPECIES.

C. album, white, May. 12 in.

C. luteum, yellow, November. 12 in.

C. purpureum, dark purple, November. 12 in.

CALTHA (kal-tha. Ranunculaceæ). Marsh Marigold. Useful waterside plants.

Hardy perennials that bloom from May to July. Divide the roots in March or July and plant in moist, heavy, rich soil. The colour of the blooms varies in the different species from yellow to gold. Height, 1–2 ft.

SPECIES.

C. palustris (Marsh Marigold), yellow, 1 ft., April, and in white and double forms.

C. polypetala, yellow, 1½ ft.

CALYCANTHUS (kal-i-kanth'-us. Calycanthaceæ). Allspice. Deciduous, aromatic shrubs with reddish-brown flowers with fruity fragrance, throughout summer and early autumn.

Culture.—Grow in ordinary soil with peat added, in sunny position.

Propagate by seeds, cuttings, and layers in summer; sucker-growths may be divided.

SPECIES.

C. floridus. Caroline Allspice, the most fragrant. Slow growing to 4 ft., camphor-scented, red flowers June to August.

C. occidentalis. A Californian species with larger leaves and flowers than *C. floridus.*

C. præcox. See CHIMONANTHUS FRAGRANS.

CALYPSO. (kal-ip-so. Orchidaceæ). Hardy terrestrial orchid. First introduced 1820. For their culture a compost of equal parts leaf-mould and peat, with coarse sand, is necessary. They should be planted in the shady parts of the rock or bog garden in October or March. They can be increased by offsets and these should be treated as old plants at planting-time.

The most popular species cultivated is *C. Borealis*, a variety with sepals and petals of rosy-purple and the lips white and brown.

CALYSTEGIA (kal-is-te-ji-a. Convolvulaceæ). Bearbind, Bindweed. Hardy, deciduous, twining and trailing perennials, closely related to Convolvulus, that are very useful for covering trellises and stakes. Unless the roots are confined, they are apt to spread and become troublesome weeds.

Propagate by division of the plants in spring or by seeds sown in the open or under glass. Any common garden soil suits them.

SPECIES.

C. hederaceæ (syn. *pubescens*) has pretty bell-shaped rosy flowers in early summer. The double form is very attractive with large flowers in great profusion for several months.

C. Sepium dahurica, rosy-purple flowers in summer. 6 ft.

C. Sepium, the common Bindweed or Bearbind, white flowers; becomes a nuisance in ordinary gardens, but may be

average guide is one inch rise to every 3 ft. width of pathway.

CAMELLIA (ka-mel'-lia. Ternstrœmiaceæ). Magnificent evergreen flowering shrubs and trees from India, China and Japan, with single, semi-single, and double waxen-petalled flowers of white to deep crimson and lustrous deep-green leathery foliage. Camellias are much hardier than is usually supposed, and their value in the garden is being more appreciated than

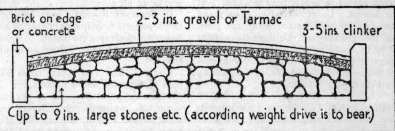

Brick on edge or concrete — 2-3 ins. gravel or Tarmac — 3-5 ins. clinker

Up to 9 ins. large stones etc. (according weight drive is to bear.)

Sound paths need careful construction and a camber in the centre to turn water.

used in the wild garden. However, its rose variety is quite useful.

CAMASSIA (kam-as-si-a. Liliaceæ). Quamash. Ornamental hardy bulbs with pretty racemes of flowers and narrow graceful foliage. Useful for the herbaceous border. The flowers are good for cutting for indoor decoration. They require a deep, light rich soil in a sunny position. The bulbs should be planted in autumn 4 in. deep and 9 in. apart in groups. Increase by offsets taken off after the leaves have withered or by seeds sown in pots under glass or in the open.

SPECIES.

The best of the species are *C. esculenta*, with spikes of pale blue starry flowers. 2½ ft. Naturalises well.

C. Cusickii forms a rosette of glaucous foliage from which rise elegant spikes of large pale lavender flowers with yellow anthers. July. 3 ft.

C. Leichtlini, beautiful spikes of creamy-white flowers and handsome dark green glaucous foliage. 3 ft. June.

The varieties of *esculenta* include *flore albo*, white, and *atrocærulea*, dark blue.

CAMBER. A well-constructed drive should be slightly raised in the centre to help dispose of surplus water, the centre being known as the camber or crown. An

formerly. Generally speaking, cold places are not suitable, owing to the Camellias blooming so early in the season. But although frost may destroy the blooms that are open at the time, the undeveloped buds will expand and again make a cheerful display. The plants themselves are perfectly hardy, especially when established, as is evidenced by the fine specimens to be found in Devonshire and Cornwall up to 25 ft. high. On the outskirts of one of the plantations in Richmond Park, Surrey, there is a fine specimen which has been there for many years and has now attained to tree-like dimensions and flowers profusely.

Culture.—Although all Camellias love a peaty soil, they prosper in an open lime-free loam if leaf-mould and peat are added to give them a start. They like semi-shade and sheltered positions, such as shaded walls and woodland conditions. Repot after buds have set; assist them to become established by syringing overhead daily. Water freely from March to September, little afterwards. Prune only when necessary to keep plants a good shape. A moist atmosphere is essential, a dry atmosphere and dryness at the root will cause leaves and buds to drop. Stand pots outside in shady position after flowering.

Take plants back into the house in September; from then until March apply weak stimulants weekly. A solution of sheep droppings and soot, soot water, or artificial manures given as a liquid, are all suitable. Winter temperature, 45°; summer, 60°.

Propagation by seeds sown in moist heat. By grafting in close propagating frame in early spring, using *C. japonica* seedlings as the stock. Also by cuttings of firm wood placed in gentle heat in sandy peat in August. Insert several cuttings round the edge of well-drained pots, and place in the greenhouse. Cuttings take from 8 to 10 weeks to root. May also be propagated by layering at the end of August or beginning of September, or by grafting in February or March.

SPECIES.

C. cuspidata (W. China). An interesting and distinguished-looking, free-growing species, 5–8 ft., with pure white flowers 1½ in. across, freely borne during May. One of the hardiest.

C. japonica (China and Japan). Flowers red, composed normally of five petals. An oil is expressed from the seed and is much used by Japanese women for dressing the hair. There are a great number of varieties of which the following are some of the most important.

C. j. Donckelaarii. One of the hardiest of all Camellias and one of the most popular. Flowers deep red with white markings. Very free flowering.

C. j. Lady Clare. One of the most handsome; bold, dark green foliage, and large single pink flowers in April and May.

C. j. latifolia. Another very hardy and reliable variety with semi-double bright red flowers.

C. j. Magnoliæflora. Foliage pale green, exquisite shell-pink semi-double flowers composed of two rows of petals, reminding one of a large-flowered pink *Magnolia stellata*. Quite distinct from all other Camellias, and always greatly admired.

C. j. Mathiona. A very old variety and still one of the finest. There are three forms: *C. M. alba* (white), *C. M. rosea* (rosy pink), *C. M. rubra* (deep crimson).

C. reticulata (China). The gem of the family and rightly known as the Queen of Camellias, and without doubt one of the most magnificent of all flowers. Flowers 5–8 in. across, according to the age of the plant. Established matured plants produce the finest blooms composed of two rows of undulated petals of a most beautiful glowing crimson-rose. Its dull surface leaves distinguish *C. reticulata* from all other red-flowered Camellias. Tender until established. Best on a sheltered or north-west wall. In Cornwall it is a great success, reaching to a height of 25 ft. A plant worthy of all care.

C. Sasanqua (China). Very hardy, but needs protection owing to its extra early flowering, February to April. Flowers fragrant, bright rose. There is a white form.

C. thea. The Tea Plant. Less hardy than *C. japonica* and *C. Sasanqua*. Not particularly attractive as a flowering shrub, the white fragrant flowers being small, about 1–1½ in. across; but of interest for its economic importance. Upper Assam is the native home of this plant although from time immemorial it has been cultivated by the Chinese and was introduced by them to N. India and Ceylon.

C. alba-plena, white; *C. imbricata*, crimson; *C. fimbriata*, white; "Countess of Orkney," "Auguste Delfosse," "Jenny Lind," and numerous other good varieties will be found in trade lists.

C. reticulata and the double varieties of *C. japonica* do not usually respond to the latter method of increase and require to be grafted.

CAMOMILE. *See* ANTHEMIS.

CAMPANULA (kam-pan'-u-la. Campanulaceæ). Canterbury Bells, Bellflower, Harebell, etc. There are few annual Campanulas of which *C. attica* 4 in., blue, and *C. ramosissima* (*Loreyii*) violet, and its white variety, *alba*, 9 in. are the only ones worth growing. Seed should be sown in spring, thinly, where the plants are to bloom. A position on a somewhat dry rockery suits them.

Campanula medium. The Canterbury Bells are the best known, and most useful of the biennial species, and of these there are several forms, such as the single-flowered, or true, *C. medium;* the cup-and-saucer types, known as *C. medium calycanthema*, and the double-flowered section,

C. medium flore pleno. The colours range from carmine to rose-pink, and lavender mauve to deep blue, also white, and come fairly true to colour and type from seeds.

Culture.—Sow end of April to early June in a prepared seed-bed outside, or in boxes in cold frame; transplant to nursery beds at 6 in. apart when three leaves have formed, and plant into flowering quarters, 2–3 in. apart, in October. A few of the stronger plants lifted and potted up into 6–8 in. pots in autumn and wintered in a cold frame, will make fine pot plants, and if put into a cool greenhouse in January–February will flower in April–May. Height, 2½–3 ft.

The most recent addition to the family is the new Covent Garden annual Canterbury Bell, a true annual which will bloom within six months of sowing. The plants are well branched, grow to a height of 2–2½ in., and give fine flowers in shades of rose-pink, white, lavender and dark blue in the greatest profusion. This new race is immensely popular for bedding or for pots, and with the help of a cold greenhouse it is possible to have plants in flower nearly all the year round.

As Border Plants. Campanulas have a great variety of form, some being tall and suited for borders or for growing in pots for indoor decoration, while others are dwarf plants and form little carpets covered with flowers in summer. They are easy to cultivate, and make a good show, varying in colour, but generally blue or white.

C. pyramidalis or the Chimney Bellflower is the form most commonly used for pots and requires special attention. Sow this early in March for strong plants the following July. Prick off the seedlings into 3 in. pots, winter them in 6 in. pots, and in spring use 8 in. pots. This plant can also be increased by suckers taken off with a heel and placed in sandy soil in a cold frame.

Most of the species are propagated by division, or by seeds sown under glass or in the open in May. When plants appear give air and shade. Campanulas will last longer in bloom if in a half-shady place, and the taller ones will require staking. Almost all species thrive in well-drained light sandy loam with grit and leaf-mould.

For baskets use *C. fragilis, C. Barrelieri, C. isophylla* (blue) and *C. isophylla alba* (white), as these are not hardy enough for many gardens. For rockwork the pale blue *C. carpatica, C. garganica* (and its white variety), *C. Portenschlagiana, C. pumila* (or *Cœspitosa*), *C. pulla,* and *C. pusilla* (with its white variety) are the prettiest. For borders, beds, etc., one of the most often used is the biennial Canterbury Bell, which has double blooms and

A dainty little Campanula for the edge of flower borders is Pumila (cæspitosa) in white or blue forms.

of which different coloured varieties may be obtained. *C. glomerata* (Clustered Bellflower) and *C. rotundifolia* (English Harebell), both blue, are easy to cultivate in any soil and are excellent border flowers. The hybrids "Standfieldi," and "G. F. Wilson," both purple, flower from June to July. They are about 6 in. tall, and are charming rock-garden plants. The height of the border Campanulas varies from 1–4 ft. The annual Campanula *Loreyi* is a particularly charming member of the Bellflower family. It is blue flowered, about 1 ft. high, and suitable for any situation, including hanging baskets.

As Pot Plants. These handsome biennials or perennials of easy culture, make extremely decorative specimens when treated as biennials. They grow from 2½-7 ft. high in a 24 pot, producing blue, mauve, pink or white flowers.

Seeds should be sown in boxes in late May or early June, being pricked out when large enough to handle. They usually go through the winter in a cool greenhouse in either a large 60 or a 48 pot, according to the time of sowing and the variety used. The soil for the larger (flowering) pots should contain good loam, old sifted manure, a good sprinkling of mortar rubble and sand. They respond to feeding when well rooted.

VARIETIES.

Varieties for the greenhouse include all the Canterbury Bells (the Single, Double and the Calycanthema or Cup and Saucer varieties), *C. pyramidalis* or the Chimney Campanula.

CAMPHOROSMA (kam-for-oz'-ma. Chenopodiaceæ). An uncommon grey-foliaged shrub about 18 in. high from the Mediterranean region. Suitable for growing in seaside gardens. Loves sun and a dry soil.

CAMPION. See LYCHNIS *and* SILENE.

CAMPSIS. See TECOMA.

CANARINA (cana-ri'-na. Campanulaceæ). Canary Island Bellflower. Greenhouse herbaceous perennial. Canary Islands, 1696.

Culture.—Compost, equal parts loam, leaf-mould and sand, with a little bone-meal and charcoal. Repot early spring. Care must be taken to give good drainage. Temperature, winter, 45°; summer, 60°.

Propagation.—By division of roots when repotting; or by cuttings of young shoots in sandy soil; place in propagator. Temperature, 65°, spring.

SPECIES.

C. campanulata, orange.

CANARY CREEPER. See TROPÆOLUM.

CANDYTUFT. See IBERIS.

CANISTRUM (kan-is-trum. Bromeliaceæ). *Kanos*, a basket, in reference to the inflorescence resembling a basket of flowers. Stove epiphytal plants with showy flowers that are attractive for two or three months.

Propagate by suckers and division and plant in fibrous peat with loam and charcoal.

Summer, 65°-85°; winter, 60°-70°.

SPECIES.

C. aurantiacum. Orange, Brazil.

C. eburneum. White and green, with ivory-white bracts. May, 2 ft.

C. roseum. Green inconspicuous flowers, 2 ft.

CANNA (can'-na. Scitamineæ). Indian Shot. India, 1570. Tropical herbaceous perennials that were formerly cultivated for their foliage only but are now so developed by careful culture that the flowers are most brilliant and of varied colours, while the leaves, which in some cases are brown, retain their beauty. Although not quite so popular as they were a few years ago, their large, brilliant flowers make them very valuable for decoration or sub-tropical bedding.

All flower from August to October, require positions in warm sunny beds or borders and rich, well-manured loam, but are really best in the greenhouse, as the plants are not quite hardy.

Culture.—Compost, 2 parts rich loam, 1 part leaf-mould, a good supply of dried cow manure, and enough sharp sand to keep it open. Repot February. Light sunny position. Water freely during the growing period. Give applications of liquid manure weekly until buds appear. After flowering, allow gradually to dry off. Store in frost-proof place, or under staging until potting time. Temperature February to May, 50°; May to September, 70°.

For greenhouse plants use a compost of equal parts of turfy loam and decayed cow manure, with a little fibrous peat and sand. Those which closely resemble Gladioli and Orchids are usually potted. They require frequent watering and an occasional feed of liquid manure when in bloom. Keep in a semi-dry state in winter in a temperature of 45°-50°. The dwarf hybrids are best for beds and continue to flower in late autumn. Water abundantly.

Propagation.—By division of roots when repotting, or by seed.

Sow seed in a case or in pots in the

greenhouse—soak previously as they are slow to germinate if put in hard—and if for beds put out in June about 2 ft. apart. If desired to increase a particular kind, divide when growth starts.

SPECIES.

New and choice varieties, many of which are brighter than orchids, are always being brought out. The best-known species are:

C. achiras, 5 ft., red blooms, and its varieties.

C. aurantiaca, 6 ft., orange.

C. discolor, 6 ft., purplish-red foliage.

C. edulis, 6 ft., purplish-yellow.

C. flaccida, 3 ft., yellow and red.

C. gigantea, 6 ft., orange, red and purple with large green foliage.

C. indica, 3–6 ft., yellow and red.

C. iridiflora, 6–8 ft., red and yellow.

C. limbata, 3 ft., red.

C. Warscewiczii, 3–8 ft., scarlet tinged blue.

C. edulis is cultivated for food, but the other varieties have only a decorative value.

Cannas as Pot Plants.

These plants are useful perennial plants for the greenhouse. Most of those grown under glass are hybrids from Canna indica and they make highly decorative pot plants, growing 4–6 ft. in height and being valuable both for the colour of their flowers (yellow, orange and shades of red), and for their highly-coloured, broad foliage, which varies from green to dark bronze-red. Some have variegated leaves.

Culture.—Seed sown in spring in gentle heat should be given plenty of tepid moisture and the resulting seedlings may be potted as they require it, using any good compost of loam, leaf-mould and sand, enriched with fertiliser or old sifted manure. Two-year-old seedlings make handsome specimens and a good proportion of high colours may be expected from a good strain of seed.

CANNABIS (kan-na-bis. Urticaceæ).

Hemp. Indian Hemp. The only species of this genus is C. sativa, the Indian Hemp: a hardy annual that is very ornamental in the garden in summer. It provides the hemp of commerce. The form usually grown in gardens, C. sativa gigantea, is an ornamental foliaged plant, and in rich soils will grow 6–10 ft. It is useful for making a quick-growing summer screen, or in groups of three to five plants in a large border or shrubbery.

Raise from seed sown in any good garden soil in April. Its foliage is attractive.

CANTUA (kan'-tu-a. Polemoniaceæ).

Very beautiful and rare evergreen shrub from Peru, needing the protection of a south-west wall.

Culture.—Soil, loam, peat and sand. Cuttings root readily in sand or very sandy soil under a bell-glass.

SPECIES.

C. buxifolia (syn. dependens). Flowers funnel-shaped, bright rose, April to May, 4 ft.

CAP.

When erecting trellis work or fences, a cap is required to disperse water from the uprights and save them from rotting. This is either wood, stone or brick, etc., according to the type of fence, and may be very simple with chamfered edges or of very elaborate design, adding interest and dignity to the fence, trellis or wall.

The usual cap or flat protective top to any upright post or column can be so dealt with as to increase its ornamental value, with no detriment to its usefulness. While a wooden post is suitably topped by a flat wooden slab, 1–1½ in. thick and 1–3 in. larger each way than the post itself, a stone post can be fitly capped by carved balls, pineapples or urns—of proportionate size and elaboration.

CAPABILITY BROWN.

A garden designer who came to the forefront in the eighteenth century, protesting against the extreme formality which was the feature of the gardens of the previous century: his theory was "Nature abhors a straight line." Working on this he destroyed many of the fine avenues and established yew hedges then existing, redesigning the gardens with curved walks and drives, undulating lawns and informal tree planting. He gained his name through his favourite saying. When called to view a site he always said it was "capable of great improvement."

CAPE GOOSEBERRY. See PHYSALIS (Winter Cherry).

CAPE PRIMROSE. See STREPTOCARPUS.

CAPE SHAMROCK. *See* OXALIS.

CAPPARIS (kap'-par-is. Capparideæ). A genus mainly consisting of stove and greenhouse evergreen shrubs. Commercially important because of the capers produced by *C. spinosa*.

Propagate by cuttings of ripened shoots inserted in sandy soil under a bell-glass in moist heat. Plant in a mixture of peat and loam. All require protection and most need moist stove culture.

SPECIES.

C. acutifolia, white flowers from June to July. 5 ft.

C. spinosa, white, June. 3 ft.

CAPSICUM (kap-si-kum. Solanaceæ). Common Capsicum, 1½ ft.

Capsicum annuum, a half-hardy annual, is the species grown for making Red or Cayenne Pepper. There are quite a number of varieties of *C. annuum*, the fruits of which vary in size, shape and colour.

VARIETIES.

Mammoth Long Red, Pigmy, Golden Dawn, East India Cayenne, Red Giant, Golden King (Sweet Pepper).

Uses.—Years ago the juices and pulp of both Capsicums and Chillies were used medicinally for allaying fevers and inflammation. Their chief use nowadays, apart from decorative work, is for adding pungency to curries, sauces and pickles.

CAPSICUMS AND CHILLIES (*Capsicum annuum* and *C. baccatum*) Solanaceæ. These closely allied South American plants are usually grown for decorative purposes.

Culture.—Their earlier cultivation is identical with that of the Aubergine. All make ornamental pot plants. Seed should be sown in February–March in heat, plants grown on in rich soil, temperature, 50°-55° till fruits formed, then place in cooler, airy, greenhouse. When 3 or 4 in. high they should be potted in 5 in. pots with a mixture of 3 parts of light loam, 1 part decayed manure, and a good sprinkling of bonemeal and sand. Good drainage is essential, and the pots should only be filled about two-thirds to allow for later top dressings.

In warm districts some of the earlier sorts will ripen their fruits if planted out on a sunny border early in June, though many prefer to leave them in the pots and plunge them to the rim, so that if necessary they may be lifted and taken under glass in the autumn to finish colouring. They can also be cultivated for the decoration of the greenhouse and conservatory.

CAPSID BUGS. Attack chiefly fruit trees; also garden crops such as shrubs, potato roots, etc. Capsid bugs on fruit trees are controlled by spraying just before the buds burst (up to the first week in March on apples) with D.N.C. wash, or with Thiol.

CARAGANA (kār-a-gā'-na. Leguminosæ). Handsome deciduous shrubs and small trees thriving in sunny positions in well-drained, damp soil, not rich.

Propagate by seeds, and by grafting.

SPECIES.

C. arborescens. The Pea Tree (Siberia), 15-20 ft. Yellow pea-shaped flowers in May.

C. chamiagu (China). New species with reddish-yellow flowers.

C. decorticans (Himalayas). Yellow flowers. June and July.

C. pygmæa (Caucasus, Tibet). A graceful pendulous species with bright yellow flowers in May.

The Caraganas are most effective grown as half-standards.

CARAWAY. *See* CARUM.

CARBENIA (kar-be'-nia. Compositæ). Blessed Thistle. *C. benedicta*, better known as *Cistus benedictus*, is the only species of this genus. It is a hardy biennial with large green leaves blotched with white and yellow thistle-like flowers. In a sunny border it is a striking plant, attaining to a height of 3 ft. or more. Sow seed in September or April.

CARDAMINE (car-da-mi-ne. Cruciferæ). Lady's Smock, Bitter Cress, or Cuckoo Flower. Hardy perennials useful in borders and the edge of shrubberies. They grow well in sun or shade, in moist rich soil, and flower from May to June.

Propagate by division in spring or autumn, when they will take well.

SPECIES.

C. pratensis, of silver-white colour, is the best known, while the double form is regarded as a better garden flower. There are less known yellow and blue varieties, but they are hardly worth cultivating. Height 12–18 in.

CARDOON (*Cynara Cardunculus*). Compositæ. This native of Southern Europe is closely related to the Globe Artichoke, and in outward appearances they closely resemble each other during their early stages. Their cultivation differs, however, for whereas the Globe Artichoke is grown for the flower heads, the Cardoon is grown for the production of edible leaf stalks.

Although introduced so long ago as 1658, the Cardoon has never become very popular amongst the masses in this country. It is grown in most large establishments for it makes a welcome change from the more usual vegetables. It is also extremely useful to those who exhibit mixed collections of vegetables.

Culture.—The Cardoon, unlike the Globe Artichoke, is always raised from seed which should be sown *in situ* at the end of April.

Trenches are taken out 18 in. wide and 1 ft. deep, and 3 in. of well-decayed manure is mixed with the bottom soil, and this in turn is covered with 3 in. fine clean soil.

At the end of April, if soil and weather conditions are favourable, 3 or 4 seeds are dibbled in, in groups 18 in. apart, down the centre of the trench, and are well watered in.

After sowing it is advisable, though not absolutely essential, to cover each group of seeds with an inverted flower-pot or a cloche until the seedlings appear. As soon as possible thin the groups to one strong plant in each. As a protection from late frosts and scorching sun it is usual to lay a few leafy branches over the top of the trench until the end of May.

The Cardoon revels in a full supply of moisture at the root, and in dry weather artificial watering must be resorted to. The plants should be fully grown by September, and upon a fine day when the foliage and the soil are dry the leaves may be gathered together and tied with raffia.

If grown for exhibition a strip of brown paper should be wound round the tied stems from the base to the top, and around this should be wound a band of hay or straw. A light stake should be placed by each plant which may then be earthed up in two or three operations in the same way as celery. Should frosty weather ensue some dry litter should be scattered over the top. The stems usually take a month to blanch, but are not lifted until required for use. If for exhibition they should be carefully lifted and sponged, and then wrapped in a damp cloth or paper until shortly before they are to be judged.

Uses.—The Cardoon is used as a boiled vegetable, and also in salads. In the former case the blanched stalks are cut into 3 in. lengths, the prickles removed, and are boiled gently in salted water for 15 minutes. This loosens the outer skin which can then be rubbed off; afterwards placing them in cold water with a little salt and boiling till tender. They may also be cooked like Celery, and when used in salads should be treated like the latter vegetable.

CAREX (kar-ex. Cyperaceæ). Sedge. Grass-like herbaceous perennials, natives of Britain, that are chiefly of value for growing on the fringe of ponds or lakes where they obtain the same conditions as in their natural habitat. A few are adapted for the garden, while some are grown in pots.

Propagate by seeds or by division of the rootstock in autumn or spring. Grow in any ordinary soil kept fairly moist.

SPECIES.

C. baccans, very effective, with red or purple berries. 4 ft.

C. paniculata, has long narrow leaves and three-sided stems.

C. pendula, has bright evergreen foliage. 4–5 ft.

C. pseudo-Cyperus, with triangular stems, is useful for growing with Water-lilies.

C. tristachya (syn. *japonica*) has leaves striped white and is grown in pots in rooms.

CARICA (kar'-i-ca. Passifloræ). Papaw Tree. Tropical fruit trees, of which the fruits are cooked and eaten by the natives of S. America where they grow. Grown in stoves in this country more for curiosity than use. An interesting point about the leaves is that they make tender any meat that is wrapped in them.

Propagate by cuttings of ripened shoots with leaves inserted in sand under a bell-glass with bottom heat. They require rich loamy soil and a temperature of 50°–60° in winter and 60°–85° in summer.

SPECIES.

C. papaya, common Papaw, green. July. 20 ft.

C. spinosa, whitish green. July. 20 ft.

C. citriformis, yellowish. July. 20 ft.

CARLINA (car-line-a. Compositæ). Named after Charlemagne.

SPECIES.

C. acanthefolia is a stemless thistle, producing one huge glistening straw-coloured flower seated centrally on a flat rosette of spring leaves. It requires poor soil in full sun, otherwise it may grow taller and so lose its character. From Carniola. *Propagate* by seed.

C. acaulis is somewhat similar to the foregoing, but on a smaller scale. The same precautions as to soil are necessary. Swiss Alps, June. From seed.

CARLUDOVICA (kar-lu-dov-i-ka. Cyclanthaceæ). Screw Pines. A genus of stove perennials of palm-like habits. some of which are evergreen while the rest are herbaceous.

Propagate by suckers and grow in sandy loam.

Winter temperature, 50°-55°; summer, 60°-80°.

SPECIES.

The leaves of all the species are set spirally round the stem, giving it a cork-screw appearance and thus giving rise to the name of the order.

C. Drudei, white. July. 4 ft.

C. funifera, white, stove evergreen climber. July.

C. latifolia, green, herbaceous shrub. July. 3 ft.

C. palmata, white flowers in July, an herbaceous shrub. July. 3 ft.

CARMICHÆLIA (kär-mĭ-kē'-li-a. Leguminosæ). Deciduous, flowering broom-like shrubs with pea-shaped flowers from New Zealand. They hate lime and love sun. Increased by cuttings in sand.

SPECIES.

C. australis. Flowers lilac, veined violet, fragrant, May.

C. Enysii. Pygmy species for rock garden, only few inches high, covered in spring with mass of small violet flowers.

C. flagelliformis (*arborea*), 3–6 ft. Flowers lilac-pink, June.

C. odorata, 3–10 ft. Flowers fragrant lilac-rose. May to September.

C. Petriei. A new species with fragrant violet-purple flowers in June and July

C. Williamsii. New species with yellow flowers.

CARNATIONS. *See also* DIANTHUS. The carnations now grown in gardens and greenhouses are chiefly of the following types :

(1) The old *Border carnation*, which has a limited flowering period in July and August;

(2) The *Perpetual-flowering carnation*, which is a hybrid between the American tree carnation and the old Border carnation, and

(3 The *Marguerite carnations*, a race of hybrids with fringed, fragrant flowers of all colours.

In addition to these there are the newer *Allwoodii*, a race of hybrids between the carnations and pinks; *Allwoodii alpinus*, a race of hybrids between the Allwoodiis and pinks, both of which are more commonly grown in the open garden than under glass. *Sweet Wivelsfield* is a cross between the old Sweet William and Alwoodii pinks—in fact so many crosses are being made by modern specialists, that it is already exceedingly difficult to trace the exact ancestry of any particular race of flowers of this genus.

Each group of carnations requires slightly different treatment, according to its habit of growth, and the various methods are outlined here for the benefit of the amateur.

Border Carnations. These are the old carnations, known here in Shakespeare's time. There seems to be a good deal of mystery attached to the rise of the various types of carnation, and certainly the family seems to be as old as civilisation itself. Theophrastus mentioned the carnation as far back as 300 B.C. when it adorned the gardens of ancient Greece. Its name "Dianthus" was derived from *Dios*, god, and *Anthos*, flower, or in plain English, Divine flower. We may imagine therefore that in olden times it was greatly esteemed.

It is further recorded that the Mohammedans made scent of carnations—that was of course before the days of synthetic scent. One of the kings of France used the carnation for medicinal purposes, and

William the Conqueror is supposed to have brought it to England.

Discussing the question of the origin of the modern carnations, one grower states that he is of the opinion that the original species just adapted itself gradually to the climatic conditions of the locality where it was grown. Those grown by the ancient Greeks resembled more the perpetual-flowering type, whilst those brought over here by William the Conqueror were nearer the border type. Judging from the ease with which the different species will cross in the hands of the modern hybridist, there seems no reason why any number of crosses should not have happened in the past; but as this question scarcely concerns the amateur gardener, it may well be left to those who wish to work out exact origins.

What concerns us to-day is that there are now two distinct types of "border" carnations, that is, carnations suitable for growing in the open garden—the true "border carnation," which has a short period of flowering round about July and August, and the "perpetual" type which flowers over a much longer period. The first is the one that Shakespeare knew, and the one which is the easiest to cultivate, being quite hardy in town, seaside, or country gardens. It can be raised from seed, but as a large percentage of the seedlings produce only single flowers, the usual practice is to grow fresh supplies from layered shoots, or from cuttings.

If seed is sown, it should be put into boxes of fairly rich soil, with a layer of leaves below to retain moisture. Some

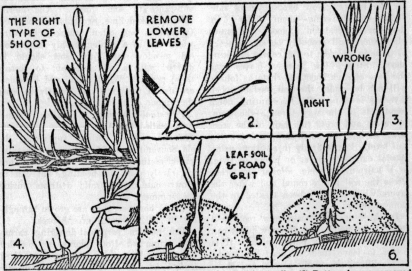

Carnations are increased by layering. (1) Side shoots laid into soil. (2) Bottom leaves removed with sharp knife. (3) Cut upwards from below a joint to make the notch. (4) Peg the layer on to the soil. (5) Place fresh soil around the layer. (6) In six weeks sever from the parent plant.

sharp sand should be added to the compost, and a goodly quantity of lime or old mortar also included. Scatter the seed thinly over the surface, and cover it lightly with fine sifted soil. Stand the boxes in the open air, covered with glass, to protect the seeds from birds, but as soon as the seeds germinate remove the glass.

Prick out the seedlings as soon as they are large enough to handle, into the soil of a cold frame, or into a special nursery bed in a sheltered position. If the seed is sown in February or March, the seedlings will possibly flower the same season, but if the seed is sown later in the summer, the seedlings will merely make fairly sturdy plants ready to produce good flowers the next year. When the plants have flowered, the grower will probably decide that some are worthless and will destroy them, but others will be worth increasing, and this can be done in the same way as ordinary purchased plants are increased.

Layering.—This is the simplest of all methods of increasing carnations of this type. First see that there is a clear space for 4 or 5 in. round the plant. Put some freshly prepared soil round, to a depth of about 2 or 3 in. This makes it easy to fix the layers. Now choose young side-shoots—non-flowering—about 4 or 5 in. long, or longer. On a good, well-grown plant there will probably be six or seven of these in addition to the centre flowering shoot. Strip a few pairs of leaves from the base of each shoot, so that the foliage will not be under the soil surface when layering is done. Cut a slanting notch two-thirds of the way through the stem, upwards, and press this part of the stem down so that the notch is open below the soil level. Peg it firmly in position, using special carnation pegs, or pieces of twig, or a hairpin, or some similar material. Press the soil firmly round and water the layers when all have been treated in the same manner.

In three or four weeks new roots will form at the notch, and the new plant can be severed from the parent plant. It is better to leave them at least six weeks before lifting the young plants, and those that are layered in July can be left until September, when they can be moved to their permanent positions in the border. Or, if the garden is very exposed, and there is a real danger of losing the plants during the winter, they can be moved to the shelter of a cold frame. They are usually so hardy that this is unnecessary, and in any case, no coddling must be given them, as the hardier they are kept during the winter, the stronger and sturdier will be the plants the next season.

Old roots from which the layers have been taken are worthless, and should be destroyed.

CUTTINGS.

Sometimes, where plants are crowded in a border, layering is impracticable, and it is easier to take cuttings. These can be merely "pulled out at a joint," in the same manner as pink pipings, and inserted in fairly sandy soil, with lime added, either in a cold frame, propagator, or in the open ground. They generally root quite easily. Cuttings can be "made" by cutting the stem immediately below a joint, and stripping off the lower leaves, and then inserting as described.

The soil in which carnations are grown in the open border should always be carefully prepared. They are fond of lime, and will not flourish without this substance in some form. Old mortar rubble, slaked lime, or chalk can be used. Carnations are often attacked by wireworm and in a garden freshly made from old meadow land, the soil should be dressed with a soil fumigant to destroy these pests. Wood ashes and bonemeal are useful dressings and greatly increase the vigour of the plants.

Perpetual-flowering Carnation, sometimes called the American tree carnation. This has almost entirely superseded the old Souvenir de la Malmaison. The cultivation of these is exactly the same. They are rarely used for bedding, but can be grown outdoors in mild districts during the summer.

Often, however, they are grown throughout in cool or heated greenhouses.

The modern perpetual-flowering carnation originated from plants of so-called Remontant carnations that were exported from France to America about the middle of last century. This type is still grown in large quantities on the Riviera, where the plants produce two crops of flowers a year; one, the autumn crop, the one of most value to the cut-flower growers, is mostly exported, the other, the spring or early summer crop, is practically wasted. In America, unlike France, these carnations had to be grown in greenhouses to have flowers during the winter months, and very soon varieties were raised to be adapted for this special method of cultivation. It was then, as it is now, usual to plant young plants out into the open during April–May, and transplant them from there to well-prepared beds or benches in the greenhouse during the latter part of the summer. Carnation-growing in those days (about fifty years ago), for the New York market, was a profitable undertaking, and numbers of growers were attracted and many raised novelties of greater or less merit. It was, however, left to that great Scotsman, Peter Fisher, to start the carnation boom in real earnest. He raised a variety which he sold in 1900 to the Copper King, Thomas W. Lawson, for 30,000 dollars. This variety was named " Mrs. Thos. W. Lawson," and because of its sterling qualities as a winter-cut flower producer, as well as the 30,000-dollar publicity, its fame quickly spread around the floral world. This variety, like some of its predecessors, was imported into England by Geo. Beckwith, of Hoddesdon, Crane Clarke, of March, and a few others. The commencement of the meteoric rise of the perpetual-flowering carnation, however, began with the introduction of that wonderful " Enchantress," also raised by Peter Fisher, of Ellis, Mass., in 1903. Thousands of carnation cuttings were shortly afterwards imported, and about 1905 the presence of the perpetual-flowering carnation made itself felt in Covent Garden. The first Carnation Show was held in the R.H.S. Hall in 1906, and the British Carnation Society, which concerns itself mainly with the cultivation of this type of carnation, was founded at the same time. (The National Carnation and Picotee Society concerns itself more with the hardy open-air plants.

A short 25 years ago, if a florist wanted 100 blooms of carnations on a certain spring, autumn or winter morning at Covent Garden Market, he would have to get up early and keep busy, and maybe would be unlucky even then. To-day he can get 100 dozen, aye 1,000 dozen, of any popular colour on any morning without much trouble. Two growers between them have sent as many as half a million blooms to market in a week. Twenty-five years ago all the carnations grown for Covent Garden might have been housed in one of our large houses of to-day. Carnation-growing has become an important industry. At a conservative estimate, six million plants are grown for cut-flower production in England, occupying about 125 acres of glass, employing 1,500–2,000 hands, using about 30,000 tons of coal and coke per annum.

The amateur gardener, however, does not expect to cultivate carnations on this scale; he merely wants to be sure that if he has a small greenhouse with, say, a hundred good plants, he can count on having a flower for his buttonhole on every day during the year, and this, with ordinary care and sufficient heating apparatus to keep the greenhouse always above freezing point, he can do.

The perpetual carnation is grown in two ways—one as a garden flower, to bloom

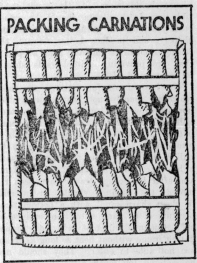

PACKING CARNATIONS

Carnation plants can be sent by post or rail if packed tightly and securely. Each root, with soil round it, should be wrapped in paper, and all should be secured so that they do not shake about in the box.

during summer, and the other as a greenhouse subject, to bloom in autumn, winter and spring. The beginner usually starts with a plant in a 3 in. pot, purchased in spring. This should be a bushy plant with from three to six shoots. Up to the middle of May it should be kept in a light, airy spot in the greenhouse, or failing this in the cold frame. Later on a sunny sheltered spot in the open garden will do well except in a very wet season.

As soon as roots appear to be growing through the bottom of the pot, repot the plant into a larger pot, and shelter it until it has established itself, when it may stand in the open garden, in the sun, until about August. After this, the plant can be put into its winter quarters, that is, on the lightest stage of a cool, well-ventilated greenhouse. Gravel, shingle, or cinders should be on the stage below the pots.

The plant so treated should flower from about September to the end of spring. A few months after it begins to flower, there will have grown from near the base several side-shoots, and from these fresh plants should be raised. It is not essential that fresh plants should be raised each year, but as young plants are more shapely, and produce better flowers, the taking of cuttings annually from all plants that are providing suitable side shoots, is recommended.

The best shoots for cuttings are those which are shapely, not dwarfed or twisted, nor too long and leggy. Generally they will be those near the base of the plant, but not the lowest shoot of all, which is often badly formed. The shoots may be pulled out at a joint, or taken off with a heel, i.e., broken from the main stem, and after the lowest leaves have been removed, the cuttings should be inserted in clean sharp sand, with a bottom temperature of 60° and a top temperature of 50°. Cuttings will root in a close propagating frame without heat so long as frosts are not able to enter. They should not be watered too much after the first few days, and should not be left too long in heat or they will make too much soft, sappy growth, so that the resulting plants will be less sturdy.

As soon as the cuttings are well rooted, they are put into 2 in. pots and stood in the greenhouse. They need light, but should be kept away from draughts. In four to six weeks they will be ready for 3 in. pots. It is at this stage that "stopping" is done. That is to say, the top centre portion of the plant is pinched out (in February, or later, according to the time when the cuttings were taken). If it is intended to develop these new plants for summer flowering in the open border, do not stop them again, but let them grow on undisturbed. If you intend to raise more plants for winter flowering, the strongest of the side shoots should be

stopped again in June or July, but only if they are growing rapidly.

Disbudding is done if the flowers are wanted as perfect specimens for exhibition, or if long-stemmed flowers are wanted for cutting; but for garden decoration there is no need to disbud, and disbudding even in the greenhouse can be dispensed with at will.

The old plants from which cuttings have been taken can be treated by one of two ways. They can be planted out in the open garden, where they will flower until the late frosts; or they can be potted into a larger pot and kept in the greenhouse another winter or longer.

The young plants in 3 in. pots, if set in the open border, will continue to flower from June until the frosts, and the next season, if cut into shape during the spring will again flower well. As a general rule, the best practice for an amateur is to raise fresh plants for the greenhouse each season, transferring the old "mother" plants to the open for summer flowering.

Soil.—The soil for carnations should be a heavy loam, to which is added sharp sand or small brick rubble for the first potting, and for the second potting wood ashes and burnt earth. For the final pots 12 parts of loam, not too finely chopped, 3 parts of old well-decayed cattle manure, 1 part of ashes, and in addition a 5 in. pot of bonemeal to each barrow-load of this mixture is recommended and the soil in the final pots should be well rammed.

Modern varieties of carnations include some that are called "Hardy Perpetual Border Carnations," as distinct from "Perpetual-Flowering Carnations." These have the hardiness of the old Border Carnation with the perpetual-flowering qualities of the greenhouse strains. In addition there are still some who grow the old Malmaisons, and the "Perpetual-Flowering Malmaisons," which are only suited to cultivation under glass. Of the various strains offered, the following are some of the most reliable varieties for the garden and greenhouse of the amateur:

HARDY BORDER CARNATIONS.

Old Crimson Clove.

Steerforth Clove—white and maroon.

Peach Blossom—pink.
Grenadier—scarlet.
Bookham White.
Border Yellow.
Gordon Douglas—crimson.
Orangeman—orange apricot.
Raby Castle—salmon.
Cottage Scarlet.
Snow Clove—white.

PERPETUAL-FLOWERING CARNATIONS.
Dilys—yellow, with pink edge.
Wanda—dark red.
Achievement—apricot.
Canadian Pink.
Arctic—white.
Laddie—light salmon pink.
Salmon Enchantress.
Red Laddie.
Orange Sunstar.
Rapture—salmon rose.
Wivelsfield Buttercup—yellow.
Sybil—violet-purple.
Wivelsfield Copper—copper-bronze and orange.

HARDY PERPETUAL-FLOWERING
CARNATIONS.
Sussex Pink.
Sussex Brilliant—white and chocolate.
Sussex Dawn—heliotrope, flaked cerise.
Hawk—white, spotted crimson.
Sussex Rosaline—yellow, red.
Highland Lassie—white, edged red.

PERPETUAL-FLOWERING MALMAISONS.
Atlantic—white, flushed pink.
Delicata—pale pink and rose.
Jessie Allwood—yellow.
Hugh Low—baby pink.
Jessie Maize—deep maize.
Mrs. C. F. Rachael—cherry.

**CARNATION AND PICOTEE
SOCIETY, THE NATIONAL.** Founded
1877, with the object of increasing interest
in the cultivation of Carnations, Pinks
and Picotees. Members are entitled to a
free copy of the Society's Annual, to
tickets for the Annual Show of the Society,
to exhibit at the Society's shows, to
enter novelties for Awards of Merit and
to advice on all matters connected with
the culture of Carnations.   *President*:
Edmund Charrington, Esq. *Hon. Sec.*:
A. E. Mustow, 10, Brinkley Rd., Worcester
Park, Surrey. *Subscription*: 5s. per annum.

CARNATION GARDENS. Why are
there not more gardens entirely devoted

to the Carnation (or Dianthus) family?
They are quite as attractive and varied
as rose gardens, but much more uncommon. Perhaps the true reason for their
rarity is that amateurs are shy of plants
that must be constantly propagated by
cuttings; but carnation cuttings and
layers root so easily that this should not
deter any amateur from making a carnation garden.

How can such a garden be planted?
First of all there are the border carnations, the old clove, and its near relatives,
of which good examples are Salmon Clove,
Scarlet Clove, Mrs. H. Swanson (pure
white), Beauty of Cambridge (yellow),
Loyalty (apricot), and Steerforth clove
(white and carmine).

These might be planted in groups in
long borders, with earlier flowering pinks
between, so that a succession of bloom is
obtained; or they could join company with
the pinks on sloping banks and dry walls,
where they could be grown without layering for two or three years, and left to
hang their full and shapely flower-heads in
delightful profusion, as they do from the
walls of old Spanish gardens.

Small beds could be given over to perpetual border carnations, and to Allwoodii,
the half-carnation, half-pink hybrids that
flower from early spring to late autumn
without ceasing.

If the garden is informal, rock edgings
make a fine home for dwarf pinks and
the tiny Allwoodii alpinus, which are
only 4 in. in height and are perpetual-
flowering.

As to soil, every kind is suitable so
long as it is made porous, reasonably
fertile, and dressed with lime. A sunny
open spot, windy if need be, but not shady,
is what carnations like. They demand
a place in the sun.

Subsequent treatment depends on the
type of plant. The perpetual border
carnations are increased by cuttings,
taken at any time between June and
September, though the plants can be left
to flower for two seasons if desired.

The Marguerite carnations, which are
raised from seed as half-hardy annuals or
biennials, must have a place among the
carnations and pinks, if only for their
wonderful colour variations.

Finally, in any Dianthus Garden, the new Sweet Wivelsfield, a hybrid between Allwoodii and Sweet Williams, should be grown. Young plants of this may be put out in early spring or seeds may be sown in March in the open for flowering in late summer.

CARNATION, MARGUERITE or MARGARET. With this may be classed the Chabaud strains. They are perennials

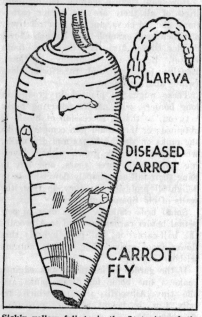

Sickly yellow foliage is the first sign of the carrot fly. The mature larvæ leave the root, breed in the soil, and the resultant fly repeats the process of infection upon the next crop.

of the perpetual class which are usually treated as annuals. They make excellent pot plants for the conservatory or may be planted in the border. They grow about 2 ft. high and contain all the shades known to Carnations: and they are also scented.

Cultivation.—Sow the seeds in heat in January and, when large enough, prick out into boxes. Pot up into small 60-size pots and about the end of April transfer to 48's using the following compost: good fibrous loam enriched with well-rotted leaf-mould and a little well-decayed

manure which crumbles freely. Open with crushed mortar-rubble, wood ash and sharp sand. Pot firmly. From seeds sown in January they commence to flower in June.

VARIETIES.

One of the best strains is Margaret Malmaison with a rich range of colours and a very high percentage of double flowers. Separate colours such as deep crimson, white, yellow, scarlet, etc., may also be obtained.

CARNATION RUST (*Uromyces caryophyllinus*). Considerable loss is often sustained by the activities of the Carnation Rust fungus. Though not a native of this country it appears to have got a strong hold, having been introduced on imported plants. The mycelium entering the plant tissues spreads and, breaking through, gives rise to small brown spots on both sides of the leaves. As the leaves die the spots ripen and countless spores are released, which only await suitable conditions to give rise to fresh outbreaks.

METHODS OF CONTROL.—In the winter and early spring when the plants are dormant they should be sprayed with a dilute Bordeaux mixture or a pale rose-tinted solution of permanganate of potash. This should be done at intervals and the foliage otherwise kept as dry as possible.

CARNATION SOCIETY, BRITISH. Founded twenty-five years ago by a band of enthusiasts who decided to form a flower society devoted to fostering the cultivation of the Perpetual-Flowering Carnation. Its aims and objects are: the extension of the culture and the improvement of Perpetual Flowering, other Carnations, and all members of the Dianthus family. This Society holds Exhibitions from time to time and awards certificates to meritorious Carnations. They collect and disseminate information likely to prove of interest and profit to the members and encourage the extended growing of these flowers. *President:* Lady Emsly Carr. *Hon. Sec.:* F. W. Alesworth, 17 Avenue Road, Isleworth, Middx. *Subscription:* 7s. 6d.

CARPENTERIA (carpen-tēr-ia. Saxifragaceæ). Beautiful evergreen flowering shrub from California, with pure white anemone-like flowers, 2–3 in. across, and showy yellow stamens, during June and July. An excellent seaside shrub for the

outh and west, attaining a height of 20 ft.
Inland, needs wall protection and perhaps
a mat or other covering in very severe
weather. Thrives at Cambridge. It revels
in humus and richness and abundance of
moisture and pure country air. Propagation by seed. Closely related to Philadelphus, differing therefrom in its evergreen
leaves and solitary style.

C. californica, the only species.

CARPINUS (kãr-pī'-nus. Corylaceæ).
Hornbeam. Deciduous trees akin to the
Beeches that thrive on poor and chalky
soils. Valuable as park trees, and for the
formation of hedges, being of rapid growth.

Culture.—Plant from November to February. *Propagate* by seeds, graft in
March.

SPECIES.

C. betulus. The Common Hornbeam
(Europe, Asia Minor and part of England).
One of our handsomest native trees, the
foliage turning yellow in autumn. Often
taken for the Beech, but far more graceful. There are several varieties, with
differing habits of growth, of which perhaps var. *pyramidalus* is the most useful.
The timber is hard, and used for making
certain parts of the pianoforte.

C. caroliniana (E. N. America).
American Hornbeam or Blue Beech.
Similar to the preceding, but not so fine
a tree. Brilliant orange and red in
autumn.

C. cordata (Japan). A slow-growing
species up to 40 ft.

C. japonica. Japanese Hornbeam.
Rare and distinct with striking corrugated
foliage. 40–50 ft.

CARPODETUS (kah-po-dē'-tus. Saxifragaceæ). A rare evergreen shrub of
graceful pendulous habit and cymes of
small fragrant white flowers. Only suitable for mild districts.

C. serratus, the only species.

CARRIEREA (kar-ē'-a-rē'-a. Bixaceæ).
A rare Chinese tree, only assuming a
shrubby form in this country, with oval
bright green, purple-tinted leaves, and
terminal inflorescences of white flowers
Sheltered position.

C. calycina the only species.

CARROT FLY (*Psila rosæ*) The
small greenish-black flies lay their eggs on
the "collar" of young carrots in summer

These eggs hatch into legless, elongate,
yellow larvæ, which enter the skin of
the carrots and by continuous tunnelling
cause rust-like patches to appear. At
this period the foliage of the plants will
wilt and die away. When full grown
the larvæ enter the soil and change to
brown pupæ, which hatch out into flies
at the end of July and early August. Eggs
are again laid and the larvæ again enter

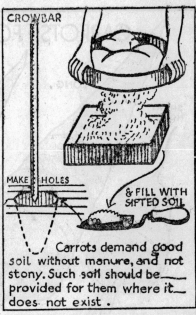

On hard, stony soils use a crowbar to make
holes for fresh compost to grow good straight
carrots and parsnips.

the roots, but the plants are now stronger
and able to withstand the attack better.
The presence of the maggot is, however,
revealed by a premature turning of the
foliage to the colours usually associated
with the autumn. When full grown they
again leave the roots, pupate in the soil,
and there remain throughout the winter till
the following spring: then the flies hatch
out.

METHODS OF CONTROL. When thinning
out the crop every care should be taken
not to injure those roots still left in, otherwise the flies will be attracted by the smell.
When once the crop is attacked, little can

be done, except the careful pulling and destruction of wilting carrots. An excellent repellant to keep the fly away is sand in which paraffin has been mixed. A quart of oil to a barrow-load of sand broadcast along the rows when the plants are up, will act as a deterrent. This should not be applied in wet weather.

CARROTS (*Daucus carotus*. Umbelliferæ). In many parts of rural England

wood ashes, and finally a dressing of air slaked lime as a top dressing, or only the short stump-rooted varieties should be grown. First-class exhibitors adopt the practice of ''boring'' to ensure long evenly-shaped roots. After the land has been prepared in the ordinary way a bar is pushed into the ground to a depth of 3 or 4 ft., and worked round to form cone-shaped holes 4–6 in. across at

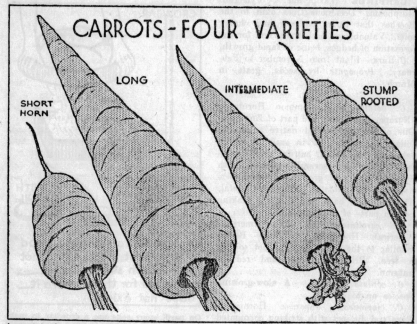

CARROTS – FOUR VARIETIES

LONG

INTERMEDIATE

STUMP ROOTED

SHORT HORN

Amongst the various types of Carrots, the Short Horn and Stump Rooted are the best for stony soils.

the wild carrot still thrives, and it is equally at home in widely separated parts of Southern Europe, and it is from such wildlings as these that the excellent garden varieties of to-day have been raised.

As a food crop it holds a most important place, and to the exhibitor it is extremely valuable as Carrots are—or should be—awarded high points.

Culture.—A light sandy loam of good depth is the ideal, though good crops of carrots are obtainable from any well cultivated garden soil. On heavy soils the site must either be especially prepared by adding sand or clean grit, burnt earth,

the top and 1 ft. apart. The holes are then filled with specially prepared soil. A few seeds are sown at the top, and these are later thinned to one in each hole.

For the earliest crops sowings of short-horn varieties may be made on a mild hot-bed from November to February. The frame should be kept closed until germination takes place, when air may be carefully admitted on all fine days. A quick, uninterrupted growth is desirable, and to this end a syringing with tepid water may be made night and morning. The plants must not be allowed to become drawn, and must be thinned to 1 in apart, and later some of the young roots may be pulled for use, leaving the remainder 3 in. apart.

In February similar sowings may be made in a cold frame, and in March the first outdoor sowings may be made on a warm dry border, providing the soil works freely and shows no sign of stickiness. These early sowings may be made broadcast, or in drills 6 in. apart.

For the main crop the land should be deeply dug in autumn, and left rough until early March. It should then break down to a nice workable tilth by lightly forking and raking.

Carrot seed should not be sown if the soil clings to the tools or rain appears imminent. It is seldom realised that if heavy rain follows a sowing and the soil is beaten down over carrot seeds they will not germinate.

Successional sowings may take place from March to May in drills 9 in. to 1 ft. apart, according to variety, and ½ in. deep. The seedlings should be thinned to 2 in. apart when three leaves have formed, and as soon as the roots are large enough to use the final thinning, to 4–6 in. apart, should be made.

Frequent hoeing during the summer is all that is necessary, and it is a good plan to draw the soil around the necks of the plants, thus preventing green shoulders.

Under all normal conditions the main crop should be lifted early in October, the leaves cut off ½ in from the root, and stored in layers of dry sand or earth in a cool frost-proof place.

Very useful young carrots are obtainable by sowing stump-rooted varieties on good soil early in July if they can be afforded ample water in dry weather.

VARIETIES.

For Frames and Warm Borders.— French Horn; Early Gem; Early Nantes; Parisian Forcing.

For Main Crop on Heavy Soils.—Chantenay; Early Market; Scarlet Gem.

For Main Crop on Medium Soils.—James Intermediate; St. Valery; Prizewinner.

For Main Crop on Sandy Soils.—Altrincham; Long Red Surrey; Wiltshire Giant White.

Uses.—As carrots are usually served as a boiled vegetable it is not generally known that they may also be glazed, made into soup and sauces, or even into jam, either alone or mixed with beetroot.

CARTHAMUS (kar′tham-us. Compositæ). Safflower. Hardy, rather coarse-growing annuals, of which the name is derived from the Arabic, meaning paint, on account of the pigments obtained from the flowers.

Raised from seeds sown in permanent positions or in boxes under glass with slight heat in spring, and planted out later. Ordinary garden soil suits them.

SPECIES.

C. lanatus, yellow. July. 2 ft.

C. oxyacantha, yellow. July, 2 ft.

C. tinctorius, orange. The Saffron Thistle.

CARUM (ka′-rum. Umbelliferæ). Caraway. These hardy biennials are of no garden value, but the seeds of Carum Carvi, popularly known as Caraway Seeds, are in general use for flavouring foods.

Sow in open ground in March or April in common soil. Formerly cultivated to a great extent in Essex and Kent; now superseded by other crops. See also PARSLEY.

C A R Y A (kär′-i-a. Juglandaceæ). Hickory. Fast growing, deciduous trees of great beauty of foliage and stately habit, allied to the Walnuts. The yellow foliage in autumn and picturesque grey trunks in winter are attractive features.

Culture.—The most satisfactory method of propagation is by seed sown singly in 6 in. pots in frame or greenhouse. Plant out the seedlings at end of May in deep well-worked loamy soil, taking particular care that the tap-roots receive no injury in the process. The seeds or "nuts" are obtainable from American nurserymen and should be wintered in boxes of moist earth.

SPECIES.

C. cordiformis. The Bitter Nut. One of the best Hickories for the United Kingdom.

C. ovata. One of the best nut-producing species.

C. Pecan. An uncommon species growing well in this country and proving quite hardy. In appearance somewhat like Ailanthus glandulosa (Tree of Heaven). This is the species which produces the famous and much-appreciated "Pecan Nuts."

CARYOPTERIS (kăr-i-op'-tĕr-is. Verbenaceæ). China and Japan. Small grey-foliaged deciduous shrubs with cymes of blue flowers in autumn and agreeably scented leaves. Fairly hardy.

Culture.—Likes a sunny open position in sandy soil. *Propagate* by soft cuttings in heat.

SPECIES.

C. Mastacanthus (China), 3 ft. Flowers violet-blue in September and October.

C. mongolica (Mongolia). The finest species, but rather tender. Flowers brilliant violet-blue. July to October.

C. tangutica (China). Similar to *C. Mastacanthus*, flowers deeper shade of violet-blue.

CARYOTA (ka-ry-o'-ta). Stove Palms. East Indian Wine Palm. East India, 1788.

Culture.—Compost: loam, leaf-mould and sand in equal parts. Repot, spring. Moist, shady position, syringe daily. Winter temperature, 55°; summer, 80°.

Propagation.—Suckers removed from plants at any time.

SPECIES.

C. mitis and *C. urens.*

CASCADE. A miniature waterfall or cascade adds greatly to the interest of a garden, the rock garden being the best place for its introduction. Stones should be arranged in a natural position for the water to fall over, variety being gained by large and small falls of water, governed by the size of the rocks.

Running water can be maintained by means of a pump, either hand or electric. (*See also* WATER GARDEN).

CASSANDRA (kăs-ăn'-dra. Ericaceæ). An evergreen shrub up to 3 ft. from N. America; with white heath-like flowers during March and April. Needs a lime-free soil and partial shade. *Propagate* by seeds and cuttings.

C. calyculata. The Leather Leaf. The only species. Formerly included with Andromeda.

CASSIA (kăs'-si-a. Leguminosæ). Deciduous and evergreen flowering shrubs. *Propagation* is by division of the root stock in spring and by seeds.

SPECIES.

C. artesioides (Australia). Only suited to mild districts. Silvery foliage.

C. corymbosa (S. America). Large corymbs of brilliant yellow pea-shaped flowers during late summer. Warm wall.

C. marylandica. (South-east U.S.A.). Hardy; flowers yellow in autumn.

CASSINIA (kăs-sin'-i-a. Compositæ). Evergreen heath-like flowering shrubs, from New Zealand, with numerous white flowers. Valuable for foliage rather than floral effect.

Culture.—Grow in sandy loam or peat. *Propagate* by late summer cuttings.

SPECIES.

C. fulvida (*Diplopappus chrysophyllus*). The Golden Heath.

C. leptophylla. The Silver Heath.

C. Vauvilliersii Of pleasing bluish-grey. Not so free flowering as the others.

CASSIOPE (Ericaceæ). Beautiful little evergreen heath-like shrubs, suitable for the north or cool moist parts of the country. They are a great success at the Botanic Gardens, Edinburgh.

Culture.—Plant in airy semi-shaded positions in damp non-calcareous soils. *Propagate* by layers and cuttings.

SPECIES.

C. lycopodioides (Japan). Dwarf. 2–3 in. Flowers lily-of-the-valley-like blooms May and June.

C. Mertensiana (Pacific Coast), 1 ft. Flowers white campanulate.

C. tetragona (Arctic regions). First introduced from Lapland, subsequently from N. America. 4–10 in. Flowers white tinged red, nodding, bell-shaped, during May.

CASTANEA (kăs-tā'-ne-a. Cupuliferæ). Sweet Chestnut. Deciduous, ornamental trees, with but little flower beauty, but valuable on account of their nuts and timber. Yields poles for fruit-gardens and hope fields, the wood being hard and strong while young.

Culture.—Plant in November, in sandy loam, non-calcareous. They like hot dry seasons and defy drought. *Propagate* by seeds sown in open ground, and by grafting for the choice fruiting kinds.

SPECIES.

C. crenata, Japanese Chestnut, 30 ft. Young trees 10–12 ft. fruit freely. Nuts small.

C. dentata, American Chestnut. Nuts of good flavour. Rare in cultivation.

C. pumila, Dwarf Chestnut or Chinquapin. Eastern N. America. Introduced 1699, but rare in cultivation.

C. sativa, Sweet or Spanish Chestnut. 100 ft. Europe, Africa and Asia Minor. Has been grown in this country for very many years, certainly prior to Norman Conquest. There are many varieties, but no pendulous form.

CASTANOPSIS (kas′-tan-op′-sis. Cupuliferæ). Golden Chestnut. California. 30–100 ft. Closely allied to Castanea, differing therefrom in its evergreen foliage and the nuts remaining on the trees for two seasons before ripening.

CASTILLEJA (kas-til-lē-ja. Scrophularineæ). A genus of herbaceous or subshrubby plants with large showy bracts. Rarely cultivated. They are of partly parasitic habit and some of the species require to be grown in the greenhouse or stove.

Increased by seeds sown in a cold frame and the tender species by cuttings of half-ripened shoots in sand, under glass, with bottom heat. Sandy loam and peat.

SPECIES.

C. coccinea, hardy herbaceous perennial with yellow flowers with scarlet bracts. July. 12 in.

C. indivisa, half-hardy, best treated as an annual. Greenish-yellow flowers with carmine bracts. 6–12 in.

C. miniata, yellow, bracts vermilion and scarlet. 1–2 ft.

C. pallida, hardy herbaceous perennial. Bracts white or yellow. June. 12 in.

CASTOR OIL PLANT (*Ricinus*). Euphorbriceæ. A rapid-growing ornamental foliage plant obtainable in many forms and growing from 3–10 ft. in a single season in any good potting soil.

VARIETIES.

Some of the best forms are Gibsonii (dark purple leaves), Scarlet Queen (orange-scarlet flowers and maroon-red foliage), and various varieties of *R. Zanzibarensis*.

CATALPA (kät-al′-pa. Bignoniaceæ). Indian Bean Tree, 15–30 ft. Hardy, deciduous flowering trees, with large attractive leaves. The flowers are very beautiful and remind one of small Gloxinias.

Culture.—Plant from November to February in well-drained rather light loamy soil. They like sun and dislike a bleak situation.

Propagate by seeds, and for the choice of distinct forms. Cuttings of young leafy shoots taken in July and placed in gentle bottom heat.

SPECIES.

C. bignonioides (Eastern U.S.A.), 25–50 ft. Flowers, white, bell-shaped, yellow and purple within, produced in long clusters nearly a foot in length during July and August. There is no more beautiful flowering tree than this in its season. Should be in every garden where trees can be grown.

C. b. aurea. A variety with leaves of rich yellow, improving in colour as the season advances.

C. Bungei (China), 20–30 ft. Small inflorescences of white flowers marked with purple and yellow.

C. Fargesii (China). A new species—pink flowers with brown spots.

C. ovata (China). Introduced from Japan, but not a native of that country. Known since 1693. Produces its flowers, white marked with red and yellow, earlier than any other Catalpa.

C. o. purpurea. Young growths purple.

C. speciosa (Central U.S.A.). Tallest-growing of genus, up to 100 ft. in nature. Flowers similar to *C. bignonioides*, but not so beautiful.

CATANANCHE (Compositæ). Blue Cupidone. Hardy perennial that likes a sunny spot in warm dry soil but will grow anywhere.

Propagate by seed or division.

SPECIES.

The blue *C. cærulea* and its blue and white variety *C. cærulea bicolor* bloom from June to August and grow from 2–3 ft. high.

CATASETUM (kat-a-se′-tum. From *kata*, downwards, and *seta*, a bristle; referring to the position of the two horns of the column. Orchidaceæ). Stove deciduous orchids. Brazil, 1818. This is a very curious and interesting genus. The flowers have an extraordinary polymorphism, sometimes two or three different forms occur on the same plant. Also it is very curious the way in which the pollen masses are ejected with violence when one of the horns of the columns is touched.

Culture.—Compost, fibrous peat and sphagnum moss with broken crocks and charcoal, well mixed together. Repot when new growth commences. They are best grown suspended from the roof of the house. A liberal supply of water must be given during the growing season, little after, as a decided rest is taken after growth is finished.

Propagate by division when re-potting.

SPECIES.

C. barbatum, green and purple.

C. marcrocarpum, yellow and purple.

C. splendens, white and yellow.

CATCH CROPS. *See* VEGETABLE GROWING.

CATCHFLY. *See* LYCHNIS.

CATCH PIT. *See* GUTTERS.

CATESBÆA (katz-be-a. Rubiaceæ). Lily Thorn. Stove evergreen shrubs having long-tubed showy flowers that are allied to Gardenias.

Take cuttings in April, and place in sandy soil in brisk heat where they root freely. For planting, use sandy loam with fibrous peat.

Summer temperature, 60°–80°; winter, 55°–60°.

SPECIES.

C. latifolia, yellow, June. 4–5 ft.

C. parviflora, small white flowers. June 4–5 ft.

C. spinosa, yellow flowers in May. 10–14 ft.

CATKIN. A cluster of stemless flowers crowded together on a single spike. In the case of the willow the male (Palm catkins) and female (silvery turning to white) catkins are borne on different plants. Male and female hazel catkins are borne on the same tree. The former is diœcious, the latter monœcious.

CATMINT. *See* NEPETA.

CATTLEYA (kat′-le′-ya. Orchidaceæ). Stove Orchids. Brazil, 1815. Named in honour of W. Cattley, a great patron of horticulture. The species of this fine genus are little grown now, but some of the best are still extremely useful to the hybridist. The hybrid Cattleyas are extremely popular. Their floriferous habit and gorgeous flowers command the attention of amateurs and professionals alike.

Culture.—Compost: Osmunda fibre with a little sphagnum moss added. Repotting should be undertaken when new roots are pushing from the base of the last made growth. Half fill the pots with clean crocks, and pot the plant so that it is well elevated above the rim of the pot. Water freely during growing-season; after growths are finished, more air and less water should be given to enable the plants to take a rest. A temperature of about 60° at night, rising to 80° or more during the day—if by sun heat—should be the aim during the growing period.

Propagation.—By division when repotting.

SPECIES.

C. Mendelii alba, sepals and petals white, lip pure white, yellow throat.

C. Trianæ-mooreana, sepals and petals splashed crimson, intensely dark lips.

Hybrids.—"Falco," sepals and petals rose, lips maroon-purple with gold veining; "Heliodor," sepals and petals apricot-yellow, lips rose-purple; "White Pearl," handsome chalky white flower with lemon-yellow throat.

CAULIFLOWER (*Brassica oleracea botrytis cauliflora*). Cruciferæ. The origin of the cauliflower is wrapped in obscurity, but strains of a sort have been known in England for well over 300 years.

In the hands of seed-growers and market gardeners it has become a most important crop, and many hundreds of acres, both at home and abroad, are devoted to its cultivation for supplying the English markets.

Like most other Brassicas there is an enormous difference in the quality of different strains of the same variety, and under no circumstances should cheap seed be bought. Good seed costs no more to raise and cultivate, and amply repays the extra initial expense by giving heavier and more uniform crops of better quality.

Culture.—Cauliflowers revel in a rich soil; in fact it can hardly be too rich, and therefore early and thorough preparation of the soil is desirable. If stable manure is unobtainable a good layer of decayed garden refuse should be worked into the bottom, plus the addition of a good general fertiliser, whilst digging two spades deep in winter. The top, left rough, should be dusted with air-slaked lime at about 4 oz. per sq. yd.

Seeds of the Early Bird, Monarch, and Autumn Giant types should be sown in gentle heat in January or early February, and in a cold frame during the end of February or early March. These sowings should produce plants for cutting from July to September. Outdoor sowings may commence in March on a warm border, and be continued at intervals until April.

The early thinning, pricking off, or transplanting of cauliflowers, as with all Brassicas, is most important if really first-class produce is required. Those raised under glass should be pricked off in boxes as soon as large enough to handle, and they can then be gradually hardened off ready for planting out in April.

The distances of planting may vary slightly with the variety, though usually they are set 1½ ft. by 2 ft. for the small early types, and 2½ ft. each way for the main crop.

During the summer hoe frequently, and during drought apply copious waterings so that the plants are not checked.

When the young "curds" or "cauliflower heads" have just formed, a dressing of nitrate of soda 1 oz. per sq. yd. well watered in, or a dressing of a good soluble manure will have a beneficial effect upon the size and quality of the crop.

Sowings of Early Bird and Autumn Giant may also be made in autumn and wintered in cold frames.

VARIETIES.

Early sowings and for forcing.—Early Bird; Snowball; All Year Round.

Main sowings.—Walcheren; Autumn Giant; Autumn Mammoth; Improved Eclipse.

Uses.—The heads should be cut whilst clean and unbroken, and prepared and used in the same manner as Broccoli.

CAULOPHYLLUM (kaul-o-fil-lum. Berberideæ). Very uncommon tuberous hardy perennials, natives of N. America, that are interesting in the rock garden. They are propagated by seeds sown when ripe, or by division of the tubers when flowering is finished.

The best-known species is *C. thalictroides*, with its yellow flowers in April,

followed by blue berries. It should be grown in sandy peat.

CEANOTHUS (sē-an-ō'thus. Rhamnaceæ). Evergreen and deciduous flowering shrubs. The deciduous species are hardy, while sheltered walls or fences are generally necessary for the evergreen section. Flowers white, pink, and various shades of blue from April to August.

Culture.—Plant in October or March in ordinary garden soil in full sun. Avoid winter planting and wet stagnant ground. Pot plants give best results, soaking well beforehand. Pruning the spring-flowering species consists of merely shortening young growths directly after flowering. The Gloire de Versailles type when on walls should be cut back to 1 or 2 in. of old wood in spring. When grown as shrubs trim to shape only.

DECIDUOUS SECTION.

C. americanus, New Jersey Tea. East and Central U.S.A. This is the oldest species in gardens (1713) and one of the hardiest. Not so showy as the hybrids raised from it. Its leaves are supposed to have been used as a substitute for tea during the American Revolution.

C. azureus (Mexico), 1818. Beautiful powder-blue flowers July to autumn. One of the parents of Gloire de Versailles, by which it is eclipsed for garden value.

C. hybridus Ceres. Beautiful rose-pink flowers.

C. h. bijou. Deep blue flowers, very free.

C. h. Gloire de Versailles. Very large panicles of rich azure blue flowers, from June to October. Perhaps the most useful hybrid. Quickly covers a wall or fence. Succeeds in the open as a bush.

C. h. Henry Defosse. The best dark blue, but not a strong grower.

C. h. Lucie Simon. Pale blue flowers.

C. h. Marie Simon. The best pink.

EVERGREEN SECTION.

C. dentatus (California), Bright blue flowers June to August.

C. papillosus (California). Flowers pale blue, very beautiful. One of the least hardy.

C. rigidus. Similar to the *C. dentatus*, but with deep purplish-blue flowers. One of the most beautiful and also one of the tenderest.

C. thyrsiflorus, Californian Lilac. Up to

30 ft. in this country. Very hardy. Flowers powder-blue during May and June in great profusion.

C. Veitchianus (California). Very rapid grower. Flowers greyish-blue. Succeeds as a bush in sheltered gardens.

CEDAR. *See* CEDRUS.

CEDAR INCENSE. *See* LIBOCEDRUS DECURRENS.

CEDAR, RED. *See* JUNIPERUS VIRGINIANA.

CEDAR, WHITE. *See* CUPRESSUS THYOIDES.

CEDRELA (sed-rē'-la. Meliaceæ). China. Handsome deciduous foliage tree with fragrant white flowers, in panicles up to 1 ft. long.

SPECIES.

C. sinensis. Known as the Chinese Cedar, but has no affinity with true cedars. The foliage resembles Ailanthus (Tree of Heaven), but is distinguished therefrom by the entire margins of the leaflets and the absence of glandular teeth.

CEDRONELLA (se-dro-nell'-a. Labiatæ). Greenhouse evergreen shrub. Fragrant resinous scented. Canaries. 1697.

Culture.—Compost: 2 parts fibrous loam, 1 part peat, 1 part sand. Repot, early spring. Winter temperature, 40°; summer, 60°.

Propagation.—By cutting of young shoots in sandy soil. Spring.

SPECIES.

C. tryphylla, deep red-purple on long spikes.

CEDRUS (sē'-drus. Coniferæ). Cedars. The most noble and imposing of all conifers, of unsurpassed grandeur.

Culture.—Plant in deep well-drained, moist loamy soil. *Propagate* by seeds sown in spring, under glass. The resultant plants are always more satisfactory than grafted ones, although it may be necessary sometimes to graft garden forms.

SPECIES.

C. atlantica. The "Atlas Cedar," of the Atlas Mountains, Algeria and Morocco. 120 ft. A most beautiful and imposing tree, with wide-spreading, horizontal branches, and needle-like leaves, green to silvery. Cones about 3 in. long. Thrives better in smoky districts than the Cedar of Lebanon.

C. a. aurea. Leaves golden or yellowish. Not so vigorous as the types, owing to its having to be propagated by grafting.

C. a. glauca. Leaves silvery, or grey-blue.

C. a. pendula. A form with very slender branches.

C. deodara (Himalayas). 250 ft. Of very elegant and graceful habit, especially when young. Not so hardy as the other species. Foliage grey, or glaucous green, branches somewhat pendulous.

C. d. aurea. The "Golden Deodar."

C. d. robusta. A variety with larger leaves, and rather pendulous habit.

C. d. pendula. A dwarf pendulous form.

C. d. verticillata. A tender form with glaucous leaves.

C. Libani (libanotica). The "Cedar of Lebanon" of Palestine, etc. Apart from its historical and Biblical associations, no tree ever introduced gives such charm and distinction to a garden, as the Cedar of Lebanon. It is very near to *C. atlantica,* but can be distinguished from that species by its twigs which are not downy as in *C. atlantica;* and the cones are more tapering. The main or leading shoot is drooping; in *C. atlantica* it is always erect. A warm dry district suits it better than a cold locality. There is a very fine specimen in a garden near Cobham, Surrey, about 120 ft. high.

C. l. brevifolia. The "Cyprian Cedar." A variety with shorter leaves.

C. l. pendula. Dwarf and pendent, 3 ft.

CELANDINE. *See* CHELIDONIUM.

CELASTRUS (se-lăst'-rus. Celastraceæ). Vigorous climbers and climbing shrubs with inconspicuous flowers, but highly decorative fruits. Useful for climbing over old trees, etc. 10–15 ft. high.

Culture.—They require a deep, loamy soil, and manure if available. *Propagate* by seeds and layers.

SPECIES.

C. articulatus (N.E. Asia). A beautiful climber with golden-yellow foliage in autumn, the branches being laden with numerous brilliantly red-coloured fruits remaining in full beauty for at least two months.

C. hypoleucus, yellow and red capsules. 20 ft.

C. latifolus, orange and red capsules. 10 ft.

C. scandens (N. America). Very fine autumn foliage with yellow fruits, exposing the scarlet seeds when ripe.

CELERIAC (*Apium graveolens rapaceum*). Umbelliferæ. This comparatively little-known vegetable is closely allied to the common celery, but unlike the latter the swollen root is the part used for culinary purposes. The leaf stalks of the plant are hollow and extremely bitter to the

rich and light is ideal. Shallow drills should be drawn at 1½ ft. apart, and along these the plants may be set at 1 ft. apart.

As the Celery Fly also attacks the leaves of celeriac the foliage should be occasionally dusted with soot or sprayed, as advised in the notes on celery culture. During dry weather copious waterings may be given, with now and again a weak dilution of soluble manure.

In August all side shoots should be carefully removed, and the soil then ridged up

Celery is a marsh plant and is grown in trenches so as to ensure adequate water supplies.

taste, and we know of no way of using them as an article of food.

Culture.—In essentials its cultivation is similar to that of celery, except that instead of preparing trenches it is planted on the flat, or in shallow depressions taken out to facilitate watering during dry weather.

Seed should be sown in fine soil in March in a temperature of 60°–65°. As with celery, only a very fine covering of top soil should be given.

As soon as the seedlings have made three leaves they should be pricked off into boxes of good light soil, 2 in. apart each way. The temperature should be gradually reduced so that they may finally be hardened off for planting out in May or June.

A sunny level position where the soil is

on either side to cover the swollen roots.

In a normal season the roots may be lifted at the end of October, trimmed of their foliage and rootlets, and stored in dry earth or sand in a frost-proof place, until required for use.

VARIETIES.

Early Erfurt; Improved Paris; Prague Celeriac; Apple-shaped.

Uses.—Celeriac is a most useful vegetable as it keeps well, and thus supplements the winter supply. The roots are peeled and chopped or sliced preparatory to boiling, like most other root vegetables. It has a distinct celery flavour, and may be cooked in the same way, or used raw in salads.

CELERY (*Apium graveolens*). Umbelliferæ. Celery has valuable dietetic properties, and is credited with being especially good for those who suffer with rheumatism. The present-day garden varieties have been evolved from the wild plant which still grows freely in many parts of the British Isles and Europe.

To grow celery correctly certainly entails a large amount of labour, but there is no other crop which can quite take its

Red, or any other reliable standard sort early in March.

Whether sown in pots or boxes, a sandy compost and only the finest covering of soil should be used, as celery seed is small and easily killed when buried too deep.

If placed in a temperature of about 60°-65° and kept damp the seeds should germinate freely in about 21 days, and when

FINAL EARTHING UP

PAPER 'COLLAR' OR CARDBOARD 'CONE'

SOIL EARTHED-UP

Celery is earthed up with soil to bleach it, or can be bleached by means of cardboard collar.

place, and there are endless ways in which it may be prepared for the table.

Culture.—Celery can be grown in any garden if the ground, and subsequently the plants, are given the right treatment. Usually the crop is grown in trenches, but self-blanching types, which may be grown on the flat, are now procurable, and the earliest crops of the ordinary types are also often grown in this way.

Sowing. — For the earliest work sow seeds of a quick-maturing variety, such as Dwarf White, White Gem, or Sulham Prize Pink, about the middle of February, and for the main crop, Exhibition White, Wright's Giant White, Lancashire Prize

three leaves have formed may be pricked out in boxes of slightly richer soil, setting them at least 2 in.—though 3 in. is better —apart each way. They should be moved to a cool house or frame as soon as possible, and kept near the glass, giving them ample ventilation upon all fine days, until they can be finally hardened off, planting out in May or June.

Trenches.—The preparation of the trenches should be undertaken in winter or early spring. This work makes a useful occupation when the weather is cold, and the ground frosty so that the necessary manure can be wheeled about the ground without using planks. Furthermore the

...ction of the frost on the opened trenches has a beneficial effect upon the soil.

If single rows are to be planted the trenches need only be 15 in. wide; for double rows 18 in. with at least $3\frac{1}{2}$ ft. between the sets of rows if more than one is grown.

The soil should be taken out to a depth of 1 ft., and the bottom well forked. On this should be placed 9 in. of rotted farmyard manure, or well-decayed garden refuse, mixed with a well-balanced general fertiliser. Those near the sea who can obtain it will find that 9 in. of rotted seaweed makes a splendid substitute for farmyard manure for this crop.

On top of the manure place 4 in. of good top soil and finish off with a light dusting of slaked lime.

Planting.—By planting-time the manure and top soil should have settled down to a nice firm consistency, but if the level of the soil in the trench is more than 3 in. below the surrounding ground it is advisable to make it up with some more good soil.

Shortly before planting water the boxes so that with careful lifting each plant will have a ball of soil around the roots; remove any side shoots which may be starting from their base, and set the plants firmly 10 in. apart down the centre of the trench if for single rows, or 15 in. apart and 12 in. asunder if in double rows.

Well water in after planting, and hoe the ground around and between the plants the following day or so as soon as the surface is sufficiently dry.

At no time should the plants get dry at the roots for they are obviously water-loving subjects. Frequent weak doses of liquid manure or fertiliser will also do much to improve the crop, and at intervals upon dewy mornings or evenings old soot may be dusted over the foliage to ward off Celery Fly. An equally effective control is to spray the whole plants with Jeyes' Fluid, one part in a hundred parts of water.

Earthing Up.—Usually eight weeks are necessary to blanch the stalks, and earthing up should not be commenced until the plants are almost fully grown. All side shoots and broken stalks should be removed, and the soil alongside the rows forked over and loosened.

Choose a day when both the soil and foliage are quite dry, and having carefully drawn the stalks together with soft string or raffia, bank 4–6 in. of fine soil firmly round the stalks. A similar amount of earthing up should be done every week under the same conditions until only the leaf blades emerge from the top. In banking up the soil it must be made sufficiently firm to hold up, but should not be beaten solid.

For exhibition produce it is advisable to surround the stalks with a brown paper collar before earthing.

In very severe weather protect the foliage by covering the top of the ridges with clean straw or old bracken.

When grown on the flat blanching may be successfully accomplished by wrapping brown paper collars around the tied plants. Even the so-called self-blanching varieties are improved by this treatment.

VARIETIES.

Dwarf White; Dwarf Pink; Exhibition White; Exhibition Pink; Lancashire Prize Red; Lancashire Prize White; Sulham Prize Pink; Bibby's Defiance; Clayworth Prize Pink; Wright's Giant White; White Gem; Aldenham Pink.

Uses.—If well grown and earthed, celery will stand in the ground until required for use. In lifting it is essential to get the spade well below the roots or the stalks will be damaged. Among the many ways in which celery may be used are raw by itself, or in a variety of special salads and sandwiches, and cooked by braising, stewed, curried, fried, or pickled.

CELERY FLY (*Acidia heraclei*). Pale transparent patches often may be seen on the leaves of celery, and if one of these is held up to the light a small maggot will be found within the upper and lower skins of the leaf. This is the larva of the celery fly which has laid its eggs upon the leaf. After the celery has been planted out, a small fly about $\frac{1}{8}$ of an inch in length, brown in colour with mottled wings, may sometimes be seen crawling rapidly over the leaves. These flies are looking for suitable places in which to lay their eggs. On hatching out the maggot immediately enters the leaf and by eating away the green portion causes the transparent areas referred to above. When fully grown the majority pupate in the soil, but some may remain within the leaf. In August a second generation of flies appear and again lay eggs. The damage done by this generation is often considerable, especially if the attack coincides with a dry period. A bad attack will cause stunted growth and stringy bitter "sticks." The winter is passed in the ground in the pupal stage.

METHODS OF CONTROL.—The most satisfactory method is to keep the flies away and so prevent egg-laying. When hardening off the plants, cover the boxes and seedlings with butter muslin. Then, directly after planting them out, broadcast soot, or spray with a dilute paraffin wash. It is as well to repeat this after three or four days. Deep trenching in the winter will bury the pupæ and prevent the fly hatching out.

CELMISIA (cel-miz-ia. Compositæ). After Celmisius, the mythical son of a nymph. Evergreen perennials from New Zealand. Hardy in the south and west. The flowers superficially resemble white ox-eye daisies. The best-known is *C. coriacea* with corrugated leathery leaves clothed with silvery down above and woolly white beneath. From the South Island. About 12 in. cuttings.

CELOSIA (se-lo-si-a. Amarantaceæ). Tender annuals growing from 9–18 in. in shades of rich red and yellow. The modern selections of compact-growing varieties have now superseded *Celosia Thomsoni* and *Celosia pyramidalis*.

Cultivation.—Seeds should be sown in good heat in early April and the resulting seedlings pricked off carefully into well-drained soil. Grow on in good heat and pot on as required in a good compost of loam, leaf-mould and sand enriched with a little complete fertiliser. At all stages of growth Celosias are very apt to damp off with "black leg," particularly when young, and again when nearly in full flower. Great care with watering is therefore essential. They flower usually in July or August.

VARIETIES.

Undoubtedly the two best varieties of *Celosia plumosa* are Red Perfection and Yellow Gem, both of which are often used in the London parks for bedding. One

of the best Cockscombs (*Celosia cristata*) is the dwarf crimson Exhibition strain.

CELSIA (sel-si-a. *Arcturis Scrophulariaceæ*). A very decorative biennial with rosettes of green leaves and bright yellow flowers rather like a Verbascum. Height 2–3 ft.

Cultivation.—This plant may be treated as a greenhouse annual and seeds may be sown either in autumn or early spring. Sown in January and grown on in gentle heat they are in flower by July. Almost any good potting soil suits them.

CELTIS (sel'-tis. Urticaceæ). Nettle Trees or Hackberries. Deciduous, fast growing trees allied to the Elms, bright yellow foliage in autumn. *Propagate* by seed. They thrive in ordinary garden soil, especially in chalky ground.

SPECIES.

C. australis (*S. Europe*), 50 ft. A rapid grower. Young growth tender. Used in Italy as street trees.

C. koraiensis (Korea). A shapely-growing tree. Fine autumn foliage.

C. occidentalis (Sugarberry of N. America), 50–60 ft. Dark purple fruits in profusion. The most suitable species for English gardens.

CEMENT. Mixed with fine sand in the proportion of one to two and brought to a semi-liquid condition, cement is used for giving a final smooth lining to lily pools, pathways, etc.

There are now coloured materials on the market which can be mixed with the cement to give a blue or green-coloured surface to pool linings, or brown and red shades to pathways.

CEMETERIES AND CHURCHYARDS. It is time something was done to beautify the drab appearance of many town and country churchyards. Where part of a churchyard is too old to be of further use as a burial ground, it is suggested that a few of the beautiful flowering cherries, almonds, etc., be planted in groups of two or three with massed planting of bulbs in the grass at the foot of the trees. One or two Mountain Ash would be fine in autumn, when their dazzling red berries are at their best, and would offer a distinct contrast to the usually heavy, rather depressing planting of yew trees.

Perennials and flowering shrubs are best for planting in permanent beds and borders where these are required. They require little upkeep to keep trim and tidy. There are several examples up and down the country where efforts have been made in this direction, and their peaceful charm calls for others to follow. One in particular, in an Essex village, is planned as a rose garden, the beds being surrounded by very trim-cut grass. Lavender hedges flank the paved path from the lych gate to the church door, and the general effect as viewed from the roadway over a low stone wall is very pleasing. The ideal to aim at should be a plain, neat effect, and straight lines to flower borders and lawns are recommended as being easy of upkeep besides being in harmony with the formal lines of the building.

CENTAUREA (cent-au'-rea. Compositæ). Cyanus or Cornflower. 2–2½ ft.

SPECIES.

C. cyanus, sometimes called *Cyanusminor*, in its various colours of rose, carmine, blue, mauve and white, is a fine annual for cutting or borders, and will grow almost anywhere. Seed may be sown in autumn or spring in clumps, in the mixed border, or in lines for cut flowers. The double-flowered forms are best.

C. moschata, Sweet Sultan, another of the family, has flowers in shades of yellow, lilac and purple; the blooms are somewhat larger than in the *C. cyanus* group and last well, both on the plants or in water. May be sown in spring where the plants are to bloom, or in boxes for transplanting; they like a fairly rich soil, and grow to a height of 2½–3 ft.

The perennials of this genus are remarkable for their beautiful silvery leaves rather than their blooms. *C. cineraria* should be raised from seed in heat in spring; other species can be grown from seed sown in the open in April, or by division in April or October. Plant out in an open sunny position in ordinary soil. There are several hundred species of these summer-flowering border plants. Some of the best are *C. babylonica* (yellow, 6–8 ft. in height); *C. dealbata* (purple-rose, 2 ft.); *C. macrophila* or Great Knapweed (yellow, 3 ft.); *C. montana* (blue, white and pink,

2 ft.); *C. ruthenica* (deep yellow, 3 ft.); and *C. scabiosa*, with purplish flowers from June to the autumn and about 18 in. high.

The more tender species should be sown in heat in spring and grown on in pots in the greenhouse; or cuttings can be inserted in the cold frame in July or August. Plant out in beds at the end of May.

CENTAURY. *See* ERYTHRÆA.

CENTAUREA
MONTANA
THE BLUE CORNFLOWER.

For cutting and for market the blue Cornflower is one of the best annuals.

CENTIPEDES. Centipedes must be distinguished from millipedes, as they are beneficial, whereas some of the millipedes are liable to do damage. As a rule the centipede is flat, has long antennæ and always one pair of legs on each segment. Millipedes, with certain exceptions, have two. *Geophilus longicornis* is perhaps the commonest, and may be found in damp places under boxes, rubbish, etc., where it seeks out and devours small slugs, slugs' eggs, and various other creatures.

CENTRADENIA (sen-tra-de-ni-a. Melastomaceæ). Stove evergreens from Central America that require to be grown in a cool stove or intermediate house.

They do well in fibrous peat and loam with coarse sand. Increased by cuttings of side shoots taken in March or April, and inserted in sandy loam under glass with bottom heat.

SPECIES.

C. divaricata, white, May. 18 in.

C. floribunda, pale red, July. 18 in.

C. inæquilateralis, rose and white, April. 12 in.

CENTRANTHUS (ken-tran-thus. Valerianaceæ). Valerian. Hardy herbaceous perennials and annuals originally from the Mediterranean, useful for borders, rockeries and garden walls. Several varieties with white, purple or crimson flowers that bloom freely from June to July. *C. ruber* or red Valerian is often naturalised on chalky soil, increases rapidly by self-sown seed and in the border its expansion needs to be checked. Will grow well in any soil, but prefers a sunny position in dry limy mould. Divide fleshy roots in March, or allow self-propagation to take place. Plant any time from November to March, and if required on walls sow in crevices and cover with a little stiff soil. Both red and white varieties. Height 18 in.–3 ft.

CENTROPOGON (sen-tro-po-gon. Campanulaceæ). Effective and beautiful stove and greenhouse perennials of which the flowers resemble Lobelias.

Propagated by cuttings of young shoots with a heel, placed in sandy soil under a bell-glass with bottom heat.

Also by division of the roots. They require moisture and heat when growing, but to be fairly dry when at rest. Grow in sandy peat and rich fibrous loam.

SPECIES.

C. cordifolius, rose flowers in November. 2 ft.

C. surinamensis, rose, November. The fruits are said to be edible despite the acid poisonous qualities attributed to the order.

C. lucyanus, the best of the genus is a hybrid between *C. fastuosus* and *Siphocampylus betulæ folius*.

CENTROSEMA (sen-tro-se-ma. Leguminosæ). This small genus consists of evergreen stove climbers that may be propagated by seeds and cuttings and are grown in any good well-drained soil.

SPECIES.

C. brasilianum, rose flowers, June. 4 ft

C. dubium hastatum.

CEPHÆLIS (se-fe'-lis. Cinchonaceæ). Stove herbaceous plants. Jamaica 1793. Ipecacuanha of the chemist shop is the *Cephælis-ipecacuanha* root. This is found growing, with long spreading roots, in the damp shady forests of Brazil.

Culture.—Compost: lumpy loam, leafmould and sand in equal parts. Repot early spring. Shady position, warm moist atmosphere. Water freely during growing season, little after. Winter temperature, 65°; summer, 80°.

Propagation.—By division, or by cuttings of firm young shoots in sand; place in propagator, temperature, 60°.

SPECIES.

C. alba, white; *C. elata*, purple; *C. ipecacuanha*, white; *C. purpurea*, white, purple fruit; *violacea*, white, violet fruit.

CEPHALANTHUS (sef-al-anth'-us. Rubiaceæ). N. America. Loves peaty soil and moisture. *Propagate* by seeds and layers.

SPECIES.

C. occidentalis (Button Bush of eastern U.S.A. and Canada). Flowers creamy-white during August. 7–8 ft.

CEPHALARIA (kef-al-ar-ia. Dipsaceæ). *Kephale*, a head, in allusion to the dense head of flowers.

The genus contains several species all of which have sulphur-yellow scabious heads on slender 3 or 4 ft. stems. The deeply-cut leaves are rather disproportionately large in comparison with the flowers. *C. tartarica* is as good as any. July. Seeds or division.

CEPHALOTAXUS (sel-al-o-tax'-us. Taxaceæ). Hardy evergreen treees and shrubs, near allies of the yew, but with larger leaves. They thrive better in semi-shade than in full sun, and will even grow well under other trees, and have no objection to calcareous soil. *Propagate* by seed and by cuttings.

SPECIES.

C. drupacea. The "Cow's Tail Pine" of China and Japan. 10–12 ft. Very like a glorified yew.

C. d. fastigata (*Podocarpus koraiana*). Resembles the Irish yew in habit.

C. de prostrata. Dwarf spreading form, suitable for a large rock garden, or can be used as a low undergrowth.

C. Fortunei (China). 10–20 ft. A handsome species with leaves about 3 in. long. *See also* CONIFERS.

CEPHALOTUS (sef-al-o'-tus). From *Kephalotus*, headed, in reference to the flower-stalk bearing a compound terminal spike. Australian Pitcher-plant. Greenhouse herbaceous perennial. Australia, 1822.

Culture.—Compost: chopped sphagnum moss and peat in equal parts, and enough sharp sand to keep it well open. Repot early spring, shallow pans most suitable, give good drainage Position shady under bell-glass. Winter temperature 45°; summer 60°.

Propagation.—Offsets in March in cool house.

SPECIES.

C. follicularie, flowers white, pitchers about 3 in. long, green, purple and pink.

CERASTIUM (cer-as'-tium. Caryophylleæ). Chickweed. A family of hardy dwarf perennials of which many are weeds and some are suitable for carpets, rockeries or paved paths. They will thrive in any soil and seed freely, but division can be done in the autumn or spring if desired. The best are *C. Biebersteinii* and *C. tomentosum*, both white-flowered with silvery foliage, about 6 in. tall, and *C. alpinum*, the alpine variety (3–4 in.), all of which flower from June to July.

CERASUS. *See* PRUNUS.

CERATONIA (ser-a-to-nia. Leguminosæ). Carob Tree. Evergreen green house tree that is scarcely worth cultivating for ornament, but is economically valuable in the countries of which it is a native. There are several interesting legends connected with these "locusts" which must not be confused with the true locust trees of N. America and the West Indies, which in turn have no connection with each other.

The brown fruit pods are supposed to have been the food of St. John the Baptist in the desert, when he fed upon "locusts and wild honey"; hence the name often given to the trees is St. John's Bread. They also fed the Prodigal Son of biblical fame when he was obliged to eat the "husks" thrown to the swine. In more modern days they were eaten by the horses of the British Army in the Peninsular War and nowadays singers eat them to improve their voices. They are used to preserve other fruits and are also supposed to be the original carat weights used by jewellers. In sheltered districts the tree is hardy, but is more successful in the greenhouse. Increased by cuttings of ripened wood in sandy soil under a bellglass and thrives in fibrous loam and sand.

C. siliqua, the only species.

CERATOPTERIS (ser-a-top-ter-is. Filices). Very interesting stove equatic fern that is usually only of annual duration, but when carefully grown may be a biennial. It succeeds best in a pot of good loam, wholly submerged in a tank of warm water in a stove. It produces spores freely, or may be propagated by the young plants that form on all the fronds.

SPECIES.

C. thalictroides, with fronds of bright green. Popularly known as the Water Elk's Horn. 2½ ft.

CERATOSTIGMA (cer-at-ō-stig'-ma. Plumbagineæ). Deciduous flowering shrubs for sunny position and well-drained soil. *Propagate* by root division in April and by cuttings struck in pots in greenhouse or frame.

SPECIES.

C. Griffithii (Himalayas). A beautiful, but rather tender species with bronzy-red foliage and bright blue flowers. Not so useful as *C. Willmottianum*.

C. Polhilli (syn. *minus*), China. A rare species with slaty-blue flowers.

C. Willmottianum (China). Hardy dwarf (3–4 ft.) shrub for sunny walls, shrubbery or herbaceous border. Flowers rich blue, plumbago-like, from July until frost. One of the finest recent introductions from China.

CERCIDIPHYLLUM (ser'-si-di-fi'-lum. Trochodendraceæ). China and Japan. Deciduous trees with superb autumn foliage of distinct and elegant appearance. The foliage resembles that of the Judastree (Cercis). In its native lands this beautiful tree reaches to a height of 100 ft., but in this country it remains shrub-like. It needs a warm climate. Worth trying in districts where late spring frosts do not prevail. Likes chalky soil.

SPECIES.

C. japonicum—Japanese form.

C. sinense—Chinese form.

CERCIS (ser′-sis. Leguminosæ). Deciduous trees of great beauty and ease of cultivation, with pea-shaped flowers during May, on old wood, before the leaves are developed.

Culture.—Plant in May as soon as the expanding buds indicate that growth has recommenced. Young plants are preferable to more mature specimens, as older trees do not transplant well. They like a moist, deep sandy loam and sunny position. *Propagate* by seed, and by grafting for new and rare species.

SPECIES.

C. canadensis. The Redbud of North America. It is not very free flowering here.

C. chinensis. The Redbud of China. The largest of the genus, growing up to 50 ft. in nature. In cultivation shrubby only. It is a tender species, and only suitable for the garden in the south-west. Glossy leaves and pink flowers in May.

C. racemosa (China), 20 ft. Hardy distinct and very beautiful species with long racemes of rose-coloured flowers. One of the very finest flowering trees ever introduced to cultivation.

C. siliquastrum, Judas Tree. S. Europe and the Orient. 30–40 ft. This tree is a very beautiful sight in April and May when all the branches are covered with a profusion of its small rose-pink pea-shaped flowers. It is more suited to southern gardens than the cold ones of the north, where it may need a south wall. There are some fine specimens around London, and at Kew the largest specimen has attained to a height of 40 ft.

The Judas Tree receives it name from the tradition which says that it was the tree on which Judas Iscariot hanged himself.

CEREUS. *See* CACTUS.

CERINTHE (ser-inth-e. Boragineæ). Honeywort. Hardy annuals with showy flowers that are most effective in large gardens where they may have plenty of room. They grow in ordinary soil, and are raised from seeds sown in spring in sunny borders.

SPECIES.

C. minor and *C. major*, both with yellow flowers. The latter is frequently grown as a bee plant.

CEROPEGIA (ker-o-pe-ji-a. Asclepiadeæ). Greenhouse trailing plants. Ornamental foliage, more curious than beautiful. India, 1804.

Culture.—Compost, fibrous loam, leaf mould and sharp sand in equal parts Repot early spring. Sunny position, pots or hanging baskets from roof of house Winter temperature, 45°; summer, 60°

Propagation.—By cuttings of young shoots in sandy soil, place in propagator temperature, 60°.

SPECIES.

C. elegans, white, brown and purple.

C. Sandersonii, green.

C. Woodii, white and purple.

C. Thwaitesii, red, yellow and green.

CESTRUM (sĕs′-trum. Solanaceæ). Showy semi-evergreen wall shrubs from South America with tubular flowers.

Culture.—Compost: 2 parts loam, 1 part leaf-mould, 1 part silver sand. Repot early spring, or plant direct into bed. Prune only for shape, to trellis or wall in February; water freely during summer months. Winter temperature, 45°; summer temperature, 60°.

Propagation.—By cuttings of young shoots taken with heel of old wood, insert in sandy soil in propagator, temperature, 60°; summer.

SPECIES.

C. aurantiacum (Guatemala). Flowers bright orange-yellow. Suitable for growing under glass.

C. elegans (syn. *Habrothamnus elegans*), Mexico. Bright red flowers in clusters, over a long period. Has survived 20° frost on east wall. May be grown under glass.

C. Newellii (Mexico). Similar to *C. elegans*, with crimson flowers.

CHÆNOMELES. *See* CYDONIA.

CHÆNOSTOMA (ke-nos-to-ma. Scrophularineæ). A genus from the Cape of Good Hope, comprising one annual and several herbaceous perennial species. The former is raised from seed sown in pots or boxes and planted out as soon as the weather permits. The latter may be raised from seed sown in heat in March, later transplanted, after being hardened off in May, to warm sunny borders at the end of May. Cuttings may be taken in August and September. These should be potted and kept in a cool greenhouse for planting out the following summer.

SPECIES.

C. fatidum, annual, white flowers in June. 1 ft.

C. cordatum, white, June. 1 ft.

C. hispidum, white, June. 1 ft.

C. polyantha, lilac, yellow, June. 9 in.

CHÆROPHYLLUM (ke-ro-fil-lum. Umbelliferæ). Annual and biennial hardy plants that are raised from seed sown in a cold frame or in the open in ordinary garden soil.

SPECIES.

C. aromaticum (3 ft.), and *C. villosum* (2 ft.), both with white flowers in July.

CHAFERS. The Large Cockchafer (*Melolontha vulgaris*). " May Bug."

The Summer Chafer (*Rhizotrogus solstitialis*).

The two chafers of most economic importance are the "May Bug" and the Summer Chafer. At the same time neither is likely to prove a very serious pest in the garden.

The "May Bug."

DESCRIPTION. *Adult.*—Head and thorax black but with short silky-grey pubescence; wing cases chestnut-brown and dusted with white when newly hatched. There are five raised lines on each wing case. Abdomen produced into a point.

Larva.—Large white fleshy grubs with brown head and considerably swollen at posterior end. There are three pairs of legs on the anterior end.

LIFE-HISTORY. — The beetles may be seen in May flying along hedgerows at dusk. Eggs are laid about the beginning of June, each female depositing several small batches in the ground at a depth of from 6–8 in. On hatching out the little white grubs feed slowly and do little damage, but in their second and third years they attack the roots of corn and grass and are often very harmful in nurseries of forest trees. During the third year they pupate, but the perfect insect does not appear until the following spring, four years from the time of egg-laying.

METHODS OF CONTROL.—Somewhat difficult to control when once in the ground; constant hoeing will help to kill and expose the white grubs to attack from birds. A dressing of naphthalene at the rate of about 6 oz. per sq. yd. will be beneficial, but it should be watered in thoroughly or, if possible, applied before rain. In lawns and grass land good results may sometimes be obtained by watering the affected area with arsenate of lead. This should be done during warm periods, but while the ground is still moist and when the larvæ are near the surface. A thorough soaking of the turf should be aimed at.

The Summer Chafer.

DESCRIPTION. *Adult.*—1¾ in. in length, head and thorax dark, wing cases yellowish-brown; the whole insect being clothed with long tawny pubescence.

Larva.—Very similar to the preceding but smaller.

LIFE-HISTORY.—The adult beetles appear in July; they may be seen in thousands on suitable nights flying round trees and shrubs. Their life is comparatively short and they soon disappear, but not before the females have laid their eggs in the ground. On hatching out the young larvæ feed upon the fibrous roots of plants, but do not touch the roots of trees. The length of life is unknown but they are, in all probability, in the larval state for about eighteen months and the pupal state for six months.

METHODS OF CONTROL.—The same as for the "May Bug."

CHAIR. *See* FURNITURE.

CHALK as a fertiliser is particularly useful on light soils, where it can be used at twice the rate of ordinary lime. It is not so good on clay soils as lime, as it does nothing to improve the mechanical condition of the soil.

Chalk is really a soft, pure limestone, a large percentage of it being calcium carbonate. It was formed under the sea. Looked at through a microscope, it is seen to be made up chiefly out of an immense number of minute shells. Tiny creatures who lived and died in ancient seas left their shells to sink to the sea-bottom and accumulate with extreme slowness. Earth movements (*see under* CRUST OF THE

EARTH) slowly raised the chalk, wrinkling
it into hills and dales. The chalk so
dominates the scenery for fifty miles and
more around London that it becomes of
great scenic importance to dwellers in
our capital. Chemically, it has too little
variety. Physically, it holds a certain
measure of water in saturation, but drains
off the excess rather speedily. Where
chalk actually comes to the surface it will
therefore only support small plants; but
the vegetation of our chalk districts varies
astonishingly. The reason is that in one
place the chalk will come to the surface,
as in the South Downs. In another place
it will be covered by 2 or 3 ft. of earth,
enough to support Beech, a shallow-rooter.
In another place, as for instance near
Berkhamsted, it will be covered by perhaps 6 ft. of earth and support Oaks. All
depends on the earthly cover.

Many beautiful things flourish on chalk
such as the Wild Clematis, that shows its
wonderful growth of "Old Man's Beard"
in the autumn; the Cambridge-blue Succory; the Rest-harrow; Tansy; Milkwort;
Rock-rose; Yellow-wort; Vervain; and
yellow and white Stonecrop; but best and
most interesting of all, various kinds of
wild Orchids, some of them comparatively
rare like the Bee Orchis, and each one a
joy to the naturalist who finds them on
his way.

Chalk is used to make sour, acid soils
more fertile. Chalk (carbonate of lime) is
not, however, so valuable for this purpose
as lime. It is useful for forming drains
and a sublayer to a pathway. Some
plants succeed better than others on a
calcareous or chalk soil. These include
Clematis, Veronicas, Thymes, Delphiniums, Anchusa, Forsythia, etc.

CHALKPLANT. *See* GYPSOPHILA.

CHAMAEROPS. *See* TRACHYCARPUS.

CHAMÆCISTUS. *See* LOISELEURIA.

CHAMÆCYPARIS. *See* CUPRESSUS
LAWSONIANA.

CHAMÆDOREA (kam-e-dor-e-a.
Palmæ). *Chamai*, dwarf, and *dorea*, a
gift, implying that the nuts of these are
easily reached. These handsome palms
require stove temperature. *Propagate* by
seed when this is obtainable, sown in
thumb pots and repotted later as necessary. Also by suckers from the roots.

Grown in rich, sandy loam. Summer
temperature, 60°–80°; winter, 50°–60°.

SPECIES.

C. elatior, green. 9 ft.

C. elegans, green. 10 ft.

C. gracilis, green, white. 10 ft.

CHAMÆLIRIUM (kam-e-lir-i-um.
Liliaceæ). Wand Lily. Dwarf hardy
diœcious plants that like a shady position
on the rockery. All the species are
herbaceous perennials from N. America.

Propagate by division of the rhizomes or
by seeds in spring. Plant in well-drained
moist soil.

SPECIES.

C. carolinianum, a graceful plant with
white or pale yellow flowers in racemes
in May and June. 6 in.

C. luteum (syn. *carolinianum*).

CHAMÆROPS (kam-e-rops. Palmaceæ). Fan Palm. Greenhouse and half-
hardy palms. Leaves fan-shaped. Will
grow outdoors in the South of England if
planted in sheltered spot. S. Europe, 1731.

Culture.—Compost: 2 parts loam, 1 part
peat, 1 part silver sand. Repot early
spring, give good drainage. Winter temperature, 45°; summer, 60°.

Propagation.—By suckers removed from
plant at any time during spring and summer. May be grown from seed in propagator; temperature, 75°–80° in spring.

SPECIES.

C. humilis. Many varieties showing
differences in the leaf formation, colour
or construction.

CHAMECERASUS. *See* LONICERA.

CHAMFER. When designing stone
stairways on a large scale, the pier caps
and side coping are sometimes bevelled or
chamfered to give dignity to the design,
and to disperse water. Coping stones of
balustrades or walls are sometimes treated
in the same way.

CHAMOMILE. *See* ANTHEMIS.

CHARDS. A term used with reference
to Globe Artichokes. After the principal
heads have been used, the plants are cut
back. New growths form which, when
about 2 ft. high, are bound with straw and
earthed for blanching. After about six
weeks the shoots are ready and are called
chards.

CHARIEIS (kar-i-e-is. Compositæ).
Cape Aster. An interesting genus of one

pecies, *heterophylla*, a pretty hardy annual, which bears daisy-like flowers on slender stems throughout the summer. Seed may be sown in April in the open, or in March in a greenhouse, or on a hot-bed. Plant out in ordinary garden soil.

There are several varieties with white, blue, violet or crimson blooms and all are useful for carpeting or for massing in the rockery.

CHEILANTHES (ki-lan-thes. Filices).

A large genus of ferns that now include several minor genera such as Adiantopsis, Allosorus, Myriopteris, and Physapteris. The numerous species come from both temperate and tropical zones.

Propagate by spores which germinate quickly in a warm damp temperature. Pot up in a compost of equal parts of loam and peat with a little sand and a few pieces of charcoal. These ferns are often regarded as difficult to grow, but with a little care they are quite successful. As many of the species have woolly or finely-powdered leaves, they require careful watering, so that the water does not touch the fronds. They die off quickly if allowed to become dry, or if stagnant water is allowed to remain in the soil. The pots should be half-filled with crocks to ensure perfect drainage. The plants are troubled by insect pests, such as snow fly and thrips, which must be prevented by fumigation or vaporising. Slugs also are troublesome, unless the pots are stood upon crushed coke, or sifted ashes over which the slugs do not like to crawl.

SPECIES.

C. argentea, greenhouse, covered with white powder, fronds, 5–8 in.

C. farinosa, powdery, fronds, 3–12 in.

C. fragrans (syn. *odora* and *suaveolens*), fronds, 2–4 in.

C. gracillima, greenhouse, fronds, 4–12 in.

C. languinosa (syn. *gracilis*), very woolly, hardy.

C. microphylla, stove, fronds 4–12 in. There are several varieties of which *micromera* is perhaps the best.

C. myriophylla, stove, *C. m. elegans*, very handsome and very much cut. Fronds, 4–9 in.

C. tomentosa (syn. *Bradburrii*), very woolly. Fronds, 6–12 in. The species

number about sixty, but the greater part of them are not in general cultivation.

CHEIRANTHUS (ky-er-an-thus. Cruciferæ). Wallflowers.

From *cheir*, hand; *antheros*, flower. Supposed to have reference to the habit of carrying the sweet-smelling wallflower in the hand as a nose-gay. Really hardy perennials, but usually treated as biennials, as they are so easily raised from seed, and old plants are liable to die out during the winter. Wallflowers are undoubtedly among the most popular spring flowers, and can be had in a good range of shades and tints of yellows, browns, and blood-reds, orange, etc.

Fire King, Grenadier, Crimson Monarch, Vulcan, Orange Prince and Gold Reef are about the best. Sow in May or June, in moist soil, keep the seed-bed moist until seedlings are through; transplant into firm soil 9 in. apart when 3–5 leaves formed. If the seedlings have a long tap-root, shorten it half-way, to induce fibrous roots. Keep soil well hoed during summer, and plant into flowering quarters in October–November.

Cheiranthus cheiri, Early Wonder, is a new section of double-flowered kinds, which bloom in 6 months from sowing, and give a good percentage of double-flowered plants. Other double-flowered forms are Double Rocket, which gives one tall spike per plant, and the double-branching varieties.

There are two good biennial species of Cheiranthus, both of which may be sown early in spring, and treated as hardy annuals, or if sown in July–August will flower during the early summer of the following season. Cutting off the seed heads as soon as the flowers fade will induce a good second show.

The species referred to are *Cheiranthus Allionii*, orange, 1–1¼ ft., and *Cheiranthus linifolius*, mauve, 1 ft.

Species for rockeries are as follows:

C. Allionii, the Siberian Wallflower, is becoming well known in cultivation as a bedding plant for its brilliant masses of orange-gold, which are well abloom in early May, and continue most of the summer. Easily raised from seed in summer to flower the following year. Best treated as a biennial.

C. alpinus, the Norwegian Wallflower,

is a dwarfish plant with flowers a clear lemon-yellow. Seed or cuttings.

C. cheiri. Harpur Crewe. A most desirable miniature double wallflower, golden-yellow and sweet scented. It grows a foot high, and produces more flowers when starved in a poor dry soil than when living richly. *Propagate* by cuttings of the new shoots in summer.

C. linifolius. A little Spanish Wallflower with lilac-pink flowers. Once established in the rock-garden it will seed itself, popping up in unexpected places year by year. Reputed to be biennial, but will last several years. 6 in.

C. mutabilis. The Changeable Wallflower. The flower changes with age from paler shades to a red-wine purple. It comes from Madeira, and is liable to disappear for good in cold winters. It is increased by cuttings. A few rooted plants should be kept in pots in a frame to replace losses out of doors.

CHEIRANTHUS KEWENSIS. *See* WALLFLOWER (winter flowering).

CHELIDONIUM (kel-i-do'-ni-um. Papaveraceæ). Celandine. *Chelidon*, a swallow, in allusion to the flowers opening on the arrival of this bird, and the plant drying up when it departs.

Hardy herbaceous perennials that thrive in any soil and are increased by division. The best known of the genus, *C. majus*, the Greater Celandine or Swallow wort, as distinct from the Lesser Celandine (*Ranunculus Ficaria*) contains a virulent poison in the shape of a yellow juice that is said to be a remedy for warts.

The double form of *majus*, *m. flore pleno*, bears yellow flowers in late summer, and is used for the wild garden. *C. m. laciniatum* is a very jagged-leaved form of *majus*.

CHELONE (ke-lo-ne. Scrophularinaceæ). Turtle head. Handsome border plants of North American origin, allied to Pentstemon and flowering in the late summer and autumn. Best position is in the sun or semi-shade in moist sandy loam with humus, but will grow in any place. Increase by seeds, by cuttings or by division of roots in spring or autumn. Plant any time from November onwards. The type is pink-blossomed but white varieties, *C. alba*, and red, such as *C. coccinea* and

C. obliqua, can be obtained. Best known is the scarlet *C. barbata* now allied to the Pentstemons.

CHENOPODIUM (ken-o-po-di-um Chenopodiaceæ). Goosefoot. A large genus of hardy annuals and perennials that are more highly valued economically than they are for their beauty.

SPECIES.

The majority of the species are weeds and of no garden value.

C. Ambrosioides is the Mexican Tea Plant, and its variety *anthelminticum* provides an oil used as a vermifuge.

C. atriplicis (syn. *purpurascens*), with purple flowers in August on 5 ft. stems, is a hardy annual that is used for decoration Its shoots are angular and reddish, and its leaves are covered with rosy-violet powder.

C. Bonus Henricus, popularly known as Good King Henry or Mercury, is frequently grown in Cambridgeshire and Lincolnshire for salads, or as a substitute for spinach.

The seeds of *C. Quinoa* are cooked and eaten in Peru and Chile, but they are not palatable to Europeans.

All the species are easily raised from seed which, however, do not ripen on the plants in England. They grow freely in any good soil.

See also MERCURY.

CHERRY. Varieties of cherries grown in English gardens have been derived from two wild species. They are *Prunus Cerasus*, the Wild Cherry, and *Prunus Avium*, the Gean. From the former come the Morello, Duke, and Kentish varieties, and from the latter the Gean, Heart, and Bigarreau. Cherries are generally grown as standards or as fan-trained trees, but it is also possible to train them as bushes or as cordons.

Soil.—As is well known, Kent is the most favourable district for cherry culture. The soil there is rich, yet on the light side. Heavy clays and light gravels are not suitable. A good depth of cultivation is necessary so that the roots may have a deep run and will not become dried out in hot weather.

Position.—Cherries mature before any other hardy orchard fruit and consequently require plenty of sunshine. A

outhern aspect is therefore best. East or
rest walls are suitable for fan-trained
weet cherries, whilst north walls are
uitable for varieties of the Morello
lass.

Distances Apart.

Standards—25 ft.
Bushes—15 ft.
Fan-trained (on walls)—12–15 ft.
Cordons—2 ft.

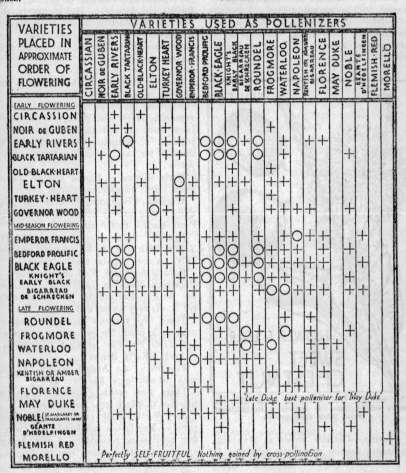

CHERRY POLLINATION TRIALS.

The varieties on the left hand were pollinated with pollen of the varieties placed at the head of the chart.

An attempt (based on many observations) has been made to place the varieties in their *approximate order of flowering.*

+ means fruit matured successfully in trials by W. O. Backhouse, M. B. Crane, C. H. Hooper and others at the John Innes Horticultural Institution, Merton, Surrey.

O means failed to mature, fruit being SELF-STERILE or because the varieties were found by M. B. Crane to be INCOMPATIBLE.

(*From the Journal of Wye Agricultural College for 1931.*)

Planting.—Ground must be prepared to a depth of 3 ft. prior to planting. Trees on walls should have a border prepared at least 4 ft. wide.

Manures.—Manure should not be given, except on the poorest ground. Dressings of sulphate of potash and bonemeal applied in alternate years during early spring at the rate of 2 oz. per sq. yd. are recommended.

FRUIT

FLOWER & LEAF
SWEET CHESTNUT

The wayside tree which in some districts bears edible nuts. It makes a magnificent trunk when fully grown.

Pruning.—Cherries grown as standards or bushes require very little pruning. It is necessary to see that such trees are provided with about six good main branches set at regular angles. This should be done as soon as possible, because heavy cutting on established trees frequently results in bleeding, or " gumming " as it is generally called.

Fan-Trained.—Duke and Bigarreau varieties should be treated as recommended for fan-trained plums. It is not generally appreciated that Morello cherries bear their best fruit on one-year-old wood. They should be treated as recommended for fan-trained apricots, being careful not to allow the young wood to become overcrowded.

Propagation.—Budding or grafting, preferably the former. For standards the wild cherry stock is used. For bushes the Mahaleb is probably the best. For fan-trained Morello trees the Mazzard is giving excellent results.

VARIETIES.

The following are the best varieties for growing as standards:

Napoleon Bigarreau. An August variety, vigorous, hardy and prolific, with large juicy fruit. Is self-sterile, and therefore requires a pollinator. Early Rivers is suitable for this purpose. Fruit red to yellow.

Early Rivers. Ripens end of June. Fruit black, an excellent flavour.

Waterloo. Beginning of July. A partially fertile variety of first-class flavour. Fruit black. Self-sterile.

Kentish Bigarreau (Amber Heart). Yellow with red flush, ripening end of July. A very popular market variety.

Suitable for South Wall (Fan-trained).—Bigarreau Napoleon (July–Aug.). Governor Wood. (Early July, pale yellow with red flush, very sweet and juicy.)

These two varieties should be planted next each other for pollination purposes.

Suitable for West or East Wall (Fan trained).—Early Rivers.

Florence. An August variety, yellow with red mottlings, fine flavour.

These two varieties should be grown together to effect cross pollination.

For North Wall (Fan-trained).—This variety—Morello—is self-fertile and therefore requires no pollinator. A very heavy cropper, the fruit being ripe in August. Valuable for preserving.

See also PRUNUS and FRUIT POLLINATION.

CHERRY AND PEAR SLUGWORM

(*Eriocampa limacina*). DESCRIPTION. *Adult.*—Black with dusky wings. *Larva.*—Olive-green in colour, but covered with a black slime. The head end is enlarged but it tapers posteriorly. These characteristics have given it the popular name of "Slugworm."

LIFE-HISTORY.—The sawflies appear in June and lay their eggs in slits along the

eins of the leaf. On hatching out the
lugworms feed upon the upper surface of
he leaves, causing pale patches which
radually turn brown, dry out and some-
imes crack. When full grown the slime
isappears and the larva becomes paler
n colour, eventually going into the ground
o pupate. A second generation appears
n late summer and the damage is then
ften more serious as the drying up of the

CHERRY, DOUBLE WHITE. *See*
Prunus Avium flore pleno.
CHERRY, JAPANESE. *See* Prunus
P. Serrulata.
CHESHUNT COMPOUND. Used
as a remedy for fungous diseases that occur
in certain popular plants such as China
Asters. It consists of a mixture of 2 parts
of powdered copper sulphate with 11 parts
of fresh ammonium carbonate, each being

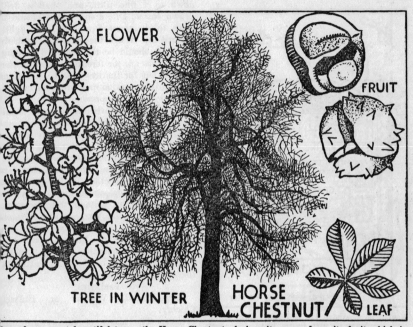

FLOWER

FRUIT

TREE IN WINTER

HORSE
CHESTNUT LEAF

One of our most beautiful trees, the Horse Chestnut, derives its name from its fruit which is
coarse or rough and not good for eating. Its buds are sticky in early spring.

leaf prevents the young wood from ripening properly. This second generation on
becoming full grown also goes into the
ground, but though they spin a tight
cocoon round themselves they do not pupate
till the following spring.
METHODS OF CONTROL.—A poison wash
such as arsenate of lead will kill the larvæ,
or one of the contact washes such as
nicotine or derris will also give good
results. It is said that lime sprinkled
under the bushes when the larvæ are entering the soil to pupate, will help to control
them.
CHERRY, BIRD. *See* Prunus.

carefully weighed and then kept in a
closely-corked glass or stone jar for 24
hours, after which 1 oz. is diluted with
2 gal. of water. It should be used immediately and should be kept away from any
metal receptacle.
CHESTNUT, HORSE. *See* Aesculus.
CHESTNUT, SWEET (*Castanea
sativa*). The Sweet, or Spanish, Chestnut
is a native of S. Europe, Asia Minor and
N. Africa. It is not grown in this country
purposely for the production of food as
it is in Italy and Spain, where millions
of bushels are gathered yearly. Most of
this produce is ground into flour.

Soil.—There is no finer specimen tree for light sandy soil. At Shrublands Park, Ipswich, there is a tree 100 ft. in height. Cold, wet soils do not suit the Chestnut.

Planting.—This may be done in the dormant season, between October and March. No special pruning is necessary.

VARIETIES.

Special varieties are not usually planted in England. Marron de Lyon is said to

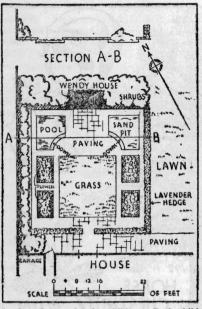

SECTION A-B

WENDY HOUSE
SHRUBS
POOL   SAND PIT
A   PAVING   B
LAWN
FLOWERS   GRASS
LAVENDER HEDGE
PAVING
GARAGE   HOUSE
SCALE ████ OF FEET

A plan of a garden for children. Each child has its own flower bed.

be one of the best. It is propagated by grafting on to seedling stocks.

Historical.—The Sweet Chestnut is supposed to have been introduced to this country by the Romans.

See also CASTANEA.

CHICORY, or Succory (*Cichorium intybus*). Compositæ. Although a native plant, it is only during the last century that the value of chicory as an article of diet has been fully realised in this country.

On the Continent it is freely grown for the sake of the root which is dried, ground and mixed with or used as a substitute for coffee.

It is now recognised that when forced and blanched chicory makes a most useful and acceptable "white" salad, and as it is obtainable in winter it is especially appreciated.

Culture.—An open position away from trees should be well broken up, and if possible should have been well manured for the previous crop. At the end of April or early May the surface should be raked down to a fine tilth, and shallow drills drawn out at 1 ft. apart. Seed should be sown thinly about ½ in. deep, and lightly covered in. When they are 1 in. high the seedlings should be thinned to 8 in. apart if the roots are for forcing; otherwise they may be left for the leaves to be cut green. The only attention required during the summer is the suppression of weeds. In October or early November the roots should be lifted and cleaned of the thongs and outer leaves, and then stored in sand in a cool, dry place, until required for forcing.

About 21 days before blanched leaves are needed, some of the stored roots should be packed closely together in boxes or deep pots, so that they are buried to the crown in fine damp soil. Stand them in a cool dark shed or cellar, and syringe occasionally with tepid water. Unless the soil becomes dust-dry give no more water at the roots, and a quantity of crisp blanched leaves should then be ready for cutting at the end of three weeks.

VARIETIES.

Large-Rooted, Witloof or Brussels Chicory.

Uses.—The leaves of chicory are used raw in salads, either green freshly gathered, or blanched. They are cut into shreds and mixed with vinegar and oil.

CHILDREN'S GARDEN. This is a feature which is becoming more important in garden design. If the garden is for small children it should be placed in view of house windows. Shade—either tree shade or a small arbour—is necessary. Dry walks and a paved area on which to play will be required as well as grass space. A small pool or rill, very shallow, will add interest, and a sand pit surrounded by paving will be an asset. Individual gardens surrounded by paving or a dry pathway will encourage children to take a real interest in plant growth. See that hese individual gardens are in a place where there is no danger of harm coming to them from balls and games, but yet are accessible to the sun and rain to permit of flower growth. A swing is also an added attraction. A hedge, trellis or shrubs should screen the garden from cold winds.

Some plants are easier to grow than others and a list is given here of those which will be most useful for the children's beds and borders. Clarkia, Coreopsis, Candytuft, Alyssum, Asters, Honesty, Kochia, Love-in-a-mist, Linum (flax), Mignonette, Nasturtiums, Marigolds, Pansies, Primroses, Wallflowers, Zinnias.

CHIMAPHILA (ki-maf-la. Ericaceæ). These little hardy herbaceous perennials remain green throughout the winter, and may be grown in a moist place in a partly shaded position in the rockery. Increased by division of the roots in October. They like a compost of peat and sand, and require to be planted in spring.

SPECIES.

C. maculata, with procumbent shoots, leathery leaves, green and white above and red beneath, and white flowers in June. Spotted Winter Green (syn. *Pyrola maculatæ*).

C. umbellata, with glossy leaves and white or pinkish-red flowers (syn. *C. corymbosa* and *Pyrola umbellata*).

CHIMONANTHUS (ki-mo-nan'-thus. Calycanthaceæ). Syn. *Calycanthus praecox*. Chinese Winter Sweet. Hardy deciduous shrub producing its very fragrant flowers in winter. About 10 ft.

Culture.—Plant in October or March in deep moist sandy loam in very sunny sheltered position, such as south wall. *Propagate* by layers in August, and by suckers and seed in spring. Pruning consists of shortening the stronger twigs, and cutting out completely the weaker and overcrowding ones. This should be done by end of February, thereby allowing time for new growths to be made, to produce next winter's flowers.

SPECIES.

C. fragrans (China). Flowers, pale yellow, stained purplish, on leafless branches, during December and January.

C. fragrans grandiflorus. A variety with larger flowers and of a better yellow,

but not so fragrant as the type. The Winter Sweet is one of those delightful old shrubs which ought to find a place upon the south wall of every dwelling-house. It blooms at a time of year when fragrant flowers are very scarce. A few twigs with the flowers on them will scent a fair-sized room with their sweetness, and last quite a long time. For foliage *Berberis Aquifolium* (*mahonia*) associates suitably.

CHINESE BELLFLOWER. See PLATYCODON.

CHIOGENSIS (kǐ-ō-gen-sis. Vacciniaceæ). Creeping Snowberry. Evergreen creeping shrub with very small leaves, and white flowers and berries. Plant in shady position in moist lime-free soil.

CHIONANTHUS (kī-ō-nan'-thus. Oleaceæ). Handsome, distinguished deciduous flowering shrubs; white flowers freely produced during June and July.

Culture.—Plant October to November in moist loamy soil and sunny position. The only pruning needed is to trim to shape after flowering, if thought necessary. *Propagate* by seeds, and layering in September. Cuttings may also be struck in close frame during July and August.

SPECIES.

C. retusa (the Chinese Fringe-Tree). One of the most attractive of flowering shrubs, grows to 30–40 ft. in China, and has been described as a "dome of soft, fleecy snow."

C. virginica (the Fringe-Tree of the eastern U.S.A.). Perfectly hardy and one of the finest flowering shrubs ever introduced from N. America. Flowers white, slightly fragrant, freely produced in May and June. Foliage bright yellow in autumn.

CHIONODOXA (Liliaceæ). Glory of the Snow. Hardy bulbs. First introduced in 1877.

Culture.—Plant the bulbs about 1 in. apart in September. They like a position in sunshine in light sandy loam and are specially suited to rock gardens, though they can also be used very effectively for edgings to a mixed border. About every three years, the bulbs should be lifted and replanted, otherwise they become overcrowded. Chionodoxas can also be cultivated in pots in a soil composed of equal parts peat, loam, leaf-mould and sand. A 5 in. pot will take 12 bulbs planted 1 in. deep. Pots should be stood outdoors in a cold frame where they can be covered with ashes until the tops begin to grow. They are best if allowed to remain in the cold frame until January, and then brought indoors to a sunny window or into a cool greenhouse. They can be increased by offsets from the bulbs replanted in the same way as the larger bulbs, or if preferred, by seeds sown ¼ in. deep in boxes of light soil in a cold frame in summer. The varieties generally cultivated are *Chionodoxa sardensis*, a rich gentian-blue with white eye, probably the best variety known at present for gardens. *C. luciliæ*, also blue and white eye, but not quite so striking as *Sardensis*.

CHIONOGRAPHIS (ki-on-o-graf-is. Liliaceæ). This pretty herbaceous perennial has a delicate flower spike, like a brush of snow. Although theoretically hardy, it should be protected in winter with a frame.

Propagate by seeds and division. Plant in loam and peat.

SPECIES.

The only species is *C. japonica*, with white flowers in May and June. 12 in.

CHIPPINGS. *See* GRANITE CHIPPINGS.

CHIRITA (kir-i-ta. Gesneriaceæ). Stove herbaceous and evergreen plants. Perennial. China, 1843.

Culture.—Compost: loam, peat and leaf-mould in equal parts, with a good supply of sharp sand and a little charcoal. Repot, March, shake out old soil slightly root-prune and pot in smaller pots, shift on into larger ones as plants progress. Liquid manure is beneficial when buds appear. Sunny position on shelf near glass. Winter temperature 60°; summer, 80°.

Propagation.—By cuttings of young shoots in sand in propagator, spring; by leaf cuttings on pans of sand in summer, in propagator, temperature, 70°, or by seed in March in propagator, temperature, 70°.

SPECIES.

C. depressa, violet.
C. Moonii, purple.
C. sinensis, lilac.
C. Walkeri, yellow.

CHIVES (Allium schœnoprasum) (Lilliaceæ). A perennial herb used for flavouring. Makes a good edging for a vegetable plot. *See* HERBS.

CHLIDANTHUS (kli-dan'-thus. Amaryllideæ). Pretty bulbous plants that resemble narcissi. They may be grown in a warm border in front of a greenhouse or at the foot of a wall, during the summer, but they so hate the wet that they need to be taken up for the winter and kept dry until April in a pot of dryish sand or light soil.

Propagate by offsets which increase so rapidly that it is rather difficult to keep bulbs of flowering size.

Grow in loam, leaf-mould and peat, with a little sand.

C. fragrans, sweet-scented, yellow flowers in June. 10 in.

CHLORA (klor'-a. Gentianeæ). Yellow Wort. This small genus of neat little plants mainly annuals. *Propagate* by seeds under glass in March, or out of doors in April. They will grow anywhere, but lengthen their duration according to the richness of the soil.

SPECIES.

C. imperfoliata (syn. *sessiliflora*), yellow, June. 1 ft.

C. perfoliata, Yellow Centaury (syn. *grandiflora*), bears flat-topped trusses of beautiful flowers in June and July. 6–12 in.

CHLORANTHUS (klor-an-thus. Chloranthaceæ). A rare, handsome flowering shrub from China and Japan with pale green leaves and small white flowers, followed by bright red fruit, remaining on the plant for many weeks.

C. brachystachys, the only hardy species.

CHLORIS (klor'-is. Gramineæ). Green Grass. Pretty annual hardy and half-hardy grasses, the former being suitable for the border, while the latter are very decorative grown in pots in the greenhouse.

Sow seeds under glass in April, or in the open in May. Grow in light sandy soil in a sunny position.

C. barbata and *C. elegans* are sometimes used as bouquet grasses by florists. 12 in.

CHLOROGALUM (klor-ō-gal-um. Liliaceæ). Soap Plant. The only grown species of this genus of bulbs allied to

Ornithogalums is *C. pomeridianum*, a pretty distinct species that is scarcely hardy enough to withstand the winter without protection.

Propagate by offsets or seeds sown in a frame in spring. The bulbs are used as soap in California. It bears white flowers veined with purple in June. 2 ft.

CHLOROPHYTUM (klor - of - īt - um. Liliaceæ). Evergreen greenhouse and stove perennials of easy cultivation. Increased by seeds, division of the roots in spring or by suckers. They grow well in rich porous loam.

Summer temperature, 60°–70°; winter, 55°–60°.

SPECIES.

C. arundinaceum. White flowers. July. 2 ft.

C. elatum (syn. *Anthericum* and *Phalangium elatum*), with white flowers in July; has a variegated variety that is used for summer bedding under the name of *Anthericum variegatum.*

C. orchidastrum. White. July. 1½ ft.

CHOICE OF SITE. This being the very first step in the making of a garden it should have careful consideration. The chief horticultural points to observe before deciding on the site will be found under ASPECT. The deciding factors in the choice of the site are usually dependent on the needs of the household, and it therefore behoves the owner to make the most of the peculiarities of his own particular plot.

CHOISYA (shwŏiz′-i-a. Rutaceæ). Mexico. Beautiful evergreen shrubs with lustrous green leaves and hawthorn-scented white flowers from December to spring and later, according to season and locality. Makes a fine hedge in mild districts, but requires a sunny wall generally, and has passed unscathed through 30° of frost in such positions around London. One of the very few Mexican shrubs hardy under such conditions.

Culture.—Plant in April or September in ordinary garden soil. The only pruning needed is to cut out old wood and trim generally, about April, if considered desirable.

Propagate by cutting of half-ripened wood placed in gentle heat, or older wood in cold frame, and by layers in August.

C. ternata. The only species, 6–10 ft. Known as the Mexican Orange Flower, so named from the flowers resembling those of the orange. A fine shrub for large pots and tubs. Associates well with *Wistaria multijuga.*

CHORIZEMA (kor-iz-ē′-ma. Leguminosæ.) Beautiful evergreen greenhouse sub-shrubs with pea-shaped flowers. Useful for training on trellises, or pillars, or wire frames. They are amongst the most ornamental of greenhouse plants.

Propagate by seed sown in a slight hotbed or warm house in March, in sandy peat and loam. Also by cuttings of short, firm side-shoots taken off at any time before midsummer and inserted in sand beneath a bell-glass. They require a compost of 3 parts of peat to 1 of fibrous loam with some sharp silver sand and charcoal.

For the best results they need to be firmly potted and to have perfect drainage. Water copiously, but do not allow stagnant water to remain in the soil. When fresh growth commences, they should be repotted and, if necessary, cut back. To induce early flowering they may be allowed rather more than normal greenhouse temperature, but when flowering begins they should be put into cooler quarters.

SPECIES.

C. angustifolium (syn. *capillipes*, *denticulatum*). Orange and red flowers in April. 1½ ft.

C. cordatum (syn. *flavum*, *Lowii* and *superbum*). Red and yellow flowers in April. 1 ft.

C. varium. Red and yellow, with a fine variety. *Chandleri.*

The other species are equally good and, by a careful selection of varieties, plants may be had in bloom during the winter and spring months.

CHRISTMAS ROSE. *See* HELLEBORUS.

CHRISTMAS-TREE. *See* PICEA EXCELSA.

CHRIST'S THORN. *See* PALIURUS.

CHRYSALIDOCARPUS (kris-a-lid-o-car-pus. Palmæ). A genus of palms now allied with Areca and represented by one species only, *C. lutescens* (syn. *Areca lutescens*). This is an elegant stove palm with light green fronds and is increased by seeds. It thrives in loam and leaf-soil in quite small pots. Height, 30 ft.

CHRYSANTHEMUM (Japanese Chrysanthemums, Ox-Eye Daisy, Marguerite, Pyrethrum, Corn Marigold, Shasta Daisy). Compositæ. Greenhouse and hardy annuals, perennials, and shrubs. The Japanese Chrysanthemum is the one most commonly called chrysanthemum.

TAKE CUTTINGS BELOW A JOINT AND REMOVE TWO LOWER LEAVES

The increase of plants by cuttings is one of the most important methods. Sandy soil, a moist atmosphere, and shade from bright sunshine are important conditions.

CULTIVATION OF HARDY AND GREEN-HOUSE CHRYSANTHEMUMS.

Japanese Varieties.—These can be purchased as plants in small pots at any time after the end of January, or if preferred, unrooted cuttings can be purchased from the end of November onwards. Those who have already some plants in pots under glass can take their own cuttings, and the method of growing throughout is as follows:

The cuttings are taken from the base of the plants as soon as they are ready, which is some time in midwinter. They are prepared in the ordinary way for insertion. (*See also* PROPAGATING PLANTS.)

The cuttings are put into shallow boxes or pots in a compost of four parts loam, one part leaf-mould, one part coarse sand mixed well together and passed through a ¼ in. mesh sieve. After the boxes are filled, put an extra layer of sand on the top, then as each cutting is put in, a little of this top sand will fall to the bottom of the hole, and if the cutting rests on this pure sand it is not likely to decay.

Water the cuttings and place them under glass or in the propagating frame, which should be at a temperature of at least 45°. On very bright days the cuttings may need a spray overhead, but as a rule they will require no further attention until the roots have formed, which will be in about the third or fourth week. The formation of roots will be indicated by the commencement of new growth at the top of the cutting. As soon as the roots have formed, harden-off the cuttings by putting the boxes into a cool greenhouse for a few days. The plants can then be put into small pots (2 in.), using a compost rather similar to that used for the cuttings but with the addition of a little extra well-decayed manure and some old mortar rubble. Wood ashes can also be added to this compost if available. The mixture should be passed through a ½ in. mesh sieve, and the coarse siftings used for the bottom of the pots, with the finer soil above. Another recommended compost is as follows: Three parts fibrous loam, one part horse manure, one part decayed tree leaves, one part coarse silver sand, a quarter part finely-ground bones, the same of dissolved bones, one part charcoal and wood ashes and a little soot.

Pot on by Degrees.

After potting, stand the plants in a cool greenhouse near the glass, but be sure they are away from sharp frosts. By the end of March the plants should be ready to put into 5–6 in. pots, the stronger plants being put into the larger pots. It is best, however, to leave the plants, until the roots actually fill the pots they are already in. The compost for the larger pots is improved if bonemeal and lime are included. One of the largest growers recommends a mixture of four parts good loam, one part decayed manure, half a part leaf-mould and quarter part coarse silver sand, and a little bonemeal and lime, mixed and stored for a fortnight before being used. Pot the plants fairly firmly and stand them in a cold frame which should be well protected at night from frosts.

It is always best to keep the frame quite close for a few days after potting, but after this a little air may be admitted, so long as frosts are not present. Plants may be sprayed overhead but should not be made too wet or allowed to remain wet over night. On the fourth day they can be watered, soaking the soil well in each pot. After this look at the plants every day, but only water those that have become dry, and water as a rule early in the day and not late in the evening. Watch for green fly, and for the leaf miner maggot. The leaf miner maggot makes light silvery-brown markings over the leaves by boring between the two surfaces of the leaf and eating out the green matter. When once the leaf miner maggot is in the leaf, it cannot be killed, except by pinching between the finger and thumb, or by cutting off the leaf and burning it. It is best, therefore, to spray with a reliable insecticide to prevent the fly laying eggs on the leaves, and the most useful insecticide for the purpose is probably nicotine. Half an ounce of nicotine to two gallons of rain water is very effective.

As soon as the plants begin to grow well, the lights should be taken from the frames to keep the plants as hardy and as stocky as possible. About the end of May the plants will be right for a final potting. This again should not take place until the smaller pots are filled with roots. The compost is similar to that used for the 6 in. pots, although the addition of a little special chrysanthemum fertiliser will help. At this stage, the chrysanthemum plants will need water about every three or four days, and they may occasionally need to be sprayed overhead on bright, warm days. The pots can be stood outside as soon as there is no danger of frost, in rows alongside the garden path or on a vacant plot of ground. It may be advisable to stand them on a bed of ashes or on boards to prevent worms and ants getting into the bottom of the pots. In any case, they should stand in full sunshine. A stake should be put into each pot, and if many pots are being grown, it is generally advisable to put a strong stick at the end of each row and to stretch a wire along the row from stake to stake so there is no danger of the pots being blown over by high winds.

"Stopping" and "Disbudding."

All side shoots should be removed as they appear and feeding, watering and spraying with insecticide must be done regularly, and as necessary. The end of July is usually early enough to start feeding with artificial fertiliser. By the beginning of August a number of the plants will show flower buds. These should be retarded for a time by leaving a few of the side shoots round the bud. Do not leave the side shoots too long or the bud will be too late and the side shoots will absorb too much of the nourishment. About the middle of August the cultivator will examine the plants and secure buds on each of the Japanese Chrysanthemums, particularly those which are intended to flower at the time of the November shows. The question of disbudding and pinching chrysanthemums is one which is a common stumbling-block to the amateur gardener. As a rule, several flower buds form at the end of each shoot and also in the axils of the upper leaves, and unless some of these buds are removed, the flowers that come will be small and possibly a bad shape. It is therefore necessary, to obtain perfect blooms, to rub off with the finger and thumb all the buds except one or two of the best and the most promising. Chrysanthemums vary considerably according to variety in the way they form their buds and flowers, and in some cases it is better to keep the top bud of the spike and in other cases it is better to keep the side buds.

The details of this stopping cannot be given here, but the growers of show chrysanthemums almost invariably give, with their lists, a key to the best methods of stopping each variety. Stopping means pinching out the tiniest possible portion of the leading shoot. The plant immediately begins to grow side shoots, that is to say, it makes an earlier "break" than it would naturally.

Some varieties should not be stopped in this way, but should be allowed to grow in a perfectly natural manner and to flower on the middle stem, but other varieties will do better if they are pinched and allowed to form three or four side shoots. When the growers talk of "securing" or "taking" buds, it means that the other buds are rubbed off and only certain ones allowed to remain. Sometimes it is the central bud which is left, which is called the "first crown" bud; sometimes this bud is pinched out and the surrounding buds are allowed to develop: these are the "second crown" buds. (Reference to the diagram under DISBUDDING will assist the amateur to understand these points). The object of all this stopping and pinching is to obtain fine large blooms but all chrysanthemums can, if preferred, be grown more naturally, to provide a large number of blooms of smaller size.

House the Plants in September.

The Japanese Chrysanthemums grown for exhibition will need to be housed as soon as the plants are ready, that is to say, usually about the second week of September. It is not at all safe to leave them out in the open beyond September as there is danger of damage by frost. When they are brought into the greenhouse, they should be immediately sprayed with a good fungicide as a preventive against mildew and light and air should be given at all times.

Never let the temperature drop below 45°, and as far as possible keep it fairly even in the greenhouse. Also, never allow the plants to become dry, particularly when the flowers are open. When the flowers commence to show colour, butter muslin is sometimes put up inside the glass of the greenhouse, under the roof, to counteract excessive moisture and also to act as a shade. It is a very useful method of avoiding "damping," and it also makes it unnecessary to shade the house on the outside.

Some of the finest modern Japanese Chrysanthemums suitable for exhibition are as follows:

Mrs. E. Alston, pure yellow.
Salmon Turner, salmon-pink.
Avon, orange-amber.

Bresil, orange-bronze.
Madame Maggie Stirling, crimson with chocolate reverse.
Mersey, clear salmon.
Orinthia, blush-pink tinged with pale yellow.
Red Cavell, red.
Rise of Day, apricot tinged red, buff reverse.
Severn, chestnut with golden reverse.
Thames, blush-mauve, silver reverse.
Trent, white.
H. J. Jones, bright chestnut shaded rose.
Lady Findlay, ivory white.
Mrs. F. C. Maples, golden yellow.

Cultivation of Decorative Chrysanthemums.

For ordinary decoration in the greenhouse and for use as cut flowers, chrysanthemums can be grown by anyone who owns a greenhouse, to provide a succession of bloom from the end of October until after Christmas. They will not need much heat; in fact, just sufficient to keep out frost. For good results the same methods can be adopted as for the exhibition flowers (already described), or, if preferred, the plants can be planted out into the open borders, lifted and potted in September and then brought into the greenhouse. The plants are generally stopped twice—the first time about the end of March and the second time at the end of June. Some are better disbudded and others better grown in natural sprays, but here again the particular habits of each plant are usually given in catalogues by the growers.

Useful varieties for the amateur's greenhouse are as follows:

DECORATIVE CHRYSANTHEMUMS.
Friendly Rival, deep yellow.
Healesville Quills, pink.
Pink Poitevene, Pink.
Arabella, silvery rose.
Balcombe Bronze, bronze with gold-tipped petals.
Cavalier, reddish-amber.
Florence Bigland, deep canary-yellow.
Gladys Pierson, golden buff.
Kenneth Hastie, crimson-maroon.
Lyoness, bronze-red.
Nelrose, silvery-pink.
Thanksgiving Pink, satin-pink.

Aurora, orange-bronze.
Bianca, terra-cotta, golden reverse.
Brightness, clear pink.
Delicata, pearly pink.
E. Reeves, golden yellow, shaded amber.
Sungold, gold, shaded chestnut.

SINGLE CHRYSANTHEMUMS.

Single chrysanthemums are becoming more and more popular, particularly for use as cut flowers. They are grown in exactly the same way as already indicated for decorative chrysanthemums. There are also other varieties known as Anemone-centred Chrysanthemums and Pom-poms, and these, too, can be grown for greenhouse decoration.

Useful varieties are as follows:

INCURVES (Petals curving inwards).
Aloma, deep yellow.
Joan Higgs, pure white.
Progress, silvery-mauve.
Romance, rich yellow.

SINGLES.

Brilliance, scarlet.
Chastity, creamy-white.
Desert Song, tawny yellow.
Futurity, pale salmon.
Splendour, chestnut flushed red.
Challenger, chestnut red, gold disc.
Daphne, silvery-pink.
Mrs. H. Woolman, bright orange-yellow.
Nona, white.
Rona, velvety purple.
Ruby Ray, bright crimson.
Valerie, terra-cotta.

ANEMONE-CENTRED SINGLES.

Aphrodite, mauve-pink.
Captivations, golden brown, yellow cushion.
Golden Nymph, straw-yellow, golden cushion.
Heloise, salmon.
Nerissa, chestnut, gold centre.
Thora, rose pink.
Wendy, amaranth.
Winsome, crimson.

POM-POMS.

Baby, deep yellow.
Bright Eyes, outer petals blush-white, orange-apricot reverse.
Buena, golden bronze.
Botton Rose, rose.
Ethel, bright red.
Hilda Canning, bronze.
Marguerite Clark, rose-pink.

Nemo, pure white.
Padoka, light salmon.
Snowball, purest white.

CHRYSANTHEMUMS GROWN OUTDOORS.

The cultivation of chrysanthemums in the open garden is practised by those who do not own a greenhouse, but it is surprising how many amateurs fail to achieve good results. The chief reason for this is the failure to distinguish between plants listed, sometimes inaccurately, as "early flowering" and those varieties which are really sufficiently early to be worth while cultivating in an open garden. Unless a chrysanthemum actually comes to full maturity before the advent of the frosts it is useless for outdoor cultivation.

Apart from this, chrysanthemum plants cannot be expected to flower well in the open garden unless they are established early in the season, so that they get the longest possible period of growth undisturbed. In the South of England they can be planted out about the middle of April, but in northern counties, the first week in May is probably early enough.

The borders to receive them should be deeply dug and liberally manured with farmyard or stable manure. Set the plants from 15–18 in. apart, and as soon as they are well established and begin to grow, pinch out the centre point of each plant; this will be about the end of May. This will make them send out a number of side shoots, and make dwarfer plants than if they were allowed to grow unchecked, but they will be more bushy and there will be more flowers on each plant.

Early staking to prevent damage by winds is also essential in the case of outdoor chrysanthemums. In cold gardens it is best to winter these in the cold frame and if only one or two small frames are available the roots can be lifted from the border and packed tightly together with just a little soil round them in the frame. Here they can remain until early spring, when the roots can be replanted as they are, or they can be watered and encouraged to make young growths suitable for cuttings. Cuttings will be rooted in the cold frame or a special propagating frame, potted up early in March, and housed in the cold frame until it is time to plant out in the open garden.

Some of the most useful varieties for outdoor cultivation are given below:

EARLY-FLOWERING DOUBLES.

Kingcup, rich yellow.
Mrs. W. D. Cartwright, rich yellow.
Pink Circle, pink.
Snowflake, pure white.
White Buttercup, creamy-white.
Autumn Gold, bright yellow.
Berengaria, deep rose-pink.
Cranford, golden yellow.
Crimson Circle, blood-red crimson.
Lichfield Bronze, chestnut-bronze.
Madame Desgrange, white.
Mrs. Jack Pearson, bronze.
Mrs. Phil Page, red.
Old Gold, golden orange.
Pink Dame, rose-pink.
Pink Domino, deep pink.
Robin, scarlet-chestnut.
Silver Queen, warm pink, silver reverse and centre.
Warrior, crimson with gold reverse.

EARLY-FLOWERING SINGLES.

Canada, salmon-rose.
Golden Gleam, rich orange.
John Woolman, rose-pink, white zone.
Mary McAlpine, creamy-white.
September Gem, clear yellow.
Stanley Baldwin, wine-crimson.

THE NEW CASCADE CHRYSANTHEMUM.

A novelty in chrysanthemums which has just recently been introduced is popularly known as the Cascade chrysanthemum. Actually, this is just a small-flowered variety of Japanese chrysanthemum which is cultivated so that it forms a floral cascade reaching from the top greenhouse shelf to the floor. This effect is produced first by pinching the plants in order to create bushy growths, and in the second place by tilting the stake to which the plant is trained, towards the north, until it is almost horizontal. This makes the side growths develop on one side of the main stem. Then, in the last stage, the stake is removed and the plant turned round so that the main stem falls in a cascade as already stated.

These plants are now supplied in separate colours and in named varieties, three of the best being:

Kaisha, bronze-red; Princess Takamatsu, white; Yusen, yellow.

Seeds of the type can also be obtained from the leading seedsmen

Cultivation of Pyrethrums.

(*Pyrethrum roseum, coccineum,* syn. Chrysanthemum). The pyrethrums have very aptly been called the "poor man's chrysanthemums," the reason being that they require no heat for their cultivation, but will grow all through the year in the open garden. They are not only perfectly hardy, but they supply cut flowers both in early spring and autumn, the flowers appearing in enormous numbers. They are bright, showy, and particularly useful for cutting on account of their fine stems. The foliage is elegant, being finely cut and of a lovely rich green colour.

The flowers of the double varieties are somewhat like China asters or chrysanthemums, while the single-flowered varieties are often called "coloured marguerites," because of their likeness to these flowers.

Pyrethrums should generally be planted in spring rather than autumn, and although they grow well in ordinary garden soil, they like a good rich loam. Well-rotted manure added to deeply-dug soil which is well drained will be very acceptable to the plants. In very dry gardens a mulch of well-rotted manure over the soil during the hot weather may be advisable.

Pyrethrums are very much liked by slugs, and the best way to protect them during the winter months is to cover the crowns with finely-sifted coal ashes.

When planting, set the plants 18 in. apart. They do not need staking, but should not be grown in positions where very strong winds will break down the flowers.

An enormous number of new hybrids have been raised during recent years, some of the best for ordinary garden decoration being the following:

SINGLE.

Agnes Mary Kelway, bright rose.
Albert Victor, crimson.
Belle of Somerset, white.
Christine Kelway, creamy-white.
Decoy, bright rosy-scarlet.
Eileen Kelway, rich pink.
Eileen May Robinson, rich pink.
Golden Rose, rosy-pink.
James Kelway, scarlet-crimson.

Kelway's Beau Geste, carmine-red.
Primrose Dame, pale primrose.
Phyllis Kelway, soft pink.
Langport Scarlet, true. Nearest carmine-red.
Lady Astor, white, tinged lilac-white.
Snow White, pure white.
The Joy Ring, deep wine-red.
White Lady, pure white.

DOUBLES.

Queen Alexandra, pure white.
Queen Mary, pink.
Melton, red.
Pericles, golden yellow, with creamy-pink guard petal.
Lord Rosebery, amaranth-red.
Roseum Plenum, rose and white.
Cleopatra, yellow and white.

C. carinatum in its single and double-flowered forms is deservedly popular and is distinguished by bands of three different colours surrounding the central eye, or disc, colours in shades of red or crimson, yellow or orange and white.

C. coronarium is obtainable only in white, primrose and golden-yellow. The flowers are mostly double; this is the species usually grown as a pot plant for market work. For this purpose, seed should be sown in February–March in a cool greenhouse, plants grown on as cool as possible, merely excluding frost, and stopping once or twice to induce branching. It is equally good for sowing outdoors in March–April. General height, 1 ft. *C. segetum* is a native British plant, and may be found growing in cornfields. Common name, Corn Marigold. There are two cultivated forms, named respectively, Morning Star, pale yellow, and Evening Star, golden yellow; both are single-flowered, and grow 2–3 ft. in height.

Cultivation of Annual Chrysanthemums.

The tricolor chrysanthemum (*C. tricolor* or *carinatum*) so popular in the cheap markets, and the *Chrysanthemum segetum*, or Corn Marigold, are among the annual varieties of chrysanthemum. These are all hardy and very easily raised from seed.

The tricolor chrysanthemum can, if preferred, be sown in autumn, and is hardy enough to stand through the winter. Such plants will flower considerably earlier than those sown in spring.

Beyond adequate preparation of the soil and occasional hoeing to keep down the weeds, no special treatment is required, but the plants must be given plenty of room to develop, and, in addition, the flower heads should be cut off immediately they fade, if the supply of flowers is to be maintained.

C. inodorum (Bridal Robe), also a hardy annual, 3–4 ft., is a species sometimes included with *Matricaria*, but

CHRYSANTHEMUM TRICOLOR AN ANNUAL VARIETY . . .

A flower that will thrive in any soil is always useful. The Annual Chrysanthemum will thrive anywhere.

may be mentioned here. It is an extremely useful bedding or edging plant with pure white, very double flowers, and feathery deep green leaves; will grow almost anywhere in sunny positions. Usually sown where to flower, but may be transplanted.

Cultivation of other Hardy Perennial Chrysanthemums.

SPECIES.

C. leucanthemum, maximum, and *uliginosum* (Ox-eye and Shasta Daisies).
Very commonly grown as ordinary inhabitants of the mixed border. They need no special cultivation apart from that

usually given to hardy perennials. Ordinary well-drained soil suits them, and as these plants increase rather rapidly, they should be lifted and divided frequently—in some cases even annual lifting is advisable. When replanting, choose the outside portions of the root stock, discarding the central worn-out parts.

C. maximum is best divided during April, although it can also be divided in the early autumn.

Some of the finest modern varieties of *Chrysanthemum maximum* are : A. J. Church ; Mayfield Giant ; Mrs. Lothian Bell; Curley Head (with incurved petals); Kenneth (fringed) ; Beauty of Nivelloise, broad white, serrated petals.

Cultivation of Marguerites.

C. frutescens. Marguerites are, on the whole, a little more tender than some of the perennial chrysanthemums and should be grown in soil which contains plenty of leaf-mould and sand. They make useful plants for bedding out in the summer, if raised from seed sown in April or cuttings taken in September (under glass). Apart from this, they are not generally grown in the open garden, but are more often used as pot plants for decoration of the greenhouse and living-rooms.

To cultivate fine pot plants for flowering in early spring, cuttings should be taken in April. These are small side shoots cut immediately below a joint and inserted, either singly in small pots or three in a 4 in. pot, in soil composed of three parts sand with a little leaf-mould.

Stand the pots in a propagating frame until the roots have formed. Then pot up the cuttings into 3 in. pots in a compost of equal parts loamy soil and leaf-mould, with one-quarter part silver sand. In August, the young plants will be moved into 5 in. pots, similar compost being used. Throughout the summer the pots should stand in full sun in the open. In September, they can be moved into the cold frame and later into the greenhouse with a temperature of not less than 50°. Sufficient (but not too much) water should be given, and when the pots are full of roots liquid manure can be given from time to time with advantage.

The plants are comparatively worthless after one season's flowering, and fresh cuttings should always be taken and the old plants thrown away.

Chrysanthemum species suitable for the rock garden are :

C. alpinum, which has brilliantly-white single marguerite flowers on short stalks. It is not of easy culture. A light gritty lime-free soil or a moraine is the best treatment.

C. articum (syn. *Zawadskyi*), has broad, fat, serrated foliage in rather lush, but low-growing tufts. Its beauty lies in the delicate rose-pink colouring of its foot-high marguerites.

C. hispanicum. From the higher parts of all the Spanish mountains. Finely cut, downy silver-grey foliage. The stems bear each a single daisy-flower of golden yellow. There is, however, a good deal of colour variation, but nearly all the forms are desirable.

All will propagate by division. *C. alpinum* requires the extra care of well-drained pots under a shade.

CHRYSANTHEMUM LEAF-MINER (*Phytomyza albiceps*). DESCRIPTION.—
The adult fly is $\frac{1}{16}$ in. in length and $\frac{1}{4}$ in. in expanse. It is dark brown in colour with reddish eyes. The larva is pale green in colour, fleshy and legless, and lives within the tissues of the leaf.

LIFE-HISTORY.—The flies hatch out in early summer and lay their eggs on the undersides of the leaves. On hatching out the small larvæ tunnel into the leaves, thus forming whitish galleries. In bad attacks the leaves may turn brown and die. When full grown the larvæ pupate within the tissues of the leaf, but after a short time the covering tissue breaks—leaving the pupa exposed. It is said there are several generations in a year, but in all probability there are only two—the second generation passing the winter in the pupal stage.

METHODS OF CONTROL.—These must be of a repellent nature, as once the maggot has got into the leaf little can be done. Spray in early June with a weak paraffin emulsion to keep the flies from laying eggs.

CHRYSOBACTRON (kris-o-bak-tron). *See* BULBINELLA.

CHRYSOCOMA (kris-ok-ō-ma. Compositæ). Goldy Locks. *Chrysos*, gold, and *kome*, hair, referring to the yellow florets.

Greenhouse evergreen and herbaceous hardy perennials. The former are propagated by cuttings of half-ripened shoots rooted in sand under a glass in April, the latter by division in March. Pot up the tender species in a compost of loam and peat and grow the hardy plants in any good soil. Winter temperature, minimum, 35°.

SPECIES.

C. como-aurea is the best of the greenhouse species, bearing yellow flowers in July. 2 ft.

C. ciliata. White, August. 4 ft.

C. nivea. Yellow, July. 3 ft.

C. linocyris, a hardy perennial, is now grown under the name of *Aster Linocyris.*

CHRYSOGONUM (kris-og-on-um. Compositæ). Golden Knee. *C. virginianum* is the only species cultivated and is a hardy herbaceous perennial with star-like golden-yellow flowers from May to June. It likes a shady spot in good ordinary soil, or a soil of equal parts loam, peat, and leaf-mould.

Propagate by seeds, but preferably by division of the roots in March or September. Height 9–12 in. Can be used for a rockery.

CHRYSOPHYLLUM (kris-o-fil-lum. Sapotaceæ). Star Apple. Stove evergreen trees of which some species bear edible fruits, while from the bark of *C. glycyphlœum* is extracted Monesia. They thrive in well-drained loam and peat and are propagated by cuttings under glass in heat.

SPECIES.

C. Cainito with white flowers in May is the West Indian Star Apple that provides dessert fruit. It has several varieties that range in height from 20–50 ft. and all bear white flowers.

CHRYSOPSIS (kris-op-sis. Compositæ). Hardy herbaceous perennials that are of coarse growth and are fit for the shrubbery or rougher parts of the garden. The small flowers are usually yellow. In their wild state they grow in poor, dry soil and only need this under cultivation. Increased by division in spring or after flowering.

SPECIES.

C. graminifolia. August. 2 ft.

C. villosa, has golden flowers. July (syn. *Amellus villosus*).

CHRYSOSPLENIUM (kris-o-sple-ni-um. Saxifrageæ). Golden Saxifrage. This large genus of hardy herbaceous perennials is of little garden value, only one or two species, such as *alternifolium* and *oppositifolium*, being useful for damp, shady corners of the rockery or the wild garden. The flowers are yellow and the leaves rather thick and fleshy. Divide in the spring or sow seed to increase stock. Plant in spring.

C. oppositifolium has golden-yellow foliage and creeps along the surface of the soil.

CHUSAN PALM. *See* TRACHYCARPUS.

CHYSIS (ki-sis. Orchidaceæ). The flowers of this Mexican genus of Orchids are very beautiful and last long in bloom owing to their firm texture. One of the few genera of Orchids that have the power of self-propagation. All are deciduous epiphytes and like to be grown in hanging baskets in the cooler part of the stove, except *aurea*, which is better in the intermediate house.

Propagate by division when growth is recommencing and plant in a compost of peat, sphagnum and potsherds. Water abundantly during the season of growth but keep the plants fairly dry when resting.

SPECIES.

C. aurea. Yellow, often flowers twice in one year.

C. bractescens. White or yellow flowers in April–May.

C. Limminghei. Yellow and purple. May–June. 12 in.

CICHORIUM. *See* CHICORY, ENDIVE.

CIMICIFUGA (cimi-cif-uga. Ranunculaceæ). Bugwort, or Snakeroot. Hardy herbaceous perennials that succeed well in half-shady borders in deep moist soil, and have white and creamy blooms from July to October. Increase by seeds or split the roots and replant in spring.

SPECIES.

C. cordifolia, C. simplex and *C. racemosa*, all about 3–4 ft. in height, are the best.

CINCHONA (sin-ko-na. Rubiaceæ). Peruvian Bark. This valuable genus of plants, originally indigenous to S. America, is now cultivated wherever possible for the sake of the medicine so useful in febrile diseases—quinine, which is extracted from the bark. The genus comprises tall evergreen trees and shrubs that require stove culture and a certain amount of care. They like a compost of fibrous loam with peat and coarse sand.

Propagate by cuttings of ripe wood in sand under a bell-glass with bottom heat.

SPECIES.

C. Calisaya. "Yellow Bark."
C. josephiana. White-flowered.

**STAR CINERARIA
A USEFUL GREENHOUSE PLANT**

Cinerarias with their rich colourings make ideal plants for rooms. Grow them in the greenhouse or frame until the buds begin to open.

C. officinalis. "Crown Bark."   18 ft.
C. peruviana. "Grey Bark."
C. succirubra. "Red Bark."   20–40 ft.
All the species bear fragrant white or pinkish flowers.

CINERARIA (ciner-ar′-ria. Compositæ). Correct name Senecio.

The Greenhouse Perennials.

Greenhouse perennials flowering from February to March, and with care from November to May, provide a range of floral colours and single and double blooms. These are best grown from seed. Sow in May or June in shallow pans in well-prepared soil. Scatter seeds thinly, cover with fine soil and place in semi-shade

at a temperature of 55°. When seedlings appear, expose to light and air, and protect from hot sun. Use a fine compost of loam and leaf-mould for seedlings, and fibrous turf with leaf-mould and sand or charcoal for potting. Finish off in 8 in. pots. Keep moist and syringe daily in hot weather. Give weak liquid manure alternately with water. One most used in the garden is *S. cruenta*, of which there are several varieties, the star-flowered or *stellata*, the cactus-flowered, and the large-flowered florists' favourite.

Cineraria maritima, a dwarf plant with silvery foliage is often used for summer bedding. It is easily kept under glass through the winter if potted up in September. Also easily raised from seed to plant out in June. Protect from greenfly and from a slug which forms a yellow streak under the skin of the leaf. It should be squeezed between the fingers. Height 1–2 ft. (*See also* SENECIO.)

Florist's Cinerarias.

(*Cruentes Senecio*). Very popular greenhouse hybrids ranging in height from 18 in. to 3 ft., according to strain. Modern strains are rich in pure self colours and in handsomely bordered varieties. The flowers are composite or daisy-like and contain shades of blue, white, mauve, rose, pink, magenta or copper-red.

Cultivation.—Seeds should be sown in early spring for winter flowering or in July for spring. Sow in gentle heat in spring or in a frame during summer. Prick off when large enough and pot on as the plants require it, flowering them in 48 or 32 size pots. The soil should be composed of good loam, peat, leaf-mould and sharp sand, to which has been added a little complete fertiliser.

VARIETIES.

"Selected Mixed" (compact habit with large flowers) "Stellata" or "Cactus" strains with smaller flowers and of full branching habit. "Blue Gem" and "Salmon Pink Star" (of intermediate habit with medium size blooms), "Matador" (copper-red).

CINNAMOMUM (sin-a-mō-mum. Laurineæ). The Camphor trees of China and Japan, with noble and aromatic foliage; flowers are greenish-white. Of economic value as producers of cinnamon.

C. camphora. The only species that can be grown outside in this country and then only in the mildest parts.

CINQUEFOIL. *See* POTENTILLA.

CIRRHOPETALUM (si'-rō-pet'-a-lum. Orchidaceæ). From *cirrhos*, a tendril, and *pitalon*, a flower leaf; in reference to the strap-shaped petals. Stove orchids. Evergreen, 1839. A genus closely allied to Bulbophyllum.

Culture.—Compost: general treatment and propagation similar in every way to Bulbophyllum, *which see.*

SPECIES.

C. Collettii, purple, April, 8 in.

C. ornatissimum, yellow and purple, October, 9 in.

C. pictuaratum, green and red, March, 8 in.

C. robustum, red, yellow, purple, June, 15 in.

CISSUS (sis-sus. Ampelideæ). A genus of stove and greenhouse climbing plants that have no pretensions to beauty except *C. discolor*, an old-fashioned favourite with handsome leaves, that is well worth a place in the stove.

Propagate by cuttings placed in sand beneath a bell-glass in either stove or greenhouse according to the species. The plants thrive in fibrous peat and loam with sand. All the species bear greenish-white flowers and should be referred to Vitis.

C. discolor has velvety green leaves prettily marked with silver (correct name, *Vitis discolor*). *See also* VITIS.

CISTUS (sis'-tus. Cistaceæ). Rock Rose. Charming hardy and half-hardy shrubs, from the Mediterranean region. Flowering profusely, and thriving in the driest positions. The colours of the flowers range from white to purple, but there is no yellow Cistus. In appearance the flowers resemble single roses and a constant succession of them appears during the early summer. They are of a fleeting character, never lasting more than a day. They hybridise very freely among themselves, and some of the hybrids are the most useful for garden purposes.

Culture.—Pot plants should be chosen as the Cistus is notoriously difficult to move, once established. They like a very sunny position, and a light dry soil.

Heavy soils should be lightened by the addition of peat or leaf-mould, etc. The plants should be sheltered from cold, cutting winds, and spring frosts guarded against. Some of the hardiest are *C. laurifolius*, *C. corbariensis* and *C. Loreti.*

Propagation is by seed sown in April and by cuttings taken in August and struck in frame. The plants should be "stopped" (i.e., the tips of the shoots pinched or cut

CISTUS—THE ROCK ROSE

The Rock Rose enjoys a light sandy soil and a sunny position. Its flowers are as soft as silk, but are not suitable for cutting.

off) in March. All dead blooms should be removed, unless seed is required. The various hybrids seldom produce fertile seed.

PRINCIPAL SPECIES AND HYBRIDS.

C. corbariensis. A very hardy and vigorous-growing hybrid, between *C. populifolius* and *C. salvifolius.* Flowers white. 3 ft.

C. cyprius. A natural hybrid found wild in Cyprus. Possibly *C. ladaniferus* and *C. laurifolus* are its parents. Flowers large crimson-blotched white, 3 in. across. One of the most beautiful, if not *the* most beautiful Cistus, hardy in this country. It will survive any ordinary winter.

Sometimes confused with *C. ladaniferus*, but easily distinguished therefrom by its flowers being produced in clusters, whereas the flowers of *C. ladaniferus* are always solitary. 6–8 ft.

C. florentinus. Found growing wild in various parts of S. Europe and Algiers, and is a natural hybrid between *C. monspeliensis* and *C. salvifolius.* Flowers white, yellow blotch. Not very hardy. 2–3 ft.

C. hirsutus. Flowers white. Fairly hardy.

C. ladaniferus. Known in English gardens since 1629. Flowers very beautiful, and larger than the other hardy Cistus, 4 in. across, white with crimson blotch. Withstands 20° frost while young, becoming tender as the plants mature. Considered to be the handsomest of the genus. 3–5 ft.

C. l. immaculatus. An old variety but scarce, with very beautiful pure white flowers. One of the few Cistuses useful for indoor decoration, lasting in water for several days.

C. laurifolius. Flowers white, 2–3 in. across. Produced from mid-June onwards. Suitable for growing in a mass. A very hardy Cistus thriving in exposed situations inland and by the sea. On hot days the leaves and stems are pleasantly aromatic, emitting an incense-like perfume. 6–8 ft.

C. populifolius. Flowers white, stained yellow at base of petal. The largest-leaved and longest-stalked Cistus. Moderately hardy, as the specific name indicates.

C. purpureus. Flowers light reddish-purple, the base of each petal being beautifully blotched with deep purple. Thought to be a hybrid between *C. villosus* and the blotched or spotted form of *C. ladaniferus.* A very beautiful and striking Cistus but unfortunately tender. 3–4 ft.

C. salvifolius. Flowers white, tinged yellow at base of petals. Inferior to other white-flowered Cistuses.

C. Silver Pink. A natural hybrid raised in a nursery at Winchester. A.M., R.H.S. Flowers pale silvery-pink in June and July. Foliage silver-grey. Very hardy. 2 ft.

C. villosus. Flowers variable in colour purple to rose, with yellow marks at base of petal. 3–4 ft.

CITRIC ACID. Made chiefly from lemon juice. Used when combined with ammonia (*see* AMMONIUM CITRATE) in determination of citric solubility of phosphates.

CITRULLUS (sit-rul-lus. Cucurbitaceæ). These rambling plants like a moist hot stove atmosphere and a rich loamy soil.

Propagate by seeds sown in heat.

SPECIES.

C. Colocynthis, "Colocynth" or "Bitter Apple," has yellow flowers and greenish-white fruits.

C. vulgaris. "Water Melon." Flowers yellow, summer, and edible fruits.

CITRUS (sit-rus. Rutaceæ). Orange, lemon, lime, citron, etc. Greenhouse evergreen shrub, ornamental flowering and fruiting. Asia, 1595.

Culture.—Compost: 3 parts rich fibrous loam, 1 part leaf-mould, 1 part dry cow manure and a liberal supply of sand, charcoal, and bonemeal. Repot early spring, good drainage must be given. Open position in cool greenhouse where a night temperature of 40° to 45° can be maintained during winter months. Prune in March. Water freely during growing-period, little after. Syringe overhead during summer, and stand plants outside in shady position. Liquid manure may be applied with benefit from May until October.

Propagation.—All kinds will propagate freely from cuttings of young shoots. Insert 2 or 3 round the edge of a 3 in. pot filled with sandy soil, and plunge in propagator, temperature 70°; June to July. Choice species are often grafted on young seedling stocks about March. The seed for these stocks should be sown in early spring, in light sandy soil, temperature, 50°–60°. Other methods are by layering in the autumn, or by budding in July or August.

SPECIES.

C. aurantium (Sweet Orange), golden rind, globular.

C. decumana (Shaddock), greenish-yellow rind, round.

C. medica (Citron), yellow rind, egg-shaped.

C. m. limetto (Sweet Lime), greenish-yellow, smooth rind, globular.

C. m. limonum (Lemon), pale yellow rind, oblong.

C. noblis major (Mandarin) reddish rind, globular.

C. n. tangerana (Tangerine), reddish rind, globular.

Nearly all of the above species have white fragrant flowers. *See also* ÆGLE.

CLADOTHAMNUS (klad'-ō-tham'-nus. Ericaceæ). Alaska, British Columbia, etc. Deciduous, compact shrub, 12–18 in. Flowers rosy in centre, margined yellow, during June and July. A rare and interesting shrub for a peaty situation in the rock garden.

CLADRASTIS (klă-dras'-tis. Leguminosæ). Deciduous ornamental trees with pea-shaped flowers, similar to Robinia. They require good loamy soil and a sunny position. *Propagate* by seeds or root cuttings.

SPECIES.

C. sinensis. Chinese Yellow Wood. 50 ft. in nature. Flowers fragrant, blush-white.

C. tinctoria. The Yellow Wood of southeast U.S.A. 50 ft. Flowers white, blotched yellow at base, fragrant. This species has reached a height of 47 ft. in Surrey.

CLARKIA (klar-ki-a. Onagraceæ), 1½–2 ft. Native of North America. There are two species in general cultivation, *C. elegans* and *C. pulchella*, both hardy annuals, of which the former is the more popular, as in its many varieties some really charming colours are to be found; the plants are of graceful habit, freely branched, and the double flowers are carried in long spikes which continue to grow as the older flowers fade. The colours now to be obtained range from white, rose, salmon, orange-scarlet, and carmine-mauve.

A really beautiful genus, well worth a place in every garden. *C. pulchella* has a limited range of colours, e.g., white, purple and crimson, and the plants are not so tall or robust as in the *elegans* group. There is also a dwarf or Tom Thumb type of *C. pulchella*, which only grows 9 in. tall, and is useful for edgings to large beds. Clarkias succeed in any ordinary garden soil, and may be sown in autumn or spring, preferably where the plants are to bloom. A few seeds sown in small pots in autumn wintered in a cold frame, potted up into 5 in. pots in March, make delightful pot plants for flowering in a cold greenhouse in May to June.

C. elegans is useful for the greenhouse as a pot plant. The double varieties are particularly attractive. Height 2–4 ft. according to cultivation. Colours vary from white, mauve and purple to red and orange-salmon.

Cultivation.—For cultivation as pot plants, seeds should be sown in boxes of open soil during the latter part of summer or in the autumn. They may be potted into 60 size pots before winter and wintered in a cool greenhouse, near the glass. They are very apt to damp off during winter unless watered with care and they "draw" very easily unless grown as cool as possible and near to the glass. In the spring they should be potted up into larger pots containing a good open compost of loam, old rotten manure and sand to which has been added a sprinkling of complete fertiliser. If necessary, a little sifted leaf-mould may also be used to open the compost. A few weeks after potting, stop the plants to make them branch freely and to promote a compact habit, unless very tall specimens are required. Continue to grow cool.

VARIETIES (DOUBLE).

Brilliant (carmine-rose); Chieftain (mauve); Firebrand (scarlet); Enchantress (salmon-pink); Orange Beauty; Purple Prince. These all do well in pots.

CLAW WEEDERS. A useful addition to the tool outfit. It is made as nearly as possible to take the place of the human hand. An ideal tool for aerating or loosening the top soil round small plants or close-growing bushes, where an "intimate" touch is necessary. These are five-pronged and are made with 7½ in. or 13 in. handles. A recent development of these weeders is a three-pronged, forged steel claw weeder which is made in handle lengths 18 in., 24 in. and 36 in. These have straight prongs bent at the end, and the centre one is longer than the two outside ones— otherwise they very much resemble the Cultivator.

CLAY. Clay is really river-mud, river-silt, tiny particles torn from the older rocks. (*See article* SOIL). Carried by sluggish rivers it spreads over wide plains. You may ask how it is that a river half a mile wide can fill with clay a plain thirty or forty miles wide. The answer is: "Easy!" In undisturbed Nature rivers wander, frequently changing their course. They fill up their first bed with silt, then

-CLEMATIS-

All the Clematises are excellent wall climbers. They need lime in the soil.

deviate to right or left and fill up another bed. And so on. Clay is chemically rich, being formed of varied particles. But it has the grave physical disadvantage that its fine, close material retains the water and will not let it run away quickly enough. Plants become waterlogged, and eventually die of drowning. Therefore a stiff clay soil should be adulterated either with sand or with ash, to make drainage. Stones will help. Never remove the pebbles from a clay bed. If you do not like the look of them, dig them underground. Clay makes a good enough soil if properly drained. In wild Nature,

our clay plains are well clothed with growing things of great variety.

Clay soil is known as heavy, and usually has a fair amount of solid clay in its composition. Such soil cracks badly in hot dry summers and is sticky and unworkable in winter. After digging in the autumn the surface should be left rough to allow the frost to break up the lumps. An application of lime will help to sweeten the soil and strawy manure, sand, etc., will help to lighten it if dug in in the autumn.

CLAYTONIA (clay-ton-ia. Portulaceæ). Spring Beauty. Dwarf hardy perennials and annuals of the Purslane order which thrive in any position and bear rose or white flowers in spring. The perennii species require moist peaty soil. Sow in March. Height 6 in.

SPECIES.

C. caroliniana, pink (perennial).

C. virginica, white (perennial).

C. perfoliata, white (annual).

C. sibirica, pink (annual).

CLEMATIS (clem-ă-tiss. Ranunculaceæ). *Klema*, a vine bower. A most important genus of flowering plants, in habit varying from dwarf herbaceous species to woody climbers up to 60 ft.

Culture.—In planting the species it should be borne in mind that in nature the flowering portions of the plant are exposed to full sun, whilst the main stem and lower parts of the plant are often shaded by other vegetation. It is therefore advisable to place the plants on the northern side of their supports. The soil should be an open loamy one, containing lime or chalk, the Clematis being essentially a plant of calcareous soils. The Clematis also thrives in peaty loam, and some of the finest plants in the country are growing in such soils. The vigorous-growing hybrids need more liberal cultivation than the species, and the soil should be trenched and well manured. This applies especially to the *Viticella* and *Jackmanii* types.

Propagation is by seeds sown in spring, by layering in summer, by grafting, and by internodal cuttings, 2–3 in. long, at pruning time, *cut at least one inch below the node.* Insert the cuttings in pots of sandy soil, place in close frame or under bell-glass. Keep the soil moist but not in a sodden condition. They may remain here until rooted, and then be given more airy conditions. Keep in frame until spring. Then pot off into single pots.

Much controversy has taken place over the merits of own root plants of Clematis versus grafted ones. Plants purchased from English nurseries are invariably grafted. If preferred on their own roots, a little soil should be removed to a depth of an inch or so, and the lower part of the stem placed therein, the soil replaced, and covered with a large stone, or the stem may be pegged down. During the season the stem so treated will take root, thereby giving additional vigour to the plant.

Pruning of the hybrids is noted under each section. The species only require the dead and useless wood to be removed in early spring, unless the plants have become ungainly or rampantly exceeded their allotted space, when they must be dealt with accordingly.

SPECIES AND HYBRIDS.

C. alpina is a lowly, rambling species, seen at its best trailing among the bushes of the rock garden, which it will not smother but will decorate in early summer with drooping flowers of light purple. Alpine woodland.

C. Armandii (China), 20–30 ft. Evergreen. Flowers creamy-white, fragrant. April. A very distinct and beautiful species, requiring wall protection in cold districts.

C. balearica (the Fern-leaved Clematis of the Balearic Islands). Evergreen. Flowers creamy-yellow, freckled with purple spots, produced during winter, thereby suggesting a sheltered spot for this species.

C. chrysocoma (China), 6–8 ft. Flowers white, tinged pink. A rare and rather tender species. Thrives in Cornwall.

C. cirrhosa (S. Europe). A dwarf-growing evergreen species similar to *c. balearica*.

C. coccinea (*C. texensis*). Texas. Purple flowers in autumn. Tender.

C. Durandii (*integrifolia* + garden hybrid). Flowers dark violet-blue, June to September.

C. Fargesii (China). Flowers large white. New.

C. flammula (S. Europe), 10 ft. Flowers white, fragrant, August to October.

C. Forrestii (China). Flowers yellowish. Rare.

C. fusca (Asia), 8–9 ft. Flowers reddish-brown.

C. indivisa (New Zealand). One of the most beautiful. Tender. Thrives in Cornwall. Flowers white, 2–4 in. across, fragrant.

C. Jouiniana (*Vitalba* + *Davidiana*), 10 ft. Flowers white, suffused pink in autumn. A suitable species for mounds and old tree trunks.

C. Jackmanii. Raised by Messrs. Jackman of Woking, 1860, and is supposed to be the result of crossing *C. Hendersonii* and *C. Lanuginosa*. Flowers 4–5 in. across, rich velvety violet-purple. The forerunner of the many well-known and popular hybrids.

C. koreana. A new prostrate Korean species with yellow flowers.

C. macropetala (China). One of Farrer's fine introductions, deserving of greater recognition than it has yet received. Flowers very refined, sapphire-blue, with a centre of narrow pure white petals. A very lovely climber suitable for trailing over shrubs or small trees.

C. montana (Himalayas), 20 ft. upwards. Flowers white, profusely produced during May.

C. m. rubens. Flowers rose-pink.

C. m. undulata. Flowers flesh pink.

C. m. Wilsonii. Chinese variety with larger flowers, white and very sweet scented, July and August.

C. orientalis (*graveolens*), Asia. Flowers are yellow in autumn, foliage glaucous grey.

C. paniculata (Japan), 30 ft. Flowers small, white, hawthorn-scented, September and October.

C. patens (Japan). The parent of a group of hybrids.

C. recta forms an erect, compact 3 ft. bush covered in early and midsummer with a mass of small cream-white flowers. Out of flower the glossy foliage is attractive. For the herbaceous border, or the back of the rock garden. It likes a limy soil, and propagates easily from division. To achieve this, it is best to remove outlying portions without disturbing the main plant. Austria.

C. Rehderiana (nutans) China. Flowers nodding, bell-shaped, primrose-yellow with the fragrance of cowslips, August to October.

C. serratifolia (Korea). Flowers bright yellow in autumn.

C. tangutica (China). The handsomest yellow-flowered Clematis. A profusion of flowers 4 in. across in late summer, followed by a mass of feathery silvery-grey fruits.

C. vitalba (Europe, including South of England). Flowers dull white, faintly scented of almonds, July to October, are followed by silvery-grey fruits, which suggest the name "old man's beard." The well-known name "Traveller's-joy" was given to this Clematis by Gerard, who writes of it as being "esteemed for pleasure by reason of the goodly shadow and the pleasant *sent* or savour of its flowers. And because of its decking and adorning *waies* and hedges where people travel, thereupon have I named it 'Traveller's-joy.'"

C. viticella (S. Europe). A very old Clematis, known to Gerard and grown by him in his famous garden at Holborn in the 16th century. Flowers, blue or purple, freely produced during summer and autumn.

C. v. alba luxurians, white.
C. v. kermesina, crimson.
C. v. Leonidas, rich purple.

Large-flowered Hybrid Clematis.
PATENS TYPE.
Large flowers, May and June. Pruning: remove dead wood and straggling or crowded branches after flowering, in July.
Lady Londesborough—silver-grey.
Lasuristern—deep blue.
Miss Bateman—white.
JACKMANII TYPE.
Large flowers from July to October. Prune to 12 in. of the older stems each spring, about February.
Comtesse de Bouchard—soft carmine-rose. One of the best.
Gypsy Queen—rich velvety purple.
Jackmanii (see also under C. Jackmanii).
Jackmanii alba.
Jackmanii superba—dark violet.
Perle d'azure—bright blue.
The President—dark plum-purple.

LANUGINOSA TYPE.
Large flowers, June to October. Prune lightly in February. This type also gives excellent results if cut to within a few inches of the ground in spring, pinching the resultant shoots when about 3 ft. high.
Beauty of Worcester—bright blue.
Blue Gem—sky-blue.
Crimson King—rich crimson.
Fairy Queen—pale flesh, pink bar.
Grand Duchess—blush-white
Henryi—white.
King Edward VII—pure violet, crimson bar.
Lady Caroline Neville—French white, pink bar.
Lawsoniana—lavender.
Mme. Boisselot—large white.
Mrs. Hope—lavender-mauve.
Nellie Moser—silvery-white, pink bar
Sensation—satiny mauve.
William Kenneth—mauve.
VITICELLA TYPE.
Blooming in masses, July to October Prune in February to the living part
Ascotiensis—azure.
Lady Betty Balfour — deep velvety purple.
Madame Grange—crimson-purple, large flowers.
Ville de Lyon—carmine-crimson.
FLORIDA TYPE.
Showy flowers in late summer. Prune as for Patens type.
Battle of Woking—silvery-mauve.
Duchess of Edinburgh—white fragrant.
Lucie Lemoine—white, double.
COCCINEA (TEXENSIS) TYPE.
Showy bell-shaped flowers in late summer. Prune lightly in spring.
Admiration—deep salmon, edged violet, white reverse.
Countess of Onslow—violet-purple, band of scarlet in centre of petal.
Duchess of Albany—bright pink, darker bar.
Sir Trevor Lawrence—crimson.

CLEMATOCLETHRA. A rare scandent shrub from N.W. China, with white clethra-like flowers. Tender.

C. integrifolia. The only species.

CLEOME (kle-ō-me. Capparidaceæ). This large genus comprises hardy annual, herbaceous and evergreen shrubs as well as greenhouse and stove plants.

Propagate the shrubby species by cut-
ngs of half-ripened shoots in sand under
bell-glass, the annuals by seeds sown in
hotbed and planted out when necessary,
nd the herbaceous perennials by division.
All like a light, rich, well-drained soil.

SPECIES.

C. arabica. Hardy annual, with yellow
owers in June. 2 ft.

C. pubescens. Hardy annual, white
owers in July. 2 ft.

C. speciosissima. Hardy annual, purple,
uly. 2 ft.

C. lutea. Hardy perennial, yellow,
uly. 1 ft.

C. gigantea. Stove evergreen shrub
ith white flowers in June. 10 ft.

C. arborea. Stove evergreen shrub,
hite, June. 8 ft.

C. heptaphylla. Stove annual, white,
uly. 1½ ft.

C. spinosa. Stove annual, white, July,
ft.

C. rosea. Stove annual, red, June.
ft.

CLERODENDRON (klē-rō-den'-dron.
erbenaceæ). A genus of flowering
hrubs and climbers, needing greenhouse
ultivation with the exception of the fol-
owing three hardy species, thriving in
rdinary garden soil and sunny positions.
Propagation is by seeds sown in heat,
nd by cuttings struck under a bell-glass
n greenhouse, and by division in spring,
nd root suckers.

HARDY SPECIES.

C. Fargesii (China), 10 ft. Flowers
vhite, star-shaped, fragrant, during August.
Succeeded by porcelain-blue fruits.

C. fœtidum (China). Flowers fragrant
ose-pink in corymbs.

C. trichotomum (China and Japan),
0–12 ft. Flowers fragrant, white with
naroon calyx, succeeded by bright blue
erries. The variety known as *montanum*
s the finest form. The leaves of all three
pecies are of unpleasant odour when
rushed, those of *C. fœtidum* being
articularly nauseous.

C. fallax is a stove plant with large,
spreading green leaves and brilliant
panicles of bright scarlet flowers which are
very showy. Height 2 ft.

Cultivation.—Seeds should be sown in
January in good heat and the young seed-

lings pricked off and potted in as they
require it; using a good compost of mature,
fibrous loam which has been opened with
leaf-mould, sand and some old manure
from the bottom of the previous year's
cucumber or tomato bed. Grown on walls
the plants bloom for the first time during
the same year.

CLETHRA (clĕth'-ra. Ericaceæ). Evergreen and deciduous shrubs with racemes
of white or cream flowers.

Culture.—Plant in well-drained peaty
soil, or loam, leaf-mould (or peat) and
sand (no lime) in half shade.

Propagation by cuttings taken in August,
3–4 in. long, with heel or piece of older
wood, and placed in gentle heat.

SPECIES.

C. alnifolia, 8 ft. Sweet-Pepper Bush
of eastern N. America. Flowers white in
late summer and autumn. A very hardy
species, thriving in ordinary soil.
Requires abundant moisture.

CLEYERA (klay-ē'-ra. Ternstrœmiaceæ). Asia. Evergreen shrub, 5–6 ft.
Propagate by cuttings placed in heat.

C. Fortunei. The only species grown in
this country. Introduced from Japan in
1860; probably a native of China.
Flowers yellow; foliage variegated.

CLIANTHUS (kli-an'-thus. Leguminosæ). Lobster Claw or Parrot's Bill.
The Red Kowhai of New Zealand, is only
hardy in very mild districts and is best
on east or west walls. It will often get
cut to ground by frosts, but springs up
again.

Culture.—Plant in well-manured, loamy
soil. *Propagate* by seed and by cuttings
in heat.

SPECIES.

C. puniceus. A very striking semi-evergreen shrub with bright scarlet flowers
2–3 in. long in clusters, during the summer.

C. p. alba, white flowers.

C. p. magnificus. The finest form, and
more vigorous than type.

The Clianthus grows and flowers well
on walls in Devonshire and the plants produce seed in abundance. Possibly plants
raised from home-grown seed might prove
more robust than those from imported
seed.

CLICKBEETLE. *See* WIREWORMS.

CLIMBING PLANTS. This term should, strictly speaking, be used only for those plants which definitely climb by means of aerial roots as in the case of the ivy, by adhesive pads like virginian creeper, or some other method. The term, however, covers also plants, such as pyracantha, which is very vigorous-growing and which by careful training can be made to cover a wall. It is interesting to note that plants also climb by means of tendrils as in the sweet pea, by means of twining leaf stems as the nasturtium, by twining stems as the honeysuckle and hop, and by prickles and thorns in the case of goosegrass and rambler roses. An understanding of the method by which a plant climbs will enable the gardener to provide adequate supports for its growth.

There is such a wide variety of plants suitable for covering tree stumps, walls, arches, pergolas, summer houses, etc., that the amateur is almost bewildered. The following lists should help to render selection more easy.

The site for a climber should be well prepared before planting is done. A frequent cause of failure of house-climbers is due to the fact that overhanging eaves prevent water from reaching the plants, and in such cases copious supplies of water should be given, especially during the summer months. When climbers are not of the self-clinging type but need fastening to the wall, special wall nails should be used for economy and the good of the plant (*see* WALL NAILS). With regard to the pruning of climbers, notes will be found on this under the various plants.

Climbers, Annual.
Hardy.

Convolvulus	Humulus japonicus
Lathyrus. Sweet	Tropæolum (syn.
Pea	Nasturtium)

Half-hardy, Tender.

Cobæa	Ipomæa
Curcubita	Maurandya
Dolichos	Porana
Eccremocarpus	Thunbergia
Grammatocarpus	Trichosanthes

Climbing and Wall Plants, Perennial.
Hardy.

Actinidia	Apios
Ampelopsis	Aristolochia
Berberidopsis	Lathyrus
Berchemia	Lonicera
Calystegia	Lycium
Celastrus	Muehlenbeckia
Clematis	Periploca
Cotoneaster	Polygonum
Cratægus	Rose
Escallonia	Rubus
Forsythias	Smilax
Garrya	Trachelospermum
Hablitzia	Tropæolum
Hedera	Vitis
Jasminum	Wistaria

Half-hardy, Tender.

Allamanda	Gloriosa
Argyreia	Hibbertia
Aristolochia	Hoya
Asparagus	Ipomæa
Bauhinia	Kennedya
Bignonia	Lapageria
Bomarea	Maurandya
Bougainvillea	Passiflora
Cestrum	Smilax
Clematis	Sollya
Clerodendron	Tacsonia
Clitoria	Tecoma
Eccremocarpus	Thunbergia
Ficus	Vitis

The cultural details and varieties of the chief climbers in this list are given under the generic name in alphabetical order.

CLINTONIA (klin-to-ni-a. Liliaceæ) Hardy herbaceous plants that are most useful for damp, shady parts of the rockery. Of the twenty species only a few are cultivated.

Propagate by division in spring and grow in peat and sand.

SPECIES.

C. andrewsiana, rose flowers in April 2 ft.

C. borealis, greenish yellow flowers followed by blue berries. Suitable for the bog garden. May, 2 ft. (*See* DOWNINGIA)

CLIPPED SPECIMENS. *See* HEDGES.

CLIVIA (kli-vi-a. Amaryllidaceæ). Evergreen bulbous plants with handsome strap shaped leaves and umbels of bright yellow or orange flowers. From the few species many beautiful hybrids have been evolved. They are easily raised from seed, which germinates readily in a warm temperature, or by division in spring. The seedlings should be potted up singly in small pots in which, provided the soil does not become sour, they may be left for years, as they grow best if left undisturbed. They require a compost of rich loam and sharp and with a little charcoal to keep the soil sweet, as the plants need copious supplies of water during the growing period.

During the flowering season they should be fed with liquid manure, and while approaching this period they may be put in moister, warmer temperature. These plants make useful pot plants for rooms because the foliage is attractive throughout the year and the flowers cover the plant in early summer.

SPECIES.

C. cyrtanthiflora. A hybrid from *miniata* and *nobilis.* Its large flowers are salmon-pink with white centres and greenish tips. Winter and spring.

C. Gardeni. Reddish-orange or yellow flowers in ten to fourteen flowered umbels. May. 1½ ft.

C. miniata, with flowers of bright yellow or scarlet, has many beautiful varieties such as: Distinction, orange, scarlet and white; President, brilliant orange; Excelsior, orange and red.

C. nobilis, red and yellow, July.

CLOCHE. This consists of small pieces of glass neatly clipped together to form a bell or tent-shaped protection for tender plants. It can be taken to pieces and packed away when not in use, and takes up very little room. It can be used to protect alpines from heavy rains and fog, to raise early lettuce, peas and straw-berries and salads. It also assists in pro-tecting root cuttings. Rows of early vege-tables can be raised by putting several cloches end to end.

CLOCK GOLF. An interesting game which can be played on a very small lawn, an area twelve to twenty feet square being suitable.

CLUB ROOT (Anbury). A fungus disease which attacks cabbages and allied crops, usually found where the soil is deficient in lime. Best cured by treating the soil in winter with gas lime at the rate of 14 lb. per rod. Affected plants should always be burnt and weeds of the Brasicca type should be strictly elimin-ated from the plot (e.g., Shepherds purse) as these are affected by the disease.

CLOSE ATMOSPHERE. A warm, moist atmosphere which is made possible in a frame or greenhouse by withholding ventilation is known as "close." It is sometimes advised to encourage the quick recovery of newly transplanted plants or to assist in the rooting of cuttings.

CLOVER. See TRIFOLIUM.

Clover. *To find a four-leaved clover is the augury of a happy, wealthy marriage.*

CLUB RUSH. See SCIRPUS.

CLUMP. A good-sized root of a her-baceous plant such as Michaelmas daisy, with several shoots is known as a clump. It can be divided to form several plants.

CNEORUM (ně-ŏr'-um. Simarubaceæ). Mediterranean region. Evergreen shrub, 1–2 ft. Flowers yellow followed by red fruits; foliage grey-green. Likes a dry position in sandy loam and peat. A tender shrub succeeding in the Southern countries with wall protection.

C. tricoccum. The only species for out-door cultivation.

CNICUS (ni-kus. Compositæ). Fish-Bone Thistle. A rather heterogeneous genus of biennial and perennial plants of thistle-like habit. Species from the genera Cirsium and Chamæpeuce are now included in this family. Increased by seeds sown in the open border in April or in heat in February, the seedlings being transplanted to pots and later planted out at the end of May after having been hardened-off. Best treated as biennials.

SPECIES.

C. Casabonæ, the "Fish-Bone Thistle" (syn. *Chamæpeuce Casabonæ),* with purple flowers in June, is often used for summer bedding, but it is not perfectly hardy in all gardens. Its leaves are deep green veined with silver and having brown spines.

C. Diacantha has bright green leaves with silvery lines and ivory-white spines. The flowers are purple. June. This is used in summer bedding for the sake of the foliage.

COAL ASH. Coal ash is of very little use as a fertiliser. May be employed, when very *finely sifted,* to lighten clay soils and make them easier to work. Unburnt coal is a source of trouble; therefore it is best to keep coal ashes for use in making paths, or for dressing lawns, rather than to use it on the soil of the borders and vegetable garden.

COBÆA (ko-be-a. Polemoniaceæ). Beautiful evergreen greenhouse climbing plants with pretty flowers, and well suited for training on trellises and pillars. For summer decoration out of doors they should be treated as annuals.

Propagate by seeds sown in heat in March or by firm side shoots taken in

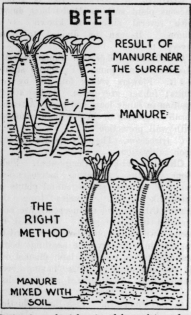

BEET

RESULT OF MANURE NEAR THE SURFACE

MANURE

THE RIGHT METHOD

MANURE MIXED WITH SOIL

Beetroot can best be stored in moist sand or sifted coal ashes in a cool, dry, damp-proof place during the winter.

spring and struck in light sandy soil in heat. In rich soil they make vigorous rapid growth at the expense of the flowers, so that it is advisable to pot them in rather dry, poor, sandy soil. Plants for outdoors must be thoroughly hardened-off before planting out.

SPECIES.

C. penduliflora. Green, December.

C. scandens. Purple flowers in May and June.

C. s. variegata has variegated leaves.

COBBLES. These small, round pebbles or stones make charming pathways for small gardens. They look well, associated with paving-stones or bricks, and give an "old-fashioned" atmosphere to a garden (*See also* PATHWAYS).

COCCULUS (kok'-kū-lŭs. Menispermaceæ). Tender evergreen shrubs and climbers of easy cultivation in ordinary soil. *Propagate* by root division, and by cuttings under glass.

SPECIES.

C. carolinus (south-eastern U.S.A.) Climber with white flowers succeeded by red pea-like berries.

C. laurifolius (Himalayas). Evergreen shrub 10 ft., with glossy dark green foliage.

C. trilobus (China, Japan). Climbing twiny shrub, attractive, with black berries with a blue bloom, and bright green foliage persisting well into the autumn.

COCKSCOMB. *See* CELOSIA.

COCO-NUT FIBRE. This material is used largely for potting indoor bulbs, being clean in use and easy to keep moist once it has been thoroughly soaked. It can also be applied as a mulch to plants in summer. Another use is as a top dressing in window-boxes, where it prevents muddy rain-splashes on the window.

CODIÆUM (ko-di-e-um. Euphorbiaceæ). Croton. Stove evergreen shrub (Jamaica, 1748). These shrubs have lovely ornamental foliage, the leaves being variegated with various colours.

Culture.—Compost: 2 parts loam, 1 part turfy peat, ½ part sand. Repot March. Keep the pots up close to the glass. Water freely during the summer. Winter temperature, 60°; summer, 80°.

Propagation.—By cuttings: insert single in small pots filled with sand (thumb size). The cuttings are taken from the ends of shoots. Place in propagator, temperature, 70°.

SPECIES AND VARIETIES.

C. Aigburthiensis, red and green.

C. illustris, green and yellow.

C. variegatum, yellow and green.

C. v. tricolor, green, yellow and cream.

C. Warreni, green and orange carmine.

CODLING MOTH (*Carpocapsa pomonella*). Apple Maggot. An extremely common caterpillar pest attacking all varieties of apples, also pears and plums. The maggot-like caterpillars, about ½ in. in length when full-grown, creamy or

1. Roses on a cottage wall.
2. Clematis montana will quickly cover a roof with a bower of star-like flowers.
3. Large-flowered Clematis—lavender, white or mauve are ideal for garden arches.
4. Nellie Moser—a good variety of the large-flowered type of Clematis.

1. Light-coloured perennials contrasted with trees and sky.
2. Purple Clematis Jackmannii associated with pink and white perennials.
3 Deep rose Phlox with pure white Watsonia.

inkish-white in colour, live inside the fruits, devouring the pulp and disfiguring the apples by their exit galleries. Attacked apples usually drop from the tree before they are ripe. The female parent moth which is inconspicuous in appearance and not often observed, lays her small, glistening, scale-like eggs, usually singly, on the skin of the young fruits or on the adjacent foliage in April and May. The

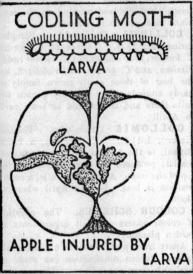

CODLING MOTH

LARVA

APPLE INJURED BY LARVA

A little moth which does great damage to the apple crop. It lays its eggs on the tiny fruitlets. The grubs hatch out and work their way inside the apples.

caterpillars hatch out about the end of May and immediately eat their way into the apple, usually through the eye. When fully fed they leave the apple by a gallery opening on the side of the fruit, and if the latter has not already fallen, they shelter in crevices and crannies on the trunk and main branches of the tree. Those which emerge from fallen apples shelter in the soil beneath the tree. The autumn and winter months are passed in this stage. About the end of March, the caterpillars moult their skins and change into a smooth, shiny, brown pupa from which the adult moths emerge in April and May. A female moth may deposit her eggs on upwards of one hundred separate apples. The earliest-hatching caterpillars some-

times pupate in the autumn and thus two broods may appear in the course of a year.

TREATMENT.—Provide shelter for hibernating caterpillars by tying strips of sacking round the trunk and destroying those which shelter there. Spray with lead arsenate after the blossom has fallen and before the calyx lobes (sepals) have closed over the eye of the young fruit. The object of the spraying is to leave a spot of lead arsenate in the eye which poisons the caterpillar as it attempts to eat its way into the apple. Winter washing with a tar-oil spray destroys many caterpillars hibernating on the bark of the tree trunks.

CODONOPSIS (co-don-op-sis. Campanulaceæ). Beautiful small perennials, natives of China and India, which grow well in any soil and are increased by seeds and cuttings. *C. clematidea* with white bell-shaped flowers in summer is useful in the border; while *C. ovata*, with slate-blue flowers, veined and spotted white and yellow inside the bell, should be planted overhead in the rock garden to obtain best effect. They bloom in July and vary from 1–3 ft. in height.

COFFEA (Coffee Tree). Rubiaceæ. Stove evergreen shrubs, with small reddish fleshy berries, which contain two seeds enclosed in the parchment-like shell. The coffee bean of commerce is borne by this tree. For its cultivation a compost of 2 parts turfy loam, 1 part leaf-mould and sand should be prepared. The best time to pot is in March. The pots should be placed in the moist plant stove. Water freely in summer when the plants should be growing in a temperature of 75°–85°, but in the winter they will need to be watered moderately. At this time the temperature should be 60°–70°.

Propagate by seeds sown in March, sowing them ½ in. deep. They should be germinated in a temperature of 85°.

Cuttings of firm shoots may also be taken. These should be inserted in sandy soil and placed under a bell-glass, the temperature for this operation being 85°. Take the cuttings in summer.

SPECIES.

C. arabica, Arabian Coffee, which bears white fragrant flowers in September. This plant attains a height of 10–15 ft.

COFFEE, KENTUCKY. *See* GYM-NOCLADUS.

COFFEE TREE. *See* COFFEA.

COIX (ko-ix. Gramineæ). *Lachrymæ*, Job's Tears. 2 ft. An ornamental annual grass, native of India: there is also a variegated form. Seeds may be sown in February in heat, or out of doors in April. A sunny position and a moist soil are best.

COLCHICINE. *See* HYBRIDISATION.

COLCHICUM (Meadow Saffron). Lili-aceæ. Hardy bulbs. *C. autumnale* and its numerous varieties form excellent subjects for naturalising in lawns or in shrubberies and borders. They like light sandy loam enriched with decayed manure or leaf-mould. Plant 3 in. deep and 3 in. apart in summer. These flowers are often called "Naked Ladies" on account of their habit of flowering before any foliage appears. The foliage grows after the flowers have died, and dies down again in June or July. They can be raised from seed sown in beds of fine soil outdoors in August or September, or, if preferred, they can be sown in pans in the cold frame at the same time. When two years old the seedlings should be transplanted, but they probably will not flower until they are 4–5 years old. (Poisonous in every part).

COLD FRAME. *See* GLASS-HOUSES.

COLEUS (ko-le-us. Labiatæ). Flame Nettle. Greenhouse perennial. Greatly prized for decoration of the conservatory, having beautiful ornamental foliage (Africa, 1774).

Culture.—Compost: 2 parts loam, 1 part leaf-mould, ½ part sand and some dried cow-manure. Pot early spring, pressing soil fairly firmly round the plants. Pinch shoots back to make plants shapely. Water freely during summer months. Winter temperature, 50°; summer, 70°.

Propagation.—By cuttings of young shoots inserted in sandy fibre at any time.

SPECIES.

C. Blumei—leaves red; this is the parent of the various varieties of the ornamental-leaved hybrids.

COLLETIA (kol-lē'-ti-a. Rhamnaceæ). *C. armata.* A Chilean species with formidable spines.

C. cruciata (*spinosa, bictoniensis*). A shrub of no floral attraction, but extremely interesting as a remarkable instance transmutation. The form *C. spino* (Chile) is noted for its smooth, rounde cylindrical spines, while *C. crucia* (Uruguay) is distinguished by havir spines flat and triangular. *Colletia cr ciata* was lost sight of soon after its intr duction. Then, to the incredulity of ga deners and botanists, this form sudden appeared in a Devon garden, raised fro seed of *C. spinosa*. Subsequently bot forms were observed growing on the sam plant in a garden in Italy.

COLLINSIA (kol-lin-si-a. Scroph larinaceæ), 1½ ft. Natives of Californi *C bicolor*, lilac and white; *C. bicolor cand dissima*, and *C. grandiflora*, violet-red, a the best of these easily-grown family c hardy annuals. Any ordinary garden so suits them and seed should be sown earl in April.

COLLOMIA (kol-lo-mi-a. Polemc niaceæ), 1–1¼ ft. *C. coccinea*, a hard annual, is the best of the genus: flower scarlet, produced in dense heads on th top of the stem. A native of Chile, a sunn position is best. Sow in April where t bloom.

COLOUR SCHEMES. The questior of colour enters into all departments c garden planning.

Apart from plants, the actual material used in garden construction can make o mar a harmonious scheme. The varying coloured stones should be used with dis cretion, as also should coloured surfacing materials available for top dressing path ways. Wood, thatch, tiles, brick, cement colouring, etc., all have their quota to add to colour in the garden, and harmony between these inanimate objects should be carefully considered. Avoid glaring white materials unless contrast is desired with evergreen foliage.

Colour schemes amongst flowers, trees, shrubs and climbers are vitally important if the best results are to be obtained from the garden design. As a general rule bright colours look best in sunshine and paler tints in the shade. White should be used in occasional bold groups to avoid a patchy effect. Grey foliage is a useful substitute for white flowers to divide one bright group from another. Grasses can also be used for this purpose. Bright colours should e kept at a distance so as to lead the eye to them. A bright colour in the foreground may mean that the rest of the garden's beauties pass unseen.

Trees have an important part to play in colour schemes. Spring-flowering cherries and plums, almonds and laburnums, trees with copper-coloured and variegated leaves, and berry-bearing trees such as the Wayfaring tree should be judiciously employed. Silver Birch and dark ever-green conifers give colour contrasts.

groups of shell pink; or blue and yellow. Start with pale shades, increase to bright and back again to pale tints; start with pinks, white and reds, increase to blues, yellows and orange and back to pinks and reds; for grouping, try Salvia Virgata, Nemerosa (purple) with Helenium July Sun (orange); Lavender with Nepeta Mussini; deep blue Delphiniums with white Madonna lilies; Cheiranthus (deep orange) with Viola Cornuta or Royal Blue Forget-me-nots. (*See also* HERBACEOUS BORDERS).

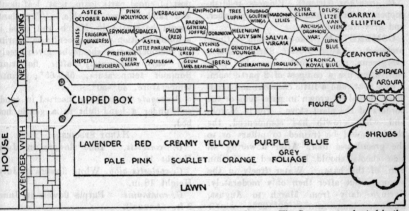

A complete design for an herbaceous border with colour scheme. The flowers are planted in the order given.

The stems of some plants are beautifully tinted. The red and yellow Dogwood and some of the willows will give winter colouring with their bare stems.

The modern shrub border is a feature to itself and arrangement and grouping for the best colour schemes is a matter of years of experience (*see* SHRUB BORDERS).

Climbers add considerably to the colour effects of a garden. Take for instance a scarlet climbing rose against a rough-cast wall; Cydonia or Pyracantha with a white background; suggestions are endless, but innumerable ideas can be gathered from noting odd corners of other people's gardens. Some of the best colour schemes come by accident. Suggestions for annual and bedding colour schemes will be found under BEDS AND BEDDING OUT.

Colour schemes for herbaceous borders will vary according to taste, but a few suggestions might be helpful. Try a blue, mauve and white border with occasional

COLUMBINE. *See* AQUILEGIA.

COLUMNEA (Gesneraceæ). Stove evergreen trailing shrubs. These plants will thrive in a soil compost of equal parts fibrous peat, sphagnum moss and charcoal. They should be planted in hanging baskets in March. They will need watering freely in the summer, but during the winter only a moderate amount should be given. Summer temperature, 60°–80°; winter, 50°–60°. Increase by cuttings of firm shoots 3 in. long. These should be inserted in compost similar to that for the adult plants with a little extra sand.

SPECIES.

C. gloriosa, scarlet and yellow.

C. scandens (climbing), scarlet, 6 ft.

C. magnifica, flame, 1 ft.

COLUTEA (kŏ-lū'-te-a. Leguminosæ). Deciduous flowering shrubs, known as "The Bladder Senna" on account of the large inflated seed pods. They are of easy cultivation in ordinary soil.

SPECIES.

C. arborescens (Mediterranean region). Flowers yellow, pear-shaped, from June until frost. Attractive to children owing to the sharp report of the pods when squeezed.

C. cilicica (Asia Minor). Flowers yellow.

C. istria (Asia Minor). Distinct with coppery-yellow flowers from late May to August.

C. media (*C. orientalis* + *arborescens*). Flowers bronzy-yellow. Likes a moist soil.

C. orientalis (Orient). Flowers, reddish-copper coloured from June to September, and grey-white foliage.

COMBRETUM ((kom-bre-tum. Cumbretaceæ). Caffre Butter Shrub. Stove evergreens, mostly climbers. For their cultivation use a compost of 2 parts loam, 1 part peat, and a little charcoal and sand. They should be grown in pots, tubs or the borders of the plant stove. Pot in March, and when growth has commenced, the shoots should be trained to pillars or to the greenhouse roof. After flowering all side shoots should be pruned to within 2 in. of the base. Water freely in the summer, but after then only moderately. Syringe daily from March to August. Summer temperature, 60°-90°; winter temperature, 50°-60°.

Increase by taking cuttings of young shoots, i.e., side shoots, taken off with a heel, inserted in well-drained sandy soil in bottom heat in summer. One of the best known species is *C. purpureum*, which is a good climber for the stove, having branching racemes of crimson flowers, blooming in September, and attaining a height of 20 ft.

Other species include *C. coccineum*, with scarlet flowers in autumn. Height 20 ft.

C. grandiflorum, with scarlet flowers in May. Height 5 ft.

COMMELINA (kom-mel-i-na. Commelinaceæ). Blue Spider-wort. Dayflower. Greenhouse and hardy annuals and perennials. The fleshy roots or rhizomes of most of the species are eatable when cooked.

The hardy kinds (annual or perennial) can be sown in the open, or in pots, in a light rich soil in spring. These plants will thrive in a well-drained, warm, sheltered bed or border. Before the

frosts the tuberous kinds should be taken up and kept like dahlias, although no over dry. Those left in the ground shoul be protected in winter with a layer o ashes or manure. In spring, those taken up and stored should be started in a littl heat and planted into the open garden at the end of May, and will bloom bette than the seedlings.

Propagate perennials also by division o the roots.

Culture of Greenhouse Plants.—A com post of equal parts loam, peat, leaf-moul and sand is most suitable. The plant should be potted in March and stood i a sunny position in the greenhouse. Durin the summer water should be given freely but only moderately after flowering Summer temperature, 55°-65°; winte temperature, 45°-50°.

Propagate by cuttings inserted in sandy soil under a hand-light in a gentle hot bed.

HARDY SPECIES.

C. coelestis. Blue flowers in July. Height 18 in.

C. coelestis alba. White flowers in July. Height 18 in.

C. communis. Purple flowers in June. 2 ft. (Annual).

C. virginica. Blue flowers in July. Height 1 ft.

GREENHOUSE SPECIES.

C. africana. Yellow flowers in May. Trailing habit.

C. elliptica. White flowers. Height 2 ft.

C. sellowiana. Blue, and its rose variety *rosea.*

C. cyanea. Blue, July, trailer.

COMPOST. Any mixture of soil is known as a compost, but especially the prepared soil used for potting plants or sowing seeds.

COMPOST PIT. Garden refuse, if treated intelligently, can be used as a valuable fertiliser. All prunings, dead bushes, etc., should be burned (*see* BONFIRE).

Any garden refuse which will decay quickly should be stacked in a heap in an out-of-the-way corner or placed in a pit dug for it. Lawn cuttings, leaves and house refuse may be used. Also any waste soil from emptied flower-pots, etc. Do *not* include diseased *growths*, which should preferably be burnt. Leave this compost through the summer, turning occasionally and adding lime to hasten decomposition.

Decomposition is hastened if even a small proportion of animal manure (farm, stable, poultry, rabbit or any kind of animal manure) can be added to the heap, as this sets up desirable bacterial action. Sufficient moisture must also be present:

particular the free use of chemical foods in place of animal manure, pointing to the fact that the Chinese have cultivated their soil for thousands of years without loss of fertility, whereas Western gardeners and farmers have left the world's surface much poorer by their system of cultivation: the Chinese, of course, return all waste products direct to the soil, and

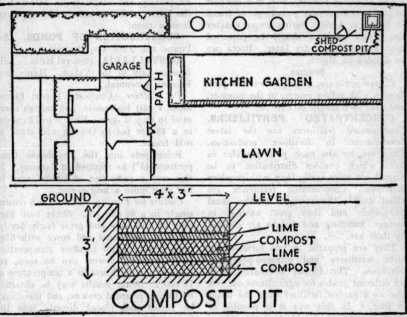

A compost pit in a corner of the garden is useful for converting waste vegetable matter into manure. Its position and construction are shown here.

many garden compost heaps fail to decay according to plan merely because they are too dry. The best method is to build each compost heap with care, treading the layers of organic refuse well down, with soil layers between them, also well trodden, and an occasional sprinkling with the watercan as the heap is built.

Well made compost should be dryish and crumbly, pleasant and clean to handle. Long straw should not be built into the heap—if it is to be used it should be chopped small first.

There are at present two opposing schools of thought concerning soil fertility. One group opposes modern methods, in

artificial fertilizers have been unknown to them. The opposite camp points to the success of soilless culture methods (*See* HYDROPONICS). We may however take it for granted that soil starved of humus does quickly become infertile, and could only be made to produce heavy crops by constant feeding and watering.

COMPTONIA (komp-tō′-ni-a. Myricaceæ). Sweet Fern, Eastern N. America. Deciduous shrubs of distinct appearance, 2–4 ft., with fern-like foliage, pleasantly aromatic. It likes shade and a peaty soil.

C. asplenifolia (syn. *Myrica asplenifolia*), The only species.

Comptonia is closely related to Myrica, but is distinguished therefrom in having flowers of the two sexes on the same plant. *See* MYRICA.

CONANDRON (ko-nan-dron. Gesneraceæ). Hardy herbaceous perennials. Dwarf herbs with the habit of Romandia, but with numerous flowers in a cyme. They thrive best in semi-shady places on the sheltered rockery, or may be kept in a cold frame in winter. Sow in a compost of peat and loam in a greenhouse or frame in March or April. During severe weather the plants outdoors should be protected with a covering of dry litter. Roots can be divided in March.

SPECIES.

C. ramondioides, which bears lilac-pink flowers with yellow centre, in the summer, and attains a height of 1 ft.

CONCENTRATED FERTILISERS. Concentrated fertilisers are the latest development in fertiliser production. They are for the most part granular in form which enables distribution to be carried out more easily than with powdery mixtures. Concentrated fertilisers are about double the strength of the usual compounds and thus great savings in cartage, handling and freight are effected by their use.

They are prepared in two forms—complete fertilisers and nitrogen-phosphate fertilisers. The former is marketed in six different grades for agricultural use and also as a garden fertiliser; and the latter in four. In this way it is possible to choose a fertiliser suitable for most soils.

Concentration is obtained by using ammonium phosphate in their manufacture and this material forms the basis of the nitrogen-phosphate group. When potash is added a complete fertiliser is obtained.

CONCRETE. Concrete for garden purposes, such as constructing a pond, is formed by mixing 1 part of cement, 2 parts of sand and 5 parts of broken brick, clinker or coarse gravel: mix thoroughly in the dry state and then mix with water to a semi-liquid condition, when it is ready for use.

CONE FLOWER. *See* RUDBECKIA.

CONSERVATORY. This is usually a structure, most frequently made of glass,

that is used for displaying plants that are unsuited to the warm atmosphere of stoves, etc., yet are too tender for outdoor culture. To further the effect and to make it natural the pots can be plunged in the soil, unlike the greenhouse, where they are left on shelves. Small plants can be shown in bowls or hanging baskets, while climbers such as Tacsonias, Roses and Passion Flowers can be used to decorate the roof. Frequently the structure is attached to the house so that it can be entered direct from a room.

CONSTRUCTION OF PONDS. *See* PONDS FOR FISH AND PLANTS.

CONVALLARIA (kon-val-lar-ia. Liliaceæ). Lily of the Valley. Hardy herbaceous perennial.

Pot Culture.—Compost: 1 part fibrous loam, 1 part leaf-mould, and enough sharp sand to keep it open. Place 8 to 12 crowns in a 48-size pot in October and stand in cold frame.

Bring pots into the greenhouse (temperature 45°) as required in January. In this way a succession of blooms may be had over quite a long period.

Culture for Forcing.—Place 6 or 8 crowns singly in a 48 size pot. Shake bulb fibre between the roots and press fairly firmly. Place in greenhouse and cover with fibre until flowers begin to show (temperature 50°). Directly flowers can be seen, remove to forcing house in a temperature of 75°–80°. Better results may be obtained by buying retarded crowns, and these may be potted and placed directly into the forcing house. Crowns are of little use after they have been forced, but may be planted in the wild garden to naturalise. Lilies of the Valley love to grow undisturbed for many years and are particularly happy in the garden if planted near a wall, tree, fence. or stone-flagged pathway, where they can enjoy a cool root run. They grow wild in great profusion on the limestone moors. For open-air culture they can be planted in September or October, the crowns being set just below the soil surface. Do not lift oftener than once in four years, and only then if the plants are becoming overcrowded.

Propagate by division of roots.

SPECIES.

C. Tayalia, white, and *mayalis flore*

pleno, double white; these are the two chief species grown.

CONVOLVULUS (kon-vol-vū-lus. Convolvulaceæ). *C. Cneorum*. South Europe. Half-hardy shrub, 1–3 ft., with large trumpet-shaped white flowers, tinged pink, contrasting pleasantly with the silvery foliage. Thrives in almost any soil, but needs a warm, dry situation under a south wall. In the open it is very liable to be injured during severe winters. Quite easily propagated by cuttings taken in summer. A very old plant in English gardens, having been cultivated since 1640.

As hardy annual, perennial climbing, and trailing plants, these plants will grow in any ordinary, rich soil. The dwarf kinds prefer to grow in the open beds and borders, while the tall kinds will grow at the base of arbours, trellises, etc. Perennial species should be planted in March. Annual species may be sown in April in the position in which they are intended to flower. They can, however, be grown in the nursery bed, and afterwards transplanted. When 2 in. high the seedlings should be planted out to 8 in. apart.

ANNUAL SPECIES.

C. tricolor. Half-hardy. Various coloured flowers in summer. Height 1 ft.

PERENNIAL SPECIES.

C. mauritanicus. Blue flowers in July. Trailing habit (greenhouse).

C. floridus. Pink, August, trailing (greenhouse).

C. glaber. White, May (stove).

C. tricolor, 1 ft., Portugal. An exceptionally easy hardy annual to grow, that will succeed almost anywhere, even in very poor soils, in sunny positions. Colour dark blue, yellow and white in a happy combination. May be sown where to flower, in autumn or spring.

See also IPOMÆA.

CONVOLVULUS MAJOR. *See* IPOMÆA.

COOPERIA (koop-er-i-a. Amaryllideæ). Half-hardy bulbous plants, opening starry-white flowers in the cool of the evening. They possess fragrance similar to that of the primrose.

A compost of equal parts loam, peat, and leaf-mould is required. They should be placed in pots in the cool greenhouse or cold frame in January or February, and until growth begins water should be given moderately. After this water freely. After September, cease to water, and during the winter the soil must be kept quite dry. Winter temperature, 40°–45°; spring temperature, 50°–55°; summer temperature, 55°–65°. Although probably hardy, these plants are best treated outdoors as half-hardy.

A deep border of sandy soil under a west wall is a suitable position; they will flower all the summer, and produce seeds.

Propagate by offsets, and by seeds sown in spring in sandy loam.

SPECIES.

C. drummondii with white and red flowers in August. Height 9 in.

C. pedunculata. White and orange flowers in August. Height 8 in.

COPING. Well-designed formal garden steps and walls are sometimes coped to give a more finished appearance, and also to protect the structures from the weather. A coping stone on treads or walls should be allowed 1–2 in. "nosing" or overlapping to give a graceful effect. The design should be uniform, and if the steps are coped, then the piers and walls should be treated in the same way. Coping is not necessary on walls in informal parts of the garden, or on walls where planting is intended on the top.

COPROLITES. Fossil remains rich in phosphate of lime. Used by Lawes in manufacture of superphosphate. *See* FERTILISERS.

COPROSMA (kop-roz'-ma. Rubiaceæ). Evergreen, half-hardy shrubs from New Zealand, for very mild districts.

Culture.—Soil, loam, peat and sand. *Propagate* by cuttings placed in bottom heat.

SPECIES.

C. acerosa. Flowers inconspicuous, followed by translucent blue berries. Fairly hardy. Suitable for the rock garden.

C. Baueri. Tall upright-growing species, with dark green Euonymus-like leaves. There is an attractive form with variegated leaves.

C. lucida. Fruit reddish-orange.

C. Petreri. Creeping species suitable for rock garden. Berries bluish-purple.

C. propinqua. Resembles *C. acerosa*, with darker blue berries.

COPTIS (kop-tis. Ranunculaceæ).
Gold Thread, Moth Root. Hardy herbaceous perennial bog plants, the roots of
which are used medicinally.

They should be cultivated in boggy
peat in a moist, shady position. They may
be planted in spring or autumn. Increase
by seeds sown in March $\frac{1}{16}$ in. deep, in
pans of fine sandy peat placed in the cold
frame, or by division of roots in October
or March. During the winter they should
be protected by lifting into the cold frame.

SPECIES.

C. occidentalis. White flowers in May.
Height 1 ft.

C. trifolia. White flowers in April.
Height 1 ft.

CORDON. Cordon fruit trees are suitable for the small garden as they take up
so little room. They have one single stem,
and are prevented from having side
branches. They are summer pruned to
encourage fruitfulness. They can be
planted 18 in. apart. There are also
horizontal cordons suitable for training on
wires.

CORDYLINE (kŏr-di-lī'-nē. Liliaceæ). *Dracæna*, New Zealand Cabbage
Tree, Australian Palm. Most striking
and handsome plants for giving tropical
appearance to the garden. Although
generally considered as suitable for only
the mild districts, they thrive in Surrey
gardens without any protection, and are
probably hardier than is usually supposed,
especially when established. *Cordyline
australis*, *C. indivisa vera*, and *C. Banksii*
have been growing in heavy soil in a
garden at Claygate, Surrey, for years,
quite unprotected. The flowers, produced
in very large panicles, are white, fragrant,
and very ornamental. *Propagation* is by
suckers, and seeds. The tops of tall leggy
specimens will root in a propagating case,
and old stems if laid in the coconut fibre
refuse of the propagating case will develop
shoots from the dormant buds. These
may be treated as cuttings.

SPECIES.

C. australis. The one most generally
cultivated.

C. Banksii. A variable species, with
red mid-ribs.

C. Baueri. Long, light green leaves,
with paler mid-rib.

C. indivisa vera. Striking variegated
foliage, main rib and side veins deep
orange.

C. i. Parrei. Long broad leaves, main
rib tinted red.

C. i. Veitchii. Similar to preceding,
leaves not so broad.

C. lentiginosa. Foliage bronzy-red.

COREMA (ko-rē'-ma. Empetraceæ).
Evergreen heath-like shrubs; thriving in
garden soil mixed with peat. *Propagate*
by seeds and cuttings.

SPECIES.

C. album. The Crowberry of Spain and
Portugal. Round white berries in autumn.

C. Conradi. Plymouth Crowberry of
eastern N. America. Very rare.

COREOPSIS (cor-e-op-sis. Compositæ). Tickseed. Late-blooming perennials with deep yellow flowers on slender
stalks, suitable for the herbaceous border
and much cultivated for cutting.

Culture.—These plants thrive in ordinary
soil and require ample water in summer.

Propagate by seeds sown in spring, by
cuttings in summer or by division in
spring.

SPECIES.

C. lanceolata with yellow flowers in
August, 2–3 ft.

C. grandiflora with yellow flowers in
August and September, 2 ft.

For annual species, *see* CALLIOPSIS.

CORIANDRUM (kor-i-an-drum.
Umbelliferæ). Hardy annuals, the leaves
of which are sometimes used for flavouring
soups, or for the salad bowl. The seeds,
which ripen in late summer, are the
coriander seeds of the confectioner.

Sow in drills, 12 in. apart, in autumn
or spring, lightly covering the seed. Any
ordinary soil and a position in full sun
is suitable.

SPECIES.

C. sativum. White flowers, June,
1–1½ ft.

Coriandrum. *Coriander seeds are used
for curries.*

CORIARIA (kŏr-i-ar'-i-a. Coriariaceæ).
Deciduous shrubs with frond-like leaves
and attractive fruits, succeeding best in
warm districts.

Culture.—Plant in loamy soil. *Propagate* by seeds, and cuttings of half-
ripened shoots.

SPECIES.

C. japonica (Japan). Low growing, leaves pale green, fruit bright coral-red, changing to black.

C. myrtifolia (Mediterranean region). Leaves and fruits poisonous.

C. terminalis (India, China). Low growing. Fruits black.

C. t. xanthocarpa. Fruits translucent yellow.

CORIS (kor-is. Primulaceæ). Montpelier Coris. Hardy biennials. These plants thrive best in sandy peat, and should be grown in well-drained beds on the sunny rockery or in pots in the cool greenhouse. Plant in March or April. Seeds may be sown $\frac{1}{16}$ in. deep in August or April in the position in which they are intended to grow.

SPECIES.

C. monspeliensis, with lilac flowers in May, and attaining a height of 1 ft.

CORK OAK. *See* QUERCUS SUBER.

CORM. Familiar examples are the montbretia, gladiola, etc. It differs from the bulb by being an underground stem, bearing one terminal bud, instead of being an underground bud. The food for the young plants is stored in the swollen fleshy stem in the corm, and in the leaves in the bulb.

CORNEL. *See* CORNUS.

CORN FLOWER. *See* CENTAUREA.

CORN SALAD, or Lamb's Lettuce (*Valerianella olitoria*). Valerianaceæ. This is a most useful salad plant for winter and spring use, when most of the other green saladings are scarce. It belongs to a class sometimes referred to as autumnal annuals, which means that they grow from seeds in the autumn and flower and seed the following year.

Culture.—Its culture is of the simplest. Seed should be sown from August to October. It is usually sown broadcast over a piece of rich soil which has been well tilled, and is merely raked in. Sometimes it is sown amongst a crop of winter onions. As the leaves are required for use the whole plant is pulled, and cleaned of the root and damaged leaves. It then merely requires washing before inclusion in a salad.

VARIETIES.

Round Leaved; Large Seeded; Golden; Italian (*V. eriocarpa*).

CORNUS (kor-nus. Cornaceæ). Dogwood. Cornelian Cherry. A horn, probably in reference to the hardness of the wood. Deciduous (mostly) and evergreen trees and shrubs (*C. capitata or Benthamia fragifera* being the exception) with white flowers. The latter are small and uninteresting, but are set in the centre of very large white and pink bracts, which give to the Cornus such a charming effect. They reach to a height of about 8–10 ft. unless otherwise stated.

Culture.—Plant in spring or autumn in loam and leaf-mould or ordinary garden soil in a sunny open position. As a rule they do not like a dry soil except *C. Mas.* Propagate by seeds sown under glass, by layering in October, and by suckers in November. Pruning consists in thinning out after flowering when necessary.

SPECIES.

C. alba (Siberia and China).

C. a. siberica. Crimson bark.

C. a. s. variegata. Creamy-white margin to leaves.

C. a. Spæthii. The most striking and beautiful of the yellow variegated cornels, retaining its attractiveness throughout the season. Bark red in winter.

The forms of *C. alba* are easily propagated by cuttings of leafless wood in the open ground in late autumn, or by layering the outer branches.

C. Mas. Cornelian Cherry. 25 ft. (Europe). Profusion of small yellow flowers in February and March, on bare branches. Berries bright red, as large as the hips of the common wild rose. Foliage bronzy-red in autumn.

C. M. aurea elegantissima. Foliage yellowish-green, tinted pink.

C. sanguinea. Common Native Dogwood. 6–12 ft. Fine autumn foliage.

C. stolonifera flaviramea (N. America). 3–6 ft. Effective in winter with its yellow bark. Cutting down yearly, produces richer-coloured bark.

COROKIA (kor-ō-ki-a. Cornaceæ), New Zealand. Evergreen shrubs with yellow inconspicuous flowers and red or yellow berries, not unlike Cornelian cherries.

Culture.—Plant in April or October in ordinary soil. Prune to shape only. Propagate by cuttings in a frame in August.

SPECIES.

C. buddleoides. Red berries.

C. Cheesemanii, 7 ft. Intermediate between *C. buddleoides* and *C. cotoneaster.* Bright yellow berries. Undersides of leaves, silvery.

C. cotoneaster, 6 ft. Red berries.

C. macrocarpa. Tender, requires wall protection except in mild districts. Pale green leaves, with silvery reverse. Berries brilliant orange-red persisting for a long period.

C. virgata. A vigorous-growing and very free-flowering species.

CORONILLA (kŏr-ō-nil′la. Leguminosæ). Crown Vetch or Scorpion Senna. Hardy and half-hardy shrubs, with pea-shaped flowers. The flowers of the rockery species are pea-shaped, usually yellow, and produced in rounded heads. A hot, dry situation is the most satisfactory.

Culture.—Plant in March or October in ordinary garden soil, in sunny positions.

Propagation.—Sow seeds in March or take cuttings of young wood in April. Wall protection is generally needed.

SPECIES.

C. cappadocica (iberica). Blue-grey shortly-trailing foliage. The flower heads are large and produced throughout the summer.

C. Emerus (Scorpion Senna), Europe. An elegant-habited shrub 7–9 ft. with pea-shaped yellow flowers, with reddish lines on the standard petals. Very long-flowering. May to October.

The name Scorpion Senna refers to the shape of the seed pod.

C. glauca. From Spain, has even bluer foliage. It forms a small bush, about 18 in. high. The flowers are crowded, conspicuous and sweet-smelling.

CORREA (kŏr-rē′-a. Rutaceæ). Evergreen shrubs from Australia with tubular fuchsia-like flowers. Only suited to the warmer parts of the country, even then needing wall protection.

Culture.—Plant in soil of peat and leaf-mould, with or without loam and plenty of sand. *Propagate* by cuttings of half-ripened shoots in sand in pots under bell-glass. Also by grafting on to *C. alba.*

SPECIES.

C. alba. White flowers from April to July. The hardiest species.

C. cardinalis (speciosa). Flowers bright scarlet, tipped green.

C. Harrisii. Hybrid or variety of *C. cardinalis.*

C. speciosa (magnifica). Pendant, prim-rose-coloured flowers produced over a very long period.

C. ventricosa. Distinct, flowers crimson, tipped green.

CORTADERIA (cor-ta-de-ria. Graminaceæ). Pampas Grass (syn. *Gynerium*). A silky plumed perennial grass with handsome curving foliage. Useful for beds if the soil is well drained and the position sheltered.

Culture.—Sow under glass in spring.

SPECIES.

G. argentea, white plumed, in late summer, 6–8 ft.

CORTUSA (kort-u-sa. Primulaceæ). After Cortusus, an Italian botanist.

C. Matthioli is a small woodland plant having soft hairy leaves like small editions of the greenhouse *Primula sinensis.* The flowers, too, are primula-like, small, and rosy-magenta.

Propagation.—From fresh seed sown in August, or by division. In a cool, shady position the plants spread rapidly.

CORYANTHES (kor-i-an-thez. Orchidaceæ). Stove epiphytal orchids. These orchids should grow in well-drained pots of fibrous peat, chopped sphagnum, and small broken potsherds, or in baskets suspended from roof of stove. Re-basket or pot in March. Growing-temperature, 75°–80°. Resting, 50°–60°. Growing-season, April to August, resting-period, August to April. Water freely from April to September, but give very little afterwards. The flowers will appear on the new growth.

Propagate by division in March.

SPECIES.

C. macrantha. Green, purple, yellow and crimson flowers in June. Height 1 ft.

C. maculata. Yellow and purple flowers in June. Height 1 ft.

C. speciosa. Yellow and green flowers in May. Height 1 ft.

CORYDALIS (kor-ĭ-dale-iss. Papaveraceæ). Fumitory. From *korudalos*, a lark. From the spur of the flower resembling that of a lark. A large family containing annual, biennial, herbaceous and tuberous plants. These attractive plants are akin to the native fumitory. All have elegant foliage superficially fern-like.

Propagate by seed or division.

SPECIES.

C. capnoides, a pale sulphur flower having a small black spot on the lip. 6 in. S. Europe.

C. cheilanthefolia. The foliage is large, the fine yellow flowers are produced in stout sprays on long stems. An attractive and hardy Chinese species. Rich, well-drained, gritty soil, in sun. 10 in.

C. Halleri, an early-flowering tuberous-rooted pink form, glaucous foliage. 4 in.

C. lutea. This is a naturalised species, often seen growing wild in the crevices of shady walls, generally near gardens from which it doubtless originally escaped. The flowers are a deep yellow. The foliage delicate and pale green. It does quite as well in sun as in shade, providing the ground does not bake hard in summer. Almost perpetually in flower. 6 in.

CORYLOPSIS (cŏri-lop'-sis. Hamamelideæ). Deciduous, hardy-flowering shrubs, from N.E. Asia, with yellow, usually cowslip-scented flowers during March and April, before the leaves. Fine woodland shrubs.

Culture.—Plant October or November in ordinary garden soil, although they respond to liberal treatment. No pruning required. *Propagate* by layers in summer.

SPECIES.

C. Goteana (Japan). New species.

C. pauciflora (Japan), 4 ft. Distinct from other Corylopsis with large open flowers. Rather tender. Very floriferous.

C. platypetala (China), 4–6 ft. Foliage bright yellow in autumn. Large racemes of fragrant yellow flowers.

C. sinensis (China), 10–15 ft. Foliage well coloured in autumn.

C. spicata (Japan), 4–6 ft. The earliest to flower. February and March.

C. Veitchiana (China), 5–9 ft. A rare species resembling *C. Willmottiæ*.

C. Willmottiæ (China), 6–12 ft. A quick-growing species, producing fragrant yellow flowers in March and April.

C. Wilsonii (China). A rare species resembling *Veitchiana*.

CORYLUS. *See* HAZEL NUT, OR FILBERT.

COSMOS (kos·mos. Compositæ). 2½–3 ft. The best form for garden purposes, *C. bipinnatus*, is a native of Mexico, and delights in a sunny position; of this there are early- and late-flowering types, and both single and double varieties. The flowers, like single anemones, are most freely produced on long wiry stems, to which the feathery foliage serves as a delicate foil. Colours: rose, crimson, pink

Cosmos with its pink and white flowers is a gay summer annual but makes foliage only in very rich soil.

and white. The late-flowered kinds should be avoided as the seasons in Britain are not long enough to bring them to perfection.

Culture.—Choose a good early-flowering strain, sow the seeds in warm greenhouse or frame in March, pot off seedlings into 3 in. pots as soon as 3–5 leaves formed; keep in good light, give free ventilation, and let the plants remain in the 3 in. pots until a flower-bud shows in the top of the stem, then repot, or plant into flowering-quarters, in poor soil: this preliminary starving will do no harm; the plants will soon recover and flower most freely.

COTONEASTER (kō-tō-nē-as'-ter. Rosaceæ). Deciduous and evergreen flowering and berry-bearing shrubs, of great value for their conspicuous and attractive clusters of berries, red, yellow, and black, and in some species richly-coloured foliage, in autumn. Of the easiest cultivation, thriving in any ordinary soil. *Propagation* is by cuttings, which strike very readily, of half-ripened wood about July, in the open or under glass.

DECIDUOUS SPECIES.

C. acutifolia (China). Vigorous, but not very attractive.

C. adpressa (China), 1–1½ ft. Suitable for rock gardens. Fruit bright red; foliage colours well in autumn.

C. angustifolia. See PYRACANTHA.

C. bullata (China), 10–12 ft. Quite one of the finest. Of little floral beauty, but most beautiful in autumn with large corymbs of brilliant red berries and scarlet leaves.

C. divaricata (China), 6 ft. Berries scarlet. Fine autumn foliage.

C. frigida (Himalayas), 15–20 ft. One of the most striking species, with large clusters of crimson berries, in some seasons persisting until February. Not such a favourite with birds as others. Quite unsurpassed as a shrub for town gardens.

C. f. Vicarii. An exceptionally fine form, with large scarlet berries.

C. horizontalis (*Davidiana*), China. 2–3 ft. Of beautiful horizontal habit: useful for covering spaces of poor ground, banks, backs of large rock gardens, etc., and always attractive wherever placed. Berries red and foliage well-coloured in autumn.

C. moupinensis (China), 8–10 ft. Often confused with *C. bullata* but distinguished from that species by its jet black berries.

C. Simonsii (Himalayas). An old favourite of gardens. An excellent hedge plant of compact habit, branches laden with bright red fruits and dark green, brilliantly tinted leaves.

C. tomentosa (Europe), 4–6 ft. Flowers pinkish, berries red.

EVERGREEN SPECIES.

C. Aldenhamensis. A garden form raised from a specially fine Cotoneaster. Forms a large bush with graceful branches growing outwards and arching downwards,

displaying the berries to the greatest advantage. Leaves large and handsome, persisting throughout the winter. Berries of big size, bright red, and most freely produced, remaining plump and shiny up to Christmas.

C. amœna (China), 3 ft. Berries bright red, persisting until mid-winter.

C. buxifolia (*rupestris*). Nilghiri Hills, N. India, 10–12 ft. Berries brilliant red. Most useful species for covering unsightly fences, etc.

C. congesta (Himalayas), 1½–2 ft. A charming species for the rock garden. Berries red.

C. Franchetii (China), 8–10 ft. Berries red.

C. Henryana (China), 10–12 ft. A fast-growing, pendulous-habited species with the largest leaves of any Cotoneaster, which become bronzy-red. Berries crimson-brown.

C. microphylla (Himalayas), 2–3 ft. Of spreading habit. Berries scarlet.

C. m. thymifolia. A diminutive form.

C. prostrata (Himalayas). Berries red.

C. salicifolia (China). Probably not in cultivation.

C. s. floccosa. Berries orange-red, extending well along the branches.

C. serotina (China). A very distinct, fine-fruiting species of graceful habit. Berries scarlet. F.C.S., R.H.S.

Those dwarf forms suitable to the rock garden are:

C. adpressa. A small-leaved deciduous form which moulds itself closely to the rocks over which it should be allowed to droop. Small white flowers in spring, followed by innumerable bright red berries closely set along the branches, persisting well into the new year if the blackbirds will allow them.

C. congesta (*pyrenaica*) has a similar but less vigorous habit of growth to *C. adpressa*, though it seems to fruit less freely.

C. humifusa has broader leaves and rambles about, rooting as it goes. Red berries in moderate quantity. Central China.

C. thymifolia makes a dwarf bush clothed with small thyme-like leaves and dark red berries. The small white flowers are attractive. This will not always survive a severe winter in an exposed position. Himalayas.

COTTON GRASS. *See* ERIO-PHORUM.

COTULA (kot-ū-la. Compositæ). From *kotule*, a little hollow or cup, referring to the shape of the flower heads. Carpeting plants with small fern-like leaves and inconspicuous flowers. Their main use is to provide a covering for bulbs or to carpet some spare corner.

Propagation.—Seeds. The difficulty is not to propagate but to repress them.

Also hardy little trailing perennials with fern-like foliage and yellow flowers in summer.

Culture.—Propagate by division of the roots in March or October. Plant out in any position in sun or shade in gritty loam, suitable for the chinks of paved walks or steps.

Best known are *C. squalida* from New Zealand and *C. potentilla* from Chatham Island. Height 1–3 in.

COTYLEDON (kot-ĭ-lee-don. Crassulaceæ). From *kotule*, a little hollow or cup; referring to hollow in the leaves of some species. Succulent or semi-succulent plants, mainly from South Africa.

Those appropriate to a collection of rock plants are: *C. chrysantha* (House Leek Pennywort), a yellow-flowered species from Asia Minor; and *C. simplicifolia*, which runs freely about and is covered in early summer with short arched stems, each bearing a number of small yellow flowers.

SPECIES.

There are also many species grown as greenhouse plants, including the following:

C. coccinea, scarlet and yellow, October.
C. fulgens, red and yellow, summer.
C. glauca, scarlet and yellow, autumn.
C. retusa, crimson and yellow, autumn.

The last three are more commonly known under the generic name of Echeveria.

COURSED. Regular-shaped pieces of stone such as pavement stone are laid so that the crevices form a straight line down the length of the pathway. This method of stone laying is known as coursed paving. One row of bricks in a wall or building is also known as a course.

COURTYARD. This was originally a paved or gravelled space, screened on two

or three sides by buildings. The same effect can be created in the modern garden by the use of trellis or hedging.

Such areas if carefully planted can be very delightful garden features and often give a note of interest as seen from a house window. Formal flower-beds in the paving, or just creeping plants in crevices will help to soften the hard outline of the stone-work. Tubs, boxes and vases are also appropriate if kept bright with flowers throughout the year. The older types of ornament such as sundials and dovecotes are the most harmonious, if one is desired for a focal point.

COW PARSNIP. *See* HERACLEUM.

CRAB. *See* PYRUS.

CRAB, Japanese. *See* PYRUS FLORIBUNDA.

CRAB, Wild. *See* PYRUS MALUS.

CRAB'S CLAW. *See* STRATIOTES.

CRAMBE. *See* SEAKALE.

CRANBERRY. There are two species of Cranberry in cultivation. The one generally seen in shops is *Oxycoccus macrocarpus*, the American Cranberry. *Oxycoccus palustris* is a native of this country. It requires a boggy situation and is not much cultivated. Well-prepared fields which can be flooded at will, produce as much as 400 bushels to the acre.

See OXYCOCCUS.

CRANE'S BILL. *See* GERANIUM.

CRASSULA (kras-su-la. Crassulaceæ). Greenhouse annuals, biennials and perennials. Sow in pots in spring in gentle heat. The perennials can also be increased by cuttings of shoots 2–3 in. long, choosing the tops of shoots that have not flowered. Take these in summer. Expose them to the air for a few days first, then pot them singly in small pots, and grow them on until the pots are filled with roots, i.e., about the end of October. Stand them on the greenhouse shelf during winter, close to the glass, and give only a little water.

In spring, stop the growths 3 or 4 in. from the pot, and take off a few of the top leaves. This encourages the formation of new shoots. Thin these to three to six, according to the strength of the plant. When the shoots are 2 in. long, move each plant into a larger pot, filled with loam and broken bricks, and stand these pots in a warm greenhouse. At the end of June, plunge them outdoors in sand in the shelter of the greenhouse, watering the sand occasionally, without actually watering the pots. Move them to the cold pit on the approach of frost, and later to the greenhouse shelf. They can be used for bedding out in the following May.

If flowers are wanted each year, only one shoot must be allowed to bloom, any others ready to flower being cut back.

SPECIES.

C. arborescens. Pink, May, 3 ft.

C. sarcocaulis. The hardest species.

C. lactea. White, September, 9 in.

For *Crassula coccinea, see* ROCHEA.

CRATÆGO-MESPILUS (krā-tē-go-mes-pi-lus. Rosaceæ). A group of deciduous trees of great interest, being hybrids natural, and graft, between the hawthorn and the medlar.

Culture.—Same as hawthorns (Cratægus).

SPECIES.

C.-m. Asnieresii. A graft hybrid between *Cratægus monogyna* and *Mespilus germanica.* A beautiful flowering tree, intermediate between its two parents.

C.-m. Dardari. Of the same parentage, but nearer to the medlar in general appearance.

C.-m. grandiflora. A natural hybrid of the same parentage, found growing wild in France. A very free-flowering tree of great beauty and elegance, and remains true to character.

CRATÆGUS (kra-tē'-gus. Rosaceæ). Thorns. Very ornamental deciduous small trees, with white flowers (usually) and berries varying considerably in form, colour, and size.

Culture.—Plant in October or November in ordinary soil. They have no objection to lime. *Propagation* is best by seeds, which may not germinate until the second year.

SPECIES.

C. Carrieri, 20 ft. Thought to be a hybrid between *C. punctata* and *C. Crusgalli*, or a form of *C. mexicana.* One of the best either in foliage, flower, or fruit.

C. coccinea, 20 ft. The "Scarlet Haw" of N. America.

C. Crus-galli. The "Cockspur Thorn" (eastern N. America). Of striking habit,

free blooming, and brilliant foliage in autumn. The fruit or berries are decorative throughout the winter, and remain so until the spring.

C. grignonensis. The bright red fruits last well into winter.

C. macrantha. Fruit bright scarlet. Distiguished by its spines, the largest of all thorns.

C. oxyacantha. The native "Hawthorn" or "May," also known as "Whitethorn," or "Quick."

C. prunifolia. Of uncertain origin. Very attractive in autumn, with beautiful deep green leaves turning to glowing crimson, and large red fruits.

CRAZY PAVING. *See* PAVING, CRAZY.

CREEPING FORGET-ME-NOT. *See* OMPHALODES.

CREEPING JENNY. *See* LYSIMACHIA.

CREPIS (kre-pis. Compositæ). Hawkweed; Hawksbeard, 6–9 in. *C. rubra* is a very pretty little annual, and would probably be popular but for the name "hawkweed." Its flowers are red or pink, and in shape somewhat resemble a common dandelion with long drooping petals. Any ordinary soil suits it. Sow in autumn for spring, or in spring for summer flowering.

CRESS, American or Land (*Barbarea præcox*). Cruciferæ. This is an entirely different plant from the ordinary garden cress which is associated with mustard, but a most useful salad for all seasons, one of its chief merits being that it is remarkably slow in running to seed.

Culture.—The seed may be sown in almost any type of soil from spring to autumn, though the best results are probably obtained from autumn sowings in a moist border. The seed may be sown broadcast or raked in, or in very shallow drills 9 in. apart. The plants form compact rosettes of leaves, and if the centre is picked out for use, further supplies of leaves will be produced.

Use.—The leaves, though somewhat hard and pungent, are an excellent addition to a salad, especially in winter and spring. They are also used for garnishing and seasoning.

CRESS, or Garden Cress (*Lepidium sativum*). Cruciferæ. This is a quickgrowing annual plant which originated in Persia, and it may safely be called one of the most popular of all small salads, and is known by everyone as the one associated with mustard and cress.

Culture.—Its cultivation is remarkably simple as it may be sown at any time and upon almost any kind of soil. As the plant runs quickly to seed, frequent successional sowings are advisable, and during hot weather the seed bed should, if possible, be situated in a moist and shaded position.

During the winter, seed should be sown thickly on the top of shallow boxes filled with an open compost, or even on sheets of clean hessian or flannel laid over a bed of fine ashes. If sown on soil the seed should not be covered, but merely pressed in and well watered. A temperature of 50°–60° is necessary in winter, and under these conditions germination may take place within 24 hours. Plenty of light should be afforded the seedlings, and if well watered at the time of sowing no further watering should be necessary before the crop is ready to cut.

For spring, summer and autumn supplies seed may be sown outside if the soil is worked down to a fine tilth. As with indoor sowings on soil, the seed should be sown thickly, and merely pressed in with a board. In the event of birds proving troublesome, a mat may be laid over the seed bed, but this should be removed as soon as germination takes place.

Varieties.—Improved Curled; Plain or Common Garden; Australian or Golden.

Uses.—The crop is cut when 1½–2 in. high, and is principally used in salads or sandwiches, and for garnishing cold joints.

CRINODENDRON. *See* TRICUS-PIDARIA.

CRINUM (kri-num. Amaryllidaceæ). Cape Lily. Stove and greenhouse bulbous plants. Deciduous. One species, *C. longiflorum*, is hardy in England, but must be planted deep enough to be protected from very severe frosts. (S. Africa, 1732).

Culture.—Compost, *see* AGAPANTHUS. Repot early spring. Give water abundantly during growing season, with applications of liquid manure at least once a week. After flowering, gradually withhold water and store plants under staging until repotting time. Temperature: stove

species, winter, 55°; summer, 80°. Temperature: greenhouse species, winter, 45°; summer, 65°.

Propagation.—By offsets at potting time. They may also be propagated by seed, but the plants take several years before flowering.

Stove Species—*C. amabile*, red.

C. speciosum, pink.

There are numerous others, but few are cultivated.

CRINUM POWELLI

A pink flower of the lily family, Amaryllis, or Crinum Powelli. It thrives best at the foot of a south wall.

Greenhouse Species.—*C. Moorei*, white and red.

C. Moorei album, white.

C. Powelli, pink.

C. Powelli rubrum, red.

Crinum longifolium and its varieties and hybrids can be grown outdoors in a south border. The border along the south side of a greenhouse is an ideal spot.

CRITHMUM (krith-mum. Umbelliferæ). Samphire. This is a hardy perennial at home at the seaside, but not easy to grow elsewhere. If sown in April (or planted at the same season), the plants will grow successfully so long as they are watered with salt water, 1 oz. to the gallon, about twice a week. A little guano should also be added to the salt water.

SPECIES.

C. maritimum. White, summer, 1 ft.

CROCOSMA (kro-kos-ma. Irideæ). Half-hardy bulbous-rooted plants, suitable for the warm south borders. One of the parents (with *Tritonia Pottsi*) of the Montbretias.

Plant in light soil, with the addition of peat and leaf-mould. Set the bulbs 6 in. deep, and 4 in. apart, with a little sand under each, or for pot culture put six bulbs 1 in. deep in a 5 in. pot. Keep moderately moist until after the flowers die.

Propagate by seeds sown in pans in sandy soil in autumn, in the greenhouse, or by offsets from the bulbs.

SPECIES.

C. aurea, orange-red, and its varieties *imperialis* and *maculata.*

CROCUS (Iridaceæ). Hardy bulbous-flowering plants. The common spring-flowering crocus is well known in gardens, and the modern forms have been derived from the *Crocus vernus.* In addition to this, there are numerous other species which can be accommodated in the amateur's garden, and these include both spring and autumn-flowering varieties. The spring-flowering crocuses are, however, the most popular, and they are particularly useful for border edgings, to naturalise in grass, to make splashes of colour on the rockery or to cultivate in special containers for indoor decoration. They prefer light rich soil, but will grow in soil of almost any type if it is fairly well drained, so that too much moisture does not collect round the corms. The ordinary spring crocus can be planted in October, November or December, about 3 in. deep and the same distance apart. Unless it is necessary for any special reason to lift the corms, they should remain where they are planted for 4 or 5 years or until they become overcrowded. Then they can be lifted in June or July. Dry them off, and then replant again as in the first instance. If it is desired to naturalise crocuses in grass, small holes should be bored 3 in. deep and 2 in. apart, and a single corm dropped into each hole,

which will then be filled up with ordinary soil. Another method is to lift pieces of turf and to fork up the under-soil, at the same time mixing with it a few handfuls of bonemeal. Press the corms into position on this sub-soil and then replace the turf, rolling it to restore the level surface.

The crocuses will grow up through the grass, and after flowering, the foliage of the crocuses will, if allowed to do so, grow to a considerable length. The grass cannot be cut while the crocus foliage remains green without damaging the crocuses, so that they will not flower next season, and crocuses cannot therefore be grown in a lawn which must be kept neat and tidy. The ideal position for crocus bulbs is on a sloping bank between two sections of the lawn or in odd positions round and under trees where a piece of the lawn can be left unmowed for a considerable time after the crocuses have ceased to flower.

Crocuses can be grown from seed which is sown $\frac{1}{3}$ in. deep in light sandy soil in the cold frame in the autumn. The seedlings will be transplanted in the August of the second year and will flower when perhaps three or four years old. The supply can also be increased by offsets, removed from the old corms in July or August, replanted 2 in. deep and 2 in. apart. These will not flower until they have been grown on for a year or two.

If it is absolutely necessary to lift crocuses after flowering, they should be lifted with some soil round the roots and either replanted in a corner of the garden or planted with the soil into shallow boxes where they can be left and watered occasionally so long as the foliage remains green. But crocuses will always flower best if they are allowed to remain undisturbed for several years, and for this reason it is inadvisable to use them as carpet plants beneath tulips, or beneath other plants which must be moved after flowering.

CROCUSES INDOORS.

Crocuses make ideal indoor decorations and they can be cultivated either in pots of soil or in bowls containing coconut fibre. If soil is used, it should be a mixture of light soil and sand, with a little leaf-mould. The corms should be planted 2 in.

below the surface, leaving about 1 in. between each corm. 10 corms can be accommodated in a 5 in. pot. After potting, stand the pots in the cold frame or under the shelter of a wall, and cover them with old fine cinder ashes until growth has begun. Then move them to a cold greenhouse, or bring them indoors into one of the house rooms, but not into a room which is artificially heated. Crocuses will not stand forcing in the early stages, and are really best grown in cool conditions throughout.

Give sufficient water at all times, but after the flowers have faded give rather less until the foliage dies. If grown in coconut fibre, shallow bowls can be used, anything above 1 in. deep being suitable. The corms can be just pressed into the moistened fibre and need not be completely covered. Keep them in a dark, cool, airy place until growth commences, after which they can be brought gradually into more light and more heat. Though, as already stated, crocuses do not like ever to be brought into very great heat.

CROCUSES IN WATER.

Crocuses are amongst the bulbs which it is quite simple to grow in water only. One of the most charming ways of growing them is to stand the corms on a saucer full of pebbles to which water has been added, so that the water reaches nearly, but not quite, to the base of the corm. It is only necessary to keep the water at this level and the crocuses will grow and flower quite well for one season, though the corms will not be much use afterwards.

CROCUSES IN WINDOW BOXES.

The purple, white and gold globes of crocus flowers make particularly charming decorations for town windows and need no special care in cultivation. Any ordinary box filled with soil, standing on a window ledge, will accommodate quite a number of bulbs if they are planted 2 in. deep and 2 in. apart. They need no sticks or any support or protection against wind. The only trouble which may arise is that sparrows are particularly fond of them and may peck the flowers to pieces. This can be prevented by stretching a few strands of black cotton 2–3 in. above the soil level of the box. The cotton is scarcely visible, and is an effective barrier to the birds.

AUTUMN-FLOWERING CROCUSES.

Autumn-flowering crocuses are cultivated in the same way as the spring-flowering varieties, except that they are planted in August or September. A useful practice is to plant both autumn and spring flowers in the grass together in a position where the grass need not be mown regularly, such as, for instance, on a sloping bank. Mixed in this way, they are also useful for the Alpine Meadow garden and for pockets in the rockery.

The autumn crocuses should not be confused with colchicum, which is commonly known as autumn crocus in many districts. (*See* COLCHICUM.)

Amongst the most useful of modern-named crocuses are:

Baron van Brunow—dark blue.
Early Perfection—dark lilac.
Purpurea grandiflora—purple.
Queen of the Blues—pure lilac.
Kathleen Parlow—pure white.
King of the Whites—pure white.
Mont Blanc—pure white.
Sir Walter Scott—violet and white stripes.

In addition, the following crocus species are offered by most traders:

C. biflorus (Scotch Crocus)—white and lilac, slightly fragrant.
C. Imperati—violet, fawn and black.
C. Susianus "Cloth of Gold"—yellow, black striped.
C. versicolor "Cloth of Silver"—white, flaked blue.
C. tommasinianus—lavender-sapphire.

CROQUET COURT. The regulation size of a croquet lawn is 35 yds. by 28 yds. Interesting games can, however, be arranged on a smaller space of lawn. (*See* sketch for lay-out, page 210.)

CROSSBAR. The transverse beam of an arch (*see* PERGOLA).

CROSSOSOMA (cros-o-sō'-ma. Dilleni-aceæ). Interesting and rare shrubs for sunny walls in warm districts, with glaucous foliage and white flowers in August, resembling *Carpenteria california*, 3–4 ft.

Culture.—Light loamy soil. *Propagate* by cuttings of half-ripened wood in summer.

SPECIES.

C. californica.

CROWEA (kro-e-a. Rutaceæ). Greenhouse evergreens. Pot in March or April in a compost of 2 parts peat, 1 part fibrous loam, and some sand. Stand on light shelves in the greenhouse. Temperature 40°–45° winter; 55°–65° September.

Prune into shape in March.

Propagate by cuttings in sand in a temperature of 65° in March or April, or graft on to *Correa alba* or *Eriostemon buxifolia*.

culture the compost should be a mixture of equal parts loam, peat, leaf-mould, decayed manure and sand.

Crown Imperials can be grown from seed, although the seedlings do not flower for some years. Varieties cultivated are the *Fritillaria Imperialis*, and its varieties, *latifolia* and *pallidiflora*.

CRUCIANELLA (kru-si-an-el-la.

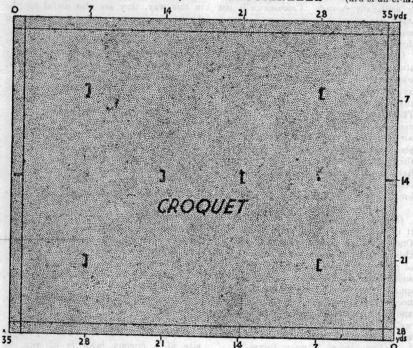

The game of Croquet is played on a lawn 105 ft. x 84 ft., with hoops placed as indicated.

SPECIES.

C. angustifolia. Red, summer, 1 ft.

C. saligna. Purple, September, 3 ft.

CROWFOOT. *See* RANUNCULUS.

CROWN. A root or rootstock having a bud from which new growth appears each year.

CROWN IMPERIALS (*Fritillaria Imperialis*). Hardy bulbs which bear tall imposing flowers on stems 3–4 ft. high. These should be cultivated in deep, rich soil well drained. They succeed admirably in shady places or in narrow borders alongside the house walls. They also make useful pot flowers in the greenhouse if one bulb is potted in a 6–8 in. pot. For pot

Rubiaceæ). Crosswort. Hardy and greenhouse perennials.

Propagate in March by seeds or division. The hardy kinds are suitable for sandy or chalky soil on dry banks or rockeries. Greenhouse species grow well in loam and peat.

SPECIES.

C. stylosa (*Phuopsis stylosa*). Rose-pink, summer, 9 in.; and its varieties, *coccinea* and *purpurea*.

C. americana and *maritima*. Both yellow, greenhouse species.

CRUST OF THE EARTH. This term explains itself: it means the outer layer of rock of the earth's surface. *See also* ROCK. This outer layer seems never to be quite still. Violent adjustments are called "earthquakes," but infinitely small adjustments seem always to be taking place, doubtless owing to conditions under the surface, of which we have as yet insufficient knowledge. Such movements might mean a rise or fall of the land surface of some country at a rate of less than 1 in. per year—a movement of almost incredible slowness—but in accordance with established facts. Sweden, for instance, appears to be rising at about an inch every two or three years. If this continued long enough it would become of great importance. When the rocks of the earth's crust break into soil, then, given suitable climatic conditions, that crust becomes clothed with vegetation. (*See also under* ROCK *and* SOIL).

CRYPTANTHUS (krip-tan-thus. Bromeliaceæ). Stove epiphytes. Pot in March in a compost of loam, peat, leaf-mould and sand in equal parts. Water freely. Temperature, winter, 65°–75°; summer, 75°–85°.

Propagate by offsets inserted singly in small pots in a temperature of 85° in April.

SPECIES.

C. undulatus. White, August, and its varieties, *ruber* and *zebrinus.*

CRYTOGRAMME (Filices). Parsley Fern. Mostly hardy ferns, preferring a moist, cool rockery, and a soil of loam and peat without lime.

Propagate by division of the roots in spring.

SPECIES.

C. crispa and its varieties *acrostichioides* and *brunoniana,* the latter being rather tender.

CRYPTOMERIA (krip-tō-mēr'-i-a. Coniferæ). The "Japanese Cedar" is a genus of one species of various forms, distinct from all other trees. Native of China as well as of Japan, and is a very valuable timber tree. The timber is highly prized by the Japanese for building purposes, taking on a high polish, and is much used for indoor decoration. In this country it thrives best in the mild, moist parts. Plant in deep, rich, moist soil, in a fairly sheltered position.

Propagate by seeds sown in March and by cuttings in August under a hand-light.

C. japonica, the type. Foliage yellowish-green, turning to dark green in winter.

C. j. araucarioides. Slender pendulous branches.

C. j. compacta. Conical, dwarf, 2–3 ft.

C. j. cristata. Dwarf compact form with contorted branches.

C. j. elegans. Bushy habit. Foliage glaucous green changing to reddish-bronze in autumn and winter. A very distinct and beautiful variety.

C. j. Lobbii. Young foliage pale green. Habit pyramidal.

CUCKOO SPIT

Frothy appearance on foliage is known as Cuckoo Spit. The insect that develops inside the protective froth is the Froghopper which sucks the sap from the plant to which it is attached.

C. j. nana. Dwarf, 2 ft.

C. j. Vilmoriniana. Very dwarf, small pointed leaves.

CUCKOO FLOWER. *See* CARDAMINE.

CUCKOO SPIT INSECT or **FROG-HOPPER** (*Philænus spumarius*).

DESCRIPTION. *Adult.*—A very variable insect nearly ¼ in. long and ranging from almost white through shades of brown to black. The majority of the brown specimens have whitish spots on the elytra. *Larva.*—Bright green with pink eyes. This stage is seldom seen as the young blow a "froth" around themselves in which they live.

LIFE-HISTORY.—The eggs are laid in rows on some woody stem. On hatching-out in the early summer they crawl up into the young green foliage and embed their beaks into the plant tissues. After sucking the sap they begin to pass this out in the form of bubbles, and in the froth so formed they go through their changes. Shortly before they come to maturity the "froth" dries, hardens and breaks away, leaving the immature adult exposed. At this stage the insects are soft and pale green in colour, but quickly assume their markings. They continue to suck the sap and may be found commonly

Providing a few main essentials are observed, cucumbers are not difficult to cultivate, and it should not be beyond the power of any amateur to grow a good crop of one section or the other.

Culture (in Glasshouses).—Seeds for the earliest crop should be sown soon after Christmas. 3 in. pots should be well "crocked," and filled with a sandy compost, and into each of these one seed should

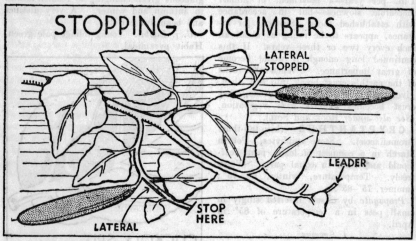

STOPPING CUCUMBERS

LATERAL
STOPPED

LEADER

STOP
HERE

LATERAL

As cucumbers make rapid growth, the laterals are stopped beyond each fruit.

on lavender, chrysanthemums, which are often badly damaged, Michaelmas daisies, sunflowers, as well as many other garden plants. In the late summer they seek out the more woody stalks wherein they lay their eggs.

METHODS OF CONTROL.—A heavy syringing with ordinary water to blow away the "froth," and then an application of a nicotine wash will soon kill them.

CUCUMBER (*Cucumis sativus*). Few salads are deemed complete without the addition of some cucumber, and it is certainly a most valuable crop for those supplying the markets. Enormous areas are devoted to its cultivation under glass, both in houses and in frames, whilst the subsection of ridge cucumbers are largely cultivated out of doors. When or how the plant was first introduced it is difficult to say, but it is claimed to be a native of the East Indies, and possibly of N.W. India.

be pressed on edge, and then covered with ½ in. more soil.

A light watering with warm water should be given, and the pots then plunged to the rim in a bed of fermenting manure, or in damp fibre situated over the water pipes.

Germination is usually fairly quick, and as soon as it takes place the pots should be moved to a shelf near the glass unless the weather is extremely frosty. The temperature during this period should not drop below 75° or exceed 85°, and every effort must be made to keep the plants short and sturdy. As the small pots become filled with roots they should be potted on into larger sizes, using a richer and more retentive compost previously warmed to the temperature of the house. A check to the young plants has a very marked influence upon the crop.

In potting on seedling cucumbers they

should be potted up to the two first or "seed leaves," and the soil made only moderately firm.

If the crop is to be grown entirely in pots, they must be moved on to larger sizes as the pots become filled with roots, until they are finally placed in 10 in. pots. In this instance they should be placed half-way down the pot, leaving the remainder for subsequent top-dressings.

The most usual method of growing them in glasshouses is in beds specially prepared and made up upon the floor along either side of a low-span roof house. Houses heated by hot-water pipes are best, as they promote a humid atmosphere, but the fallacy that bottom heat is essential has long been exploded.

The most suitable compost is a mixture of equal parts good turfy loam, roughly broken up and well-rotted strawy manure to which has been added a 4½ in. potful of old soot, and a similar quantity of steamed bone flour to each bushel of the mixture.

If the subsoil is gravel or chalk, or the border is otherwise well drained, the surface should be thoroughly firmed, and the prepared beds or mounds placed immediately on top. If they are to be grown on stages, a base may be made with slates laid over the wooden slats, and then a layer of old turves with the roots uppermost.

Beds on the ground are usually ridge shaped, 18 in. high and 2½ ft. through at the base. On stages it is usual to make a mound of about half a barrowful of soil for each plant.

A day or two before planting, stand the young plants in their pots on the mounds to acclimatise them to the different temperature. To plant, turn the specimen out of its pot without damaging the roots and carefully insert it up to the bottom leaves. The soil around the roots should only be moderately firmed, and a soaking of tepid water should immediately follow planting. A useful distance is 2½ ft. apart.

A light cane should be put in at planting time, and the plant trained up to the bottom wire. A series of these should run horizontally along the roof 9 in. apart and 9 in. from the glass.

All side shoots, tendrils, fruits, or male blooms should be rubbed out so as to have a clear single stem up to the first wire, along which the first pair of side shoots should be trained, the later ones being similarly trained along the higher wires. The main stem should be allowed to grow on to the top wire, and should then have its tip removed, but the laterals and sub-laterals should be stopped by removing the growing-point at every second leaf beyond a female flower.

The careful removal of tendrils and male flowers, the tying in and stopping of laterals and sub-laterals, must be attended to at least every other day, and as soon as the root tips are seen emerging from the side of the beds a top-dressing of about 2 in. of compost must be given.

Unless the weather is abnormally warm, no ventilation need be given. A thin coat of shading sprayed over the glass will prevent scorching. The plants—especially the under sides of the leaves, should be forcibly syringed with tepid water twice a day, and the floors and walls also thoroughly wetted to promote a humid atmosphere. Such a process is known as "damping down." The temperature should not fall below 60°.

The fruits should be cut as soon as ready, which is before the withered blossom falls from the end.

Cucumbers, Ridge. Very satisfactory results can be obtained from ridge or outdoor cucumbers during a normal season, their principal requirements being an abundance of organic matter with moderate supplies of water, so that the soil is uniformly moist throughout their growth.

On light soils they may be grown on the flat, but on cold heavy land carefully prepared raised beds should be made.

Holes or trenches about a yard wide, and of any length, may be taken out to a depth of 1 ft. In these should be placed farmyard manure or decayed garden refuse and lawn mowings, heaped a foot above the general level and trodden quite firm. The top of the heap should be made flat, and the whole covered with the best of the soil which was taken out. This work should be done at the end of April, and towards the end of May seeds are to be sown in groups of three at intervals of 2 ft. along the centre of the bed. An inverted flowerpot placed over the seeds will quicken germination, and the pots may afterwards be put on as protection at night until the fear of late frosts is past. It is, of course, an advantage to raise under glass, and to harden-off for planting outside, where the necessary facilities are available.

Every inducement should be given to encourage healthy growth. Strong shoots that are not carrying fruits should have the growing point removed and lateral shoots should be stopped one leaf beyond a fruit. Only in very warm weather is syringing likely to be necessary, and then it should be carried out in the evening with tepid soft water. Occasional feeding with weak soluble manure following rain will prove very beneficial.

VARIETIES.

Under Glass.—Rochford's Disease Resister; Telegraph; Every Day.

Ridge or Outside.—Bedfordshire Prize; Stockwood Long; Gherkin.

Uses.—In this country cucumbers are generally eaten raw in salads and sandwiches, or as a single dish with fresh salmon, or pickled, but on the Continent they are often boiled, and used in the preparation of most appetising dishes. It was introduced into England in the time of Edward III.

CUCUMBER COLLAR ROT (*Hypochnus cucumeris*). This disease, which occurs now and again in this country is caused by a fungus, the mycelium of which works into the tissues of the plant at about ground level. This causes moisture to be cut off from the plant with the result that the bine becomes sickly, wilts, turns yellow and the stem collapses.

METHODS OF CONTROL.—It is more than probable the fungus is introduced in leafmould, and if collar rot has ever been experienced it is as well to treat the soil with Kainit. If any plants show sign of attack, immediately water them with sulphate of potash.

CUCUMIS. See CUCUMBER AND MELON.

CUCURBITA (ku-kur-bi'-ta. Cucurbitaceæ). Native of the Orient. Gourd. *C. pepo* is the "ornamental" fruited gourd. The fruits are of the most quaint shapes, colours and markings, and the plants, which grow rapidly, may be effectively used to trail over old tree stumps, trellis or rustic fences. They like a fairly rich soil, with plenty of water when in active growth. Sow in frame in April, plant out in June, or sow where to grow in May.

See also GOURD, PUMPKIN and VEGETABLE MARROW.

CUDRANIA (kūdrăn-ea. Urticaceæ). Deciduous hardy tree, 20 ft. Native of China, with small insignificant flowers. Thrives in ordinary soil. The leaves are used in China for feeding silkworms on, after the mulberry leaves are finished.

ONLY SPECIES.

C. tricuspidata (syn. *triloba. Maclura tricuspidata*). Known as the "Chinese Silkworm Tree."

CULTIVATOR. This tool has three or five prongs of crucible spring steel separately adjustable and removable for light or heavy work. Can be used to do the work of hoe, fork, or rake, and is in fact a miniature hand-plough, or pulveriser. It is fitted with 4 ft. or 4½ ft. ash handle. For bigger and heavier work than is met with in the ordinary garden there is a larger cultivator on wheels, in every way similar to a small plough, except that the plough is interchangeable with cultivator teeth, hoe blades, rakes, or seed drill.

CUMINUM (Umbelliferæ). Half-hardy annual, with aromatic seeds used as flowering. Sow the seeds in May, where required, in ordinary soil. Gather the seeds in July and August. The plants are best grown in full sunshine.

SPECIES.

C. cyminum. White or pink, 6 in.

CUNNINGHAMIA (kun-ning-hā-mi-a. Coniferæ). An evergreen tree of great beauty, with glossy bluish-green foliage and round cones. Only really happy in the mild parts of the country. 30–50 ft. Representative of a very ancient type of vegetation, and found in a fossil state. Plant in light soil, in a sheltered position. *Propagate* by seeds.

SPECIES.

C. Konishii Formosa. A rare species with shorter leaves than the next species.

C. sinensis. The "Broad-leaved Fir" of China. Foliage approximating to emerald green, sometimes glaucous, ageing to darker green, and becoming bronzy in autumn.

CUNONIA (Saxifragaceæ). Greenhouse evergreen tree. Plant in equal parts sandy loam and peat, and keep in a light airy greenhouse. Temperature moderate. Prune into shape in spring. Water freely during summer.

Propagate by cuttings in sandy soil under a bell-glass in summer.

SPECIES.

C. capensis. White, August. Will grow to a good height under the right conditions.

CUPANIA (Sapindaceæ). Stove evergreen trees. Pot in March in equal parts peat and loam, and grow in moist stove. Prune to keep the habit dwarf. Winter temperature, 55°-65°; summer, 60°-85°.

Propagate by cuttings under a bell-glass in a temperature of 85° in summer.

SPECIES.

C. anacardioides, 20-30 ft.

C. americana. Downy.

C. elegantissima, 15-20 ft.

CUP FLOWER. *See* GRAMMATO-CARPUS.

CUPHEA (ku-fe-a. Lythraceæ). Mexican Cigar Flower. Greenhouse evergreen flowering plants. These plants may be grown in 5-6 in. pots in the greenhouse in a compost of dry rich soil, or they may be grown in a similar soil in beds outdoors in the summer.

Pot in March or April and plant outdoors in June. Water moderately in winter and spring, but freely afterwards. Summer temperature, 60°-70°; winter temperature, 50°-55°.

Propagate by seeds sown in a light rich soil in a temperature of 65°-75° in spring or by cuttings of young shoots inserted in a sandy soil in the same conditions in spring or in August.

SPECIES.

C. æquipetala. Purple flowers in June. Height 2 ft.

C. cyanea. Yellow and red flowers in July. Height 2 ft.

C. Hookeriana. Vermilion and orange flowers in July. Height 2-3 ft.

C. ignea (syn. *C. platycentra*). Scarlet, black and white flowers in July. Height 1 ft.

C. ignea alba. White flowers.

C. lanceolata. Blue flowers in July. Height 18 in. (Annual).

C. micropetala. Scarlet, white and red flowers in July. Height 1 ft.

C. miniata (syn. *C. Llavea*). Bright red flowers in summer. Height 2 ft.

CUPRESSUS (kū-pres′-sus. Coniferæ). Cypress. Evergreen trees of considerable beauty and interest for mild districts. According to the latest classification both Chamæcyparis and Retinospora are included in this genus. They may be distinguished by the branchlets always being flattened, while the true Cypress have rounded branchlets.

Culture.—Plant in April or September in rich loamy or peaty soil, in a position sheltered from cold winds. *Propagate* by seed sown in April, also by cuttings taken in August and placed in frame.

SPECIES.

C. arizonica. The "Arizonian Cypress," extending from Arizona to N. Mexico, 30-40 ft. and upwards. One of the hardiest. Of a symmetrical pyramidal habit and glaucous foliage.

C. Lawsoniana (*Chamæcyparis Lawsoniana*). "Lawson's Cypress." Oregon and California, up to 200 ft. The most useful and hardy of all cypresses. Succeeds in exposed positions, hedging or as tall screens, etc. May be grown in the shade of other trees. First raised at Lawson's nursery in Edinburgh in 1854, since which date many forms have been raised in various parts of the country with great variety of foliage and habit, some being very distinct. They are best increased from cuttings taken in late summer. The most distinct and noteworthy forms are enumerated hereunder. Likes good loamy soil and a moist climate. If the soil is poor, watering should be resorted to during dry spells, with occasional supplies of manure water.

C. L. albo-spica, creamy-white variegation. Habit pyramidal.

C. L. Allumii. Of conical-like habit and very glaucous-blue foliage.

C. L. argentea. Compact habit. Leaves silvery-grey.

C. L. argenteo-variegata. Compact, slow-growing variety, with leaves mottled white.

C. L. Fletcheri. A perfect glaucous-blue pyramid. Slow growing up to about 4 ft.

C. L. F. nana. A dwarf form very suitable for rock garden.

C. L. lutea. The "Golden Lawson's Cypress." Erect habit.

C. L. "Silver Queen." Foliage silvery grey-green.

C. L. Stewartii. A distinct form, with bright yellow young shoots.

C. L. "Triomphe de Boskoop." A vigorous-growing, very glaucous-blue form. One of the finest.

C. L. Westermannii. Distinct yellow foliage, rather pendent habit.

C. L. Wisselii (Conica). A curious form of columnar habit and very glaucous foliage. Not so attractive as some of the other forms, the growth being too sparse.

C. macrocarpa. The "Monterey Cypress." of California, 60–90 ft. Very well-known hardy, fast-growing species, most valuable as trees for shelter in wind-swept areas. Although it succeeds well inland (it has exceeded 40 ft. in Surrey), this species is seen at its best in warm seaside districts. Makes a beautiful hedge and bears clipping well. Foliage rich dark green. In light sandy soils (which this cypress prefers to a heavy clay soil) will grow as much as 3–4 ft. in a season. If grown as an isolated specimen it should be firmly staked, as owing to its rapid growth it is liable to be blown over by high winds. When grown as a hedge, pot plants are essential, and these, 12–18 in. high, give the best results. They may be planted 18–24 in. apart, at the end of April, or early May. The plants should be well watered if necessary before planting. Assuming that the plants are put out in spring, as advised, they may be allowed to grow at will until after the second winter. In the spring following the second winter, the taller plants may be reduced by a foot or so, others may only need tipping. The sides may also be trimmed. They will require to be clipped about the end of April each year, and possibly again in August. The hedge should slightly taper towards the top. Never clip the hedge in winter, or after August.

C. m. lutea. Like *C. m. fastigiata* in habit, but with a beautiful suffusion of golden yellow in the leaves and shoots.

C. nootkatensis (Chamæcyparis nootkatensis). Thujopsis borealis. The "Yellow Cypress" of western N. America. 120 ft. A rapid grower with dark green foliage. Branchlets inclined to pendulous. Cones glaucous.

C. n. glauca. Foliage glaucous.

C. obtusa (Chamæcyparis obtusa, Retinispora obtusa). Known as the "Hinoki" of Japan, 100–120 ft. Foliage dark green above, paler beneath, and with a thin line of glaucous bloom on the margin. Likes a moist-free soil. A very choice timber tree, producing a firm, fine white wood. This is one of the conifers used by the Japanese for making their famous dwarf trees, those little marvels of skill and patience, which are so much admired for their exquisite and wonderful "form."

C. o. Crippsii. A beautiful slow-growing form of very elegant habit and golden foliage.

C. nana. Dwarf, compact form for the rock garden.

C. pisifera (Chamæcyparis pisifera. Retinispora pisifera). The "Sawara Cypress" of Japan. A remarkable species with sharp-pointed leaves, of a dark green colour, 70 ft. upwards. On poor soils the growth is apt to be thin, which may be improved by clipping over in spring, especially when young. Occasional doses of manure water greatly assists.

C. p. aurea. Golden foliage.

C. p. ericoides. Dwarf, compact, foliage bronzy-red in autumn.

C. p. filifera. Dense growth of whip-like branchlets.

C. p. aurea. A golden-leaved form of preceding.

C. p. gracilis. A very elegant form.

C. p. nana. Very dwarf.

C. p. plumosa. Of dense conical habit.

C. thyoides (Chamæcyparis sphæroidea), the "White Cedar" or "White Cypress" of cold, swampy parts of eastern N. America. 50 ft. upwards. Distinct, slow-growing, and very hardy. Not for chalky districts.

CURCULIGO (kur-ku-li-go. Amaryllideæ). Stove evergreens, with ornamental foliage. Strap-like, recurved leaves. Pot in February or March and stand in moist plant stove. Use a compost of equal parts lumpy peat and loam and a little silver sand. During the winter water should be given in moderate quantities, but freely at other times. Summer temperature, 75°–85°; winter temperature, 55°–65°.

Increase by suckers or offsets inserted

in small pots of sandy soil in March in a temperature of 85°.

SPECIES.

C. recurvata. Height 3–4 ft.

C. recurvata variegata, variegated foliage.

CURCUMA (kur-ku-ma. Scitaminaceæ). Stove fleshy-rooted perennial. Most of the species possess aromatic, stimulating properties in the roots or rhizomes, and seeds similar to those of the common Ginger. They are objects of some beauty from their coloured bracts. Some species yield Arrowroot. Use a compost of 2 parts peat, 1 part loam, and a little sand, and stand the pots in a warm greenhouse. Pot in February. It is essential that the pots should be well drained. Summer temperature, 65°–75°; winter temperature, 60°. During the growing season, water plentifully. When the foliage dies down dry off the tubers.

Increase by division of roots or by offsets and treat as tubers.

SPECIES.

C. amada. Yellow flowers. Height 1–2 ft.

C. ferruginea. Yellow flowers. Height 1 ft.

C. latifolia. White and yellow flowers. Height 12 ft.

C. longa. Yellow flowers. Height 12 ft.

CURRANT. *See* RIBES.

CURRANT, BLACK (*Ribes nigrum*). Saxifragaceæ. The original wild Black Currant is a native of Europe and Siberia and possibly of Britain.

Soil.—A good rich soil is preferable as the Black Currant is a heavy feeder. A sunny position is essential to obtain fruit of good flavour.

Planting.—Allow 5 ft. apart each way. May be carried out between November and March.

Pruning.—Prune newly-planted bushes hard back in order to obtain a good supply of young wood. The following September thin out the young shoots, leaving only the strongest ten or twelve, and opening out the centre of the bush for ready access of sunshine. Subsequent pruning should be done every autumn by cutting out as much old wood as possible consistent with leaving a good supply of young wood, which bears the fruit. Old wood does not bear. In districts where birds are a nuisance, pruning is deferred until spring.

Manures. — A mulch of well-decayed manure should be given each May.

Propagation.—Black Currants strike easily from cuttings of young wood, about 6 in. in length, inserted in shallow trenches of sandy soil during November. Tread in the base of the cuttings firmly to a depth of 5 in.

Pest.—The worst pest is Big Bud (*q.v.*).

Varieties.—Boskoop Giant. One of the earliest to ripen, but not a heavy cropper. Thin-skinned and therefore not a good market variety unless picked before ripe.

Seabrook's Black. An excellent cropper, and very resistant to Big Bud.

Laxton's Grape. Very large berries of excellent flavour. Strong growing.

September Black. A useful late variety.

CURRANTS, RED AND WHITE.

Ribes vulgare. Red Currant.

Ribes vulgare album. White Currant. Saxifragaceæ.

The same soil, situation, distances apart as suggested for the Black Currant may be applied; the only difference in cultivation lies in pruning and method of making cuttings.

Pruning.—Fruit on both red and white varieties is borne on the old wood. The aim must be to grow a tree with 5 or 6 main branches, keeping the centre well open. Short lateral growths must be spurred back to within 3 or 4 buds, and leaders should be cut back by half their length, always cutting to an outside bud. (For definitions of "lateral" and "leader," *see* instructions for pruning under APPLE). Be certain to make all cuts clean to a bud, always removing any dead wood, or Coral Spot fungus may appear. Prune in autumn.

Culture as Cordons.—Red and White Currants may be grown as cordons on a north wall. The flavour is not so good, but the fruit hangs for a long time, extending the season.

Pests.—Most dangerous pests are Aphis and Currant Sawfly.

Propagation.—Make cuttings as suggested for Black Currants, only longer— about 9 in. is the correct length. Before inserting them remove all buds save the top 4, and put in 5 in. deep, making certain that the base of each is securely trodden into position.

Varieties.—RED: Laxton's No. 1. The finest Red Currant in cultivation. A free grower, constant cropper, with enormous bunches and large individual fruits of good colour.

RED DUTCH: Enormous cropper, bearing regularly. Bright-coloured fruit.

WHITE: White Versaillaise. The best white variety.

CURRANT SAWFLY. *See* GOOSEBERRY AND CURRANT SAWFLY.

CYANAMIDE. A valuable nitrogenous fertiliser, but one to be used with care since it causes painful sores if allowed to come in contact with broken skin. Cyanamide should not be applied as a top-dressing because, until it has been for some time in contact with the soil, it is liable to kill all vegetation.

Cyanamide is made by passing nitrogen over calcium carbide—the material used in acetylene-gas outfits.

CYANANTHUS (cyan-an-thus. Campanulaceæ). Hardy herbaceous plants with flowers of great beauty.

Culture.—Propagate by seeds or cuttings, the former being sown in heat in spring, the latter made from young growths and inserted in sandy soil in the open or under a hand-light in April or May. Plant out in a sunny position in sandy moist soil and protect from wet in winter with a mulch of sand, or squares of glass.

SPECIES.

C. lobatus with trailing hairy stems, lobed leaves with large blue flowers in August, 4 in.; *C. incanus*, with blue-throated flowers in August and September. A rarer and more beautiful species is *C. longiflorus*, with rich blue flowers on short stems. All are suitable for the rock garden or for carpeting.

CYANELLA (si-a-nel-la. Liliaceæ). Half-hardy bulbous plants. Fragrant flowers. A compost of two parts sandy soil, one part leaf-mould or decayed cow manure should be put into well-drained pots 4½ in. in diameter. The bulbs should be planted in October, putting them 2 in. deep and allowing 5 bulbs to each pot. They should be covered with coconut fibre refuse until growth begins. Water moderately. During the winter keep the bulbs dry.

Propagate by offsets in November.

SPECIES.

C. capensis. Blue flowers in July. Height 1 ft.

C. lutea. Yellow flowers, July. 1 ft.

CYATHEA (si-a-the-a. Filices). Tree Ferns. Stove and greenhouse evergreen Ferns. (W. Ind. 1793).

Culture.— Compost: Equal parts fibrous loam, peat and silver sand. Repot early spring, shady position, stove, or green-

CYCLAMEN

Dainty flowers of Cyclamen are easily cultivated in the cool greenhouse.

house, particularly during summer months. Syringe trunks daily during hot sunny days. Winter temperature, stove, 55°; greenhouse, 45°.

Propagation.—By spores sown on the surface of peat or sand, in shallow pans or trays; place in propagator and keep shaded. Temperature, 75°.

Stove Species.—C. arborea.

Greenhouse Species—C. dealbata, C. medullaris.

CYCAS (si-kas. Cycadaceæ). Sage Palm. Stove plants. Ornamental leaves (China, 1737).

Culture.—Compost: 2 parts loam, 1 part leaf-mould, 1 part sand. Repot early spring. Water freely during summer; moderately at other times. Winter temperature, 55°; summer, 80°.

Propagate by suckers inserted in small pots of sandy loam. Temperature, 75°.

SPECIES.

C. circiralis ; C. glauca ; C. revoluta.

CYCLAMEN (Primulaceæ). Sowbread. The hardy kinds of cyclamen deserve to be more widely cultivated than they are

producing a number of rosy-pink flowers followed by large silver-marbled foliage, is another useful variety.

Cyclamen for the Greenhouse.

Cyclamen persicum (C. latifolum) is a very popular tuberous-rooted greenhouse plant. Height 1–1½ ft. with various colour varieties. The flowers turn back their petals and are white, mauve, magenta,

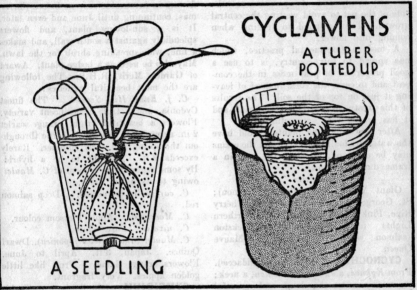

CYCLAMENS
A TUBER
POTTED UP

A SEEDLING

Although a moisture- and shade-loving plant the Cyclamen needs careful potting. The tops of the tubers should not be below the soil surface.

at present. They will grow quite well in fairly rich soil containing plenty of leaf-mould, and are particularly happy in a shady pocket of the rockery, or in turf under trees.

The tubers can be planted in August or September 2–3 in. apart and 1½ in. deep. A top-dressing of heavy manure and rich soil annually after the leaves die down will prove of great benefit.

Amongst the various hardy cyclamen the variety *C. europæum*, which has scented flowers of crimson-red in autumn, is one of the most easily grown. *C. coum* should be chosen for the shadiest side of the rockery. This flowers in February and March and makes a valuable addition to the winter garden. *C. neapolitanum,*

salmon, scarlet or cherry-red. They are highly decorative for flowering early in the year. The foliage is often beautifully mottled with silver.

Cultivation.—Seeds should be sown in August in boxes of open soil, placing them in a cool greenhouse or cold frame to germinate. Do not expose the seedlings to too much hot sun. It is best to place the seeds carefully when sowing and so avoid further handling until the plants have made two or three leaves, when they may be lifted from the boxes and potted into small pots. Cyclamen like an open soil at all stages of growth and will not do well unless they have it. They are lovers of lime and a certain amount of crushed mortar-rubble is essential to success. Grow on gently during winter in a warm greenhouse and, for the final pots, give plenty of drainage covered with coarse leaf-mould. The soil should be composed of turfy loam which has passed through a ¾ in. sieve, to which has been added well-rotted cow manure, crushed mortar-rubble and a little sharp sand. If the loam is not too strong, a little complete fertiliser may be added. Do not press the soil firmly and always water at the side of the pot to avoid wetting the central growth. They respond to feeding when coming into flower.

A modern Continental practice, which has spread to this country, is to use a good proportion of peat moss in the compost and to cover the corm instead of leaving it just on top of the soil. The results of this treatment justify further trial, and it has proved very successful.

After flowering, the plants should have the water gradually withheld and the corms may be dried off, standing the pots in a frame during summer.

VARIETIES.

Giant White, Bath Beauty (salmon); St. George (silver-leaved salmon); Cherry Ripe, Pink Pearl, Giant Scarlet, Northern Lights (carmine-rose); Mrs. Buckston (salmon with frilled petals); Mauve Queen.

CYCNOCHES (sī-nō'-kes. Orchidaceæ). From *Kyknos*, a swan, and *auchen*, a neck; in reference to the long and graceful curved column. They are commonly called "The Swan-neck Orchids." Very handsome deciduous, stove orchids. 1830.

Culture.—Compost: General cultivation and propagation, similar to Catasetum.

SPECIES.

C. auleum, yellow.

C. chlorochelum, yellow.

C. Loddigesii, white and purple.

C. ventricosum, green and white.

CYDONIA (sī-dō-ni-a. Rosaceæ). Quince. Deciduous and very ornamental spring-flowering shrubs, with large cup-shaped flowers, white, orange and red, followed by decorative fruits, edible when cooked, but very unpleasant in a raw state. Quince jelly is especially good.

Culture.—Plant October or November in ordinary soil. Pruning consists in cutting out old wood and shortening the side shoots

in June. *Propagate* by seed, layers, suckers and cuttings in June.

SPECIES.

C. cathayensis (lagenaria Wilsonii). China. Flowers white flushed pink. Fruit very large, 4–6 in. long, and fragrant.

C. japonica (Chænomeles lagenaria. Pyrus japonica). China and Japan. Up to 20 ft. One of the most admired of early-flowering hardy shrubs. It bears its red flowers in favourable seasons before Christmas, continuing until June and even later. It is a sun-loving plant, and flowers splendidly against a south wall, and makes a fine, wide-spreading shrub for the lawn. May also be used as a hedge plant. Award of Garden Merit, R.H.S. The following are the most beautiful varieties:

C. j. Knap Hill Scarlet. The finest Cydonia, and a truly magnificent variety. Flowers a beautiful bright orange-scarlet 2 in. across, and very freely borne throughout the spring and early summer. Rarely exceeds 3 ft. Thought to be a hybrid. By some regarded as a form of *C. Maulei,* owing to its dwarf habit.

C. cardinalis (princeps). Deep salmon red.

C. Moerloesii. Apple blossom colour.

C. nivalis. Pure white.

C. Maulei (Chænomeles japonica). Dwarf Quince. Japan, 3 ft. April to June. Flowers orange flame. Fruit like little golden apples. Very fragrant.

CYMBIDIUM (sim-bid-ium. Orchidaceæ). From *Kymbe* a boat, referring to the recess in the lip. Mostly greenhouse terrestrial orchids (E. Ind., 1789). The Cymbidium hybrids have become very popular, and are now grown by almost every gardener with a small greenhouse. The graceful flower spikes and handsome foliage make them very desirable as decorative plants.

Culture.—Compost: good rich loam and fibre in equal parts, with some broken pots to keep it open. Repot March. Syringe overhead with clear water daily during warm bright weather; this will greatly help to keep away Red Spider, their worst enemy. They thrive in a temperature round about 55° at night, with a rising day temperature by sun heat, plenty of fresh air, and less moisture in the atmosphere than most orchids enjoy.

Propagation.—By division when re-potting.

SPECIES.

C. alorfolium, purple.

C. Devonianum, purple.

C. Finlaysonianum, white and crimson.

C. giganteum, yellow and purple.

C. Lowianum, yellow and maroon.

C. Tracyanum, yellow and crimson.

The hybrids are extremely numerous and a good trade list should be consulted for best varieties.

CYMBOPOGON (sim-bō-pō-gon. Grammæ). Ornamental stove flowering grass. Pot in March in a compost of 2 parts loam, 1 part leaf-mould and sand, and stand the pots in stove. Water freely in the summer, but moderately afterwards. Summer temperature, 75°–85°; winter temperature, 55°–65°.

Propagate by division in March.

SPECIES.

C. Martinii (syn. *Andropogon Schoenanthus*). Lemon-scented foliage. 2 ft.

CYNARA (*Cardunculus*). *See* CARDOON.

CYNOGLOSSUM (sīn-o-glos-sum. Boragineæ). Hound's-tongue. Hardy perennials and alpines. Rather coarse-growing plant from China, but very effective when in bloom.

Propagate C. Wallichi by division. *C amabile* is best treated as a biennial, raising a fresh stock each year from seed sown in cold frames in spring.

Compost: Well-drained loam with leaf-mould and sand. A position in the herbaceous border is the most suitable, or plant in sunny beds and rock gardens.

SPECIES.

C. amabile is the best of the genus. Blue flowers, June, 2 ft. Sow in June for flowering the following season.

C. Wallichi. Sky-blue flowers in summer. Height, 8 in.

See also OMPHALODES.

CYPELLA (si-pel-la. Iridaceæ). Half-hardy bulbs suitable for greenhouse culture or for positions in a sunny, well-drained border.

Outdoors they can be planted from September to January, 4 in. deep and 2 in. apart. Treat them the same as Ixias. In pots they should be grown in sandy loam with peat or leaf-mould, and decayed cow manure. Cover with coconut fibre until growth begins. Water moderately until the flowers fade, and gradually dry off the bulbs afterwards. Temperature always a little above freezing.

Propagate by offsets.

SPECIES.

C. Herbertii. Red, 1 ft.

C. peruviana. Yellow, spotted red.

C. plumbea. Blue.

CYPERUS (sī′-per-us. Cyperaceæ). Umbrella Plant. Ornamental sedges for greenhouse, or for margins of lakes. Plant the hardy species in heavy loam with rotted cow manure, any time from October to March.

Plant greenhouse species in a compost of good fibrous loam, leaf-mould and sand. Give water liberally when the plants are growing.

Propagate by seeds in a temperature of 55°–65° in March or by division of the roots in March or April.

SPECIES.

(Hardy).

C. esculentus, of which the long underground tubers are edible. 2–3 ft.

(Greenhouse Species).

C. aristatus (annual). Green, 6 in.

C. alternifolius and its varieties *gracilis* and *variegatus*.

C. giganteus, 10 ft., scented.

CYPHOMANDRA (sif-ō-man-dra. Solanaceæ). Tree tomato. Shrubs for the cool stove.

Propagate by cuttings inserted in sand in close bottom heat, in spring or early summer. Prune plants into shape in March. Water moderately from October to March and freely in summer.

SPECIES.

C. betacea, with purple and green fruits, large, egg-shaped and edible. These are ripe in August and September.

CYPRESS. *See* CUPRESSUS.

CYPRIPEDIUM. The stove and greenhouse varieties are very popular and interesting. They are of easy culture, mostly winter flowering, and the heavy texture of their flowers makes them almost immune from fogs. N. America, 1731.

Greenhouse Culture.—Compost: fibrous loam and Osmunde fibre in equal parts and a little chopped sphagnum moss. Some of the tessellated-leaved species prefer a lighter compost, and sphagnum moss should be substituted for loam. Repot March or April. Good drainage essential. A moist growing atmosphere should be maintained, and shade from direct sunlight during the summer should be given. Overhead syringing during bright days will help to keep down thrips. A night temperature of 55° rising to 75° or 80° in the day during the summer and 50° rising to 65° during winter.

LEAVES

CYPRESS

The Cypress are small evergreen trees suitable for lawn specimens. The variety Macrocarpa is used for hedges, but is not hardy in all districts.

Propagation.—By division when repotting.

SPECIES.

C. barbatum, white and purple.
C. Boxallii, green and purple.
C. Charlesworthii, rose and white.
C. Rothschildianum, yellow, purple and brown.
C. venustum, green and red.
C. villosum, brown and purple.

The hybrids are numerous and rich in colour; only a few can be given. For others, *see* good catalogue.

Varieties.—Aramis, sepals and petals, marble-brown, the former spotted on lower

half. Dorsal sepal large, basal portion green, upper portion rosy-white, spotted rose-purple with white margin.

Catherine Hardy, rubrum, lower sepals, petals and pouch claret-red, dorsal sepal same colour, lower half deeper shade with white margin; this is probably the finest red Cypripedium in cultivation.

F. W. Sander, petals greenish-brown, pouch a deeper shade, dorsal sepal centrally lined rose-purple with deep white margin.

Helene, petals and pouch honey-yellow, dorsal sepal of same colour, with purple spots on a green base and white margin.

CYRILLA (sī-ril'-la. Cyrillaceæ). Leatherwood. Eastern North America. 4 ft. A deciduous late summer-flowering shrub. Flowers white, very small. Thrives in a mixture of peat and loam. No lime.

CYRTANTHUS (sir-tan-thus. Amaryllidaceæ). Allied to the Scarborough Lily of cottage windows. All greenhouse bulbs, some with evergreen leaves and therefore requiring water all the year round. Pot in a strong friable loam, in well-drained pots, in November, putting the bulbs 2 in. deep. Temperature 50°–55° in winter and 60°–65° in summer. Deciduous kinds may dry off entirely during the winter.

Propagate by offsets in November.

SPECIES.

C. angustifolia. Orange, autumn, 1 ft.
C. carneus. Red, summer, 1 ft.
C. collinus. Red, June, 1 ft.
C. sanguineus. Bright red, June, 1 ft., and its orange-red variety *glaucophyllus.*

CYSTOPTERIS (sis-to-ter'-is. Filices). Hardy deciduous ferns, slender in growth, and suited to moist positions on the rockery. They like deep, rich, sandy loam, containing pieces of limestone or mortar. Plant in spring, and water moderately in dry weather.

In pots they like a soil of two parts loam with one part leaf-mould and some sand or mortar. They will grow in the cold greenhouse or frame, and can be repotted in March.

Propagate by spores sown on the surface of fine sandy soil, covered with a sheet of glass, in a cold frame, at any time when ripe spores are available. Or the plants can be divided at potting time.

SPECIES.

C. bulbifera. 6–12 in. Fronds three times divided.

C. montana. Triangular fronds.

C. fragilis. Fronds two or three times divided. The last two are British.

CYTISUS (sit-i-sus. Leguminosæ). This is a very popular, sun-loving deciduous shrub, with a great wealth of pea-shaped flowers, from white to crimson. Of very diverse habit of growth, ranging in height from creeping alpines to 15 ft. Native of Europe, Asia and N. Africa.

They can be propagated easily from seed or by cuttings of half-ripened wood in sand.

Culture.—Plant in October in ordinary garden soil. Grafted plants are necessary for certain Brooms in shallow, chalky soil. Pruning should take place after flowering to prevent "legginess," for the spring-blooming species; the late-flowering ones are left until February or March. *Propagation* is best by seed, also by cuttings and grafting. Cuttings should be taken in August: 1½–3 in. long, with a "heel," and dibbled in a very sandy soil in frame or under a bell-glass. In the following spring they should be potted singly in small pots. They should be placed in their permanent places early.

SPECIES AND HYBRIDS.

C. albus. White Portugal Broom, 7 ft. Award of Garden Merit, R.H.S.

C. Ardoinii. Flowers yellow. 4–5 in. Useful for rock garden. Silvery-green foliage, May. Mediterranean.

C. Dallimorei. A Kew hybrid. *C. Scoparius Andreanus* + *C. albus.* Flowers deep rose, flushed claret. Likes good soil. Requires to be grafted on laburnum. 8–9 ft.

C. decumbens (prostrata). Flowers rich yellow during May and June. 4–6 in.

C. Donard Seedling. Flowers quaintly coloured red, rose, yellow and white.

C. Dorothy Walpole. A new variety with flowers of a rich velvety crimson.

C. hirsutus. Flowers buff, stained brown. 2 ft.

C. junceum. See Spartium junceum, the Spanish Broom.

C. præcox. Warminster Broom. Hybrid *C. albus* + *C. purgans.* Flowers sulphur-yellow. One of the finest of May flowering shrubs. Its seedlings revert to *C. albus.*

C. scoparius, common Yellow Broom. 3–5 ft. May.

C. s. Andreanus. This very beautiful variety, with yellow and crimson flowers, was discovered by Mr. E. André in Normandy. It should be grafted on laburnum in spring. Very variable from seed.

D

DABOECIA (do-boĕ-si-a. Ericaceæ).
St. Dabeoc's Heath, Connemara Heath,
Irish Heath. One of the most valuable
and beautiful dwarf flowering shrubs,
growing about 12–18 in. high, with glossy
leaves and spikes of large bell-shaped
flowers, white to purple, in the greatest
profusion from June to November. It
makes an admirable edging to large beds,
and is very charming in the mass. Very
useful for indoor decoration. The more
the flowers are cut the more freely the
plants grow. The Daboëcia is near to
Erica (Heath), differing therefrom in its
non-persistent corolla.

Culture.—Plant in lime-free soil, either
all peat, or light sandy loam with leaf-
mould.

Propagation is by seed, and for the
varieties by cuttings. Pruning consists
in going over the plants in early spring,
removing all flower-spikes.

D. polifolia. Rosy-purple.

D. p. alba. Large snow-white globular
flowers, held well above the green foliage.

D. p. tricolor. Red, white and crimson
flowers on the same plant.

D. p. purpurea. A very fine variety
with beautiful reddish-crimson flowers, in
the best forms.

DACRYDIUM (dak-rid'-i-um. Coniferæ). Exceptionally graceful and beautiful trees from New Zealand and Tasmania.
Economically important owing to the hardness of their timber. They thrive on a
mixture of loam and peat.

Propagate by cuttings of young wood
in sandy peat under a bell-glass or close
frame.

SPECIES.

D. cupressinum, the "Rimu" or "Red
Pine" of New Zealand. One of the most
attractive and graceful trees of the world,
with long pendulous branches.

D. Franklinii, the "Huon Pine" of
Tasmania. A very beautiful and graceful
species with slender pendulous branches.

DACTYLIS (dak-til-is. Gramineæ).
Rough Cocksfoot. Gardener's Garters.
Rather coarse-growing strong grasses of
which only one species is grown to any
extent, *D. glomerata*, which bears

flowers in June and July. Its dwarf
form, *glomerata variegata*, with prettily
variegated leaves that give a light
silvery effect, is often used for summer
bedding. It forms small tufts and should
not be allowed to flower, as this spoils the
effect. This is not as hardy as the type,
and some plants should be wintered in a
cold frame.

Propagate by seeds and division and
plant in a damp shady place.

DADDY-LONG-LEGS (The Crane
Fly). *See* LEATHERJACKET.

DAFFODIL. *See* NARCISSUS.

DAHLIA (Compositæ). Although in
England it is generally pronounced dā-lia,
in all other countries it is pronounced
dah-lia, as in the name of the Swedish
botanist *Dahl*, after whom it was named.
Half-hardy, herbaceous, tuberous-rooted
perennials.

SELECTION OF POSITIONS FOR GROWING,
PREPARATION OF SOIL AND
CULTIVATION.

Position.—This depends on the space
available and the objects of growing, etc.,
as to whether dahlias should be grown in
separate beds of distinct colours, borders
of dahlias entirely, or groups in front of
shrubberies, or whether in herbaceous
borders or in a separate position for
cutting purposes.

Soil and Preparation.—Dahlias will
grow well on a wide range of soils, but if
the soil be heavy and inclined to be waterlogged it would require attention as to
draining, and it is most important to
prepare the ground in the autumn or
winter by breaking up the soil fairly deep
and, if at all poor, to apply plenty of
manure.

By breaking up deeply and allowing air
and frost to penetrate, the soil greatly
improves by planting time. If possible
farmyard or stable manure should be
dug in in the autumn, but a heavy coat of
manure is not necessary unless specially
large flowers are needed for exhibition
purposes.

Plants and Planting.—Assuming that
the amateur is commencing, he should
carefully consider what effects or purposes

FLOWERS FOR CUTTING

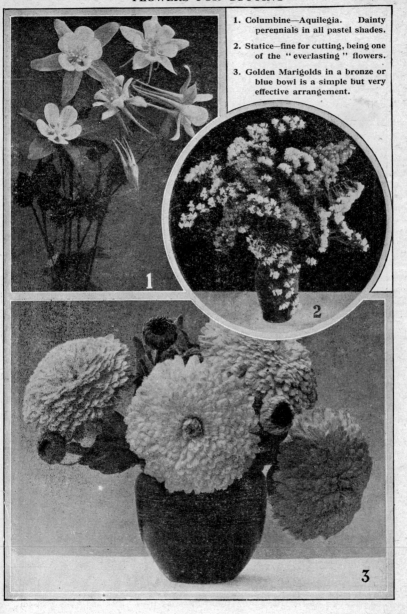

1. Columbine—Aquilegia. Dainty perennials in all pastel shades.

2. Statice—fine for cutting, being one of the "everlasting" flowers.

3. Golden Marigolds in a bronze or blue bowl is a simple but very effective arrangement.

1. Cistus — Rock Rose, mostly yellow with chocolate blotch. Good for sandy soils.

2. Ceanothus — blue flowers throughout the summer. Useful for covering walls.

3 Japanese Cherry (Hisakura). Dwarf flowering trees. Pink and white blossom.

he has in view to select and produce varieties most suitable for this purpose. Results depend very largely on the care with which the varieties are selected so as to get the best blending or contrast of colours, and it is also most important to select the right heights for various positions, otherwise a short variety might struggle for existence behind a tall and strong grower and be practically lost to sight. Obtain plants from the most reliable source of either rooted cuttings or plants established in small pots. These should be obtained in March or early April. This will give time to pot them into larger pots if desired and to grow on in a cool greenhouse or frame. By this means you obtain strong plants by the time it is safe to plant out. This is usually about the end of May or early in June, according to the season. This method enables the grower to obtain earlier flowers than by planting out only small cuttings.

Planting.—It is essential to mark out on the ground where each plant is to go before planting. The distance apart varies from 18 in. in the case of Mignons to 4-4½ ft. in the case of the largest growers. It is also a good plan to provide and drive in stakes before planting (except in the case of Mignons, which need no stakes). The plants can then be at once tied to the stakes and the danger is avoided of injuring the plants by driving in the stakes afterwards. It is most essential to consider carefully the height of the plants so as to avoid the unsightly appearance of stakes standing above the plants.

Slugs frequently attack the young plants immediately after planting, and it is a great safeguard to sprinkle a little soot around each plant. This is not only a safeguard but has manurial value as well.

Manure.—If the ground has been well prepared and manured in winter, or is naturally in a good condition, it will not require more manure at the time of planting; but otherwise it is helpful to the plants in starting to apply a small quantity of artificial manure. Sprinkle this over the hole when planting, thus mixing it with the soil.

Attention During Growth.—As the plants grow, care should be taken to tie up all shoots to the stakes. Disbudding may also be adopted where specially large blooms are required for exhibition, but this is not necessary for ordinary garden decoration, or for cutting purposes. All seed pods should be regularly removed in order to keep the plants in full flower. During dry weather in the early stages of growth some watering will be required from time to time, and this may be done with clear water or, better still, with liquid manure, and if this cannot be easily obtained it may be made by soaking soot or cow manure in a tub or tank, or artificial manure may be applied to the surface around the plants before watering.

Pests and Diseases.—Fortunately these are few in the case of dahlia. Black Fly will sometimes attack young plants in the early stages of growth, but this is easily checked by spraying with an insecticide. In some places earwigs attack the blooms and eat the young growth. The old remedy for this was to place inverted flower-pots on the top of each stake and to examine these every morning to destroy any earwigs that might take refuge there, but this is unsightly and is now very seldom necessary, as in cases of attacks by earwigs the plants may be dusted with tobacco powder or sulphur.

Wasps sometimes attack the plants in August and gnaw round the stems. The best remedy for this is to place wide-mouthed bottles amongst the plants about half-filled with some kind of jam and water, with a little raspberry vinegar added. The wasps soon collect in these. The bottles may be periodically examined and the wasps removed.

Seedlings.—Some growers take an interest in growing plants from seed, but this requires a good deal of space and is disappointing if definite colours and sizes are required. You may get some interesting varieties amongst them, but so many will be only common varieties of the mixed types, that if any definite colours, types or sizes are required it is far more satisfactory to plant only carefully selected plants.

Seeds may be sown in March in pans or boxes in a greenhouse or frame and the young plants, when they are large enough, potted and planted out in the usual way. It is best to give them a side place from which selections may be made and propagated for another season.

Lifting and Storing.—When the plants are cut down by frost in the autumn, cut off the tops and leave these lying on the roots for a week or so—this encourages eyes to ripen round the crowns—then lift them and clear from soil. Place them in boxes with dry soil, sand or peat, packed tightly about the roots. Store in a fairly dry place safe from frost. They usually require no further attention until February or March. If it is desired to propagate any of them, take out and clean the tubers, and plant them in soil in a green-house and take off, as they grow, cuttings about 3 or 4 in. long. Place these in pots in heat, when they soon form roots and may be potted ready for planting out.

If not required to increase them, the roots may be taken from the store, cleaned and planted where desired in open ground early in April, with a little ashes over their crowns in case of late frost.

DAISY. *See* BELLIS.

DAISY BUSH. *See* OLEARIA.

DAISY GRUBBER OR FORK. These are made with either two or three prongs. They all serve the same purpose—that of uprooting daisies or similar weeds in the lawn—and are most effective when the lawn is thoroughly damp. The prongs are inserted either side of the weed, and the handle is pulled towards the ground, which movement raises the weed.

DALECHAMPIA (dal-sham-pi-a. Euphorbiaceæ). Stove evergreen climb-ing plants, mostly with inconspicuous flowers of greenish-white colour.

They do well in a mixture of equal parts of peat and loam with a little sand, and are propagated by cuttings a little dried at the base inserted in sandy soil under a bell-glass.

SPECIES.

The principal species is *D. roeliziana*, which has yellow and rose flowers. All are natives of Brazil.

DAMASONIUM. *D. stellatum*, a native species, is the only representative of this genus. Should be treated like

Alisma or Water Plantain. Bears white and yellow flowers in the summer. 1½ ft. (syn. *Alisma Damasonium*).

DAME'S VIOLET. *See* SWEET ROCKET.

DAMNACANTHUS (dam-na-kan-thus. Rubiaceæ). A Japanese half-hardy slow-growing miniature shrub with fragrant white flowers, followed by round scarlet fruits. Likes a mellow loam, peat and sand.

SPECIES.

D. indicus.

DAMPING OFF. A term used by most gardeners when seedling plants suddenly wilt and die. It is most com-monly found in the hot-house, but occa-sionally damping off will occur out of doors. The two fungi which cause these diseases are quite distinct.

OUT OF DOORS.—Seedling cabbage will at times "go down" under the attack of a fungus known as *Olpidium brassicœ*. The plants are attacked at ground level, become weak, fall over and wilt.

METHODS OF CONTROL.—As overcrowd-ing, excess of moisture and dull weather are likely to bring about the disease, plants should be given as much room as possible in order to get the maximum of light and sunshine.

INDOORS.—*Pythium de baryanum* is the cause of the damping off of seedlings in hot-houses.

METHODS OF CONTROL.—As neglect is the chief cause of this fungus getting hold of seedlings in hot-houses, the remedy is obvious. Overcrowding in too damp and stuffy atmosphere is a sure method of bringing about an attack. Give plenty of ventilation.

DAMSON. The damson is believed to be a variety of the plum, *Prunus com-munis*. It is grown as a half-standard or standard, and in all respects cultivation should be carried out as suggested for the plum. The fruit is not much used for dessert, but certain varieties have a very excellent flavour when preserved.

Propagation.—Budding or grafting on the Myrobalan stock.

VARIETIES.

The Merryweather is the best variety, bearing the largest fruit, which is well flavoured.

Bradley's King is another excellent variety which becomes quite sweet when ripe, and is suitable for dessert purposes. *See also* PLUM.

Damson. *A Damascene plum, from its place of origin.*

DANÆA or DANAE (dan-ē-a. Liliaceæ). *D. racemosus, Ruscus racemosus.* The Alexandrian Laurel, known in gardens as *Ruscus racemosus*, is an extremely useful, elegant-growing shrub, 2–4 ft. high, with beautiful glossy bright green foliage, almost indispensable in the house as well as in the garden. The sprays are most valuable for winter indoor decorations, either by themselves or associated with flowers, and last for a long time. The foliage, or "leaves," are, strictly speaking, but flattened branches (*cladoles*), resembling leaves and performing the same functions. Flowers greenish-yellow, small, and of no floral beauty, followed by decorative red berries; but these latter are not borne very freely in this country.

Culture.—Plant in moist soil in semi-shade. *Propagate* by seeds; or by division in spring.

SPECIES.

D. lauris.

DAPHNE (daf-ne. Thymelæaceæ). Garland Flower. Greenhouse and hardy evergreen and deciduous flowering shrubs. Fragrant flowers. Italy, 1752.

Culture (greenhouse species).—Compost: loam and sandy peat in equal parts. Suitable for cool house where temperature can be maintained at about 36°–40° during winter nights. Repot February. Stand outdoors during summer months.

Propagation.—By layering in early spring, or by grafting on *D. laureola* (the Spurge Laurel) at the same time.

GREENHOUSE SPECIES.

D. odora, fragrant reddish-purple flowers.

HARDY SPECIES.

Culture of outdoor species.—Plant in sandy peat, or sandy soil containing plenty of leaf-mould. Some of the drooping species are useful for the front rocks of rockeries, other species are at home in the border or shrubbery. Plant in autumn or spring.

The hardy species cultivated in borders and shrubberies include:

D. blagayana, white, flowering in March.

D. cneorum, the "Garland Flower," pink, May flowering. Only 1 ft. high.

D. collina, rose, March to June, 2–3 ft.

D. neapolitana, rose-purple, spring.

D. petrœa, pink, June, 2–3 in.

D. alpina, white, May, 6–18 in. Deciduous.

D. mezereum, red or white flowers; also makes a good pot plant for the cool house.

DAPHNE A FRAGRANT SPRING FLOWERING SHRUB

Daphne mezereum, which blooms in February. This is magenta or white. All the Daphnes are sweetly scented. Cneorum is the variety which is covered with pink blossoms in spring.

CULTIVATION ON ROCKERIES.

These are among the most ornamental of small shrubs in the rock garden.

D. blagayana has creamy-white flowers at the extremities of long bare shoots in early spring. It is usual to cover these shoots with stones, or it may be inter-planted with some low-growing plant such as a dwarf heather, which will serve the same purpose of protection. The soil should be a stony sandy peat.

Propagation can be done by layering.

D. cneorum, the Garland Flower, has fragrant, circular heads of crowded bright

pink in May. Evergreen. 1 ft. Austria.
It is best propagated by layers.

D. mezereum is the deciduous bush often
found in cottage gardens. The barest
branches are smothered with fragrant
pink blossoms very early in the year,
followed by red berries. It will grow to
a height of 5 ft. or so. Its propagation is
usually by seed, a lengthy process since
it is of very short growth. The young
plants flower quite early in their existence,
but some years are needed to form an
effective bush. Layering is difficult owing
to the upright habit of the bush. Cuttings
seldom root. This variety thrives in
ordinary garden loam. It is found in
woods throughout Europe and Russian
Asia. It is included among the native
plants of Britain, but its occurrence in a
truly wild state is very rare and confined
to certain southern counties only.

D. laureola, the Spurge Laurel, is a
native of Britain, fairly common in woods
in chalk districts. The leaves are dark
green and glossy, the inconspicuous yellow-
green flowers clustered in the axils of
the leaves at the extremities of the
shoots. The flowers emit a strong
fragrance, perceptible for a considerable
distance on still evenings. This variety
is often used as a grafting stock for the
choicer kinds.

DAPHNIPHYLLUM (daf-nē-fil'-um.
Euphorbiaceæ). Vigorous and imposing
evergreen shrubs with rhododendron-like
leaves, pale green above and glaucous white
beneath. Flowers inconspicuous. Useful
for woodland, or moist shady positions.
Propagate by cuttings of half-ripened
wood in July. Thrives in chalky soils.

SPECIES.

D. macropodum.

DARLINGTONIA (darling-tō'-nia.
Sarraceniaceæ). Californian Pitcher Plant.
A curiously formed half-hardy perennial
of which the only cultivated form is
D. californica, with peculiar hollow hood-
shaped leaves with green, yellow or red
flowers in spring. *Propagate* by division
when growth commences and plant out in
light spongy soil of fibrous peat and
chopped sphagnum in any moist place.
Expose to direct sunlight and protect
from frost and cold winds in winter.

DARWINIA (dar-win'-ea: named after

Dr. Darwin, a noted authority on Botany.
Myrtaceæ). Greenhouse evergreen shrubs.
Australia, 1820.

Culture.—Compost: fibrous loam and
peat, with liberal supply of sand. Suitable
for the cool house. Repot early spring.
Prune March or April. Water freely
during the summer. Winter temperature,
40°; summer, 55°–60°.

Propagation.—By cuttings of young
shoots in sandy peat, when pruning.
Stand in shady position in greenhouse.

SPECIES.

D. fimbriata, rose.

D. macrostegia, crimson.

DASYLIRION (das-i-li-ri-on. Liliaceæ). Greenhouse evergreens that are
raised from seeds and thrive in rich sandy
loam perfectly drained.

SPECIES.

D. acrotrichum (*D. gracile*), white. 8 ft.

D. Hookeri, purple flowers.

DATE PALM. *See* PHŒNIX.

DATISCA (da-tis-ka. Datisceæ). A
hardy, herbaceous, diœcious perennial
with graceful stems, pinnate leaves and
yellowish-green flowers; will grow in any
soil. *Propagated* by seeds or division.

D. cannabina, grown chiefly for its
foliage.

DATURA (da-tu-ra. Solanaceæ).
Thorn Apple. A genus of beautiful
annuals and shrubs that are invaluable
for decoration in the greenhouse or conservatory. The shrubby forms frequently
classed as Brugmansias are pretty grown
in bush form or on pillars. The annuals
are useful in borders and may be planted
out in summer. When grown in tubs or
pots they do well outdoors in summer.

Propagate the annuals by seeds sown in
a hotbed or a warm house in March and
grow on the seedlings until they are fit
to plant out. To increase the shrubby
species take cuttings or side shoots with
a heel and strike in sandy loam with a
brisk bottom heat. Sandy soil suits all
the species and they must have occasional
doses of liquid manure during the summer.

SPECIES.

D. arborea is a handsome greenhouse
shrub with flowers in August.

D. chlorantha, greenhouse shrub with
yellow flowers in May. 10 ft. *D. c. flore
pleno*, a fine double form.

D. fastuosa, blue or white flowers in July. Annual. Its varieties, *rubra*, red, and *flore pleno*, double, are good.

D. Metel is an annual with white flowers.

D. sanguinea, a scarlet-flowered greenhouse tree. August. 10 ft. This has a yellow form, *bicolor*.

D. suaveolens is a lovely greenhouse shrub with large fragrant flowers in August.

These plants are also known as Angels' Trumpets, and grow to 2½–3 ft. *D. cornucopia* is a desirable plant; the foliage is very similar to that of the tobacco plant (nicotiana), and the large trumpet-shaped flowers, dark purple in colour, are freely produced during summer. Sow in heat in March; plant into good soil in sunny position in May (Oregon).

D. stramonium (Thorn Apple). A native; is a hardy annual medicinal plant. Flowers white, trumpet-shaped, seeds enclosed in a thorny capsule. Soil, sandy loam; position, sunny and dry. (Perennial Daturas now included under BRUGMANSIA.)

The flowers of all species are fragrant and usually followed by curious fruits.

The plants are very poisonous, but this does not prevent them from being grown, as they are so attractive.

DAUCUS. *See* CARROT.

DAVALLIA (da-valea. Filices). Hare's-foot Fern. Stove and greenhouse ferns. Evergreen. The rhizomes of the fern, clothed with a light brown down when protruding over the side of the pots, look very much like a hare's foot. Canaries, 1699.

Culture.—Equal parts loam and peat, with enough silver sand to keep it open. Repot early spring. Position: pots suspended from roof of house, partial shade during bright sunny weather. Stove temperature: winter, 55°; summer, 80°. Greenhouse: winter, 40°–45°; summer, 60°.

Propagation.—By division when repotting, or by spores sown in pans of sandy peat at any time. Place in propagator, temperature, 60°.

STOVE SPECIES.

D. aculeata.
D. alpina.
D. dissecta.

D. heterophylla.
D. pallida.

GREENHOUSE SPECIES.

D. bullata.
D. canariensis.
D. Mariessii.
D. Tyermanni.

DAVIDIA (dā-vid-ia. Cornaceæ). Japan, 8–12 ft. Deciduous trees of unique appearance when in flower, the latter being subtended by the two enormous white bracts, which constitute the remarkable beauty of the Davidia, and give to it the name of the Ghost Tree. The fruit is like a green plum.

Culture.—Plant in deep loamy soil. It has no objection to chalk but is impatient of dryness at the root. *Propagate* by cuttings of the side twigs when the wood is becoming firm.

SPECIES.

D. involucrata (China). Leaves whitish, mulberry-like and scented when bruised.

D. Vilmoriniana (lacta). The first Davidia to be introduced to European gardens, and considered to be practically identical with the preceding. It was discovered in 1869, in China, by the Abbé David, after whom the genus is named, but not introduced to Europe until 1897, when seeds were sent to France by Père Farges. Only one seed germinated. It was subsequently found by Wilson, as the chief object of his earliest journey to China for Messrs. Veitch in 1899–1902.

DAVIESIA (dā-vē-sea: named after the Rev. H. Davies, a Welsh botanist. Leguminosæ). Australian Hop. Greenhouse flowering shrubs. Evergreen. Australia. 1805.

Culture.—1 part rich loam, 1 part leaf-mould, ½ part sharp sand. Water freely during summer, little at other times. Winter temperature, 45°; summer, 65°.

Propagation.—By cuttings of young half-ripened shoots in the spring; insert in light sandy soil in propagator. Temperature, 60°.

SPECIES.

D. alata, yellow. *D. cordata*, yellow.

DAY LILY. *See* HEMEROCALLIS.

D.D.T. *See* PAGE 252.

DEAL. This is the wood of the pine or fir. It is used in the construction of garden arches and pergolas and occasionally for garden seats. It has to be treated with a preservative and is not to be recommended so much as oak or teak except that it is a much cheaper wood.

DEBREGEASIA (deb-re-gē-sea. Urti-caceæ). Deciduous shrub or small tree from the Himalayas, China and Java, with most striking, long, lance-shaped leaves, whitish beneath. Flowers small, followed by fruit resembling yellow raspberries.

SPECIES.

D. longifolia. The only species in cultivation.

DECAISNEA (de-cais-nea. Berberi-daceæ). Remarkable deciduous shrubs with elegant pinnate leaves and unique blue bean-like fruits. Plant in rich loamy soil. *Propagate* by seeds.

SPECIES.

D. Fargesii. (China), 10 ft. Leaves 2–3 ft. in length. Long (12–18 in.) panicles of yellowish-green flowers, followed by greyish-purple or blue pods of fruit, resembling broad beans. Quite hardy.

DECEMBER WORK IN THE GARDEN.

Flowers.

Shelter beds of bulbs by a mulch of litter over surface.

Press back young plants of carnations and wallflowers into the soil after each severe frost.

Protect Christmas Roses and Iris stylosa with hand-lights.

Finish Rose planting.

Plant masses of Michaelmas daisies where large borders are to be filled.

Examine stored bulbs and tubers. Remove any that appear to be diseased and destroy them.

Sweep and roll lawns occasionally.

Collect all rubbish and burn it. Use the ash over the flower-beds. When the ground is hard and frosty, manure may be wheeled from one part of the garden to another as required. All digging should be completed before the end of the year.

Herbaceous borders can be renovated when the ground is neither too wet nor frosty.

Plants should not be divided this month but they may be lifted if a large ball of soil is left round the roots. Dig in well-decayed manure before replanting.

Bulbous flowers begin to send up their leaves and as soon as they appear, the surface soil should be forked between them and dried bracken or litter put over the beds, if unsheltered, to prevent damage by frosts.

Coarse sand or cinders will protect the roots of liliums, hardy fuchsias and early-flowering gladioli from frost.

Order lilies for pot and garden cultivation. Supplies begin to arrive from Japan in January.

The Shrubbery.

Deciduous climbers of all kinds can be planted except when frosts are severe.

Thorough preparation of the soil is necessary as the plants will be placed in their permanent position, and the subsoil cannot afterwards receive treatment.

Clean up the soil beneath evergreens.

Bulbs for naturalising can be planted as the weeds are cleared.

Remove unwanted shrubs and prepare the site, by deep digging and manuring, to receive the newer varieties in spring.

The Rock Garden.

Rock plants lifted out of their soil pockets by frosts, should be pressed back. Place a layer of stone chippings on the surface round the plants.

Examine all protected plants, and wipe surplus moisture off the glass of cloches.

Keep a look out for slugs if the weather is mild. They will make for the tender plants.

Protect alpine plants by horizontal sheets of glass raised a few inches above the plants.

Fruit.

Wall fruits should receive attention. Pruning should be done, and the shoots that are retained should be nailed to the wall.

It is not wise to prune on very frosty days.

The walls should be washed with soft soap, sulphur and paraffin before the plants are renailed to them.

Prepare the ground for trees to be planted.

Fruit trees should not be planted in mid-winter, except during mild spells.

Cut down newly-planted grape vines to within 12 in. of the soil.

Spray tree trunks with caustic winter wash.

Raspberries should have suckers removed.

Order new fruit trees if not already done. Delay in planting is the cause of many losses.

Vegetables.

Frost should not harm cabbage, broad bean seedlings, etc., unless the plants are lifted out of the ground. After a frost, the earth should be pressed round the stems of the seedlings.

Celery should be earthed up for the last time.

To obtain early potatoes, set a few tubers in shallow boxes this month and plant in the cold frame in the New Year. Blanch endive by covering with pots and adding a surround of litter. Cover Seakale for forcing. Clear herb beds of weeds and dead tops.

Trench celery beds when the crop is finished and prepare them for onions.

Examine potatoes, carrots, beet, and onions in store and destroy any that show signs of decay.

Under Glass.

Choice dahlia roots may be placed in heat at the end of the month for flowering in May.

Chrysanthemums, after flowering, should be cut down to within a few inches of the soil level.

Weak growths should be cut out from the base.

Put a layer, an inch thick, of leaf-mould and sifted loam, over the soil surface in the pots, and water frequently (without allowing them to become sodden) to encourage fresh growths.

When the new shoots are 3 in. high they will be ready to make cuttings for next season's plants.

Plants from the mixed border may be lifted into the greenhouse; in a frost-proof greenhouse, lilies can be potted now. For early supplies, tomatoes and beans may be sown in pots.

The first batch of strawberries for forcing should be brought into the greenhouse.

Temperature is an important factor in the greenhouse this month.

Air the greenhouse in the mornings to keep it free from unnecessary dampness. Air on the side away from winds.

During dull and cold weather watering should almost cease. Keep the stages clean and burn all dead leaves to prevent mildew.

Force Rhubarb; this can be done in the greenhouse. Lift one or two roots, with plenty of soil round them.

Plant them in boxes, cover with more soil, and a layer of coconut fibre.

Stand the boxes under the greenhouse stages, and keep them watered as neces-

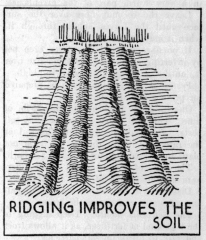

RIDGING IMPROVES THE SOIL

Leave heavy land in ridges after digging to expose the soil to the action of frosts.

sary. Early stems of good colour will then be available before any other fruit is ripe.

Rhubarb can also be forced in the open, by covering the stools with inverted boxes, or pots. A layer of strawy manure over and around the boxes will assist.

Beautify the greenhouse by lifting some of the plants from the mixed borders and bringing them on quickly under glass.

Lift them with plenty of soil round the roots, and pot them very carefully so that they receive no check.

Suitable plants for such treatment are: Andromeda; Azalea; Deutzia; Dielytra; Hydrangea; Solomon's Seal; Spiraea; Violets.

In addition to these, Cinerarias and Primulas should be almost ready to flower, and their pots should be stood in the lightest part of the greenhouse, to hasten the opening of flower buds.

Bulbs in fibre are showing flower stems.

Give them more water, light, and more warmth, and some will then flower by Christmas-time.

Force Lilies of the Valley. Pot up the crowns now in pots or boxes of fine leafy soil.

The tips should be just covered with soil, and a thick layer of coconut fibre added to give protection. Let the crowns be quite close together, and stand the boxes in a very warm part of the greenhouse.

Leave the coconut fibre over the surface until the leaves appear through it, when it may be removed.

If no fibre is available, cover each pot by inverting another of the same size over it, until the leaves are 3 or 4 in. high.

Pests. A soil fumigant can be prepared for present use as follows:

One lb. crude naphthalene and 14 lb. of lime. This will prove a cure for most soil pests. It should be dug into the soil at the rate of 1 lb. to the sq. yd. Do not plant in treated soil for at least a month.

The eggs of several insect pests hibernate on the trunks of fruit trees now.

Dissolve 2 lb. of caustic soda in 10 gallons of water and spray the trees.

The Soil this month. Deep digging is the best kind of fertiliser, as it allows frost and rain to break up soil particles.

Dig all vegetable matter into the soil now as trenching is done.

Manure heavy soils, using basic slag at the rate of 2 or 3 oz. to the sq. yd.

Do not apply artificial fertilisers to light sandy soil until the spring.

Add road grit, long strawy manure and leaves to heavy soil, mixing well into the under layer.

Add cow manure, heavy stable manure, leaves and vegetable matter to light soil, placing it at the bottom of the trench.

Keep the top soil at the surface, as this is more fertile.

Prepare soil composts. Winter is a good time to get soil ready for seed sowing, etc., so that time is saved when outside work presses.

Two parts of loam (decayed turves), 1 part of decayed leaves and 1 part of sand passed through a ½ in. mesh sieve, and well mixed makes an ideal compost for most seeds.

Store it in boxes, protected from rain.

Renew labels. Prepare wooden labels for seed sowing, and other temporary uses in the garden.

It is wise to use permanent labels, with names that cannot be erased or defaced, for all permanent subjects such as fruit trees.

Also prepare tying material, a line for seed sowing, stakes of various sizes, and other oddments in readiness for the rush of seed time.

DECIDUOUS. Trees and shrubs which shed their leaves each autumn are known as deciduous. The leaves of some plants such as Guelder Rose and Virginian Creeper turn beautiful rich tints before falling.

(*See also* EVERGREEN).

DECUMARIA (dek-u-mar-i-a. Saxifragaceæ). Semi-evergreen self-clinging climber, sending out aerial roots like ivy. Tender, requires a sheltered wall except in the warmer districts. *Propagate* by cuttings of firm shoots.

D. barbara (South-eastern U.S.A.). Flowers white in June and July. Climbs to a height of 30 ft. in nature.

D. sinensis (China). Similar to preceding.

DEHISCENCE. Opening of pod or fruit to disperse seed.

DELL. On undulating ground it is sometimes possible to shape an existing valley or dell and so bring it into the garden scheme. Such a feature is a great acquisition to a garden if carefully planted. Screened by flowering trees and shrubs it could be converted to a wild garden (*which see*). If, however, it is near the house, a rhododendron or shrub dell would be more appropriate, or possibly a rock-garden treatment would give the best results.

DELPHINIUM (Larkspur). Ranunculaceæ. Annual, biennial and perennial plants, some of which have thick fleshy roots. Different species of Delphiniums have come to this country from Central Europe, North America, California, Madagascar and China. They vary in height from 6 in. to 4 ft. and the colours include all shades of blue, violet, purple, lavender and white, while some species are a soft yellow and one is red.

The common perennial delphiniums, which are so useful for the back of the herbaceous borders, prefer a good loamy soil, enriched with lime and animal manures. They will, however, grow in any soil so long as measures are taken to supply deficiencies. The first and most important thing is deep digging, which must be done whether the soil is light or heavy in texture. For a depth of fully 3 ft. the soil should be thoroughly broken up. If it is light, plentiful supplies of decayed leaves and old manure should be incorporated with it, and if the soil is heavy, long strawy stable manure will be the best addition. Lime is an essential to the health of the delphinium and a dressing of this should always be given, the amount varying according to the condition of the natural soil.

If it is desired to grow delphiniums on shallow soil over chalk, very large quantities of decayed manure must be mixed with the top 18 in. of soil. The delphinium is very susceptible to drought, and unless there is plenty of animal manure above the chalk the roots are almost certain to get dry in the hot summer weather.

For gardeners in town districts, where stable manure cannot easily be obtained, the best preparation of the soil for delphinium culture would be to add liberal quantities of bone meal, and if the soil seems light and dry, to dig in hop manure.

PLANTING.

The best time to plant border delphiniums is in February. Autumn planting is quite satisfactory in some gardens but on the whole February is the best month of the year for the work.

Young plants should be set very firmly in the soil, with the crowns below the surface. This prevents the drying out of the new roots. As slugs are inclined to be troublesome amongst delphiniums, especially in the winter months, it is advisable at planting time to spread finely-sifted coal ashes over the crowns.

For ordinary garden decoration, the plants can be as close together as 2 ft., but for exhibition spikes 3 ft. should be allowed between each.

As soon as the young shoots appear above the ground the soil between the plants should be lightly forked, and a top dressing of old stable manure, leaves or grass clippings should be put over the soil surface. This will help to preserve the moisture during dry spells or when there are cold winds. The plants should at no time be allowed to become dry, and if weeks of dry weather occur it is advisable to soak the ground thoroughly about twice a week. When the flower spikes begin to form, feed with liquid manure to help the plants to make tall, tapering spikes. As with most strong-growing perennial plants, delphiniums send up a large number of spikes from each root, particularly the second and third year after planting. If these are all allowed to grow, the flowers will be only of inferior quality. As soon as the spikes are a few inches high they should be thinned out, allowing only three the first year, and five to seven the second year, of the strongest shoots to each crown, for exhibition plants, or half a dozen to each plant if required only for garden decoration.

STAKE FIRMLY.

The modern delphinium grows to such a height that it is hardly ever safe to leave the spikes without artificial support, otherwise they are almost certain to fall to the ground in high winds or heavy rains. The exhibition spikes should have a stick to each spike, but with other plants it will be sufficient to place three or four sticks round the clump and to run a string round these sticks to hold the spikes in position. As the flowers fade, cut the stems down to the ground. If the food supplies are maintained, the delphiniums will then send up further stems to flower during the late summer months.

Slugs, in winter, are probably the chief trouble to which delphiniums are subject, and almost every grower has his own special remedy for dealing with the pest. To cover the crown, as winter approaches, with a small heap of finely-sifted coal ashes is one method, the ashes being renewed from time to time as necessary. Another method is to remove all the dead and dying vegetation from the crowns of the plants at the beginning of the winter, and to strew liberal quantities of mortar rubble over the crowns. This prevents the plants from becoming waterlogged and consequently from rotting, as well as keeping slugs at bay. Another method is to cover the crowns with sharp river sand, with a top dressing of some good insecticide.

Among diseases, the only ones which worry the delphinium cultivator are Black Spot (*Bacillus delphinii*), and Black Rot (*Scloritium Rolfsii*). Both may be combated by applying a liquid solution of 1–80 each of mercuric chloride and nitrate of soda. Occasionally mildew will put in an appearance, but it can easily be checked by spraying with a very weak solution of lime sulphate.

EXHIBITION HINTS.

When Delphiniums are to be staged at a flower show, they will, of course, have been grown as directed above, with a single stick to each spike. A few days before the show is to be held, give the delphinium border a thorough soaking with water. This will help to open out the top buds of the spikes, and will also keep the flowers in a better condition than if they are allowed to dry out and consequently drop off. The water should not be given overhead, but the ground should be properly drenched. Cut the flowers in the early morning before the sun is up. Only those spikes with opened or partly-opened flowers from the base to the top of the spike should be cut, as there should not be unopened buds on an exhibition spike. Cut the stem as long as possible, but do not cut it straight across. Slice it diagonally. Cut in this manner, the base will not rest tightly on the bottom of the vase, and the spike will be able to drink in more water. As soon as the spikes are cut, take off most of the leaves, and stand the spikes into deep water, allowing the water to come up almost to the base of the flowers. At the same time keep the flowers themselves as dry as possible. If the spikes have to travel before they reach the show, leave them in water as long as possible beforehand. If the spikes have to be taken a very long distance, it will be necessary to obtain long boxes in which to pack them, and egg cases will probably be the best containers. Wrap each flower spike in a sheet of tissue paper, and lay spikes side by side at the bottom to make one layer. Put more paper over this and pack the next layer with the heads in the opposite direction. Do not make too many layers or the bottom ones may be crushed

by the weight of the top ones. As soon as the flowers arrive at the hall, stand the stems in pails of water so that they do not get a chance to dry out before the actual staging is done.

VARIETIES.

The popular garden delphiniums are hybrids between several species, such as *D. elatum; D. cheilanthum,* and *D. formosum.*

There are over 1,000 good named hybrids in commerce to-day, and the British Delphinium Society annually adds to its list of approved varieties a number of the latest introductions. Some which can be recommended for use in the amateur's garden are: —

SINGLE: *Afghan Queen,* medium sky blue; *Ann Hathaway,* porcelain blue; *Blue Danube,* rich medium blue; *Constance,* gentian blue, white eye; *Lady Augusta,* brilliant gentian; *Mrs. Townley Parker,* pale blue.

SEMI-DOUBLE: Advancement, blue and mauve; *Blue Gown,* brightest ultramarine; *Cambria,* light lavender and purple; *Hewitt's Superb,* lavender mauve; *Jenny Jones,* rich purple and blue; *Millicent Blackmore,* blue and mauve; *Monarch of Wales,* blue and mauve; *Mrs. Newton Lees,* mauve and pale blue; *Pompadour,* brilliant Reckitt's blue; *Rose Marie,* rich deep violet; *Welsh Boy,* gentian blue.

DOUBLE: *Lady Eleanor,* double pale blue. *Mrs. Foster Cuncliffe,* double mauve.

RANUNCULUS FLOWERED: *Lady Bath, Lady Betty, Rosette.*

Belladonna delphiniums are rather more dwarf than the ordinary border delphiniums and more graceful in growth, therefore generally preferred for house decorations. They come quickly into bloom from seed and can in fact be raised and flowered as annuals.

Good varieties are: Belladonna Semi-Plena, sky-blue, semi-double; Blue Bees, pale blue, white eye; Capri, sky-blue; Lamartine, dark blue; Moerheimi, white; Theodora, medium blue shaded mauve; Wendy, dark blue.

In the rock garden, *D. nudicaule* is a small plant with bright scarlet flowers, suitable for the moraine. California. 1½ ft. *D. californicum* is larger, even brighter, and easier to grow. On the other hand its stature may be anything up to 3 ft. so that it is out of place in a small rock garden, though well enough in a border.

See also LARKSPUR.

DENDROMECON (den - dro - mē′ - kon. Papaveraceæ). Californian Poppy Bush. Deciduous shrub from California, with glaucous leaves, and fragrant poppy-like yellow flowers, 2 in. across. Thrives on warm south wall, in a well-drained loamy soil, lightened by sand and mortar rubble. *Propagate* by cuttings consisting of three joints inserted singly in quite small pots in very sandy soil, and placed in gentle heat. Will attain to 12 ft. or more in mild districts.

DENTARIA (den-tar-ia. Cruciferæ). Tooth Wort. Hardy herbaceous perennials that are rarely grown. The species are often included with those of Cardamine.

D. bulbiferæ is the best of the species, with pinnate leaves and purple or white flowers in racemes in spring.

D. diphylla, with white flowers in May, is a pretty subject for damp, shady places.

DEODAR. *See* CEDRUS.

DERRIS. A new and very efficient insecticide, obtainable in powder form to be used dry or in solution. It forms the basis of many commercial preparations.

DESFONTAINEA (dā - fŏn - tā′ - ni - ă. Loganiaceæ). An exceptionally beautiful evergreen flowering shrub from Chile and Peru, attaining a height of 10 ft. and more, and similar in appearance to a holly, with tubular scarlet and yellow flowers. Thrives best in moist warm districts or the south-west, but also does well in the home counties and has withstood nearly 30° of frost. It likes a position facing south in semi-shade and peaty soil. Flowers from July to autumn. The fruit is about the size of a cherry containing many small black seeds which afford the best means of increase. Also by cuttings.

SPECIES.

D. spinosa. The type.

D. s. Hookeri. A beautiful variety very superior to the type, distinguished by its lighter coloured leaves and much larger and brighter coloured flowers.

DESIGN OF PONDS. *See* PONDS FOR FISH AND PLANTS.

DESMODIUM (dez-mo-di-um. Legu-

minosæ). Tick Trefoil. Stove and green-house or hardy shrubs.

Propagate by young side shoots firmly rooted in sand under a bell-glass for the tender shrubs, by division for the hardy perennials, and by seeds for all the species. Plant in soil composed of two parts of fibrous loam to one of leaf-mould with plenty of sand. The outdoor plants thrive

The Deutzia is a shrub which will thrive in any soil. It is a delightful flower for cutting and needs very little attention.

in light rich soil in a sunny position and are best planted in March.

SPECIES.

D. canadense is a good hardy plant for the shrubbery. Purple flowers in July, 3–4 ft.

D. paniculatum, purple flowers in July and *D. rotundifolium*, white flowers in the same month, are useful perennials.

DESMODIUM PENDULIFLORUM. *See* LESPEDEZA SIEBOLDII.

DESTRUCTORS. *See under* INCINER-ATORS.

DEUTZIA (doit-zi-a. Saxifragaceæ). Handsome hardy deciduous early-flowering shrubs from Asia, with abundance of flowers varying from white to rosy-pink during June.

Culture.—Plant in autumn in rich well-drained ordinary soil in a partially shaded position. After flowering thin out well and cut away weak and old wood. *Propagate* by cutting of soft wood about end of June in a frame with gentle bottom heat.

SPECIES.

D. discolor (China). Flowers white to pink, May and June, 5 ft.

D. gracilis (Japan). Only suitable for mild seaside districts or cold house, being very subject to spring frosts. Flowers white in spring.

DEVIL IN A BUSH. *See* NIGELLA.

FLOWER

SEED PODS

SCATTERING SEEDS

BROOM

When the seeds of Broom ripen, the fibre in the pod causes it to burst and scatter the seeds. Botanists call this dehiscence. All the Brooms are excellent plants for light soil.

DEW PONDS. High up on the Downs are age-old ponds used to provide water for cattle, and so constructed that they never dry out. Originally they were used as a permanent water supply on a fortified hill-top. Such ponds are of interest if introduced into the garden, and although they originated so many years ago that the secret of their construction is rather vague, yet the following formula can be taken as fairly reliable. The ponds may be any desired diameter, but the first step is to dig out the centre to a depth of 5 ft., sloping outwards to the edges, banking up

the last 18 in. to the ground level. The pond is then lined with clay, and covered with straw. Puddled lime is then placed on the straw and it must not be allowed to mix with the clay. Earth is then rammed down over the lime to make the bed of the pond.

Such a pond takes six months to fill by natural means, but in the garden it may have a small quantity of water placed in it to hasten filling.

The scientific explanation is that the layer of straw prevents heat passing from the earth below to the pond water. The water, being cold, causes condensation of the moisture-laden night air. Evaporation during the day also cools the pond water and so helps condensation.

DIANELLA (dī-a-nel'-la. Liliaceæ). An evergreen with rush-like leaves, and small white or blue flowers, in long panicles up to 2 ft. long, succeeded by blue berries. Rather tender. Soil, loam and peat. *Propagate* by seeds and division.

SPECIES.

D. intermedia (New Zealand). Flowers white; berries dark blue.

D. Tasmanica (Tasmania). Flowers blue followed by large blue berries.

Dianellas are suitable for growing in pots in the cold house in a compost similar to that used for Agapanthus. Repot in early spring. Water freely during growing period, little after

Propagate by division when repotting.

DIANTHUS (carnations, pinks, etc.). These include hardy perennials and biennials. Some of the latter group are practically annuals since they will if sown early under glass, flower the same season. The genus has attracted the attention of modern hybridists and new races are constantly being offered. They include flowers of almost every colour, many with fringed petals and all fragrant. Most of them are hardy and suitable for cultivation all the year round outdoors.

CULTIVATION OF THE BIENNIAL SPECIES AND HYBRIDS.

The Sweet Williams are amongst the oldest and best known of the biennial species of Dianthus. They are very simply raised from seed sown out of doors in any ordinary soil. The seed should be sown in summer and thinned or transplanted as soon as possible. In autumn the plants can be set 12 in. apart each way in the open border where they are to flower.

Sweet Wivelsfield, a new annual or biennial raised by crossing Sweet Williams with the Allwoodii Pinks, can be cultivated in precisely the same manner, and will be found particularly useful for bedding schemes.

The Chinese Pink is also easily grown from seed in the same way as the other biennials.

The perennial border Pinks are usually propagated by cuttings, though they also will be found easy to raise from seed. A full description of their cultivation is given under PINKS, the same treatment being suited to all the perennial pinks.

Allwoodii, the new hardy race of hybrids resulting from a cross between the perpetual Carnation and the hardy border Pink, are also cultivated in very much the same way as the ordinary perennial Pinks. They will succeed in almost any situation except under the drip of trees or in an absolutely sunless border.

They are propagated by cuttings or layers, rooted in early summer and planted out in the garden in August or September. After planting they are prevented from flowering by pinching out the tops. The plants then remain dormant during the winter months and commence to flower in the spring or early summer. General cultivation is the same as for all hardy flowers, but on the approach of autumn, plants which have been growing and flowering freely all through the summer should be trimmed back so that no long stems or growths are left. Keep the plants very firm in the soil during the winter months, and if there is the slightest tendency to over-dampness in the soil, top dress it with gritty material so that the moisture cannot collect round the collar of the plants.

The Allwoodii Pinks are excellent for growing in many other places than in the open border. They can be grown in 6 in. pots in a similar soil to that used for Carnations, and can be forced for early bloom in March or can be grown to provide flowers until late December. They are also excellent plants for window boxes,

for dry walls and rockeries, and for hanging baskets.

The miniature Alpine Dianthus—*Dianthus alwoodii alpinus*—is a new race obtained by crossing *Allwoodii* with *Dianthus alpinus* and others, and then inter-crossing the progeny. They are cultivated in precisely the same manner as the Allwoodii Pinks.

Carnations are for the most part descendants of the species *D. caryophyllus*, but these too are being constantly crossed by growers, and new varieties with differing habits are being produced. For a fuller description, with varieties and culture, *see* CARNATIONS.

DIAPENSIA (di-a-pen-si-a. Diapensiaceæ). Extremely rare prostrate shrub, from Lapland, that forms cushion-like tufts.

Propagate by division or seeds and grow in moist peat and loam in a cool spot on the rockery. Water well in dry weather. The plants miss the covering of snow that provides a warmth for them in winter, so it is as well to protect them in a frame, or keep a few reserve plants in the cold greenhouse in pots in winter to maintain a supply.

SPECIES.

D. lapponica is the only species commonly grown. A choice evergreen, with pure white flowers, $\frac{1}{2}$ in. across, in July. 1–3 in.

D. barbulata (syn. *Pyxidanthera barbulata*).

DIASCIA (di-as-ki-a. Scrophulariaceæ). Greenhouse annuals with slender erect or diffuse stems. Grow as half-hardy annuals and sow seed in a frame or hot-bed in spring to be planted out later in May or June in light friable soil.

SPECIES.

D. Barberæ, with rosy-pink flowers in July, is a useful plant for greenhouse decoration or for summer bedding. 1 ft.

DIBBERS. This tool is very useful for planting or transplanting of any kind when it is necessary to make a suitable hole in the soil. It is just like the **D** handle of an ordinary spade or fork cut off about 1 ft. down and then pointed. It can quite easily be made at home from an old spade handle, with the aid of a saw and a penknife or chisel. Some dibbers are iron shod to make them more effective in gravel soil. These tools should not be too pointed at the end—in fact definitely rather blunt. If the dibber is too pointed it allows an air space in the soil beneath the plant or bulb, which is liable to cause decay, through the accumulation of water. Dibbers are very cheap to buy.

DICENTRA (di-cent-ra. Fumariaceæ). *Di*, two; *kentron*, a spurr. These were formerly known as Dielytra, by which

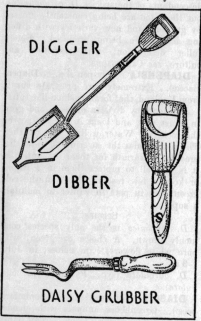

DIGGER

DIBBER

DAISY GRUBBER

Three handy tools : the digger is for clay soil; the dibber for planting seedlings, and the daisy grubber is for removing weeds from lawns.

name they are still often catalogued by nurserymen.

SPECIES.

The principal one, which must be familiar to almost everyone with garden interests, is *D. spectabilis*, or Bleeding Heart.

D. eximia and *D. formosa* are much alike and produce rosy hanging hearts in little clusters, flowering the whole summer. Both grow about 6 in. and inhabit N.W. America.

D. spectabilis (Bleeding Heart) is altogether on a larger scale, and would be more suitably placed among the larger

plants of the border or in the front of the shrubbery. The hanging, heart-shaped flowers are rose-pink; the foliage bluish-grey. It makes a good plant for gentle forcing for early spring bloom.

DICHÆA (di-ke-a. Orchidaceæ). Stove orchids distinguished by the way in which the sheaths of the double rows of leaves cover the slender long stems.

Propagate by division. Grow in hanging baskets with ample drainage in a mixture of chopped sphagnum and peat. Being epiphytes they may be grown on wood blocks.

The only grown species is *D. picta*, with green flowers spotted with purple.

DICHORISANDRA (di-kor-i-zan-dra. Commelinaceæ). This genus of handsome stove perennials includes plants that are highly valued for their beautiful foliage as well as for their flowers. Increased by seed sown in light peaty soil in pans in a stove in spring. Also by division of the plants when growth is commencing. Plant in a compost of fibrous loam, peat and leaf-mould with a dash of sharp sand. Summer temperature, 60°–80°; winter, 45°–55°.

During the summer they must be stood in shady positions and some of the taller plants may be put out under the shade of palms or other tall subjects.

SPECIES.

D. mosaica, of which the leaves are marked with white, like mosaic work, while the flowers are whitish blue. 2 ft.

D. m. gigantea has very much larger leaves.

D. pubescens tæniensis has leaves striped white and bluish-white flowers.

D. thyrsiflora has blue flowers in autumn and winter. It is easily the handsomest of the order, and under favourable conditions it has been known to rise to 10 ft. in height with many branches, each ending in a spike or thyrse of thickly-set sky-blue flowers. When it begins to flower it may be put into a warm conservatory where it will last in bloom for two months.

D. undata has wavy leaves marked with silvery grey.

DICKSONIA (dik-sŏ′-nea. Filices). Tree Fern. Stove and greenhouse tree ferns. 1786.

Culture.—Compost, general culture, propagation, etc., the same as for Cyathia.

STOVE SPECIES.

D. Schiedoi, D. Lathami.

GREENHOUSE SPECIES.

D. Calcita, D. squarrosa.

DICOTYLEDONS. One of the two classes into which flowering plants are divided, characterised by the embryo having two seed leaves while the leaves are

SPECIES.

D. albus or *D. albus purpurea* (*Fraxinella*), with white and purple flowers respectively in May. A Caucasian form is larger and finer.

DICTYOSPERMA (dik-ti-os-per-ma. Palmæ). Tropical palms with several slender stems rising from one rootstock, and graceful leaves. In Mauritius and Madagascar in their natural habitat they

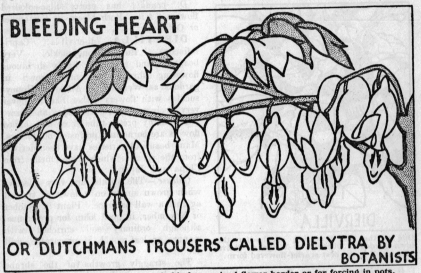

BLEEDING HEART

OR 'DUTCHMANS TROUSERS' CALLED DIELYTRA BY BOTANISTS

Dielytra is a spring flower suitable for a mixed flower border or for forcing in pots.

net-veined and the flowers have their organs in pairs or fives or multiples of these numbers. Opposite to Monocotyledons.

DICTAMNUS (dic-tăm'-nus. Rutaceæ). Bastard Dittany, Burning Bush, Fraxinella.

Fraxinella.—Pretty hardy border flowers remarkable for inflammable resin on the stems, which will flame without injuring the plants if a lighted match is applied when the flowers are in full bloom.

Propagate by seeds sown as soon as ripe, or by the fleshy roots which if cut into pieces in spring will produce new plants much quicker than seedlings. Once planted, leave undisturbed. They require rather dry light soil and, although slow-growing in most gardens, will thrive rapidly in warm soil.

grow to a height of 20 or 30 ft., but under cultivation they rarely attain more than a few feet. They thrive in a moist stove in rich loam.

SPECIES.

D. album, with leaves 6–7 ft. long. 15 ft. Its varieties are *furfuraceum* and *rubrum.*

D. aureum. Leaves, 3–4 ft.

D. fibrosum, with leaves 4–5 ft., yields the Piassava Fibre.

DIDYMOCARPUS (did-i-mo-kar-pus. Gesneraceæ). Tropical herbaceous perennials that are closely allied to Streptocarpus. Most of the species are stemless, resembling Primroses in habit, with umbels of pretty flowers of various colours. Coming from the regions of Cochin China and Ceylon, they require a moist stove culture.

Propagate by seeds, cuttings of young side shoots in sand with bottom heat, and division in spring. Use a mixture of peat and sandy loam to grow them.

SPECIES.

D. *crinita.* White, July. 6–8 in.

D. *humboldtiana* (syn. *primulæfolia*). Leaves like those of primroses and lilac blue flowers in September and October. 4 in.

DIERVILLA

One of the best flowering shrubs for the town garden is Diervilla or Weigelia. " Eva Rathke " is the best scarlet-flowered form.

D. *malayana.* Yellow flowers in July. 4–6 in.

DIDYMOCHLÆNA (did-i-mo-kle-na. Filices). Stove ferns of which only one or two species are grown. The best, D. *lunulata*, is to be found throughout the tropical regions. It is very ornamental with large fronds 3–4 ft. long. It succeeds in 2 parts of peat to 1 of loam and is increased by the spores formed on the fronds. Lesser species are D. *sinuosa* and D. *truncatula.*

DIELYTRA. *See* DICENTRA.

DIERAMA (dee-er-am-a. Iridaceæ). Wandflower. Pretty bulbous plants from S. Africa that are only half-hardy in most places in England. They may be grown in pots or bowls, or else in a well-drained sheltered border near a south wall or in front of the greenhouse. The bulbs should be planted in November or February 3 in. apart and 3 in. deep in sandy loam. In

very cold weather they should be protected with bracken or litter. Increase by offsets.

SPECIES.

D. *pulcherrimum* (syn. *Sparaxis pulcherrima*), has sword-shaped leaves and long graceful flower stems bearing drooping blood-red flowers. It has white, red and striped varieties. The flowers are useful for cutting. 3–6 ft.

D. *pendula* has pretty lilac-coloured flowers. 4 ft. Both bloom in September or October.

DIERVILLA (di-er-vil-la. Caprifoliaceæ). Bush Honeysuckle. Very beautiful and attractive hardy deciduous flowering shrubs frequently grown in gardens as Weigelas. Allied to Honeysuckles with flowers rather like foxgloves very freely produced during May and June.

The many pretty tubular or bell-shaped flowers are borne in a profusion of clusters. Many beautiful varieties have been derived from the species, which come chiefly from China and Japan.

Culture.—The shrubs are very effective when grown singly on a lawn or trained against a wall or fence. Plant in October or November, in good loam for preference, although ordinary soil enriched with manure or leaf-mould, if procurable, will do.

The straggly growths of the shrubs should be cut back and dead and weak wood should be cut out in winter. For these shrubs pruning consists in cutting out old and straggly wood after flowering.

An annual top dressing of well-decayed manure applied in autumn will greatly benefit the plants, while in summer they need plenty of water and doses of liquid manure when the shrubs are flowering freely.

Propagate by soft wood cuttings in June in a frame; also cuttings of ripened shoots taken with a heel and inserted in a frame in sandy soil or outdoors in October root quickly, or the shoots can be layered in summer.

SPECIES.

D. *florida* (*rosea*, *amabilis*). China. Flowers deep rose. One of the parents of the many fine hybrids, which generally surpass the species in effectiveness in the garden. May and June. 8 ft.

D. f. candida. Flowers pure white.

D. hybrida Abel Carriere. Soft bright rose.

D. h. Eva Rathke, bright crimson, late flowering.

DIGGING. A spade is the best implement to use for digging a fresh site, the fork being reserved for turning ground which has been recently dug.

In the case of heavy soil it may be easier to use both tools for the first trenching.

Take out a trench a "spit" deep and wide and wheel the soil to the place where he work will finish. Fill in with soil from the next "spit" width of trench and continue until the soil from the first trench fills in the last "spit" width. Put the spade into the soil in as upright a position as possible and thrust it well down into the soil, using the foot if necessary. A basket or truck is useful for receiving perennial weed roots, rubbish, etc., which may be turned up in digging. Never dig in wet weather.

Heavy soils are best dug in the autumn and the surface left rough so that the weather can take action on as large a surface as possible. Light sandy soils are best dug in the spring. Start at the top of a sloping site and work downhill. A small wooden or iron scraper is a very useful tool for keeping the spade clear while in use.

DIGGING FORKS. *See under* Forks.

DIGGING SPADES. *See under* Spades.

DIGITALIS (diji-tā-lis. Scrophulariaceæ). Foxglove. Showy hardy perennials and biennials that are highly valued for borders and of which the best known is the biennial *D. purpurea* or common Foxglove. By careful choice of a site the majestic grace of wild Foxgloves can be reproduced in the garden, but they cannot be induced to flourish in uncongenial spots. A semi-shaded somewhat damp position is quite suitable, though, like lilies, Foxgloves appear to prefer to reach up into sunshine. Good modern varieties for sowing are: Grant Primrose, rich cream or buff flowers, effective at the edge of a shrubbery; Monstrosa, with large bell-shaped terminal flowers, white or rose;

Giant Spotted, different colours; Shirley, flowers vary from white to dark rose; White, almost entirely white. The seed is best sown in the autumn, and plants may take 18 months to flower, or more in some cases. The plants can also be increased sometimes by division.

Most of the species are perennials, but the new *Lutzii* and Canary Hybrids will bloom the first year from seed sown in

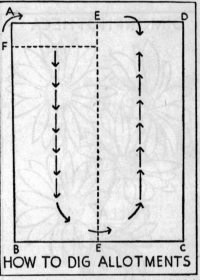

HOW TO DIG ALLOTMENTS

The plot is divided into two, E E, a trench is opened and the soil in the trench at F is placed between E D to fill up the trench when the plot is dug.

February or March, in a cool greenhouse, and planted out in May. A cool, moist soil and a position in partial shade is best.

DILLWYNIA (dil-win-i-a. Leguminosæ). Greenhouse evergreen shrubs with pea-shaped flowers of orange or yellow frequently blotched with red and heath-like leaves.

Propagate by cuttings of firm side shoots rooted in sand under a bell-glass, in August. Also sow seed in peaty soil in heat in March. Pot up in fibrous peat with plenty of coarse sand. They must be carefully watered to ensure success. Summer temperature, 55°–75°; winter, 40°.

SPECIES.

D. cinerascens. Yellow and red, spring. 1–2 ft.

D. ericifolia (heath leaved). Yellow and red, spring. 1–2 ft.

D. floribunda. Similar to preceding.

D. hispida. Orange and red, spring. 1–2 ft.

DIMORPHANTHUS. *See* ARALIA.

DIMORPHOTHECA (di-mor-fo-the-ca. Compositæ). Stars of the Veldt. Cape

DIMORPHOTHECA

A HARDY ANNUAL FROM SOUTH AFRICA.

" Star of the Veldt," or Dimorphotheca, a half-hardy annual, bears a profusion of orange flowers in the summer.

Marigold. Shrubby and annual half-hardy plants that are not much grown. They are both pretty and showy plants for summer bedding.

Easily raised from seed sown under glass in heat in spring and planted out at the end of May in loam and leaf-mould. They like a fairly light soil in a sunny position, and under such conditions seeds may be sown in April, where the plants are to bloom, but should be grown cool, and in good light, or the plants will get leggy. The perennials also by division or cuttings struck in heat under glass.

SPECIES.

D. aurantiaca (orange-coloured) is th type, but the newer *D. A.* hybrids ar wonderfully fine, giving a wealth of daisy like flowers in a fine variety of colours

DIONÆA (Di-onæ´-a. Droseraceæ) Venus's Fly Trap. Interesting greenhouse perennials. Insectivorous. Leaves margine with hair-like teeth, very sensitive. Grow chiefly as a curiosity. 1778.

Culture.—Compost: peat and sphagnum moss in equal parts, with an addition o some small broken crocks. Repot March Good drainage essential. Pots should b stood in pans, the space between the po and sides of the pans filled with moss and kept in a wet condition. Place unde bell-glass, leaving one side slightly raised Winter temperature, 40°; summer, 55°.

Propagate by division of plant whe repotting.

SPECIES.

D. muscipula, white.

DIOSMA (di-oz-ma. Rutaceæ). *Dios* divine, *osme,* smell, refers to the pleasan scent that characterises these plants Heath-like greenhouse evergreen shrub from S. Africa. This is one of the oldes genera that have come to us from th Cape, but the most showy of the specie have now been transferred to other orders

Propagate by cuttings of half-ripe shoot in August or young shoots in April and strike in sandy peat in a warm frame Use good fibrous peat with a liberal dash of silver sand. When potting use as smal pots as possible, at the same time withou starving the plants. Pot firmly and stop back young shoots to obtain a bushy growth. The plants only need a tempera ture from which frost is just excluded. In summer the pots may be plunged out o doors.

SPECIES.

D. ericoides. White, spring. 2–3 ft.

D. album (*Coleonema album*).

D. crenata (*Barosma betulina*).

D. fœtidissima (*Barosma fœtidissima*).

D. speciosa (*Adenandra umbellata*).

D. oppositifolia (syns. *hirsuta, vulgaris*)

DIOSPYROS (di-os´-pir-os. Ebenaceæ). Deciduous trees, with leaves more or less oval in shape, and in some species large and Magnolia-like. Although of no floral beauty, the Diospyros have long been

ultivated in Eastern countries for their
edible and ornamental fruits. They need
a warm, sunny wall, and a loamy soil
with peat added. No regular pruning is
needed.

Propagate by seed, except the named
varieties, which are grafted on seedlings.

SPECIES.

D. Kaki, Kakee or Chinese Persimmon
China, 20–40 ft. Distinguished from
other species by its large leaves, up to
in. long. Fruit yellow, 3 in. wide by
in.; in appearance like a yellow tomato.

D. Lotus, Date Palm (China), 30 ft.
Perfectly hardy and has been grown in
English gardens since the 17th century.
Fruits yellow or purplish, but never ripen
in this country sufficiently to become
edible, but remain very astringent.

D. Virginiana, Persimmon (Eastern
U.S.A.), 40 ft. upwards. Rather tender
when young, but becomes perfectly hardy
after a few years. There is a fine specimen at Kew between 60 and 70 ft. high.

D. costata and *D. Mazelli* are two
varieties of Persimmon, with transparent
yellow and red fruits respectively. Much
grown in the Channel Islands.

DIOSTEA (dī-os'-tea. Verbenaceæ).
Deciduous shrub from Chile resembling
the Spanish Broom in growth, with
clusters of pale lilac verbena-like flowers
during June. 12–15 ft. Plant in light,
loamy soil.

Propagate by cuttings in July, in cold
frame.

SPECIES.

D. juncea (syn. *Lippia juncea, Verbena juncea*).

DIPELTA (dī-pel'-ta. Caprifoliaceæ).
Deciduous shrubs originating from China,
with sweetly-scented flowers resembling
Weigela (*Diervilla*). They thrive in open,
moist, loamy soil.

Propagate by cuttings.

SPECIES.

D. floribunda. Flowers pink, with
yellow throat, in May and June. Very
beautiful. Likes a semi-shaded position.
8–10 ft.

D. ventricosa. Very similar to above.

D. yunnanensis. A rare species with
paler coloured and more slender flowers.

DIPHYLLEIA (di-fil-le-i-a. Berberideæ). A pretty, hardy herbaceous plant

with only two leaves and heads of white
flowers.

It is best treated as an alpine and grown
in a moist shady part of the rockery in
peaty soil. Increased by division or by
sowing the blue berries when ripe.

SPECIES.

D. cymosa. May, white. 1 ft. Umbrella
Leaf.

DIPLADENIA (dip-la-de-nia. Apocynaceæ). Beautiful evergreen climbers
that when trained on balloon-shaped
trellises or pillars in a stove make lovely
objects, suitable for exhibition purposes,
while when grown in a border and trained
to the roof fewer plants are shown off to
greater advantage.

Increase in spring by cuttings of young
ripe shoots which root readily in sandy
peat under glass. Plant in a compost of
2 parts of fibrous peat to 1 of loam with
coarse sand and charcoal. Repot in
early spring when new growth is just
commencing. As they are from the
tropics of S. America they require
a stove temperature. After potting or
planting keep them in 65° or 70° by day
and only a few degrees below that at
night. During the spring and summer
they should be frequently syringed to
keep down red spider and given plenty
of water. After the flowering season is
over—which may last from May to
October—they may be kept in a cooler
house and allowed less water. If planting
is extended over a period of a few weeks
flowers will appear consecutively and thus
prolong the flowering season.

When trained to trellises the young
shoots must be tied in as soon as possible
as otherwise they become entangled.
During the winter the side branches
should be spurred back almost to the
old wood.

SPECIES.

D. atropurpurea (syn. *Echites atropurpurea*). Purple flowers in summer. 12 ft.

D. amabilis. Rose and crimson flowers
in summer. 12 ft.

D. boliviensis. White and yellow,
summer. 9 ft.

D. brearleyana. Crimson, summer.
14 ft.

D. eximia. Rosy-red, summer. 10 ft.

D. Sanderi. Rose, summer. 12 ft.

D. Thos. Speed. Rosy-crimson flowers with a white throat and a golden eye. 12 ft.

DIPLOPAPPUS. *See* CASSINIA.

DIPSACUS (dip-sa-cus. Dipsaceæ). Teazel, and Fuller's Teazel. Britain. Hardy biennial, 4–6 ft. *D. Fullonum* is supposed to have originated from the more common *D. sylvestris*, and differs from the latter in the seed heads, the scales of which are hooked at the end, and provide the teazel heads used in cloth mills for raising the nap on cloth. Both species are more suitable for growing in the wild garden or shrubbery where they can be allowed to ripen their seeds and become naturalised.

DIPTERONIA (dip-ter-ōn'-ea. Aceraceæ). Deciduous tree allied to Acers, with foliage resembling those of the Tree of Heaven (*Ailanthus glandulosa*). Flowers insignificant, followed by fruit in large clusters like the fruits of the wych-elm. Quite hardy, thriving in loamy soils.

Propagate by cuttings in July and placed in gentle bottom-heat.

SPECIES.

D. sinensis (China). The only species in cultivation. 25 ft.

DIRCA (dir'-ka. Thymelæaceæ). Leatherwood. Deciduous shrub, allied to the Daphnes, with yellow flowers in March, and exceedingly tough and flexible wood. It is a moisture-loving plant and needs a deep peaty soil, or loam with peat added.

SPECIES.

D. palustris (eastern N. America).

DISA (di-sa. Orchidaceæ). Very beautiful terrestrial orchids from S. Africa. Although numerous species have been described very few are successfully grown as they are difficult to establish. Their growth commences in late autumn and continues in winter so that they are unable to obtain sufficient light. This impediment is removed to some extent by growing them just under a ventilator which should be kept open except in the very coldest weather.

Propagate by offsets or division when growth is recommencing. Pot up in a soil composed of equal parts of peat and sphagnum with a basis of broken crocks and, only if it is the best quality, fibrous loam.

The latest advice about repotting to perform this operation in Augus previously December and March ha been given as the right months. Whe potting the plants entirely fill the po so that the plants are well raised in th soil and the collar keeps dryish. Unt roots have formed water sparingly an carefully, but when they are well esta lished water copiously and syringe i bright weather. Once they reach th flowering period give liquid manur occasionally and keep the plants on th coolest stage of the stove. When th flowers are over the plants must re thoroughly. If insect pests appear di the plants in liquid insecticide.

SPECIES.

The species of this genus are di tinguished by tuberous rootstocks, leaf succulent stems and flowers with sepa that are much larger than the petals, an the under sepal is shaped like a hood.

D. grandiflora is one of the best of th species. Originally growing in spong peat on the edges of pools on Tabl Mountain it proved difficult to grow i England, but it is now successfully grow in several houses. It has scarlet and gol flowers in June and July. 2 ft.

VARIETIES.

D. g. pittacina. Yellow, crimson spots

D. g. superba. Scarlet.

D. nervosa. Rosy, June. 2 ft.

D. racemosa. Rosy-crimson and yellow flowers. June. 1½ ft.

D. pulchra. Lilac and purple flower in June. 2 ft.

Good hybrid forms are *D. Veitchii* rose, and *D. Luna*, rose.

DISANTHUS (dis-an'-thus. Hama melidaceæ). Deciduous shrub from Japan with foliage like that of the Judas-tre (*Cercis seliquastrum*) changing in autum to claret red, suffused orange. Flower dark purple, of no importance.

SPECIES.

D. cercidifolia. The only species Thrives remarkably well in Ireland, wher there are some very fine specimens Rather tender when young. Likes a peaty soil, such as Heaths grow in.

DISBUDDING. A term applied to the thinning out of unwanted growths. In the case of exhibition blooms such as roses chrysanthemums, dahlias, etc., the buds are removed to leave fewer but finer flowers.

DISCARIA (dis-kār′-i-a. Rhamnaceæ). Deciduous shrubs, formidably armed with spines, and numerous small bell-shaped flowers. They require a sheltered sunny position, in ordinary garden soil. *Propagate* by cuttings in July in frame.

SPECIES.

D. Toumatou, the "Wild Irishman" (New Zealand). Varies from a bush of 2 ft. to a tree 25 ft. high.

DISEASES. *See* FUNGOUS DISEASES.

DISTYLIUM (dis-til′-e-um. Hamamelidaceæ. Evergreen shrub from China and Japan with reddish Hamamelis-like flowers in April, contrasting well with the dark glossy green leaves. 3–4 ft. in the open, up to 15 ft. on sheltered north wall. Very good on chalky soils.

SPECIES.

D. racemosum. The only species.

DITCH. A trench used either for drainage or to mark a boundary. A hedge and ditch separating two plots of land must be kept trimmed by the owner on whose land the hedge is planted. If, however, the adjoining owner has been trimming the ditch and hedge for twenty years with the knowledge and consent of his neighbour, he gains a right thereto.

A ditch requires clearing of any rubbish and overhanging growths removed once a year. This is usually done in the autumn. Acts of ownership decide to whom a hedge belongs when there is a ditch on both sides.

DITTANY. *See* DICTAMNUS.

DIURIS (di-ur-is. Orchidaceæ). From *dis*, double, and *oura*, a tail, in reference to the tail-like sepals. Stove terrestrial orchids.

Propagate by division. The pots should be half filled with crocks and the plants placed in sandy peat or leaf-soil and sand.

SPECIES.

P. alba. White and rose flowers in August. 1 ft.

P. maculata. Yellow spotted brown. March. 1 ft.

P. punctata. Purplish-blue flowers. 1–2 ft.

DODECATHEON (do-de-kath-e-on. Primulaceæ). Literally Twelve Gods. The name was anciently applied by Pliny to

a plant whose identity is at present unknown. Shooting Stars. These plants are from North America. They form tufts of light green leaves, from the centre of which spring stems up to 8 in., bearing a number of small flowers with reverted petals, after the manner of cyclamen. The styles in this case are protruding. The plants succeed best in moist and rich soil and, if agreeable to their position,

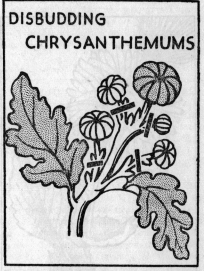

DISBUDDING CHRYSANTHEMUMS

To obtain large Chrysanthemums remove side buds, called by gardeners "taking the crown bud."

make luxuriant clumps. Very useful for damp shady corners of the rockery.

Propagate by division in spring or after flowering, or by seeds sown when ripe in pans in a cold frame.

SPECIES.

D. Meadia with light purple cyclamen-like flowers has several varieties with white, crimson-lilac and orange flowers. The best known of the varieties are as follows:

D. M. Clevelandii, which is the only kind that likes a dry soil and has violet or blue flowers in May. 1 ft.

D. M. elegans. Deeper coloured and more numerous flowers than the type. 1 ft.

D. M. giganteum. Earlier flowering and taller than the type. 1½ ft.

D. M. splendidum. Deep crimson flowers with an orange ring.

DOG'S TOOTH VIOLET. *See* ERY-THRONIUM.

DOGWOOD. *See* CORNUS.

DOLCHOS (dol-i-kos. Leguminosæ). A large but unimportant genus of hardy and tender shrubs, trees and herbs, mostly with twining stems.

Propagate by seeds for all species and by cuttings in brisk heat for the stove ones

DORONICUM

Doronicum or Leopard's Bane is welcome in the spring garden for its golden flowers. They are suitable for cutting.

or in a cool frame for the half-hardy species.

SPECIES.

D. Lablab, greenhouse, rosy purple, twining (syns. *lignosus, purpureus, Lablab vulgaris*). 12 ft.

DOMBEYA (dom-be-ya. Sterculiaceæ). Stove evergreen shrubs and trees.

Propagate by cuttings of young shoots taken in spring and inserted in sand over bottom heat. Plant in a compost of 2 parts of loam to 1 of peat with sand.

SPECIES.

D. acutangula. 16 ft., red.

D. mollis. 30 ft., pink.

D. viburniflora. 13 ft., white, February

DOODIA (doo'-di-a. Filices). Green house ferns. N. S. Wales, 1808.

Culture.—Compost: 1 part loam, 1 par leaf-mould, ½ sand with small broke charcoal. Repot early spring. Shad position. Winter temperature, 40° summer, 60°.

Propagation.—By spores sown on sand peat in propagator, temperature, 70°.

SPECIES.

D. aspera, D. caudata, D. lunulata D. media.

DORONICUM (dŏr-ŏn'-icum. Com positæ). Leopard's Bane. Early flower ing hardy perennials that are useful fo beds and borders.

Culture.—Propagate by division i spring or autumn and plant out in a goo well-manured garden soil or by th waterside in moist shady places. Cu down the shoots that have flowered an dress with manure to obtain a secon blooming.

SPECIES.

D. austriacum and *D. caucasicum,* bot about 1 ft. high, with bright yellow bloom in April and May, are the best known fo gardens. The variety of *D. plantagineum* known as Harpur Crewe, is taller an more beautiful, but shorter lived. Arnica, the well-known remedy fo bruises, is obtained from leopard's bane

DORYANTHES (dory-an'-thes Amaryllidaceæ). From *dory,* a spear and *anthos,* a flower—commonly called the Spear Lily. Greenhouse flowering plants palm-like foliage. N. S. Wales, 1800.

Culture.—Compost: equal parts sandy loam and leaf-mould. Repot spring Position: light, airy, lofty conservatory Winter temperature, 50°; summer, 65° to 70°.

Propagation.—By suckers removed, and placed in small pots in the greenhouse, a any time.

SPECIES.

D. excelsa, scarlet; *D. palmeri,* red.

DORYCNIUM (dor-ik'-ni-um. Legu minosæ). Deciduous shrub, with numer ous flowers, white shaded pink and resembling a Broom in appearance. produced from June to September. Leaves clover-like with a silvery sheen.

SPECIES.

D. hirsutum (S. Europe). Thrives in full sun, in quite poor dry soil.

DOUBLE DIGGING. In this process the soil is moved to a depth of two spits. By this means the soil is better aerated and roots can penetrate more easily. Thus it will be seen that the extra labour required is worth while if good results are hoped for.

Start at one end of the plot and open out a trench 2 ft. long and one spit deep, wheel this soil to the other end of the plot as in ordinary digging. With a large fork break up the subsoil in the trench another spit deep, incorporating with it farmyard manure, decayed refuse and anything which will help to improve the soil. Turn the next 2 ft. of soil over into this trench, leaving a second trench open. Thus the soil is broken up to a depth of two spits but the original layer of soil is kept on the surface of the plot.

DOUGLAS FIR. *See* PSEUDOTSUGA.

DOUGLASIA (dug-la-si-a. Primulaceæ). Pretty and rare little hardy plants that resemble Androsaces.

Propagate by seeds and division in spring. They like a compost of loam, peat and sand. In winter they should be covered with glass to protect them from damp.

SPECIES.

D. lævigata, has rosy pink flowers in spring and autumn. 1 in.

D. nivalis. Purple flowers in June. 3 in.

D. vitaliana (syn. *Androsace vitaliana*, by which name it is usually known in gardens, and *Arctia vitaliana*).

DOVE COTE. A well-built dove cote in a paved court giving on to both house and garden is attractive, but may have disadvantages. Well-fed pigeons, provided with plenty of grit, will, however, leave the mortar of the walls alone, and doves do no harm to a garden: thus these common objections vanish, while the fancy varieties of birds, fantails, etc., bred in the cote, become so tame as to become a constant source of entertainment.

The cote itself can be constructed of wood or of stone and should be sufficiently thick and strong to keep out the cold. Moreover, it is essential that the centre post on which it is mounted should be amply solid and firm to prevent damage in high winds. A wall cote, especially if on a south wall, does not need such thick material, but it is less picturesque. The windmill or tower-cote of olden days that housed hundreds of birds have given place to the smaller type which requires less space for its setting.

DOVE, RING. *See* WOOD PIGEON.

DOWNINGIA (down-in-gi-a. Campanulaceæ). These very beautiful hardy

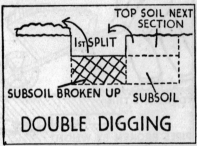

In double digging, the top soil, which is usually the most fertile, is kept at the top, the subsoil being merely broken up.

annuals, suitable for pots or borders, are synonymous with Clintonia. Raised from seed sown in a frame in March or in the open in May.

SPECIES.

D. elegans, blue and white flowers in July. 6 in.

D. pulchella, with white, blue, or yellow flowers in July, is a pretty subject for hanging baskets. 6 in.

DRABA (dra-ba. Cruciferæ). Whitlow Grass. Charming little rock plants that form dwarf tufts covered with bloom in spring and produce a lovely effect in sunny positions.

They are of easy growth in the ordinary soil of the rock garden.

Propagate by seeds sown in a frame in spring and the perennials by division. They make interesting pot plants and many look well inserted in crevices of the rockery. Plant in ordinary soil with some grit and sandy peat.

They may also be propagated by cuttings.

SPECIES.

D. aizoides forms spiny tufts covered with yellow flowers in spring, 3 in. A native of the Swiss Alps, it has established itself on the rocks and walls in the neighbourhood of Penarth Castle, Swansea.

D. Aizoon. Yellow, 3 in.

D. bruniæfolia forms wide mats of foliage with golden-yellow blossoms. Caucasus.

D. dedeana. Hairy leaves and white flowers.

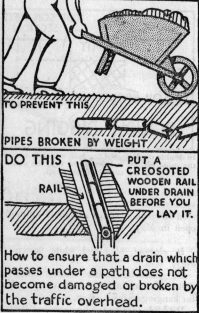

TO PREVENT THIS

PIPES BROKEN BY WEIGHT

DO THIS   PUT A CREOSOTED WOODEN RAIL UNDER DRAIN BEFORE YOU LAY IT.

RAIL

How to ensure that a drain which passes under a path does not become damaged or broken by the traffic overhead.

Land drains are easily damaged by heavy weights.

D. imbricata. A most attractive species with sprays of golden flowers rising above tufts of dark green foliage. 3 in. March.

D. pyrenaica. The "Rock Beauty" with white flowers in May (syn. *Petrocallis Pyrenaica*).

There are several other species but they are almost similar to those listed above, having chiefly yellow flowers in spring-time and averaging about 3 in. in height.

DRACÆNA (dracæ'-na. Liliaceæ). Dragon Blood-tree, so called, because when this plant is cut or wounded, the milky juice quickly dries into a hard gur having the same properties as the su stance called Dragon's blood. Stov ornamental evergreen. East Indie 1640.

Culture.—Compost: two-thirds pea one-third sandy loam. Repot sprin give good drainage. Light, airy position Water freely during summer month Winter temperature, 50°; summer, 70 to 75°.

Propagation.—By cuttings of the mai stem, cut into lengths of about 2 in., ar inserted in pots of sandy soil in the spring by root cuttings in sandy soil in propagate during same period; by offsets at an time; or by seed sown in March in pots (sandy soil and placed in propagator. A these methods of propagation need temperature of 70° to 75°.

SPECIES.

D. fragrans, leaves green.

D. lindenii, leaves yellow and green.

D. goldieana, leaves green and white.

D. Sanderiana, leaves green and white are those chiefly grown, but others ar obtainable in commerce.

See also CORDYLINE.

DRACOCEPHALUM (drā-kǒ-cěph-a lum. Labiatæ). Dragon's Head. Prett summer flowering hardy herbaceous per ennials with tall spikes of bloom, tha are suitable for the rock garden or th mixed border.

Culture.—Increase by seed or divisio in spring and plant in light garden soil

SPECIES.

D. altaiense, with bright green leave and clusters of red-spotted tubula flowers of deep blue, in July, 1 ft.

D. austriacum, with tall spikes o purplish flowers in July, 1 ft.

D. ruyschianum and its Japanese form resemble *austriacum* but are mor showy.

D. grandiflorum, the most beautiful o all, with dense clusters of intensely blue flowers about 2 in. across, flowering from June to August, is the best for rock gardens, 6 in.

D. moldavicum is a hardy annual member of the genus, the remainder being perennials. It is of easy cultivation in any ordinary garden soil, and should be sown where to flower. Height 1-1½ ft.

tems freely branched, flowers violet in
long spikes, July to August. A good plant
for the mixed border.

DRACUNCULUS (dra-kun-ku-lus.
roideæ). Unusual half-hardy plants very
similar to the Arum.

Propagate by division of the tuberous
roots. They require rather rich but not
heavy soil.

SPECIES.

D. creticus. Spathe purple-brown.
D. vulgaris. Spathe purple-brown, June.
Both are synonymous with *Arum
Dracunculus.*

DRAGON'S HEAD. *See* DRACO-
CEPHALUM.

DRAINAGE. A naturally sloping site,
or a gravelly, stony or sandy soil will
probably not require draining, but a heavy,
clayey, waterlogged soil will never give
satisfactory results until adequately
drained. If water stands on the surface
soil for more than two hours after heavy
rain, drainage is required.

Pipe drainage is the method commonly
employed, but this is of no use in a case
where the subsoil is of a nature imperme-
able to water. Deep digging and trenching will be necessary in a case such as this
to allow the water to drain away from the
surface.

On a site with an even slope parallel
trenches should be dug 15–20 ft. apart
and 30–36 in. deep. On a site with a
central depression, dig a central trench
with lateral trenches coming into it every
15–20 ft. at an angle of 60°. See that
the trenches are deeper at the outflow
than at the head. The main pipe may
be 3–4 in. in diameter and the laterals
2–3 in. Lay the pipes evenly by means
of a straight-edge and spirit-level, with the
joints touching. Agricultural and garden
drain pipes are about 1 ft. in length.
Pack rubble, gorse, stones, etc., around the
joints and fill in the excavated soil. Do
not ram the soil back into position but
allow it to settle down naturally. A
ditch or sump will have to be arranged to
carry the water away.

A sump is prepared by digging a hole at
the lowest part of the garden and partially
filling with broken bricks, crockery, rubble,
etc., and replacing the soil.

In small gardens where the expense and

trouble of pipe drainage is not advisable,
the trenches when dug—as for pipe drains
—may be filled in with rough material in
the same way as the sump. This rubble
should be about 9 in. in depth, and then
covered with a layer of old turves turned
upside down. The excavated soil can
then be replaced. This method will be
found to be quite effective although not
so lasting as pipe drainage. A sump is

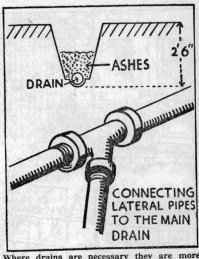

Where drains are necessary they are more
effective if covered with ashes or clinker.

necessary in a small garden which is not
surrounded by a ditch, or the surplus water
will flow into neighbouring gardens.

DRAWN. Plants and seedlings become
drawn through being overcrowded and
having insufficient light. They become
pale in colour and tall and weakly. Such
seedlings will never make good plants and
should be avoided when buying seedlings
from nurserymen. Greenhouse plants are
also affected in this way by being placed
too far away from the glass.

DRESS is the term given to applying
manure or other substance to the ground.
The substance itself is usually termed a
"dressing."

DRILL. A term connected with seed
sowing. A garden line should be stretched
across the ground as a guide, the
drill being made alongside it either with
the edge of a hoe or a piece of wood,

according to the size of the seed for which it is intended; for example, seed potatoes or annual seeds. Drills running north and south allow the maximum of sunlight on to the seedlings, which is an advantage. Sowing in drills is more economical than broadcasting, and weeding is greatly facilitated.

DRIMYS (drim'-is. Magnoliaceæ). Very handsome and desirable trees, only

D. colorata (New Zealand). Flowers yellowish-green, foliage yellowish-green, mottled red. Rare.

D. Winteri (S. America). By far the finest of the genus. Leaves large and of a very pleasing glaucous green. Flowers ivory-white, deliciously scented of jasmine, very freely produced in May. Has withstood nearly 30° of frost inland (Hants and Sussex), and is between 8 and 9 ft.

Here is a novel treatment for the garage entrance with random square paving set in grass. Simple oak trellis is used to screen the garden and to give support to climbing roses.

really satisfactory in the milder parts of the country. In South Cornwall it has exceeded 50 ft. It is important to train it properly, i.e., the leader must be left, but all side growth kept shortened back for the first few years, otherwise the plant develops a very ungainly habit. It thrives against a warm wall, in rich sandy loam, but not in a windy position. Does not object to chalky soils. *Propagate* by cuttings in cold frame.

SPECIES.

D. aromatica (Tasmania and Victoria). Flowers white in April and May.

high and as much through. Near Falmouth it has attained to 50 ft. *Drimys Winteri* takes its specific name from Capt. Winter, who brought home some of its bitter aromatic bark in one of Drake's ships from the Magellan Straits in 1578.

DRIVE. A carriage-way to a house or building. It needs careful designing in relation with the house and garage in order to ensure easy access to both. Meaningless curves should be avoided. Winding drives are sometimes necessary and beautiful, especially on a sloping site, or where a turn in the drive will open up a fresh vista cross the garden. Planting of some sort, other flower borders, an avenue, or groups of flowering shrubs will soften the hard outline of the drive and bring it into the garden picture. In planning, care should be taken to see that all corners are easily negotiable by cars and that ample room is allowed either for reversing or turning. (*See* FORECOURT.)

In small gardens the straight drive is nearly always the most pleasing. If it is constructed of glaring white concrete by the builder, planting—such as lavender hedges, a grass verge with flower borders, etc.—should be undertaken as soon as possible to soften the hard lines. For Drive Construction *see* PATHWAYS.)

DROSERA (dro-se-ra. Droseraceæ). Sundew. Curious insectivorous plants that are usually found growing in damp peaty soil at the edge of marshes. The plants are covered with glandular hairs that give them the appearance of being studded with dewdrops. They are generally propagated by seeds, sometimes by division of the crowns. Root cuttings of *D. binata* if placed between layers of sandy peat will root under a bell-glass. The plants should be potted in peat with a layer of live sphagnum on top of the pot in which the plant is put, and the pot may be plunged in a pan of water to keep the soil as moist as in their natural home, or they may be well and frequently watered. Although some of the species are hardy, being found in England, they all do well if grown in the greenhouse.

SPECIES.

D. binata. White, June, 6 in. Pretty perennial.

D. filiformis. Purple, July. 1 ft. A pretty N. American perennial.

D. peltata. White, and its varieties, *foliosa*, white; *gracile*, pink.

D. rotundifolia is a charming native species with white flowers in July. This is remarkable in full sunshine when the "dewdrops" glisten like numerous little stars.

DROSOPHYLLUM (dros-o-fil-lum. Droseraceæ). The solitary species of this genus, *D. lusitanicum*, is a greenhouse plant with linear leaves and bright yellow flowers. The dew-like drops found on the leaves are very viscid and flies which settle

on them are held tight and killed by this matter, their substance being absorbed by the leaves as nutriment for the plants.

It likes light sandy loam, kept fairly dry, and is propagated by seeds.

Summer temperature, 60°–80°; winter, 40°–50°.

DRYAS (dry-ās. Rosaceæ). Mountain Avens. Dwarf alpine, evergreen trailing hardy perennials with shrubby stems and oak-like leaves of rich green. The flowers of white or yellow resemble single dog-roses very full of yellow stamens.

Culture.—Propagate by division in spring, by cuttings or by seeds sown in heat in March. They thrive on exposed places in the rock garden where they can root deeply.

SPECIES.

The best are *D. Drummondii* (syn. *D. chamædryfolia*), a trailer with golden yellow flowers from June to July that is best in gritty loam, and *D. octopetala*, with white flowers in June and July.

The seed vessels are clothed with downy filaments like Clematis, and if left undisturbed these plants will spread into large clumps. Height 3–4 in.

DRYPIS (drip-is. Caryophyllaceæ). The only species is a dwarf hardy evergreen, of which the leaves are armed with spines.

Propagate by seeds or by cuttings under a handlight in early summer. They need a dry situation in a compost of equal parts of loam, peat and coarse sand.

D. spinosa. Pale blue flowers in June. 9 in.

DUCKFOOT. *See* PODOPHYLLUM.

DUNG. *See* MANURE, FARMYARD.

DUNNOCK or Hedge-sparrow. Wrongly called hedge sparrow, this bird (which is really an Accentor) is one of our most useful garden allies. Its food consists of injurious insects (caterpillars and weevils), and some slugs, to the extent of 44 per cent., the remainder of its food consisting chiefly of wild fruits and seeds, earthworms, neutral insects, etc.

DUSTING. Lime, soot, sulphur, etc., are "dusted" on the ground to ward off or eradicate insect pests.

DUTCH GARDEN. The style of gardening known as Dutch became popular in England in the time of William and Mary.

Actually the Dutch in Holland to-day call their formal sunk gardens English, so the term is very misleading. The actual words, however, convey the idea of a neat, trim garden, speaking of dignity and repose. This is achieved by means of formal beds surrounded by clipped box edgings, the beds being set in paving or gravel and the whole garden secluded by means of thick, evergreen formal hedges. These hedges are clipped to form curious shapes of animals, birds, etc., and the theme of topiary or clipped specimen shrubs is carried out throughout the garden. Topiary work is introduced to the flower beds at the expense of flowers. The garden is frequently sunk below the main garden level to add to the idea of seclusion.

DUTCHMAN'S PIPE. *See* ARISTOLO-CHIASIPHO.

DWARF SHRUBS. Although on large rockeries shrubs of many kinds can be accommodated, it is as a rule unwise to use the free-growing type of shrub which is more general in the shrubbery or in the mixed shrub border. There are certain Conifers and other evergreens, as well as a number of deciduous shrubs, which are particularly appropriate in the rock-garden.

In addition to the ordinary rock-garden there are the miniature rock-garden, Japanese garden, Alpine Meadow garden, and the Alpine garden made in a pig trough or stone sink, all of which types require diminutive, slow-growing shrubs,

in order to create landscape effects i a tiny space.

DYCKIA (dik-i-a. Bromeliaceæ) Succulent plants like small Pine Appl plants. They should be grown in th greenhouse in a mixture of loam, peat an lime rubbish. Increased by suckers Allow plenty of water in summer but littl in winter and perfect drainage.

SPECIES.

D. altissima. Orange flowers in Sep tember. 2 ft.

D. frigida. Orange, February. 1½ ft.

D. rariflora. Orange flowers in June 2 ft.

DYER'S WEED. *See* RESEDA LUTEOLA

D.D.T. A widely publicised insecticide which is not, however, a cure for all insect troubles. It is, for instance, useless against red spider and almost useless against aphides on account of its slow action. It does not destroy insect eggs.

As a spray or dust, D.D.T. is an effective control for greenhouse thrips, plant bugs, scale insects, leaf-eating caterpillars, ermine moth, beetles, pea and bean weevil, woodlice, cockroaches; dog and hen fleas are controlled by 5 per cent. dust.

Amounts required are very small. An ounce of D.D.T. is enough to kill at least 3,000,000 caterpillars.

It must always be prepared according to the detailed instructions supplied by the manufacturers.

When used as directed D.D.T. preparations can be regarded as non-poisonous.

E

EARWIG (*Forficula auricularia*). Of
he seven British species of earwig
uricularia is the commonest; in fact so
>mmon is it that it needs no description.
LIFE-HISTORY.—The adults hibernate
uring the colder months. During the
ummer eggs are laid in small cells in the
round, under stones or decaying vegeta-
.on. A most interesting fact in the life-
istory of this insect is that the females,
fter laying their eggs, "sit" on them, and
-hen the young have hatched they nurse
hem until they are able to fend for them-
elves. The early stages are passed in the
round, but in late summer when the
najority are mature they crawl up trees,
hrubs and plants, hiding themselves by
lay in any dark corner there may be.
Vhen feeding at night they do damage not
nly to flowering plants such as dahlias,
>ut also to fruit. Of late years they have
•ecome very troublesome in apple orchards,
loing considerable damage to the fruit by
>iting holes round the stalk.
METHOD OF CONTROL.—A poison bran
nixture made as follows will often give
;ood results. Sodium fluoride, 12 oz.,
vheat bran, 12 lb., water, 6 quarts. A
ittle molasses may be added, but not more
han two quarts. This mixture should
>e sprinkled in infested places during early
summer and late autumn. Grease-band-
ng of fruit trees will prevent them crawl-
.ng up, and matchboxes suspended by a
>iece of wire and left half-open will catch
many adults if placed among dahlia plants.
The contents of these boxes should be put
into a pail of water each morning.

ECCREMOCARPUS (ek-kre-mo-kär'-
pus, Bignoniaceæ). Semi-woody climbers
of rapid growth; require wall protection;
may be treated as annuals. Seeds freely;
should be sown in February in heat. Pot
up seedlings and plant out in May.

SPECIES.

E. punicea. Flowers scarlet.

E. Scaber. Flowers tubular, orange-
scarlet, 1 in. long.

ECHINACEA (ek-in-ā-cea. Compositæ). Hardy herbaceous perennials of easy
culture, closely allied to the Rudbeckias.
Culture.—Easily propagated by summer-

sown seed or by root division in March
when they should be planted in ordinary
light rich loam.

SPECIES.

E. purpurea bearing large rosy-purple
flowers with drooping petals and bronzy
golden centres and its hybrid forms with
various shades of rose-coloured flowers (all
forms blooming from July to September)
are the best, and are suited for borders
or beds. Height 3–4 ft.

ECHINOCACTUS. *See* CACTUS.

ECHINOCEREUS. *See* CACTUS.

ECHINOCYSTIS (e-ki-no-sis-tis.
Cucurbitaceæ). Hardy annual climber
from U.S.A. Sow in heat in spring and
plant out in May against a wall or trellis.

SPECIES.

E. lobata, greenish-white, summer,
8–10 ft.

ECHINOPS (ek-i-nops. Compositæ).
Globe Thistle. Useful hardy perennials
that may be used in the border or in the
wild garden. The flowers have curious
spherical heads that are spiny before opening and are well liked by bees.
Culture.—They are easily increased by
division of the tufts or by cuttings of the
roots in spring, and succeed in any good
garden soil in a hot sunny site.

SPECIES.

E. bannaticus, with branching stems of
purplish-blue flowers that bloom in July
and August; about 3 ft. high. *E. exaltatus,*
a tall white July-blooming plant about
6 ft. in height.

E. humilis, a dwarf form with blue
blooms in June, 12–14 in.

E. niveus, with white flowers in September, 18 in.

E. Ritro, has heads of metallic blue and
its several forms which bloom from June
to August are among the best of this genus.

ECHINOPSIS. *See* CACTUS.

ECHITES (echi'-tes. Apocynaceæ).
Stove climbing and flowering shrubs.
Evergreen. Jamaica, 1733.
Culture.—Compost: 1 part lumpy loam,
1 part peat, and enough sand to keep it
open. Repot early spring. Prune after
flowering, cutting away the old flowering
shoots. Train up trellis or over wire to

roof of house. Winter temperature, 50°; summer, 75°.

Propagation.—By cuttings of young shoots in sandy soil, place in propagator, temperature, 65° to 70°.

SPECIES.

E. paniculata, yellow; *E. umbellata*, yellow.

ECHIUM (ek-i-um. Boragineæ). Viper's Bugloss. Hardy annuals, biennials and evergreen shrubs. Useful plants for hot, dry gravelly places in the wild garden.

Propagate by seeds sown in flowering position in September or by division. Also by cuttings and layering for the shrubby species.

SPECIES.

E. creticum. Red flowers in long racemes. July.

E. fastuosum. Half-hardy shrub, with deep blue flowers. May.

E. vulgare. "Viper's Bugloss." An attractive native plant that attains 3 ft. in height and bears flower-stems like a branching candelabra with violet flowers. The species are numerous and are very similar to the type plant.

E. creticum and *E. vulgare*, both hardy biennials, are the best. Both will succeed in poor dry soils, and are good "Bee" plants.

EDGE TRIMMER. For some years past this machine has been on the market, but it has never been really popularised. In method it is very similar to a mowing-machine, and for trimming and cutting the edges of the lawn saves a lot of time with edging iron and shears. A land roll, of about 4 in. diameter and 6 in. wide, works—with a direct drive from a spindle—a star-shaped rotary blade. This roller and blade can be pushed backwards or forwards each way, coming in contact with a stationary, triangular and slightly concave blade. This forms the cutting edge, and whereas the roller is actually on the lawn, the blades are just over the edge, and cut all that they come in contact with. It is fixed on to a stout ash handle about 5 in. long. These machines are made by several well-known proprietary firms, and are sold also in cheap forms.

EDGEWORTHIA (edg-wŏrth-i-a. Thymelaceæ). Deciduous shrub, closely allied to the Daphnes. Sandy loam and peat. *Propagate* by cuttings.

SPECIES.

E. chrysantha (syn. *E. papyrifer* *Daphne chrysantha*). China and Japa 3–4 ft. Flowers yellow, fragrant, pr duced in February. The branches are s flexible as to allow them being tied int a knot, as one would a piece of string.

EDGING IRON. This is a half-moo shaped steel tool, sharpened on the curve edge, and is really the only effective wa of straightening up the edges of lawns o beds. The best and surest method c finishing with a straight line—when thi is desired—is to lay down a length of lin or string, drawn taut, and fixed on peg or reels at either end of the propose straight line. Then stand above this lin on the lawn and use the iron as guillotine. A treaded iron is used wit advantage in heavy soil.

EDGING SHEARS. *See under* SHEARS

EDGINGS. Edgings are required t raise borders to retain the soil and kee it from slipping on to the pathways Lengths of deal about 1 in. thick, creosoted are satisfactory and cheap. They will las several years, but should be removed befor rotting sets in, or they will encourag insect pests. Tile and patent metal borde edgings are not really in harmony wit garden flowers, and bricks set at an angl seem hard and unfriendly. Bricks se lengthways with ends touching are no so conspicuous and are quite satisfactory

A strip of grass 1 ft. to 2 or 3 ft. wid makes a charming edging, acting as a foil to the bright colours of the flowers This is known as a grass verge. Clipped Box-edgings are suitable in the forma garden but entail a fair amount of upkeep.

Plants suitable for living edgings include Violas (especially cornuta), London Pride, Thrift, Perennial Candytuft, Cerastium tomentosum, Campanula pusilla and pumila, Echeveria (for very formal planting), Pinks, dwarfs, etc. (*See also* LISTS).

EDRAIANTHUS (ed-rai-an-thus. Campanulaceæ). This genus is very near to Campanula. The purple flowers are borne in clusters on stems of 2–3 in. It is of reasonably easy culture in a deep light soil and sunny position. The period of bloom is not long—two or three weeks in June or July as most.

Propagate by seed.

SPECIES.

E. caudatus, for stony soil in full sun, is deep purple.

E. graminifolius. Foliage slightly downy, purple flowers large and freely produced.

EDWARDSIA. *See* SOPHORA.

EHRETIA (ēh-rē′-ti-a. Boraginaceæ). Deciduous Asiatic tree, hardy after juvenile stage is passed. Thrives in N.E. position in ordinary loamy soil.

SPECIES.

E. acuminata (China and Japan). 20 ft. Flowers white, fragrant, during July.

E. macrophylla (China). Similar to above, flowering in August.

EICHORNEA (eik-or-nea. Ponteriaceæ). Tiny aquatics that require a tank in the warm house, or stove. To propagate divide the rhizomes in spring.

SPECIES.

E. speciosa, with blue flowers in summer.

ELÆAGNUS (el-ē-ag′-nus. Elæagnaceæ). Oleaster. Evergreen and deciduous shrubs and small trees. Perfectly hardy, thriving in ordinary garden soil; the silvery-leaved species develop a better colour on light sandy soil than on rich ones. *Propagate* by grafting for the evergreen species, and by seeds for the deciduous species.

SPECIES.

E. augustifolia (S. Europe and W. Asia). Deciduous; cultivated in English gardens since the 16th century. A very telling tree with its silvery-white, narrow, willow-like leaves and white twigs, especially when associated with dark-leaved evergreens. The flowers are yellow, tubular. 15–20 ft.

E. glabra (China and Japan). Evergreen. The large green leaves are very silvery beneath. 15–20 ft.

E. macrophylla (Corea and Japan). Evergreen. Leaves silvery on both sides. Flowers silvery, shaped like a fuchsia, in October and November. 8–12 ft.

E. pungens (Japan). Evergreen. Often confused with *E. glabra.* Leaves glossy dark green, under-surface dull white. Flowers pendulous, silvery white, Gardenia scented, appearing in October and November, followed by red fruit.

E. umbellata (Himalayas, China, etc.).

Semi-evergreen. A very handsome and distinct species, with very attractive silvery foliage, and fruit, changing to red.

ELÆOCARPUS (el-ē-o-kar′-pus. Tiliaceæ). Australia. A rare shrub, for the mildest districts only, bearing racemes of small white-fringed flowers, succeeded by turquoise-blue berries.

ELDER. *See* SAMBUCUS.

ELEUCHEROCCUS. *See* ACANTHOPANAX.

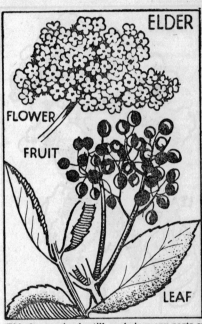

Elderberry wine is still made in many parts of the country. The golden-leaved variety is a quick-growing shrub.

ELISENA (e-li-se-na. Amaryllideæ). Handsome greenhouse bulbs with flower scapes nearly a yard high and 6–8 flowers, rather like a Peruvian daffodil. *Propagate* by offsets planted in sandy loam. For potting use more than half sand with light loam.

SPECIES.

E. longipetala. White. May.

ELM. The wood of the English elm tree can be put to good use in the garden. Polished and planed, but with its edges left naturally wavy, it makes charming bench seats for informal parts of the garden. If left unpolished the wood mellows to a very pleasing grey shade. Elm boarding can also be used in the construction of garden houses. *See* ULMUS.

ELODEA. *See* WATER PLANTS.

ELSHOLTZIA (el-sholtz´-i-a. Labiatæ). China. Deciduous semi-woody shrub, with small purplish-pink flowers, August–November, and mint-scented leaves. **3 ft.** Plant in rich loamy soil in full sun. *Propagate* by young cuttings.

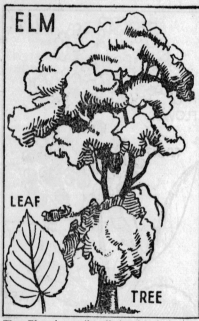

The Elm is easily distinguished by the asymmetrical leaf. There are two common kinds—the Wych Elm and English Elm.

EMBOTHRIUM. Fire Tree of Peru, Chilean Fire Bush, Chilean Honeysuckle. One of the greatest treasures of the garden. A glorious shrub or tree, reaching to 40 ft. in Cornwall, with brilliant crimson-scarlet honeysuckle-shaped flowers, produced in the greatest profusion during May and June, creating a striking and colourful display unsurpassed by any other evergreen flowering tree capable of being grown outside in this country. It is generally regarded as only suitable for the milder districts, but the variety sent home by Comber recently, has been grown successfully around London and in Buckinghamshire, passing quite unscathed through nearly 30° of frost.

Culture.—Soil, leaf-mould, peat and coarse sand. *Propagate* by seeds and cuttings; sometimes by suckers. Some of the old wood may be cut out after flowering.

SPECIES.

E. coccineum. The species most generally grown.

E. longifolium. A distinct and very free growing form with narrow wavy leaves 6–9 in. long, flowers similar to preceding. This is the hardy form referred to above.

EMILIA (em-i-li-a. Compositæ). This genus is synonymous with Cacalia, the Tassel Flower. The plants bear brilliant orange-scarlet flowers arranged in clusters to suggest a tassel. Although native to India they are fairly hardy and may ever withstand the winter if seed is sown in September, but an April sowing is preferable provided the plants are transplanted when still quite small as they hate disturbance. They are useful for borders or cutting. Sow in heat in spring.

SPECIES.

E. flammea (syn. *Cacalia coccinea*) scarlet-orange flowers in July. **2 ft.**

E. sonchifolia. Purple, July.

EMMENANTHE (emmen-an-the. Hydrophyllaceæ). Whispering Bells. California, 1–1¼ ft. *E. penduliflora* (yellow) is a half-hardy annual, very pretty, rather difficult to grow. Seeds germinate irregularly. Should be sown in March in gentle heat, and in poor sandy soil. Plant out in May in a sunny position.

EMPETRUM (em-pe-trum. Empetraceæ). Crowberry. An evergreen heathlike shrub about 1 ft. high, common throughout the mountainous regions of the northern hemisphere, including this country. Flowers very small, pinkish in March, followed by black berries. Plant in sandy, peaty soil.

SPECIES.

E. nigrum.

E. scoticum. Of dwarf habit and smaller leaves.

ENDIVE (*Cichorium Endivia*). Compositæ. Endive is another vegetable which has come to us out of the East; how long ago it is difficult to say, but certainly before the reign of "Good Queen Bess."

There are two distinct types, the round-leaved and the curled or cut-leaved, both of which are in demand where salads are appreciated. The round-leaved or Batavian type is the hardier of the two.

Culture.—It is possible to have a regular supply right through the summer by making three small successional sowings at 10-day intervals, commencing early in April. These should be sown in shallow drills set 18 in. apart, and the plants thinned early to 15 in. apart.

Similar sowings in June and July will ensure an autumn supply, and for winter and spring two sowings should be made in August and September on a warm border or in cold frames.

A deeply-dug and heavily-manured soil is ideal for this crop. Little attention beyond hoeing is required, though copious watering may be necessary in very dry weather.

Three or four weeks before the endive is required for use, the plants should be covered with boxes or large flower pots with the drainage hole blocked up. This will ensure well-blanched specimens, though good blanched hearts are obtained by merely gathering the leaves together with a loose tie of raffia.

VARIETIES.

Digswell's Prize, Fraser's Broad Leaved, White Curled.

For winter use.—Batavian and Green Curled.

Uses.—The blanched leaves are used raw in salads, or cleaned and shredded, then boiled till tender and, after draining, simmered for half an hour in a little milk and butter with a pinch of salt. A tablespoonful of fine sago is then dissolved in a cup of warm water, and mixed with the endive, and the whole is served hot.

ENKIANTHUS (en-ki-an'-thus. Ericaceæ). Deciduous shrubs from Asia, producing Lily of the Valley-like flowers during May. Foliage very attractive in autumn.

Culture.—Plant in moist soil containing leaf-mould or peat in full sun. *Propagate* by seed and by cuttings.

SPECIES.

E. campanulatus (Japan), 4–10 ft. Flowers creamy-yellow, veined and tipped with red. Leaves golden and red in autumn.

E. c. albiflorus. Flowers pale primrose fading to nearly white.

E. c. recurvus. A new species, with cup-shaped flowers.

E. Palibinii (Japan). Near to *campanulatus*, distinguished by its rich red flowers.

E. perulatus (japonica) Japan, 6 ft. Flowers white, pitcher-shaped in May.

ENDIVE FOR WINTER SALADS

TIE UP, AND COVER WITH A BOX OR POTS FOR BLANCHING

Endive is a useful winter salad, but must be blanched before use.

Foliage in autumn beautiful golden yellow One of the first twelve shrubs to plant for autumn colours.

EOMECON (e-o-me-con. Papaveraceæ). Morning Poppy. The only species is a very pretty hardy perennial with white flowers in May. It likes a damp, peaty soil in some low-lying spot and is increased by division in spring.

E. chionantha, 2 ft., cyclamen-like leaves.

EPACRIS (epā-cris. Epacridaceæ). From *epi*, upon, and *akros*, the top. The genus is usually found on tops of hills in Australia. Greenhouse flowering shrubs. Evergreen. Australia, 1803.

Culture.—Compost: sandy fibrous peat. Repot spring, giving attention to the drainage. Stand outside in sunny position during summer months, but care must be taken to well plunge the pots in ashes. Plants should be pruned well back to base after flowering. Winter temperature, 45°.

Propagation.—By cutting of the ends of young shoots in spring or summer. Insert 4 or 5 round the edge of a 3 in. pot, filled with sandy peat, place in propagator, temperature 60°.

SPECIES.

E. delicata, white.

E. d. hyacinthiflora, red.

E. longiflora splendens, red, white margin.

Numerous hybrid varieties are in cultivation.

EPHEDRA (ef-ĕd-ra. Gnetaceæ). "Shrubby Horn-Tail." A group of deciduous, very curious shrubs of little or no garden value, but interesting as being a connecting link between ordinary flowering plants and conifers, inhabiting dry and inhospitable regions of parts of Europe.

Species.—*E. distachya* is the only species available.

EPICATTLEYA (ep-i-cat-ley-a. Orchidaceæ). This genus of orchids is the result of hybridising Epidendrums with Cattleyas. It gives several pretty plants showing strongly the influence of the parents, Epidendrums. Culture suitable for either parent is successful.

SPECIES AND HYBRIDS.

E. guatemalensis. Rosy-crimson flowers in March and April. 1¼ ft.

"Mrs. James O'Brien." Rich purple. January.

EPIDENDRUM (epiden′-drum. Orchidaceæ). From *epi*, upon; and *dendron*, a tree. Tree Orchid. Stove and greenhouse epiphytal orchids, best treated as cool and intermediate growing plants.

Culture.—Compost: two-thirds peat, one-third chopped sphagnum moss, with a little sand and charcoal added. Repot early spring. Good drainage essential. Best suspended from roof of house in pots or hanging baskets. Water moderately at all times. Plants like a decided rest period. Winter temperature, 50°; summer, 70°.

Propagation.—By division of plant before active growth commences.

SPECIES.

There are about 500 species of this genus known to science, but the majority are not worth cultivation. The few given here are amongst the best.

E. atro-purpureum, brown, white and purple.

E. Endresio-Wallisii, yellow, white and purple (hybrid).

E. fragrans, white (sweet scented).

E. O'brienianum, yellow and carmine.

E. oncidioides, yellow and brown.

E. radicans, yellow and orange.

E. virens, green.

E. vitellinum, orange, scarlet and yellow.

E. Wallisii, yellow crimson and white.

EPIGÆA (ep-i-ge′-a. Ericaceæ). May flower. An evergreen creeping shrub of N. America, appreciating woodland conditions. Clusters of white or rosy-tinted fragrant flowers from mid-March to May. It likes a peaty soil, or leaf-mould and although a cool, shady position is usually advised, it more often thrives in full sun. The protection of a hand-light in late winter and early spring is advisable.

Propagate by layers.

E. repens, the only species.

EPILÆLIA (ep-i-le-li-a. Orchidaceæ). As a result of fertilising Epidendrums with the pollen of Lælias, interesting bigeneric plants have been raised. These require the treatment meted out to Cattleyas.

SPECIES AND HYBRIDS.

E. Charlesworthii (*E. radicans* + *L. cinnabarina*). Orange and scarlet flowers in July. 1½ ft.

E. hardyana (*E. ciliare* + *L. anceps*). Violet and white flowers in November. 1 ft.

E. radico-purpurata (*E. radicans* + *L. purpurata*).

EPILOBIUM (epi-lo-bium. Onagraceæ). Willow Herb. French Willow. Handsome hardy herbaceous perennials, of which the dwarfer species are grown to advantage in the rock garden, while the rest are useful in the water garden.

Culture.—*Propagate* by summer-sown seeds or by division in spring. They are easily grown in light rich loam in sun or shade. In a border they spread too rapidly and become a troublesome weed.

E. angustifolium, has purplish-crimson flowers on long willowy stalks. There is also a white variety, July, 4–6 ft.

E. Dodonaei (syn. *angustissam* or *Fleisheri*) with purple blooms in June and July, 2 ft.

E. hirsutum or "Codlins and Cream" with purplish flowers from July onwards does best in a moist border or in the water garden, 4 ft.

E. nummularifolium with pinkish-white flowers in July and August and *obcordatum* with rosy-purple flowers in the same months are both trailing species suitable for the rock garden. These plants are apt to overcrowd smaller plants so they should be given plenty of room. They are very useful in the wild garden.

EPIMEDIUM (ĕpi-mē-dium. Berberiaceæ). Barrenwort. Attractive dwarf perennials with delicate leaves on slender stems.

Propagate by division of the roots in spring or autumn and grow in a shady position in sandy loam with some peat.

These plants form a useful and bold edging for beds and grow so close that they keep out weeds.

SPECIES.

E. alpinum with crimson or yellow flowers from April to July, 9 in.; *E. macranthum* with blue and white flowers in spring has remarkable veined leaves and is the finest of all the species.

E. pinnatum bears long clusters of yellow flowers and large pinnate leaves; blooms from May to July, 1–2 ft.

EPIPHRONITIS (ep-i-fron-i-tis. Orchiaceæ). The only member of this genus is a bigeneric hybrid resulting from the crossing of the tall *Epidendrum radicans* with the dwarf *Sophronitis grandiflora*. It requires a similar culture to that given to Sophronitis with a little more warmth in winter.

E. Veitchii. Orange, scarlet and yellow flowers in June and July. 1 ft.

EPIPHYLLUM (ep-i-fil-lum. Cactæ). Fleshy-leaved stove plants that are highly decorative.

Propagate by cuttings dried at the base before insertion in loam and leaf-mould or by grafting upon *Cereus speciosissimus*, the scions being attached to the stock by

spines without being tied, and placed in gentle heat. They require perfect drainage and a soil composed of loam, leafmould and mortar rubbish. Start the plants in growth in February in the warmest part of the stove and later lower the temperature. In winter place the plants in the driest part of the stove and only allow sufficient water to prevent them from drying off. The flowers are borne upon the edges of the leaf-like branches.

SPECIES.

E. delicatum.

E. Gærtneri. Orange or scarlet flowers in April.

E. russellianum. Rosy flowers in May. There are several beautiful varieties with red, rose or violet-coloured flowers

EPISTEPHIUM (ep-i-ste-fi-um. Orchidaceæ). A South American genus of Orchids comprising very few species and usually represented by *E. Williamsii*, a stove terrestrial orchid that likes fibrous loam and sand with ample drainage. It has rosy-mauve or yellow and white flowers in summer. 1½ ft.

EQUISETUM (e-qui-se-tum. Equisetaceæ). Horsetail. A genus of graceful native plants usually found growing by the waterside or in damp boggy places. Useful for filling up bare patches at the edges of water or lakes; but they spread so rapidly that they become troublesome and must be kept down by intensive cultivation.

Propagate by division.

SPECIES.

E. maximum, Giant Horsetail (syn. *Telmateia*); *E. sylvaticum*. Both are leafless herbs that have two distinct periods of growths. The first is the fruiting stage, when they only throw up single stems. In the second they have strong graceful stems borne in whorls.

ERANTHEMUM (erän-themum. Acanthaceæ). Greenhouse flowering plants. E. Ind., 1796.

Culture.—2 parts loam, 1 part peat and sand. Repot early spring. Good drainage essential. Light airy position in greenhouse. Water freely during summer months. Prune hard back to base after flowering. Winter temperature, 50°; summer, 70°.

Propagation.—By cuttings of young

shoots in sandy soil in the spring. Place in propagator, temperature 70°.

SPECIES.

E. andersonii, white and purple.

E. elegans, scarlet.

E. Cooperii, white and purple.

ERANTHIS (eran-this. Ranunculaceæ). Winter Aconite. Pretty early-blooming perennial with yellow flowers surrounded by a whorl of leaflets. This hardy

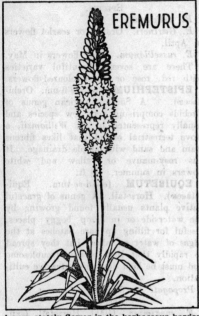

EREMURUS

A very stately flower in the herbaceous border is Eremurus robustus. It has tuberous roots like the dahlia and will grow ten feet high or more in good soil.

plant will grow in any soil in a shady position. *Propagate* by seeds or by dividing the tuberous roots which are planted in autumn to produce flowers in the following January. Height, 3 in.

The best place to use Winter Aconites is in the wild garden or shrubbery. To be quite successful, plant as early as it is possible to obtain the tubers. Do not lift, but leave the plants to their own devices until they are established.

SPECIES.

Eranthis hyemalis, the "Winter Aconite."

ERCILLA (ĕr-sil'-la. Phytolaccaceæ). An evergreen Chilean climber with aerial roots like ivy, and dense spikes of white flowers. March to April.

E. volubilis. The only species.

EREMOSTACHYS (er-e-mo-stak-is. Labiatæ). Pretty hardy perennial with flowers arranged in long whorled spikes.

Propagated by division in spring or autumn or by seeds sown in a frame in April or May, and grown in any ordinary garden soil.

SPECIES.

E. laciniata is the only species with pale rosy flowers in a 12 in. long inflorescence. July. 1½ ft.

EREMURUS (ĕr-e-mū-rus. Liliaceæ). Fox Tail. Lily. Stately herbaceous perennials of Eastern origin bearing long spikes of flowers throughout the summer.

Culture.—These plants require careful handling and planting as the roots are rather brittle and extensive. Plant several inches deep in rich well-drained soil, preferably in a position facing south, at any time from October to March, spread the roots out flat and leave the crowns 6 in. below the surface; cover with a light dry compost and dress annually with the same material. Protect from cold in winter with a covering of leaf-mould or coconut fibre. To raise from seed sow when ripe under glass and prick out the seedlings into a cold frame, where they should remain for a year; they can then be transferred to a bed or border, where they will flower after about two years. All these plants need protection from cold winds and in the first stages of growth from slugs.

SPECIES.

E. Aitchisonii with dense spikes of pale reddish flowers in June, 3–5 ft. in height.

E. Bungei (syn. *aurianticus*) with yellow flowers in July and its sub-varieties *Pallidus* and *superbus* are good. 2–4 ft.

E. himalaicus with white spikes in July is one of the prettiest and most easily grown, 2–6 ft.

E. robustus with silvery rose flowers in June is the strongest. 6–9 ft.

E. Elwesii, pink or white, is a more beautiful form of *E. robustus*.

E. Altaicus and *E. spectabilis* have yellow flowers in June and July.

In addition to these there are many

hybrids giving shades of cream, buff, pink, salmon and orange which are later flowering, and thus prolong the flowering season.

ERIA (e-ri-a. Orchidaceæ). Low-growing stove orchids with only a few species of any horticultural value. They should be grown in a compost of fibrous peat and sphagnum in deep pans or baskets with good drainage. During the summer they must have an abundance of water but during the winter only enough to keep them from drying off.

SPECIES.

E. bratescens with white and crimson flowers in May. 8 in.

E. extinctoria with white and purple flowers in April and May is one of the smallest orchids in cultivation.

E. flava. Yellow and purple. April–May 1 ft.

E. hyacinthoides.

E. obesa. White and pink flowers. February. 1 ft.

E. stellata. Yellow and red, summer. 2 ft.

ERIANTHUS (er-i-an-thus. Gramineæ). Beautiful perennial grasses that do well in a warm, dry, sunny position in a rich soil.

Propagate by seeds or division. *E. Ravennæ* is often used to obtain a sub-tropical effect.

SPECIES.

E. Monsteiri, 9 ft.

E. Ravennæ, 6 ft.

E. saccharoides, 8 ft.

ERICA (ĕ-rī′-ka. Ericaceæ). Heath. Erica is the typical genus of the order Ericaceæ, and consists of a very large number of species, mostly natives of the Cape of Good Hope. The hardy ones, dealt with herein, are of European origin, five being natives of the British Isles. These heaths are all evergreen and distinct from other hardy shrubs by the smallness and abundance of their leaves. In stature they range from semi-prostrate species up to a height of 20 ft. Generally speaking, they will not thrive in calcareous soils, except *carnea, mediterranea, darleyensis, cinerea,* and possibly a few others. The ideal soil is light, sandy peat, but ordinary sandy loam with the addition of peat or leaf-mould answers admirably. If the soil is too rich the plants become lanky, thereby losing much of their character.

Propagate by seeds, sown in very sandy peat in spring. If possible, get some soil from where heaths are growing wild; but cuttings are preferable. They should be taken in July and August—just tiny pieces about ½–1 in. in length. It is an operation requiring both patience and care. Take a pot and place therein 3 in. of small crocks; upon these place a few dead leaves, half-decayed leaf-mould, or fibrous peat. Then try and obtain some soil from a heather district, where heaths are growing, pass it through a very fine-meshed sieve; and then add more fine sand. Place this mixture in the pot, to a depth of about 1 in. and then add 1 in. of clean, coarse silver sand on top. Water the pots thoroughly, and ram the sand firm.

The reason why soil where heaths are growing is recommended is because such soil contains the parasite that lives on and about the roots of heather, and is essential to its well-being. The months of April and June are the best months to take cuttings of *E. carnea* and its varieties, when the young tips of the shoots have made sufficient new growth. And these young shoots should be pulled downwards so that each comes off with a tiny heel, at the clearly defined junction between the old and young growth. Cuttings of the other heaths are best taken in early August, or at any time during the summer.

The pots containing the cuttings should be placed in a cold greenhouse, or garden frame, and attended to in the ordinary way. Remove at once any cuttings that become mildewed, or show signs of damping off. When the little rooted cuttings have bushy roots as long as their respective tops, they are ready to pot in small separate pots, and kept therein until ready to be placed in their permanent quarters. *Propagation* by division, although the plants are more imposing to start with, is rarely satisfactory; indeed one may safely say that it is never satisfactory.

SPECIES, VARIETIES AND HYBRIDS.

E. arborea (S. Europe, etc.). Tree Heath, 6–15 ft. A very beautiful heath tree, with a profusion of white flowers, scenting the air with their honey-like fragrance during March and April. In favourable districts exceeds 20 ft. Briar root tobacco-pipes are made from the roots of this species, and not from the briar rose, as is so generally supposed. The word "briar" is a corruption of the French *bruyère*, the French name for the plant.

E. australis (Spain and Portugal). Spanish Heath, 3–4 ft. Flowers bright rose; in great profusion during April and May. Not absolutely hardy.

ERIGERON SPECIOSUS SUPERBUS.

For cutting and for ease of culture the Erigeron is one of the best hardy flowers.

E. a. Mr. Robert. Similar to type in height and habit. Flowers pure white, foliage paler green.

E. carnea (Alps of Europe), 6–10 in. Valuable for its early flowering. February to April. Flowers deep rosy-red. Award of Garden Merit, R.H.S.

E. c. King George. Dark red, early, very fine. Award of Garden Merit, R.H.S.

E. cinerea (W. Europe, etc.). Fine-leaved Heather, Scotch or Grey Heather. In England, this and *E. tetralix* are called heather, and *E.* (*Calluna*) *vulgaris* is called Ling; in Scotland this is reversed. *E. vulgaris alba* is the white Scottish Heather.

E. darleyensis (*E. carnea* + *E. mediterranea*). Rosy-red flowers from November to May. Of cushion-like habit. 18 in. high. A plant for every garden. Award of Garden Merit, R.H.S.

E. mediterranea. The Mediterranean Heath, a misnomer, as this species is not found growing wild in the Mediterranean region, but is a native of parts of S. France, Spain, and the mountainous boggy parts of Mayo and Galway, Ireland.

E. tetralix. Cross-leaved Heath (N. and W. Europe and Britain). Rose-coloured flowers in drooping terminal clusters, all facing from the centre of the plant. June to October. 6–18 in. Will thrive on very wet ground.

E. vagans. Cornish Heath (S.W. Europe and Cornwall). Flowers pinkish rose. July to October. 1–1½ ft. Like other late-flowering heaths, the parts that have flowered should be cut over in spring occasionally. Practised too often, the size of the racemes suffers.

ERIGERON (ē-rij'-eron. Compositæ). Fleabane. Hardy perennials resembling asters that are very useful in town gardens as they are easily cultivated.

Culture.—Easily raised from seeds sown in summer, or by dividing the roots in autumn or spring when they should be planted. They flourish in any soil and the dwarf species are suitable for the rock garden.

SPECIES.

E. alpinus with pale blue flowers in summer; *E. aurantiacus* with orange flowers from May to July; *E. mucronatus* a charming prostrate species with purple or pink and white flowers on each stem are all suitable for the rockery. The best of the taller kinds is *E. speciosus* that will grow in any soil and has purplish-lilac flowers in June and July, on tall stems; *E. grandiflorus* a rare species with solitary violet flowers in July, 6 in.; *E. glaucus*, a rare species with glaucous leaves has a central flower of deep lavender hue with large yellow disks in July below which are several strong lateral growths which flower after the central bloom has faded; *E. Philadelphicus* has numerous small rosy flowers from May to November, 12 in.; *E. multiradiatus* has thready petalled violet flowers from June to September, 18 in. The border plants are frequently grown for cutting.

ERINACEA (e-rin-ā-sea. Leguminosæ). Hedgehog Broom. Dwarf mound of stiff spiny growth with purplish blue flowers in April and May. Suitable for a sunny nook in the rock garden, or at foot of sunny wall. *Propagate* by cuttings or layers. Also by seeds when obtainable.

E. pungens the only species.

ERINUS (e-ri-nus. Scrophularineæ). Pretty little alpines that are valued for crevices in the rock garden or in walls owing to the early season of flowering. They like a light dry soil and are best propagated by seeds sown in the flowering position in spring or autumn. In wet and cold districts they should be kept in a cold pit in winter or planted in a vertical position in the rockery.

SPECIES.

E. alpinus (Pyrenees), with purple flowers in May, is the only one grown, and has white and rose varieties. 4 in. In Britain it has established itself on the Roman wall at Hexham.

Other species from the Cape of Good Hope are rarely grown.

ERIOBOTRYA (ĕr-i-ō-bot'-ria. Rosaceæ). The Loquat or Evergreen Medlar of China and Japan. A very striking evergreen shrub or small tree with very large, handsome dark green glossy leaves. 6–10 in. long. Flowers white, hawthorn-scented, but rarely seen in this country. Thrives in calcareous soils. Best raised from seed.

SPECIES

E. japonica. Up to 15 ft. in the open, in mild districts; twice that height against a wall. Around London it reaches to about a third of that height (5 ft.) and has withstood 30° of frost.

E. prinoides. A Chinese form of the above.

ERIOCEPHALUS (er-i-o-sef-a-lus. Compositæ). Shrubby greenhouse evergreens from S. Africa. *Propagate* by cuttings in spring and grow in a compost of sandy loam and peat.

SPECIES.

E. africanus. White, winter. 4 ft.
E. racemosus. Yellow, March. 3 ft.

ERIODENDRON (er-i-o-den-dron. Malvaceæ). Tall-growing stove trees allied to the genus Bombax. To increase, sow seeds in a hotbed. They should be grown in rich sandy loam. Summer temperature, 60°–80°; winter, 35°–40°.

SPECIES.

E. anfractuosum. 100 ft.

ERIOGONUM (er-i-og-o-num. Polygonaceæ). Pretty hardy annuals and perennials that are best planted in the rockery between large stones in a sunny position. Use sandy loam. Increase by division or seeds sown in a cold frame in spring.

SPECIES.

E. compositum. perennial, white flowers in June. 1 ft.

E. corymbosum, perennial, rose, white or yellow. June.

E. umbellatum, has yellow flowers in umbels. June. 1 ft.

ERIOPHORUM (er-i-of-or-um. Cyperaceæ). Cotton Grass Pretty plants that are best grown in moist peaty soil in bog gardens or by the waterside.

SPECIES.

E. polystachion, the Cotton Grass of British swamps. 1 ft.

E. alpinum. 1 ft.

E. vaginatum. 1 ft.

ERIOPHYLLUM (er-io-fil-lum. Compositæ). From *erion*, wool, *phyllon*, leaf. (Syn. *Bahia lanata*.)

E. cæspitosum. Large yellow daisy flowers; divided leaves covered with silvery down. 6 in., June. N. America.

ERIOPSIS (er-i-op-sis. Orchidaceæ). A small genus of stove orchids that are very attractive when flowering, although rarely grown. Give the same culture as Cattleyas and grow in peat and sphagnum.

SPECIES.

E. Helenæ, orange.

E. rutidobulbon, purplish-brown flowers. August.

ERIOSTEMON (er-i-o-ste-mon. Rutaceæ). Greenhouse evergreen shrubs that flower abundantly in spring and early summer. They are excellent for conservatory decoration but do well planted in a bed or border. Increase by cuttings of young shoots taken in April and inserted in sandy peat with bottom heat.

Plant in a compost of 3 parts of sandy peat to 1 of loam and sand. Provide ample drainage and pot firmly.

SPECIES.

E. buxifolius, pink, May. 4 ft.
E. ericifolius, red, June. 3 ft.

E. myoporoides, white, September. 3 ft.

E. pulchellus, rosy, May. 3 ft.

ERITRICHIUM (er-i-trik-i-um. Boragineæ). Hardy perennial and annual plants, of which the best known, *E. nanum*, has been found difficult to grow. Those who have succeeded with it recommend that it should be planted in a sunny fissure of the rockery, where it will be kept dry from September to January.

ERYNGIUM

Sea Holly or Eryngium thrives in a sandy soil and loves the seaside.

After this period it should be watered without wetting the foliage. The other species are easily grown.

Propagate by seeds sown under glass in spring or by division and cuttings for the perennials. Use a soil of fibrous peat, leaf-mould and grit in equal parts.

SPECIES.

E. nanum, blue flowers in June that cover the cushiony growth of leaves. 2 in.

E. rupestre, blue, July. 1 ft.

E. strictum, annual or biennial, blue. July. 1½ ft.

ERODIUM (ĕr-ō-dium. Geraniaceæ). Heron's Bill. Pretty hardy plants resembling Geraniums but smaller and of southern origin. Many species have silvery fern-like fragrant leaves.

Culture.—Suited for chalky banks, the rockery or for borders. They are propagated by cuttings in July or seeds in spring and should have a warm dry position in sandy loam.

SPECIES.

E. amanum, a tufted plant with silvery leaves and pure white flowers from May to August, 6 in.

E. chamædryoides bears white flowers veined with pink from May to September and likes a position sheltered from rain and wind. 3 in.

E. chrysanthum resembles *E. amanum* but has lemon-yellow flowers.

E. guttatum (syn. *E. petræum*), a rare plant with white flowers veined with violet and silky white leaves, 6 in.

E. macradenium, a hardy Pyrenean plant with flowers of pale violet, tinged with a darker colour, from June to August, 6 in.

E. Manescavi, the most showy, with strong flower-stalks bearing seven to fifteen blooms of crimson-purple from May to September, 18 in.

E. trichomanefolium with deeply-cut silvery-grey leaves has flowers of pinkish-white veined with rose from May to October, 6 in.

ERYNGIUM (ĕr-inj'-ium. Umbelliferæ). Sea Holly. Delightful hardy herbaceous plants of which the stems are singularly beautiful and surmounted by brilliant involucres. The leaves have great diversity of form, ranging from the great succulent foliage of *E. pandanifolium*, that will last throughout the winter, to the small thistle-like foliage of *E. dichotomum*.

Culture.—They require a good, well-drained sandy soil as damp injures them more than cold. Propagate by root cuttings, or by seed, which should be sown in pans and placed in a cold frame. The seeds germinate in spring and will be ready to plant out the following year. Self-propagation often takes place.

SPECIES.

E. alpinum, of which the stems and blooms are blue, with flowers in July and August, has very developed feathery bracts; *E. oliverianum,* resembling *alpinum,* and *giganteum,* with a silvery-grey involucre formed of several spiny leaves, as well as *alpinum,* are suitable for the rockery; *E. amethystinum,* the bluest of all the genus, has forked stems of bright blue; *E. oliverianum,* with many highly-coloured flower heads of rich blue, is excellent for the border, 2–4 ft.; *E. planum,* with branching stems bearing many pale blue flowers, is useful for cutting and borders, 3–4 ft.

Other good species are *E. Bourgatii, E. palmatum,* and the hybrid *E. Zabelii.*

All the border species flower from August to September.

ERYSIMUM (ĕr-ĭs-imum. Cruciferæ). Hedge Mustard. Fragrant dwarf perennials like wallflowers that are easy to cultivate and give a continuity of bloom of bright colour.

Culture.—Propagate by division of the roots in spring or by seeds which, if allowed, will sow themselves. Plant in sunny, rocky soil. If raised at intervals they bloom practically all the year.

Species.—*E. ochroleucum,* a tufted plant with yellow flowers from April to June, 12 in.; *E. pumilum,* a small plant rarely cultivated, with pale yellow fragrant flowers that are large in relation to its size, 1 in.; *E. rupestre,* with sulphur-yellow flowers in June, is a neat alpine, 6 in.

The best and most useful as a garden plant is the hardy annual, *E. perofskianum,* 1¼ ft. The flowers are of rich orange, somewhat similar to *Cheiranthus Allionii,* but not so large. Sow March to May where the plants are to flower. Thin to 6 in. Will grow and flower well almost anywhere.

ERYTHRÆA (e-rith-re-a. Gentianeæ). Centaury. Pretty annual, biennial and perennial plants for the rockery. All are propagated by seeds sown in spring, and the perennials by division. They like a light soil.

SPECIES.

E. diffusa, perennial, likes a shady position with plenty of water in summer. It bears pink flowers in June. 6 in. (syn. *E. Massoni*).

E. Centaurium, the Common Centaury, is a native annual that grows freely on dry limestone banks. It has rosy flowers in June. 3–12 in.

E. linarifolia, biennial, pink, June. 3 in.

E. Mehlenbergia, rich pink, white-eyed flowers in May. 8 in.

E. venusta, annual, pink, August. 9 in.

ERYTHRINA (ĕ-rith-rĭ-na. Leguminosæ). Coral Tree or Cockscomb. Very

DOG'S TOOTH VIOLET OR ERYTHRONIUM

A bulb with quaint flowers, mainly lilac, is the Dog's Tooth Violet. It enjoys a cool, shady pocket in the rock garden and blooms in spring.

beautiful semi-woody deciduous shrub from Brazil, with flowers like a waxen sweet pea of a deep bright scarlet colour during the summer. In most districts it requires the protection of a warm wall.

ERYTHRONIUM (Dog's Tooth Violets. Liliaceæ). Hardy bulbous perennials first introduced in 1596. The Dog's Tooth Violet makes a very valuable addition to the semi-wild garden, or any part of the garden where it can be allowed to grow without disturbance. The plants like best a soil composed of equal parts of loam, peat and leaf-mould, but they will grow easily in any ordinary soil so long as it contains some leaf-mould. The bulbs should be planted 2 in. deep and 2 in. apart in March, and top-dressed every year after flowering, with some well-decayed manure. The variety generally cultivated is *E. dens-canis*, which is rose-coloured in spring.

There are also varieties which have white or purple flowers. The foliage of

MIXED ESCHSCHOLTZIAS

The Californian Poppy or Eschscholtzia likes sunshine and will grow in any country garden. It comes easily from seeds.

these plants is marbled and very attractive in the rock garden.

ESCALLONIA (ĕs-kal-lō-ni-a. Saxifragaceæ). Evergreen, hardy and half-hardy shrubs, of vigorous growth, glossy green leaves and a wonderful profusion of flowers, ranging from white, pink and deep rose to crimson. When the plants become established they withstand all but the severest winters, especially if planted against walls and fences. The soil should not be too rich; just ordinary sandy loam, without manure of any kind. *Propagate* by cuttings of half-ripened wood during August placed in pots of

sandy soil, in frame or in gentle bottom heat. There is one deciduous species, which is also the hardiest, viz., *E. Philippiana*. Among the hardiest of the evergreen section the *exoniensis*, *langleyensis*, *rubra* and *illinita*. For seaside districts they are almost unsurpassed, forming perfect shelter hedges.

SPECIES.

E. C. F. Ball. Hybrid of fine branching habit and bright carmine-red flowers from May to autumn.

E. Donard Seedling. Hybrid of semi-weeping growth and showy pale pink flowers, fading to white, and delightfully fragrant of hawthorn.

E. edinensis (Edinburgh). Hybrid with arching branches, smothered with pink flowers during summer.

E. Ingrammi, 12 ft. Deep rose.

E. langleyensis (*E. Philippiana* + *E. punctata*). Hybrid of drooping habit, flowers bright crimson. 5 ft.

E. macrantha (Island of Chiloe), 6–10 ft. Beautiful glossy foliage, and bright rosy-crimson flowers from June onwards. Around London and further north fence or wall protection is necessary. In the warm south-western maritime districts it makes a superb hedge and successfully withstands strong winds and even gales.

ESCHSCHOLTZIA (e-skoltz-i-a. Papaveraceæ). Californian Poppy. 1 ft., spreading, or tufted. California. Many colours. Probably the easiest to grow, and most popular of all the Californian native flowers. Very hardy, easy to grow, succeeding almost anywhere in ordinary garden soil, and may be sown spring or autumn where to bloom. As cut flowers they last well in water and are sufficiently light for table decorations. The buds are covered with a shield shaped like a clown's cap, which is pushed off entire as the buds develop. The best time to cut for decorative purposes is when the "cap" is half-way off; the flowers will open in a few hours and last for several days.

There are species of spreading habit as *E. aurantiaca*, and others of tufted or upright growth as *E. The Geisha*, also varieties with double or semi-double flowers, of which Carmine Queen is a good representative. *E. cæspitosa* is a dwarf, small-flowered, yellow form, very useful for rockeries.

ESPALIER. A term formerly applied only to the frame used chiefly to support fruit trees and now applied to the trees themselves, which are trained with one vertical and several horizontal branches at right angles to the former.

EUCALYPTUS (ū-kă-lip′-tus. Mystaceæ). Gum Trees, Iron Barks, etc. Hardy and half-hardy trees and shrubs from Australia and Tasmania, generally of very rapid growth, and in the case of some species, attaining to a greater height than that of any other trees.

E. Gunnii. Cider tree. Very hardy, having reached to 80 ft. in this country. Young leaves beautiful glaucous blue.

EUCHARIDIUM (u-ka-rid-i-um. Onagrarieæ). Attractive hardy annuals, useful for beds and borders. Raised from seeds sown in a hotbed in March or in the open in April or May. All are desirable annuals and will succeed in ordinary garden soil. May be sown in spring or autumn.

SPECIES.

E. Breweri, lilac, purple or white flowers in June. 9 in.

E. concinnum, purple, June. 1 ft. White variety, *album.*

E. grandiflorum, rosy-red flowers in June. 1½ ft.

EUCHARIS (eucha-ris. Amaryllidaceæ). Amazon Lily. Stove bulbous, evergreen flowering plants. 1851.

Culture.—Compost: 2 parts rich loam, 1 part leaf-mould, 1 part sand, dried cow manure, broken charcoal, and a liberal supply of bonemeal. Repot June, give good drainage, and press soil firmly around and between bulbs. Repotting should only be done every 3 or 4 years. Top-dress established plants with rich soil annually. Water freely during growing period, but little during rest period. Applications of liquid manure, or artificial manure, very beneficial after flower stem appears. Syringe freely while growing. Winter temperature, 60°–65°; summer, 75°–80°. The essentials of success in the cultivation of eucharis are a brisk temperature, a moist atmosphere, and a rich compost.

Propagation.—By offsets removed from the old bulbs, and planted singly in small pots of sandy loam when re-potting.

SPECIES.

E. amazonica, white.

E. Masterii, white.

E. Sanderii, white and yellow.

E. Stevensii, white and yellow.

EUCOMIS (u-ko-mis. Liliaceæ). Strong-growing bulbs from the Cape of Good Hope that if planted out in front of a greenhouse in a sheltered spot will survive the winter, but are best grown in the greenhouse. Increase by offsets and plant the bulbs for outdoor culture 6 in. deep and 12 in. apart in September in light rich loam. Protect with a covering of leaves in winter. Water well and give liquid manure during the growing season, but keep the bulbs fairly dry while they are resting.

SPECIES.

E. bicolor, a curious early autumn-flowering plant. The green foliage is broad and flattish with faint black spots on the under surface, while the stem is blotched with purple and the flowers are arranged in dense heads and of a purplish-claret colour shaded with green. 1 ft. July.

E. punctata, of which the leaves are spotted with purple beneath and the creamy-white fragrant flowers are borne in cylindrical trusses. August, 2 ft.

EUCOMMIA (ū-ko′-mia. Trochodendraceæ). Chinese Gutta-percha Tree. Deciduous tree from 20–30 ft. high, elm-like in appearance with large leathery leaves and inconspicuous flowers. Highly valued by the Chinese for the tonic properties of its bark. It also furnishes a poor grade of rubber. Quite hardy, and thrives in almost any soil, including calcareous. Distinct from all other trees, and has not been found growing wild, so far as is known.

E. ulmoides, the only species.

EUCRYPHIA (ū-krif′-i-a. Rosaceæ). Evergreen flowering shrub of exceptional beauty and interest, ranking among the finest Chilean plants that can be grown in our gardens, and when established never fails to flower regularly and very freely. There are some very fine specimens in the south-west and some good ones in the Midlands. Plant in a position sheltered from winds, and in a mixture of loam and peat. It likes a cool root run, and should either be mulched or receive a carpet of some dwarf-growing shrub, such as dwarf heaths, etc. This is an important cultural detail, and if attended to will probably prevent young plants suddenly collapsing without any apparent reason, as they are liable to do. *Propagate* by layering and by seeds. Seedlings should be given sandy peat soil.

SPECIES.

E. pinnatifolia (Chile), 12–15 ft. Flowers of four petals, pure white with a profusion of golden anthers, in August. Foliage pleasantly tinted in autumn. One of the real treasures of the garden.

E. p. flore pleno. A form with extra petals.

EUGENIA (ū-jē'-ni-a. Myrtaceæ). Very attractive evergreen shrubs, closely related to the Myrtus, thriving in sandy peat or loam and peat. *Propagate* by cuttings in close frame or under bell-glass.

SPECIES.

E. apiculata (*Myrtus Luma*), Chile. A most desirable shrub with white, very fragrant flowers, glossy green foliage and cinnamon-red bark. Fairly hardy against a wall, does remarkably well near the sea, and attains to tree-like dimensions.

E. Chilensis (*Rhaphithamnus chilensis*).

E. Ugni (*Myrtus Ugni, which see*).

E. zeylanica. Flowers, white, handsome long leaves.

EUGENIA APICULATA. *See* MYR-TUS LUMA.

EUGENUA LUMA. *See* MYRTUS LUMA.

EULALIA (ēu-lā-lia. Graminæ). Zebra-striped Grass. Hardy perennial grass that looks very well in a clump on the lawn or in a border. It thrives in ordinary soil and is increased by division in spring. The brownish-violet flower panicles curve gracefully and the flowers have long silky hairs at their base which give a feathery appearance to the plant. Height, 6–8 ft.

EUONYMUS (ū-on'-i-mus. Celastra-ceæ). Spindle-tree. Very useful foliaged evergreen and deciduous shrub from China and Japan, devoid of floral beauty,

but attractive in the autumn with richly-coloured foliage in some species, and the beauty of its fruits.

Culture.—Plant evergreen section in April or October, and deciduous section from November to March. No pruning is necessary. *Propagate* by seeds, and by cuttings of the previous year's growth at almost any season if a little bottom-heat be available.

SPECIES.

Deciduous Section.

E. alatus (China and Japan). 6–9 ft. One of the most distinct, and one of the finest autumn shrubs for foliage effect, the leaves turning to pink and crimson.

E. europæus, Spindle-tree (Europe, including Britain). Interesting in winter when laden with rose-pink fruits.

E. yedoensis (Japan). 10 ft. Foliage changes in autumn to yellow and red, fruit rosy-pink, remaining long after the leaves have fallen.

Evergreen Section.

E. radicans (Japan). A creeping species suitable for covering poor ground in shade or sun. If trained up wall or house-front it will reach to 20 ft. and more. May also be used as an edging to paths. It can be increased by pulling old plants apart and replanting. Even the smallest pieces will root.

EUPATORIUM (ū-pa-tŏri-um. Compositæ). Hemp Agrimony. Mexico. Coarse herbaceous perennials useful for either border or shrubbery, or evergreen flowering shrub with corymbs of fragrant white flowers during August and September, that are only fit for warm and seaside gardens. The former are easy to culti-vate, quite hardy, and will succeed in good garden soil in a sunny spot.

SPECIES.

E. ageratoides blooming in Septem-ber, *E. altissimum* and *E. aromaticum* which is fragrant and blooms in July. All have numerous white blossoms in flat heads, 3–5 ft. high; *E. purpureum* with clusters of purplish flowers and *E. macu-latum*, its pink variety, are grand wild garden plants.

E. Weinmannianum, best for the green-house.

EUPHORBIA (Spurge. Caper spurge), Euphorbiaceæ. Poinsettia. Stove and hardy flowering shrubs or herbs. Cape of Good Hope, 1695. This is a large family, few of which only are grown, and widely differing in their habits, the remainder not being worthy of cultivation.

Culture (established plants).—Compost, 3 parts fibrous loam, 1 part dried cow manure, 1 part peat, ½ part sharp sand. Start into growth in greenhouse at the end of March or beginning of April. Temperature, 50°. When new shoots appear, take plants out of old pots, shake the soil from the roots, slightly root prune, and repot into pots just large enough to take the roots with a little compost. Prune shoots back to one or two buds from their base at the end of April, and place in stove, temperature, 65°–70°. Repot into flowering pots when root growth is well established. Place outside in sunny frame during the summer months. Remove to the greenhouse in September to a temperature about 60°, gradually move into stove to temperature 70°–75° for flowering. After flowering period place back into greenhouse, temperature 45°, and cease watering. Store plants on their side under staging. Syringe daily during growing period, and a little weak liquid manure, applied weekly until flowers appear, will be very beneficial.

Propagation and culture from cuttings.— Cuttings should be taken in May from young shoots about 3 in. long. Insert in small pots of sandy peat, plunge in fibre to the rim in the propagator, temperature, 70°–75°. When well-rooted, pot on into 48's, place plants on a shelf near the glass. As soon as the roots are showing well to the side of the pots, repot into final pots for flowering, and treat exactly the same as advised for old-established plants.

SPECIES.

E. *capitata*, the smallest of the group, bears small capitate bracts and blooms in August, 3 in.

E. *Cyparissias*, with bright yellow flowers in July, has beautiful foliage, 3 ft.

E. *Gulgeni*, scarlet.

E. *heterophylla*, 2 ft. Sometimes called Mexican Fire Plant; is not very suitable for British gardens. The principal feature is a cluster of scarlet "bracts" or leaves at the top of the stems, but the seasons

here are not long or hot enough to bring them to perfection.

E. *lathyris*, 2 ft., or Caper spurge, is a most unique-looking plant. The long pointed leaves are produced at right angles to the stems, giving a particularly rigid appearance. It is now naturalised in Britain and is reputed to have been introduced by the Romans with their building materials brought from

EVENING PRIMROSE

Evening Primroses are either biennials or perennials. They usually open their blooms in the evenings and are very fragrant.

Italy. It may be a remarkable coincidence, but it is found in most districts in which there are traces of Roman occupation. It provides capers for flavouring, is useful for wild gardens or rough places.

E. *marginata*, 1½ ft., has attractive variegated foliage, green and white, and is effective in the mixed border.

E. *pulcherrima*, scarlet.

E. *splendens*, scarlet.

GREENHOUSE SPECIES.

Chief amongst these are the Poinsettias, E. *pulcherrima*. The flowers are insignificant the real charm being in the beautiful scarlet bracts.

HARDY SPECIES.

None of the hardy perennials and annuals are very desirable plants, while some are weeds. They can be used in the wild garden. They are of easy culture and thrive in any soil. *Propagate* by division or by seeds.

EUPTELEA (trochodendraceæ). Deciduous tree with fine foliage, especially in autumn.

Culture.—Ordinary garden soil. *Propagate* by cuttings and by layers.

SPECIES.

E. *Davidiana* (China). 20–30 ft. Young foliage reddish in spring.

PLANTING
EVERGREENS

SACKING
REMOVE AT LAST MOMENT
BEFORE FILLING IN HOLE.

Evergreens usually have sacking tied round the ball of soil when they arrive. They need moist weather for success in planting. Showery weather in April or September is the best time.

E. *polyandra* (Japan). 20 ft. Leaves turn yellow and red before falling.

EURYA (ū'-ri-a. Ternstrœmiaceæ). Dwarf compact flossy-leaved evergreen shrub, with inconspicuous white flowers, followed by black fruit as large as a peppercorn. Only half-hardy. Grow in peaty loam.

Propagate by cuttings placed in gentle heat.

EURYBIA. *See* OLEARIA.

EURYCLES (u-ri-klez. Amaryllideæ). Stove bulbs that do well in rich loam and leaf-mould and require a culture similar to that given to Pancratiums.

Propagate chiefly by offsets, occasionally by seeds. They require a hot temperature and plenty of water when growing and to be kept drier and cooler during their resting period in winter.

SPECIES.

E. *Cunninghamii*, white, July. 1 ft.

E. *sylvestris* (syn. *amboinensis* and *australasica*), white, August, 1½ ft.

EUTOCA (u-to-ca. Hydrophyllaceæ),

1 ft. E. *viscida*. Flowers rich blue, produced in great profusion over a long period; will thrive in good soil and likes sunny position. A good plant for bees.

EVENING PRIMROSE. *See* ŒNOTHERA.

EVERGREEN. Opposed to deciduous. A term given to any plant which retains its leaves throughout the year. In addition to the many evergreen hedge shrubs such as privet, lonicera nitida, etc., there are many evergreen trees, flowering shrubs and alpine plants. A good selection of evergreens should be included in the garden planting schemes to ensure protection and interest throughout the winter months.

EVERLASTING FLOWERS. The term applied to those species whose flower scales or bracts are of a strawy

HELICHRYSUM
EVERLASTING
FLOWER

The petals of everlasting flowers contain a large quantity of silica, which enables them to be kept in a dry state during the winter.

texture, and retain their natural colours for a long time after being cut and dried. Examples: Acroclineum, Helichrysum (*which see*), Rhodanthe, Xeranthemum.

EVODIA (ē-vŏ-di-a. Rutaceæ). Deciluous trees from China with aromatic foliage and a profusion of clusters of bright red fruits.

SPECIES.

E Hupehensis. Of easy cultivation,

EXOCHORDA

The Pearl Bush or Exochorda is a white-flowered shrub blooming in May. It likes a sheltered position, but is not particular as to soil.

thriving in quite poor soils; also in chalky districts.

EXACUM (Gentianaceæ). Beautiful greenhouse annuals, biennials and perennials.

Cultivation.—Sow in autumn or early spring in pans or boxes and place in a warm greenhouse. Prick off into well-drained soil and pot up as required, using a compost of loam, peat and silver sand. *Propagate* perennials also by cuttings.

SPECIES.

E. zeylanicum macranthum. Height, 18 in. Beautiful mauve-blue flowers with yellow anthers, usually flowering in December. Related to the Gentians of the rock garden.

Exacum affine is a smaller plant (9 in.) with bright rosy-mauve flowers, which are sweetly scented.

EXOCHORDA (ex-o-kŏr′da. Rosaceæ). Flowering shrubs, from N. Asia.

Culture.—Plant in rich loamy soil and a sunny position. *Propagation* is best by seeds. Cuttings of rather soft wood placed in heat may root, but they are uncertain.

SPECIES.

E. Giraldii (China). 6–8 ft. Beautiful white flowers in May, $1\frac{1}{2}$ in. across.

E. Wilsonii (China). 8–12 ft. high and as much in width. Flowers large pure white, almond scented.

E. Korolkowii (*Albertii*) Turkestan. 8–12 ft. white flowers in April. Excellent on chalky soils.

E. macrantha. Hybrid between *E. racemosa* + *E. Korolkowii*. Very beautiful during April and May. Also does well on chalky soils.

E. racemosa (*grandiflora*). The "Pearl Bush." China. One of the most beautiful of May-flowering shrubs, with pure snow-white inflorescences up to 18 in. long and 8–10 in. wide. Thin cut branches immediately after flowering. Not suitable for chalky or limy soils.

F

FABIANA (fab-i-ā′na. Solanaceæ). Chile, 8–10 ft. An exceedingly beautiful evergreen heath-like branching shrub with pure-white narrow tubular flowers in May and June. Rather tender, but succeeds well in upland and mild districts; easily grown in light sandy soil; also does well in chalky districts. *Propagated* by

Culture.—Plant in October or November. No pruning necessary. *Propagation* by seed, except the named varieties, which need to be grafted in spring.

Species.

F. sylvatica. Common beech. Native of this country and Europe. Few trees are more pleasing and attractive than our

The Beech tree is one of the finest wayside trees. The copper-leaved form is grown in gardens for lawn decoration. Kept clipped it makes beautiful russet winter hedges.

cuttings taken about August, and placed in gentle heat, or under bell-glass in frame.

Species.

E. imbricata. The only species of note.

FAGUS (fā′gus. Cupuliferæ). Beech. Deciduous trees of noble dimensions, thriving particularly well on calcareous soils. They do not mind the shade of other trees growing nearby, and make good shade and shelter trees themselves. The purple-leaved forms are very ornamental in the garden. The beech also makes a very good tall hedge, retaining most of its leaves throughout the winter. An excellent seaside tree.

native Beech, well grown, either as an isolated spreading specimen, or associated with others in a group, or plantation, and drawn up by them, exhibiting its tall smooth, column-like trunk.

At Ashridge Park, Herts, the famous Queen Beech has attained to a height of about 140 ft. The following is a selection of the most popular varieties.

F. s. cuprea. Copper Beech.

F. s. pendula. Weeping beech.

F. s. purpurea. Purple beech.

F. s. p. pendula. Weeping purple beech.

FAIRY RINGS. Circles formed by fungi, frequently *Agaricus arvensis* which, starting by one spore, spread underground and become richer every year owing to the nitrogen left by the decease of the first spores, and the grass nearby attains a rich deep green for the same reason. At the outer edge of the circle appears a ring of Toadstools, the fungus in its fruiting stage.

While pretty in a meadow they are not exactly desirable in a garden, and can be removed by syringing with a dilution of 1 lb. of sulphate of iron in 3 gallons of water.

FAIRY WALLFLOWER. *See* ERYSI-MUM.

FALLOW. Ground is said to be fallow when it has been dug or ploughed, but left unsown for a period.

FALSE BROME GRASS. *See* BRACHY-PODIUM.

FALSE CHAMOMILE. *See* BOL-TONIA.

FALSE DRAGON'S HEAD. *See* PHYSOSTEGIA.

FALSE HELLEBORE. *See* VERA-TRUM.

FALSE INDIGO. *See* BAPTISIA.

FALSE LUPIN. *See* THERMOPSIS.

FARADAYA (far-a-da-ya. Verbena-ceæ). White flowered stove climbers. *Propagate* by cuttings inserted in sand under a bell-glass or by seeds and plant in good loam.

SPECIES.

F. papuana. F. splendida.

FARSETIA (far-se-ti-a. Cruciferæ). Rarely grown hardy annuals and herbs that resemble Alyssums and have hoary foliage.

Propagated by seeds sown in a frame in spring and the herbaceous plants by cuttings.

SPECIES.

F. ægyptia. White. July. 1 ft.

F. clypeata. Yellow. June. 1½ ft.

F. suffruticosa. Violet flowers in May. 1 ft.

FASTIGIATE. Used of trees that grow in a pyramidal shape owing to the branches being almost erect and parallel. Notably the Lombardy Poplar.

FATSIA (fat'-si-a. Araliaceæ). A striking evergreen tree or shrub from Japan; 6–15 ft. high, rich dark shining leathery leaves 12–16-in. across. Flowers white in large branching panicles during autumn, succeeded by black pea-like fruits. Likes a sheltered half-shaded position. First rate for seaside gardens. Perfectly hardy. Plant in ordinary garden soil. *Propagation* by cuttings placed singly in small pots, and rooted in mild bottom heat.

SPECIES.

F. japonica (*Aralia Sieboldii*). A tropi-cal-looking shrub or small tree. Mis-takenly called the Castor Oil Plant.

Fatsia, or Aralia Sieboldii, is a useful evergreen plant either for the cool greenhouse or in sheltered places outdoors.

F. j. Moseri. A form with larger leaves.

F. j. variegata. Leaves blotched white.

FEBRUARY WORK IN THE GARDEN.

THE FLOWER GARDEN.

Build new arches and pergolas. Attend to paths and to border edgings. Keep the lawns well swept and rolled, and as soon as the weather turns warm, begin to use the mower.

Divide and replant herbaceous plants

whenever there is a favourable opportunity.

Delphiniums in particular should be planted this month.

Place Dahlia tubers in boxes, sprinkle them with soil and a little water to induce growth of new shoots.

Stir the surface of bulb beds with a fork as soon as the shoots show above the ground.

Sow China Asters, Balsams, fibrous Begonias, Coleus, Petunias, Phlox drummondii, Lobelia, Stocks, Tobacco plants, and all other half-hardy annuals to be used for summer beds and borders. These should be sown in boxes of prepared soil and placed in the frame over a hotbed or in the warm greenhouse.

Plant out autumn-rooted cuttings of Carnations. Where a special Carnation border is being arranged, set the plants 12 in. apart each way.

Mulch rose beds with a thick layer of decayed leaves or old manure.

Divide London Pride, and plant out Polyanthus, Primrose, Anemones and Runanculus as edgings to borders.

Plant Lily-of-the-Valley crowns in a position where they can be left undisturbed for some years. They like to run alongside a wall or stone path.

Lift and divide Montbretia, if this was not done in November.

Plant Honeysuckle, Jasmine, Virginia Creeper, Clematis and other hardy climbers.

Sow Sweet Peas in small thumb pots in the frame. A dusting of red lead over the seedlings will prevent the attack of mice.

The Rock Garden.

Parts of the rock garden that are unsatisfactory can be re-made this month.

If possible avoid building any part of the rockery under the drip of trees.

Build the desired shape with rough material first. Then commence from the bottom to build stones and soil, making the stones quite firm and leaving large soil pockets for the accommodation of rock plants.

Use plenty of lime in the soil except where the lime-haters are to be grown.

Plant the rock plants firmly and top

dress with granite chippings or similar material round each of the plants. This prevents them from becoming too damp, which is a frequent cause of decay among the more tender plants.

If frost continues give slight protection to rock plants which are coming into flower. Cloches are useful, but a few twigs and some dried leaves over small plants will often provide adequate protection.

Make Miniature Gardens now. In the smallest of gardens a charming piece of mountain scenery can be made in an earthenware trough. For ease in tending raise the trough to table height on some kind of support. See that drainage is provided.

Old sinks make good trough gardens, and these have, of course, an outlet for surplus water.

Put rough material such as mortar rubble, old broken bricks, broken crocks, or large stones at the bottom of the trough. This assists drainage. Cover this with leaves, coarse manure, or some other material which will prevent the soil from washing down through the stones and clogging the drainage holes. Add more soil in which plenty of lime and sharp sand are present, and build the miniature landscape with stones and this fine soil. Lime must be omitted if heaths are to be grown.

The Shrubbery.

Some of the shrubs can be pruned this month. Cut back old wood. Clean the soil by forking in the leaves.

Many shrubs make new and unwanted stems from the base. These should be layered to form new plants. Climbers such as the late-flowering Clematis jackmanii can be cut back now to within a few inches of the old wood, or in the case of young plants to within 10 in. of the base. (*See* pruning list below.)

Prepare stocks for grafting Rhododendrons.

Prune the following shrubs as required: Actinidia, Ailanthus glandulosa, Artemisia, Buddleia variabilis, Bupleurum fruticosum, Cæsalpina japonica, Cassinia, Celastrus, Ceanothus americanus, C. azureus, C. Gloire de Versailles, C. Indigo, Cestrum, Clematis davidiana, C. flammula,

C. jackmanii, C. Lanuginosa, C. Viticella, Colutea, Coriaria, Cyrilla, Desmodium, Eccremocarpus scaber, Elscholtzia, Ercilla volubilis, Ficus, Fuchsia, Hedera, Hedysarum multijugum, Hydrangea aborescens, H. grandiflora, H. paniculata, Hypericum calycinum, H. moserianum, Indigofera gerardiana, Itea virginica, I. ilicifolia, Lespedeza, Lippia citriodora (Aloysia), Lupinus aboreus, Marsdenia, Menispermum, Microglossa, Myricaria, Paulownia imperialis, Pentstemon, Periploca græca, Piptanthus, Polygonum baldschuanicum, Rhus, Romneya, Rosa (species), Sambucus, Schizandra, Spiræa, Stauntonia, Tamarix pentandra, Tecoma, Teucrium, Vitex, Vitis.

Hoeing should be carried out whenever the weather permits.

Climbing roses should be trimmed and trained.

The care of climbing plants which form permanent covering for house walls, etc., should be entrusted to the care of skilled gardeners only. At this season many need pruning and others must on no account be cut back until they have flowered.

Climbers which will flower on the new wood made last season are among those to be left unpruned now. Tie in the branches so that the flowers will show to the best advantage when they open.

FRUIT.

Weed strawberries. Lightly fork the surface soil and give a light dressing of manure.

Use prunings from currants and gooseberries as cuttings.

Tie and nail fruit trees grown on walls.

Peaches, nectarines, and Morello cherries flower on the young wood, which should be spared as much as possible.

Cut away shoots which grow at right angles to the wall and tie in the side shoots as evenly as possible over the wall surface.

In favourable weather fruit trees in sunny sheltered gardens will show by their swelling buds that the flowering season is almost here. Prepare fish netting or other form of shelter beforehand so that open blossoms will not be killed by sudden frosts. A light fish-net stretched over peach trees gives a surprising amount of protection. Wall fruits particularly should be given this attention.

Train loganberries on to wires stretched between poles, laying the stems horizontally along the wires.

Stocks for grafting may be headed back this month.

Scions for grafting should be taken from the parent tree and placed in earth under a north wall.

Damsons are best pruned this month, also quince trees.

All fruit trees tied to stakes should be examined. Untie the stake and remove the sacking or other wrapping from the trunk of the tree.

If "mussel scale" is present paint the attacked portion with lime sulphur. The scale is shaped like a mussel shell and is about an eighth of an inch long, and brown in colour. After treatment the sacking and ties should be replaced. Unless these are attended to each season, the tie often becomes too tight and causes serious damage to the tree.

VEGETABLES.

The secret of success in the vegetable garden is to sow early.

Seeds sown this month must be protected during the late winter frosts, and should therefore be sown in a sheltered position in the garden, or under glass.

Where seeds are sown in the open, cloches or twigs can be used to give protection.

Seeds for present sowing include cabbage, early cauliflower, leeks and Brussels sprouts under glass, and broad beans and peas in the open.

Plant shallots now.

Press the small bulbs half-way into the soil.

They should be 8 in. apart in the rows, and the rows should be a foot or 15 in. apart.

Soil preparation should be similar to that for onions.

Deep digging and a firmly-levelled bed are needed, and a light dressing of kainit should be given just before planting, say an ounce to four square yards.

Tomato culture.—To be successful with tomatoes grown in the open garden, obey the following rules:

Sow early in the year, towards the end of this month.

Select suitable varieties.

Keep the plants sturdy.

Thick stems, short-jointed and with dark green foliage should be developed before the young plants are put in their permanent positions.

These can only be obtained by correct ventilation and feeding.

Prepare the soil of the tomato-beds by deep digging.

This is best done early, so that the under-soil has time to settle a little before the plants are put in.

Seedlings are first thinned out when just large enough to handle, to about ½ in. apart.

When they have made two rough leaves, they are pricked out to about 2 in. apart in boxes or put singly into small pots.

Soil 3 in. deep is needed at this stage, and this should be prepared in advance.

UNDER GLASS.

Cauliflowers and lettuces that have been wintering under frames should not be coddled.

The frames should only be closed when the weather is frosty.

Early lettuces can be pricked out on rich beds in frames.

Onions sown in boxes last month will require thinning out.

Hotbeds made up last month need daily watching to keep up the heat.

When a lowering of temperature becomes dangerous to the plants, add more manure round the sides of the frames, and keep them well covered with mats at night.

Globe artichokes, vegetable marrows and tomatoes can all be sown on a hot bed for early supplies.

Potatoes can be planted for very early supplies, and early carrots and salad crops can also be raised.

Prepare soil composts for the rush of seed sowing next month.

Tuberous begonias should be started under glass.

Start bulbs in small pots on the surface of rich loamy soil. Plant with the hollow side on top. Pot up into larger pots when growth has begun. Nurse with care; frosts are fatal. A temperature of 40°–50° should be maintained at night. Watering should be attended to carefully.

Bedding-out plants should be propagated now.

Dahlias should be started in heat.

Fuchsias should be given a little bottom heat after repotting.

Geranium roots which have been stored should be subjected to bottom heat and cuttings taken.

Cuttings can also be taken of double petunias, coleus, heliotrope and perpetual-flowering carnations.

PESTS.

Mice and sparrows often raid a newly-sown row of peas or broad beans.

The best remedy is to soak the seeds in water overnight before sowing, dry them on a sheet of paper and sprinkle over a few spots of paraffin. Shake the seeds up and then dust on sufficient red lead to give a pink colour. This makes the seeds both poisonous and distasteful. When the seedlings appear, special pea guards, which are sold by nurserymen, or tiny twigs placed among the seedlings with a few strands of black cotton intertwined, will be very effective as a guard against birds.

Birds are so useful for the quantities of grubs and snails they devour that they should not be driven from the garden.

Set pans of water for them, and also arrange a bird-table for scraps.

Under glass, mildew is the worst spring trouble.

The following precautions should be taken:

Avoid draughts to young seedlings.

Avoid stagnant atmosphere by adequate ventilation.

Remove decayed leaves and vegetable matter from cuttings and old plants.

Omit leaf-mould from soil used for delicate seeds.

An ounce of potassium sulphide (liver of sulphur) dissolved in three gallons of tepid water makes an effective spray if mildew appears on vines or roses, as it frequently does.

CARE OF ROOM PLANTS.

Only a little water is needed for most room plants at this season.

Move bulb bowls into light and give
ore water.

Watch for signs of new growth on ferns
d aspidistras, and repot if necessary
hen this is seen.

Ferns like soil made from two parts
am and one part leaf-mould or peat with
leavening of sharp sand.

Wash and dry old pots before use.

Sponge the leaves of aspidistras and

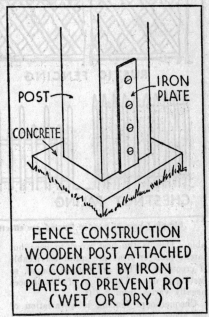

WOVEN FENCING MAKES AN
EFFECTIVE SCREEN AGAINST
WIND & INTRUDERS

**Shelter is provided on wind-swept sites by
woven or wattle fencing.**

palms with tepid soapy water and syringe
off with clear water.

A few weeks of greenhouse treatment
will refresh jaded room plants.

FEEDING PLATFORM. This can be
constructed separately from, or in conjunction with, a nesting-box. It is usually
made very simply of a flat wood top raised
on a post, either fixed in the ground with
supporting struts, or made with a solid
base, so that it can be moved from place
to place when necessary. A thatched roof
above the platform makes it more useful
and can add to its beauty. Biscuit-meal
should be soaked and spread, corn can be

scattered, and marrowbones and coconut
suspended from these feeding platforms.

FEIJOA (fī-jo′-a. Myrtaceæ). Beautiful evergreen shrub from Brazil with dark
green, roundish leaves, light grey beneath,
white fuchsia-like flowers, waxy in substance, and numerous protruding crimson
stamens during late summer and autumn.

A very striking and attractive flower,
and richly perfumed; followed by large,
yellow, egg-shaped edible fruits. Thrives
in chalky soils. Generally grown against
a wall, and regarded as only half-hardy,
but has withstood 30° of frost without
injury.

F. sellowiana, the only species.

POST

IRON
PLATE

CONCRETE

FENCE CONSTRUCTION
WOODEN POST ATTACHED
TO CONCRETE BY IRON
PLATES TO PREVENT ROT
(WET OR DRY)

**Where wooden posts have to bear heavy strains
they need to be set in concrete.**

FELICIA (fe-lis-ia. Compositæ). King-
fisher Daisy. *F. Bergerianus.* South
Africa, hardy annual, 6 in. A charming
dwarf daisy with green, turf-like foliage.
The stems are flat-growing (procumbent),
and the flowers are carried singly on 6 in.
stems well clear of the leaves. The colour
is an enchanting shade of gentian blue,
and but for the fact that the blooms open

late in the morning and close early in the afternoon, this would be one of the most delightful annuals of recent introduction. Sow in April in light soil where the plants are to bloom, or sow in March under glass, and plant out in May.

FENCES. A fence is used to mark a boundary (*which see*) and also to give protection and privacy.

Close wooden fencing is one of the best types for giving privacy and is very dur-

temporarily in various parts of the ga den to protect young shrubs during t winter.

Split pale or Chestnut fencing is a che type of fencing, quite useful and econom cal although fairly temporary. The pal are spaced 3 in. apart and secured means of strong wires. Main posts, t bottoms of which should be charred creosoted to prevent rot, are spaced 10 apart.

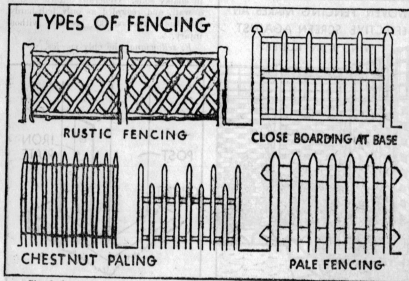

TYPES OF FENCING

RUSTIC FENCING

CLOSE BOARDING AT BASE

CHESTNUT PALING

PALE FENCING

Simple forms of wooden fencing are effective for training Roses and other climbers.

able. Oak is the best wood to use; but larch, pine or deal are quite serviceable if creosoted. They are not, of course, so lasting as oak. The height of these fences usually varies from 3–7 ft.

Chequerboard fencing is a variation of the above, being much more pleasing and artistic for use in the garden; it is supplied in various lengths and heights ready for fixing. This woven type of fencing also makes a very good screen on wind-swept sites.

Wattle hurdles are a very cheap and economical form of fence, less artistic than chequerboard, but serving equally well as wind-screens. They are very useful for protecting a newly-planted hedge, and are supplied in sections suitable for placing

Rustic fences made of hazel, larch o spruce are useful in the less formal part of the garden for screening. The bar should be left on, and it is best to notc the pieces together as well as nailing them.

Larch poles form economical screens an take up very little room. The poles ar trimmed, leaving one branch on either side a foot or so from the top. The pole are then placed 6–8 ft. apart and climbers planted against them will soon form an effective screen.

Wire netting is inartistic but service-able, especially for keeping out rabbits. For this purpose it should be sunk 9 in. below the ground level, and 3 in. of this should be turned outwards in the direction

om which the rabbits are known to
proach. Main posts should be about
ft. apart, and straining posts every
0 ft. and at each corner. The cost of
ire netting rises in proportion to the
nallness of the mesh.

Iron palings are ugly and unsuited to
e garden, although they may be neces-
ry in some cases. They should be
inted periodically to keep them in good
ndition.

To heighten an existing fence, trellis
ork or strands of wire are quite suitable.
hese are held in position by means of
on or wooden uprights fixed in the
round, against the existing fence. Wood,
iron chains linked from post to post,
so answer the same purpose when clothed
ith climbers.

FENDLERA (Saxifrageæ). Decidu-
us shrub, 3–6 ft., from south-western
.S.A., producing white or rose-tinted
owers during May and June. Requires
very sunny position against a south wall.
ropagate by cuttings placed in gentle
eat and by seeds sown under glass in
pring.

F. rupicala, the only species.

FENZLIA. *See* GILIA.

FERNS, HARDY. There are between
hirty and forty species of ferns which are
ound wild in Great Britain, and which
hould therefore prove hardy under cultiva-
ion.

These include the old favourites: Hart's
Tongue, Parsley Fern, Hard Fern,
Maidenhair, Wallrue, Spleenwort, Lady
Fern, Prickly Shield Fern, Male Fern and
Polypody. They are all very beautiful
and no doubt most people possess one or
more of these ferns, since they are commonly sold and exchanged by hawkers at
house doors. Nurserymen now have new
varieties of many of these, but unlike the
flowering plants, ferns are not much
altered in cultivation, and the commonest
varieties will give almost the same effect
in a garden as the rarer sorts.

They vary considerably in form.
Wallrue is a very tiny species, not more
than two or three inches high, which grows
wild in walls, bridges, and rocks in the
country; but it hates smoke and will not
grow in towns. Most of the others are
less particular, in fact the Male Fern is

often the only vegetation to be found in
sunless town gardens.

Of the many half-hardy ferns which
are suitable for cultivation indoors, one
of the most useful is *Pteris cretica*, cousin
to the common bracken, of which there are
many varieties. *Adiantum capilus veneris*
(Maidenhair) and *Asplenium bulbiferum*
are two others suitable for growing in
pots, but the Maidenhair Fern will not
grow if gas is burnt in the room. It pre-

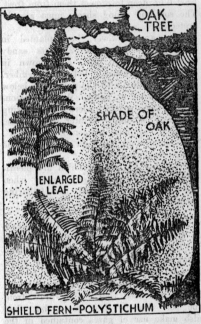

For the shady garden Ferns of all kinds are
useful. They love the shade of oak trees and
benefit from oak-leaf soil mixed with the soil
before planting.

fers a rather moist atmosphere, and
succeeds well if grown almost entirely
under a large bell-glass. In this manner
it will provide buttonhole foliage of
excellent quality.

Most ferns like plenty of decayed leaves
mixed with the soil, in addition to sand.
A useful compost is made by mixing leaf-
mould, loam and sand in equal proportions.
Some varieties, e.g., *Blechnum spicant*
and *Adiantum pedatum*, like lime rubble
in the soil. Clean drainage is essential
to all, for although ferns like moisture,

stagnation is fatal. Pot ferns should always have broken crocks at the bottom of the pot. Broken charcoal and lime rubble mixed in the soil used for potting Maidenhair Ferns will keep them healthy.

FERN TROWEL. *See under* TROWEL *and* FORKS.

FERRARIA (Black Iris). Iridaceæ. Half-hardy bulbous plants. Deciduous. They may be grown in the open borders, but in this case they must be planted at least 6 in. deep to protect them from frost. The soil and young shoots must also be protected.

They are, however, best planted in pots in a compost of 2 parts sandy loam and 1 part peat, and grown in the cool greenhouse. Pot in November. Place the bulbs with the point just below the surface 1–2 in. apart. Water occasionally in the winter, moderately in spring and early summer. Winter temperature, 40°–45°; summer temperature, 50°–60°. The bulbs must be kept dry after the foliage has withered.

Propagate by offsets, which are plentifully produced, or by seeds sown when ripe or kept dry until the following spring.

SPECIES.

F. undulata. Brown and purple flowers in March and April. Height, 6–8 in.

FERTILISERS. What they are and what they do. All plants live and grow in very much the same way as we do. That is, they need food, air, water and light. The food they mostly draw from the soil through their roots, but they also make use of gases contained in the air, principally oxygen and carbon dioxide (carbonic acid gas). The foods in the soil they can only take up in solution. Thus the nitrogen in an old boot and that in farmyard manure both have to pass into solution before the plant can use them. No solid particle, however small, is capable of passing into the roots. Furthermore, these foods have to take the particular form which the plant requires before they become, as we say, "available" for the plant.

The only difference, therefore, between fertilisers and manures like dung, shoddy, wool waste, leather scrap and the like, is that the latter are made by natural means

and the former artificially. Thus it mak no difference to the plant in what origin form its foodstuffs are presented, sin before it can use any of them they mu all become uniform. It is because of tⁿ latter fact that, so far as plant food concerned, artificial fertilisers have a gre advantage over so-called natural manur or "organics" such as dung, shoddy, wo waste, leather scraps, etc. These manur usually take a considerable time befoⁿ they break down into the forms require by the plant; artificial fertilisers, on tⁿ other hand, are specially made to ⁿ immediately available as soon as they aⁿ applied.

A SHORT HISTORY.

Apart from the early experiments of tⁿ alchemists little was known about tⁿ behaviour of plants and the foods they re quired until the beginning of the nineteenth century, when at last it becam possible to say with some certainty tha all plants require nitrogen, phosphates an potash for their livelihood. Lime also i essential, but is omitted at this stag because it is not one of the fertilisers but kind of assistant in their work. (For short account of lime and the work it does *see* LIME.)

In 1843 John Bennet Lawes founded tⁿ first agricultural research station in the world at his home at Rothamsted, Herts Here, Lawes and his assistant, the chemis Gilbert, began experiments on the re quirements of plants, upon which it may well be said rests the whole of our present day agricultural knowledge.

In those days the multitude of excellent fertilisers which we now have was quite unknown. Nitrogen was only obtainable in the form of sulphate of ammonia which, moreover, unlike the *neutral* sulphate of ammonia of to-day, was of the quality now called "ordinary" and contained a certain percentage of free sulphuric acid. Phosphates existed, apart from guano and bone products, only as superphosphates. Indeed, it was by the manufacture of this material (from the treatment of coprolites—fossil remains rich in phosphates of lime—with sulphuric acid) that Lawes built up the fortune which enabled him to endow Rothamsted.

Later an alternative source of phosphate

pply was provided by the discovery of homas and Gilchrist that a lining of ne and magnesia in the great vessels ed for holding molten iron during its nversion into steel, removed the phos- norous impurities with great efficiency. rom time to time this lining was renewed nd the old one ground into a powder. his powder, known as basic slag, was und to exert a beneficial influence on oils. Indeed, slag is still perhaps the

most popular fertiliser for grassland improvement. It may perhaps be of interest to note in passing that, in Germany, basic slag is still known as "Thomasmehl."

With the finding of the great beds of natural potash salts in Alsace Lorraine, a full supply of all the three essential plant foods was guaranteed to farmers all over Europe.

Since those early days, the attention of scientists and inventors has been

		PARTICULARS REQUIRED					
		Limits of Variation Allowed					
Fertiliser	Particulars Required	N. %	Sol. P_2O_5 %	Insol. P_2O_5 %	P_2O_5 %	K_2O_5 %	Remarks
Basic Slag.	Amount of P_2O_5				1	1	
	Amount of fertiliser that will pass through a prescribed sieve.						$\frac{1}{20}$ of amount stated to pass through sieve.
"Compound" Fertilisers, i.e., mixtures of any fertilisers, or of two or more fertilisers.	Amounts of N., sol. and insol. P_2O_5 separate and K_2O_5.	0·3	0·5	0·5		0·3	If N. and P. content 4% or less.
		0·5	0·5	0·5		0·5	If N. and P. content over 4% and not over 5%.
		·75	0·5	0·5		·75	If N. and P. content over 5%.
Nitrate of Lime.	Amount of N.	0·5					
Nitrate of Soda.	Amount of N.	0·3					
Potassium Salts, including Kainit, Muriate of Potash and Sulphate of Potash.	Amount of K_2O_5.					1	If K_2O_5 content not over 15%.
						2	If K_2O_5 content is over 15%.
Sulphate of Ammonia.	Amount of N. and of free acid.	0·3					Free acid: $\frac{1}{8}$ of quantity stated.
Superphosphate.	Amount of soluble P_2O_5.		0·5				

N.B. Never mix Superphosphate of Lime with Nitrate of Soda.
Never mix Basic Slag and Sulphate of Ammonia.
Potash manures increase quality and assist resistance to disease.
Phosphoric manures provide fruitfulness and early ripening.
Nitrogenous manures increase growth and cause darker green foliage.

constantly devoted to improving the various plant foods and, more particularly, nitrogen. They can now all be obtained in a variety of forms. Nitrogen is available as sulphate of ammonia, nitro-chalk, nitrate of soda, cyanamide, nitrate of lime, ammonium phosphate, and urea; phosphates as superphosphates, basic slag, potassic mineral phosphate, ground rock phosphate, basic mineral phosphate and many others; potash as sulphate and muriate (chloride) and in the form of mixed salts.

It will be noted that many of the above fertilisers, such as ammonium phosphate, nitrate of potash and potassic mineral phosphate, contain two plant foods in the form of a single substance. More recently still, further advances have been made and it is now possible to obtain concentrated complete fertilisers which, granular in form, contain fixed proportions of all three essential ingredients.

The most expensive of all fertiliser ingredients—nitrogen—is now obtained direct from the air. At Billingham, Stockton-on-Tees, there is a vast factory for the manufacture of this "synthetic" nitrogen, which has only one rival for size and efficiency in the world.

Sale of Fertilisers.

By the Fertilisers and Feeding Stuffs Act, 1926, certain particulars must be given to purchasers of fertilisers on or before delivery, or as soon after as possible, in the form of a statement. This does not apply where the purchaser requests that two or more articles shall be mixed before delivery. Nor is it applicable when the quantity sold is 56 lb. or less and is taken by the purchaser from a bulk on which the required particulars are displayed.

The penalties for failing to give the required statement or for giving wrong information are, on summary conviction, a fine not exceeding £5 for the first offence and similarly £10 for the second and subsequent convictions.

The Act requires the Council of each County or County Borough to appoint an agricultural analyst and inspectors. The inspector has the right at all reasonable times to enter a fertiliser merchant's premises within his borough or county and to take samples. The sample is analysed by the agricultural analyst and if the seller or the purchaser objects to the analysis they may submit a sample to the Government Chemist for examination payment of a small fee.

Inspectors must regard all information they obtain as confidential and heavy penalties follow disclosure.

The particulars required in this connection will be seen from the table on page 281.

Fertilisers—Quantities Needed.

It has been estimated that a garden of half an acre, partly lawn, partly flower border, partly vegetables, and with a few fruit trees, will need the following supply of fertilisers, or their equivalent in the form of commercial mixtures, for a year's supply: 4 cwt. basic slag; 2 cwt. super phosphate; ¼ cwt. kainit; 28 lb. nitrate of soda; ½ cwt. sulphate of ammonia. This may be regarded as a generous allowance and not a hard and fast guide, as naturally all soils need different treatment.

Fertiliser Fish Meal or Fish Guano.

Fish waste such as heads, tails and non-edible spines, steamed and pressed to remove oil and then ground up and bagged for fertiliser. It has its uses on light soils and in market garden produce but is too expensive for general application.

FERULA (Giant Fennel). Umbelliferae. Hardy herbaceous plants with elegant deep green, fern-like foliage. Will grow in any ordinary soil in the open, at the edge of shrubberies, borders or ponds. Good specimen plants for lawns and summits of rockeries or banks. Plant November to March.

Propagate by seeds sown in a light soil in autumn outdoors and transplant the seedlings the following summer. Also by division of roots in October or November.

SPECIES.

F. communis (Giant Fennel). Yellow, June. Height, 8–12 ft.

F. glauca. Yellow, June. Height, 6–8 ft.

F. tingitana. Yellow, June. Height, 6–8 ft.

FESTUCA (Fescue Grass). Gramineae. Hardy perennial grass which grows in any ordinary soil at the edgings of flower-beds or borders. Plant in spring or autumn

pot culture a compost of 2 parts good
l, 1 part leaf-mould, and sand, will be
uired. The pots should be placed in
cold or warm greenhouse near the
ndow. Pot in March or April. Water
derately in winter but freely at other
es.

Propagate by seeds sown outdoors in
ril, or by division in March or April.

SPECIES.

F. ovina glauca, glaucous green, bristly
ves. Height, 6 in.

FEVERFEW. See PYRETHRUM.

FICUS. See FIG.

FIELD BOOK. A book used for writing
wn the measurements taken in a field
rvey. Each page is divided into three
lumns, the centre column being used
the chain lengths and those either side
noting offsets and any general informa-
n—such as the presence of a tree or
ream.

FIG (Ficus Carica). Morads. The fig
a native both of West Asia and the
editerranean, and has been cultivated in
rope for countless generations.

Culture.—In this country, except in the
ildest localities, this fruit requires the
elter of a wall in order to mature its
uits. It is seldom killed outright by
ost, and even if cut down during cold
eather, young shoots generally appear
ice more during the following season.

Soil.—The poorest soil is best. The fig
rives excellently in a gravel path, where
is far more likely to fruit well than in
ch garden soil. Mortar-rubble or chalk
ould be added.

Planting.—Plant during October, 8 ft.
part.

Pruning.—Naturally, the fig produces
ree crops of fruit a year. In this
untry the only crop which matures
at of doors is the last one, formed during
e autumn (when the little figs are about
e size of peas). These fruits mature the
llowing summer. They are to be found
t the extremities of shoots during Sep-
ember. At this time there are also in
idence much larger fruits, which cannot
ossibly ripen before winter, and therefore
ust be removed. No pruning is neces-
ary, as the cutting away of shoots
bviously incurs the removal of next year's
ruit.

Manuring.—Manuring should never be
necessary. Watering should be done in
periods of extreme drought.

Propagation.—The best means of propagation is layering, which should be done
in May. Alternatively, cuttings may be
struck with ease if placed under glass in
bottom heat during early spring.

Culture under Glass.—Figs may easily
be grown under glass and are best treated
in large pots. The variety generally used
for earliest work is "St. John's" which,
if placed in bottom heat during late
October, produces ripe fruit by March.
Other varieties such as "Brown Turkey"
and "Grizzly Bourjasotte" may be started
in March without bottom heat. All pot
figs should be "stopped" on each branch
at five leaves, and watering should be carefully regulated. Pots standing on ashes
require frequent moving, otherwise they
root into the ashes. Pot plants should be
repotted every other year, using a good
loam, leaf-mould, a little manure, and
plenty of mortar-rubble.

Varieties for out of doors: The best
and one of the hardiest is "Brown
Turkey."

FIGURE. See STATUARY.

FILBERT. See HAZEL NUT.

FINGER-AND-TOE DISEASE (Plasmodiophora brassicæ). This disease,
otherwise known as "Club Root" and
"Anbury," must not be confused with the
damage caused by the gall weevil. In this
case we get swollen masses of root tissue,
whereas in the other we get round marble-
like balls. The spores pass the winter
in the soil. About the time young plants
are put out minute flagellated creatures
appear from the spores and these are
known as "flagellulæ." These enter the
cells of the root and become amœbulæ."
After a short time these amœbulæ fuse
together and become "plasmodium." This
plasmodium is at first a yellow, stringy
slime which fills the plant cells, but after
a time it dries up and by October has
changed into countless little spores. On
the break-up of the plant tissue these
spores are liberated into the soil, where
they remain until the following year when
the minute flagellulæ are born. This
disease may be found on cruciferous flowering plants as well as vegetables.

METHOD OF CONTROL. — Pull up and *burn* all diseased plants and dress the ground heavily with lime, which should be powdered as finely as possible. After this application the ground should be left for at least six months and then a crop not likely to be attacked planted.

FIR, DOUGLAS. *See* PSEUDOTSUGA DOUGLASII.

FIRMIANA. *See* STERCULIA.

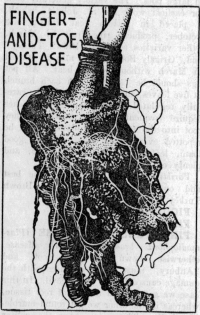

FINGER-AND-TOE DISEASE

One of the worst diseases of the cabbage family is the "Finger-and-Toe," Plasmodiophora brassicæ. It causes swellings on the roots of cabbages, turnips, etc.

FISH PONDS. *See* PONDS FOR FISH AND PLANTS.

FITTONIA (Acanthaceæ). Greenhouse evergreen trailing plants, with dark green or bright green leaves with red or pure white veins. Cultivate in a compost of equal parts peat, loam and sand in shallow pans, or pots, or the surface of beds in the shady part of the plant stove. Water moderately in winter but freely afterwards. Winter temperature, 55°-60°; summer temperature, 65°-80°.

Propagate by cuttings of firm shoots inserted in sandy soil in temperature of 75°-85° in spring or by division of plan in spring.

SPECIES.

F. argyroneura. Leaves, green vein white. Height, 6 in.

F. gigantea. Leaves, green veined re 12-15 in.

F. Verschaffeltii. Leaves green wi red, 8 in., and its variety *Pearcei*, t leaves of which are glaucous on the unde sides.

FITZROYA (fitz-roy'-a. Coniferæ Extremely interesting and elegant eve green trees of pyramidal habit. Th soil should be light and rich and we drained. Cuttings taken in summer w root under glass in sand, or very sand soil.

SPECIES.

F. patagonica, "The Patagonia Cypress," grows to 80 ft. in nature, bu is of bushy habit only in this countr Fairly hardy, but only really at home i the West.

FIXTURES, LEGAL ASPECT OF.

Fixtures removable by Tenant.

1. Fixtures comprising stock-in-trad such as the plants and glasshouses of market gardener, but not building an fixtures of a permanent or substanti nature.

2. Agricultural fixtures are dealt wit under special by-laws which must b consulted.

3. Those for ornament or convenience but the right of moving these depends upo circumstances. Those which are obviousl not permanent and can be moved withou injuring the property provided they ar not part of the premises, may be taken Generally speaking this applies to thing that have been provided at the expens of the tenant and are removable by takin out screws or nails. Those fixture attached by mortar or cement are usuall regarded as permanent. If any damag is done in removal the tenant must mak it good, and if he has taken down a fix ture to replace it with one of his own h must, upon removal, return the old fixture or its equivalent to its former position.

Time Limit For Removal of Fixtures.

The right to remove fixtures expires a the end of the tenancy, and after this th tenant cannot remove them without the consent of the landlord, but once this has been given the landlord forfeits all claim to them.

If the landlord attempts to prevent the tenant from removing fixtures which belong to the tenant, the latter can ask for an injunction restraining the landlord from interfering, but the landlord is entitled to prevent the tenant from taking that which is not legally his. If either exceed his rights in preventing the other from taking his own property he may be liable for assault.

Sale on Credit of Fixtures.

An outgoing tenant if selling his fixtures to an incoming tenant should stipulate for cash payment, for once he has left the property and the fixtures are not paid for, he cannot sue for payment for his goods, as the fixtures left behind are not the property of the incoming tenant but of the landlord. Also the tenant cannot claim for improvements that he has made to the property or for any permanent structure that he has erected and is unable to remove at the expiration of the tenancy.

FLAG. Plants which become dry at the roots soon flag, or droop, the stems losing their stiffness. (*See* WATERING.)

(*See* IRIS. *For* SWEET FLAG *see* ACORUS.)

FLAGSTONE. A large flat stone similar to those used for street pavements. Thus a garden path constructed of large flat stones—such as York stone—could be termed "flagged" as opposed to brick, cobble, or crazy pathways.

FLAME FLOWER. *See* KNIPHOFIA.

FLAX. *See* LINUM.

FLEABANE. *See* ERIGERON *and* INULA.

FLEA BEETLE, THE (*Phyllotreta nemorum*). This pest is a frequent cause of the failure of sowings of cruciferous plants such as turnip, cabbage, broccoli, kale, cauliflower, Brussels sprout and radish, particularly in droughty weather, when the surface of the soil tends to become dry and dusty. The adult beetles measure only about one tenth of an inch in length. The body is oval, dark-coloured and shiny with a colour varying from blue-black to greenish-black. The greater part of the back is covered by the ensheathing wing cases, each of which is marked by a broad longitudinal yellow stripe. The thighs of the hindermost pair of legs are very well developed and give the beetles the power of leaping like fleas. When it is found that the seed leaves of cruciferous seedlings become filled with round holes, the presence of these beetles may be suspected, but as these tiny beetles jump from the plant and conceal themselves in the dust on the slightest disturbance, they frequently escape notice. In the autumn, the adult beetles find shelter beneath fallen leaves, under the bark of trees, in chinks of old timber and fence palings and in the hollow stalks of grass and stubble. On the first fine warm days of the spring they leave their winter quarters and make their appearance in the garden as early as March, but May and June are the months of their greatest activity as garden pests. They are able to fly considerable distances and the certainty with which they will discover crops of a suitable food plant is amazing. The female beetles lay their eggs on the under sides of the young leaves of the food plants. These eggs hatch in about ten days and the small yellow maggots eat their way into the substance of the leaf. They become fully fed in about six days and then drop to the soil where they bury themselves and pupate, to emerge again as adult beetles after the lapse of a fortnight or more. Several broods may develop in the course of a season and the beetles continue to feed until the autumn.

TREATMENT.—Large numbers of the beetles may be trapped by pushing between the drills, boards or sheets of cardboard, the upper surface of which is smeared with some sticky substance, such as tar or treacle; but, best of all, one of the grease-banding materials used for fruit trees. Dressings of basic slag, scattered along the drills and freely dusted over the surface at the time of sowing, give some protection, but promising results have been obtained recently by the use of dusting powders containing some of the modern insecticides of vegetable origin.

FLINT. Flints are common in the clays and sands near the chalk. All true flints began their lives in the chalk when it was being formed under the sea. Flints are masses of hard grains, joined firmly together by Nature's chemistry. Many began as fossil sponges. The sponge mesh can still be seen in these. In some flints, fossil shells are embedded; in some of the London gardens such shells can be discovered in the flints.

FLOWER GARDEN. *See* HERBACEOUS BORDERS, FORMAL GARDENING, etc.

FLOWERING RUSH. *See* BUTOMUS.

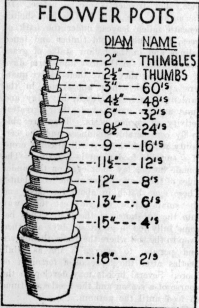

FLOWER POTS

DIAM	NAME
2"	THIMBLES
2½"	THUMBS
3"	60's
4½"	48's
6"	32's
8½"	24's
9"	16's
11½"	12's
12"	8's
13"	6's
15"	4's
18"	2's

Comparison of the potter's and gardener's descriptions of flower pots. For example, 3 in. gardener's pot is equivalent to a potter's " 60." Glazed varieties may be used if desired.

FLOWER POTS. These are made in several sizes to meet the varying requirements of plants (*see* sketch). Special shallow pots are made for Orchids; while those for Seakale and Rhubarb are like bell-glasses with a lid attached to the knobby handle so that they are placed over these plants, and when they need cutting it is only necessary to remove the layer of manure put over them for forcing, and the plant is easily accessible. All pots should be well scrubbed with soapy water, as dirt is conducive to disease, and new pots should be soaked for several hours. Glazed pots are

favoured by some florists, but they are more expensive than the old porous pots.

FOAM FLOWER. *See* TIARELLA.

FONTANESIA (fon-tă-nē'-zi-a. Oleaceæ). Deciduous shrubs with privet-like leaves, easily grown in ordinary soil. *Propagate* by cuttings.

SPECIES.

F. Fortunei (China). 10–15 ft. Flowers creamy-yellow in August.

F. phillyræoides (Orient). 6–10 ft. Subevergreen; flowers greenish-white in June.

FORCING. By placing plants in a high temperature they may be forced, to bring them to maturity earlier than their normal season. The temperature should be raised gradually so as not to shock the plant by sudden changes. Both flowers and vegetables can be treated in this way.

FORECOURT. A space immediately

CUTTINGS OF FORGET-ME-NOTS INSERTED IN A BOX OF SANDY SOIL.

Special varieties of Forget-me-nots can be increased by means of cuttings kept moist in sandy soil but many species will propagate themselves freely if allowed to do so.

in front of a house entrance, and connected with the drive and garage. The most convenient shape is the circle with the central portion grassed, the drive continuing right round this. To allow motor traffic a complete turn the grass area should be sixty feet in diameter. An arrangement whereby cars can reach the front entrance and reverse to the garage can be planned to occupy a much smaller space. The aesthetic treatment will of course vary according to the type of house and garden.

FORERIGHT (Forthright). *See* Breastwood.

FORESTIERA (*Adelia*). Oleaceæ. Dwarf shrubs bearing olive-like fruits. Requires a very hot sunny position.

Species.

F. acuminata. Small dark green leaves; fruit purple.

F. neo mexicana. Fruits purple.

FORGET-ME-NOT. *See* Myosotis.

FORKS. These must be divided into their two kinds—digging and small hand forks. Both of these are of different types, as follows:

(i) Digging Forks.—These are made in several sizes, according to the number of prongs—usually four, but on the larger ones, five. They are used for general-purpose digging and are generally strongly made, with square prongs, and a strapped handle.

Border or Ladies' Forks are just as above, but smaller and lighter, and are sometimes made with oval prongs to make the digging easier.

Potato Forks are very much the same as the digging forks, but they have broad and usually diamond prongs, according to quality: broad, so as to dig up all the potatoes on a root, and diamond-sectioned, so as to give greater rigidity. Obviously, these forks are also very useful in light soil, because they gather more soil at a time.

Provided that the fork is made by some well-known maker who would stand by his product in the event of a flaw in the metal, which is unavoidable sometimes, and provided also that the fork is made of forged steel throughout, personal taste and requirements will dictate which to buy.

(ii) Hand Forks.—Generally speaking, the differences here depend on whether they are made of stamped or forged steel. The former are always cheap to buy, not so nice to use, liable to bend under strain, and the handles are liable to come off. If it is just to do one or two pots or small beds, then a stamped fork might suffice, but otherwise it pays to buy a forged fork which is just like a miniature digging fork.

Both kinds can be obtained with different handle lengths, approximately 6 in., 15 in. and 48 in. They are used for planting, transplanting, and anywhere that you cannot with safety reach with the clumsier digging fork. The longer the handle, the less you have to stoop—which is worth considering.

FORKS (HAND), STAINLESS STEEL. *See under* Stainless Steel.

Despite the advice to dig with the spade, most gardeners use the fork. Here is a selection of four to cover different garden operations.

FORMALDEHYDE. A good soil fumigant. Four ounces of formaldehyde in a gallon of water used to soak the soil in seed boxes, before sowing, will prevent "damping-off."

FORMAL GARDENING. It is only in exceptional cases that an entire site can be treated formally throughout. One exception is the case of the tiny town garden or suburban front garden which is not large enough to lend itself to any informal treatment.

Formality should never be forced into a garden. Its one object should be to link the formal architectural lines of the house with the natural beauties of a site. If there are no natural beauties, as in the case of hundreds of gardens which are bounded by straight fences or walls, a suitable planting of shrubs and small trees will screen the hard boundaries and reproduce a little of the gracefulness of Nature even in restricted space. Other than this, formality is most suited to the

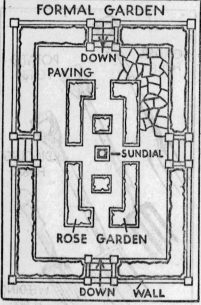

FORMAL GARDEN

DOWN

PAVING

SUNDIAL

ROSE GARDEN

DOWN WALL

A sunk garden suitable for the seaside where shelter from winds is desirable. The rose beds are 5 ft. wide.

type of plot where one can never quite forget the nearness of the house.

The formal garden, however, is usually part of a larger garden, and designed to be a special garden feature. Such a feature can be placed near the house, below the terrace, in a dip in the ground or an old pit, or in an odd corner of the garden. Its main axial lines should link with an important house window or pathway, and in a large garden of this type it may be possible to introduce three or four cross axial lines. The design should be kept as simple as possible, both in its outline and arrangement of flower beds. For ease of upkeep the flowers should be set in pav-

ing or gravel, but grass may often be introduced to soften the stonework, so long as it is not placed where it will be greatly trodden on, or has many edges to keep clipped. See that all parts of the garden are in proportion, making the flower beds slightly wider than the pathways. One or two ample beds will give a much better effect than several small beds. If a focal point is desired, a pool is often used as a substitute for an ornament. The garden should be suitably enclosed either with a hedge or wall, etc., and may often be sunk below the main level of the garden. The extreme degree of a formal garden verges on the Dutch garden (*which see*). Flowers which accommodate themselves to planting in formal beds are chiefly roses, irises, carnations, etc. The formal garden can of course be used for a spring display of bulbs, followed by annuals or bedding plants. Antirrhinums, Zinnias, Stocks, etc., lend themselves to this treatment.

FORMULÆ. The following formulæ are applicable to the gardener rather than the large commercial fruit-grower:

FUNGICIDES.

Fungus diseases are of two kinds, endophytic and ectophytic, those living within the plant tissues coming under the first heading and those living exposed coming under the second heading. Fungicides may be roughly divided into two types, those containing copper and those with sulphur. Copper is perhaps mostly used for fungi of the endophytic types, while sulphur is used for moulds and those of ectophytic type. It must be remembered that certain plants are more susceptible to copper than to sulphur, therefore treatment for fungus diseases must be undertaken with care.

Bordeaux Mixture: The manufacture of this should not be attempted at home by the amateur. It may be bought in paste form to be diluted as stated by the makers. It is always liable to cause a certain amount of russeting on apple and must not be used on Cox's Orange Pippin, Beauty of Bath, Duchess Favourite, Gladstone, Lady Sudeley, Millar's Seedling. Those who have large orchards to deal with, however, should see notes on Burgundy Mixture. The above trees should be sprayed with lime-sulphur at normal strength with the exception of Cox's Orange Pippin, which will only stand half-strength.

INSECTICIDES.

Carbolic Emulsion: A repellent for use against such pests as celery and carrot fly.

Carbolic acid	...	...	1 pint.
Soft Soap	...	...	1 lb.
Water	...	...	10 gal.

Dissolve the soap in some of the water already heated, churn in the carbolic, and then make up to 10 gal.

Caustic Soda: A somewhat obsolete method of winter washing, but nevertheless a very effective method for destroying moss and lichen and scale insects.

| Caustic Soda | ... | ... | 3 lb. |
| Water | ... | ... | 10 gal. |

Wear goggles and protect all exposed parts of the body when applying.

Hellebore Wash: Less poisonous than arsenate of lead and therefore often used for destroying caterpillars on quick-ripening fruit, now being superseded by nicotine and derris washes.

| Hellebore Powder | ... | 12 oz. |
| Water | ... ... | 3 gal. |

The powder remains in suspension, therefore the wash should be kept agitated while spraying. Its sticking powers can be improved by the addition of 4 oz. of flour.

Lead Arsenate: Used for all biting insects, but should not be applied to any fruit or vegetable just before gathering. Rather than manufacture at home, the amateur is advised to buy arsenate of lead paste. Quantities and dilution will be found on the tin.

Lime-Sulphur: This should be purchased in concentrated form from a reliable manufacturer. Use and dilute according to instructions supplied with it.

Nicotine Wash: For all insects such as aphides, pyella, and young caterpillars.

Nicotine	...	...	...	¾ oz.
Soft Soap	...	...	...	1 lb.
Water	...	...	...	10 gal.

Add the Nicotine after dissolving the soap, stirring well the while. Very poisonous and should be treated with the same care as arsenate of lead.

Paraffin Emulsion: For use as a repellent especially against certain vegetable pests.

Paraffin	...	...	...	1 pint.
Soap	...	...	...	1 lb.
Water	...	...	...	1 gal.

Dissolve the soap in the water after warming it, then slowly churn in the paraffin. Thorough emulsification may be obtained by means of a syringe. Bottle this stock solution off. For use, take one part of emulsion to from 10 to 20 parts of water, according to the hardiness of the plants to be treated.

Quassia Wash: A somewhat obsolete but, at the same time, an effective method for destroying greenfly.

Quassia Chips	...	...	1 lb.
Soft Soap ...	...	...	1 lb.
Water	...	...	10 gal.

Boil the chips in some of the water for two hours; dissolve the soap in hot water; strain off the chips, thoroughly mix the two liquids, make up to ten gallons.

Copper Sulphate: One pound of copper sulphate crushed and dissolved in ten gallons of water makes a good lethal spray for slugs. It can be used to soak the soil round plants subject to attack. The same mixture, used as a soil drench round roses, prevents the reappearance of Black Spot. It should be sprayed freely on the roses and soil in January.

FORSYTHIA (for-si'-thi-a. Oleaceæ). Deciduous flowering shrubs, producing a beautiful effect with long arching leafless branches, wreathed with a profusion of golden-yellow flowers, like little golden bells, from end to end, during March and April. Useful planted in the shrubbery or as a single specimen; can also be treated as a climber, thrives on a north wall. Perfectly hardy. Plant in autumn, in rich loamy soil. Cut well back after flowering. *Propagate* by cuttings taken in June or July in frame; also by layering.

SPECIES.

F. europæa. The Albanian Forsythia, 4–6 ft. Flowers pale cream.

F. intermedia. 6–9 ft. Hybrid (*F. suspensa* + *F. viridissima*). More suitable as a single specimen than for growing against walls, etc.

F. i. densifolia. A distinct form with shoots densely crowded with the flowers.

F. i. spectabilis. 6–10 ft. A seedling form, with extra large flowers of a deep yellow, and more abundantly produced

K

than in other forms. Unsurpassed as a specimen on a lawn. The most beautiful Forsythia, and worth a place in any garden. Easily increased by suckers, which are freely produced. Award of Garden Merit, R.H.S.

F. i. vitellina. Of erect habit and deep yellow flowers.

F. ovata (Korea). Flowers primrose-yellow.

F. suspensa (China). 8–10 ft. Of ram-

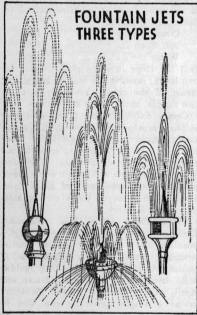

FOUNTAIN JETS THREE TYPES

Fountains give life to the garden. Here are three types of jets. They look best in the centre of a pool where sunshine catches the falling water.

bling habit and pendent branches. Suitable for training against a wall. Flowers golden-yellow in late March and April.

F. s. atrocaulis. Branches and shoots dark purplish.

F. s. Fortunei. Vigorous, of stiffer growth, with erect or arching shoots.

F. s. Sieboldii (China). Of bushier habit, and with pendent branches reaching to the ground, and taking root there.

F. viridissima (China). 5–8 ft. A sturdy, erect species flowering after the other Forsythias some time in April.

FOTHERGILLA (fother-gil'-la Hamamelidaceæ). Deciduous shrub from southern U.S.A., with fragrant flowers during May and April.

Culture.—Plant from October to March. They like a soil of moist, sandy loam and peat. *Propagate* by cuttings in late summer, by layering in autumn or by seeds in sandy peaty soil in heat in spring.

Species.

F. Gardenii (alnifolia). 3 ft. Flowers white, fragrant, before the leaves; during March and April. Leaves alder-like, turning in autumn to dark red and scarlet, persisting for some weeks. Dislikes a heavy soil, preferring one of sandy loam and peat.

F. major. 6–9 ft. Fragrant. White flowers in spring and occasionally again in autumn. Leaves grey and bluish-white beneath, tinted bright golden-yellow before falling.

F. monticola. Of more spreading habit than the preceding, and the under surface of leaves not so white. Foliage very attractive in autumn, turning to shades of orange-scarlet and crimson.

FOUNTAIN JETS. *See* Water Garden.

FOXGLOVE. *See* Digitalis.

FOXTAIL LILY. *See* Eremurus.

FRAGARIA. *See* Strawberry.

FRANCOA (Bridal Wreath). Saxifragaceæ. A half-hardy greenhouse perennial with sprays of white flowers about 2–2½ ft. Very decorative and related to the saxifrages of the rock garden.

Cultivation.—Should be treated as a biennial for conservatory decoration, sowing the seeds in early spring in gentle heat to flower during the summer of the following year. The soil should be composed of good loam, enriched with leafmould and a little complete fertiliser, being well opened with sharp sand.

Species.

F. ramosa, white. *F. soncifolia,* pinkish-purple.

FRANKENIA (Sea Heath). Frankeniaceæ. Hardy evergreen flowering plant, of creeping habit. These plants thrive best on dry sunny rockeries or borders in a light sandy soil. Plant in October or April.

Propagate by seeds sown in April in

cold frame, by division of plants in October or April, and by cuttings.

SPECIES.

F. lævis. Rose flowers in July and August. 3 in.

FRAXINELLA. *See* DICTAMNUS.

FRAXINUS (frax'-in-us. Oleaceæ). Ash. Deciduous trees of rapid growth; valuable for their stately form and fine foliage. Some are valuable for timber.

Culture.—Plant in November in good rich soil, preferably one containing plenty of lime or chalk. Ash thrive remarkably well in calcareous district, but will "do" in almost any soil; but where they are grown for timber, rich soil is necessary. Pruning consists in thining out branches when needed. *Propagate* by seed sown in frame in autumn or outside in spring. When about two years old transplant the seedlings to a nursery bed, where they should remain until large enough to be planted in their permanent positions. Grafting is used for the garden varieties.

SPECIES.

F. excelsior. Common Ash. 100–140 ft. Native of this country, also Europe and the Caucasus. A very valuable timber tree, producing wood of great toughness and durability.

F. e. aurea. Golden Bark Ash, young shoots yellow, older bark yellowish.

F. e. a. pendula. Forms a fine flat umbrella-shaped head.

F. ornus. Manna Ash of S. Europe. 50–65 ft. White flowers very freely produced in May.

FREESIA (frē'zia. Iridaceæ). Greenhouse bulbous plants, deciduous. From the Cape of Good Hope.

Modern freesias are descendants of the white *Freesia refracta*, the rosy pink *Freesia Armstrongii*, discovered in South Africa in 1898, and the yellow *Freesia aurea.* A short time ago freesias were known only as modest flowers of creamy-buff colouring, valued chiefly for their fragrance, which has been likened to the scent of apricot jam. To-day a greenhouse can be filled with freesia blooms of blue, gold, pink, mauve and cream. Some of the new hybrids are almost scentless, but as one of the old scented varieties will perfume the whole green-house, one can afford to substitute colour for perfume in some of the pots. Freesias need no artificial heat for cultivation in this country. They grow in the open in Cornwall, and they would succeed outdoors in any warm sheltered position, with some slight protection such as coconut fibre spread over the soil during the coldest months.

The first pottings of the early varieties for cultivation in the cold greenhouse can be made during July, and freesias can be potted up at intervals right on to December. By this method, a succession of bloom is obtained through the first four months of the year. The earliest freesias for potting come from abroad. British-grown freesias in new colours are not usually obtainable until about the middle of August.

Equal parts of sandy loam, leaf-mould and well-crumbled cow manure make a good compost for freesias. One of the most successful raisers of modern varieties never uses stable manure, but relies on a mixture of three parts good loam, one part sandy loam, and two parts coarse silver sand, with a little bone meal.

Plant the corms 2 in. deep in the pots. Place these in a cold frame until the plants begin to grow, i.e., about six weeks. Do not cover them with ashes or fibre in the way that most spring flowers can be covered. When growth commences, remove the pots to the greenhouse shelf, where they should stand near the glass. As the flower buds appear, a dose of liquid manure can be given, and at this stage it may also be desirable to add thin sticks for the support of the flowers.

Freesias, as already stated, can easily be increased from seed, and home-saved seed will often be found to be most satisfactory. It can be sown in August or September, immediately it is ripe, or it can be saved and sown at other times. To obtain the best results, soak the seeds for twenty-four hours before sowing. Use 5 in. pots, and soil consisting of well-sieved sandy loam and leaf-mould. Stand the pots in a cold frame exposed to the rays of the sun, and when the seedlings appear thin them to five or six in each pot. They would object to transplanting, and must be grown in the same pot until they flower.

After the tops have died down, however, the corms should be allowed to dry off. Offsets can be replanted separately in order to increase the stock. These offsets will of course be true to type, and if the variety of freesia is particularly good the offsets should be carefully labelled when they are planted.

FRENCH MARIGOLD OR TAGETES

Many people dislike French Marigolds because of their quaint odour, but they are free-flowering and gaily coloured and make splendid edgings to summer borders.

FREMONTIA (frē-mon′-ti-a. Sterculiaceæ). Deciduous, or semi-evergreen shrub from California, bearing large cup-shaped, orange-yellow flowers, 2 in. across, throughout the summer months. Leaves in shape like a Mallow.

Culture.—Plant in poor soil and full sun. Best against a wall, especially in cold northern gardens. *Propagate* by seeds, and by cuttings in spring under a hand-glass or bell-glass. A few young plants should be kept growing on in pots, as it is not a long-lived plant, although under

favourable conditions it will reach to a height of 25–30 ft.

F. californica. The only species. Discovered in 1846 by Col. Frémont.

FRENCH GARDENING is a form of gardening which has been practised in Great Britain for some time. It is an intensive form of gardening dealing chiefly with crops such as cucumbers, melons, tomatoes, chicory, mushrooms, lettuces, beans, turnips, carrots, radishes, etc. The top spit of soil is manured until it becomes a black mould. The crops, planted in this soil, are forced under frames and cloches. A reliable book should be consulted on the subject by those interested commercially in this form of gardening. (*See* INTENSIVE CULTURE.)

FRENCH HONEYSUCKLE. *See* HEDYSARUM.

FRENCH MARIGOLD. *See* TAGETES.

FRINGE-TREE. *See* CHIONANTHUS.

FRITILLARIA (Fritillary). Liliaceæ. Hardy bulbs suitable for borders or for naturalising in turf. All fritillaries succeed well in ordinary deep rich soil. They should be planted from 4–5 in. deep and 6–8 ft. apart in autumn. A top-dressing of decayed manure annually after the flowers fade will assist them. Fritillaries do not like frequent disturbance, and should be left alone for at least four years without transplanting. They can, if preferred, be grown in pots in the greenhouse in soil composed of loam, leaf-mould, decayed manure and sand. They can also be raised from seed, but the seeds do not flower for some years. Of the species cultivated *F. meleagris* or *Snake's Head Fritillary* is mostly used for naturalising, particularly in wild parts of the garden. Others are: *F. coccinea* with red flowers, *F. Elwessii*, green and brown. (*See also* CROWN IMPERIALS.)

FRITILLARY. *See* FRITILLARIA.

FRONDS. A term used only of ferns to describe the parts that correspond to leaves.

FROST. Frost is the gardener's foe and friend. It breaks up his heavy soil and leaves it loose and friable ready for sowing and planting in the spring. This is caused by the moisture in the soil expanding when thawed. But frost will harm his plants unless preventative measures are taken.

Tender plants should be protected during the winter months by means of cloches or wattle hurdles. Straw or bracken spread round the base of tender bush roses and climbers will be useful. Frozen plants should not be exposed to the sun, but should be syringed with cold water. Greenhouse plants can be protected by spreading sheets of newspaper over them at night.

FRUIT CULTURE. General Remarks. —The great truism that a thing which is worth doing at all is worth doing well, is severely applicable to fruit culture.

There is nothing very difficult in the cultivation of fruit, which can and ought to be grown in every garden. In these times the value of all kinds of fruit as diet is far more appreciated than it was a century ago. The science of fruit-growing has advanced with great rapidity. Twenty years ago trees were planted and fruit was not expected to be borne in economical quantities for many years. To-day, thanks to the splendid research work by our experimental stations, stocks which have a dwarfing and immediate fruit-bearing influence have been produced, and there has been a considerable saving, not only in the time during which a tree takes to come into bearing, but also in the space which each tree requires for full expansion. These remarks apply to all hardy orchard fruits. The cultivation of soft fruits has never been difficult. Currants, gooseberries, raspberries, and other hybrid berries require only fair soil, firm planting at the correct distances apart, and strict attention paid to correct pruning. Strawberries are not difficult providing that a reliable strain is purchased in the first place, and attention paid to the small cultural details outlined.

The following points should be carefully considered by those who contemplate fruit culture.

(1) **Purchase of Stock.**—It is of the utmost importance that the original stock should be purchased from a suitable source. If a nurseryman cannot guarantee that his orchard trees are worked upon particular named root-stocks, he should not be consulted. It is as well to place the matter in the hands of a reliable man. If he be informed as to soil and situation he will be in a position to assist not only in the selection of varieties, but also to inform as to what stocks are the most suitable. It is also important to purchase soft fruits from a reliable source. This remark most particularly applies to strawberries. Growers who specialise in the culture of this fruit are in a position to offer vigorous, disease-free and fruitful strains, and in order to encourage the sale of such stock only, the Ministry of

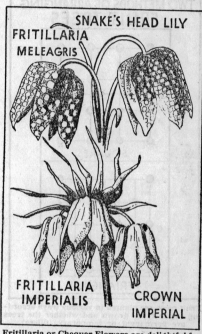

Fritillaria or Chequer Flowers are delightful for naturalising in grass. Crown Imperial adds colour to the mixed flower border in early spring.

Agriculture yearly visit nurseries and issue certificates to those stocks which are of sufficiently high standard.

(2) **Planting.**—Always plant firmly. More trees are lost every year through insecure planting than from any other cause. A mulch of strawy manure following planting protects roots against drying out during cold March winds, and assists trees in making a good start.

(3) **Spraying.**—The importance of spraying cannot be over-estimated. Most

amateurs shrink from carrying out any programme at all, because they do not understand the various uses of the different sprays. Trees are frequently left until they are terribly afflicted with some pest or disease, when the trouble becomes doubly difficult to eradicate. Pests and diseases are fully dealt with elsewhere, but it should here be mentioned that "prevention is better than cure." At least two sprayings

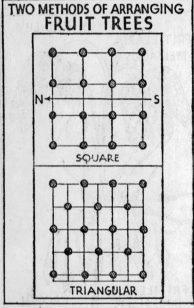

TWO METHODS OF ARRANGING
FRUIT TREES

SQUARE

TRIANGULAR

Fruit trees are planted in various ways according to the types grown and whether the trees are permanent or temporary (fillers).

should be given in fruit gardens every year. This is no mere waste of time, but a common fairness to one's own trees and to those of neighbour:, and probably also to all commercial growers who have to depend upon clean fruit for a livelihood. The importance of the following two sprays should be looked up and their uses thoroughly understood.

(a) *Tar Distillate Washes.* Applied during December and January to apples, pears, plums, cherries, currants, of all kinds, gooseberries and raspberries. This wash controls greenfly in the egg stage, eggs of harmful caterpillars, apple suckers,

Capsid Bug (to a certain degree) and also appears to control American Gooseberry Mildew to a certain extent.

(b) *Lime Sulphur Wash.* This is principally used on apples and pears as a preventive against Black Scab. It also controls Red Spider, Bud Mite of black and red currants, Apple Canker, Brown Rot, Blossom Wilt and Coral Spot fungus. It is not suggested that the use of this spray will eradicate the above diseases once they are apparent. Its use is suggested as a preventive measure, and is most important. For fuller details *see under* SPRAYING.

(4) **Pruning.**—Correct pruning is most important. If the instructions given are carefully carried out, regular crops of good fruit should be produced. Bear in mind the two important points:

(a) Vigorous trees are not fruitful ones. Prune them lightly to tone down their vigour.

(b) Stunted and weakly trees may fruit themselves to death. Prune them hard and remove some of the fruit spurs during the winter pruning.

(5) **Thinning.**—Thinning of fruit is a most important point. It has not been dealt with under each separate fruit in order to save space and prevent repetition. Failure to thin fruit is the cause of intermittent cropping. Whilst a tree matures its crop it is also forming its fruit blossoms for next year's crop. If a very heavy crop is borne one year it may take one or even two seasons to get over the exhaustive effects. For this reason, trees which are not thinned settle down to biennial or triennial bearing. It is far better to have a reasonable crop each year than to have a heavy one in one year and none the next. Thinning should be done gradually in the case of apples and gooseberries. Some of the last of these to be removed are useful for culinary purposes. For the final thinning apples and pears should not have more than two fruits to each spur, and spurs which are allowed to bear should not be nearer than 6 in. apart. The thinning of grapes and peaches is dealt with under the headings of each. Unless required for exhibition, raspberries, strawberries and currants need not be thinned. In "heavy" plum years it is sometimes necessary to

remove half the crop. Vigorous trees do not require such severe thinning as those which grow less strongly.

(6) **Manuring.**—Correct manuring calls for careful discretion. Heavily-bearing trees which do not make much growth, always benefit by an annual mulch of decayed manure, which should be applied a fortnight before flowering. Vigorous trees should not be manured. Potash in

appearance, this is undoubtedly the cause of the trouble. In these instances, nitrate of lime should be applied in early spring at the rate of 1 oz. per square yard. *See also* PROPAGATING PLANTS AND FERTILISERS.

FRUIT, GRADING AND PACKING. The last generation has seen in this country an enormous advance in the methods employed for grading and packing. Com-

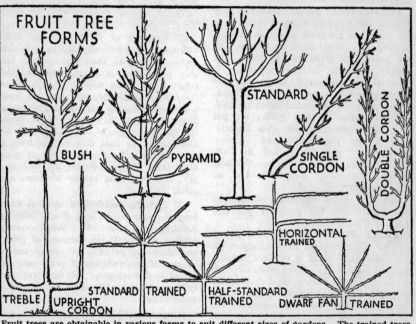

FRUIT TREE FORMS

BUSH

PYRAMID

STANDARD

SINGLE CORDON

DOUBLE CORDON

HORIZONTAL TRAINED

TREBLE UPRIGHT CORDON

STANDARD TRAINED

HALF-STANDARD TRAINED

DWARF FAN TRAINED

Fruit trees are obtainable in various forms to suit different sizes of gardens. The trained trees are best where space is limited, but they need more care and attention.

some form should be given at regular intervals, especially in light soils, which are naturally deficient. Sulphate of potash is one of the most readily available forms and should be applied in spring at the rate of 1 cwt. to the acre, or ½ oz. to every square yard. Potash plays a vital point in all fruit production, increasing colour, size, flavour, and keeping qualities. It also makes trees more resistant to disease. Old-established orchards growing in grass are frequently starved for want of lime in some form, even in districts overlying chalky ground. If little growth is made, and the foliage has a yellow and sickly

mercial growers in this country found that the competition provided by colonial and foreign fruit, which was marketed in attractive form, made it necessary to do the same style of packing. This has been a move very much in the right direction.

English fruit is well known to be the finest procurable, but it is up to the growers to see that it is put on the market in good condition. Grading machines are used now by all up-to-date growers of apples. There are different types of machines, some grading by weight, others by size.

Packages are divided into two classes. Returnable ones generally consist of wicker baskets which carry either one or one-half bushel. The non-returnable ones are made of wood, and are now generally considered to be the best. The sizes for non-returnables are standardised. A national mark scheme is now under force for apples and pears. Full particulars of this scheme are obtainable from the Ministry of Agriculture, Whitehall Place, London.

An authorised grower assumes very definite and statutory responsibilities as to the quality of his fruit, and each package bearing the national mark must agree with the particulars given on the label, and comply with the defined standards.

Cherries, strawberries and plums are also governed by a national mark scheme. Plums are generally packed in wicker half-bushels, whilst the best grades are put into 12 lb. non-returnable chip baskets. Cherries are similarly packed. Gooseberries may also be packed in half-bushels or in 12 lb. chips, but the best dessert fruit should be put in 1 lb. or 2 lb. punnets.

Red and black currants, blackberries and loganberries are generally put into 4 lb. or 6 lb. chip baskets.

FRUIT POLLINATION. This is a subject which deserves more consideration than one might think it requires, because botany teaches us that practically all fruits in order to mature, need the transfer of pollen from the stamens to the stigma or stigmas, and that fertilisation of the ovule or ovules is in most cases essential. Granted good cultivation, drainage, control of fungus diseases and insects, fruit production is still dependent on efficient pollination and favourable weather. Favourable weather is mild, sunny and calm with occasional warm showers. Frost may destroy the open blossoms; but a more frequent cause of a short crop is dull, windy weather with low temperature and frequent heavy rain, thus preventing the insects visiting the blossoms; this was apparently the cause of most of the small fruit crops in 1932.

We may divide our hardy fruits into at least four classes with particular reference to pollination.

(1) Those that are **Perfectly Self-fruitful** with their own pollen, but which still need the transfer of the pollen from stamens to stigmas by insects, include: gooseberries, red, white, and black currants (the pollen of these fruits is glutinous and globular), strawberries, raspberries, blackberries and a few plums (such as Pershore Yellow Egg, Pershore Purple or Martin's Seedling and Victoria), Morello cherry and peaches. These can each be planted alone, and a good crop may be expected provided the weather is favourable and there are sufficient pollinating insects.

(2) Varieties of fruit that are **Self-unfruitful,** or practically so, i.e., do not mature fruit with their own pollen, but only with pollen of another variety; the result is the same whether the pollen is from the same flower, same tree, or from a tree of the same variety growing at a distance because they are all of the same family. The degree of self-sterility may be absolute or one fruit may mature from a thousand or a hundred blossoms as with May Duke cherry. Fruits that mature, say, one fruit from twenty blossoms are called.

(3) **Partially Self-fruitful,** such as Conference among pears; Irish Peach, Miller's Seedling and Rev. W. Wilks among apples; about half the varieties of plum, one third the varieties of apples and a quarter of the varieties of pears may be placed in this category. All these varieties fruit more abundantly with pollen of another variety.

(4) **Incompatible Varieties.** A few varieties of plums and a good many varieties of cherries will not mature fruit with pollen of certain other varieties. In England it is considered that in apples and pears all varieties will cross-pollinate efficiently; but in America three or four varieties of apple are found to be incompatible, and in Sweden two or three kinds of pears.

It seems quite probable there is some preference in pollen and that some varieties are better pollenisers than others; thus Cox's Orange Pippin fertilises Bramley's Seedling well, but Bramley appears to be a bad polleniser for Cox; Cox in many cases seems to be a good polleniser for other varieties. I have recently been told of an orchard composed of Bramley and Newton which, although the trees are well-grown, healthy and blossom well, do not crop well. Doyenné du Comice pear seems to be a specially good polleniser for other varieties.

In germination trials of pollen, Gravenstein apple gave a very feeble germination, and the same with Alexandre Lucas and Pitmaston Duchess among pears.

The advice in planting an orchard is to choose two or three varieties that flower about the same time, and avoid planting very early- with late-flowering kinds (e.g., Irish Peach has its petals fallen before Crawley Beauty commences to flower) and *change the varieties every two or three rows.*

The smallest number of the polleniser variety recommended is every third tree in every third row.

With a garden there may be trees that act as good pollenisers in adjoining gardens; but if this is not the case in apples, pears, plums and cherries, the result will probably be better if trees of different varieties are planted rather than several trees of a single variety.

The most successful fruit garden I know is four acres of land enclosed by a circular wall 10 ft. high, against which a large number of varieties of the different fruits are trained. This gives the trees various aspects, which influences the relative time of flowering. Bush and espalier trees are grown in the centre and, last but not least, three strong hives of bees are kept. Here all varieties seem to fruit well. This garden wins prizes for apples and pears at the Royal Horticultural Society's shows than any other in Britain.

In a garden it may be of advantage, and will certainly be of interest, if some of the blossoms are *pollenated by hand* with pollen of another variety, using either a camel's-hair brush, a rabbit's tail affixed to a stick, or forceps holding the stamens. An espalier pear tree, rather shaded, that had not borne for years, was thus treated and yielded a good crop.

It is certainly worth while hand-pollenating peach trees grown out of doors; they flower so early that few insects are generally about. The *peach* is self-fruitful so fruits perfectly with pollen of same tree.

Apples. Among the most *Self-fruitful* may be mentioned:

Early. Irish Peach, Keswick Codlin, Golden Spire, Egremont Russet, Stirling Castle, Devonshire Quarrenden.

Mid-season. Benn's Red, Christmas Pearmain, Miller's Seedling, Cellini, John Bownie Crab, St. Everard, Rev. W. Wilks.

Late. Lord Derby, Crawley Beauty.

Among those that are usually somewhat *Self-fruitful* are:

Early. Tower of Glamis, Bismarck, White Transparent, Warner's King.

Mid-season. Lord Grosvenor, Ribston, Baumann's Red Winter Reinette, Lord Hindlip, Early Victoria, Worcester Pearmain, James Grieve, Charles Ross, Gladstone, Sturmer Pippin, Pott's Seedling, Bramley, Ecklinville, Peasgood, Lady Sudeley, King of the Pippins, Allington, Encore.

Late. Rival, Grenadier, Annie Elizabeth, Chelmsford Wonder, Newton Wonder, Orleans Reinette, Golden Noble, American Mother.

Amongst apples that are practically *Self-unfruitful* may be mentioned:

Early. Manx Codlin, Brownlee's Russet, Duchess Favourite.

Mid-season. Beauty of Bath, Norfolk Beauty, Early Julian, The Queen, Cox's Orange Pippin.

Late. Blenheim Orange, Lane's Prince Albert, Barnack Beauty, Red Joaneting, Wellington, May Queen, Gascoigne's Scarlet, King Edward VII, Graham's Royal Jubilee, Court Pendu Plat.

Because an apple is classified as self-fruitful it is not necessarily more valuable —or a self-sterile variety less valuable—on that account, but it is more important to inter-plant the latter. However, both in America and in Britain it is found that no variety can advantageously be planted alone in block, but that all varieties fruit better if they are intermixed.

In the case of Cox's Orange when planted alone in block it has been found to crop very little, but the yield has been wonderfully increased after interplanting Worcester Pearmain, or regrafting trees or boughs with this variety; it is, however, quite likely other kinds flowering about the same time would do equally well, but the fact that Cox and Worcester fruit well together is ascertained.

Pears. The following gives an idea of the more self-fruitful pears, those that are occasionally self-fruitful and those that seem to be self-unfruitful, placed in approximate order of flowering.

The more Self-fruitful.—Doyenné Boussoch, Conference (the most self-fruitful pear), Marie Louise d'Uccle, Hacon's Incomparable, Hessle, Marguerite Marillat.

Others that mature fruit with own pollen to a smaller extent are:

Doyenné d'Été Jargonelle, Beurré Diel, Verulam, Brown Beurré, Beurré Superfin, Duchesse d'Angoulême, Beurré d'Amanlis, Souvenir du Congrès, Bergamot Esperen, Durondeau, Petite Marguerite, Uvedale's St. Germain, Bellissime d'Hiver, Louise Bonne de Jersey, Chalk Triomphe de Vinne, Williams' Bon Chrétien, Dr. Jules Guyot, Winter Windsor (stewing), Marie Louise, Glou Morçeau, Pitmaston Duchess, Doyenné du Comice, Swan's Egg, Blickling.

Varieties that appear to be *Self-unfruitful* include: Madame Treyve, Thompson, Princess, Conseilleur de la Cour, Vicar of Winkfield, Marie Benoist, Beurré Clairgeau, Belle Julie, Beurré Superfin, Olivier de Serres, Grosse Calebasse, Clapp's Favourite, Emile d'Heyst, Catillac (stewing), Fertility, Josephine de Malines, Winter Nelis, Beurré Capiaumont, General Todleben.

Like apples, it would be unwise to plant a block of any single variety of pear, not even Conference: they should be planted with another pear—not too far off—in flower at the same time.

For pollenating Doyenné du Comice (our finest pear, called "Angel's Food" in Covent Garden) the following are found to be good pollenisers: Fertility, Glou Morçeau, Triomphe de Vienne, Hessle, Emile d'Heyst. Doyenné du Comice seems to be a good polleniser for other varieties such as Glou Morçeau, Louise Bonne of Jersey, Catillac, Emile d'Heyst Williams' Bon Chretien.

Plums. Among the *most Self-fruitful plums* may be mentioned (placed in approximate order of flowering): *Early*—Red Mirabelle or cherry plum, Prince of Wales,

Merryweather Damson, Langley Bullace, Monarch, Black Bullace, Denniston's Superb; *Mid-season*—Early Transparent, Bradley's King of Damsons, Victoria, Golden Transparent, Pershore Yellow Egg, Pershore Purple or Martin's Seedling, White Bullace, White Magnum Bonum, Czar, Rivers' Transparent Gage, Shepherd's Bullace, Kentish Bush and Gisborne's Early.

Of those *less Self-fruitful* may be mentioned: *Early*—Yellow Mirabelle, Bittern, Mallard Curlew, Blue Rock, Utility, Reine Claude de Bavay; *Mid-season*—Rivers' Early Prolific, Early Orleans, Farleigh Damson, Burbank's Giant Prune, Belgian Purple, Cambridge Gage, Cox's Emperor, Prince Englebert; *Late*—Oullin's Golden Gage, Stint, Belle de Louvain.

Whilst among the *Self-unfruitful* may be mentioned: *Early*—Grand Duke, Jefferson's Gage, Black Diamond, Coe's Golden Drop, Count Althann's Gage; *Mid-season*—President, Admiral, Old Greengage, Wyedale, Late Orange, Bryanston Gage; *Late*—Washington Gage, Pond's Seedling, and Sultan.

The above list is obtained from research by the John Innes Horticultural Institute, the Royal Horticultural Society, and by personal research.

All plums, except perhaps Pershore Yellow and Pershore Purple Egg plums, crop best among other varieties. It is of special importance to inter-mix other varieties among the plums enumerated as self-unfruitful, as among these are the notably shy-bearing varieties.

Suggestions as to good cross-pollenisers: Rivers' Early Prolific with Prince of Wales, Czar or Monarch. Pond's Seedling with Czar, Kentish Bush or Belle de Louvain. Belle de Louvain with Czar or Kentish Bush. Monarch with Rivers' Early Prolific, or Prince of Wales. President with Czar. Victoria with Czar. Golden Gage with Pershore Purple.

Cherries. A great deal of valuable research on the pollination of cherries has been made at the John Innes Horticultural Institute at Merton, Surrey, by several experimenters, especially Mr. M. B. Crane. These experiments have been made under glass. Mr. Cecil H. Hooper has made his experiments in cherry orchards, and the following are examples of a few varieties. (*See also* the JOURNALS OF POMOLOGY AND HORTICULTURAL SCIENCE.)

VARIETY AND GOOD POLLENISERS.

Early flowering :

Novi de Guben + Early Rivers, Black Tartarian, Turk.

Early Rivers + Turk, Baumann's May, Governor Wood, Bigarreau de Schrechen, Waterloo.

Black Tartarian + Noir de Guben, Turk, Governor Wood.

Old Black Heart + Early Rivers, Bigarreau de Schrechen.

Turk + Early Rivers, Emperor Francis, Waterloo.

Elton + Knight's Early Black, Black Eagle, Monstreuse de Mizel.

Governor Wood + Turk, Knight's Early Black.

Early Rivers + Novi de Guben, Napoleon Noble.

Emperor Francis + Turk, Knight's Early Black, Governor Wood.

Mid-season flowering :

Monstreuse de Mezel + Emperor Francis, Black Eagle.

Bedford Prolific + Governor Wood, Turk, Elton, Frogmore, Waterloo, Noble.

Black Eagle + Turk, Frogmore, Napoleon, Amber or Kentish Bigarreau.

Knight's Early Black + Bigarreau de Schrechen, Baumann's May, Waterloo, Noble.

Bigarreau de Schrechen + Knight's Early Black, Black Eagle, Roundel, Napoleon, Turk.

Late flowering :

Roundel + Napoleon, Amber Bigarreau, Florence, Emperor Francis.

Frogmore + Roundel, Amber Bigarreau, Noble, Black Eagle.

Waterloo + Knight's Early Black, Amber Bigarreau, Black Tartarian, May Duke.

Napoleon + Waterloo, Amber Bigarreau, Florence, May Duke, Bigarreau de Schrechen, Black Eagle.

Amber or Kentish Bigarreau + Frogmore, Florence, Napoleon, Waterloo, Roundel.

Florence + Amber Bigarreau, Waterloo, Napoleon.

May Duke + Late Duke, Frogmore, Black Eagle.

Noble (St. Margaret or Tradescant's Heart) + Frogmore, Bedford Prolific, Napoleon, Geante d'Hedelfingen, Morello, Kentish Red.

Geante d'Hedelfingen + Florence, Noble, Napoleon, Black Eagle.

Flemish Red + Morello, Kentish Red.

Kentish Red + Morello, Flemish Red.

Morello is perfectly self-fruitful, no gain by cross-pollination.

The following varieties are found by Mr. M. B. Crane and Mr. W. J. C. Laurence to be incompatible, i.e., do not cross-pollinate one another and should not be planted together without other varieties.

Group I. Bedford Prolific, Black Eagle, Black Tartarian, Early Rivers, Knight's Early Black, Roundel.

Group. II. Bigarreau de Schrechen, Frogmore, Guigne de Winkler, Waterloo.

Group III. Windsor, Napoleon, Emperor Francis.

Group IV. White Bigarreau, Amber or Kentish Bigarreau and Lugwig's Bigarreau.

Group V. Late Black, Bohemian Black, Turk or Turkey Heart.

For the results of more recent research and experiments, see the John Innes leaflet "The Fertility Rules in Fruit Planting," published by the John Innes Horticultural Institution in December, 1940.

Insect Visitors to Fruit Blossoms. Closely related to the structure of fruit flowers and their pollination and fertilisation is the study of the insects that visit them and their habits. The pollination of the blossoms and the production of fruit is found by experiment and observation to be almost entirely dependent on insects. Although there are many insects that visit these blossoms, the more important belong to the Bee family, their special value being their furry bodies, their search for nectar and pollen, and the fact that they keep to one class of flower each journey; they are therefore specially valuable in cross-pollinating. Hive bees, bumble bees, and the smaller wild bees are most valuable insects.

In many parts, especially if the acreage of fruit is not large, there may be sufficient of wild bees, especially if there are woods, common and hedge banks where they can make their nests; but high cultivation often destroys their natural homes. Certainly on most fruit farms there are not sufficient pollinating insects for the requirements, and it is wise to have some hives of bees interspersed among the plantations, so that the bees can come out when weather is genial. It is marvellous the amount of pollinating that can be done in a short time if bees are on the spot. Even if there are several varieties in an orchard, if the weather is unfavourable and pollination is entirely dependent on wild insects, the crop will be extraordinarily small; whereas if there are one or more strong hives of bees the result is much better.

Many examples of these facts might be quoted. One garden that for ten years had hives of bees had far better crops of fruit then, than during the last three years without bees. It is said that fruit may be grown even in smoky districts if bees are kept. The recommendation is one strong hive of bees per acre. The cherry and gooseberry crops are specially increased by bees.

FUCHSIA (fū-shi-a. Onagraceæ). Deciduous flowering shrubs of great beauty and brilliancy during summer and autumn. In the milder districts, like the Isle of Wight and Cornwall, Devonshire, etc., they become one of the most brilliant features of the garden. The plants will often get cut down to the ground, but shoots spring freely from the old stools in spring. fuchsias grow in ordinary garden soil, and cuttings root quite readily under glass.

SPECIES.

F. coccinea (Brazil). Large violet carolla, red sepals.

F. macrostemma (magellanica). South American. Beautiful long scarlet calyx and purple petals. This is the type of the garden fuchsias.

F. m. corallina (*exoniensis*). Showy flowers with bright red sepals and purple petals.

F. m. gracilis (minor). Flowers red and purple from July to frost.

F. m. pumila. A dwarf compact variety of pyramidal habit, purple flowers, suitable for rock garden.

F. parviflora (Mexico). Flowers coral red passing to crimson. Needs protection in all but mildest districts.

F. reflexa. Dwarf species with cerise flowers. Needs protection in cold districts.

F. Riccartonii. The hardiest of all fuchsias, and in mild districts much used as a hedge plant. Flowers crimson and purple, freely borne throughout late summer and autumn, making a most striking feature in the garden at that season.

FULLER'S TEAZLE. *See* DIPSACUS.

FUMIGATING. A method used in greenhouses to exterminate certain pests such as white fly.

The two principal methods are by nicotine and cyanide, but as fumigating materials conveniently put up may now be purchased from any reliable manufacturer, we need not go into the method of preparation. The only thing necessary when purchasing the material is to state the cubic contents of the house. It must be remembered that if fumigation is to be effective the house should be air-tight, also it should be remembered the fumes are poisonous and the house must not be entered while full of fumes. After fumigating it is as well to open the door for a period before entering. Watering should be dispensed with for 24 hours before fumigation, as moisture may cause scorch. On no account should conservatories with doors leading into dwelling rooms be fumigated as the poison is likely to find its way into the house.

FUMIGATION. The vaporisation in plant houses of preparations usually containing nicotine for the purpose of cleansing and disinfecting. A periodical fumigation, at about fortnightly intervals, is beneficial, as it prevents any pests from becoming established.

FUNGOUS DISEASES. The lowly plants known as "Fungi" cause many diseases in plants. They grow from spores and if conditions are suitable they are liable to attack plants at any time.

A few of the main causes of fungous diseases are: Weak constitution of the plants; excessive moisture; overcrowding; absence of sufficient potash manure.

Certain plants are very susceptible to attack; for example, potatoes and wart disease; but the main diseases are dealt with under the crops and plants on which they are most likely to be found.

As to cures the best is of course prevention. When certain elementary precautions are taken the plants are much more likely to be immune.

Keep all plants clean; burn diseased leaves and twigs; keep down weeds which are frequently disease carriers; maintain proper balance of fertilisers in the soil.

When plants are grown under glass ventilate according to their requirements and observe the same precautions as for the hardy plants. Once the plants are attacked the following remedies should prove beneficial:

Liver of sulphur, 1 oz. to 3 gal. of water. The solution is sprayed over the foliage. Potassium permanganate diluted to a pale brandy colour. Bordeaux Mixture (see FORMULÆ) is a most effective control of "blight," the fungous disease so often found in potatoes.

Lime in sufficient quantities is also a valuable asset in the soil. To prevent "damping off" in seedlings the soil should be sterilised by using Formaldehyde in the proportion of 4 oz. to 1 gal. of water or by pouring boiling water over the soil and allowing it to cool before use.

Above all the old dictum of the gardener, "get your garden clean and keep it clean," will be invaluable advice to follow.

FUNKIA (Plaintain Lily). Liliaceæ. Hardy herbaceous flowering plants with ornamental foliage. Deciduous. Fragrant flowers and large, deep green or variegated white and yellow leaves. Any ordinary soil enriched with decayed manure in open, sunny, well-drained borders will do for their cultivation. Plant in spring or autumn. Top dress annually with decayed manure. Cultivated in pots these plants require a compost of 2 parts loam, 1 part well-decayed manure and river sand. Plant in pots in spring and stand in the cold frame during the winter, and in the greenhouse during summer. Water moderately in winter, freely in summer. Make an application of liquid manure while the plants are flowering.

Propagate by division of crowns in spring or autumn.

SPECIES.

F. Fortunei. Lilac flowers in July. Height, 18 in.

F. lancifolia. Lilac flowers in August and its varieties *alba* (white), *albo* marginata (leaves edged silvery-white), *undulata* (leaves waved) and *variegata* (leaves blotched with white). Height, 9 in.

F. ovata (syn. *F. cærulea*). Blue flowers from May to July, and its varieties *aurea* (golden-leaved) and *marginata* (leaves edged creamy-white, and much variegated). Height, 1 ft.

F. Sieboldiana (syn. *F. cordata*). White and lilac flowers in summer. Height, 2 ft.

F. subcordata (Corfu Lily; syn. *F. grandiflora*). White flowers in August. Height, 1 ft.

FURNITURE, GARDEN. What is the best type of garden seat? The answer is by no means simple for every garden differs in appearance and use, and the possibilities among modern productions are immense.

Steel furniture has now made its appearance. It is light, easily portable, and takes up only a little room. Some steel chairs are of the nesting pattern. They fit one inside the other, like nests of tables, and a complete set takes up the space of one ordinary chair.

Other types of garden seats, such as canvas, are also useful where accommodation is limited. Canvas furnishings include many different colours.

Wickerwork is universally popular, because of its lightness and portability. The willow wicker garden furniture is the cheapest kind. In this material, which harmonises with every garden scheme, tables, chairs, baskets, shelters, fences and a variety of other useful articles are made. It is not satisfactory unless it can be kept under cover when not in use, as otherwise strands of the cane tend to decay and chairs that have to support heavy weights then collapse.

A better-finished article is made from thin whole cane, woven to comfortable designs. These chairs are more comfortable than any other type of garden seat, are very lasting in wear, and so neat and artistic that they can be used both indoors and out.

The more permanent types of garden furniture should have a definite place in the garden design. They are generally heavy and unwieldy, and therefore should not have to be moved. The site for permanent seats will have been chosen when the plan of the garden is first made, and, before the seat is actually placed, some attention should be given to the surround. For instance, if a seat of permanent type is placed direct on a lawn, the grass will soon wear away from the spot beneath the seat, and a muddy and unsightly patch will be the result.

Slabs of stone, crazy paving, or a patch of gravel would prevent this, but if the gravel patch is the choice, care must be given to its level. The surface should be slightly above the elevation of the grass, so that water never stands on it. A slight fall in gravel from front to back is the most effective way of preventing the collection of water.

The site for the seat will determine to some extent the size and design of the seat itself. For instance, as the terminal of a garden walk, a straight seat of solid appearance, painted or stained, would be appropriate.

A stone seat would be suitable if near a stone-edged pond, or on a stone terrace.

Such a seat will be more ornamental than useful in this cold climate, unless the seat is sufficiently near the house for an ample supply of garden cushions to fill it.

Under a tree, a circular seat might find a place, and under a group of trees on a lawn, furniture of somewhat unconventional character could be grouped. Of this unconventional furniture, several new kinds are now on the market.

There are other informal kinds of chairs —the old monk chairs, for instance, so designed that one could never go off to sleep in them without toppling over! A plain bench, such as one meets in well-designed wild gardens, has also a use in some other positions.

Solid, everlasting furniture is made in designs that are both elegant and restful from the weathered oak and teak of old battleships. In the same material are fashioned tea-wagons, garden tubs, rose trellises, and a number of other articles for garden use. These are quite the most lasting of all wooden types, and need no staining or preservative. Their appearance is improved if they are rubbed over occasionally with a little linseed oil, but otherwise no labour is required in their upkeep.

FURZE. *See* ULEX.

G

GAGEA (Yellow Star of Bethlehem).
Liliaceæ. Hardy deciduous bulbous plants.
Should be grown in sandy soil in sunny
borders or in turf. Plant from August to
November, placing the bulbs 3 in. deep and
3 in. apart. Leave undisturbed until the
lack of flowers shows that they are overcrowded.

Propagation is by offsets treated as
bulbs.

SPECIES.

G. lutea (syn. *G. sylvatica*). Yellow
flowers from March to May. Height,
6 in.

G. stellaris (syn. *G. villosa*). Yellow,
May, 6 in.

GAILLARDIA (gaill-ārd-ia. Compositæ). Blanket Flower. Attractive annuals
and perennials with gaily coloured flowers
that last for a long time both on the
plants and when cut.

Culture of Annuals.—Sown under glass
in March–April, and planted out in May
in fairly rich soil, will provide a fine display in borders or for cutting for several
months. The perennial forms belong to
another group.

Culture of Perennials.—They succeed in
a warm, sunny site in ordinary dry soil,
and where heavy frosts occur they should
be wintered in a light frame. *Propagate*
by division or by cuttings.

SPECIES.

G. aristata, with narrow deeply-cut
leaves and orange-yellow flowers blooming
in August. Perennial. Height 18 in.
This species has given rise to a large number of hybrids which bloom at the same
time as *aristata*, such as *Aurora*, orange-
yellow; *grandiflora*, a strong plant with
yellow flowers; Masterpiece, red and sunset, brilliant crimson with yellow margin.
Height 2–4 ft.

G. picta, 1½ ft., yellow and scarlet.
G. picta Lorenziana, double flowers, red
and yellow. *G. picta* (Indian Chief), with
flowers of an unusual shade of bronzy-red,
are the best of the annual kinds.

GALANTHUS (Snowdrop. Fair Maids
of February). Amaryllidaceæ. Hardy
bulbous flowering plants. They like ordinary rich soil, and will grow as edgings to
beds, in groups on shady or sunny borders,
on banks or rockeries, and in turf. They
should be planted 2 in. deep and 1 in. apart,
September to December. The bulbs should
be left undisturbed until they show signs
of deterioration.

The snowdrop can also be cultivated in
pots, in a compost of 2 parts ordinary
soil, 1 part leaf-mould, and sand. They
should be planted 1 in. deep and 1 in.

GAILLARDIAS VERY SHOWY BORDER PLANTS

**Golden and red flowers of Gaillardia are showy
in the border and useful for the cut-flower bowl.**

apart in the pots any time from September
to November, and placed in the cold frame
or outdoors, covered with cinder ashes,
until they begin to grow. Grow them in
the cool throughout. Water moderately
until after flowering, then gradually cease.
The bulbs should be planted outdoors the
following season. They can be increased
by offsets, treated as bulbs, or by seed,
although the seedlings will not flower until
they are about three years old.

The double snowdrop is not so well liked,

but the flowers will last much longer, and they are very useful for cutting.

SPECIES.

G. *byzantinus*, with large showy white flowers. This is one of the earliest-flowering varieties.

G. *nivalis*, single snowdrops.

G. *Elwesii*, giant snowdrops, very large and snow-white.

GALAX (Wand-plant; Carpenter's Leaf). Diapensiaceæ. Hardy herbaceous perennials best grown in bog gardens. May be treated as alpines.

In moist sandy peat these will thrive on the ledges of the moist rockery, or on the margin of rhododendron beds.

Propagate by seeds sown in peaty soil in cold frame in spring or by division in spring or autumn.

SPECIES.

G. *aphylla*. White flowers, July. Height, 6 in.

GALAXIA (Iridaceæ). Greenhouse bulbous plants. Deciduous. Compost for cultivation 2 parts sandy peat, 1 part light loam. Pot August to November in well-drained pots, and stand in cold frame or greenhouse. Place bulbs just below the surface, allowing one bulb in a 5 in. pot or three in a 6 in. pot. Cover pots with ashes till growth begins. Water moderately when growth commences, freely afterwards. Keep dry after flowering. Repot annually.

Propagated by seeds sown ⅛ in. deep in well-drained shallow pans or boxes in August or September in the cool greenhouse, or frame. Also by offsets treated as bulbs, from August to November. They can be grown outdoors in sheltered gardens if protection is given to the roots in winter.

SPECIES.

G. *graminea*. Yellow, July. Height, 6 in.

G. *ovata*. Yellow, autumn. Height, 6 in.

GALE. *See* MYRICA.

GALEGA (gă-lē-ga. Leguminosæ). Goat's Rue. Useful hardy herbaceous perennials for the border, the mixed border or the wild garden. Provide flowers for cutting, and when fully developed the plants become bush-like and covered with pea-like bloom.

Culture.—Any soil in sun or shade will suit these vigorous plants, which are propagated by division at any time between March and November, or by seeds. Stake early and securely. No watering or feeding is required except in the hottest weather.

SPECIES.

G. *officinalis*, with lilac-blue flowers from June to the end of the summer, and its pink (*carnea*) and white (*alba*) varieties are the best known. Height, 2–4 ft.

G. *Hartlandii*, probably a variety of *officinalis* with a profusion of pale blue and white flowers and variegated leaves. Blooms all through the summer. Height, 4–5 ft.

Other well-known varieties are *orientalis* dwarfer than the type, with bluish-purple flowers, and His Majesty. Height, 2–3 ft.

GALIUM (Rubiaceæ). Hardy perennial herbs, used mainly for rock gardens. Possess more or less the dyeing qualities of Madder. Grow in ordinary soil in sunny borders or rock gardens. Plant October to March.

SPECIES.

G. *olympicum*. White flowers, summer. Height, 2–3 in.

G. *purpureum*. Brownish-red flowers, summer. 9–12 in.

G. *mollugo*. White flowers, summer. Height, 3 ft.

GALLS. Growths caused on certain plants due to the presence of fungi and insects. Well-known examples are the rose-galls and oak-apples.

GALTONIA (Spire Lily). Liliaceæ. Hardy bulbous flowering plants. Deciduous. Ordinary rich well-drained soil in the open sunny border is ideal for these plants. Plant October to March and leave undisturbed as long as possible. Place bulbs 6 in. deep and 6 in. apart.

For pot culture prepare a compost of 2 parts loam, 1 part decayed manure and silver sand and plant in cold or warm greenhouse. Pot October to December for spring flowering, or February to April for autumn flowering. Allow one bulb in each well-drained 6 in. pot, planting so that the apex just shows through the surface soil. Cover with ashes in cold frame till growth begins. When leaves appear water moderately, and freely when in full growth. After flowering they should be

:ept nearly dry. Occasionally a weak
olution of liquid manure may be given to
>lants in flower. Bulbs will not flower a
.econd time in pots.

Propagate by offsets treated as bulbs in
.utumn. Also by seeds sown $\frac{1}{8}$ in. deep in
.hallow boxes of sandy soil in spring or
.utumn and put in a cold frame. Seedlings
lo not flower until they are four or five
/ears old.

The principal species is *G. candicans*,
generally listed in catalogues as *Hyacinthus candicans* or " Cape Hyacinth."

GAMMEXANE dust is a formulation
of the gamma isomer of benzene hexa-
chloride (666). It has remarkable insecticide properties, already in use against
such pests as ants in restaurants, flies in
stables, styes, in the house, etc., against
poultry lice, cockroaches and many others.
As with other modern insecticides, Gammexane will be available to the general
public in prepared forms for different purposes, and should be used strictly in accordance with instructions given by the
manufacturers. Gammexane is already
used in the preparation of Flea Beetle
Powder, and is also an ingredient in Abol
Ant Killer. It is being tried out as a cure
for wireworms, leatherjackets, asparagus
beetle, carrot fly, onion fly and earwigs,
and there is great promise that these and
other pests will succumb to treatment that
can be used by the amateur gardener.
Insecticides containing Gammexane will
be prominent among the contributions of
Imperial Chemical Industries to the world
of horticulture in the near future. Gammexane is not, and will not be available
to the public as a " pure " product, and
the apparent slowness of its development
is due, as with D.D.T. (see page 252) to
the care taken to ensure that its effects
are not harmful to warm-blooded animals.
It is known to be toxic to fish (as is Derris), but will not be generally distributed
without full instructions as to its use.

GARCINIA (Guttiferæ). Stove evergreen fruit-bearing tree with ornamental
foliage. The edible fruits are chestnut-
brown in colour and are the size of an
orange. Grow in a compost of 2 parts
peat, 1 part loam and sand in pots or light
boxes, in light part of plant stove. They
should be potted from February to March

and pruned during the same period.
Summer temperature, 60°–90°, with moist
atmosphere; winter temperature, 55°–65°.

Propagate by cuttings of ripe shoots
inserted in sand in a close propagating
case with strong bottom heat.

SPECIES.

G. Cambogia (Gamboge tree). Yellow,
November. Height, 30 ft.

G. Mangostana. Red, June. Height,
6–10 ft. (The Mangosteen).

GARDEN DATA. There are several
facts which are constantly needed in gardening for which it is sometimes difficult
to find a quick reference. A few are
given here to aid the gardener in his
calculations.

LONG MEASURE

12	inches	=	1 foot
3	feet	=	1 yard
5½	yards	=	1 pole
22	yards	=	1 chain
40	poles	=	1 furlong
10	chains	=	1 ,,
8	furlongs	=	1 mile
3	miles	=	1 league

SURVEYOR'S MEASURE

1	link	=	7.92 inches
25	links	=	1 rod
100	,,	=	1 chain
1	chain	=	66 feet
80	chains	=	1 mile

SQUARE MEASURE

144	square inches	=	1 square foot
9	,, feet	=	1 ,, yard
30¼	,, yards	=	1 ,, rod, pole
			or perch
40	,, poles	=	1 rood
4,840	,, yards,		
or 4	roods	=	1 acre
640	acres	=	1 square mile

CUBIC CONTENT OF A GREENHOUSE.
It is sometimes necessary to be able to
gauge this before fumigating. Multiply
the length by the breadth by the height
of the straight vertical walls. Add to this
the area of the triangular portion formed
by the sloping roof. This is gained
by multiplying the length and breadth as
before by the height of the triangle between
the apex of the roof and the commencement of the straight vertical walls and
dividing by two.

AREA OF A CIRCLE. The formula for
this is πR^2. Thus, if a circle is 10 ft. in

diameter its area would be determined as follows:

$\pi = \frac{22}{7}$. R^2 = half the diameter squared. $\frac{22}{7} \times 25 = 78\frac{1}{2}$ square feet approximately.

A LOAD OF SOIL is approximately a cubic yard or cartload. It weighs approximately 1 ton. It is safer to order by the ton than by the load, although weights vary according to the condition of the soil,

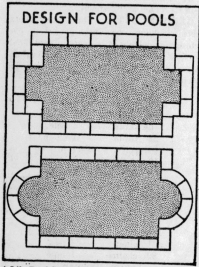

DESIGN FOR POOLS

A Lily Pool is a permanent and most pleasing feature in the garden and needs careful designing to secure a pleasing result. The formal type is best suited to the rectangular garden.

wet or dry. A load of sand is about $1\frac{1}{4}$ cubic yards.

GARDEN DESIGN. Remodelling the Garden. An old garden sometimes presents more problems than a new site. The garden is frequently in a half-wild state, and more often than not is badly designed. First of all, make a thorough inspection of all existing features. Draw out a rough plan of the garden as it is and also a plan of the garden as you wish it to be when redesigned. Note all the plants, shrubs and other trees which are worth saving. Dig up the movable plants which you wish to keep, and heel them in in a corner of the garden.

Tall shrubs which cannot be moved should be cut back drastically if they are "leggy" and "scraggy" at the base. If they are very rank and overgrown, grub them out and start afresh with new varieties.

Trees also may need thinning and pruning, and, if overcrowded, remove one or two, leaving room for the remainder to grow to full maturity.

Carefully examine all wooden structures such as fences, arches, etc. Treat with preservative where necessary, and do not retain anything which shows signs of decay at the base. All this work can be done in the winter, especially in the case of trees and shrubs, as they should be pruned before the sap begins to rise.

If the existing lawn has become very rank, close cutting and rolling several times during the winter—so long as the ground is not sodden or frosty—will help to bring it into shape. If it is desired to move a lawn from one part of the garden to another, economy can be effected by cutting the existing lawn into turves, either 1 ft. × 3 ft. or 1 ft. × 3 yds., and rolling them up for removal to the new site. Do not let them stand for more than a day or two, certainly not more than a week, or they will dry out and go brown. Thus it is best to prepare the site for the new lawn before dealing with the old.

The same applies to moving large trees and shrubs. Prepare the new hole before moving the plant so that it can go straight into its new home with little chance of the roots being damaged or drying out.

The existing stone on pathways can often be used to make new paths in a different part of the garden. Measure up the amount of stone which is worth using, and allow for this when ordering more. Take care to order the same type of stone, or the patching will be too obvious. (For suggestions as to methods of using up odd scraps of path materials, *see* the illustrations under PATHWAYS.)

GARDEN DESIGNING. The art of creating a garden in which every feature fits harmoniously into its appointed place and all parts of the garden are linked together to form a pleasing whole. Such a result is only achieved by considering the natural characteristics of the site, having thorough knowledge of the plants and materials at one's disposal, and an understanding of the needs of the household. The scheme should be worked out on paper first to a scale, so that the site with its various features may be considered as a whole. This is the work of the garden architect who has years of experience to guide him in his designing. The amateur gardener can, however, do for his own

bloom. Moist atmosphere at all times. Plants 2 or 3 years old produce the best flowers. Winter temperature, 60°; summer, 80°.

Propagation.—By cutting of young shoots, insert in pots of sandy peat in propagator; temperature 75°, early spring.

SPECIES.

G. florida, white; *G. florida flore pleno*, double white; *G. florida radicans*, white.

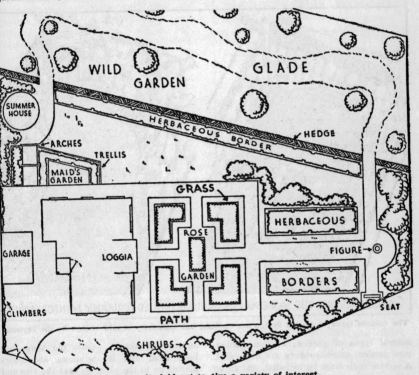

A garden site laid out to give a variety of interest.

plot what the architect can do for the larger site, if he will study his ground carefully before any constructional work is done. (*See* GARDEN PLANS.)

GARDENIA (gar-de-ne-a. Rubiaceæ). Cape Jasmine. Stove evergreen flowering shrubs; fragrant (China, 1754).

G. florida was at one time a very popular buttonhole flower.

Culture.—Compost, 2 parts loam, 1 part each of peat, leaf-mould and sand. Repot early spring, syringe daily except when in

GARDEN LAYOUT. Without obtaining the permission of the landlord a tenant may not alter materially the formation or layout of an established garden and may not cut down or destroy trees and hedges.

GARDEN PLANS. Treatment of an odd-shaped plot. House buyers fight shy of corner plots, because of road charges, but the keen gardener often desires the extra ground that is here available. Sometimes, however, the plot is of an awkward shape, and much ingenuity is needed in its design.

A simple rule, if somewhat obvious, is to plot the largest garden feature first, where there is most room for it, and then to work in the remaining spaces as they suggest themselves. If the plot is only ornamental, stone paths winding among banks of shrubs may surround either a grass plot or a small formal garden. If

sidered at the same time as the house This is unfortunately rarely the case an the unfortunate gardener is left to struggl with the problem of conspicuous man-holes etc., which could have been avoided if the house position had been fixed with du regard to the plan of the proposed garden If the garden is not large enough to cal in the services of a garden architect, a useful home-made plan can be drawn ou

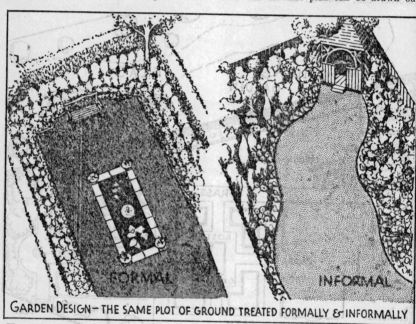

GARDEN DESIGN—THE SAME PLOT OF GROUND TREATED FORMALLY & INFORMALLY

The various types of garden design are endless, but simplicity should always be the keynote.

several types of garden, kitchen garden, rose garden, and shrubbery are demanded, a service path must be included, and in an odd or triangular plot, this is usually best near the outer boundary. A rose screen will hide it from the other parts of the garden.

Planning the Garden. There is great practical value in a plan. It is because so many people start gardening without a plan that disappointments arise. The plan enables the gardener to look ahead and to foresee all likely labour and expense. First of all obtain a plan of the boundaries of the site and the position of the house if existing. The perfect result is more easily obtained when the garden is con-

on squared paper. Once the house has been fixed and its windows and doors plotted on to the plan, go over the site and plot down all trees, variations in the ground level, offending features such as nearby houses which need screening, etc. When all these data have been collected the garden can be planned to its very best advantage.

Keep the design of the garden simple and consider upkeep charges all the time. If the design consists of several parts such as a service area, kitchen garden, main lawn, plot these out in outline on the plan and rearrange the areas until they are definitely in the most convenient places.

ormal treatment is necessary near the ouse to be in keeping with the hard rchitectural lines. The kitchen garden ould be easy of access from the service rea and kitchen door, being connected by dry pathway. Informality can be introduced on the boundaries. If the garden small, this treatment will help to hide ormal fences and, if a large garden in rural setting, will help to link the garden ith the neighbouring countryside.

Consider the views from doors and windows. Every view should be a complete cture and be pleasing at all seasons. hese views will govern the design to uite a large extent, especially in the maller garden. Allow for borders close gainst the house for the cultivation of imbers and dwarf plants.

Take into account natural features. Never destroy a tree if you can help it, or ditch, pond or stream. These are so are in gardens that they should be conerved wherever possible. Trees near the ouse are a problem, however, but careul topping will often save the need for heir removal.

When planning, keep at the back of your ind the kind of shrubs, flowers, etc., hich it is intended to grow in the various orders. This will guide you in deciding he widths of the beds and will help to ive a more balanced proportion to the whole design when seen in elevation.

If the whole scheme is set down on aper it can be carried out at once, or the ork spread over several years. It should e remembered, however, that permanent hrubs and trees take several years to each maturity, so they should be planted s early as possible. (*See also* Garden Design.)

If the owner of the garden has very ittle time to devote to its management, nd he can only afford to employ a partime gardener, the garden design should ontain those features which require little pkeep. These would include.

(1) Permanent planting.

(2) The use of compact-growing plants, like Lavender and Rosemary.

(3) The introduction of paved walks.

(4) The use of tar-surfaced paths.

(5) The introduction of rock gardens (of a certain type).

(6) The establishment of a wild garden.

(7) The elimination of all glass structures.

Instead of relying upon annuals and summer bedding flowers, the main planting should consist of perennials, with shrubs and flowering trees. Amongst these the mixed shrubbery border is, perhaps, the most labour-saving of all, and here a choice should be made of shrubs which require little or no pruning. (*See* Pruning.)

GARDEN ROOM. This is a feature which all are not able to enjoy. One room of the house, preferably facing south or west, can sometimes be converted into a garden room. There should be a doorway giving direct access to the garden, french doors being the ideal. Plenty of window space is desirable. The room should include light cane furniture and many cushions so that they can quickly be carried into the garden during the hotter days. A table with a washable top suitable for arranging flowers is useful, also a substantial mat at the door to prevent garden soil being carried into the house. Vases for arranging flowers and scissors for cutting, could be kept in the room, also gardening books.

An old conservatory can easily be used as a garden room if the staging is removed. Pot plants stood about the room would add interest during winter months, and having plenty of light should do well if tended carefully.

GARDEN SHELTERS. A well-furnished garden encourages every member of the household to live an open-air life. In this climate of alternating warm and chilly days, even at midsummer, it is impossible to be really happy and comfortable in the garden unless there is plenty of shelter.

A garden shelter must be weather-proof, with a roof that will keep out rain, and walls that will keep off keen winds. If it is of the fixed type, it will be all the better for blinds, or doors and windows that can, on occasion, be used to close the side that opens to the sunshine.

If these points are ensured by the nature of the structure, its position can then be at any convenient point in the north or east of the garden, so that the shelter faces south or west. This allows midday and evening sun to enter.

If a shelter is to fulfil all these requirements in a fairly exposed garden, great care must be taken in selecting the right type.

Specialists offer many intriguing designs in timber and in asbestos sheeting. The warmest type is that constructed of

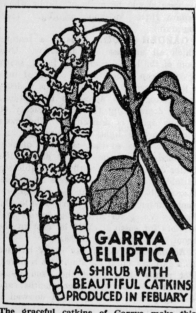

GARRYA ELLIPTICA
A SHRUB WITH BEAUTIFUL CATKINS PRODUCED IN FEBUARY

The graceful catkins of Garrya make this shrub valuable for the spring garden. It is also a good screen plant.

weatherboards or elm boarding on the outside, lined inside with asbestos sheeting and panelled overlays.

A roof covered with Norfolk reed thatching, or heather thatch, makes a garden house of the cosiest kind imaginable, that will last many years without needing repair. These thatched shelters have a rural appearance which harmonises with almost every kind of garden. Where thatch is not desired, tiles that match the house and outbuildings will give most satisfaction.

Elm is a wood that stands up well to our variable weather. With age and exposure it takes on a soft, silver-grey

tone which is very delightful. It is usual sawn into boards with the natural wa edges left untrimmed, and these edg have a decorative appearance that is lac ing in the straight lines of ordina weatherboards.

Some shelters are made to turn on t same principle as that used for locomoti turntables. The rollers revolve betwe an upper and a lower steel track, t upper one being below the floor of t shelter, while a lower one is fixed on sleeper foundation. The result is that t weight is on the actual rollers, and n on the pins or axles as in the case castors.

These revolving shelters need speci care as regards their position in the garde Whichever way they are facing, the vie must please, and for this reason, a som what central position in the garden indicated. At the same time, an esse tial point for all shelters is that they shou be readily accessible in all weathers, wi a clean, dry approach, and the centre a lawn is therefore not the best place.

A good position would be on a sligl elevation, with a paved or gravel surroun An outer ring of flower beds and shrub through which would break paved wall that lead to the house and to other par of the garden, could be arranged, so tha there would be colourful pictures on a sides.

In the case of fixed shelters, also, corner of a plot, from which a genera view of the garden is obtained, can usuall be raised easily above the lawn level i order to create a site for the shelter. Thi gives a vista both ways in a small garde —from the house to the garden shelter and vice versa.

GARDENS, HEATHER. *See* Heathe Gardens.

GARDENS, HERB. *See* Herb Gar dens.

GARDENS, IRIS. *See* Iris Gardens

GARDENS, JAPANESE, *See* Japan ese Gardens.

GARDENS, SPANISH. *See* Spanis Gardens.

GARRYA (găr′-ri-a. Cornaceæ). Ever green shrubs or small trees with flower produced in catkins during February.

Culture.—Plant in May in ordinary

rden soil, in a sunny sheltered position. ropagate by layering and by cuttings in ugust in a frame. Pruning consists of tting out dead wood and trimming the ng shoots in May. In cold midland and orthern gardens they will require wall rotection.

SPECIES.

G. elliptica (California). An excellent easide shrub; inland needs protection of all. Foliage like that of evergreen oak nd the many drooping catkins, up to 5 in. in length, are very attractive in idwinter. The male form is the one to lant.

G. macrophylla (Mexico). A robust-rowing shrub or small tree, with no ttraction beyond the very large striking oliage. Rather tender when young.

G. Thuretii. Hybrid between *G. elliptica* + *G. Fadyenii.* Of very rapid growth nd upright habit and dark green glossy eaves.

GAS LIME. When fresh, gas lime is , powerful insecticide, and can be freely used on vacant land. It should be not used later than November if crops are o be grown the following season, and not nore than a $\frac{1}{4}$ lb. to a square yard should be applied. If the gas lime has been stored for a time, it can be used even on growing crops without injury.

GASTERIA (Liliaceæ). Greenhouse evergreen succulent plants with thick, fleshy, prickly leaves, spotted with white or purple. Use a compost of 2 parts loam, 1 part peat, with old mortar, broken bricks and river sand. Pot in March or April in well-drained pots in the sunny green-house or window. Water moderately in summer. Summer temperature, 55°–65°; winter, 40°–50°.

Propagate by seeds sown in well-drained pots or pans of sandy soil, in temperature of 65° from March to August.

SPECIES.

G. brevifolia. Red flowers, July. **3 ft.**
G. Croucheri. Red and white flowers, August. 2 ft.
G. disticha. Scarlet flowers, July. 2 ft.
G. verrucosa. Red Flowers, July. 2 ft.

GATEWAYS. Gateways are used in garden design to separate the garden from the roadway; to divide one part of a gar-

den from another; to keep out cattle and give a degree of privacy.

Gates to entrance drives should be set well back from the roadway if a dignified treatment is required. A pair of gates is usually required for such a position, while a side gate for pedestrians is very useful. The width of the gates will of course vary with the width of the drive. For a 4 ft. entrance pathway a simple gateway about

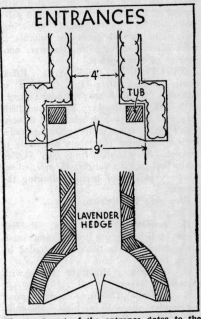

The treatment of the entrance gates to the garden needs careful planning. A nine-foot gateway looks best with a recessed entrance.

3–4 ft. high is in keeping. It should be of the same material and in the same style as the fencing which marks the front boundary.

To divide one part of the garden from another a gate 3 or 4 ft. wide is suitable. Rustic work or trellis gateways are pleasing, while a wrought-iron gate is charming between clipped evergreen hedges. If the gateway screens the path-way to the tool-shed, see that the gate posts are far enough apart to allow free passage of the mower, roller, etc. Gate posts should be set in concrete or else soil rammed round the tarred end of the post.

For heavy posts 18 in. of the length should be below the soil surface. Gate piers made of some local material—brick, tile or stone—can be made to form an interesting garden feature if fitted with appropriate caps. Such piers on varying scales can be used either in connection with entrance gates or those inside the garden.

Teak and Oak are suitable woods for gates, but they should be treated with linseed oil to preserve them. Painted gates look well in "garden green" colouring, and white painted gates are suitable in some places; white gates, however, need greater care in upkeep.

GAULTHERIA (gaul'-te-ri-a. Ericaceæ). Named after Dr. Gaulther of Canada. N. American procumbent shrubs with dark green leathery leaves and little sprays of small pink or white bell flowers. Their main value is for planting under trees where other plants are not likely to succeed. They dislike lime. *G. Shallon* is the best-growing variety. *G. procumbens* has very pretty red berries following the flowers.

Propagate by division.

SPECIES.

G. cuneata (China), 9 in. Reddish stems, polished green leaves, and small lily-of-the-valley-like flowers, succeeded by white berries.

G. depressa. Miniature form with thyme-like leaves.

G. Forrestii (China). Prostrate-growing species up to 18 in. high. Insignificant flowers followed by a profusion of plum-coloured berries.

G. procumbens (N. America). A beautiful carpeting species, 6 in., thriving in shade and under trees. Numerous pink flowers during July and August, followed by bright red fruits during the autumn and winter. The dark lustrous green leaves turn to a reddish tone in winter. A very attractive and desirable little shrub, with a variety of popular names such as "creeping wintergreen," "box-berry," and "partridge-berry," the latter name owing to the fondness of partridges for the berries. An oil is expressed from the plant which possesses tonic properties.

G. trichophylla (China). A very striking exquisite little prostrate species, forming large mats where happy. Leave quite small, indeed "tiny," bell-shape pink flowers, followed by very large blu fruits; in the best forms the colour ma be described as lapis-lazuli blue. Apprec ates woodland conditions.

GAURA (gaw-ra. Onagraceæ). *G lindheimeri*, 3 ft. Flowers white, tinte rose, buds tinted purple. An elegan slender branching plant very suitable fo the mixed border. It is perennial on som soils, but as it is always liable to die ou during the winter, is best raised from seed each spring. Sown March unde glass, planted out May; will flower from July to autumn.

GAUZE FLOWER. *See* GYPSOPHILA

GAYA. *See* PLAGIANTHUS.

GAYLUSSACIA (gā-lus-săk'-i-a. Vac ciniaceæ). Evergreen and deciduous, peat loving moorland shrub, with brilliant red foliage in autumn and showy berries.

Culture.—Plant in moist peaty soil *Propagate* by seeds; and layers in autumn.

SPECIES.

G. brachycera. Box Huckleberry. (Eastern U.S.A.), 6–12 in. A rare charming little treasure with box-like leaves, vivid crimson when young, ageing to dark glossy green. Flowers white, striped pink. A shade-lover.

G. frondosa (glaucum). U.S.A. Leaves glaucous, flowers purplish-green, June and July, berries blue, very palatable.

G. resinosa (baccata), Black Huckleberry (North America), 3–5 ft. A rare deciduous species with pale red flowers in June, followed by the best-flavoured of all edible Huckleberries.

G. ursina (Carolina, U.S.A.) 3–5 ft. Deciduous species with milk-white flowers, tinged red, followed by very dark purplish-black berries of insipid flavour.

GAZANIA (gă-zā-nia. Compositæ). Treasure Flower. Showy half-hardy perennials suitable for hot sunny borders in summer, and often grown in chalky beds at the seaside for display of blazing colour. *Propagate* by cuttings of shoots in March and August, inserted in sandy soil under a bell-glass.

SPECIES.

G. splendens is the most usually grown and bears orange flowers from June to October. Height 12 in. Also useful for

he cool greenhouse. These flowers are
receiving the attention of the hybridists,
and shades of cream, yellow and orange
re available, while new and better kinds
may be expected in the near future.

GELSEMIUM (jel-sē-mi-um. Logan-
aceæ). A choice, half-hardy, climbing
shrub, needing a wall in half-shade.
Leaves glossy green, 2 in. long, and sweet-

GAZANIA

The orange blooms of Gazania make this half-
hardy perennial a showy flower for window-
boxes or flower-beds. It thrives in chalky soil.

scented yellow jasmine-like flowers in
spring.

Culture.—Plant in loam with decayed,
dried cow manure, if available. *Propagate*
by cuttings in sandy soil under a hand-
light.

G. nitidum the only species.

GENISTA (jen-is-ta. Leguminosæ).
Broom. Beautiful deciduous flowering
shrubs, allied to Cytisus, growing from a
few inches high to upwards of 20 ft.
Flowers yellow (except *G. monosperma*,
which has white flowers), pea-shaped and
very freely produced.

Culture.—Plant in October in dry light
soil, in full sun. Pruning consists in
thinning out old wood and trimming into
shape immediately after flowering. The
later-blooming species should not be
pruned until February or March, when
they may be cut hard back. The following
species should not be pruned, but kept in
shape by "stopping" or pinching the
shoots: *G. ætnensis*, *G. cinerea*, *G. virgata*.
All dead bloom should be removed.
Propagate by seeds sown in frame, and by
cuttings of half-ripened wood in a frame
during August. The young plants should
be grown on in pots, until ready for their
permanent positions.

SPECIES.

G. ætnensis, Etna Broom, 15–20 ft.
(Sardinia and Sicily, on the slopes of
Mount Etna up to 6,000 ft.). A shrub of
great beauty and value producing its
golden-yellow flowers at a time (July and
August) when few other hardy shrubs
are in bloom. Useful for planting at the
back of shrubberies. Although a native
of warm climes, it is perfectly hardy.

G. hispanica. Spanish Gorse. 1–2 ft.
Grows in the form of a rounded cushion,
hidden with numerous rich golden flowers
in May and June. One of the indispen-
sables.

GENTIANA (gent-i-an-a. Gentianaceæ). After Gentius, an ancient king of
Illyria. Gentia. The gentians are of
the greatest value in the rock garden for
their conspicuous blue flowers, though apt
to be pernickety in their requirements.
Unless otherwise stated, all varieties
require an ample—but not stagnant—
moisture in a well-drained sunny position.

G. acaulis is the best known and the
easiest to grow, but not always the
easiest to flower. The blooms are large,
trumpet-shaped and almost stemless, of a
rich shining blue—gentian-blue in fact.
An admixture of brick rubble in the soil
will prove beneficial, and there are some
who roll them heavily with the garden
roller in autumn to encourage in some
mysterious way the production of spring
bloom. March to June.

The *G. acaulis* of gardens does not
appear to be met with outside cultivation.
According to Farrer ("The English Rock
Garden") the name covers at least five
allied species.

G. cruciata has clustered heads of 4-holed flowers of a rather dull blue in August. 1 ft.

G. Farreri, a native of Tibet, bears on trailing shoots enormous upturned trumpets of an extraordinarily vivid Cambridge blue. The plant in flower is quite the most striking of the whole range of rock

HOW TO INSERT CUTTINGS

SAND

Before inserting cuttings place a layer of sand over the soil.

garden flora. No enthusiast should rest till he has established it. It flowers with exuberance in a cool rich soil. August to September.

There are some remarkably fine clumps in the Botanic Garden at Edinburgh.

Propagate by division.

G. Lagodechiana. Large blue flowers speckled with white in the interior of the throat, borne in clusters on somewhat floppy stems, 4 in. Cuttings or division. July to September.

G. lutea is a tall yellow-flowered variety of the Alpine meadows, more suited to the wilder parts of the garden. 3 ft. May to June.

G. Purdomi has narrow leaves and large

trumpets of sapphire-blue with whi speckled throat. 4 in. China.

G. septemfida has procumbent shoo bearing clustered heads of clear soft blu Caucasus, 4 in.

G. sino-ornata produces a long succe sion of brilliant azure-blue trumpets c mats of narrow, pointed foliage througho October and November. 4 in.

G. verna has a reputation for breakin hearts and pockets, but in reality it i not difficult if pot-grown plants are used The soil should be made of leaf-mould c peat and coarse sand. Well watered du ing the growing season, it undoubtedl does best in association with other plant and is best planted where its roots ca:

GERANIUM IBERICUM

The Geranium or Cranesbill makes the flower border gay for several months.

mingle with those of other small plants of equal growth. The star-shaped flowers are sky blue, white at the centre. In mountain pasture generally, in Central and Southern Europe, but found also in the West of Ireland.

GEONOMA (Palmaceæ). Stove Palm, with feather-shaped, pale green leaves.

or culture use a compost of 2 parts peat, part loam, with sand and charcoal. Pot February or March and place in moist ady part of the plant stove. Water eely at all times. Syringe daily. Winter mperature, 55°–60°; summer, 65°–80°. *Propagate* by seeds which should be wn 1 in. deep in March in a tempera-re of 85°. Also by offshoots from the ase of plants inserted in small pots in a mperature of 80°–85°. This can be done any time.

SPECIES.

G. acaulis, 5 ft.
G. gracilis, 6 ft.

GERANIUM (ger-a-nium. Gerani-ceæ). Cranesbill. The true geraniums

3-IN. POT →

TO MAKE THEM BUSHY, AUTUMN ROOTED CUTTINGS AS ABOVE SHOULD BE PINCHED OUT.

When growth begins in the spring, Geranium cuttings are pinched to encourage bushy growth.

are hardy herbaceous plants suitable for border or rock garden. Often confused with Pelargoniums (*which see*).

Culture.—Sow in March or April in the open, or increase by division from October to March. They will thrive best in warm well-drained soil in a sunny open site and the dwarfer kinds do well in the

rockery in gritty soil. A dressing of granite chips in autumn will help them to survive the winter.

All species flower from June to October. There are many varieties but they mainly resemble one or other of the following.

G. anemonæfolium. Large, much-cut foliage. Large crowded sprays of bright

GERANIUM CUTTINGS CAN BE ROOTED IN THE GARDEN IN AUGUST

No flower is more generous with its blooms than the Geranium, and it is easily increased by cuttings.

pink. Being a native of the Canary Islands it requires a sunny situation, and is liable to disappear for good in a hard winter. As it produces seed freely, a few seedling plants in pots should be kept in reserve under glass to replace possible winter losses. It is worth the extra trouble. 18 in.

G. argenteum, a well-known inhabitant of rock gardens, has rose-pink blossom and silvery foliage. Tyrol and Apennines. 6 in.

G. armenium has rich purple-red flowers, and grows about 2 ft., flowering from May to August. It is one of the best. Armenia.

G. cinereum, a Pyrenean species with silvery leaves and purplish-red flowers.

G. Endressi. Vivid chalk-pink, the flowers being produced in great profusion. This variety spreads rapidly through under-ground runners and should be kept away from small plants, which will otherwise be engulfed. 1 ft. Pyrenees.

G. Fremonti, from N. America, has dark lilac flowers with purple veins. 18 in.

G. grandiflorum has clear blue, white-eyed flowers of large size. 1 ft. N. Asia.

G. ibericum, from S. Europe, is perhaps one of the most commonly seen in gardens. The magnificent violet-blue flowers are produced in great masses, while the foliage, ornamental at any time, turns a brilliant red in the autumn. 2½ ft.

G. Lowei is a biennial, in that it flowers in its second year and then dies. Its

DWARF GERANIUM GROWING ON WALL

The dwarf Geraniums are excellent plants for the dry wall or rock garden. They thrive in any soil.

chief claims to attention are the very fine, dark purple-green leaves borne on red stems, the whole eventually taking on brilliant autumn tints. These leaves are much cut and divided, resembling large editions of our native Herb Robert. The pink flowers are pretty, but not equal to others described here.

G. macrorrhizum. Vivid aniline-pink flowers and bracts. The leaves are strongly aromatic and become highly coloured in autumn. South Europe, 1 ft.

G. phæum. The Dusky Geranium is an unusual chocolate-brown, more quaint than beautiful. In Britain it is said to be wild in Westmorland and Yorkshire. Meadows of central and western Europe. 1 ft.

G. pratense is the well-known geranium of our roadside ditches, but for all that well up to garden standard. The flowers are violet-purple, a shade or so lighter than *G. ibericum*. In cultivation it grows about 2 ft. It flowers in spring and summer, but the flowering season is short and ends abruptly, the whole plant going out of bloom with a snap, as it were, leaving no straggling blooms behind.

G. Pylzowianum. A choice and dainty little plant for poor, light, and stony soil in the rock garden. Here it will run cheerfully about, popping up here and there to display its large clear rose-pink flowers. Introduced by Farrer from Tibet.

G. sanguineum, a low-growing species of semi-creeping habit. The colour of the flowers is a vivid but crude purple-red. Southern Europe to the Caucasus, local in Britain.

G. s. album, its white variety, 6 in.

G. s. Lancastriense is a form of the above but infinitely more attractive. The whole plant is smaller, with the exception of the flesh-coloured purple-veined flowers which are comparatively large. It was originally found in the Isle of Walney Lancashire. For the rock garden.

G. Traversi has woolly, silver-grey foliage and light pink flowers. An attractive plant for the rock garden. New Zealand.

G. T. var. *R. Pritchard* is minus the silver sheen, but has a very effective and bright rose-pink flower and is seldom out of bloom during the summer. 9 in.

G. Wallichianum, for the rock garden, is 6 in. high with large flowers of pale blue. Himalayas.

GERANIUMS, BEDDING. *See* PELARGONIUM.

GERARDE. John Gerarde was a "Master of Chirurgerie" in London in the early part of the 17th century, but it is not in this capacity that we remember his name. In 1630, or thereabouts, he published a book entitled "The Herbal or General Historie of Plants gathered by John Gerarde of London, Master in Chirurgerie." Since that date, although his was not the first book to be published the same subject, references to his work e frequent, and when desirous of estab- shing the antiquity of the culture of a ant his book is consulted. In spite of is, all that he says cannot be taken riously as he with every appearance of ncerity quotes the old legend of barnacles anging into tree geese. However, for ose who can enjoy the quaint language d quainter idiom, Gerarde's "Herbal" ill provide amusing reading, and will ve some idea of the esteem in which owers were held in his day and of the eans at their disposal for growing them.

GERBERA (ger-be-ra. Compositæ). arberton Daisy. Greenhouse perennial. , Africa, 1888.

Culture.—Compost, 2 parts sandy loam, part leaf-mould or peat, ½ part silver and. Repot early spring. A winter mperature of 45° suits them, but they ould go into the cool house during the ummer months.

Propagation. — By cuttings of young hoots from the base of the old plant, or y seed.

SPECIES.

G. Jamesoni, brilliant scarlet. Since the ntroduction of *G. Jamesoni* the hybridists ave given us many various-hued varieties, or which see any good trade list.

GERMANDER. *See* TEUCRIUM.

GERMINATION. There are three actors which cause seeds to germinate or tart into growth. These are moisture, eat, and oxygen or air. Light is rarely ecessary; in fact in many cases the seeds enefit if placed in the dark during germi- ation.

As a general rule the most vigorous eeds, which will germinate most easily, re those of the preceding year. Seeds if ept dry will, however, last several years, lthough their vitality decreases each ear. (*See also* SEEDS, and SEED TESTING.)

GESNERA (ges-ner-a. Gesneriaceæ). Named after Conrad Gesner, a celebrated otanist of Zürich. Greenhouse tuberous- ooted perennials. Jamaica, 1793.

Culture.—Compost, 2 parts loam, 1 part each of leaf-mould, dried cow manure and sand. The tubers should be started in leaf- mould and sand with a little bottom heat, and then potted on in February up to June or a succession of flowering plants to last

from early summer until the following spring. Water freely during growing period, and give applications of liquid manure once or twice a week after buds appear. After flowering, allow plants to dry off, and store pots under staging until repotting time. Winter temperature, 50°; summer, 65°-75°.

Propagation.—By cuttings of young shoots in sandy peat in spring, by leaves pegged on the surface of pots of sandy peat—both in propagator, temperature, 75°—or by seed.

SPECIES.

G. cardinalis, scarlet and white.

G. Douglasii, red and yellow.

G. maculata, purple, spotted.

G. Lindleyi, scarlet and yellow.

G. refulgens, violet and white.

GETHYLIS (Cape Crocus). Amarylli- daceæ. Greenhouse bulbous plants, deciduous. Plant August to November in well-drained pots in a compost of equal parts peat, loam and sand. Plant in 5 in. pots, allowing one bulb to each pot and placing the point just below the surface. Plunge in ashes in cold frame or greenhouse until growth commences, when they should be watered moderately until the flowers fade. When the foliage has died down, keep quite dry until potting time. Repot annually. Winter temperature, 35°-45°.

Propagate by seeds sown in cold frame or greenhouse in spring. Sow ½ in. deep in well-drained pots of sandy soil. Also by offsets treated as bulbs at potting time.

SPECIES.

G. afra. Red and white flowers, summer. Height, 6 in.

G. cilaris. White flowers, summer. Height, 6 in.

G. lanceolata (Apodolirion lanceolata). White flowers, summer. Height, 1 in.

G. spiralis. White flowers, autumn. Height, 9 in.

GEUM (gē-um or jē-um. Rosaceæ). Avens. Easily grown herbaceous peren- nials for borders or rockeries, that will provide excellent flowers for cutting.

Culture.—Sow seed in the open in April, or propagate by division in March or October. Plant in any good light well- drained soil and blooms will be obtained all the summer.

SPECIES.

G. chiloense (*coccineum*) with scarlet flowers in July and its variety *grandiflorum* with same characteristics, height, 18 in.; *G. chiloense*, Mrs. John Bradshaw, is the best and most usually grown, with large flowers of brilliant scarlet; Lady Stratheden is a lovely golden yellow, a good companion to Mrs. Bradshaw.

G. Heldreichi with pale orange flowers from May to August and its variety

GEUM
"MRS. BRADSHAW"

The scarlet Geum, Mrs. Bradshaw, and its golden companion, Lady Stratheden, are flowers of the continuous blooming variety.

splendens, which is superior to the type with broad leaves and brighter flowers and is hardly ever out of bloom; height, 18 in.

G. rivale, the native Water Avens with handsome foliage and small nodding orange flowers, suitable for damp places in wild gardens, 18 in.

G. reptans, a creeping species with flowers of golden yellow and pinnate leaves, 4 in.

G. montanum, with yellow flowers, 9 in., and *G. Rossii*, with feathery pinnate leaves and yellow flowers. All are suited to the rock garden and flower from May to July.

There are many other species such a *japonicum* (yellow) that possess the colouring and form of one or other of the varieties given.

GILIA (jill-ia. Polemoniaceæ). *G achilleæfolia*, purple. *G. androsacea*, pinkish purple (syn. *Leptosiphon*), 6 in.; *G capitata*, blue, 1½–2 ft. *G. dianthoide* (syn. *Fenzlia*), 6 in. *G. tricolor*, three coloured orange, purple, and white, 6 in. are the best of the annual species. Al are natives of California and succeed bes in a fairly light sandy soil. *G. coronopi folia*, 3 ft., scarlet shades, is a beautifu half-hardy perennial, requiring the protec tion of a cool greenhouse during the winte months.

GILLENIA (Rosaceæ). Hardy herba ceous perennials. Will grow in any com mon soil in moist shady beds or borders Plant October to December or in March Flowering stems should be cut down in September.

Propagate by division of roots in spring.

SPECIES.

G. stipulata. White flowers in June. Height, 1–2 ft.

G. trifoliata. Red or white flowers in July. Height, 1–2 ft., and its variety *major*, which is 3 ft.

GILLIFLOWER. The old name for Wallflower. *See* CHEIRANTHUS.

GINKGO (gink'-ko. Coniferæ). The Maidenhair Tree—so called on account of the peculiar fan-shaped leaves resembling those of the maidenhair fern (Adiantum)— is one of the most distinct, and indeed unique, of all conifers. Unlike coniferous trees in general, its attractive dull green foliage is deciduous, assuming a clear yellow tone before falling in the autumn.

The ginkgo is an extremely interesting relic of the very distant past—indeed of prehistoric times. It is well represented in a fossil state, and no doubt occupied an important place in the vegetation of a very much earlier period of the world's history. Although not actually found growing wild in any part of the world, it is thought probable that China may have been its original home.

The ginkgo was introduced from Japan early in the 18th century, and it is markable that no variation has taken place in its original characteristic. It makes a fine lawn tree, and is valuable for small gardens. It thrives in ordinary garden soil, and flourishes in town gardens. *Propagate* by seed. To preserve a fine pyramidal form, the trees should be pruned in the autumn.

G. biloba, the only species.

GLACIAL DEPOSITS. Traces of the Ice Age, which is supposed to have ended about 30,000 years ago, are found in very many parts of Great Britain. Ice-age soils are very variable; the action of glaciers is capricious. You may find in one spot a heavy clay, containing many stones; not far away, pockets of sand and gravel; in another spot, a real rock-jumble. But the stuff will have been so well pounded as to be on the whole very serviceable to vegetation. The glaciated soils of East Anglia, especially of North Norfolk, are good examples. The botany will vary according to the variations of the soil; no single rule applies. But if you happen to know that you are working on old glacial soils, be sure to keep any strange stone that you may dig up. Norwegian rock has been found quite near to London, brought by glacial agency. A good find may fall to the lot of anyone, and the romance is undeniable.

GLADE. A glade is an open space forming a walk through woodland. If the woodland contains many trees it is sometimes possible to open the glade in such a way that these trees form an avenue. On the other hand, woodland consisting mostly of shrubby subjects will have groups of shrubs here and there either side of the main walk, the breaks in the woodland giving delightful glimpses of various parts of the garden. Such an effect can be achieved by careful planning and planting, but will of course take several years to reach maturity. In the case of old woodland which is being developed in this manner, it may be found that the effect in winter is bare, scraggy trunks. In such a case evergreen flowering shrubs should be carefully interplanted.

The walk through a glade is usually of grass, but this is frequently ruined by the drip of trees. To avoid this the walk should be well drained, pipes being laid each side of the walk, and the centre slightly crowned. The pipes should be laid fairly deep to avoid obstruction by tree roots. Plants such as Hypericum and Ivy can be substituted for grass if desired. Glades are chiefly a feature of the larger gardens, as their greatest beauty is seen when they are used to link the garden with distant countryside views.

GLADIOLUS (Corn Flag, Sword Lily). Liliaceæ. Most of the gladioli are natives of S. Africa and grow in great profusion near the Cape of Good Hope, on Table Mountain, etc. The *Primulinus* species are called Maids of the Mist, because their native haunts are the banks of the Zambesi River, where they grow in the spray of the Victoria Falls. This is probably the reason for the hood which the top petals of the flowers form. The hood protects the pollen from the spray. Most of the gladioli will grow in the open garden, although a few species are generally grown in the greenhouse, but even these will thrive in warm sandy soil outdoors, if planted fairly deeply. All the gladioli make fine pot plants, potted either in autumn or spring. They will not force until the roots have filled the pots, and are generally best grown throughout in cool conditions. In ordinary gardens the culture of the gladiolus is similar to that of most other bulbs. It prefers deeply-dug, well-drained soil containing plenty of sand as well as some leaf-mould. The soil should be dug at least 18 in. deep, more if possible, and well-decayed manure should be worked in to the bottom 12 in.

Planting can be done in succession from the second week in March to the second week in May at fortnightly intervals. This ensures a continuity of flowers throughout the summer and autumn months. The corms should be planted at least 6 in. apart and will display much better if they are massed together instead of being dotted singly along the borders.

Generally speaking, the gladiolus does not need staking, although exhibition blooms are generally protected from the effect of high winds by tying the flower spikes to a thin cane. When used for ordinary decoration, however, the flower spikes will not need staking if the corms are planted 6 in. below the soil. Shallow planting encourages the flower spikes to topple. When planting in rather heavy soil, put a small portion of sand underneath each corm at planting time. This will assist drainage and prevent the development of disease. Apart from this, the gladiolus needs no special treatment to secure good blooms. When growing gladioli for exhibition, a weekly dose of liquid manure can be given as soon as the flower spikes appear, and will prove beneficial. This should only be given when the soil is wet, and if there is no rain, the border or pots should be soaked with water before the application of the liquid manure. Exhibition growers sometimes adopt artificial means in order to delay the opening of the bottom flowers on the spike while some of the upper flowers are maturing. This practice makes it possible to exhibit flower spikes in which nearly all the flowerets are fully open. In the garden, however, the chief value of the gladiolus is that when once the lower flowerets on the spike begin to open there will be a constant succession of opening flowers for some weeks, and gardeners would not wish to have all the flowerets open at the same time, as this would considerably shorten the season of colour.

Gladioli from Seed.—Gladioli are so easily raised from seed and also so easily cross-fertilised, that many amateurs have been attracted to the ranks of hybridists. Practically all seedsmen offer good strains of gladioli which can be sown about the beginning of April outdoors. The seeds should be sown in drills about 6 in. apart and covered with ½ in. of fine sifted soil and sand. The seedlings appear looking rather like grass, and should be grown on till the autumn, when they can be lifted and stored in the same way as older corms. They will possibly flower the next season. Enthusiastic amateurs will probably prefer to make their own crosses and to keep records of the parentage of all seedlings, and this is quite simple. It is best to start by acquiring a few corms of varieties of modern gladiolas. When these are in bloom the most distinctly-coloured flowers will be selected as the male parents, while only flowers of good form should be chosen to be the seed bearers. The pollen of the seed bearer will be removed before the

anthers burst, and the pollen from the selected male parent will be used to fertilise the flower as soon as the anthers open. The plant will be numbered and entered in a "stud" book, for future reference. When the seed is ripe, it should be covered, and kept in a dry place until the following spring. Then it will be sown as already described, and will probably flower either the next year, or in the third year.

After Flowering.—When gladiolus bulbs have flowered for the season they should be allowed to die down naturally in the borders. As soon as the foliage is quite brown, corms should be lifted, and if they are of named varieties they should be tied together in bunches, carefully labelled and hung in a dry shed. If preferred, the corms can be cleaned and stored in dry sand. Some of the corms will be found to have small offsets attached to them when they are lifted, and these small corms can be stored in the same way as the large ones and replanted the following spring, or they may be immediately replanted—in a prepared bed of good soil, over old manure and with plentiful drainage material—and allowed to grow on for two years, until they reach the size of flowering corms. They will, of course, be true to type, and therefore should be carefully labelled if the original stock was of named varieties.

Diseases.—There are one or two rather troublesome diseases amongst the gladiolus. Scab (*bacterium Marginatum*) is one of the most common. As a rule, however, the gladiolus will be free from disease if the corms are healthy when obtained, so long as the soil is well drained and contains plenty of sand. Pests sometimes attack the corms, wire-worms and other soil pests being troublesome, but these also can be easily kept down by any ordinary soil fumigant, or by watering the soil with a weak solution of permanganate of potash at planting time. If corms are discovered which are already attacked by dry rot, it is best to burn them entirely, in order to prevent the infection spreading to other corms.

GLAND BELLFLOWER. *See* ADENO-PHORA.

GLASSHOUSES. A glasshouse can best be described as the nursery from

1. Growing exhibition Melons. A warm greenhouse is needed.
2. Grapes staged for show : note careful thinning.
3. A well-arranged fruit exhibit. Colour, shape and finish count ·or points

1. Elk Horn Fern—suitable for the warm greenhouse.
2. Polypody (Polypodium vulgaris).
3. Hart's Tongue—has many garden varieties with fringed fronds.
4. Polypody over water of dripping well.
5. Shuttlecock Fern—a dainty hardy fern.

which all plants are obtained. Without one it is only possible to produce a very small proportion of the plants required for normal consumption.

Glasshouses are extremely varied in type and design, but the following will serve as a very good guide to the prospective purchaser in determining the one best suited for his own particular needs.

The Span-Roofed Plant House.—This is readily adaptable for all general plant and as much wider up to 20 ft. as may be necessary to give the extra accommodation and head-room in the centre.

Ventilation is obtained by ventilators each side of the ridge and also at the sides.

The Span Forcing House.—Is primarily intended for propagation and growing of bedding-plants of the dwarf order, the amount of air space being considerably reduced as compared with the plant house. This tends towards economical running of

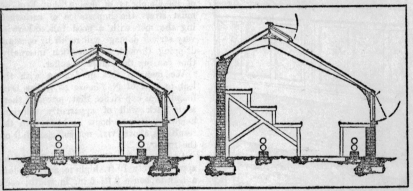

The two best types of greenhouses. The span-roof with central pathway, and the three-quarter span, with tiered staging.

culture. The aspect should be N. and S. (the ridge running N. and S.). The door should preferably be at the S. end on account of the naturally warmer aspect, and the heating boiler placed at the opposite, or N. end.

The length of the house is largely determined by the size of the garden which it will be required to stock with plants, the number of flowering plants, and amount of cut flowers which the gardener will be called upon to produce.

The width is determined by the variety or particular types of plants to be grown. The span-roofed type is a house of a width varying from 9–12 ft., and is usually designed for all general flowering plants such as Gloxinias, Petunias, Primulas, etc.

Should taller plants also be required, such as Carnations, a wider house is desirable which will give sufficient space for a centre staging, in which case the width is increased to 15 ft. as a minimum,

the heating installation and a higher temperature is obtained more rapidly by the action of the sun's rays.

Ventilation is obtained by ventilators each side of the ridge and also by means of box ventilators built into the brick walls at the sides.

This type of house is usually confined to a width of 12 ft., but in some cases as wide as 14 ft. is permissible.

Staging.—The lattice-wood type is the most universally used, but the moisture stage which is shown in the sketch is very useful where greater humidity is required to be maintained over a longer period without attention.

Some gardeners, however, favour the lattice-wood stages in the winter months by virtue of the fact that the movement of air so essential to successful culture is more easily maintained.

The "Three-quarter-Span" Plant House.—This type is intended for an aspect facing S. (the ridge running E. and W.).

L

The back wall may be an existing boundary wall, or an old garden wall on which fruit trees have been trained. The height may vary from 5–8 ft., assuming the width of the glasshouse to be from 10–15 ft.

This type of house is naturally rather warmer than the span type, as there is a greater area of glass exposed to the direct rays of the sun at any one time.

¾ SPAN PLANT HOUSE

To hold moisture on the greenhouse stage small pebbles or crushed coke are laid over the staging.

The cubic capacity is rather larger to counteract this effect, but again the N. atmosphere is kept away by the back wall, so the general result is equalised.

Ventilation.—Is obtained by ventilators on the long south roof at ridge, also by the front sashes.

Staging.—This is similar to the span type, but a 3- or 4-tiered stage can be fixed on the back wall for easy and decorative display of the plants, at the same time allowing the plants to be nearer the glass than would be the case if a flat back stage were fixed.

The back stages are sometimes made portable for easy removal, so the Chrysanthemums, etc., can be housed for blooming in the autumn.

Another use for the back wall can be made by planting Peach or Fig trees in the adjoining soil and training them on the wall. It must be appreciated, however, that the trees will require a resting period, during which time the house cannot be used successfully for other plant work.

The Lean-to Plant House.—This type is the best known, probably on account of its simplicity of design; but here we must stress the importance of constructing the roof with a good fall, otherwise very serious damage will result by constant dripping through condensation internally, thus causing the plants to suffer.

We mention this in dealing with the lean-to type of glasshouse as it has been found from experience that, provided there is a back wall of apparently sufficient height, a lean-to house is built with the results as above, viz., not sufficient fall on the roof.

As a general guide a back wall must be approximately 10 ft. high to accommodate a lean-to house 9 ft. 6 in. in width, each 12 in. extra in width of the house demanding 6–7 in. extra height for the back wall.

The above figures assume a height at eaves or front gutter line of 5 ft.

The lean-to house is characteristically the same as the ¾-span, the only fundamental difference being the larger cubic air space, and the aspect should be S.

It is well to mention here that all glasshouses should be built in the sunniest part of the garden. Care must be taken in each case to build the house unobscured by tall trees which would shade it from morning, midday, or evening sun, the only concession being possibly the midday sun, but even this is desirable at certain times of the year, and during unseasonable periods of weather.

Shading of Glasshouses.—We have dealt with the normal types of plant houses desirable for the garden, together with the aspects suited to the various types, and we consider the question of mechanical shading one of importance.

Blinds of the chain and lath type are the most durable and satisfactory, and are easily manipulated by means of pulleys and cords. They can be laid either flat on the roof or supported clear, the latter method being recommended for delicate plant culture as a current of air is allowed to pass between the blind and the glass, thus keeping the glass clear of condensation. Again, this method allows the blinds to pass over the ventilators, and ventilation can thus be obtained when the blinds are down.

Storage of Rain-water.—Plants thrive better when watered with rain-water as opposed to well or hard water, and for this provision should be made to store the water collected from the roofs of the glasshouse in tanks situated inside the house. This also ensures the water being somewhat tempered.

Greenhouse Heating.—The artificial heating of a glasshouse is most important, and, in fact, one of the essential additions for satisfactory maintenance of equable temperature and atmospheric conditions inside the house.

In dealing with the various methods of warming the inner air of a glasshouse, the most universal is the low-pressure hot-water system, the hot water being conducted through cast-iron pipes of 2, 3 or 4 in. diameter, the latter being the size usually found the most satisfactory and economical.

In dealing with the heating of a glasshouse the following example will be found to work out approximately correct:

Size of house, say, 20 ft. long × 11 ft. wide; roof span, 5 ft. to eaves, 8 ft. to ridge, 2 rows of 4 ft. pipes each side of the house and across the boiler end will maintain a temperature of say 50° with outside temperature at freezing point. These figures are based on the assumption that the aspect is normal, and not subject to excessive N. or E. winds. The boiler should be of a type easy to stoke, easy to keep clean of clinker, and easy to keep free of ashes.

The Beeston Boiler is designed especially for the purpose, and made in sizes capable of dealing with houses up to approximately 50 ft. long.

Houses are frequently divided by means of a partition; thus one portion can be maintained at a higher temperature, the other part being used for hardening-off, in which case valves are placed in the hot-water piping to shut off the heat from the cooler portion if required.

Another system of heating lately sprung into prominence is the electric tubular heating system, which has proved eminently suitable for glasshouse work as it can be thermostatically controlled, thus automatically regulating the amount of artificial heat given off by the tubes.

The running cost is naturally in excess of the coke- or coal-fired boiler, but the lack of attention and increased efficiency go far to outweigh this disadvantage.

The gas boiler is also very convenient when it is not feasible to attend to the coke-fired boiler, and the gas boiler is also free from smoke or fumes, thus overcoming this nuisance, which is acute in some localities.

Oil fuel is only suitable for the larger types of heating installations, but the time may come when it will be adapted for the small systems.

Garden Frames are certainly one of the essential accessories to every well-equipped garden. They are a necessity where a gardener is employed, if he is to obtain the results that are generally expected of him. In particular they are useful as adjuncts to the greenhouses, and relieve them of surplus plants during the spring when seedlings are becoming crowded and need more room. It is impossible to give the seedlings more room in the already overcrowded greenhouse, and equally impossible to plant them outdoors until they have been hardened-off, a process which can be most easily done in the cold frame.

All garden frames are more or less orthodox in design, but the following points should be borne in mind when selecting one for any particular purpose or site.

A Single-light Frame is the most popular, chiefly on account of its simplicity in design. The light is made to slide on runners so that it can be easily manipulated. This type of frame is generally placed so that it can be worked easily from all sides. The same type is also made with a hinged light, in which case the back can be against the wall. It is never desirable to make a hinged light more than 4½ ft. from front to back, as otherwise there may be some difficulty in obtaining access to all parts of the frame.

The Span Frame is a very useful type, also placed so that it can be worked from all sides. The lights of this are usually hinged to fold over. This type is usually lighter to handle and often preferred for this reason.

The Three-quarter Span Frame is to all intents and purposes a miniature greenhouse. It is particularly useful for storing taller plants, and bringing on carnations.

Heated Frames. Any of the ordinary types of garden frames can be heated artificially, though this naturally increases the initial outlay, as well as the running costs. It is more common to provide heat for the cold frame by making a hotbed of new stable manure, and it is surprising the amount of heat which is generated in this manner.

A hotbed may be made in October, using a quantity of stable manure not more than three weeks old. It requires nearly a load of manure to make a hotbed for one large frame. This is piled into a suitably-sized, flat-topped heap and covered with a good thick layer of fine soil, over which the frame is placed. If a larger hotbed is being made it is advisable to turn over the manure a few times at intervals of two or three days, and to mix with it an equal quantity of leaves, so that the heat generated will not be too great when the hotbed is made. It is always necessary to make the bed measure about 18 in. more each way than the length and breadth of the frame, and after the frame is placed in position the light should be left off for a time to allow rank steam and undue heat to escape. This can be done before the top layer of soil is put over the manure.

The important thing to remember when heating a frame in this manner is that the heat should never be too great when the frame is first brought into use. The heat should have dropped to 75° before any actual planting is done in the soil of the frame, although seeds may be raised in pots and boxes stood in the frame while the temperature is still a little higher than this.

In order to maintain the heat in the frame some sort of cover must be used over the glass during frosty weather, and the best form of cover is a mat which exactly fits the lights. The heat of the hotbed should last for a couple of months; but it is advisable to keep a thermometer in the frame and if the heat begins to drop below 70° to pile more fresh stable manure round the sides of the frame. When the temperature drops again, some of the old manure from the sides can be taken away and fresh added, so that the temperature is kept up.

Artificial Heat. If it is preferred to use some form of artificial heater for heating the frames, a small oil-stove can be purchased which will prove satisfactory if attended to regularly, or it may be possible in many cases to heat the frame with the same apparatus which is used for heating the greenhouse. This arrangement is generally made where a large number of frames is used, some being heated and others left unheated for hardening-off purposes.

Where a number of frames are used they are often placed on a brick foundation, which replaces the ordinary wooden sides. In such cases a small boiler and a 2 in. flow and return pipe can be used which will be found sufficient to keep out any frost likely to be experienced in this country. In the artificially-heated frame, cucumbers and melons can be grown in plenty. Early lettuces, radishes and other salad crops for use at all times can be raised, and such vegetables as French beans and cauliflower can be grown under glass for use when outdoor supplies are unobtainable. The frames can also be used for forcing celery, chicory, endive and rhubarb.

Frames are also very much used to bring on bedding plants, raise half-hardy annuals and to shelter alpines during cold foggy weather, as well as for the cultivation of violets and other flowers which it is desired to bring into flower early in the year.

GLAUCIUM (glau-se-um. Papaveraceæ). Horned Poppy or Horn Poppy. These are hardy perennials but flower easily the first year from seeds sown in the open in April. The flowers are large, like single poppies in shape and of various colours. A peculiar feature is the long horn-like seed-pod, often over a foot in length. *G. flavum*, yellow, 2 ft., *G. flavum tricolor*, orange-scarlet and black, 3 ft., *G. leiocarpum*, bright orange-red, are the best. All like a sandy soil, and a warm sunny position.

GLEDITSCHIA (gleditsch'-i-a. Leguminosæ). Honey Locust. Deciduous trees with exceptionally beautiful and striking foliage resembling the "Mimosas." Of no floral beauty.

Culture.—Plant in good loamy soil. *Propagate* by seed sown in spring, 1 in. deep, after soaking for some time in tepid water.

Species.

G. Delavayi (China). Subject to late spring frost.

G. japonica, 60–70 ft. Perfectly hardy.

G. triacanthus. The Honey Locust of Central North America, introduced as far back as 1700. The best species for this country, and is notable for its beautiful fern-like foliage, which becomes bright yellow in autumn, and for its formidable spines up to 12 in. long. A good town tree.

G. t. elegantissima. A beautiful pyramidal form.

GLEICHENIA (Umbrella Fern). Filices. Ornamental stove ferns with brown spores. Feather-shaped fronds and creeping stems. Grow in a compost of 2 parts fibrous peat, 1 part fibrous loam, with a little charcoal and sand, in well-drained pans in the shady stove or greenhouse. Pot in early spring. Water moderately in winter but freely otherwise. Temperature in winter, 45°–65°; summer, 55°–75°.

Propagate by division in spring, or by spores sown on surface of sandy peat in well-drained pots under glass at any time.

Species.

G. circinata. Height, 6 ft.

G. dicarpa. Height, 6 ft., and its varieties *alpina* and *longipinnata*.

G. dichotoma. Height, 6 ft.

G. flabellata. Height, 5 ft.

G. rupestris. Height, 5 ft.

GLOBE DAISY. *See* Globularia.

GLOBE FLOWER. *See* Trollius.

Globe Flower. *Used in the old Peak district custom of "Dressing the Wells"— because of its gay colour—to pick out such* sayings as "Water is the Gift of God."

GLOBE THISTLE. *See* Echinops.

GLOBULARIA (glob-u-lā-ria. Selaginaceæ). Globe Daisy. Dwarf perennials that form dense tufts and do well in the rock garden or border.

Culture.—Propagate by division in autumn or spring, or by cuttings in summer. Plant in sandy loam in rather moist well-drained position.

Species.

G. cordifolia is the best known, with small leaves, trailing prostrate stems and blue flowers in June, height 3 in. Also a white variety of *G. cordifolia*.

G. tricosantha with large whitish-blue flowers from April to July is the only variety of Eastern origin, height 6 in.

G. nana, nudicaulis, and *vulgaris*, the latter with dark green shiny leaves. All bear bright blue flowers from April to July.

GLORIOSA (glor-i-o-sa. Liliaceæ). From *Gloriosus*, glorious, referring to the beautiful flowers. Stove tuberous-rooted climbers. E. Indies, 1690.

Culture.—Compost: peat and loam in equal parts, with enough sharp sand to keep it open. Repot when required in January or February, but this should be only done if pots become too crowded. Water freely during summer; after flowering allow plants to dry off and keep dry until following January. Winter temperature, 50°; summer, 75°–80°.

Propagation.—By offsets at any time.

Species.

G. superba, brilliant orange and red flowers, which are curiously contorted, is the chief one grown.

GLOVES. These protect not only from dirt which grimes into the skin, but also from minor cuts and scratches which may prove dangerous. When examining the quality of gardening gloves, bear in mind not only how long they are to last, but also what use they are going to be put to. Canvas gloves will keep out some dirt, but not water, or thorns. Leather will keep out most dirt, some water, and thorns. Genuine horse-hide and mule skins will keep out dirt, water and thorns. They are made with and without gauntlets.

GLOXINIA (Gesneraceæ). A handsome bulbous greenhouse perennial with rosettes of broad downy leaves and a central mass of very showy trumpet-shaped flowers. The plants are about 1 ft. high and the flowers very varied and beautiful. Some are self-colours of crimson, purple, rose, violet, etc., while others are edged with white or have white throats surrounded with a rich colour.

are ready, pot off into small pots. Watering should be done with care and the plants grown on steadily until they are ready for 5 in. (48) or 6 in. (32) size pots. The final compost should consist of mellow, turfy loam, a little peat, charcoal and sand. In the later stages of growth they may be fed occasionally to advantage. Particular care must be taken to avoid wetting the flower buds.

GLOXINIA

Gloxinia needs a warm greenhouse for its culture and should never be dry at the roots, but the buds must not be wetted when watering is done.

Others are spotted or marbled, and there are strains which are elegantly frilled at the edge. Gloxinias are amongst the most popular plants for the warm greenhouse. They are closely related to the Gesneras.

Cultivation.—Seeds sown in September or in January will produce flowering plants by the following August or September. Seeds should be sown in pans or boxes of well-drained soil, only pressing the seeds into the surface of the soil or just covering them. Dip the pans into tepid water and, after moisture has risen to the surface, place in 70°-75° to germinate. Prick out into fresh boxes of soil when large enough and, when they

The modern varieties have been derived from the *Gloxinia speciosa*. If it is desired to raise more of specially good plants, leaf cuttings can be taken as advised for Begonias.

Gloxinias of named varieties can also be obtained as tubers. After the flowers die in autumn, the tubers are generally stored in sand for the winter months, and during the dormant season they can be purchased from leading nurserymen.

Some of the best of modern varieties are: Her Majesty, Pure White; Royal Crimson; Pink Beauty; Firefly; King George V; Meteor.

GLYCYRRHIZA (gli-sir-rhi-za.

Leguminosæ). Liquorice plant. Hardy herbaceous flowering perennial, with ornamental foliage and edible roots.

Cultivate in rich sandy soil in an open sunny position. Set the plants in rows 18 in. apart in the row and 3 ft. between the rows. The foliage should be cut down in November and creeping stems removed close to the root. The roots will be ready for use during the third year.

Propagate by division of the creeping stems in February.

SPECIES.

G. *glabra*, the Spanish Liquorice. Blue-flowered.

GLYPTOSTROBUS (glip-tos-trō-bus. Coniferæ). China's Deciduous Cypress. Deciduous trees from China resembling Taxodium, thriving best in warm districts. They grow best in rich well-drained soil.

Propagation is best by seed.

SPECIES.

G. *sinensis* (*heterophyllus*, *pensilis*). The "Deciduous Cypress" of China. A rare and graceful tree.

GNIDIA (ni-di-a. Thymelaceæ). Greenhouse evergreens. Pot in March in a compost of 2 parts fibrous peat, 1 part of loam, and 1 part silver sand. Keep them shaded in summer and in a temperature of 40°–50° in winter. The soil should be kept moist at all times, but stagnant water will very quickly ruin the plants. The water used should be rain-water, not tap water.

Propagate by cuttings of young shoots, 2–3 in. long, inserted in sandy peat under a bell-glass, in spring.

SPECIES.

G. *argentea*. Silvery, 2 ft. June.
G. *denudata*. Yellow, 18 in. Summer.
G. *polystachya*. Yellow, 4–6 ft.
G. *pinifolia*. White, 2 ft. Spring.

GOAT'S RUE. *See* GALEGA.

Goat's Rue *is so called as it is supposed to increase their milk.*

GODETIA (go-de-she-a. Onagraceæ). 9 in. to 2 ft. Various colours. A very popular and useful class of hardy annual which will succeed almost anywhere, making a fine show in beds or borders all summer; are also good for growing in pots in cold frames during winter for early flowering under glass.

Godetias are extremely valuable as pot plants for the cool greenhouse or conservatory. They produce an abundance of brightly-coloured flowers of the most pleasing shades. Few flowers have been improved more than godetias in recent years and the double-flowered varieties, both the tall and the dwarf, are the most suitable for pot cultures.

Cultivation.—Sow in a mixture of leaf-mould, loam, and sand which is well drained. After-treatment is exactly similar to that given to Clarkia in pots. *See* CLARKIA.

SPECIES.

G. *Schamini flore pleno* and its varieties have fine double flowers in long sprays, in salmon-rose and pink shades. Height, 2 ft.

G. *Whitneyii azaleaflora*, 1¼ ft., is more compact growing and has large double flowers of bright satiny-rose. In the single-flowered forms of G. *Whitneyii*, we have some of the most brilliant colours and shades to fit in with almost any colour-scheme—Crimson Glow, Firelight (crimson), Rosamond (pink), Scarlet Queen and perhaps best of all, the new variety, Sybil Sherwood, pink and salmon-rose, in a delightful combination. There are very many others offered in seed catalogues, all of which may be described as "good for gardens large or small." Sow in ordinary garden soil, March to May.

Tall Double (2–2½ ft.).—Beauty, crimson-scarlet shaded pink; Carmine; Cherry Red, Crimson, Mauve, Rich Pink; Rosy Morn, and Flesh Pink.

Dwarf Double (18 in.). — Pink Pearl; Cattleya, mauve; Sweetheart, rich cream-pink; Double Azaleaflora, pink with dark blotch; Cornelia, pale cream-pink.

See ŒNOTHERA.

GOETHEA (gō-te-a. Malvaceæ). Stove evergreens. Pot in March in a mixture of fibrous loam and sand. Stand in a shady part of the stove.

Propagate by cuttings inserted in sandy soil under a bell-glass with bottom heat. A shady position is desirable at all times for these shrubs, and they should be syringed freely during the summer months.

SPECIES.

G. *cauliflora*.
G. *makoyana*, 2 ft. Rose coloured.
G. *strictiflora*, 18 in. Yellow-red.

GOLDEN FEATHER (*parthenifolium aureum*, *Pyrethrum*). It is used as an edging to summer beds or for carpeting. It has golden foliage, and is treated as an annual, the seeds being sown in heat under glass in spring. The seedlings are planted out at the end of May. They require to be frequently pinched to make them dwarf and compact. The seeds being very small, they should be sown very thinly. In the second season, if allowed to remain in the ground, they become straggly and are practically weeds.

GOLDEN KNEE. *See* CHRYSOGONUM.

GOLDEN ROD. *See* SOLIDAGO.

GOMPHIA (gom-fi-a. Ochnaceæ). Button flower. Stove evergreens, all with yellow flowers and ornamental foliage. Pot in February or March, in sandy loam with a little peat. Summer temperature, 60°–85°; winter, 50°–55°.

Propagate by cuttings taken of firm young shoots, in sand under a bell-glass in spring.

SPECIES.

G. *angustifolia*, 4 ft.

G. *decora*, 2–3 ft.

G. *guyanensis*, 4 ft.

G. *theophrasta*, 10 ft.

GOMPHOCARPUS (gom-fo-kar-pus. Asclepiadaceæ). Greenhouse evergreens. Use a compost of sandy loam and fibrous peat and grow in a temperature of 40°–50° in winter; 55°–75° in summer.

Propagate by seeds sown in hotbed in spring, or by cuttings or small side shoots under a bell-glass.

SPECIES.

G. *physocarpus*. Bladder-fruited.

G. *textilis*. White-violet. 3 ft.

GOMPHOLOBIUM (gom-fo-lo-bi-um. Leguminosæ). Trailing evergreens, suitable for the greenhouse. Pot in February or March in compost of 2 parts rough peat, 1 part rough loam with some charcoal and sand. Maintain winter temperature of 40°–50°.

Propagate by cuttings of young shoots about 2 in. long in sand under bell-glass in April or May.

SPECIES.

G. *grandiflorum*. Yellow. 2 ft.

G. *latifolium*. Yellow. May. 2 ft.

G. *polymorphum*. Purple, red, or yellow. 12 in.

GOMPHRENA (gom-fre-na. Amaranthaceæ). Globe Amaranth. Everlasting flowers for greenhouse cultivation. Annual. Sow the seeds in pots of light sandy soil in March, and in a temperature of 75°. Transplant and pot on as required, finally growing the plants singly in 5 in. pots. Keep them near the glass and in a temperature not less than 55°. Liquid manure as the flowers form will assist. The flowers are dried when fully open, for use in winter.

SPECIES.

Chiefly G. *globosa* and its varieties which include purple, red, white, and yellow flowers. There are also perennial and shrubby species of this genus, but they are not usually cultivated.

Colours: Rose, orange, yellow, pink, purple, etc. Native of Australia.

GONGORA (gon-gor-a. Orchidaceæ). Stove epiphytal orchids. Evergreen. These prefer a compost of sphagnum moss, fibrous peat, broken pots and charcoal, and should be grown in baskets in a sunny part of the stove. Summer temperature, 60°–90°; winter, 55°–65°. Give plenty of water, and syringe during summer.

Divide the pseudo-bulbs and put into fresh baskets in February.

SPECIES.

F. *atropurpurea*. Purple-brown, and its varieties *major* and *picta*.

G. *bufonia*. Variegated.

G. *Charlesworthii*. White, barred with purple-brown.

G. *maculata*. Yellow spotted, and numerous varieties of this.

GOOD KING HENRY. *See* CHENOPODIUM.

GOODYERA (good-ye-ra. Orchidaceæ). Rattlesnake Orchid; Adder's Violet. Hardy terrestrial and greenhouse orchids. They are very decorative on account of their ornamental foliage. Leaves of bronze, chocolate, olive-green, purplish-green, reddish-crimson, variegated with white or yellow.

Culture of hardy species.—For the cultivation of these plants the soil compost should consist of two parts peat, leaf-mould and sand. They should be planted on the shady side of the rockery, or in a shady border where good drainage is ensured. The best time to plant is March or April.

They need plenty of water in dry weather.

The plants may be increased by cuttings of shoots removed with the roots attached. These should be inserted singly in small pots of peaty compost under bell-glass in a temperature of 45°-65° in the spring.

Culture of greenhouse species. — The plants should be grown in a compost of two parts fibrous peat, one part loam and sand, in well-drained pots or shallow pans which should be placed in the shade in the greenhouse. They can be potted in February or March. They should then be watered freely to September, and after this month only moderate watering should be maintained.

Species cultivated.—G. Dominii, leaves velvety bronze and greenish-white, hybrid (stove species).

G. *macrantha*, pink and white, June (greenhouse). G. *pubescens*, leaves veined silver, white flowers in July (hardy species).

GOOSEBERRY (*Ribes Grossularia*). The wild Gooseberry is a native of Europe and Western Asia, being frequently found in this country in hedges and thickets. It is interesting to note how selection and cultivation have increased the size of the fruit, the wild one weighing no more than a ¼ oz., whilst present-day show specimens weigh over 2 oz.

Soil. — The gooseberry likes a fairly moist soil of an open nature. Heavy clays which bake hard in periods of drought are not conducive to good culture. A light loam with a high precentage of silt is ideal. Heavy soils should therefore be lightened by adding sand, mortar-rubble, strawy manure, or decayed garden refuse.

Position.—As with all fruits, a sunny position is best, and essential for the production of colour and flavour.

Planting.—Planting may be carried out between November and March, and the distance should be 5 ft. apart each way.

Pruning.—Fruit is borne on one-year-old wood, therefore the object of pruning must be to keep the bushes as vigorous as possible, so as to maintain a plentiful supply of strong and healthy young growth. Fruit is also formed on spurs produced on the older wood, but such fruit is of inferior quality. If it is found impossible to get the bushes to produce sufficient young

wood each year, some of the old wood must be retained, and the young side-shoots or laterals from it must be cut back to two or three buds. Hard pruning must always be practised in the centre of the bush. Gooseberry bushes are never kept sufficiently open in the centre. This is necessary for the proper ripening not only of the fruit but also of the wood which is to produce next year's fruit. Leading shoots need only to be slightly shortened. Prostrate-growing kinds should be pruned to an inside bud. Prune in September.

Manures.—Poor ground must be heavily manured prior to planting, as gooseberries are heavy feeders. An annual mulching should be given in May. Light dressings of sulphate of potash in spring are also recommended.

Propagation.—Cuttings root easily in the open ground. Employ the method recommended for currants (black) (*q.v.*).

Pests and Diseases.—The worst disease is American Gooseberry Mildew. Gooseberry Sawfly is also a troublesome pest.

Cordon Culture.—One of the best methods of culture, especially where birds are troublesome, is to grow gooseberries as cordons. They should be planted as such in rows at a distance of 18 in. apart, and each should be trained to a 6 ft. cane. When the fruit is ripe the rows may easily be netted. Pruning consists of pinching back all side-shoots to four or five leaves early in June. In September they must be further shortened to three or four buds. The leading shoots should not be pruned. The best variety for cordon culture is Lancashire Lad.

VARIETIES.

Red.—Lancashire Lad, excellent market variety; Lord Derby, good flavour; Whinham's Industry, the best flavoured red. Succeeds in semi-shade.

Green.—Keepsake, large fruits, good flavour; Lancer, the best all-round variety, good flavour, late; Langley Gage, very excellent flavour, fruit small.

Yellow.—Golden Drop, very sweet, but rather subject to mildew; Leveller, the heaviest cropper, an excellent market variety.

White.—Whitesmith, the best white for cropping, vigour and flavour; quite one of the best varieties.

It is interesting to note that the name of this fruit owes its derivation to the fact that our forbears used it for making sauces, which were served with meats and in particular with goose. Gooseberries were also used in making broth, and Gerarde says, "they are very profitable to such as are troubled with an hot burning ague."

GOOSEBERRY MILDEW, AMERICAN (*Sphærotheca mors-uvae*). A fungus

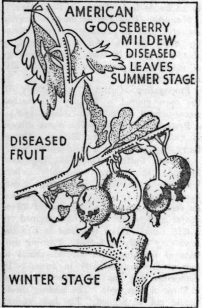

AMERICAN
GOOSEBERRY
MILDEW
DISEASED
LEAVES
SUMMER STAGE

DISEASED
FRUIT

WINTER STAGE

Gooseberries suffering from American gooseberry mildew should be reported to the Ministry of Agriculture. It is a notifiable disease.

of American origin introduced into this country in 1906, though it had previously been recorded from Ireland in 1900.

The fungus first appears in May as a fine, cobweb-like film on the young leaves and fruit. This soon becomes "mealy" and is then easily carried and spread from bush to bush, with the result a fresh infestation is set up.

A second form, brownish in colour, soon appears and this affects not only the fruit, which is covered with a felt-like covering, but also the tips of the young shoots. It is in this stage that the winter is passed.

METHODS OF CONTROL. — Like most fungous diseases, the American Gooseberry Mildew thrives in moist atmospheres, therefore the bushes should not be overcrowded. Over-manuring with highly nitrogenous manures is also liable to help the fungus. As soon as the wood is ripe in September tip the shoots and burn all diseased prunings. The best wash for the amateur gardener can be made of the following:

1½ lb. of washing soda, 1 lb. of soft soap and 10 gal. of water. This should be applied at 10-day intervals, beginning just after the fruit has set. Should the weather be abnormally wet, more frequent applications must be resorted to.

A much more powerful wash made from 2 lb. of soda and sprayed on in February will help considerably in keeping the fungus in check.

GOOSEBERRY AND CURRANT SAWFLY. (*Nematus ribesii*.)

DESCRIPTION.—*Adult.*—Nearly ¼ in. in length, head and thorax black, abdomen dull orange-colour.

Larva.—¾ in. in length when full grown; greenish in colour with small raised black points, arranged in rings round the abdomen.

Eggs.—Yellowish in colour and placed in rows along the veins of a leaf.

LIFE-HISTORY.—The adults appear, as a rule, early in May, but in some years they hatch out at the end of April. Eggs are laid on the underside of the leaves and from these caterpillars hatch in from five to twelve days. At first they remain on a rib of a leaf, eating out small holes on either side, but as they grow they gradually spread all over the bush. The damage done is characteristic, for they devour the whole of the green tissue, leaving only the veins. This loss of leaf often causes the fruit to wither and drop off. When full grown the larvæ turn yellow, drop to the ground and pupate. It is not known how many generations are produced in a year—it is possibly only one—but as that is spread over several weeks it would appear there were several. The winter is passed in the larval state within a tight cocoon in the ground.

METHOD OF CONTROL.—Poison washes such as arsenate of lead should be used with caution, owing to the fruit being of a comparatively quick-ripening nature. Dusting or spraying with one of the vegetable insecticides such as hellebore, pyrethrum, or derris gives equally good results with less danger of poisoning the fruit. Hand picking may be resorted to on a small scale. As soon as the small shot holes appear the leaf should be picked.

GOOSEBERRY APHIS (*aphis grossulariæ*). *Winged females.*—Green to slatey-grey with pale cornicles. The abdomen has well-developed lateral tubercles.

Winged males.—Head and thorax dark, abdomen dark green with pale lateral tubercles.

LIFE-HISTORY.—Eggs are laid in the autumn on the gooseberries and these hatch the following spring, the young rapidly growing up into "Mother queens." Fresh wingless generations are now born asexually until June, when winged forms appear which fly away to viburnum and other plants. In the autumn they become winged again, returning—fully grown—to the gooseberry.

METHODS OF CONTROL.—Any reliable aphicide sprayed on the bushes immediately the greenfly shows itself and before it has had time to curl the leaves, will keep it in check.

GOOSEBERRY DIE-BACK (*botrytis cinerea*). The attack may take one of four forms. The fruit only may be attacked, in which case the berries rot after showing a browning of the skin.

Again, the leaves may be attacked, in which case the symptoms are as follows: The edges become discoloured, and if the attack is bad the leaves gradually assume a yellowish tint and may fall off, but leaf-fall does not always follow. The young twigs may become attacked, in which case the wood does not ripen and the diseased shoots if left on cause a re-infestation the following year. There is also a danger of the fungus being spread by cuttings. Lastly, the whole branch may wilt and die away after the leaves and even the fruit have developed

METHODS OF CONTROL.—Cut away and burn all wilting branches as soon as they appear. Collect and burn all fallen leaves showing symptoms of attack. Should the fruit be attacked it can be picked and

destroyed, though it is safest to cut out as much as possible of the branch which holds them. In the autumn prune away all dying tips. It is of the utmost importance that all such infested material be burned. As a preventive, spray before the buds burst with a copper sulphate solution, 4 lb. to 100 gal. of water.

GORDONIA (gor-dō'-ni-a. Ternstrœmiaceæ). Evergreen shrubs and trees with beautiful flowers and laurel-like foliage,

GOOSEBERRY SAWFLY

A tiny grub, the Gooseberry Sawfly, often strips the bushes of the leaves. The sawfly is only half an inch across the wings.

requiring sheltered positions in soil of peat and sand or leaf-mould and sand and a little loam. *Propagate* by layers and seed.

SPECIES.

G. anomala (Himalayas). A tender species with large creamy-yellow flowers in autumn. Rare.

G. Lasianthus (Georgia and Florida). A hardier species with fragrant white flowers.

GORSE. *See* ULEX.

GORSE, SPANISH. *See* GENISTA HISPANICA.

GOURDS, ORNAMENTAL. *See* CUCURBITA.

GOURDS AND PUMPKINS (*Cucurbita Pepo* and *C. maxima*). Cucurbitaceæ. The popularity of these very ornamental plants has waned rather during the past decade, and one now rarely hears of Pumpkin Pie or sees as huge specimens as were grown by our great-grandfathers, and as described in the story of Cinderella.

They are more largely grown in America, where they are grouped with the vegetable marrows and known as "Squashes."

When not required for food, many of the Gourds and Pumpkins are admirable subjects for covering arches and trellis during the summer, on account of their rapid

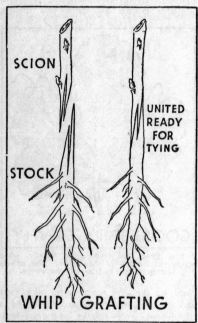

SCION

STOCK

UNITED
READY
FOR
TYING

WHIP GRAFTING

Grafting is generally limited to fruit trees. The grafts are fixed on when the sap begins to move.

growth, large flowers, and ornamental fruits.

Culture.—Single seeds should be sown in small pots of light soil in a temperature of about 60° in early May. When well-rooted they should be potted on into 5 in. pots of good rich compost, and grown steadily along, gradually hardening-off in cool house and cold frame until they are ready and safe for planting out at the end of May or early June.

So long as a good supply of water is available in dry weather, good fruits can be grown on any soil. A hole should be dug out and filled with well-decayed

manure trodden firm and covered with 6 in. of good light soil.

Set out the plants carefully at least 4 ft. apart and protect from frost until the end of June.

VARIETIES.

Yellow Hundredweight, Turk's Cap, Green Giant, Hubbard's Squash.

Uses.—Gourds and Pumpkins may be cut and cooked whilst green, in the same manner as Vegetable Marrows. If allowed to ripen and colour, they can be kept through the winter in a cool, dry place, and parts of them may be sliced off and used from time to time.

GRAFTING. Healthy fruit trees which produce an inferior crop of fruit may be grafted with another variety. Nurserymen use trees known as stocks, which form strong, fibrous roots, and by grafting on to them a good variety of apple, pear, etc., they are able to raise strong healthy trees. The shoots or scions of the good variety are best prepared in the winter, so that their buds remain dormant and are not using up the energy which will be required to complete the graft. Cut the scions from wood of the previous year's growth and store them through the winter in moist sawdust or a damp cloth. Cut the scions about 4 in. long with about 3 buds and a slight notch as shown in the sketch. In the spring, prepare the stock with a similar notch, open the cut and slip the scion in in such a way that the cambium, or the layer just inside the outer bark, of both stock and scion is touching. Wax all exposed cut surfaces and tie round with raffia. This method is known as whip-grafting or tongue-grafting.

Other methods are cleft-grafting and crown-grafting. These methods are employed for large trees. For cleft-grafting a branch is sawn back and the stump slit 2 or 3 in. across the top. A wedge-shaped scion is then placed at each side, waxed and tied in.

In crown-grafting, the stump is slit down either side for about two inches and with a straight cut slipped into the slits. They are then waxed and tied. Crown-grafting is sometimes known as inlay or bark grafting. *See also* PROPAGATING PLANTS.

GRAMA GRASS. *See* BOUTELOUA.

GRAMMANTHES (gram-man-thes. Crassulaceæ). Half-hardy annuals, and best suited to greenhouse culture. Sow thinly in well-drained pots containing a mixture of lime rubble and sandy loam in equal parts. The seedlings can be grown in pots on the greenhouse shelves, or, if preferred, they can be transplanted to the open ground. They are best in a sunny pocket of the rockery if grown outside.

SPECIES.

G. chloræflora. Orange and red, summer, 3–4 in.

G. gentianoides. Pinkish red, 6 in.

GRAMMATOCARPUS (gram-ma-to-karpus. Loasaceæ). Cup Flower. Twining, half-hardy annual. Seeds should be sown in March in gentle heat, and later hardened-off and planted outdoors in the same manner as *Cobæa scandens.* Any ordinary soil will do. These plants are suitable for vases or for low fences. They need sunshine in plenty.

SPECIES.

G. volubilis. Deep yellow, July and August, 3 ft.

GRAMMATOPHYLLUM (gram-ma-to-fil-lum. Orchidaceæ). Queen of the Orchids. Stove epiphytal orchids, allied to Brassia. Pot in a basket of sphagnum and fibrous peat, with the plants well raised above the basket. Summer temperature, 60°–90°; winter, 55°–65°.

Propagate by division of the pseudobulbs in February or March.

SPECIES.

G. elegans. Brown, yellow edges.

G. multiflorum. Brown-green.

G. rumphianum. Yellow, blotched brown.

G. speciosum. Yellow-brown.

GRANITE. This is one of the world's most handsome rocks. It is highly crystalline. Sawn and polished slabs of granite are seen in the shop fronts in all our large towns and make a brave show. It is an igneous rock; it welled up, hot, from the lower levels of the earth's crust, but it did not burst its way through in the manner of the true volcanic rocks. Granite moorlands exist in Cornwall, Devon, the Lake District and Scotland. Wales is rather poor in true granite, though "semi-granites" are to be found. Granite is, roughly spreaking, two-thirds quartz, and

when it breaks up, gives us large stretches of sandy moor. The botany of this resembles that of the sandstone heights (*see* SANDSTONE), though the rock scenery is, on the whole, grander and wilder. Where the rock has little soil upon it we find interesting members of the Stonecrop family, Crassulaceæ.

GRANITE CHIPPINGS. These are

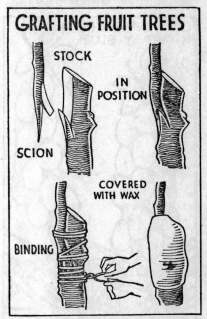

GRAFTING FRUIT TREES

STOCK

IN POSITION

SCION

COVERED WITH WAX

BINDING

Diagram showing how a new variety can be grafted on to an older tree. It is then bound in place with raffia, and covered with wax.

used to spread between alpine plants to prevent the soil from drying out. Flint chippings should not be used as they are not porous. In their natural state, the alpines grow rapidly so that surrounding ground is practically covered by their leaves. Thus granite chippings help new plants to have more natural conditions until they have spread sufficiently to cover their allotted area.

In towns where alpines are apt to die off during the winter through fogs and excessive moisture, a thin layer of granite chippings on the rockery will absorb excessive moisture and protect the plants.

GRAPE (*Vitis vinifera*).

Soil.—A good rich friable soil is best. Select a good loam and chop it down carefully with a spade, making certain to remove all wire-worms which generally exist in such soil. To each barrow-load of soil add 1 lb. of bonemeal and a shovelful of mortar rubble. If the loam is on the heavy side, add some good coarse sand. Farmyard manure should not be added.

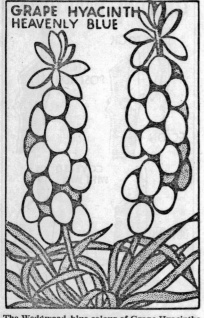

GRAPE HYACINTH HEAVENLY BLUE

The Wedgwood-blue colour of Grape Hyacinths is an effective carpet beneath Golden Forsythia.

Planting.—October is the best month for planting. Allow a distance of 5 ft. apart for training the vines on the usual system. This is known as the "spur system," and gives the quickest and most satisfactory results.

Pruning.—Treatment of young Rod. A young vine when first planted should be cut back to 5 ft. The following growing season, tie in the strongest leading shoot for further development of the rod. Tie in side shoots horizontally. These should be interspersed alternately on each side of the main rod, and should be approximately 9 in. to 1 ft. apart. In autumn,

shorten all these laterals to two buds, and shorten the leader to 5 ft., making the rod now 10 ft. in length.

The following spring, thin the laterals from the spurs on the older wood to one, leaving the strongest. Do not allow any fruit to set. The next year the same treatment should follow. If the vine is very vigorous, one or two bunches of fruit may be carried.

An Established Rod.—As soon as all foliage has dropped, pruning should be done. All shoots emanating from spurs should be cut back to two buds. Keep a look out for young buds which may break on the older wood of the spur, and prune to these wherever possible, so as to keep each individual spur as short as possible. Following pruning, the rod should be "bent," taking the top of the rod down from the wires and securing it close to ground level. This ensures even breaking.

Disbudding.—More young shoots are invariably produced than is necessary. A rod well set with spurs does not require more than one shoot from each. Rub out the weaker ones to encourage healthy growth from those selected to remain.

Stopping.—Each shoot should be pinched at three or four leaves beyond the flower bunch. Any secondary shoots, or sub-laterals which appear between the main rod and the flower bunch, should be rubbed out. Those produced beyond the flower should be stopped at one leaf.

Tying In.—It is frequently necessary to support laterals which are carrying fruit. Vine wood is very brittle, and easily breaks.

GRAPE HYACINTHS. *See* MUSCARI.

GRASS BANK. This is the cheapest way of retaining soil as regards the first costs, but the difficulty of upkeep usually makes a wall more pleasing in the long run. To every 2 ft. width the bank should rise 1 ft. This proportion gives a convenient angle for mowing. A bank less steep than this looks too flat, and anything more steep causes the bank to dry out during the summer, leaving the grass bare. A drain running along at the foot of the bank may be necessary if this position is found to be waterlogged. (*See* BANKS.)

GRASS OF PARNASSUS. *See* PAR-
NASSIA.

GRASSES, ORNAMENTAL. *See*
AGROSTIS, AVENA, BROMUS, HORDEUM,
PHALARIS, etc., *also* ORNAMENTAL GRASSES.

GRASS VERGE. A strip of lawn varying from 1 to 3 ft. wide makes an excellent foil for flowers. The soil should be
thrown well back from the grass so that
both edges of the verge may be kept well
clipped. This of course is the disadvantage
of the verge; it needs constant attention
and unless kept well trimmed it is not
an asset.

A verge may be formed by sowing grass
seed, but turf is usually the best method,
as the firm edges are then formed immediately. To neaten a badly-worn grass verge
or a piece which has been jagged, cut
turves about 1 ft. square from the outer
edge and reverse them, turning the ragged
edges to the centre. Fill in the gaps with
fine soil and grass seed, and roll and water
well. This is only necessary in very
extreme cases, as careful use of the edging
iron should be sufficient to keep the verge
in good repair. (*See* EDGINGS.)

GRAVEL. As gravel contains many
stones of fair size, it is obviously brought
together by currents or forces of strong
action — either river torrents or glacial
action. Binding the stones more or less
together there is usually a "matrix," or
bed of reddish sand. Gravels in Nature
are very limited in choice of chemicals.
They therefore attract a peculiar vegetation. The botanical family of "Leguminosæ"—the bean and pea family, with the
gorse and broom and the clovers—has the
power of bringing into the soil the nitrogen
of the atmosphere. This is done by the aid
of certain microbes at their roots. You
will find, then, that in gravelly soil the
leguminous plants predominate. Very
often they alone can tackle the problem of
nutrition set up by so special a soil. But
the family may be represented by a great
variety of charming members. Some of
our London gravel-pits offer quite a
fascinating study of this botanical order.
(*See* PATHWAYS.)

GRAVES, PLANTS SUITABLE FOR.
White.

Anemone japonica	Candytuft
Campanula	Crocuses
Grape Hyacinths	Roses, dwarf
Hyacinths	Saxifrage, London
Lily of the Valley	Pride
Lobelias, dwarf	Scilla campanulata,
Love-in-a-Mist	and S. nutans
Madonna Lilies	Snowdrops
Narcissus	Solomon's Seal
Ornithogalum	Veronica spicata
Primula	Viola

Colours.

Anemone japonica	Iris, English and
Aubretia	Spanish
Campanula	Lobelias, dwarf
Candytuft	Love-in-a-Mist
Cheiranthus Allionii	Montbretia
(Siberian Wall-	Narcissus
flower)	Nepeta
Chionodoxa	Potentilla
Crocus	Primula
Daffodils	Roses, dwarf
Dianthus (Pinks)	Saxifrage, London
Euonymus radicans	Pride
Fritillarias	Scilla
Geranium ibericum	Thyme
Heuchera	Viola
Hyacinths	Winter Aconite

Evergreens.

Cupressus. Fletcherii	Lavendula. Laven-
and F. nana	der
Cytisus, dwarf	Rosemary
Euonymus radicans	Santolina. Laven-
Genista, dwarf	der Cotton

Also any of the evergreens listed under
dwarf shrubs.

GREASE-BANDING. A method de-
vised originally for the control of Winter
Moth.

It consists of placing round the tree
trunk a sticky substance which will prevent the ascent of the tree by the wingless
females. This material should first of all
be smeared on grease-proof paper which
has been securely tied to the tree both
top and bottom. Too much care cannot be
taken in this tying, as slovenly work will
only enable the moths to crawl under
the paper. The grease is now applied by
means of a piece of flat wood or specially-
prepared comb supplied by the makers.
Grease-banding should be completed by the
20th of October and periodical inspections
made when all dead leaves, dead moths
and foreign matter should be removed, as
these only form bridges for any moth still
hatching out in the ground. The grease

itself should be purchased from a reliable firm who specialise in such material, and it should be of such quality that it will not film through sun or wind, nor should it run through excessive heat. The ideal grease should remain "tacky" throughout the winter.

In the spring the grease should either be re-combed or, better still, fresh bands should be put on. These bands will catch all caterpillars and insects which attempt to re-climb the tree after being dislodged by wind and other causes. Grease may be applied direct to old trees but not to young ones. At the same time, banding first with paper is strongly recommended as the continual application of grease to the bark makes trees unsightly.

GREAT BELLFLOWER. *See* PLATY-CODON.

GREAT REED. *See* ARUNDO.

GREEK MALLOW. *See* SIDALCEA.

GREEK VALERIAN. *See* POLEMO-NIUM.

GREENHOUSE. *See* GLASSHOUSES.

GREENHOUSE ANNUALS (G.A.). This term denotes that the subjects so indicated are annuals and require greenhouse treatment; or in such instances as Cinerarias, Calceolarias, Primulas, are best treated as annuals as they are so easily raised from seeds (*see also* SEEDS), and the young plants are so much better than old ones. The culture of these is dealt with in their respective sections.

GREENHOUSE HEATING. *See* GLASSHOUSES.

GREENHOUSE MANAGEMENT. *See* MANAGEMENT OF THE GREENHOUSE.

GREENHOUSES, SUMMER-HOUSES, ETC. In erecting any building that will back on to and be higher than the fence or wall of a neighbour, it is sometimes necessary to obtain permission from the District Surveyor, and always necessary to consider the rights of the owner of the neighbouring property, as the erection of such a building is sure to affect such property.

GREENHOUSE, TYPES OF. *See* GLASSHOUSES.

GREEN MANURING. The amateur gardener is not greatly concerned with the problem of green manuring, except in the following way. Where manure from

stables is unobtainable and the soil lacks humus, the compost pit—which contains all the leaves, weeds, and plant tops from the garden—has to supply the deficiency. This can often be easily supplemented by growing mustard, or vetches, from seed on land left empty after the earliest crops, and digging the plants in during the winter. If mustard is used, the soil will need a nitrogenous manure next season; but vetches (or lupins) will add nitrogen to the soil. Experiments in the growing of fruit entirely without animal manure have proved quite successful, and gardeners to whom the use of animal manure is objectionable can rest assured that green manuring, supplemented by the use of chemical fertilisers, will keep their soil in satisfactory condition.

GREVILLEA (gre-vil'-le-a. Prote-aceæ). Handsome flowering shrubs from Australia, needing sheltered positions in a soil of peat, leaf-mould and sand, or a sandy loam with peat added. *Propagated* by cuttings of half-ripened shoots about July, and placed in a bottom heat.

Cultivation.—If sown early, useful plants may be obtained in one season. Seeds should be sown in pans of peaty compost and germinated in brisk heat. They may be potted up into 3 in. pots when large enough, and eventually into 5 in., 6 in., or 8 in. pots. The compost for the final pots should contain good loam, opened with good peat and sharp sand.

SPECIES.

G. alpina. A low, compact-growing species, similar to *G. rosmarinifolia.* Flowers crimson.

G. rosmarinifolia, 6–7 ft. Flowers deep rosy-red from May to July. A splendid seaside shrub.

G. sulphurea (*juniperina* var. *sulphurea*), 6 ft. Flowers pale yellow. Hardiest species.

GRIFFINIA (grif-fin-i-a. Amarylli-daceæ). Stove bulbous plants. Pot in peat and loam, with a little dried leaf-mould, in June or July. Press down the compost firmly, and keep in a tempera-ture of 60°–80° while growing, and 55°–65° while at rest. Repot every third or fourth year.

Give plenty of water and syringe freely during summer, but allow to dry almost entirely while resting.

Propagate by seeds sown in sandy soil and a temperature of 85° in March, or by offsets from the bulbs after repotting.

SPECIES.

G. blumenavia. Pink and white, 1 ft.

G. hyacinthina. Violet-blue, 1 ft. (Blue Amaryllis).

G. ornata. Purple-lilac, 1 ft.

GRINDELIA (grin-de-li-a. Compositæ). Hardy or half-hardy; mostly perennials. Sow seeds in heat in early spring, or in the case of *G. ciliata,* in autumn.

Propagate perennials also by division and cuttings. Ordinary soil and plenty of sunshine are the simple needs of these plants. In sheltered gardens they grow in the open; in others they like the protection of the greenhouse.

SPECIES.

G. angustifolia. August, 1 ft. Yellow.

G. ciliata. August, 18 in. Biennial. Yellow.

G. grandiflora. July, 4 ft. Orange. Biennial.

G. integrifolia, 3 ft. Yellow.

G. robusta. 18 in. Yellow.

G. inuloides. Evergreen, 5 ft. Yellow.

"GRIPIT" CLOCHE. This little gadget will take any size, shape or thickness of glass and protects seeds and seedlings from frost, rain, cats and birds. Can be used to make a continuous or single cloche and will last a lifetime. It is heavily galvanised, and the great advantage is that all the odd pieces of glass can thus be turned to good use.

GRISELINIA (gris-el-in-ia. Cornaceæ). Evergreen shrubs or small trees, best suited for maritime districts. They like deep, rich, light soil. *Propagate* by seeds and by layering.

SPECIES.

G. littoralis (New Zealand), 10–25 ft. The New Zealand Kupuka Tree. A very interesting species of olive-like appearance, making a very attractive hedge in seaside gardens. As a single specimen it may reach a height of 20 ft. or more. A fairly hardy species, only injured in very severe winters.

G. l. variegata. Leaves variegated silver.

GROUNDSEL. *See* SENECIO.

GUANO. Bird and other animal droppings collected from districts of low rainfall. Some Pacific and Atlantic islands still possess considerable deposits. Contain nitrogen and phosphates.

GUELDER ROSE. *See* VIBURNUM OPULUS STERILE.

GUERNSEY LILY. *See* NERINE.

GUEVINA (guev-ē-na. Proteaceæ). Evergreen shrubs for favoured districts. They like a peaty soil and shade. *Propagate* by seeds and cuttings.

SPECIES.

G. avellana (Chile). Handsome deep green glossy foliage, fragrant cream flowers, followed by edible nut-like fruits.

GUM-TREE. *See* EUCALYPTUS.

GUNNERA (gŭnn-era. Haloragaceæ). Hardy perennial plants with striking foliage and small insignificant flowers.

They are easily cultivated in rich soil and a shady position, and will do well by the waterside or in a shrubbery. In winter protect the crowns with a mound of leaf-soil, coconut fibre, or coke ashes. *Propagation* is best effected by root division in spring, but they can be raised by summer-sown seed. Give a mulch of well-rotted manure each spring.

SPECIES.

G. scabra (*chilensis*) with small red flowers and leaves that often measure 5 ft. across.

G. manicata resembling *scabra* but with more kidney-shaped leaves and longer spikes of flowers.

GUTTERS. When a drive or pathway is constructed on a steep slope gutters are required at the sides of the path to carry away surplus water after a heavy shower. These may be constructed of cement, brick, tile or cobble, etc., and should be about 6 in. wide. Loose materials such as cobbles should be cemented into place for security and also to prevent the growth of weeds. These gutters should connect with the drains by means of catch pits placed at regular intervals either side of the pathway. Thirty feet is an average distance apart except in the case of steep gradients, when they should be more frequent. The catch pits are holes built round with bricks, uncemented, and covered with iron gratings approximately one foot by eight inches. The bars of these gratings should be curved towards the centre.

GUZMANIA (guz-man-i-a. Brome-liaceæ). Stove herbaceous perennials with ornamental bracts.

These like a rich soil containing plenty of peat and leaf-mould. Pot them in March, in well-drained pots, and water freely at all times. Summer temperature, 60°–80°; winter, 55°–65°.

Propagate by offsets.

SPECIES.

G. lingulata. Yellow-white, with purple-red bracts; summer.

G. tricolor. Green-scarlet, 1 ft. April.

GYMNADENIA (gim-na-de-ni-a. Orchidaceæ). Stove and hardy terrestrial orchids closely allied to Habenaria. They should be grown in a compost of fibrous loam and peat with sand in a sunny position.

HARDY SPECIES.

G. albida. Alpine species, rare in this country, spikes of white flowers.

G. conopsea. Rosy-mauve with long slender spur. Fragrant.

G. odoratissima. Strongly scented rosy-lilac flowers.

G. rupestris. Japanese species, very beautiful.

GREENHOUSE SPECIES.

G. macrantha, dark brown, purple-lilac.

GYMNOCLADUS (gim-no-klā-dus. Leguminosæ). Deciduous trees with handsome pinnate foliage. They like a rich loamy soil. *Propagate* by seeds.

SPECIES.

C. canadensis (Kentucky Coffee, U.S.A.). A tree up to 60 ft. in this country with most beautiful foliage; leaves 3 ft. long and 2 ft. wide, turning clear yellow in autumn. One of the handsomest of all hardy trees.

GYMNOGRAMME (gim-no-gram-me. Filices). Gold Fern; Silver Fern. Stove and greenhouse ferns. The ferns are highly prized for hanging baskets, where their beautiful colouring can be best seen to advantage. W. Indies, 1790.

Culture.—Compost: equal parts loam, peat, leaf-mould and sand. Repot early spring, give good drainage. Water freely during summer months, and shade from hot sun. Winter temperature, 50°; summer, 70°.

Propagation.—By spores sown on the surface of sandy peat, place in propagator,

temperature 70°, or by division of plants when repotting.

SPECIES.

G. calomelanos, and its varieties *chrysophylla* (Gold Fern); *peruviana cirgyrophylla* (Silver Fern); *schizophylla*, pretty silvery fronds; and *sulphuria*, golden fronds.

GYMNOLOMIA (gim-no-lo-mi-a. Compositæ). Hardy or greenhouse perennials. Useful for cut flowers.

Sow in pots of loam, leaf-mould and sand. Increase also by division.

SPECIES.

G. connata, 4 ft. Yellow. October.

G. multiflora. Yellow, 18 in: Generally grown as an annual; will grow outdoors in sheltered gardens.

G. triplinervia, 3 ft. Yellow.

GYNERIUM. *See* CORTADERIA.

GYNURA (gi-nu-ra. Compositæ). Stove herbaceous plants, mostly perennials.

Use a compost of loam, leaf-mould and sand. Pot in March, and grow in a shady part of the stove.

Propagate by cuttings inserted in sand in heat.

SPECIES.

G. aurantiaca. Orange; stems, leaves, and bracts covered with purple hairs. 2 ft.

G. bicolor, 3 ft. Yellow.

G. divaricata, 18 in. Purple, straggling. July (biennial).

G. sarmentosa. Dull orange, trailing.

GYPSOPHILA (jyp-sōph'i-la. Caryophyllaceæ). Chalk Plant. Gauze Flower. Graceful hardy plants, the dwarfer species being good for rock gardens, while the taller plants are excellent for borders and for cutting as they bear numerous sprays of lace-like tiny flowers. Much used by florists.

Culture.—They thrive in dry well-drained light limy soil but will grow in any well-worked garden soil. *Propagate* by seeds sown as soon as ripe or by root division made before growth commences. Plant out in permanent position and leave undisturbed for several years. Give a mulching of well-rotted manure in spring and autumn. Cut some of the flowers early as they bloom in such profusion that the plants are weakened if the flowers remain on for long.

Species.

More than fifty species have been described. Best known is *G. paniculata* with clouds of white flowers most useful for cutting, 3 ft.; *G. acutifolia* with panicles of rose or white flowers, 4 ft.; *G. cerastioides*, a prostrate plant with white flowers veined with red; *G. repens*, a rock variety with pale rose flowers, 6 in.; *G. Stevenii*, with slightly larger flowers of white or rose, 1–2 ft.

All bloom from May to September.

In the annual varieties the flowers are fully ½ in. across and most lavishly produced on thin hair-like stems, making good subjects for cutting to mix with other flowers. They are of the easiest cultivation. Sow March to July. A succession of useful material may be had for several months. Any ordinary garden soil is suitable.

G. elegans, pink; *G. elegans alba* (white), *G. alba grandiflora* and *G. carminea* (rose) are the pick of the annual species, which must not be confused with the perennial species, *G. paniculata*. 1 ft.

G. Bristol Fairy is easily the best of the modern forms. It is a variety of *G. paniculata*, and has pure white flowers larger than in any of the other forms. It is very free flowering and blooms from July to September.

GYPSUM. Calcium sulphate. Is of little use in horticulture and garden practice but, if cheap, is worth applying to the manure heap from time to time. It will considerably increase the value of dung by reducing the loss of nitrogen.

H

HABENARIA (Butterfly Orchis, Rein Orchis). Orchidaceæ. Hardy and stove terrestrial orchids. Valuable for the fragrance of the flowers.

These should be planted in a soil of equal parts leaf-mould, peat and sand, or leaf-mould and loam, in partially shaded borders, and kept moist. In June a mulch of leaf-mould, coconut fibre refuse,

gradually, as they need very little during the resting period. Increase by division at potting time.

HARDY SPECIES.

H. bifolia. The Butterfly orchid with white flowers tinged with green on lip and spur.

H. chlorantha, variety of *bifolia.* The Greater Butterfly.

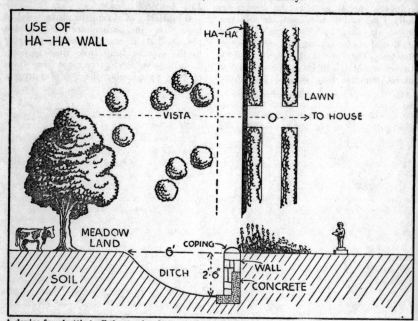

A device for shutting off the garden from cattle without the use of a fence is known as the Ha-ha. It is really a ditch retained by a dry wall.

or short grass should be given. They need plenty of water, especially if they are in a dry situation. These plants are best left undisturbed and they should only be replanted when they show signs of deterioration. Some species should be grown in pots in the greenhouse in a compost of one half of equal proportions of fibrous peat, loam and fresh-chopped sphagnum moss, and the other half of fine crocks and coarse silver sand. They should be potted when growth commences, and watered freely until they are well advanced. Then decrease water supplies

H. viridis. Frog orchid. Greenish-yellow, lip sometimes marked brown. Likes full sun.

GREENHOUSE SPECIES.

H. cornea, pink and white.

H. pusilla, green and scarlet flowers.

HABERLEA (hā-ber-lēa. Gesneraceæ). Tufted herbaceous perennials suitable for the rockery or for edging borders.

Culture.—Propagate by division of the crowns in spring or autumn, or by seeds sown as soon as ripe. Thrive in peaty soil, but require a little protection in winter.

SPECIES.

H. rhodopensis is the only species much grown. Each rosette of deep green leaves bears several flower-stalks with two to four blossoms of lilac colour with yellow throats, from June to July, height, 4–5 in.

Varieties of *H. rhodopensis* are *H. Ferdinandi; H. Coburgi*, with larger flowers and *H. Virginalis*, with pure white flowers.

HABLITZIA (ha-blitz-i-a. Chenopodiaceæ). Hardy herbaceous climbers that will grow in any ordinary soil. Plant in October or March at the base of a naked tree, on south or west trellis, arbour, wall or fence. Cut the stems down to the ground in October.

Propagate by seeds sown in spring in sunny places. Plant just below the surface. They may also be sown in a similar soil in boxes placed in the greenhouse in March, the seedlings being transplanted outdoors in May or June. Also by division of roots in October or April.

SPECIES.

H. tamnoides. Green, in summer. Height, 8–10 ft.

HACQUETIA (hak-kwe-tia. Umbelliferæ). A curious little hardy perennial plant usually known by the generic name, Dondia. It should be grown on a sunny rockery in sandy loam, and once planted it should be left undisturbed, as it is slow growing.

Propagate by division of the roots before growth starts in spring.

SPECIES.

H. epipactis, is rather similar to an Astrantia, having three lobed leaves and yellow flowers in umbels. Spring blooming. 3–6 in.

HÆMANTHUS (he-man-thus. Amaryllidaceæ). Greenhouse bulbous plants. Brilliant flowers, deciduous. S. Africa, 1722.

Culture.—Compost: 2 parts loam, 1 part peat, ½ part sharp sand. Repot only every 3 or 4 years, but remove a little of the top soil and replace with new annually. Water freely during growing period. After flowering gradually withhold water, dry off, and store pots under staging. A little liquid manure may be applied to plants in flower. Winter temperature, 50°; summer, 70°.

SPECIES.

H. cinnabarinus, red; *H. coccineus*, scarlet; *H. multiflorus*, scarlet, are the best.

HA-HA. A hedge, wall or fence sunk so as to be inconspicuous from the garden, with a ditch on the outside to prevent the intrusion of cattle.

Such a boundary gives uninterrupted views of surrounding country.

HAKEA (hā-ke-a. Proteaceæ). Tender foliage shrub from Australia, requiring warm sheltered gardens. In Cornwall they grow luxuriantly in the open. Plant in fibrous loam and peat.

Propagate by seeds sown under glass, and by cuttings under a bell-glass in spring.

SPECIES.

H. saligna. The Willow-leaf Hakea. Flowers white in April.

H. suaveolens. Pinnate foliage. Flowers white during summer.

HALESIA (hāl-zi-a. Styracaceæ). Snowdrop Trees. Deciduous shrubs or small trees bearing clusters of large pendulous, snowdrop-like flowers.

Culture.—Plant in October or November in sandy loam in a sunny or half-shady sheltered position. Pruning consists in thinning out overcrowded branches. *Propagate* by seeds and layers.

SPECIES.

H. carolina (*tetraptera*), Silver Bell or Snowdrop Tree (south-eastern U.S.A.). Undoubtedly one of the most handsome of all hardy flowering shrubs. Of spreading habit, soon reaching to a height of 6–10 ft. and flowering freely in May.

H. diptera. Leaves larger than preceding species; not so free flowering.

HALF-HARDY ANNUALS. Among these some of our most beautiful summer flowers are to be found, as for instance Anagallis, Asters (*Callistephus*), Ten Week Stocks (*Matthiola*), the stately Zinnia, and the exotic-looking Salpiglossis, and no garden can be considered complete without some representatives of this glorious family, most of which are very easy to grow.

Cultural Notes for H.H.A.'s—The best results are obtained by sowing under glass in February–March in a temperature of 50°–55°. A compost made up of loamy soil 2 parts, peat as used for bulb fibre 1 part, coarse sand 1 part, is very suitable; mix all thoroughly and pass through a ¼ in. sieve. Use pots or boxes of a suitable size, place some drainage material in the bottom, cover this with 1 in. of the coarser material, and fill up to within ½ in. of the top with the sieved compost. Use the compost in a moist condition, make the surface smooth, even, and moderately firm. Sow the seed thinly and evenly over the surface and just cover with fine soil. A light dewing overhead with a fine rosed watering-can will complete the operation. When sown, place the pots or boxes on a moist base and cover with sheets of glass; turn the glass over each day to dispel superfluous moisture, until the seedlings are through, then remove it entirely and stand the seedlings in good light near the roof glass to prevent drawing. Take care that the soil does not become dry, standing the pots, etc., in water nearly to the rim is better than overhead watering. As soon as the young plants are large enough to handle transplant into other boxes, compost as before, and at about 2 in. apart each way. Avoid at all times a close, stuffy atmosphere by judicious ventilation, and aim at getting sturdy plants ready to put out into their flowering quarters as soon as danger of damage by frost is past. The term Half-Hardy Annuals indicates that the types are not sufficiently hardy to be sown out of doors early in the season, although good results may sometimes be obtained by sowing out of doors on light soils in May. So treated they should be sown where they are to flower. Some of the most favoured kinds are *Acroclineum roseum*, *Ageratum*, *Alonsoa*, *Brachycome*, *Callistephus* (Asters), *Cosmos*, *Dimorphotheca* (Star of the Veldt), *Gaillardia picta*, *Helichrysum* (Everlasting Flowers), *Ipomœa*, *Kochia*, *Lobelia*, usually treated as H.H.A. *Petunias*, *Ricinus*, *Stocks* (Matthiola), *Nemesia*, *Nicotiana* (Tobacco Plant), *Phlox Drummondii*, *Salpiglossis*, *Salvia*, *Schizanthus*, *Statice sinucata*, *Tagetes*, *Ursinia*, *Venidium*, *Verbena*, *Zinnia*.

HALF-HARDY BIENNIALS. This is a group the members of which will not stand the winter out of doors in Britain,

and require the protection of a greenhouse from which frost can be excluded. Seed should be sown in pots in spring or summer, and the plants grown on in cold frames, or out of doors in sheltered districts for the summer months; taking them into the greenhouse in early autumn before frosts are likely to occur.

Examples. — *Calandrinea umbellata; Celsia cretica; Gilia coronopifolia.*

HALF-HARDY BULBS. This refers to those subjects which have a bulbous root-stock and which are liable to be killed by frost if left in the open ground during winter.

Examples.—Gladioli, Tigridia, etc.

HALF-HARDY PERENNIALS. The Dahlia is a good example of this section, the members of which have a perennial root-stock which is liable to be killed by frost if left in the open ground during the winter. They can be raised from seed sown under glass in March. The roots should be lifted in autumn and stored in a dry frost-proof place for the winter.

HALIMODENDRON (hal-i-mo-den'-dron. Leguminosæ). Deciduous handsome grey-foliaged shrubs, with small pea-like flowers. Thrives on poor soils, but not chalky ones. *Propagate* by grafting on common laburnum; also by seeds, cuttings and layers.

SPECIES.

H. argenteum (syn. *Robinia Halimodendron*), Salt Tree of Siberia, 6 ft. Flowers pinkish during June and July.

HAMAMELIS (ha-ma-mē'-lis. Hamamelidaceæ). Witch-Hazels. Deciduous shrubs and trees, flowering profusely in winter and early spring.

Culture.—Plant in October or November, in moist, well-drained loamy soil, with additions of peat and leaf-mould. Pruning consists in merely thinning out the branches in April if overcrowded. They are also very effective, kept to a single stem. *Propagate* by seeds sown in frame, by layering in late summer and by grafting. The best stock for grafting is *H. virginiana*.

SPECIES.

H. japonica, Japanese Witch-Hazel (China and Japan). A spreading species, 10 ft. Flowers pale yellow, fragrant, during January and February.

H. j. arborea. Differing from type in the deeper yellow of the petals, and the more tree-like habit of growth, attaining to 20 ft.

H. mollis, Chinese Witch-Hazel. The handsomest of the genus. Leaves deep green, changing in autumn to golden yellow; flowers rich golden yellow, very fragrant, commencing to open in December and continuing until March. Most effective grown as a standard. Award of Garden Merit, R.H.S.

HAND-LIGHT. *See* CLOCHE.

HANGING BASKETS. These are used for hanging in conservatories, win-

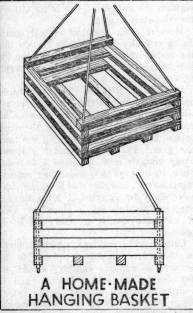

A HOME·MADE HANGING BASKET

Hanging baskets filled with ivy, geraniums and other flowers can be grown where there is no garden.

dows, corridors and greenhouses, and, if filled with a pleasing combination of plants, can be very beautiful. They are made of galvanised wire, wood and sometimes terra-cotta.

They should be lined with moss before being filled with good soil and it is usually advisable to plant some trailing plants round the edges, as these add considerably to the charm of the basket.

HARD-CORE. The name applied to the layer of brick-bats, rubble, etc., used to form the foundation of a drive or pathway.

HARDENBERGIA (har-den-ber-ji-a. Leguminosæ). Greenhouse herbaceous and shrubby climbers that may be trained to pillars and trellises and grown in pots or, preferably, in a border.

Propagate by seeds sown in gentle heat in spring, but more commonly by cuttings

Hanging flower-baskets should be lined with moss before being filled with soil.

of young side shoots taken in April and inserted in sand. Soil, 1 part each of loam, peat, manure, with a good dash of sand. Almost all the species flower early in the year. During very sunny weather they need to be shaded.

SPECIES.

H. comptoniana, purple, March.

H. monophyla, purple, April.

HARDENING OFF. Plants raised in a greenhouse need to become gradually accustomed to outdoor conditions before being planted out in the garden borders. This is done by taking seedlings or tender plants from the greenhouse and placing in a cold frame and after a few days moving them to a sheltered position out of doors. This process of hardening off is necessary so as to avoid checking the growth of the plants by sudden changes of atmosphere.

HARD TENNIS COURTS. There are roughly two types of hard tennis court which are popular at the present time. One is the type with asphalt or concrete surface, and the other of some loose material such as burnt clay. The former is not very satisfactory, being tiring to the feet, and if the subsoil sinks the surfacing cracks and is difficult to repair. The latter type needs occasional sweeping and rolling but is more resilient and dries quickly after rain. Hard-court firms are, however, constantly introducing new surfacing materials in red and green shades. They are aiming at a type which will give a perfect drainage, require no upkeep, and of suitable colouring and surround to fit in harmoniously with the general garden scheme.

Much has yet to be done in connection with this last point. A hedge of some quick-growing evergreen such as *Cupressus macrocarpa* or *Thuya lobbii* does much to soften the hard outlines of tennis court surround netting. A trellis screen well covered with climbers is also suggested. In any case the court should be reached by well-made pathways giving direct access to the house and linked up with the main garden design. A well-planned shrub and tree border or some flower borders add to the beauty of the court surround and are restful to the eyes of the players.

Whichever type of court is chosen, the construction does not vary to any great extent. The first step is thoroughly to clear the ground of weeds and rubbish, strip the ground of any existing turf and, if thought necessary, dress the site with a good weed-killer to prevent the further growth of any perennial weeds.

The site should then be levelled, allowing for a steady fall of not more than 6 in. from end to end of the court to assist drainage. If the soil is very heavy, drains may be necessary, but on light soils the clinker foundation should be sufficient. An edging of bricks should then be set in cement around the court to retain the foundations. On top of the levelled,

consolidated soil spread a layer of clean boiler ash, thoroughly roll and allow for the finer of the coarse ashes to be on the surface. A layer of fine sifted ashes—approximately 1–2 in. thick—should then be thoroughly rolled on to the boiler ash foundation. The surfacing material which has been selected is then applied about 2 in. thick, sprayed with a bituminous colouring material, and the playing lines either marked out with white paint or lead tapes.

Iron netting posts are usually 9 ft. high, spaced 10 ft. apart, and inserted 2 ft. into the ground. String netting or galvanised wire link-netting is stretched between the uprights, gates being allowed for where necessary.

Moss is often prevalent on old courts owing to faulty drainage. To remedy this the surface should be treated with caustic soda, mixed at the rate of 8 lb. to 15 gal. of water.

HARDY ANNUALS. The term hardy annual is applied to those races of plants which are born, i.e., grown from seeds, produce flowers, and die during the same season, their life cycle occupying less than one year. For general garden purposes hardy annuals must be given a foremost place, their range is so wide, their requirements so few, and they can be grown most successfully by everybody. Even for uncongenial positions and in almost any kind of soil some species or other will be at home.

Culture.—The positions, whether clumps in the mixed border or places to be devoted to annuals entirely, should be dug during the winter months, and if a little well-rotted manure can be spared dig it in then, leaving the surface rough. Hardy annuals need no protection. Sow the seeds out of doors in March or early April in the positions where the plants are to bloom. To sow: on a drying day in spring, break down the surface soil to a fine tilth and rake smooth, draw drills 1 in. deep and 6 in. apart for large seeds such as Lupins, Lavatera, etc., and $\frac{1}{2}$ in. deep for smaller seeds as Clarkia, etc. Sow thinly and cover with fine soil, the amount of covering to afford, as a general rule, to be three times the diameter of the seed. The following kinds will succeed ractically anywhere: *Adonis autumn-lis*, *Agrostemma cœli-rosa*, *Alyssum mari-imum*, *Amaranthus caudatus*, *Bartonia urea*, *Calendula* in variety, *Calliopsis* in ariety, *Centaurea cyanus* (cornflower), *Chrysanthemum tricolor*, *Clarkia elegans*, *Delphinium ajacis* (Rocket Larkspur), *Delphinium consolida* (Branching Lark-pur), *Eschscholtzia* in var., *Gilia capitata*, *Godetia* in variety, *Gypsophila elegans alba*, *Helianthus annuus* (Annual Sunflower), *Iberis* (Candytuft), *Lavatera trimestris* in ar., *Linum grandiflorum* (Scarlet Flax-lower), *Lupinus Hartwegii*, *Malope grandi-flora*, *Matthiola bicornis* (Night-Scented Stock), *Papaver* (Poppies, Shirley and Opium), *Reseda* (Mignonette), *Tropæolum majus* (Tall Nasturtium), *Tropæolum nanum* (Dwarf Nasturtium), *Viscaria occulata*. Many other kinds will be found in the general list of plants, including Sweet Peas, for which special cultural notes have been written.

HARDY BIENNIALS. Hardy bien-nials are those types, the seed of which is sown in the spring or summer of one year so produce plants for the following season's display. Some of the most popular kinds such as Wallflowers, are really of a perennial nature, but give best results if created as biennials.

Culture.—A good guide to sowing is to sow for the following season's display at the time the current season's plants are at their best. A position shaded from the midday sun is best. Rake the seed bed fine, draw shallow drills a few inches apart, and if the soil is dry, water the drills prior to sowing. Sow thinly and evenly, and just cover with fine soil. A few sheets of newspaper laid over the seedbed and kept in position by stones on the corners will help to keep the soil moist until the seed-lings are through. Transplant to 6 in. apart each way as soon as large enough. Plant into their flowering quarters in autumn.

Examples.—Canterbury Bells; Forget-me-nots; Double Daisies; Wallflowers.

HARDY BULB. Hardy bulb is the term used to indicate those plants which have a bulbous root-stock, and may be left permanently in the open gardens.

Examples.—Daffodils; Narcissi; Tulips; Snowdrops, Muscari, etc.

HARDY PERENNIALS. This term refers to those plants which last for many years—an exceedingly large group and among the most popular of which are Achillea; Campanula; Delphinium; Erige-ron; Gaillardia; Helenium; Hollyhock; Phlox; Michaelmas Daisies, etc. These are invaluable for growing in the "Her-baceous Border," and many types are very suitable for the rockery. The cultivation of the different genera, and the best purpose for which they are adapted, are dealt with under their respective headings.

HAREBELL. *See* CAMPANULA.

HAWKSBEARD. *See* CREPIS.

HAWKWEED. *See* HIERACIUM.

HAWORTHIA (ha-worth-ia. Liliaceæ). A genus of succulent plants that respond to the treatment given to Aloes. The leaves are small and arranged in rosettes, while the flowers are inconspicuous and of a greyish-white or greenish colour.

SPECIES.

The species are numerous and only a few of the best are given.

H. albicans, leaves 2–3 in., edged white. July.

H. arachnoides, August.

H. attenuata, July.

H. atrovirens, May.

H. clariperla, June.

H. fasciata, August.

H. mirabilis, July.

H. reticulata, June.

H. retusa, June.

H. tortuosa, July.

H. viscosa, June.

Several of the species are synonymous with some of the Aloes.

HAWTHORN. *See* CRATÆGUS OXY-CANTHA.

HAZEL NUT, or FILBERT (*Corylus avellana*). The Hazel Nut, or Filbert, is a native of Europe, and is frequently to be found in our hedgerows and woods. The size and flavour of the nuts as culti-vated have been much improved by means of selection.

Varieties known as Cob Nuts are those with short husks, whilst those with long husks are called Filberts. The Barcelona nut is a variety widely grown in Spain.

Soil.—The hazel nut will grow on any type of soil. A light, well-drained loam produces the best results. On heavy soils there is a tendency to make too much growth with a consequent loss in bearing qualities.

Position.—Although not essential, a sunny position with a southern aspect is best.

Planting.—This may be done at any time between November and March. Allow a distance of 10 ft. apart each way.

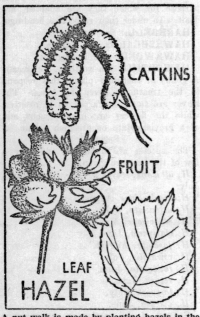

A nut walk is made by planting hazels in the form of an avenue. The little red star-like female flowers appear with the male catkins in early spring.

Pruning.—Young bushes should have all shoots shortened back by about one-third of their length, in order to encourage side shoots which bear the fruit. Summer prune these laterals in August to 6 in. and cut them back hard in late winter as soon as the catkins, or male flowers, have withered. The cut should be made to a female flower bud, which may be readily distinguished by the production of crimson styles at this period. It sometimes occurs that the shorter laterals bear these female flowers terminally, in which case they should be left unpruned.

VARIETIES.

KENTISH COB.— The best variety for garden cultivation. Nuts large and flavour good.

KENTISH FILBERT.—Excellent flavour, but does not produce many catkins, and is consequently not very fertile. "Prolific Filbert" should be planted as a pollinator.

PROLIFIC FILBERT.—A heavy cropper. The nuts are small but of excellent flavour.

Propagation.—The best means is to take off suckers in autumn and plant them in nursery rows until large enough for planting permanently. Seedlings may be raised from the nuts sown in autumn when ripe but they seldom produce such good bushes as the parent.

Pests.—The maggot which is frequently found in mature nuts is that of the Nut Weevil. Prevention is best secured by shaking the trees in summer, and burning all nuts which have holes bored in them.

Hazel (Corylus). *In Norse sagas sacred to Thor—and thus a protection from lightning (Thor's bolts). In the Tyrol to this day it is used for making "lightning conductors."*

In Sweden its nuts bestowed invisibility upon the one who picked them with the prescribed ceremony, and, in addition, "no witch's charm could do him harm." Hazel wands have been the "divining rods" for water-finding and even for finding hidden treasure from time immemorial.

HEATH. } See ERICA, *also* CALLUNA
HEATHER. } *and* DABOËCIA.

HEATHER GARDENS. It is increasingly popular to grow one kind of flower in a garden by itself. The most common gardens of this kind are rose gardens. The latest vogue is to devote a garden entirely to the culture of heaths. A heather-garden has much to commend it. It is possible to select various kinds of heather so that there is always one, or perhaps more, varieties in bloom throughout the year. Of course, if a mountain site is available this makes the construction of the heather-garden at once easy and appropriate.

The inspiration for the heather-garden cannot be found in a book. It must be taken direct from nature. The rocky

illsides and sweeping moorlands offer
many suggestions for the design of a
eather-garden.

If a stream is available, this will, of
course, be employed to enhance the beauty
f the picture.

The paths through the mountain
heather-garden should be similar to those
ound in nature, simple "sheep-tracks"
hat wind to and fro and provide unexpected views. They may be carpeted
vith various plants which are found on
he mountain-side, such as thymes, hill-
ide grasses, etc.

The best time of the year for planting
he heather-garden is during September
or October, provided there is showery
weather at the time of planting.

Ericas, grown in pots, are obtainable
or planting at any time of the year, but
here is much to be said for autumn
planting.

There are many kinds of heathers which
can be used according to the amount of
space available. They vary considerably
in height, as will be seen from the following list.

Erica arborea	.	.	.	3 to 6 ft.
,, australis	.	.	.	3 ,, 6 ,,
,, carnea	.	.	.	¾ ,, 1¼ ,,
,, ciliaris	.	.	.	1 ,, 1½ ,,
,, cinerea	.	.	.	1 ,, 1½ ,,
,, codonodes	.	.	.	3 ,, 6 ,,
,, mediterranea	.	.	.	1½ ,, 3 ,,
,, scoparia	.	.	.	3 ,, 6 ,,
,, stricta	.	.	.	1½ ,, 3 ,,
,, tetralix	.	.	.	¾ ,, 1¼ ,,
,, vagans	.	.	.	1½ ,, 2 ,,
,, (Calluna) vulgaris	.	.	1 ,, 1½ ,,

A good guide for distance apart is the
height of the plant, i.e., plants of 1 ft. in
height should be planted 1 ft. apart.

Once planted, the heather-garden is not
costly in upkeep, in fact it can be left to
its own devices, the only attention required being to control certain varieties
which outgrow their allotted space.
Should any of the varieties seed themselves, the seedlings would have to be
thinned or removed to prevent the area
from becoming too crowded.

The following are hardy heathers,
suitable for stocking the garden :

Erica carnea.
,, c. præcox.

Erica c. Vicelli.
,, cinerea coccinea.
,, Darleyensis.
,, D. rubra.
,, vagans Lyonesse.
,, v. grandiflora.
,, v. St. Keverne.
,, mediterranea rosea.
,, Tetralix plena.
,, vulgaris alba.
,, v. Alportii.
,, v. flore pleno.

HEBE. *See* VERONICA.

HEBENSTREITIA (hēben-streit-ia.
Selaginaceæ). *Comosa.* Half-hardy perennial with spikes of white flowers spotted
orange. Sow outside in ordinary soil in
April.

SPECIES.

H. comosa, 12 in.

HEDERA (hed'-er-a. Araliaceæ). Ivy
Evergreen climbers, unrivalled for covering old trees and buildings and useful
in many other ways. Some of the
varieties are very beautiful. To enjoy
ivies in their fullest beauty, it is necessary
to give heed to position, soil and training,
especially to the choice and more delicate
varieties. *H. mederensis variegata,* for
instance, may be successfully used as
edgings to a bed of shrubs; or it may be
used to cover an old root-stump, arbour,
etc. Flowers usually appear in October
followed by berries of black, red and yellow. It is generally supposed that ivy is
injurious to trees when allowed to climb
them, but this is only when the ivy has
reached the leafy shoots of the trees it is
allowed to climb over. No harm results
if the ivy is confined to the trunk and
main branches.

Culture.—The spring months are the
best for planting. Plants grown in pots
may be put out at any time. Poor soil is
best for the variegated forms, so as to
bring out the variegation. *Propagate*
by cuttings taken in late summer, and
placed in a shady border, root readily
and quickly. If the shoots are weak, the
plants will be strengthened by cutting
down to the ground after the first year.

SPECIES.

The common Ivy (*Hedera Helix*) has
been grown for many years, and has produced under cultivation so many varieties

that their name is legion. The following are some of the most distinct and useful species and varieties:

Hedera canariensis (maderensis), algeriensis Canary Island Ivy. A large-leaved species.

H. c. variegata (Gloire de Marengo). Leaves dark green at centre merging into silvery-grey; bordered white.

H. Helix, the native "Common Ivy."

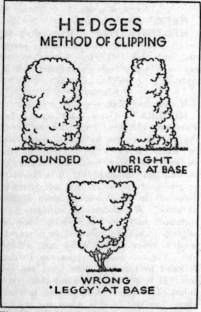

HEDGES
METHOD OF CLIPPING

ROUNDED   RIGHT WIDER AT BASE

WRONG 'LEGGY' AT BASE

The ideal hedge should be feathered close to the ground. A mixture of Thorn and Beech is very attractive if clipped with a wide base.

H. H. elegantissima (marginata rubra). Beautiful variety with small green leaves margined silvery-white, tinted pink.

HEDGE MUSTARD. *See* ERYSIMUM.

HEDGES. *Planting.*—A hedge once planted must remain for many years, and thorough preparation of the soil is of vital importance. If it is a boundary hedge the method of working should be as follows: First mark out a 3 ft. width of ground where the hedge is to be. Next attend to the drainage, if necessary. An agricultural drain 2 ft. beneath the surface may be advisable. In other cases it will be sufficient to excavate a ditch along one side and build a mound for the hedge with the soil taken from the ditch. If the natural soil is poor, add more good soil or enrich the existing soil by digging in well-decayed manure and bonemeal. Lime is, of course, also advisable except in the case of certain plants to be grown in peaty soils.

Hedge planting may be carried out at any time between early September and the middle of May; but, generally speaking, the earlier in winter the hedge is planted the more quickly will it establish itself.

The really evergreen hedges, such as holly and yew, are best planted in September or May and not during the coldest months.

It is advisable to cut hedge evergreens back at least one-third at the time of planting, otherwise there is so much evaporation of moisture from the leaf surface that the plants may wither before the roots are able to take hold of the soil. It also helps evergreens if they are syringed overhead daily for a short time after planting, unless the weather is showery. Do not be alarmed if the leaves of the newly planted evergreens begin to fall; this is a good sign and means that nature is restoring the balance between the injured roots and the plant tops. It is a bad sign if the leaves shrivel and remain on the plants. If this happens, cut the plant back still more and keep it moist and shaded.

Distance apart.—The distance apart of hedge plants is largely determined by the size and condition of the plants obtainable. Plants well furnished with branches to the ground line are best. Leggy plants with naked lower parts will never be satisfactory. Common privet is set from 1 ft. to 18 in. apart. Thorn is set even closer than this; but hollies and yews may be placed as much as 18 in. apart. Naturally, the closer the plants are set the more quickly will the hedge become thick and serviceable; but if time is not a serious consideration, a good hedge can be made much more cheaply by setting the plants farther apart and feeding them well to encourage rapid growth. Although the choice of garden hedges generally depends entirely on the wishes of the owner, a little care must be exercised in the case of garden hedges bordering on the fields and farmland. A few types of hedges are injurious to stock. Yew, for instance, is well known to have poisonous properties, and as a rule cupressus and thuya should be avoided. Thorn is generally best, as it makes a good hedge which cattle will not break. Beech, Hornbeam and Maple are also suitable subjects for boundary hedges.

Pruning.—The pruning of young hedge plants is particularly important. It is always a mistake to let them grow high too quickly. Encourage them first to make dense bottom growth—the tops can be left to take care of themselves; otherwise the tops become thick while the bottoms are thin, and this cannot be rectified without drastic pruning which causes considerable delay.

Whitethorn and Myrobalan plum are best cut down to within 6 in. of the ground level twelve months after planting. This makes them form a number of strong shoots, and the resulting hedge is very thick at the bottom. As a rule, more clipping is needed with young hedges than with older ones.

Very formal garden hedges need continual clipping during the summer months. Privet, Lonicera nitida, Box and other small-leaved evergreens can be cut with shears to a definite shape. Clipping is then necessary very frequently through the growing season. The Portuguese Laurel and similar large-leaved hedge plants can also be trimmed rather formally, but it is much better to use secateurs for the work, so that the leaves do not get cut in half.

Informal hedges are as a rule cut immediately after flowering, though in the case of informal rose hedges and others, where the fruits are ornamental, some discretion must be exercised.

The old garden hedge that is becoming straggly may need to be pruned back very severely to reduce its size. This severe pruning should be done in March or April, if possible, as the pruning will be immediately followed by a long growing season, during which the hedge will be able to recover.

Some of the best hedge plants are as follows:

Austrian Pine.—A dense shelter hedge or wind-break for exposed places. Plant two or three rows, with the plants 8 ft. apart.

Beech.—Deciduous, but clipped hedges hold the brown leaves all through the winter. Makes a fine contrast if used with dark green holly. The copper beech also makes a good hedge but is more expensive.

Barberry.—Both evergreen and deciduous forms of Berberis are useful as hedges. *B. Darwinii* and *B. stenophylla*, both spring flowering, make good evergreen hedges. *B. verruculosa*, *B. Wilsonae*, *B. Thunbergii* also make good dense, impenetrable hedges. These three bear yellow blossoms and coloured fruits.

Box.—Dwarf hedges up to 5 ft. Most useful of all evergreens for topiary work.

Butcher's Broom (*Ruscus aculeatus*). About 18 in. high. Evergreen. Female plants with red berries. Excellent for a position under trees.

Cistus.—For informal hedges up to 4 ft. high. Good in sunny positions and poor soil.

Cotoneaster Simonsii.—For seaside districts. Ornamental berries.

Cupressus.—*Lawsoniana* or *C. macrocarpa*. The latter is too tender for the north of Britain.

Heaths.—Several tall forms of Erica are useful for informal hedges in lime-free soil.

Escallonia.—White- or red-flowered varieties. Useful in the south and south-west counties.

Euonymous japonicus.—Gold- and silver-leaved varieties. Good seaside plants.

Fuchsia riccartonii.—Good for seaside districts.

Hawthorn.—The best cheap hedge.

Holly.—Probably the best evergreen hedge, but slow growing.

Hornbeam.—Useful on heavy ground.

Laurel.—Good shelter hedge for all purposes.

Laurustinus.—Winter-flowering hedge.

Lavender.—A useful dwarf hedge. Specially effective on the top of rock banks.

Lonicera nitida.—4-5 ft. hedges. Clip constantly from the earliest stages.

Myrobalan, or Cherry Plum.—Used with the purple-leaved plum makes a fairly good hedge.

Daisy Bush (Olearia Haastii).—For almost any position. White flowers in

July. Forms a hedge 6 ft. high and 2–3 ft. through.

Privet.—Too common to need any description. The golden-leaved form mixed with the green form makes an attractive hedge.

Roses.—Sweet Briars. Grüss an Teplitz, Zéphirin Drouhin, Rosa rugosa and its varieties and others make useful hedges if encouraged to form bushy plants.

HEEL

SHRUB CUTTINGS SHOULD BE TAKEN WITH A HEEL

SHOWING HOW ROOTS FORM FROM HEEL

When a cutting is taken off with a small piece of the older wood from a shrub or plant, the older portion is called the heel.

Thuya (Arbor vitæ).—Evergreen, and sometimes golden-leaved.

Veronica.—Several varieties are useful for small informal hedges, particularly near the sea.

Yew.—Green or gold-leaved. Makes the finest possible shelter hedge, but is best for situations within a garden and not for boundary hedges.

Other trees suitable for screening are: Acacia (common); Common Chestnut; Fruit trees (in variety); Laburnum vulgare; Larch, European; Lime; Mountain Ash; Poplar, Lombardy; Poplar, Balsam; Poplar, Black; Silver Birch; Sycamore.

HEDYCHIUM (he-dik-i-um. Scitamineæ). Beautiful herbaceous plants from the tropics, that bear their flowers in huge trusses and have handsome leaves.

Propagate by division of the roots before repotting them in spring. Cut the crowns with a sharp knife, allowing one or two eyes to each portion of root. Insert these in sandy loam or coconut fibre over bottom heat. When growth has started they may be treated similarly to Cannas. Pot up in a compost of equal parts of loam, leaf-mould and manure with a little sand. During the growing period they require plenty of light and water, and to satisfy the latter demand the pots can be stood in water, as they are almost sub-aquatics.

SPECIES.

Very few of the species are grown, and amongst these *gardnerianum* is the most popular. Although the plants revel in heat, some of them are almost hardy in the south-west of England.

H. coronarium, with white fragrant flowers from May until July, is a stove plant. Its variety *flavum*, with orange fragrant flowers, although a stove or greenhouse plant, may be grown outdoors in very sheltered districts such as Cornwall and Devon. 5 ft.

H. gardnerianum, lemony-yellow fragrant flowers in summer, is nearly hardy in the districts mentioned above. 3–5 ft.

H. flavosum, yellow fragrant flowers, July. 2–3 ft.

H. Greenii.

HEDYSARUM (hē-dis-ar-um. Leguminosæ). French Honeysuckle. Deciduous, sun-loving shrubby Vetch with racemes of red flowers from June to September. Will thrive in almost any soil.

Culture.—Propagate by root division in spring and plant in open sunny borders in ordinary loam; also by seeds.

SPECIES.

H. capitatum, with rose-coloured blooms from June to July, height, 2 ft.

H. coronarium, with flowers of deep red from July to August, height, 2–3 ft.

H. microcalyx, with bright purple flowers, height, 18 in.

H. Multijugum (Mongolia). Beautiful

in autumn with numerous rosy-red (rosy-magenta to some people), pea-shaped flowers, with a patch of yellow at base of each petal; of rather ungainly habit, which may be corrected by pegging down the branches, which causes them to break into new growth at their base.

H. neglectum, with rosy-purple flowers from June to August, 12 in.

H. obscurum, with flowers of bright crimson, 6–18 in.

HEDYSCEPE (he-dis-se-pe. Palmæ). The only species of this genus is *H. canterburyana*, 30 ft., a handsome stove palm that is synonymous with *Kentia canterburyana* and requires the culture given to Kentias.

HEEL. When a cutting, formed of the side shoot of a plant, is detached with a small piece of the main branch attached, the cutting is said to have a heel. Shrub cuttings are often taken in this way. The best way to sever them from the parent plant is to break the side shoot with a downward pull from the main stem. The presence of the "heel" will then be noticed.

HEELING-IN. A method of protecting roots of plants from drying out while waiting to be planted. A trench is dug into which the roots are placed, the stems being placed at a convenient angle against the slope of the trench. The roots are then completely covered with soil. Plants can safely be left like this for several weeks so long as the weather is not too frosty.

HELENIUM (hē-lē-nium. Compositæ). Sneeze-weed. Hardy herbaceous perennials that are useful for the border or shrubbery, are easy to cultivate and in autumn bear excellent flowers for cuttings.

Culture.—Propagate by division in spring or autumn, or by seeds sown in March or June. The taller species require staking but little feeding or watering is needed. Plant in ordinary garden soil in a sunny site.

SPECIES.

H. autumnale with heads of bright yellow flowers from July to October (height, 6 ft.) and its many varieties, *H. a. grandiflorum,* *pumilum*, and *magnificum* all with masses of bright golden flowers (height, 2–3 ft.) *cupreum* with coppery coloured flowers, and *striatum* with flowers of yellow striped with red (height,

5 ft.). Riverton Gem is another fine variety of *autumnale*.

H. bigelovii has rich golden flowers with brown centres from August to September. Height, 18 in.

H. Bolanderii resembles *Bigelovii*, but with black disked flower.

H. Hoopesii has orange flowers with black disks. Height, 2–3 ft. This is of rather coarser growth and earlier flowering.

HELENIUM

Helenium in yellow or bronze colours is a useful autumn border flower.

HELIANTHEMUM (heel-i-an-the-mum. Cistaceæ). *Helios*, the sun; *anthemum*, flower. Sun Roses. Of the greatest value for clothing dry, sunny banks, where but little else will grow. The number of these brilliant-flowered little bushlings is now so great that it is not possible to give a list of the garden varieties. New names are constantly being introduced, though not invariably applied to new varieties, and an up-to-date choice will be better made from the descriptions in nurserymen's catalogues. Nearly all these are varieties of our native species, *H. vulgare*, the yellow-flowered plant of our chalk downs. This itself is quite worthy of a place. Helianthemums will grow in gardens under almost any well-drained conditions in which the sun plays a part. The main flowering period is May and early June, though odd flowers will linger till August. To keep the bushes under control and check any tendency to straggling, they may be clipped back in early July to the required size. This

HELIANTHUS

The perennial Sunflower is useful for cutting and makes a bold display in the mixed flower border.

operation will not adversely affect the flowering in following year; it may even lead to an increased production of bloom.

Culture.—Plant in sandy loam, or ordinary garden soil, well drained; if possible add ample lime-rubble. No pruning is needed, but all dead blooms should be regularly removed and the plants kept in shape by "stopping" or "pinching" in March. *Propagation* is by seed sown in April, layering in August, or cuttings of half-matured wood in August, and placed in a shaded frame. The young plants should be grown on in pots until needed for

planting out. A sunny position is their principal need.

HELIANTHUS (hĕl-i-an-thus. Compositæ.) Sunflower. A genus of hardy annuals and perennials. The latter are popular flowers for borders and make a splendid show of colour in the garden in the autumn.

Culture.—Propagate by division of the root stocks in autumn or spring or by seed sown in March or summer. They will grow in any soil in a sunny position, and as the tuberous roots spread rapidly they quickly fill bare patches in the garden, although in the border they should be lifted occasionally as they exhaust the soil and deprive other plants.

SPECIES.

H. annuus is the tall-growing "Sunflower," 8–9 ft. Of this there are double-flowered forms—*H. a. fistulosus* is representative. The variety "Russian Giant" is extensively grown on the Continent for its seeds. Grow in a comparatively poor soil, and the plants will flower most freely.

H. cucumerifolius, 3 ft. Commonly known as Miniature Sunflowers, are very useful for borders or cutting. Flowers yellow, black disk. Its varieties *Stella* and *Orion* have long, twisted petals. Sow March–April, in ordinary soil where the plants are to flower. Give plenty of room.

H. giganteus or *altissimus*, a coarse kind with small yellow flowers. Height 10 ft.

H. multiflorus, a favourite species of which there are many varieties both single and double, such as Bouquet d'Or and Soleil d'Or.

See also ARTICHOKE, JERUSALEM.

HELICHRYSUM (hĕl-i-krīs-um. Compositæ). Everlasting Flowers. A genus of half-hardy or hardy annuals or perennials with flowers that if gathered early and hung head downwards in a cool dry place will retain their beautiful colouring throughout the winter.

Culture.—Plant in ordinary garden soil, with leaf-mould; if the soil is heavy, add sand.

Propagate the perennials by division in spring, or take cuttings in April and plant in gentle heat. They like a well-drained gritty loam in a sunny position.

1. Double herbaceous borders in the height of their summer glory.
2. Foxgloves in mixed colours are useful for the shady border.   (J. Carter & Co.)
3. Lupins massed in variety   If seed pods are removed fresh flowers form.

1. Cordon apples as they are grown in the nursery.
2. Gooseberries may also be grown as cordons.
3. Top branch self-pollinated—no plums set ; bottom branch cross-pollinated—set well.

(R.H.S.)

SPECIES.

H. anatolicum (plicatum). Asia Minor. Leaves silvery-white, flowers bright yellow in July.

H. bellidioides, a creeping plant with heads of white flowers from July to September, height 4 in.

H. frigidum, a small tufted plant with heads of white, flowers at the same time as *bellidioides.* It is not quite hardy and should be covered with glass in winter.

H. Rosmarinifolium (Ozothamnus rosmarinifolius). The Tasmanian Snow in Summer. About midsummer every twig bears clusters of white flowers, practically covering the whole plant in a snow-white sheet of bloom. The flowers should be cut before they have opened sufficiently to show the central disk, and dried by hanging them up in a room free from dust. They may be taken down in a few weeks, and used for indoor decorations. No water should be put in the vases. It is only hardy in the warmer counties, needing wall protection in other parts.

HELICODICEROS (hel-i-kod-i-ker-os. Aroideæ). A hardy tuberous-rooted perennial that is more curious than beautiful. The leaves form a sort of horn at the base of the plant.

Propagate by division. Plant in light rich soil. In cold localities it needs protection in winter.

SPECIES.

H. crinitus, dark purple spathe (syn. *Arum crinitum*), 1 ft., April.

HELIOPHILA (he-li-of-i-la. Cruciferæ). A charming half-hardy annual from The Cape with beautiful racemes of sky-blue flowers which have a small white eye. Like *Ursinia anethoides,* this plant has been re-introduced of late years, and is much in vogue for the cool greenhouse. It looks well when grouped with *Ursinia.* Height, 12–15 in.

Cultivation.—Sow thinly out of doors in April, and thin out to 6 in. apart, or sow the seeds in January in gentle heat and after germination prick out into fresh boxes of soil when large enough. Pot on into 60-size pots in a compost of leaf-mould, loam and sand and flower in 48-size pots, using for the final pots a similar soil compost which is rather coarser and enriched with a sprinkling of some complete

fertiliser. The plants require cool treatment as the season advances and plenty of sun. They can be transplanted to the open as bedding plants if desired. They flower during June and July.

HELIOPSIS (he-li-op-sis. Compositæ). A small genus of hardy annuals and perennials, of which the latter are the only ones seen. The annuals are rarely cultivated.

HELIOTROPE

" Cherry Pie " or Heliotrope, is a tender shrub which can be grown outdoors in the summer. It needs protection from frosts.

Propagate by division and seeds. Plant in any ordinary garden soil in a very sunny position. They respond to the same culture as Helianthus.

SPECIES.

H. lævis, orange-yellow flowers from July to September. Useful for cutting. 5 ft.

H. scabra, yellow, 3–4 ft., autumn.

H. s. imbricata, dwarf form, golden yellow. 3 ft.

H. s. pitcheriana, golden yellow, autumn. 5 ft.

HELIOTROPIUM (he-li-o-trop-i-um. Boraginaceæ). Heliotrope. Cherry-Pie.

M

Greenhouse flowering shrubs. W. Indies, 1752. Although not brilliant or showy, the Heliotrope is very pleasing to the eye and is numbered amongst our most richly-perfumed flowers. It is easy of culture and should find a place in every greenhouse or conservatory. May be planted outdoors in June, where it makes a valuable addition to the bedding plants, or better still, planted in the little "Scent

CHRISTMAS ROSES

The shade of trees and a leafy soil are the simple needs of a Christmas Rose.

Garden," where its wonderful perfume will be fully appreciated.

Culture.—Compost: 2 parts loam, 1 part leaf-mould, 1 part sand with the addition of charcoal and bonemeal. Pot early spring. Sunny position in greenhouse. May be grown as bush, standards, or trained to pillars or walls of house. Winter temperature, 45°; summer, no artificial heat required.

Propagation.—By cuttings of young shoots in light sandy soil in propagator, February, temperature, 65°; or in August in the greenhouse. Those taken in August generally strike more easily and

make the better plants. May be grown from seed.

SPECIES.

H. peruvianum, lilac (very fragrant) there are many varieties, but Lord Robert (beautiful dark mauve) is probably best

HELIPTERUM (he-lip-ter-um. Compositæ). Pretty half-hardy "everlasting" flowers that do well in pots or in the border in summer.

Propagate by seeds sown in the flowering position in April or in pots in the greenhouse in March, the seedlings being pricked off later 4 or 5 in a pot. The herbaceous and shrubby species are also increased by cuttings inserted in sand under a bell-glass.

SPECIES.

H. humboldtianum (syn. *H. Sandfordii*) yellow, annual. July, 1 ft.

H. Manglesii, with pretty pink or purple flowers, is an annual often sold under the name of *Rhodanthe Manglesii*, and is most commonly grown in pots. 1–1½ ft. Its varieties, *flore pleno* and *album*, are good doubles.

H. roseum (syn. *Acroclinium roseum*) pink, July, 2 ft.

HELLEBORUS (hĕll-eb-ōrus. Ranunculaceæ). Christmas Rose. Hardy perennial plants that are highly valued for borders as they bloom in winter and early spring and have beautiful foliage and stems, as well as flowers. The flowers of the Christmas Rose and the Lenten Rose are excellent for cutting, and if the stems are split when placed in water will last for several weeks.

Culture.—Plant in March. Propagated by seeds sown under glass in winter, or by division of the roots in March. They like a rich moist soil and often fail on a poor dry one. If grown among ferns, the fronds will protect the flowers from rain and the stalks will grow longer. For early flowers plant in a sunny position and use hand-lights in winter. Give occasional doses of weak liquid manure when in bloom and a mulch of good manure when flowering is over. Once planted leave undisturbed as the plants require three or four years to mature.

Hellebores are good for growing in pots for early winter flowering. Force gently and place outside in summer in a shady position. Give plenty of water. They are sometimes grown in warm pits where they will produce many blooms if well watered and given plenty of air.

H. niger, the Christmas Rose, with white flowers from November to February. 12 in. Several varieties of this exist with pink, purple or white flowers, such as *altifolius*, *angustifolius* and *præcox*.

HELONIAS (he-lo-ni-as. Liliaceæ). Hardy herbaceous perennials from N. America that like a moist, shady situation in fibrous loam and peat. Increase by division in spring, after which the plants are slow to grow, or by seeds sown at the same time.

SPECIES.

There are only about four species in the genus, of which the best is *H. bullata*, a graceful plant with rosy-purple flowers in spring and early summer. 1 ft.

HELWINGIA (Cornaceæ). Deciduous shrub from Japan. 3–4 ft. high, of no garden value, but of botanical interest only.

HELXINE (helks-ine. Urticaceæ). Wall Pellitory. A creeping, carpet perennial common on walls and in damp places in south-west England. Useful as a soil covering in pots and on walls, but often becoming a weed in rockeries.

SPECIES.

H. solierolii. 1 in. high, green.

HEMEROCALLIS (hĕm-ĕr-o'-căl-lis. Liliaceæ). Day Lily. Hardy attractive herbaceous perennial plants that are useful for borders or for the water garden, and are of much value in spite of the short duration of the flowers as they provide a continuity of bloom.

Culture.—Propagate by seeds sown in spring under glass, or preferably by division when growth is commencing. Plant in any good garden soil in a sunny position and provide plenty of moisture.

SPECIES.

H. aurantiaca, and its larger variety *H. a. major*, bear deep orange flowers from August to September. Height 3 ft.

H. Dumortierii and its variety *Sieboldii* have orange and orange-pink flowers from July to August. Height 1–2 ft.

H. flava, the native Day Lily, bears free-flowering clear yellow blooms that are good for cutting. Height 2–3 ft.

H. fulvo and its double form bear

coppery-coloured flowers shaded with crimson from June to August.

H. hybrida includes several hybrids such as Apricot, Citrina with pale lemon-coloured flowers, Gold Dust and Sovereign. Height, 2–3 ft.

H. Middendorffii resembles *Dumortierii*.

H. minor is the dwarfest of all and bears golden-yellow flowers from August to October. Height, 12 in.

DAY LILY

A useful plant for town gardens is the Hemerocallis, or Day Lily, so called because it opens a fresh flower each day.

H. Thunbergii, a late-blooming sort with rich orange flowers. Height, 2 ft.

HEMIPTELEA. *See* ZELKOVA.

HEMITELIA (hem-i-tel-i-a. Filices). Stove and greenhouse tree ferns. Evergreen. Jamaica, 1824.

Culture.—For compost, general cultivation and propagation, *see* BLECHNUM.

SPECIES.

(Stove).

H. Horrides, 8–10 ft.; *H. Walkeræ*, 4–6 ft.

(Greenhouse).

H. capensis, 6–10 ft.; *H. Smithii*, 8–12 ft.

HEMLOCK SPRUCE. *See* TSUGA.

HEMP AGRIMONY. *See* EUPATORIUM.

HEN AND CHICKENS. This name is given to a freak growth which sometimes appears on marigolds and on double daisies. It consists of a central normal flower with tiny satellite flowers surrounding. It is often seen in seasons when the weather is abnormal, and also results from abnormal

HERBACEOUS BORDERS. These flower borders, consisting largely of herbaceous perennials, have become a feature of almost every garden, whether large or small. There are good grounds for their popularity. Once planted they need not be disturbed for three to five years, and if varieties are selected carefully, they give a wealth of bloom for many months of the year.

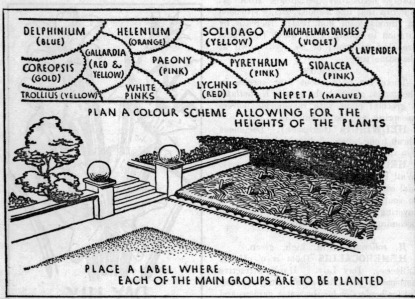

Above is a remarkable colour-scheme for the herbaceous border. Dwarf kinds are placed near the front.

food supplies. Some strains of seed appear to be particularly more liable to this peculiarity than others.

Bellis perennis prolifera is the striped double daisy, generally known as the "Hen and Chickens" daisy.

HERACLEUM (he-rac'leum. Umbelliferæ). Cow Parsnip. Hardy biennials and perennials which are too coarse to be worth while growing in flower borders but are extremely useful for the wild garden.

Culture.—Propagate by division or by seeds, and plant in any poor soil.

H. giganteum and *persicum*, both with umbels of white flowers from June to September, are the most commonly used. 7–10 ft.

They may be placed against a wall, fence, or hedge boundary, or they may be used to mark a division between one part of the garden and another. A smooth lawn is the best setting for a herbaceous border, but if space is limited a paved pathway with a grass verge is pleasing and really more practical.

A narrow path, possibly only 18 in. wide between a boundary and the back of a border, will give room to attend to the staking of tall plants without treading on the border.

Arrange the plants in groups of three, five or more to a clump. This method gives bright displays without patchiness. As a general rule place tall varieties to the back of the border; but the ideal to be aimed at should be that no plant hides another, and each has ample room to show its beauty.

To fill blanks in the border the first year use bulbs, annuals such as chrysanthemums, and dahlias. After the second year these should not be necessary. If the border is backed by a wall, introduce a few flowering and evergreen climbers to form a soft background. Flowering and evergreen bush shrubs, used in moderation, will fulfil exactly the same purpose for the border which has no architectural background.

When planting the border, place labels on the prepared site where each group is to come. This allows for proper spacing and ensures that the plants are planted without delay as soon as unpacked. During the summer keep the border hoed and stake the plants *before it is necessary*.

When renovating the border in the autumn of the third or fifth year, take out all the plants for a certain length, keeping them carefully labelled. Dig over the border, incorporating manure or lime if necessary, divide the roots and replant as required. Tackled in this way the whole border can be cleared gradually without leaving plants long exposed.

Finally, make a note of your failures. Note down during the summer the plants that are not doing well and find out whether they require a special soil condition which, with a little extra care, you can give them. Note down also good and bad colour associations and remedy the defects when renovating.

HERBACEOUS BORDERS, PLANTS FOR.

The plants selected for any herbaceous border should provide something of interest all the year round. The following brief selection would be suitable, but would be added to in most cases according to the personal tastes of the designer.

January.—Iris reticulata, Iris stylosa, Snowdrops.

February.—Snowdrops, Scillas, Anemone blanda, Crocus, Hardy Cyclamen, Iris alata.

March.—Fritillarias, Narcissus, Primulas, Doronicums, Muscari, Iris nudicaulis, Arabis.

April.—Arabis, Aubrietia, Doronicums, Alyssum saxatile, Primulas, Wallflowers, Tulips, Centaurea.

May.—Oriental Poppies, Iris (various), Lupins, Columbines, Campanulas, Geum.

June.—Delphiniums, Roses, Carnations, Pinks, Gypsophila, Linaria, Pæonies.

July.—Heleniums, Heuchera, Lilies, Chryanthemum maximum (the large Ox-eye Daisy), Anchusa italica, Achillea, Phlox.

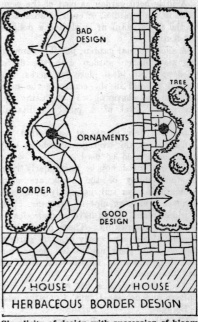

HERBACEOUS BORDER DESIGN

Simplicity of design with succession of bloom are the important features of the herbaceous border.

August.—Coreopsis, Scabiosa, Pyrethrum, Montbretias, Hemerocallis, Dictamnus, Rudbeckias, Spiræa, Gladioli.

September.—Rudbeckias, Statice, Chrysanthemums, Gladioli, Colchicum, Anemone japonica, Phlox, Linaria.

October.—Aster amellus, Aster (Michaelmas Daisy), Chrysanthemums, Sunflowers, Gladioli, Physalis (Winter Cherry).

November. — Kniphofias (Red Hot Pokers), Hydrangea paniculata, Schizostylis.

December.—Red Hot Pokers, Iris reticulata, Christmas Roses, Winter Heliotrope, Winter Aconite.

HERBACEOUS PERENNIALS.

Plants with a root-stock which lasts several years, increasing in size yearly. Fresh growth springs from the root-stock yearly.

HERB GARDEN. There are a number of herbs which are best grown together. They are frequently required in the house, and for this reason they should be planted near paths where they can be cut at all seasons of the year.

A little herb garden as part of the vegetable or fruit garden, or even as an annexe to the flower garden, is always a delightful feature.

A small formal garden, possibly connecting the kitchen garden with the flower garden, is an ideal place for herbs, and an old sundial in the centre is the most suitable and charming way of raising this above the level of a purely utilitarian section.

Since a few plants of each kind are sufficient for the average household, only small beds need be used.

The soil need not be particularly rich, in fact, many of the herbs are more aromatic in poor soil, especially if the site receives a fair amount of sunshine. The world of plants which have aromatic leaves is always interesting. These plants have become almost a necessity in every garden, not only for their use in the house, but for their romantic associations with all our literature.

The following is a list of herbs. For culture and use *see* HERBS, CULINARY, etc.

Borage	Parsley
Chervil	Rosemary
Chives	Rue
Fennel	Sage
Lavender	Savory
Marjoram	Tarragon
Mint	Thyme

HERBS, CULINARY. Angelica (*Angelica officinalis*). Umbelliferæ. A perennial herbaceous plant used for flavouring. Raise from seed sown in March in permanent places. Shady position.

Anise (*Pimpinella anisum*). Umbelliferæ. An eastern annual herb grown for the flavouring properties of the seeds and leaves. Sow in April in drills 1 ft. apart in sunny position, and thin to 6 in. apart when seedlings are large enough to handle.

Aniseed. *See* ANISE.

Balm (*Melissa officinalis*). Labiatæ. Hardy herbaceous perennials with aromatic foliage. Sow seeds thinly in shallow drills in sunny position in March. For winter use gather stems when flowers open and dry off.

Basil, Bush (*Ocimum minimum*). Labiatæ. Except for being more dwarf, this is very similar to Sweet Basil, and should be treated in the same way.

Basil, Sweet (*Ocimum basilicum*). Labiatæ. An annual herb used for flavouring many dishes. Sow early in April in light soil in temperature, 60°–65°. Prick off when large enough to handle and grow on close to glass. Ventilate freely, and harden-off for planting at the end of May. When fully grown pull up the plants and tie in small bunches for drying in an airy shed. Some plants may have the top cut off and the roots potted up for producing a supply of young green shoots under glass during winter.

Borage (*Borago officinalis*). Boraginaceæ. Largely grown as a Bee plant, and also used as a flavouring for liquors, notably claret-cup. Sow seeds in March in sunny position where to remain, and finally thin to 1 ft. apart.

Caraway (*Carum carui*). Umbelliferæ. A member of the Parsley family grown for the seeds for flavouring confectionery. Sow seeds in well-prepared soil in drills 1 in. deep and 1 ft. apart, in April. Well firm the soil after sowing, and keep well hoed throughout the summer. Cut down to ground in autumn. Seeds the second year.

Chervil (*Anthriscus cerefolium*). Umbelliferæ. A hardy annual herb used for garnishing, and for flavouring salads and soups. Sow at monthly intervals from March to October, choosing shady position for summer crops, and a south border for winter. Sow broadcast or in drills ½ in. deep, and finally thin the seedlings to 6 in. apart.

Chives (*Allium schoenoprasum*). Liliaceæ. A perennial native herb possessing a mild onion-like flavour. Used for flavouring. Sow seeds in March in same manner as Onions. Plant bulbs in March, 6 in. apart, in rows 1 ft. asunder. Divide in autumn or spring, and replant on fresh ground every third year.

Coriander (*Coriandrum sativum*). Umbelliferæ. A native annual herb grown for its seeds for use in confectionery, or its leaves for flavouring salads and soups. Sow seeds in shallow drills 1 ft. apart in March or September. Keep well hoed and harvest in August.

Dandelion (*Taraxacum*). Compositæ. A perennial herb, a native of Europe. In this country it is usually looked upon as a weed, but on the Continent, and particularly in France, improved strains are largely cultivated for the production of leaves, either green or blanched, for salads. Seed should be sown in March or April in a prepared seed bed and pricked out in May into good rich soil, spacing the plants 15 in. apart. In the autumn large pots may be placed over the plants to effect blanching. Dandelion is hardier and more productive than most Endives, and when well grown is not unlike the latter in flavour.

Dill (*Anethum graveolens*). Umbelliferæ. An annual herb which is gradually dropping out of cultivation. At one time it was largely used for medicinal purposes and for flavouring dishes. Seed should be sown in April in shallow drills 1 ft. apart where the plants are to stand. Thin to 9 in. apart when the seedlings are an inch or two high, and hoe frequently and water copiously in dry weather. The leaves may be picked as required for use, or dried for the winter. The seeds are also used for flavouring.

Fennel, Bitter (*Fœniculum vulgare*). Umbelliferæ. An ornamental perennial herb grown chiefly for its seeds, which are used for flavouring liquors. Seeds may be sown outside from April to August, and the plants will thrive on almost any soil, and in practically any position.

Fennel, Sweet (*Fœniculum officinale*). Umbelliferæ. A biennial herb of Southern Europe cultivated as an annual for the thick fleshy leaf-stalks. In Southern Italy the stalks are broken and eaten raw, and are considered a delicacy. Seeds may be sown *in situ* in spring and autumn to provide a succession of produce.

Finnochia (*Fœniculum dulce*). Italian or Florence Fennel. Umbelliferæ. This is an Italian annual herb quite distinct from the preceding species. The plant is dwarf in habit and produces very large fleshy leaf bases, which attain almost the size of a hen's egg. These are usually boiled for use and have a delicate flavour not unlike Celery. Sow thin in shallow drills 15 in. apart in April and September for successional crops. Thin the seedlings to 6 in. apart and slightly earth up the leaf bases as they commence to swell.

Garlic. Bulbs should be planted in February, or early in March, just deep

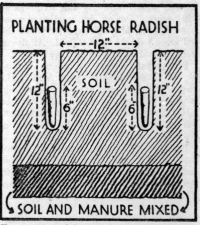

To secure straight succulent roots of Horse-radish the soil needs deep digging and manure.

enough to make them firm, but should not be quite covered with soil. 6–9 in. should be allowed from bulb to bulb, and 12 in. between the rows.

Horse-Radish (*Cochlearia armoracia*). Ground should be trenched in late autumn to a depth of 2–3 ft. Plant in February.

Mercury, French (*Mercurialis annuus*). Euphorbiaceæ. A little-known plant which is relished by some people when served as a vegetable in the same manner as Spinach. Sow in open in March, thinning the seedlings to 1 ft. apart. Earth up in spring to obtain blanched shoots for cutting like Asparagus. The leaves may be used in place of Spinach.

Mint. Mint grows from pieces of root and requires a moist soil in a not too sunny corner of the garden.

Parsley (Carum Petriselinium). Umbelliferæ. One of the most popular of all garden herbs, and one which is in demand almost all the year round for garnishing and for flavouring.

Although parsley will grow almost anywhere it is a crop which amply repays generous treatment. The ground should be deeply dug and manured in time for it to settle before the first sowing in April. Successional sowings may be made during June and August. Parsley makes an excellent edging in the kitchen garden, and the seeds may be sown in shallow drills along the margins of paths and borders, finally thinning the seedlings to 9 in. apart. During dry weather copious waterings should be given, after which the soil around should be well hoed. All flower stems should be cut off as they appear.

Pennyroyal (*Mentha pulegium*). Labiatæ. A member of the mint family, the leaves of which are used for seasoning. It grows best on heavy soils, and may be raised from seed sown in moist sandy loam and afterwards increased by division of the roots.

Purslane (Portulaca oleracea). Portulacaceæ. An annual herb introduced from India. It is used as a salad plant in the raw state or cooked after the manner of spinach. Seeds may be sown broadcast from the middle of April to the middle of August in light soil in a sunny position. Sow thinly, lightly rake in and keep well-watered during dry weather. When the young shoots are 2–3 in. lòng they are ready for use and should be cut off close to the ground.

Rampion (*Campanula rapunculus*). Campanulaceæ. A fleshy-rooted biennial herb, the leaves and roots of which are eaten raw in salads. The seeds are extremely small and should be mixed with sand to ensure even distribution when sowing in May either broadcast or in shallow drills 10 in. apart. As soon as possible the plants should be thinned to 10 in. apart each way, and should be kept well hoed and watered during dry weather.

Rosemary (*Rosmarinus officinalis*). Labiatæ. A perennial shrubby herb which flourishes best upon chalky soil. The plants are well clothed with small leaves, glossy green on top and grey beneath, and with many clusters of grey-blue flowers at the ends of the stems they make quite attractive features in a herb or kitchen garden. The leaves are very aromatic, and are used for seasoning.

Seeds may be sown $\frac{1}{2}$ in. deep in drills 1 ft. apart in an open sunny border from April to June, transplanting to their permanent quarters in the autumn, or a stock may be obtained from hard-wooded cuttings 8 in. long inserted in a sheltered border in September.

Rue (*Ruta graveolens*). Rutaceæ. A small bushy herb of perennial habit, which originated in Southern Europe. The leaves are very pungent and bitter, and are used for seasoning certain dishes. It grows readily from seed sown $\frac{1}{8}$ in. deep in fine soil outside in April or May, or by cuttings or division of the roots in late summer.

Sage (*Salvia officinalis*). Labiatæ. A very well-known herb, the leaves of which are largely used either green or dried for various "stuffings" or seasonings.

The plant is remarkably easy to cultivate, and may be raised from seed sown in shallow drills in April or from cuttings taken from old plants in April and inserted in a semi-shady border of good light soil. For winter use, leafy stems should be cut towards the end of summer and hung in bunches in a dry, airy place.

Savory, Winter and Summer (*Satureia hortensis* and *S. monta*). Labiatæ. Summer Savory is an annual, and Winter Savory a perennial. Both originated in Southern Europe and were introduced into English gardens about 1575. In both cases the leaves and young shoots are used for flavouring.

Both types may be raised from seed sown in shallow drills 6 in. apart in April; afterwards thinning to 1 ft. apart in the rows. When growth finishes in the autumn cut off close to the ground and hang up in a dry shed for winter use.

Skirret (*Sium sisarum*). Umbelliferæ. A hardy perennial with clusters of cylindrical, fleshy roots possessing a sweet flavour. It is used in the same manner as Salsafy and Scorzonera.

Seed should be sown in drills $\frac{1}{2}$ in. deep and 18 in. apart in April, afterwards thinning the seedlings to 1 ft. apart in the rows. Lift the roots in October, and after twisting off the leaves store in sand for winter use as is done for beet.

Tansy (*Tanacetum vulgare*). Compositæ. This is a very old-fashioned herb with aromatic leaves used for seasoning. It is a native of the British Isles, and grows well almost anywhere. Seeds may be sown thinly on a warm border in spring, or the perennial roots may be lifted and divided every second or third year in March.

Tarragon (*Artemisia Dracunculus*). Compositæ. This herb is now most often used as a flavouring for Tarragon vinegar and less frequently for salads and soups. It is a perennial and thrives in a rich, light soil which is well drained in winter. When seeds are obtainable they should be sown in shallow drills on a warm border in April or the tufts of roots may be increased by division.

Thyme (*Thymus vulgaris*). Labiatæ. This is probably one of the oldest and most generally used kitchen herbs. It is a small, slender, shrubby plant clothed with small leaves, dark green on top and grey beneath and bears clusters of pale pink flowers at the ends of the stems.

It grows easily from seed sown on a warm border in April or May. If thinned or pricked off in the seedling stage they may be planted out in their permanent places in autumn. Cuttings taken in summer also root readily and old plants may be divided.

HERBS, MEDICINAL.

Aconite (*Aconitum napellus*). Monkshood. Ranunculaceæ. A hardy perennial, the roots of which are similar in appearance to those of horse-radish, but are extremely poisonous.

Agrimony (*Agrimonia eupatoria*). Rosaceæ. Slender perennial. Native herb. Roots have astringent properties, and yield a yellow dye.

Chamomile (*Anthemis nobilis*). Compositæ. Hardy perennial herb. The flowers are used for making tea. Sow seeds outside, April to July. Divide roots in March.

Colt's-foot (*Tussilago farfara*). Compositæ. A perennial creeping herb. Native of the British Isles, and a troublesome weed in some districts. Sometimes used in the preparation of cough medicine, and the leaves used for making cigars, and for smoking to relieve asthma.

Horehound (*Marrubium vulgare*). Labiatæ. A hardy perennial herb used for making a home-brewed ale, and also for the alleviation of coughs and colds. Sow in shady border outside in spring, and the following spring transplant 18 in. apart in a fairly dry sunny position.

Hyssop (*Hyssopus officinale*). Labiatæ. A dwarf perennial shrubby herb with aromatic foliage used for making a medicinal tea. It is supposed to be beneficial for lung complaints. It is usually hardy in this country, and may be raised from seed sown in the open ground in April and planted out in July.

Lavender (*Lavandula vera*). Labiatæ. Small shrubs almost too well-known to describe. They are grown for the fragrance of the flowers, which may be cut and dried, and also for the oil which they yield. Hundreds of acres are devoted to the commercial cultivation of Lavender for distillation purposes. Lavender thrives best on a chalky soil, and a stock of plants may be raised from seed sown outside in shallow drills on a sunny border in April.

Marigold, Pot (*Calendula officinalis*). Compositæ. A popular old English herb which was used for promoting perspiration in the treatment of fevers. Seeds sown outside in April germinate readily, and may be transplanted to 1 ft. apart. The flowers when fully open are picked, dried, and stored for use as required.

HERMINIUM (Musk Orchis). Orchidaceæ. Hardy terrestrial orchid with musk-scented flowers.

For the culture of the musk orchid a compost of light turfy loam, with plenty of chalk or old mortar and leaf-mould added, should be prepared. A position on the sunny rockery or in a limestone moraine is most suitable, but it will also grow in pots in the cold frame. If wild roots are to be planted it is better to do this immediately the flowers have faded. Grown roots should be potted in early spring and division can also take place in the spring.

SPECIES.

H. monorchis, Musk Orchid, which has a small green flower, and the distinct perfume of musk.

HERNIARIA (her-ni-ar-i-a. Illecebraceæ). Rupture Wort. This genus is usually represented by the low-growing hardy herb, *H. glabra*, that is extensively used for carpeting and for forming a background for other plants. As it is perfectly hardy it may be left out of doors during the winter, unless it is desired to change the plan of the bed, and the room left by tender subjects lifted for the winter can be taken up by hardy bulbs.

Propagate by divisions and cuttings made in autumn. The ground should be firm, to ensure the beds giving a dense effect.

HERON'S BILL. *See* ERODIUM.

HESPERANTHA (hes-per-an-tha. Iridaceæ). From *hesperos*, the evening, and *anthus*, a flower — Evening Flower. Greenhouse bulbous plants, flowers fragrant, opening in the evening. S. Africa, 1787.

Culture.—Compost as for HÆMANTHUS. Pot November, 3 or 4 bulbs to a 4½ in. pot. Place in cold frame and cover with ashes or fibre; when growth commences remove to greenhouse, temperature, 45°. Water freely until flowering period is over, then gradually dry off. Store bulbs until following season in a dry position.

Propagation.—By offsets.

SPECIES.

H. cinnamomea, violet and white; *H. pilosa*, red and white; *H. radiata*, red and white.

HESPERIS. *See* ROCKET.

HESSEA (hes-se-a. Amaryllideæ). Syn. *Periphanes*. Greenhouse bulbs that are propagated by offsets or by seeds. They like a soil of sandy loam with a little leaf-mould and plenty of water during growth, but none during the resting period.

SPECIES.

H. crispa (syn. *Strumaria crispa*), pink. April to August. 3 in.

H. gemmata, pale yellow. August. 1 ft.

HETEROMELES (het-er-o-me-lez. Rosaceæ). Handsome evergreen shrub with holly-like leaves. Closely allied to Photinia, known as the Toyon or Tollon of California, thriving well in warm counties, including Surrey, but not in the London area. The pure flowers are produced freely in clusters during August, followed by berries, and are used in California at Christmas as we use holly.

H. arbutifolia, the only species.

HEUCHERA (heu-chera. Saxifragaceæ). Alum Root. Hardy perennials that are highly valued for their long graceful sprays of brilliant flowers which resemble those of London Pride, and provide flowers for cutting all through the summer.

Culture.—Propagate by division of the crowns in spring. Lift the old clumps and divide carefully. Place the divisions in a nursery bed of sandy soil in a warm sheltered position and leave for a year. If planted at once in permanent positions they do not succeed. They like a warm sunny soil of medium quality and plenty of air and light. In town gardens they die off very quickly.

SPECIES.

H. sanguinæ, with flowers of rosy-carmine and its varieties *grandiflora* and *splendens*, which are both larger and richer coloured than the type, are the best suited for all gardens.

H. brizoides, with pale pink flowers suitable for cutting; height, 2 ft.

H. Edge Hill, with pink freely-flowering blooms, height, 18 in.

H. micrantha has yellowish flowers, height, 2 ft.

A very good hybrid is *tiarelloides* with feathery pale pink flowers, height, 2 ft. All bloom from May to August.

HIBBERTIA (hib-ber-ti-a. Dilleniaceæ). Evergreen greenhouse trailers and climbers that may be grown in baskets or on pillars. The flowers form a fine contrast to the dark green or purplish leaves.

Propagate by cuttings of half-ripened shoots in a propagating case. Plant in sandy loam with a little peat. The climbers should not be tied too tightly or their beauty will be spoilt.

SPECIES.

H. Cunninghamii. July. 3 ft.

H. fasciculata. Summer. 3 ft.

H. dentata. Dark leaves. Spring to autumn. 10 ft.

H. perfoliata. May. 3 ft.

All bear yellow flowers.

HIBISCUS (hi-bis-kus. Malvaceæ). South Africa, 1½–2 ft. *H. Africanus* is synonymous with *H. trionum*. Hardy annual. Flowers yellow with a distinct purple eye. Sown out of doors, where to flower, April. Will flower from July onwards. There is a variety of *H. trionum* with white flowers flushed with pink. The genus also contains a deciduous flowering shrub, sometimes known as the Tree Holly-hock. Hardy in all but cold districts, where it may need wall protection owing to its late flowering. Commences to flower in the south from August onwards.

Culture.—Plant in March in ordinary garden soil, well drained, and in a sunny position. *Propagate* by layers and cuttings or by seed sown in spring. The choice and rare varieties are sometimes grafted on the commoner ones. Plants that are overgrown should be pruned in early April. They may be kept in shape by "stopping." The Hibiscus may also be cut back each year to a formal shape, as is practised at Versailles. In Italy it grows to over 20 ft. high, but in our uncertain climate 10 ft. is a good height. It is a very old plant in English gardens, and was grown by Gerarde in the 16th century.

SPECIES.

H. Syriacus. Although named after the country of Syria, it has never been found growing wild in that country, and the type is unknown. The following comprise the most distinct and beautiful garden forms:

H. s. amplissimus—double rose.

H. s. amplissimus cœleste—single, deep blue.

H. s. amplissimus cœruleus plenus—double blue.

H. s. amplissimus Duc de Brabant—double blue.

H. s. amplissimus Jeanne d'Arc—double white, exterior rose.

H. s. amplissimus monstrosus—single, large white, dark centre.

H. s. amplissimus rubis—single, ruby red, very fine.

H. s. amplissimus totus albus—single pure white.

HICKORY. *See* CARYA.

HIDALGOA (hid-al-go-a. Compositæ). *H. Wercklei*, a pretty climbing plant with scarlet ray florets and yellow disk florets, is the only species of this genus that has been introduced. It climbs by its leaf-stalks and blooms freely. Though not quite hardy it may be grown out of doors in summer, but must be brought in before

the frost comes. *Propagate* by cuttings and plant in good loam.

HIERACIUM (hī-er-ā-cium. Compositæ). Hawkweed. Hardy herbaceous perennials with yellow flowers, that are often beautiful when wild but are rarely worth growing in the garden. *H. villosum* and *H. aurianticum*, the latter having orange flowers, are both summer-bloomers and can be grown in the border or rock garden, height, 12–18 in. *Propagate* by seeds or division; plant in ordinary garden soil.

HIEROCHLOE (hi-er-ok-lo-e. Gramineæ). Hardy perennial fragrant grasses that are increased by division and seed. Called Holy Grass because it was used in churches on feast days. Grow in any soil.

SPECIES.

H. alpina. Green. July. 1 ft.

H. borealis. Brown. May. 2 ft.

H. redolens. Green. Summer. 2–3 ft.

HINDSIA (hind-si-a. Rubiaceæ). Greenhouse evergreen shrubs from Brazil. *Propagate* by cuttings in sand with bottom heat. Grow in loam, leaf-mould and sand. Summer temperature, 60°–85°; winter, 48°–55°.

SPECIES.

H. longiflora (syn. *Rondeletia longiflora*). Blue, August, 2 ft. *H. l. alba*, white, May.

H. violacea. The best of the species with violet-blue flowers in May. 3 ft.

HIPPEASTRUM. *See* AMARYLLIS.

HIPPOCREPIS (hip-po-kre-pis. Leguminosæ). Horseshoe Vetch. *Hippo*, horse, *crepis*, a shoe, referring to the shape of the seed pod.

Annual and perennial plants that are all hardy with the exception of *H. balearica*, which must be protected in winter.

Propagate by seed sown in the open border in spring or by division at the same season. A light sandy soil is best.

SPECIES.

H. balearica, shrub. Yellow flowers in spring. 2 ft.

H. comosa. Perennial trailer. Yellow. April. 6 in.

H. multisiliquosa. Annual. Summer. Yellow. 1 ft.

HIPPOPHAE (hip-pof'-ā-ē. Elæagnaceæ). Deciduous, willow-like, berry-bearing shrubs or small trees, growing particularly well in seaside districts.

They also thrive in inland gardens especially at the margin of water.

Culture.—Plant in October or February in ordinary garden soil. *Propagate* by seed sown in the open and by suckers or layers in autumn. Root cuttings may also be taken in spring.

SPECIES.

H. rhamnoides. See Buckthorn (Asia, Europe, Britain), 30–40 ft. Leaves grey-

FOUR TYPES OF HOES

CANTERBURY HOE

TRIANGULAR HOE

DUTCH HOE

DRAW HOE

No tool is more important in the garden than the hoe, of which there are various types for different purposes.

ish-green, silvery underneath. Flowers small in April. Berries orange-coloured, usually in colour by September, and being disliked by birds, they remain in beauty over a very long period. Both male and female plants should be obtained.

H. salicifolia (Himalayas). 40 ft. and over. Leaves broader than preceding, but not silvery. Berries smaller and paler.

HIPPURIS (hip-pur-is. Halorageæ). *H. vulgaris* is the best-known species of this genus. It resembles Equisetum in habit and is best grown by the waterside. Commonly known as the Mare's Tail and indigenous to Britain, Europe and N. America.

Propagate by division in spring.

HOEING. Hoeing is practised to clear the ground of weeds and to aerate the soil. For cleaning neglected ground and removing large weeds the draw hoe is the most useful tool. During the spring and summer there is nothing which will benefit the plants so much as systematic hoeing. By the use of the Dutch hoe the ground round the plants is broken up, allowing for the easy admission of air. Hoeing carefully practised almost does away with the need of watering, especially in established beds and borders. If the surface soil is caked hard, the sun very quickly draws from the soil the particles of moisture raised to the surface by capillary attraction. If the surface soil is broken, capillary attraction is checked, with consequent good to the plants. After the soil has been beaten down by a heavy shower, it should be hoed so that the full benefit of the rain is felt by the plants, and they are not left to dry out rapidly as soon as the sun appears.

HOES. These tools are primarily for weeding purposes, but are also very useful for aerating or loosening the top soil. They can be divided into two classes— the drag hoe and the thrust hoe.

THE DRAG HOE, as the name implies, is dragged towards the user. The blade can be had in many shapes, such as straight or curved along the bottom edge, V-shaped bottom edge, or completely triangular. The neck between the blade and socket can be had short or long—the latter is usually curved and called "swan-necked."

THE THRUST HOE is pushed away from the user with the blade parallel with the ground and cuts under the weeds and top soil. This hoe also has several varieties, chief amongst them being the Dutch Hoe. This is a steel blade anything from 4–8 in. long attached to the socket by two arms fixed at either end of the blade, and forming a small angle with the socket.

There is also the PAXTON HOE, which is just like a Dutch Hoe, except that the blade is fixed directly on to the socket. A variation of the Paxton has a V-shaped front edge. It is possible to buy a Dutch Hoe frame and separate blades of different lengths which are slipped into the sockets of the prongs.

THE SPUD HOE is a stiff 2–3 in. push hoe, and is particularly useful for cutting up weeds, thinning out onions and similar crops, and aerating the soil between plants.

All hoes can be bought with or without handles.

HOHERIA (Malvaceæ). Very handsome evergreen shrubs or small trees from New Zealand, with attractive foliage and white flowers. Hardy in mild parts of the country, but generally needs a wall or a sheltered site. Plant in good fibrous loam. *Propagate* by cuttings and seeds.

SPECIES.

H. populnea (*Sinclairii*), 10–30 ft. Distinct species with pure white flowers borne in bunches during September and October.

H. sexstylosa. Upwards of 12 ft. Handsome species with pure white flowers during July and August. The hardiest hoheria.

H. s. lanceolata. A variety producing a wonderful profusion of snow-white flowers in July.

HOLBŒLLIA (Berberidaceæ). Handsome evergreen climbing shrubs of rapid growth, bearing fragrant flowers. Thrives well in the genial south-western districts. Plant in sandy soil. *Propagate* by cuttings of half-ripened shoots placed in gentle bottom heat.

SPECIES.

H. coriacea (China). Flowers small, white to purple.

H. latifolia (Himalayas). Male flowers white, female flowers purple, and very fragrant. The flowers should be hand fertilised. The side growth must be kept spurred to induce freedom of flowering.

HOLCUS (hol-kus. Gramineæ). Soft Grass. Annual and perennial grasses of which *H. mollis* is the best-known wild species, while *H. lanatus albo-variegatus* is the only species ever used in gardens. Increased by seeds and the perennials by division of the tufts in spring. Any soil will do, but a loamy one is preferable.

HOLLY. *See* ILEX.

HOLLY FLAG. *See* SANTOLINA.

HOLLYHOCK (Malvaceæ. Althea-rosea). Hardy border perennials. The well-known border hollyhock attains a height of well over 6 ft. They thrive well in almost any soil when once established, but they prefer deep, loamy soil, and a soaking with liquid manure occasionally when the flower spikes are developing. When preparing the soil, trench it three spits deep and work in plenty of decayed manure. If planted singly, they should be 3 ft. apart each way, or they can be planted in groups of three with a distance of 12 in. from plant to plant. They should be planted out in April.

The surface soil should be mulched and the plants staked. Give plenty of water in dry weather. Immediately the flowers fade they should be removed. If the plants are required for exhibition, the tops of the spikes should be cut off as soon as the lower blooms show signs of expanding. Offshots can be removed from the base of the plants in June. After flowering they should be cut down to within 6 in. of the ground.

Propagation of hollyhocks takes place by seeds sown 1 in. deep and 6 in. apart on a south border in June. Pinch out the seedlings to 12 in. apart in July. On warm soil, the seedlings may be transplanted into their flowering position in September.

In cold or wet soils they should be potted in winter or autumn in cold frames and planted out in April. They may also be increased by cuttings of young shoots growing from the base of the flower stems, inserted singly in pots and plunged in a gentle hotbed.

Hollyhocks are best raised annually from seed, as old plants are more subject to "Red Rust," or "Hollyhock Disease." It is possible now to obtain double-flowered varieties in separate colours which will come true from seeds, and this method should always be adopted in gardens where the disease is at all troublesome. Good named varieties are:

"Golden Beauty," "White Queen," "Prince of Orange," "Rose Queen," "Crimson King."

See also ALTHÆA.

HOLLYHOCK RUST (*Puccinia malvacearum*). The growth of hollyhocks is often seriously affected by the development of small yellowish-brown areas upon the foliage and stem. These areas are usually raised, and with suitable weather conditions cover the leaf to such an extent that the leaf ceases to play its part, becomes yellow in colour and perhaps dies right away. The result is, the whole plant is stunted and unsightly and the flowers are small. It is said if a plant is attacked in the seedling stage and is able to grow away, it will be immune in the future.

METHOD OF CONTROL.—Spray in spring and summer with permanganate of potash

The silvery seed pods of Honesty make an attractive winter decoration and the plants thrive in partial shade.

solution (pale rose colour), at intervals of 10 days.

HOLODISCUS. *See* SPIRÆA.

HOMERIA (ho-me-ri-a. Iridaceæ). Greenhouse bulbous plants. 1793.

Culture.—For compost, general cultivation and propagation, *see* HESPERANTHA.

SPECIES.

Collina, red and yellow; *collina aurantiaca*, orange, red and yellow; *miniata*, red.

HONESTY. *See* LUNARIA.

HONEYSUCKLE. *See* LONICERA.

HOP. *See* HUMULUS.

HOP, HORNBEAM. *See* OSTRYA.

HOP-TREE. *See* PTELEA.

HORDEUM (hor-de-um. Graminæ). Squirrel Tail Grass. An ornamental

annual grass. *H. jubatum* is the best for decorative purposes. Sow in March in any ordinary garden soil, preferably in a rather dry position.

HOREHOUND. *Used now, as of old, for the cure of coughs and consequent relief of lung troubles.*

HORMINUM (hor-mī-num. Labiatæ). Pyrenean Clary. Pretty hardy tufted perennial that is worth growing in the border or rockery.

Propagate by seeds sown in summer, or by division in autumn or spring and grow in warm dry soil. *H. pyrenaicum* is the only grown species of the genus and has purple-blue flowers from June to August; height, 10 in.

The evergreen Honeysuckle (Lonicera sempervirens) makes a delightful smother growth for the cottage porch. It is a twining plant and needs wire supports.

HORNBEAM. *See* CARPINUS.

HORNED POPPY. *See* GLAUCIUM.

HORNED RAMPION. *See* PHYTEUMA.

HORNS AND HOOFS. From 12–14 per cent. nitrogen is found in a good sample of this kind of manure. It is also obtainable mixed in varying proportions

with bonemeal or bone-flour. This fertiliser is useful for greenhouse work.

HORSE CHESTNUT. *See* ÆSCULUS
HIPPOCASTANUM.

HORSE MINT. *See* MONARDA.

HORSE RADISH. *See* HERBS.

HORSE TAIL. *See* EQUISETUM.

HOSE. It is not advisable or economical to buy cheap hose. Just for a
few odd feet to fit cans, etc., the cheap
hose will probably do, but where any
greater length is required, a cheap hose
will be a perpetual source of trouble and
annoyance by bursting or kinking.

ALL-RUBBER HOSE.—This is a black,
corrugated all-rubber hose made with
$\frac{1}{2}$ in., $\frac{5}{8}$ in. or $\frac{3}{4}$ in. bores, which does not
kink; but, on the other hand, it has no
canvas to strengthen the walls, and is
therefore not to be recommended for any
great length.

CANVAS-WRAPPED HOSE.—This hose is
made by wrapping canvas round a thin
rubber pipe and finally moulding the whole
in more rubber. It is usually made with
$\frac{1}{2}$ in. or $\frac{5}{8}$ in. bores, and finished red or
grey. It cannot be recommended for
lengths of more than 60 ft. Not being
corrugated, it will kink, but on the whole
will stand more pressure than the all-
rubber.

GENUINE NON-KINK.—This is quite the
best hose, and is made in several qualities
according to the process. Generally speaking, it is made of three rubber pipes with
two canvas wrappings in between and all
vulcanised into one. The outside is corrugated and cannot kink. It is made with
$\frac{1}{2}$ in., $\frac{5}{8}$ in., $\frac{3}{4}$ in. or 1 in. bores.

When buying, remember that the greater
the length required, the larger the bore
should be, otherwise there will be loss of
pressure at the extreme end. Half-an-
inch bore will be all right up to about
100 ft., $\frac{5}{8}$ in. bore up to about 200 ft. and
above that, $\frac{3}{4}$ in. bore.

Care of Hose.—As hose is chiefly composed of rubber, it should never be left
out in the hot sun. Likewise it should be
emptied of all water after use, otherwise
decay is likely to set up. Dragging the
hose over gravel should be avoided as
much as possible, and when not in use, it
should be rolled on to a reel or hose-
hanger, and stored under cover, preferably

in the dark. With care a good hose should
last five to twenty years, according to
use and the initial price paid.

HOSE FITTINGS. First of all, the
tap end. There are several ways of
making a tap joint thoroughly leak-proof.
If your tap is screwed, then the only way
is to buy a tap union to screw with the

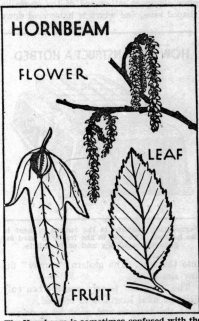

HORNBEAM

FLOWER

LEAF

FRUIT

**The Hornbeam is sometimes confused with the
Beech, from which it differs by having duller
foliage and serrated leaves.**

correct thread and size; see that it has
also a leather washer, otherwise it will
leak. The best way of getting the size
is to put a piece of paper, plasticine or
putty against the tap and take an imprint.

If a tap is plain, then there is only one
method that can be recommended as
thoroughly leak-proof. This is made by
looping the union over the tap and forcing
the end of the tap into the union by
tightening a winged bolt on to the neck of
the tap. The hose is fixed to the union
by a zinc claw-like clamp, whose teeth are
hammered into the hose all round.

There is a type which is pushed on to
the tap, but this is inclined to blow off;
and yet another new type is fixed by a

clamp that expands *inside* the tap and, therefore, lessens the bore with subsequent loss of pressure.

Should a hose burst at any time, a "repairer" or "coupler" is wanted. The old-fashioned way of inserting a brass tube and binding it at either end with copper wire has been surpassed by the new claw clamp at either end of the specially-shaped tube, and which is hammered down

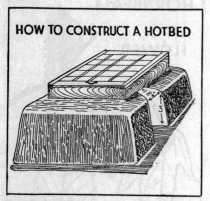

HOW TO CONSTRUCT A HOTBED

Fermenting manure is the source of heat in the hotbed. The soil in the frame is used for growing seedlings and early salads.

into the hose. The modern "coupler" fits any size hose.

The "coupler" is very useful when only half the total length is to be used.

At the extreme end must be some sort of branch to spray the water. The best branch is that with a separate rose and jet, fitted with a full-bore tap. The cheaper ones invariably have the rose fitted over the jet, which is not removable. Thus, when using the rose, the water must first go through the jet with subsequent loss of real spray.

The spray nozzle is a very useful all-round form of hose branch. By turning the outside casing, and thus moving it up or down, the setting of the nozzle opening is altered, making it large and open for a jet and partially closed for a spray or mist. This is therefore a dual-purpose nozzle which will give anything from a jet to a fine-mist spray.

It is imperative that all hose fittings should be of a non-rusting metal, such as brass.

HOSE REEL. This is a most important item if a hose is to have long life. The cantilever type is the best. It can be obtained with wheels for ease in transport.

HOTBED. There are several uses to which a hotbed may be put in a garden. It may be used for raising early flowers and vegetable seedlings, for striking cuttings, for forcing early vegetables and for growing melons and cucumbers.

Fresh stable manure, containing a percentage of stawy litter, is the material used. The quantity required is approximately two loads to a single light frame. Dry grass or tree leaves can be used with manure if sufficient quantity is not obtainable. The manure should be stacked in a conical shape and left for two days. The whole heap should then be turned so that the fermenting material in the centre is on the outside and vice versa. If the manure is very hot it should be sprinkled with water from the rose of a can as the layers are stacked back into place. Any lumps of soil should be broken up and the strawy litter shaken out with a fork. After two days this process should be repeated. After a further two or three days the manure should be ready for forming into the bed. The size of the bed should be sufficient to allow 1 ft. to 18 in. in width all round the frame which will be placed on it. 4 ft. is an average depth. Of course, the deeper the bed the more heat it will produce. Form the bed in a sheltered position, and if the site is well drained the bed can be placed in a pit dug for it. This will help to conserve the heat, but should not be done if water is likely to stand in it. Tread each layer of soil firmly down as it is put into place, and lightly sprinkle with water. Place a stick in the centre of the bed, about 3 ft. down, and withdraw occasionally to test the heat. When the stick can be grasped comfortably in the hand, place the frame in position and spread a layer of garden soil, about 4 in. deep, over the bottom of the frame. Hang a thermometer inside the frame and close the light. If the thermometer shows more than 75°, damp the bed down again and leave the light slightly open to allow the vapour to disperse. A hotbed properly constructed in this way in the spring should last for about two months, after which time the sun's heat should be sufficient to keep the temperature up. If a hotbed shows signs of drying before its work is finished, fresh manure packed round the sides will sometimes be effective in raising the temperature again. When finished with, the hotbed manure can be used for dressing the garden.

HOTHOUSE. See GLASSHOUSES.

HOTTONIA (hot-to-ni-a. Primulaceæ). Water Violet. Hardy aquatic perennials that do well in lakes or ponds where the water is not more than 1½ ft. deep. Plant in a heap of rich loam in the water or in a basket and place the latter in water.

Propagate by division in April.

SPECIES.

H. inflata. White, July. 1 ft.

H. palustris is the best of the genus with beautifully cut fern-like foliage, which is usually under the water, and lilac-blue flowers which rise well above the water. June to August. 1-2 ft.

HOUSELEEK. See SEMPERVIVUM.

HOUSTONIA (hous-to-nia. Rubiaceæ). After Dr. Houston, an English botanist. *H. cærulea,* a small N. American plant of creeping habit with small pale blue flowers. It needs a shady position in loose sandy soil, though Farrer ("The English Rock Garden") says that the finest masses he ever saw were growing under a dense hazel-covert in wet and heavy calcareous loam. There is likely to be some difficulty with it if the position chosen for it is not just right.

HOVEA (ho-ve-a. Leguminosæ). Greenhouse evergreen shrubs from Australia, usually with purplish pea-shaped flowers. They are not often grown but are highly ornamental. The leaves are small, alternate and oval or lanceolate, while the flowers are borne in great profusion.

Propagate by seeds that have been moistened in hot water before being sown in a hotbed, or by cuttings of half-ripe shoots inserted in April or May in sandy peat under a bell-glass in a close frame. Pot up in fibrous peat with plenty of sand and some charcoal to keep the soil sweet. The plants must be stopped when young and as the growth is slow frequent changes of pots are not necessary. Watering must

be done carefully as they must never have too much water yet must not become dry. They should have as much fresh air as possible with very little fire heat, and the pots should be stood on cool ash.

SPECIES.

H. Celsi. Deep blue flowers from March to May. 3 ft.

H. longifolia. March to May. 6 ft. (Syn. *lanceolata pannosa,* and *villosa.*)

H. splendens. 2 ft.

H. trisperma. March to May. 3 ft.

HOVENIA (hō-vē'-ni-a. Rhamnaceæ). Deciduous tree up to 30 ft. (much higher in nature). China. Not a native of Japan, but largely grown there, and known as the Japanese Raisin Tree. After the decay of the flowers the flower-stalks swell into a sweet, fleshy mass, and are eaten by the natives. Of more botanical interest than of garden value.

H. dulcis is the only species.

HOWEA (how-e-a. Palmæ). Stove palms from Lord Howe's island that make tall stems with large leaves divided into several segments.

Propagate by imported seeds and plant in good loam. They are largely grown for house decoration under their synonym, Kentia, in which case they need liquid manure. They are troubled by Scale which is removed by sponging the leaves. They require a minimum temperature of 40°-45°, but are better when given 5 or 10 degrees more of heat.

SPECIES.

H. belmoreana (syn. *Kentia belmoreana*).

H. forsteriana (syn. *Kentia forsteriana*).

HOYA (hoy-a. Asclepiadaceæ). Wax-Flower. Asia, 1802. Warm greenhouse climbing and flowering plants.

Culture.—Compost: 2 parts peat, 1 part loam and sand. Repot and prune into shape in February. Train to roof of house or up pillars and trellis. Sunny position. Syringe well in summer to keep down greenfly and mealy-bug. Water freely during summer, but very moderately during the winter. Winter temperature, 50°; summer, 65°-70°.

Propagation.—By cuttings of well-ripened shoots from preceding year's growth, inserted in pots of sandy soil in propagator. Temperature, 70°, spring and summer.

SPECIES.

H. bella, white and purple. *H. carnosa*, pink.

HUDSONIA (hud-so-ni-a. Cistineæ). Hardy evergreen shrubs with yellow flowers and tiny heath-like leaves.

Propagate by cuttings in sand under a hand-light or by layers in spring and

CAPE HYACINTH

A summer-blooming hyacinth which can be grown amongst other plants to ensure succession of bloom—Cape Hyacinth (Galtonia candicans).

autumn. Grow in sandy peat in a moist situation.

SPECIES.

H. ericoides. June. 1 ft.

H. tomentosa. Summer. 1 ft.

HUMEA (hu-me-a. Syngenesia). Incense Plant. A greenhouse biennial with aromatic scented foliage and tall, gracefully drooping racemes of rosy-purple flowers, the habit of which resembles a decorative grass. Height, 4–8 ft., according to cultivation.

Cultivation.—Seeds should be sown in spring or early summer to produce plants for flowering the following summer. When large enough for the final pots, they require a good rich soil which should be composed of mature and mellow loam, old decayed manure which crumbles freely and which has passed through a ¾ in. sieve, a little leaf-mould, sand and bonemeal. In the spring of the year following sowing, the flower spikes will begin to grow, and the plants may require additional feeding while the rapid growth is taking place. The plant often remains several months in flower.

SPECIES.

H. elegans, and the larger form, *H. e. gigantea.*

HUMULUS (hū-mulus. Urticaceæ). Hop. Attractive twining annuals and perennials most useful for covering trellis or pergolas, etc. Hops do almost as well in the town garden as in the country.

Culture of perennials: Propagate by division of roots in spring or by seeds. Plant in deep rich soil as the plants are gross feeders. The roots are apt to spread and cause trouble amongst other plants, so do not plant near shrubs.

SPECIES.

H. japonicus, the Japanese Hop and its variety with variegated foliage. Both these are annuals which can be grown early from seed sown outdoors in May.

H. Lupulus the common perennial Hop, apart from its commercial value for brewers, is worth growing for garden decoration, as the fruits are very pretty. There is also a golden-leaved form that is very ornamental.

HUMUS. The dead organic matter in soils. *See* MANURE, FARMYARD.

HUNNEMANNIA (hun-e-man-ea. Papaveraceæ). Mexico, 1½ ft. A near relation of the Eschscholtzia, but not quite hardy. Sown in March under glass— plants put out in May. Will flower the same season. May be sown outdoors May–June, but the plants will need protecting in winter. *H. fumariæfolia* is the only species yet introduced.

HUNTSMAN'S HORN. *See* SARRACENIA.

HUTCHINSIA (hutch-in-sia. Cruciferæ). Pretty hardy perennials of which the only grown species is *H. alpina*, with tufts of bright green and umbels of white flowers from April to May. Resembles a minute Candytuft.

Culture.—Propagate by seeds in spring and plant in light sandy soil in a sunny position. It is best suited to a rockery; height, 6 in.

HYACINTHUS (Hyacinth). Liliaceæ. Fortunately for the novice, there are not nearly so many types and varieties of hyacinths as there are of daffodils or tulips. Hyacinth cultivation is also comparatively simple. The chief varieties on the market are: (1) The ordinary *Bedding* or *Exhibition Hyacinths* which throw up the solid candles of colour that are so effective when massed. (2) The *Miniature Hyacinths*, which are much smaller, having smaller bells and a looser habit of growth than the large Bedding Hyacinths, and (3) the *Roman Hyacinths* which are of about the same size as the Miniature Hyacinths but of different type. The so-called Roman Hyacinths are grown chiefly in France while the Miniature Hyacinths come from Holland.

There are also bulbs which are commercially known as "prepared" or "treated" hyacinths, which are used exclusively for forcing. These are so treated that the bulb ripens earlier and consequently they come into flower earlier. They cost a little more than the ordinary bulbs but are well worth the extra cost, because of the ease with which they can be brought into flower by Christmas.

How to Choose Bulbs.

When buying hyacinths the novice should note that the best bulbs are not necessarily the largest bulbs. A solid bulb, firm and of heavy weight, and particularly firm on the underneath side, is better than a large, flabby bulb.

In spite of its legendary origin, this flower is not a water-loving plant. It certainly likes plenty of moisture, but hyacinths are not waterside plants, and do like well-drained soil in which to grow. This may seem surprising to many who have seen the hyacinths growing in glasses of water indoors, but it must be remembered that in this method of cultivation the bulb itself does not come in contact with the water. It is only the fine roots which penetrate down into the water.

If the soil of a garden is naturally somewhat low and wet, it is best to raise the flower-beds above the general level when preparing for hyacinths. Or it may be possible to use the hyacinths on a sloping bank, where they will be particularly effective.

It is not at all necessary to use these flowers always in formal designs as they are equally delightful in informal groups or large drifts, but if a formal garden is to be planted there is probably no other spring-flowering bulb which can be used more effectively. Hyacinths like a very sunny position, although they will grow and flower fairly well even in complete shade.

It is as a rule inadvisable to plant hyacinths beneath trees, but almost any other situation will give satisfactory results. They should be slightly protected from driving winds and if the garden is inclined to be wind-swept, some shelter should be provided in the form of a row of dwarf evergreens, or a shelter-bank of soil.

HYACINTHUS CANDICANS. *See* GALTONIA.

HYBRIDISATION. The process by which the pollen from one flower is placed on the stigma of another for the purpose of raising new varieties or species. When species are " crossed " in this way the off-spring is known as a hybrid. If hybrids are crossed their offspring are termed varieties. A study of Mendelism should be made by those who wish to hybridise systematically.

The effect of a substance called colchicine on plant life is of interest to the hybridist. This substance acts on the nucleus of the cells, preventing the halving of the chromosome numbers: plants resulting grow into giant forms.

HYDRANGEA. (Saxifragaceæ). Greenhouse and hardy flowering shrubs. Deciduous.

SPECIES.

H. arborescens grandiflora (U.S.A.). 4 ft. The hardiest species. Flowers white, July to September.

H. hortensis. The Common Hydrangea (China and Japan). Up to 8 ft. Hardy in all but the cold northern gardens. Flowers pink or blue. Blue flowers are produced by planting in a soil free of all lime, and by watering freely with a solution of alum; one teaspoonful to the gallon of rain-water; or with 3 oz. of aluminium sulphate to one gallon of water. The pink-flowered kinds are much improved by a dressing of sulphate of iron, broken up into small pieces and placed around the roots and allowed to dissolve, in autumn and spring. Hydrangeas like a certain amount of shade, and the Hortensis section will thrive under trees or in almost any position and soil. (*See below* for detailed cultivation.)

Culture.—Hydrangeas known in gardens are chiefly of the species *H. hortensis* and hybrids. *H. paniculata*, the autumn-flowering Hydrangea, often grown in beds and borders, can also be grown as a pot plant. This needs somewhat different treatment from that given to *H. hortensis*. It should be potted in February or March, having been previously pruned to within an inch of the base. During summer it will be watered freely, but after October water will be almost entirely withheld, so that the plants rest. Liquid manure can be given with benefit when the plants are showing flower buds.

In the open, *H. paniculata* will be planted in late autumn or in March. Prune to within an inch of the base in February and top dress with decayed manure. Water freely if the weather is dry.

Hydrangea hortensis and its hybrids, are beautiful water-loving deciduous plants that are suitable for growing in pots 5–12 in. high. They are natives of China and Japan. The flowers grow in large trusses (cymes, corymbs, or panicles) and are remarkable for the reason that they produce quantities of sterile florets constituting the showy part of the flower. It is towards increasing the number and size of these that the aim of the cultivator is directed. The flowers of the Hydrangea will last for many weeks in good condition. They should be cut off when they become green with age.

The plants are easy to cultivate, and if the instructions given below are followed, good results should be obtained. They grow best on warm soil and in seaside districts.

As the name implies, the plants need plenty of water and they grow splendidly out of doors in full sunlight, but grown under glass they must be shaded from very bright sunlight or the flowers will burn and not last so long as they should.

The cuttings for propagation should be rooted in very sandy soil and taken in spring (February to March). The first potting compost should be a light one—2 parts loam, 1 part peat and 1 part leaf mould with a good sprinkling of sand. The soil for the next potting should be of a somewhat stiffer texture and the following mixture is recommended: 3 parts loam, 1 part peat, 1 part leaf-mould and ½ part coarse sand. They should be potted moderately firm, and have plenty of drainage. They should also be watered carefully when first potted, but as soon as they are well established, they must be watered freely, and fed judiciously. Autumn cuttings should have an even temperature of 40° F.

When the plants have finished flowering, cut back the *old* wood slightly, leaving the strongest-growing shoots for next season's flowering. Decrease the water until they commence growing, then repot in soil as before. When growing freely stand out of doors until autumn. It is absolutely necessary for the current season's growth to be well matured and ripened or they will not flower satisfactorily. Then return to cold house that is kept free from frost.

Treatment of plants out of doors.—As soon as they have finished flowering they should be thinned, leaving the strongest of the growing shoots for next season's flowers. Shoots that have flowered may be cut back slightly to make the bushes shapely (but not heavily pruned). These shoots will flower again off the old wood, but the growths that have not flowered will, if not cut, provide the largest trusses. At this time a liberal watering with Hydrangea fertiliser will help to swell the new buds.

Blueing plants out of doors.—Hydrangeas are pink naturally and only obtain their blue colour by treatment. The blue varieties will require further treatment with blueing powder if the colour is to be maintained the following year (that is unless the ground is known to contain a quantity of iron), otherwise they will probably revert to the pink shades or flower a very washy pale blue. Treatment should commence in August. First apply plain water, then water with blueing powder added at the rate of 1½ oz. to 2 gal. of water or with a solution of alum as previously advised. Repeat this operation three times at intervals of three weeks, and in the following summer when plants are in full growth give one or two more applications. At this stage Hydrangeas would benefit by watering with fertiliser, but in the case of the blues there should be a plain watering between the blueing and fertiliser.

Blueing plants in pots.—Add to each bushel of soil ½ lb. of blueing powder, mix well and pot as before directed. To intensify the blue, as soon as the plants are well rooted and growing freely, water once a fortnight with ½ oz. of the blueing powder to each gallon of water. The powder should be dissolved in hot water. The plants that are being blued should only be fed with manure once a week, and not at the same time as when being watered for blueing.

No plant should have manure or blueing powder given when the plant is dry. An hour or so after they have been well watered is best.

All varieties of Hydrangeas that have been treated for blue should, the first and third week in August, have a small tea-spoonful of the blueing powder sprinkled round each plant and well watered in. This intensifies and fixes the colour when they flower the next season.

It should be noted that watering the plants with blueing powder just as they are coming into flower will have little or no effect unless the plants have been previously treated as above.

HYDROCHARIS (hi-drok-ar-is. Hydrocharideæ). Frog-Bit. *H. Morsus-ranæ*, the only species of the genus, is a native aquatic that is common in shallow muddy water. It has white flowers in summer and kidney-shaped leaves that float on the water, but is of no horticultural value.

HYDROCLEIS (hi-dro-cle-is. Alismaceæ). The only species of this genus is *H. Commersonii*, better known as *Limnocharis Humboldtii*, a half-hardy aquatic from Brazil. This has round leaves which float on the water, and yellow flowers in summer. The tuberous roots can be divided in spring. It does well in shallow ponds or may be sown in tubs that are sunk in the ground out of doors during the summer, and are brought in in the autumn.

HYDROPONICS. The name given to the method of plant cultivation in which water and soluble chemicals alone are used in place of soil. In America soilless culture of plants is already practised as a commercial proposition: in Britain experiments are still in progress though some measure of success has already been attained in the cultivation of carnations, tomatoes, cucumbers, and other plants.

Briefly, the principle is this: if some form of anchorage for the roots can be given (moss and wire netting, pure sand, gravel, etc., are used by different cultivators), and if enough air, water, and soluble plant food can be supplied to the roots, plants can be grown without ordinary soil. Water and soluble chemicals reach the roots more readily, and can be absorbed with ease, and growth is consequently speeded up.

Those who wish to experiment on their own are referred to the numerous small books and pamphlets on the subject that can be obtained from any bookseller.

HYMENANTHERA (hī-men-an-thē'-ra. Violaceæ). Evergreen shrubs or trees, with small flowers and attractive berries.

Culture.—Plant in ordinary garden soil. Propagate by cuttings and by seeds.

SPECIES.

H. Chathamica (New Zealand). Handsome pale green lance-shaped leaves. Berries white.

H. crassifolia (New Zealand). Of prostrate habit, and a profusion of white pearl-like berries.

H. dentata angustifolia (New Zealand). Berries white.

HYMENOCALLIS (hī-men-o-kal-lis. Amaryllidaceæ). *Hymen*, a membrane, and *kalos*, beautiful, referring to the membranous cup inside the flowers.

A large genus of bulbous-rooted plants that closely resemble Pancratiums and in fact some of the species of this genus have been grown as Pancratiums and *vice-versa*. It comprises stove, greenhouse and almost hardy bulbs, the last being often grown under the name of Ismene.

Propagate by offsets taken off at potting and inserted in sandy soil, or by seeds which are large and green, thus differing from those of Pancratiums which are black. The hardiest of the bulbs may be grown out-doors in summer and taken up for the winter and the bulbs stored in dry sand. Pot up every second year in rich sandy loam and top-dress annually with new soil. The tender species must be kept moist throughout the year. When attacked by Mealy Bug, which is partial to them, the plants must be sponged with a nicotine wash or paraffin emulsion.

HYPERICUM MOSERIANUM WILL GROW IN THE SHADE

Hypericum, the "Rose of Sharon," one of the best shrubs for growing under trees. It has golden flowers with stamens in five bundles.

Species.

H. calathina (syn. *Pancratium calathinum*), the Sea Daffodil of Peru. Fragrant green or greenish-white, trumpet-shaped flowers in March and April. Nearly hardy. 1½ ft.

H. macrostephana. Stove, white, fragrant. February, 2 ft.

H. ovata (syn. *amoena* and *Pancratium amoenum*). White, fragrant. October, Stove. 1–2 ft.

H. speciosa. White, stove. Sweet. July, 1½ ft.

HYMENOPHYLLUM (hi-men-o-fi-lum Filices). Filmy Ferns. Hardy, greenhouse and stove ferns with very attractive, delicately-cut fronds, as the popular name implies.

Propagate by spores which, however, are rarely successful in germinating, or by division of the rhizomes, a slow process and not always sure. Some of the species will succeed on blocks and only need to be packed with a little sphagnum when starting them. Other species are grown in pots in sandy peat with live sphagnum. They need plenty of water and must be kept almost at saturation point all the year round. Only soft water should be used. They will stand being grown in towns better than many ferns of a hardier appearance.

Species.

H. Tunbridgense with its variety *Wilsonii* and *H. unilaterale* are native species that may be grown outdoors with a little protection in winter. The fronds are from 1–3 in. long and ½–1 in. broad.

Other species include *H. æruginosum, caudiculatum, ciliatum, abruptum* (syn. *brevifrons*), *hirsutum* and *pulcherrimum*, all suited to stove culture.

H. bivalve, tricoideum and *javanicum* do well in the greenhouse.

HYOPHORBE (hi-o-for-be. Palmæ). Handsome stove palms that are not frequently grown. They have large leaves which in a young state are often tinted with maroon.

Propagate by seeds and pot firmly in a mixture of 3 parts of loam to 1 of cow manure with some sand.

Species.

H. amaricaulis, trunk and leaf-stalks maroon coloured. Leaves 4–6 ft. long.

H. commersoniana (syn. *indica* and *Areca lutescens*).

H. Verschaffeltii, the best of the genus with leaves 4–6 ft. long and white midribs.

HYOSCYAMUS (hi-o-sy-amus. Solanaceæ). Henbane, 2 ft. Of no garden value. Chiefly grown as a medicinal herb. Ordinary soil. *H. niger*, the common Henbane, is a native of Britain.

HYPERICUM (hi-per'-i-kum. Hypericaceæ). Deciduous and evergreen shrubs, chiefly valuable for their flowering during late summer and autmn. Of the easiest culture in ordinary garden soil. The Hyperikon of Dioscorides, one of the earliest Greek botanists. St. John's Wort. A race of plants found in one form or another over a large portion of the globe. Their flowers are bright yellow, often large, with a central tuft of prominent stamens. In size they range from small plants which would be lost anywhere but in a rock garden, to large bushes 6 ft. or more in height. The best known is H. calycinum, the garden St. John's Wort or Rose of Sharon, useful in covering dry banks. An attraction of many of the rock-garden forms is the large size and number of the flowers in comparison with the low stature of the plant. They are easily propagated by seed, division, or cuttings of young shoots in sand.

H. calycinum. Evergreen. " Rose of Sharon," " Aaron's Beard " (Orient), 12–15 in. Flowers bright yellow, 3–4 in. across. June to October. Cut to ground-level in April. One of the most useful species for covering dry and shaded situations.

H. moserianum. Evergreen. A hybrid between H. patulum + H. calycinum. 1–1½ ft. Flowers golden yellow, from July to frost. Sometimes killed back in severe winters. Should be protected by leaves, etc. Most useful for ground cover. It has the dwarf habit of H. calycinum, but the petals instead of being spreading have the overlapping cup-shaped form of patulum. It is more ornamental than calycinum, but seems to spread less rapidly.

H. patulum is a handsome flowering shrub from Nepal. The W. Chinese form, H. p. Henryi, is even better. The large cup-shaped flowers, produced in great abundance, are of a beautiful golden yellow, 4–6 ft. June.

HYPOXIS (hip-ox-is. Amaryllideæ). Pretty bulbs from the Cape of Good Hope that are not often grown.

Propagate by division and plant in sandy loam.

Species.

H. hemerocallidea. Yellow (syn. elata).

HYSSOPUS (his-so-pus. Labiatæ). Hyssop. Hardy evergreen shrubs of which the species H. officinalis sometimes grown as a bedding plant was formerly much used for herb potions. Apart from the medicinal use the flowers are very pretty. Raise from seed or cuttings inserted in light sandy soil in spring.

There are several varieties with white, red or blue flowers.

I

IBERIS (i-ber-is. Cruciferæ). Candy-tuft. A large genus of annual, biennial, and perennial herbs. The perennials are mainly evergreen and are useful for the rock garden where, if the conditions are good, they will flower early in the summer and form a mass of bloom.

Culture.—Propagate by cuttings made after flowering and placed in sandy soil

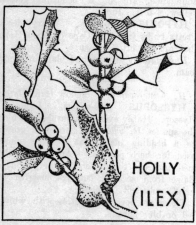

Holly in its green, gold or silver forms is effective as a shrub or hedge plant.

under a hand-light during the summer months. They will thrive in any friable well-drained garden soil, and should be kept fairly dry during the winter.

SPECIES.

I. corræfolia, the best of the hardy ever-green candytufts with white flowers in June, is suitable for the rockery or for the front of the herbaceous border; height, 3–6 in.; *I. semperflorens* and *I. semper-virens* are both suitable for the herbaceous border as well as the rockery.

Annual Candytufts.—*I. coronaria* is the tall-growing species with white flowers in long dense spikes. Its varieties, Little Prince, 6 in., and Miniature Gem, 3½ in., are exceptionally good dwarf edgings, or on the rockery. *I. umbellata* and its varieties in many colours, 9 in., produce their flowers in flat heads or corymbs, and are fine subjects for beds or borders. Rose

Cardinal is a very popular variety with bright rose flowers. All grow easily in ordi-nary soil; sow in spring or autumn.

ICE PLANT. *See* MESEMBRY ANTHEMUM.

ICHNEUMON FLY. *See* BENEFICIAL INSECTS.

IDESIA (ī-dē'-si-a. Bixaceæ). Decidu-ous, free-growing, ornamental trees from China and Japan.

Culture.—Plant in ordinary garden soil Propagate by seed. Cuttings will strike in heat but are difficult.

SPECIES.

I. polycarpa. Leaves dark green, glau cous beneath. Flowers yellowish-green followed by berries or fruits like a bunch of grapes, each about the size of a pea, at first green, ageing to red.

ILEX (ī'-lex. Aquifoliaceæ). Holly Deciduous and evergreen trees and shrubs, with flowers of no floral interest being grown for their glossy dark green foliage and red or other colour berries.

Culture.—Plant in May or September in well-drained loamy soil in sun or shade. The necessary pruning should be performed with secateurs in April. In the case of hedges, prune in May or August. *Propa-gate* by seed sown in shallow drills in the open about March. The seeds may lie dormant for two years. Cuttings taken in August root readily in cold frame.

SPECIES.

(Unless otherwise stated, the berries are red.)

I. Aquifolium, Common Holly (Europe, Asia and Great Britain), up to 80 ft. Makes a magnificent hedge, either by itself or mixed with Box and Yew. It is in-different to smoky, impure air, and makes one of the most useful evergreens for manu-facturing towns. As a rule, the sexes are on different plants, but some are bi-sexual. If a good crop of berries is desired, both male and female varieties should be grown.

I. A. ferox argentea. Silver-leaf form.

I. A. Hodginsii (altaclarensis Hodginsii). Hybrid. Female broad-leaved form.

I. A. Madame Briot. Leaves margined gold. Berries freely.

ILLICIUM (il-lis'ium. Magnoliaceæ).

nise Trees. Evergreen aniseed-scented
hrubs or small trees, allied to Magnolias
or lime-free peaty soils. *Propagate* by
ayers.

SPECIES.

I. anisatum (religiosum), China and
apan. 3–6 ft. Leaves pleasantly aromatic. Flowers yellow, 1 in. across, from
March to May. Likes semi-shade. Hardy
n all but cold districts.

IMBRICATED. When the petals of a
lower overlap each other the flower is said
o be imbricated, e.g., scarlet pimpernel.

IMMORTELLES. The French name
'or "Everlasting Flowers" (*q.v.*). *See*
XERANTHEMUM.

IMPATIENS (im-pa-shi-ens. Geraniaceæ). Zanzibar Balsam. Half-hardy
annuals of spreading habit with very showy
red, rose or vermilion flowers. Height,
10–12 in. The plants are usually at their
best during the latter part of summer.

Cultivation.—Seeds should be sown in
boxes or pans of light, well-drained soil
in early spring and placed in gentle heat
to germinate. The resulting seedlings
may be pricked off into fresh boxes of
soil in the usual way and, when large
enough, potted up singly into 3 in. pots.
They should be repotted when necessary
into 5 in. pots and a compost of rich
loam, leaf-mould and sharp sand should
be used, enriched with a sprinkling of
some complete fertiliser. Grow in a
temperature of about 60°.

SPECIES.

I. balsamina is an exceptionally easy
beginners' plant for pots. Seed sown in
spring in cool house and potted off singly
into 3 in. pots, re-potted into 5 in. pots in
sandy loam, will grow into well-flowered
specimens 1–1½ ft. tall and last a long
time in full beauty. May also be bedded
out in June.

I. glandulifera is a tall-growing hardy
annual species which delights in a moist
position in semi-shade. It seeds very
freely, and one sowing will usually be
sufficient for it to naturalise itself. 4–5 ft.
Syn. *I. Roylei*. Native of Ceylon.

I. Holstii is a strong-growing and free-
flowering species with flowers of vermilion-
red. It is the best Impatiens to grow
for general purposes. The *I. Holstii* hybrids contain many lovely shades of colour.

I. Sultani is bright rose and there are
also many other good hybrids.

INCARVILLEA (in-car-vill-ea. Bignoniaceæ). After P. Incarville, a botanical
correspondent of the botanist Jussien.
1743. In spite of the exotic splendour of
the large trumpet flowers and the luxuriant
foliage, most of these Chinese plants are
perfectly hardy. That most commonly
seen, and the showiest, is *I. Delavayi*,
bearing large rose-coloured gloxinia-like
flowers on stout stems. 18 in. July.

INCARVILLEA
DELAVAYI

**Incarvillea Delavayi is a stately border flower
about 18 in. high with flowers of rosy carmine.**

I. grandiflora runs *Delavayi* close in
beauty (some prefer it). It is more suitable
for the rock garden, being altogether more
compact. Rose-purple, 6 in. July.

Propagate all varieties by seed or
division.

INCENSE PLANT. *See* HUMEA
ELEGANS.

INCINERATOR. This is an ingenious
device for burning rubbish, and making
use of what is apparently useless. It
takes the place of the old bonfire, which
merely burnt the rubbish and made a

nasty smoke. The incinerator burns almost any kind of rubbish by slow combustion and whatever smoke there is, is protected to a large extent from the wind and is therefore more or less controlled. The slow combustion turns the rubbish—wet or dry—into an especially valuable stimulant, which is beneficial to fruit trees, etc. The general principle of all incinerators is much the same;

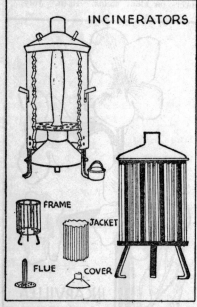

INCINERATORS
FRAME
JACKET
FLUE
COVER

Woody garden refuse should be burnt and the ashes saved, to be applied as required to the garden soil. There are various types of incinerators similar to the above.

galvanised jacket and cover with an iron frame and centre flue. The better quality ones usually have a separate loose lining, which gives longer life; but in the cheap range there is one made in four separate parts. The advantages are obviously that as one part wears out you can replace without having to buy a complete new incinerator.

INDIAN CORN. *See* ZEA.
INDIAN CRESS. *See* TROPÆOLUM.
INDIAN PINK. *See* DIANTHUS.
INDIAN POPPY. *See* MECONOPSIS.
INDIAN SHOT. *See* CANNA.

INDIGOFERA (in-di-gof'-er-a. Leguminosæ). Indigo. Deciduous shrubs, with elegant acacia-like foliage. Plant in ordinary soil in full sun. *Propagate* by seed and by cuttings taken any time during summer. Keep the young plants in pots until spring.

SPECIES.

I. decora alba (*floribunda alba*), China and Japan. Flowers white, pea-shaped in long racemes, during July and August. The plant dies down to the ground in winter.

I. Gerardiana (*dosua, floribunda*), Himalayas. 3–4 ft. in open, more against a sunny wall. Flowers, purplish-rose from June to September.

I. Potaninii (China), 5 ft. A choice, very shrubby species with long arching branches of clear pink flowers on panicles 10 in. long, from early June to August.

INDOOR PLANTS. *See* ROOM PLANTS.
INSECTICIDES. Preparations to destroy insect pests. *See* FORMULAE, D.D.T., and GAMMEXANE.
INSECTIVOROUS PLANTS. This is a class of plants, interesting rather than beautiful, which trap insects for food. The best known are Sundew (*Drosera*), Pitcher plant (*Nepenthes*), Venus fly trap (*Dionæa*), Butter Wort (*Pinguicula*) and Bladder Wort (*Utricularia*). The leaves or some equivalent part secrete a sticky fluid which, once the fly is on the leaf, decomposes it into a form suitable for the plant to absorb. All these plants prefer a moist atmosphere and boggy conditions.

INTENSIVE CULTURE. Briefly speaking, the practice of intensive culture is undertaken in the vegetable garden in order to secure three successive crops of vegetables during the twelve months from the same plot of ground, without the aid of glasshouses or of heat. Obviously this result cannot be obtained unless each crop is grown very quickly to maturity, and this implies that the soil must be in excellent condition, that the plants shall never be set back by drought or by the shock of transplanting, and that constant attention shall be given to the various operations of cultivation such as hoeing, weeding, etc.

This method of cultivating vegetables has for some long time been adopted on the Continent, but it was probably not until the Great War that it became at all general in England. Certainly during that time a good deal of knowledge concerning the best varieties for early and late sowing, etc., was gathered, and it is this knowledge which makes it possible for the three crops to be produced by the amateur gardener.

The first and most important thing to do is to improve the soil through deep digging and adequate drainage. (*See also* Soil *and* Fertilisers.)

In France, which is the home of intensive culture, special hotbeds are built up and the manure of these beds is renewed from time to time as it becomes exhausted. It is, however, sufficient to dig in at first plenty of well-decayed manure, and afterwards to supplement this with artificial fertilisers. It is also important that no crop should be ruined by the presence of insect pests, and dressing the soil with a reliable soil fumigant during the winter months is also advised as a preparation for intensive culture.

With regard to the crops.—Assuming that the plot is comparatively sheltered from cold winds and the soil in excellent condition, the ordinary vegetables may be sown at the usual time, that is in March and April. The earliest-maturing varieties of each vegetable should be sown in order that the crops may mature before July or August, when another crop can be sown on the same site. In addition to this, a system of rotation of crops must be arranged, and this means that the vegetables will be divided into three groups—the green crops, root crops and the legumes (peas and beans). Onions, shallots, and other bulbs can form a fourth if preferred, where the plot divides more easily into four sections. The plot will also be divided into three (or four) and each of these groups of vegetables will be grown on the different plots in turn. The actual selection of the vegetables to be grown must naturally depend on the demands of the household, but a suggested rotation would be as follows:

Plot No. 1.—Potatoes, Parsnips, Carrots, Jerusalem Artichokes and Beetroot.

Plot No. 2.—Peas and Beans. These leave the soil richer in nitrates.

Plot No. 3.—Cruciferous Crops—Cabbage, Savoy, Cauliflower, Broccoli, Brussels Sprouts, Kohl Rabi, Kale, Turnips, Radishes, Seakale.

Plot No. 4.—Onions, Leeks, Garlic, Shallots.

The peas and beans will be grown on Plot No. 1 in the second year, cruciferous crops the third year, and bulbs the fourth, and so on.

The most important thing with regard to

WASH EACH LEAF IN TURN

TRIM ENDS OF LEAVES

To keep indoor plants in good health the leaves should be washed once a week with tepid water.

intensive cultivation is the selection of varieties of vegetables which can be sown as late in the year as July or August and still mature before the frosts arrive.

As far as possible inter-cropping will be practised; that is to say, early salads will be grown between larger vegetables, and young plants or seeds of the later crops may be put into the intervening spaces between the rows, even before the early crops have been gathered, but the chief concern will be the crops sown in July or August.

In some cases also it will be necessary to let these crops stand through the winter, but some will be ready by October. The

best varieties for these late sowings are as
follows :

Beetroot.—Globe, Crimson Ball, Egyptian, Turnip-rooted Crimson Globe. These
will stand all winter with only a little
protection and will provide tender little
roots of a suitable size for salads.

Carrot.—Champion, Scarlet Horn, Scarlet Model, Intermediate.

Onions.—White Leviathan, Giant Lemon
Rocca, Giant Red Rocca, Ailsa Craig.

Lettuce.—All-the-year-round and Hardy
Hammersmith.

Turnip.—Golden Ball, Orange Jelly.

Salads.—Endive, Mustard and Cress,
Winter Radish and Corn Salad (as "catch
crops").

Cabbages.—Ellam's Early, Harbinger.

Savoy.—Earliest of All. Dwarf Green
Curled.

Kohl Rabi.—Earliest Purple or Earliest
Green.

Another point with regard to the modified French gardening that the British
gardener can adopt, is the protection of
crops when weather conditions are
specially unfavourable. For this, the
finest arrangement is the use of cloches,
which can be obtained in adaptable form
for use on long rows or over single plants.
It is also advisable to prepare accumulations of litter such as bracken, or dried
leaves, bushy twigs cut from trees or
shrubs at pruning time, sacks, wire netting, or any other material which can be
pressed into service quickly to protect rows
of seedlings from cold frosty winds.

Apart from these precautions, extra
care should be taken where quick results
are needed to ensure that water is never
lacking, that the plants do not get choked
or starved by the presence of weeds, and
that the soil is kept loose and friable on
the surface by constant hoeing. By such
simple precautions, the amount of produce
obtained from a small vegetable plot may
easily be trebled.

INTERCROPPING. *See* ALLOTMENTS
and VEGETABLES.

INULA (ĭn-ula. Compositæ). Fleabane. Hardy herbaceous plants, of easy
culture and able to grow where many
plants fail. Some have large showy
flowers and handsome leaves and are
suitable for the wild garden or for pro-

tecting more tender plants in the border or
rockery.

Culture.—Divide the roots in spring and
plant at once in their permanent position,
or sow seed. They grow anywhere but
prefer deep rich soil, and are benefited by
mulchings of manure, and liquid manure
in summer.

SPECIES.

I. glandulosa with narrow petals but
large flowers and its variety *grandiflora*,
height, 1–2 ft.; *I. helenium* with very
large leaves, *I. hookeri* and *I. christi* are
all suitable for borders and produce deep
yellow flowers in July and August. *I.
royleana* flowers later than the rest of the
species. *I macrocephala* bears long spikes
of flowers and has fine leaves. The flowers
in all these species are 2–3 in. across, and
the plants vary from 1–4 ft. in height;
I. acaulis, short stemmed with large
flowers, and *I. ensifolia* are suitable for
the rock garden.

IODINE. Much publicity has been
given in recent years to fertilisers containing this mineral. Although its value in
animal feeding mixtures is beyond all
doubt, there is no evidence to show that
iodine is of the slightest value to plants.
All trials carried out to test this point have
so far given purely negative results.

IONOPSIDIUM (i-o-nop-sid-i-um.
Cruciferæ). Violet Cress. *I. acaule*, the
species usually grown, is a charming little
hardy annual with violet-colour flowers.
Once seed is sown in some shady spot the
plant sows itself and comes up year after
year. It succeeds in almost any soil provided it is not too light and sandy. Height,
2–3 in.

Sometimes referred to as *Cochlearia
acaulis*

IONOPSIS (i-o-nop-sis. Orchidaceæ).
Stove epiphytal orchids that are very
pretty although only one species, *I. paniculata*, is generally grown. They are best
attached to a block of wood with a little
live sphagnum and fibrous peat and hung
up close to the glass. They need plenty
of water at all times.

Propagate by pieces which have to be
continually imported not only to increase
but to keep up the stock.

SPECIES.

I. paniculata. White or rosy flowers. 6 in.

I. utricularioides (syn. *tenera*). White and pink.

IPOMÆ. *See* MORNING GLORY.

IPSEA (ip-se-a. Orchidaceæ). Stove orchid allied to Paxtonia. Grow in rough peat with a little fibrous loam. Summer temperature, 60°–90°; winter, 55°.

SPECIES.

I. speciosa. May.

IRESINE (i-re-si-ne. Amarantaoeæ). Stove and half-hardy ornamental foliage plants. Leaves mostly lance-shaped, and were very popular in the old carpet-bedding days. 1864.

Culture.—Compost: loam, peat, leaf-mould and sand. Sunny position in stove. Repot early spring, in good drainage. Water freely in summer, but little in winter. Winter temperature, 55°; summer, 75°.

Propagation.—By cuttings of young shoots in sandy soil, early spring. Temperature, 70°.

SPECIES.

I. Herbstii, leaves dark crimson; *I. H. aureo reticulata*, leaves gold and red; *I. Lindenii*, blood red.

IRIS (Flag or Fleur de Lys). Iridaceæ. Hardy evergreen bulbous and tuberous-rooted perennials. Irises are often called the poor man's orchid, doubtless because the form of the flower is quite as striking as that of any orchid, and the colours are also quite as showy. At the same time irises grow so freely and increase so rapidly that their cultivation is one of the cheapest forms of flower culture.

The bulbous-rooted irises include the Spanish, English, and Dutch (so called) irises, and also some of the winter-flowering irises such as *Iris alata* and *tingitana*. The cultivation of the Spanish, English and Dutch is almost identical.

They can be grown in the open garden in ordinary soil, if planted in sunny beds or borders in September or October. The bulbs should be about 3 in. deep and 6 in. apart.

They are excellent subjects for deep pockets in the rockery garden, or they can be used in the mixed border. The mixed border is better on the whole than using these irises in formal beds, because they are best if the foliage is allowed to die naturally after the flowers have faded, and in the mixed border the dying leaves can be hidden by other foliage. The iris bulbs can be left where they are year after year, until they become overcrowded. None of them need any special cultivation apart from keeping down weeds, and staking should not be necessary.

Pot Culture of Bulbous Irises.—The Spanish and English iris can be cultivated in pots, and so also can the winter-flowering irises *tingitana* and *reticulata*. They should be grown in soil composed of equal parts of loam, leaf-mould, and silver sand. Place them in a cold frame until top growth shows, then move them to a cool greenhouse, but do not attempt to force them unduly. They will grow quite well if allowed to remain in the cold frame until they are actually in flower. Watering is particularly important in the pot culture of Winter Iris. If the soil is moist at the time of potting, no water should be given until after the growth has commenced. Then it should be given fairly freely as required until after the flowers fade, when water should be given only in very sparing quantities.

Japanese Irises.—The Japanese irises are the ones suitable for waterside planting. They are particularly effective by the side of informal pools in the rock and bog garden, but they can also be used for planting in any situation in the garden where the soil is moist and boggy. They should be planted in October or March and during the growing season they will appreciate frequent doses of liquid manure. Otherwise their cultivation is of the simplest.

The Tuberous or Rhizomatous Irises.—This group includes the irises known as "bearded," and those called "beardless," and also the "cushion" irises, each of which requires slightly different treatment at the hands of the gardener. The *bearded irises* are those of which the outer falls or petals are beautifully bearded or crested. These are all perfectly hardy and easily cultivated in almost any kind of soil. They are usually planted in the early autumn, at which time they are easily increased by breaking off pieces of the root stock, together with a few of the fibrous roots, and planting each piece separately in the border. Any ordinary soil suits them, but it must contain some lime. Also these plants revel in full sunshine. When planting, do not bury the rhizome, but let it lie on the surface to be "sun-baked." The fibrous roots must, of course, be covered with soil.

The newest portions of the root stock make the best plants, and if the root stock is split up into many portions, care should be taken to see that each has an "eye," or growing portion, from which the new plant will develop. Irises that are allowed to become overcrowded will not produce good flowers, and it is often worth while to lift them every two years. The common purple Flag, or German Iris, is the most widely grown of this group, but amongst modern hybrids there are now so many beautiful colours that the iris should not be represented in any garden only by the purple Flag.

Beardless Irises.—This group of irises prefers a rather heavy soil as a rule, although some like a peaty loam. Possibly the one best known to gardeners is the *Iris sibirica*, which when once established grows almost like a weed, and *Iris unguicularis* (*stylosa*) which blooms in midwinter, and is often grown both in the open garden and in the cool greenhouse to provide cut flowers for the winter table. The following species amongst the beardless section prefer moist soil on the margins of ponds or streams for their cultivation: *Iris sibirica*, *I. ochroleuca* and *I. pseudacorus*. Most of the others will grow in ordinary rich soil in sunny borders or rockeries. They can be planted in October or March.

Cushion Irises.—These require more care and attention in their cultivation than most of the other irises. A raised bed should be prepared against a south wall. The ideal soil is a light rich loam, and with this should be mixed plenty of old mortar rubble. Plant in October, and if possible protect with cloches or a cold frame during the winter.

The roots should be lifted in July and stored in dry sand in a warm shed or greenhouse until October, when they will be replanted. This section contains some of the most interesting of all the irises, although, on the whole, they are not so showy as border flowers as are the bearded irises.

Seed Sowing.—Nearly all the irises can be raised from seed sown in sandy soil in a cold frame, as soon as it is ripe. When the seeds come through they are only like fine grass, and care must be taken in transplanting them. They may take up to several years before they arrive at the stage of flowering.

The bulbous species can also be cultivated by offsets, removed in autumn.

IRIS GARDENS. Nothing can surpass an Iris Garden for colour and splendour. There is nothing else in any garden to compare with the rich plum-coloured draperies and gossamer crowns of Prosper Laugier, contrasted with the silky textures of Silver Mist.

September is the best month for moving June-flowering irises, and as these are the main group used for bold picturesque effects a new iris garden is best made then. A formal garden is sometimes the home of the irises, a separate colour being used in each of the centre beds, and a varied selection of bulbous and rhizomatous irises in the long borders.

The comparatively short flowering period of most irises is rather a drawback to this method, as the beds are colourless during the greater part of the year.

With regard to the principles of design in a formal iris garden, the same rules apply as to the general layout of formal gardens. It is worth noting, however, that formal beds of irises look better contrasted against stonework than against grass. Thus one of the best settings for irises is in a paved, sunk garden.

Irises also look charming planted informally, and a long wide border planted with groups of varieties of iris, planned to give a succession of bloom, is a wonderful sight during the summer. Such a feature is of course only advisable when the garden is large enough to allow of other borders and shrubberies to give colour during the autumn and winter.

Certain types of irises such as *sibirica* and *Kæmpferi* are suited for planting informally by the waterside or in the bog-garden.

Informal iris gardens, if possible by a pond or stream, are to be preferred to those of formal type. Any ordinary soil, with the addition of lime, will do for the bearded irises. The bulbous species prefer a sandy loam mixed with leaf-mould or peat. Japanese irises like full sun, as do the other groups, but they revel in the moist or marshy soil and are usually grown right at the water's edge.

ISATIS (eye-say-tis. Cruciferæ). *Isazo,* to equal, from its supposed power to smooth roughness of the skin. Woad.

I. glauca. A useful border plant, producing clouds of yellow flowers on

thalictroides of which the foliage is like that of Maidenhair Fern. It looks very attractive when grown in clumps in the rockery or herbaceous border. Increase by seeds sown when ripe or by division of the clumps in autumn. Plant in any fairly rich good soil.

ITEA (ĭ'tēa-a. Saxifragaceæ). Deciduous and evergreen shrubs or trees with fragrant white flowers.

Culture.—Plant in rich soil, in moist

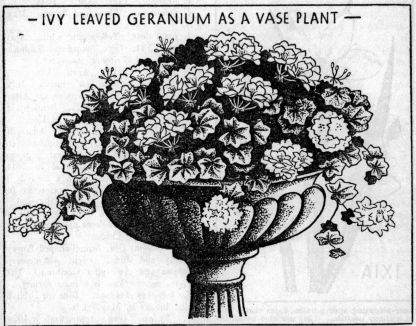

— IVY LEAVED GERANIUM AS A VASE PLANT —

When Ivy-leaved Geraniums are grown in vases they need constant feeding and should have the dead flowers removed to keep up the supply of bloom.

long stems. An extremely decorative plant for the back of the border. Being biennial, it dies after flowering, but is very easily raised from seed which can be sown where the plants are to bloom. It looks best when planted in groups. Thin out to 10 in. if sown in its flowering position. Once established, self-sown seedlings will usually be found round the parent plants. These can be transplanted as required.

ISOPYRUM (i-so-pi-rum. Ranunculaceæ). The principal species of this genus of elegant dwarf perennial herbs is *I.*

position. *Propagate* by seeds sown in spring, or by suckers.

SPECIES.

I. ilicifolia (China), 4–6 ft. Evergreen. Flowers greenish-white in August, holly-like leaves. Likes semi-shade. Often supposed to be tender, but has withstood nearly 30° of frost in Hampshire.

I. virginica (N. America), 3–5 ft. Flowers creamy-white, fragrant. July to September. Some of the older stems should be cut out now and then, to afford light and space for new ones constantly coming up from the base of the plant.

IVY. *See* HEDERA.

IXIA (ix-i-a. Irideæ). Half-hardy bulbs from the Cape that bear long spikes of beautiful flowers and resemble Babianas, Sparaxises and Tritonias.

Propagate by seeds sown in shallow pans of sandy soil in spring or by offsets which quickly form flowering plants. Although not quite hardy they may be grown outdoors in a sunny border that is

IXIA

Late-blooming spring bulbs, Ixias thrive best in a sunny position. They are also useful for rockeries.

well drained. Plant in rather light soil about 4 in. deep and during the winter cover the bulbs with some material that will help them to throw off water from heavy rains. Otherwise pot up in October and keep in a cold pit protected from frost and heavy rain until roots have formed when they may be moved to the greenhouse. In any case once the flowering is over the leaves should be allowed to die a natural death as this is conducive to good bulbs for the following year. If they must be lifted from the ground as soon as the flowers are over they should be left where the leaves will die slowly and not be dried up at once. After the leaves have withered the plants may be left in or out of the soil.

SPECIES.

Many of the species formerly included with Ixias are now transferred to other genera.

I. flexuosa. Pink. April. 1½ ft.

I. maculata. White and brown. May. 1 ft.

I. paniculata. Yellow and white. April onwards. 1 ft. (Syn. *longiflora, Gladiolus longiflora* and *Tritonia longiflora.*)

I. patens. Purple. April. 1 ft.

I. speciosa. Purple and crimson. July. Amongst the named varieties are Afterglow, Beauty of Norfolk, Bridesmaid, Emperor of China and Queen of Roses.

IXIOLIRION (ix-i-o-lir-i-on. Amaryllideæ). Hardy bulbs from Syria that in spite of their charming flowers are rarely grown although they were introduced in 1844. They are easily reared as they flourish in any fertile soil, but have a preference for loam with leaf-mould and a little sand.

Propagate by seeds when obtainable or by offsets. Plant in September or October.

SPECIES.

I. montanum. Blue funnel-shaped flowers in May and June. (Syn. *Alstroemeria montana* and *Amaryllis montana.*) 1 ft.

I. m. macranthum is a good variety.

I. kolpakowskianum. Blue or bluish-white flowers in May. 1 ft.

I. Pallasii (syn. *tataricum*). Blue. Summer.

The flowers are useful for cutting and last well in water.

IXORA (ix-or-a. Rubiaceæ). Stove evergreen flowering shrubs. E. Indies, 1690.

Culture.—For general cultivation, propagation, etc., *see* BOUVARDIA.

SPECIES.

I. coccinea, scarlet; varieties, *Fraseri* and *superba*; *I. Duffi,* scarlet; *I. D. grandiflora.*

J

JABOROSA (jab-or-o-za. Solanaceæ). Herbaceous perennials allied to Mandrake. *Propagate* by division of the rootstock or by cuttings under hand-lights. Plant in well-drained sandy loam.

SPECIES.

J. integrifolia. White. July to September. 1 ft.

JACARANDA (jak-ar-an-da. Bignoniceæ). Mimosa-leaved Ebony-tree. Stove evergreen flowering trees. Foliage fernlike. The species mimosæfolia grown chiefly for foliage. W. Indies, 1800.

Culture.—Compost: sandy peat, 2 parts, fibrous loam, 1 part. Pot and prune into shape in the spring. Light part of stove, and as it will grow from 4–8 ft. high it must have plenty of room overhead. Winter temperature, 55°; summer, 75°.

Propagation.—By cuttings of well-ripened shoots in sandy peat in the summer; place in propagator, temperature, 70°.

SPECIES.

J. ærulea, J. filicifolia, J. mimosæfolia. All have blue flowers.

JACKDAW. Although this bird has a mischievous reputation, it must be regarded as being distinctly beneficial. Of its food 89.5 per cent. consists of injurious insects (including wireworms, beetles, larvæ of moths and cockchafers), and to a lesser extent slugs and snails, millipedes, ticks, etc. A considerable portion of its food is of a neutral nature, and the harm done by its slight depredations on cereals, roots, fruit, etc., is well counterbalanced by the good.

JACK TREE (artocarpus integrifolia). *An Indian Bread-fruit tree.*

JACOBÆA. *See* SENECIO.

JACOBINIA (jak-o-bin-i-a. Acanthaceæ). Stove shrubby perennials allied to Justicia. Indigenous to S. America.

Propagate by cuttings inserted in sandy soil. Pot up in a mixture of loam, peat, and leaf-soil with a little dried cow manure and sand. They need plenty of water, but no moisture should be allowed to remain near the roots of young plants. The growing shoots must be pinched back and the plants kept near the glass.

SPECIES.

J. chrysostephana. Yellow flowers in winter. 3 ft. (Syn: *Cyrtanthera chrysostephana.*)

J. magnifica. Rosy. August. 1–15 ft. Good varieties are *J. m. carnea*, flesh colour, 3–9 ft.; and *pohliana*, red, autumn. 3–9 ft.

JACOB'S LADDER

Jacob's Ladder or Polemonium is a useful blue perennial about 2 ft. high for the mixed flower border.

Some of the species are synonymous with those of Justicia.

JACOB'S LADDER. *See* POLEMONIUM.

JAMESIA (jăm'-si-a. Saxifragaceæ). Western N. America. Deciduous compact-growing shrub, 3–5 ft., with white flowers in June and July. Thrives in open, not too rich soil, sunny position. *Propagate* by cuttings.

J. Americana, the only species.

JANUARY WORK IN THE GARDEN.

FLOWERS.

Finish all path-making and constructional work, such as archways, pergolas. etc.

Trench or fork borders and beds.

Prepare labels and seed-pans or boxes.

Sow seeds of annual carnations under

N

glass. Remember that the best seed gives the highest percentage of double flowers.

Press back soil loosened round roses, wallflowers, etc., by frost.

Coconut fibre is a useful substance among flowering plants at this season. It can be used to cover the soil between dwarf roses, over Montbretias and other bulbous plants, and also to protect the crowns of delphiniums, pæonies, pyrethrums, etc.

Coconut fibre is also used over the surface soil of flower boxes on window-sills and roofs. It serves a double purpose by protecting the plants and preventing muddy splashes on windows when heavy rains occur.

Order seeds early and wisely. A little of the best quality will give more pleasure than large quantities of inferior seed of which most has to be wasted. Avoid clashing colours and prepare a scheme for the whole season before making any choice of varieties.

Trim laurel hedges and keep all lawns rolled, unless the weather is very wet, in which case rolling should cease.

Well-decayed manure, that is, manure in a dry crumbly condition such as it adopts after several months' storing, makes a fine mulch for pæonies. Cover the crowns of the plants with this and leave it to be washed in by heavy rains.

As the manure disappears, and the days get warmer, the pæonies will develop young buds. These should grow into strong heads of bloom. To help them, dress the ground with fertiliser as soon as they show, hoeing it lightly into the surrounding soil.

In the Shrubbery.

Cut back all cherry and Portugal laurel. Prune wall climbers. Shake snow from evergreens to prevent breakage. Thin out dead wood, and clean up the shrubbery.

Shrubs which can be pruned this month, or as soon as it is possible from the new growth to distinguish the living wood from the dead, include: Abutilon vitifolium, Ailanthus glandulosa, Artemisia (Lad's Love), Buddleia variabilis, late-flowering Clematis, Fuchsias, winter Jasmine, Lavender, climbing Knotweed, Sambucus, Grape vines (outdoors).

Order new roses, bush, standards, climbers, etc. Meanwhile prepare the ground to receive them.

Dig to a depth of 2 ft., putting draina material below, and improving the textu of the upper soil by adding humus to lig soil, and straw and road grit to clay.

The modern roses do not need stiff cl but grow best in ordinary rich loam.

Add lime to the soil after digging.

Prepare rose stakes for each new ro ordered. Even the bush roses, prun hard back, may often be staked with a vantage, and standards and climbe invariably need a stake at plantir time.

The Rockery.

Renovate rock gardens and add fres soil if needed. Remove weeds from thic carpets of arabis, aubrietia, etc. Give dressing of lime except where heaths ar other lime haters are grown.

Rock gems wake quickly from wint sleep when sunny days arrive. Look car fully to see if they have been lifted fro the soil by frosts, or if the surface so has been washed away from the crown Top dress where necessary with gritty soi and press the lifted plants back into the pockets.

Wood ashes sprinkled among dwarf bul in the rock garden will act as fertilise and also add a little warmth.

Fruit.

Prune soft fruits. Cut away old thi shoots from black currants, thin youn shoots from red and white currants an from gooseberries.

Burn prunings and store the ashes dr for dusting among the seedlings, unles cuttings are wanted, when pieces 8–12 ir long, cut below a joint, can be inserted

Thin main branches of apples, and an that overcross. Stake and secure youn trees.

Spray with caustic wash to destro insects.

Clean out and thin raspberry canes, ti them to supports, and mulch the surfac soil with manure.

Dress strawberries with manure.

Top dress the soil round loganberries.

Nail up wall fruits.

Prune outdoor grapes.

Force rhubarb.

Spray winter wash well into the bar of fruit trees. Wear old clothes and gloves Spray with the wind.

Fruits to plant this month.

Bush apples ... ... 9–12 ft. apart.
Apricots (wall) ... 18 ,, ,,
Cherries ... ... 15–20 ,, ,,
Currants ... ... 5–6 ,, ,,
Damsons ... ... 15–20 ,, ,,
Gooseberries ... ... 5–6 ,, ,,
Loganberries ... ... 8–10 ,, ,,
Peaches (wall) ... ... 12–15 ,, ,,
Pears, pyramids ... 8–12 ,, ,,
Plums ... ... 20 ,, ,,

(*See also* FRUIT CULTURE.)

In purchasing plants for a new fruit garden, arrange for all the soft fruits to be grown in one section.

Build a cage over this portion to keep birds away from the fruit.

The framework of the cage can be made of thin wooden supports creosoted to prevent them from rotting.

Over these stretch a cover of small-mesh wire netting or old fish netting.

Make the wooden supports for the cage sufficiently high to allow fruit pickers to stand upright inside.

VEGETABLES.

Finish digging for frost and weather to work the soil before spring planting.

Mushroom culture can begin now. Turn fresh manure over two or three times until the rank heat has escaped. When well rotted, it can be mixed with oak or chestnut leaves and packed in layers, well trodden so that it is firm all over. As soon as the bed is prepared it can be spawned. Pieces of spawn 1 in. or 2 in. square are used and pressed into the bed at intervals of 8 in. all over the surface. Soil is used to cover the whole of the bed which is often made in the form of a mound with sloping sides. Thin canvas over the top, with litter packed over this to keep the bed warm, completes the work. A simple bed of this kind will produce a surprising crop.

EARLY POTATOES.

Potatoes can be grown for early use by placing the tubers to sprout now. Towards the end of the month they can be planted in the cold frame, and if a very warm sheltered border is also available a few can even be planted outdoors.

EARLY PEAS.

To obtain these, sow early-maturing varieties only, in a sheltered position.

As soon as the young plants begin to show, sprinkle lime and soot among them to keep away the slugs.

Put in twigs immediately after sowing. They break the wind and give a little shelter in addition to providing for the growing plants.

Protect globe artichokes with litter, leaves or soil.

Protect chicory and endive from frosts.

Break over a few broccoli leaves to protect the heads.

Celery needs a little protection. Bracken, straw and fern are excellent protection materials.

Plant out cabbages on a sheltered border if seedlings are available.

Force asparagus crowns, early potatoes and seakale.

UNDER GLASS.

Greenhouse chrysanthemums should be throwing up plenty of young shoots suitable for cuttings. Cuttings 3–4 in. long should be inserted in sandy soil and covered with a bell-glass until they have rooted.

Do not add leaf-mould to the soil in which the cuttings are inserted.

Greenhouse plants generally need less water during the winter months, but all plants should be well supplied with moisture when they begin to throw up flower stems or to open buds.

Use water at the same temperature as the greenhouse or the plants will be chilled. Rain water is best.

As soon as possible after the New Year, seed-sowing in the greenhouse can begin. Seed boxes can be used, or if there is a border of soil in the greenhouse, some seeds can be sown direct in this.

Prepare a Compost for Seed-sowing.—An ideal mixture of soil for seed-sowing in the greenhouse or cold frame consists of two-thirds loam (decayed turf) and one-third leaf-mould, with a good sprinkling of sharp sand.

The sand is necessary to keep the soil open. For seedlings that damp off easily, like primulas, omit leaf-mould and add more sand.

Mix well together and rub the mixture through a quarter-inch mesh sieve. Level the surface of this so that it comes just below the rim of the box or seed pan.

Cover fine seeds with the same soil or

pure sand rubbed through the finest sieve you have.

A piece of zinc gauze fixed to a wooden frame makes an ideal soil sifter for very fine seeds.

Seeds to sow in the greenhouse.—Sow a row or two of carrots and a few rows of lettuces with radishes between. The radishes will be ready to pull before the lettuces mature.

Sow onions in boxes.

Sow mustard and cress in boxes.

Sow now annual carnations, schizanthus, cyclamen, amaryllis, begonias, gloxinias, grevillea, verbena, antirrhinums, petunias.

Sow cauliflowers, leeks, melons, Alpine strawberries.

Order Lilies.—During this month lily bulbs arrive in large quantities from Japan. If these are shrunken on arrival they should be placed in the greenhouse in boxes, packed with moist coconut fibre. They will quickly plump up and be in good condition for planting in the open in late February or March. Japanese bulbs which arrive this month include:

Lilium auratum.—Golden lily.

Lilium batemanniæ.—Reddish-apricot.

Lilium hansonii.—Orange-brown.

Lilium henryi.—Orange-red.

Lilium cordifolium.—Hemoracallis.

Lilium leichtlini.—Citron-yellow.

Lilium tigrinum.—Tiger lily.

General care of the greenhouse now.— Give air whenever possible, especially to cinerarias, and other growing plants. Ventilate on the side away from the wind. With lighter days the house will need more light. The glass of the greenhouse should therefore be kept clean inside and out.

Paint-work should also be scrubbed with disinfectant soap, and, if necessary, repainted. White paint adds light to the interior.

While repainting is being done, hooks and supports for the training of climbing greenhouse plants can now be renewed. Greenhouse stages should receive attention, and the floor boards should be repaired where necessary.

PESTS.

Soil pests. Frost alone does not destroy all soil pests. Deep digging, which brings soil pests to the surface, places them at the mercy of the birds and frosts. In addition, a soil fumigant dug into vacant land now will effectively destroy soil pests.

Wash all fruit-trees with caustic winter wash. This will destroy all hibernating insects in the crevices of the bark, and also rid the tree of moss, lichen, etc. Add a fungicide to the spray if fungoid diseases are to be destroyed at the same time. Fruit-trees can be sprayed now with a tar-oil wash, to destroy eggs of pests, but if this is used, a caustic soda wash will not be needed.

Dig into the soil of flower-beds, vegetable garden, and fruit plantation a good soil fumigant. Only vacant land or soil between trees and plants can be dressed. Avoid crowns and roots of plants.

Keep grease bands in a sticky condition.

Order spring and summer insecticides, nicotine wash, soft soap, paraffin, etc.

Turn vacant soil a second time, between frosts. Grubs will be either frozen or eaten by birds.

CARE OF LAWNS.

Lift turf where hollows or hummocks appear, and after levelling replace the turf and roll well. A mixed top dressing of sifted soil, manure and decayed leaves revives a lawn like magic. Use three barrow loads to a rod (30¼ sq. yds.). The dressing will disappear before the spring, and a soft velvety lawn will appear. Soot and fine dust are also good fertilisers, and these should be applied during showers.

In very wet weather roll gravel walks. Renew worn-out gravel. Fork the surface and destroy weeds first.

COLD OR WET WEATHER TASKS.

Prepare pea and bean sticks.

Order seeds and plan the season's garden on paper.

Clean up the tool shed.

Coat lawn mowers and other tools with vaseline or thick grease to prevent rust.

Get tools sharpened and repaired if necessary.

Prepare labels, stakes and potting soil.

Give a little protection to tender plants; it works miracles. Evergreen branches, fern leaves, or litter, among tea roses, tree lupins, fuchsias, hydrangeas and other tender plants will often save their lives in severe seasons.

Fertilisers to apply in January.

Lime or chalk (general) 3–8 oz. per. sq. yd.
Bonemeal   ,,   2–4 ,, ,, ,, ,,
Basic Slag (for fruit) 4–8 ,, ,, ,, ,,
Kainit (root crops) 2–4 ,, ,, ,, ,,

These are best applied to the surface soil after digging.

JAPANESE GARDENS. These gardens are divided into two classes: One, which is called a formal garden—Shin, Giyo, So, styles—generally consisting of

In the background a more rugged effect is created to give a natural aspect to the garden, and to produce the effect of a long-distance scene. There are two distinct styles of well. One, which is made entirely of wood—an ornamental well—(*Kazarildo*) is more commonly used than the stone well.

Large stones or rocks can be used to substitute the well if so desired. An important thing to note is the presence

JAPANESE GARDENS

1. Informal type of Japanese garden with well.
2. Large stones can be used to substitute the well if desired.
3. Stones are placed near the well to serve as stepping-stones and to drain waste water drawn from the well.

waterfalls, lakes, etc., and the other, an informal garden, is generally a flat garden, without any particular form, such as the one given in the drawing.

Informal Garden.

The illustration shows an excellent (informal) flat garden which is admirably suited for any small space—such as a town garden—or it would make a very charming roof garden.

The foreground shows a garden well—which is a very important feature in Japanese gardens—and a willow tree, one of the main features of the garden.

of small pebbles (Goro Ishi) which are arranged by the side of the well, and in between the stepping-stones. These serve to drain off the waste water, drawn from the well, as well as adding to the general scenery. This particular spot is called in Japanese Mizu Hake Dokoro, which means draining of waste water.

It is usual to find an ornamental water-basin erected a little distance away from the well. There are two different types of water-basins. One is the ornamental water-basin (Tsukubai), which is used in ordinary gardens; and the other is called the Crouching water-basin (CHIYOZYBACHI), which is always to be found in a tea garden. There are various shapes of water-basins; the one given in the picture is named FUJI GATA, after the shape of the famous sacred mountain in Japan, Fuji Yama.

The tall trees at the back of the water-basin are named upright Spirit trees. These trees are specially picked for their

JASMINUM OFFICINALE

A good plant for towns is the white Jasminum Officinale.

height and strength to fill their respective positions. On the left of the trees is a simple shaped stone lantern (SOWA GONOMI), which is used not only as an ornament but for lighting purposes if the garden is lighted up at night. Thus the stone lanterns should be placed *prominently* so as to give the proper illumination to the garden. It is worthy to note that screening the stone lantern are a few small trees which give the effect of distance.

Great care must be used in placing the stepping-stones, as it is extremely difficult to place them in their proper positions,

because if an unnecessary stone is placed it spoils the whole effect.

The Japanese landscape garden in general is composed mostly of small shrubs, evergreen, miniature and large pine trees. Flowers are not used to a great extent except such as rock plants, water reeds, and irises, which fit in with the rocks and water.

Such trees as oak and ash have been introduced with great success to give added colouring in the autumn.

JAPANESE HYACINTH. *See* OPHIO-POGON.

JASIONE (jas-i-ōn-e. Campanulaceæ). An ancient name used by Theophrastus. The Jasione all resemble miniature fluffy Scabious. All are bright or deep blue.

Propagate by seeds or division.

J. humilis is one of the smallest grown. 4 in. high.

J. montana. The Sheep's Bit, is frequently seen in banks and hedges in the less cultivated districts of Great Britain.

JASMINE. *See* JASMINUM.

JASMINE NIGHTSHADE. *See* SOLANUM.

JASMINUM (jas-mī-num. Oleaceæ). Jasmine. Deciduous and evergreen climbers and shrubs, with white or yellow flowers, usually fragrant.

Culture.—Plant in good, rich loamy soil from October to March. Prune shoots that have flowered. *Propagate* by cuttings of ripe wood placed in frame, and by layering.

SPECIES.

J. nudiflorum, the "Winter-flowering" Jessamine (China). One of the most useful and beautiful of winter-flowering shrubs. Will grow anywhere in any soil. Looks especially well associated with *Berberis Aquifolium,* either growing or as "cut flowers." Award of Garden Merit, R.H.S.

J. officinale, "Common White Jessamine" (Persia, China, India). Exquisitely fragrant white flowers, from June to frost.

J. o. affine (*grandiflorum*). A fine large-flowered form.

J. primulinum (China), 6–10 ft. Most beautiful species, with a profusion of soft yellow flowers about 1½ in. across, from May onwards. Supposed to be tender, but has survived without injury nearly 30° of frost on a south wall in Hampshire.

JEFFERSONIA (jef-fer-son-ia. Berorideæ). Named in honour of the President of the United States. Hardy herbaceous perennials that grow in any well-drained and rather sandy garden soil.

Propagate by seeds or by division in spring.

SPECIES.

J. binata (syn. *diphylla*) with white flowers in May is the only species. 6 in.

JOB'S TEARS. *See* COIX.

JUDAS TREE. *See* CERCIS.

JUGLANS (jug'-lans. Juglandaceæ). Walnut. Deciduous trees with handsome foliage. Valuable as a fast-growing shade tree, and for the edible nuts. Certain species valuable as timber trees. Plant in October in well-drained loam (but they are not particular as to soil) in a sunny open position. They should always be grown from seed (nuts), which should be sown 4 in. deep in the open as soon as ripe, and never be allowed to become dry before sowing. The plants will be ready for their permanent positions when 3 or 4 years old. Named varieties are propagated by grafting on the common walnut.

SPECIES.

J. nigra, Black Walnut of N. America. A fast-growing species with exceptionally long leaves. A very valuable timber tree in its native country.

J. regia, Common Walnut (E. Europe, Asia Minor, Afghanistan). Has been grown in this country for many centuries but its date of introduction is unknown. As a timber tree it is very valuable, and is much used for gunstocks, veneering and furniture; but it is chiefly grown for its nuts, and for its soft unripe fruit, which is made into what is known as "Pickled Walnuts." *See also* WALNUTS.

JULY WORK IN THE GARDEN.

THE FLOWER GARDEN.

Sow seeds of Brompton Stocks, which are best treated as biennials. Sow the seeds in the open border or in the cold frame and when they are a few inches high transplant them to their permanent position, leaving 8–12 in. between the plants.

Bud roses. If any named varieties have reverted to briars, bud them with a choice variety already in the garden.

Plant Colchicums. (Autumn Crocuses.)

Chrysanthemums require attention. Plunge the pots into soil or ashes. This saves watering. Tie, disbud, and keep a watch for greenfly.

Feed Dahlias.

Sow Primulas, and Meconopsis (Baileyi and Wallichii).

Layer carnations, and water if necessary.

Perennial flowers like Delphiniums, Phloxes, and Anchusas will give a second crop if faded blossoms are removed.

Take cuttings of Hollyhocks.

Ivy cuttings inserted in the cold frame will root readily this month.

Lift tulips and dry them. A few of the species like to be left undisturbed, but most of the named early, cottage, and Darwin tulips prefer to be lifted.

Towards the end of the month clumps of Irises can be lifted and replanted, if the soil is moist.

Gather Sweet Peas regularly to prevent seed-pods forming. Pick in the evening or early morning before the sun has dried the dew. After a hot day, syringe the Sweet Peas with water. Hoe the soil round the plants.

Attend to the staking of autumn-flowering plants such as Sunflowers, Heleniums, Michaelmas Daisies.

Fuchsias and Geraniums should be watered regularly.

Pansies may be sown outdoors in boxes.

Feed roses with liquid manure diluted to a pale straw colour. Unless fed they will not give a satisfactory second crop of flowers.

Increase pinks by cuttings or "pipings," i.e., short pieces pulled out at a joint and inserted as cuttings. Insert in sandy soil and keep moist until the roots have formed.

Take cuttings of all the early flowering carpet plants such as Arabis, Aubrietia, etc. Pieces pulled off and inserted in sand, with no trimming or other preparation, will root readily if kept moist overhead. Shade them if a cold frame is not available.

Sow seeds of summer-flowering perennials such as Chrysanthemum maximum, Lupins, etc. Sow in lines in a shady border, and transplant when large enough to handle, leaving 6–12 in. between the plants.

THE ROCK GARDEN.

Remove faded flowers from the rock garden. This is a good month to increase early-flowering rock plants by means of cuttings. Fine silver sand is a good medium to strike small cuttings and a bell-glass or a cloche is advisable. Shade cuttings from the sunshine by covering the glass with lime wash. As soon as the cuttings are rooted, remove the glass and transplant into pockets in the rock garden.

The bright pink of the Catchfly *Silene compacta* is very useful in the new rock garden, where colour is desired and more permanent plants have not yet spread to their full extent. Seeds sown now on any bare patches in the rockery will make a mass of bloom next summer. Sow thinly in pockets of sandy loam. Iceland Poppies are fine plants for rock gardens, and flourish as true perennials in pockets of warm, sandy loam. To avoid possible complete loss of plants during the winter, sow seeds now.

THE SHRUBBERY.

Now is the time to clear up this part of the garden. Prune back shrubs that have flowered, except those varieties which flower on stems growing from the tips of old shoots. Clean the soil by hoeing and forking, keeping a sharp watch for self-sown seedlings of Foxgloves, Honesty, or other woodland plants. Such seedlings can be left where they are or transplanted in groups wherever desired.

Layer Rhododendrons.

Trees and Shrubs to prune in July:

Azara; Buxus; Carpinus; Deutzia; Discaria; Eleagnus; Euonymus japonicus; Evodia; Griselinia; Hedera; Kadsura; Laurus; Ligustrum; Lonicera; Magnolia; Michelia; Osmanthus; Robinia hispida.

Keep climbers trained.

Quick-growing climbers like Clematis and Roses need attention at least once a week.

FRUIT.

Fruits of all kinds make rapid growth this month. Trained trees can have a number of the surplus shoots removed.

Where summer pruning is practised, this should be done this month. For the most part it is best left alone unless they are pruned by an expert. Espalier and cordon trees must be attended to, or they will lose their shape. Reduce the shoots to induce the formation of fruiting spurs.

Budding fruit trees is done this month in the same way that roses are budded.

Gooseberries and Red Currants may need to have the young wood thinned out.

Pears should be examined. Some of the fruits will appear unhealthy. These should be removed and only the best allowed to mature.

Strawberries require constant attention. Cut away runners not wanted. Layer others. Clean up the beds, and take away all rubbish to the bonfire.

Thin shoots of Morello cherries.

Cut away Raspberry canes not required.

Mulch and water wall fruit-trees.

If apples are thick on the trees, thin the bunches to 2 or 3 at each joint.

Protect soft fruit from birds by means of netting stretched over a framework of wood.

Dress stone fruits with sulphate of potash, 2–3 oz. per sq. yd., hoed into the surface soil.

Moisture is necessary for the development of all fruits. In dry weather conserve the soil moisture by constant use of the hoe between soft fruits, standards, and bush trees.

VEGETABLES.

Continue to plant out winter greens, allowing between Brussels sprouts and Broccoli 30 in. apart each way. Kale and Sprouting Broccoli can be planted between rows of early Potatoes. Take advantage of any showers for this work.

Liquid manure builds up strong crowns of Rhubarb and Seakale.

Plant Leeks. Make drills 3 in. deep and 2 ft. apart, and plant the seedlings in deep holes. Stimulate with liquid manure or a dusting of sulphate of ammonia.

Make sowings of Spring Cabbage. Sow the seeds thinly in drills 1 in. apart. If the soil is dry, water a few hours before sowing the seeds.

There is still time to sow carrots such as Early Horn, and Sutton's Globe Beet. Sow in drills 15 in. apart.

When ripe, Eschallots should be harvested.

Lift Early Potatoes as the tops turn yellow.

Spray Late Potatoes with Bordeaux mixture as needed.

Water Runner Beans if the weather is dry.

Make a sowing of Parsley for winter use.

It is possible to obtain a crop of Peas in autumn by sowing early-maturing varieties now.

After the crops have been gathered, all cabbage stalks, bean stalks and pea haulms should be removed.

The head of Globe Artichokes should be cut when about three parts open.

Mint and other sweet herbs should be cut for drying.

Mushroom beds should be made in the open.

All loose soil covering Shallots should be pulled away.

The tops and side-shoots of Tomatoes must be pinched out.

An abundance of tepid water should be given to Marrows.

Dust soot and lime along the celery rows to keep off the celery fly as well as slugs. Celery and Leeks require plenty of liquid manure just before they are earthed up. Earthing-up of both crops should be done in gradual stages. Begin with the Leeks, drawing a little earth towards the plants at regular fortnightly intervals. The earliest celery should be ready for the first earthing up at the end of this month. This also should be attended to at regular intervals.

Mulch vegetable Marrows and other gross feeders that suffer from drought. Cow manure, short litter, and grass clippings and leaves make useful mulches.

Watch newly-sown French Beans for the appearance of red spider. Plenty of water over and under the leaves will cure this trouble.

Bend a leaf or two over the heads of Cauliflowers that are nearly ready for use, to protect them.

Hoe constantly between all growing crops, to conserve moisture.

UNDER GLASS.

Copious watering will be required by all plants under glass. Air can generally be given at night without risk. Plants that have finished flowering should be cut down. If the greenhouse has not already been cleaned, an attempt should be made this month.

Carnations and Chrysanthemums in pots will need staking and tying.

Sow annuals for greenhouse decoration. Cinerarias, Mignonette, etc.

Browallia speciosa major is a charming greenhouse plant of the easiest possible culture. Seeds should be sown this month.

Sow Cyclamen seed.

Peaches and Nectarines under glass need constant watering, and it is essential to keep the staging watered two or three times a day. Syringe the foliage with clean water every evening to keep down red spider. Should greenfly or "leaf-curl" put in an appearance, spray at once with an insecticide. Transplant Primulas and Cinerarias sown last month into small pots, and place in a semi-shady cold frame. Pot up Freesias. After potting, the bulbs should be plunged in a cold frame in ashes or fibre refuse until growth commences. Sandy loam and dried cow manure make an ideal compost.

When Azaleas have flowered, stand the pots outside in a sunny position to ripen the wood. Plunge the pots in ashes or soil, and keep the roots watered.

Give full sun to succulents.

Take cuttings of Pelargoniums and Hydrangeas. Bud or graft Citrus, Camellias and Azaleas.

When summer-bedding plants have been taken from the frames, there is no need to let them lie idle until the autumn. When not actually in use they should be cleaned, and the opportunity can be taken to repair the woodwork or broken glass, and repaint the frame.

Ridge cucumbers or tomatoes can be grown during the summer months in the frames. If not required for these crops, use the frames to raise seedlings of perennial plants, or to root cuttings.

The advantage of a frame in summer is not that it shelters from cold nights so much as that it shelters from hot days. Wash the glass over with whitewash, or use sheets of paper as well as the glass, so that the brilliant sun rays are softened, and do not scorch the seedlings or cuttings.

In addition, moisture is conserved under the frame lights.

Pests in July.

To destroy wireworms.—Traps made by inserting pieces of carrot in the soil are useful for ridding the soil of this pest during the growing season. The traps should be examined each day. Soil fumigants are also effective, but not so safely applied while plant growth is active.

A Weed Killer.—An effective weed-killer for summer use can be made by mixing a pint of creosote with a gallon of hot water. Sprinkle this over the path with a rosed water-can and it will kill all weeds within 24 hours. Care should be taken to see that the mixture does not touch the border plants or lawns.

Leaf Miner. — Little silver streaks in chrysanthemum leaves are the work of this grub. It will cause considerable damage if allowed to go unchecked. An occasional spray with quassia and soft soap is effective and affected leaves should be picked off and burned.

The leaf-cutting bee eats semi-circular pieces (from the leaves of roses particularly), and the only way to prevent this is to spray the foliage with quassia extract to make it bitter.

Mildew may appear now on roses. This is best dispersed by spraying the foliage with liver-of-sulphur solution, 1 oz. to 3 gallons. Dissolve first in a little warm water, and then mix with cold water. The best method of treatment for green and black fly is spraying with a good insecticide. Spray each week while the trouble lasts.

This month the lackey moth deposits a band of eggs on the twigs of apple trees. Search for them, and remove them, otherwise considerable damage will be done by the grubs when they emerge.

Staking and tying are important duties this month. Plants grow so rapidly that this work should be attended to at least twice weekly. Climbers should be tied in frequently, or they quickly become entangled, and grow twisted. Climbing roses with heavy trusses of flowers sometimes break away from the trellis or pillar unless they are very securely tied. Border perennials of the Michaelmas daisy type should be supported with several stakes,

placed round the clumps, with a string run round the whole. If a few stems are left outside the string, and tied separately to the stakes, the supports will be hardly noticeable. Never tie many stems to one stake.

Herbs and Potpourri.—This is the month to gather herbs. Gather them when the flowers have not yet opened, and dry them for winter use. Potpourri can be made now, and a simple way to make this from the home garden, where flowers can only be gathered a few at a time is as follows. Take as many fresh rose leaves as you can, some lavender, and lemon-scented verbena foliage. Dry them in the sun. Put them into layers with a sprinkling of bay salt between each layer. Stir occasionally, and add to the mixture from time to time as the garden flowers mature. Each gathering must be well dried before being added. When about three months old, add some cloves, half a wineglass of brandy and a wineglass of eau-de-Cologne. Also add a small packet of patchouli.

Among the ingredients which can be gathered this month as occasion arises are marjoram, lemon geranium and bergamot leaves, carnation petals, and lemon balm.

JUNE-BERRY. *See* Amelanchier.

JUNE WORK IN THE GARDEN.

Flowers.

Climbing roses and bush roses, standards and dwarf polyanthus roses are all in flower during this month and next, and need feeding with occasional doses of liquid manure at this season to get the best from them. Use a little and often.

Apply when the soil is wet, after a shower or after watering, but always be careful to keep the water away from the foliage.

Be generous with the blooms. The more you cut the more you will have. When cutting, sever the stem low down. This encourages finer blooms when the second crop is ready.

Watch for the appearance of mildew on roses. Spray with liver of sulphur, or dust flowers of sulphur over the plants to destroy this.

Hardy annuals need attention during the growing season. Thin out ruthlessly, as crowded plants never give the best results.

Give support to such flowers as Shirley Poppies and Cornflowers. A few twigs pushed in between the growing seedlings will be sufficient. Stake Carnations.

Newly-planted seedlings of half-hardy annuals may need water if the weather is dry.

Dahlias should be planted in beds and borders as soon as the danger of frosts is over. At frequent intervals they will need liquid manure. Strong inch-square stakes are needed for tall Dahlias. Thin stakes are useless.

Anchusas, Delphiniums, Doronicums, Lupins, etc., should be cut down as the flowers fade, the roots being mulched with manure and watered regularly.

Most of the biennials and hardy perennials such as Pansies, Hollyhocks and Delphiniums, can be sown now. They may be sown in a shady part of the garden. Sow the seed thinly, in shallow drills, allowing enough room between the rows to use the hoe.

Keep the weeds down by hoeing until the plants are large enough to transplant to permanent quarters.

Seeds to be sown this month, on nursery beds outdoors, include:

Alyssum saxatile, Anchusa, Aubrietia, Aquilegia, Coreopsis, Chrysanthemum maximum, Cheiranthus, Delphinium, Gaillardia, Iberis, Linum perenne, Lupin, Lychnis, Phlox (perennial), Statice, Sweet Rocket, Honesty, Wallflowers, Canterbury Bells.

THE SHRUBBERY.

Prune intelligently. Here are hints that will be specially useful at this season of the year:

Shrubs that flower on the *tips* of the shoots, such as lilacs and rhododendrons, rarely need much pruning. When the shrub is overgrown or "leggy," however, it will need pruning to make it shapely again. Such pruning should be done with this class of shrub immediately after the flowers have faded.

Shrubs that flower on stems that *were new growths last season* are treated differently.

Look at the Forsythia, for instance, and note that the long new stems of last year's growth have been a mass of flower this spring.

If such shrubs are pruned hard back now, it will encourage them to make plenty of new stems during this summer, and there will be plenty of flowers next year.

The third class of shrub is that which flowers on *short spurs* along the old wood. Leave these severely alone for the present. They will be cut back during the winter.

THE ROCK GARDEN.

In new gardens where large spaces on the rockery have to be filled, take the opportunity now of increasing carpet plants.

Arabis, Aubrietia and the Mossy Saxifrages all increase easily by means of cuttings. Shoots about 3 in. long make good cuttings. Insert in sandy soil under a hand-light, or in any position where they can be kept moist and shaded.

A sheet of glass can be made to serve by those who have no frame. Make a hole in the border 5 in. deep, and an inch or two smaller in area than the glass. Scatter a handful of sand over the bottom and insert the cuttings close together, stripping off the lower leaves of each one. Water overhead. Lay the glass over them, thus excluding all draughts, and shade with a sheet of newspaper held in position by stones.

The cuttings will root in a few weeks, and as soon as they begin to make new growth, the glass can be removed.

Every variety of pink can be accommodated on the rockery. They are sun-lovers, and given a gritty soil, with plenty of lime and sunshine, they will flower profusely. Seeds of all varieties of pinks can be sown now in boxes of sandy soil in the cold frame. Cuttings of short side shoots can also be inserted under glass.

Among the rockery pinks suitable for increase by seeds or cuttings during June are: *D. deltoides*, *D. chinensis*, *D. cœsius*, *D. heddewigii* (*biennial*).

FRUIT.

Wall fruits need watching this month. Give them a few pailfuls of water at the root.

Apricot, peaches and nectarines should have breast wood cut out, and any badly-placed side shoots should also be removed. All shoots that grow at right angles to the wall must be cut away. Syringe the leaves morning and evening with extract of quassia to keep off insect pests. Be certain that sufficient water reaches the roots.

A net will be needed to keep the birds from pecking cherries and other wall fruits, and also strawberries as soon as they begin to ripen.

Gooseberries should be thinned out. The green gooseberries are best for preserves, and if only a few of the choicest fruits are left on each bush, they will make fine dessert fruit later.

Strawberry plants exhaust themselves in three years. They are at their best the first season. A good plan is to remake a third of the strawberry plantation yearly. Begin now by carefully pegging down one or two of the best runners from each plant. Remove all you do not need, otherwise they exhaust the strength of the parent plant.

When the part of the plantation to be remade has yielded its full crop, trench it, adding manure, decayed leaves, and other material according to the nature of the soil. River sand added to stiff clay soil, and cow manure added to light poor soil will be of assistance. This work can be done while the layers are establishing themselves, and as soon as favourable weather (i.e., showery) comes, the rooted layers can be set out in rows to form the new plantation. The site of early potatoes will be a good place for the new strawberry patch. The plants will be 18 in. apart and the rows 2½ ft. apart. The time of fruiting varies according to variety.

Loganberries appreciate a mulch of manure round the roots. They need plenty of moisture, and repay generous feeding.

All trees require mulching.

All superfluous growths on fruit trees of every kind should be thinned out and stopped.

Over-vigorous shoots on young trees should be cut back.

Heavily laden trees will need support.

Greenfly should be attended to, insecticide being used where necessary.

Cherry trees should have the shoots stopped and nets arranged to save the fruit.

Young side shoots of currant bushes must be pinched back.

Pear, plum and cherry trees will need disbudding.

All surplus and weak raspberry canes should be pulled to ensure a good crop.

VEGETABLES.

Cease cutting asparagus in the middle of this month.

Plant out celery in trenches. Deeply-dug soil, enriched with well-decayed manure, is essential for the successful cultivation of this crop. It is a moisture lover, and needs humus in the soil to retain water.

Radishes and lettuces can be planted between the celery trenches, to mature before the celery is blanched.

Sow first early peas. These mature rapidly and will be ready for table when the peas previously sown are over.

Plant out tomatoes—if possible, against a south wall or fence.

Plant out ridge cucumbers on a sunny slope.

Plant vegetable marrows in the open. They will act as useful smother plants for old hotbeds and untidy corners.

Plant out Brussels sprouts, broccoli, cauliflowers, kale and savoys whenever there is a favourable opportunity. Between rows of early peas, or in their place when the crop has been gathered, the greens will all be at home. If the weather is very dry "puddle" the plants in.

Parsley, spinach and radish can all be sown this month.

Celeriac can be planted out this month. This is an excellent crop on many soils where cultivation of celery is difficult.

Endive makes a good salad crop in the cold months of the year. Sow seeds of the fine curled variety now on a bed of good rich soil, made firm with the back of the spade. Sow ¼ in. deep in drills 4 in. apart. If the weather is dry, water the seed bed before sowing. Plant out as soon as possible on to a soil rich but not too heavy. The plants should then be 1 ft. apart. Delay in planting out will cause a large percentage of the plants to bolt.

A little liquid manure should be given to early cauliflowers, a leaf being broken over each flower to shade it.

Lettuces should be watered copiously in dry weather. They are then not so likely to run to seed.

Mushroom beds may be made in the open and will bear in August.

Onions (autumn sown) should be given a final top dressing of nitrate of soda.

Peas should be picked off regularly. Late varieties will need staking.

Potatoes may still be earthed up.

Runner beans need supports.

Dress Seakale with salt.

Shallots should be dressed with nitrate of soda.

Vegetable marrow plants which were planted out last month should be stopped to encourage sturdy growth.

Sow turnips, in shallow drills 1 ft. apart. Dress the soil first with soot and wood ashes. Cover the seeds lightly by raking. A shaded bed is essential, and in sunny gardens shade should be provided by pushing in a few leafy twigs near the rows of seed. Do everything possible to keep the seedlings cool and moist, and protect them from the turnip-fly by dusting soot and lime along the rows occasionally.

UNDER GLASS.

Plenty of air should be given.

Fumigation and syringeing for insects should be attended to.

The greenhouse must be shaded unless the roof is covered with creepers.

Damp the floor to keep the atmosphere moist.

All faded blooms should be removed.

Artificial heat should no longer be needed, unless the weather turns very damp and cold.

Azaleas and Camellias should have a steady growing heat all the time they are making wood.

Heaths and tender shrubs may be hardened off and stood outdoors.

Dahlias, half-hardy annuals, Geraniums, Pentstemons, Cannas, etc., are leaving the shelter of the greeenhouse and frame this month for the open border. Fill their places with seedlings such as Cinerarias, or Primulas, which are ready for potting.

All seedlings should be pricked out as soon as the second pair of leaves has formed, and thenceforward given as much room as possible.

Pot up Chrysanthemums. 9–10 in. pots will be needed. But it is best to repot frequently, allowing the plant roots to fill the smaller pots before they are put into larger ones.

Calceolarias of the herbaceous type can be sown now under glass. Prick off the seedlings when the second leaf shows. Shade them carefully from the sun and keep an even temperature.

Japanese Primulas can be raised from seed sown now. Sow in the greenhouse in sandy soil, and prick off as soon as possible. Buy a good strain of hybrids, and when the seedlings flower for the first time destroy ruthlessly any that have undesirable colouring. The colours vary from blush-white to crimson and maroon, but occasionally seedlings produce muddy-coloured flowers that are almost worthless.

The Himalayan Cowslip, or Primula sikkimensis can also be sown. This is excellent for moist gardens.

As soon as Grapes have grown to the size of green peas, they should be thinned out. Use a pair of sharp pointed scissors. Feed the roots with weak liquid manure.

Tomatoes remaining under glass must be kept strictly to a single main stem and all side shoots should be pinched out.

To ensure fertilisation of plants under glass, brush a rabbit's tail or piece of down over the flowers, to distribute the pollen. If time cannot be spared for this, tap each plant with a cane now and again, to ensure pollination.

Slugs show a fondness for young Dahlias. Put a few lettuce seedlings between the Dahlia plants. As the slugs like lettuce even better than Dahlia, this will induce them to leave the Dahlias alone.

Where slugs are numerous, spraying the plants and soil with Bordeaux mixture will be efficacious. Thrushes and blackbirds destroy large quantities of slugs during the breeding season and should be encouraged. Poison traps such as scooped-out potatoes smeared with arsenate of lead give good results; but poison should be used with great discretion, especially where animals are kept.

Clean cultivation, keeping the surface soil loose and free from weeds, is the best way to keep down insect pests.

Damping-off disease is encouraged by allowing seedlings to become too crowded or too damp. A gritty soil is a good preventive, and sharp sand should always be added where seedlings are pricked out.

Plants affected by "damping-off" should be pulled and burned, and a dressing of flowers of sulphur should be given to the soil.

Give more air and light to the remaining seedlings, and only water sparingly. Watering the soil beforehand with a solution of 4 oz. of formaldehyde to a gallon of water will effectively prevent damping-off.

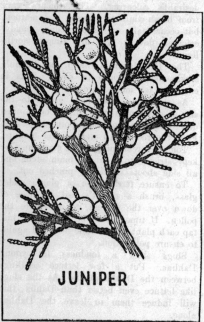

JUNIPER

The Juniper family are evergreen and are rather formal in growth. Some kinds are useful for lawn planting or where formality is required.

Ponds that are not sweet are very objectionable. To keep them clean put in pieces of charcoal, removing them from time to time and putting in more. Also grow water plants. The scum can be destroyed where there are no fish by adding copper sulphate. A pound to 100,000 gallons of water can be used. This will not make the water unfit for drinking.

MANURE MULCHES.

The conservation of water in the soil is a summer problem. The solution is in giving surface mulches, but these should be put on only after showers or watering.

The use of the hoe is also important and will do much to prevent the soil from drying out. The oftener hoeing is done the easier is the operation, and the more beneficial to the plants.

Liquid manure will also be needed in all parts of the garden from now on. To make, suspend a bag full of stable manure and soot in a tub of water. Dilute to a pale straw colour when used.

Nitrate of soda is a quick-acting stimulant, which makes new growth very rapidly on crops of all kinds. Used now on cabbages and other green crops, just as they begin to get away, it makes a remarkable difference, producing succulent growth in a short time.

Used on fruit it has the same tendency. If the tree is not growing as much as is wanted, or if the foliage is sickly, a little nitrate of soda may be given, but if plenty of growth is made and fruit is scarce, no nitrate should be used.

All fertilisers should be used in small, rather than large, quantities, and never given until the plant has reached the stage when it can usefully accept them.

JUNIPER. *See* JUNIPERUS.

JUNIPERUS (jū-nip-er-us. Coniferæ). Beautiful and attractive evergreen shrubs and trees of very diverse habit of growth from quite prostrate or creeping species up to tall-growing trees. Junipers like a well-drained loamy soil, with lime. They flourish in chalky districts. *Propagation* is best by seed, which may lie dormant for a year or more before germinating. Cuttings may be taken at the end of summer and placed in a shady border and covered with a hand-light or bell-glass.

SPECIES.

J. chinensis, "Chinese Juniper," 60 ft. Perfectly hardy, of pyramidal habit, but may become shrubby in very exposed situations.

J. c. aurea, "Young's Golden Juniper." A compact slender-growing form with golden foliage.

J. c. japonica (*plumosa*). Of dwarf bushy habit.

J. c. "Coffin Juniper" of China. This is the sacred Juniper of the Chinese. Its wood is used to make the coffins of the mandarins. The branches are pendent and leaves glaucous. This remarkable species was discovered and introduced by the late Reginald Farrer; and has not yet received any specific name.

J. communis. The "Common Juniper" of very wide distribution in both the new and old worlds. Very hardy and accommodating, thriving almost anywhere, especially so in chalky districts. The berries are used to flavour gin.

J. c. compressa. A minute-growing, cone-shaped form; a perfect little gem for the rock garden. Very slow growing.

J. c. hibernica (stricta). The "Irish Juniper," like a miniature Italian Cypress.

J. c. nana. Foliage glaucous of compact growth, 1 ft.

J. drupacea. The "Syrian Juniper." A distinct species of columnar habit.

J. excelsa. The "Grecian Juniper." Of columnar habit, and scale-like leaves.

J. horizontalis (Sabina procumbens; Sabina prostrata). The "Waukegan Juniper" of N. America. A trailing species with bluish-green foliage, turning to plum colour in autumn.

J. Oxycedrus. The "Sharp Cedar of the Mediterranean region. Rare in cultivation. Similar to *J. rigida,* with longer leaves.

J. recurva. The "Weeping Juniper" from the Himalayas. Slender shoots of sage-green. Flourishes best in warm moist parts of the country.

J. Sabina. The Common Savin. Europe. One of the most useful of junipers, especially good on chalk soils. Very hardy and vigorous.

J. S. tamariscifolia. The "Spanish Savin." A prostrate form suitable for rock garden.

J. S. variegata. Young foliage tipped creamy-white.

J. virginiana. The "Red Cedar" or "Cedar Pencil Juniper" of N. America. Very hardy and accommodating. Specially good in chalky districts. Of erect, pyramidal habit reaching to a height of over 70 ft. in parts of this country.

J. v. Canaertii (Cannartii). Of neat pyramidal form with bronzy-green foliage and glaucous blue grape-like berries.

J. v. glauca. A beautiful form with silvery foliage, changing to green.

J. v. globosa. A dwarf, dense, rounded alpine form, with bright green foliage.

J. v. pendula. Branches horizontal, tips pendulous.

JUSTICIA (jus-tis-i-a. Acanthaceæ). Stove flowering and ornamental foliage plants. E. Indies, 1759.

Culture.—Compost: equal parts loam, peat and sand. Repot spring, good drainage essential. Prune hard after flowering. Pinch shoots back occasionally to obtain bushy growth. Winter temperature, 65°; summer, 75°.

Propagation.—By cuttings of young shoots in pots of light sandy soil in spring; place in propagator, temperature, 70°.

SPECIES.

J. calycotricha, yellow; *J. carnea,* pale rose; *J. formosa,* purple.

K

KADSURA (kad-sū'-ra. Magnoliaceæ). Climbing evergreen shrubs related to the Magnolia, rather tender, generally requiring shelter of a warm wall.

Propagate by cuttings taken in summer in frame.

SPECIES.

K. japonica (*chinensis*), Japan and Korea. Flowers cream coloured, followed

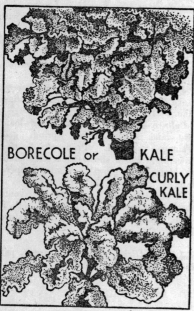

BORECOLE or KALE

CURLY KALE

Kale or borecole is one of the most useful vegetables for winter. It is a good crop to succeed early potatoes.

by bright red berries. The foliage assumes attractive red shades in autumn.

K. j. variegata. Leaves variegated, creamy white.

KÆMPFERIA (kemp-fe-ria. Scitaminaceæ). Stove herbaceous perennials, flowers fragrant, leaves lance-shaped, flaked with white above, purple beneath.

Culture.—Compost: 2 parts fibrous loam, 1 part peat, ½ part sharp sand. Repot early spring. Water freely during growing period; after flowering, gradually

dry off and store under staging. Winter temperature, 50°; summer, 70°–75°.

Propagation.—By division of roots when repotting.

SPECIES.

K. Gilbertii, K. Kirkii, K. rotunda.

KAINIT. This is a soluble salt obtained from the refuse of iron works, containing chlorosulphate of magnesium with potassium. A good sample will contain about 12½ per cent. of potash. It makes a good fertiliser on any soil for fruit and vegetables when applied at the rate of 2½ lb. to a square rod.

KALE. *See* BORECOLE.

KALMIA (kal'-mi-a. Ericaceæ). Evergreen shrubs, from N. America, bearing a profusion of beautiful flowers. The foliage is regarded as being poisonous to animals, and *K. angustifolia* is known in the United States as "lamb-kill."

Culture.—Plant in peaty soil, or loam containing leaf-mould, no lime. *Propagation* is by cuttings in October in a frame, or layer in October. Seeds may be sown in frame in spring.

SPECIES.

K. angustifolia, Sheep Laurel (eastern N. America), 3 ft. Flowers saucer-shaped, deep rosy-red, very freely produced in June.

K. a. rubra. The finest form.

K. glauca (*K. polifolia*), Pale Laurel (eastern N. America), 1–2 ft. Flowers pale rose in late April and May.

K. latifolia, Calico Bush (eastern North America), 4–6 ft. Leaves glossy green, flowers bright pink, in large clusters. One of the most exquisitely beautiful flowering shrubs hardy in this country. Likes the semi-shade of distant trees in southern gardens.

KANSAS FEATHER. *See* LIATRIS.

KAULFUSSIA (kaul-fuss-ia. Compositæ.) S. Africa. (Syn. *Chareis*.) *K. amelloides,* blue, is a pretty little edging plant with blue, daisy-like flowers. Sow in April where to bloom, ordinary garden soil.

KEEL. The name given to the lower pair of petals in flowers belonging to the leguminosæ family; for example, Sweet

Peas. This keel is used as a landing-stage by bees in search of honey and serves its purpose in the pollination of the flower.

KELP. Seaweed. Much prized as a basal manure for early potatoes on the Cornish coast and in the Scilly Isles.

KENNEDYA (ken-ned-i-a. Leguminosæ). Greenhouse evergreen trailing and climbing shrubs and sub-shrubs with pea-like flowers. Cuttings of short side-shoots inserted in sand and kept close for a fortnight, after which they are given more heat, will root or they may be increased by seeds. Use peat and sandy loam. They should be watered freely during the flowering period and when this is over the shoots should be cut back to within 2 in. of the old wood.

KENTIA PALM

The Kentia Palm is one of the best of room plants. Leaf-sponging and careful watering are important.

SPECIES.

K. coccinea. Scarlet. June. 10–15 ft.

K. inophylla. Scarlet. June.

K. nigricans. Dark purple and green. Summer. 10–20 ft.

K. prostrata. Scarlet. Spring. Is useful for baskets. Several species are now classified with Hardenbergias.

KENTIA (ken-ti-a. Palmæ). Umbrella Palm. Greenhouse palms, also suitable for living-rooms. Leaves feather shaped.

Culture.—Compost: equal parts loam, peat and silver sand. Repot early spring, give good drainage. Water moderately and syringe plants at least 2 or 3 times a week. Winter temperature 45°–50°; summer, 65°–70° with shade.

Propagation.—By seed sown at least 1 in. deep in sandy peat. Place in propagator, temperature 70°. Early spring.

KENTISH COBNUT

Where a garden is large enough a Nut-walk is a delightful feature. The Kentish Cobnut can be grown as a small tree in the fruit garden.

SPECIES.

K. australis, K. Belmoreana, K. Canterburyana and *K. Forsteriana.*

KENTISH COBNUT. *See* HAZEL-NUT.

KERRIA (kĕr′-ri-a. Rosaceæ). Deciduous shrub, with arching branches of rich yellow flowers during April and May.

Culture.—Plant from October to March in ordinary garden soil in sunny position. They do well against south or west walls. *Propagate* by cuttings of young shoots in frame in autumn, or by division of roots in autumn. Cut out old wood in June.

SPECIES.

K. japonica (China), 6 ft. The only species.

K. j. flore-pleno, 12 ft. The old-fashioned double-flowered variety. Does well on a north wall.

K. j. variegata (*picta*). Leaves margined white.

KETELEERIA (ket-e-lee′-ri′a. Coniferæ). Evergreen trees up to 100 ft.

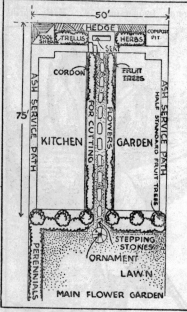

The kitchen or vegetable garden need not be ugly, if it is properly designed and planted.

Natives of China and Formosa. Very near to Abies, distinguished therefrom by the male catkins being produced in umbels.

SPECIES.

K. Davidiana. A remarkable species, like a huge Abies.

KICKXIA (kicks-i-a. Apocynaceæ). Stove trees with smooth leaves. Increased by cuttings inserted in sand over bottom heat, or by seed. Soil, loam, leaf-mould and sand.

SPECIES.

K. africana. Yellow. Valuable rubber tree. *K. elastica.* Yellow.

KIELMEYERA (kel-mi-er-a. Ternstroemiaceæ). Stove trees and shrubs. Showy flowers in racemes. Cuttings in sand in heat.

SPECIES.

K. excelsa. White. July.

KING'S SPEAR. *See* ASPHODELINE.

KITAIBELIA (kit-i-be-li-a. Malvaceæ). Hardy and half-hardy perennials of coarse growth fit only for shrubbery.

Propagate by seeds and plant in loamy soil.

SPECIES.

K. vitifolia. Half-hardy. White. Summer. 2 ft.

KITCHEN GARDEN. ÆSTHETIC TREATMENT. By careful planning this feature need no longer be banished to the far garden boundaries, but can be made to work in with the complete garden scheme, so as to be beautiful as well as useful.

A flowering evergreen hedge surround would add beauty to the main flower garden and provide shelter for the kitchen garden crops. Roses trained on pillars with lavender hedges at their feet would form an effective surround in the smaller garden.

By the introduction of several well-made paths the area could be broken up into small plots, thus facilitating cultivation and the gathering of crops in wet weather. Such a treatment of the layout gives scope for the gardener with imagination to beautify his kitchen garden. Narrow borders either side of the pathways could be planted with flowers suitable for cutting. A feature such as a well would be both beautiful and useful placed in the centre of the main walk, and surrounding borders filled with flowers such as pansies, honesty and marigolds would add an old-world touch without detracting from the efficiency of the garden. Such a feature could easily be linked up with the main garden design. A smaller border near the entrance to the garden could be allocated to sweet-smelling herbs. If the garden is small specialise on the more valuable crops, such as salads, peas, onions, asparagus, etc., and leave cheaper crops, such as potatoes, to be purchased.

KLEINIA (kli-ni-a. Compositæ). Candle Plant. Greenhouse perennial, ornamental foliage. 1759.

Culture.—Compost: equal parts peat,

leaf-mould and sand. Repot early spring, good drainage essential. Position, sunny part of greenhouse. Winter temperature, 45°; summer, 60°.

Propagation.—By cuttings of young shoots in the greenhouse at any time during the summer. Cuttings do best if allowed to dry for a few hours before inserting in sandy soil.

SPECIES.

K. articulata (candle plant), yellow; *K. fulgens*, orange and red; *K. Galpini*, orange; *K. repens*, white.

KNAPWEED. *See* CENTAUREA.

KNEELING MATS. These rubber mats are very useful to the gardener in

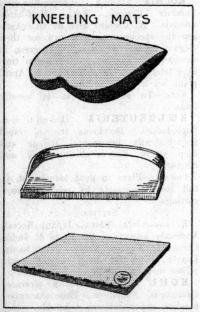

KNEELING MATS

Kipling says " Half that a gardener's work is done upon his knees," but there is no reason why it should not be done comfortably. There are three types of mats now made for the purpose.

that they keep the knees dry and clean. They can be obtained in various qualities and thicknesses, according to price.

KNIPHOFIA (knī-fō-fia. Liliaceæ). Red-hot Poker. Torch Lily. Brilliant hardy herbaceous perennials with long stiff flower stems and graceful curving leaves. They make a grand display of

colour against shrubs, and the smaller forms are excellent for the border.

Culture.—Propagate by seeds sown in sandy soil in the frame, by division of the root-stock or by suckers. The plants like a deep rich light soil in full sunshine and plenty of water in summer. In autumn tie the leaves together above the plant in a column to prevent winter rain lying in the crowns.

KNIPHOFIA ROYAL STANDARD (RED HOT POKERS)

Red-hot Poker or Kniphofia gives brilliant colour to the flower border in late summer. It likes to be undisturbed for several years.

In very cold districts it is advisable to lift and winter the plants in a frame or to cover their roots with leaf-mould or coconut fibre.

SPECIES.

K. aloides, the commonest and best known of the species, bears spikes of flame-coloured flowers from June to October and has given rise to a great number of hybrids, such as Empress with scarlet flowers, *floribunda*, free flowering, *nobilis* with serrate leaves and scarlet flowers in August, and *glaucescens* with long flower spikes.

K. burcelli has a purple-spotted stem

and bright green leaves while the flowers
are bright red, height, 3 ft.

K. caulescens is smaller than *aloides* but
is more robust and has rich crimson spikes
that change gradually to white tinged
with green. Its glaucous blue-grey foliage
is attractive all through the year. It
flowers in September, height, 4–5 ft.

K. comosa, a rare species with yellow

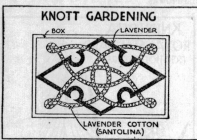

KNOTT GARDENING

BOX   LAVENDER

LAVENDER COTTON
(SANTOLINA)

**A corner of the Knott Garden at Hampton
Court.**

flowers and dense rosettes of narrow
pointed bright green leaves, height,
2 ft.

K. leichtlini bears red and yellow flowers
from August to October, height, 3 ft.

K. macowanii is one of the best of the
species, but is not quite hardy. It has
many spikes of coral or flame-coloured
flowers in August and September and
is only 18 in. in height.

K. modesta, a rare kind with white
flowers, 1 ft.

K. nelsoni, a dwarf species bearing very
many orange flowers during the summer,
2 ft.

K. rooperi has flowers of red and yellow
nearly all the year in mild districts, height,
4 ft.

K. tuckii with large heads of brilliant
red flowers that fade to yellow, and
glaucous foliage, 3–4 ft.

Many hybrids exist but they do not
depart much from the typical forms.

KNOTT GARDENING. A form of
gardening introduced into England in
Tudor times. Elaborate and intricate
designs of interlacing bands and ribbons
are worked out in lavender, rosemary, box
and similar dwarf shrubs or in inanimate
materials, such as tiles or bricks. The
beds between these spaces are filled with

Old English flowers, such as pansies
honesty, sweet williams, etc., and bulbs
About 1520 the craze for effect reache
such a pitch that coloured sands and stone
were used to the exclusion of flowers. Th
best example of knott gardening now
existing is at Hampton Court. This wa
laid out in 1924, but it was designed on th
old records of garden writers in the time
of Elizabeth. Although such a garden
would make an interesting feature of a
garden design, it should be remembered
that much care and skill would be
required to keep it trim and in good
condition.

KNOTWORT. *See* POLYGONUM.

KOCHIA (kok-i-a. Chenopodiaceæ)
Summer Cypress, 3 ft. Half-hardy
annuals. *K. Childsii* and *K. tricophyllo*
are the species usually grown for their
elegant foliage, which is bright green in
summer and has delightful autumn tint-
ings later. Sow in cold frame in April
plant out in June, ordinary soil.

Note.—To sow in heat is usually
fatal.

KŒLREUTERIA (kol-rōi-tē′-ri-a.
Sapindaceæ). Deciduous tree of rapid
growth, with ornamental foliage and
deep yellow flowers during July and
August.

Culture.—Plant in good loamy soil, in
full sun. *Propagate* by seeds or root-
cuttings.

SPECIES.

K. paniculata (China, Japan, Korea).
Variously known as the Pride of India,
China, or Varnish Tree. Quite hardy.
Leaves up to 2 ft. long, turning bright
yellow in autumn.

KOHL RABI (*Brassica olearacea
Caulorapa*). Cruciferæ. This is a rather
peculiar and uncommon vegetable, which
cannot be highly recommended as a food
plant for human beings, though as a
cattle food it is excellent.

In appearance the plant resembles a
turnip with leaves growing from its sides;
in point of fact it is the stem, which becomes abnormally enlarged and spherical
in shape, which is used.

In flavour it is something between the
turnip and the cabbage and may possibly
be a derivative from these two types of
Brassica.

Culture.—Seeds should be sown in April, transplanted when large enough to handle to a rich, well-dug site, spacing them 18 in. apart and 2 ft. asunder. Little attention beyond hoeing is required during the summer.

Varieties.—White; purple; green.

Uses.—The roots should not be allowed to grow larger than a tennis ball if flavour is the main consideration. The roots may be lifted and stored in dry sand for winter use, and this practice is preferable to leaving them in the ground. It is prepared and cooked in the same way as the ordinary turnip.

KOLKWITZIA (kolk-ūt-si-a. Caprifoliaceæ). Deciduous shrub, with Abelia or Weigela-like pink flowers, with yellow throat, during May and June.

Culture.—Plant in ordinary garden soil, with addition of peat or leaf-mould.

K. amabilis (China), the only species. A very charming plant when happy, but it does not thrive everywhere.

KOSTELETZKYA (Malvaceæ). The only commonly grown species of this genus of hardy and greenhouse herbs and shrubs is *virginica*, a hardy perennial with rosy-pink flowers in August on stems 2–5 ft. in height. *Propagate* by seeds or division.

L

LABELS. The amateur gardener does not as rule bother much about labelling his plants, but all trees, shrubs and roses should be labelled to guide the pruner, who might easily cut away all his flowering shoots if he is not sure which shrub variety he is dealing with. Metal tabs stamped with the name are cheapest and

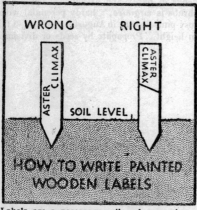

Labels are a necessary evil and convenience. Use a blacklead pencil on white newly-painted labels.

most satisfactory in the long run. They may either be placed in the ground or wired round a branch. In the latter case they should be examined periodically to see that the wire is not strangling the branch. Wooden labels painted white and written with Indian ink or indelible pencil are sold in various sizes. These are cheap but not at all permanent. Avoid using large conspicuous labels for places such as those in the rock garden. There are also many patent types on the market from which the gardener may take his choice. Zinc and celluloid are amongst other materials from which these labels may be made.

LABICHEA (la-bi-ke-a. Leguminosæ). Greenhouse evergreen shrubs all with yellow flowers.

Cultivate in a compost of equal parts peat, loam and sand. Pot in March in well-drained pots and stand in a light, sunny greenhouse. Prune into shape in February. Water moderately in winter but freely afterwards.

Winter temperature, 45°-55°; summer 55°-65°. Give plenty of air in summer

Propagate by half-ripened shoots in summer, inserted in sand, and placed under a bell-glass.

SPECIES.

L. lanceolata. Spring. Height, 4-6 ft.

LABURNUM (là-bur'-num. Leguminosæ). Hardy deciduous trees bearing racemes of yellow flowers in May and June Plant in November in ordinary garden soil Pruning consists of cutting back weak shoots after flowering. Remove old wood in winter. Pick off all seed pods as formed *Propagate* by seed sown in frame in the spring, or by budding and grafting during August and September.

SPECIES.

L. Adamii (France). Up to 25 ft Similar in habit to *L. vulgare*. Racemes yellow, tinted purple, 5-7 in. long. Some growths "sport" back and thus flowers of parent trees (generally *Cytisus purpureus* or *L.vulgare*) can be seen on the same tree

L. vulgare (Common Laburnum Golden Rain). Central and S. Europe 20-30 ft. One of the best laburnums for English gardens, having a wide, spreading, bushy habit. Racemes, 6-10 in. long.

L. v. Alschingeri (East Europe). Geographical form with large glossy leaves.

L. v. Vossii. The finest of all laburnums having abundant racemes of bright yellow flowers 18-21 in. This variety does not retain its seed pod. Award of Garden Merit from R.H.S.

LACE WING FLY. *See* BENEFICIAL INSECTS.

LACHENALIA (lak-e-na-li-a. Liliaceæ). Cape Cowslip. Greenhouse bulbous plants. S. Africa, 1752. These are pretty, free-blooming plants and very suitable for the cool greenhouse.

Culture.—Compost: 3 parts fibrous loam, and equal parts leaf-mould and sharp sand. Pot autumn; place 4 or 5 bulbs in 6 in. pot or several round the edge of a hanging basket. Sunny position on shelf or suspended from roof of house. Water freely during growing period and give weak liquid manure when flower spikes begin to show. After flowering stand outside in sunny frame and gradually cease watering. Repot annually. Winter temperature, 40°–45°.

Propagate by offsets at potting time.

SPECIES.

The best are *L. pendula*, red, green and purple; *L. Nelsoni*, yellow; *L. tricolor*, yellow, green and red; and *L. violacea*, violet and green.

LADYBIRD. *See* BENEFICIAL INSECTS.

LADY'S SLIPPER ORCHID (CYPRIPEDIUM).

LADY'S SMOCK. *See* CARDAMINE.

SPECIES.

The species are numerous and only a few can be mentioned: *L. anceps*, rose, crimson, purple and yellow; and its varieties, *alba*, white; *Amesiana*, white and purple; *Barkeriana*, purple; *Sanderiana*, white and crimson. *L. Perrinii*, red and white, *L. pumila*, rosy purple, and *L. superbiens*, rosy-purple and yellow, are other good species.

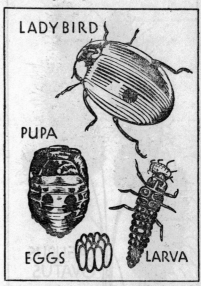

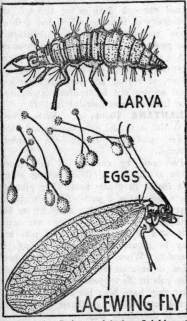

The Lacewing fly is one of the beneficial insects. It feeds on greenfly.

The Ladybird goes through a cycle of changes and is the gardener's best friend. She and her progeny feed on green flies.

LÆLIA (le-li-a. Orchidaceæ). Stove Orchids. Mexico, 1833. Named after Lælia, a vestal virgin, alluding to the delicacy of the flowers. A genus closely allied to Cattleya, with a wonderful richness of colouring. Mated with the more perfectly shaped Cattleya, they helped to produce the Lælio-Cattleya hybrids.

Culture.—For compost, general culture, etc., *see* CATTLEYA.

LÆLIO-CATTLEYA (le-li-o-kat-le-a. Orchidaceæ). A race of orchids obtained by the intercrossing of the genus Cattleya with those of the genus Lælia. It is one of the most popular sections of home-raised orchids. By these handsome, floriferous and beautifully-coloured gems, the house may be kept bright the whole year round. The varieties are so numerous that only one or two of the best can be mentioned here, and an up-to-date trade list should be consulted.

Audrena nobilior. Sepals and petals rose magenta, lip bright crimson with yellow eyes at base and gold lines in throat.

Cynthia grandis. A magnificent variety; sepals and petals white, lips deep rose-purple with gold veining.

General Maude splendens. Sepals and petals rich mauve-purple, lips royal purple, with ruby-crimson shading and gold veining in throat.

Mrs. Kitty Wallace. Sepals and petals rose-purple, lip deep maroon with yellow lines in throat.

LAGENARIA (laj-en-aria. Cucurbitaceæ). Bottle Gourd. Climbing *L. vulgaris*

LAGURUS OVATUS

Hare's-tail grass or Lagurus is an annual grass suitable for arranging with sweet peas and other flowers, or it can be dried and used for winter decoration.

has curious bottle-shaped fruits. For culture *see* CUCURBITA.

LAGURUS (lay-gu-rus. Gramineæ). Hare's-tail Grass. 1 ft. Channel Islands. Sow outdoors in spring. Ordinary soil.

LAMARCKIA (lam-ark-ia. Gramineæ). Golden Grass, 1 ft. N. Africa. Treat as for Lagurus. Hardy annual.

LAMIUM (la-mīum. Labiatæ). Dead Nettle. A large genus of annual and perennial herbs, of which only a few are of any value in the garden as the rest are weeds. The troublesome Red Dead Nettle belongs to this family.

Culture.—Ordinary soil will suit these plants, which are raised from cuttings.

SPECIES.

L. maculatum and its golden-leaved variety are the most frequently grown for spring bedding. They are both compact dwarf plants with purple flowers. *L. Galeobdolon* is a rarer species with whorls of yellow flowers from May to July. 18 in.

LANDSCAPE ARCHITECTURE Landscape architecture is the art of designing open-air spaces, for any purpose compatible with æsthetic treatment.

An extensive knowledge and training is required before one can qualify to become a fellow of the Institute of Landscape Architects. This can be obtained through Articles or through the University of Reading, which has a three years' course in Landscape Architecture. The profession is open to men and women.

A knowledge of architecture, geometrical drawing, freehand drawing and colour, surveying and levelling, horticultural science and horticulture is required. The Institute was founded in 1929.

LANTANA (lan-ta-na. Verbenaceæ). Beautiful stove and greenhouse shrubs that flower profusely during the summer months.

Propagate by cuttings of side shoots taken at the end of the flowering season and rooted in gentle heat. For planting use a compost of 2 parts of loam and 1 of peat or old manure from a mushroom bed with some sand. These plants are easily cultivated in the greenhouse in pots and may be planted out in beds during the summer. When the cuttings have been taken in autumn they should be struck in 3 in. pots in the following spring and later, after they have been pinched back, transferred into 6 in. pots. Their chief enemy pest is the Mealy Bug.

SPECIES.

L. camara. Stove. Violet flowers in June. Prickly stem. 6–10 ft.

L. nivea. Snowy white flowers all through the summer. Fragrant. Its variety *mutabilis* is yellow-flowered.

L. trifolia. Red or purplish-red flowers in August. 4 ft.

LAPAGERIA (lap-a-jĕr'-i-a. Liliaceæ). Chilean Bell-flower. A magnificent climbing or twining shrub, with dark green leathery leaves and very showy, rich, rosy-crimson flowers, pendulous, bell-shaped, and very waxy in substance. Quite one of the most glorious of all climbing plants. Discovered early in the 19th century in Chile. Named after the first wife of Napoleon—Josephine de Lapageria. The plant is not hardy in the general sense, but succeeds out of doors in many parts, and has been growing for a number of years against a north wall in a garden not far from Oxford, one of the coldest towns in the country.

Culture.—The soil need not be deep, 18 in. being ample, but moist, well drained and very porous. A mixture of coarse granite or grit (not limestone), sand and peat; and kept open by stone chippings, broken sandstone, and especially clinkers. The roots of Lapageria have a peculiar fondness for clinkers. The shoots should be carefully trained to strings in preference to wire; on no account use galvanised wire as the shoots have a great aversion to its nearness. The flowers appear about July or August and continue for many weeks. They may be obtained in clusters or in long trails. If garlands are desired, the shoots should be left to lengthen; but if the strong shoots are pinched when they begin to show broad leaves, clusters of many flowers will result; sometimes as many as a dozen may be seen hanging together. Pruning consists in removing the shoots that have flowered unless needed to extend the plant. Weak growths may also be cut away. *Propagate* by layering. They may take a year or more before rooting and being ready to lead a separate existence. Strong growths cut from the plants and placed in a warm close frame or propagating case will also root. Seed germinates freely in a warm house. Slugs are keen on the young shoots which spring from the base.

L. rosea. The only species. There are several garden varieties, some larger and finer than others.

L. r. alba. Pure white flowers.

LAPEYROUSIA (la-pe-ru-si-a. Irideæ). Half-hardy bulbs of little importance horticulturally.

Propagate by offsets.

SPECIES.

L. corymbosa. Blue and white flowers in May. 9–12 in.

L. grandiflora. Red flowers with a yellow eye.

L. fissifolia. Rose and pink flowers in August. 6–9 in.

LARCH. *See* LARIX.

LARCH APHIS (*Chermes laricis*). There is some divergence of opinion on the life-history of the Larch Aphis, but the common theory is that it hibernates in the

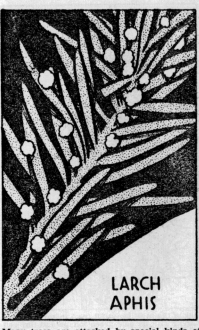

LARCH
APHIS

Many trees are attacked by special kinds of Aphis and one has chosen the Larch. Spraying with insecticide is the best remedy. It is similar to woolly aphis in appearance.

female state on the trunk of the trees under a covering of a white cottony wool. In the spring these females move, and having taken up suitable positions they lay their eggs, which are glued together. On hatching out the young *Chermes* quickly grow, giving rise to further generations. As each individual covers itself with wool, the tree soon becomes unsightly, and, with the constant sucking of the sap, the needles are weakened, turn yellow and fall off; young trees may be killed outright.

METHODS OF CONTROL.—Treatment should be undertaken in the winter, when much good may be done by spraying with a paraffin emulsion. This wash should be applied with force in order to penetrate the wool and so reach the insect.

LARCH POLES. The tall, straight trunks of the common larch tree are largely used in garden work as supports for climbing plants. The wood being very durable, these trees are admirably suited

One of the most beautiful trees in spring is the Larch, with its pale green foliage and tiny red stars. A useful tree for shelter belts on sandy soils.

to such a purpose. The poles are lopped of all side branches unless a few at the top are retained to form a thicker screen. The bark is then stripped from them (as it harbours insect pests) and the wood is treated with a preservative such as creosote. Every description of rustic fencing and screening can be made from larch wood.

LARDIZABALA (lar-diz-a-ba-la. Berberideæ). The only species, *L. biternata*, is an almost hardy climbing shrub with dark purple flowers in October.

Propagate by cuttings of half-ripe shoots inserted in sand under a bell-glass. Plant in equal parts of peat and loam.

LARIX (lăr-ix. Coniferæ). Larch. Deciduous trees of distinct and ornamental appearance, and producing timber of very high quality. The larches are exceedingly attractive in spring with the young shoots of a soft, pale green, and the fascinating red-coloured flowers which develop into attractive glaucous red-coloured cones in early summer. The larches like a well drained good loamy soil, and plenty of moisture. They are best increased from seeds, sown out of doors. The rare and choice kinds are grafted in spring on seedlings of the common larch.

SPECIES.

L. europæa (*decidua*). The "Common" or "European Larch," up to 140 ft. Native of South and Central Europe. A tree of very great economic importance owing to its very valuable timber. Few, if any, trees excel the Common Larch in its quiet beauty and soft tenderness of young green foliage in the spring. The exquisite flowers are worthy of close study.

L. Kæmpferi. See PSEUDOLARIX.

L. leptolepis (*Kæmpferi*). The "Japanese Larch," 80–100 ft. Very distinct and useful as an isolated specimen in the garden or park. Immune to "Larch canker," and exceptionally valuable on that account. The timber is of a coarser grain than that of the European Larch.

LARKSPUR. The annual Delphiniums are usually known as Larkspurs in trade lists. *D. ajacis*, blue hardy annual, 2½ ft., is the common Larkspur, a native of Britain, and has given rise to many of the modern cultivated forms with single or double flowers in a variety of shades of blue and rose, and dwarf or "nanum" types of similar colours, 1½ ft.

D. consolida, or tall-branching Larkspurs, 2–2½ ft., are particularly good garden plants, being very free flowering and easy to grow. There are some beautiful shades of rosy-scarlet, salmon-pink, rose and pink now obtainable as "named" kinds, such as *coccineum*, Exquisite Rose, Exquisite Pink, La France, etc., all of which are well worth growing. This section makes fine pot plants from seeds sown in autumn, and the plants wintered in cold frames.

D. grandiflorum, 1½-2 ft. Native of Siberia. White, pale blue and dark blue, are the Butterfly Delphiniums, fine subjects for bedding or pots, and flower over a long period.

Culture for all the species mentioned here is very simple. They like a fairly rich well-drained soil. Seed should be sown thinly in spring, and the seedlings thinned out to 9 in. to 1 ft. apart. *See also* DELPHINIUM.

The taller-growing annual larkspurs (varieties of *Delphinium consolida*) are those which are popular as pot plants for conservatory or greenhouse decoration. The tall branching sections and stock-flowered grow 3 ft. or more, but there are also modern selections of intermediate growth, such as the Emperor class and the Hyacinth-flowered; the latter is earlier flowering than the others. The flowers are shades of white, blue, mauve, pink or carmine and resemble a Delphinium.

Cultivation.—Seeds should be sown in boxes in a cold frame during the latter part of August or in early September, in boxes of well-drained soil. The seedlings may be pricked out when large enough to handle, and subsequently potted up singly into large 3 in. pots containing a compost of good loam, leaf-mould and sand. They may be set out in a cold frame, and about the middle of January or in early February they will be ready for potting into 6 in. pots. For these pots use a compost of fibrous loam, leaf-mould and some old manure, which crumbles freely. Open the mixture with a little sharp sand and crushed mortar rubble. When well rooted they may be brought into the greenhouse and they make attractive specimens in April or May. The greatest difficulty with larkspurs in pots is the watering, especially when they are coming into flower. They may be regarded as difficult in this respect and they often have a habit of developing "black leg" just as they promise well. Watering should only be done when the plants actually require it, ascertaining the moisture in the pots by tapping them and not by the appearance of the surface soil.

VARIETIES.

Stock-flowered branching – Ageratum Blue, La France (salmon), Blue, Rosy Scarlet, Exquisite Pink, White Spire,

Miss California (salmon-rose), and Flesh Colour.

Emperor (Double Intermediate, 18 in.) —Azure Blue, Violet Queen, Brilliant Carmine, Dark Blue, Pink Delight, White.

Hyacinth-flowered—Brick Red, Dark Blue, Lilac, Deep Blue, and White.

LARVA. The primary condition of an insect on issuing from its egg. Usually applied to grubs, caterpillars and maggots, but sometimes used in reference to the undeveloped phase of invertebrates that undergo changes in their form.

LASTHENIA (las-thee-nea. Compositæ), 1 ft. *L. glabrata.* Pretty annual with daisy-like flower, bright yellow in colour. Prefers a light sandy soil in a sunny place. Native of California. Sow outdoors end of April.

LATANIA (la-ta-ni-a. Palmæ). Bourbon Palm. Handsome palms that are much used for decoration when small.

Propagate by imported seeds sown in strong bottom heat. They should be planted in good rich loam, with some bonemeal. When mature they need a good deal of room. Summer temperature, 60°–90°; winter, 55°–60°.

SPECIES.

L. borbonica, 20 ft. Sometimes known as *Livistona chinensis.*

L. rubra (syn. *Commersoni*). 7 ft.

LATEX. A milky fluid secreted in the stems of some plants which prevents damage by insects, as when the stem is injured the fluid clots and the insects cannot pass over it.

LATHRÆA (lath-re-a. Orobanchaceæ). Parasitic plants which require to be grown near the trees upon which they feed. The showy flowers are all that appear upon the surface, the leaves and stems are underground. Sow the seed in a boggy place beneath the host plant. The plants take two to three years to mature and flower in June.

SPECIES.

L. clandestina with purple flowers, 6 in.

LATHS. Narrow strips of wood used in trellis work. They vary in size and thickness according to the strength required.

LATHYRUS (lath-i-rus. Leguminosæ). Everlasting Pea. Sweet Pea. Hardy

annuals and perennials. Mostly climbers.
Seeds of any of the annuals may be sown
in ordinary rich soil, well manured.
Under glass sow the seeds in light soil in a
temperature of 55°–65° in March. Seedlings can be transplanted to the open in
May. Water freely in dry weather. Feed
with liquid manure, and remove seed pods
as they form to increase the quantity of
flowers.

EVERLASTING
PEA

**The Everlasting Pea with its carmine flowers
or the variety White Pearl are easily raised
from seeds. They are best grown against
fences or pillars.**

Perennial species may be sown in light
soil in March or April in a temperature of
55°–65°, or the roots may be divided
in spring. During summer give light
applications of liquid manure, and water
freely in dry weather. Cut back the
stems nearly to the ground in October,
and top dress with decayed manure in
March.

ANNUAL SPECIES.

L. odoratus (Sweet Pea). Various
colours. Height, 6–10 ft.

L. tingitanus (Tangier Pea). Purple and
red in the summer. Height, 4–6 ft.

PERENNIAL SPECIES.

L. grandiflorus. Rosy crimson flowers in
the summer. Height, 5 ft.

L. latifolius or *Sylvestris platyphyllus*
(Everlasting Pea), with red, crimson, and
violet flowers. Height, 8–10 ft.

L. latifolius albus, with white flowers.

L. magellanicus (Lord Anson's Pea).
Purple flowers from June to September.
Height, 6–8 ft.

L. rotundifolius. Rosy-pink flowers in
summer. Height, 6 ft.

L. undulatus (syn. *Sibthorpii*). Rosy
purple flowers in May and June. Height
2–3 ft.

L. splendens. Carmine-red flowers in
summer.

See also SWEET PEA.

LAUREL. *See* PRUNUS LAUROCERASUS.

LAURELIA (lau-re-lia. Monimiaceæ).
Chile. Evergreen tree with dark handsome
leaves having a spicy fragrance when
crushed. Flowers of no importance. The
outstanding feature of the plant is the
seeds with a tuft of long brown hairs which
enables them to be dispelled by the wind
for quite long distances. Only suitable
for the mildest districts. At Falmouth it
has attained to over 50 ft.

SPECIES.

L. aromatica.

LAUREL, PORTUGAL. *See* PRUNUS
LUSITANICA.

LAURUS, BAY (Lauraceæ). Hardy
and tender trees of which Laurus nobilis,
the Sweet Bay, is the best known. Plant
in autumn or spring in a sheltered
position. Young plants are more susceptible to frost than established specimens. Increase by cuttings, layers, or
seeds.

LAURUSTINUS. *See* VIBURNUM
TINUS.

LAVANDULA (la-van-du-la. Labiatæ).
Lavender. Evergreen shrub, long prized
for its delightful old-world fragrance.
Makes a charming dwarf hedge. Flowers
during July and August. Likes a sunny
position. *Propagate* by cuttings and
division. Quite large branches removed
from parent plant will root readily.

SPECIES.

L. dentata. Dark purple, 1–2 ft.

L. spica. Old English Lavender, 3–4 ft.

L. s. alba. White.

L. s. Folgate Variety, dwarf, similar to
Munstead variety, but paler in colour.

L. s. gigantia (Grappenhall variety),
3 ft. Robust growing, late flowering.

L. s. nana (compact). Dwarf French,
9 in.

L. s. nana. Munstead Dwarf, 1 ft., dark owers, early.

L. s. Stæchas. Distinct variety, dark urple.

L. s. vera. Dutch Lavender. Foliage ore silvery than others.

LAVATERA (lav-a-te-ra. Malvaceæ). Iallow. Asia Minor, 3 ft. *L. trimestris,* hardy annual, is the type and has ose-purple flowers, while its varieties, *. trimestris alba, L. t. rosea-splendens* nd *L. t. Sunset* are white, rose, and deep ose respectively. They are of the easiest ultivation and will succeed almost any- where in ordinary soil.

Tree Mallow. South Europe. 6–8 ft.)eciduous shrubs having mallow-like owers, produced in great abundance uring summer and autumn.

Propagate by seeds and cuttings.

SPECIES.

L. arborea. S. Europe and Great 3ritain. Flowers pink, veined purple.

L. cachemiriana (Himalayas). Pink.

L. olbia rosea (S. Europe). Beautiful clear rosy-pink.

LAVENDER. *See* LAVANDULA.

LAVENDER COTTON. *See* SANTO- LINA.

LAWNS. Britain is famed the world over for its green lawns. And scarcely a garden in the British Isles is without a lawn of some size. The average lawn is not merely a collection of similar plants: there may be half a dozen types of grass in each, and obviously some grasses are more suitable for certain districts and soils than others. In the main, however, the lawn of the small garden is made on the same principle, wherever it may be.

Let us take the operations of lawn making in order.

Levelling.—It is not necessary to have all the instruments which would be used by landscape contractors when making a small lawn in an amateur's garden. The levelling can be done quite simply; but in the first case it must be decided weather the lawn is to be made in the horizontal level or whether it is sufficient to level it in the general plane, that is to say, to leave the lawn sloping according to the natural slope of the land.

In some cases it may be desirable to make the lawn in two or three sections,

with a retaining wall between each so that terraces are formed. Where a horizontal lawn is required it is necessary to obtain a wooden straight-edge—i.e., a piece of wood about 8 or 10 ft. long and 1–2 in. wide and 6 in. deep.

A good spirit-level and a quantity of pegs of even length are also needed. If the site slopes considerably, excavations will, of course, have to be made in order to

LAVATERA

Although not suitable for cutting, the Mallow or Lavatera in its various forms is one of the showiest of annuals. It is one of the best pink flowers.

obtain a horizontal surface, and before any final preparation of the soil is commenced some attention must be given to the drain- age. It will always be found that the wettest part of a lawn made on a sloping site is at the end where the greatest amount of excavation has had to be done.

Where the site only slopes slightly, the method of levelling is as follows:

First make a mark on each of the pegs about 6 in. from the top. Drive one into the soil at the highest end of the plot, so that this mark is on the ground level. Other pegs can be driven in at distances of 6 or 8 ft. apart and by resting the board across them, with the spirit-level on the board, it will be easy to discover how great the fall of the lawn is, and to level it as desired.

If it is immaterial whether the lawn is dead level horizontally, the straight-edge alone can be used, and moved from place to place in order to test the general level of the surface.

Drainage.—Amateur gardeners who make lawns often forget that grasses are

either be led to a main drain or to som portion of the garden where the water ca find a natural outlet. Another point t remember is that the soil immediatel over the drain should be light and porous not sticky impervious clay.

Sowing.—The surface soil of the lawr area must be well prepared before any attempt is made to sow seeds.

The best lawns are those made from

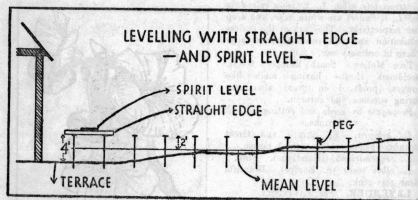

LEVELLING WITH STRAIGHT EDGE — AND SPIRIT LEVEL —

SPIRIT LEVEL
STRAIGHT EDGE
PEG
4′
2′
TERRACE
MEAN LEVEL

The simplest method of making a level surface is to use a wooden straight-edge with pegs and a spirit-level.

plants, and to remain healthy they need a soil which is not only rich in plant food but which is also well drained so that air can penetrate to the roots.

If stagnant water remains in the soil during wet weather, that is to say if the soil seems muddy and sticky for some time after rain has stopped, some extra drainage should be provided before the lawn is made. A simple way of draining a small lawn is to cut a trench across the soil about 15 in. deep and wide, fill the bottom of this trench with old bricks, coke breeze, or other rough material, and then replace the soil. A simple trench of this sort will drain the soil for about 15 ft. each side of the trench.

Where this form of drainage is not sufficient it may be advisable to put in a few agricultural drain-pipes on the herring-bone principle. If the ground slopes, the centre pipe will be allowed to slope in the same direction as the surface. If it does not slope at all, the centre pipe should be put down the centre of the lawn, sloping a little to one end. All drains should

seed; but they are only satisfactory if the soil is fertile, in good mechanical condition and free from weeds and pests. If there is no hurry for immediate results, it is a good practice to grow potatoes one season on the soil, and to make the lawn in September, as the cultivation of the potato crop breaks up the ground and cleans it of weeds. Alternatively, the ground can be dug in autumn, left rough and bare all winter, and sown in March or April.

The average amateur is not concerned with the types of grasses used for lawns, as the mixture supplied by the nursery-man can now be relied on to give satisfaction. It is always worth while to tell the nurseryman exactly what the seed is to be used for, as special mixtures are sold for town gardens, bowling greens and sports greens, etc. The best results are obtained from autumn-sown seeds, the middle of August to the end of September being a good time for sowing.

Soil preparation consists of breaking the surface soil to a fine tilth. The underneath soil should also be well broken, so that the drainage is good. If the natural soil is of sticky clay, it is advisable to add road grit, sharp sand and old decayed leaves which have been passed through a sieve. If the natural soil is poor and sandy, decayed manure will assist in obtaining moisture and plant food. Be careful to preserve the proper relation of soil to subsoil, especially if excavations are made. The darker, more fertile, soil should always be kept on the surface.

Choose a dry day for sowing seeds and sow from 1–3 oz. of seed per square yard. One oz. will do for making a lawn in rural districts, where there is no hurry; but 2 or 3 oz. will make a good lawn more quickly, and the larger quantity of seed should always be used wherever circumstances are not congenial, such as in town gardens. An easy method of sowing seeds is to mark off strips about a yard wide and to measure out the seed in small quantities, according to the amount to be sown. Sow very thinly, going over the ground two or three times in order to ensure even sowing. To prevent raids by birds, mix the seed before sowing with a little Sanitas or carbolic powder. This will give it a distasteful odour and birds will leave it alone.

Having scattered the seeds over the surface, take a fine-toothed rake and lightly scratch the surface not more than ¼ in. deep, and then scatter a little fine soil over the whole. The top-soil should only be just sufficient to hide the seeds. Pass a light roller over this to make the surface firm. Obviously this cannot be done unless the weather is fairly dry. In fact the whole operation of seed sowing must be done on a dry day.

All seeds need moisture before they can germinate, and if the weather should remain dry it is worth while to water the newly-sown lawn if this is possible. The new grass may appear in ten days, or may take three weeks. As soon as it begins to grow and is about one inch high, a light roller should be passed over the surface again on a dry day. The effect of rolling this very young grass is to make it thicken or "tiller" as the farmers would call it.

No cutting need be done until the grass is about 2 in. high; then it is *not* necessary to use a scythe. If your lawn mower is

very sharp it can be adjusted so that the blades are 1½ in. from the ground and used on the new lawn. It will "top" the newly-sown grass, and a week later the grass can be cut and rolled again, and afterwards cut once a week, or more often if required.

The secret of success in cutting the newly-sown lawn is to use a sharp machine and to keep an eye on it to make sure

To sow grass seed evenly, sow both ways.

that the young grasses are not being pulled out by the roots.

One of the most important things about a lawn from seed is to keep a sharp watch for weeds. If there are weed seeds or roots in the soil, they will germinate and grow even more quickly than the grass, and unless they are removed at once they will quickly spread and ruin the new lawn.

Lawn from Turf.—The advantage of using turf for lawn-making is that an established lawn suitable for rough use, sports, etc., can be made more quickly than when seed is sown. Disadvantages are that the turf is generally costly and very seldom obtainable free from weeds.

The finest sea-washed Cumberland turf makes excellent lawns, weed free, and of very fine texture, but it is very much more costly than a lawn made from seed. However, where turf is obtainable fairly weed-free and a lawn is desired quickly, the amateur gardener may prefer to use this method of lawn-making.

The levelling of the soil must be done in the same manner as for the lawn from seed, but there need be no particular attention paid to the fertility of the soil at the time of making the lawn.

For the best lawns turf is cut a foot square and 2 in. thick and trimmed in a gauge box to a thickness of 1½ in. Such pieces of turf can be laid with dead accuracy by expert workmen. In laying, the surface is lightly disturbed. The turf is then placed in position, packed level with

Rake the soil level, lay the turf and press it down well with a wooden beater.

fine sifted soil where necessary, and then gently beaten down with a turf mallet. It is not desirable to beat the turf too heavily, particularly if the soil is of a sticky nature. If the turf seems a little poor after laying, dress it with a finely-sifted soil, mixed with a little grass seed at the rate of about 4 lb. of seed to a barrow-load of soil. Brush this well into the turf, filling up the cracks. Turf so treated will very quickly become thick and velvety. If quantities of sand or sifted ashes are obtainable, good results can be obtained on heavy land by spreading this 1 in. thick on the soil surface before the turf is laid.

Kinds of Turf.

(*a*) **Cumberland Turf.**—The best kind of turf obtainable. Very fine and thick.

(*b*) **Moorland Turf.**—Sometimes nearly as good as Cumberland turf, but the moorland or heath turf varies considerably and should be inspected before purchase.

(*c*) **Meadow Turf.**—Generally inferior because it is full of weeds, coarse grasses and dormant weed seeds. It is fairly cheap, particularly if local supplies are obtainable, and with care and attention will eventually become a good lawn.

Fertilisers.—To keep grass in healthy condition it needs the ordinary plant foods in correct proportion, i.e., nitrogen, phosphates and lime. The lime itself is not a food, but it assists the decomposition of the vegetable matter in the soil and is therefore an essential for most plants.

Peruvian guano is specially good for lawns. Sulphate of ammonia and superphosphate of lime in the proportions of one to three make a good spring fertiliser, and the easiest method of applying them is to mix them with a quantity of finely-sifted soil and scatter them over as a top-dressing in March. 2 oz. of this fertiliser is sufficient for each square yard. In the autumn, 1 oz. per square yard of basic slag or bonemeal can also be given to the lawn. Basic slag encourages clover, and where this is disliked slag should not be used. Sulphate of ammonia in small, frequent doses during the growing season will discourage clover.

Special lawn fertilisers are of course sold, and these are excellent for the small garden owner.

Weeds on Lawns.—Lawn sand can be purchased from any nurseryman and by its use weeds destroyed. It can, if preferred, be mixed at home. Sulphate of ammonia 2 lb., sulphate of iron 1 lb., and 7 lb. of sand or fine soil, mixed well together and scattered over the lawn on a dry evening will kill the weeds. Its immediate effect will be to turn the lawn black, but in a very short time the grass will grow again, more rapidly than the weeds. It may, however, be necessary to remove some of the larger weeds by hand, and the grasses should be stimulated by the application of fertilisers and by constant cutting and rolling.

Spot Treatment.—It is sometimes desirable to treat weeds on lawns by tackling them individually. If about a saltspoonful of lawn sand is dropped on to each of the weeds over the lawn on a dry day, they will disappear, and the remainder of the grass will not be temporarily disfigured. Some weeds, such as Plantains, Dandelions, etc., are particularly difficult to eradicate, and liquid weed-killers,

Dog's-tail, etc., cannot be applied to lawns.

It has been found in recent experiments that a few applications of a mixture of

3 parts sulphate of ammonia,
1 part calcined sulphate of iron, and
20 parts sand

used at 4 oz. per square yard, result in the disappearance of the following weeds: Wild White Clover, Red Clover, Bird's-foot Trefoil, Yellow Suckling Clover, Field

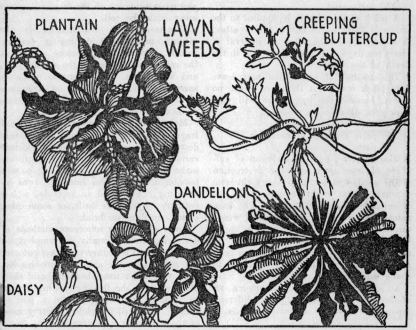

PLANTAIN LAWN WEEDS CREEPING BUTTERCUP DANDELION DAISY

Weeds on lawns are kept in check by hand weeding if only a few are present. Use lawn sand for daisies and flat-leaved weeds. Constant cutting and the use of a suitable fertiliser also keep down weeds.

together with a patent ejector, are sold for their destruction.

The Board of Greenkeeping Research (St. Ives Research Station, Bingley, Yorks) gives the following advice with regard to weeds on lawns:

"The improvement of lawns lies in the eradication of all weeds and the retention of the finer grasses, such as certain species of Agrostis and Festuca, which some agricultural workers might rank with the weeds. It follows that any treatment for weed-eradication which simultaneously encourages such grasses as Rye-grass and

Speedwell, Creeping Buttercup, Yarrow, Daisy, Mouse-ear Chickweed, several species of Moss, Pearlwort, Ribwort, Plantain, Selfheal.

Of these, Pearlwort, Creeping Buttercup, Mouse-ear Chickweed and Yarrow are the most resistant, but can eventually be eradicated.

The success of this treatment depends essentially on fine weather. If rain follows an application, half the potency of the chemicals is lost. The number of applications will depend on the state of weediness of the lawn, but the treatment should be continued at roughly fortnightly intervals. When the weeds have disappeared, the sand in the mixture should be replaced by compost.

Tap-rooted weeds, such as Broad-leaved Plantain, Dandelion and Cat's Ear, are best eradicated by means of a mixture compounded as follows:

35 parts sulphate of ammonia,
15 parts calcined sulphate of iron,
50 parts sand.

A pinch of this should be applied to the crown of these weeds during fine weather. A second application after an interval of about ten days, will generally result in the death of the weeds.

This method of eradication may leave ugly black scars, but this need cause no alarm, because the bare areas will ultimately be filled in by grasses.

A mixture of:

50 parts sulphate of ammonia,
50 parts sand,

is also effective, but the inclusion of sulphate of iron accelerates the destruction of the weeds and counteracts any chlorotic appearance that might accompany the use of sulphate of ammonia alone. The bare patches left after the destruction of weeds can also be renovated with a seeds mixture, but great care should be taken not to attempt this until the chemicals have been washed away, as they are injurious to young seedlings.

A substance known in commerce as Methoxone is a weed killer of different type. Its action is selective, that is it destroys only certain weeds.

Dressings of coke breeze or charcoal reduce worm infestation.

Lawn Pests.

Worms.—The common earthworm, though it does not destroy the grass, is regarded as a pest because it covers the surface with worm casts which, even when they are rolled down, do considerable damage by smothering the finer grasses. Watering the surface of the turf with lime and water will bring the pests up in large quantities, when they can be swept off and moved to some other part of the garden, where they will do no harm.

The end of August to the beginning of December, and the end of March to the end of May, are the breeding seasons of earthworms and it is at these times that they are most easily brought to the surface.

Leather-jackets.—These destructive pests are particularly prevalent in Cumberland turf and if steps are not taken to prevent damage they may easily destroy hundreds of pounds' worth of turf in two or three days.

The leather-jacket grub eats the grass at the roots, the grass suddenly turns brown and when rubbed with the fingers it comes away with the soil.

Treatment with naphthalene is the modern method of destroying leatherjackets. Prepared naphthalene applied at the rate of about 2 oz. to the square yard and watered in, is sufficient to penetrate several inches, and will bring thousands of dead and dying grubs to the surface while others will die in the soil.

Moles.—Moles can be trapped by special traps, but they are more effectively destroyed by gassing. Pieces of calcium carbide dropped into the runs will quickly make an end of these pests. It is also possible to drive them from the runs by inserting rags soaked in creosote, a few ordinary naphthalene balls, or some other strong smelling material.

Ants.—There are numerous methods of destroying ants. Usually the simplest for the small lawn is to invert a flower-pot over the spot where the ants are troublesome. In a very short time the ants build their nests up into the flower-pot when it can be removed and dropped into a pail of water. This will completely destroy most of the ants with little trouble.

Fungoid diseases.—Healthy turf, well fed with complete fertiliser and kept in good condition by constant attention, is seldom troubled with fungoid diseases. If it is, a light dose of carbonate of lime or spraying with a weak solution of potash will easily effect a cure.

Care of the Lawn.

The best lawns are never allowed to grow more than 1 in. long. This means constant cutting almost daily in the growing season. The reason for keeping grass short like this is that the longer it is allowed to grow, the more possibilities there are of the coarser grass overwhelming the finer grasses. Also long grass grows erect instead of prostrate and is therefore less like a thick matted carpet. On a lawn which is not used for games and not too near the house for the clippings to become a nuisance, there is no need to use a box when cutting. In fact, the lawn which is cut frequently without a box will need far less artificial fertiliser to keep it in condition, since the clippings are taken down by worms into the soil, and act as plant food.

Rolling is also an important part of lawn care, but rolling should never be done when the ground is either too wet or too dry, or when frosts are about. Whenever the soil is just slightly moist, and frost is absent, the roller should be used, even in winter. (*See also* ROLLERS, MOWERS, etc.)

Lawn Renovation. — Even the most cared for lawn at times gets worn and patchy from use or other causes. One of the most common defects is raggedness at the edges. This is often a special trouble where wide grass walks are cultivated. The best way to repair the broken edge is to cut out a piece of turf about 15 in. square, and turn it round so that the straight edge from the middle lies along the outer side. The broken part can then be repaired by filling up the cracks with a mixture of soil and grass seed, beating this level, and watering it well.

Bare patches on lawns are easily repaired by lightly stirring the surface of the bare soil with a fork. Then sow fresh grass seed and just cover it with fine soil. Roll or beat this level, and water if the weather is dry.

Care must be taken in the case of fine lawns to sow grass seed of the same variety as that already existing in the lawn, otherwise the new grass will look patchy.

In the case of a lawn used for cricket, tennis, or other games, that probably becomes bare in certain places, groundsmen often keep a spare plot of turf similar to that of the main lawn. This they can use from time to time to repair patches on the sports ground, and as the new turf is exactly similar to the old, repairs carried out in this manner are almost invisible.

A Thin Lawn.—Sometimes the newly-sown lawn of the amateur gardener looks thin and poor in the spring, after one season's use. If soil and grass seed are mixed—4 lb. of grass seed to a barrow-load of soil—and spread over the lawn as a top-dressing during showery weather, the grass will soon become thicker. This dressing should be brushed into the turf and the lawn well rolled several times during the following weeks.

Lawns on Heavy Clay.—A lawn on heavy clay soil is often considerably improved in texture if dressed with coke

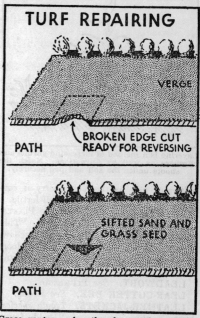

Grass verges and paths often need repairing. Use new turf or reverse a section and turn straight side to the edge.

breeze or charcoal passed through a quarter-inch mesh sieve. Ordinary ashes from the domestic fires sifted in the same manner are also useful on clay. This material should be evenly spread over the surface and well rolled. The dressing will also have the effect of reducing worm infestation.

LAWN MOWERS. *See under* MOWING MACHINES.

LAWN SHEARS. *See under* SHEARS.

LAWN SPRINKLER. *See under* SPRAYING.

LAWSONIA (law-so-ni-a. Lythraceæ). Stove tree from Egypt and the East Indies.

Cultivate in a sandy peat and turfy loam. Increase by cuttings of ripened shoots inserted in sand under a bell-glass in strong heat.

SPECIES.

L. *alba*, white.

L. *a. purpurea*, purple. Height, 12 ft.

LAXTONBERRY. A hybrid between a Raspberry and Loganberry. Not much

Layering is a method of increasing shrubs and climbers as well as Carnations. Notch the shoots under the soil and peg securely.

cultivated now as the Veitchberry is considered a better plant. Not self-fertile.

LAYERING. *See* PROPAGATING PLANTS.

LAYIA (lay-e-a. Compositæ). "Tidy Tips." California. 1½ ft. Flowers yellow, edged with creamy-white. Sow indoors in April, ordinary garden soil. A sunny position is best. Hardy Annual.

LEADWORT. *See* PLUMBAGO.

LEAF-CUTTER BEE. *See* ROSES.

LEATHER-JACKETS. *Tipula species.* At least three species of "Daddy-Long-Legs" are liable to do harm to roots when in the larval stage, and as the life-history of each is somewhat similar it would be as well to give a general life-history.

LIFE-HISTORY.—Eggs are laid in late summer or autumn, the females depositing anything up to 300 just below the surface of the soil. These eggs hatch out in late September and the small leather-jackets begin to feed upon any roots they may come in contact with. If the weather is mild much damage may be done in November and December by the growing larvæ, but should there be a cold spell they burrow deeper into the ground, and there remain for more favourable conditions. One point of interest and importance in the life-history is the fact that on warm nights they come to the surface and may then be seen by the aid of a lamp. On becoming full-grown in the spring they pupate, the perfect "Daddy-Long-Legs" hatching out in the summer.

METHODS OF CONTROL.—Of the many suggested remedies undoubtedly a poison bait will give the best results. This is made up of 20 lb. of bran, 1 lb. paris green, to one gallon of water. Though effective in itself the addition of about ½ pint of treacle will often improve it. After thoroughly mixing, it should be broadcast over the area affected; 20 lb. should be sufficient for one acre.

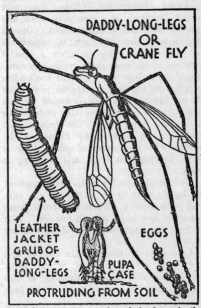

DADDY-LONG-LEGS OR CRANE FLY

LEATHER JACKET GRUB OF DADDY-LONG-LEGS

EGGS

PUPA CASE

PROTRUDING FROM SOIL

One of the worst enemies of the lawn is the Leather-jacket. The best remedy is a soil fumigant and to encourage the birds.

The larvæ or grubs of those two-winged flies, popularly known as "Daddy-long-legs" (*Tipula*), attain their maximum activity in the spring and early summer, when they are often the cause of serious damage to lawns. In the garden nothing comes amiss to them, but they show a preference for runner beans, lettuce, cabbage, potatoes, peas and strawberry plants. In the flower-garden they commit their ravages on Dahlias, Carnations, Chrysanthemums and many other perennials.

Treatment.—The application of soil insecticides. *See* WIREWORMS.

LEAVES, FALLEN. Dead leaves of all kinds should be collected and stored in a corner of the garden. When decayed they make excellent mould for use in potting plants, and for digging into a flower border. Allotment holders who can arrange with the local council to have leaves from the street tipped on to vacant plots could use two or three loads to each 10-rod plot. They can be dug in at once, or left in stacks to decay, and used in spring when forking over the ground after the winter digging. The latter plan is always safer in case there should be any tarred grit among the leaves. Clean the leaves from paths as they fall. They are then no more trouble for a year, as very few trees make any considerable growth until the warmer weather comes again.

LEDUM (le′-dum. Ericaceæ). America and Greenland. Hardy evergreen shrubs. Plant in May or September in peat or sandy loam, free from lime. *Propagate* by seeds, layers and cuttings.

SPECIES.

L. intermedium. Neat habit, pink flowers in clusters.

L. latifolium. Labrador Tea. 2–3 ft. Pink, flowering in April and May.

L. palustre (Marsh Ledum). 2–3 ft., with small leaves and pink flowers.

LEEA (le-a. Ampelideæ). Dwarf shrubs of which the grown species are remarkable for the variety of colouring in the foliage.

Propagate by cuttings kept in a close propagating case with slight bottom heat. They must at all times be kept well moistened but must never be allowed to suffer from over-watering. A suitable compost is made of leaf-mould and peat with some sand.

SPECIES.

L. amabilis. This is the best of the genus having pinnate leaves that are bronzy coloured above and red beneath, with a white central stripe. Its variety *L. a. splendens* is better than the type. 3 ft.

LEEK (*Allium Porrum.* Liliaceæ). The Leek is an exceedingly popular vegetable, and has been so for many

hundreds of years. The Israelites, the Romans, and later the ancient Britons all favoured the leek as a wholesome article of diet, and referred to it in their various writings or records.

Whilst the leek is grown in all parts of the country it is especially popular in the North, and in Wales; in fact it is the national emblem of the Principality, and

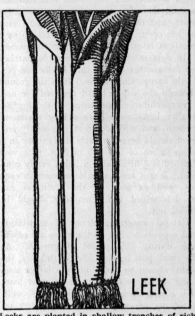

Leeks are planted in shallow trenches of rich soil. They are earthed up to bleach the stems.

forms the badge of one of its most famous regiments.

As an exhibition vegetable the leek is ideal. Perfect specimens can be produced without great experience, and when well grown and staged the points awarded are high.

Culture.—Leeks for the general crop should be raised from seed sown in the open ground in March, being transplanted to their permanent places in May or June.

The soil for leeks should be well dug and liberally manured. For all ordinary uses it is not necessary to prepare and plant in trenches, for excellent specimens may be obtained by planting on the flat in the following manner.

A garden line should be used to get straight rows 1½ ft. apart, and along these at intervals, holes 1 ft. apart should be made with a blunt-ended dibber. The young plants are then lifted from the seed bed, the tips of the roots and of the leaves are trimmed off, and one is set in each hole so that only an inch or so of the leaves stands out. A little water given from a water-can will wash sufficient soil around the roots to enable them to get a start, and the remainder of the hole may be left open, until they finally fill up as a result of later hoeings amongst the plants.

In September the plants can be earthed up for another 3 or 4 in. Leeks are perfectly hardy, and may be left in the ground through the winter until required for use.

For exhibition specimens of the highest quality leeks must have a long season of growth, and will require to be highly fed. Seed should be sown early in January in a temperature of 55°–60° in 3 in. pots well drained and filled with a light, sandy compost. 3 or 4 seeds should be sown in each pot, and as soon as the strongest can be determined the remainder should be pulled out.

Careful watering, plenty of ventilation and a position close to the glass are essentials during this period of growth. As the small pots become filled with roots, the plants should be potted on to a larger size, using a compost of 2 parts of good loam and 1 part each of good leaf soil, well-rotted manure and sharp sand. After re-potting they should again be placed near the glass and kept in a steady temperature of 55°.

Culture.—As the plants increase in vigour the tips of the leaves should be taken off, and the plants must be gradually hardened-off, planting out in April.

During the winter or early spring the trenches should be dug out 18 in. wide and 2 ft. deep. The bottom should be forked over, and then covered with 4–6 in. of good farmyard manure, and finally 15 in. of good top soil to which some old soot, mortar rubble and bonemeal has been added.

At planting time the plants should be carefully knocked out of the pots to leave the ball of soil intact, and should be planted moderately firmly in a single row

at 18 in. apart down the centre of the trench.

Every attention must be given in order to encourage rapid growth, and to this end a syringing twice daily with tepid soft water should prove useful, and at no time must the plants suffer from lack of moisture at the roots. As soon as growth is active doses of weak soluble manure and soot water may be given alternately at intervals of 10 days, until the end of September.

Unlike Celery, Leeks are blanched in stages as they grow and not at the end of the season when growth is practically finished.

An effective and not too difficult method is to place a stiff brown-paper collar or sleeve about 6 in. long over each plant soon after they are set out, and to put two small canes on either side as guides and supports. A little dry soil can then be drawn round the bottom of the collar. As the plants grow the collars should be raised and the bottoms filled round with more soil. To keep the latter in position a plank should be set on edge on either side of the row, thus forming a sort of box, and enabling a greater length of blanched stem to be obtained.

VARIETIES.

The Lyon, Prizetaker, Standard Bearer, Holborn Model.

Uses.—Many delectable dishes may be made with Leeks. They are often boiled but are much nicer when braised in a good stock with a suspicion of cloves, and afterwards served on toast with a covering of white or brown sauce. Boiled or braised Leeks are also delicious when eaten the same way as Asparagus with a vinaigrette sauce.

LEIOPHYLLUM (lī-o-fil'-lum. Ericaceæ). Eastern N. America. 9–18 in. Small evergreen shrub, with white or rose-pink flowers, profusely borne in early summer.

Culture.—Plant in loam and peat. Likes a moist position. *Propagate* by cuttings in July or August in sandy peat with bottom heat.

L. buxifolium. Sand Myrtle. Clusters of small flowers, pink tipped.

L. b. prostratum. A low-growing shrub suitable for rockery.

LEONOTIS (lē-o-no'-tis. Labiatæ). Lion's Tail. A beautiful and interesting flowering shrub for cultivation in very mild districts.

Culture.—Plant in rich loam. *Propagate* by cuttings placed in bottom heat.

SPECIES.

L. leonurus (South Africa). Scarlet flowers in winter.

LEONTICE (le-on-ti-se. Berberideæ). Some of the Leontices may be grown as hardy herbaceous plants in sheltered districts, but usually they are better grown in a greenhouse.

Propagate by seeds or offsets of the tuberous roots. Plant in damp loam and peat.

SPECIES.

L. Albertii, browny-yellow flowers in April. 8 in.

L. Leontopetalum, yellow flowers in spring. 1 ft.

LEONTOPODIUM (le-on-to-po-di-um. Compositæ). Edelweiss. Lion's foot. *Leon*, lion; *pous*, foot. Referring to the shape of the flowers.

The only species is a hardy herbaceous perennial with grey leaves. Increased by seeds and division in spring. Although theoretically it grows anywhere, it is difficult to establish in some places, but once it has taken it is most persistent. It likes to have plenty of sun.

SPECIES.

L. alpinum, which bears little yellow flowers in May and June, is scarcely a showy plant, but because it is so essentially an alpine plant gardeners like to have it for their rockery, where in the sun it will flower as freely as on its native Alps. 3–6 in. There are several varieties but they are pretty much alike.

LEOPARD FLOWER. *See* BELAMCANDA.

LEOPARD'S BANE. *See* DORONICUM.

LEPECHINEA (le-pek-in-i-a. Labiatæ). Hardy herbaceous perennials that are allied to the Mint family.

Propagate by division in spring or by seeds sown in a cold frame in soil composed of 3 parts of loam to 1 of peat.

SPECIES.

L. clinopodifolia or *Mentha dahurica*, and *spicata* with yellow flowers in July. 12 in.

LEPIDIUM. *L. sativum* is the common cress so well known in conjunction with mustard. There are three kinds, the curly-leaved, used for salads, the plain-leaved that is the most commonly cultivated, and the broad-leaved that is rarely grown.

L. draba is the "devil's cabbage," which is one of the most persistent of weeds and can be destroyed by using a dilution of copper sulphate at the rate of ½ lb. to 1 gal. of water.

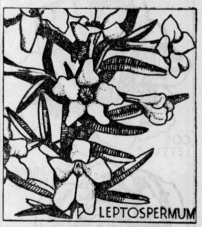

The lilac flowers of the Leptospermum appear in winter. They enjoy a sheltered position outdoors or can be grown in a cool greenhouse.

LEPTODERMIS (lep-to-der'-mis. Rubiaceæ). Only suitable for mild districts. Shrubs with ornamental leaves. Flowers in small clusters.

SPECIES.

L. kumaonensis, Himalayas. A rare species with white flowers.

LEPTOSIPHON (lep-to-si-phon. Polemoniaceæ). 6 in. Various colours. Hardy annual. Natives of California. The flowers are 2 in. long, narrow, tube-like, very dainty and elegant and set off by the dark green bristly foliage. A sandy loam suits them best. Pretty subjects for edgings. Sow in April where to flower. *L. androsaceus* (lilac-purple), *L. aureus* (orange-yellow), *L. hybridus* (orange and yellow shades) and *L. roseus* (rose-pink) are the best varieties.

LEPTOSPERMUM (lep-to-sper'-mum. Myrtaceæ). Australia and New Zealand.

6–8 ft. Evergreen shrubs. Tender:
require wall protection, except in south-
western districts.

Culture.—Plant in loam and peat.

Propagate by cuttings in May under a
bell-glass, or seeds in March.

SPECIES.

L. lævigatum. White.

L. Liversidgei. Very distinct, white.

L. pubescens (*lanigerum*). White, large
silvery leaves. July–September.

COS LETTUCE

CABBAGE LETTUCE

**Of the two common types of lettuces, Cabbage
are the most tender, while the Cos lettuces
have a nutty flavour.**

L. scoparium. White flowers in June.
Thrives in almost any soil.

L. s. Boscawenii. Pale pink, compact
bush, 6–8 ft.

L. s. Chapmanii. Bright rosy-red
flowers, very floriferous. Compact.

L. s. prostratum. Prostrate growing;
suitable for rock gardens. Hardier than
the erect-growing forms.

LEPTOSYNE (lep-to-sy-ne. Compositæ). Annual and perennial plants resembling Coreopsis that are grown for cutting.
They thrive in ordinary soil in a sunny
position and are propagated by seeds sown

outside in spring, by cuttings in summer
or by division in spring.

SPECIES.

L. maritima is the only species that
is much grown for borders and produces
large yellow and orange flowers in late
summer and autumn. 12 in.

LEPTOTES (lep-to-tez. Orchidaceæ).
Stove orchids that are increased by
division in spring. When planting, the
pot should be nearly filled with drainage,
with some fibrous peat and old moss.

Summer temperature, 60°–85°; winter,
55°–60°.

SPECIES.

L. bicolor, white and red flowers, April.

L. b. glaucophylla, milky green leaves
and purple flowers, February.

L. concolor, white, February.

LESCHENAULTIA (les-ken-aul-ti-a.
Goodenovieæ). A genus of greenhouse
evergreens from Australia with several
beautiful species.

Propagate by cuttings of young shoots
rooted in sand under a bell-glass. They
do well in a compost of 3 parts of peat to
1 of loam with some sand and charcoal.
At all times they must be well drained
and have some shade with plenty of air.
The minimum temperature in winter must
not be less than 40°.

SPECIES.

L. biloba, blue flowers, June and July.
1 ft.

L. b. major is a larger and better form
of *biloba.*

L. formosa, scarlet flowers, June. 1 ft.

LESPEDEZA (les-pe-de′-za. Leguminosæ). Bush Clover. China and Japan.
Hardy deciduous, free-flowering shrubs,
with large racemes of pea-like flowers in
late summer.

Culture.—Plant in loamy soil, open
position. *Propagate* by cuttings, division,
and seeds when available.

SPECIES.

L. bicolor. 3–6 ft. Rosy-purple. August
and September.

L. Sieboldii (syn. *formosa*). Light purple
flowers in racemes 2 ft. long. Starts into
growth very early. Cut away dead stems
in spring.

LETTUCE (*Lactuca sativa*). Compositæ.
Although lettuces were not introduced into
this country until during the reign of Queen

Elizabeth, they were cultivated for use many thousands of years before in Egypt and Persia, and later in southern Europe.

To-day they form a most valuable crop to both the amateur and professional grower. Large areas are devoted to their commercial cultivation in this country and also in France and Holland, where very early crops are more easily obtained, and in California, where thousands of acres are grown for human consumption or for seed.

Culture.—Lettuces may be grown on any soil, but all types respond readily to good cultivation, and well-tilled land in good condition is essential for the production of crisp, tender and well-flavoured produce.

The earliest sowings must be made in shallow boxes in a moderate temperature under glass early in February, followed by two or three further sowings at intervals of ten days to provide a succession. For these early sowings, and also for winter supplies, the Cabbage types are more reliable than the Cos.

When large enough to handle, the tiny lettuce plants must be pricked off into other boxes to allow them to develop sturdily until ready for hardening-off, and finally planting out on a warm, sheltered border.

Normally the first outdoor sowings may be made on a warm border at the end of March. The land should have been well dug and manured some time previously, so that only a good raking is required to obtain a fine tilth in which to sow the seeds.

The best method is to draw shallow drills 1 ft. apart, sowing the seeds thinly and giving only a light covering of soil. When an inch or so high and during showery weather, the surplus seedlings may be carefully lifted and replanted on other vacant ground.

Successional sowings should be made at intervals right through the summer, but it is rarely safe to transplant after early June as the check to the plants induces them to run to seed.

About the middle of September seeds of a good hardy variety may be sown very thinly in a sheltered spot or skeleton frame, where they may be allowed to remain until lifted and moved to a good warm border in February or March.

Their cultivation under glass is possible at all seasons if afforded rich moist soil, a moderate temperature which goes to neither extreme, and plenty of ventilation upon all fine days to ensure the best possible results.

Although there are so-called self-folding cos varieties on the market, it is really advisable to tie all of them. This should be done when the plants are about three parts grown, and the tie should be sufficiently loose for the heart to develop.

Varieties.—CABBAGE: Continuity; Wonderful; Tom Thumb; All-the-Year-Round.

Cos.—Hardy Winter White; Brown Bath; Hicks Hardy White; Mammoth White Cos.

Uses.—Used fresh and raw in salads and sandwiches, and as a single dish with vinegar, oils and condiments.

LEUCADENDRON (lū-ka-den-dron. Proteaceæ). Silver Tree. South Africa. 15 ft. Tender, requires mild and sheltered position in rather dry soil of loam and peat.

Greenhouse Culture.—Compost: equal parts sandy loam and peat with several pieces of large charcoal to keep it open. Pot early spring. Water moderately during the summer, but very sparingly in the winter, as the plants will not thrive in a damp cold house. Winter temperature, 45°; summer, 65°.

Propagate by cuttings of well-ripened shoots in sand during the summer. Stand in ordinary greenhouse close to glass. Temperature about 60°.

SPECIES.

L. argenteum. Yellow, globular flowers. This is the Cape Silver Tree, and the only one worth cultivating. 12–15 ft.

LEUCOCORYNE (lu-ko-kor-i-ne. Liliaceæ). Glory of the Sun. Half-hardy bulbs that are thought by those who have seen them in their natural habitat to be amongst the most beautiful of bulbous plants. They resemble Chionodoxas in form, size and colour, but the flowers are in umbels of 3–7. They are deliciously fragrant and last well when cut. In very warm localities they might be grown out of doors, but are best in the cool greenhouse (50°–60°). The treatment after flowering is the same as that given to Freesias, the bulbs being dried and kept

in the sun, while during the growing period
they need the same culture as Ixias.

Propagate by offsets, and seeds.

SPECIES.

L. alliacea. White or lilac flowers in
June.

L. ixioides. Blue or white. August.
1 ft.

LEUCOJUM (lu-ko-jum. Amaryllidaceæ). Snowflakes. Hardy bulbs. The

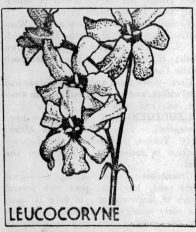

LEUCOCORYNE

Leucocoryne (Glory of the Sun) is a half-hardy
bulb with lilac flowers. They are fragrant and
excellent for cutting.

Snowflakes are very ornamental, generally
bearing white and green flowers on stems
about a foot high. They do well in shady
borders or rockeries, and can also be
naturalised in grass. The bulbs should be
planted 4 in. deep and 3 in. apart in
autumn, from August to November. As
a rule the bulbs do not flower the first
year after planting, and when once
established they should not be lifted unless
it is necessary.

They can be propagated by offsets.

Varieties generally cultivated are:
L. æstivum, Summer Snowflake, white
bells touched with a spot of green;
L. vernum Carpathicum, Spring Snowflake, white flowers, tipped green.

LEUCOPHYLLUM (lu-ko-fil-lum.
Scrophulariaceæ). *L. texanum.* Violet.
Greenhouse branching shrub, propagated
by cuttings of immature wood in sand

under a bell-glass. Soil: loam, leaf-mould
and sand.

LEUCOPOGON (lu-ko-po-gon. Epacri-
deæ). Evergreen shrubs from Australia
that require greenhouse culture. They
provide the native currants.

Propagate by cuttings of young shoots
rooted in sandy peat under a bell-glass.
They should be planted in peat and loam
with silver sand and some charcoal to
keep the soil sweet. Winter temperature,
38°–45°.

SPECIES.

L. amplexicaulis. 3 ft.

L. Fraseri. New Zealand. Very dwarf.

LEUCOJUM

The Snowflake or Leucojum is like a large
Snowdrop. The white flowers are tipped with
green.

Tiny leaves, and white fragrant flowers,
followed by apricot-coloured berries.

L. lanceolatus, white flowers, May. 10 ft.

L. Reichei, white. 5 ft.

LEUCOTHOE (lū-koth'-o-ē. Ericaceæ).
America. Hardy evergreen and deciduous
shrub, with white pitcher-shaped flowers
in racemes. Thrives well in good loamy
soil, in semi-shade. *Propagate* by cuttings
in August.

SPECIES.

L. Catesbœi. A handsome species with long arching branches, bearing many racemes of flowers in May. Foliage lustrous green, assuming beautiful crimson tints during the autumn and winter.

L. C. Rollisonii. Similar to above, but with smaller leaves.

L. Davisiœ. 1–3 ft. Distinct evergreen shrub, with white flowers produced on erect racemes, 2–4 in. in June. Thrives well in and around London.

L. racemosa. 4–6 ft. Deciduous shrub producing abundant racemes of flowers, 2–4 in. during June. Thin out old wood to promote growth.

LEVELLING. Levelling is the term given to the operations by which it is possible to ascertain the varying levels of a piece of land or to the practical levelling of land, that is, reducing it to a horizontal plane.

Scientific levelling is the work of a surveyor or other qualified person. It is carried out with a level, or theodolite, staff, and other instruments. Ordinary garden work, such as levelling a tennis lawn, can be carried out at home with a few pegs, a straight-edge, and a spirit-level. Drive in a peg so that the top is level with the ground at the highest corner of the plot. Next drive in another ten feet from the first, placing the straight-edge with the spirit-level across the two. Next drive a third ten feet from the second and level the second and the third as before. Continue in this way until the lowest part or the end of the plot is reached. Now it is easy to see that the length of the last pole above the ground is equal to the fall of the ground from A to B, say 4 ft. If this is divided by two, the mean level is thus obtained. Now at the lower end drive the peg in another 2 ft., i.e., down to the mean level. A mark made on the peg before it is driven in will serve as a guide. Proceed across the plot as before, but from the lower end, reducing the pegs to the mean level. When the point is reached where the soil has to be excavated to bring it down to the mean level, it can be dug out horizontally, the excavated soil being used to bring the lower portion up to the mean level. The whole will be level with the tops of pegs.

N.B.—Levelling should always be done with the subsoil, as the top layer is by far the most fertile. Therefore, the first operation in levelling is usually to remove the top 6 in. of soil and wheel it clear of the site, to be replaced later, if desirable.

LEWISIA (lew-is-ia. Portulaceæ). Beautiful little perennials that are useful for the rockery and do well in a soil composed of light sandy loam with brick

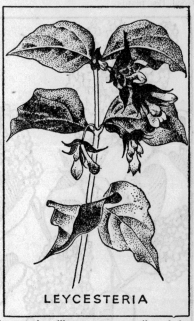

LEYCESTERIA

Leycesteria will grow on any soil, and does well by the sea. It has curious white and purple flowers in summer.

rubbish, in a sunny position with good drainage. They are increased by seeds sown under glass in spring or by division in the same season.

SPECIES.

L. rediviva, so called because it has been known to revive after being dried off, has rosy flowers in summer. 4–6 in.

L. Tweedyi, with pink flowers in July and August and leaves bronzy on the lower side, needs protection in winter.

LEYCESTRIA (lāy-ste-ri-a. Caprifoliaceæ). Himalayas. Hardy deciduous shrub, 4–5 ft., with purplish flowers followed by small dark berries.

Culture.—Ordinary soil in sunny position. Useful as game coverts, the berries being liked by game. *Propagate* by seed sown in frame, or open ground.

L. formosa the only species.

LIATRIS (li-a-tris. Compositæ). Blazing Star. Kansas Feather. Handsome border plants with long spikes of flowers that open from the top downwards in succession, and pointed succulent leaves. Good Bee plants.

LILAC

The well-known Lilac, Syringa vulgaris, blooms in spring and does well in town gardens.

Culture.—Propagate by division of the roots in spring. For best results plant in March, although autumn planting is successful in warm districts. They should have a light sandy soil and ample water at the flowering season or the spikes will be small. In cold exposed districts they should be lifted in October and the roots placed in coke dust in a frame until March, when they may be replanted.

SPECIES.

Pycnostachya, an attractive plant with rich purple flowers on an inflorescence that is from 1–2 ft. long and flowering from August to September, 3–4 ft.; *Scariosa* (syn. *Serratula scariosa*), bears purple flowers in July and August, 3 ft.; *L. elegans* is probably the favourite plant of the family and like *acidota*, *punctata*, *spicata* and *tenuifolia* has purple flowers in August and September. The height of these plants varies from 2–4 ft. All are useful for the perennial or mixed border.

LIBERTIA (li-ber-tia. Iridaceæ). Hardy and half-hardy perennials that are useful alike for the rock garden and border and have long grassy leaves in dense tufts from which grow graceful spikes of bluish-white flowers.

Culture.—Grow in a light, dry, friable soil in a sunny position and propagate by spring division or by seeds sown in spring. Winter the seedlings in a frame.

SPECIES.

All bear whitish flowers in April and May. *Formosa, grandiflora* and *ixioides* are not quite hardy and require a winter covering of litter or ashes. *Paniculata* is a very pretty species. The height of all is about 18 in.

LIBOCEDRUS (lib-ō-sē′-drus. Coniferæ). Very ornamental evergreen trees resembling and closely allied to Thuya. They thrive in a rich light soil, moist, but well drained. Dead branches should be removed. *Propagation* is best from seed sown as soon as ripe, in sandy soil indoors. Cuttings may be taken in August, and placed in a close frame.

SPECIES.

L. chilensis. The "Chilean Cedar." A distinct and beautiful tree, with leaves of an unusual shade of soft green. In Devon specimens have attained to a height of over 50 ft.

L. decurrens. The "Incense Cedar" of western N. America, up to 150 ft. Of a columnar or narrowly pyramidal habit of growth, reaching to 70 ft. in this country. Leaves of a dark glossy green. Ideal as a specimen, adding distinction to any garden.

L. d. variegata. A variety of which pieces of various sizes are entirely yellow.

LICHENS. These are amongst the lowest forms of plant life, yet are most interesting and, incidentally, ubiquitous. Under their many guises lichens are found upon old stonework as greyish-greeny matter that is familiar to everybody, on rocks, on rocky matter high up on mountains and in the Arctic regions as the staple green food of the reindeer. When found growing on fruit trees they may be appreciated æsthetically, but this is counteracted by the harm they do in impeding the growth of the trees. They can be removed by spraying the infected trees with a mixture of 1 lb. of caustic soda with 1 lb. of commercial potash, each being dissolved separately and then mixed together with sufficient water to make 10 gal. Thick gloves should be worn when spraying and the spray must be kept from falling on the face of the gardener. A preventative is to dust the branches when damp, with lime. Physiologically they are of great interest, as they show a symbiotic union between fungi and algæ, which can live apart but when together form lichens. The fungi envelop the algæ which manufacture the food for both. They are prepared by spores from the fungi and cellular division of the algæ. The best means of prevention lies in keeping the soil around the trees well drained.

LICUALA (lik-u-a-la. Palmæ). Handsome rather small palms from the East Indies. They need a stove atmosphere at all times and some of the species do well if their pots are plunged in a tank of water during the summer.

They should be potted in rich sandy loam. Summer temperature, 60°–80°; winter, 60°. Seed should be sown in small pots or shallow pans and given bottom heat.

SPECIES.

L. grandis, yellow, spring. 10 ft.

L. peltata, white and yellow, summer. 6 ft.

L. spinosa, whitish green, 6 ft.

LIGUSTRINA. *See* SYRINGA.

LIGUSTRUM (li-gus-trum. Oleaceæ). Privet. Hardy, deciduous, and evergreen shrubs from Japan, China and Australia, ranging from 2–10 ft. Thrive in any garden soil, and easily propagated from cuttings.

SPECIES.

L. Delavayanum. 5–6 ft. Evergreen, with large panicles of white flowers. A showy elegant plant.

L. ionandrum. 7 ft. Evergreen. Distinct, with large glossy leaves, and stiff, rigid growth, berrying freely.

L. japonicum. 6–8 ft. Evergreen, with white flowers and large leaves.

L. lucidum. 10–18 ft. Evergreen, very large leaves and white flowers in August and September.

L. ovalifolum. Semi-evergreen, the most useful for hedge-making.

L. o. aureum (syn. *elegantissima*). Golden Privet. Useful for hedges, but not so quick-growing as type.

L. vulgare. Common Privet.

LILIES: ARRANGING BULBS FOR PLANTING

Lilies thrive in a well-drained soil with a liberal dressing of sand before planting.

LILAC. *See* SYRINGA.

LILIES (*Lilium*). Liliaceæ. Hardy or half-hardy bulbous flowering plants, the first of which were introduced in 1596. There are over 200 species and innumerable hybrids. They have been classified into main groups according to the shape of the flowers and habit of the plants, but so far as the amateur gardener is concerned, the only classifications he need recognise are the distinction between hardy bulbs and those suitable for greenhouse culture, and a further distinction between lilies which will grow in lime and lilies which are lime-haters. A number of lily bulbs which are sold in this country come from abroad, some from China and Japan, others from the Continent, but a good many of the lilies which are most valuable in our gardens are now grown in British nurseries. Lilies are natives of waste places all over the northern hemisphere. They thrive generally in regions where there is plenty of moisture in the air, mountainous districts, or in river valleys

LILIUM GIGANTEUM GROWS WELL IN THE WILD GARDEN

A deep, rich, moist soil with a background of trees and partial shade are the best conditions for the giant lilies.

or near the great oceans. Since the ambition of the gardener is, as nearly as possible, to reproduce the natural conditions for each kind of plant, it is as well for him to remember these facts, for they will remind him that lilies do not like too rich food, but that they do appreciate moisture in the atmosphere. The majority of lilies do not like lime in the soil, although some of them will tolerate it. They like leaves, but with the exception of a few cases, they dislike bog peat, because of its acidity.

It is a mistake to enrich soil for lily culture with fresh animal manure, as this is inclined to breed fungoid diseases as well as to introduce pests which may ruin the bulbs. Where lilies are to be cultivated, the soil should be deeply dug, so that it is well drained, and if leaf-mould cannot be obtained, some very old, well-rotted manure may be dug into light soil. When planting, each bulb should be surrounded with a little sharp sand, about ¼ in. thick under and over; to keep off slugs and excessive wet, and ward off disease.

Hardy lilies are planted either in autumn or spring.

In the case of swamp lilies, it should be remembered that in native surroundings they grow on the banks of small streams or on the edges of lakes and ponds, but that *only the roots* penetrate directly down into the wet mud. Lily specialists therefor advise that in swamp gardens these lilies can be grown best by planting them on an inverted flower-pot under 4–5 in. of soil, and surrounding with gritty sand.

LILIES. DIVIDING CLUMP FOR TRANSPLANTING

Madonna Lilies occasionally need lifting. Select the best bulbs for replanting.

With regard to the depth at which to plant lily bulbs, this varies according to whether they are stem-rooting or whether they only grow basal roots. Those that grow stem roots need to be planted a little deeper, that is fully 6 in. below the surface soil, while the others need only be about 4 in. deep. It is also important to draw a little soil round the stems of the plants as they grow, for the roots tend to grow above the surface level.

Without exception, lilies growing wild are found in association with shrubs or with grasses, and in cultivation it is always found that they appreciate the shelter and shade of low-growing shrubs or other plants near their roots. They do, however, like to lift their heads into the sunshine, and the ideal position for lilies is therefore amongst dwarf shrubs at the edge of a shrubbery.

Varieties in commerce include the following hardy lilies, which are useful for the average garden:

L. auratum. Stem rooting. The Golden-rayed Lily of Japan. The variety Crimson Queen, really a hybrid, is one of the best.

Backhouse hybrids. Stem rooting, cross between *L. martagon* and *L. Hansoni.*

L. Brownii. Stem rooting. Creamy white, outside shaded chocolate-brown.

L. canadense, likes peat and is good to grow amongst Azaleas and Heaths.

L. candidum. White Madonna Lily of old cottage gardens. Will grow almost anywhere, but likes some lime in the soil. Plant not later than September.

L. croceum. The Orange Lily.

L. Hansoni. Stem rooting. Golden yellow, spotted with brown.

L. Henryi. Stem rooting. One of the best for growing among shrubs. The flowers are deep orange-yellow. Very striking. Does not mind lime.

L. longiflorum. Stem rooting. White. One of the best lilies for forcing.

L. Martagon. Splendid lilies for a shady garden, particularly the white form.

L. regale. The royal lily. The finest of all garden lilies. Stem rooting. Does well on limestone soil. Flowers white inside, wine-coloured on the outer side.

L. speciosum. Stem rooting. White and rose forms.

L. tigrinum. The old orange-red Tiger Lily. Stem rooting.

L. umbellatum. Stem rooting. Orange. Very easily grown.

L. Willmottiæ. A marvellous lily that will grow 8 ft. high and may bear as many as seventy flowers of the *Martagon* type. There are innumerable hybrids of the varieties mentioned, and also other varieties which are useful in the garden and greenhouse, particulars of which will be found in trade catalogues.

LILY, ARUM. *See* RICHARDIA.

LILY OF THE VALLEY. *See* CONVALLARIA.

LIME. It is not easy to convey in non-technical language the functions of lime in the soil. Though not exactly a food, plants cannot thrive without it: lime has been called the key which unlocks the storehouse of plant foods in the soil, and

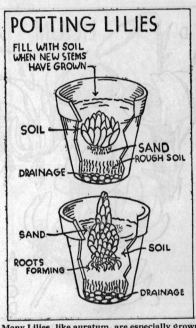

Many Lilies, like auratum, are especially grown in pots.

perhaps this description is as good as any that we can give.

ITS FUNCTION IN THE SOIL.

We have seen that very few plant foods are "available" to the plant in the state in which they are originally present in the soil. In soils lacking in lime the necessary changes do not occur and the plant is therefore unable to make use of all materials that are actually ready and waiting for it, as it were, in the soil. Roughly speaking, plant food materials combine with lime in the soil in such a way that the unneeded part of them forms a compound with it and the essential plant food is left "on its own" for the use of the crop.

Most cultivatable land contains a certain amount of lime but it is constantly being lost in a variety of ways. Every time farmyard manure or most fertilisers are applied, lime is used up in order to allow them to exert their influence. Every crop and every shower of rain removes some more. In addition, lime tends to sink in the soil and eventually passes

Lime is available in many forms in the British Isles.

Hand-picked Lump Lime.—The first selection from the kilns.

Small Lime.—The lime passing through the screens during the selection of hand-picked lumps.

Hydrated Lime.—A very fine powdered lime made by treating hot lump lime with

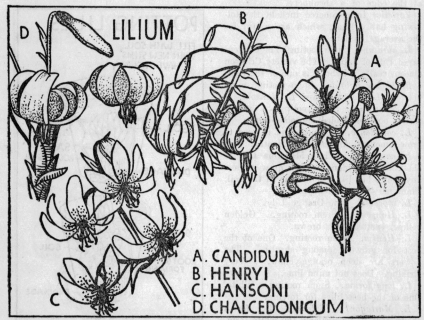

Lilies need no praise. They love partial shade when they come above the soil and later to get their heads in the sunshine. They thrive amongst low-growing shrubs with plenty of decayed leaves in the soil.

beyond "root range" where alone its influence is of any benefit.

Lime provides physical benefits as well as chemical. On clay soils it causes minute particles to adhere together, making the land more porous and easier to work. It is no exaggeration to say that adequate dressings of lime will in time turn stiff, sour land into a condition such that it can be worked with ease.

Lime, then, is of paramount importance, and any scheme of garden improvement designed for high production will fail unless attention is given to the lime needs of the soil and any deficiency remedied.

water. Excellent for lime spraying, garden use, or anywhere where a quick-acting lime of great purity is required. A form of this is sold under the name of "Limbux."

Ground Limestone.—Raw quarry lime ground fine in mills. A very safe way to apply lime, but not recommended if quick results are required, since ground limestone is in the slower acting carbonate form and its full effects are not felt until a few months after application.

Stamford Lime.—Lime from famous quarries in Lincolnshire. Although Buxton Lime is the world's standard, it is sometimes unprocurable on account of freight charges or other causes. In such cases, especially on the East Coast or in East Anglia, Stamford Lime should always be given the preference unless lime is being kilned in the immediate locality, when this can be used.

See also TILIA.

LIME AND SULPHUR. A valuable fungicide for both winter and summer use.

be proved to have once been coral reefs. In the Pennines, where limestone hills lie beside sandstone hills, the change in the vegetation is most dramatic. On the sandstone, bold patches of Heather and Bilberry; on the limestones, chiefly short turf, with some small fancy plants and herbs dotted about. Heather will not grow on limestone. Some of the old

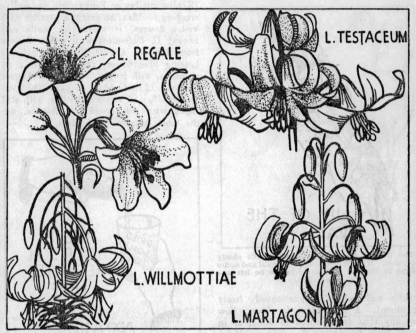

The purple and white Martagon lily is the best of all the lilies for the shady garden. Regale is one of the finest lilies of recent introduction. Willmottiæ has bright orange flowers, while Testaceum (The Nankeen Lily) is pale yellow.

The home-made article is troublesome to prepare and often very unsatisfactory; it is best, therefore, to purchase the concentrated preparation from a reputable firm and use in accordance with the manufacturer's instructions.

LIMESTONES. These were always formed under water, and almost always sea-water, though in just a few cases under lakes. They are doubtless being slowly formed under the ocean to-day. They are made up largely of microscopically minute shells, in just the same way as chalk. But all the other British limestones are older than chalk and harder. Some can

Derbyshire farmers put it the wrong way round and say: "Limestone will not come under the heather." The Ash-tree loves the limestone valleys, and grows there in great beauty. Hence the popular Welsh folk-song, "The Ash Grove." Gorges are often found between limestone hills, as at Cheddar and Monsal-dale.

LIME-WASHING MACHINES. *See* under SPRAYERS.

LIMNANTHEMUM (lim-nan-the-mum. Gentianaceæ). Aquatic and marsh plants with white or yellow flowers allied to Villarsia and requiring similar treatment. Increased by seeds and division.

L. humboldtianum needs to be put in a warm house in winter. The other species are hardy.

L. peltatum (syn. *Villarsia nymphæoides*).

LIMNANTHES (Lim-nan-thees. Geraniaceæ). California. *L. Douglasii* is the only species worth growing. Flowers

LILY OF THE VALLEY

The Lily of the Valley thrives in the shady garden. It loves plenty of leaf-mould and some lime in the soil and also likes to be left undisturbed.

white and yellow, saucer-shaped, freely produced. A good plant for bees. Sow at any time from March to June, or in September for spring flowering. Moist position.

LIMNOCHARIS (lim-no-kar-is. Alismaceæ). Stove aquatics from Brazil that require a tank of warm water or may be grown in the shallow part of an aquarium.

Propagate by seeds, by division or by their runners.

L. emarginata (syn. *flava* and *plumieri*). Yellow flowers, July. 1½–2 ft.

L. Humboldtii (syn. *Hydrocleis Commersonii*).

LINARIA (li-na-ria. Scrophularineæ). Toadflax. Useful hardy herbaceous annuals and perennials that resemble Antirrhinums and vary from dwarf plants to large border plants, good for cutting.

Culture.—The perennials are propagated by division in spring or after blooming and by seeds sown in spring. They are not particular as to soil.

L. alpina, a pretty summer-blooming perennial with purple and orange flowers, and its white and rose varieties are excellent for the rockery; *L. Cymbalaria* (Kenilworth Ivy or Pennywort), the native creeping toadflax, an evergreen trailer with violet flowers, is useful for walls and banks; *L. Dalmatica* with yellow flowers from June to August, 2 ft.; *L. galiodes* bearing blue flowers in July, 18 in.; *L. purpurea*, with purple flowers from August onwards, 12 in.; and *L. vulgaris*, the common toadflax of woods and fields, with stiff stems with sulphur-coloured flowers, are the most suitable for borders.

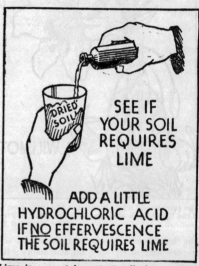

SEE IF YOUR SOIL REQUIRES LIME

DRIED SOIL

ADD A LITTLE HYDROCHLORIC ACID IF NO EFFERVESCENCE THE SOIL REQUIRES LIME

Lime is a most important soil element. To test for its presence use dilute hydrochloric acid.

Annual Linarias are useful in annual or mixed borders. Modern strains come true to colour in white, gold, mauve, pink and combined crimson and gold colours. They are from nine inches to a foot in height and are as useful for table decorations as for the border.

L. aparinoides, 1 ft., mixed colours, *L. bipartita*, 1 ft., purple and white, *L. marveeana*, 1 ft., violet-purple, *L.*

ureo-reticulata, 1 ft., purple and orange, are the best.

LINDELOFIA (lin-del-of-i-a. Boraineæ). Hardy perennials that thrive in any fertile soil and are increased by seeds or division.

SPECIES.

L. longifolia, blue flowers, May. 2 ft.
L. spectabilis, purple flowers, June ½–2 ft.

LINDEN. See TILIA.

LINDERA (lin-der-á. Lauraceæ). Spice Bush. North America and Japan. Spicy, aromatic, deciduous shrub bearing small yellow flowers and purplish berries. Requires a non-calcareous soil, thriving especially in bog or lake-side.

L. Benzoin (syn. *Laurus Benzoin*). 8–12 ft. Yellow flowers, followed by dark red or purple berries. Leaves, when crushed, emit a very strong, spicy and rather unpleasant odour. Hardy in southern gardens.

LINDSAYA (lind-se-ya. Filices). A genus of handsome stove or greenhouse ferns that are rarely grown in spite of their charm, as they are difficult to keep in good condition.

Propagate by spores sown when ripe or by division when they have rhizomatous roots. They should be planted in loam and peat with some sand and need to be grown in a moist atmosphere with good drainage and plenty of water. Thrips are very troublesome and should be combated by fumigating and constant syringing.

SPECIES.

L. adiantoides, 6 in. Resembes Maidenhair.
L. elegans. 1 ft.
L. ensifolia. 1 ft.
L. reinformis. 6 in. The fronds are kidney shaped. There are several other species.

LING. See CALLUNA.

LINNÆA (lin-nē'-a. Caprifoliaceæ). Twin Flower. Canada. A fast-creeping evergreen a few inches high with pink Abelia-like flowers. Suitable for damp, non-calcareous positions in the rock garden.

L. borealis the only species.

LINSEED-OIL PLANT. See LINUM.

LINUM (li-num. Lineæ). Flax. Linseed-oil plant. Free-flowering hardy annuals and perennials that are of great beauty in borders and rock gardens, the best known being the scarlet hardy annual, *Linum grandiflorum rubrum*.

Culture.—The herbaceous perennials are propagated by division in spring, by cuttings of the young shoots, or by sowing seed in pots under glass in the same

The Linden or Lime has pale green leaves and sweet-scented flowers in early spring. It sheds its leaves rather early. A pleasing tea is made from the bracts of the flowers.

season. They like a light rich soil, but are not particular provided it is not stiff and damp, and although known to be sun-lovers they do quite well in semi-shade.

The annuals can be cultivated in ordinary soil in any sunny bed or border. The seeds should be sown broadcast, or in lines, where the plants are to flower, as they do not like the shock of transplanting. Sow them as thinly as possible and thin them out as soon as they are large enough to handle.

The scarlet flax is a favourite for use in the annual border, and is particularly effective if used as an edging immediately behind white Sweet Alyssum, or Candytuft. As the flax flower closes during dull, rainy weather it is best to grow it with some other edging plant. The annual flax also makes a good pot plant.

The shrubby flax (Tree Flax), native of the Mediterranean regions, is an evergreen shrub with bluish leaves and a profusion of golden-yellow flowers in May and June. It grows up to 2 ft. high. It will do well in any good garden soil in a good sunny position. This species can be increased by cuttings of young shoots inserted in sandy soil in the propagating frame in summer.

Seed pods should be picked off before they ripen, as otherwise the plants will be short-lived.

SPECIES.

SHRUB.—*L. arboreum* (Tree Flax).

L. alpinum for the rock garden, with pretty blue flowers from June to August, height 6 in.; *L. flavum*, a showy plant with masses of yellow flowers; *L. hirsutum*, with pink flowers; *L. maritium*, resembling *L. flavum*, yellow; *L. monogynum* bears large white flowers; *L. narbonense*, an invaluable border plant with large deep flowers; and *L. perenne*, a very hardy species with slender stems and clear blue flowers, an excellent plant for a hot dry place. These are the best of the border species and bloom from June to September. Their height varies from 1–2 ft.

ANNUAL.—*Linum grandiflorum* and its varieties *coccineum*, *splendens* and *rubrum*. *L. usitatissimum* (Common Flax).

LIPPIA (lip'pia. Verbenaceæ). Chile. Deciduous shrub, principally grown for its lemon-scented leaves. Flowers of no importance. Tender. Best planted against a warm wall. Assumes bush-like proportions up to 12 ft. in Channel Isles and in southern gardens.

Culture.—Compost: equal parts loam, leaf-mould and sand. Prune hard back in February. When the new growth appears repot. Water freely during the summer, but little required in the winter. Winter temperature, 45°.

Propagate by cuttings taken with heel of the old wood when shoots are about 3 in. long. Insert in sandy soil in the greenhouse in March, temperature, 55°.

SPECIES.

Only one species is grown to any extent that is *L. citriodora* (syn. *Aloysia citriodora*), 2–5 ft.

LIQUIDAMBAR (liquid-am-bar. Hamamelidaceæ). Deciduous trees, with maple-like leaves. Flowers of no importance.

Culture.—Plant in ordinary soil in a sunny position. *Propagate* by seeds, which may take a year to germinate, also by layering. Protect young plants from late frosts.

SPECIES.

A. formosana (*acerifolia*). China and Japan. 10–20 ft. Maple-like dark red leaves, changing to green. Very hardy.

L. orientalis (Imberbe). Oriental Sweet Gum. Asia Minor. Slow-growing tree up to 20 ft., with distinct five-lobed leaves turning yellow in the autumn. The inner bark of this tree is used in the manufacture of the preparation known as Friar's Balsam.

L. styraciflora (Sweet Gum). U.S.A. A beautiful tree with corky bark.

In the autumn the leaves turn to beautiful shades of crimson and orange. The timber is known and imported as Satin Walnut. Requires a moist, loamy soil and sunny position. A specimen near Ashford has attained a height of 80 ft.

LIRIODENDRON (lir-i-o-den-dron. Magnoliaceæ). Tulip Tree. Deciduous trees, with flowers of large size and very distinct foliage.

Culture.—Plant in May in good rich soil in sunny position. *Propagate* by seed sown in frame during May and by grafting in March. Cut out dead wood in autumn

SPECIES.

L. chinensis (China). 60 ft. Slow growing.

L. tulipifera, Tulip Tree. N. America. A tree of pyramidal habit, of large size, reaching to nearly 200 ft. in its native haunts. Flowers greenish-white, tulip shaped, during June and July.

L. t. aureo-variegatum. Leaves edged with yellow.

L. t. pyramidale. Growth erect, similar to a Lombardy Poplar.

LIRIOPE (lir-i-o-pe. Hæmodoraceæ). Hardy plants of Chinese origin with spikes of violet flowers among curving green

eaves in autumn. Readily increased by
division of the roots in spring, and best
suited to a loamy soil.

SPECIES.

L. spicata (syn. *graminifolia* and *Ophio-
pogon spicatus*).

LISTERA (Tway Blade). Orchidaceæ.
Hardy terrestrial orchids. Natives of
Britain. Will grow in loam and leaf-
mould in a shady position.

SPECIES.

L. ovata, green flowered. 1 ft.

LITHOSPERMUM (lith-o-sperm-um.
Boraginaceæ). Gromwell. The feature of
this race is the beautiful metallic-blue
of the flowers of many of the species. All
are suitable for the rock garden. They
like a gritty, sandy loam and a sunny
position, and in spite of many statements
to the contrary, do not really object to
lime.

L. graminifolium has dark grass-like
leaves in tufts with 9 in. stems topped
with branching heads of sky blue. From
N. Italy, where it forms on some of the
hills one of the principal members of the
plant associations. It will propagate from
seed, cuttings or layers. June.

L. intermedium has a somewhat shrubby
growth. The leaves are grass-like with
spreading heads of brilliant deep blue in
June.

L. petræa is rare in its native haunts in
Greece, but less so in garden catalogues.
In sunny positions, such as a sheltered
crevice, it forms a neat bush with pale
blue to purple flowers. 6 in. Seed or
cuttings.

L. prostratum with its variant *L. p.
Heavenly Blue* is that without which any
rock garden will seem unfinished. The
large spreading mats are covered in May
and June with flowers of deep or
"heavenly" blue. It is commonly reputed
to be a lime-hater; nevertheless, it is found
growing wild among the limestone rocks of
Biarritz. It is advisable to cut this plant
back after flowering, otherwise the mat
will evolve a bare centre with succeeding
years.

Propagate by cuttings, which may give
some trouble if not carefully tended. They
need shade and moisture till rooted, provided this moisture is not allowed to
become stagnant.

L. purpurea-cœruleum, the creeping
Gromwell, is the heartiest grower and will
spread in all directions unless controlled.
It is listed as a British species, being
rarely found in Wales, and certain southern
counties of England. Although this is a
plant of the woodland species, especially
on the Riviera, in the British climate
it gives a much better display in full
sunlight.

L. rosmarinifolium (Italy and Greece).
1 ft. Flowers similar to above. Indifferent
to chalk.

The Tulip tree or Liriodendron is too large for
small gardens but makes a fine ornamental
tree where space permits.

LITTONIA (lit-to-ni-a. Liliaceæ). A
small genus of bulbous-rooted herbaceous
perennials from S. Africa. The only
species grown, *L. modesta*, that forms
succulent branches that climb by tendrils
from the end of the leaves, has drooping,
bell-shaped, orange-coloured flowers in the
axils of the leaves in early summer. It
grows best in a compost of leaf-mould with
peat and sand.

LIVER OF SULPHUR. A mixture of
sulphides of potassium, formerly used as a
plant fungicide, but now replaced by other
fungicides. It is very uncertain in its
action.

LIVISTONIA (liv-i-sto-ni-a. Palmaceæ). Greenhouse palms. Ornamental
fan-shaped foliage. Australia, 1824.

Culture.—For compost, general cultivation and propagation, *see* KENTIA.

SPECIES.

L. Australis, *L. chinensis* (syn. *Latania borbonica*).

LLAVEA (lla-ve-a. Filices). *L. cordifolia*, a greenhouse fern which is found difficult to grow, so is rarely found in cultivation. The most suitable soil is loam and peat with finely-broken bricks. It needs plenty of air, but must not be syringed.

LLOYDIA (loyd-i-a. Liliaceæ). Small hardy bulbs of which there are very few species that are found in Europe, Siberia and America. The flower stems rise from amongst a few radical leaves and bear a solitary flower. Increase by seeds or division and plant in a sunny position in well-drained sandy soil.

SPECIES.

L. alpina (syn. *striata*). White flowers in June. 6 in.

L. rubroviridis. Greeny-red flowers. May–June. 6–9 in.

L. triflora is an exception to the rest, having three flowers on one flower stalk.

LOASA (lo-a-sa. Loasaceæ). Cajophora. Chile. Climber, 2–3 ft. Flowers orange-scarlet. A rather uncommon half-hardy annual, quite at home on a low fence in a sunny position. It is not a pleasant subject to handle as the leaves and stems are clothed with coarse, stiff hairs which have similar properties to those of the "stinging nettle."

LOBELIA (lō-bē-lia. Campanulaceæ). A large genus of hardy and tender annuals and perennials that range in size from dwarf African lobelias for edging beds, etc., to large border plants. Introduced from America in the 17th century. Only a few species are in general cultivation, but a great number of varieties and hybrids have been developed.

Culture.—The herbaceous perennials are best propagated by division of the tufts or by cuttings. For the latter, pot up the old plants in autumn and place in a cold greenhouse where they have plenty of light and air but are kept dry.

In February or March treat them to gentle heat to induce growth and take off the young shoots and plant in sandy soil where they soon root. The dwarf lobelias, chiefly varieties of *L. erinus*, are grown as annuals, being sown in light soil in March in a warm house and kept under glass until required for bedding. A light sandy soil is best for the dwarf plants, but the taller kinds like a rich friable soil in a position where they can obtain plenty of water.

The taller half-hardy species can be cut down at the beginning of winter and have their roots covered with coconut fibre or ashes, or they can be lifted and wintered in a frame. A top dressing of leaf-mould in July and occasional doses of liquid manure are of great benefit. If the centre spike of flowers is taken off before it has finished flowering, the side shoots will be larger and stronger.

SPECIES.

L. cardinalis has bronzy green, lance-shaped, smooth leaves and an 18 in. long inflorescence of brilliant cardinal-red rising above erect stems. It flowers in July and August, 3–4 ft.

L. fulgens, with downy leaves, resembles *L. cardinalis*, but has larger flowers and blooms from May to September, height, 1–3 ft.

L. laxiflora, a tender slender-stemmed plant with red and yellow flowers, height 3 ft.

L. syphilitica, and its white and rose varieties, are hardier than most and may be left out in winter. It is a good bog plant and flowers from July to September, height, 2 ft.

L. tenuior is the trailing variety used for hanging baskets and window boxes, etc.

Excellent hybrids are Crimson Beauty from *cardinalis*, and Queen Victoria, with handsome purple leaves, and the free-flowering Firefly from *fulgens*. The latter is sometimes attacked by a kind of rust which shows itself in spots on the main fleshy roots. All soil must be shaken off the roots and they must be well washed before the spots are cut out with a sharp knife.

Replace the plants in free sandy soil with a slight bottom heat and very soon new fibre will have formed.

The dwarf *L. erinus*, with blue flowers, is known to all gardeners and has many varieties with single and double flowers of white and various shades of blue.

Barnard's Perpetual.

Cobalt Blue.

Emperor William.
Blue Stone.
Oxonian.
Carmine Gem.
Tricolor (with carmine spot on blue or ink ground, height 6 in.).
Prima Donna (wine colour).
Drury Blue (deep blue).
Mrs. Clibran (blue, white eye).

These compact-growing kinds are much used for edgings.

Lobelias are admirable pot plants for conservatory decoration. The variety known as *Lobelia ramosa* (*tenuior*) *compacta* is specially desirable, being compact and upright in habit (about 10 in. to 1 ft. in a size 48 pot) and covered with large flowers of bright cobalt blue with white centre. This plant deserves growing far more frequently than it is at present.

Cultivation.—Seeds should be sown in January in pans or boxes of open soil and placed in good heat to germinate. The seedlings should be pricked out when large enough to handle and grown in heat. Pot up into 3 in. pots and eventually into 5 in., in which size pot they will flower about July. The final compost should be light, well-drained and open. Loam, leaf-mould and sand enriched with a sprinkling of a complete fertiliser are ideal.

Varieties of *L. ramosa* are also obtainable in rose and white colours.

LOGANBERRY. The origin of the Loganberry is uncertain. It was raised by Judge Logan in America, and introduced to this country in 1897. Should be planted and pruned as recommended for the Blackberry. This is an excellent fruit for dessert when really ripe, but its greatest use is for bottling purposes.

LOGGIA. This name is applied to a room which is attached to a dwelling house, but is almost completely open to the air. It varies from the garden room in that it has no glass or wooden doors to keep out inclement weather. Such a feature may be built at the same time as the house or it may be added years later. In either case extremely careful consideration should be given to the relation of the garden design to the loggia. The axial lines of the garden layout must have a definite relation to the lines of the house,

otherwise the result as viewed from the loggia will be inharmonious. The columns which support the loggia roof can sometimes be used as supports for scented climbing plants, thus making the loggia a more definite link between the house and the garden. The loggia should be built of materials which will be in harmony with the main house design and should not contain anything which will be harmed by the weather. Thus a floor of brick or tiles is more practical than one of wood, and light cane furniture which can be moved into either the house or garden as desired is more suitable than heavy articles of furniture.

LOISELEURIA (lōi-se-lū-ri-a. Ericaceæ). Alpine Azalea. Sub-arctic regions. Procumbent evergreen shrub, with small clusters of bell-shaped flowers.

Culture.—Plant in a peaty non-calcareous soil, in a cool, moist, shaded position. Not suitable for hot, sunny gardens unless specially cared for.

SPECIES.

L. procumbens. 3–6 in. Light pink, nearly white flowers in May.

LOMARIA (lo-mar-i-a. Filices). Handsome stove and hardy ferns that are popular in nearly all gardens. The genus is closely allied to Blechnum and requires the cultivation given to all FERNS (*q.v.*).

SPECIES.

L. attenuata, has deep green fronds, 1–3 ft. long. Stove or warm greenhouse.

L. boryana (syn. *magellanica* and *zamioides*). Fronds 1–2 ft. Greenhouse.

L. ciliata, with fronds 9–12 in. long, is useful for house decoration. It is very much like *L. gibba*, and has varieties larger than the type.

L. discolor. Long narrow fronds.

L. Germainii, with fronds 2–3 in. long, is very similar to *L. alpina* and both make good window plants.

L. gibba, with fronds from 1–3 ft. long, is perhaps the most popular of all and does well in a stove or warm greenhouse, It has several good varieties.

L. Spicant is the British hardy fern that may be grown out of doors or in a cool house.

There are many species which are sometimes classified with Blechnum and sometimes with Lomaria.

LOMATIA (lō-ma'ti-a. Proteaceæ). Chile, Peru. 20 ft. Evergreen shrubs or small trees with large glossy fern-like leaves, blue-white beneath and Brevillea-like flowers in May and June. For southern gardens. Plant in loam and peat.

SPECIES.

L. ferruginea (*pennatifolia*). Large fern-like leaves, with red and white flowers borne on racemes, May and June.

L. longifolia (Australia). Distinct. Narrow-leaves, flowers yellowish.

L. obliqua (Chile). Distinct. Leathery foligae.

L. silaifolia (Australia). Elegant foliage, with racemes of white flowers in May and June.

LONAS (lo-nas. Compositæ). A hardy annual that will grow in any fertile garden soil that is not too heavy. Increased by seeds sown in April.

The solitary species is *L. inodora* with yellow flowers in July and August.

LONDON PURPLE (an impure arsenate of copper, a waste product of dye-works). Formerly used as a contact-spray for the destruction of caterpillars and leaf-eating insects. Now replaced by arsenate of lead.

LONICERA (lon-i-sēr'-a. Caprifoli-aceæ). Honeysuckle. Hardy, deciduous and evergreen shrubs and climbing plants.

Climbing Section.—The well-known climbing, fragrant honeysuckle, bearing clusters of sweet-scented flowers, of varying shades. Of great utility for covering pergolas, fences and summer-houses, etc., thriving well in good loamy soil and shady positions. *Propagate* by cuttings in late summer, or by layering and seeds.

SPECIES.

L. japonica (Japan). Evergreen. A strong climber, with fragrant white flowers ageing yellow.

L. j. aurea reticulata (*brachypoda*). Tender, leaves variegated golden-yellow, shy flowering.

L. j. flexuosa (*repens*). Bronze foliage and fragrant reddish-yellow flowers.

L. j. Halliana. A pubescent variety with very fragrant white to yellow flowers.

L. Periclymenum, Common Honey-suckle, Woodbine.

L. P. belgica, Early Dutch Honeysuckle. Purplish-red and yellow flowers.

L. P. serotina, Late Dutch Honeysuckle. Late flowering than type. These tw varieties are the most popular of all honey suckles.

L. sempervirens, Scarlet Trumpet Honey suckle (southern U.S.A.). Deciduous, witl orange to yellow flowers. Tender.

Deciduous Shrubby Section. This group of honeysuckle consists of flowering shrubs thriving well in ordinary garden soil and attaining a height of 6–8 ft. In season they produce a prolific quantity of berries. *Propagate* by seeds or cuttings in gentle bottom heat during July or August.

L. fragrantissima (China), 6–12 ft. Of branching habit and creamy-white fragrant flowers from December to March. Perfectly hardy, but best on south or west wall. Partially evergreen.

L. Maackii (*Manchuria*). Flowers pure white, ageing yellow, followed by red berries. A very rapid grower.

Evergreen Shrubby Section. Thriving in any garden soil, useful for planting as undergrowth, under trees, and in other dark, damp places of the garden. *Propagate* by cuttings in July and August.

L. nitida (China). Dark, glossy small leaves, makes a very beautiful close hedge. Most easily propagated. Any pieces put in open ground root quite readily. Flowers fragrant, creamy-white.

L. pileata (China). Low-spreading habit, with dark, shiny foliage, and yellowish-white flowers, followed by purple berries.

L. p. yunnanensis (Yunnan), 5–6 ft. Erect habit, similar to *L. nitida*, with yellow flowers followed by purplish berries.

LOPEZIA (lo-pe-zi-a. Onagrariaceæ). Attractive little annuals, rather like fuchsias, from Mexico. Seed may be sown in the open in April or under glass in March and the seedlings planted out in May. Light, good garden soil suits them.

SPECIES.

L. cordata. Purple flowers in August. 1½ ft.

L. coronata. Red. August. 1½ ft.

L. hirsuta and *L. grandiflora* are very similar to *coronata*.

LOPPING SHEARS. *See under* PRUNERS.

LOROPETALUM (lo-ro-pēt-a-lum. Hamamelidaceæ). China, 5–6 ft. Evergreen shrub requiring wall protection, except in the mildest parts of the country. White witch-hazel-like flowers during February and March.

Culture.—Plant in peaty soil in a sunny position. *Propagate* by cuttings.

L. chinensis, the only species, making a lovely show when in bloom.

LOTUS (lō-tus. Leguminosæ). Bird's-foot Trefoil. This genus comprises several forms of plants from prostrate herbs to small shrubs but scarcely any of the species are grown in gardens. The hardy herbaceous forms of the common Bird's-foot Trefoil are, however, useful for banks or for the rougher parts of the rock garden and *Bertholetii*, *Jacobæus*, and *Gebelia* are greenhouse perennials that make fine basket plants.

Culture.—They are easy to grow and are propagated by cuttings inserted in July out of doors, or by root division in spring. Plant in ordinary garden soil and for the greenhouse plants use equal parts of loam and leaf-mould with a little sand.

SPECIES.

L. corniculatus, a double form of the native plant with trefoil foliage and masses of golden-yellow flowers in summer, is the best for the rockery, height 3–6 in. The greenhouse varieties have red or purple flowers in summer.

LOTUS, SACRED. *See* NELUMBIUM.

LOVE APPLE. *See* LYCOPERSICUM and TOMATO.

LOVE-IN-A-MIST. *See* NIGELLA.

LUCULIA (lū-kū′-li-a. Rubiaceæ). China and Himalayas. Tender, suitable for only the mildest localities, where it is quite a free grower.

Culture.—Plant in loam and peat. *Propagate* by cuttings taken about end of June in sandy soil and kept close in warm frame. They require attention in regard to shade and moisture or but few will strike.

SPECIES.

L. gratissima (Himalayas). Flowers in large trusses, pink and very fragrant, and remain perfect for about a month.

L. Pinceana (China). Even more fragrant and larger flowers than preceding.

LUFFA (luf-fa. Cucurbitaceæ). Vegetable Sponge. Ornamental annual Gourds from the Tropics that require to be grown in a stove. They are easily raised from seed sown in brisk heat and require a culture similar to that given to melons. When in fruit they are most remarkable as the seeds are enclosed in a peculiar fibrous network which, when dried and softened, is used as sponge and is known as loofah. They grow in a mixture of 3 parts of loam to 1 of leaf-mould and need plenty of water.

SPECIES.

L. acutangula.

L. ægyptiaca. Fruit 5–12 in. and club-shaped. This is grown in many parts of the tropics.

LUNARIA (lu-nar-ia. Cruciferæ). Honesty. "Moonflower." 2½ ft. Native of W. Asia. The flowers are produced in terminal heads and on branches on the main stems during May and June, but the plants are usually grown more for the seed heads than the flowers, as the dull silvery, semi-transparent divisions of the seed vessels are much prized for winter decorations. Cut when fully ripe and store in a dry place for a few days to harden. The outer, loose portions of the seed vessels can then be easily removed. A moist rich soil is best. Sow outside from May–June, plant into flowering quarters in autumn. *L. biennis*, lilac-purple, and its white form, *L. b. alba*, are the varieties usually grown.

LUNGWORT. *See* PULMONARIA.

LUPINUS (lū-pī-nus. Leguminosæ). Lupin. Hardy and half-hardy annuals and perennials of which more than a hundred species have been described, but with only a few that are much grown, as these with their hybrids provide a great variety of charming plants for borders or beds.

Culture.—Both annuals and perennials are best propagated by seeds which can be sown out of doors at any time from March to August and the seedlings pricked off and planted in the usual way.

The perennials may be increased by division of the root stock, only strong clumps being chosen and the soil specially enriched or the pieces will fail to root. All lupins will grow in any soil, but they are better for a rich well-drained soil in a sunny position with little or no lime. They require a heavy annual dressing of manure as well as ample supplies of liquid manure in dry weather when the flower spikes are blooming. Once planted the lupins should not be moved. Stake the plants early and to prolong the flowering season take off dead spikes as soon as it is conveniently possible.

SPECIES.

L. *arboreus*, Tree Lupin, a hardy evergreen that with a few years of growth becomes a large and handsome bush covered with fragrant yellow and red flowers in summer. L. *a. albus*, its white variety, is very fragrant and it has many hybrids of various colours such as Daisy Hill, pale blue, and Luteus, yellow. Height, 4–7 ft.

L. *polyphyllus*, is the commonest and best known of all. A handsome perennial with beautiful leaves and pyramidal spikes of inflorescence. If in deep rich soil it flowers in autumn as well as in summer. Its dark blue flowers last well when cut but are a little too heavy to be used for this purpose. Many varieties with pale blue, white and pink blooms have been raised from this species. Somerset is a cross between *arboreus* and *polyphyllus*, and has yellow flowers, 3 ft.

All flower from May to October and are from 1–4 ft. in height.

Apart from their decorative use lupins can be used as a green manuring crop as they have the power of obtaining nitrogen from the air, and some varieties are used as a cattle food.

Useful varieties among the newer hybrid (polyphyllus) lupins are as follows:

"Chocolate Soldier," a striking flower which at first sight appears to be brown. At close quarters it is seen to have flowerets half cream and half dark purple, the purple being overshot with a brown sheen; "Pink Pearls," a thick rope of pearly-pink flowers; "May Princess," purple; "Downer's Delight," deep red; " Icicle," white; "Blue Sky"; "Mrs. Benedict Hoskyns," amber with a suspicion of gold; "Malvina," a dark purple, almost an indigo shade.

As free-flowering annuals which thrive almost anywhere, even in poor stony land, they are seen to best advantage in fairly good garden soil. Best sown in April or early May.

LYCHNIS (lĭk-nĭs. Caryophyllaceæ). Rose Campion. Easily cultivated hardy annuals and perennials with showy flowers that are useful for rock gardens and borders.

Culture.—All species are propagated by seeds but the double forms are only increased by root division in spring or after flowering. They thrive in light ordinary garden soil and the perennials are excellent for cutting.

SPECIES.

Several of the species have double flowers and one of these, L. *Viscaria* with pink or rose flowers, is a fine early-summer bedding plant; L. *chalcedonica* the most popular of all, bears dense scarlet heads which need support as the stem is so fragile that it is apt to break off from the root stock. There are also white and scarlet double forms, the best being *alba plena* and *flore plena*. L. *coronaria* has brilliant magenta-rose flowers in July and August, and silverish woolly leaves on branching stems. It is very effective when in masses by itself, but is apt to be devastating when its colour is allowed to conflict with that of other border plants; height, 2–3 ft. There are several varieties, of which *atrosanguinea*, with rosy-purple flowers, and *oculata* are the best; L. *fulgens*, with salmon-pink flowers, height, 6–12 in., and L. *grandiflora*, a later-blooming plant with scarlet flowers, height, 8–12 in., are border plants. The best of the rock plants are L. *alpina*, with dense heads of rosy flowers, and L. *lagascæ*, with its varieties bearing rosy flowers, height, 3–6 ft.

L. *flos-cuculi*, or Ragged Robin, and L. *flos jovis*, or Rose Campion, are native plants that are best suited to the water-side in wild gardens.

Nearly all species bloom from June to September.

LYCIUM (lĭs′-i-um. Solanacea). Box Thorn. Hardy, deciduous shrub, allied to the Deadly Nightshade, having small flowers, followed by ornamental berries, thriving in ordinary but well-drained garden soil. *Propagate* by seeds, when obtainable, or by cuttings and layers. A good shrub for seaside planting.

SPECIES.

L. *chinense* (*barbarum*). China. Quick grower, with large oval leaves and small purple flowers, followed by scarlet-orange

erries. This species gives a beautiful
ffect planted against a wall.

L. halimifolium (*europæum*). S. E.
Europe and Asia. 8–9 ft. Similar to *L.
hinense*, having lilac-purple flowers, fol-
owed by a profusion of red berries.

LYCOPERSICUM (li-ko-per-si-kum.
Solanaceæ). The only species of this
genus is the Tomato or Love Apple which
s dealt with under its best-known name.

LYCOPODIUM (li-ko-po-di-um. Lyco-
odiaceæ). Club Moss. Formerly an
extensive genus of stove, greenhouse, and
hardy plants, there are now very few
species grown, and the genus is interesting
chiefly to botanists on account of its past
mportance. The plant usually known as
Lycopodium is really *Selaginella kraus-
siana*. The explosive powder known as
Lycopodium powder is manufactured from
the spores of the plants.

The species still in cultivation are propagated by cutting tips of young branches
and inserting them in well-drained peat
and sand in a temperature of about 70°
with moisture in the atmosphere and at
the roots. Also by spores, sown in pans
of well-moistened soil and kept in a close
frame. The plants should be potted up
in a compost of 2 parts peat to 1 each of
sphagnum moss and sand with a little
live sphagnum on the surface of the soil.
The best containers are baskets of teak
only 3 or 4 in. deep in which the plants
can be hung up near the light. During the
spring and summer they need plenty of
water but during the winter very little,
as the baskets attract the moisture in the
air.

SPECIES.

L. clavatum. British Club Moss. Wolf's
Claw. 1–3 in.

L. Selago. British Fir Club Moss.
3–4 in. Erect.

L. alpinum, may be used for carpeting.
2–3 in.

LYCORIS (li-kor-is. Amaryllideæ).
Greenhouse bulbous plants allied to
Vallotas. They are increased by offsets
and by seeds and grow well in equal parts
of loam and leaf-mould with sand. The
pots must be well drained.

SPECIES.

L. aurea, the Golden Spider Lily of
America, bears yellow flowers in August

and September before its leaves appear
and needs stove culture. It must be
rested during the winter. 1 ft.

L. sanguinea, with dark red flowers in
July and August and *L. squamigera*, with
pink or lilac-blue flowers at the same
period, will do quite well out of doors
in a dry, sheltered position by a south
wall.

LYGODIUM (li-go-di-um. Filices).
Climbing Fern. Greenhouse climbing
ferns. Fronds, twining. *L. dichotomum*
needs stove. E. Indies, 1793.

Culture.—Compost: peat, loam, leaf-
mould and sand in equal parts. Best
planted out at the foot of the pillars, or
trellis, in the spring. Winter temperature, 45°; summer, 65°.

Propagate by spores (*see* ADIANTUM).

SPECIES.

L. dichotomum, *L. japonicum*, *L. palmatum*.

LYONIA (li-ō'-nia. Ericaceæ).
N. America, 3–8 ft. Hardy, deciduous
shrub, with flowers borne on panicles
3–6 in. long and oval leaves.

Culture.—Plant in moist sandy loam or
peat. *Propagate* by seed, or by cuttings
taken with a heel during August and
September.

L. ligustrina (*Andromeda ligustrina*,
paniculata). N. America, 3–6 ft. Panicles
of lily-of-the-valley-like small white flowers
in July and August. The large leaves are
finely coloured in the autumn.

LYSICHITUM (lis-ich-i-tum. Araceæ).
From *lusis*, the act of loosening, *chiton*,
a tunic. The spathe is open to reveal the
spadix.

L. camtschatcense. This remarkable
yellow Aroid is a plant of the bog, where
it produces great yellow blooms resembling
stemless Arum Lilies, or perhaps giant
"Lords and Ladies," among large grey-
green leaves. It can be seen to great
effect in the Castle Gardens at Exeter,
where it appears to be growing on low
mounds of mud just emerging from the
surrounding water. It can also be grown
in tubs filled with semi-liquid mud and a
foundation of well-rotted stable manure,
but its luxuriance will, of course, be
curtailed by the restricted root-run.

Propagate by division. Japan to
N. America.

LYSIMACHIA (lĭssy-măk-ia. Primu-laceæ). Loosestrife. Creeping Jenny. A large genus of hardy annuals, biennials and perennials with a few unimportant half-hardy greenhouse plants. The taller forms are effective in borders, in shrubbery margins or in the wild gardens, while the dwarfs are useful spreading rock plants.

Culture.—Propagate by division of the root-stock in March or October or by summer-sown seed. They need little care provided they get plenty of water and thrive in any soil in a sunny or half-shady position.

SPECIES.

L. clethroides, with drooping spikes of large white flowers, is one of the best of the border species, 2–3 ft.

L. ephemerum with glaucous leaves but otherwise resembling *clethroides, japonica* and *punctata* both with spikes of yellow flowers, are all good border plants, height, 2–3 ft.

L. Nummularia, Creeping Jenny or Moneywort, is a prostrate creeping ever-green plant that is perfectly hardy and is an excellent subject for window boxes and hanging baskets in town as well as for the rock garden, or for carpeting the wild garden. This and its golden-leaved variety *aurea* bear yellow flowers that spring from the joints of the shoots.

For potting these plants use two parts of loam to one of leaf soil with a little sand, and allow free drainage.

L. vulgaris (Loosestrife) like *Nummularia,* a useful native plant, is often planted by the waterside. It has yellow flowers, is 3 ft. in height, and is distinct from the purple Loosestrife or *Lythrum salicaria.*

LYTHRUM (ly-thrum. Lythraæ). Purple Loosestrife. Fine hardy or half-hardy perennials of showy appearance and easy culture.

Culture.—Propagate by seeds or division in spring or autumn and plant for prefer-ence in March, in ordinary soil, in a sunny site. Give an annual dressing of manure as the plants are gross feeders. They are best suited to bogs or the waterside and are easily transplanted.

SPECIES.

L. salicaria, the common Purple Loosestrife, with rosy-purple flowers, is only suited to naturalisation in damp half-shady places, but *rosea* with erect branch-ing spikes of rosy-pink flowers and *superba* with rosy-purple flowers are good hardy perennials for herbaceous or shrub borders, height, 2–4 ft.

L. Virgatum is very like *salicaria rosea;* height, 2–3 ft. All bloom from June to August.

M

MAACKIA (māăck'-i-a. Leguminosæ). Asiatic regions. Hardy, compact, deciduous tree, having pinnate leaves 8–10 in. long, with white pea-shaped flowers in July and August.

M. amuriensis (*Cladrastis amuriensis*). White flowers, in erect spike, 4–6 in. long.

M. a Buergeri (Japan). A more robust and vigorous variety.

MACKAYA (mak-a-ya. Acanthaceæ). The only species of this genus, *M. Bella*, is now referred to botanically as belonging to the order Asystasia. It is a beautiful greenhouse shrub with racemes of rosy-lilac flowers veined with purple.

Propagate by seeds or cuttings of half-ripe wood taken in summer and inserted in a close frame or under a bell-glass. Plant in light sandy loam. The flowers spring from the points of the previous season's growth, so that any pruning must be done immediately after flowering. It should be kept dry from November to April but should have plenty of water and liquid manure during the summer. Summer temperature 70°–80°; winter, 50°–60°.

MACLEANIA (mak-lā-ni-a. Vacciniaceæ). Greenhouse evergreens that are usually trained to pillars or walls.

Propagate by cuttings of the points of the shoots inserted in sandy soil under glass. Plant in loam with fibrous peat and sand. Winter temperature 40°–48°.

SPECIES.

M. pulchra. Yellow and scarlet flowers in spring. 10–12 in.

M. longiflora. Red flowers in May.

M. speciosissima. Scarlet and yellow flowers in spring. Good basket plant.

MACLURA (mak-lū'-ra. Urticaceæ). Osage Orange (U.S.A.), 40 ft. Hardy, deciduous tree, having thorns 1 in. in length, with inconspicuous flowers, followed by inedible orange-like fruit of a yellowish-golden colour. Trees of both sexes should be planted.

Culture.—Plant in ordinary soil. *Propagate* by seeds when obtainable, or by root cuttings and layers.

SPECIES.

M. aurantiaca. Male.

M. a. inermis. Female.

MACROZAMIA (mak-ro-za-mi-a. Cyadaceæ). Handsome foliage plants with long thick leaves that rise from a thick trunk. The male and female flowers resemble scaly cones. The leathery, shiny leaves last a long time. They may be grown at the cool end of the stove or in an intermediate house.

Propagate by suckers, which are sometimes formed, or by seeds which are rare. Trunks are imported and these soon establish themselves in a stove. A suitable soil is made up of lumpy loam with plenty of sand. They require a fair supply of water all the year with good drainage. Scale is liable to attack them and this must be kept down with frequent sponging.

SPECIES.

M. Fraseri. Pendulous leaves.

M. Hopei. Very beautiful.

M. perowskiana, spiralis, plumosa and *tenuifolia*, with twisted leaves.

MADEIRA VINE. *See* BOUSSIN-GAULTIA.

MADIA (ma-di-a. Compositæ). Hardy annuals allied to Sphenogyne. Sow in heat in March or outdoors in April. Plant in any garden soil, preferably in a shady place where the sun cannot give them a rusty appearance.

SPECIES.

M. corymbosa with white flowers in September.

M. elegans, yellow flowers. August. 1½ ft.

M. sativa. Yellow. July. 1 ft.

MADONNA LILY. *See* LILIES.

MADWORT. *See* ALYSSUM.

MAGNOLIA (mag-nō'-li-a. Magnoliaceæ). Deciduous and evergreen shrubs and trees, with magnificent foliage, and flowers produced in succession from March to June, and occasionally in the autumn. Perhaps no trees or shrubs give to a garden such distinction as a collection of magnolias.

Culture.—Magnolias are of easy cultivation if moved at the right time. They should never be moved while dormant, as the thick fleshy roots are apt to decay if disturbed and damaged while the trees are at rest. Spring is the most suitable time for transplanting, when the leaf buds are moving, but before they actually unfold. This may be about April, according to climatic conditions. The soil should be deep and of a good loamy nature. If the soil is shallow and poor, capacious holes should be dug to a depth of 18 in. at least, and 3 yds. in diameter, and filled with fibrous loam, and if possible

MAGNOLIA
SOULANGIANA

The flesh-pink flowered Magnolia is a tree which increases in beauty from year to year.

peat or leaf-mould. The more delicate-rooted species such as *M. parviflora* and *M. stellata* should certainly have a proportion of peat mixed with the soil. The magnolia likes a fairly sheltered position, with protection from the early morning sun. *Propagation* is by seeds, layering and grafting. The seeds should be sown singly in small pots, under glass, and as soon after gathering as possible, as they do not retain their vitality for long after they are ripe. Layering is satisfactory, but grafting should not be practised unless necessary. It should be the last resource.

SPECIES.

M. conspicua (*denudata*), Chinese Yulan

or Lily tree, 30 ft. Flowers pure white and fragrant.

M. Delavayi (China). Evergreen. A magnificent species, with grand foliage, with leaves up to 14 in. long and 8 in. wide. Flowers creamy-white and fragrant and about 8 in. across.

M. grandiflora, Laurel Magnolia, 40–80 ft. Evergreen, and perfectly hardy, although often grown against walls. A noble magnolia with huge glossy leaves up to 14 in long, and spicily fragrant, creamy-white flowers nearly 1 ft. across.

M. Lennei. A beautiful occidental hybrid magnolia, thought to be *M. conspicua* + *M. obovata*, var. *purpurea*. Leaves 8 in. by 5 in. Flowers of a beautiful rich rose-purple outside, and with white interior, produced from late April, lasting through May, and occasionally again in the autumn.

M. parviflora (Japan and Korea), 7–15 ft. A very beautiful species with drooping fragrant flowers, 4 in. across, produced intermittently from May to September.

M. soulangiana. A very fine and hardy hybrid (*M. conspicua* + *M. obovata*). Flowers white, stained purple, from April to June.

M. stellata (*Halleana*). Japan, 10–15 ft. Flowers fragrant, pure white changing to pink, hiding the bare branches in March and April. Young bark very aromatic.

MAGPIE OR CURRANT AND GOOSEBERRY MOTH (*Abraxas grossulariata*). DESCRIPTION. *Adult.*—The full-grown moth is about 2 in. in expanse; white in colour but freely speckled and blotched with black. The amount of black varies considerably, but there is always a yellowish to orange transverse stripe near the apex of the upper wing. *Caterpillars.*—About 1½ in. in length and of the same colouring as the moth, namely, white with a row of black spots down the back and two rows of smaller spots on each side, divided by an orange line. *Pupa.*—Black in colour with yellow rings on the abdomen, suspended in a light hammock-like web.

LIFE-HISTORY.—The moths hatch out at the end of June, and may be seen on calm evenings fluttering about their haunts. Eggs are laid on the undersides of the leaves in July and August. The young caterpillars on hatching out feed for a short time and then go into hibernation. In the spring they come out and at once attack the leaves, often doing considerable injury. They pupate at the end of May or the beginning of June.

METHODS OF CONTROL.—Derris washes have given good results, and are safer to use than arsenate of lead. Much good may be done by hand-picking when the larvæ appear in the spring.

MAHALEB. *See* PRUNUS MAHALEB.

MAHARAJAH PALM. *See* BACTRIS.

MAHONIA. *See* BERBERIS.

MAIANTHEMUM (ma-yăn-the-mum or mi-an-the-mum. Liliaceæ). Twin-leaved Lily-of-the-Valley. Only one species of this genus is grown, *M. convallaria* (syn. *C. bifolia*, *Smilacina bifolia* and *S. canadensis*). A pretty little plant with white flowers in June; useful for carpeting the rock garden; likes a fertile soil in a shady position. *Propagate* by division in April or September.

MAIDENHAIR FERN. *See* ADIANTUM.

MAIDENHAIR TREE. *See* GINKGO.

MAINTENANCE OF PONDS. *See* PONDS FOR FISH AND PLANTS.

MAIRIA (mā-ri-a. Compositæ). Herbaceous perennials requiring winter protection. *Propagated* by seeds and division and grown in any fertile soil.

SPECIES.

M. crenata with lilac-blue flowers in April; *taxifolia* with yellow flowers in June, 12 in.

MAIZE. *See* ZEA.

MALABAILA (ma-la-bā-la. Umbelliferæ). Hardy perennials with yellow flowers. *Propagated* by division or by seeds in spring and grown in any fertile soil.

SPECIES.

M. opopanax and *pimpinellæfolia*, both June and July flowering; 2–4 ft.

MALCOMIA (mal-co-mia. Cruciferæ). Virginian Stock, 6 in. *M. maritima* (red) and *M. m. Crimson King* are worth growing as separate colours, but for general purposes a mixture of *M. m.* hybrids is to be preferred. The seed is cheap, and the most common mistake is to sow far too thickly, and in consequence the plants grow spindly and are soon over. Sow very thinly and thin out to 3 in. apart for best results. May be sown at any time from March to August. A good edging plant for town gardens.

MALLOW. *See* LAVATERA *and* MALVA.

MALOPE (mal-o-pe. Malvaceæ). Mallow. Showy annuals with large, wide, open flowers in crimson, ruby, white and rose, somewhat similar to the Lavateras in general habit, and requiring the same

MAGNOLIA STELLATA (HALLEANA)

A white-star-flowered Magnolia, vaulable because it blooms in early spring before the leaves appear. It only makes a small tree.

treatment. For general garden purposes the Lavateras are superior.

MALUS. *See* PYRUS MALUS.

MALVA (māl-va. Malvaceæ). Mallow. Weedy-looking hardy annuals and perennials of which some are useful for wild gardens and a few for borders.

Culture.—The perennials are propagated by root division in spring or autumn or by seed. The annuals are raised from seed sown in gentle heat in March, the seedlings being potted singly in rich light soil and hardened off gradually before being planted out in June. Give them water in dry weather. Easily cultivated.

SPECIES.

M. crispa, an annual, is grown for its foliage rather than its white or purple flowers; height, 2–3 ft.

M. moschata, the Musk Mallow, together with its white variety, is the prettiest with rosy-pink flowers from June; 2–3 ft.

M. sylvestris, with pink and violet flowers, is only suitable for the wild garden, but medicinally it is of use for its soothing qualities.

MALVASTRUM (mal-vas-trum. Malvaceæ). From *malva*, a mallow; *astra*,

MALLOW

The Musk Mallow is a hardy perennial about two feet in height with rose flowers. It thrives in most soils.

a star. A genus closely allied to Malva, consisting of greenhouse and perennial herbs which are too weedy to be of great value. Dwarf species are suitable for rough places in the rock garden.

There are a number of these, but the one most likely to give satisfaction (the others being inclined to weediness) is *M. coccineum*, a trailing plant best placed when hanging over a high declivity. At its best it forms a large trailing mass of small bluish-grey divided leaves, their axils spangled with small mallow flowers of rich orange-scarlet. It must have full sun and good drainage. N.W. America.

July. (The family is now included in *Sphæralcea.*) *Propagate* by cuttings.

Culture.—The perennials require the same treatment as Mallows. The free-flowering evergreens are increased by cuttings placed in sandy soil under a bell-glass or frame and reared in the greenhouse in fibrous loam with peat and a little sand

SPECIES.

M. asperrimum with red flowers and tridactylites with pink flowers in July and August are greenhouse varieties; height, 3 ft.; *coccineum* with red flowers and *lateritium* with numerous salmon-pink flowers are quite good border or rockery plants, height, 6–9 in.

MAMILLARIA. *See* CACTUS.

MANAGEMENT OF THE GREENHOUSE. To obtain a supply of flowering and choice foliage plants through the dreary dull days of winter, it is not necessary to have a long range of greenhouses or large and imposing structures. A quite small house will give endless enjoyment to the enthusiastic gardener and a supply of plants for the home.

The reason so many people fail with their greenhouses is not so much that they cannot grow plants, but that they try to grow too many and do not study sufficiently the requirements of individual plants, and in consequence have a medley of plants growing together needing different treatment, often overcrowded, and doomed from the start. It is much better to get the advice of a good nurseryman and allow him to choose a number of suitable plants and only sufficient to allow each ample room to develop fully. The greatest difficulty encountered by the majority of people is the use of ventilation and keeping the correct atmospheric conditions. Once these two important things are mastered, the management of the house is greatly simplified.

Ventilation.—To give ventilation during spring, summer, autumn and the sunny days in the winter is absolutely necessary. All plants, like human beings, to keep healthy and vigorous require their full share of fresh air. For this purpose hinged lights are arranged at the top and sides of the house that may be opened and shut, according to the amount of

1. Nemesis—multi-coloured flowers for bedding and greenhouse. About 1 ft. high.
2. Phlox Drummondii—useful in new rock gardens for quick display, and for bedding.
3. Zinnias—brilliant flowers for summer bedding. Unusual and pleasing form.

1. Helianthus—Sunflowers, give a late summer display.
2. Jacobæa—this double variety is excellent for cutting.
3. Verbena—brilliant colours, suitable for summer bedding.

entilation needed and the prevailing
weather conditions. Never open top and
ide ventilators together except during
he very hot days of summer, as the cold
ir entering by the side will meet the cold
ir entering at the top and will be forced
own on to the plants, perhaps causing
rreparable damage. Again, the lights
hould never be opened up against the
wind, or the plants on the shelves will
uffer and perhaps be blown down, not
nly getting broken themselves but
ausing damage to any others that may
e underneath them. The closing down
f the ventilators at night must depend
ntirely upon the season of the year.
n the summer they may be left open or
artly open, but at other times it is a
ood rule to close them an hour or two
efore sunset, so that the heat generated
rom the sun may be conserved, and help
o keep up the temperature through the
ight.

Atmospheric conditions.—The cause of
o many failures can generally be traced
o bad atmospheric conditions. All
lants require a certain amount of
moisture in the air, but this does not
nean that they must all be syringed
verhead daily, or be drenched with water
underneath. If all specimens requiring
imilar treatment are grown together in
he one house the amount of moisture
equired can easily be regulated. It may
be found necessary to damp the staging
as well as the floor of the house during
the summer, but in the winter it will
generally be found that the air is sufficiently charged with moisture for the
plants' requirements. It is useless trying
to grow plants that need the cool, fairly
dry atmosphere of the mountain, with
cacti that require a dry hot atmosphere,
or with tropical species that thrive in
dense humid conditions. Remember that
excessive moisture in the winter will
encourage the attacks of fungous diseases
and mildew, while extreme dryness in
the summer provides the happy hunting-
ground for all insect pests.

Temperature.—Sudden changes in the
temperature are very harmful. It can
be regulated by the use of the ventilators,
gradually opening them in the morning
a little at a time until the sun has reached

its height, then reversing the process and
closing them down by stages until they
are finally shut. Every care must be
taken to keep the night temperature
correct in the winter: remember it only
needs one frost to completely spoil a
house of valuable plants. The winter
night-temperatures of the various houses
are given here, and must not be allowed
to fall below the lower figures. Stove,

MAMILLARIA

One of the most dainty of the cacti family is
Mamillaria. The delicate blooms appear
amidst the spines.

55°–65°; warm house, 50°–60°; cool house,
45°–50°. A great deal may be done in
the unheated house by covering the plants
at night with sheets of brown paper.

Watering.—There is a golden rule—
never water a plant unless it needs it—
and this rule must be strictly adhered to.
So many people fail to do this, and get
into the habit of watering just for the
sake of using the watering-can. A good
method by which to tell when a plant
needs water, is to tap the pots with a
stick. Those requiring water will give
out a hollow bell-like sound, but those
that are wet enough will sound heavy and
dull. By over-watering a plant the soil
becomes sodden, soon it is sour, the
roots will then refuse to function and
the plant will die. On the other hand
the soil must not be allowed to become
dust-dry, or it will shrink away from the
sides of the pot. Once this has happened
it is very difficult to get it well watered
again. Plants will need most water in

P

the spring and summer as they are then in full growth and a lot will be lost in evaporation. But during the winter very little will be required. Most of the plants are then in a dormant condition, only needing sufficient moisture to keep them just alive.

The Cold and Alpine House.

Few gardeners really make the best use of the unheated greenhouse, thinking that it is only fit for a few flowers or tomatoes during the summer months. If the right selection of plants is made it is quite possible to have a pleasing show almost all the year round. Alpines alone provide unlimited scope, as the beautiful silvery-grey and green foliage of the Saxifraga and Sedums, and the richly-scented Thymus, make them welcome through the dull days of winter for their decorative value, while in the early spring come their delightful little star-like flowers as a kind of herald that a new season has really commenced.

Arrangement.—These alpines can be grown in well-drained pots and pans, or a miniature rockery may be constructed on the greenhouse staging, where the plants could be arranged with pleasing effect, especially if a dwarf conifer, like *Retinospora pisifera aurea*, be used in conjunction to give it a more natural appearance.

MANDEVILLA (man-de-vil'-la. Apocynaceæ). Argentine. Half-hardy, elegant climbing shrubs, with large fragrant pure white flowers in clusters during the summer. Thriving in peat or leaf-mould and loam, in full sun.

Greenhouse Culture.—Compost: loam and peat equal parts with a liberal supply of sand and charcoal. Should be planted out in February at foot of pillars or trained up trellis. Sunny position. Prune hard back to base of shoots directly after flowering. Winter temperature, 40°; summer, 60°.

Propagate by cuttings of well-ripened shoots during the summer. Insert them in sandy soil in propagator, temperature, 70°.

SPECIES.

M. suaveolens, white fragrant flowers. The only species grown in the open in this country.

MANDRAGORA (man-drag-or-a Solanaceæ). Mandrake. From *mandra*, a ox-stall, and *agauros*, cruel, alluding to the poisonous effects on cattle when given them by accident with their food. The has always been credited with variou legendary qualities, amongst others th the roots resembled the human form an cried out when being pulled from th ground. The roots are still sold as cure for certain ills.

The plants are hardy herbaceous pe ennials that may be increased by seeds c by division, and grow in any rich, fairl light soil in a rather shady position.

SPECIES.

M. autumnalis. Bluish-purple flower in September. Supposed to be th mandrake of the Old Testament.

M. officinarum, the common mandrak sometimes known as Devil's Apples Blue or white flowers in May.

MANETTIA (ma-net-ti-a. Rubiaceæ) Stove evergreen shrubby and herbaceou climbers allied to Bouvardia. The flower are very showy and some of the specie make good pillar plants while others loo well trained to wire balloons.

Propagate by cuttings of young shoot taken in spring and struck in sand in hea or by division of the fleshy roots. Late pot on in a mixture of peat and loam wit a little sand. They flower best when little pot-bound, so that rapid potting o is not advisable.

Winter temperature, 45°–50°; summer 60°–85°.

SPECIES.

M. coccinea. Scarlet. June.

M. cordifolia. Showy scarlet flower from August to November.

M. luteo-rubra (syn. *bicolor*). Scarle and yellow flowers from February to June and when planted in a border in the stov will flower practically all the year.

MANURE, FARMYARD. This manure is perhaps the most important of the raw materials used in the garden. It is a com plete plant food containing nitrogen phosphoric acid and potash. Many gardeners imagine it to be the cheapes of all plant foods, but this is certainly no the case. Unless it is made with care an the animals producing it are fed on rich foods, its direct fertilising value is small.

Undoubtedly the greatest advantage obtained from dunging land is that organic matter or humus is thus added to the soil. A stiff soil is rendered easier to work and a light soil more retentive of moisture. This makes it warmer and more friable and greatly assists the working of those minute organisms called bacteria which are responsible for many of the chemical changes which result in crop improvement.

Too much farmyard manure, however, sours the soil, the effect produced being analogous to that produced by the excess of humus in bogs and on moors.

The best way to use well-made rich farmyard manure is to follow the procedure of the forester when thinning. "Early, lightly and often" is a golden rule. Crops grown with heavy dressings of dung alone seldom reach their maximum productivity. Farmyard and stable manure should be used carefully, the gardener applying supplementary dressings of nitrogen, phosphates and potash where he thinks they will do most good.

Farmyard manure should always be stored carefully and not left exposed to rains. The following data illustrate the need for this. In three months, the total loss of nitrogen from a quantity of manure stored in a compost heap under cover was 4 per cent. only. During the same period the loss from manure stored loose under cover was 7 per cent.; from manure stored loose in the open the loss was 43 per cent. All manure heaps should therefore be stored dry, and covered with a layer of soil.

MANURE, LIQUID. This is more beneficial than dry manure when a quick result is required, and its application is advisable when plants are about to flower or are flowering and when trees are fruiting and vegetables are in pod. The times when it should be used and the kinds of plants, etc., will be found under the individual subjects.

The best materials are the following: Nitrate of soda or sulphate of ammonia, 1 oz. to 3 or 4 gal. of water; guano used in the same manner is of great value for pot plants.

Sheep manure soaked in water.

Liquid from stables and cow-houses, which should be collected in a large tank and for pot plants, fruits and borders or the rose garden should be diluted to the colour of weak tea, while for fruit trees, etc., it may be used much stronger.

Soot water, prepared by soaking 1 lb. of soot to 3 gal. of water.

One of the most fertile of manures is made from cow-dung, of which ½ bushel should be put in 20 gal. of water, allowing it to stand for a day, after which the manure can be drawn off and a second 20 gal. of water poured on after the residue has been well stirred. In a small garden where this is not obtainable, house slops can be used, well diluted for crops and stronger for fruit trees.

Perhaps the best and most effective way to make liquid manure is to suspend a bag in a barrel of rain water. Put farmyard manure, poultry droppings, and soot in the bag, as obtainable. The liquid should always be used in dilute form, usually a pale straw colour; never used when the soil is dry. During drought, soak the soil well before applying any liquid fertiliser. Remember the golden rule, "Never feed a sickly plant," that is to say, do not give fertilisers until the plant roots are established, and the plant is in normal health.

MANURE, POULTRY. The droppings from a chicken farm are valuable manure. They double in value by being allowed to dry in the air, and if then stored in sacks, or boxes, will be found to be about three times as rich as farmyard manure. Do not use more than 1½ lb. per square yard, and never let it come into actual contact with seeds or seedlings. Pigeon manure is even richer than ordinary poultry manure, and may be used at half the rate.

MANURES, MIXING. In using special fertilisers, the amateur gardener should beware of mixing them unless quite certain of the result. Basic slag should never be mixed with superphosphate of lime; neither should nitrate of soda be mixed with other chemicals. As a general rule, it will be found better to apply each fertiliser separately at different seasons, and mixing should only be done in accordance with definite instructions.

See FERTILISERS.

MANZANITA. *See* ARCTOSTAPHYLOS.

MAPLE. *See* ACER.

MARANTA (ma-ran-ta. Scitamin-aceæ). Arrow-root. Stove herbaceous perennials, with beautifully marked and coloured foliage. Guiana, 1803.

Culture.—Compost: 2 parts loam, 1 part leaf-mould and sand. Repot early spring, and give good drainage. Shady position. Water freely during summer months and syringe daily. Little water required in

MAPLE
LEAF & FLOWER

The Maples are a useful group of trees, some of which have scarlet and golden foliage.

the winter. Winter temperature, 55°; summer, 95°.

Propagate by division when repotting, place divisions in propagator, temperature, 70°.

SPECIES.

M. abundinaceæ variegata, leaves green and white; *M. bicolor makoyana*, leaves green, blotched darker green; *M. Chantieri*, leaves grey and dark green.

MARATTIA (ma-ra-ti-a. Filices). Handsome large ferns from the tropics that are found growing in such a humid atmosphere that they require to be treated as sub-aquatics in a moist stove. The pots should be stood in water or they will suffer from drought in warm weather. It is only possible to grow them in a very large house where they can have plenty of overhead room. Apart from their decorative value the genus is useful, as the crowns are cooked and eaten in the West Indies and Brazil. The best means of

increasing is to take off the fleshy scale at the base of frond stems and to plac them in sphagnum in heat. The scale soon form roots and side growths lik bulbs which eventually produce plants For planting use a compost of 3 parts o loam to 1 of cow manure with some roa grit, which should be mixed together fc some months before use. The plant should never be allowed to want for water but when they have become dejecte through lack of it, a thorough soaking an a few hours in the shade will put then right, although if allowed to become dr more than once they are unlikely t recover. During the summer they shoul have liquid manure and soot water, bu during the winter they need no stimulants The chief enemies are scale bug, which ca be kept down by sponging, and thrips which have to be fumigated.

SPECIES.

M. alata. Fronds 4–6 ft.

M. Ascensionis.

M. attenuata. Fronds 3–5 ft.

M. cicutæfolia.

M. fraxinea. Fronds 6–15 ft. Ha several varieties, including *purpurascen* and *elegans.* The latter will do well in cool house.

M. kaulfussii. Quadripinnate fronds 3–4 ft.

MARBLE. Technically speaking marble is only a hard and handsom variety of limestone, and is quarried among the limestone hills. Several really fine marbles are found in Great Britain especially in Devonshire, Derbyshire and Durham.

MARCH WORK IN THE GARDEN.

THE FLOWER GARDEN.

All herbaceous perennials should b planted at once.

Finish rose planting.

Prune, train and tie up climbers.

Sow hardy annuals such as Clarkias Larkspurs, Malope, Mignonette, Nigella Californian poppy, etc., during mild weather.

Sow Sweet Peas outdoors.

Plant hardy flowers such as Carnations Pinks, Gladioli, etc.

Transplant Pansies, Violas and Snap dragons into their flowering quarters.

Violas are effective as a carpet under dwarf Roses. Plant 6 in. apart.

Stir the soil amongst Wallflowers, Forget-me-nots, Bulbs and other spring flowers.

Remember to sow flowers for cutting. These will be valued later on.

On a warm south border, Roses may be pruned during March. In most districts, the last week is the safest time. Prune strong-growing kinds lightly and weak ones more severely.

Leave Tea Roses until the first week in April, as they are more tender than the hybrid perpetuals, and new growths are therefore more likely to be damaged by frosts.

After flowering, bulbs in bowls will still need some water. It is best to take them from the bowls, remove faded blooms, and plant in an odd corner of the garden to ripen.

THE ROCK GARDEN.

New rock gardens must be planted without delay.

Plant as soon as possible, Saponaria, Californian poppies, Gilia diathoides (rock pink), Campanulas, Gentians, Iberis lithospermum, Dianthus, Thymes and Veronicas. Primulas raised under glass can be planted out now on the rockery. Choose sites according to the habit of each variety. Some prefer partial shade, some like full sun. Some must have moist conditions and should be planted at the foot of the rockery, or where water forms pools.

Anemones are fine subjects for the rock garden, but should be chosen according to the soil.

Beware of slugs among the young shoots of rock plants. A zinc collar placed round each plant will be most effective, and this can also be surrounded by soot, lime, sifted coal ash, or finely broken granite as an extra precaution. Traps, and applications of slug-killer (*See* SLUGS) should also be used with discretion.

THE SHRUBBERY.

Look over all evergreen shrubs and cut out dead wood. Where necessary use the pruning knife to restore symmetry to the bushes.

Plant new evergreens while the weather is still showery.

Ferns for the edge of shrubberies may be planted this month.

Rhododendrons get old and straggly in time. Cut such plants back severely now.

Look out for suckers of the original stock and remove them entirely or they will soon outgrow the grafted variety. If new plants are being ordered, ask for them on their own roots wherever possible.

One season's flowering is lost by pruning

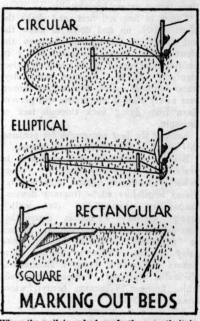

MARKING OUT BEDS

When the soil is raked perfectly smooth it is easy to mark out flower beds by means of pegs and a piece of string.

Rhododendrons, and only very overgrown plants should be cut back.

Azaleas should receive the same treatment.

Lilies of various kinds will grow between shrubs such as Azaleas. Some can still be purchased for outdoor planting including: *Lilium auratum, L. Davidii, L. Henryi, L. longiflorum giganteum, L. regale, L. speciosum* (white or red), *L. tenuifolium, L. thunbergianum, L. tigrinum*

Thumb and finger prune young flowering trees, i.e., rub off undesirable buds before they develop. If old wood is cut, gumming often results.

Prune the following shrubs, where necessary :

Clematis, Hedera (ivy), Lavender, Rhododendron, Salix, Rose species.

Plant evergreens. Make a deep hole larger than is apparently necessary for the roots. Break up the subsoil. If the soil is poor, add a quantity of animal manure or other humus, and also a double handful of bonemeal. Spread the roots out to their fullest extent horizontally.

Throw in fine soil first, and shake the plant gently, up and down to allow the soil to fill in the crevices between the plant roots. Tread the plant firmly in position and stake it immediately after planting. If the weather turns dry, water overhead daily. Wet tiffany thrown over newly planted evergreens will prevent them from dying back through lack of moisture.

Some of the best evergreens for planting this month in the ordinary garden are:

Berberis stenophylla, yellow flowers in profusion ; Berberis darwinii, orange flowers ; Ceanothus rigidus, blue flowers ; Cistus laurifolius white fragrant flowers ; Cotoneaster angustifolius (for walls), orange berries ; Escallonia macrantha, rosy-red flowers ; Laurustinus, flowers in midwinter ; Olearia haastii, white daisy flowers, Phillyrea decora, white flowers and purple berries ; Rosmarinus officinalis, rosemary ; Veronica traverssii, white flowers ; Viburnum henryi, white flowers, red fruit.

Fruit.

Any unplanted fruit trees should be put in their permanent positions at once.

Protect apricots and peaches on walls by the use of netting. This keeps several degrees of frost from damaging the blooms.

Grafting is done this month. An expert should generally be called in to do this, but amateurs may like to experiment with one or two trees, and full instructions for those who wish to try their hand will be found elsewhere in these pages.

Make new strawberry plantations.

Limewash fruit trees before the blossoms open, to keep down pests such as green fly.

As soon as the warm days come, look out for weed seedlings, and hoe between the fruit trees to destroy them.

Hoeing also makes the soil sweeter, allows air to penetrate to the plant roots, and brings soil pests to the surface to be eaten by birds.

Gooseberries and currants sprayed with paraffin emulsion are immune to attacks of red spider and brown scale.

Cut back autumn-fruiting raspberries to within an inch of the ground and give a top dressing of well-decayed manure.

Summer-fruiting raspberries need tying to supports.

Prune back trees planted last autumn.

Stake all standard and half-standard trees.

Vegetables.

Most of the main crop vegetables are sown this month.

When the weather is suitable sow broad beans, broccoli, cauliflower, cabbage, and brussels sprouts in lines or boxes for transplanting later.

Sow carrots, leeks, parsnips, spinach, swede, garden turnips and early potatoes.

Sow mustard and cress, lettuce, radishes and onions for salads.

Sow pickling onions.

A hotbed is useful for early tender vegetables. To make it, use a heap of manure. Pile it up, stand a frame over it and add a depth of a foot of light rich soil. Wait a few days before sowing seeds to allow excess heat to escape. Sow the seeds in boxes and stand them over the heap, lodged on bricks.

Salads and the tender vegetables, broccoli, cauliflower, celery, cucumber, and also tomatoes and alpine strawberries can be sown on such a hotbed.

Make a new bed for globe artichokes.

Sow seeds of parsnips, kohl rabi, marrowfat peas, spinach and turnip, where they are to grow.

Watercress does not need running water. Seeds can be sown now in moist trenches.

Potatoes should be planted now, or early next month.

Divide and replant chives.

Under Glass.

Clear away bulbs that have been forced. They can be planted in the borders, and will flower again after two years. A useful place for them is in the wild garden.

Plant out pansies and violas from frames.

Start begonias by placing them in moist soil or fibre, in the greenhouse.

Take cuttings of chrysanthemums, and also make new plants by detaching suckers with pieces of root attached.

Sow seeds of cinerarias and primulas.

Half-ripened side shoots of Genista fragrans can be inserted as cuttings now. Keep them close until they have rooted.

Cuttings of the winter cherry (*solanum capsicastrum*) should be ready for potting up.

Dahlias should be placed in moist soil in the greenhouse to encourage shoots. These will be removed and inserted as cuttings.

The root stocks of cannas should also be encouraged to send out shoots, by watering. When growth commences pot the roots in good soil.

The greenhouse should be plentifully stocked with plants for summer bedding.

Give adequate ventilation to tomatoes, melons, cucumbers, marrows, leeks, celery and all vegetables under glass. The hardier they are kept, so long as they are not checked by frosts, the sturdier the plants will be, and the better the crops.

Sow half-hardy annuals such as asters, ten-week stocks, petunias, salpiglossis, verbena, etc. Violets from the cold frame may be transplanted into the semi-shady borders.

Thin and disbud peaches, leaving one peach to each square foot of wall space.

Hardy ferns may be raised in the greenhouse from spores (the brown dust on the back of the leaves).

Any plants that are large enough at this season can be pricked out into pans of rich, gritty soil. Ferns that have been repotted are best kept in the greenhouse until they have recovered from the shock. The dry air of a living-room is more likely to affect them when their roots have just been damaged than at any other season. It does all room plants good to be given a "greenhouse holiday" occasionally.

PESTS.

The big-bud disease of blackcurrants is easily recognised, and the affected buds (which are round instead of pointed) should be picked out and burnt. Dusting the opening buds of the blackcurrants with dust from sifted coal ashes, is a good preventative; or lime and flowers of sulphur applied in the same way whilst the insect is migrating is also effective.

Get ready an insecticide so that immediate steps may be taken when the green fly appears. Paraffin emulsion should be syringed on to the plants, being careful to spray both sides of the leaves and stems.

Two kinds of weevils attack peas occasionally at this season. One remedy is to dust the leaves of the plants with soot while they are wet. Another way to treat them is to lay tarred boards alongside the rows early in the morning, and when the sun is shining shake the plants over them. The weevils will be thrown on to the tar, where they will stick.

MARGUERITE. *See* CHRYSANTHEMUM.

MARGYRICARPUS (mär-gĭr-i-kar'-pus. Rosaceæ). Pearl Fruit (Chile). Small hardy evergreen shrub, with inconspicuous flowers, followed by small white berries of an acid flavour. Thrives in not too rich soil, in sunny position.

M. setosus. Prostrate, with finely-cut leaves. Thrives very well in East Anglia.

MARICA (mar-i-ka. Irideæ). Tender bulbous plants that rather resemble Irises, with flowers that only last for a day, thus giving rise to the name of the genus, which is derived from *maraino*, to flag or droop.

Easily cultivated and propagated by division of the rhizomes after flowering. The divisions may be started off in a close frame and later planted in turfy loam with leaf-mould and sand. Although requiring stove or greenhouse treatment, they do well in a rockery if planted under glass.

SPECIES.

M. brachypus. Yellow flowers striped with brown. Stove. 1½ ft.

M. cœrulea. Blue or yellow flowers barred with brown and orange. May to June. Stove. 2–3 ft.

M. Northiana. White and yellow flowers with red spots. June. Stove. 4 ft. The variety *splendens* is larger and better.

MARIGOLD. *See* CALENDULA *and* TAGETES.

MARJORAM. *See* ORIGANUM.

MARJORAM, POT (*Origanum onites*). Labiatæ. A very common perennial herb, the leaves of which are used for seasoning. It is quite hardy, and although strictly a perennial it may be treated as an annual.

Seed may be sown in spring or autumn in shallow drills along the margin of paths or borders where it will form a useful edging for years without further attention. When the growth for the year has finished cut them off close to the ground, and hang in bunches in a dry airy shed until required for use. *See* HERBS, CULINARY.

MARJORAM, SWEET (*Origanum marjorana*). Labiatæ. This again is a peren-

MARIGOLD AFRICAN

LEGION OF HONOUR

FRENCH

Three types of Marigolds. They are very showy half-hardy annuals for the summer garden.

nial herb, which is invariably grown as an annual. It originated in the East, and was brought to this country about 1573.

Sow in hollow drills 9 in. apart outside in April, and when large enough thin the seedlings to 9 in. apart in the rows. The young leaves are used for flavouring, and the mature growths are cut and stored for winter use in the same manner as Pot Marjoram. *See* HERBS, CULINARY.

MARL. Earthy deposits rich in carbonate of lime. If such a pit is in the neighbourhood, its contents should be used for all liming requirements in the garden.

Marling was a practice greatly favoured by our forefathers and their habit largely explains their success under the handicaps provided by the age in which they lived.

MARROW. *See* VEGETABLE MARROW.

MARRUBIUM (mar-ru-bi-um. Labiatæ). Of the thirty odd species in this genus only one, *M. vulgare*, Horehound, is useful. Hardy herbaceous perennials, with white or pinkish flowers. Thrive in any soil and increased by seeds, or cuttings.

MARSH MALLOW. *See* MALVA.

MARSH MARIGOLD. *See* CALTHA.

MARTYNIA (mar-tin-ea. Pedalineæ). *M. fragrans*, a native of Mexico, is a unique and handsome half-hardy annual for the mixed border. The flowers, crimson-purple in colour, with red or orange markings in the throat, resemble those of the Foxglove, and are freely produced on long spikes in summer and autumn. Sow in a warm greenhouse in March, plant into well-drained soil in a sunny position in June.

MARVEL OF PERU. *See* MIRABILIS.

MASDEVALLIA (mas-de-val-li-a. Orchidaceæ). Named after Dr. Masdevall, a Spanish botanist. Greenhouse evergreen orchids. A genus remarkable for its diversity of form and colour in flowers. The structure of the flowers differs from that of most of the other genera in which the lip is developed at the expense of the other segments, for in Masdevallia the sepals are the most developed and the richest coloured parts of the flower. This is probably the easiest genus to grow, and thrives in a cool house. Brazil, 1835.

Culture.—Compost: equal parts sphagnum moss and peat, with a liberal supply of broken crocks and several larger pieces of charcoal. Repot January and February when new growth commences. Give water freely during the growing season. During the winter little will be wanted, but plants should never be allowed to become quite dry at the roots. Syringe daily during the summer and shade from hot sunshine. Winter temperature, 45°; summer, 65°.

Progagate by division when repotting.

SPECIES.

M. amabilis, rose, crimson, and yellow; *coccinea*, scarlet, and its varieties *Hardyana* and *alba*.

M. chimæra, yellow and purple, and its varieties *Mooreana*, *Roezlii* and *Wallisii*.

M. tovarensis, white.

M. veitchiana, vermilion.

There are several hybrids, for which a good catalogue should be consulted.

MASTERWORT. *See* ASTRANTIA.

MATRICARIA (mat-ri-kar-i-a. Compositæ). A large genus of annual and perennial herbs, mostly weeds and scarcely worth cultivating. Some of the plants sold as Matricarias are really Pyrethrums, but the double form of *inodora*, *i. plenissima*, is grown. Easily raised from seed and the perennials by division. Grow in any garden soil.

SPECIES.

M. inodora, the Scentless Mayweed, with white flowers from June onwards, seeds so freely that it easily becomes a nuisance.

M. i. discoidea has fragrant leaves.

M. i. plenissima, the double white May Weed, summer flowering, 1 ft. *Propagate* by cuttings, and division of roots.

MATTHIOLA (ma-ti-ol-a. Cruciferæ). *M annua*. Stocks, Ten-week. Half-hardy annual. Brompton, East Lothian, half-hardy biennials. Intermediates, half-hardy annuals or biennials, South Europe. The annual kinds, and also the intermediates, if to be treated as half-hardy annuals, should be sown towards the end of March in cool greenhouse and planted out in May, or they may be sown out of doors in a prepared seed bed at the end of April, for planting into flowering quarters as soon as large enough. They like a sunny position, and soils rich in organic matter should have a dressing of lime—4 oz. per yard—applied in March. The kinds most preferred are those bearing double flowers, and it will be noted that the plants with double flowers do not produce seeds; the seeds are saved from the plants bearing single blooms, and such seeds will give a good percentage of doubles. In this connection it may be mentioned that Ten-week Stocks, of a good strain, will give 85 per cent. of doubles; Intermediates or Beauty of Nice types, 75-80 per cent.; Bromptons, 70-75 per cent.; East Lothians, 60-65 per cent. The Intermediate or Beauty of Nice types are fine for pot culture to flower under

glass in April and May, and when this flowering is over, if planted in good soil in the open garden, will soon break into fresh growth and flower again from July to autumn. Sow in June or July in cold frame, pot off singly as soon as 4-5 leaves are formed, and into flowering pots, 4½-5 in. size, in October. Grow as cool as possible; merely excluding frost is sufficient. Give free ventilation and do not over water.

A grower's tip: When pricking out seedling Stocks, discard those which have a thick tap root, as they are usually singles. The doubles commence to make fibrous roots earlier than the singles.

M. Bicornis, the Night-scented stock, 1 ft., is a native of Greece, and only resembles the Stock family in the shape of its flowers, which are of a purple colour, and remain closed during the day-time. It is a very desirable annual for sowing in moist soil in out-of-the-way places, and gives off a delightful perfume at night.

MAXILLARIA (max-il-lar-ia. Orchidaceæ). Stove terrestrial Orchids. A genus very closely allied to Lycaste. Mexico, 1825.

Culture.—Compost. Equal parts sphagnum moss and peat. Re-pot when growth commences, etc. Good drainage and care in the use of the water-can is most essential as they resent being too wet at the roots. Winter temperature, 50°; summer, 65°.

Propagate by division after flowering.

SPECIES.

M. meleagris, yellow and brown.

M. grandiflora, white and yellow.

M. luteo-alba, white and yellow.

M. Sanderiana, red and white.

M. tenuifolia, yellow and purple.

M. venusta, white and yellow.

The only known hybrid in this interesting genus is *Lyoth*, sepal and petals white, lips buff-yellow, inner surface white, spotted red below.

MAY. *See* CRATÆGUS.

MAY APPLE. *See* PODOPHYLLUM.

MAYTENUS (mã-te'-nus. Celastrinæ). Chile. Hardy evergreen shrub with myrtle-like leaves and flowers of no importance.

Culture.—Plant in sandy loam. *Propagate* by cuttings under a bell-glass, or layers in autumn.

M. chilensis, 10 ft., the only species grown.

MAY WORK IN THE GARDEN.

The Flower Garden.

Early bulbs such as Hyacinths are over, and their place can be taken by summer flowers. Lift the bulbs carefully and replant them in an odd corner of the garden where they can die down naturally. They will then be fit to flower next season. Daffodils, Hyacinths and Tulips can all be treated in this way.

If preferred, Daffodils may be left undisturbed, as can Snowdrops, Crocuses, Scillas and Muscari.

Unless the ground was manured the previous autumn it should receive a dressing of well-rotted manure now, but this should be well forked in before any planting is done. Well-rotted manure is dry and crumbly and not wet and "steamy," as it is when it comes straight from the stables.

If manure is not obtainable, use 3 oz. to the sq. yd. of the following mixture: 1 lb. each of steamed bone-flour, sulphate of ammonia and sulphate of potash, with 3 lb. of superphosphate of lime. Fork this into the top soil before planting summer flowers.

Seedlings of the hardier border plants such as Sweet Alyssum, Antirrhinums, Stocks and Lavateras, should be transplanted from the cold frame.

The distance apart will depend on the height of the mature plants. Most annuals need to be at least 6 in. apart. Dwarf Nasturtiums should be left at least 8 in. to 1 ft. apart.

Some varieties of annuals which are grown for mass effect can be left unthinned. A few of these are Night-scented Stock and Virginia Stock, and Scarlet Flax, particularly if these are grown as border edgings.

Bedding plants, such as Geraniums, Calceolarias, Lobelia, etc., should be hardened by allowing as much light and air as possible in readiness for planting out at the end of the month. Gladioli may still be planted where they are to bloom.

Spring perennials like Primroses, Polyanthuses, Daisies and Aubrietia can be lifted to make way for the summer flowers. Divide up the old plants, and set in a reserved part of the garden to grow on during the summer.

Dahlias may be planted out at the end of the month if the weather is favourable. Use the new Star Dahlias such as Lemur, Prince Henry, Ada, Paisley Gem, Coltness Gem, Lady Eileen, as bedding plants for massed colour effects. Geraniums and Fuchsias can also be planted out towards the end of the month.

Sow biennials. The secret of success lies in sowing early. Sow the seeds in the open garden in drills and allow 12 in. between each drill, sowing the seeds thinly. Seeds suitable for present sowing are Canterbury Bells, Honesty, Wallflowers, Coreopsis grandiflora, Evening Primrose, Foxgloves, Mullein, Meconopsis, Acquilegia, Asters, Auriculas, Brompton Stocks, Cobæa scandens, Delphiniums, Eccremocarpus, Forget-me-nots, Gypsophila.

Stake herbaceous plants.

Prepare borders for bedding plants and bed out as weather and aspect permits.

Mulch Hollyhocks.

Plant Chrysanthemums, Stocks, Asters, etc., at the end of the month.

Spray Roses to prevent blight, and to keep down greenfly.

Plant out Abronia, Begonias, Calceolarias, and Dahlias from pots under glass.

Sow the first batch of Wallflowers in boxes.

Treat Hydrangeas coming into flower with weak doses of liquid manure. Plant out those that have been forced as soon as the weather permits.

Dust Roses affected with mildew with flowers of sulphur.

Treat wall trees with weak liquid manure, and see they are moist at the roots.

Remove superfluous buds and thin out foliage from centre of bushes and standards to admit light and air.

Sweet Peas may be sown in the open air for a succession to those raised under glass.

The Rock Garden.

As each flower fades on the rock garden, it should be cut away, unless seed is wanted, and any unsightly leaves removed. Some rock plants bear fruits which are quite as pretty as the flowers; for instance,

Dryas octopetala. The dead flowers in such cases must be left to develop.

Water-loving plants such as Mimulus and Primulas may need water this month if the weather is dry. Rare alpines can be grown successfully in pots if these are filled with small stones and grit. More protection can be given to the rare varieties if grown in this way, as they can be placed under glass for the winter months.

Seeds from rock plants should be saved, as many plants can be raised this way. Sow immediately the seed is ripe. Sow in pans of gritty soil, covering either not at all, or with the finest possible cover of sand.

Amongst the rock plants that can be raised easily from seed sown now are: Aubrietia, Silene compactus, Primulas, Campanulas (various), Yellow Alyssum, Cheiranthus, Arabis, Cerastium.

The Shrubbery.

The following shrubs are in flower now, and should be pruned as soon as the flowers fade.

Berberis, Diervilla, Forsythia, Prunus, Rhododendrons, Lilacs, Broom, Philadelphus, Ribes, Buddleia, Magnolia conspicua, Syringa.

Tie Clematis and other creepers as they grow, to prevent the growths from becoming entangled.

The Vegetable Garden.

Asparagus seedlings will now need thinning, but the work cannot be completed in one operation, as some of the seedlings may not be through the soil. At the final thinning leave the plants 1 ft. apart. Keep the permanent beds free from weeds.

A further sowing of Broad Beans may be made in the open.

The globe varieties of Beet sown in the frame last month should be thinned out to 8–10 in. apart. Sow seeds for the outdoor main crop if a sowing was not made in April. Where sowing was possible in the previous month and the seedlings have appeared, thin out the latter and hoe between the rows.

Those sown in specially prepared holes should be reduced to three plants at each station and finally to one, which should be as near the centre as possible.

Plant out the seedlings of Broccoli which were pricked out in March, in well-prepared soil. Make a further sowing in the frame.

A further plantation of Brussels Sprouts may now be made.

Seedling cabbages raised in boxes in a cold frame will now be ready for planting out on ground which has been heavily manured. Hoe frequently.

Sow Cardoons in prepared trenches as for Celery. This vegetable needs plenty of water in dry weather.

Carrots sown in January and February should be thinned as required for use. Those sown in the open in prepared "holes" should be thinned to three at first and then to one at each station. Those in drills should be thinned out to 8 in. apart.

During the first half of the month, make more sowings of Early Giant, Autumn Giant and Mammoth cauliflowers. Sow the seeds in a skeleton frame and keep the bed well watered. Give a dusting of soot occasionally.

Continue to plant out from previous sowings as the plants become ready. All established batches should be supplied liberally with liquid manure and mulched with long stable litter.

Prepare Celery trenches and transplant seedlings.

Successional sowings of Lettuce should be made, and given plenty of water. When the seeds are large enough, thin out the seedlings and make further plantations with them.

Mushroom beds may now be made in the open.

Sow Peas during the month, for August and September use.

Make successional sowings of Tomatoes. Plants in bearing should be fed liberally with liquid manure.

Make frequent sowings of Turnips and cover them with short mown grass, which is an excellent method of warding off the turnip fly.

Earth up early Potatoes.

Thin out seedlings of Parsley to 6 in. apart.

Divide and replant Mint.

Sow seeds of ornamental Gourds and Pumpkins outdoors and treat as for vegetable marrows.

Fruit.

Fruit trees grown on walls need syringing thoroughly after hot days to keep down red spider and other pests. Stone fruits such as Apricots, Peaches and Nectarines grown on walls need thinning. The number of fruits left will depend on the strength of the tree. Generally it is best to leave one fruit to each square yard of wall.

Dress strawberries with superphosphate, 2 oz. to sq. yd., and water it in.

Place clean straw between strawberry plants to keep the fruit clean. Runners not required for making young plants should be cut off.

All fruit trees on dry ground will benefit by a mulch of manure round the roots. The fruit should be thinned out to half a dozen on newly-planted trees.

Morello cherries can be disbudded.

Raspberry suckers should be thinned out. Only those which will be needed to replace the old canes should be left, unless it is desired to make new plantations.

Thin Gooseberries.

Remove grease bands from standard trees.

Attend to grafts.

Commence summer pruning.

UNDER GLASS.

Harden off all plants by slow and gradual processes.

Do nothing suddenly.

Give air daily to frames and greenhouses.

If a cold wind comes, give air on the side of the house away from the wind.

Close the ventilators sufficiently at night to keep out several degrees of frost.

Shade seedlings from scorching sunshine.

Give more water if the weather is fine, and less if it is cool and sunless.

Lift out boxes of seedlings daily on to the paths, putting them back in the frames at night, until the weather is quite settled and the seedlings are hardy.

On the first appearance of "damping-off," dust the seedlings with flowers of sulphur; give them more air and less water.

The same treatment applies to plants affected with mildew.

Pot up Chrysanthemums and perpetual-flowering Carnations.

Repot Azaleas.

Sow Cinerarias. These are among the showiest of greenhouse flowers and a small packet of seed provides many pots of bloom for house decoration.

Tomatoes for winter should be sown now.

Tomatoes in the greenhouse beginning to show fruit should be fed with weak doses of liquid manure and be top-dressed with dry fertilisers.

Harden off greenhouse shrubs ready for planting out.

Vegetable marrows may be planted out under hand-lights.

Malmaison Carnations should be layered this month.

Any vacant parts of the greenhouse should be thoroughly cleaned in readiness for the next plants. Wash with disinfectant soap, and repaint as necessary.

The temperature should remain at 45° F. by night and 65° F. by day for most half-hardy plants and shrubs.

Water must be given regularly, and a moist atmosphere maintained by means of damping the floors, syringing, etc.

Plenty of air and shade must be given where necessary.

A sharp look-out for insect pests must be kept.

Climbing and trailing plants, which are too tender for outdoor cultivation, add charm to the greenhouse. Some of these include:

Abutilon megapotamicum, Climbing asparagus, Bougainvillea, Heliotropium, Hoya, Solanum jasminoides, and S. Wendlandi, Swainsonia, Tecoma.

French Beans sown in pots last month should be planted in the cold frame, allowing them plenty of room, two rows to each 4 ft. frame, or light, being sufficient. Cauliflower (Magnum) under glass should be ready for cutting at the end of the month, and the light may be removed entirely.

Remove from the greenhouse Arum Lilies that have flowered and plant in trenches out of doors.

PESTS.

Gooseberries and Currants attacked by the Magpie moth or Gooseberry Sawfly should be sprayed with arsenate of lead, or hellebore powder should be dusted on the foliage when it is damp.

Spray Raspberries attacked by the Beetle, with arsenate of lead.

MAZUS (ma-zus. Scrophulariaceæ).

Dwarf hardy creeping perennials suitable for the rock garden or border edging.

Culture.—They thrive in well-drained soil in a sunny position and are propagated by division in spring.

SPECIES.

M. pumilio with large pale violet flowers from May to July. Will grow in sandy loam in crevices of flagged paths or rockeries; height 2 in.; *reptans* with spotted mauve flowers from June to July, 2 in.

MEADOW RUE. *See* THALICTRUM.

MEADOW SAFFRON. *See* COLCHICUM.

MEADOW SWEET. *See* SPIRÆA.

MEALY BUG (*Dactylopus longispinus*). DESCRIPTION. *Adults.*— About ⅛ in. in length, reddish in colour, but covered with a white mealy substance. The sides of the body are furnished with long spines. At times a troublesome pest in hot-houses, attacking vines and various greenhouse plants. The larvæ move about sucking the sap of the plant, which they weaken, and they also cause indirect damage by exuding a sticky substance which, adhering to the plant, collects dust and foreign matter generally, so choking up the pores and making the plant unsightly. When full grown the females lay their eggs under the woolly covering and these eggs quickly hatch, giving rise to a fresh infestation of lice. There is only a partial hibernation when they hide away in crevices and under pieces of bark, and at such times are most difficult to eradicate.

METHODS OF CONTROL.—A difficult pest to fight, but much good will be obtained by carrying out one or other of the following methods.

On Vines.

PARAFFIN JELLY WASH.—After the fruit is picked, but while the leaves are still on, thoroughly spray with a wash made as follows:

Soft soap	...	...	1 lb.
Washing Soda	...	...	2 oz.
Water	...	...	1 pint.
Paraffin	...	...	½ gal.

METHOD OF MIXING.—Make a fire, preferably well in the open, boil up the water and stir in the soap; when dissolved add in the washing soda. After this has dissolved and while still over the fire, gradually add the paraffin with care, stirring awhile. When thoroughly mixed continue to heat for about 10 minutes, still stirring; take off the fire and allow to cool until a jelly is formed. This has now to be further diluted.

Take 15 gal. of hot water and pour a little on the jelly, stirring thoroughly as it dissolves, and gradually add the remainder of the water till all traces of the jelly have disappeared. When the liquid has cooled it is ready for use and spraying should be done thoroughly. Again in the winter the house should be cleared as much as possible and thoroughly sprayed with the above wash, particular attention being paid to crevices.

Other Plants.

As it is inadvisable to spray all and sundry with the paraffin jelly wash, fumigation with nicotine or hydrocyanic acid gas should be resorted to.

MEALY PLUM APHIS. *Hyalopterus arundinis*, Fab. DESCRIPTION. *Adults.*— Both winged and wingless forms are green with darker lines and mottlings. The cornicles also are dark green and very small. The whole aphis is covered with a whitish powder. *Young.*—Yellowish-green, also covered with a whitish powder.

LIFE-HISTORY.—The winter is passed in the egg state on the trees, the eggs being placed near the buds. In the spring these hatch out and grow slowly, the resulting "mother queens" giving rise to fresh generations. In June they begin to increase rapidly and cover the underside of the leaves. Winged forms appear and they fly off, some to settle on other plums, but the majority go off to rushes and water grasses, where they remain until the autumn, when a fresh winged generation returns to the plums. It will thus be seen that whereas we may find this aphis on the plum all the year round, the majority spend part of their life on rushes and such-like plants.

METHODS OF CONTROL.—Tar distillate washes during the dormant period to destroy the eggs. In the spring a nicotine or derris-containing wash will kill the early stages, but such washes must be applied with some force and before much "meal" has been found.

MECONOPSIS (mec-on-op-sis. Papaveraceæ). Himalayan Poppy. Hardy herbaceous annuals, biennials and perennials with showy flowers like poppies.

Culture.—They are easily cultivated in any good garden soil although they prefer a light rich gritty one in a sunny or half-shaded position. The annuals and biennials are propagated by seeds and the perennials by division of the roots in March or by seeds sown in a frame in the same month. All species are benefited by

MECONOPSIS
BAILEYI

A newcomer from Tibet, Meconopsis Baileyi, enjoys a moist shady corner in the garden.

occasional doses of liquid manure during the flowering season, which sometimes is not until three years after planting.

SPECIES.

M. cambrica, the Welsh Poppy, is the only really perennial species, with graceful leaves and yellow flowers from May to September. Is a good border and rock plant, but seeds so profusely that it will overcrowd other plants. Its double variety is better because it lacks this profusion of seeds.

M. aculeata with bright green leaves covered with silvery hairs and blue flowers.

M. nepalensis, the Nepal Poppy, with

purple flowers in autumn, *M. paniculata* with yellow flowers, and "Wallichii" the Satin Poppy-wort, with attractive blue flowers, are best in borders and, like the rock plants, are biennials. All bloom from June to August and are 2–5 ft. in height. The best of all recent introductions is *M. betonicifolia*, or *Baileyi* Bailey's variety, the flowers of which are a glorious Cambridge blue, with golden stamens in the centre. This is a splendid plant for the shady border.

M. racemosa, similar to *aculeata* but with leaves arranged in rosettes.

M. simplicifolia with solitary blue flowers is suitable for rock gardens.

MEDICAGO (med-i-ka-go. Leguminosæ). A large but unimportant genus. Increased by seed sown at any time in spring.

SPECIES.

M. arborea has a woody stem and yellow flowers from May to November, 2–8 ft.

M. Echinus, the Calvary Clover, so called from the blackish-purple spots on the leaves. Yellow flowers in June. 6 in.

M. falcata, a perennial, will do well anywhere on banks or rockeries. Yellow flowers in summer and prostrate stems.

M. sativa, with violet flowers, is grown for fodder.

MEDINILLA (med-in-il-a. Melastomaceæ). A fairly large genus of stove shrubs distinguished by large hanging bunches of rosy flowers and leathery leaves rising from peculiarly winged stems.

Propagate by cuttings of side shoots taken with a heel in spring, or young shoots may be used provided they are not allowed to damp off. Insert in sandy soil with a little peat with brisk bottom heat. Plant in good loam with peat and leaf-mould. As they are apt to suffer from over-potting, they may be kept in quite small pots and repotted every three years. The soil must be kept from becoming sour and waterlogged.

Winter temperature, 45°–55°; summer, 60°–85°.

SPECIES.

M. javanensis. Pinkish-rose flowers in December. 4 ft.

M. magnifica. Rosy-pink. May. 3–4 ft.

M. sieboldiana. Whitish-rose. Winter to spring. 3–4 ft.

M. speciosa. July. 2–4 ft.

MEDITERRANEAN HEATH. *See* ERICA.

MEDLAR (*Mespilus germanica*). The Medlar is a low-growing tree of somewhat artistic appearance owing to its crooked habit. It is a native of Europe and Asia Minor, and although found wild in the southern counties of this country, most probably it is not indigenous.

Soil.—Practically any soil is suitable, but excessively dry positions should be avoided.

Planting.—At any time between October and March.

Pruning.—The only pruning necessary is to make certain that the young tree is properly set with main branches. Following this no pruning is necessary. Owing to the twisted growth it is impossible to prevent branches from crossing.

Propagation.—The Medlar may be raised from seed, which takes two or more years to germinate. The better method is to graft upon the Pear or Quince Stock.

Gathering Fruit.—Fruit should be gathered at the end of October. It is not ready until "bletted," which means that a certain amount of decay must be present.

MELALEUCA (mel-a-lū´-ka. Myrtaceæ). Australia. Tender shrub, for mild districts, resembling the Calistemon with "bottle-brush"-like inflorescences.

Culture.—Plant in peat, leaf-mould and sand. *Propagate* by cuttings under bell-glass, in May.

SPECIES.

M. armillaris—white flowers.

M. ericifolia—creamy-white flowers.

M. hypercifolia—scarlet flowers.

M. Wilsonii—mauve flowers.

MELIA (mē´-li-a. Meliaceæ). "China Tree," of the Himalayas. Half-hardy, deciduous shrub of little decorative value.

M. Azedarach (*Arbor Sancta*). Flowers lilac-mauve, followed by small nuts, used for the making of Rosaries. The nuts have a natural hole through the middle which facilitates the threading.

MELIANTHUS (mel-i-an´-thus. Sapindaceæ). "Honey Flower" (South Africa). Half-hardy deciduous shrub, of compact habit, with bluish-green leaves.

Culture.—Plant in a light rich soil. *Propagate* by seeds or cuttings.

M major, 4–10 ft. Much used for sub-tropical gardening on account of its glaucous foliage.

MELICOPE (mel-i-kō´-pē. Rutaceæ). New Zealand. Semi-evergreen shrub, for very mild districts.

Culture.—Plant in loam and peat. *Propagate* by cuttings.

SPECIES.

M. ternata. Handsome foliage and greenish-white flowers.

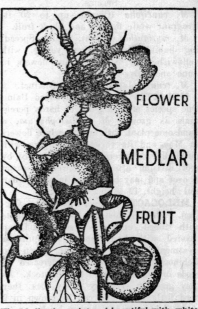

The Medlar is quaint and beautiful with white flowers in June and pretty autumn foliage. The fruit is used when it begins to decay.

MELISSA, Balm (Labiatæ). A herb with fragrant foliage. Species cultivated: *Melissa officinalis.*

MELILOTUS (meli-lot-us. Leguminosæ). Melilot. A plant that grows wild in the British Isles and is much sought after by bees. It grows on roadsides and banks and flowers in late summer. It is a perennial but usually lives only two years; is worthy of more cultivation in gardens. Seed may be sown in any common soil, and will grow best in sheltered places. Increase also by cuttings.

SPECIES.

M. alba, white, July. Height, 2–10 ft.

M. leucantha, white, July. Height, 4 ft.

M. officinalis, yellow, July. Height, 1–4 ft.

M. suaveolens, yellow (fragrant), July. Height, 3 ft.

MELIOSMA (měl-i-ŏs-ma. Sabiaceæ). China and Japan. Deciduous shrubs, with handsome foliage, and small white flowers in pyramidal panicles 6–9 in. long, followed by small black berries. Thriving in a good loamy soil and a sunny position.

SPECIES.

M. cuneifolia (China), up to 20 ft. Fragrant white flowers and black fruit.

M. myriantha (Japan), 20 ft. Spreading habit. Tender when young, with yellowish-white, very fragrant flowers in June and July.

M. tenuis (Japan). Rare. Distinct.

MELITTIS (Labiatæ). Bastard Balm. One species of this genus of hardy perennials is grown, *M. melissophyllum*, a handsome plant with creamy-white flowers in May and its variety *grandiflora* with purple-lipped flowers. It is propagated by root division after the flowering season is over and may be planted in any garden soil; height, 12–18 in.

MELOCACTUS (mel-o-kak-tus. Cacteæ). Melon Thistle. Succulent plants with ribbed, unbranched stems and cap covered with hairy spines. Require a treatment similar to that given to Echinocactus (*see* CACTUS). Increased by seeds or grafting on to Cereus stock. As they grow in very dry sandy rock, they need little water and can be grown in 2 parts of loam to 1 of broken brick.

SPECIES.

M. communis. Rosy-red. 12–20 ridges. 1–1½ ft. Other species are rarely grown.

MELON (*Cucumis Melo*). Cucurbitaceæ. The fruits of this plant are eaten as dessert, but it may be grown with such plants as Cucumbers.

It was introduced about 1570, and is supposed to have originated in the warmer parts of Asia, though no wild types can now be found.

There are now endless varieties in more or less general cultivation, and in colour, shape, and size they vary considerably.

MELON CACTUS. *See* MELOCACTUS.

MENDELISM. A theory of heredity based on researches and generalisations by Johann Gregor Mendel, an Austrian priest and teacher, showing that the characters and the parents of cross-bred offspring reappear in certain proportions in successive generations according to definite laws. Those who wish to hybridise plants should certainly make a study of the theory from a modern scientific work.

MENISCIUM (me-nis-ki-um. Filices). Stove ferns with remarkably beautiful veining on the fronds. In their natural habitat they are found growing by the sides of streams and are of vigorous growth. Under cultivation they need to be treated as sub-aquatics.

Propagate by spores, which germinate freely, or by division of the crowns in spring. A soil composed of loam and peat with charcoal and broken brick is the most suitable.

SPECIES.

M. reticulatum. Fronds 2–4 ft. long. There are good, well-marked varieties such as *macrophyllum* and *oligophyllum*.

M. simplex. Fronds 6–9 in.

M. Thwaitesii. Fronds 8–10 in.

MENISPERMUM (mē-ni-sper'-mum. Menispermaceæ). "Moonseed" (North America). Deciduous climber, with peltate leaves, and racemes of flowers followed by moon-shaped seeds, hence its name. Good climber for summer-house or wall: should not be planted near slow-growing plants having vigorous underground suckers. Does well in any garden soil. *Propagate* by division.

SPECIES.

M. canadense, 12–15 ft. Inconspicuous greenish yellow flowers on slender racemes followed by black fruit. Useful for covering damp and shady walls.

M. dauricum. Similar to above, with smaller leaves.

MENTHA (men-tha. Labiatæ). Mint. A large genus of hardy herbaceous aromatic plants chiefly grown for their culinary uses, although a few species are useful in the rock garden or for carpeting.

Culture.—Propagate by division of the roots in March or by cuttings and plant in moist sandy soil or stiff moist loam. The beds should be remade in alternate years and the plants set 9 in. apart. To force the plants place in good soil at a temperature of 60° and give them plenty of water.

SPECIES.

M. requieni, a pretty little creeping rock plant with pale purple flowers, gives off a strong scent when the leaves are bruised.

M. piperita is the Peppermint used in medicine and confectionery, *viridis* is the spearmint used in kitchens, and *pulegium* the pennyroyal, of which the variety *gibraltarica* is used for carpeting the rock garden.

MENTHA PULEGIUM. *See* HERBS, CULINARY.

MENYANTHES (men-yan-thēz. Gentianaceæ). Buckbean or Bogbean. The only species of this genus cultivated is *trifoliata*, a pretty native plant with white flowers in May. It would prove an ornament in the water garden or in a boggy patch, and may be propagated by cuttings struck in mud in summer.

MENZIESIA (men-zī-ē'-si-a. Ericaceæ). North-east America. Deciduous shrubs with oval leaves, and bell-shaped flowers borne in clusters in May. Thriving in peaty soil. *Propagate* by seed.

SPECIES.

M. ferruginea. Small creamy-white bell-shaped flowers.

M. pilosa (globularis), 3–6 ft. Erect habit, with a profusion of yellow flowers tipped with orange.

MERCURY (Chenopodium Bonus Henricus). Dog's Mercury is the poisonous weed, *Mercurialis*. *See also* HERBS, CULINARY.

MERENDERA (mer-en-de-ra. Liliaceæ). Hardy bulbs requiring the same culture as Colchicum.

SPECIES.

M. bulbocodium (syn. *Colchicum montanum*). Rose or lilac flowers in autumn. The variety *bulbocodioides* has larger flowers. 3–6 in.

M. caucasica. Rosy-purple flowers in May. 3 in.

M. Eichleri. Very like *caucasica*, but with appendages to flower segments.

M. persica. Lilac flowers, fragrant. November. 2 in.

MERTENSIA (mer-ten-sia. Boragineæ). Hardy herbaceous free-flowering perennials that are suitable for the front of the border or for the rock garden.

Culture.—They like almost any soil, but thrive best in a peaty one and are increased

by summer-sown seed, by cuttings raised under a hand-light, or by division of the roots in March at which time they must be planted.

SPECIES.

M. alpina (syn. *lanceolata*), a dwarf plant for edging, with slender stems bearing pale blue flowers.

M. echioides, a rare plant with deep blue flowers, 6–12 in.

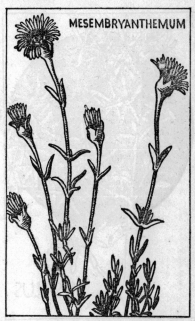

Mesembryanthemums are a group of fleshy-leaved plants with bright flowers that thrive in sandy soils.

M. maritima, a procumbent plant which is frequently destroyed by slugs.

M. pulmonarioides, the Virginian Cowslip, is the best known with graceful racemes of rich blue flowers, 18 in.

M. Sibirica has pretty foliage and racemes of flowers which are pink when opening, but change to lavender. 18 in.

All the species flower from May to July.

MESEMBRYANTHEMUM (me-sem-bry-an-themum. Ficoideæ). Ice-plant. South Africa. *M. crystallinum*, 1½ ft., spreading, a half-hardy annual, is a curious plant. The leaves and stems are covered with large grains (papútæ) which glisten and give the appearance of a granulated coating of ice. Flowers insignificant. Sow in the greenhouse in March. Plant outdoors in June; ordinary soil, sunny position. *M. tricolor*, 3 in., flowers white, yellow and red in concentric rings. A pretty plant for a dry, sunny rockery; the flowers close at sundown, and remain closed on dull days. Sow in April where to flower. *M. criniflorum*, 3 in., various

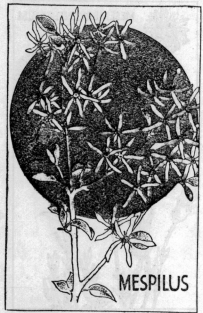

The Mespilus is a showy flowering tree. It is used in the mixed shrubbery.

colours, is probably a selection from *M. tricolor*, and should be given similar treatment.

MESPILUS, SNOWY. *See* AMELANCHIER.

MEUM (me-um. Umbelliferæ). The only species that is ever cultivated, and that but rarely, is *M. athamanticum* with white flowers and very feathery leaves. It is a hardy perennial and is increased by seed or division. It may be grown in any garden soil, and is useful for dry banks or in the rock garden.

MEXICAN ORANGE BLOSSOM. *See* CHOISYA.

MEZEREUM. *See* DAPHNE MEZEREUM.

MICE. *See* SOIL PESTS.

MICHAELMAS DAISY. *See* ASTER.

MICHAUXIA (mi-kaux-si-a. Campanulaceæ). Persia, 4–5 ft. *M. campanuloides*, a hardy perennial, white, tinted purple, is an interesting plant for the mixed border, in ordinary soil. These plants should be sown in April on a warm border, and planted into flowering quarters in October.

MICONIA (mi-ko-ni-a. Melastomaceæ). Stove trees and shrubs with beautiful leaves and, usually, white flowers. They are, however, rarely grown in this country. They can be grown in loam and peat with sand and charcoal, and are increased in spring by cuttings rooted in peat in a propagating case with brisk bottom heat.

SPECIES.

M. flammea, with large glossy leaves.
M. grandifolia, large leaves.

Although not so showy as many annuals the Mignonette is worthy of a place if only for its sweet fragrance and its use as a cut flower.

M. hookeriana. Olive-green leaves with a silvery mid-rib. Its variety, *trifasciata*, has three silvery ribs.

M. magnifica. Leaves are large and bronzy green, while the mid-ribs are prominent and the stem hairy.

MICROGLOSSA (mī-krŏ-glos'-sa. Compositæ). Tree Aster (Himalayas). Deciduous shrub, having erect growths, with long slender leaves and clusters of flowers in late summer. *Propagate* by division or cuttings in heat.

M. *albescens* (*Ampherabis albescens*, *Aster cabulicus*). Lilac-blue flowers in July.

MICROMERIA (mi-kro-me-ria. Labiatæ). From *mikros*, small, *meris*, a part, referring to the flowers.

A group of small-flowered Labiates, whose leaves emit a pungent and pleasant smell. (They are now often included in *Satureia*.)

M. *croatica*, a tiny pink-flowered bushling with wiry stems, is most worthy of notice. Croatia, 4 in. June.

MIGNONETTE. *See* RESEDA.

MIKANIA (mi-ka-ni-a. Compositæ). A large genus, chiefly comprising stove evergreen climbers allied to Eupatorium and requiring similar treatment.

MILFOIL OR YARROW

A useful perennial for dry soil is the Yarrow or Milfoil.

SPECIES.

M. *Sanderi.* Large bright green leaves.

M. *scandens.*

MILDEW. Fungous diseases that attack the leaves of plants. So called from the mealy appearance of the foliage.

Preventatives.—Dust the plants with flowers of sulphur which by being brought into direct contact with the mildew is most effective, or spray with liver of sulphur, 1 oz. to 3 gal. of water (*see* FUNGOUS DISEASES). Under glass ventilate freely.

MILFOIL. See ACHILLEA.

MILKWORT. See POLYGALA.

MILLEPEDES. Usually cylindrical and, except for the first four segments, with two pairs of legs on each segment. The first, second and fourth have only one pair, the third having none.

Like the wood lice and centipedes,

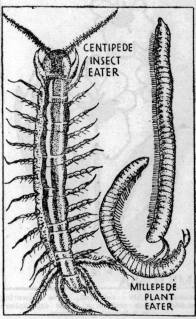

CENTIPEDE INSECT EATER

MILLEPEDE PLANT EATER

Centipedes are useful and Millepedes are harmful in the garden. Centipedes have one pair of legs to each segment. Millepedes have two pairs to each segment.

millepedes live in damp, dark places, usually coming out at night when they may do damage to seedlings and plants in general. At certain periods of the year they migrate, and have then been known to do considerable damage to strawberry plants. The chief pest is *Blanjulus gettulatus*, the small snake millepede. It is pinkish in colour and has a double row of red spots down the back. The larger black species in this country act more as scavengers and rarely damage crops. They feed mostly on decayed vegetation.

METHODS OF CONTROL.—The application of a soil fumigant will act as a repellent.

MILTONIA (mil-to-ni-a. Orchidaceæ). Named after Viscount Milton. Stove epiphytal orchids. The richness of colouring, floriferous habit and decorative value of the recently raised hybrids are a great tribute to the modern hybridists, and

MILTONIA

Miltonia—richly coloured, free-flowering orchids which require a moist atmosphere in a heated greenhouse.

have made this genus exceedingly popular. Brazil, 1830.

Culture.—Compost: use 3 parts well-chopped fibre to 1 part sphagnum moss. Repot when new growth commences. Pots should be half-filled with broken crocks, as plants are notably shallow-rooting. Shady position. Water freely during growing period. A moist atmosphere and an equable temperature of 60° night and day should be aimed at.

Propagate by division when repotting.

SPECIES.

M. candida, red, yellow and brown.
M. flavescens, white, yellow and brown.
M. Regnellii, rose, purple and white.

M. spectabilis, rose and purple, and its variety, *spectabilis rosea*, rose.

M. vexillaria, white, rose and yellow.

Miltonia hybrids. These are very numerous and exceedingly beautiful. One or two of the best only can be given.

Beau Brummell—Aureole, a perfect flower, sepals bluish-white, petals tinged purple, lips broad and round, bluish-white, with dark crimson mask at base, from which radiate heavy lines the same colour.

Eleanor Dixon, white throughout with faint flush at base of petals, lips flushed rose and deep purple mask.

Lucia, sepals and petals blush-rose with purple at base, lip flushed crimson lake, with a brown and yellow mask.

Sheila, sepals and petals rose-purple, former with narrow white margin, lip rose-magenta with yellow mask.

MIMOSA (mi-mo-sa. Leguminosæ). Sensitive Plant. S. America. *Mimosa pudica*, 1 ft. The leaves are sensitive to the slightest touch; usually grown as a pot plant for cool greenhouse.

Greenhouse Culture.—Compost: 2 parts loam, 1 part peat and sand. Pot early spring. Water freely during the summer, moderately at other times. Winter temperature, 50°; summer, 70°.

Propagate by cuttings of young shoots in sandy soil during summer. Temperature, 65°, but is best treated as an annual and raised by seed sown in light sandy soil in the spring, temperature 65°.

M. pudica (Sensitive Plant) is the only one grown to any extent.

See also ACACIA DEALBATA.

MIMULUS (mĭm-u-lus. Scrophulariaceæ). Monkey Flower. Musk. Hardy and half-hardy annuals and perennials that are effective as bedding plants in shady places or as edgings to borders.

Culture.—The annuals are propagated by seeds sown in heat in February and planted out after hardening, the perennials by seeds or by division and cuttings. They thrive in rather moist soil, and the seeds should be sown in a very fine sandy seed bed. In cold districts it is advisable to lift plants and winter them in a frame.

SPECIES.

M. cardinalis is a good scarlet species with masses of flowers from June to August. 1–3 ft.

M. moschatus the common yellow old-fashioned, sweet-scented Musk, is a creeping perennial that is most often grown in pots in the greenhouse, but is sometimes used for bedding. 6 in. Since it lost its scent, unaccountably, it is not much grown.

MINA (mi-na. Convolvulaceæ). Half-hardy annual. Climbing. Similar in habit to Japonica. Scarlet flowers in racemes. A rapid grower. Sow where to bloom in ordinary garden soil.

MINT or SPEARMINT (*Mentha viridis*). Labiatæ. This herb is known under various names, such as Spearmint, Common Mint, Garden Mint and Green Mint. It is a perennial herb with creeping root-stocks, and has been used for culinary and medicinal purposes for many hundreds of years.

It is extremely easy to cultivate, and may be planted in any odd corner where it can enjoy shade during a part of the day.

A stock of plants may be raised by cuttings of young shoots placed in sand under bell-glass during summer, or by dividing and replanting small pieces of the root. Plants may also be obtained from seed sown in gentle heat in March or outside in well-prepared soil on a shady border during April and May. In either case the plants should be allowed to become well established before cutting is commenced. In the autumn a little good soil mixed with well-decayed manure should be spread over the plants as a top dressing.

See also MENTHA.

MIRABILIS (mir-ăb-i-lis. Nyctagineæ). Marvel of Peru. Hardy perennial and greenhouse plants that are best treated as half-hardy annuals in most cases.

Culture.—If seed is sown in heat in spring the seedlings can be hardened-off for planting out at the end of May, and will produce quite sturdy plants. They should be planted in a sunny position in rich light loam, but are not particular as to soil. They may be treated in the same way as Dahlias and the tuberous roots lifted and stored in winter. In spring the plants should be re-started in pots.

SPECIES.

M. jalapa, The Marvel of Peru, the most familiar of the species, grows rapidly into a small bush covered with fragrant flowers of white, rose-yellow, crimson and purple and even striped, all appearing on the one plant. Also remarkable for the flowers being at their best in the evening. 2–3 ft.

M. longiflora, with long tubular pink, white, or violet flowers, is a hardy perennial in a warm site. 2 ft.

MIMULUS OR MUSK

The Monkey Flower is a moisture-loving plant and thrives by the side of a pond or stream. Its gay colours of gold and scarlet are a joy to the waterside.

M. multiflora is similar to but dwarfer than *jalapa* and has bright fragrant purple flowers in large clusters. In warm borders it is a hardy perennial.

The plants flower in July and August.

MISCANTHUS (mis-kan-thus. Gramineæ). Eulalia. China and Japan, 5–10 ft. Handsome quick-growing, ornamental grasses, giving a sub-tropical effect to the garden, producing in late summer plumes borne on long, slender stems. Thriving in ordinary damp soil and sunny position. *Propagate* by division. Suitable for planting in bog and lakeside and also

for pot culture in the greenhouse. Pot
or plant in March or April.

SPECIES.

M. japonicus (Japan). Slender bright
green leaves.

M. j. variegatus (*folstriata*). Alternate
green and silver variegation.

M. j. zebrinus. A very attractive variety
with zebra-like markings of green and gold.

MISTLETOE GROWING ON AN APPLE TREE

The Mistletoe can be grown on old apple or
poplar trees simply by pressing seeds of the
Mistletoe into a notch of the bark.

M. sinensis (China and Japan). Fine
arching slender leaves.

MISTLETOE. *See* VISCUM.

MITCHELLA (mitch-el'-la. Rubiaceæ).
Creeping evergreen, similar to *Linnea
borealis*. Quick-spreading habit, with
Abelia-like flowers. Plant in non-
calcareous, loamy soil, in shady position.
Propagate by division.

M. repens, the only species.

MITELLA (mi-tel-la. Saxifrageæ).
Mitre Wort. Hardy herbs with small
white flowers. Useful for rockeries or
borders in moist peaty soil.

Propagate by division and more rarely
by seed.

SPECIES.

M. diphylla. April. 6 in.

M. nuda. June. 6 in.

MITRARIA (mit-rar'-i-a. Gesneriaceæ).
Chile. Half-hardy evergreen shrub with
bright orange-scarlet flowers, like suspended pentstemons, 1 in. long. It likes
sandy peat, but has been seen growing
on a wall in Cornwall and flowering freely.
The wall was cool and shady. *Propagate*
by division in spring or cuttings in slight
heat during spring and summer.

M. coccinea. The only species.

MITRIOSTIGMA (mit-ri-os-tig-ma.
Rubiaceæ). A genus of two species of
stove shrubs allied to Gardenias and needing the same culture.

SPECIES.

M. axillaris (syn. *Gardenia citriodora*).
White fragrant flowers in spring. 5 ft.

MOCK ORANGE. *See* PHILADELPHUS.

MOHRIA (mohr-i-a. Filices). Frankin-
cense Fern. Greenhouse evergreen ferns.
Fronds feather shaped. S. Africa, 1842.

Culture.—Compost: 2 parts peat, 1 part
coarse sand and brick rubble. Repot early
spring, good drainage essential. Shady
position. Winter temperature, 40°;
summer, 65°.

Propagation.—*See* ADIANTUM.

SPECIES.

M. caffrorum. Tripinnatifid fronds (syn.
thurifraga).

MOLES. *See* SOIL PESTS.

MOLINIA (mo-lin-i-a. Gramineæ).
Hardy grasses of tufted habit that are
found growing wild in all parts of Britain,
particularly on bleak, damp moors. The
principal species is *M. cærulea*, of which
the variegated variety is used as an edging
plant. Increased by seeds and the variety
by division.

MOLOPOSPERMUM (mol-op-o-sper-
mum. Umbelliferæ). The only species
is an elegant hardy perennial with fern-
like leaves. Suitable for naturalising in
the shrubbery. Increased by seeds sown
as soon as ripe or by division of the roots
in spring. It likes a deep rich soil, but
is quite content with a poorer one. It
bears yellow and white flowers in May and
has yellowish-brown fruits. 3–5 ft.

MOLTKIA (molt'-ki-a. Boraginaceæ).
Albania. 1–2 ft. Semi-evergreen compact
shrub, having long slender leaves with

clusters of violet-blue flowers in June. Thrives best in a light well-drained soil in sunny position. *Propagate* by cuttings during summer.

M. petræa (*Lithospermum petræum*). The only species.

MOLUCCA BALM. *See* MOLUCELLA.

MOLUCELLA (mol-u-sel-la. Labiatæ). Molucca Balm. Hardy and half-hardy annuals that thrive in sandy loam. Increased by seeds sown in heat in spring and planted out in May.

SPECIES.

M. lævis. White flowers in August; is excellent for skeletonising. 1–1½ ft.

M. spinosa. White.

MOMORDICA (mo-mor-di-ka. Cucurbitaceæ). Ornamental stove climbing annuals and perennials with white or yellow flowers and curious fruits that are most interesting when ripening. They can be raised from seed like other tropical gourds, or they may be imported. They like a rich soil and can be trained to pillars or to trellises as well as to the roof of the house.

SPECIES.

M. Balsamina. Balsam Apple. Yellow flowers in June and roundish yellow fruits.

M. Charantia. Yellow. Yellow fruits oblong, with red seed.

M. chinensis. Fruits larger than foregoing, and silvery.

M. cochinchinensis. Large yellow flowers. Fruits yellow and round or oval.

M. muricata. Flowers yellow. Fruits golden yellow with red pulp and white seeds.

MONARDA (mon-ar-da. Labiatæ). Horse Mint. Showy hardy plants with long slender corollas arranged in whorls at the top of the stems, and fragrant leaves.

Culture.—These plants are easily grown in any fertile garden soil that is fairly moist. *Propagate* by division of the roots in March or by seeds sown in spring.

SPECIES.

M. didyma (Oswego Tea, Bee Balm or Sweet Bergamot) is the best known, with scented leaves and whorls of scarlet flowers which give rise to a second inflorescence.

Its white (*alba*), purple (*purpurea*) and rosy-scarlet (*rosea*) varieties are equally good for damp borders. 2–3 ft.

M. fistulosa, Wild Bergamot, of which the variety *mollis* is superior to the type, with lilac-coloured flowers from July to August. 2 ft.

M. citriodora, with lemon-scented leaves and yellow flowers in August. 2 ft.

MONARDELLA (mon-ar-de-la. Labiatæ). Hardy annual and perennial herbs with sweet-scented foliage. They bear a

MOCK ORANGE

Mock Orange, wrongly called Syringa. Where there is plenty of room the Mock Orange is one of the most useful flowering shrubs. It flowers on the young shoots made the previous year. Botanists name it Philadelphus.

marked resemblance to Monardas and succeed under much the same conditions.

Propagate by root division.

SPECIES.

M. candicans. White, summer, annual. 1 ft.

M. macrantha. Scarlet, autumn. Foliage very fragrant.

MONEYWORT. *See* SIBTHORPIA *and* LYSIMACHIA.

MONKEY FLOWER. *See* MIMULUS.

MONKEY NUT. *See* ARACHIS.

MONKEY PUZZLE. *See* ARAUCARIA.

MONKSHOOD. *See* ACONITUM.

MONOCHÆTUM (mon-o-ke-tum. Melastomaceæ). Greenhouse shrubs that are rather difficult to cultivate. They grow in a soil composed of 2 parts of fibrous peat to 1 of leaf-mould and plenty of sand. Increase by cuttings taken in spring and rooted under a bell-glass over bottom heat.

SPECIES.

M. alpestre. Red. Leaves and stem tinged with red.

M. hartwegianum. Bright red flowers in winter arranged in panicles (syn. *dicranantherum*).

M. humboldtianum. Reddish-purple flowers in early winter.

M. sericeum. Mauve flowers in spring. Its variety *multiflorum* bears more flowers.

MONOCOTYLEDONS. One of the two classes of flowering plants. Marked by the possession of only one seed leaf (as distinct from Dicotyledons) and parallel-veined leaves.

MONSTERA (mon-ster-a. Aroideæ). Stove evergreen climbers that do well in pots standing in water, as they are very thirsty subjects. They may be increased by cutting up the fleshy stems and planting them in coconut fibre in a close frame. Use loam that has stood for some time with cow manure with half as much leaf-mould.

SPECIES.

M. acuminata. The Shingle Plant. Leaves 8–10 in. long.

MONTBRETIA (Iridiaceæ) (also called Tritonia). Hardy South African bulbs from which many modern varieties have been raised chiefly from Tritonia or *Montbretia Pottsii* and Crocosma. Plant in autumn or spring in ordinary border soil. Lift annually in autumn, and replant the largest bulbs three or four inches apart in order to get the best flowers. Good varieties are:

Fire King—rich reddish-scarlet.

Croesus—large, rich yellow.

Golden West—rich golden yellow.

Messidor—pretty shade of citron yellow.

MOONWORT. *See* SOLDANELLA *and* BOTRYCHIUM.

MOORHEN. This shy bird is of considerable assistance to mankind, as its food, though mainly of a neutral nature, includes a proportion of injurious insects and their larvæ, including wireworms. It also does good work in the destruction of pond snails upon which the liver-fluk breeds. The bulk of its food consists of seeds and fruits of weeds and grass.

MORÆA (mo-re-a. Irideæ). Pretty bulbous plants rather like Irises and suitable for the greenhouse or conservatory. They like sandy loam and must be kept away from frosts. Some authorities include in this genus Helixyra, Dietes and Vieusseuxia. Increase by offsets.

SPECIES.

M. bicolor. Yellow and brown flowers in summer. 2 ft.

M. edulis. Violet flowers in May. 4 ft.

M. elegans. Vermilion. May. 1½ ft.

M. glaucopsis. White, black spotted flowers in May. 2 ft. (syn. *Iris Pavonia* and *Vieusseuxia glaucopsis*).

M. robinsoniana. The Wedding Flower. White. June. 6 ft.

M. spathacea. Yellow. March. 1 ft. (syn. *Dietes Huttoni*).

M. tricuspis. White with purple spots. May. 1 ft.

M. tripetala. Blue. June (syn. *Vieusseuxia tripetaloides*).

MORICANDIA (mo-ri-can-dia. Cruciferæ). *M. sonchifolia*, 1–1½ ft., was introduced into England from China many years ago, but it is only recently that its merits have been recognised. It is a very pretty plant for blooming from January to March in a cool greenhouse; easily raised from seeds sown in June or July in a cold frame. Pot up the seedlings singly and pot into 4½–5 in. pots in October, and place them in the greenhouse, where they will commence to flower early in January. Loam 2 parts, old manure 1 part, sand 1 part, is a suitable compost. Flowers, pale violet-blue.

MORINA (Dipsaceæ). Hardy and half-hardy perennials that make excellent border plants.

Culture.—Propagate by seeds sown in heat in early spring or by division of the roots after flowering, and plant in light warm soil in a sheltered position.

SPECIES.

M. coulteriana (syn. *brevifolia*) bears pale yellow flowers in spikes in July, and, like *M. persica* (syn. *wallichiana*), which has tall spikes of red or white flowers, should be lifted in autumn and wintered in a frame. 1–3 ft.

M. longifolia, with tufts of evergreen leaves and whorls of purple flowers in July, is a hardy plant that is useful both for the border or a warm place in the rockery. 2 ft.

MORISIA (mor-is-ia. Cruciferæ). After Professor Morris.

M. hypogæa (syn. *monanthus*). Has a flat rosette of much-divided glossy leaves from whose centre emerge short-stemmed yellow flowers which, after blooming, turn and bury their seed capsule in the earth. This is an elegant plant in poor, sandy or moraine soil, but any attempt at over-feeding will result in few flowers and a coarse vegetable growth. Easily propagated from runners. May. Sardinia.

MORMODES (mor-mo-dez). Orchids. Deciduous epiphytal orchids only differing from Catasetum in the column of the flower. The thick flowers are borne in spikes on fleshy stalks that rise from buds on the sides of the pseudo-bulbs, while the lance-shaped plaited leaves emerge from the pseudo-bulbs.

MORNING GLORY (Convolvulaceæ). Ipomæa. Stove greenhouse and hardy herbs, shrubs and climbers.

Propagate by seeds, and the shrubs and perennials by cuttings in sand in heat. Soil, for the garden species, may be any fairly rich compost; for the stove plants, equal parts of loam, leaf-mould, manure and sand. Plant in beds or borders in the stove or in pots. Prune in February or after flowering.

SPECIES.

I. Bona-Nox. White, summer, climber.

I. Horsfalliæ. Rosy flowers in winter. Increased by layering.

I. purpurea (syn. *Convolvulus major*). Purple, summer.

I. versicolor (syn. *Mina lobata*). Hardy annual. June. Rosy crimson and yellow flowers.

MORUS (mor'-us. Urticaceæ). Mulberry. China and Japan. Deciduous trees, up to 30 ft. high, with large leaves and small flowers, followed by the well-known fruit.

Culture.—Plant in October in warm well-drained loamy soil, in sunny position. *Propagate* by cuttings in September.

SPECIES.

M. alba. White Mulberry. fine large fruit. It is the beautiful foliage of this tree upon which the silkworm is fed.

M. a. pendula. Weeping habit, forming an umbrella-like head, reaching to the ground.

M. nigra. Common or Black Mulberry. Ragged and picturesque habit. (*See also* MULBERRY.)

M. rubra. Red Mulberry. Of little value.

Morning Glory is a delightful climber for the balcony garden. It twines round wire supports.

The Mulberry has been grown from time immemorial in Oriental and South European countries. Although the White Mulberry thrives well in the South of England, only small success has so far followed the various attempts to establish the silkworm industry in this country.

MOSCHOSMA (mos-kos-ma. Labiatæ). *M. riparium*, a greenhouse perennial, bears large racemes of whitish flowers with purple anthers and opposite nettle-like leaves. It is at its best in December and January.

Cuttings of young shoots root readily and require the same treatment as for Salvias.

MOSS. Low-tufted flowerless plants which belong to the cryptogamous order, Musci, which in turn is divided into four sub-classes, Bryaceæ, Phascaceæ, Andrea-ceæ, and Sphagnaceæ. Like ferns they are remarkable for alternate arrangement of the generations, one having sexual organs while the other is non-sexual. The first named is a creeping or erect, simple or branching plant, while the second is a leafless plant bearing spores by which the genus is continued.

When moss appears on lawns it shows

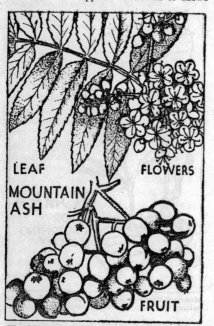

LEAF   FLOWERS

MOUNTAIN ASH

FRUIT

The Mountain Ash is easily recognised by its scarlet berries in autumn and its preference for chalky or limestone districts.

that the soil is poor and too damp and shaded. To remedy this the surface may be raked during the winter while a top dressing of rich soil and soot will be bene-ficial. Shade from nearby trees should be removed if possible. Moss on gravel walks can be destroyed by dressings with salt in dry weather or with a solution of copper sulphate. *See also* SPHAGNUM.

MOUNTAIN ASH. *See* PYRUS.
MOUNTAIN AVENS. *See* DRYAS.
MOUNTAIN EBONY. *See* BAUHINIA.
MOWERS, LAWN. Buy a mower according to the size of your pocket and garden; but, for the sake of a few shillings,

always make sure that it is the new pro-duction of a well-established firm for which spare parts can always be obtained. Do not buy any "seconds" or "throwouts" from mass production, or foreign mowers. British steel and engineering is acknow-ledged best. Whilst it is obvious that a really good first-class side-wheel mower will give longer wear and greater satis-faction than a cheap roller-type mower, yet it must be remembered that the former always leaves a verge of uncut grass on the edge of the lawn which has to be finished off with the lawn shears. The roller-type machine, with its enclosed gear-box and ball bearings, cuts right to the edge of the lawn and saves extra work.

Points to look for in a Mower.

(*a*) *Your own point of view.*—Ball bear-ings are essential to an easy-running mower. If they are self-aligning, then even when ageing the mower will still run smoothly and be as near a pleasure to push as any mower can be. The handles should be adjustable to the height of the user and the grass-box easy to put on or take off. The adjustments should be of the hand-wheel type both on the cutting cylinder adjustment and that for height of cut, thus obviating the use of spanners. In the case of the side-wheel machine the land wheels should be of large diameter, thus making for easier work.

(*b*) *Your lawn's point of view.* — The adjustments between lower blade and cut-ting cylinder should be so perfect as to be almost a micrometer adjustment, so as to *cut* the blades of grass and in no way scrape them. One of the chief disadvantages of a cheap machine is that the blades on the cutting or rotary cylinder are not all in perfect alignment and this makes accurate adjustment almost impossible.

The *land rollers* should be in at least two separate parts, so as not to scrape the lawn when turning. There is one maker who puts a mechanism similar to the differential gear of a car in the land rollers, as this point is considered to be so essen-tial to the easy running of the machine and the care of the lawn.

The *gears* or *chain drive* should be en-closed so that when covered with grease and oil the latter cannot drip on to and spoil the lawn.

For a very perfect lawn such as a putting, golf, or bowls green, or even a well-established old lawn, an eight-bladed cylinder is advised so as to avoid any possible "ridging" as sometimes occurs on a slow-revving cylinder.

The often forgotten necessity of an easy-running and long-lasting mower is a supply of good quality machine oil always at hand. The correct time to have the machine overhauled is any time out of season—not the rush of the season—and then have it sent by some well-established ironmonger direct back to the makers, who know how to do it properly.

MOWERS, MOTOR. When purchasing a motor-mower the essential point to be remembered is that the size of a motor-mower must be in proportion to the acreage of grass to be cut. Thus, the cutting cylinder would soon wear out if a 12 in. mower were used to cut two acres of grass regularly. As regard the engine, the amateur can rest assured that no well-known maker would spoil his good name as a mower manufacturer by using a bad engine.

MOWING. This is a very important operation in the care of lawns, but modern mowing machines have made the task very easy compared with the old method of scything. Lawns should be mown once a week in wet weather and fortnightly in dry summer weather. An occasional cutting during the winter is advised to keep the lawn in good condition. This is frequently neglected, with the result that the first cutting in the spring is difficult and leaves the lawn in a poor state. If the grass is short the clippings need not be collected, but can be allowed to fall and act as a mulch. Mowing should be done when the grass is dry and scything when it is damp.

For small gardens a 10 in. hand machine is a useful size, other sizes increasing by 2 in. in width. The chain-driven machine fitted with ball bearings is the most serviceable type of hand machine.

Motor mowers are advisable for lawns more than a quarter of an acre in area. These machines are obtainable from 14–20 in. in width.

When mowing, cut the lawn up and down one time and back and across the next time. Always clean the mower after use, brushing it to clear it of clippings, etc., and oil it.

Always sweep the lawn before mowing, especially during the winter months, or the mower will deteriorate rapidly.

MUEHLENBECKIA (mūhl-en-bek'-i-a. Polygonaceæ). Australia and New Zealand. Deciduous and evergreen shrubs and climbers, having inconspicuous greenish-white flowers followed by small nuts. Thriving in any garden soil. *Propagate* by division or cuttings.

SPECIES.

M. axillaris. Deciduous prostrate shrub with small leaves on wiry stems.

M. complexa. Deciduous, slender climber, having round dark leaves and small waxy-white flowers. Suitable for covering tree-stumps, etc.

M. varians. Similar to preceding, with larger leaves.

MULBERRY (*Morus nigra*). The Mulberry is a native of Oriental parts, more particularly Persia. It is a deciduous tree up to 30 ft. in height.

Soil.—Although this tree prefers a moist soil, a light rich loam suits it best. Trees planted on heavy ground frequently refuse to ripen their fruits.

Planting.—From October until March.

Pruning.—No pruning is necessary other than providing for the proper formation of the main branches during the early stages of growth.

Propagation.—The best means is layering. This should be done in spring. Another method consists of cutting off a branch and inserting it during autumn in some good light soil, where it will probably take root. When rooted the lower branches should be removed in order to make a clean stem. The fruit is ripe from August onwards, and should not be gathered until fully ripe.

Historical.—Our forefathers ate Mulberries to give them appetites. Gerarde also says: "The barke being steeped in vinegar helpeth the tooth-ache: of the same effect is also the decoction of the leaves and barke."

See also MORUS.

MULCHING. A layer of material such as grass mowings spread on the surface above the roots of a plant helps the soil to retain its moisture by preventing rapid evaporation. Thus the plant roots are prevented from drying out. This method, largely practised by gardeners, is known as mulching. It forms a useful substitute in many cases for hoeing or watering. Manure is the best material to use as a mulch, as it definitely feeds the plant, but spent hops, leaves, etc., are equally good for keeping the soil moist. The material used should be spread evenly over the surface soil around the plant for the distance to which it is estimated the roots extend. A mulch in the flower border may be covered with a thin layer of soil to render it less unsightly. A mulch is most beneficial if applied after a shower.

In the case of shallow-rooting plants such as raspberries, a spring or early summer mulch is advisable to protect the roots from being scorched. Strawberries benefit from a strawy litter mulch, which will also protect the ripening fruits from being bruised and made dirty by the soil. A mulch of straw over vine roots which are outside the greenhouse will protect them from frosts.

MULLEIN. *See* VERBASCUM.

Mullein. *Known as the "Hag Taper," was much in use in witchcraft. Its leaves were used by the Ancient Greeks as lamp-wicks, and its stalks, soaked in suet, were the Romans' "funeral tapers."*

MURIATE OF POTASH. The commercial name for chloride of potash, usually sold as a basis of 50.5% pure potash.

MUSA (mu-za. Scitaminaceæ). Banana. Stove herbaceous perennials. Ornamental foliage and fruiting. Tropics, 1690.

Culture.—Compost: 2 parts rich fibrous loam, equal parts dry cow manure, leaf-mould and sand. Plant into well-drained tubs in the early spring and place in lofty, sunny position in stove. Copious supplies of water must be given during the growing season, moderately afterwards. Syringe daily at all times. A lively heat and moist atmosphere is essential. Winter temperature, 65°; summer, 75°-90°.

Propagate by suckers from the parent plant; placed in pots in the same compost as for established plants, plunged to their rims in fibre in the propagator with bottom heat temperature, 75°.

SPECIES.

M. cavendishii, 10 ft.

M. sapientum (Banana), 10–20 ft.

M. sparadisiaca (Plantain), 10–20 ft.

M. ensete may be used for garden decoration during the summer months. The tubs should be plunged to their rims in a sunny sheltered border.

MUSCARI (Grape Hyacinths). Liliaceæ. Hardy bulbs. Grape Hyacinths can be cultivated in any part of the garden, being equally suitable for groups in the mixed border, for edgings, for the sunny rockery, for naturalising in wild gardens, and also for indoor cultivation.

They should be planted if possible in a deep sandy loam and they will succeed in practically any soil. Small bulbs should be planted 2 in. deep, and larger bulbs rather deeper, allowing from 2–4 in. between the bulbs, and planting them either in a straight line or in masses. They can be planted at any time from August to November. Every third year the bulbs should be lifted, sorted and replanted.

If grown in pots, a mixture of two parts sandy loam, one part leaf-mould and one part sharp sand should be used. From 6 to 12 bulbs in a 5 in. pot, according to the size of the bulbs.

They are best stood in a cold frame under a layer of cinder ashes until growth commences, and then either in the cold frame, or in a very cool position indoors until the flowers have actually formed. After this they can be brought into the house rooms for decoration or can stand on the shelves of the greenhouse. Weak liquid manure during the flowering period will prove of assistance.

New plants can be raised from seed sown in light sandy soil in boxes or cold frames in September. Seedlings do not flower until they are 3 or 4 years old. The chief varieties cultivated are: *M. comosum,* tufted, with blue flowers in April, commonly called "Tassel Hyacinth"; *M comosum monstrosum,* bearing pale blue flowers in April, commonly known as "Feathered Hyacinth"; *M. azureum,* light blue; *M. plumosus,* mauve plume-like heads; *M. conicum,* "Heavenly Blue," fragrant, gentian blue.

MUSHROOMS (**Agaricus Campestris**). Fungi. Doubtless many consumers of mushrooms would scarcely recognise the common mushroom as it grows naturally in lawns or pastures. It is, however, easy to distinguish the common *Agaricus* from other fleshy fungi, and it may, therefore, at the outset be well to note some of the

upon this stalk there is supported the relatively large expanded part known as the cap or pileus. The cap is in reality a very essential part, producing, as noted later, the spores or propagative structures. The diameter and thickness of the pileus

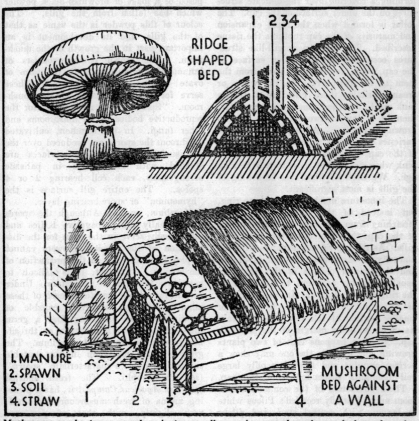

RIDGE
SHAPED
BED

1 2 3 4

1. MANURE
2. SPAWN
3. SOIL
4. STRAW

MUSHROOM
BED AGAINST
A WALL

Mushrooms can be grown anywhere in grass, cellars or in covered mushroom beds made under trees.

important characteristics of a typical form of the cultivated mushroom.

Characteristics of the Common Edible Mushroom.

Cap, Stem and Ring.—The field mushroom is interesting not only in appearance but in life history as well. The full grown mushroom (sporophore) is of the stout-stemmed umbrella type (*see* Photograph). It consists of a centrally-placed stalk, and

vary considerably in the different varieties, and with the conditions under which the plant is grown, but the diameter of the cap is usually about equal to the height of the stalk, and the thickness of the cap is about equal to the diameter of the stalk. The upper surface of the cap gives the main colour tone to the plant, and this, too, varies in the different varieties, from almost pure white or cream to purplish grey or dark brown.

The stem is usually cream or white, and near the cap end it is encircled by a ring or collar of tissue, known as the annulus. The annulus is the remnant of that tissue which in the younger plants connects the stem with the periphery of the cap, thus forming a covering over the delicate structures on the under surface of the cap. The collar is formed when the rapid expansion and maturity of the cap ruptures the tissue described. The lamallæ or gill-like structures occurring on the under surface of the cap, reach, for the most part, from the stem to the periphery. In the white or cream varieties these gills are distinctly pink until after the formation of the collar, then in a day or two they turn a deep brownish black. Among some of the varieties possessing a brown upper surface of the cap, the gills may be only greyish-pink when young, but these turn dark with age. We shall see that this darkening of the gills is most significant.

The immature mushrooms show no ring, but instead of this there is a "veil" stretching from the stem to the periphery of the cap, thus protecting the developing gills. As the cap rapidly expands with the maturity of the plant, the veil is broken and the greater portion of this structure usually remains adherent to the stem as the ring above indicated. In some varieties of the common mushroom, a larger or smaller portion of the veil may maintain its union with the margin of the pileus or cap. It often happens that of two plants growing side by side, the one may show a perfect annulus and the other only large veil remnants suspended from the cap.

These characters of the common mushroom may be briefly recalled: Pileus white to brown, with central stem and pileus convex: gills pink or pinky-brown, becoming brown-black: a characteristic annulus, ring or collar near the upper portion of the stem, and no other stem appendages at all.

The Production of Spores.—If one should take a full-grown mushroom after the under-surface of the cap has become exposed by the breaking away of the annulus, twist the stem until it breaks away from its attachment to the cap, or cut it off short, and then place the cap—gill surface downward—on a sheet of white paper,

there will be found in the course of twenty-four hours, more or less, a print.

To avoid draughts of air, a vessel may be inverted over the preparation. The print obtained is a fairly good reproduction of the projected form of the gills, being composed of a mass of brownish-black powder which has fallen from the gills. The colour of this powder is the same as that of the gills, and its development is an important part in the growth of the mushroom. The brown powder consists of innumerable minute cells in the form of ovate bodies, termed "spores." These serve for the reproduction of the mushroom. "Spore" is the designation for the reproductive bodies of all mushrooms and other fungi. In the common, cultivated mushroom the spores are produced over the gill surface only. These surfaces are studded with erect cells in palisade arrangement, each cell bearing 2 or 4 spores. The entire gill surface is the "hymenium" or spore-bearing layer.

Mycelium, spawn.—Although the spores are normally the propagative bodies and undoubtedly serve in the open for the distribution of the species, growers cannot employ these directly in the production of mushrooms. In fact, it is difficult to germinate them in the laboratory. Under certain favourable conditions, each of these minute cells is, however, capable of germinating and producing first a germ tube, ultimately a filamentous or thread-like growth, known as the mycelium. The growth of the mycelium in any suitable substratum yields a characteristic "spawn" (*see* Photograph). The fresh undried spawn of *Agaricus Campestris*, has a pleasing aroma of fresh mushrooms combined, very slightly, with that of powdered almonds.

Stages of the Mushroom.—When, in any favourable compost or other substratum, the spawn has developed sufficiently, and the conditions for fruiting are satisfactory, minute cushion-like areas of growth appear on the large threads. These become spherical in form and thus there arise the snow-white pin heads, the first unmistakable signs of mushroom growth. Under suitable conditions these pin heads grow fairly rapidly in size and are soon recognised as "buttons," ultimately as mature mushrooms. Under the best conditions for commercial mushroom production, a week or ten days will elapse between pin-heads and maturity. Commercial mushrooms are graded highest if picked just before the veil breaks.

The mycelium, or spawn, running through the substratum in all directions, absorbs the necessary moisture, as well as the organic and inorganic food materials required for its growth, and at the same time there accumulates a considerable surplus. This accumulation of food materials is shown by the rapidity with which mushrooms are produced, once the process is started.

Suitable Places for Mushroom Growing.

The main factors to be taken into consideration when choosing a situation for the growth of mushrooms are temperature and moisture, and, consequently, any situation in which these conditions may be so controlled as to accord with the requirements specified, should be satisfactory.

In France, mushrooms are grown in subterranean quarries, which now constitute a very extensive array of artificial caves, especially under Paris. These caves are responsible for the enormous development of the mushroom industry in that country.

The suburban caves are from a few feet to 50 ft. beneath the surface. They vary usually from 5–25 ft. in width, and from 5–20 or more feet in height. The caves are well ventilated by means of chimneys or chutes. The change of air is often facilitated by small charcoal fires beneath these air-chutes, and occasionally by the use of special ventilating devices. Entrance to the caves may be, on the one hand, through an open quarry more or less readily accessible, or it may be through a hole only a few feet or more in diameter, by means of a ladder, with a windlass for lifting or lowering materials. It may be noted that in England mushrooms are grown either in specially constructed houses, in cellars, barns; outhouses or in caves, and in the open air.

For temporary use, a mushroom house may consist of a very simple boarded shed or unused barn. It is necessary to provide a heater of some type, since the winter is the important season for mushroom work. Many commercial mushroom houses which pay well are not particularly elaborate.

As a permanent investment for mushroom-growing, the house should be built with due consideration for convenience, durability and economy. Perfect drainage is a factor of the first importance. To obtain this may be complicated by the fact that for convenience in heating, as well as for more uniform temperature considerations during the warmer parts of the season, it is often convenient to construct the house over an excavation which may be at least several feet lower than the natural surface. In constructing this type of house, arrangements should be made for the utmost convenience in unloading the compost and for cleaning out the old beds. The greatest economy is attained by the construction of houses high enough to accommodate the beds in tiers of from two to four.

It is necessary to allow about $2-2\frac{1}{2}$ ft. free space between the beds in tiers, and since the bed is at least 8–10 in. deep somewhat more than 3 ft. in height must be allowed for each bed. The better class of mushroom house is built with double walls, fresh shavings being packed between these. More expensive houses may be made of hollow brick or concrete. There will always be a moist atmosphere in the house, and the contact of moisture-laden air with cold walls may, of course, produce constant "sweating." A sufficiently sloping roof provided with air space will correct, to a large extent, this difficulty. It is usually advisable to place the ventilators in the roof, as this method assures less inconvenience from direct draughts.

When beds are to be prepared in caves, cellars, or merely on the floors of the buildings used, the matter of preparing for the beds is a very simple one. When every foot of space is to be used, the construction of supports for the different tiers will require particular attention. The upright supports for beds in tiers of three or four should not be less than 2×6 in., and these should be placed about 4 ft. apart. Supports made of gas piping are now largely used, and these, of course, are perfect from a sanitary point of view. Wall beds should seldom be more than 3 ft. across, but beds approachable from either side may be 6 ft. across. Paths need not be wider than 2 ft.

Open-air Culture.—In the South of England the extremes of temperature during the winter are not so great as to prohibit culture in modified hotbeds, or cold frames. Culture frames (minus glass) are used, and these are covered with sheet iron or boards upon which finally a layer of straw is placed, if necessary.

Method of Composting the Manure.

There is no substitute known for stable manure as a compost for commercial mushroom production. In selecting manure for mushroom work, only that which is recognised as of the highest quality should be taken. Considerable bedding straw should be present with the manure. The straw of the various grains seems to possess distinct advantages over that of other grasses, probably on account of a certain resistance to complete fermentation or decay, yielding a highly porous substratum which maintains an excellent physical condition in the beds. Avoid any manure from veterinary hospitals, or from stables which use freely any type of disinfectants. The ideal is manure from grain-fed, and worked horses, bedded with rye straw.

The Fermentation Process.—Beginning with good materials, the essentials are adequate moisture all the time and sufficient forking over, or turning, to effect equal ferment action and uniformity throughout. The manure contains many soluble organic substances which invite a vigorous development of mould fungi, if it is not fermented. During the fermentation process, the common mould fungi do not, as a rule, develop profusely, but bacterial and direct chemical action is facilitated. The result is such a stage in the decomposition of the material, as will favour the growth of mushroom spawn rather than the mycelia of moulds.

If fresh stable manure is secured, it should be thrown into piles not more than 4 ft. high and of any extent desired. It is unsatisfactory to make one great pyramid, or many small heaps. At first the manure should be thoroughly wet throughout.

Subsequently, it will be necessary to maintain it in a moist state, and to turn or fork over the pile three or four times, or oftener, depending upon the condition. Under ordinary circumstances, if the manure is well moistened, it may be properly fermented in three weeks or somewhat less, being turned at intervals of from three to five days. The presence of shavings or sawdust may necessitate a longer fermentation interval, and the longest fermentation period will be required when there is much resin in the shavings. At each turning it should be seen that there is sufficient moisture throughout the pile, and it is usually necessary to water during the turning process, in order that the moisture may reach all parts. A temperature of 140° to 150° F. between the first three turnings may be considered advantageous. If there is little moisture, the manure will "burn" easily and will require a much longer period of fermentation.

The difficulty of fermentation is increased if only a small quantity of compost is to be prepared. In this case it dries out quickly and a certain amount of "burning" is apt to occur. Special attention to the moisture and compactness of the material is then required, but whether it "burns" or not, the best type of fermentation is obtained when the temperature remains for several days at a time above 125° F. "Burning" indicates a fairly high temperature combined with a rapid drying out. In a properly-arranged compost pile, the greatest "burning" will occur just beneath the surface.

During composting, the manure should lose practically all objectionable odour, and there should be no unpleasantness after the preparation of the beds. Other unmistakable signs of sufficient composting are the oleaginous "feel," the pliability and the uniform colour of the straw. Usually the temperature declines to about 120° or 130° F. As soon as the compost is ready, it is advisable to make the beds and spawn when the temperature has dropped to about 70° F.

It is preferable to have the compost made under cover, particularly if prepared during midsummer or during freezing weather. Manure which has been piled

1. Lavatera—the Rose Mallow forms a large bush from spring-sown seed.
2. Phacelia—blue-flowered, compact habit, growing 9 in. high.
3. Viscaria—forms brilliant clumps of colour 1 ft. high.
4. Clarkias—useful for filling gaps in the borders.

1. A May-flowering Iris.
2. Iris graminea—a dwarf-growing species. Scented reddish flowers.
3. A specimen June-flowering Iris.
4. Clumps of Irises brighten the herbaceous border.
5. A succession of bloom can be maintained using Iris species.

in the open, or otherwise subjected to leaching, will have lost much of its value. In short never use for compost anything but the best fresh stable manure from grain-fed horses.

The Quantity of Compost required.—In estimating the amount needed, it is advisable to take into consideration the age, moisture content and compactness of the product, as well as the amount of straw content. The more straw content, the greater the loss of bulk after composting.

A Quick Method.—Where it is impossible to ferment the manure, and yet it is desired to grow mushrooms in a small way for home consumption, some measure of success may be attained by the following procedure: Free the fresh manure from long straw, mix thoroughly with one-third as much light garden loam, moisten if required, then let it stand three or four days before preparing the bed. Spread the material in the space for the bed, or in a box in layers of about 2 in. deep, firmly stamping down each layer until a bed 8 in. deep is prepared. Observe the temperature at intervals, and for spawning and subsequent care of the bed, follow the directions given later for beds of the usual type.

Substitutes for stable manure are not generally found to be successful for mushroom cultivation.

Moisture and Temperature.

It is advisable to have a more or less uniform temperature of the air, in the mushroom house, the best being from about 54° F. to 58° F. The amount of heat and the amount of cold which may permanently injure a bed will be determined very largely by the extent of the growth already made, and by the conditions of moisture. A mushroom bed will not be rendered useless by being heated to 70° F. or more, for brief periods, and it will withstand a low temperature, or even being frozen, for a considerable period of time. Any severe changes, however, either retard growth or act more injuriously. A high temperature of say 72° F. for 24 hours is fatal to the pin heads, and injurious to the spawn. If other organisms could be largely eliminated from the mushroom bed, it would be found that mushroom production would be possible at a

considerably higher temperature. However, as a high temperature stimulates the growth of other organisms such as insects, fungi and bacteria, and many of these either crowd out or directly attack the mushroom mycelium or the young pin heads, it is distinctly safer to work at the lower temperatures. However, pure cultures of *Agaricus Campestris* grow well up to 85° F. so long as sufficient moisture is present. This is positive proof that the conditions for growth in *pure cultures* are different from what they are in the mushroom bed, and this difference is largely due to the elimination of certain "biological" factors and enemies.

Moisture.—The moisture factor is one which should be considered as next in importance. With an atmosphere saturated with moisture, and with water dripping from the walls everywhere, the environment would be anything but favourable. On the other hand, the atmosphere should always contain a fairly high relative humidity, 60 to 75 per cent. being satisfactory. A gradual but slow evaporation from the surface of the beds is altogether desirable, and as a rule this can be easily regulated by controlling ventilation. The undesirable extremes, therefore, so far as moisture and ventilation are concerned, would be on the one hand, caves in which there could be no circulation of air, and, on the other, exposure to drying winds.

Light.—Light has no directly injurious effect upon the quality or productiveness of the cultivated mushrooms. Sunlight is, of course, accompanied by heat, and where the sun shines directly into a window, the temperature is appreciably raised. In cellars, therefore, which admit the sunlight through many windows, the temperature factor might be variable, and, during bright weather, too high for successful work. Mushrooms can be, and are indeed, grown in greenhouses, both under the benches and on the benches, under proper conditions of temperature and moisture.

Making, Spawning and Care of Beds.

There are two types of beds, namely: the flat bed and the ridge bed.

Flat Bed.—May be used in ordinary beds, outhouses, cellars or mushroom houses where the beds are made on the floor only and in mushroom houses or deep cellars, etc., where it is desirable to make use of the floor space and at the same time to arrange shelves in tiers. It will be readily understood that the shelf-bed system will often allow one to multiply the amount of available space four or five times.

The Ridge Bed.—This system permits of a more effective sanitation, and apart from slightly increasing the floor space, it does, to some extent, increase the yield possibilities.

Whatever the type of bed employed, the compost is taken into the area designed for the beds, and immediately arranged and "firmed" with a compressing board, to prevent it from becoming loose and dry. The flat bed should be made about 8–10 in. deep, that is, after suitable compression it should be of this depth.

The ridge beds may be arranged in groups of two, and it is usual to leave between each group of two a floor space of about 10 or 12 in., which will be reduced to about 9 in. after the process of casing. Each ridge bed should be about 20–24 in. wide at the base, tapering gradually to a top which should not be more than 6 in. across. They may be from 12–14 in. high. These dimensions will give to the ridge beds a gentle slope from crest to floor, which will permit of the production of heavy clusters. If the slope is much steeper, the mushrooms developed will be smaller, since they will not only be subject to more rapid drying out, but the clusters will also pull away more or less readily from their attachment to the spawn below, and thus will not reach the maximum size possible.

Between making and spawning beds.— The compost must remain moist when made into beds. If there is rapid drying at the surface, it must be sprinkled, but in a suitable cellar or mushroom house little attention to watering should be necessary during this interval. A sure test of sufficient moisture is to compress some of the compost in the hand. Under such pressure it will not be easy to squeeze from a properly prepared compost, any drops of water, yet the hand will be quite moist. This usually denotes a water content of about 65 per cent. For a few days after the preparation of the beds, the temperature may rise, but if so, it will quickly decline again. Spawning should not be carried out until there is a fall to 70° or 75° F.: in fact, spawning at 75° F. is permissible only when the temperature is unquestionably declining. 70° F. is preferable when one is prepared to maintain, during the growing period, a temperature of 55° F. in the houses. If beds are spawned at lower than 50° F., growth will be very slow. In spawning, lift the compost and insert the piece of spawn deep enough so that it may be covered fully 1 in. with manure, taking care to press the compost well around the piece of spawn, to prevent air-holes occurring. It is inadvisable to "case" or cover the bed with soil until it is seen that the spawn is running well. Casing consists in covering the bed throughout with a layer of earth (preferably virgin soil) 1–1½ in. deep. A pure sand or heavy clay soil is undesirable: the former loses moisture too easily, and the latter (especially where artificial heat is employed) is subject to baking. Such soil as is usually found just beneath a grass sod, is excellent.

Care after Casing.—The only factor to be considered after casing, besides temperature, is that of moisture of the bed and air. It is fatal to drench the bed with water, as in this case the spawn is destroyed, but on no account should the bed be allowed to dry out, otherwise the spawn will not grow near the surface of the bed and will not, therefore, produce mushrooms. The casing soil should be well moistened by repeated sprinkling with lukewarm water—not by a sudden drenching—as soon as the beds are cased. The beds should then be kept *merely moist*. If the casing soil is kept moist, there will be little danger of the beds drying out. When the mushrooms begin to appear, more water may be given.

The Growing Period.

All conditions being favourable, a bed of straw-manure compost should produce mushrooms within four to eight weeks of spawning. However, if shaving-manure compost is used, the beds may take twelve weeks to bear. In the same way, even with the best spawn, the growth will be slow if the manure is inadequately fermented, if the temperature is low, or if the moisture conditions are unsatisfactory.

Flushes of Growth.—When the mushrooms begin to form, they usually appear first almost directly over the inoculum of spawn inserted, so that under uniform conditions, the first patches of buttons will be regularly distributed. As these clusters all push toward maturity simultaneously, it may be called a "flush" of fruiting (*see* Photograph). When these are picked, a little fresh earth should be placed where necessary, and the bed sufficiently watered. It may be a week or more before a second flush of buttons occurs.

Period of Production.—This varies from a few weeks to several months, depending upon conditions. After a bed has apparently ceased to bear, it should not at once be discarded, but examined first, as sometimes an application of water—heavier than usual—may cause it to yield an additional supply.

Care during Production.—Beds which are yielding heavily will, undoubtedly, require considerable water so long as mushrooms are evident. The water applied should be of the temperature of the bed. Obviously one must beware of water if ventilation is poor and evaporation practically nil: indeed, there is then nothing more disastrous than too much water. If the bed shows sign of cracking through change from a moist to a dry atmosphere, some type of covering may be necessary. The simplest cover method is to spread newspapers over the bed. When the condition is likely to be permanent, a framework may be made to extend 6–12 in. above the bed, with cheese cloth or unbleached cotton over the frame. In this connection it is necessary to call attention again to the fact that such coverings should never be used where they retain so much moisture that the effect is to induce a "stemmy" development of the mushrooms, at the expense of the caps. In open-air culture, matting is often used over the frames—thus retaining moisture and preserving a more uniform temperature.

Between Crops.—Immediately the beds in a mushroom house or cellar have ceased to produce, they should be removed and the house thoroughly cleaned and fumigated or sprayed. None of the old compost, soil, etc., used in the beds, should be employed in any subsequent mushroom crop. The old compost is, however, quite suitable for flowers, lawns and gardens, etc. When the beds have been destroyed and the old compost removed, all wooden supports and boards, as well as the walls and floors of the house, should be thoroughly cleaned. For preference the boards should be taken from the house or cellar, and as soon as dry, white-washed with a lime-wash made from good stone lime, or thoroughly sprayed with strong copper sulphate solution. Where possible the walls of the cellar should also be sprayed with one of these washes.

Food Value of Mushrooms.

Doctors—particularly continental doctors, who have better opportunities for observing the advantages of a mushroom diet—are increasingly favouring an "Eat more Mushroom" campaign. They say: "Mushrooms should be an item of diet which everyone eats regularly, just the same as in the case of bread and meat. If the true food value of mushrooms was generally realised, there would be as much demand for them as there is for potatoes to-day. They are, though, infinitely superior to potatoes, being capable of far more variations in cooking, so that they can be introduced twice into even the same meal, without risk of monotony. From the scientific standpoint, their high mineral value makes them a first-class foodstuff, especially for invalids, while their high percentages of glycogen, their oily and sugary elements, make them equivalent to other vital constituents of our daily diet. Their large albuminoid content has led them to be called 'vegetable meat' because they combine the essentials of meat without its indigestibility."

MUSK. *See* Mimulus.

MUSK MALLOW. *See* Malva.

MUSSAENDA (mus-sen-da. Rubiaceæ). A genus of stove evergreen shrubs and sub-shrubs with a few herbs. Resemble Bouvardia. Cuttings taken in spring. Plant in equal parts of loam and peat with a liberal dash of sand.

SPECIES.

M. erythrophylla. Sulphur-yellow flowers with scarlet bracts.

M. macrophylla. Orange flowers in May. 8 ft.

M. speciosa. Red. August.

M. uniflora. White.

MUSSEL SCALE (*Lepidosaphes ulmi*).

DESCRIPTION. *Scale.* — About ⅛ in. in length, brown in colour and shaped like

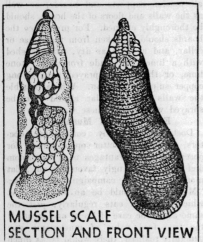

MUSSEL SCALE
SECTION AND FRONT VIEW

The Mussel Scale is one of the most injurious scale insects. It attacks apples and other fruits.

a mussel shell. *Female.*—White legless body under the scale. *Eggs.*—Minute oval bodies, white in colour and under the scale. *Male.*—About $\frac{1}{16}$ in. in length with long antennæ and a pair of comparatively large wings. Very rare. *Larva.*— About $\frac{1}{90}$ in. in length with six legs.

LIFE-HISTORY. — The larvæ hatch out from the eggs under the scale and in the early summer crawl out and wander over the twigs and branches of the apple. Having found a suitable position, they bury their beaks into the bark and become stationary. If they are to become females, they now begin to form a scale over themselves, and when they are completely covered, they begin to lose their limbs and form by a process of "degeneration." On the other hand, a very small percentage are destined to become males, in which case they develop, eventually

growing wings. They then seek out the females under the scales and fertilise them. In a short while the females commence egg-laying, and as this process proceeds they gradually shrivel up. Their skins, with the eggs, may be found under the scale during the winter months.

METHODS OF CONTROL.—Tar-oil winter washes in the dormant season will destroy the scale.

MUSTARD (*Brassica alba.* Syn. *Sinapis alba*). Largely used with Cress for salads.

Culture.—Make successional sowings from March onwards in the border in fine rich soil. Cover with boards or mats until the seeds germinate and water plentifully. Gather when 1 in. high.

Indoor Culture.—Sow on surface of soil in shallow boxes; cover with a sheet of paper or board.

MUTISIA (mū-tis-i-a. Compositæ). S. America. Evergreen half-hardy climbers.

Culture.—Plant in a well-drained light soil. *Propagate* by cuttings placed in gentle heat in spring and by seeds.

M. Clematis (Peru). Scarlet flowers.

M. decurrens, with beautiful flowers of a bright orange-scarlet or vermilion colour. 4–5 in. across, resembling a fine Gazania or *Cerbera Jamesonii.* In favourable gardens in warm districts it thrives in the open, rambling through some deciduous shrub of twiggy growth. It likes a porous, open soil perfectly drained. When happy the plant suckers freely and they should *not* be removed.

M. illicifolia. The holly leaved Mutisia, with lovely pink blooms.

MYOSOTIDIUM (my-ō-sō-tid-ium. Boragineæ). New Zealand Forget-me-not. The only species of this genus, *M. nobile,* is a rather short-lived half-hardy perennial with large glossy leaves on erect stems and many white blue-centred flowers in May. *Propagate* by seeds or by division in spring, and plant in a shaded place in good moist garden soil or in a peaty compost. 2 ft.

MYOSOTIS (myo-sō-tis. Boraginaceæ). Forget-me-not. The charming and popular Forget-me-not, a common British plant that has always been known in gardens, is included in this genus of annual, biennial and perennial plants. They are useful in the greenhouse as well as in beds, borders and rockeries. They are particularly valuable in spring, as the early flowering varieties commence to flower in March.

Culture.—All the species may be propagated by seeds sown in the open in spring, or they may be allowed to sow themselves, which they do freely. The perennials, several of which are treated as biennials, are also increased by division of the rootstock in spring and by cuttings placed under a hand-light or bell-glass in summer. They grow well in moist soil in shady places but are quite successful in any position in ordinary garden soil.

SPECIES.

M. alpestris, a compact biennial plant with lovely blue flowers that are fragrant in the evening, is best in the rockery as its natural habitat is moist rocks. It is sometimes regarded as a variety of *sylvatica*. Its varieties "Queen Victoria," "Royal Blue," and "Star of Love," which are all larger and better than the species, are best for bedding with bulbs as they are of dense habit and bear rich blue flowers which last well into the summer but gradually lose their colour in the hot weather.

M. dissitiflora has large flowers of sky blue that continue until midsummer. 6–12 in.

M. palustris, the true Forget-me-not, a native of British marshland, bears spreading stems with numerous pale blue flowers. With its varieties *grandiflora* and *semperflorens* (the latter having a long flowering season), it is suitable for water gardens, for edging moist beds, shrubberies, etc.

M. sylvatica, the wood Forget-me-not, is very like *dissitiflora* and is suitable for wild gardens, while it has white, pink and striped forms that are cultivated for beds and borders.

M. versicolor, a tiny native plant that is found in the crevices of limestone rock, with very small dainty flowers, can live in a mere dusting of soil and will grow well on walls. In sufficient soil it becomes quite big.

MYRICA (mǐ-rǐ'-ka. Myricaceæ). Sweet Gale Bayberry. America. Deciduous and evergreen shrubs, with fragrant leaves; flowers borne in catkins.

American varieties produce a white wax-coated fruit. Thrives in any good non-calcareous garden soil. *Propagate* by seed and layers.

SPECIES.

M. asplenifolia. See COMPTONIA.

M. cerifera. Semi-evergreen shrub, 20 ft., aromatic foliage with wax-covered fruit.

M. Gale. "Native Sweet Gale." A fragrant foliaged dwarf shrub, 2–4 ft., with flowers in catkins during May and June.

MYROBALAN. "Cherry Plum." *See* PRUNUS CERASIFERA.

MYRRH. *See* MYRRHIS.

MYRRHIS (mir-his. Umbelliferæ). Sweet Cicely. Myrrh. The British Myrrh *M. odorata* is a hardy perennial that was formerly much used as a pot herb and for salads.

Propagate by cuttings, seed or division. Grows in any soil. It is suitable for growing in the mixed border or in the wilder parts of the garden and bears fragrant white flowers in May with delicately-cut leaves. Plant in autumn or spring.

MYRTLE GRASS. *See* ACORUS.

MYRTUS (mir'tus. Myrtaceæ). Myrtle. W. Asia. 10–15 ft. Evergreen shrub, suitable for mild regions with wall protection. Small white or pink flowers followed by small black, red and white berries. Thriving in good soil in sunny position. *Propagate* by half-ripened cuttings in slight heat. Adaptable for training to walls or fences.

M. communis. "Common Myrtle" (S. Europe). Fragrant flowers during July and August. Held sacred as a symbol to the goddess of love by the ancient Britons.

M. c. microphylla. Distinct small-leaved variety.

M. c. variegata. Variegated foliage.

M. Luma (Eugenia apiculata). Chile. Cinnamon-red bark and cream coloured stems. Fragrant flowers from July to September. Likes sandy peat.

M. lusitanica tarentina (Jenny Reitenbach). Compact habit, with small leaves similar to *M. communis.*

N

NANDINA (nan-di'-na. Berberidaceæ). China. 4–6 ft. Evergreen shrub having highly-coloured fern-like leaves, and white flowers borne in panicles during June and July, followed by coral-red berries. Hardy except in the coldest districts.

When applied as a soil fumigant, naphthalene should be sprinkled on the surface and then dug in to a depth of 6 in. or more. To facilitate even distribution, it may be mixed with twice its weight of fine sand, sifted soil or ashes. It should be

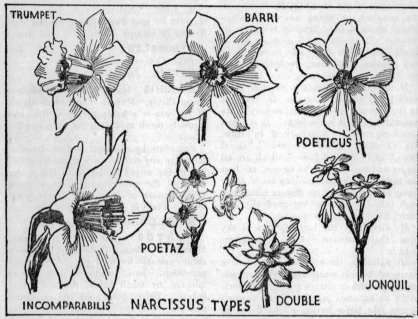

There are many thousands of Daffodils and Narcissi in cultivation, but they can all be grouped according to type, of which the above are the principal groups.

Culture.—Plant in good sandy loam, with peat and leaf-mould. *Propagate* by cuttings placed in bottom heat.

N. domestica. The only species.

NAPHTHALENE. A white crystalline compound with a characteristic odour. A product of the distillation of coal tar. The pure product is a glistening white solid, sold in the form of flakes or lumps, or moulded into balls, cakes or sticks (often termed "camphor-tar" or "carbon"). It is used extensively either alone or admixed with other substances as a soil fumigant for the destruction of soil pests, such as surface caterpillars, grubs, wireworms, sawfly larvæ, insect pupæ and root-infesting aphides.

applied at the rate of 1½–2 lb. to each rod of ground to be treated.

NARCISSUS (Daffodils, Jonquils, Pheasant's Eye. Amaryllidaceæ). Hardy, bulbous perennials. The amateur gardener often inquires what is the difference between a Narcissus and a Daffodil. The answer is, of course, that Narcissus is the family name, which includes Daffodils, Jonquils, and all other varieties of the same genus. "Daffodil" is more often used for the trumpet varieties of Narcissus, that is, the varieties which have a long trumpet, but it is also used sometimes for the short-cup yellow varieties. "Narcissus" or "Pheasant's Eye" are more common names for the white-flowered short-cupped varieties, while the Polyanthus varieties are generally called Jonquils. Like most common names, however, these vary considerably among different growers.

CLASSIFICATION OF NARCISSI GROUPS.

The following is a brief guide to the classification of Narcissi, which will help the novice:

(1) *Yellow, White, or Bicolor Trumpets*: These have trumpets as long as, or longer than, the perianth segment.

(2) *Yellow and Bicolor Short Cup or Incomparabilis*: In these the cup is not less than one-third, but less than equal to the length of the perianth segments.

(3) *Yellow and Bicolor Barrii*: In these the cup should be less than one-third the length of the perianth segments. They have as a rule bright-coloured cups, and perianths bright yellow or white.

(4) *Large and Small crowned Leedsii*, or *Eucharis-flowered*: Here the outer petals are white, with white or pale yellow or cream cups, sometimes tinged pink.

(5) *Triandrus*: With short cup, and reflexed outer petals.

(6) *Cyclamineus*: Pale yellow with darker and very narrow trumpet.

(7) *Jonquil flowered, Tazetta or Polyanthus*: All bunch-flowered and white or yellow with yellow cups.

(8) *Poeticus or Poet's Narcissus*: Petals white or yellow, with red eye.

(9) *Double*.

NARDOSTACHYS (nar-dos-tak-is. Valerianaceæ). Hardy perennial herbs suitable for cultivation on the rockery. These may be grown in ordinary soil, and can be increased by cuttings taken in summer, and inserted under a hand-light.

SPECIES.

N. jatamansi, pink, August. Height, 1–1½ ft.

NARTHECIUM (nar-the-si-um. Liliaceæ). Bog Asphodel. Iris-like herbaceous plants of dwarf habit adapted for growing in the mixed border.

Propagate by division in spring and grow in a cool border in sandy peat or sand and leaf-mould.

SPECIES.

N. ossifragum with yellow flowers in July, 3 in., and its variety *americanum* with narrower leaves.

NASTURTIUM. *See* TROPÆOLUM. Nasturtium is the botanical name of the common Watercress.

NAVELWORT, VENUS'S. *See* OMPHALODES.

NECTARINE. *See* PEACH *and* NECTARINE.

NEGUNDO. *See* ACER NEGUNDO.

NEILLIA (nē-il'-li-a. Rosaceæ). 5–8 ft.

The common Nasturtium thrives in poor soil, but must have sunshine to produce plenty of flowers.

Hardy deciduous shrubs, similar to Spiræas, with racemes of small flowers.

Culture.—Plant in a moist situation in ordinary soil. *Propagate* by cuttings in frame.

SPECIES.

N. longiracemosa (China). Racemes of lovely pink flowers.

N. opulifolia (*Spiræa opulifolia. Physocarpus opulifolius*). N. America. Flowers white, tinged pink.

N. o. lutea (*aurea*). Leaves a beautiful shade of yellow in spring.

N. sinensis. Rosy-pink flowers in June.

N. Torreyi (*Physocarpus monogynus*)

California. Small foliage with white or light-pink flowers.

N. thibetica (China). Attractive foliage and small pink flowers.

NELUMBIUM (ne-lum-bi-um. Nymphæaceæ). Sacred Bean; Water Bean; Egyptian Lotus. Handsome aquatics with very attractive flowers and leaves. Formerly prized by the Egyptians as the symbol of fertility and embodied by them

NECTARINE

Those who dislike the "flannel" skin of the Peach should grow Nectarines. They thrive outdoors on a south wall.

in much of their literature and works of art. In the Far East the plants are still regarded as sacred. According to Homer in his Odyssey that wanderer of wanderers, Ulysses, came upon an island where the inhabitants ate the fruit of the lotus and had no further desire for aught but the lotus. Some of Ulysses' sailors, having eaten of this fruit, refused to help him to return home and had to be carried on board by force. In N. America the roots of *N. luteum* are eaten.

In Britain they are almost hardy, but only in very favoured places can they be planted in the open. The best way to

grow them is to plant them in tubs which can be plunged out of doors in summer and taken in for the winter, or they may be kept in a tank in a cool house with a temperature of 45°–50°.

They should be planted in loam with well-rotted manure about 1 ft. below the surface of the water.

Propagate by seeds sown under glass in winter or by dividing the roots when growth is commencing.

SPECIES.

N. luteum. The yellow flowers of this species are rather like Tulips. Edible roots.

N. speciosum, with white flowers edged with rose, has many good varieties such as *album grandiflorum*, large white flowers; *album plenum*, *album striatum*, striped with red; *Osiris*, bright red; *pekinense rubrum*, double red; *pygmœum*, dwarf red; *roseum grandiflorum* and *roseum plenum*.

NEMASTYLIS (ne-mas-ti-lis. Irideæ). Half-hardy bulbs requiring the same culture as Gladioli, *q.v.*

SPECIES.

N. cœlestina. Blue. July. 2 ft.

N. geminiflora. Yellow, blue and black flowers, very ephemeral. Summer, 6 in.

NEMESIA (ne-me-si-a. Scrophularineæ). Half-hardy annuals from S. Africa, 6–12 in. Seed should be sown under glass, end of March, plants grown cool, and planted into flowering places end of May, or may be sown outside in light soil in May. They succeed best in a moderately light soil and in a sunny position flower most freely, making splendid bedding plants. *N. strumosa* is the best type, and the varieties Aurora (carmine and white); Fire King (scarlet); Orange Prince (rich orange); Blue Gem (Forget-me-not blue); and the Triumph Mixed in a fine range of all colours, give a wealth of rich colouring unobtainable in any other class of summer bedding plants. There are a number of other Nemesia species, some with long-spurred flowers, but they are sparse flowering and not of much service in the garden.

NEMOPHILA (ne-mof-il-a. Hydrophyllaceæ). North America. *N. insignis*, a most accommodating hardy annual plant. Seeds may be sown in August and September for spring flowering, or in April to June for summer display. A

SPECIES.

N. oleander (Oleander or Rose Bay), red;
Varieties, *Henri Mares*, rose-pink (double);
Madonna grandiflorum, cream (double);
N. splendens, red (double).

NESÆA (nĕ-sē'-a. Lythrarieæ).
America, 4 ft. Deciduous shrubs of compact habit, narrow leaves, and small
flowers produced from July to September.
Need protection in cold districts.

Culture.—Plant in ordinary soil. *Propagate* by seeds or cuttings.

SPECIES.

N. salicfolia. Small yellow flowers.

NETTING. Netting for fences. Fish
netting is used by the gardener to protect
fruit from birds, and also to save the
blossom of wall-fruits from frost. Where
much fruit is grown netting can be used
to form fruit cages. These are made of
wooden supports and cross laths with netting about 1 in. mesh stretched across.
In the arrangement of fruit trees all soft
fruits such as bush cherries and plums,
currants, raspberries, strawberries, etc.,
should be grouped together for convenient
caging, as a protection from birds.

See FENCES.

NETTLE TREE. *See* CELTIS.

NEVIUSIA (nev-i-us-i-a. Rosaceæ).
N. America, 4–5 ft. Deciduous hardy
shrubs; small leaves and white flowers.

NEW ZEALAND FLAX. *See* PHORMIUM.

NEW ZEALAND FORGET-ME-NOT.
See MYOSOTIDIUM.

NICANDRA (ni-kan-dra. Solanaceæ).
Hardy annual from Peru. A rather
coarse-growing plant with pale blue bell-shaped flowers. Sow in open in April,
ordinary soil, transplant when 3 in. tall,
giving ample room. *N. Physaloides* is
the only species grown. 3 ft.

NICOTIANA (nĭ-cō-tiā-na. Solanaceæ). Tobacco Plant. Apart from the
species *Tabacum*, which is commercially
important on account of the tobacco obtained from its leaves, a few plants of this
genus of half-hardy perennials are used
for decorative purposes and grown as
annuals.

Culture.—Seed should be sown in heat
in February and the seedlings pricked out
into pans. In June they should be planted
in the open in warm rich loam in a

sheltered position, and the plants staked.
If surrounded at soil level with soot, the
plants will be kept free from slugs, which
like the succulent stems.

Species.—*N. alba* (syn. *affinis*) is the
most widely grown and produces large
white flowers, which are sweetly scented at
night, when they are more open than in the
day. They last in bloom for several months

NICOTIANA

The Tobacco Plant is a good annual for the
shady border and is at its best in the evening
time.

in the greenhouse, and until the frost cuts
them down when grown outside. Height,
2–3 ft.

N. sylvestris, with white, and *N. Sanderæ*, with rose or magenta flowers, are
good border plants. 3–4 ft.

N. tomentosa is sometimes grown for its
foliage, which is large and beautiful, while
its flowers are white or pink. 9–15 ft.

A small-flowered Nicotiana hybrid now
obtainable, is more decorative than the
older type, but just a little less fragrant.

NICOTINE WASH. *See* FORMULÆ.

NIEREMBERGIA (nē-rem-bēr-gia.
Solanaceæ). Half-hardy perennials mostly

with creeping or diffuse stems. Suitable for rock-work or for growing in pots.

Culture.—Propagate by seeds sown in heat in spring or autumn or by cuttings and division in spring. They like a soil similar to that given to Petunias, i.e., composed of three parts of sandy loam to one of manure, with a little sand. They like an ample supply of water and the variety *rivularis* is best grown in pots standing in

Nierembergia rivularis is a dainty trailing plant for moist parts of the rock garden Unfortunately it has no common name.

water. In cold weather allow the plants to rest completely in the greenhouse, only giving them sufficient water to prevent them from withering. In spring, repot all plants whether for bedding out later or for indoor culture.

SPECIES.

N. gracilis is usually grown as a half-hardy annual. Its flowers are white streaked with purple and have yellow centres. It blooms from July to September. Height, 9 in.

N. rivularis is more suitable for damp places and will form a dense carpet in the moister parts of the rock garden, or will grow well in pots. Its flowers are white tinged with yellow or rose. Height 3 in.

NIGELLA (ni-gel-la. Ranunculaceæ). South Europe. "Love-in-a-mist" or "Devil-in-a-bush." Very pretty hardy annuals with flowers in white and varying shades of blue, partly hidden by feathery leafy bracts; will succeed in ordinary garden soil, sown where to flower in March to May, and thinned to 6–9 in. apart. Very useful for cut flowers. *N. damascena* (dark blue), *N. d. Miss Jekyll* (pale blue or white), *N. hispanica* (dark blue with red-purple stamens) are desirable kinds.

NIGHT-SCENTED STOCK. *See* MATTHIOLA.

NIGHTSHADE, DEADLY. *See* BELLADONNA and POISONOUS PLANTS.

NITRATE OF SODA. A valuable nitrogenous fertiliser. Occurs in natural deposits in Chile as "caliche," from which it is washed out and evaporated as a fairly pure salt.

A very pure form is now made synthetically in England.

NITRIFICATION. The roots of plants can only absorb water and salts in solution. Thus they are not able to make use of the free nitrogen of the air until it has been changed into soluble nitrates. Their change, which is brought about by soil bacteria, is known as nitrification. Bacteria flourish in warmth, moisture and darkness. These conditions can be provided for them by thorough cultivation of the soil.

NITRO-CHALK. A fertiliser combining the advantage of sulphate of ammonia and nitrate of soda. Also contains lime.

Nitro-Chalk is probably the most efficient top-dressing in the world, since the nitrate nitrogen it contains acts on the crop immediately; this quick action being followed by a gradual feeding process lasting throughout the growing period.

The lime content of Nitro-Chalk, although in no sense taking the place of dressings of pure lime, is yet sufficient to check the development of such diseases as "finger and toe" and to give a good start to barley and sugar beet on sour soils. Like many fertilisers, Nitro-Chalk cannot be obtained in quantities of less than 1 cwt.

NITROGEN. A colourless, odourless gas upon which the whole life of the world depends. All living tissues are largely made up from it and probably only the discovery of synthetic processes for recovering it from the air and fixing it into nitrogenous fertilisers has saved the world from ultimate starvation. No plant can grow without it and it is the one element almost invariably deficient in soils. *See also* PLANT FOODS.

NOLANA (no-la-na. Convolvulaceæ). Hardy annual trailing plants from Peru. *N. atriplicifolia* (syn. *N. grandiflora*) is the species usually grown. Suitable for sowing on a sunny rockery where its blue, bell-shaped flowers are seen to best advantage. May be grown as an edging plant or in baskets in cool greenhouse. Sow outdoors April to May.

NOLINA (no-li-na. Liliaceæ). Greenhouse and half-hardy bulbous plants sometimes known under the generic name of Beaucarnea.

Propagate by division or seeds. Plant in leaf-mould and sand.

SPECIES.

N. erumpens, *N. georgiana*, white, summer. 2–3 ft. *N. recurvata*. White flowers and drooping leaves. 2–3 ft.

NORWAY MAPLE. *See* ACER.

NOTHOFAGUS (noth-ō-fā-gus. Cupuliferæ). Southern Beeches. S. America and Australia. Deciduous and evergreen trees, with small flowers, followed by three-cornered nuts, similar to beech nuts but smaller. Suitable for the milder parts of the country, and thriving in a moist non-calcareous soil.

Propagate by layers.

SPECIES.

N. antarctica, Antarctic Beech (S. America). Deciduous, attaining large proportions when established, with small leaves on branches 3 ft. long.

N. Cunninghamii, Cunningham's Beech (Tasmania). Evergreen, glossy-leaved species, for the milder districts, in semi-shade.

N. Dombeyi (Chile). Evergreen, slender growths and glossy green leaves.

N. procera (Chile). Deciduous, quick-growing, corrugated leaves colouring in autumn to a beautiful yellow.

N. Solandri (New Zealand). Evergreen, with narrow oblong foliage.

NOTHOPANAX (noth-ō-pan′-ax. Araliaceæ). Panax. Evergreen trees, with elegant ornamental foliage, thriving in well-drained soil. *Propagate* by stem or root cuttings, with gentle bottom heat.

SPECIES.

N. arboreum, Whauwhaupaku of New Zealand, having 5–7 lobed leaves, requiring sheltered position.

N. Davidii (China). Very hardy,

NIGELLA

A blue hardy annual with delicate foliage. It is called Love-in-a-mist or Devil-in-the-bush. If you hold the flowers sideways you can see the devil's horn which becomes more conspicuous as the seed-pods form.

resembling the so-called Castor Oil plant, with large lobed leaves.

NOTOSPARTIUM (nō-tō-spar-tium. Leguminosæ). New Zealand, 4–8 ft. Deciduous, almost leafless shrub, producing in July racemes of beautiful pink, pea-like flowers. Protect during frost.

Culture.—Plant in light loam, in a well-drained soil, in semi-shade. *Propagate* by seeds.

N. Carmichaeliæ. Pink Broom. Graceful habit, having rush-like branches, and racemes of lovely pink flowers.

NOVEMBER WORK IN THE GARDEN.

THE FLOWER GARDEN.

Plan the new flower garden this month. Cut the outline of the beds before digging. Dig new beds deeply, turning the soil over to at least 10 in. deep. 18 in. below the surface the soil should be broken up sufficiently to ensure good drainage.

Give a good dressing of lime over the soil after digging.

Immediate plantings can be made in mild weather of Wallflowers, Polyanthus, and Darwin tulips.

Where sheltered positions can be given, Sweet Peas may be sown this month. They can be sown in pots if a cold frame is available, and kept under glass till the spring. Open out trenches for the sowing of exhibition Sweet Peas next year. Trenches should be at least 18 in. deep, preferably 2 ft. Loosen the bottom soil and leave the trenches open until Christmas.

Order farm manure if available, and if not, keep all the leaves and other vegetable refuse stored in a heap or pit to be dug into the bottom of the trenches when they are filled in. This is especially necessary on land that has a tendency to dry out.

Good varieties of Sweet Peas for autumn sowing, to provide plentiful supplies of cut flowers for the house, are:

Charity, crimson; Constance Hinton, white; Apple Blossom, pink; Mrs. Tom Jones, blue; Powerscourt, lavender; Warrior, maroon.

Tulips can be planted this month, together with Arabis, Forget-me-nots, Wallflowers, and Polyanthus.

Lift Dahlias and Gladioli. Store in dry, frost-proof shed or attic. Protect all plants of doubtful hardiness.

Plant Pæonies in deeply-trenched and well-manured ground. Also plant Ranunculus.

Give shrubby Calceolaria cuttings plenty of air in order to maintain a sturdy growth.

Cut down Chrysanthemums that have bloomed, and keep the soil in the pots moist to induce a good production of shoots for cuttings.

Hollyhocks should be propagated from the whole stools or by eyes from the flowering stems, but should not be forced. Pansies may be potted off as a reserve for filling up vacancies or for making new beds in the spring.

The Spanish and English Iris may still be planted outdoors. Lilies of the Valley may also be planted. Anemone (tubers), Canterbury Bells, Primroses, Pansies, Sweet Williams, Violets and Wallflowers may still be planted out.

The stock of cuttings should be sorted, and those which require similar treatment during the winter should be placed together in separate frames.

Plant roses, but only when the ground is fairly dry. If the soil is too wet, heel in the new trees and await a favourable opportunity for planting.

THE SHRUBBERY.

Roses and deciduous shrubs should be planted when the leaves are absent.

Make holes wider and deeper than are at first needed. Spread the roots out when planting. Do not let them hang down into the holes. Cover with fine soil and give the plant a shake to ensure that the soil particles surround all the roots.

Put in a sufficiently strong stake before filling in the soil. Tread the soil firm after planting.

Tie a label with the name, etc., on to the stake. After the first frost, examine newly-planted shrubs, and press back any weather-loosened soil round the stem.

Scented deciduous shrubs to plant now include:

Daphne mezereum, Abelia rupestris, Viburnum fragrans, Chimonanthus fragrans, Lonicera fragrantissima, Lilac.

Dwarf evergreen shrubs suitable for the rock garden for present planting include: Thuya orientalis, Cotoneaster congesta, Rosemary officinalis, Cupressus obtusa nana, Rododendron oleofolium, Picea excelsa gregoryana.

Roses are frequently treated with animal manure in large doses. This is good, but should be supplemented by a good dressing of lime during this month.

Half a pound to one square yard is the maximum amount, and where isolated specimens are grown, this quantity for each will not be too much.

Rhododendrons thrive best in a position sheltered from north and east winds, and where they obtain some shade. They need a soil deficient in lime, and prefer a moist, peaty loam, and will grow in most town gardens.

Plant hardy hedge shrubs such as Aucuba, Box, Euonymus, Laurel, Yew, Privet and Lilac.

VEGETABLES.

One important matter in the vegetable garden this month is to collect all fallen leaves. These are useful for hotbeds and for making leaf-mould.

As much digging as possible should be done during dry weather. Leave the surface rough.

Cut down the stems of Globe artichokes. Remove decaying leaves and protect the crowns from frosts with stable litter.

Strong suckers can be severed from the parent crown and potted up for wintering in cold frames. Remove in mild weather.

Lift and store Jerusalem artichokes in sand.

Cut down asparagus to the ground, and give a good dressing of short stable manure over the bed.

Where the soil is light and warm, a few broad beans of the variety Early Mazagan, or long-pod varieties, may be sown. If a cold frame or a greenhouse is available, seeds can be sown in pots, 4 to an 8 in. pot, or they can be sown in the open in drills 3–4 in. deep, allowing 2 or 3 ft. between the rows.

The first sowing of early peas can be made this month, in warm soil. Little Marvel, Edwin Beckett and Quite Content are good varieties for this purpose. These should not be sown in the open until early spring if the soil is cold and heavy.

Heel over broccoli towards the north, and well cover the stems with soil.

Lift cauliflowers not yet ready and heel them in, either in cold frames, or in some place well protected from frosts. The leaves should be tied loosely together in a point over the crowns. Finish earthing up celery and leeks.

Lift chicory roots and plant them in boxes of soil in the greenhouse or shed. Keep them dark to provide young white shoots for the salad bowl.

Cover parsley beds with litter so that they are not frosted, otherwise there will be difficulty in lifting the roots.

Admit air to the cold frame where lettuce is grown. Remove decayed leaves and stir the surface soil to prevent damping off.

Asparagus should, if not already done, be cut down, and the bed dressed with well-rotted manure.

Beetroot and carrots should be lifted. Endive should be blanched in successive batches.

Parsnips should be covered with a little litter, unless dug up and stored in sand.

Seed potatoes should be gone over carefully and any diseased specimens burnt. If left, they rapidly contaminate good ones. All roots to be stored should be taken up before the end of the month.

Scorzoneras must be left in the ground until wanted.

Spinach will continue to grow if thinned properly.

Horse radish may be planted this month. Plan next year's cropping in the vegetable plot. Continue to dig and trench.

Ridge up celeriac, parsnips and turnips.

Cut leaves of rhubarb and seakale and cover for the winter.

Plant leeks for late supplies.

FRUIT.

During this month the greater part of planting and transplanting of fruit trees should be carried out.

Currants and gooseberries should be planted now, and should be encouraged by thorough preparation of the soil. They thrive best and give the finest results if grown in rich well-drained loam.

Early and late varieties should be planted to give a succession of fruit. Plant 5 ft. apart, and prune back moderately hard after planting.

Good varieties for the amateur gardener to plant now are:

Currants.

Cherry, early red; Red Dutch; Mammoth, red, late; Boskoop Giant, black, early; September Black; White Dutch.

Gooseberries.

Crown Bob, red, early; Lord Derby, red, late; Golden Gem; Yellow Ball, early; White Lion.

If not already done, old wood should be cut away on Black Currants, leaving stems of one season's growth for next year's fruit.

On clay or stiff soil apply a $\frac{1}{4}$-$\frac{1}{2}$ lb. of basic slag and 1 or 2 oz. of Kainit to each bush.

On light soil, wait until spring to apply artificial fertilisers, otherwise they would be washed out of the soil before the plant roots are active.

Various fruit trees and bushes may be attended to with a knife.

Untie peaches, apricots, nectarines, etc., on walls, if necessary, and wash the walls with soft soap, sulphur and paraffin.

Figs on walls should have their superfluous shoots thinned out, the points of the wood selected for bearing being pinched out.

Strawberry plantations should have some short strawy manure spread between the rows.

When pruning dwarf trees, decide the exact forms the trees are to assume when full size and prune accordingly.

UNDER GLASS.

The secret of success with plant cultivation under glass in winter is to give sufficient ventilation and to keep out frosts. The temperature should be kept at from 40°–45° F. at night. All dead leaves should be removed.

The staging and floors should be kept scrupulously clean. It is advisable to spray the staging and floors with a weak solution of permanganate of potash, which forms a good disinfectant.

Water should be reduced to a minimum during cold spells.

Plump crowns of Lily of the Valley potted this month will, if treated liberally, give a succession of flowers during the winter months.

Pot them 1 in. apart in 5 or 6 in. pots in a compost of sandy loam and leaf-mould. The tips of the crowns should just protrude above the soil surface. Stand the pots in the cold frame and water them well. After a few days, bring them into the greenhouse.

It is best to bring batches into greater heat, at fortnightly intervals, so as to provide a succession of blooms.

Watch Auriculas in pots, for the presence of worms, and treat with lime water if they are troublesome.

Calceolarias and Cinerarias should be moved into larger pots as required.

Pansies for winter blooming should be kept in the warmest part of the greenhouse.

Remove all dead leaves from scarlet Geraniums. The shoots should be thinned out and trained, and late-blooming plants should be removed into their flowering pots.

Pot Spiræa *japonica* for forcing, also Dielytras.

Pot another batch of bulbs for late blooming in the greenhouse.

Keep the greenhouse, furnished with Chrysanthemums, nicely warm in wet and foggy weather. Give plenty of air on suitable days.

Give arum Lilies a temperature of at least 55°, otherwise they will not bloom.

Force Hippeastrums.

Take a few pots of Roman Hyacinths from their cover of fibre or ashes, and gradually accustom them to the light before introducing them to the warm greenhouse for flowering.

Sow Cyclamen seed.

Pot up shrubs for forcing.

Cut back Chrysanthemums after they finish flowering, to encourage young shoots which will make cuttings.

Azalea mollis and Azalea indica are really hardy plants, but they can be obtained earlier in bloom if grown in the greenhouse.

A few suitable plants for cold-frame cultivation are Clivia, Cytisus, Deutzia, Oxalis, Pelargonium, Primula sinensis and Arum lily. These may be supplemented with bulbs and annuals such as Schizanthus.

It is not too late to insert cuttings in the cold frame of Violas, Pansies, Pentstemons, Snapdragons and Calceolarias.

Cuttings of shrubs such as Forsythia, Berberis, golden Privet, golden-leaved Elder, etc., may also be rooted in the cold frame, where they may remain until planting time in spring.

Rhubarb may be lifted and forced, and Seakale may be treated in the same way towards the end of the month.

French beans may be sown in 8 in. pots in a temperature of not more than 65°.

Lettuce, Mustard and Cress, Radishes and small salading may be sown now.

Plant Cauliflower seedlings.

Pot Tomato seedlings.

Finish pruning vines, Nectarines, Peaches, etc., and top-dress.

THE SOIL NOW.

Now is the time to improve the fertility the soil. Deep digging is the best rtiliser.

be given with the slag to the lawn and the fruit garden.

During wet weather, when it is impossible, or undesirable, to work outside, the following jobs will need attention:

Labels require to be renewed occasionally where a large collection of plants is kept. Old or used labels that are still

Nymphæa (Water Lilies) can be grown in water from 9 in. to 3 ft. in depth, according to the variety chosen.

Basic slag, 4–8 oz. to the square yard, is the best for soils deficient in lime, but containing plenty of humus.

Farmyard manure is good where humus is lacking, and if this cannot be obtained use leaves, decayed vegetable matter, ash manure, spent hops, or some other material which will hold moisture and ood in the soil.

Bonemeal is the best fertiliser for shaded gardens, where too much humus is not advisable. Three oz. to a square yard is a good dressing.

Half an oz. sulphate of potash to the square yard may be added at the same time as basic slag on the perennial borders.

One oz. of kainit to the square yard can

quite sound may have the old names shaved off with a sharp knife. If painted afresh they will serve again and be as good as new.

Tidy up the sheds. This will include arranging potting soils and composts in their proper places, clearing the old caked soil from the floor, arranging tools, sticks, pots, tying material, broken pots and crocks, etc., so that they are easily found when wanted.

Tools should be cleaned and sharpened if required, and put in order. A special place should be allocated for each.

Plants requiring potting may be tackled on a rainy day. Surface them if required by taking off a little of the old top soil of pot plants, and replacing it with a corresponding layer of new, fresh soil. This is a good way of refreshing plants that are not flourishing. At the same time the plants can be examined for the presence of pests of all kinds.

The foliage of many smooth-leaved plants is improved by being washed over gently with a soft sponge and soapy water. A little insecticide should be added, to keep the insect pests at bay.

There is nearly always some plant or other that may need cuttings taken on a wet day; these can be inserted under glass.

Stages and glass in the greenhouse may be washed down with plenty of warm soapy water.

Empty pots that are dirty should be laid in soak in a tub, and cleaned at leisure. Pots with plants in should also be scrubbed outside to clean off green slime and dirt.

Broken pots may be smashed into crocks of various size, for drainage purposes, to be stored until wanted.

All garden work to be done outside should be listed on paper, and the most urgent jobs marked to receive preference as soon as the weather allows outdoor work again.

NUPHAR (nu-far. Nymphæaceæ). Hardy little aquatics allied to Nymphæas. They may be grown in ponds, tanks or tubs with a little soil, and have 1–3 ft. of water over the roots.

Propagate by division in spring or by seeds sown when ripe. Use rich loam with a little manure for planting.

SPECIES.

N. luteum with yellow flowers in June

is known as the "Yellow Water Lily" o "Brandy Bottle" in many parts o England.

NUTS. *See* ALMOND, CHESTNUT, etc.

NUTTALIA (nut-tä'-li-a. Rosaceæ) California, 6–8 ft. Deciduous shrubs, wit sweet almond-scented flowers borne o stiff erect racemes, produced from Januar to March on leafless stems, and followed b handsome, showy purple fruits. Hardy thriving in a well-drained soil. *Propagat* by seeds or division.

N. cerasiformis. There are male an female forms and both should be planted

NYCTERINIA (nik-ter-in-ia. Scro phularineæ). S. Africa. *N. capensis*, 1 ft white, night-flowering, sweet-scented, an *N. selaginoides*, 3 in., white and orange both half-hardy annuals, are the bes species. They like a sandy, peaty soil an a sunny position. Sow outdoors, May early June. Good for borders.

NYMPHÆA. *See* WATER PLANTS.

NYSSA (nis'-sa. Cornaceæ). N. America, China and Himalayas. Decidu ous hardy trees, with large leaves, and flowers of no importance, followed by small fruits.

Culture.—Plant in a good loamy soi in a moist position. They like woodland conditions with roots shaded from sun.

SPECIES.

N. aquatica, Tupelo Gum (N. America) Handsome glossy-leaved species, turning to beautiful yellow-orange tints in autumn

N. sylvatica (*multiflora*), N. America 10–15 ft. Pyramid habit, having flowers of a greenish colour in June, with larg glossy leaves, turning crimson, ageing to bright yellow, in autumn.

O

OAK. *See* QUERCUS.

OCHNA (ok-na. Ochnaceæ). Stove evergreens that except for one species are all yellow-flowered.

Propagate in summer by cuttings of half-ripened shoots inserted in sand in bottom heat. The soil that suits them best is sandy loam with peat and a little charcoal.

SPECIES.

O. atropurpurea. Dark purple flowers in spring. 4 ft.

O. lucida. Bright flowers. 5 ft.

O. multiflora. Attractive black and crimson berries. 5 ft.

OCIMUM (os-i-mum. Labiatæ). Basil. Half-hardy annuals and shrubs of which the only really useful member is the common Basil or *O. basilicum* (*see* HERBS).

Propagate by seed sown under glass or in a warm border in May in rich soil.

SPECIES.

O. canum. White; July. 1 ft.

O. basilicum.

OCTOBER WORK IN THE GARDEN.

THE FLOWER GARDEN.

Herbaceous plants of all kinds can be planted now.

Old-established borders can be rearranged and replanted when necessary.

Sever Carnation layers and plant them in well prepared soil.

As soon as Dahlia tubers have been cut down by frost, lift the tubers. Dry and clean them before storing.

Lift Gladiolus corms, tie them in bunches and hang in a frostproof shed for the winter.

All half-hardy bedding plants should be taken from the ground and put in a safe place for the winter.

Summer-sown flowers should be planted out at the same time that bulb planting is done.

A few plants that are useful for carpeting the ground of bulb beds are, Wallflowers, Silene compacta, Polyanthus, Arabis and Aubrietia.

Double Daisies, Pansies and Violas may be planted as edgings to borders.

All spring flowering bulbs can be put out this month, including Daffodils, Hyacinths, Crocuses, Snowdrops, Fritillarias, Lilies, Grape Hyacinths, etc.

The mixed border needs renovating entirely every three years, and October is the best month for the work. Lift out every plant, leaving a ball of soil intact round the roots, so that those plants which do not need division are disturbed as little as possible. If the border is a large one, it is worth while to dig a trench in another part of the garden and heel the plants into this while the border is dug.

Double dig the whole of the ground, keeping the top soil still at the top, but breaking up the hard pan of soil underneath. Keep a trench open as the ground is dug, and throw into it all the dead tops, annual weeds, leaves and rubbish from the garden.

A layer of farmyard manure forked into the bottom of each trench before the next width of soil is turned on to it assists the plants by retaining moisture during dry spells. A dressing of lime, 4 oz. to the square yard, and basic slag, 2 oz. to the square yard, will improve the fertility of the soil.

Replant according to a prepared plan, putting the larger, taller plants at the back and the dwarf ones at the edges, with occasional variations of this procedure so that the border is not too monotonous.

A few slender-leaved plants such as Montbretias and Iris give relief to the bushy round-leaved plants. Grey foliage of Lavender or Sage adds variety of colour to the winter border.

Pæonies can still be divided and replanted in good soil.

Lilies should be planted without delay.

Roses can be increased by cuttings taken now.

Bush roses planted now give better results than those planted in spring. Plant in deeply-dug and well-manured soil.

Biennials such as Canterbury Bells, Wallflowers, and Forget-me-nots should be planted out in their permanent positions, if possible.

Six good plants for successional flowering which could be purchased this month and planted immediately in the mixed border, would be: Doronicums; Lupins; Iris, "Lord of June"; Delphinium, "Blue Butterfly"; Phlox, "Starlight"; and Helenium autumnale.

Withhold water from tuberous Begonias in pots, dry off and store in boxes in frostproof situation for the winter.

Lift Begonias and Cannas.

Phloxes, Ragwort, Roses, Salvias, c now be struck.

Take shrubby Calceolaria cuttings.

Renovate defective lawns by layi turf. Finish mowing for the season a top dress the lawn with fine soil a decayed manure.

THE ROCK GARDEN.

Top dress the surface of the soil rou alpines with stone chippings, or if the are unobtainable use sharp sand.

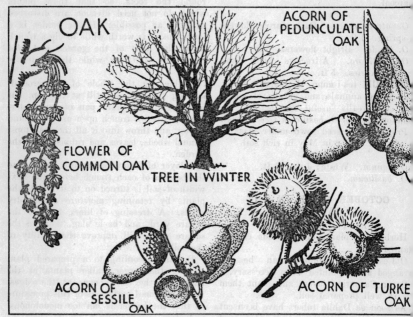

Three of the commonest Oaks are the English, Turkey and Sessile Oaks. They are usually prese on land where clay and heavy loam abound.

Transplant Anemone japonica, Papaver orientalis, etc., if necessary.

Sow Sweet Peas for early flowering.

Dig and manure ground intended for Sweet Peas, next season. Leave the surface rough.

Divide and plant out Montbretias in open borders.

Dahlia and Hollyhock seed should be gathered.

Eranthis (Winter Aconites) may be planted, or propagated by offsets now.

Cuttings of Anagallis, Bouvardias, Calceolarias, Cerastiums, Periwinkles,

Put slug traps every few yards protect the plants and to prevent the slug from becoming numerous. Shelter wooll leaved plants by placing a small pie of glass over them, supported by wires sticks.

Shelter the tenderest subjects wit cloches.

Plant small bulbs in drifts whe colour will be lacking in the spring ro garden. Those suited to this purpo are Muscari, Crocus, Snowdrop, Narcissu Chionodoxas, Scillas.

This is a good time to renovate th

established rock garden. Go over each pocket and remove decayed leaves. Stir the soil surface between the plants and add a top dressing of fresh soil where this is thought advisable. Where plants have overgrown their allotted space, they should be lifted and divided. Replant the best pieces and discard the rest, or use it for raising fresh plants from cuttings.

THE SHRUBBERY.

Deciduous shrubs may be planted now. If they arrive from the nursery during the frosty weather, put them into some moist earth or keep them covered with damp sacks in a greenhouse where they will not get frosted, until the weather is suitable for planting.

Trees and shrubs of many kinds, including roses, can be propagated quite easily from cuttings taken at this season. Cuttings should be of well-ripened wood of one season's growth. In most cases, the cut is made at, or immediately below, the joint.

Clematis and coloured willows are exceptions. They will root more easily if the cut is made midway between the joints.

Strip all the lower leaves from each cutting, and insert it two-thirds of the way up to the stem in sandy soil. Keep them close and moist until the roots have formed.

The following are a few of the shrubs which can be planted this month and which need a minimum of attention from the cultivator:

Berberis Darwini, Forsythia, Hamamelis mollis, Hippophæ, Hypericum moserianum, Leycesteria formosa, Olearia haastii, Ribes sanguinea, Syringa.

Plant hardy creepers and ivy.

THE VEGETABLE GARDEN.

Summer crops can be cleared away and the plot prepared for the next crop.

Lift and store all the roots except parsnips and Jerusalem artichokes.

Top-dress asparagus with 6 in. of well-rotted manure.

Asparagus foliage should be well ripened before being cut down.

Plant out cabbage seedlings. Draw a little soil up round the stems of all the plants to protect them during the winter.

A few roots of chicory should be placed in the mushroom house and brought along steadily for salading.

Earth up late celery.

Bring unripened tomatoes on stems indoors and hang up to ripen.

Cut marrows and bring under cover.

Lift beet, carrots, onions and potatoes.

Beet should not be stored unless the leaves have been twisted—not cut—off.

Store carrots and beet in sand for winter use.

Clear off stems of late peas and beans and burn. Remove pea and bean sticks and store for future use.

Lift a root or two of mint, place in a box of soil, and grow on in greenhouse for a winter supply.

Endive growing outside should be lifted and planted thickly in a cold frame. Blanch as required, by placing a mat over the glass.

Lettuces should be treated in the same way as endive, except that they should not be blanched.

The main crops of onions should now be thoroughly dry. Remove any rubbish from them and spread the onions thinly on shelves in an airy shed, or string them together and hang them in the shed out of the way of frosts.

Parsley seedlings should be pricked out in rows 6 in. apart in cold frames.

Place some litter over a portion of the parsnip bed, so that it may be possible to lift the roots as needed, even if the ground becomes frosted elsewhere.

Rhubarb crowns should be lifted and placed in the mushroom house, or under the greenhouse stages, so that a supply of stems may be ready by Christmas.

Turnips sown early are now ready to be lifted and stored for winter use. Keep later sowings well hoed and draw a little soil over the roots.

Earth up celery and leeks.

Corn salad and early peas may be sown on a warm south border.

Radishes and spinach may still be sown.

Cucumbers for winter use may be sown in heat.

The roots of horse radish may be lifted and stored.

By the end of the month all the fruits on outdoor tomatoes will be ripe or ready to gather, and the plants may be taken up and burned. If allowed to rot on the surface the tomato disease is often encouraged.

FRUIT.

Gather all fruit as soon as it ripens. To test the ripeness of apples, lift them in the hand; if they separate easily from the stem, gather the crop at once. Apples and pears which are allowed to drop become bruised and unsuitable for storing. Store these fruits on shelves in a frost-proof place, where air can circulate freely, and they will keep many months, according to the variety.

October is the best planting month for most fruit trees. The fine roots are able to take hold of the soil before the cold months of winter arrive and the plants are then ready to take advantage of the first warm days of spring.

Orchards should be carefully looked over for signs of diseased trees. Trees suffering from cankers should be cut right out if beyond remedy, but in any case the affected portions should be removed.

Cuttings of gooseberries and currants can be inserted in sheltered positions now.

Make new plantations of raspberries, which can easily be made from suckers detached from the old plants. Plant them 3 ft. apart each way and after planting keep the soil hoed between the roots to prevent weeds establishing themselves.

Loganberries, veitchberries, etc., can all be planted now.

The soil for new fruits should be immediately prepared. Moderately light soil is best for most fruits, but any ordinary soil in which vegetables thrive will do. Heavy soils are agreeable to gooseberries, raspberries and loganberries. Damp soils are suitable for black currants.

Trench all land intended for fruit-growing to a depth of 2 ft.

Add road grit, sharp sand, strawy manure and leaves to clay soils; heavy manure, leaves and vegetable refuse to light soils. Lime in moderation is liked by all fruits.

Basic slag and crushed bones are best fertilisers for heavy soil.

Bone-flour and superphosphate of lime are good for light soils.

Transplanting may take place, or old trees may be lifted so that the soil may be replenished.

Begin to root-prune those trees which require it.

Grease banding should be done at once.

Apricots, cherries, currants and gooseberries should be pruned this month.

The old fruit, leaves, and the naked old wood of figs should be cut away to make room for the new shoots.

Loganberry stems which have borne fruit must be cut away to ground level. Train the new stems to the supports spacing them out well so that they get light and air.

All strawberry runners should be removed from the plants.

Outdoor grapes should be pruned.

Cut out all weak and useless canes and shorten back good ones to two or three buds from the base.

Vines that are losing their leaves should have plenty of air.

Plums and pears may be planted against walls facing west.

Untie peaches, apricots, nectarines, etc., from walls if necessary, and wash the walls with soft soap, sulphur and paraffin.

UNDER GLASS.

Ventilate freely on warm days. Be on the look out for night frosts.

Wipe off moisture that collects on glass. This may prevent "damping off."

Make up hotbeds for growing winter cucumbers, etc.

Pinch out tops of annual seedlings, such as Clarkia, Sweet Peas, Schizanthus, etc., to make bushy plants.

Take cuttings of shrubby Calceolarias and insert in cold frames ready for bedding out next year.

Disbud perpetual-flowering Carnations and Chrysanthemums.

Pot up retarded Lily-of-the-Valley crowns for forcing.

Repot arum Lilies.

Repot Lilies dried off in frames, and keep them in a cool greenhouse for the winter.

Pot up hardy and half-hardy plants for indoor decoration.

Bring pot roses into the greenhouse.

Pot Pansy cuttings for winter blooming indoors.

Flowering shrubs that are intended for forcing should be potted up now. Do ot force plants that were forced last season. To retain their vigour they should only be forced in alternate years.

Suitable shrubs for forcing are: Azalea mollis, Ceanothus, Chimonanthus fragrans, Clematis, Cytisus andreanus, Kalmia latifolia, Lilacs, Magnolia stellata, Pieris floribunda, Roses (*see* ROSES), Viburnum carlesii.

Bulbs in bowls and pots should be brought gradually into more light and heat as soon as the tops begin to grow.

When the ashes are removed, wash the outside of the pots and cover the soil surface with a layer of clean shell.

Great care must be taken when watering Pelargoniums as the leaves must be kept dry. No syringing or sprinkling should be done.

Begonia tubers may now be stored.

Cuttings of Pansies may be potted up for indoor flowering.

Take Cinerarias grown on in frames, into the greenhouse.

Stand seedling Primulas on top shelves near the glass. Continue to give cool treatment; they do not need a great heat.

Freesias in pots may be transferred to greenhouse, where, without undue forcing, they will supply early bloom.

All late-flowering Chrysanthemums should now be under glass. They need plenty of air on warm days.

Thin out the wood of climbers on greenhouse roofs, walls and pillars.

Place potted Fuchsias and Heliotropes under greenhouse staging, away from drip, in moderate temperature, to remain there all winter.

Put cuttings of Violas, Pansies, Calceolarias, Pentstemons in boxes and stand in a frame or under handlights.

Young cauliflower plants may be lifted into frames and the leaves tied over the heads of those nearly ready for use.

Other smaller plants may be lifted with a good ball of soil, and replanted in deep frames so as to be safe from frost.

Mustard and cress may be sown for succession.

Tomatoes may now be sown.

PESTS.

Any fruit trees showing signs of canker should be looked over carefully, and cut down and burnt if beyond remedy.

Grease bands should be placed round the trunks of fruit trees as a protection against the female moths of various injurious insects, crawling up to the branches to lay their eggs.

Hoe the ground round the trees whenever possible in order to bring pests to the surface for the birds to eat.

ODONTADENIA (o-don-ta-den-i-a. Apocynaceæ). Stove climbing shrubs that

ODONTIODA

Many hybrid Orchids, such as Odontioda, have wonderful colouring.

are increased by seeds or cuttings, and thrive in loam and sand.

SPECIES.

O. speciosa. Yellow and orange fragrant flowers in autumn. 10 ft.

ODONTOGLOSSUM (o-don-to-glossum. Orchidaceæ). From *odous*, a tooth, and *glossa*, a tongue, referring to the tooth-like parts on the lip. Greenhouse orchids. This wonderful genus is rich in fine species from which our hybridists have produced a splendid race of hybrids. *Guatemala*, 1837.

Culture: Compost: use 3 parts well-chopped fibre, 1 part sphagnum moss. Repot when new growth is 3 or 4 in high, fill the pots at least two-thirds with well-broken crocks. The pseudo-bulbs should rest above the compost. Water freely during the summer and moderately in the winter; roots must never be allowed to become dry. A moist atmosphere must be maintained at all times. Shading from hot sun is essential spring and summer. Winter temperature, 45°; summer, 60°.

Propagate by division when repotting.

Orchids with bulbous stems should not be over-watered, but they like plenty of moisture in the growing season. Odontoglossum likes a cool greenhouse.

SPECIES.

The cheapest and most popular species is *Crispum* and its varieties, white, rose, crimson, etc., which can be found in almost every amateur collection. Others are *citrosmum*, rose, white and yellow; *Edwardii*, purple and yellow; *luteo-purpureum*, yellow and brown, and its varieties; *pulchellum*, white and yellow; *Uro-Skinneri*, yellow, brown and rose.

ODONTOGLOSSUM HYBRIDS.

These hold the premier place amongst all orchids. They are more robust than the species, and their wonderful colour-ing makes them ideal for choice decora-tion. Their varieties are so numerous and beautiful that a good home-raiser's trade list should be consulted. To give an idea of their beauty one or two varieties are here described:

Alector-perfectum. A perfect-shaped flower. Central portion of sepal and petals densely spotted with rose-mauve, the outer portion white, deeply serrated. Lip flat, spotted with rose and a distinct frilled margin of mauve.

Imperator-Olympic. The whole flower is cœrulean-purple, shading to violet at tips of sepals and petals, lip large and flat, barred with violet-purple on a mauve ground.

Royal Ascot. Sepals and petals chest-nut-red with overlay of violet purple, white margin with lilac spots. Lip broad, blotched chestnut-red with white margin.

Xanthinum. Sepals and petals pale yellow with larger orange blotches, lip white ground with a central orange blotch.

ODONTONIA (o-don-to-ni-a. Orchid-aceæ). A comparatively new race of orchid hybrids, from *Miltonia + Odonto-glossum*. They may be cultivated under the same condition as *Miltonias* or *Odontoglossums*. Many of them have remarkable colouring.

Aglaon. Sepals and petals purple-crimson with rose and white markings and margin, lip broad, lower portion mauve on a white ground with a central blotch of rose-purple, yellow crest.

Avril Gray. Sepals and petals blotched reddish-purple on a white ground with white margin, lip blush-mauve, apical portion chestnut-red, with yellow crest.

Baroness Schröder. Sepals and petals claret-red, labellum pale rose richly lined with purple and having a distinctly rayed disk.

ŒNOTHERA (ē-nō-thē-ra. Onagrari-aceæ). Evening Primrose. Godetia. A popular genus of brilliant flowers consisting of annuals, perennials and biennials, several of which, in spite of their name, are open in the day. Although originally from America they are thoroughly naturalised in many parts and are com-mon cottage-garden plants. They make excellent border plants and the dwarfer kinds are useful for rock-work.

Culture.—The cultivation of these plants is an easy matter as they sow themselves freely and grow in any warm soil, but preferably a sandy one. The annuals are raised from seed sown out of doors in spring, the biennials from seed sown as soon as ripe, and the perennials from seed, from cuttings placed in a cold frame in spring or from divisions of the roots.

SPECIES.

The annuals are known under the name of Godetias. They were formerly separated from Evening Primroses on account of their being open all day, and because of the differences in colour of the flowers.

O. biennis, the common Evening Primrose, is a biennial plant with large pale yellow fragrant flowers. Its variety *grandiflora* (syn. *lamarckiana*) is larger and makes a fine effect in masses in the wild garden. Height, 2–5 ft.

O. cæspitosa (syn. *eximia* and *marginata*) bears large white flowers that are very fragrant in the evening. 1 ft.

O. fruticosa with golden yellow flowers that are open all day. Its varieties *major* and *Youngii* are larger. 1½–2 ft.

O. missouriensis, with prostrate downy stems of a reddish colour and large clear yellow flowers that are sometimes 5 in. across, is a valuable border plant and is very showy among the taller subjects for the rock garden. 12 in.

O. glauca and its variety *Fraseri*, which is an improvement on the parent form, both with free-blooming yellow flowers, are among the best of the garden plants. 1–2 ft.

O. amæna (*Godetia amæna*) is a pleasing little annual with rosy, crimson-spotted flowers. It has given rise to a large number of garden Godetias such as *Crimson King* (crimson), *Duchess of Albany* (white), *Duke of York* (red), and *Schaminii* (double, with continuous rose-pink bloom).

O. whitneyi (*Godetia grandiflora*) has cream, scarlet and white forms that provide a continuity of blooms. 12–18 in. The Godetias make good pot plants and for May bloom in pots the seed should be sown in September.

All the species flower during the greater part of the summer and several of the annuals will provide flowers for cutting.

OIL. It is most important to have a tin of oil always handy. All working parts of mowers, rollers and such-like machines need oil. If, after use, the ordinary tools are cleaned and wiped over with an oily rag, they will last much longer and look much nicer.

OLD MAN. *See* ARTEMISIA.

OLD MAN'S BEARD. *See* CLEMATIS VITALBA.

You can easily recognise the Oleander. Its leaves occur in whorls of three and it has small gardenia-like flowers. It is half-hardy, with double pink flowers.

OLEA (ŏl'-ē-a. Oleaceæ). Olive. Asia Minor and Syria, 6–10 ft. Half-hardy evergreen trees of rugged habit and slow growth, with oval leathery leaves, glaucous or silvery beneath. Flowers white. *Propagate* by cuttings in gentle heat.

SPECIES.

O. europæa. The Fruiting Olive (S. Europe and Asia Minor). Leaves greygreen. Only suitable for the mildest districts of southern England. Has borne fruit in South Cornwall.

O. fragrans. *See* OSMANTHUS FRAGRANS.

OLEANDER. *See* NERIUM.

OLEANDRA (ol-e-an-dra. Filices). Yellow-spored stove ferns.

Propagate by spores and division. Plant in loam, peat and coarse sand.

SPECIES.

O. articulata. Evergreen. Fronds, 6–12 in.

O. neriiformis. (Like the Oleander.) Fronds, 6–18 in.

O. Wallichii. Fronds, 6–12 in long.

OLEARIA (ŏl-ē-ar'-a-a. Compositæ). Daisy Bushes. Australia and New Zealand, 4–8 ft. Small hardy and half-hardy evergreen shrubs, with clusters of white to creamy-white aster-like flowers in July and August.

Culture.—Plant in a light loamy non-calcareous soil. *Propagate* by moderately-ripened wood placed in gentle heat, or in frame.

SPECIES.

O. Haastii (New Zealand). The hardiest of the genus, producing masses of starry-white flowers during summer months.

O. macrodonta (New Zealand). Hardy species, having withstood nearly 30° of frost near London. Holly-like leaves, and flowers in clusters, 3–8 in. across.

OLEASTER. *See* ELÆAGNUS.

OLIVE. *See* OLEA.

OMPHALODES (ŏmpha-lō-des. Boraginaceæ). Navelwort. Pretty hardy annual and perennial herbs that are useful for the border or rockery.

Propagate by seed sown in spring in the open or under glass and the perennials by division as well in the same season. The plants like a shady position in ordinary garden soil.

SPECIES.

O. linifolia, known as Venus's Navelwort. Hardy annual with white flowers from May to August. Suitable for borders. 6–15 in.

O. lucillæ with lovely lilac-blue flowers from June to August, and glaucous grey foliage, succeeds in well-drained soil in the rock-garden. Protect this species from slugs by means of rings of perforated zinc placed round the plants.

O. verna, the Creeping Forget-me-not, is a dwarf plant with flowers the colour of Forget-me-nots spotted with white. It is useful for borders and, owing to its early season of blooming (March to May), for the spring garden. 6 in.

O. nitida is a rarer species with loos tufts of light leaves and panicles of whit flowers in May and June.

ONION (*Allium Cepa*). With the sing exception of Potatoes, it is probable tha Onions are more used in the kitche during the course of a year than any othe vegetable.

The wild onion originated in Centra Asia and references to its dietetic qualitie and cultivation can be traced right dow from the time of the ancient Egyptians.

It still remains a very popular vegetable yet the quantity produced in the Britis Isles falls far short of the requirements and enormous quantities are importe every year.

Culture.—SPRING SOWN: No crop give a better yield for the labour expended on it yet it is a lamentable fact that althoug their cultivation is not difficult, it is all too frequently attempted in a very half-hearted manner, so that disappointment in th crop is a natural result.

The onion is a sun-loving subject and delights in a well-tilled deep soil that has been in cultivation for several years. It is rarely successful on land that has been recently broken up.

During the winter months the land should be deeply dug and well manured, and if the soil is of a heavy, retentive nature, or the subsoil wet and cold, raised beds are preferable to beds on the flat.

Some of the finest onions in England are grown every year by an ardent amateur who has trenched the whole of his onion bed 3 ft. deep and buried at the bottom all the old iron rubbish he could collect; bedsteads, old bicycles, wire netting, barbed wire, pots and pans, have all gone in to make a perfect and permanent drainage system just below the normal working depth.

Simple raised beds can be made by marking out beds 8 ft. wide with alleys 2 ft. wide betweeen. The soil from these alleys can then be taken out to a depth of 6 in. and soil spread evenly over the beds. The alleys can afterwards be used for lettuces, spinach, or turnips.

The onion is a crop which normally requires a long season of growth, and the best results are obtained by sowing the seed in boxes during February or early March in a temperature of 50°–55°. If this is unobtainable, they may be sown in a cold frame covered with matting at night.

A light compost should be used to fill the boxes and thin sowing is desirable. Care must be exercised in watering, and germination should take place in about 7 to 10 days.

For Exhibition work the seedlings are either potted singly into small pots as soon as they are large enough to handle, or two or three seeds are sown in each pot, and the seedlings thinned down to one at an early date.

If sown sufficiently thinly in the boxes they may stand till planting time, but if crowded they should be given an extra move into other boxes.

The hardening-off process must be gradual and thorough, so that by early May they may be in a strong enough condition to set out in their permanent positions 4–6 in. apart in rows 1 ft. asunder.

If sowing under glass is impracticable, the first sowing outdoors may be made as early in March as soil and weather conditions will allow. During the winter digging the soil will have been left rough. The surface should be lightly forked over on a drying day, and then raked and trodden several times until a very fine tilth of 2 or 3 in. is obtained.

Drills about 1 in. deep should be drawn 1 ft. apart and given a dressing of old soot. It pays to sow onion seed outside rather thicker than usual, and no waste is entailed, as the surplus seedlings can be pulled early for use. After covering the seed the bed should be well firmed with the feet, or even have a light roller run over it; then the surface may be finished off by a very light raking.

As soon as the seedlings appear, the surface soil should be stirred with a dutch hoe or cultivator, and during May the seedlings may be thinned out during overcast weather, leaving them 4–6 in. apart, except for pickling kinds, which may be left, as small bulbs are desired. It is a wise plan to follow this thinning by earthing up the remaining plants with about 1 in. of soil. To a certain extent this prevents the ravages of the Onion Fly.

If this pest is usually troublesome in the garden, the plants and surrounding earth should be sprayed frequently with Jeyes Fluid (1 part in 100 parts water).

When the plants are growing freely a dressing of nitrate of soda at the rate of 1 oz. per square yard may be given during showery weather, and once or twice during the growing period a dressing of soluble manure at 2 oz. per square yard should be hoed in along the rows.

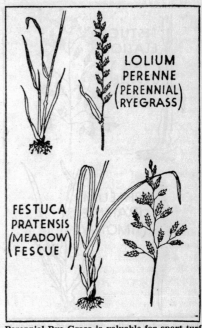

LOLIUM PERENNE (PERENNIAL RYEGRASS)

FESTUCA PRATENSIS (MEADOW FESCUE)

Perennial Rye Grass is valuable for sport turf in combination with the other sorts. For fine lawns rye grass should be left out of the mixture.

Throughout the summer the soil must be kept well hoed, for a mulch of fine soil does much to conserve the soil moisture and keep the plants growing steadily; furthermore, it encourages early ripening, which is a most important factor in this climate.

During September the tops that have not fallen over should be gently bent down, and if growth still continues the bulbs may be partly lifted or "wrenched," so as to disturb the roots and check the growth.

Culture.—SPRING-SOWN: As the foliage yellows and shows signs of withering, the crop should be lifted and moved to an open, dry shed to finish off. During settled weather they may be laid or hung in the open, but it is not advisable to leave them on the ground after lifting.

AUTUMN-SOWN: These are usually known as Tripoli Onions, and are most useful for supplementing the supply.

Sowing should be done in August in drills in a sheltered position. The soil

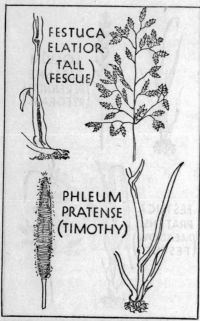

Fescues and Timothy grasses are commonly found in lawns and are suitable where hard wear is given.

for the seed bed need not be rich, but must be thoroughly prepared. Little attention is required during the winter beyond an occasional hoeing and weeding.

The final plot must be carefully prepared as advised for the spring sowing, and all should be ready for the plants to be set out in February.

The plants should be lifted carefully and transplanted 4–6 in. apart in rows 10 in. to 1 ft. asunder, according to the variety. Only sufficient of the plant to keep them standing should be inserted, and the surrounding soil must be made quite firm.

Some plants are almost sure to produce flower heads. These should be cut off cleanly through the solid part at the top of the stem just below the bud.

During the summer the same cultivation as recommended for the spring-sown crop will suffice.

VARIETIES.

Spring Sowings. Flat types.—White Spanish; Rousham Park Hero; Giant Zittau; Red Wetherfield.

Globular.—Brown Globe; Bedfordshire Champion; James Long Keeping; Paris Silver (pickling).

Autumn Sowings. Flat types.—Red Italian; Giant White Italian; Giant Rocca.

Globular.—Ailsa Craig; Up-to-date; Walker's Exhibition.

Uses.—When pulled young and green the pungent flavour of onions makes them agreeable for use in salads or for use with cheese or there are numerous recipes for their use in a cooked state or pickled.

At one time a raw onion rubbed on the affected part was considered an effective remedy for wasp or bee stings.

ONION FLY (*Hylemia antiqua*). A two-winged fly, grey in colour and not unlike the common house fly, lays its eggs around the young onions when they are about 2–3 in. high. The resulting maggots, after eating their way into the developing bulb and completely hollowing it out, pass on to the next. One maggot often destroys three or four onions before it becomes full grown and pupates. A second generation of flies appears in late July or August. These again lay eggs which hatch into maggots. Instead of the plant drying right out as when attached at the young stage, the stem falls over and becomes yellow and limp. At the same time bacteria may enter the bulb, causing a rapid rotting of the root. When full-grown the larvæ leave the bulbs to pupate in the soil.

METHODS OF CONTROL.—When once onions are attacked there is nothing that can be done, except to pull them up and burn them. As a safeguard against attack, bring the plants through the early stages as rapidly as possible by applying suitable cultural methods. When they are 2–3 in. high, spray with a paraffin

ulsion, 1 part emulsion to 25 parts of
ter. The emulsion may first be made
dissolving ½ lb. of soap in 1 gallon of
water and then churning in 1 pint of
raffin oil. This is then diluted as stated.

ONION SETS. These are small onion
ıbs of the size of a large marble, and are
ually sold by measure.

They are extremely useful in those
rdens where the Onion Fly makes seed-
g onions a precarious crop.

The site for a bed of onion sets should
prepared as for seed. Planting may
done from March to May—the earlier
e better—by merely pressing the sets
o the soil to half their depth at dis-
nces of 9 in. apart in the rows and 1 ft.
ınder.

Their later cultivation and uses are the
me as for seedling crops.

ONOCLEA (on-ok-le-a. Filices).
tractive hardy ferns which are usually
nd growing by the side of streams or
nds in rich soil, and under cultivation
ed the same conditions. They are easily
opagated by their creeping stolons which
ay be taken off in spring or autumn. A
il composed of 1 part of leaf-mould to 3
loam is suitable.

SPECIES.

O. germanica. Ostrich Fern. 2–3 ft.
ery ornamental.

O. orientalis (syn. *Struthiopteris
ientalis*).

ONONIS (ō-nō-nis. Leguminosæ). Rest
arrow. A large genus comprising hardy
ıd tender annuals, biennial and perennial
erbs with a few shrubs. Only a small
ımber are desirable garden plants, among
ese being the native "Rest Harrow."

They are propagated by seeds sown in
pring, the perennials also by division of
ıe root in spring or autumn. Any fertile
oil suits all the species except *arvensis*,
rhich likes a high position in well-
rained soil.

SPECIES.

O. arvensis is one of the prettiest of
vild plants with racemes of pink flowers
rom June to August and is worth cultivat-
ng for the wild garden or for the rockery
vhere it forms dense tufts. Height 6 in.

O. fruticosa, a dwarf shrubby kind with
ich purple flowers from June to August.
½–2 ft.

O. natrix (Goat Root) has yellow flowers
veined with red. 1½ ft.

O. rotundifolia is a sub-species with
bright rosy flowers and is easily cultivated.
Flowers throughout the summer. 1½–3 ft.

O. spinosa (syn. *campestris*) bears
purple-pink flowers, and its variety *alba,*
white, from July to August. 12 in.

Most of the remainder of the genus are
not worth growing.

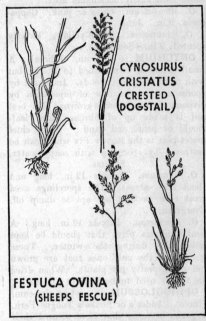

The Crested Dogstail is a grass for hard wear
and is good for chalky soils. The Sheep's
Fescue is also a suitable grass for chalky soils
and for first-class lawns.

ONOPORDON (o-no-por-don. Compositæ). Cotton Thistle. Europe. Stately
Border plants with silvery foliage and
stems, and bright blue flower heads,
8–10 ft. The foliage is elegantly cut, or
laciniated. Sow where to grow, in good
soil, in spring. Most effective as single
specimens.

O. acanthium, hardy perennial, July.
4–5 ft.

O. illyricum, hardy biennial, July. 6 ft.

ONOSMA (on-os-ma. Boraginaceæ).
From *onos,* an ass, *osma,* smell. The ass

is said to appreciate the smell. Golden Drop.

The species are all characterised by curly racemes of drooping, pear-shaped flowers and grey, often rough, narrow foliage. They absolutely demand a hot, dry position or the winter wet will overcome them. They propagate from imported seeds or from cuttings under glass. There are a great number of species, but those most easily obtainable are:

O. albo-roseum, white or pink. Cappadocia, 9 in. June.

O. tauricum, lemon-yellow, sweetly scented, 9 in. Sow June.

ONYCHIUM (o-nik-i-um. Filices). A small genus of ferns allied to Pteris, but with more finely cut fronds. Increased by spores and in the case of *japonicum* by division of the numerous crowns. The best soil is made up of fibrous loam, leafmould or peat, and sand. Their chief insect pest is the Snowy Fly which can be destroyed by sponging with soapy water.

SPECIES.

O. auratum. Fronds 12 in. long and about 8 in. across. The sporelings need great care as they are apt to damp off. Evergreen.

O. japonicum. Fronds 12 in. long. A semi-deciduous plant that should be kept rather dry during the winter. These species are the only ones that are grown and make pretty pot plants. When dried the fronds used to be kept in albums.

OPHIOGLOSSUM (of-i-o-glos-sum. Filices). Adder's or Snake's Tongue Fern. A genus of ferns that have secured their popularity not so much by their beauty as by their curious formation. The spores form long narrow spikes that have given rise to the name of the genus.

Propagate by division and grow in loam and sphagnum moss with sand. They need plenty of water, but are quickly ruined by anything approaching stagnant conditions.

SPECIES.

O. palmatum. Fronds 8–20 in. Greenhouse. Epiphytal.

O. vulgatum. The common Adder's Tongue. Spike 1 ft. Fronds 3–8 in. Several varieties.

OPHIOPOGON (of-i-ō-pō-gon. Hæmodoraceæ). Snake's Beard. Herbaceous

half-hardy perennials with racemes small flowers and narrow leaves. The are useful for pot culture or for borde: but are not very ornamental.

Culture.—They are propagated b division in spring and should be grow in a sandy soil. In winter they shoul be kept under glass.

SPECIES.

O. intermedius, *O. jaburan*, of whic there is a variegated variety, and (*japonicus* are the best known. The vari gated form is the best for pot culture All flower from June to August with viole flowers. 1–1½ ft. *O. japonicus* is know as the "Japanese Hyacinth."

OPHRYS (Bee Orchis, Fly Orchis Spider Orchis). Orchidaceæ. Hard terrestrial orchids.

Culture.—Outdoor. These plants wi] thrive in a dry, sunny rockery in a soi of two parts loam, one part chalk or broke: limestone, and one part leaf-mould. Plan from August to November, covering th surface soil between the plants with piece of chalk or limestone, or mulch with layer of coco-nut fibre refuse.

SPECIES.

O. apifera (Bee Orchis). Sepals green tinged with pink, with velvety-brown li| with yellow markings.

O. arachnites (Late Spider Orchis) Yellow-green sepals, lip of black-browi marked with yellow.

O. aranifera (Spider Orchis). Sepal: yellow-green, with dull brown lip witl paler markings.

O. Bertoloni (Looking-glass Orchis) Pink sepals, velvety-brown lip, spotted with carmine, with central blotch cobalt blue.

O. bombylifera (Bumble Bee Orchis). Small species, green sepals and purplish-black lip with grey-blue blotch.

O. lutea (Wasp Orchis). Brown lip broadly margined with yellow, giving striking appearance.

O. Muscifera (Fly Orchis). Purplish-brown lip with bluish central spot. Likes peat in the soil.

OPUNTIA. *See* CACTUS.

ORANGE. *See* CITRUS.

ORCHARD, DECORATIVE TREATMENT. For cultural details *see* FRUIT. For fruit cages, *see* NETTING. An orchard on

small scale can be introduced with good
ffect into a medium-sized garden. For it
 be an æsthetic feature, grass should be
rown under the trees with naturalised
ulbs grouped in it. Definite vistas should
e arranged between the trees, and, with
he addition of a seat, the orchard quickly
ecomes a useful extension of the flower
arden. A ring of soil should be kept
ear to pass round the base of the trees
or the first two or three years. This area
an be planted with annuals which take
ttle nourishment from the soil and add
o the beauty of the orchard before the
owering and the fruiting seasons.

ORCHID (Hardy). Hardy terrestrial
rchids, that is, the orchids which are
rown in the soil of the open garden, are
ot difficult to cultivate. Generally speak-
ng, they are more suited to the rock gar-
en than to borders, and as they all like
lenty of moisture from the time growth
ommences until they are actually in
ower, a position in the sunny pockets of
he rock and water garden is admirably
uited to these beauties. After flowering
hey prefer drier conditions and the tubers
an then be lifted and ripened. Many of
he species do not flower in nature every
eason, and naturally will not do so in
ultivation. The soil surface all round
he orchids can be covered with small
rowing plants, as these tend to prevent
he soil drying too rapidly, and also pre-
ent stagnation.

The following hardy orchids are in
ommerce and can be obtained easily for
ultivation by the amateur. It will be
een that they cover a very wide range
nd include some interesting genera.
Fuller particulars of their cultivation are
given under each genus elsewhere in this
ook.

Orchis foliosa—rich purple. (Madeira
Orchis.)

O. fusca—purple spotted hood, sepals
brown. (Brown Man Orchis.)

O. incarnatus—lilac-pink with red vein-
ngs. (March Orchis.)

O. maculata—lilac spotted with purple.
(Spotted Orchis.)

O. Mascula—purplish-crimson. (Early
Purple Orchis.)

O. militaris—red with paler hood
(Military Orchis.)

O. papilionacea—bright red hood, pink
lip spotted red. (Italian Butterfly Orchis.)

O. pyramidalis—rich rose. (Pyramid
Orchis.)

O. simia—rosy-purple hood, pink lip.
(Monkey Orchis.)

O. tridentina—white lip heavily spotted,
purple and pink hood. (Toothed Orchis.)

O. Ustalata—white, crimson spotted.
(Burnt Orchis.)

SWEET ORANGE

The orange, which can be grown in a cool
greenhouse, carries flowers and fruits together.

Spiranthes autumnalis—white. (Lady's
Tresses Orchis.)

OREODAPHNE. *See* Umbellularia.

ORGANIC FERTILISERS. Fertilisers made from any living matter and
containing the element carbon as an essential ingredient.

ORIGANUM (ō-rīg-anum. Labiatæ).
Marjoram. Hardy sub-shrubs and herbaceous perennials, very few being of any
value in the garden save for the herb
Sweet Marjoram.

Culture.—Propagate by seeds, cuttings
and by division.

SPECIES.

Among the very small number of plants that are worth growing are *Dictamnus*, a shrubby species with pink flowers and woolly leaves, on account of which it requires a little protection in winter.

O. hybridum, which bears little pink flowers from June to August.

O. pulchrum like *hybridum*, with pink flowers. 12 in.

AGROSTIS
STOLONIFERA
(FIORIN)

POA
NEMORALIS
(WOOD MEADOW GRASS)

Wood Meadow grass is one of the lawn grasses which enjoys a partially shady position and is valuable for sowing under trees.

O. vulgare the "Common Marjoram," with purple flowers which is a good wild garden plant, and *aureum* its golden-leaved form which is very pretty. Both these should find a place in every old-world garden.

ORNAMENT. *See* SCULPTURE FOR THE GARDEN. VASES, PEDESTAL, SUNDIALS, etc.

ORNAMENTAL GRASSES. Apart from their decorative value in the garden ornamental grasses are invaluable for use in the house where they may be used with cut flowers or individually. If cut before they are quite mature they will make excellent subjects for drying and for use

with Everlasting flowers. The major are hardy annuals, but the tender grass may be equally effective. A good selecti can be made from the following list:

Agrostis laxiflora and pulchella, t Cloud Grass.

Aira flexuosa and pulchella, the A Grass.

Avena sterilis. Oat Grass. Animat Oat.

Briza maxima and gracilis. Quaki Grass.

Bromus brizaeformis and aureus. Bron Grass.

Coixlachryma. Job's Tears. Silv grey.

Dactylis glomerata. Cock's Foo Gardener's Garters.

Eragrostis elegans. Love Grass.

Eulalia japonica. Zebra Grass.

Gynerium argenteum. Pampas Grass.

Hordeum jubatum. Squirrel's Tail Barley Grass. (Purple.)

Lagurus ovatus. Hare's Tail Grass.

Panicum. Panick Grass.

Pennisetum longistylum.

Stipa pennata. Feather Grass.

Zea variegata. Maize or Indian Corr

ORNITHOGALUM (or-nith-og-al-um Liliaceæ). Star of Bethlehem. Hard and greenhouse bulbs that make good po plants.

Propagate by offsets and seed and us sandy loam for the hardy species an loam and peat for the rest. The hard species should be grown in a warm border

SPECIES.

O. arabicum. Fragrant white flowers often as many as 20 on one flower-stalk June. Protect in winter. Bulbs must b well ripened-off after flowering.

O. lacteum. Satiny white flowers wit yellow anthers. Greenhouse; the flower when cut remain fresh for some time $1\frac{1}{2}$ ft.

O. nutans. Elegant racemes of silvery white flowers. Valuable for cutting and for naturalising in woodland. 1 ft.

O. thyrsoides. Yellow flowers. Green house. $1\frac{1}{2}$ ft. Several varieties, *aureum* and *flavissimum* being the best.

O. umbellatum. Pure white starry flowers. Hardy. May. *Splendens* is ar exceedingly good variety with larger flowers. $1\frac{1}{2}$ ft.

ORNUS. *See* FRAXINUS ORNUS.

OROBUS (or-oh-bus. Leguminosæ.)
From *oro*, excite, and *bous*, an ox. Bitter
Vetch. Small pea-like flowers; generally
low, bushy growth.

O. aurantiacus has flowers of rich old
gold, the stems weakly erect. It is not
always easy, though if well grown it forms
a very attractive plant by reason of the
unusual colour of the flowers.

Propagate by seed.

O. vernus, the early spring-flowering
Vetch, is a neat bushy plant of 6 in. to 1 ft.
in height with lilac and purple flowers.
This plant if lifted and potted in winter,
kept in warmth and well watered, forces
admirably.

Propagate by seed or division.

ORONTIUM (o-ron-ti-um. Aroideæ).
Hardy aquatic perennials that are best
grown in baskets sunk in the water.

Propagate by division. Soil, loam.

SPECIES.

O aquaticum. May. 6 in.

O. japonicum (syn. *Rohdea japonicum*).

OSIER. *See* SALIX.

OSMANTHUS (ōz-man′-thuz. Oleaceæ). Asiatic regions and U.S.A. Evergreen shrubs or small trees allied to Olea,
having long oval leaves, and white to
yellowish flowers borne in clusters, followed by small oval fruit not often seen
in this country.

Culture.—Plant in good loamy soil.
Propagate by cuttings in July with gentle
bottom heat.

SPECIES.

O. aquifolium (*illicifolius*). 10 ft., sometimes more in milder regions. Slow-growing species, having holly-like leaves with
clusters of small, sweetly-scented flowers
in September and October.

O. Delavayi (China). 6 ft. Densely
covered with stiff leathery leaves and
fragrant, pure white flowers like
Jessamine. Likes semi-shade. One of the
best hardy evergreens.

O. fragrans (*Olea fragrans*). Japan.
Only half-hardy, needing wall protection,
except in mild districts. The flowers are
minute but astonishingly fragrant, and
scent the air for yards around. There are
two forms, one with white flowers and one
with orange-coloured flowers, the latter
being the more fragrant.

OSMOSIS. The mixing in plants of
liquids of varying densities by means of a
semi-permeable membrane, in order to
provide food in such a form that it can be
easily assimilated.

OSMUNDA (os-mun-da. Filices).
Royal Fern. Greenhouse and hardy ferns.
These ferns are very stately, and the
cluster of sporangia at the tip of the fronds
very much resembles flowers and has

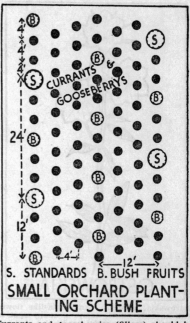

S. STANDARDS B. BUSH FRUITS
SMALL ORCHARD PLANT-
ING SCHEME

**Currants and gooseberries (fillers) should be
removed after five to seven years to allow for
full development of the fruit trees.**

earned for them the name of "Flowering
Ferns."

Culture.—Compost: equal parts fibrous
loam, peat and sand. Repot spring.
Shady moist position. Water freely in
summer, moderately other times. Winter
temperature, 40°; summer, 60° to 65°.

Propagation.—*See* ADIANTUM.

SPECIES.

Bipinata, 2–3 ft.; *cinnamomea*, 2–4 ft.

OSTEOMELES (os-te-ŏm-e-les. Rosaceæ). S. America and Asia. Evergreen
shrubs of distinct, handsome appearance,
having small 8–15 lobed, fern-like leaves,

with white flowers borne in clusters during June. Only hardy in mild S.W. districts.

Culture.—Plant in good garden soil. *Propagate* by seeds or cuttings in gentle heat.

SPECIES.

O. Schwerinæ (anthyllidifolia). China. 6–8 ft. Elegant silvery foliage, with white fragrant flowers like Hawthorn, followed by dark red to black fruits.

OSTROWSKIA

Ostrowskia, a pretty Campanula-like flower with an ugly name, enjoys a sunny spot in the perennial border.

O. s. microphylla. Smaller and more compact than type.

O. subrotunda (China). Distinct rare species, of compact habit, with clusters of flowers in June.

OSTROWSKIA (os-trof-ski-a. Campanulaceæ). *O. magnifica* is a handsome hardy perennial that should be grown in a sheltered sunny place in rich soil, while in very cold districts it should be grown as a cold greenhouse plant. Needs the same treatment as Campanulas. The large light blue flowers are very ephemeral, but follow so swiftly on the heels of their predecessors that there is continual bloom throughout July and August. 3–5 ft.

OSTRYA (ōs'-trĭ-a. Corylaceæ). Hop Hornbeam. Hardy deciduous tree, similar to the common Hornbeam (*Carpinus*), having oval leaves, with catkins 3 in. long followed by clusters of seed-pods; very striking when coloured in autumn.

SPECIES.

O. carpinifolia (*Vulgaris*). S. Europe and Asia Minor. 50–60 ft. Handsome species with seed-pods of beautiful autumnal tints.

O. virginica (Ironwood). N. America. 30–50 ft. Very hard-timbered species, the wood being used for tool-making. Similar in habit to *carpinifolia*.

OSWEGO TEA. *See* MONARDA.

OTHONNA (o-thon-na. Compositæ). Ragwort. Annual, perennial and ever green greenhouse plants, mostly from the Cape of Good Hope.

Propagate the annuals by seeds, the perennials by division, the tuberous-rooted species by division, and the shrubs by cuttings. Grow in 3 parts of loam and 1 of sandy peat and provide good drainage.

SPECIES

O. amplexifolia. Yellow, June. Shrubby 1½ ft.

O. carnosa. Yellow, summer. Shrub. 1 ft.

O. pinnata. Yellow. May. 1 ft.

O. tagetes. Annual. Yellow. 1 ft. May

O. tenuissima. May; 1½ ft. Shrub.

O. tuberosa. Tuberous-rooted. August Yellow. 2 ft.

OTHONNOPSIS (oth-onn-op-sis. Compositæ). From *Othonna* and *opsis*, like resembling the genus Othonna. Barbary Ragwort.

O. cheirifolia. An Algerian plant with broad, flat, grey strap-shaped leaves, and yellow daisies for flowers. It has an unusual exotic appearance and is quite hardy. Cuttings in spring or autumn 1 ft. June.

OURISIA (oo-ris-ia. Scrophularineæ). Hardy creeping perennials that are excellent for ledges in the rock garden. They were regarded as plants of difficult culture until they were grown in moist cool rich loam in a shady position, where they succeed quite well. *Propagate* by division or by seeds.

SPECIES.

O. coccinea is the most usually grown

and has scarlet flowers in summer. 9–12 in.

OUVIRANDRA (ou-vi-ran-dra. Naiadaceæ). Lattice or Lace Leaf Plant. Stove aquatics from Madagascar with exquisitely cut leaves like fine lace. In their natural habitat they grow by the sides of streams; need to be grown in a tank in the stove. As they are not fond of the light when growing they should be kept under the staging, if possible, or in a dark corner.

Propagate by seeds or division. The best soil for a rooting-medium is sandy loam and the water should be at a temperature of 70° all the year round.

SPECIES.

O. bernieriana. Pink. August. 2 ft.

O. fenestralis. White. August. 2 ft.

OVARY. The unripened seed-pod. It is placed just below the stigma and style and contains the ovules which, when ripened, are known as seeds. In plants where the ovary is below the petals it is called an inferior; when above the petals a superior ovary.

OVULES. The name given to unripened seeds while they are still in the ovary.

OXALIS (ox-a-lis. Geraniaceæ). Wood Sorrel. Cape Shamrock. A large genus of hardy annuals, hardy and half-hardy perennials, half-hardy bulbs, greenhouse herbaceous perennials and a few stove evergreens. The majority of the plants are low-growing and are excellent subjects for rock work or for growing in pots in the greenhouse.

Culture.—The annuals are propagated by seeds, the perennials by seeds and division, and the evergreens by cuttings. The pot species should be grown in light sandy loam with peat or leaf-mould, and the garden kinds in any light soil in a warm dry place.

SPECIES.

O. corniculata, Horned Wood Sorrel, is a very pretty hardy annual bearing yellow flowers from August onwards. It should be planted in wild gardens or in bare stony places, and will reproduce itself abundantly by means of seeds discharged to some distance from the plant by its elastic-valved capsules. Its variety *rubra* has dark purple leaves. 4 in.

O. adenophylla is a rare and beautiful species with pink flowers with a dark eye from May to July. It is quite hardy and is best in the rock garden. 4 in.

O. enneaphylla produces lovely erect white flowers amongst pale green glaucous foliage. Like the foregoing it is best in the rockery and is increased by division of the tubers when dormant. May to September. 6 in.

O. bowiei (syn. *purpurata*), known as the Cape Shamrock on account of the shape of the leaves, is one of the best of the grown species. It bears bright rose flowers with yellow centres in umbels from August to September. Half-hardy. 6 in.

O. cernua, the Bermuda Buttercup, with yellow flowers in spring and deep green leaves, is very decorative when grown in shallow pots or pans in the greenhouse, as the foliage and flowers droop down and cover the pans.

O. deppei is another greenhouse plant with red flowers in spring. Or it may be planted on the rockery in March and lifted in September. Its tubers are sometimes eaten as a vegetable on the Continent, but rarely in England.

O. floribunda is a useful half-hardy plant with rose flowers also white and bluish varieties.

O. acetosella, the Wood Sorrel, a hardy perennial, is the most suited to a shady place in the perennial border and bears white flowers from May onwards. 3 in.

All of the bulbous and tuberous rooted species are grown in the greenhouse, and if kept fairly dry during the winter and given as much sun as possible, will bloom in early spring. They require a temperature of 40°–45°.

OX-EYE. *See* BUPHTHALMUM.

OXYCOCCUS (ŏx-i-kok′-kus. Vacciniaceæ). Cranberries. World-wide distribution. Prostrate evergreen shrubs, having small pink flowers followed by round red berries.

Culture.—Plant in a moist peaty soil. *Propagate* by division or layers.

SPECIES.

O. macrocarpus (*Vaccinium macrocarpum*). "American Cranberry." Slender wiry stems, with racemes of pink flowers, followed by fruit of acid taste. Largely cultivated in America for fruit preserving;

also much used for sauce with roast turkey.

O. palustris (Vaccinium Oxycoccus). Small Cranberry of Britain. Smaller habit than preceding, with pleasantly-flavoured berries.

OXYDENDRUM (ŏx-i-den'-dron. Ericaceæ). Sorrel Tree. East N. America. 50 ft. Hardy deciduous trees, with long oval leaves assuming beautiful tints in autumn, and white bell-shaped flowers borne on racemes in July and August. Thriving in good peaty, non-calcareous soil in semi-shaded position. *Propagate* by seed when obtainable.

O. arboreum (Andromeda arboreum). The only species.

OXYTROPIS (ox-i-tro-pis. Leguminosæ). Hardy herbaceous perennials.

Propagate by seeds sown in flowering-position as the plants do not transplant well. Also by division or cuttings, the former in spring and the latter in summer. They do well in a rock garden where they can be exposed to the full sun.

SPECIES.

O. cyanea. Bluish-purple flowers in June and July. 6 in.

O. floribunda. Purple. May.

O. campesiris. Yellow. July. 6 in.

O. Lambertii. Flowers that vary from blue to white or purple. May to August. 1 ft.

O. montana. Blue or yellow. June to July. 6 in.

O. pyrenaica. Short racemes of purple barred with white. Summer. 6 in.

O. sulphurea. Creamy-yellow flowers. 6 in.

OYSTER-SHELL BARK SCALE (Aspidiotus ostreæ-formis). An insect, the scale of which somewhat resembles a minute oyster shell, and which infests the currant, cherry, peach, plum, apple, pear and other fruit trees and has also been found on heather (Calluna). The best control is to spray infested plants with a winter wash of 2 gal. of paraffin, 1½ lb. soft soap, 6 lb. caustic soda and 28 gal. of water. Mix the paraffin and soap with hot water to a creamy emulsion before adding the caustic soda, and use immediately after the soda has been added.

OYSTER PLANT. *See* MERTENSIA.

OZOTHAMNUS. *See* HELICHRYSUM.

P

PACHYSANDRA (pak-i-san'-dra. Euphorbiaceæ). China and Japan. Low-growing creeping evergreen, suitable for covering bare places under trees, etc., with dull green leaves, and white flowers on erect stems produced in April.

Culture.—Plant in a moist soil, in either a shady or sunny position. *Propagate* by cuttings during summer months.

P. terminalis (Japan). 6–8 in. The only cultivated species. Forms a low, compact shrub, with clusters of greenish-purple flowers.

PACHYSTIMA (pak-i-sti'-ma. Celastraceæ). N. America. Evergreen shrubs, of low, compact habit, having tiny, inconspicuous flowers followed by small white fruit. Of but little garden value. Adaptable for small nooks in rock garden.

Culture.—Plant in moist non-calcareous, peaty soil or sandy leaf-mould in shady position. *Propagate* by cuttings.

SPECIES.

P. Canbyi. 1 ft. greenish-white flowers from May to August.

P. myrsinites. 6–18 in. Reddish flowers, and small white fruit.

PADUS. *See* PRUNUS.

PÆDERIA (pe-de-ri-a. Rubiaceæ). Asia. Tender, climbing shrub up to 18 ft., having white, tinged purple, tubular flowers produced during summer. *Propagate* by cuttings in sand with gentle heat.

P. chinensis, the only cultivated species, requires protection in colder regions.

PÆONIA. *See* PEONY.

PALIURUS (pal-i-ūr'-us. Rhamnaceæ). S. Europe to W. Asia. Hardy deciduous shrubs, or small trees, having long spines and small greenish-yellow flowers followed by peculiar flat-shaped, small fruits. Will make a good hedge if clipped.

Culture.—Plant in good loamy soil. *Propagate* by seeds when obtainable or by cuttings and layers.

P. Spina Christi (*P aculeatus*). "Christ's Thorn." Reputed to be the species from which the "Crown of Thorns" was made. Flowering in July and August, followed by disk-like fruit, giving the plants an unusual appearance.

PAMPAS GRASS. *See* CORTADERIA.

PAN. A shallow vessel, usually earthenware, in which seeds are sown.

PANAX. *See* NOTHOPANAX.

PANCRATIUM (pan-krat-i-um. Amaryllidaceæ). Greenhouse bulbous flowering plants. Fragrant. South Europe, 1579.

Culture.—Compost: 3 parts loam, equal parts dried cow manure, leaf-mould and sand. Repot spring, but this should only be done every 3 or 4 years as plants flower better when pot-bound. Water freely during the summer, after flowering, gradually withhold water until plants become quite dry. Give weak liquid manure during growing period. Winter temperature, 50°; summer, 65°–75°.

Propagate by offsets when repotting.

SPECIES.

P. canariense, white; *P. calanthinea,* white; *P. maritimum,* white. The last may be grown ouside in a warm border.

PANICUM (pan-i-kum. Gramineæ). Hair Grass. 1½–2 ft. North America. There are a number of annual and perennial species, and *P. capilare,* the hair-panicled grass, is the best known of the annual species. Sown in March it will produce its elegant inflorescence in August. Good for drying.

PANSY. *See* VIOLA.

PAPAVER (pa-pa-ver. Papaveraceæ). Poppy. Poppies rank amongst the most brilliant of hardy flowers and are great favourites with gardeners despite the short duration of the flowers. They range from the tiny alpine to tall border species and include both annuals and perennials.

Culture.—*Propagate* the annuals by seeds and thin the seedlings as soon as they are fit to handle. Later thin them to 1 ft. apart to obtain really good plants. The perennials are also propagated by seeds and by division of the roots, the pieces being placed in sandy loam in a frame until they have rooted. All poppies seed freely, and as they dislike transplantation the capsules should be picked off to ensure that the following year's crop will not be too closely sown.

If the dead flowers are taken off the flowering season should last a deal longer.

The perennials should be carefully staked, and as they hate to be disturbed they should only be lifted every three or four years. A mulch of old hotbed manure is useful for preserving the moisture in the roots and may be applied in June. All the plants like a rich moist soil in full sun-

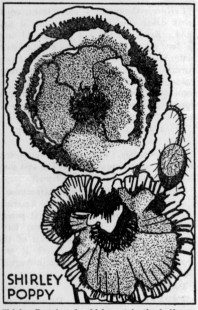

SHIRLEY POPPY

Shirley Poppies should be cut in the half-open stage. They were raised by the late Rev. W. Wilks, in the village of Shirley.

shine, and although they are supposed to thrive in any soil, in a light dry one they only live for a short time.

Species.—*P. Rhoeas* is the scarlet or common field Poppy, of which the well-known strain, Shirley Poppy, provides a great variety of colours ranging from creamy pink to crimson. There are also several double forms, chiefly known as German, French and Ranunculus Poppies. All are annuals. They are about 2 ft. in height.

P. somniferum is the opium poppy that has been grown for the sake of the drug since time immemorial, but it is used only for garden decoration in England. It is an annual that is naturalised in several parts of the country, and has large flowers of various colours and greyish foliage. The flowers are useless for cutting and have a rank smell, but make a bold show when grouped together. The single forms include Maid of the Mist, white with fringed petals, and Danebrog, a handsome plant with scarlet and white flowers. The double forms are much more numerous, the best being perhaps the Pæony-flowered Poppies, so called from their likeness to pæonies in form and size. They last longer than the singles and range in colour from bright crimson to white. Carnation Poppies, with fringed petals, are another double form derived from *somniferum*. The flowering season of these varieties lasts throughout the summer. Height 2–4 ft.

Pavoninum is the Peacock Poppy, an annual with scarlet flowers, black-blotched at the base of the petals. 18 in.

Orientale, the Oriental Poppy, is a fine hardy perennial with deep scarlet flowers about 6 in. across. It has numerous varieties and has engendered many hybrids, chiefly with red flowers that bloom from May to June. *Bracteatum* is a variety, better than the original, with larger flowers and large leafy bracts. 2–4 ft.

Nudicaule (syn. *radicatum*), the Iceland Poppy, is a useful perennial, usually grown as a biennial. It bears yellowy-orange or white flowers. Its dwarf forms are excellent little rock plants. 6–18 in.

Alpinum, the smallest of the Poppy genus, is grown as a biennial and has yellow, rosy-orange or white flowers in summer. It is best suited to rock-work. 6 in.

The flowers of the Iceland and Shirley Poppies are highly valued for cutting and should be gathered early in the morning, when they are only half open, to ensure the blooms lasting. The Oriental Poppies are very effective in town gardens and will last quite well during the winter.

Cultivation of Iceland Poppies.—The modern Iceland Poppies are specially valued as cut flowers, and in order to obtain good quality flowers on long stems, that will display well, the following cultural methods should be adopted:

Sow the seed outdoors during the first week of July. Sow very thinly, and cover very lightly with fine soil or sand.

When the plants can conveniently be put into their flowering quarters in September or early October, this will be found the best practice; but failing this they can be wintered where they are sown, and moved to the borders in early spring, say about March.

All old flowers and seed pods should be removed from time to time, as this will lengthen the flowering period and improve the quality of the flowers.

These Poppies like a light rich soil, and will not come through the winter successfully in cold wet ground. Of the newer modern strains, "Gibson's Improved Orange," and "Sandford's Aurora" are particularly attractive.

Amateur gardeners are recommended always to grow these afresh annually, instead of trying to keep old plants. Where the garden soil is uncongenial, and plants cannot easily be raised from seed, small plants can be purchased each spring in the same way as summer bedding plants, and if used as bedding subjects they will give every satisfaction.

The Rev. W. Wilks, a former secretary of the Royal Horticultural Society, and Vicar of Shirley, found a common or field Poppy with different coloured flowers from those of the type, saved the seeds, made careful selections over a period of years, and finally produced a practically new race, with colours ranging from white, blush-pink, salmon and rose, to scarlet. Further improvements have been made, and the present-day strains of Shirley poppies are of great beauty. The flowers are good for cutting, and if cut in the bud stage, and the ends of the stalks put into boiling water, or seared with a hot iron, will open in water, and last several days.

PARADISEA (par-ad-is-ea. Liliaceæ). St. Bruno's Lily. Hardy bulbous plants. Increase by division.

SPECIES.

P. liliastrum. White flowers spotted with green (syn. *Anthericum Liliastrum*). June. 2 ft.

P. l. major. Larger than the type.

PARAFFIN EMULSION. *See* FORMULÆ.

PARIS (par-is. Liliaceæ). Hardy herbs with creeping rootstocks that may be divided to increase the plants. Also increase by seed. Grow in any fertile garden soil.

SPECIES.

P. polyphylla. Greenish-yellow flowers. May. 1 ft.

P. quadrifolia. Yellowish-green. April. 1 ft.

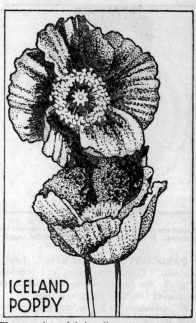

ICELAND POPPY

The pure tints of their yellow, orange and white forms make the Iceland Poppies hard to beat as cut flowers. They are best treated as biennials but some varieties should be raised annually from seed or purchased as bedding plants.

PARIS GREEN (Aceto-arsenite of copper). An emerald-green compound formerly used as a stomach poison for the destruction of caterpillars and other leaf-eating insects. It is preferable to use arsenate of lead (*q.v.*) which has practically replaced the older compound.

PARNASSIA (par-nass-ia. Saxifrageæ). Grass of Parnassus. Hardy herbaceous perennials that are usually regarded as only useful for the bog or water garden, but are really quite good in moist shady places in borders or rockeries.

They are *propagated* by division in spring or by seeds sown at that time or in late summer.

SPECIES.

Caroliniana and *asarifolia*, both with white flowers, are pretty in borders; while *palustris*, with white flowers on erect stems and tufts of green foliage, is the best of the species. Useful in the rock garden as well as the border. Height 6–9 in.

SEED HOPPER

(H.M.B. patent)

A neat contrivance which no bird-lover should be without. It ensures a clean and plentiful supply of food.

PAROCHETUS (par-ok-e-tus. Leguminosæ). From *para*, near; and *ochetos*, a brook, the conditions under which it is frequently found. Shamrock Pea.

P. communis is a low, creeping plant, with trifoliate leaves and large pea-shaped flowers of a beautiful azure blue. It likes a moist, sheltered situation; it will not always survive a winter in spite of the earnest assertions to the contrary by nurserymen's catalogues. 2 in. Summer. Nepal.

Propagate by division.

PARONYCHIA (par-on-i-ki-a. Illecebraceæ). Nailwort. Whitlow Grass. Thought to be a cure for whitlows. Hardy herbs of tufted habit.

Propagate by seeds sown in spring. Grows in any light garden soil.

SPECIES.

P. argentea. Bracts and stipules silvery while the rest of the flowers is white. Summer. 9 in. In Algeria a beverage

known as Sanguinaire is obtained from this plant.

P. serpyllifolia. White, July. 4–6 in.

PARROTIA (pa-rot'-ti-a. Hamamelidaceæ). Deciduous trees, having almost round leaves, and small flowers produced during April and May.

Culture.—Plant in good moist, loamy soil, not allowed to get dry. *Propagate* by seeds, layers, or cuttings.

SPECIES.

P. jacquemontiana (*involucrata*). W. Himalayas. 5–6 ft. Flowers with conspicuous white bracts. Foliage assumes yellowish tints during autumn.

P. persica. Persia. 30–40 ft. Very effective during autumn when foliage colours to gold and yellow. Prune back lower branches when young, otherwise it is liable to remain stunted.

PARSLEY. *See under* HERBS, CULINARY.

PARSNIP (Peucedanum sativum). The Parsnip is a native and European plant known to have been used for food in this country during the time of the second Roman occupation. It is an extremely hardy vegetable, and one which, fortunately, will grow on almost any type of soil.

Culture.—For all ordinary purposes excellent roots can be grown on well prepared ground which was well manured for the previous crop. The addition of fresh manure to ground for parsnips cannot be recommended, as it results in badly-shaped and many-thonged roots. For exhibition work, tapering holes 6 in. wide at the top are bored to a depth of 3 ft.; these are filled with a good sandy compost that has been passed through a ½ in. sieve, and a few seeds are sown in the centre.

Parsnips require a very long season of growth, and should be sown as soon as soil and weather conditions permit.

They also require more room than is usually afforded them, and it is a good plan to draw the drills 15 in. apart, and to sow 5 or 6 seeds in a group at every foot, alternating them in rows.

Whichever plan is adopted, the seedlings must be thinned out to single plants as soon as the strongest can be determined. Frequent hoeings during the summer constitute the only other operations necessary.

Parsnips are sufficiently hardy to stand in the ground during the winter, but as frost sometimes makes it impossible to lift the roots when they are wanted, and as they may be stored satisfactorily in sand, as advised for carrots, we prefer the latter method with at least part of the crop. Another point in favour of this is the fact that the ground is left vacant for winter digging.

SPECIES.
P. cœrulea. Vigorous climber, with lovely fragrant blue flowers produced from June to September.

P. c. Constance Elliott. A white form of this type.

P. racemosa (princeps). Brazilian Red Passion Flower, having flowers of a vivid scarlet.

PATHWAYS. There are many kinds

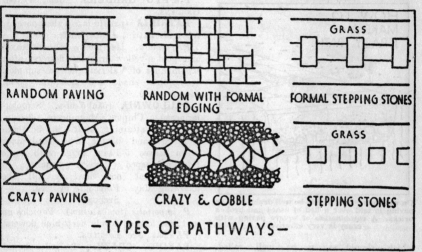

—TYPES OF PATHWAYS—

RANDOM PAVING

RANDOM WITH FORMAL EDGING

GRASS
FORMAL STEPPING STONES

CRAZY PAVING

CRAZY & COBBLE

GRASS
STEPPING STONES

Neat well-made pathways give an orderly appearance to a garden.

VARIETIES.
Hollow Crown, Magnum Bonum, Tender and True, Student.

Uses.—Generally used as a boiled vegetable, or for flavouring soups and broths.

Parsnip. *Was brought annually to the Emperor Tiberius from the Rhine district.*

PARTHENOCISSUS. *See* VITIS.

PASQUE FLOWER. *See* ANEMONE PULSATILLA.

PASSIFLORA (păs-si-flor'-a. Passifloraceæ). Passion Flower. Brazil. Semi-evergreen climbers, having flat, open, fragrant flowers, 3–4 in. across. Require protection and a south wall in cold districts north of London. Will thrive in ordinary garden soil. *Propagate* by seeds sown in heat, or cuttings. It derived the name Passion Flower from Spanish priests connecting parts of the flower to episodes in the "Passion of Christ."

of surfacing for garden pathways, but the construction does not vary to any great extent. Except in very small gardens, pathways should not be less than 2 ft. wide, 4 ft. being a good average width, and 9 ft. and over suitable for drives. In the tiny garden, stepping-stones sunk flush with the grass level will often be found to be more pleasing than a path.

The site for the proposed path should be marked out with pegs and the soil removed to a depth of 18 in. in heavy soils, 9 in. being sufficient on light soils. If the site requires draining, a pipe down the centre of the pathway is sufficient for 4 ft. paths, drains at either side being necessary for a drive or 9 ft. path. If the soil does not easily become water-logged, the foundations should be sufficient to carry away water without additional drainage. The ground should next be cleared of any perennial or long-rooted weeds. If these are not eradicated they will push their way up through the path and be a perpetual nuisance. Fill in about a third to a half of the excavated area with large clinkers, brickbats, hard rubbish, stones, etc. All but the last 2 or 3 in. should then be filled in with coarse gravel or smaller clinkers. This foundation should then be well rolled. The path is then ready for a top layer of *gravel*,

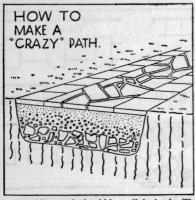

HOW TO MAKE A "CRAZY" PATH.

On wet soils a path should be well drained. The paving is laid over a bed of ashes and broken bricks. A combination of square paving with crazy is very effective.

which should again be well rolled, but not when the gravel is wet or it will adhere to the roller. For *paved pathways* the foundations need not be so deep, but they must be rammed down firmly and tested with the straight edge and spirit-level before commencing to lay the stone. A 2 in. layer of sand should be spread over the hard core to make a bedding for paving, which should be laid with the edges fitting as far as possible, leaving no crevices more than 1 in. wide. Such a path is suitable for planting with dwarf alpines. If the path is to bear much traffic the stones may be set in mortar to tie them together and keep the whole firm.

Solid pathways of cement, asphalt, etc., need careful preparation as for paving, for once laid it is difficult to repair any defects caused in the surface by an uneven and slipping foundation. The material should be run in between boards, and in the case of cement may be marked with the spade when almost set, to imitate the crevices in paving stone. The boards may be removed or not, as desired, when the cement is absolutely dry. Brick pathways need preparing in the same way as for paving, the bricks either being set in mortar or sand swept in between them. There are many ways of combining stones with bricks, grass, etc., to form serviceable pathways. Some suggestions are given in the sketch. *See also* CAMBER, DRIVE, GUTTERS.

PATIO GARDENS. *See* SPANISH GARDENS.

PATRINIA (pat-rĭn-ia. Valerianaceæ). After M. Patrin, a Siberian traveller.

P. palmata. Has glossy palmate leaves and golden-yellow fragrant flowers, after the manner of Valerian, in late summer. It requires shade and moisture. 6 in. Japan. Seed.

PAULOWNIA (pâul-ŏ′-ni-a. Scrophulariaceæ). China. Magnificent deciduous trees attaining 40 ft. in Southern England, and having five lobed dark green leaves 5–10 in. long, with large Foxglove-shaped flowers, forming in autumn, but not flowering till the following May. *Propagate* by seed.

SPECIES.

P. imperialis (tomentosum). Panicles up to 12 in. long of lovely deep blue flowers.

PAVIA. *See* ÆSCULUS.

PAVING, CRAZY. Irregular-shaped pieces of stone of fairly even thickness, say 1–2 in., make useful "crazy" pathways, which are dry and serviceable. They may be planted in moderation with small, creeping Alpines. (*See* PATHWAYS for construction.)

PEA (*Pisum sativum*). Apparently the garden vegetable pea of to-day has been developed over the course of several centuries from a wild type found in Eastern Europe or Western Asia. Records are on hand of its cultivation in England during the reign of Henry VIII, but so much progress has been made during the last twenty years that the varieties now in common use are far superior in size, flavour, fruitfulness and vigour.

Culture.—No vegetable crops respond more readily to generous treatment than Peas, and the land in which these are to be grown should be thoroughly prepared during the winter months. In large establishments, it is usual to devote special plots to this crop, and to prepare the land to suit their requirements by double digging and heavy manuring. In smaller gardens this is rarely possible, and the need may be met by taking out trenches for the rows at distances of 8–12 ft. apart, and growing other crops in the spaces between the rows. This method applies to all but the earliest dwarf types, which can be grown in rows 2 ft. apart, and the bed double-dug right over.

For all other types, the trenches should be made 15 in. wide and 2 ft. deep, forking up the bottom soil and working into it a good dressing of manure. The surface soil should be broken up and shovelled back into the trench, mixing in with it as the work proceeds a liberal dressing of manure, wood ash, and bonemeal, at the rate of 4 oz. per yard run. The returned soil will fill the trench above the usual level, but by planting-time it should have settled down. If manure is unobtainable, decayed garden refuse, lawn mowings, etc., may be used together with a good all-round fertiliser. If the soil is at all deficient in lime, a dressing of air-slaked lime should be scattered over the top at the rate of 4 oz. per square yard as soon as the digging is finished—which should not be later than the end of February.

Except in the most favoured districts, early March is quite soon enough for the first outdoor sowings, and then only round-seeded types should be used.

The surface should be lightly forked over and broken down, and, when sufficiently dry, drills 4–6 in. deep should be drawn the full length and width of the trench.

To prevent attacks by birds and mice, slightly damp the seeds with paraffin and dust them with red lead, then space them evenly 3 in. apart in 3 or 4 lines down the trench. The stronger plants and heavier crops obtained from thinly-sown rows make the extra trouble involved well worth while; furthermore, it means a great economy in seed over the old method of indiscriminately scattering handfuls of seeds along the row.

The seeds should be pressed in and finally covered with about 2 in. of soil, so that the finished row is now somewhat below the surrounding level of the ground.

This gives a certain measure of protection from cold winds to the seedlings as they emerge through the soil, and is also an advantage in June and July if the weather is extremely dry and watering becomes necessary.

As soon as the seedlings are 3 or 4 in. high, those varieties which require staking should have the sticks placed along either side of the trench and about 3 in. from the

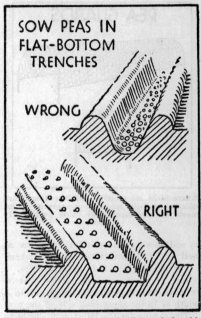

SOW PEAS IN FLAT-BOTTOM TRENCHES

WRONG

RIGHT

Peas must have room to develop and, for this reason, are best sown thinly in flat-bottomed trenches.

outside rows. Twiggy hazel sticks are best, and the tops when trimmed off should be struck in to train the shoots up to the bigger wood. The angle of incline of the stakes should be very slight, so that the top of the row of sticks is little narrower than the bottom. When sticks are unobtainable peas can be grown on wire netting or coarse fish netting. All supports should be at least 6 in. taller than the recognised height of the variety.

Birds sometimes do considerable damage to the growing plants and to the pods, but a few strands of black cotton stretched along and amongst the sticks is usually sufficient to keep them off.

To maintain a succession, it is a good plan to sow another row as soon as the seedlings from the previous sowing show through the soil. When growing for exhibition, three sowings of the same variety should be made at intervals, allowing 100, 90, and 80 days respectively, as the actual timing is largely influenced

PEA GUARDS

Where birds are troublesome Pea Guards are effective until the seedlings are staked. 3/4 in. mesh is recommended as being particularly suitable.

by soil, locality, and weather conditions, as well as by the cultivation afforded them.

For mid-season and late varieties, a mulch or top-dressing of strawy manure or lawn mowings should be placed to a width of 18 in. along each side of the row.

The sowing for the latest crop should be made early in June. One or two round-seeded varieties, and especially Cooper's Standwell, may be sown in November to stand outside through the winter for early crops. For these sowings thicker seeding is advisable.

VARIETIES.

Early.

Earliest of All (r), 2 ft.
Pilot (r), 3 ft.
Early Round Gradus (r), 3 ft.
Little Marvel, 1½ ft.
William Hurst, 1 ft.
Bedford Champion, 3 ft.

Second Early.

Universal, 2 ft.
Stratagem, 2 ft.

Telegraph (r), 5 ft.
Admiral Beatty, 4 ft.
Senator, 3 ft.
Fillbasket (r), 3 ft.

Main Crop.

Alderman, 5 ft.
Duke of Albany, 5 ft.
Quite Content, 5 ft.
Ne Plus Ultra, 6 ft.
Autocrat, 4 ft.
The Gladstone, 3½ ft.

(r) denotes round-seeded varieties—the others are wrinkled.

Garden peas are usually boiled and eaten at once, but can also be bottled or dried for winter use.

Pea Guards. These are usually a dozen in a bundle with two ends and are made of 1 in. or ¾ in. mesh galvanised wire netting with wire supports either end and bound along the length. Useful for protecting seeds and seedlings—such as peas —from the birds; and ¾ in. mesh is particularly recommended as birds can just get through the 1 in. mesh.

Pea Moth or Maggot (*Grapholitha pisana*).

DESCRIPTION. *Adult.*—About ½ in. in expanse; wings, greyish and shining with a series of small yellow spots along the upper edge of the upper wing. *Larva.*— About ½ in. in expanse; yellowish, with a brown head.

LIFE-HISTORY.—The moth appears in early summer and lays its eggs on the pods as soon as the flowers begin to fall. On hatching out the small caterpillars first of all tunnel into the pod, but as soon as the peas develop they eat their way through and commence feeding on the seed. When full grown they leave the pods, fall to the ground and there pupate in a slight cocoon.

METHODS OF CONTROL.—No very satisfactory method of control has been discovered; subsequent attacks, however, may be lessened by pulling up and burning all haulm as soon as the peas are gathered and digging in a soil fumigant at the rate of 4 oz. per square yard. When peas are being shelled all "maggoty" pods should be put aside and burnt and not thrown on to the rubbish heap as is so often the case. It is said a dusting of soot, just as the blossom is falling, will check egg laying, the soot acting as a repellant.

PEA, SWEET. *See* SWEET PEA.

PEACH AND NECTARINE (*Prunus persica*). As the nectarine is merely a variety of the peach, and as both fruits require precisely the same treatment, they may be dealt with together. It is interesting to note that nectarines are frequently raised by the sowing of peach seeds, and *vice versa*. The only difference between the two is that the peach has a downy skin, whilst that of the nectarine is smooth.

The peach has been grown for so many centuries and over so wide an area, that its country of origin is a trifle obscure. It is generally supposed to have come originally from China, where it was recorded over two thousand years before its introduction to the Romans.

Out-of-Doors Culture.—In this country, the only satisfactory means of culture out of doors is as a fan-trained tree on a wall. The wall should preferably have a south aspect, although in warm and sheltered localities a west or an east wall is suitable.

The Border. Correct preparation of the border is essential to success. This should be at least 6 ft. wide, preferably 8 ft. No other plants should be put in this border. The soil must be prepared to a depth of 2–3 ft. Heavy soils are valueless, and must be entirely removed and replaced with a good light loam. Should there be any tendency to water-logging, draining must be efficiently arranged. If the soil is light, it may possibly have a gravel subsoil, which must be removed, and good soil replaced. It is useless to endeavour to grow peaches if the soil in which they are planted becomes either waterlogged or dried out. When preparing the soil for the border add mortar rubble at the rate of one barrow-load per ton of soil. If the soil is of poor quality yet good texture, it should be enriched with a little manure.

Distance Apart. Fan-trained trees should be planted 15 ft. apart.

Planting. This should be done in October. Peaches start early into growth, and planting should not be deferred until after this month.

Pruning. The chief point in successful cultivation lies in correct pruning. This may appear complicated, but is easily

grasped with a little thought. Peaches fruit on one-year-old wood, and on no other class of wood at all; therefore it is necessary to see that, year by year, the entire space which the tree covers is furnished with such wood. Consider starting with a young tree as supplied by the nurseryman. Early in the season buds begin to break throughout the entire length of each young shoot. Some of these buds produce flowers, others produce shoots. Two things have now to be done. First the fruit must be brought to perfection; and secondly a supply of fresh wood must be made to take the place of the current season's fruiting wood, which by the end of the season will be useless, since two-year-old wood never produces flowers. Since this two-year-old wood is useless, it becomes obvious that it should be cut out as soon as possible. It has finished its purpose as soon as the fruit is gathered. It would be useless, however, to remove an entire shoot which has just fruited if this shoot is set with young wood which is going to supply next year's fruit. The method employed to obviate this difficulty is to pinch out almost all of the young shoots on fruiting wood during the growing season, leaving only the two strongest at the base of each fruiting branch. It is also necessary to leave one at the extremity to draw the sap up past the fruit. It then becomes possible to cut away fruiting wood after the fruit is gathered, the cut being made carefully to the two young shoots which are to be left. These remain to provide next year's crop.

The process may be summarised thus: During the growing season, gradually pinch out all the laterals from each piece of fruiting wood, saving only the basal two, and the leader at the extremity. In January, cut out all old wood which has borne fruit, making the cut as far down as the two basal young shoots which were left. These are then tied in to take the place of the removed wood.

Thinning. Young trees should not be allowed to carry more than half-a-dozen fruits. On matured trees allow one fruit for every square foot of tree surface. Thinning may be done gradually, using the last to be removed for preserving.

Watering. The Peach border must

never be allowed to dry out. Do not water little and often, but when signs of dryness appear give the whole border a thorough soaking. Syringing with water is recommended daily after the fruit is set.

Culture under Glass. The ideal house for Peach culture should be sunny, well ventilated, and must have a suitable border thoroughly drained as advised for outdoor culture. Strong heat must not be used to cause premature opening of the flowers. It is necessary only to exclude frost. A warm temperature of 45°-50° is best at flowering time. Plenty of air must be given at this time. The following temperatures should be kept up as nearly as possible: after setting, 55°-60°; after stoning, 65°-75°; swelling, 75°-80°.

Syringing. This should be done daily after the fruit is set until it begins to ripen, when it must be discontinued. After the fruit is gathered, continue again until the leaves have fallen.

Thinning. See under CULTURE, OUT-OF-DOORS.

Watering. See under CULTURE, OUT-OF-DOORS.

Pollination. At flowering time, pollen should be transferred from one variety to another with a rabbit's tail in order to ensure a good set of fruit.

Pruning. The same process should be applied as that recommended for outdoor culture, with the exception that old wood may be cut out as soon as the leaves have dropped.

Propagation.—Budding or grafting on Plum stock; preferably the "Mussel."

VARIETIES.

PEACHES: *Barrington.*—A large-fruited variety of good flavour; very hardy and prolific.

Bellergarde.—A prolific bearer suitable for out of doors; healthy grower.

Dymond.—A first-class variety, excellent for outdoor culture. It has large fruits of good flavour and bears well.

Hale's Early.—One of the earliest, ripening out of doors by the end of July. A good variety for the north.

NECTARINES: *Early Rivers.*—Very large fruit, ripening at end of July. Rich flavour and fine cropper.

Lord Napier.—One of the best for indoors

or out. The skin is thin and requires shading under glass when ripening.

Pineapple.—One of the richest-flavoured varieties and a good cropper. Recommended for outdoors in the warmest localities only.

Pests.—The worst pests are: Peach Scale, Aphis and Red Spider.

Diseases.—Peach Leaf Curl and Mildew.

PEACH APHIS. *Anuraphis amygdali.*

DESCRIPTION. *Adult.*—Head and thorax dark, abdomen ranging from greyish-green through dull rusty-yellow to almost black. The yellowish forms have black spots of varying size and it is the increase in size and consequent coalescence of these spots which give rise to the green form.

Larvæ. The young are at first pale yellow in colour, but gradually the pigment forming the spots in the adult is developed, so making them darker in appearance.

LIFE-HISTORY.—This is the common aphis of peaches and nectarines both under glass and out of doors. The young hatch out in the spring and quickly smother the shoots, the leaves of which are rolled up into tight masses. If the attack is really severe these leaves will dry out and fall off. In June many become winged and fly away to some unknown plant, while others remain on the peach right throughout the year. In the autumn there is a tendency for the offspring of those which left the peach to migrate back again, when eggs are laid on the small branches and twigs.

METHODS OF CONTROL.—Much care must be taken in selecting a wash for peaches; undoubtedly the best used are those of vegetable origin such as quassia, nicotine, etc.

PEAR (*Pyrus communis*). The wild pear, from which garden varieties have been selected, is a native of Europe and North Asia, and possibly of this country also. The fruit was cultivated by the Romans, and from that time has always claimed the special attention of gardeners. There are now probably over one thousand different varieties in cultivation in this country alone.

The pear is generally grown in one of the following forms—cordon, espalier, bush, half-standard, standard. Of these the cordon and the bush are the most popular, as they produce fruit more quickly than the other forms.

Soil. A rich and fertile loam is necessary for the cultivation of the best quality pears. The situation should not be too dry. On very light soils trees should be ordered that have been worked on pear stock, whilst for heavy soils the Quince stock must be stipulated.

Situation. Pears are more particular as to situation than are apples. They flower a fortnight earlier, and the young growth is more tender. The fruits are liable to be blown down by heavy gales. A sheltered spot is therefore essential. At the same time a full share of sunlight is essential to the production of well-flavoured fruits. Undoubtedly the best method of culture is to grow the fruit as a cordon, trained to a wall. As such trees do not take up much room, they may be put in at 2 ft. apart.

Distance apart. Cordons, 2 ft.; Espaliers, 15 ft.; Bushes, 10 ft.; Half-standards, 15 ft.; Standards, 25-30 ft.

Planting. Planting should be done at any period between November and March. The ground should be free from frost, and should be in a sufficiently dry condition to permit thorough treading.

Pruning. The same treatment as suggested for apples should be applied to pears. In the earlier stages of the formation of the tree it is important to prune lightly those specimens which are making strong growth; otherwise they will take some time to settle down to fruiting. Conversely, young trees which make little growth and which bear comparatively heavily, should have most of the fruit removed and be treated severely with the knife. For the rest, spur-pruning and the treatment for leaders as recommended for apples may be applied. Summer pruning is advisable for espaliers and cordons.

Propagation.—Pears are grafted either on wild pear stocks or on the Quince stock. The former is a vigorous stock and should be used for standard trees grown on poor soils. The Quince stock tones down the natural vigour and produces early fruiting. It is the only stock for the smaller-trained trees. Owing to its use it now need no

longer be said that "He who plants pears plants for his heirs."

VARIETIES.

(Dessert in order of ripening.)

Loxton's Superb.—August; a new variety of great merit. Large and well-flavoured.

Colmar d'Eté.—Early September; small fruit, but very sweet and good flavour.

Williams Bon Chrétien.—September. This pear is too well known to need much description. Unfortunately many inferior varieties are sold under its name, not only on street barrows but in shops also. The "Bartlett" pear used for canning is the same variety. Is not so much grown commercially as it should be owing to its susceptibility to "Black Scab," a disease which cripples and cracks the fruit. This disease is easily controlled by using Bordeaux mixture.

Emile d'Heyst.—October; an easily-grown and regularly-cropping pear which should be planted in every garden. Very sweet and juicy.

Louis Bonne of Jersey.—October. Another easily grown variety of very excellent flavour. Thrives in most situations.

Doyenne du Comice. The finest flavoured pear of all, but not too easily cultivated in this country. Beurre Superfin is very similar and more easily grown, although a type subject to the ravages of scab. (*See* WILLIAMS.)

Duchesse de Bordeaux.—January. A late pear of excellent quality, its only fault being a tendency to over-crop in the younger stages. Fruit must be well thinned, and mulches of manure given in order to build up a strong specimen.

CULINARY

Catillac.—December–April. A very old variety and the best for culinary purposes.

PEAR LEAF BLISTER MITE (*Eriophyes pyri*). ADULT MITE.—About $\frac{1}{20}$ of an inch, cylindrical but tapering at the posterior end, from which two long bristle-like processes spring. The two pairs of legs are placed near the head.

LIFE-HISTORY.—The mites are concealed under the bud scales in the winter, but they do no apparent damage. In the spring, however, they crawl out and enter the young leaves. After a time they cause galls or swellings to appear on the leaves. These, on account of their colour, which is bright pink at first, are very conspicuous. As time goes on the leaves begin to crack, the galls harden and turn brown. In the autumn and before leaf-fall, the mites leave their summer quarters and return to the new buds. This mite is usually commonest

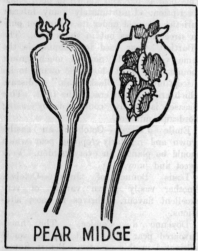

PEAR MIDGE

The tiny midge lays its eggs on the young pears, causing them to drop off in June.

on wall pears, and if allowed to multiply will not only do damage to the foliage but will also cause swellings on the young fruit, which is prevented from developing and ripening.

METHODS OF CONTROL.—Winter treatment is useless. Spray with a lime-sulphur wash, 1 in 20, in the autumn and before the leaves have fallen.

PEAR MIDGE (*Diplosis pyrivora*). DESCRIPTION. *Adult.*—About $\frac{1}{16}$ of an inch in length, dark grey in colour, with long legs. The abdomen of the female is drawn out into a long ovipositor. *Larvæ.* —About $\frac{1}{7}$ of an inch long. Yellowish-white in colour, with brown head. They are able to "jump" by means of a spring-like process.

LIFE-HISTORY.—The flies hatch out from the ground about the time the buds are beginning to show colour. As these

swell, eggs are deposited in them by means of the long ovipositor with which the female is provided. As the blossom falls, these eggs hatch and the young larvæ enter the developing fruit. This, instead of being checked, grows rapidly, becomes swollen and cracks, falling off about the end of June. On reaching maturity the larvæ leave the fruitlets and enter the ground to pupate, in which state they pass the winter.

METHODS OF CONTROL.—Sprinkling Kainit under the trees about the time the buds are beginning to show, will control the fly. Also young chicks, placed under the tree, will keep down the flies and so prevent egg laying.

PEAT. Peat accumulates chiefly where there are wet hollows in the moorland. It consists of many generations of vegetation, each overlying the one that has died before it. Sphagnum moss is often the main ingredient. As decaying vegetation tends to become black, peaty soils are blackened and can be known by this coloration. Although if properly mixed in, dead vegetable matter makes good manure, in the case of peat an acidity is set up which makes an absorption difficult, and plants fail for want of nourishment that they can assimilate. Under these circumstances, two enterprising plant families have acquired carnivorous habits. The Sundew and the Butterwort both trap small crawling insects in the sticky hairs of their leaves and proceed to digest them. Sundew has a very red rosette of leaves. Butterwort has yellow leaves. Either may be easily found on peaty moorland. They will accept and digest small particles of ham if dropped on their leaves, but remain quite indifferent to grains of sand. These are two of the most interesting of all our native plants. Butterwort is, quaintly enough, to be found in the utmost abundance on the moors lying around Buttermere, in the Lake District.

PEDESTAL. It is important, when choosing a pedestal as a base for a vase, figure, or other garden ornament, to select one which is in harmony with the object it is to support, both in its design and form. Do not place together an ornament and pedestal whose *motifs* of decoration differ considerably. If used with taste and in the right place, a pedestal can sometimes stand alone in a garden, relying upon its simiplicity for its effect.

Pedestals may look very old and weatherworn, while really quite new, if made of a stone which quickly weathers. This type should be chosen for old-world gardens. *See also* ACROLITH.

PELARGONIUM (Geraniums, Zonal Pelargoniums). Geraniaceæ. Greenhouse and hardy herbaceous evergreen, shrubby and tuberous-rooted perennials. Flowering and ornamental foliage.

Zonal Pelargoniums used for Summer Bedding.—Thousands of Zonal Pelargoniums used for bedding, popularly called Geraniums, are raised every year to replace the plants which amateurs fail to keep through the winter months. It should, however, be possible for most amateur gardeners to keep a stock of Geraniums through the winter, and also to increase the stock, if treated as follows:

In about July or August, or as soon as suitable side shoots are available on the plants; cuttings of these should be inserted either singly in 2 in. pots or half a dozen round the sides of a 5 in. pot. These cuttings should be taken off with a cut made immediately below the joint, and the lower leaves on the cutting should be removed. The soil used for the cuttings should contain a good proportion of sand. The cuttings will root fairly quickly if they can be kept moist overhead and if the soil is very light and open. The pots are best stood in a cold frame, covered closely with glass, and then shaded until the roots have had time to form. After this the pots can remain in the cold frame all the winter, or kept in the cool greenhouse, air being given when possible, but all frosts being excluded.

Give only the minimum of water. As soon as the weather begins to turn warm in the spring, the plants will need a little more water, and they will then begin to make top growth. When this happens, they can be put into larger pots containing a compost of two parts good loam, one part coarse sand, one part either leaf-mould or well-decayed manure. To this may be added 1 oz. superphosphate, or 2 oz. bonemeal to each bushel of soil.

Thus potted, they will make excellent bedding plants for use in the summer borders, to be set out about the first week in June. The chief thing to remember in keeping Pelargoniums during the winter months is to keep the atmosphere fairly dry, otherwise the plants damp off, and this disease having once started amongst a batch of cuttings, very few, if any, will be saved.

Greenhouse Cultivation.—For greenhouse cultivation, Zonal Pelargonium cuttings are usually taken in the spring, and inserted in sandy soil in a warm greenhouse. These plants are not allowed to bloom during the summer. If flower trusses appear, they are pinched out immediately, and treated in this way, the plants will make a fine display during the winter months, provided the atmosphere can be kept up to a minimum of 60° at night.

When the plants are well growing and flowers are opening, they can be watered with liquid manure, or with nitrate of soda, using a quarter of an oz. to a gallon of water once a week. This should only be given when the soil is already moist. Sulphate of ammonia can be used instead of nitrate, and soot water can be used together with the animal manure.

Soot water will be helpful in adding colour to the foliage and flowers. Firm potting, plenty of sunshine and nipping the main shoots in order to induce bushy growth are the secret of success with the cultivation of these plants.

Almost exactly the same treatment is given to the ivy-leaved Pelargoniums. These are usually grown in hanging baskets or ornamental vases and tubs. They can be either trained to stakes or allowed to droop over the sides of the baskets and vases. Show and fancy Pelargoniums and scented-leaved varieties are also cultivated in the same way. There is also a herbaceous type (*P. endlicherianum*) which can be grown outdoors throughout the year, provided the soil is warm and sandy, and the position fairly sunny and sheltered. These are often grown on rockeries and will benefit from a covering of coco-nut fibre during the winter months.

Amongst the large-flowered Zonal Pelargoniums used for exhibition, the following are useful varieties. They show how varied are the colours obtainable:

Achievement, soft salmon pink.

Aldenham, richest crimson.

Barbara Hope, pale salmon pink, white eye.

Cassiope, salmon pink.

Cymbric, purple blooms; dwarf habit.

Dr. Leon Petit, clear violet, shaded magenta, upper petals orange-red.

Flame, flame colour.

Fraicheur, white, picotee edge.

General French, soft scarlet shaded deeper at base of each petal.

General Wolseley, clear rosy-red.

Joyful, deep salmon centre, white margin.

Mars, crimson, lighter in upper petals.

Mme. Rozaine, double white.

O. W. Holmes, orange-salmon.

Paul Crampel, single scarlet; large trusses.

Sir E. Treves, deep crimson, large white eye.

See also GERANIUM.

PELECYPHORA (pel-le-si-for-a. Cacteæ). Hatchet Cactus. A genus of only one species, *P. aselliformis* and its varieties *concolor*, *cristata* and *pectinatus*. Allied to Mamillarias. For culture *see* CACTUS. The type has white or rosy flowers on a short stem.

PELLÆA (pel-le-a. Filices). Cliff Brake Fern. Handsome ferns of which the greater number respond to greenhouse culture and many resemble Cheilanthes in habit.

Propagate by spores, also by division when the plants have rhizomatous roots. Plant in a soil composed of 2 parts of peat to 1 each of loam and mortar rubbish.

SPECIES.

Many of the species are best grown in hanging baskets from which the pendent fronds are seen to advantage. They should not be exposed to strong sunlight or the fronds will turn yellow. If attacked by thrips the plants must be fumigated and those with leathery fronds can be sponged.

P. adiantoides (syn. *Pteris adiantoides*). Fronds bipinnate. 1½–2 ft. long.

P. cordata. Spear-shaped leathery fronds, 12 in. long, 4–6 in. across. Several varieties.

P. falcata. Spear-shaped fronds, 6–15 in. long, 1–2 in. broad. Almost hardy.

P. hastata. Bi- or tripinnate leathery fronds, 1–2 ft. Makes a good room plant.

P. rotundifolia. Fronds, 6–12 in. long, 1–2 in. broad. Pinnate, very leathery.

Many other species which only differ from the foregoing in small details of construction.

PELTANDRA (pelt-an-dra. Aroideæ). Arrow Arum. Hardy perennials that do well in shallow water or in boggy soil.

Propagate by division in spring.

SPECIES.

P. virginica. Large pointed leaves. 1 ft.

PELTARIA (pel-tar-i-a. Cruciferæ). Herbaceous perennials bearing white flowers. Increase by seeds or division in spring, and grow in any light soil.

SPECIES.

P. alliacea. June. 1 ft. Plant has a scent like that of garlic.

PENNISETUM (penny-setum. Gramineæ). Feather Grass. *P. longistylum*, 1½ ft., a half-hardy annual. *Abyssinia* is the best. Sow under glass in March, plant out in May. The downy plumes 4–6 in. long are freely produced in August.

PENNYROYAL. See HERBS, CULINARY *and* MENTHA.

PENTAPTERYGIUM (pen-tăp-té-rij-i-um. Vacciniaceæ). Himalayas. An exceedingly beautiful but tender epiphytal evergreen shrub, requiring protection of wall. Has bright red flowers, hanging from the underside of pendent branches. Thrives in moist peaty soil. *Propagate* by cuttings in sand under bell-glass or in frame.

SPECIES.

P. serpens. 2–10 ft. The finest and most showy species.

PENTAS (pen-tas. Rubiaceæ). Stove herbs and sub-shrubs from S. Africa. Cuttings of young shoots root readily in sandy soil in a propagating case. Pot up in a mixture of 2 parts of loam to 1 of leaf-mould with sand. Pinch back the young plants and keep in rather small pots. These plants are invaluable for the stove during winter when in flower.

SPECIES.

P. carnea. Flesh-pink flowers in autumn and winter. If plants are raised from cuttings in early spring they can be had in flower during the summer.

P. c. kermesina. Rosy flowers tinted with violet. 1½ ft.

P. c. quartiniana. Very free flowering.

PENTSTEMON (pent-ste-mon. Scrophulariaceæ). Beard Tongue. A beautiful genus of hardy and nearly hardy perennials, some of herbaceous and some of sub-shrubby habit. With their large bell-shaped flowers on tall graceful stems they make magnificent bed and border plants. The hybrid forms which are included in so many gardens are chiefly derived from *Cobaea* and *Hartwegii* and are very fine.

Culture.—Propagate by seeds sown in gentle heat, harden-off as soon as possible and plant out in April or May. The named varieties are best propagated by cuttings taken in autumn and struck in sandy soil in a cold frame. They should be wintered in the frame and planted out in spring. If the plants are too full of bloom to allow of strong shoots for cutting, the flower stems should be removed in late summer and a top-dressing given to encourage the young shoots. All are best propagated annually. They like a rich, well-manured and well-drained soil in a sunny position, and plenty of rotten manure should be forked in before planting. In cold districts they need protection from frost and a sheltered position.

The best of the border species are *barbatus* (syn. *Chelone barbatus*), with spikes of scarlet or carmine flowers; *Cobaea*, a tender plant that is parent to a great number of garden hybrids and has purple, yellow or white flowers; *Hartwegii*, a free-flowering scarlet spiked species and a prolific parent of hybrids, which has excellent flowers for cutting; and *gentianoides*, with purplish-red flowers, which is also responsible for hybrids. 1½–3 ft.

The dwarfer forms are fine rock garden plants, chief amongst them being *azureus*, a neat form with narrow greyish leaves and purple flowers and its variety, *Jeffreyanus*, with reddish stems and rich blue flowers; *Cœruleus*, a sub-shrubby species, of which the flowers—when fully open— deepen to a rich blue; and *Menziesii*, a sub-shrub with numerous purple and rosy flowers. 6–12 in. The species and varieties are many, and give a tremendous variety

of colouring. The flowering season starts in June, and usually lasts until October or until the frosts spoil the flowers. *Hartwegii* is so hardy that it has been known to flower in November.

PEONY (Pæonia). Ranunculaceæ. Hardy herbaceous and shrubby perennials. First introduced into this country in 1548. A great many species are known, but in gardens those cultivated are chiefly the herbaceous *P. officinale*, and shrubby *P. moutan*, with their hybrids.

The soil for the cultivation of these plants should consist of two parts loam, one part decomposed cow manure. Peonies like plenty of sun, and a situation not too near shrubs and trees. A border at the edge of a shrubbery, facing south or west is, however, suitable, as the plants welcome shade from the very early morning sun, which sometimes damages growing tips in spring when frosts are frequent. Hard, caked subsoil will often cause weak growth and lack of flowers. It is essential in a stiff soil that the ground should be worked to a depth of 18–24 in., and if there is any tendency to sourness, a dressing of lime should be given. Manure is desirable, since a Peony plant once established may be left in undisturbed peace for twenty years. Moreover, manure helps to retain moisture, and peonies never thrive if they are thirsty. Stable manure must not come into direct contact with the roots, but should be worked into the soil, and should not be too fresh when used. A good artificial manure composed of 5 oz. of bone-meal and 2 oz. of sulphate of potash, applied to each sq. yd., supplemented by humus in some form, makes an excellent dressing.

Too deep planting will often injure the plants. If the roots are to be divided, do this in September, i.e., at planting time. First clean them of soil, and with a sharp strong knife sever pieces of root 6–8 in. long with two or three "eyes" to each. When replanting, see that the crown is not more than 2 in. below the surface. Plant 2–4 ft. apart, to allow for development.

The plants dislike transplanting, and will often not flower until the third year after a move.

A disease called Botrytis (blight) will sometimes attack Peonies, but this need cause no alarm. A spray with Bordeaux mixture would quickly cure the disease, should it appear.

The newer hybrid Peonies are so beautiful that they defy description. Some are full skirted like the old red Peony of cottage gardens. The richly-scented rose balls of Bunch of Perfume and nearly white Lady Alexandra Duff are still favourites. Kelway's Glorious was not long ago rated as the second best Peony io the world by the American Peony Society. This is a variety with very full crinkled petals of glistening white, and a fragrance no other peony can surpass. The single Peonies, like huge dog roses of red, white, pink and purple, with vivid gold centres, are no less imposing than the doubles. Mafeking, dark-petalled and mint-scented, Queen of the Belgians, a creamy-white flower resembling a water lily, and peach-pink Pride of Langport are typical single varieties.

Still newer are the "Imperial" Peonies, resembling shapely bowls, filled almost to the brim with clusters of silky threads, some in close tassels and rosettes, and others in tangled disorder. The colours of these vary from "Moonlight's" white bowl of cream and green to the rich rose goblet of gold called "British Empire," but probably the finest of all is one called "Globe of Light." This is a silver rose goblet, in the centre of which there is a cushion of pale rose and gold threads all crumbled together, while a translucent light seems to glow over the whole, as if it came from the flower itself.

Apart from the herbaceous Peonies there are also Tree Peonies, which are worthy of a position in sheltered sunny shrubberies or borders. These also should be planted in September, though they can be planted in March with some success.

It is advisable to mulch them in spring with a thick layer of cow manure, and protect them in very severe weather with litter, such as bracken or dry leaves. Tree Peonies usually begin to flower three years after planting.

PEPEROMIA (pep-er-o-mi-a. Piperaceæ). Annual and perennial plants with fleshy leaves, many being very desirable foliage plants. The flowers are mostly inconspicuous. Useful for baskets, or for trailing on tree stumps or wall of stove.

Propagate by cuttings which will root at any season if inserted in heat with plenty of ventilation. Grow in fibrous peat and loam. Although they are not so thirsty as the majority of stove plants, they need syringing constantly and like a shady position.

SPECIES.

P. maculosa. Leaves green, petioles purple.

P. marmorata. Broad leaves marbled white.

P. metallica. Red veins on the underside.

P. nummulariæfolia. Leaves small and round. Good basket plant.

P. Sandersii. Green and white leaves. Compact habit.

PEPPER. *See* PIPER.

PERAPHYLLUM (pir-a-fil'-lum. Rosaceæ). North America. Distinct hardy deciduous shrub, having narrow, grey lanceolate leaves and clusters of three small white flowers, followed by edible yellowish berries. Does not flower freely in this country and very seldom berries.

Culture.—Plant in ordinary soil in sunny position. *Propagate* by layers.

P. ramosissimum. The only species. Usually not more than 3 ft. high, with spreading branches and hawthorn-like flowers during April and May.

PERENNIAL. Any plant which lives for more than two years is a perennial. There are two types. Herbaceous perennials which are fleshy, e.g., delphiniums; and woody perennials, which includes deciduous and evergreen trees and shrubs, roses, etc. Some perennials are hardy and some are not.

PERESKIA (per-es-ki-a. Cacteæ). American or Barbadoes Gooseberry. For cultural details *see* CACTUS.

SPECIES.

P. aculeata. Globular fruit. October. 5–7 ft.

P. Bleo with red flowers is frequently grown for providing stocks for grafting other genera.

P. zinniæflora. Rosy-red flowers. 2 in. across.

PEREZIA (pe-re-zia. Compositæ). Blue. Hardy annual or biennial. 3 ft., ndes. An interesting, rather than beautiful, plant for the mixed border; ordinary soil. Sown March where to flower, will bloom the same season.

PERFUME GARDEN. Scented plants should be included in all garden-planting schemes, but if room permits, a small section devoted entirely to scented plants is very pleasing. Such a corner should be fairly near the house, or in any case

violets, Czar and Victoria Regina are the best while many are beautifully scented and a selection of these beautiful plants should be made.

As regards the design of the garden, informality seems to be more in keeping than straight, hard lines. A seat should be included for the better enjoyment of the garden, and the path may well be sparingly planted with minute thymes,

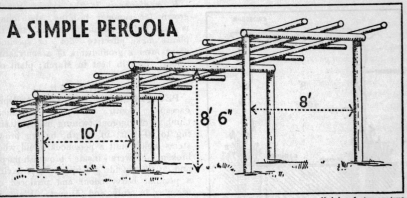

A SIMPLE PERGOLA

A pergola is used for dividing one part of the garden from another, or as a division between two gardens; also as an interesting cover-way to a garden path. It forms a support for all kinds of climbing plants.

should be of easy access by means of a pathway of stepping-stones. Many flowers diffuse their sweetest perfumes after sundown, so that a dry track across dew-laden grass is advisable if the best use is to be made of this feature. The garden could be enclosed by scented rose-hedges or, if by walls, these should be clothed with scented climbers. *See* PORCH. For the back of the borders rose species such as *Rosa damascena* and *centifolia*, also Sweet Brier, would be useful. Many of the Lilies, especially the white Madonna, are delightfully scented. Lily of the valley and the belladonna are other useful flowers. Many Carnations, especially the old clove Carnations, are worth including, also the garden Pinks. Some of the bulbs such as Hyacinths and Narcissus, are scented, whilst Heliotrope, Wallflowers, Cheiranthus, Mignonette, Sweet Alyssum, etc., should not be forgotten. Evening Primrose, Night-scented Stock and Nicotiana, the Tobacco plant, are some of the best for evening perfume. Amongst

which so deliciously scent the air when they are trodden upon.

PERGOLA. A covered walk formed by climbing plants trained over posts or trellis work. This feature, introduced from Italy many years ago, has become very popular amongst English gardeners. It can be used very effectively in a garden design if it is introduced with an object, that is, if it leads to some definite part of the garden or feature of interest. After all, it is only a covered pathway, and nothing is more annoying than to get to the end of the path and have to come back the same way. It is not advisable to erect pergolas over grass pathways, for the turf quickly becomes worn and dank. Large flat stones placed at convenient intervals can be used down the centre with good effect if a substantial path is not required. A border for Lavender, Bush Roses, Lilies, etc., down the outside of the pergola saves innumerable small beds in the turf round each post and adds to the beauty of it.

There are many materials suitable for
pergola construction, varying from rustic
poles to substantial stone or brick and
tile erections. Whatever material is used,
it should harmonise with the other
garden features, and should be strongly
constructed or it will not be able to stand
the weight of foliage.

A substantial wooden pergola would
consist of oak uprights 6 in. square, about

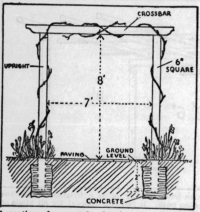

A section of a pergola showing the method of
construction.

8–10 ft. high, allowing 18 in. to 2 ft.
cemented below the ground; the uprights
should be spaced about 6–8 ft. apart.
Runners or bearers parallel to the path are
then nailed to the tops of the posts; these
should be about 6 in. by 4 in. in size.
Crossbars about 4 in. by 3 in. are nailed
across, spanning the path, the ends projecting 12–18 in. to give a good finished
effect. To strengthen a rustic pergola the
uprights may be placed in pairs.

A pergola on three or four sides of a
small garden gives a delightful cloistered
effect where it is desired to completely
block out surrounding views. Arches
should be constructed in the same way as
pergolas. Climbing plants for pergolas
need not be restricted to roses, but can
include winter-flowering and berry-bearing
climbers to add interest throughout the
seasons. *See* CLIMBING PLANTS.

PERILLA (per-il-la. Labiatæ). Half-
hardy annuals chiefly used for summer bedding. India. Foliage plants.

Propagate by seeds sown in heat i
March, the resulting seedlings bein
pricked out and hardened off before bein
planted out at the end of May. Gro
in light rich soil. The flowers should b
picked off to allow further developmen
on the part of the foliage for which plant
are grown.

SPECIES.

P. arguta. July. 1–3 ft.

P. nankinensis is the species usuall
grown for summer bedding, the foliag
is dark bronzy-purple in colour, and th
plants make effective "dot" or specimer
plants over a groundwork of a contrastin
colour. Sow in heat in March; plant ou
in June.

P. ocimoides. July. 1–3 ft.

PERIPLOCA (pe-rip-lo-ka. Asclepia
daceæ). South Europe. Deciduou
climbers of vigorous twining habit, attain
ing to 20–30 ft. in length, having brow
stems which emit a poisonous liquid whe
broken. Flowers inside brownish-purpl
and on the outside greenish-yellow, havin
a peculiar heavy odour and produced o
racemes in July and August. Plant in
any ordinary soil in sunny position.
Propagate by division.

P. græca, "Silk vine." Slender habit,
suitable for climbing over pergolas, etc.
The only cultivated species.

PERISTERIA (peri-ste-ri-a. Orchidaceæ). Flower of the Holy Spirit. Dove
Flower. From the dove-like appearance
of the column. Handsome orchids with
fleshy bulbs and broad leaves. The flowers
are fragrant and large.

Propagate by division and plant in equal
parts of loam and fibre. Allow plenty of
water when the plants are growing but
little when they are resting.

SPECIES.

P. elata. The Dove Orchid. Flowers
white spotted with purple. Fragrant, 3 in.
across. Summer. Leaves 2–3 ft. long.

P. pendula. Flowers yellow and white
spotted purple. Autumn. Leaves 12–15 in.

PERIWINKLE. *See* VINCA.

PERMANGANATE OF POTASH.
This simple and inexpensive substance is
becoming more and more important to the
gardener. It is found to be one of the
finest of remedies for all kinds of fungous
diseases. It is also one of the best of

nsecticides. And as it is harmless to plants when used in a weak solution, there should certainly be a supply ready to hand in every garden shed.

Among the various uses to which it is put may be mentioned the following:

To Destroy Slugs. A few crystals of permanganate of potash scattered along each side of a row of seeds will effectively prevent damage from slugs. They are very soluble, and need renewing after rain.

To Prevent Damping-off. The soil in which seeds are to be sown is soaked with a weak solution before use.

Cuttings are sometimes stood in water slightly coloured with permanganate of potash for a few hours before being inserted in the ordinary way. This reduces the possibility of decay before the roots form.

To Prevent Rhizome Rot. The rhizomatous roots of June irises are sometimes attacked by a disease which causes them to rot. Watering them with weak solution of permanganate of potash is a good preventive. If the rot is present, lift the roots, cut away all decayed portions, dip the remainder in the solution, and also water the soil with the solution before replanting. This will, in most cases, effectively end the trouble.

Permanganate of potash crystals should as a rule be added to water to make it just a pale rose colour.

The solution used at this strength will not harm any plant life, and all fungous diseases may be treated with it.

PERNETTYA (per-net′-ti-a. Ericaceæ). South America. Extremely showy and very hardy evergreen berrying plants. Flowers white in May, followed by a profusion of large marble-like berries ranging in colour from white to purple, and lasting from autumn to the following spring. Valuable for indoor decoration during the Christmas season.

Culture.—Plant in cool, moist non-calcareous soil in full sun. *Propagate* by seeds, division and cuttings.

SPECIES.

P. ciliarsi. (Syn. *Gaultheria furens*).

P. mucronata. 2 ft. Forms a dense bush with a profusion of crimson berries.

P. m. alba. Lovely white berries.

PEROWSKIA (per-of′-skia. Labiatæ). Himalayas and Afghanistan. Half-hardy deciduous shrubs, attaining 3–5 ft., with foliage of a lovely shade of silvery white, and a sage-like odour, having flowers borne on slender racemes, 6–12 in. Thrives in good loamy soil and the sunniest position possible. *Propagate* by cuttings in July. Cut out old wood in spring.

P. atriplicifolia. The only species. Flowers of a lovely shade of violet-blue, harmonising with the silvery foliage, during August and September.

PERSICA. *See* PRUNUS PERSICA.

PERSIMMON. *See* DIOSPYROS.

PERTYA (per′-ti-a. Compositæ). China. Hardy deciduous shrubs, having dark green leaves, tasting like Quassia, with small pinkish-purple flowers, during June and July.

P. sinensis. The only species. Of more botanical interest than garden value.

PERUVIAN LILY. *See* ALSTROEMERIA.

PETASITES (pet-a-sites. Compositæ). Hardy herbs with woolly leaves and fleshy rhizomes. Increase by division and grow in any garden soil.

SPECIES.

P. fragrans. The Winter Heliotrope. White fragrant flowers in February. 6 in. Often grown as a pot plant in the cool conservatory.

P. frigidus. White. May. 6 in. (syn. *Tussilago frigida*).

P. officinalis. Bog Rhubarb. Butter Bur. White flowers from March to May. 1–5 ft. Excellent for naturalising by the sides of ponds or streams where in rich soil the leaves become so large that they are quite tropical in appearance (syn. *Tussilago Petasites*).

PETREA (pet-re-a. Verbenaceæ). Stove shrubs and twiners from S. America.

Propagate by cuttings in shady soil with bottom heat and use for potting a compost of 3 parts of turfy loam to 1 each of leaf-mould and manure with a little sand.

SPECIES.

P. arborea. Violet-blue flowers in June. 12 ft.

P. volubilis. Purple Wreath. Purple flowers in July.

PETROCALLIS (pet-ro-kall-is. Cruciferæ). Rock Beauty. The genus is allied to Draba. Tight cushions of wedge shaped, minute green leaves and lilac flowers. It flowers most freely in poor, stony, light soil or under moraine conditions. 1 in. May. Pyrenees. Multiply by division or seed.

PETTERIA (pet-tēr'-i-a. Leguminosæ). Dalmatia. Hardy deciduous shrubs attaining 6 ft. Similar to laburnums, having lovely fragrant yellow flowers. Thrive in ordinary soil. Seed pods should be removed before they mature.

P. ramentacea. Dalmatian Laburnum (*Cytissus Weldenii*), 6–8 ft. The only species cultivated. Very attractive in spring, with racemes of fragrant yellow flowers during May and June.

PETUNIA (pe-tu-nia. Solanaceæ). These brilliant half-hardy perennials are frequently grown in hanging baskets and pots as well as in beds.

Outdoor Culture.—Propagate by seeds germinated in heat in March and prick off the seedlings as soon as they are fit to handle. They are afterwards potted singly and pinched back to make compact plants. The double varieties are also propagated by cuttings of young wood in spring, or of mature shoots in autumn in a warm greenhouse. Those for outdoor culture must be hardened off in May prior to planting out and like a sunny position in fairly rich light soil.

SPECIES.

P. Nyctaginiflora and *P. violaceæ*, (the former an annual with white flowers, and the latter a perennial with purple or violet flowers) have given rise to a large number of named varieties with both single and double forms which can be obtained from seedsmen.

Petunias make excellent greenhouse plants. Some of the taller varieties have beautiful blooms 5 in. across which are elegantly frilled or fully double. Of easy culture, they are among the most suitable plants for the amateur's greenhouse.

Cultivation.—Seeds should be sown in February or March in gentle heat, the resulting seedlings being pricked out when large enough and potted on into 3 in. size pots when they require it. They may be flowered in 5 in. or 6 in. pots and the soil should be composed of fibrous loam, leaf-mould, sand, and a little well-decomposed manure. Use rough leaf-mould as drainage. In the double-flowered strains the smaller seedlings are often the best.

Varieties.—Grandiflora Mixed (colours of purple, rose magenta and white); Grandiflora fringed double; Violet Queen Clematis Blue; Queen of Roses. Dwarf varieties include Silver Queen (lilac) and Rosy Morn.

PHACELIA (fa-ce-lia. Hydrophyllaceæ). A genus containing a large number of species, a few of which are desirable garden plants of value for edgings, or massing in the mixed borders, where they may be sown as late as the end of May (earlier if desired) to give a wealth of blue flowers in 6–8 weeks from sowing. The best are *P. campanularia* (rich gentian-blue), 9 in., *P. congesta* (blue), 1 ft., *P. Pariyi* (dark violet), 1 ft., and *P. tanacetifolia* (blush-rose), 1½ ft. Mexico.

PHÆDRANASSA (fe-dra-nas-sa. Amaryllideæ). Queen Lily. Stove and greenhouse bulbs with showy flowers in umbels.

Propagate by offsets taken off when the parent bulbs are resting. Pot up in loam and leaf-mould with sufficient sand to keep the soil porous.

SPECIES.

P. Carmioli. Red. Stove.

P. Lehmanni. Scarlet. Stove.

PHÆNOCOMA (fe-no-ko-ma. Compositæ). The only species is a greenhouse evergreen shrub with showy flowers that last for two or three months. Increase by cuttings in sand with slight bottom heat. Pot up into fibrous peat with silver sand in spring and ensure perfect drainage. Keep the plants near the glass and allow plenty of air. Winter temperature, 40°–48°.

P. prolifera. Crimson or rosy-purple flowers in summer. Leaves small. 3–4 ft. (syn. *Helichrysum* and *Xeranthemum proliferum*).

PHALÆNOPSIS (fal-e-nop-sis. Orchidaceæ). Stove epiphytal orchids. From *phalaina*, a moth, and *opsis*, resemblance, referring to the appearance of the flower, commonly called Moth Orchid. An interesting genus, which includes some of the most beautiful orchids, with flowers in long graceful spikes. Manila, 1836.

Culture.—Compost: fibre and sphagnum moss in equal parts. Position: teak baskets suspended from roof of house.

Plant in baskets, keeping the crowns well raised, in the early spring when growth commences. For successful cultivation plenty of heat and moisture is necessary from March to early autumn. During the rest period water only sufficiently to keep roots from becoming dry. Shade from hot sun spring and summer. Winter temperature, 55°; summer, 80°.

Propagate by division when repotting.

SPECIES.

P. amabilis, white and yellow and its varieties; *esmeralda*, rosy-purple; *Lowii*, purple, white and yellow; *Sanderiana*, pink, purple and white; *schilleriana*, purple, rose, white and yellow; *violacea*, violet and rose.

PHALARIS (fal'-ar-is. Gramineæ). Northern regions, including Britain. Hardy grasses, having long, slender leaves, making lovely border plants, and one variety being suitable for edging.

Culture.—Plant in any moist garden soil. *Propagate* by division in spring.

SPECIES.

P. arundinacea. 3–5 ft.

P. arundinacea variegata. Ribbon grass, having striped variegated leaves.

P. elegantissima. 1½ ft. Fine for edging.

PHASEOLUS. *See* BEANS.

PHELLODENDRON (fel-ō-den'-dron. Rutaceæ). China and Japan. 40 ft. Hardy deciduous trees, their large handsome foliage turning to yellow in autumn, but of no floral beauty.

Culture.—Plant in good loamy soil with chalk added, if possible. *Propagate* by cuttings placed in gentle heat during July.

SPECIES.

P. amurensis, Amur Cork Tree, having a cork-like bark, with pinnate leaves 10–12 in. long, of a dark green colour.

P. japonicum. Large pinnate leaves and 4 in. racemes of yellowish flowers.

P. j. chinense. Very similar to type, having larger leaves.

P. sachalinense. Quick-growing species with dull green leaves.

PHILADELPHUS (fil-a-del'-fus. Saxifragaceæ). Popularly called "Mock Orange" or "Syringa." Deciduous flowering shrubs, producing during June and July a wonderful display of fragrant blossom.

Culture.—Plant in good loamy soil in sunny position. *Propagate* by cuttings placed in gentle heat.

SPECIES.

P. coronarius (Europe and Asia Minor). Yellowish-white flowers, 1 in. across, with a most insistent fragrance. A very old inhabitant of English gardens.

This species was cultivated by Gerarde, who quaintly writes of its flowers: "They have a pleasant sweete smell, but in my

RIBBON GRASS

Phalaris a. variegata, a pretty ornamental grass, about 3 ft. high, is commonly called Ribbon Grass and Gardener's Garter.

judgement troubling and molesting the head in very strange manner. I once gathered the flowers and laid them in my chamber window which smelled more strongly after they had lain together a few howers, but with such a pontick and unacquainted savor, that they awaked me from sleepe, so that I could not take rest till I had cast them out of my chamber."

P. Delavayi (China). Fragrant white flowers in May and June.

P. grandiflorus (U.S.A.). Strong grower, sometimes 12 ft., with large odourless white flowers.

P. hybridus. Under this heading are all the best new and old hybrids, mostly raised by M. Lemoine, of Nancy, France.

P. h. Albatre. Double white fragrant flowers.

P. h. Avalanche. Branches pendent, with profusions of medium-sized fragrant white flowers.

P. h. Belle Étoile. Flowers sweetly scented, white with centre tinged purple.

P. h. Boule d'Argent, 4 ft. Clusters of fragrant pure white flowers.

P. h. Bouquet Blanc. Erect growths and racemes of double white flowers.

P. h. Conquête. Large pure white double flowers.

P. h. Dame Blanche. Fimbriated, pure white, semi-double flowers.

P. h. Enchantment. Erect habit, double white flowers.

P. h. Virginal. The best double-flowering variety, having racemes of fragrant pure white double flowers.

PHILESIA (fī-lě'-zi-a. Liliaceæ). Chile. Dwarf evergreen shrub. Dark green leaves, glaucous white beneath and beautiful crimson, lapageria-like flowers of very waxy texture, from June to August. Hardy in most districts. In Cornwall attains a height of 4–5 ft. In colder districts it likes protection in winter.

Culture.—Plant in sandy soil: keep moist. *Propagate* by suckers, and cuttings of the young tips of the branches.

P. buxifolia. The only species grown.

PHILLYREA (fĭl-ĭ-rē'-a. Oleaceæ). Evergreen shrubs and small trees, having large leaves and fragrant white flowers borne in clusters, followed by bluish-black small fruits.

Culture.—Plant in any good garden soil in semi-shade or sunny position. *Propagate* by cuttings of new growths taken in July.

SPECIES.

P. decora (*Vilmoriana*). Black Sea. Large oval leaves and sweetly-scented flowers in April, followed in autumn by oval purplish fruits.

P. latifolia (Mediterranean seaboard). Strong grower, attaining 20 ft., having clusters of small white and fragrant flowers, similar in foliage to the Evergreen Oak.

PHILODENDRON (fil-o-den-dron. Aroideæ). A genus of ornamental stove trees, shrubs and climbers, of which many are useful for clothing pillars, walls, etc The leaves are large and fleshy and frequently curiously cut.

Propagate by cutting up the thick stems into pieces, each having two or three nodes These root quickly in a close propagating case. Soil, equal parts of peat and loam with some charcoal and perfect drainage.

SPECIES.

P. andreanum. Leaves 2–3 ft. long Metallic green. Good climber.

P. gloriosum. Leaves deep green, white veins and pink margins. Climber.

P. grandifolium. Leaves long, green spotted purple.

P. Lindenii. Leaves heart-shaped, yellow when young and metallic green later.

P. melanochrysum. Leaves dark green tinged with gold.

P. tripartitum. Leaves divided in three.

PHLOMIS (flŏ'-mis. Labiatæ). Vigorous evergreen shrubs, having oval, dull green, sage-like leaves, with clusters of bright yellow flowers. Height 6 ft.

Culture.—Plant in a fairly light soil in dry, sunny position, sheltered in all but the warmest districts. *Propagate* by cuttings.

SPECIES.

P. chrysophylla (Syria). Having foliage of a yellowish tinge.

P. fruticosa, "Jerusalem Sage" (S. Europe). Having weakly-scented leaves like giant sage, followed by bright yellow clusters of flowers produced in autumn.

PHLOX (flox. Polemoniaceæ). A valuable genus for any garden, as the spring-flowering dwarf plants are useful for the rockery, or for edging beds and borders ; the half-hardy annuals are beautiful bedding plants, and the later-flowering perennials are brilliant border plants.

Culture.—Propagate the annuals by seeds sown in heat in February or March. Transplant the seedlings carefully to 3 in. apart in boxes, and continue to grow in heat until the end of April, when they are hardened-off and then planted out in May. The seeds may also be planted in the open in April or May.

The perennials are propagated : (1) By seeds sown as soon as ripe in heat, wintered in the greenhouse and planted out the following May, after being hardened-off. (2) By cuttings of the young shoots which, if placed in a frame in gentle heat, will root more quickly than in the open. (6) By division of the roots, care being taken to use only the outside young part of the clumps, as the woody old part is useless. It is advisable to divide the plants occasionally as they bear their best flowers in the third or fourth year. Both annuals and perennials require a rich and loamy soil, and are benefited by a mulch of manure during the flowering season, and by weekly doses of liquid manure. Provided they have plenty of water they do well in the sun, but the blooms last longer and the colour is better if grown in partial shade. The rock garden species can be increased by cuttings of young shoots inserted in sandy soil under glass, or the trailing shoots can be covered with sandy soil in summer, and by the following spring roots will be found on the shoots. If the weakest of the young shoots are removed early in spring, much stronger plants and larger flowers will be obtained.

SPECIES.

P. Drummondii, the best known of the half-hardy annuals, with red, purple or white flowers, is the progenitor of nearly all the annual garden varieties, of which the best are perhaps *cuspidata*, with pointed petals; *fimbriata*, with fringed petals; *grandiflora*, and *nana*, a dwarf form. They bloom from July to October. 9–18 in. The perennials are divided into two groups, the first derived from *p. suffruticosa*, being early flowering, and the rest, chiefly crosses between *paniculata* (*Decussata*) and *maculata*, are late flowering, and more valuable on that account. Hybrids listed in modern catalogues are far superior, and new ones are being constantly produced.

Some of the best of the modern varieties of Phlox are:

Border Gem—deep violet.
Deutschland—orange-red.
Europa—snow-white.
Le Mahdi—rich violet-blue.
Mrs. Oliver—soft rose, white eye.
The King—purple.
William Ramsay—dark purple.

The rock garden species are very effective when in flower, with their tufts of spreading foliage and various colours. The best are: *P. amoena*, rose flowers in May and June; *divaricata*, with lavender flowers and a white variety, *alba*, *procumbens*, lilac-blue, June; *reptans*, creeping, purple or rosy-coloured flowers; *stellaria*, white or silvery star-like flowers; and *subulata*, an April-blooming rose-pink trailing plant which has many varieties, with white (Little Dot, *Nelsonii*), lilac (Fairy, and *Lilacina*), rose (*compacta*, *rosea major*), and purple, rose or crimson (*atropurpurea*) flowers in spring. These

PHLOX

No flower is more showy in summer than the Phlox in its many richly coloured varieties.

plants vary in height from 6 in. to 1 ft. They should be planted in spring, in sandy, gritty loam in a fairly dry position.

PHŒNIX (fe-nix. Palmaceæ). Date Palm. Stove Palms. Leaves feather shaped. 1597.

Culture.—For culture and propagation, *see* KENTIA.

SPECIES.

P. canariensis, 6–10 ft.; *P. dactylifera* (Date Palm), 20–30 ft.; *P. reclinata*, 20–30 ft.; *P. repicola*, 10–20 ft.

PHORMIUM (for'-mǐ-um. Liliaceæ). New Zealand. Evergreen shrubs or small trees, attaining 9 ft. in height, having handsome glaucous leaves, sometimes 3–6 ft. long, and lovely 3 ft. spikes of bronze-red flowers.

Culture.—Plant in any good loamy soil protecting young plants from frost. *Propagate* by division when possible. For the sub-tropical garden, they are indispensable; also giving a good effect if planted by the waterside.

SPECIES.

P. Cookerianum (Colensoi). Has shorter, broader leaves than Tenax.

P. tenax, New Zealand Flax. The best ornamental species. In warm regions in S. England flower spikes attain 12 ft. long.

P. t. alpinum. Smaller-growing than type.

P. t. Powerscourtii. Having larger leaves than type.

P. t. purpureum. Foliage a lovely shade of bronze-purple.

P. t. variegatum. Having foliage variegated sulphur-yellow.

P. t. Veitchii. Similar to variegatum but with a bolder type of variegation.

PHOSPHATE ROCK. Occurs in many parts of the world. Is quarried and ground fine for direct application to soils as "ground mineral phosphate," or may be treated with acids to form superphosphate and similar fertilisers.

PHOSPHATES. *See* PLANT FOODS.

PHOTINIA (fo-tin-ĭ-a. Rosaceæ). Half-hardy evergreen and deciduous shrubs allied to the Cratægus, having small leathery leaves, with clusters of hawthorn-like flowers in April and May, followed by red haw-shaped berries or fruits.

Culture.—Plant in good loamy soil and sunny position. *Propagate* by seeds or cuttings of nearly-ripened wood placed in gentle heat.

SPECIES.

P. arbutifolia. See HETEROMELES ARBUTIFOLIA.

P. Beauverdiana (China). Rare hardy deciduous shrub, growing up to 20 ft., having foliage of lovely autumnal tints and bright red berries.

P. B. notabilis. Elliptical, tomentose leaves.

P. Benthamiana (China). Distinct evergreen, narrow-leaved species, requiring protection in most districts.

P. Davidsoniæ (China). Distinct, rare hardy evergreen, having in spring young growths of a pleasing shade of red.

P. serrulata. Evergreen. Handsome red foliage in spring and profusion of small white flowers in clusters.

P. villosa (*variabilis*), sometimes known as *Pourthiæa arguta* (China and Japan), 8–15 ft. Deciduous shrub or small tree with striking red foliage in autumn. Prefers non-calcareous soil.

PHOTOSYNTHESIS. *See* ASSIMILATION.

PHYGELIUS (fī-jē'-li-us. Scrophulariaceæ). S. Africa. Deciduous shrub in warm districts, but of semi-herbaceous habit in most parts of England, requiring wall protection. Attains about 2 ft.

Culture.—Plant in good soil and full sun. *Propagate* by cuttings in gentle heat.

P. capensis. Tubular flowers of a striking crimson, produced in panicles 12–18 in. long during late summer and autumn. Will make a good wall-climber if trained.

PHYLLAGATHIS (fil-la-gath-is. Melastomaceæ). Beautiful dwarf stove shrubs. Increase by leaf cuttings rooted in a close propagating case. Soil, 1 part of leaf-mould and sand to 2 of peat.

SPECIES.

P. rotundifolia. July. Pink inconspicuous flowers. Showy leaves, of rich green tinged with red and dark red on the under side. 6–9 in. long, 4–6 in. across.

PHYLLOCACTUS (fil-lo-cac-tus. Cacteæ). Stove epiphytal succulents with large soft hued flowers that are rather ephemeral, but are produced in such rapid succession that the plants are not bare for a long period. In some cases they will do well in a greenhouse or even in the window of a room. For culture, *see* CACTUS.

SPECIES.

P. Ackermannii. Spineless flat stems. Flowers rich crimson, 6–8 in. across. 4–6 ft. Many varieties.

P. crenatus. Fragrant creamy-white or orange flowers. Parent of many hybrids.

P. grandis. Creamy-white flowers that open after sundown.

P. latifrons. Cream or white flowers, 8–10 in. across, 8–10 ft. high.

P. phyllanthoides. Many rosy or white flowers. 1–3 ft.

PHYLLODOCE (fil-ō′-dō-sē. Ericaceæ). Dwarf evergreen shrubs not exceeding 1 ft.; similar in habit to heather with bell-shaped flowers borne in small clusters during May, thriving best in damp peaty soil and a damp atmosphere. Suitable for the lower slopes of the rock garden. *Propagate* by seeds or preferably by well-ripened cuttings placed in peaty soil during July and August.

SPECIES.

P. aleutica (Asia and N.W. America). Spreading habit, 6–12 in. high, with cream-coloured flowers, during May and June.

P. Breweri (the Heath of Sierra Nevada, California). A most charming species of spreading habit, 6–12 in. high. Flowers sweet-scented, saucer-shaped, wine-red during May and June.

P. coerulea (*taxifolia*, *Andromeda coerulea*). Europe and Asia. A dwarf species, 9 in. high, with dark glossy leaves and pitcher-shaped bluish-purple flowers.

P. empetriformis (*Menziesia empetriformis*) the Heath of Vancouver. Clusters of rosy-purple urn-shaped flowers produced in spring.

P. glanduliflora (Columbia and Alaska). Rare, erect-growing species, with sulphur-yellow flowers, ageing to white during June and July.

PHYSALIS. (phy-sā-lis. Solanaceæ). Winter Cherry. Hardy and half-hardy perennials. Chiefly grown for the sake of the inflated calyx, which is beautifully veined and bright red in autumn. The fruits may be cut and used with dried grasses for winter decoration.

Culture. — The plants can be raised annually from seeds, or can be increased by division in spring. They require to be grown in a warm, sunny position in light rich soil.

Species.—Only three species are much grown: *Alkekengi*, the Winter Cherry, a hardy perennial with white flowers and scarlet berries, 18 in.; *Franchetti*, a much stronger and hardier plant that is displacing the Winter Cherry in favour, has white flowers and large red "fruits"; *Peruviana*, the Cape Gooseberry, is a half-hardy plant with whitish flowers and fruits. The fruits of *Peruviana edulis*, which are yellowish, make a jam that is a real delicacy, and are also eaten as a dessert fruit, while those of *Alkekengi* are also eatable.

PHYSIANTHUS. *See* ARAUJIA SERICOFERA.

PHYSOCARPUS. *See* NEILLIA.

PHYSOSTEGIA (fi-sos-tē-gia. Labiatæ). False Dragon's Head. A genus of hardy herbaceous perennials that are allied to Dracocephalum and bear

PHYSALIS

WINTER CHERRY

The orange inflated calyces of Winter Cherries are dried for use as winter decoration.

spikes or racemes of flowers that are useful for cutting.

Culture.—Propagate by division of the creeping rootstocks or by seeds sown in spring. Will grow in any soil in the sun.

Species.—*P. virginiana* is the best of the species with flesh-pink or purplish flower spikes, and has both white (*alba*) and pink (*rosea*) varieties; also *speciosa*, which is a finer variety with larger spikes of pink flowers, 1½–4 ft. All flower from July to September.

PHYTEUMA (fi-teū-ma. Campanulaceæ). Horned Rampion. Pretty hardy perennials with many flowers in peculiar spiky heads. Valuable for borders or rock work. *Propagate* by seeds or by division in spring, and all grown in any soil, except *comosum*, which has purple or blue flowers in July, and likes a gritty soil in a moist crevice in the rock garden.

Species.—Halleri, violet blue, May, 6 in.; *humile*, blue, July, 4 in.; *Sieberi*, a Pyrenean species, with blue flowers in July, 4–6 in.; *Scheuchzeri*, dense heads of deep blue flowers, July and August, 6–12 in.; and *spicatum*, either white or blue, May and June, 1–2½ ft.

PHYTOLACCA (fi-tō-lacca. Phytolaccaceæ). Poke weed. Very few of this genus of hardy and greenhouse perennials are grown. They are suitable for the shrubbery or for the wild garden. *Propagate* by seeds or by division and plant in ordinary soil.

Species.—P. decandra, the Virginian Poke Root, forms quite a bush, and has white or lilac flowers from June to August, which are followed by purple berries like blackberries. The foliage tints beautifully in autumn and the roots are poisonous, 3–10 ft.; *acinosa*, sometimes considered as a variety of *decandra*, has reddish stems and black berries in spikes after the flowers have faded.

PICEA (pis´-e-a. Coniferæ). Spruce Firs. The "Spruce Firs" are handsome evergreen trees mostly of a pyramidal habit of growth in a young state, becoming pendulous in the course of time. They are distinguished from the "Silver Firs" (Abies), by their round needle-like leaves and by the cones being usually pendent, instead of erect as has been explained under ABIES.

P. excelsa. The "Common Spruce" is remarkably rich in dwarf and pygmy forms; indispensable for rock gardens.

Culture.—Plant in October or November, or in March or April. While they thrive in almost any soil, the finest specimens are to be found in deep sandy loam. They prosper in the pure air of the country better than under town conditions. *Propagation* is by seed sown in spring. They should be transplanted to nursery rows when a few inches high. The various "forms" do not come true from seed and have to be grafted on seedlings of the **type.** Cuttings may also be tried.

SPECIES.

P. alba (glauca). The "White Spruce" of N. America. Very hardy, flourishing in quite cold and exposed positions. 60–100 ft.

P. a coerulea, more glaucous than type.

P. albertiana (glauca albertiana). Western N. America, allied to *B. alba*, but a finer tree, with bluish-green foliage.

P. a conica. Forms a perfect cone of about 3 ft. high. Makes a good specimen for rock gardens.

P. Breweriana. "Brewer's Weeping Spruce," of N. California. Up to 100 ft. in nature. Of remarkable pendulous habit as it reaches maturity.

P. Engelmanni (western N. America). 80 ft. In cultivation a small pyramidal tree, with glossy green leaves.

P. E. glauca, leaves silvery-glaucous.

P. excelsa (Abies Picea). The "Common Spruce" or "Christmas Tree." (Europe). 100–150 ft. Of more use as a forest tree than for the garden. Valuable as a timber tree, especially in Norway. The wood is known in this country as "white deal." The following are the most distinct and useful of the garden forms of this species.

P. e. aurea, leaves with golden suffusion.

P. e. Maxwellii. Of cushion-like habit, and bright green leaves.

P. e. Merkii. Of dwarf spreading habit nearly twice as broad as it is high. Dark green foliage.

P. e. nana. A "wee" pygmy with dark green foliage.

P. e. nidiformis. Low-growing, spreading habit.

P. nigra. The "Black Spruce" of N. America, 20–30 ft. and upwards. Grown in this country since 1700. Leaves dark blue, green and purple cones. A very useful species, growing in almost any kind of soil, wet or dry. The cones of this species remain on the trees for a considerable period, sometimes persisting for 30 years.

P. pungens (Parryana). The "Colorado Spruce," up to 100 ft. in nature, and sometimes exceeds that height. Leaves glaucous green, and very prickly.

P. p. glauca. The "Blue Spruce."

P. p. Kosteriana. A superb form and the bluest of all the forms of Blue Spruces.

Leaves covered with a beautiful blue-white bloom.

PICKEREL WEED. *See* PONTEDERIA.

PICOTEE. *See* CARNATION.

PIER. A structure used to strengthen a wall. It should be constructed of the same material as the wall or steps with which it is associated. It is usually 1–2 in. larger on all sides than the wall it strengthens. It is necessary at the beginning and end of a wall and either side of a flight of steps. On long, high walls it may be necessary at lengths along it. Buttresses serve the same purpose in very substantial walls. They add considerably to the finished appearance of a garden, and may be beautiful as well as useful, especially if wells are left in the centre for lavender, hydrangeas, etc.

PIERIS (pi-er-is. Ericaceæ). N. America and S.W. Asia. Hardy, deciduous and evergreen shrubs or small trees, having racemes of Lily-of-the-Valley-like flowers, during spring.

Culture.—Plant in damp light loam or peaty soil in half-shady position with protection from March and East winds. *Propagate* by seed or layers.

SPECIES.

P. floribunda (U.S.A.), 4–6 ft. Evergreen. Panicles of white pitcher-shaped flowers during March and April.

P. japonica (Japan). Long narrow leaves and pendent racemes of pink flowers ageing to white during March and April.

PIGEON HOUSE. *See* DOVE-COTE.

PILEA (pi-le-a. Urticaceæ). Artillery Plant. Stove perennial herbs. Interesting plant with fine fern-like foliage, flowers insignificant. 1793.

Culture.—Compost: 2 parts loam, equal parts leaf-mould and sand. Repot early spring. Semi-shady position. Winter temperature, 55°; summer, 75°.

Propagate by cuttings in pots of sandy soil in spring, placed in propagator, temperature, 70°; or by division of plant when repotting.

SPECIES.

P. muscoso. If water is sprinkled on this species when in full bloom, explosions follow like the crackle of miniature artillery.

PILLAR. *See* PEDESTAL.

PIMELEA (pi-mel-e-a. Thymelæaceæ). Rice Flower. Greenhouse trees, shrubs and herbs from Australia.

Propagate by cuttings of young shoots taken with a heel rooted in sandy peat in spring. Cover with a bell-glass and keep in an intermediate house. Imported seed can be obtained. Soil, 3 parts each of fibrous peat and loam with silver sand for older plants and peat and sand only for the younger plants. Pot up firmly and ensure good drainage as the plants need plenty of water at all times. Liquid manure may be given before flowering, and after flowering the plants should be cut back to the old wood. Syringe to keep down red spider and only stop back young shoots that spoil the form of the plant.

SPECIES.

P. ferruginea. Globular heads of rosy flowers in May. 1–2 ft.

P. rosea. Pink or white flowers. Close to *ferruginea* but more slender. 2–3 ft. June.

P. spectabilis. Flowers in globular heads, white tinged with pink. May. 3–4 ft.

P. suaveolens. Yellow. April. 1–3 ft.

PIMENTA (pi-men-ta. Myrtaceæ). Wild Clove. Allspice. Stove trees with sweetly-scented foliage that is often used for sauces, especially in Spain. Increase by cuttings of ripe shoots in sandy soil in a close frame. Soil, leaf-mould and sandy loam. Pot firmly and give plenty of water with ample drainage. Regular syringings are beneficial.

SPECIES.

P. acris. Flowers white tinged with pink. Berries aromatic and large as peas. Wild Clove or Black Cinnamon.

P. officinalis. White flowers in May and June. Leaves very fragrant (syn. *vulgaris* or *Eugenia Pimenta*). Allspice, Pimento Bush.

PIMPINELLA (pim-pi-nel-la. Umbelliferæ). Anise. For culture, *see* HERBS, CULINARY.

PINCHING. An important garden operation in which the tips of growing shoots are removed by hand while they are tender and soft. This is done to preserve the symmetry of the plant and make it bushy, and to promote the growth of fruit and flower rather than leaf buds.

Edging plants need pinching back during the summer to prevent them straggling over the edges. This should not be done too early in the summer, or strong sub-lateral shoots will be formed. Another name for this operation is stopping.

PINE. *See* PINUS.

PINEAPPLE. *See* ANANAS.

PINGUICULA (pĭn-gwick-ŭla. Lentibulariæ). Bog Violet. Butterwort.

PINKS SINGLE

Pinks are delightful for dry walls, for the sides of crazy paths, for edgings to flower borders, or as groups in the rock garden.

Insectivorous greenhouse and hardy perennials with fleshy leaves.

Propagate by seeds sown in damp peat and leaf-mould, by leaf cuttings kept in a close, cold frame and by division of the roots. The hardy species do well in the bog garden or in moist nooks in the rockery. The pot plants can be grown in well-drained peat and sphagnum. All require ample water all through the year.

Species.—*Alpina*, white with yellow lip, May, 3 in.; *grandiflora*, violet-blue, May to July, 3–6 in.; *lusitanica*, lilac, June to October, 6 in.; *orchidioides*, half-hardy, purple, October, 3–4 in.; *caudata*, the best

of the species, with rosettes of leaves and bright carmine flowers, is a greenhouse plant and *vulgaris* is the common hardy plant of English fields, with violet flowers from May to July. Known as Bog Violet or Butterwort, 4–6 in.

PINK (*Dianthus plumarius, etc*). Caryophyllaceæ. A genus of hardy plants closely allied to carnations and picotees, which are useful for borders or edgings and for the rock garden, as the glaucous evergreen foliage is always attractive. They are old favourites for cottage gardens and for cutting.

Culture.—Propagate by seeds sown in boxes in the open in April and May, the resulting seedlings being ready by the following September to plant in their flowering quarters; or by cuttings removed with a heel, or cut immediately below a joint, or pulled out at a joint and struck in sandy soil in a frame in July. These cuttings, or "pipings," root readily and are fit to plant in September (which is the best month for planting) in pots or the border in a compost of loam and well-decayed manure. They are also propagated by division when lifted in September or by layering in July. Pinks hate to be disturbed. The ground may however be limed and an annual dressing of manure given. Old clumps are apt to become bare in the centre; they should then be split up and planted in fresh soil. If it is desired to bring on the border plants, pot them in September and winter in a cold frame. Pinks like a sunny position in a sheltered place, but are not particular as to soil. Those for the rock garden are easily grown in a sunny position in a sandy soil.

SPECIES.

The perennial species of border pinks raised from *Dianthus plumarius* include many varieties, among the best of which are the Show or Laced Pinks, such as "Chantilly," white, maroon centre; "Empress of India," white, laced purple; "Reliance," red, laced white; and "Favourite," clear bright pink, rich darker-coloured centre.

It is advisable to consult a specialist's catalogue to obtain the best and latest of the varieties. All flower throughout the summer and are about 12 in. in height.

The culture of other perennial pinks is similar, and species in common cultivation include: *D. alpestris*, *D. alpinus*, *D. deltoides* (Maiden Pink), *D. neglectus*, *D. superbus*, and many others.

PINUS (pī'-nus. Coniferæ). Pine. The pines are unquestionably the most important of all conifers. They are of very great economic value, not only as timber trees, but also as producers of tar, turpentine and various resins. *P. Sylvestris* produces tar by distillation. Black pitch is the residue of the distillation. The leaves of *P. larico* are made into "Pine-wool" and used for stuffing cushions, etc. *P. longifolia* is a valuable producer of timber, resin, and turpentine. *P. Pinea*, or Stone Pine, produces edible seeds, used in cake-making, and in other culinary ways.

It may be interesting to note that the leaves of pines are invariably in bundles or clusters of from 2 to 5, except in *P. monophylla*, which has one only, as its name implies. The flowers are also borne in clusters, the male flowers at the bottom, and the females at the tips of the branches. These female flowers, or inflorescence, evolve into the fruit, generally known as the "cone." At maturity the scales covering the cones open, thereby releasing the seeds. In most species this period of maturity is reached at the end of the second year.

Culture.—Plant in September or May, when about 2–3 ft. high. Pines will grow in almost any soil, but they like a light sandy, or peaty soil, and an open sunny position. On gravelly soils some very fine specimens are sometimes produced. *P. Pinea* and *P. Pinaster* will grow well in quite shallow sandy soil, and thrive in such soil near the sea. *P. Banksiana* and *P. ponderosa* will grow in the driest of soils. *P. rigida* likes a moist, even swampy soil. *P. Lambertiana* will prosper in the bleakest and most wind-swept positions. Propagation is best from seed sown in the spring. The seedlings should be frequently transplanted to encourage an abundance of their fibrous roots, preparatory to planting them in their permanent positions. Grafting is practised for the choice varieties which do not come true from seed.

SPECIES.

P. Cembra. The "Arolla Pine" from Central Europe and Siberia, up to 100 ft. Of pyramidal outline. Leaves in fives; slightly glaucous and fragrant in summer.

P. excelsa. The "Bhutan Pine," or "Himalayan Blue Pine" of the Himalayas. A very elegant and beautiful tall-growing tree, up to 150 ft. Young shoots blue-green. Leaves in fives, greyish-green, up to 7 in. long. Cones 10 in. long; a superb species.

P. Laricio. The "Corsican Pine" of Corsica, Spain, Greece, etc. A noble species up to 150 ft. Leaves in pairs, dark green. Valuable as a forest tree in this country. Excellent on very light, sandy soils. It does not transplant well. Trees not exceeding 1 ft. give the best results. Makes a stately and imposing specimen.

P. montana (Mugo), the "Mountain Pine" of Europe, 60–80 ft. A very hardy species, thriving almost anywhere in any soil. Leaves in pairs.

P. Pinaster maritima, Hamiltonii, the "Maritime Pine" or "Cluster Pine" of the Mediterranean region. Leaves in pairs. Does remarkably well in sandy soils of seaside districts.

P. Pinea, the "Stone Pine" of Southern Europe, 100 ft. Leaves in pairs.

P. ponderosa, the "Western Yellow Pine" of western N. America. Leaves in threes, glaucous green. 5–10 in. long.

P. Strobus, the "Weymouth Pine," so called from this species having been planted extensively by Lord Weymouth about 200 years ago. It does not take its popular name from the town of that name. 60–90 ft. Leaves in fives, of a glaucous appearance. Cones up to 8 in. long.

P. sylvestris, the "Scotch Pine." A species of very wide distribution, growing wild in most parts of Europe (including Britain), extending to Asia. Grows to over 100 ft. in height, with a reddish-tinged trunk, and grey-green leaves in pairs.

PIPER (Piperaceæ). Pepper. From *pepto*, to digest. Although an extremely large genus, very few species are grown, and these only for their commercial value.

Propagate by cuttings of half-ripe shoots rooted in sandy soil and grown in loam, leaf-mould and sand.

SPECIES.

P. Betle. Betle Pepper and Betle Leaf. The latter is chewed in the East as the tobacco leaf is sometimes chewed here.

P. nigrum. Provides pepper. Black pepper is obtained when the outside husk is left on the seed and white when the husk is removed.

PIPES. For agricultural pipes, which are usually earthenware, *see* DRAINAGE.

Iron pipes 1 in. in inside diameter are usually used for carrying clear water from taps to other parts of the garden. Lead pipes are more lasting and also more expensive than iron.

Greenhouse heating pipes are usually made of cast iron, in 9 in. lengths, with a 4 in. inside diameter.

Gutter piping, which should be fixed to the eaves of all glasshouses, etc., is made of half pipes usually 4 in. in diameter.

Galvanised iron rain-water pipes vary from 3 in. to 6 in. in diameter. The mouths of these pipes should be covered with a wire guard.

Any pipes which are exposed to frosts should be covered with straw, or sacking bands.

PIPINGS. Young shoots of carnations, pinks, etc., which are used for propagating. The shoots should be cut about 3 in. long, off the current year's growth, and the lower leaves removed. These pipings, which are best cut when flowering is finished, should be inserted in a shady border in sandy soil and covered with a hand-light until they root. Overhead watering should be given.

PIPTANTHUS (pip-tan-thus. Leguminosæ). Himalayas and China. Evergreen shrubs, attaining 12 ft., with long dark green leaves, glaucous beneath, and racemes of yellow flowers in May and June.

Culture.—Plant in well-drained soil in a sunny and sheltered position. *Propagate* by seeds sown in gentle heat or by cuttings. If trained, they will make handsome wall climbers.

SPECIES.

P. nepalensis (Thermopsis Laburnifolia). "Evergreen Laburnum," with bright yellow laburnum-like flowers on erect racemes in May.

P. tomentosus. Similar to preceding

species, with silky down on young leaves and shoots.

PIQUERIA (pi-que-ri-a. Compositæ). Hardy herbs and greenhouse shrubs of no horticultural value.

PISTACHIO-NUT. *See* PISTACIA.

PISTACIA (pis-ta-si-a. Anacardiaceæ). Pistachio-nut. Mastic Tree. Asiatic regions. Handsome deciduous trees, attaining 20 ft., and requiring protection in cold districts. Flowers inconspicuous; foliage assumes lovely colourings in autumn.

Culture.—Plant in ordinary garden soil, and propagate by layers and cuttings. From the trunk of these trees is obtained the resin used by Arabs as chewing gum.

SPECIES.

P. chinensis (Chinese Pistachio). China. Very elegant leaves, beautifully coloured in autumn.

P. mutica. Rare species from Caucasus. Should be hardy.

P. terebinthus (Turpentine Tree). Asia Minor. Flowers of no interest but leaves emit pleasant resinous smell. Turpentine is made from the bark.

P. vera. Levant. Deciduous; the "Pistachio Nut Tree." Grows up to 20 ft. Flowers in April.

PISTIA (pis-ti-a. Aroideæ). The only species is a curious stove aquatic that floats on the surface of the water and has bright green leaves about 2 in. long. The flowers are green, small and of no account

Propagate by offsets.

SPECIES.

P. Stratiotes. Water Lettuce, Tropical Duckweed.

PISTILLATE FLOWERS. Female flowers which contain pistils only, no stamens. The pistil includes the style, stigma and ovary.

PISUM. *See* PEA.

PIT. A sunken construction differing from a frame in that it is usually built upon walls, and from a greenhouse in that it is very much smaller. Heated pit are used for melons, cucumbers, etc.

PITCAIRNIA (pit-kar-ni-a. Bromeliaceæ). Stove perennial herbs and shrub of which many species are very attractive and some have spiny leaves.

Propagate by division or suckers in spring and grow in sandy peat and loam

Winter temperature, 50°–55°; summer, 60°–85°.

SPECIES.

P. andreana. Yellow and red flowers. July. Leaves long and white on under side.

P. corallina. Flowers red, spring. Leaves spiny, 4–5 ft. long.

P. fulgens. Bright flowers in May. Leaves 2–3 ft. long.

P. tabulæformis. Leaves in rosettes and prostrate on the ground, 5–6 in. long. Spineless.

Practically all of the species have red flowers and differ mainly in their leaves.

PITCHER PLANT. *See* NEPENTHES.

PITTOSPORUM. (pit-tos'-por-um. Pittosporaceæ). The Tree Daphne. Ever-green free-growing shrubs and small trees from New Zealand and Australia, etc., with very conspicuous foliage, and in most species very attractive and fragrant flowers. Generally regarded as on the tender side, but some of the species are fairly hardy and some perfectly hardy. At Goodwood in Sussex there are some remarkably fine, dense hedges of *P. tenuifolium.*

Culture.—Plant in ordinary loamy soil. They are easily cultivated. *Propagate* by seeds and by cuttings of half-ripened wood placed under bell-glass or in frame.

SPECIES AND VARIETIES.

P. eugenioides (New Zealand). "Tarata." A very beautiful species with elegant light green waved foliage and purple stems. The yellow flowers are so fragrant as to perfume the air for some distance around.

P. e. variegatum. Foliage silvery stained pink.

P. tenuifolium (*nigricans. Mayi* of gardens). New Zealand. "Kohuhu." This beautiful species is perhaps the hardiest of all the Pittosporums. Habit pyramidal, height up to 30 ft. Foliage pale shining green on black twigs, most useful for cutting, remaining fresh for many days. Flowers dark chocolate, scenting the garden with their delicious honey-like fragrance. Makes a very choice and charming hedge.

P. t. Silver Queen. Foliage silvery, wood black.

PLACEA (pla-se-a. Amaryllideæ). Beautiful bulbs from Chile that are closely related to the Narcissus, but are rarely grown as there seems to be some difficulty in getting them to thrive.

Propagate by offsets or seeds and plant in light rich soil. Good results have been obtained from planting in a soil made up of 3 parts of rotted cow manure with 1 of sand. The plants rest from August to December and flowers are borne in May. During the growing period they need plenty of water, but scarcely any when they are at rest.

SPECIES.

P. Arzae. Yellow and purple flowers. 9–12 in.

P. grandiflora has white flowers striped with crimson.

P. ornata. Pure white flowers lined with vermilion.

PLACENTATION is the name applied to the manner in which the seeds are arranged in the ovary.

PLAGIANTHUS (plă-gi-an'-thus. Malvaceæ). Cotton Tree, Ribbon Tree. Deciduous trees and shrubs from Australia and New Zealand with attractive foliage and very beautiful white flowers. All more or less tender, but in suitable districts of easy cultivation. They like a stony soil, with peat and sand added. Propagation by cuttings.

SPECIES.

P. betulinus (New Zealand). A fast-growing elegant tree up to 40 ft. in its native country. In Hampshire it reaches to 20 ft. and over and has withstood nearly 30° of frost.

P. divaricatus (New Zealand). 3–6 ft. A slender-growing species with narrow leaves and very small fragrant yellow flowers. Grows wild in salt marshes.

P. Lyallii (*Gaya Lyallii*). New Zealand. 30 ft. Possibly the most beautiful flowering tree or shrub ever introduced from New Zealand. Extremely attractive when in bloom in July with clusters of white flowers, almost translucent, 1½ in. across. Suggestive of large cherry-blossom. Leaves deeply lobed when young, 3 in. long.

P. L. glabrata. The finest form.

PLAGIOSPERMUM. *See* PRINSEPIA.

PLANE. *See* PLATANUS.

PLANERA (plă'-ner-a. Urticaceæ). Water elm. A very rare deciduous tree up to 40 ft. Found in swamps of south-eastern U.S.A.

P. aquatica. The only species.

PLANNING THE GARDEN. *See* Garden Plans.

PLANTAIN. *See* Weeds.

PLANT ASH. The ashes from the garden bonfire are valuable, though it should generally be recognised that vegetable matter allowed to decay and form humus is of more use in the soil than is the ash. Weeds, which have developed seeds should be burnt to prevent the spread of the seeds to the cultivated land, and tap-rooted weeds are also best consigned to the bonfire as they are pulled out during digging. Ordinary plant ash contains potassium (as K_2O usually), magnesium, iron, phosphorus, and sulphur. Sometimes it also contains sodium, chlorine, silicon and manganese. The most important constituent so far as the gardener is concerned is potash, and as this is highly soluble, ashes should always be kept dry until they are actually used. Ashes spread on the surface round young Carnations, Delphiniums, etc., keep slugs at bay, in addition to providing a little food; while ashes added to the trenches in which potatoes are being set will be extremely useful.

PLANT FOODS. The Functions of Nitrogen, Phosphate and Potash. When plants receive the foods which they want and which are not present in the soil, they grow big and strong and, as we say, yield well. It follows that if we can find out just what each plant likes best and give it those foods, we shall always have the best possible results, subject, of course, to good cultivation and the right sort of weather.

It has been found that generally speaking, each of the plant foods, nitrogen, phosphates and potash, help the plant in a particular way. Nitrogen makes for a large growth of leaf which, in turn, builds up a heavy root or a well-filled fruit. Phosphates help the plant to ripen and also, in the early stages of growth, assist in the formation of roots and top shoots. Potash assists the plant to build up the reserves of food, such as the root of parsnips, radishes, etc., and the tubers of potatoes, which the gardener wants.

Thus *balance* in manuring is all important. Excess of one necessary ingredient is wasteful if there is a deficiency of either of the other two.

See also Manure.

PLANTING. This is an extremely important garden operation which is usually very badly done. The first rule of the planter is *plant firmly.*

Trees, Shrubs and Roses.—A circle of soil should be removed from the proposed planting site. Place the tree in position, spread out the roots, and test if the circle is large enough to allow all the roots to be spread out round the base of the tree without touching the circumference. Remove tree and take out soil until this ideal is obtained. Cut away with a sharp knife any roots which have been broken in transplanting. Place the tree in position and sprinkle a little fine soil over the roots. Gently shake the tree so that the soil settles well down among the fibrous roots. As additional soil is added tread it down firmly. Place the stake in position so that it settles between the roots and tie to the tree and then complete the filling in of the hole (*see* Staking).

Herbaceous Plants and Alpines. Small plants can be planted with a trowel, large ones with a spade. Make a hole sufficiently large to contain the roots without crowding. Tread the soil down firmly. If planting with a trowel ram the soil down round the plant with the handle.

From the time the plants are dug up either in the nursery or garden, the roots should either be covered with a light layer of soil or sacking. If the roots become dried out the plant suffers a severe check. If some time must elapse between digging up and replanting, heel the plants in. *See* Heeling-in.

PLATANUS (plăt′-a-nus. Platanaceæ) Plane. Deciduous, very handsome and striking large-growing trees, with leaves resembling large-leaved maples. The bark peels off in large flakes. White "planes" make imposing park trees. They are most appreciated for street or town planting being remarkably resistant to a smoky atmosphere, and will tolerate any amount of pruning.

Culture.—Plant in November in rich

deep, well-drained soil in sunny position. Soil of an alluvial nature gives the best results. *Propagate* by seed sown outside in drills, 1 in. deep in March. The hard fruit should be broken before sowing the seeds. The resultant young plants require to be shifted every other year until about seven years old, in order to produce fibrous roots. The lower branches may be layered. Cuttings of shoots about 10 in. long, with a "heel," taken in autumn and placed under a hand-light will root readily.

SPECIES.

P. acerifolia. The well-known "London plane." This has never been found in a wild state. May be a form of *P. orientalis* or a hybrid between that species and *P. occidentalis.* One of the largest, frequently over 100 ft. high. Leaves up to 10 in. wide, a little less in length.

PLATYCERIUM (plat - i - ser - i - um. Filices). Stag's-horn Fern. Stove and greenhouse ferns. Fronds resemble stag's horns. N. S. Wales. 1808.

Culture.—Compost made up of equal parts fibrous peat and sphagnum moss mixed with enough broken charcoal and crocks to keep it open. Plant in suspended pans half-filled with broken crocks in the early spring. The plants should be well packed in with the compost, and one or two strands of copper wire fixed across the top of the pan to keep it in position. Water freely spring and summer, moderately at other times. Shady position. Winter temperature, 55°; summer, 75° for stove species. Greenhouse species: winter temperature, 45°; summer, 70°.

Propagation by offsets when replanting or by spores (*see* ADIANTUM).

STOVE SPECIES.

P. grande (a very fine species), and *P. Wallichii.*

GREENHOUSE SPECIES.

P. alcicorne (Elk's-horn Fern) and its varieties *Hillii* and *majus.*

PLATYCODON (plăty-cō-don. Campanulaceæ). Chinese Bellflower. Only one species of this genus is grown. *P. grandiflorum*, a handsome hardy perennial that thrives in well-drained, deep, sandy loam, in an open position. It is propagated by division in spring, or by seeds, and is excellent for the border or rock garden. In wet, heavy soil, it will not survive the winter. The purple flowers are bell-shaped, and the buds before opening are like small balloons; hence the name by which they are sometimes known is Balloon Flower. There are several good varieties: *album*, white; *album plenum*, semi-double; and *Mariesii*, dwarfer than the type, with larger flowers of rich blue. 6–18 in.

PLATYSTEMON (platy-ste-mon. Papaveraceæ). Sometimes called Californian Poppy, but the term is usually applied to Eschscholtzia. California.

P. californicus (yellow), a hardy annual trailer, is the only species introduced, and is a very pretty little plant for rockeries or sunny places. May be sown spring or autumn. Ordinary soil.

PLATYTHECA (plat-i-thek-a. Tremandreæ). *P. galioides* is the only species of this small genus of Australian heath-like shrubs. Increase by cuttings of young shoots taken in July and rooted in sand. Use sandy peat for potting and water carefully. The plant bears pale blue flowers in May. 1 ft.

PLEACHING. A method of restricting trees to a small space, forming a green alley-way instead of an avenue. The side branches of the trees are trained to interleave with each other, the trees being planted about 6 ft. apart. The front and back branches are removed so that all the energy goes into the side branches. This work is usually done in the autumn, after leaf-fall.

PLUM (*Prunus communis*). The wild plum is frequently seen in the hedgerows in this country, but it is not a true native. Such trees are garden escapes. The plum is a native of Russia and Central Asia.

Soil.—The chief essential for successful cultivation is a soil which has been worked deeply and which is well drained. The plum, in common with all other stone fruits, likes a constant supply of moisture at its roots, yet at the same time the sub-soil must never become stagnant.

Situation.—The common kinds of plum succeed quite well as bushes or standards in the open, although owing to the comparatively early season of flowering a sheltered position is best. The choicest varieties are best grown as fan-trained specimens on east or west walls. Cordons are also grown.

Distances Apart.

Cordons on walls—2 ft. apart.

Fan-trained—12 ft. apart.

Bushes in the open—15 ft. apart.

Half-standards—20 ft. apart.

Standards—25 ft. apart.

Planting.—Plant and mulch as recommended for the apple.

Pruning.—Standards, Half-standards and bushes. The initial treatment for freshly planted trees should be much the same as that recommended for other standard fruit trees (*see* APPLE). Once the head of the tree is formed, there should be no need for further pruning Excessive vigour frequently becomes evident in the younger stages, in which case the tree should be lifted, root-pruned and replanted. If leading shoots are excessively vigorous the tips should be pinched in summer.

Fan-Trained.—Careful treatment of trained specimens is necessary. Young trees from the nursery should be supplied with six or more shoots which should be spread at equal angles to form the branches. All side shoots from these main branches should be summer-pruned during July, pinching them back to about six leaves. Many growers prune the upper half of the tree some days before the lower, which encourages an even distribution of sap. Plums have a habit of concentrating their energy on the upper branches, and it is only by maintaining an ample supply of foliage on the lower branches that this tendency can be checked.

In winter these shoots must be pruned back to two or three buds in order to form fruiting spurs.

Leading shoots should never be pruned hard, but should be shortened back in winter only to remove unrefined wood. Any strong shoots appearing from the lower parts of the tree should be kept pinched back. Root-pruning is frequently necessary on fan-trained specimens.

Cordons.—Cordon plums are not frequently grown, but they produce fine fruit. Pruning should be done as recommended for fan-trained trees. If the tree becomes excessively vigorous, root-prune and allow two or more shoots to develop as leaders on established trees. Suckers on all plums should be removed immediately upon appearance.

Manures.—Mulching at flowering time is recommended for well-established trees which are bearing well. Young, stronglygrowing trees should not be fed.

Propagation.—Budding or grafting upon the St. Julien or Mussel stock. The Myrobalan is also now extensively used, and is probably the best.

Pests.—The worst pests are Scale, Plum Sawfly, Plum Aphides and Red Spider.

Diseases.—The outstanding disease which is causing havoc in many plumgrowing districts is Silver Leaf.

VARIETIES.

There is one outstanding variety which should be grown in all gardens where plums are to be planted; this is Victoria It ripens in early September, is a regular and heavy cropper; quite self-fertile and in all ways reliable. It is rather subject to silver-leaf disease, and also suffers badly from red spider when grown on a wall, unless frequently syringed. Two other varieties grown widely on commercial plantations are the Czar and Pershore, which ripen in August in the order named. Both are self-fertile and are excellent garden varieties. Their flavour is scarcely good enough to warrant description as dessert varieties although they are invaluable for culinary purposes.

Denniston's Superb Gage. A mid August dessert variety, self-fertile, of excellent flavour and cropping qualities.

Greengage. One of the finest flavoured of all plums, this variety requires careful handling. It is self-sterile and therefore needs other varieties close at hand to ensure pollination. It generally requires root-pruning. Birds seem particularly addicted to the buds in winter. Ripens in early September.

Coe's Golden Drop Gage. Another self-sterile delicious variety ripening at the end of September. Does best on a wall.

Out of the countless numbers of varieties

the above are the best. As long ago as 1597, John Gerarde said: "My selfe have sixty sorts in my garden, and all strange and rare; there be in other places many more common, and yet yearly commeth to our hands others not before known."

See also PRUNUS.

PLUM APHIS, LEAF-CURLING (*Anuraphis helichrysi*).

DESCRIPTION OF ADULTS.—Stem mother, purplish-brown in colour; wingless female, olive-green; winged female, bright green with black head and thorax; winged male, small and dark in colour.

LIFE-HISTORY.—The small black shining eggs are placed either singly or in groups around the buds, usually at the base. These hatch in the early spring and rapidly grow into the "stem mother." She gives rise to young asexually, with the result that hundreds of young are born. These, in turn, rapidly grow up into wingless viviparous females which again give rise to young. Thus we have three generations on the plums and damsons in the spring. The foliage becomes covered with aphides and soon begins to curl and, in bad attacks, to die. Not only is this direct damage serious, but they indirectly do harm by excreting honey dew. About the end of May they all become winged, and fly off to herbaceous plants and can then be found on Forget-me-not, Yarrow, Ragwort, Artemisia, etc. Here they remain until the autumn, when they return to the plums to lay eggs.

METHODS OF CONTROL.—Tar oil winter washes in the dormant season will control the eggs, otherwise nicotine or derris-containing washes in the spring, before they have had time to curl the leaves and protect themselves.

PLUMBAGO (plum-bā-go. Plumbaineæ). Leadwort. Useful free-flowering, showy, hardy or greenhouse perennials, the latter of rather shrubby habit, and with branches inclined to ramble, while the former are popular in most gardens. Propagate the herbaceous species by division in autumn or spring and the tender species by cuttings of young shoots in a warm propagating case in spring. Cut back the pot plants after flowering, to induce growth of new shoots,

on which the following season's growth is produced, and pinch them back in the case of the bushy species. Climbers are trained in a single stem in the same way as vines. Water well and syringe in hot weather, but keep dry in winter. The greenhouse species like a compost of two parts of loam to one of leaf-mould with sand, while the border plants do well in any soil.

PLUM APHIS

Greenfly often attack plums and damsons, causing the leaves to curl and die. Antiseptic washes both in Winter and Spring will help to control the breeding and hatching of these damaging insects.

Species.—*Capensis*, with blue flowers, in late summer and autumn, is a favourite for use as a rambler on a greenhouse or pillar, or grown in pots and trained to a balloon-shaped wire trellis. It may also be used for summer bedding.

Rosea and its variety *superba* will flower during the winter and spring in a temperature higher than that given to *capensis*. These are perhaps better treated as annuals, as cuttings rooted in spring make good flowering plants the following winter.

Larpentæ (syn. Ceratostigma), blue, and *micrantha*, white, are hardy summer-flowering species useful for the border. Height, 2 ft.

For other Hardy Species *see* CERATO-STIGMA.

PLUMB-BOB. A plum-bob is merely a piece of lead, usually pear shaped, attached to a length of strong thin cord. It is used to ascertain whether a building,

POA (po-a. Gramineæ). Hardy grasses that are of more agricultural value than horticultural. Increase by seeds.

SPECIES.

P. annua is largely used for forming lawns and does well beneath trees.

P. trivialis does best under glass.

PODOCARPUS (pŏd-o-kar'-pus. Coniferæ). A genus of evergreen trees and shrubs allied to the Yew, and bearing

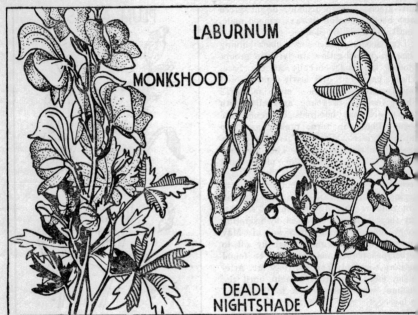

Poisonous plants : The seeds of Laburnum, the roots of Monkshood, and the berries of Deadly Nightshade are often eaten with fatal results.

wall, or other object is perpendicular. It is very useful when erecting greenhouses, walls, or other garden fixtures. To use it hold the end of the string to the wall with the thumb, when the string will hang perfectly perpendicular and flush with the side of the wall, if it is upright.

For convenience the plumb-bob is used with a frame. In this the string hangs along the groove running from the top of the frame to the hole which accommodates the bob.

PLUME POPPY. *See* BOCCONIA.

PNEUMATIC SPRAYERS. *See under* SPRAYING.

plum-like fruits. They thrive in a mois loamy or peaty soil. *Propagate* by seeds or cuttings of half-ripe wood.

SPECIES.

P. alpina (Tasmania and Victoria). A ideal rock garden shrub with small Yew like leaves.

P. macrophylla. A fairly hardy specie from China and Japan known as th "Kusamaki." Leaves bright green 5-7 in long. Dislikes lime or chalk. In Japan it i used as a hedge plant, and clipped int various quaint shapes, the same as w clip Yew. In Ireland it reaches to wel over 20 ft.

P. nivalis (New Zealand). Dwarf, compact-growing shrub.

P. Totara (New Zealand). A hardy species with bronzy foliage.

PODOLEPIS (po-dol-epis. Compositæ). *P. acuminata*, 1½ ft., is an uncommon hardy annual with yellow flowers. *P. aristata*, 1 ft., is somewhat similar, but has small, pink ray florets round the central disk. Natives of Australia and require a light sandy soil in a sunny position. Sow under glass, March, plant out, June, or sow outside where to flower, April–May.

PODOPHYLLUM (pō-dō-phyll-um. Berberideæ). Duckfoot or May Apple. Hardy herbaceous perennials with large deeply-lobed handsome leaves.

Propagate by seeds sown in sandy peat in a cold frame or by division in spring. They like a peaty soil in a moist, shady position, in the wild garden or by the side of a stream.

Species.—P. Emodi. has beautiful leaves spotted black and cup-like white flowers, followed by large red berries. 1 ft.

Peltatum bears glossy leaves and waxy white flowers, resembling Christmas roses, succeeded by pale yellowish berries. Both flower in May, and the berries, which are edible, are ripe in June. 6–9 in.

POINCIANA (poin-si-a-na. Leguminosæ). Stove evergreen trees and shrubs.

Propagate by seed sown in heat in spring in light sandy soil; also by cuttings of young shoots inserted singly in pots of sand in summer under a bell-glass. Grow in rich fibrous loam. Winter temperature, 55°–65°; summer, 70°–85°.

P. regia. Crimson, summer. Very long seed pods. 15–30 ft.

POINSETTIA. *See* EUPHORBIA.

POLEMONIUM (pō-le-mō-nium. Polemoniaceæ). Jacob's Ladder. Greek Valerian. Very desirable hardy perennial herbs that are as pleasing in the rock garden as in the border. *Propagate* by seeds in spring, or by division in October or March, in which months they may be planted. They do best in light, well-drained soil, and the rock plants like a mixture of leaf-mould and gritty loam.

SPECIES.

P. Cœruleum (Jacob's Ladder), a native of moist woodland, is the best known, and has dense tufts of pinnate leaves,

with panicles of clear blue flowers. 2 ft. Some of the best of its many varieties are: *album*, white, with various coloured foliage; *campanulatum*, bright blue; and *dissectum*, white; *P. flavum*, a rare plant with pale yellow flowers, 2–3 ft.; *Richardsonii*, considered by some a variety of *humile*, blue, is a useful rock plant; *humile*, blue, is a very dwarf species not growing more than 6 in. high.

POLIANTHES (pol-i-an-thes. Amaryllideæ). Tuberose. Greenhouse bulbs that will flower out of doors in warm districts in light sandy soil. Increase by offsets, although they are usually raised from seed.

SPECIES.

P. tuberosa. White. August.

P. t. flore pleno. Large flowers.

POLIOTHYRSIS (Bixaceæ). China. Deciduous tree with a terminal inflorescence of white flowers.

P. sinensis. The only species.

POLLARD. To cut out the main central branch of a tree to make it bushy, and restrict its growth.

POLLINATION. *See* HYBRIDISATION.

POLYANTHUS. The name given to many different hardy primulas all of which may be cultivated in the same manner as primroses. The winter flowering primula "Wanda," is one of the most striking of recent introductions but many other species and hybrids well worth growing, will be found listed in catalogues.

POLYGALA (pŏ-lig'a-la. Polygalaceæ). Milkwort. Evergreen creeping shrubs, with pea-like flowers and box-like leaves.

Culture.—Plant in peat and lime-free loam. *Propagate* by cuttings placed under a hand-light. Also by seeds.

SPECIES.

P. Chamæbuscus (Europe). Forms a mat 6–12 in high covered with bright yellow pea-shaped flowers from March to May. Likes a cool moist position. Easily increased by removing the suckers which form naturally.

P. C. purpurea (grandiflora). Flowers purple and yellow.

P. myrtifolia grandiflora (Dalmaisiana). South Africa. Flowers bright purple, very attractive. Not quite hardy. In mild districts flowers continuously.

P. rhodoptera (Europe). Flowers carmine, during April and May.

P. Vayredæ (Pyrenees). Flowers deep purple, during March and April.

POLYGONATUM (poly-gŏ-nā-tum. Liliaceæ). Solomon's Seal. Pretty hardy perennials with graceful arching stems and flowers borne in the axils of the leaves, suitable for almost any part of the garden, and naturalising well in half-shady places. They practically grow themselves as the rootstocks spread, and they are not particular as to soil, growing in any moist site. They may be propagated by summersown seed, but division of the roots is much more satisfactory.

SPECIES.

The common Solomon's Seal, *P. officinale* with drooping white flowers, is the best known, and thrives in town gardens or may even be grown in pots and subjected to forcing. It mixes well with ferns, or other vigorous-growing plants. May to June. 2–3 ft.

A better species is *P. latifolium*, with broad leaves and clusters of drooping white flowers, and its variety, *commutatum, P. biflorum*, with flowers in pairs, *multiflorum, oppositifolium* and *roseum*, the latter with rosy flowers, while the rest are white, are all quite useful species. 2–4 ft.

POLYGONUM. (pŏ-lig'-ŏ-num. Polygonaceæ). Evergreen shrub, and deciduous climbers of great vigour, unrivalled for quickly covering fences, sheds, or old trees. The flowers are produced in such profusion as to entirely envelop the plant, and are a striking feature during summer and autumn.

Culture.—Plant in rich loamy soil in full sun. *Propagate* by cuttings taken in summer of the current year's growth with a "heel" and placed in gentle heat. Cuttings of leafless wood taken in February will also root.

SPECIES.

P. affine (syn. *Brunonis*), a dwarf species with spikes of rosy flowers and bronzy leaves, and *vaccinifolium* a prostrate plant, are pretty rock garden plants. 6–12 in. All of these species are perennials, while most of them are white-flowered and bloom in summer and autumn. The taller plants range in height from 3–12 ft. while the rock plants are only a few inches.

P. baldschuanicum (Bokkara). A very beautiful and rampant climber with large panicles of flowers, white flushed pink, produced with wonderful prodigality through the summer and autumn.

P. Orientale, sometimes listed as Persicaria. India. A robust-growing plant, in good soils will sometimes grow to 10 ft. The stems are much branched, and the purple-red flowers are freely produced in long racemes in August. A good plant for rough places or the wild garden.

P. vaccinifolium (Himalayas). A creeping shrub forming a mat some yards in circumference, thriving in any limefree soil. Flowers rose-colour, from August to late autumn.

POLYPODIUM (pol-i-pod-i-um. Filices). Oak Fern. Greenhouse and hardy ferns. This is probably the largest of the Fern genera, mostly evergreen.

Culture.—For compost, cultivation and propagation, *see* ADIANTUM.

POMEGRANATE. *See* PUNICA.

PONDS FOR FISH AND PLANTS.

Choice of Site and Design.—To be fully effective, a garden pond must harmonise with its surroundings, and be in true proportion to the garden or part of the garden in which it is situated. A pond is required either to be decorative, i.e., grow water-lilies and nelumbiums, to contain fish, or to fulfil both purposes, the latter being more general. Since water-lilies and flowering aquatics require a good deal of sunlight and fish require shade, choice of site should, where possible, compromise in each respect. Where not possible, favour should be given to the sunny position. The essentials of a fish pond are:

(*i*). An open but not too exposed a position, preferably protected on that side from which the prevailing cold winds come;

(*ii*). A generous surface area in proportion to depth to allow of a maximum of absorption of atmospheric oxygen;

(*iii*). Differing depths of water to allow of correct cultivation of aquatic plants, and the comfort of fish in summer and winter, and breeding (*See* CONSTRUCTIONAL DETAILS);

(*iv*). A position which does not admit of the access of too many dead leaves, particularly of trees not associated with water;

(v). A position which does not allow of the access of surface water polluted by sewage or undesirable organisms or harmful inorganic matter.

Design. This may be formal or informal. In the first case, the pond is of regular and even-sided outline, often of decorative finish, and should be associated

with water dripping into a larger pond below, the sides of an informal pond should not be above ground level. Those of a formal pond, on the other hand, will often look better when from 6–18 in. high above ground level.

An informal pond judiciously placed will sometimes form a charming contrast in a conventional garden, particularly to fill an awkward corner; but a formal pond

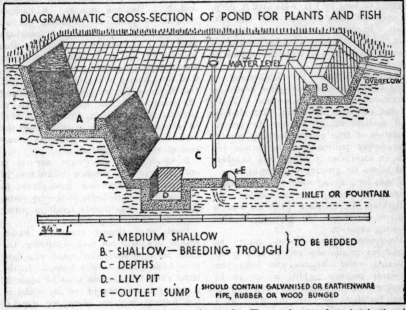

DIAGRAMMATIC CROSS-SECTION OF POND FOR PLANTS AND FISH

WATER LEVEL

OVERFLOW

A

B

C

E

D

INLET OR FOUNTAIN.

3/4" = 1'

A.- MEDIUM SHALLOW
B.- SHALLOW — BREEDING TROUGH } TO BE BEDDED
C.- DEPTHS
D.- LILY PIT
E.- OUTLET SUMP { SHOULD CONTAIN GALVANISED OR EARTHENWARE PIPE, RUBBER OR WOOD BUNGED

Fish are always interesting and give life to garden ponds. They need water of varying depth as is shown above.

with conventional gardens to harmonise with the lay-out of lawns and flower beds. The edges are usually of shaped fascia, or ornamental artificial stone, coloured tiles, etc.

The informal pond is of irregular shape often forming part of a rock or crazy-paved garden. To enhance the charm of a rockery pool, it should be built direct into the rockery, the pathway—usually of crazy paving—only partly surrounding it. The edges of an informal pond are generally bounded by slightly overhanging crazy paving, built-in rockery, or are flush with a lawn.

Except when it is in the form of a basin

can rarely be harmonised into unconventional surroundings. The effect is too artificial.

Construction. The usual medium for pond construction is concrete. Where the ground is of a heavy, clayey consistency and known to be impervious to water, i.e., an area of natural drainage, plain excavation with a little decorative rockwork or walling stone will be all that is necessary to construct the pond. Such conditions in gardens are rare, but if there is any doubt, concrete should be used in the first place to prevent trouble afterwards and complete drying in very dry weather.

A pond should be made with the

intention of retaining the original filling of water with as little addition as possible. This should always be borne in mind whether fountains or water-drips are built or not.

To obtain the best results from a pond, the surface area must be in generous proportion to its depth. For example, a body of water disposed 2 ft. long by 2 ft. wide and 6 in. deep will support considerably more life than the same capacity of water 1 ft. long by 1 ft. wide by 2 ft. deep, or even 2 ft. long by 1 ft. wide and 1 ft. deep. In other words, a pond that is 3 ft. deep should have a surface area of no less than 6 ft. by 6 ft. and other depths in similar proportion.

Varying Depths. For fish-keeping, a pond should have at least three depths, a maximum of $2\frac{1}{2}$–$3\frac{1}{2}$ ft., a medium of $1\frac{1}{4}$–$1\frac{3}{4}$ ft. and a shallow of 9–12 in. The shallow and medium depths are for the accommodation of true aquatic aerating plants. The deeper portion provides retreat for fish, in exceptionally hot or cold weather, and allows for growing of water-lilies.

Ponds for growing water-lilies need have only two depths, one for actual lily cultivation (*see* WATER PLANTS), and a shallow depth for the growing of true aerating aquatics.

Protection against frost must be considered in the construction of a pond. Freezing water expands and exerts an outwards pressure, which is apt to be disastrous to perpendicular walls; it is wise, therefore, to build the walls at a slope in an even-sided pond, or basin-shaped in round or oval ponds. Where this precaution is disregarded for the sake of appearance, and perpendicular walls are built, they should be very robust and reinforced.

It is not difficult to construct a concrete pond, but to ensure success the work must be carried out carefully and thoroughly. The excavation, which must be of the internal dimensions plus the thickness of the sides and bottom, should be well and firmly rammed to form a solid foundation. The thickness of the concrete and the proportion of its ingredients will depend upon the size of the pond. For a naturally firm foundation and a capacity not exceeding 400 gal. ($6\frac{1}{4}$ gal. of water

per cube foot of space), the thickness of the sides need not exceed 3 in. and the bottom 4 in.; where the capacity is between 400 and 1,600 gal. the sides should be 4–5 in. and the bottom 6–7 in. Ponds larger than this should receive the attention of an expert concreter, the thickness of the sides and bottom being modified by the use of reinforcement.

The best mixture consists of equal parts of sharp sand, $\frac{1}{4}$ in. granolithic chippings and best Portland cement. A cheaper mixture for ponds not exceeding 400 gal. can be made of 2 or 3 parts of sharp sand to 1 of cement. When the area exceeds 80 sq. ft., a second foundation should be laid, consisting of 1 part cement, 2 of sand, and 4 of broken bricks for half the thickness, the finishing thickness being completed with an equal mixture of cement, sand and $\frac{1}{4}$ in. grano, reinforced in between with 1 in. wire mesh. Only the best cement should be used, as cheap cement is not economical.

Successful and water-tight concrete is only assured by absolute cleanliness in mixing, and by extreme thoroughness in mixing of the ingredients in the dry state. Badly mixed constituents result in porosity and " blotting-paper" concrete.

Ponds with sloping inward or basin-shaped sides will not need shuttering, but those with perpendicular sides will have to be built behind wooden frames. In the latter case, the concrete must be made of a creamy consistency to run in, whilst in the former, without being too dry, it should hold together.

The bottom and walls should be built in one whole as the job proceeds, when it is easier and safer to proceed if the job has to be left.

Fountain and inlet pipes should be built in as the work proceeds. Although it is not required to change or empty the water, provision for this should also be made by including a drain-away sump, composed of an earthenware or galvanised pipe with a suitable wooden or rubber bung, particularly where it is impossible to syphon out the water to a lower level.

An important consideration, after construction, is to eradicate poisonous constituents from the new concrete; to introduce animal life immediately is fatal.

This danger can be eliminated by natural weathering and permitting the pond to stand unused—but filled with water—for a fortnight or three weeks, with periodic renewals of water and scrubbings. A more desirable method is by applying a special liquid substance which immediately and chemically neutralises the solubles, making the pond safe for plant and animal life immediately after drying, and also improves the concrete.

Planting. To keep fish, a pond must be naturally mature, and such maturity can only be attained by *not* changing the water, and by growing true aquatic plants. True aquatic plants are those which have their leaves under water and which grow only in that medium. Fish and other animal life in the process of respiration breathe out carbon dioxide, and this waste gas is absorbed into the water which becomes greyish and smells unpleasantly, particularly if the capacity of water is at its limit for holding animal life. Fish obtain the oxygen they breathe from the water, which absorbs a certain amount from the atmosphere. It is not often that the size of a garden pond is sufficient for enough atmospheric oxygen to be absorbed to support fish life, and therefore oxygen must be added artificially by aeration, or naturally by the use of plants. Plants, in the process of assimilation and under the influence of sunlight, absorb the carbon-dioxide from the water, use the carbon element and free a large percentage of the oxygen. When there are sufficient plants in a pond to keep the water clean and the fish healthy, the pond is said to be "balanced," and is almost entirely self-supporting. Apart from their natural aerating qualities, true aquatics also encourage the propagation of microscopic plant and animal organisms, which are essential in the pond, and which can never find a place if the water is continually changed or running. The study of "balance" and maturation of ponds is very involved and too lengthy to discuss here. It will be seen, however, that true aquatics are essential in both fish and lily ponds to assist in keeping the water in good condition.

The medium and shallow depths of a pond should be properly bedded for the reception of their plants, the bed being composed of a layer of loam, or inverted turf about 2 in. thick, covered with 1–2 in. of fairly coarse white sand, preferably Bedford sand The deep part need not be bedded, for water lilies can be accommodated in boxes or baskets (*see* WATER LILIES) and sunk into position, or, as illustrated, sumps can be built in the pond to accommodate them. It is easier to fill the pond before planting, as more often than not aquatic plants are supplied without a rooting system, which they rapidly form when placed in water. The stems of plants to be cultivated, some singly, and some in bunches, according to species, can be leaded and gently eased into the sand, when they will make their roots about the lead, which helps to keep them in place until established.

A useful tip when filling a pond is to run the hose into a bowl and not direct into the sand. Filled this way, a pond is perfectly clean to start with, and settles down much quicker.

So far as the well-being of the pond is concerned, the true aquatics are the most important plants, and some or all of the following should find a place: Elodea *canadensis* (Anacharis), *E. densa* or *Crispa*, Fontinalis *antipyretica* (Willow-moss), Myriophyllum *spicatum* or species Milfoil, Ranunculus species, Potamogeton species, Callitriche species, Ceratophyllum (Hornwort). Many of these are British water plants and grow rather rampant, to which some people raise objection. It is better, however, to have to prune strenuously a healthy-growing plant, and have a clean, wholesome pond, than to have only an inadequate service from some of the semi-aquatic and indigenous plants that are often recommended. Professional advice should be taken as to the most suitable of plants for different purposes and districts, and to combine satisfactorily with the growing of decorative aquatics. For fish-keeping only, the following are a good combination in the medium and shallow depths:

Shallow.—Fontinalis *antipyretica* (b); Callitriche *obtusangula* (b); Ranunculus; Myriophyllum.

Medium.—Elodea *canadensis*, E. *crispa*, E. *densa* (do well in company with

Nymphæas), Potomageton, Ceratophyllum.

Fuller details of the plants in question are given under WATER PLANTS.

Fish for Ponds. Fish life should not be added immediately the pond has been planted, for this does not give the plants a chance to establish themselves, apart from the fact that the water is organically and chemically unsuitable. At least a fortnight should elapse from planting, and if one can be patient enough and a month or two is allowed, the fish will do all the better when introduced. It is usually more satisfactory to buy large fish rather than small, and their size should not be less than 5 in.

The maximum accommodation of a pond can be ascertained on the rule of 1 gal. of water per inch of fish, i.e., a 400 gal. pond will accommodate at the most forty 10 in. fish, eighty 5 in. fish, etc.

A pond should only be stocked up to 50 per cent. of its maximum capacity, leaving a safety margin for hard winters or excessively hot weather, when the amount of atmospheric oxygen is considerably decreased. It gives a new pond a better chance if fish are added a few at a time, rather than stocking to full capacity at once.

Whilst coarse fish are interesting to the angler and the naturalist, the most popular for garden ponds are decorative fish. These include the Goldfish (*Carassius auratus*), or Golden Carp, as they are known, in a great variety of colour, from pure reds and yellows to variegated red and black, yellow and black, and albinos. Pure yellows are sold as Canary or Primrose Fish. The variegated fish will sometimes change colour two or three times, either to their pure ground colour, or more deeply black. Golden Orfe (*Leuciscus Orfus*) and Golden Tench (*Tinca aurata*) are highly-coloured and favoured pond fish. The former is a long-bodied graceful fish, orange-yellow on the back and upper part of its sides, shading to a silvery tint beneath, the latter a pure yellow, often with chocolate-coloured patches. The Japanese Golden Carp (*Cyprinus Hi-Goi*) is a pure-tinted fish with scales smaller than the ordinary Goldfish and Barbels. All these fish may be associated together in a charming and

pleasing variety, but it is wiser to keep them apart from the ordinary coarse fish of our ponds and streams. Roach, Dace and Bream, particularly from rivers, do not always acclimatise themselves to a garden pond, and may introduce fungoid diseases. Carp, Tench and Gudgeon, when taken from slow-moving or still water will do quite well, but in limited surroundings, suffer during hot and stormy weather, whilst Minnows will thrive in all but the breeding season. Sticklebacks will thrive and breed under most conditions, but are rather ferocious when breeding and will not hesitate to attack other fish.

Hard-and-fast rules cannot be given for the feeding of fish as regards quantity. The Carps are omnivorous and will eat animal and vegetable food. They may be fed upon special fish meat meals, small biscuit meal, crushed vermicelli, occasional fresh ant eggs, or specially-prepared fish foods which contain dried ingredients with a high protein content, and are therefore preferable for ordinary purposes. Orfe and Tench have a preference for carnivorous food, and, apart from the insect life they will gather from the water, should be fed upon small red worms. They can, however, particularly in aquaria, be induced to take to the same foods as given for Goldfish. The appetites of fish are keenest in warm weather and during the summer months, and in the winter are negligible. In the very coldest weather, fish are naturally torpid and eat little or nothing. When a pond has been established two or three years, it usually contains a great quantity of microscopic and semi-microscopic organisms upon which the fish feed, and if the pond is a large one, it may be self-supporting in this respect, as such organisms propagate very rapidly. When fish are left to fend for themselves, they do not become tame so readily as those which are regularly fed artificially, and for this reason, even if the pond is well stocked with natural food, a little daily tit-bit will not come amiss.

To breed fancy fish is the ambition of most pond-keepers, and for this purpose a shallow portion is recommended. This part of the pond should be densely planted with either *Elodea canadensis* (Anacharis),

Callitriche, Starwort or Fontinalis (Willowmoss), in which the fish will deposit and fertilise the spawn. Fancy fish breed from April to August. It is not unusual for fry to appear in ponds where fish of a good size are kept, in this country, but the difficulty is in rearing them through the early months of their existence. Apart from natural enemies, which are many, the vagaries of our

water containing salt and Epsom or Glauber salt in the proportion of 2 oz. of the first and 1 of the latter per gal. and changing the solution every 12 hours until the cure is effected. During treatment, successive changes of water should be kept at the same temperature, as nothing is more harmful to fish life than sudden temperature changes. The woolliness of fungus is actually a fruiting stage

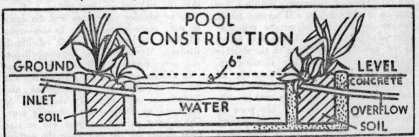

POOL CONSTRUCTION

GROUND LEVEL
6"
CONCRETE
INLET
SOIL WATER OVERFLOW
SOIL

A pool can be constructed to cultivate both aquatic and bog plants. The overflow from the pool keeps the bog garden in a permanently moist condition.

climate, particularly in the Midlands and North, are not conducive to the health of small fish, and most of them die in the first autumn.

A healthy fish can be told by the vigour and steadiness of its movements, and the fact that its dorsal fin is erect and tail fully spread. Providing a pond is matured, adequately planted and not overstocked, disease should be rare and losses very few. If guaranteed cold-water-bred and acclimatised, fish can be purchased in the first place, the risk of disease will be lessened even more, although in proper conditions imported fish will rapidly become acclimatised with only a small percentage of loss. It is usually a case of the survival of the fittest, and those that do survive are very hardy fish.

Fungus, which appears as a white woolliness, is the main cause of trouble, growing about the gills and suffocating the fish. The disease, however, is incidental to the fish having been injured, or being indisposed through the pond not being in a proper condition. Fungus occurs naturally in the breeding season when fish are constitutionally weak. Taken immediately the woolly patches appear on any part of the body, it can be treated and cured by keeping the fish in a vessel of

of the disease, which has been in the fish for some time before it appears. For this reason, any fish showing laxity or unbalance in swimming, should be given treatment immediately.

A good plan is to keep a well-planted aquarium or tub as a "hospital." Any sick fish can be removed to this and left on its own, and, fed with natural living food, will require no other attention. A good hospital diet is Water Fleas (*Daphnia*), which can be obtained from all reputable dealers. Tail rot and congestion, in which the fins and tail are streaked red with congested blood and begin to rot away, may be treated with the salt and Epsom solution, the fish afterwards being removed to an outdoor aquarium at a steady temperature for some weeks. The disease is caused by sudden temperature variation. A minor ailment is constipation, when the droppings, instead of leaving the fish, cling behind it in a solid mass. It should succumb to the "hospital" and live-food treatment. If not attended to, it will lead to bladder trouble, when the fish will not be able to swim on an even keel, and eventually be unable either to rise or sink in the water.

Maintenance.—Once a pond has been planted and stocked in proper proportion, the less it is interfered with, the better it will be. The water should not be changed, to induce the growth of microscopic organisms which have a far-reaching effect upon the pond. The success of a pond is a matter of natural adaptation, and, like a garden, it is not achieved in a few days. It is twelve months or more before a pond can be said to be matured, and in attaining maturity, the water must pass through several phases of coloration. Within a few months of planting, it will become green, due to the presence of minute vegetable cells (*algæ*), and this will change to brown or red, varying in density with the weather conditions, and periodically clearing up. When the pond is fully matured, all discoloration will have disappeared and the water will be clean, but with a rich, aleish colour. The sides of the pond by this time will have a brown or green furry growth upon them. This is filamentous algæ, a primitive type of plant life, and it is highly productive of oxygen—apart from housing indescribable numbers of larval and microscopic organisms. The fish will feed greedily upon it. Other species of this algæ unfortunately give trouble and have earned the name "blanketweed." These too are filamentous and of a rich green, with the unpleasant habit of growing in a thick, slimy mass around the plant life. The usually recommended methods of extermination are by the use of copper sulphate and permanganate of potash. The proportions of either, however, to be effective, are dependent upon the species of the algæ, and should be applied only at the direction of a specialist. In any case, more harm than good is done by the use of chemicals in a pond, and it is wiser to keep a good eye for the appearance of the " blanketweed" and remove it regularly with the fingers or a stick.

When adding water to a pond to replace evaporation, it should be done in the late evening or early morning. A fountain that is used for effect should have a fine, many-holed rose that will break up the water into small globules, having the advantage of gathering atmospheric oxygen and at the same time not unduly altering the temperature of the water. A fine-jet fountain is very useful in sultry or stormy weather,

and will be greatly appreciated by the fish.

The decomposition of a few leaves in the water during the autumn, provides a good manure basis for the following year, but in excess may disturb the "balance" of the pond and give rise to a bacterial phase of life. Where there are many trees, therefore, a wire-mesh screen should be placed across the pond when the leaves fall, so that the majority are kept out.

As to whether the plants will die down or not, depends—in many species—upon whether the pond is well sheltered. Elodeas, Myriophyllums, Ceratophyllums, and some species of Callitriche will persist —in a dormant state, certainly—when not too much exposed. Potamogetons and Ranunculus will generally die down to the roots, to reappear the following year. The deepest part of the pool will provide good shelter for the fish when the surface is frozen, but nevertheless, when practicable, the ice should be kept broken. A shelter of wattles or straw half-covering the pond will provide retreat for the fish in severe weather, and this plan can be easily adopted where the freezing of the surface leaves very little water beneath.

PONTEDERIA (pon-te-der-i-a. Pontederiaceæ). Pickerel Weed. Hardy and stove aquatics allied to Eichornea, *q.v.* Increase by division and plant in mellow loam in a tub.

SPECIES.

P. coerulea. Blue. July. **2 ft.**

POPLAR. *See* POPULUS.

POPLAR, BALSAM. *See* POPULUS BALSAMIFERA.

POPLAR, BLACK. *See* POPULUS SEROTINA.

POPLAR, GOLDEN. *See* POPULUS SEROTINA AUREA.

POPLAR, GREY. *See* POPULUS CANESCENS.

POPLAR, LOMBARDY. *See* POPULUS NIGRA ITALICA.

POPLAR, WHITE. *See* POPULUS ALBA.

POPPY. Of all garden flowers none is more widely grown than Poppies, and this is particularly true if one includes in the title "Poppies" all those genera to which this common name is given. For in addition to the true Poppies—*Papaver*, of various species—there are the Californian Poppies or *Eschscholtzias*, the Welsh or Himalayan poppies, *Meconopsis*, the Mexican Poppy, *Hunnemannia*, *Glaucium* or Horn Poppy, and the Tree Poppies or *Romneya*, all of which are commonly called Poppies.

Poppies have been known for many centuries, and just as they are to-day chiefly associated in our minds with corn-

able in separate colours to come true from seed, and the Oriental Poppies that are perennials, and are also obtainable in white, salmon-pink, and red shades. The Californian Poppies or Eschscholtzias are also now obtainable in a great variety of separate colours.

The new *Meconopsis Baileyi*, or blue poppy from Tibet, is becoming very popular because it provides a welcome

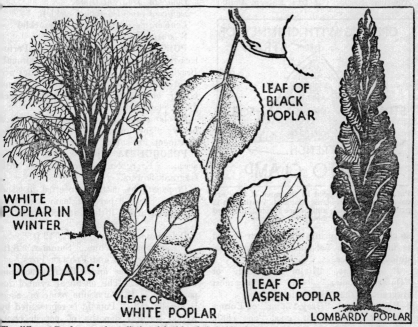

LEAF OF BLACK POPLAR

WHITE POPLAR IN WINTER

'POPLARS'

LEAF OF WHITE POPLAR

LEAF OF ASPEN POPLAR

LOMBARDY POPLAR

The different Poplars are best distinguished by their habit of growth, and by the shape of the leaves. The Balsam Poplar has sweet-scented foliage.

fields, so it appears they were associated in the past, for the Poppy had the place of honour on the brows of Ceres, the goddess of the fruits of the earth.

The poppies of the cornfields are the species *Papaver rhœas*, while the Shirley Poppies are various coloured poppies of the same species, which were raised in the garden of the Rev. W. Wilks at Shirley. The species of Papaver which have received the greatest attention from the hybridists are the *Rhœas* Poppies (which include the Shirleys and also the black-blotched scarlet Poppy *umbrosum*), the *Nudicaule* or Iceland Poppies, now obtain-

pale blue colour in the half-shady border. Full details concerning all these will be found under the various genera, PAPAVER, ESCHSCHOLTZIA, MECONOPSIS, HUNNEMANNIA, ROMNEYA.

POPPY, MALLOW. *See* CALLIRHOE.

POPPY, TREE. *See* ROMNEYA.

POPULUS (pop′-ū-lŭs. Salicaceæ). Poplar. Deciduous, exceptionally fast-growing trees, allied to the willow. Useful for making wind-breaks. Some species are useful timber trees.

Culture.—Plant in November in moist loamy soil. In dry soils they are not long lived, and less so in chalky ones as a rule.

Propagate by cuttings of matured wood in the open in October. Also by suckers.

SPECIES.

P. alba pyramidalis (Bolleana). "White Pyramidal Poplar." Very similar to "Lombardy Poplar."

P. angulato "Carolina Poplar." Leaves glossy green, young shoots angular or ribbed.

P. balsamifera. " Balsam Poplar" of N. America. 100 ft. The true Balsam Poplar,

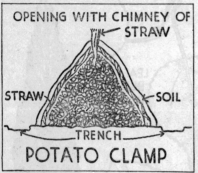

OPENING WITH CHIMNEY OF STRAW

STRAW

SOIL

TRENCH

POTATO CLAMP

Potatoes can be stored in the open if they are covered over with straw and soil. Ventilation is provided at the top, and before storing, diseased specimens should be removed.

so charming in spring when the air around is filled with a balsamic odour from the unfolding leaves.

P. candicans. "Balm of Gilead," or "Ontario Poplar." One of the most fragrant of the "Balsamic" group.

P. canescens. "Grey Poplar" of Europe and Britain. Quite good on chalk soils. A very vigorous species and provides good timber.

P. lasiocarpa (China), 40–60 ft. A very beautiful species with such large leaves (over 1 ft. long) as to need protection from strong winds. The mid-rib and stalk are of a rich red colour. Increased by cuttings, quite large pieces rooting easily.

P. nigra italica, Lombardy Poplar. Of pyramidal form. Makes an effective wind-break.

P. serotina, Black Italian or Swiss Poplar, 100 ft. and over. A hybrid of *P. nigra*; exceptionally vigorous. Very pretty bronzy foliage in spring.

P. s. aurea. Leaves golden yellow.

P. tremula, our native Aspen Poplar,

50 ft. Leaves greyish-green, with an almost perpetual quiver reminding one of the line, "To tremble like an aspen leaf."

PORCH. This is a feature which helps to link the garden with the house, if it is used as a support for climbing plants. Scented climbers are the best to use.

Chimonanthus fragrans (winter sweet)
Jasminum nudiflorum.
Jasminum officinale.
Lonicera fragrantissima.
Lonicera japonica (honeysuckle).
Lonicera periclymenum (honeysuckle)
Wistaria longi-racemosa.

PORTULACA (port-u-lak-a. Portulaceæ). Trailing half-hardy annual Brazil. *P. grandiflora* and its varieties are beautiful free-flowering subjects for sunny borders or rockeries. Sow in March under glass, plant out in June. 3 in.

P. oleracea is the common Purslane, a hardy plant, much in favour on the Continent for salads and pickles.

POSOQUERIA (po-zo-ker-i-a. Rubiaceæ). Evergreen stove shrubs with fragrant flowers.

Propagate by cuttings inserted in sand in heat. Soil, 3 parts of loam with 1 of leaf-mould and a little peat and sand.

SPECIES.

P formosa. White. July. 12 ft.

P. macropus. White. Summer. 6 ft.

POT. *See* TUB *and* FLOWER POTS.

POTASH. *See under* FERTILISERS *and* PLANT FOODS. The chemical symbol for potassium is K. Potassium oxide or, as it is usually called, Potash, is represented by K_2O. Natural deposits of potash occur largely in Alsace Lorraine, Spain, and parts of the United States. A concession has obtained evaporating rights in the Dead Sea to obtain potash salts.

Potash occurs naturally as rock salt, kainit and sylvinite. The higher grades, muriate and sulphate of potash, are produced by refining processes. Muriate is usually prepared by refining carnallite—a low grade of kainit, and sulphate of potash by treating muriate with sulphate of magnesia.

POTATO (Solanum). The potato is such a familiar item in the daily diet that it needs no description. It is perhaps the most important of the vegetable crops and as such occupies by far the largest place in kitchen gardens and in allotments.

History.—The importation of the plant is usually accredited to Sir Walter Raleigh, who is supposed to have brought it from America, but later authorities claim that Mr. Herriot was responsible for its introduction. In any case it was grown in England at the end of the sixteenth century, as Gerarde in his "Herbal" refers to it as the "Potatoe of Virginia" and mentions that he grew it in his garden by the waterside in London. However, for about two centuries it continued in obscurity until its food value was discovered, especially in Ireland, where it was often the only constituent of a meal. From that time onwards great attention has been paid to its culture, and many improvements have been effected in its quality.

Culture.—Soil. As they are so universally grown it is obvious that they will grow in any soil, but the character of the soil plays a great part in determining the quality of the tubers. Damp, badly-drained ground might in a dry year provide a good crop, but in a wet season potatoes grown on such a soil would be the first to be attacked by fungoid diseases.

The ideal soil is a light, well-drained medium, neither wholly clay nor wholly sand, and the best position is a sunny, open one, slightly elevated if at all possible.

Before planting, the soil, if not suitable, should be prepared by working deeply in the autumn so that it can be left open during the winter to benefit by the frosts and rain. In most cases it is best to apply manure in the autumn, although for early crops on a light fine soil this can be done in the spring. A well-worked soil will need no manure, but when used it should take the form of chemical manure rather than animal, although if the soil be deficient in humus natural manure is better.

Planting.—This can be done with a potato dibber, but the better method is to make drills.

For early potatoes make drills 5 or 6 in. deep. For second and main crops make the drills about 4 in. deep. The early crop may be planted 2 ft. apart with the tubers 1 ft. apart. The later crops should have 2½ to 3 ft. between the rows and 1½ ft. between each tuber. In any case the maximum of room should be allowed as the health of the tubers, which are really underground stems, depends upon the development of the overhead part of the plant. When growing for exhibition, and size is a consideration, double the space given may be allowed, but for ordinary purposes the distances given are ample.

Seed.—When buying "seed" the variety chosen must be left to the judgment of the grower. It is, however, wise to procure seed from different districts every three or four years. For some time Scottish seed has been regarded as the best, as it is thought that immature tubers give the best crop, and the "seed" from Scotland, owing to the shorter summer, does not have the same chance of growing to its full extent as the English tubers, which are allowed to fully ripen before being lifted.

The size of the tubers is another important matter. If large it is necessary to buy a greater weight to plant a given area. If too small they will only throw up miserable shoots and produce a poor crop.

It has been found that the best for seed weigh about 2 or 3 oz., and can pass through a riddle with a 2 in. mesh. By the Seeds Act buyers are protected against those who sell "seed" over size. By this Act the seller has to give his name and address, the class of potato he is selling, i.e., Class 1 English, Irish, Scotch "once grown" out of Scotland ; Class 2, all others. Name of the variety and the size of the seed. If above the stated size the buyer should write to the Ministry of Agriculture, Whitehall. When tubers are sold as "grown" they can be any size.

Cut Sets.—In the case of tubers that are too large for planting, they may be cut in half, allowing sufficient "eyes" to each piece, and the portions left in a damp shady place for 48 hours before planting so that a cork-like layer forms over the cut surface and thus prevents rot.

Time of Planting.—This varies with the district and the variety grown. For ordinary culture the first week in April is usually the best time, although in favoured districts they may be planted in March and in cold places this operation is sometimes deferred to the middle of May. Old gardeners have a maxim "plant late potatoes early and early potatoes late." Contradictory as this sounds the advice is good, as the precocious early potatoes are through the ground very quickly and are more likely to be cut down by late frosts.

Earthing. This is most important as the tubers will turn green if allowed to grow in the light.

For early varieties earthing should be done as soon as the tops show above the ground, or they are likely to be injured by frost. By using a draw-hoe, weeds can be destroyed while earthing up. Care should be taken to see that there is not a trough at the top of the ridge, or moisture will collect in it and assist the spread if not cause disease.

Early potatoes.—Sound seed of a reliable variety should be obtained for early potatoes and this should be packed in trays one layer deep and with the "rose end" (the end where the eyes are clustered) upwards, in January. The trays can be stood in the full light where there is no danger from frost. By the time they are wanted for planting it will be found that they have made a number of short sprouts. All but two of these should be rubbed off and the tubers planted in the prepared ground in the first week in March. When the tops show, protect with litter and earth up. The potatoes should be ready to lift in June.

Potatoes in pots and frames.—The earliest potatoes can be grown in pots or frames. For the former choose sprouted tubers and allow two sets to a pot. Use light rich soil and start in a warm temperature, later removing to a cooler place and affording all the light possible. When grown in frames these should be placed on beds of leaves and spent manure. The plants must have enough head room to avoid touching the glass. Ventilation is given daily, the lights being opened 1 in. on the coldest days and anything up to 4 in. when the weather is mild. When the weather permits, remove the lights altogether by day and replace by night. When it is impossible to have a warm frame, a cold frame will forward the crop,

and if lights are not available a frame alone, covered with mats at night, will help to bring on the crop. In any case, tubers grown in this fashion need a rich soil and should be planted at the beginning of March.

Lifting and Storing.—When the tops of potatoes turn yellow the plants should be lifted and if not required for immediate use they can be stored. Lifting should be done when the soil is fairly dry, so that the tubers come out clean. Early crops are taken up for sale as soon as they are large enough to sell, and when the tops are yellow. Crops for seed should be lifted before they are quite mature, as the subsequent crop is better raised from undeveloped tubers.

Potatoes for storing must be left in the ground until the haulm has died down.

For storing, the tubers must be clean and free from disease. They can be kept in any dark frost-proof place and when only a few are grown they can be left in the sun for a few hours after lifting and then placed in a dark corner of a cellar and covered with a few sacks until required for use.

Where, however, there is a good number to store, this is usually done by means of a "pie" or a potato clamp. This may be sunk in the ground but a better method is to make a heap of the best of the potatoes in the driest part of the ground, cover this with straw, hay or old newspapers, and over the whole pile place a layer of soil smoothed with a spade. This soil is taken from the ground around the clamp and thus a ditch is formed that will carry away any surplus moisture from the "pie."

Ventilate the clamp by pushing a handful of straight straws through the top of the soil to the potatoes. In February or sooner, they should be examined and any that are diseased should be taken out. If shoots have formed these should be rubbed off.

Potatoes and Disease.—This has been the subject of much research both on the part of growers and of the Ministry of Agriculture. The worst of all, the Wart disease, is now effectively controlled and growers are trying to produce disease immune varieties.

Growers should, however, remember

that if reliable seed is bought, and the land is kept clean by burning weeds and affected tops, the crops are less likely to be attacked.

Varieties.—When choosing varieties, it is best to consult either the seller of seed or your neighbours, to find out which does best on your own particular soil, as this is an important factor in the successful cultivation.

Early Varieties.—In this group are included the varieties that are suitable for forcing.

Di Vernon. A thick fine kidney. Immune to Wart Disease.

Herald; Midlothian Early; Sharpe's Express; Witch Hill Early.

Second Early.—Arran Comrade; Catriona; Great Scot; King Edward VII; Majestic; The Ally.

Late Crop or Main.—Arran Chief; Field Marshal; Kerr's Pink; The Bishop.

Coloured Varieties for Exhibition.—Arran Rose. A pink kidney. Immune; The Cardinal. (Early). A bright kidney. Disease-immune; Mauve Queen. A bright mauve-coloured round.

POTATO DISEASE (*Phytophthora infestans*). DESCRIPTION. From the beginning of June to the middle of July if the weather is warm and damp, brown patches begin to appear on the edges of the leaves of potato. These rapidly spread and if the weather is still favourable to their growth, the whole of the leaf and stem will become affected, the haulm often dying right back and so checking the development of the root. The spores which are now ripe may get into the ground and set up an attack on the tubers. This is not always noticeable at first, but after a time the potato will begin to decay and fail to keep.

METHODS OF CONTROL.—Potatoes should be sprayed with Bordeaux Mixture in June, either in the early morning or in the evening but not when the sun is full on them.

A second spraying should take place at the end of July. Potatoes thus sprayed will continue growing for a longer period, thus allowing further growth of the roots.

In a bad attack where spraying has not been carried out, the diseased haulm should be carefully cut away and the potatoes left

in the ground to ripen. Though this method will save the root from actual attack, they will be small in size.

POTENTILLA (pō-ten-til′-a. Rosaceæ). Cinquefoil. Deciduous shrubs with attractive foliage, and very charming single rose-like flowers during summer until late autumn.

Culture.—Plant in good garden soil, not dry. *Propagate* by seeds. Cuttings

POTATO BLIGHT

EARLY STAGES

LEAF MARGINS DISCOLOURED

Brown patches on the leaves are the first signs of potato blight. It is controlled by spraying with Bordeaux mixture in summer.

of late summer wood root readily in sandy soil in frame.

SPECIES.

P. fruticosa (*moyesii*), shrubby Cinquefoil, 2–4 ft. A native of England and Ireland and many other parts of the northern hemisphere. The following comprise the various "forms" and hybrids known as *fruticosa*. The type has bright yellow flowers.

P. f. mandshurica. Flowers white.

P. f. nana argentea (*Beesii*). A delightful silver-foliaged form of *Vilmoriniana*, with rich yellow flowers.

P. f. Veitchii. White flowers, otherwise similar to type.

P. f. Vilmoriniana (China). Flowers creamy-white, and very attractive silvery-grey foliage.

DWARF SPECIES.

Culture.—They are of quite easy cultivation, thriving in any good, well-drained garden soil, with sand for the rock plants. They are propagated by seeds sown in

FILLING POTS WITH SOIL

LEAVE ROOM FOR WATERING

GOOD POTTING COMPOST

ROUGH POTTING COMPOST

DRAINAGE

Pot plants should have clear drainage to promote healthy growth.

light loam in spring or by division of the roots in spring and autumn and by cuttings struck in a frame in autumn. Water well in dry weather and give the hybrids a richer soil than that used for the other plants. The old wood should be thinned out in September.

The species are numerous, and for border plants a nurseryman's catalogue should be consulted to obtain the best. They are usually about 2 ft. in height and give a tremendous range of colours.

Among the best of the dwarf species for edging beds or borders and for the rockery are:

P. alba, white, single, April to July, 6 in.

P. alpestris, large bright yellow flowers and hairy green leaves, May to July, 6–12 in.

P. ambigua, yellow, May to September, 3 in.

P. pyrenaica, golden yellow, July to September, 8–12 in.

P. rupestris, large white flowers, June and July, 12 in.

P. reptans, yellow, and its double variety. June, 4 in.

P. splendens. March, white, 6 ins.

POTERIUM (pō-tē-rium. Rosaceæ). Burnet. Only a few of this small genus of hardy perennials are worth growing, as some are of weedy appearance. They have no preferences with regard to soil, but will grow anywhere. *Propagate* by seeds or division.

SPECIES

P. canadense, a handsome border plant with pinnate, feathery, glaucous leaves, and long slender spikes of white flowers which are good for cutting.

POT MARIGOLD. *See* CALENDULA.

POTTING. In this operation, dirty flower pots should never be used, or the roots will tend to cling to the pot and be broken in the process of removal. Clean the pots with warm soapy water and a scrubbing brush, and allow them to dry thoroughly before use. New pots are best soaked in cold water before use.

Plants usually need repotting when roots show at the drainage hole. Place some broken crocks at the base of the new pot, tip the plant out carefully, retaining a ball of soil round the roots and replant in fresh soil well pressed down with the fingers. Leave a small space free of soil at the top of the pot to allow for watering. Always plant firmly.

Seedlings from boxes are usually transferred to 3 in. pots and then on to 5, 7 and 9 in. as required.

After repotting, water carefully until the roots have freely rooted again. The term "potting off" refers to moving a seedling from a box to a pot and "potting on" or "shifting" moving a pot plant to a larger pot. *See* POTTING SOIL *and* FLOWER POTS.

POTTING SOIL. A soil compost, suited to most plants grown in the greenhouse, and also suitable for raising seedlings of half-hardy flowers, should be mixed and stored until needed. You will find this saves considerable time when daylight is scarce and the seed-sowing rush has begun.

A good mixture for most purposes is made of: ½ part fibrous loam (old turves are splendid); ¼ part leaf-mould; ½ part coarse sand, ⅛ part well-decayed manure. Rub all this through a half-inch mesh sieve, watching it at the same time for signs of wireworms in the old turf.

Keep also handy a supply of charcoal and lime or old mortar rubble to use in the pots as required.

POURTHIÆA. *See* PHOTINIA VILLOSA.

PRATIA (pra-ti-a. Campanulaceæ). After M. Prat, a French Officer.

P. angulata forms a mat of angular, fleshy leaves. The star-shaped flowers are white, succeeded by purple berries. This New Zealander requires a somewhat sheltered, moist soil, and cannot be regarded as hardy under all conditions.

As with many other of the New Zealand flora in this country, a few pot plants should be held in reserve. These are easily obtained from cuttings. 3 in. June.

PRICKING-OUT. The operation of transplanting seedlings from boxes, pans, etc., in which they were sown. It should be done before the plants get overcrowded. Sometimes the seedlings are pricked-out into other boxes and sometimes straight into the flower borders. If the seedlings are very small, a pointed piece of wood should be used to lift them with a small ball of soil retained round their roots. The best way to plant young seedlings is to make a hole with a piece of wood or small dibber, insert the seedling, place the dibber in the soil ½ in. away and lever it over towards the plant. This presses the soil firmly against the roots without their actually being touched by the wood. Seedlings should be carefully watered and inspected once or twice for the first day or two to see that they are upright. Tightly press down the soil round the base of the plant if the seedling is seen to be leaning to one side.

PRIMROSE, EVENING. *See* ŒNO-THERA.

PRIMROSES—NEW AND OLD. In these days of gardening enthusiasm, an unfailing demand exists for the newest creation of hybrid, and also for plants whose origin goes far back into bygone centuries. Double Primroses touch both extremes, new crosses are being introduced fairly freely, though to get any worth having is another matter, while there are other varieties such as Jackanapes, or the "Franticke Cowslip" which grew in Shakespeare's England.

The rarer kinds are costly; but to those who wish to start them, a word of cheer: among the least expensive are the most effective and the best doers.

Some sort of classification is perhaps advisable. First, there are the homely and attractive varieties, such as Arthur De Moulin, like a Parma violet, and the most profuse of bloomers—it will carpet the ground as does Aubrietia; Marie Crousse, violet flecked with white; Salmonea, soft rose, a generous grower; Red Paddy, the compact crimson—once upon a time to be found in most cottage gardens; and the double white, sulphur and lilac, the latter known as "Quaker's Bonnets."

Second, the rarer kinds: Rose du Barri, a vivid pink, brighter than Salmonea and more difficult to please; Burgundy, claret-purple; Cloth of Gold, lovely despite its rather ragged flower; the peerless Madame de Pompadour; and, rarest of all, Double Blue, a deep delphinium shade. The last two certainly justify the high price their growers ask for them. They have no equals. Pompadour is a rich velvet red, hard to get and, alas, easy to lose. Double Blue is on the market now and has been shown in the fortnightly shows of the R.H.S. It is a useful variety for the amateur as it increases easily.

The third class are collectors' pieces, such as Rex Theodore, Harlequin, Pantaloon, all old varieties, rare and interesting, but scarcely rewarding their cost; in fact, they are best left to the collectors.

Then, fourthly, there is the double poly-anthus type, represented by Prince Silverwings, a blue-purple, silver-laced; Curiosity, three or four shades in one bloom, like a coloured marble; and Tortoiseshell, the gem of the lot, a rosette-like flower of orange and terra-cotta.

There is yet another class, the Bonac-cord Doubles, produced before the war by Cocker, of Aberdeen fame. These are a distinctive type, of compact growth, with erect, well-formed flowers. Cocker's cream is perhaps the best. This race was fast disappearing, but with the revival in the demand for double primroses, they have been successfully cultivated and will soon be as well known as they deserve to be.

No article on Primroses would be complete which failed to mention the

Hose-in-hose varieties, double-deckers, of endless shades, as they come from seed and hybridise themselves. Lady Lettice and Lady's Favourite are two well-established kinds.

More interesting than these are the Jack-in-the-Greens or Galligaskins, to use their Irish name. These are single primroses, but they grow an Elizabethan ruff or frill of green leaves round the blooms.

PRIMULA WINTERI

The dainty little Primula Winteri has lavender flowers and powdered leaves. It enjoys a semi-shady spot in the rock garden.

When the blooms fade, the frills remain and grow larger. To this class belongs the enchanting Jackanapes.

Where to grow and how to grow primroses are questions not easy to answer. Their natural home is in the rich damp soil of Ireland, yet, they flourish also in north-easterly Aberdeenshire. Undoubtedly they like leaf-mould and dislike very light soil, but leaf-mould in itself will not keep them growing in a dry season. There is a theory that primroses dislike all manure; this is a fallacy. On the contrary, some varieties, notably Prince Silverwings, require well-manured ground. Primroses seem to change their character

with their situation, so advice is difficult to give; but it is safe to say that if bonemeal and leaf-mould are added to the soil before planting, they should do well. They like deep, firm planting. Even so, they will show a tendency to throw themselves out of the ground in spring. This is fatal for their well-being, as they are surface rooters, but it can be corrected by a top-dressing of sifted leaf-mould. Partial shade in summer and division of roots at least every two years are also essentials for success.

After all, they are really not very exacting, certainly not in proportion to the pleasure they give, and to their effect in May and June.

PRIMULA (prim-u-la. Primulaceæ). Primula, a diminutive of *Primus*, first. This genus has been the subject of perhaps more attention than any other of recent years, probably because, following the botanical explorations of Farrer, Frost, Kingdom Ward and others in the interior of China and the Burmese Hinterland, many new varieties have been brought into cultivation. At one time Primulas had a reputation for difficulty, but this was really due to a lack of appreciation of the simple cultural needs of the plants, which may be roughly divided into two classes; the large-growing Asiatic group which likes a rich, cool, moist soil, and the smaller-sized European group, which require full exposure to the sun.

For convenience they will be dealt with in these groups.

The Asiatic Group. These consist largely of the strong-growing types which have been described as Cabbage Primulas and are represented by *P. japonica* as being the best known and the easiest to grow. Cultural requirements of this group are satisfied by a good moist loam to which farmyard manure may be added with advantage, preferably about 6 in. below the crown, for Primulas are long-rooted. Actual contact of the manure with their crowns should be avoided. Failing a naturally damp situation, a shady one will do instead, provided that the ground is not sucked dry by the roots of trees. With every care the Primula family is very far from being immortal Plants should not be expected to last more than three years, though many will do so.

Propagation can also be effected by division of the crowns after the plant has flowered.

P. Beesiana. Rich bright magenta with yellow eye. Candelabra section. 18 in. Yunnan.

P. Bulleyana. Rich whorls of fierce red-gold, turning with age to serene, clear yellow. Candelabra section, 18 in., May. W. China.

P. denticulata and *P. d. cashmeriana.* One description will do for both, bearing in mind that *P. d. cashmeriana* is the finer form. Huge, tight, round heads of crowded lilac-purple in early spring. This will grow in any garden soil; its size and luxuriance increasing with its appreciation of its position. One of the most useful subjects for early spring flowering. There is a good white form, *P. d. alba.*

P. Florindæ. A giant among primulas. Loose heads of dangling mealy-amber bells, ambrosially scented, on 4–5 ft. stems above lush foliage of brightest green. Recently introduced from China. This makes a most excellent waterside plant. It can be seen well grown in the beds bordering the lake in St. James's Park, London. Sikkimensis section.

P. japonica. Richly-coloured flowers, ranging from purple-red in the species through various shades in the hybrids to creamy-white. The stout 18 in. flower stalks rise from fat cabbages of lush green leaves. This is the primula most frequently seen in gardens where the family is not a speciality. Candelabra section, June. Japan.

P. sikkimensis. Loose heads of fragrant, hanging lemon-yellow bells on powdered stems, arising from tufts of oval, saw-edged corrugated leaves. One of the most beautiful and easily grown, reaching perfection at the bog-side, but not disdaining more ordinary garden conditions. 18 in. to 2 ft. May. Himalayas.

European Section. It is mostly Primulas of this section which are responsible for engendering that inferiority complex which seizes the inexperienced gardener when he first dares to contemplate their cultivation. Who is he to succeed where so many have failed? The failures, however, are due to a misunderstanding of their requirements.

The idea that Primulas welcome shade, true enough of the leafy Asiatic kinds in many cases, is with this section an erroneous one. What they want is sun and plenty of it, with their roots in a good fibrous loam, and this in general should be the treatment accorded to the following species.

P. acaulis is our native Primrose. It is now united botanically under the name *P. veris* with the Cowslip (*P. veris*) and the Oxlip (*P. elatior*), thus reverting to the original classification of Linneus. The Primrose is found in Central Europe, being particularly abundant in Britain. It is not recorded from N. E. Europe. It is a parent in a whole range of hybrids, the best of which is dealt with in some detail below.

P. Allionii. This has a reputation for being one of the most difficult (it is certainly one of the most expensive). It should be firmly wedged in chinks in a deep limestone soil, perfectly drained, for the slightest suspicion of stagnant moisture will kill it, and there is every probability that it will succeed without trouble. It is worth some effort, for its great rose-pink flowers, completely hiding the small sticky leaves, are of outstanding beauty. 4 in. April. Maritime Alps.

Propagate by seeds or cuttings made from pieces pulled off the crown.

Primula Auricula. The numerous types of Auriculas now grown are all forms of the common auricula or Bear's Ear, a native of the European Alps. It has been grown in gardens for more than two centuries, but its popularity dates from the time when it was taken up by the workmen of the North.

The different forms are divided into Show and Alpine, and those that cannot be included under either of these heads are termed "fancies."

Show Auriculas.—These are sub-divided into "green-edged," in which the flower should be absolutely circular, smooth-edged, with the truss of blossom borne on a stout stalk. The richer the green of the outside of the flower the better, while inside the flower is a sort of white paste made of dense, meal-like matter known as farina, and the centre is filled by a yellow eye. "White-edged," in

which the outside of the flower is covered
with farina so that the green is hidden.
Grey-edged varieties have insufficient farina
to cover the green and so occupy a position
between green-edged and white. Fancies
mingle the characteristics of the groups
and are not much appreciated by florists.
In addition to the attractiveness of the
flowers, the foliage is very pretty, as it is
covered with farina so that in some cases
it seems to be covered with fine snow.

Alpine Auriculas.—These, owing to the
conditions under which they grow, have no
farina on the flowers or leaves and
are more vigorous than the greenhouse
plants.

Culture.—For both alpines and show
plants a good compost is made of fibrous
loam, well-decayed manure, leaf-mould
and sand. The alpines will also grow in
any garden soil.

Propagation.—New varieties can be
raised from seeds which are usually produced from plants cross-fertilised from
other plants of the same type, e.g., green-
edged with green-edged and not with white
edged. To cross-fertilise, remove the
anthers before the pollen is ripe and dust
the chosen pollen on to the stigma when
the flower is fully open. The seed will
ripen in July and may be sown at once or
kept for some months until spring. As
the seeds are rather erratic in their germination, and sometimes do not appear
until about two years after planting, the
pots containing the seed should be kept.
When the seedlings are large enough to
handle, they should be potted singly and
gradually potted on until they reach 4 or
5 in. pots, when they will bloom.

Perfect blooms will often be given by
thus crossing the plants. In judging the
merit of a variety, although it may appear
to be good it must not be what is known
as a "pin-eyed" form (i.e., having the
stigma taller than the anthers). Named
varieties can be raised from offsets, taken
about February and after being potted,
kept close under glass until they have
rooted.

During the winter the Auriculas need
no special care. In February they begin
to show signs of life and by March should
be flourishing. Repotting should be done
after flowering and the plants kept close

for a few days after this operation. The
pots must be well drained and the plants
carefully watered.

Primulas in the Greenhouse. Several
species of Primulas are suited to greenhouse cultivation, and each species has a
great variety of selected colours. They
are perennial or biennial, but all of them
are treated as biennials. They vary in
height from 9–15 in.

PRINOS. *See* ILEX.

PRINSEPIA (prin-sep-i-a. Rosaceæ).
Plagiospermum. Deciduous flowering
shrubs of spreading habit, lanceolate
leaves and yellow flowers.

Culture.—Plant in ordinary garden soil,
with leaf-mould. *Propagate* by cuttings.
SPECIES.

P. sinensis (Manchuria), 3–6 ft. Flowers
light yellow, nearly 1 in. in diameter,
followed by red plum-like fruits.

P. utilis (Himalayas). Similar to preceding, but with white flowers.

PRITCHARDIA (pritch-ar-di-a. Palmaceæ). Stove Palms. Leaves fan-
shaped. 1870.

Culture.—For compost, cultivation and
propagation, *see* KENTIA.
SPECIES.

P. aurea, 4–10 ft.; *P. Martii*, 4–10 ft.;
and *P. Thurstonii*, 4–10 ft.

PRIVET. *See* LIGUSTRUM.

PROPAGATING PIT OR FRAME.
See MANAGEMENT OF THE GREENHOUSE.

PROPAGATING PLANTS. Nature
increases plants in several different ways,
and it is chiefly Nature's methods which
are adopted by gardeners. There are some
exceptions. For instance, nothing in
Nature is quite like grafting or taking
cuttings. The principal methods which
Nature uses are reproduction by seeds or
spores, and the formation of new roots
from some other part of the plant, i.e., the
formation of offsets and runners, and the
rooting of the tips of long branches of
such plants as brambles.

Seed Sowing is the method most
generally employed for the raising of new
plants. New seedlings are generally
supposed to be more healthy and vigorous
than plants continually raised from
cuttings. There are good reasons to
support the theory that vitality is lost by
continuous vegetative reproduction. For

instance, potatoes seem to lose their resistance to disease after a few generations, and there is consequently a need for new varieties raised from seeds to take the place of older worn-out kinds. Seeds are the basis of a very important industry throughout the world, and there are many wholesale houses responsible for the distribution of the world's supply of seeds. Certain seeds are best grown in certain districts and the growers work in conjunction with the wholesale firms. Purity of seed strains is often obtained by limiting each grower to the production of a certain strain of seeds. Seed testing is also another important side of seed production and is compulsory in the case of vegetable seeds and usually practised in the case of flower seeds.

Several points should be borne in mind when the gardener is raising plants from seeds. It pays to buy good seed, and also to buy fresh seed each year. If any seeds are used that have been left over from a previous season, a few should be tested for germination before the rest of the seeds are sown, so that there is no waste labour. Any plant which produces seeds can be successfully raised from seed if given natural conditions. So many of our plants come from other countries, however, that special conditions must be given them here if the seeds are to germinate.

Hardy annuals are merely sown outdoors where they are to bloom. The hardy biennials and perennials are also sown in the same manner. Half-hardy annuals are generally sown in boxes of prepared soil in a heated greenhouse or frame, the seedlings being transferred to the open garden for the summer months only. Trees and shrubs can also be raised from seed and for this the cold frame is usually the most suitable, as a very even temperature can be maintained in this and also the supply of moisture can be regulated. Greenhouse plants are often raised from seeds sown in pans or boxes either standing on the greenhouse stages or more often in a special propagating frame. It is important when raising seeds under glass to see that no moisture hangs about in the atmosphere, and that proper ventilation is given. Cleanliness is also important. Bottom heat, that is pipes or

hot air underneath the seed pans, is of great assistance in keeping the soil warm while germination actually takes place.

Ferns are raised from spores, usually sown on pieces of turf or peat in shallow pans, and kept moist by covering them with a piece of glass. The pans are generally plunged into a bed of moss which is kept moist at all times. (For fuller details, *see* SEEDS, SEED TESTING, etc.)

The common Privet, when not cut back, makes a beautiful shrub in fruit or flower.

Cuttings. We have no record of the first man who discovered that he could increase plants by cuttings. The discovery was probably accidental. Perhaps it was noticed that sticks of willows and other trees driven into the ground to form a boundary fence took root and became new plants. Thus the idea of increasing plants from cuttings grew. This method is now universally adopted for increasing many kinds of plants. Its particular value is in the case of plants which cannot be raised from seed to be true to type. For instance, the Paul Crampel geranium, whose marvellous colour is so much appreciated for formal flower beds, is always increased by cuttings. If seeds were saved of this variety it is quite unlikely that many of the seedlings, if any, would be of the same colour, and it is exactly the same with many other named varieties of plants.

The general rule concerning cuttings is to cut immediately below a leaf joint, as roots develop more easily just at this point. Internodal cuttings, that is, cuttings severed midway between two joints, are better in a few exceptional cases, such as willows and clematis. Cuttings root best in moist conditions and generally in pure sand. Very little nourishment is needed to root a cutting; soil containing much humus would be fatal, as they would probably decay before the roots formed.

Cuttings should be shaded from bright sunshine and kept constantly moist until the root growth begins. In the case of plants which only root with difficulty, they can be very greatly assisted by the use of bottom heat. In a greenhouse this can be provided by putting a propagating frame over the hot-water pipes. Those who have to root all their cuttings in the open ground will generally find that the best season to insert them is towards the end of the month of August, and this is because the soil is warm, and autumn showers and mists will help to prevent the cutting from drying instead of rooting.

Leaf Cuttings. Roots will often form on a plant not only from the joints of stems but also from the leaves. Plants such as Begonias and Gloxinias are often increased by means of leaf cuttings. A fleshy leaf is taken and laid flat on a box of moist sandy soil. Small notches are made in the veins of the leaf to encourage the formation of roots, and the leaf is pegged down on to the moist surface.

A sheet of glass is put over the box, or the pan is put in a frame, so that the whole is kept moist at all times. It is also shaded from bright sunshine. After a short time new little leaves begin to show. The large leaf can then be divided and the small plants, which will be found to have roots, can be potted up.

If a large leaf of Bryophyllum is laid on a damp surface in a warm greenhouse and kept moist in the same way as already described for Begonia leaves, it will throw out young plants all round the edge.

Some of the ferns also have the habit of producing new small plants from leaves of the older plant.

Root Cuttings. Quite a number of the fleshy-rooted plants can be increased very easily by means of root cuttings. These include such things as Seakale, Horseradish, blue Anchusa and the large perennial poppies. For instance, if an Oriental poppy of a particularly fine colour is in the garden, and it is desired to make a bold show of these plants, the poppy should be lifted at the end of the summer, when it is resting. It will be found that there are numerous fleshy roots about the thickness of the little finger, and if portions of these about as long as a finger are cut, and planted in fairly open soil, in pots or in the open border, they will each make a new plant. It is also common knowledge that dahlias and potatoes can be increased by cutting the tubers into various portions, allowing one eye to each. Potato tubers are not strictly roots, but they are regarded as such by the gardener.

Division of Roots.—The easiest of all methods of increasing plants is the division of roots which every gardener practises each autumn and spring. Rank-growing perennials of the Michaelmas daisy and ox-eye daisy type spread extensively underground. The spreading roots send up new stems, or suckers, in the same way as trees and shrubs do. Any plant which sends up fresh shoots some distance from the parent plant can be increased by the simple method of digging up these fresh shoots, with some root attached, and replanting them elsewhere. But many plants which do not send up suckers can also be divided to make fresh plants. Primroses, for instance, are often increased in this way, particularly where they are of unusual colouring or double flowered.

In general, this dividing of plants is understood by every gardener, but there are a few rules which are often disobeyed, and cause trouble. One is, to use only clean tools in the work of division. A sharp clean knife for such roots as primroses, where they do not break easily in the right manner, and a spade for large overgrown clumps of Michaelmas daisies, are the best tools.   Clumps difficult to divide can be best split up by using two hand-forks driven into the centre of the clump, after lifting. The forks should be back to back, and it will be found that by levering them apart, the clump will divide satisfactorily.

Another point to remember is that the outside portions of a strong clump always make the best new plants. If in any doubt take the youngest, most recently-developed part of the root. Older portions are worn out, and will not make such good plants.

All cuttings, divided roots, and transplanted seedlings need special care and attention, and the wise gardener keeps a nursery plot in reserve for these young plants. The nursery plot, will, if properly stocked whenever there is a favourable opportunity, provide ample plants— climbing, shrubbery, and herbaceous—to replace losses that occur from time to time in the borders and shrubbery.

In such a reserve garden, the soil should be sandy, well drained, and clean, i.e., not weedy or pest-ridden. It should also be shaded from bright sunshine, at least in part.   A small hand-light or frame, so that a moist atmosphere is maintained round certain types of cuttings, is also needed. The best time for taking cuttings of all kinds is in the autumn, when the sap is on the move and the soil is still warm. Failing that, the spring will be found satisfactory. But the gardener does not want to be restricted, and likes to take cuttings whenever there are suitable growths available on his plants, and he therefore provides himself with the frame or hand-light so that he can create artificially the warmth and moist atmosphere of autumn at any season.

The nursery plot will be used, too, for growing on the bulbils that form in the leaf axils of lilies, and offsets from other bulbs. Often these are very small at first, but if grown in the nursery bed for one or two seasons, they make strong bulbs for use in the borders. Planted in the mixed flower border direct, these smaller bulbs would probably be lost before they had time to reach the flowering stage.

Ringing. Knowing that plants will, if

encouraged, develop roots from any part of the stem, the gardener puts his knowledge to account in various ways. Extra fine delphiniums are, for example, often produced by allowing more stems to grow from the base than are actually wanted to flower.   Then about July, these stems are laid down on the surface of damp light soil, in the shade, and a little soil scattered over them. Roots form at

WINTERING FUCHSIAS

GRADUALLY WITHHOLD WATER AND DRY OFF. LAY POTS ON SIDES IN FROSTPROOF PLACE TILL SPRING.

GREENHOUSE STAGING

Winter is the rest time for many plants. Fuchsias can be kept without water until spring.

each joint and the separate rooted pieces can be cut off and replanted, each to make a fresh border plant.

But even more interesting than this is the method adopted by gardeners to restore symmetry to room plants of the type of "Aralia," commonly called the "Castor-oil Plant." This frequently becomes tall and leggy after a number of years of cultivation, and in this state is unsuitable as a room decoration.   To shorten the stem, and at the same time preserve the fine head of foliage, roots are encouraged to form at a point only a short way below the leaves. To do this, a ring of bark is first removed, using a sharp clean knife.

Then this portion of the stem is surrounded by damp moss or soil, in which new roots can form.   An ordinary flower-pot, split into two vertically, is generally used. This is supported on wires so that it is on the level of the ring round the stem.   The two halves are secured on either side of the stem, and the pot is filled with soil.   Roots rapidly form, and when this has happened, the lower portion of the stem is cut, leaving a new plant in the divided pot. This is repotted and grown on in the ordinary way.   The old root can be discarded, or allowed to grow a fresh head of foliage.

Layering. The same principle governs the processes of layering.   Here again the plant is encouraged to form roots at a certain point before the new plant is detached from its parent.   A number of plants layer themselves naturally.   The strawberry, for example, sends out numerous "runners" or long stems which develop little plants at the end, and at various parts along the stem where this touches the ground and new roots can form.   There are many other plants, especially among the rock garden plants, that behave in the same way.   Tall climbing plants also do the same thing if any of the stems bend over to the ground. Brambles spread in this manner through neglected woodlands.   The gardener uses the method of layering, because, like ringing, it allows the new plant to draw nourishment from the old roots while it is making a start in life for itself.

Carnations are usually layered in gardens where there are no special facilities for rooting cuttings, and this simple form of layering may be outlined.   The plants make a number of side growths each season, in addition to sending up a flowering stem.   It is these side shoots that are layered.   First a quantity of fresh soil is put round each plant.   This should be open soil, with leaf-mould and some lime in its composition.

Each stem to be layered is prepared by stripping off a few of the lower leaves and cutting a slanting notch in the stem, upwards.   The stem is bent into the soil at this point, and pegged there firmly with the soil pressed well round the new plant. It is not completely severed from the old

plant for about six weeks, by which time the roots will have formed and the new plant will be growing well.   In dry weather there is less danger of failure with layering than with cuttings, since the young plant can call on the roots of the old one to supply moisture.

Numbers of woody shrubs, and other plants difficult to strike as cuttings, can be successfully increased by the amateur in this manner.

Budding and Grafting. The operations of budding and grafting are extremely useful methods of increasing a stock of plants of special varieties.   They are employed to save time.   The principle is the same in both cases.   A bud, or eye, or short terminal stem is taken from the special variety—rose, ornamental shrub, tree, fruit, etc.—and transferred to a well-established plant of some commoner kind. Two advantages result: The new shoot receives the support of an established root, and therefore develops with rapidity, and it also in many cases takes on increased vigour, because the stock plant is naturally of a more vigorous type than the fancy variety.

Budding is the simpler of the two operations, and one which can be undertaken by any amateur with every hope of success.   It is chiefly practised in the case of roses, but it can also be employed successfully with young trees.   Those who live near enough to woods to obtain saplings of wild cherry, for instance, can easily bud them with ornamental varieties, or fruiting cherries, if one of these is at hand to furnish the buds.

For budding roses the tools wanted are a budding-knife (which is a very sharp knife, with a flat blunt handle that will lift the bark from the stem without damaging either) and some raffia.   A supply of twigs carrying leaves with buds in the axils is taken from the "scion," i.e., the rose which it is desired to propagate.   It is best to keep these moist and no more should be cut than can be used at one time.   If they come from another garden, keep the ends in water until the budding is done.

A bud can be inserted in any part of the stem, so long as the bark can be raised easily when cut.   Bush roses are budded just below the ground level. Standards in two or three places round the stem, 4 or 5 ft. up. The bud is removed from the scion by cutting behind the bud in a curve, so that an oval piece of the bark is removed with the bud and leaf. Cut off the leaf near the stem. The small piece of leaf-stem remaining makes a good handle for the bud. Take out any woody portion of the stem that lies at the back, but do not damage the bud in the process. If you do, take another bud. Make a T-shaped cut in the bark of the stock, lift the edges of the bark, and quickly insert the prepared bud, replacing the lifted edges of bark, and binding the whole securely with raffia. The tip of the bud, and the small portion of leaf-stalk, will just be visible after the operation is complete. Swelling of the bud, instead of shrivelling, is a sign that it has "taken," and the raffia should then be loosened sufficiently to prevent damage to the stem. Before growth begins the following season, all the stem of the stock above the bud must be cut away, and any buds below the "scion" should be rubbed off and not allowed to grow. Otherwise they rob the new shoot of nourishment.

Grafting is the term applied to the moving of a short stem from one plant to another, instead of moving only one dormant bud, as in budding. The graft has more than one bud, and is therefore a quicker method of propagating new varieties of fruit. It must be taken from young wood of not more than one year's growth. Generally the best plan to adopt is to cut off the grafts in January, to keep them moist by putting the ends into the soil in some cool corner of the garden, and to insert the grafts about March or April. In spring the sap is more active, and the trees to be grafted will be ready to supply food for the young graft immediately.

Whip grafting is the most common form. To do this, a slanting cut is made in both the stock and the scion in such a way that they will fit together exactly. Often a tongue is also cut in each, so that they join more neatly and firmly. When they have been neatly fitted together, the join is surrounded with some special material which will hold them firm. Raffia bound round the join and covered with special grafting wax is a common method. The wax excludes air, and so prevents the cuts from drying. Other forms of grafting are done in much the same way except that the cuts are made differently. Cleft grafting means making a cleft in the head of the stock (usually an old tree, cut down) and inserting the scion in this. Saddle grafting is when the stock is cut to a point, and the scion cut with a V-shaped notch which sits down over the stock. Rind grafting is when the scion is cut in slanting fashion, with a second cut part way across, so that a shoulder is left. This rests on the cut surface of the stock as the graft is pushed down. These grafts are inserted, two or more in the same stock, near the outside, or "rind." Grafts can also be inserted in the side of a tree to fill the place of a branch that has been damaged. In all cases the principle is the same, that is, the *cambium layers* of both stock and scion must meet, and air must be excluded until the union has taken place. (The cambium layer is the layer between the bark and the pith of the tree. It is only present in dicotyledonous plants.) If the two stems to be united are of the same size, the cambium layer will meet naturally, but if one is larger than the other, care must be taken to see that the graft is put to the side so that these layers do actually meet in one place. Otherwise union will not take place.

Inarching. This is somewhat similar to grafting, but is not often practised. When done, it is usually with vines. The stems from two plants—stock and scion—are brought together, a piece cut from the bark of each, and the join sealed over as in grafting. The scion is not cut from its parent roots until after the union is complete.

Other forms of grafting, such as root grafting, and the grafting of herbaceous plants, are sometimes done, but only by expert gardeners for special purposes.

Effect of Grafting. As already stated, grafting is done to save time, and gives extra vitality to a plant that is desirable on account of its special colour and form, but may not be so strong and vigorous as others of the same genus. It has its uses but also its abuses, since grafted plants in the amateur's garden sometimes show a great tendency to revert to the common stock. (With bush roses, the throwing up of many suckers from the stock may be the result of too-shallow planting.) The effect of grafting depends, too, on the varieties used. For instance, experiments with the grafting of fruit trees on different stocks have shown that the influence of the stock is consider-able. In some rare cases the stock and

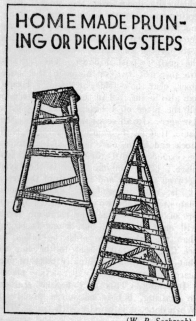

HOME MADE PRUN-ING OR PICKING STEPS

(*W. P. Seabrook*)

Where an orchard is cultivated a step ladder is needed for fruit gathering.

scion characteristics come out simul-taneously in the new growths; for instance, in the case of Adam's Laburnum, yellow, purple, and both colours mixed appear in the flowers, and this is said to be due to the combination by grafting of *Laburnum vulgare* (the common yellow) and the purple-flowered *Cytisus purpureus*. In the case of fruits, the influence is generally felt in the habit of the plant, and dwarf types are created by selection of suitable stock plants.

PROPAGATOR. A box placed inside the greenhouse: used for propagating by means of cuttings and seeds. If it is to

be a fixture it should be built to include part of the heating pipes, which should be covered with a good depth of coconut fibre. It is also possible to have a propagator which can be moved out of the greenhouse when not required, if space is limited. The boxes of seeds or cuttings should be plunged in fibre in the box and covered with glass, the glass being covered with paper to shade it from the sun for the first few weeks until the cuttings are rooted. Subsequent care is the same as for propagating frames.

PROSOPIS (pros-ō'-pis. Leguminosæ). Deciduous evergreen trees or shrubs, mostly grown under grass in this country, except the following:

. *P. juliflora* (South America). Deciduous, fine Acacia-like foliage and white flowers in July.

PROSTANTHERA (pros-tan-thē'-ra. Labiatæ). Evergreen, half-hardy shrubs, with very beautiful flowers in spring.

Culture.—Plant in perfectly-drained soil, loam, peat and sand, against sunny wall.

Propagation by half-ripened shoots under bell-glass..

Species.

P. lasianthos (Victoria). Flowers white, tinged red in June.

P. rotundifolia (Australia). A very beautiful species with aromatic foliage and a profusion of heliotrope flowers from May to June.

PROTEA (pro-te-a. Proteaceæ). Green-house evergreen flowering shrubs.

Cultivate in a compost of fibrous loam, silver sand, charcoal, freestone, broken pots and peat. Allow for ample drainage. Pot firmly in March. Water moderately in the summer, but after this keep the plants just moist. In the warmer weather the pots may be stood outdoors in a sunny spot, but when in the greenhouse they should be near the window and in direct sunshine. Take cuttings close to a joint, and insert in sandy soil. Young shoots make best cuttings.

Species.

P. cordata. Purple flowers in spring. Height 18 in.

P. grandiflora. White flowers in May. Height 6–8 ft.

PRUNELLA (prü-nell-a. Labiatæ). Self Heal. Small hardy perennials useful

1. The Shirley Poppies—brilliant coloured perennials.
2. The Pæony—Queen of the May—flowering perennials.
3. Alstrœmeria—Peruvian Lily, handsome plants for a sheltered corner

1. Greasebanding. An operation to control pests. (Cooper, McDougall and Robertson Ltd.)
2. Staking—the support should be adequate but almost invisible.
3. Raising seeds—using sandy soil, fine-rose can, and small stick for pricking out.

for the rockery or the front of the herbaceous border, with flowers arranged in whorled spikes. *Propagate* by division in April or October or by seed sown in the open in April. Plant out in moist, fairly rich soil. The common Self-heal or *Prunella vulgaris* is not worth growing, but it was formerly of medicinal value as an astringent in cases of internal bleeding.

P. grandiflora, with spikes of rich purplish-blue flowers and brown bracts, and its varieties, *alba* white and *rubra* red, are the best known, while *vulgaris laciniata* purple is worth growing. Height 6–12 in.

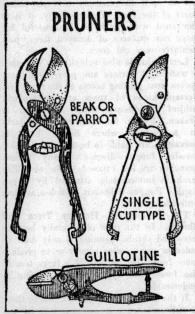

PRUNERS

BEAK OR PARROT

SINGLE CUT TYPE

GUILLOTINE

There are various types of pruners or secateurs. They are much more convenient for the amateur than the pruning knife.

PRUNERS OR SECATEURS. There are many arguments for and against the three main methods of design: the single cut, double cut or parrot beak, and the anvil or guillotine type pruners. The advantage of the first is that if you keep your fingers on the handle operating the blade, and the blade always nearest the root, you cannot in any way bruise

that part of the tree or flower that is expected to grow again—and that is most important. The branch or stem that you have cut off would be the only part that would be bruised, and that does not matter. With the parrot-beak pruners you are rather liable to squeeze the stem of the flower until finally it is cut, which bruises both sides of the cut. Similarly it is impossible to make a clean cut all along

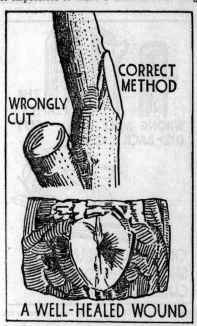

CORRECT METHOD

WRONGLY CUT

A WELL-HEALED WOUND

Careful pruning will prolong the life of trees.

the edge of the blades. But the advantage of this type of pruner is that if you are liable to change hands or turn your hands over you do not have to worry about which blade is nearest the root. The anvil type of pruner is excellent for general use, but as it must obviously bruise when the stem is, so to speak, guillotined, then it cannot be recommended for delicate pruning.

Budding-knives are quite distinct from pruning-knives, and each have a different use, as their names imply. It is merely a matter of taste and use as to whether you use a pruner or a pruning-knife. A budding-knife has one very sharp blade,

T

and either on the back of the blade or the end of the knife a blunt end for lifting the bark after the cut has been made.

Lopping-shears are in reality very large pruners usually of the parrot-beak type and on long handles for lopping or pruning branches of trees up to about 1 in. diameter. Above this diameter a pruning-saw should be used, and in that case it is best to get one with the teeth

THE PERFECT CUT

WRONG WILL DIE-BACK

OLD WOOD PRUNED & SHOWING SHOOTS OF CURRENT YEAR

Pruning should be done with due regard to the plant's habit of growth.

leaning towards the handle, so that when on a ladder with one hand holding the branch to be sawn and the other holding the saw, it is much safer to pull than to push.

PRUNING. When to Prune. The best time for the beginner to think about pruning trees and bushes is when they are in full leaf. Overcrowding is emphasised much more then than when the trees are bare of leaf. Also, it does no harm to a tree to have one or two branches cut away while they are in full leaf, in fact it often considerably assists the plant to be pruned at this season as it allows more sunshine to penetrate into the heart. Regular pruning to be done when leaves have fallen.

The first kind of pruning which an amateur gardener has to do is, often, the pruning of old neglected trees or shrubs that he wishes to bring into the scope of a new garden design. In this, the first and most important thing is to cut away any branches that are suffering from disease. Good sharp tools are required for this, and they must always be kept clean or disease will be spread from one tree to another.

It is also useful to have a pot of creosote handy to paint over the cut portion of the tree. Various other materials can be used for painting cuts, but creosote is anti-septic and does not injure the tree or shrub. Care should be taken, of course, not to spill the creosote over the other parts of the tree. Tar, specially, if it is thickened with pitch, is also useful for large cut surfaces of decayed trees, par-ticularly very old trees.

Lead paint is also valuable as it makes a watertight surface and prevents disease spores from gaining access to the branches. Certain kinds of trees are particularly subject to disease when a branch is broken. Plums, for instance, particularly in a district where Silver Leaf is prevalent, are liable to be attacked by this dreaded fungus disease if any broken branches are left exposed to the air. The larch is immediately attacked by Larch Canker Fungus if broken branches are left untreated.

The Pruning of Healthy Trees and Shrubs. In the case of normally healthy trees and shrubs, pruning is only done in order to create more beauty or to produce more fruit. In the case of a large tree of the forest tree type, drastic pruning is undesirable.

If the tree has been planted where there is sufficient space to accommodate it, and if care was given to it in its early stages, it should seldom need pruning when it is mature. With all pruning the rule is to practise "finger and thumb" pruning as much as possible, that is to say, to rub off shoots that are not wanted before they are large enough to need secateurs or knives to cut them.

When a tall forest tree does need prun-ing, as for instance, when it becomes rather too big for its site, an effort should be made as far as possible to retain the natural symmetry of the tree. It is best, for instance, to remove a portion from each branch, particularly in the case of a tree of pyramid shape, so that when the tree is again full of foliage, it does not look badly proportioned. In fact, the careful pruner will *leave a tree looking as if it had not been pruned at all.*

When a side branch of a tree is shortened, it should always be shortened back to a point where a secondary branch is growing from it, otherwise a stump is left which becomes unsightly and eventually decays. This method of reducing an overgrown tree is much better than cutting back the whole top of the tree and allowing it to form a new head, a practice which makes it very unsightly for a few years after pruning.

Small ornamental trees, such as almond trees, require comparatively little pruning. Beyond exercising discretion and removing or shortening branches so that the tree does not become very badly disproportioned, pruning may be entirely neglected.

Evergreen trees such as conifers are often best left entirely unpruned, and certainly no pruning should be done by inexperienced gardeners. In the case of a young tree it sometimes happens that two leaders appear instead of one at the top of a tree. These can be reduced to one. The appearance of more than one leader is usually caused by some damage to the leading original shoot. Some conifers, particularly when they are older, will not replace damaged shoots by new leaders, and it is very unwise to cut back the top of a tree which it is intended to grow as a specimen. Conifers and evergreens grown as hedges are of course clipped in the usual manner. (*See* HEDGES.)

Flowering Shrubs. All shrubs cannot be pruned alike, the reason for this is that some flower on old shoots and some on new ones; for instance, Forsythia flowers on young shoots made *during the previous year.* Buddleia blooms on the new shoots made *the same year.* The winter-flowering *Daphne mezereum* flowers on old stems, and does not grow much each season. The pruning of all these would be different; Daphne is not touched, unless it becomes necessary to thin out some of the old branches. The Forsythia can be cut back in spring *immediately after flowering,* to encourage the growth of new strong shoots to flower again the next spring. The Buddleia is cut back to the old wood at the *end of February,* so that the new wood growing through the summer will be strong and sturdy, and will carry fine trusses of flowers. Most flowering shrubs fall into one or other of these three categories.

In some cases the same shrub may be treated in either of two different ways. For instance, in the case of *Forsythia spectabilis,* it may be left unpruned for many years, if preferred, or it may be cut back fairly hard each year as soon as the flowers are over. In the one case a large mass of flowers is produced, and in the other, extra long sprays carrying finer individual blooms will result.

It should be remembered in pruning that the first stem which will grow on the branch that is left will come from the top bud. This should always be in the mind of the pruner when the knife is used, for by examining the buds on the stem and choosing one which is pointing in the direction in which he wants it to grow shapely trees and shrubs can be encouraged. For instance, when roses are pruned the cut is made immediately above the bud which is on the outer side of the bush, and points in the direction in which the new shoot is desired.

It is just as important to cut away the whole of the piece of stem above a bud in the case of small twigs as it is to prune back to a side branch in the case of larger trees. A stem should either be cut right back to the main branch, or else cut so close to a bud that there is no portion left to die and to harbour disease.

Another point to remember when pruning flowering shrubs is that the symmetry of the shrub is fully as important as the actual number of flowers. It is neither attractive nor conducive to good health for a tree to be allowed to grow in a one-sided manner.

Dead wood in a tree or shrub is also a source of trouble if allowed to remain, and shrubs that are pruned in late winter may often with advantage be left until the buds are actually breaking into growth before the knife is used, in order that the dead wood can be clearly distinguished from the living.

PRUNUS (prü'-nus. Rosaceæ). A very large and attractive genus of evergreen and deciduous trees and shrubs, of very great beauty and usefulness. Included therein are Almonds and Peaches, Apricots, Plums, Cherries, etc., and they are described under these headings. All the deciduous species which flower before the leaves appear, are seen to best advantage against a background of evergreens.

Culture.—Plant during October or November in deeply-dug well-enriched soil, containing a good proportion of lime. They do exceedingly well in chalky districts and also in town gardens. Pruning consists in cutting out dead wood and weak shoots.

Propagation is effected by seed, by budding during summer, and also by grafting.

GROUP I—FLOWERING ALMONDS, APRICOTS AND PEACHES.

P. amygdalus (communis). Deciduous. Europe and Asia, 20–30 ft. The well-known single pink Almond producing its delightful flowers in leafless branches, towards the end of March and April.

P. a. dulcis. The "Sweet" or Edible Almond.

P. persica. The Peach has been cultivated from the most ancient times. The following is distinct and beautiful varieties, flowering after the Almonds. They should all have a background of evergreens for their great beauty to be seen to the best advantage. They like a warm soil, and sheltered positions.

P. p. Clara Meyer. Flowers double rose-pink.

GROUP II—FLOWERING PLUMS.

P. cerasifera, "Myrobalan" or "Cherry Plum" of Western Asia. Very beautiful with its leafless branches covered with small white flowers in March. Makes an excellent hedge.

P. spinosa flore pleno. The double-flowering form of the common sloe. Most beautiful when in bloom.

GROUP III—CERASUS (FLOWERING CHERRIES).

P. avium. Our native "Wild Cherry," "Mazzard" or "Gean." Very attractive with its masses of single white flowers during April and May. Fine for the woodland garden.

P. a. flore pleno (multiplex). The double-flowered form. One of the most beautiful of flowering Cherries. Not suitable for small gardens, growing as it does to a height of 50 ft. and over. The pure white flowers are very double and last well. Award of Merit, R.H.S.

P. cerasus. The "Wild Dwarf Cherry" of Europe, including Britain. One of the parents of our edible dessert cherries and the Morellos, 10–20 ft. Flowers white, in clusters. Fruit red to black.

P. Sargentii (serrulata sachalinensis), Korea and Japan. A species of exquisite beauty. Flowers delicate rose or shell-pink. Young wood greyish-brown, becoming dark chocolate-brown the second year. Foliage in autumn various shades of orange and crimson. This is "the" one, where there is only room for one Japanese Cherry. It likes a woodland soil, well drained, and a cool position.

P. serrula tibetica (China), 15–20 ft. Of little floral beauty, but very beautiful in autumn when the golden-brown coloured bark peels off, revealing a polished bark beneath.

P. s. fugenzo (Veitchiana). Better known in gardens as "James H. Veith," and was found by the man it takes its name from in a nursery in Japan. It is one of the finest—some think *the* finest—of all the Japanese Cherries. The flowers are 2 in. across, and of a very beautiful deep rose-pink.

P. s. autumnalis (Miqueliana). A remarkable and beautiful variety with semi-double, almond-scented, pale pink flowers, produced intermittently from November or earlier, until April. Own root plants are recommended in preference to grafted ones. Award of Garden Merit, R.H.S.

P. Mahaleb (Cerasus Mahaleb). The "St. Lucie Cherry," of Central and South Europe. 30–40 ft. Young plants do not flower very freely, but when established this is one of the most beautiful of flowering-trees, filling the air for yards around with the fragrance of its sweet-scented white flowers. A fast-growing tree; should be planted in soil not too rich. Used as a stock for grafting edible Cherries on,

P. Padus. The "Bird Cherry," is a native of Britain, and is widely distributed over Europe and Asia into Japan. A most handsome native tree with spikes of white fragrant flowers in April and May.

GROUP V—LAUROCERASUS (CHERRY LAUREL).

Prunus caroliniana. The "Wild Orange" of southern U.S.A. A rare evergreen, with beautifully-coloured foliage. Only suitable for very mild districts.

P. ilicifolia. The "Spanish Wild Cherry" of California. Supposed to be tender like the preceding, but has withstood nearly 30° of frost in Hampshire (inland). The leaves are glossy, holly-like, about 2 in. long. Flowers white.

P. Laurocerasus. The "Cherry Laurel" or "Common Laurel" of Europe and Asia Minor. Evergreen shrubs up to 20 ft. high and twice as wide if left unpruned. Not recommended for planting in shrubberies, its vigorous hungry roots robbing the ground unduly of nourishment needed by its neighbours. It bears clipping and pruning well, and is used for hedges, covering banks and sloping ground, etc.

P. lusitanica. The well-known "Portugal Laurel," quite indispensable as an evergreen or small tree. Wonderfully effective grown as a standard and left unpruned. Native of Portugal and Spain, where it may reach to a height of 40 ft. Flowers white, about ½ in. across. Leaves dark green and very glossy. Hardy in all but the very coldest parts. If the soil is well drained, will withstand 30° of frost. A very old plant in English gardens, having been introduced in 1648.

See also ALMOND, APRICOT, PEACH AND NECTARINE, PLUM.

PSEUDOLARIX (sū-do-lar′-ix. Coniferæ). A monotypic genus very near to Larix (Larch).

P. Fortunei (amabilis, Kæmpferi). A hardy deciduous and very beautiful tree from China. 100–130 ft. Leaves, in spring, of a tender, yellowish-green, turning to a rich golden yellow in autumn. Requires a lime-free soil.

PSEUDOPANAX (sū-do-pan-ax. Araliaceæ). Evergreen shrubs. New Zealand. Require same treatment as Aralias.

P. ferox. Long sword-like leaves, 2 ft. long. Tender.

PSEUDOTSUGA (sū-dot-su′-ga. Coniferæ). A noble genus of handsome trees allied to Abies, but differing therefrom in the narrower leaves and persistent cone-scales. It thrives best in fairly good loamy soil well drained and free from lime or chalk and in a district where the rainfall is abundant.

SPECIES.

P. Douglasii (*taxifolia*). The "Douglas Fir" of western N. America, also known as the "Vancouver" or "Oregon Douglas Fir," and the "Green Douglas Fir." 200–250 ft. high and a trunk of 8–12 ft. in diameter. Of great value as a timber tree.

P. D. cæsia. The "Grey Douglas Fir." A hardy variety, with greyish-green leaves.

PSORALEA (sor-ā-lē-a. Leguminosæ). Scurvy Pea. Evergreen flowering shrubs, grown mostly in the greenhouse, but in warm districts they may be cultivated in the open.

Cultivate in a soil compost of sandy peat and fibrous loam. Good drainage is essential. Pot in February or March and stand in the sunny greenhouse with plenty of ventilation. Prune in February. During the summer months water should be given freely, but after this period only moderate quantities should be given. Take cuttings of firm shoots 2–3 in. long and insert in moss and pure sand. Place these under a bell-glass and stand in a shady part of the greenhouse. This should be done in May or June.

SPECIES.

P. aculeata. Blue and white flowers in summer. Height 3 ft.

P. glandulosa. White and blue flowers. May–September. Height 4 ft.

P. pinnata. Blue flowers in summer. Height 6 ft.

PTELEA (tĕl′-e-a. Rutaceæ). Canada and eastern U.S.A. Deciduous low-growing trees with large trifoliate leaves and clusters of elm-like fruits in the autumn. Both leaves and twigs, when crushed, are aromatically suggestive of hops. Plant in ordinary garden soil.

Propagate by seeds and layers.

P. trifoliata. The "Hop Tree." Flowers greenish-white in June, exceedingly fragrant, reminding one of the best scented honeysuckle.

PTERIS (ter-is. Filices). Brake Fern. Greenhouse and hardy ferns. A large genus, comprising several of our most popular ferns for table decoration. *Longifolia* is the one chiefly grown for market purposes, and has become very popular for growing in small ornamental bowls.

Culture and Propagation. See ADIANTUM.

SPECIES.

P. cretica and its varieties, *albo-lineata*, *Mayi* and *Wimsetii*, are all good, and the last two named are crested.

P. ensiformis Victoriæ, nicely variegated.

P. quadriaurita, and its varieties *argyræa*, fronds having white centre, and *rubricaulis*, red centre.

P. serrulata, graceful, and its variety *cristata* with crested fronds.

P. tremula, and its varieties, *elegans*, *flaccida* and *Smithiana* are all excellent for decorative purposes.

PTEROCARYA (tero-car-i-a. Juglandaceæ). "Wing Nut." Deciduous, hardy trees, allied to Juglands (walnut), with ornamental pinnate leaves, and long slender spikes of small nuts.

Culture.—Plant in deep, moist, loamy soils.

Propagate by seed.

SPECIES.

P. caucasica (Persia and the Caucasus). An excellent tree for swampy ground. Leaves up to 2 ft. long.

P. c. dumosa. A dwarf, shrubby form with narrow leaves.

P. rhoifolia. The "Wing Nut" of Japan, with leaves about 1 ft. long. In nature a very large tree up to 100 ft. in height.

P. stenoptera (*sinensis*). A Chinese species of vigorous and rapid growth.

PTEROCELTIS (tĕr-ŏ-sel′-tis. Urticaceæ). A deciduous tree from Central China, of botanical interest only, the flowers being inconspicuous and of little beauty.

P. Tatarinowii. The only species.

PTEROCEPHALUS (ter-o-ceph-al-us. Dipsaceæ). *P. parnassii* is a low-growing plant with greyish leaves and heads of pink, scabious-like flowers in summer and autumn. It is easily propagated by cuttings or seed. 3 in. Greece.

PTEROSTYRAX (tĕr-ŏ-sti′-rax. Styraceæ). Deciduous trees or shrubs from China and Japan, formerly included under Halesia.

P. hispida (Japan and China), 20 ft. and upwards. Very graceful and attractive tree in June and July with pendulous panicles of white fragrant flowers.

PICKEREL WEED. *See* PONTEDERIA.

PUERARIA (pū-er-ār′-i-a. Leguminosæ). Fast-growing climbers from China and Japan. Plant in loam and peat.

Propagate by seeds and by cuttings.

SPECIES.

P. thunbergiana. The "Kudzu Vine" of China and Japan, with violet-purple flowers. Only half-hardy.

PULMONARIA (pul-mon-ā-ria. Boragineæ). Lungwort. A useful genus of hardy herbaceous perennials with hairy, white-spotted leaves that form dense tufts. They are useful for making pretty groups in shady woodland or for the mixed border. Increase by division or cuttings in spring or autumn and plant out in these seasons in permanent position in ordinary light, rich garden soil.

SPECIES.

The best of the species are:

P. angustifolia, of dwarfish habit with pretty violet-blue flowers in April and May, 9 in., and its bluer variety *azurea*.

P. officinalis, the common native plant known as Bethlehem Sage with reddish flowers that turn to blue.

P. saccharata, a very attractive species with red flowers and decorative foliage, 12 in.

Several species are now dealt with under Mertensia (*which see*).

PULTENÆA (pul-ten-e-a. Leguminosæ). Greenhouse evergreen flowering shrubs. Pot in March in 2 parts fibrous peat, 1 part equal proportions silver sand and charcoal, and stand in a light, airy greenhouse. The pots should be well drained and the plants set firmly. These points are essential. Water freely in summer, but moderately after this period, using only soft water. During the warmer weather the plants may be stood in the open during the daytime. Take cuttings of firm shoots in summer and insert in sandy soil under a bell-glass in a temperature of 55°–65°. Seeds may be sown in March or April on the surface of sandy peat. They should be placed under bell-glass in a temperature of 55°–65°.

SPECIES.

P. obcordata. Yellow, April. Height, 3 ft.

P. rosea. Pink, spring. Height, 1 ft.

P. stricta. Yellow, spring. Height, 3 ft.

P. villosa. Yellow, spring. Height, 3 ft.

PUMPKINS. *See* GOURDS.

PUMPS. Where it is desired to have cascades and pools of running water and there is no existing spring, the problem is difficult. A supply run from the water main is very expensive, and by far the best method is by means of pumps. These may be hand-worked or run by electricity. There is now on the market a type of electric pump which is fairly inexpensive, and capable of providing a running stream. The pump may be run from the public lighting supply or from the house-lighting set. It has a capacity of 150–650 gallons per hour, depending upon the pumping conditions. It is suitable for lifting water to a head of 50 ft. including a suction lift up to 22 ft. It possesses the advantage of being self-priming. The pump can be used to provide a running rock-garden cascade. A tank concealed in a part of the rock garden is utilised. Water flowing from it by gravity is returned by the pumps from the water supply at the lower end.

With this arrangement a float switch may be fitted to the tank, effecting a saving in power should the pumps deliver more water than is required by the stream.

PUNICA (pū-nica. Lythraceæ). Pomegranate. Deciduous trees or shrubs up to 25 ft. high, of great antiquity. It has been grown in the south of Europe, Persia, Palestine, etc., from very remote times, for its juicy refreshing fruit. The fruit is rarely borne in this country out of doors, but the tree is grown for its very attractive and distinguished-looking foliage, and beautiful scarlet blossoms, in summer and autumn.

Culture.—Plant against a south wall in loam and leaf-mould, adding grit if the loam is heavy.

Propagate by seeds, grafting and cuttings.

SPECIES AND VARIETIES.

P. granatum (Persia and Afghanistan),

the "Common Pomegranate." Very beautiful scarlet flowers from June to September.

P. g. albo-plena. Flowers double white.

P. g. rubro-plena. Flowers double red.

P. g. nana. A compact dwarf form, very free flowering.

PURPLE LOOSESTRIFE. *See* LYTHRUM.

PURSLANE. *See* PORTULACA.

PUSCHKINIA (Striped Squill). Liliaceæ. Hardy bulbs first introduced in 1810.

These can be grown in ordinary light sandy soil in any well-drained border or rockery. They have small hyacinth-like spikes with pretty pale blue flowers. The bulbs should be planted 4 in. deep and 1 in. apart in November, and protected with a covering of coconut fibre over the surface during the winter. When the flowers fade, the coconut fibre can be removed, as the sunshine on the surface soil will help to ripen the bulbs. Every two or three years they may need to be lifted and replanted.

They can be propagated by offsets or by seeds sown ⅛ in. deep in shallow, well-drained pans.

SPECIES.

P. scilloides (syn. *libanotica*). White striped with blue flowers in spring, 6–8 in.

P. s. compacta, dwarfer.

PUTTING GREEN. A putting green is a possibility in most gardens which have a stretch of lawn in them because the number and length of the holes may easily be varied to suit the size of the lawn available.

Most lawns, however level in appearance, are sufficiently undulating to provide varied and interesting runs from the tees to holes. The length of the holes may be varied from ten to, say, sixty feet; while, if the lawn is large enough, drives or full-length shots may be possible.

Plates for tees, and holes with numbered flags, can be purchased from any store, or, with a little ingenuity, can be made from sheet metal, or even cocoa tins and rods.

If a more hazardous course is required, mounds of earth arranged naturally, in the form of bunkers, may be introduced, and arranged to cover two or three holes.

All that is needed to play the game are two or three teeing irons and golf balls.

PYCNOSTACHYS (pik-nos-tak-is. Labiatæ). Greenhouse perennial. Sow the seeds in spring in a compost of loam, leaf-mould and sand and stand in the warm greenhouse. Give plenty of water during the growing period, but little at other times.

Propagate by division cf roots in spring.

PYRETHRUM - DOUBLE

Pyrethrums are showy flowers useful for cutting. They enjoy a rich sandy soil, well drained, with plenty of sunshine, and they resent disturbance.

SPECIES.

P. Dawei. Blue flowers in winter. Height, 4–6 ft.

PYRACANTHA (pī-ra-kan'-tha. Rosaceæ). "Evergreen Thorns," some of which were formerly placed under Cratægus and Cotoneaster. Flowers white, followed by an abundance of yellow or scarlet fruit. They thrive in almost any soil and if planted against east or north walls or fences reach to about 15–20 ft.

Propagate by seeds, and by cuttings of half-hardy leafy twigs taken in late summer.

SPECIES.

P. angustifolia (Cotoneaster angustifolia). China. Leaves narrow. Clusters of orange-yellow fruits throughout the winter, on into spring.

P. coccinea (Cratœgus pyracantha). South Europe. Fruits brilliant coral red.

P. c. Lalandei. The well-known and popular variety with orange-red berries and fruit in abundance.

P. Gibbsii (China). Perhaps the finest of all. Fruit or berries vivid red, persisting until March.

P. G. yunnanensis (crenulata yunnanensis). A horizontally-branched variety, with an abundance of berries, orange-red, ageing to bright crimson, retained until the turn of the year.

P. Rogersiana (crenulata Rogersiana). China. Of bushy habit, with berries similar to the preceding.

P. R. flava. Berries chrome-yellow.

PYRENEAN CLARY. *See* HORMINUM.

PYRENEAN PRIMROSE. *See* RAMONDIA.

PYRETHRUM. *See* CHRYSANTHEMUM *and* GOLDEN FEATHER.

PYROLA (py-rō-la. Ericaceæ). Winter-green. Dwarf-growing hardy perennial herbs of the Heath family with spikes of flowers like those of Lily of the Valley, that make pretty garden plants worthy of a place in the rockery or border edging.

Propagate by seeds sown in summer or by division in March, and plant in gritty, peaty loam in a semi-shaded site.

SPECIES.

P. rotundifolia, with racemes of sweet-scented white flowers, is the best known.

P. r. arenaria, found on sandy sea-shores, is dwarfer and differs from the former through having several bracts below the inflorescence.

P. chlorantha, elliptica, minor and *secunda,* with yellow, white, red and white flowers respectively, are all good summer-blooming plants, 3–6 in.

PYRUS (pīr'-us. Rosaceæ).

GROUP I—MALUS (FLOWERING CRABS).

The Flowering Crabs are quite in the first rank among ornamental trees, few, if any, being more beautiful, when they are smothered in April and May with their exquisite blossoms. They are quite hardy and very adaptable. They thrive in good garden soil.

Propagate by grafting on to the various apple and crab stocks used by nurserymen for grafting garden apples.

SPECIES AND VARIETIES.

P. aldenhamensis. Hybrid. One of the most beautiful of flowering crabs, with foliage, flowers, fruit, and wood all tinged red in varying degrees of tone. Very similar to *P. Eleyi.*

P. Eleyi. A first-class hybrid between *P. Niedzwetzkyana* and *P. spectabilis*, with larger flowers than *P. Niedzwetzkyana*, and opening later than that species. An attractive soft-red colour. Fruit 1½ in. long, red-purple, resembling large Morello cherries. Young foliage of a coppery colour. The Royal Horticultural Society have honoured this very beautiful hybrid with an Award of Merit, when in flower, a First-class Certificate, when in fruit, and also the Award of Garden Merit.

P. floribunda (*Malus floribunda; pulcherrima*). Japan. 20–30 ft. Thought to be a hybrid from the Siberian Crab and perhaps *P. Toringo.* Quite one of the most beautiful, and by many regarded as *the* most beautiful of all flowering Crabs. Its beauty is at its height when half the pale pink flowers 1½ in. across are expanded, while the other half are in the bud stage, and of a rich crimson. May and June.

P. f. atrosanguinea, is more richly coloured, and the foliage a brighter green. Habit somewhat pendent.

P. Malus. The Wild Crab of W. Europe and N. W. Asia; and although not worth a place in the garden is of interest as being the origin of the cultivated garden apples, and is the type of the Malus group. The following are the most distinct varieties:

P. M. Dartmouth. Flowers white, followed by plum-like fruits covered with reddish-purple bloom.

P. M. John Downie. One of the finest of all Crabs. In spring the branches are laden with large white flowers, succeeded by a profusion of clusters of bright orange-scarlet fruit over 1 in. in length.

The Whitebeam members of this group, do not possess the floral beauty of the Crabs, their flowers being mostly dull white and somewhat fugacious. Their chief attraction is when the fruiting stage is reached, the fruit being in large clusters, and of a bright red colour. The Mountain Ashes are distinguished from all other Pyrus by their much-divided leaves, which impart to them a gracefulness that is usually lacking in other varieties.

They all do well in chalky or limestone districts.

SPECIES.

P. alnifolia (Korea and Japan). 20 ft. A very attractive species bearing corymbs of oval bright red fruits. The Alder-like leaves become finely coloured in autumn.

P. americana. The "Mountain Ash" of

The Crab Apple with purple foliage and bright fruits—Pyrus Eleyi—adds colour to the shrub border.

America is a near relative of our own "Rowan Tree," and bears clusters of bright red fruit.

P. Aria. The "Common White Beam" of Britain is a handsome native tree, 30–50 ft. high, sometimes attaining to bush form only. Leaves bright green, vivid white beneath, very attractive when loaded with its bright red or scarlet fruit. Thrives in chalky districts and in and around large towns.

P. Aucuparia. The "Mountain Ash" or "Rowan Tree," native of many parts of this country, more particularly in the north.

P. A. pendula. The "Weeping Mountain Ash."

P. Sorbus (*P. domestica*). The "Service Tree" of S. and E. Europe, and also of this country, although very rare here. 30–50 ft. and upwards. In some parts of this country it has exceeded 60 ft. In Surrey it has exceeded 70 ft. While less attractive as an ornamental tree than its ally, the "Mountain Ash," it has beautiful foliage of a soft green, colouring well in the autumn.

GROUP III.—PEARS.

P. communis. The "Wild Pear" of Europe and N. Asia, and although found growing wild in Britain, it is regarded as a doubtful native; 30–40 ft., sometimes up to 60 ft. Of no garden merit, but of interest as being the origin of our garden pears. Its timber is excellent, being heavy, tough and very durable. Flowers are white, 1–1½ in. across.

P. germanica. The "Medlar." *See* MEDLAR.

P. salicifolia. A very beautiful and ornamental tree with silvery willow-like leaves and white or cream-coloured flowers, opening simultaneously during April. After the flowers fall, the leaves retain their charming silvery appearance for some weeks, ultimately becoming green on the upper surface. The fruit is of no special consequence.

GROUP IV—ARONIA OR CHOKEBERRIES.

P. arbutifolia. The "Red Chokeberry" of eastern N. America. 5–10 ft. Flowers white, or rosy-white, ½ in. across, produced in late May, followed by clusters of scarlet berries, persisting well into the winter. Foliage turns a brilliant crimson in autumn.

See also APPLE, PEAR.

Q

QUAKING GRASS. *See* BRIZA.

QUASSIA. *See* FORMULÆ.

QUERCUS (quer′-kus. Cupuliferæ). Oak. A very large and important genus of deciduous and evergreen trees and shrubs. Two are natives of Britain, *Q. pedunculata* and *Q. sessiliflora* and produce very valuable timber. Of the 300 or so species known to botanists, over 60 are in cultivation.

Culture.—Plant in October in deep, rich, loamy soil. They will prosper on chalk if the loam is deep, and if the soil is of a woodland nature so much the better.

Propagation of the rare varieties is by grafting, otherwise seed is the usual and best method of increase. The acorns ripen in the autumn (of the same year that they are formed), and should be sown as soon as ripe. If autumn-sowing is inconvenient, the acorns must be kept in sand, or they will soon lose their vitality if allowed to become dry. The young trees should have the lower branches gradually removed, and the leading shoots kept clean.

EVERGREEN OAKS.

Q. Ilex. The "Holm Oak," or common "Evergreen Oak" of the Mediterranean region. One of the finest evergreen trees capable of being grown outside in this country. It is really a noble tree, attaining to a height of 70–90 ft., with an abundance of foliage. The young leaves are covered with a whitish down, which soon falls away from the upper surface, leaving it a dark glossy green. The underside of the leaf is grey, and remains so, until the leaves fall, during May and June. The shedding of the leaves at that time of year is its one defect, especially in gardens which are kept neat and tidy. It stands clipping and pruning well, and may be clipped into pyramids or other shapes. It also makes a beautiful hedge if carefully trimmed. The Holm Oak likes a warm, rather light, well-drained loam, although it will grow in almost any kind of soil. It thrives in warm districts better than in cold ones, and is particularly happy in maritime districts.

Q. suber. The "Cork Oak," 60 ft. Its bark is thick and corky, and from it is made the cork of common use. The acorns of this species are nearly 1 in. long, and take two seasons to reach maturity. This latter peculiarity and the corky nature of its bark, distinguish *Q. suber* from all other evergreen oaks.

QUAKING GRASS

Quaking Grass, a charming ornamental grass for the flower border and vases.

DECIDUOUS OAKS.

Q. Cerris. The "Turkey Oak" of S. Europe and Asia Minor. 120 ft. and upwards. Very hardy and quick growing, and of elegant habit. Thrives well in this country, and is excellent on chalky soils. As a timber tree it is inferior to the "English Oak."

Q. coccinea. The "Scarlet Oak" of N. America. 70–80 ft. Leaves up to 6 in. long, turning to a brilliant red in autumn and remaining on the tree until November and even into December.

Q. c. splendens. "Knap Hill Scarlet Oak." The finest form in regard to magnificence of autumn colour, but of slower growth than the preceding.

Q. palustris. The "Pin Oak" of the eastern U.S.A. 70–100 ft. Leaves glossy green on both surfaces, often turning deep red or scarlet in autumn, but inferior in this respect to *Q. coccinea.*

Q. pedunculata. The "Common" or "English Oak." Up to 100 ft. One of the longest-lived of all trees. Highly valuable as a timber tree. Its wood is extremely durable, and for floors, doors, panelling, and general house-building is still unsurpassed, and, of course, formerly it was in great demand for ship-building. *Q. pedunculata* is very widely distributed over Europe to Asia Minor. The following is one of the most distinct varieties:

Q. p. concordia. A slow-growing form with bright yellow leaves.

QUINCE. *See* CYDONIA.

QUINCUNX. A method of arranging fruit trees for planting, used in large orchards. Four trees form a square and the fifth tree is planted in the centre.

QUISQUALIS (quis-qua-lis. Combretaceæ). Rangoon Creeper. Climbing, deciduous flowering stove shrub.

Pot in February and cultivate in a compost of two parts loam, one part peat and a little sand, in well-drained pots or in a bed where the shoots can be trained to climb. After flowering the shoots should be pruned fairly close. During the summer, plenty of water should be given, and the plants syringed daily, but at other times the plants should be kept nearly dry. When taking cuttings of young shoots, a part of the old stem should be attached. Insert in sandy soil under a bell-glass in a temperature of 75°–85° in spring.

SPECIES.

Q. indica. White flowers, turning red in summer. Fragrant. Height, 10–15 ft.

R

RADISH (*Raphanus sativus*). From the time of the Egyptians and the Ancient Greeks, the Radish has been a most popular vegetable, but there is no definite record of the actual date of its introduction to this country. The historic herbalist, Gerarde, tells of its cultivation in the time of Queen Elizabeth, but the varieties then in use were undoubtedly much coarser and of poorer quality than the many fine salad types which are obtainable to-day.

The radish as a garden plant has been derived from the wild species whose native habitat is scattered over the temperate regions of Europe and Asia.

Culture.—Radishes, to be crisp and sweet, must be grown quickly, and the soil should be light, warm and moderately rich. As with most other root crops, the addition to the soil of fresh manure shortly before sowing is inadvisable, as it induces the formation of coarse, badly-shaped roots.

It is possible to obtain a supply of radishes all the year round if facilities are available for growing the winter crops under glass. Elaborate structures are not necessary, and a simple hot bed covered with 6 in. of good soil and surmounted by a frame will suffice.

The seeds may be sown in shallow drills 6–9 in. apart, or broadcast and lightly covered with more soil. In the latter case, the seedlings should be thinned to 3 in. apart when 1 in. or so high to ensure all of them obtaining sufficient light and air.

No coddling should be attempted, and plenty of fresh air should be admitted on all fine days. During severe weather, and when sharp frosts appear imminent, the lights should be covered at night with sacking, or old bracken, or straw.

Some of the better sorts may be pulled for use about 20 days from sowing, and it is therefore better to make small successional sowings, and have a constant supply of young crisp roots than to depend upon only two or three large sowings.

Following the sowings on hot beds, cold frames may be brought into use as the season advances, and in March the first sowings may be made outside.

Owing to their short period of growth, radishes may with advantage be sown in rows between the more permanent crops. Some growers also adopt the practice of sowing a few radishes with the slow germinating seeds, such as parsnips and onions. As the radishes appear in a few days they clearly mark the line of the drills, and enable hoeing to commence at an early date.

In hot, dry soil, summer radishes often show a tendency to "bolt" or run to seed, and where this trouble is experienced, seed beds for summer crops should be selected in deeply-dug soil with a northern aspect.

The varieties, Black Spanish and Winter Rose, sometimes listed as Winter Radishes, should be sown in July and August, but lifted when mature and stored in sand, like other root crops, until required for use.

VARIETIES.

FORCING: Wood's Early Frame; French Breakfast; Sparkler; Delicacy.

GENERAL USE: Long Cardinal; Early Rose; Olive-shaped Scarlet.

WINTER: Black Spanish; China Rose.

Uses.—Generally sliced raw in salads or eaten with salt as a single dish.

RAFFIA. A material used for tying plants, similar to bass except that it is the fibre of a different tree from that of bass.

RAGGED ROBIN. *See* LYCHNIS.

RAGWORT. *See* SENECIO.

RAIN-WATER. Has a distinct advantage over tap-water for garden purposes, in that it is more nearly at the temperature of the atmosphere, and contains a percentage of nitric acid which is beneficial to the plants. It also contains less lime than tap-water.

RAMONDIA (ră-mŏnd-ia. Gesneraceæ). Pyrenean Primrose. Charming hardy perennials, useful for shady nooks in the rock garden or border. They form compact plants with rosettes of crinkly leaves close to the ground, with short flower stems.

Propagate by seeds sown under glass in spring, or by division of well-established plants only, as the seedlings grow slowly, and small plants do not divide successfully In good sandy loam and peat, and well-watered, Ramondias will form interesting subjects in crevices in the rock garden; should be planted on a northern aspect.

SPECIES.

R. pyrenaica, a dwarf plant found in the valleys of the Pyrenees, with orange-centred, purple-violet flowers in summer, and its very rare white variety *alba*, are the best of the genus.

R. Heldreichii and *serbica*, of which there is a variety with darker flowers—*s. Nathaliæ*—resemble pyrenaica in colouring. 3–6 in.

RANDIA (ran-di-a. Rubiaceæ). Stove evergreen flowering shrubs of climbing habit. Cultivate in a compost of loam, peat, well-decayed manure and charcoal. Pot in February or March in pots or beds in which good drainage has been assured, and place in the plant stove. Prune in February or March. Give a moderate amount of water in winter, but freely afterwards, and except when in bloom, the plants should be syringed daily. Healthy plants in flower may be given weak doses of liquid manure. Young plants give better blooms. Take cuttings of firm young side-shoots in spring and insert in sandy peat under a bell glass in a temperature of 75°–85°.

SPECIES.

R. macrantha. Yellow, summer. 20–30 ft.

RANDOM PAVING. The name given to formal rectangular pieces of stone which are laid in a random fashion, i.e., not coursed. It differs from crazy paving in that the slabs have right angled sides. Many types of stone are suitable for this kind of paving, perhaps the commonest, although not the cheapest, is York paving. The cost of paving is governed chiefly by railway and cartage rates, so that if local stone is obtained this is always preferable to that from a distance. In any case local stone is more likely to be in harmony with the house and garden buildings than that from a different county. A rough guide for quantities is that a ton of paving will lay from 10–12 square yards of surface area. The variance is of course due to the thickness of the stone. A good average thickness is 1½–2 in. (*See* PATHWAYS.)

RANUNCULUS (ra-nŭn-culus. Ranunculaceæ). Crowfoot. Buttercup. A large genus of annual and perennial hardy plants that range from the stately florist's forms to the lowly buttercup. When speaking of Ranunculus as a garden flower, the florist's forms are meant. The tall plants have now gone out of general favour as cut flowers.

Culture.—Most of the species thrive in partial shade in moist, deep, rich loam, rather heavy for the border plants, but with sand and leaf-mould for the alpines. The dwarf growers are splendid for the moraine, when grown in loam with sand, and well-decayed animal manure. *Propagate* the perennials by division and leave the plants in position for several years. The tuberous-rooted species should be planted with the claws downwards 2 or 3 in. deep and a few inches apart, early in spring. Surround them with sand and charcoal. The annuals, of course are propagated by seeds.

Species.—The florist's varieties are chiefly derived from *asiaticus*, a pretty plant with single flowers of various colours. Its varieties raised from seed are often double, and are divided for identification into three classes—the French, the tallest and largest-flowered; the Persian, providing the finest blooms that are first to flower; and the Turban, combining qualities of both. They may be propagated by offsets from the tuberous roots, and like a soil composed of two parts of loam to one each of leaf-mould, sharp sand and manure. If the natural soil is unsuitable, it is best to make up a bed and allow it to settle before planting. Planting may be done in October, provided protection is given, or more safely in February. The plants must never be allowed to become dry, but watering must be done carefully after the sun is off the beds. For really perfect blooms they should be shaded by an awning, but this is unnecessary when growing ordinary flowers for cutting. The tubers should be lifted when the leaves turn yellow. Named varieties can be obtained from a seedsman.

Other good border plants of this family are *R. acris flore pleno*, the familiar yellow Bachelor's Buttons (the double form of the common buttercup), and *aconitifolius flore pleno*, a double form of *aconitifolius*, with white flowers in early summer, which is the old favourite, Fair Maids of Kent, otherwise known as "Fair Maids of France,"

or White Bachelor's Buttons. 18–30 in.
There are several useful rock-garden plants
in the genus, such as *alpestris*, three-lobed
leaves and pure white flowers; *amplexicaulis*, large snow-white flowers with golden
centres; *glacialis*, a plant from Northern
icy regions, that reminds one of melting
ice, having thick fleshy leaves and rosy-
tinted white flowers on semi-procumbent
stems.

R. montanus, with golden flowers.

R. parnassifolius, a rare species with
woolly leaves and white flowers.

R. pyrenæus, narrow leaves, branching
stems bearing white flowers, 6–9 in., are
useful for the border, while *R. aquatilis*
(white) and *Lingua*, the Greater Spear-
wort (yellow) are useful in the water
garden. All the plants bloom throughout
the summer.

RAOULIA (rah-oul-ia. Compositæ).
The Raoulias form compact mats of tiny
foliage, grey in the case of *R. australis*, and
bright emerald green in *glabra*. The
flowers are inconspicuous. They are useful
for covering bulbs perhaps, and *R. australis*
has some decorative value. Coming from
New Zealand and Tasmania, they may
succumb in winter, unless planted in a
well-drained, dry, sunny place.

RAPE CAKE. The residue from the
seeds of cotton, linseed and rape—after
the extraction of oils—is often used as
manure. Rape dust contains about 5 per
cent. of nitrogen, with a little potash and
phosphate. It is generally used as an
ordinary nitrate manure.

RAPHANUS. *See* RADISH.

RAPHIOLEPIS (raf-i-o-lĕp'-is. Rosaceæ). Indian Hawthorn. Evergreen
shrubs, fairly hardy, with sweet-scented
flowers and leathery leaves.

Culture.—Plant in loam, or loam and
peat, with some grit or sand.

Propagate by cuttings of the half-
ripened shoots placed in sand under a
bell-glass in a cold frame, and by seeds
sown in frame.

SPECIES AND HYBRIDS.

R. Delacourei (*R. japonica* + *R. indica*),
3–5 ft. A delightful, pink-flowered hybrid.
All but hardy, except in cold districts,
where it needs wall protection. May.

R. indica (*salicifolia*), China. Narrow
leaves and pink flowers. A more graceful

shrub than the next species, but less
hardy. March–June.

R. japonica (*umbellata; ovata*), Japan
and Korea, 4–6 ft. Dark green, leathery
leaves, and fragrant white flowers ¾ in.
across during June. Quite hardy near
London, but usually likes a fairly sheltered
spot.

The Raphiolepis are seen at their best
in seaside districts.

RASPBERRY. *Rubus Idæus.* The
wild Raspberry which is a native of this
country and of Europe, North Asia and
Japan has been the source of cultivated
varieties of this fruit. It is frequently to
be found in woods in this country.

Soil.—The Raspberry will do well in any
soil which has been deeply worked and
which is not too stiff and heavy. Sandy
and peaty soils are excellent, but should
be well enriched with manure, as this
fruit is a coarse feeder. Heavy soils
should be lightened with sand, lime,
rubble and decayed garden refuse.

Situation.—Any situation except a most
bleak one is suitable.

Planting.—Raspberries should be planted
in rows. A stake should be firmly secured
at either end and wires stretched at a
height of 2 ft. and 4 ft. The canes are
tied to these. The rows should be 5 or
6 ft. apart, and the plants 3 ft. apart in
the rows. The best time for planting is
October or November, and if one-year-old
canes are being put in they should be
planted in groups of three about 9 in. apart
instead of singly.

Pruning.—Pruning is a simple operation.
The first year after planting, cut each
young cane down to within 4 in. of the
ground as soon as growth commences.
The following autumn, cut away all canes
save the four strongest, which must be left
to bear next year's fruit. In subsequent
years, prune in October, cutting away all
the previous year's wood which has
fruited, and tying in the strongest six
young shoots. The above instructions
apply to summer-fruiting varieties. On
some soils, more particularly light sandy
ones, it is possible to make some varieties
bear on current season's wood. In this case
the clumps should be cut down to ground
level in spring, before growth commences.

Manuring.—The importance of manuring

prior to planting has been mentioned. It is advisable in subsequent seasons to give a mulch annually. This should consist of well-decayed manure, and should be applied in spring. Failing this an application of sulphate of potash should be given in early spring at the rate of 2 oz. to the square yard.

Propagation.—This is done by means of digging up suckers and offsets. Care

HOLE CAUSED BY LARVA

LARVA

RASPBERRY BEETLE

The Raspberry Beetle lays its eggs in May on the flowers. An inspection of the canes then will save trouble with the fruit.

should be taken not to injure the roots of the parent plant. October is the best time for removal.

Pests.—Raspberry Beetle.

VARIETIES.

Autumn-Fruiting.

Lloyd George: Probably the best raspberry of all. May be cut to the ground each spring and treated as an autumn-fruiting variety, or may be treated as a summer-fruiting variety. Very vigorous and fertile.

Hailsham: Large-fruited variety of deep colour. Vigorous and fertile.

Summer-Fruiting.

Lloyd George (*see above*).

Park Lane: The finest-flavoured variety, but is too soft for market culture.

Red Cross: An early variety with large fruits of an excellent flavour.

Royal: One of the largest-fruited rasp-

berries in cultivation. Excellent flavour. Vigorous and a good cropper.

RASPBERRY BEETLE (*Byturus tomentosus*). DESCRIPTION. *Adult.*—About ⅛ of an inch long, black in colour but densely clothed with golden scales. These however become somewhat bleached with age, giving the beetle a greyish appearance. *Larva.*—About ¼ of an inch long, creamy-white, with dark brown patches on the back. Three pairs of legs, on the first three segments, and no more. The last segment is drawn out into two horn-like processes.

LIFE-HISTORY.—The adult beetles hatch out in the spring and are first to be found on hawthorn and apple blossom. Then they migrate to the raspberries and loganberries, where they may do much damage by eating out the buds and generally damaging the flowers. As the fruit forms, eggs are laid, and on hatching out the young "maggot" lives for a period on the berry before eating its way in. Having entered, it destroys the "plug," causing the fruit to lose its firmness and keeping qualities. When the berries are ripe the full-grown larva falls to the ground where it pupates, remaining in the soil until the following winter.

METHODS OF CONTROL.—The old method of jarring the canes over tarred boards has given place to dusting with derris preparations just as the beetle appears on the buds.

RASPBERRY MOTH (*Lampronia rubiella*). DESCRIPTION. *Adult.*—The moth is a little more than ¼ in. in expanse, chocolate-brown in colour, with yellowish spot on the upper wing. *Larva.*—Pink in colour with a black head, and about ¼ in. in length when full grown.

LIFE-HISTORY.—The moth hatches out in May or early June and lays its eggs in the blossom; these hatch out in from 7 to 9 days and the young caterpillars feed for a short time upon the blossoms, but do no great damage at this period. About the beginning of July they crawl or let themselves down to the ground, where they spin a cocoon round themselves wherein they remain till the spring. They come out during warm days in March, crawl up the canes and enter the stems through the buds. Here they live till full-grown, with the result that the canes become sickly and eventually die. Pupation takes place within the cane, the moth appearing about the time the buds open.

METHODS OF CONTROL.—Cut out and burn all canes inclined to wither and, as a precaution, in late winter following smear a grease-banding preparation on the canes and supports. This may appear a laborious method, but it gives excellent results, as the young caterpillars on coming out from their winter quarters stick to the grease. A number may be killed by a thorough cultivation of the ground in the autumn.

RATS. See SOIL PESTS.

RATTAN PALM. See CALAMUS.

REDBUD. See CERCIS.

RED HOT POKER. See KNIPHOFIA.

RED VALERIAN. See CENTRANTHUS.

RED SPIDER (*Trombididæ*). These mites are to be found both in glasshouses and out-of-doors and though there are several species the damage done to plant life is very similar. By the constant rasping of the leaf tissues and absorption of the sap the foliage becomes pale and sickly and may drop off. As a rule the winter is passed in the egg stage, though one or two species hibernate in the adult stage. As soon as the weather becomes warm in the spring and the buds open, the eggs begin to hatch and the adults wake up. Those that have hatched from the egg grow quickly, mature and lay more eggs in the autumn, whereas those that have passed the winter as adults give rise to a fresh generation which remains in the adult stage throughout the next winter.

METHOD OF CONTROL.—Lime-sulphur is an excellent control for all members of the mite tribe. There may be difficulties in its application to such trees as peach trees in hot-houses, then a mixture of ordinary flour and water can be used.

REDWOOD. See SEQUOIA.

REHMANNIA (reh-man-ni-a. Scrophulariaceæ). A half-hardy perennial of easy culture, which flowers within nine months of sowing the seed. Height, 3–4 ft. Clear bright pink tubular flowers are carried at the leaf axils; the throat of the flower is somewhat paler.

Cultivation.—Sow in autumn or early spring in gentle heat; prick off the seedlings when large enough and pot them on as they require it. They should be

flowered in a 48 or 32 size pot in a compost composed of loam, leaf-mould and sand, which has been enriched with some old manure. Use rough leaf-mould as drainage.

Species.—*R. angulata*, red and orange; *R. elata*, rose purple and yellow.

REINECKIA (ri-nek-i-a. Liliaceæ.) The only species is a hardy herbaceous perennial with ornamental foliage.

Propagate by division of the creeping rhizomes and plant in any good soil. Suitable for borders or rockeries. Lift every three or four years and water plentifully in hot weather.

SPECIES.

R. carnea, with flesh-pink fragrant flowers in April. 2–6 in.

REINWARDTIA (rin-wardt-i-a. Liniaceæ). Winter Flax. Stove or greenhouse evergreen flowering shrubs of dwarf habit. Very ornamental. Pot in spring and grow in a compost of loam, leaf-mould and sand. Place in the warm stove or greenhouse, but during the warm weather they may stand in a sunny, cold frame. Water moderately in winter, but freely afterwards. Syringe twice daily from spring to autumn. When in flower, weak stimulants may be given. For bushy growth nip off the young shoots in June. Take cuttings in spring and insert in sandy soil in a close frame.

SPECIES.

R. tetragyna. Yellow, winter. 3 ft.

R. trigyna (syn. *Linum trigynum*). Yellow, autumn. Height, 2–4 ft.

RESEDA (rĕs-e-da. Resedaceæ). Mignonette. A genus of hardy annual, biennial and perennial herbs, of which only a few are of any value, the best being the old favourite for herb gardens, *Reseda odorata*, the sweet-scented mignonette.

Culture.—The perennial mignonette is commonly grown as an annual, seed being sown in the sun in spring, and thinned out to 12 in. apart when large enough. For pot culture sow under glass in spring or autumn in a compost of two parts of loam to one of manure and some sand. Thin to four plants in a pot and grow near the glass or in a frame. For garden plants use ordinary soil with some lime rubble.

SPECIES.

R. alba, a white-flowered, silvery-leaved biennial, May; and *R. odorata*, yellow or white, the Italian originator of the popular scented plants and its several varieties, with white, golden or red spikes of flowers. *R. o. Machet* is the form now most commonly in use for pot culture.

R. Luteola, the Dyer's Weed, yellow, is sometimes confused with Dyer's Woad, *Isatis*, beloved of the ancient Britons.

The species provide flowers for cutting throughout the summer and until late in the autumn, and *R. odorata*, on account of its fragrance, is widely cultivated in the South of France for supplying winter flowers for the North.

REST HARROW. *See* ONONIS.

RESTIO (res'-ti-o. Restiaceæ). A tender South African evergreen shrub with graceful arching growth, 4–6 ft. long, known as "Mare's Tail."

RESTREPIA (res-trep-i-a. Orchidaceæ). Named in honour of J. Restrep, a naturalist. Greenhouse epiphytal orchids. A genus very similar to Pleurothallis, and requiring the same cultural treatment.

SPECIES.

R. elegans, purple, yellow and white; *maculata*, yellow, purple and crimson; *pandurata*, white and crimson.

RETAINING WALL. *See* WALLS.

RETINOSPORA. *See* CUPRESSUS *and* THUYA.

RHABDOTHAMNUS (rab-do-thamnus. Gesneriaceæ). A monotypic genus from New Zealand.

R. Solandri. Dwarf, slender, small-leaved shrub with handsome tubular orange, red-striped flowers throughout the summer.

RHAMNUS (rhăm'-nus. Rhamnaceæ). Buckthorn. Evergreen and deciduous trees and shrubs of but little garden value. Flowers of scarcely any beauty. The fruits or berries are more interesting, becoming reddish as they ripen. Some species yield yellow and green dyes, and the bark and fruit of others possess laxative properties.

Culture.—Plant in ordinary soil.

Propagation is best by seed, also by layers. Cuttings of some of the species will root, others are difficult.

SPECIES.

R. Alaternus (S.W. Europe). Evergreen shrub up to 10 ft. Leaves smooth, glossy

green. Berries black. Cuttings root readily. Very hardy.

R. californica. The " Californian Buckthorn," 15 ft. Berries purple. Evergreen.

RHAPHITHAMNUS (rhaf-i-tham'-nus. Verbenaceæ). Evergreen shrubs suitable for mild climates by the sea. Inland it needs the protection of a south or west wall. Flowers pale blue in April and May; succeeded by attractive blue berries. In Cornwall it has exceeded 20 ft. and is nearly as high in Sussex. It likes a deep, loamy soil.

Propagate by cuttings, and by seeds.

R. cyanocarpus, the only species.

RHAPIS (rha-pis. Palmaceæ). From *rhapis*, a needle, referring to the sharp-pointed leaves. Greenhouse palms, leaves fan shaped. China, 1774.

Culture.—See KENTIA.

SPECIES.

R. flabelliformis, 3–4 ft. (green), and its variety, *variegata* (green and white).

RHAZYA (ras-ya. Apocynaceæ). Hardy evergreen sub-shrub, similar to the Periwinkle (Vinca), but more erect in habit. Planted in spring it will grow in any ordinary soil on sunny, well-drained slopes or in the rock garden. Sow seeds in spring, using shallow pans for the purpose.

SPECIES.

R. orientalis, blue, in late summer. Height, 9–12 in.

RHEUM. *See* RHUBARB.

RHEXIA (rhex-i-a. Melastomaceæ). Deer Grass. Meadow Beauty. Erect herbs and sub-shrubs increased by division in spring. Plant in sandy peat or loam and leaf-mould.

SPECIES.

R. ciliosa. Purple. Perennial. Summer. 1–1½ ft.

R. virginica. Purple. Summer. 6–12 in.

RHIPSALIS. *See* CACTUS.

RHODANTHE (ro-dan-thee. Compositæ). Australia. Elegant daisy-like everlasting flowers in shades of rose. Sow in sandy soil April, outdoors, or in March under glass for transplanting. *R. maculata* and *R. Manglesii* are the half-hardy annual species usually grown. 1–1½ ft. Good for drying.

RHODOCHITON (rho-do-ki-ton. Scrophulariaceæ). Greenhouse evergreen climber. Pot March to May in a compost of loam, leaf-mould and silver sand, and place in well-drained pot or boxes or in the beds or borders where the shoots can be trained up trellis, or the rafters of the greenhouse. Water plentifully in summer, but moderately at other times. When the plants are in flower, stimulants should be given. Cut back moderately in February. Sow seeds in ordinary soil in March, and transplant when 1 in. high, allowing one to a 2–3 in. pot. Take cuttings of shoots in summer and insert in sandy soil under a bell-glass.

SPECIES.

R. volubile (syn. *Lophospermum atrosanguineum*). Red, purple, summer. 10–15 ft.

RHODODENDRON (Ericaceæ). Greenhouse and hardy evergreen and deciduous flowering shrubs. The genus Azalea is now included with the Rhododendron. *R. ponticum*, parent of hardy kinds, first occurred in 1763. *R. indica* (Indian Azalea) in 1808.

They vary in height from 6 in. to 50 ft. and the colours include practically every colour in flower life except a brilliant blue.

The foliage of rhododendrons is ornamental and of very great variety, so much so, in fact, that annually at the Royal Horticultural Society's Show, an exhibit is made of rhododendron leaves showing both the top and underneath sides of each variety of leaf, and this exhibit never fails to attract attention from visitors.

The rhododendron is so important in the gardening world to-day that special attention to the many species of rhododendrons, including the cream of the new species introduced from China, Tibet, Burma and by such skilful and discriminating collectors as Farrer, Forrest, Rock and Kingdom Ward, during the last few years, is well worth while. These collectors are sent out from this country by a syndicate of enthusiastic amateurs, and our gardens to-day owe much to their efforts.

SPECIES.

R. arboreum (Arboreum Series). Himalayas. 30–40 ft. Only hardy in the south and west. Parent of many of the well-known hardy hybrids. Colours range from white to deep ruby-red. The following are some of the most distinct varieties:

R. bullatum (Edgeworthii Series). China.

One of the most beautiful species, being the Chinese form of Edgeworthii. Leaves bright green and handsomely veined, with a thick woolly tomentum beneath. Flowers 3 in. across, white flushed pink, and deliciously fragrant, during May and June. Only suited for the warmer parts of the country. Very beautiful in a cold greenhouse. The habit is straggling and may reach to a height of about 8 ft. Flowers freely in a young state.

R. calostrotum (Saluenense Series). Burma. Beautiful dwarf species, about 1 ft., with attractive grey leaves and bright magenta-purple flowers during April, and sometimes again in the early autumn. An excellent shrub for the rock garden. May be kept quite dwarf by pinching. Likes moisture. Quite hardy.

R. ferrugineum (Ferrugineum Series). 3–5 ft. The Alpine Rose of Switzerland, with small, rosy-crimson flowers. A good rock-garden plant. Best in a mass.

R. hippophæoides (Lapponicum Series). 2-3 ft. Flowers lavender-blue, in great profusion. Easily grown in moist loam and sand. Best in a group. Award of Garden Merit, R.H.S.

R. keleticum (Saluenense Series). An ideal rock garden rhododendron, with deep purple-crimson flowers.

R. ponticum (Ponticum Series). Spain and Portugal and Asia Minor. The well-known pale purple rhododendron, naturalised in various parts of this country.

R. racemosum (Virgatum). China. A very desirable rhododendron with small grey-green leaves, and numerous bright pink flowers (sometimes white) during May. There are two forms, one growing to 3-4 ft., and the other, a more recent introduction, and sent home by Forrest from China under No. 19,404, only grows a few inches high. The flowers are a brighter pink, and very freely produced about the end of April and the early part of May. Valuable for the rock garden or front part of a border. Very effective in a mass.

Azalea Series of Rhododendrons.

EVERGREEN SECTION.

Dwarf, slow-growing shrubs, with masses of gorgeously-coloured flowers, of the greatest value for rock gardens.

R. amœna. Japan. Very slow-growing,

up to 3 ft. The flowers are bright rosy purple.

R. balsaminæflora (*rosæflora*). Japan. A dwarf, spreading bush with very small leaves, and double flowers of a beautiful salmon-red colour.

R. ledifolia. China and Japan. 5–6 ft. Flowers white, fragrant, very freely produced in May.

R. macrantha. China and Japan. Up to 6 ft. Flowers deep salmon.

R. malvatica. Semi-evergreen shrub with flowers of a pale crimson.

R. Maxwellii. 4 ft. Flowers carmine, 3 in. across.

DECIDUOUS SECTION.

R. Kæmpferi (Japan). Flowers brilliant orange-red.

R. occidentalis (western N. America), 8 ft. Flowers fragrant, white with yellow blotch, 2–3 in. across, produced during June and July. Parent of late-flowering garden hybrids.

R. pontica (*flavum*), Asia Minor. The Common Yellow Azalea, valuable for its very fragrant, bright yellow flowers and beautifully-coloured autumn foliage. About 8 ft.

R. Vaseyi (Carolina), 12–15 ft. A very beautiful species, with pale pink flowers in early May. Award of Garden Merit, R.H.S.

Azaleas of Garden Origin.
MOLLIS SECTION.

Deciduous flowering shrubs of the greatest value for associating with evergreen rhododendrons; the latter forming a perfect background for their gorgeous flowers and brilliant autumn foliage. They thrive in the same soil as rhododendrons, but will stand more exposed positions. The flowers should be removed immediately they are past, and on no account allow seed pods to form, unless seed is wanted to increase the stock. The following are some of the most distinct. They may be grown in bush form or as standards.

Mrs. Arthur de Warelles, cream.

Mrs. L. J. Endtz, fine yellow.

Ruby, crimson.

Therese, orange pink.

Robespierri, bright deep pink, very large flower. New.

MOLLIS + SINENSIS.

Anthony Koster, bright golden yellow.

Frans van der Boom, deep salmon.

Hugo Koster, salmon red.

HARDY GHENT (single).

A little later flowering than the preceding.

Coccinea speciosa, deep orange-red.

Daviesii, finest white.

Fanny, bright pink.

Gloria Mundi, vermilion.

Nancy Waterer, yellow.

Pallas, red.

HARDY GHENT (double).

Byron, pink.

Freya, nankeen.

Il Tasso, red.

Narcissiflora, pale yellow.

Norma, bright rose.

Phoebe, pale yellow.

RHŒO (rē-o. Commelinaceæ). Greenhouse herbaceous perennial. Plant in the spring in a compost of loam, leaf-mould and sand, equal parts, and suspend in baskets from the greenhouse roof. Keep the plants in partial shade. Water plentifully in summer, but moderately after. Take cuttings of young shoots in summer and insert in light soil under a bell-glass.

SPECIES.

R. discolor (syn. *Tradescantia discolor*). Creeping. White in summer.

R. d. vittata (syn. *Tradescantia variegata*). Leaves striped with pale yellow.

R. concolor, leaves wholly green. Less common in cultivation than *R. discolor*.

RHUBARB (*Rheum hybridum*). There is a good deal of speculation about the actual parentage of the present-day types of rhubarb, and it is more than probable that they have been derived during the course of years from several species whose habitat is southern Siberia, and which were introduced about 1573.

By many it is regarded as fruit and used as such, though it is the leaf stalks which are eaten, and it is invariably grown in the kitchen garden.

Culture.—Rhubarb is a long-suffering plant, and will generally manage to produce some sort of a crop in any soil or position. The ideal is a deeply-dug, well-drained loam which remains cool and comparatively moist in summer. The plant is essentially a gross feeder, and will amply repay good treatment and liberal feeding. A stock of plants may be raised from seed, though some variation may occur in the seedlings and no stalks should be pulled for the first two years. The seed should be sown in drills in prepared beds outside from March to April–May. The seedlings should be left in the drills until the following March, when they may be planted in their permanent places.

The more usual method is to obtain good single "crowns" or roots in February and March, and to plant either in groups of three at 1½ ft. apart between the crowns and 5 ft. between the groups, or in single rows 1½ ft. apart and 4 ft. asunder.

The crowns must be planted firmly in the soil so that only the topmost bud is just showing on the surface. After planting, lightly fork out all footprints and mulch with a little strawy manure.

No stalks should be pulled during the first season after planting, and in later seasons gathering should cease after midsummer, so that the remaining stalks may strengthen up the crowns for the following year. If flower-heads are produced they should immediately be broken off at the ground level.

In the autumn the old brown leaves should be cleaned up, and a covering of old bracken or strawy litter placed over the crowns and kept in place with canes bent over so that their two ends are in the soil.

This winter covering may be dispensed with, but the crop is later the following year.

Forcing.—A few roots should be lifted annually for forcing indoors. Any dark room or cellar having a steady temperature of 50° or so will suffice.

The crowns should be lifted as soon as growth ceases in the autumn, and are best left on the top of the ground exposed to wind and frost for a few days. They are then quicker in starting into growth when placed in a warm temperature.

The lifted crowns may then be packed in large pots, boxes, or even in beds on the ground with only sufficient soil between them to fill in the spaces. Afterwards they should be given a good watering, and further light sprayings if they appear to be drying off. Under this treatment good stalks should be available in from 4 to 6 weeks.

Early crops are also obtainable by covering selected crowns in the open ground with special earthenware pots or even old barrels and boxes, and surrounding these with a thick layer of fresh stable manure to provide warmth. Coverings such as these should be removed in April, but the manure may be left as a mulch around the plant.

VARIETIES.

Myatt's Victoria; Linnæus; Champagne.

Both the leaves and large flower panicles of "Burning Bush" are tinted purple.

Uses.—The fleshy stalks are cut into pieces and made into pies, tarts, and preserves. An excellent home-made wine is often brewed from the juice of the stalks. There is a certain acidity about rhubarb which makes it unsuitable for those who suffer from rheumatism.

RHUS (rhūs. Anacardiaceæ). Sumach. Deciduous trees and shrubs notable for their brilliant autumn foliage. Flowers insignificant.

Culture.—Plant in ordinary garden soil, without manure being added, unless size of foliage is desired in such species as R. *typhina* and R. *glabra*. The poorer the soil the more superb is the colouring.

Propagate by seed when obtainable; also by ordinary cuttings of the simpleleaved species, and by root cuttings of the others.

SPECIES.

R. *Cotinus* (*Cotinus coggygria*). The "Venetian Sumach" of parts of Europe,

extending to the Himalayas. A deciduous
shrub about 12 ft. high, and as much
in width. During July the very characteristic inflorescence turns to a pale
flesh colour, later becoming a smoky-grey.
The flower stems gradually elongate, and
assume such a hairy appearance after
flowering as to cause this species to be
commonly known as the "wig-tree," and
sometimes as the "smoke-plant." The

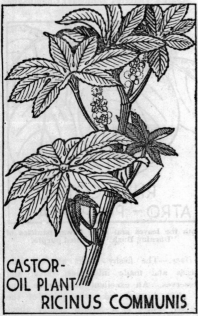

CASTOR-
OIL PLANT
RICINUS COMMUNIS

**Beautiful foliage plants with large, handsome
leaves, crimson and purple in some varieties.
Castor-oil is extracted from the seeds.**

foliage turns yellow in autumn. Must
not be confounded with *R. cotinoides.*

R. C. atropurpurea. The "Burning
Bush." Flowers, leaves and young wood
purple.

R. C. folius purpureis. A very attractive shrub with wine-coloured foliage
throughout the season, seen at its best
with the sun shining through it. Cut
sprays are most useful for indoor decoration, and last a considerable time in
water.

R. typhina. The "Stag's Horn Sumach"
or "Vinegar Tree" from North America.
A deciduous small tree up to 25 ft. high, of

gaunt appearance, but very attractive in
autumn when its large leaves are brilliantly
coloured, and remain so for a long time.
Ordinarily the leaves are 1–2 ft. long, but
if the plant is cut down to almost ground-
level in the spring and the resultant
growths reduced to one, or at the most
two, leaves 3 ft. long will be produced.

R. t. laciniata. Has handsomely-cut
leaflets, colouring well in autumn.

RHYNCOSPERMUM. *See* TRACHE-
LOSPERMUM.

RIBES (rī-bēz. Saxifragaceæ). Currants and Gooseberries (*which see*). Evergreen and deciduous shrubs, thriving in
ordinary garden soil.

Propagate by cuttings and by seed.

SPECIES.

R. alpinum. The "Alpine Currant." A
native of Britain and of the cooler countries
of the Old World. It is especially plentiful
in parts of Yorkshire, where it grows to a
height of 15 ft. It succeeds in shady
positions.

R. a. aureum. Young leaves yellow.

R. americanum. The "American Black
Currant." Foliage very attractive in
autumn.

R. Gordonianum. An interesting hybrid
between *R. aureum + R. sanguineum,* but
inferior to its parents.

R. sanguineum. The well-known North
American flowering currant. A very
attractive shrub with rosy-red flowers in
spring.

R. s. albidum. Flowers creamy-white,
tinged pink.

R. s. atrosanguineum. Flowers deep
crimson.

RIBBON GRASS. *See* PHALARIS.

RICHARDIA (rich-ar-di-a. Aroideæ).
Arum Lily. Named after L. C. Richard,
a French botanist. Greenhouse herbaceous perennials.

Culture.—Compost: 2 parts rich fibrous
loam, equal parts leaf-mould and sharp
sand. Repot annually in the autumn and
stand in cold frame until October, when
they should be removed to the greenhouse; temperature, 40°. Water moderately until early spring, then freely,
giving weak stimulants to plants showing
flower spathe. After flowering period is
over the plants should be stood outside
until following autumn, and must never

be allowed to become dry during the hot weather. A sharp look-out must be kept for signs of greenfly, as these plants are very subject to attack by these pests.

SPECIES.

R. africana is the one chiefly grown, and is much prized for its white bloom for church and other decorations at Easter. There are one or two varieties, but Godfrey's, although small, is probably the best. Other species are: *R. albo-maculata*, white, leaves spotted white; *R. Elliotiana*, yellow; *R. Pentlandii*, yellow; *R. Rehmannii*, purple.

RICINUS (re-ce-nus. Euphorbiaceæ). Castor-oil Plant (Palma Christi). Africa. Half-hardy annual foliage plants. Sow in March singly in small pots, in heat, pot on into 4½ in. pots, May, plant out June. Good as "dot" specimens or centre plants in flower-beds, giving a rich, exotic effect. They like a fairly rich soil, and plenty of water when growing freely. *R. communis* is the species from which castor-oil is obtained: foliage green, 3–5 ft. *R. barbonensis* is very robust, growing to 8–10 ft. in rich soil (green foliage). *R. Gibsonii* has dark red foliage and stems. 4–6 ft. *R. Cambodgensis* grows 4–5 ft. Leaves and stems blackish-purple.

See also CASTOR-OIL PLANT.

RIDGING. A process used on heavy soils to make them friable. When digging in the autumn, the soil is left in parallel ridges so that a large area is exposed to the action of frost.

RINGING. A method employed to encourage fruitfulness in fruit trees. It is a very old practice, which is now employed under more scientific conditions. Ringing is effective in preventing the dropping of unripened apples and bringing trees into bearing. It has also been known to bring pears, which have flowered without fruiting for several years, into bearing.

To ring a tree, remove two half rings of bark about three-quarters of an inch wide, the rings being about 4 in. apart and on opposite sides of the stem. The cuts end so that a line drawn vertically up the trunk would touch the ends of the two half rings. In extreme cases, when the tree fails to crop, the ends of the half rings may be made to overlap. Ringing should be done during flowering time. As the ring

joins up, it should be reopened the next spring. All freshly made rings should be painted with white-lead paint of the consistency of thick cream. This excludes fungus spores and woolly aphis. If desired, ringing can be localised and applied to individual branches.

RISER. *See* STEPS.

ROBINIA (rŏ-bin'-i-a. Leguminosæ). Deciduous trees and shrubs from N.

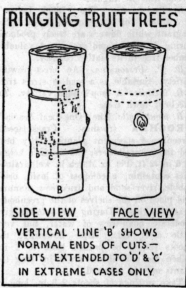

RINGING FRUIT TREES

SIDE VIEW   FACE VIEW

VERTICAL LINE 'B' SHOWS NORMAL ENDS OF CUTS.— CUTS EXTENDED TO 'D' & 'C' IN EXTREME CASES ONLY

The modern method of controlling excessive growth is to cut rings out of the bark. It is easier than root pruning.

America, very ornamental both in leaf and flower. The latter are pea-shaped and borne in pendulous racemes during the summer months. The leaves are of an elegant fern-like appearance and of a bright green.

Culture.—Plant in October in light, well-drained soil in a sunny, sheltered position.

Propagate by grafting and by seed.

N.B.—The wood of all Robinias is very brittle and they need protection from strong winds.

SPECIES.

R. hispida. The "Rose Acacia" of the south-eastern parts of the U.S.A., 6–8 ft. An exceedingly attractive tree with drooping panicles of large rose-pink flowers during June and July. Perhaps there is no more beautiful flowering tree at that time of year.

R. Kelseyi. Of American nursery origin, but of unknown parentage. Possibly a true species. A very beautiful sight in June with its bright rose-coloured flowers, and young bronzy leaves.

R. neo-mexicana (luxurians). Flowers pale rose, produced in June, and often a second time in August.

R. Pseudacacia. The "Black Locust" or "Acacia" of the eastern U.S.A. The fragrant white flowers are freely produced during June. A rapid grower. A valuable timber tree in its native country.

R. P. Bessoniana. An erect-growing variety. Suitable as a road or street tree.

R. inermis. A mop-headed variety. An excellent town tree.

R. monophylla. The "One Leaf Acacia."

ROCHEA (rō-shea. Crassulaceæ). Greenhouse succulent plants. They bear red and white flowers, and attain a height of 6 in.–2 ft. Pot in March in well-drained pots containing a compost of loam, brick rubble, river sand and dried cow manure, and place on the shelves of the greenhouse near the glass. During the summer give moderate quantities of water, but very little after this. After flowering, the shoots should be pruned back to 1 in. When the new shoots are 1 in. long the plants may be repotted.

Take cuttings of shoots 2–3 in. long in summer and lay them in the sun for a few days so as to dry them at the base. After this they may be inserted in pots of sandy soil and stood in the greenhouse. At this stage, the plants need little water.

Sow seeds in March or April in pots of sandy soil, covering them with a light dressing of sand only. The seedlings need very little water and should be kept close to the glass.

SPECIES.

R. coccinea. Scarlet, July. Height, 1 ft.

R. jasminea. White, spring. Height, 6–9 in.

R. versicolor. White and red, spring. Height, 2 ft.

R. odoratissima. Pink, June. Height, 1 ft.

These plants are allied to Crassula (*which see*).

ROCK. The word "rock" is used popularly, and also by geologists, to mean the solid material of the earth's crust. But whereas ordinarily "rock" implies something hard, to a geologist clay, loam, sand and gravel, if found as they occur naturally, are also called "rock." For the difference between rock and soil, *see* SOIL. Rocks are divided into two great classes—Igneous (which means formed in heat) if they have been forced up from the under layers of the crust; or Sedimentary if they are composed of portions of the older rocks torn to pieces and re-arranged. "Newer" rocks are always formed out of "older" rocks as, except for a few meteorites, the earth is not receiving new material. The best-known types of igneous rock are the granites and the basalts or lavas. The sedimentary rocks include clay, loam, sand, gravel, limestone, chalk, marble. (*See also* CRUST OF THE EARTH.)

ROCK CRESS. *See* AUBRETIA.

ROCK FORGET-ME-NOT. *See* OMPHALODES.

ROCK GARDEN CONSTRUCTION. A rock garden is, or should be a part of the garden specially designed and set aside for the cultivation of alpine and rock plants. A well-designed and well-built rock garden provides for plants of widely varying needs, both as to soil and aspect. There are some alpines which demand a cool northern position, whilst others must have as much sun as possible. Some, again, look best and grow best when planted upon steep cliff-like formations, whilst others should have small level pockets. Lastly, there are some plants which are most suitably placed in open meadow-like expanses. To grow a full and representative collection of alpines, therefore, the rock garden should be made in an open position, so that by the formation of hills, valleys, cliffs and undulating plains every aspect may be had, and the varying types of alpines may be put where they will both look best and grow best.

In choosing the site for a rock garden it is not always possible to find the ideal open position. It may happen that the only available site is a bank, sloping due south or due north. In such cases the only thing is to make the best of existing circumstances and concentrate on the cultivation of plants suited to the enforced aspect. Where a southern slope is the only possibility, good gardening can be done, for there is a wide selection of sun-loving alpines to choose from, and under such circumstances it would be a mistake to attempt the cultivation of shade lovers. To enjoy a rock garden to the full, one

Perhaps the most beautiful rock of all is the *Waterworn Limestone* of Westmorland and north-west Yorkshire. It is blue-grey in colour, and may be had in pieces up to any size it is possible to handle. It is found in an endless variety of beautiful shapes, and in skilful hands it "builds" well.

Tufa is another lime formation, which is especially good for the small or medium-sized rock garden, whose owner wishes to

Water, rock, turf and other suitable plants are easily fashioned into a living picture. No item should be overdone in planting a rock and water garden. A balanced and natural composition should be the aim.

must feel that the plants are enjoying it too. Never choose a position under or near trees as a site for a rock garden, unless you wish to specialise in woodland species. Drip, shade and encroaching tree roots are among the worst enemies of the general run of alpine plants.

Choice of Rock.—The choice of rock is an important matter. The first consideration should be the suitability of the rock from the view-point of the plants' well-being, and in this connection a porous rock is infinitely preferable to a non-porous rock. Then there is the question of beauty, good form and pleasing colour.

The average size of the rocks must also be considered. For a big rock garden some large rocks are desirable if bold picturesque effects are to be made, and certainly a big bold rock building can be made a lovely home and setting for such alpines as the Silver Saxifrages, Rock Primulas, etc. Lastly there usually arises the unfortunate question of cost, and on this point it is impossible to give advice— except that one should buy the best one can afford.

grow some of the smaller and more difficult lime-loving saxatile alpines. Tufa being highly porous, and usually rather soft, it is possible to drill holes in it in which plants of the saxatile species will grow to perfection. Other forms of limestone are *Purbeck*, which may be had in good water-worn shapes, *Oolitic* limestone and *Magnesia limestone*. These last are to be had in rough quarried pieces. They are of good colour, porous, and therefore congenial to plant life.

Kentish Rag is a brown sandstone, porous and of good colour, but care must be taken to find a type which does not break under frost, a common fault with this otherwise desirable stone.

Millstone Grit is a fine rough-quarried rock. It is porous, and plants do well on it, but it weathers rather slowly.

Granite is one of the least satisfactory rocks, with the exception perhaps of "dressed" stone from old buildings! There is something stark and forbidding about granite. It weathers slowly, and having very little porosity, it is less encouraging to plant life than most rocks.

It is difficult to tell how to build a rock garden, as difficult almost as to tell how to paint a landscape or a portrait. But here are a few basic principles which should be observed, and the rest is a question of artistic ability, coupled with a knowledge of alpine plant requirements, and a gift for interpreting rock formations as they occur in Nature. Almost every type of

RODGERSIA

The Rodgersia are perennial plants for a moist position.

rock has a "grain" not unlike the grain in wood, and it is important to lay such rock with the grain running as it ran in Nature, stratified either horizontally, or tilted at an angle throughout the garden. If stratified rocks are laid at all angles, some horizontally, and some upended, they at once give an unnatural and chaotic appearance. In the waterworn limestone the grain of the stone is less marked than in many others, but every piece of such stone has its natural "bed" on which it has lain out on the moors, and on which it should lie on the rock garden.

In making a rock garden of the hill-and-valley type, the first thing to do is to map out roughly the lie of the principal contours, and it is convenient that the principal paths should follow the floor of the valleys. Working on level ground it is possible to create quite impressive contours by sinking the valley paths and throwing up the excavated soil to form hills; but, in doing this, much depends upon the skill and judgment used in the matter of scale and proportion. Too wide a valley will dwarf a hill; whilst a valley made to the right scale is capable of enhancing the apparent size of a hill.

Having roughly carved out the soil into the desired contours, the work of rock building proper may be begun. It is best to start building at the lowest point of the deepest valley, and from there to work gradually outward and upward. Choose every stone for each position with the utmost care; place each on its natural bed and no other; and, as you build, keep two principles always in mind—the placing of the group of rocks you are at the moment working on in such a way as to make congenial homes for your alpine plants, and making the general trend of your building create a pleasing and convincing geological composition as a whole.

ROCKET, SWEET (Cruciferæ). Hesperis, Dame's Violet. Sweet-scented hardy perennials and biennials, with a few annuals of no particular value. The plants are useful for the mixed border or rockery.

Culture.—The annuals are propagated by seed, the biennials by seed sown in the open in May, and later planted outdoors, and the perennials by seed and by division of the crowns, the plants being kept for a few months in the reserve garden and planted out in the following March, in any light soil, in a sunny position.

Species.—The true rockets are varieties of *Hesperis matronalis*. The original single-flowered form is pinkish in colour, but the double white and purple forms are more valued for borders and cutting.

RODGERSIA (rŏdgĕr-sia. Saxifrageæ). Hardy herbaceous perennials that are chiefly valued for their foliage; suitable for the moist border or the edge of water.

Culture.—Very easily propagated by division of the thick rootstock. They like a light, loamy, fibrous soil, or peat only, in a boggy or swampy place.

The best-known species is *podophylla*, with fleshy underground stems, and minute creamy-white flowers in panicles, borne high above the large palmate, bronzy-tinted leaves. 3–4 ft.

Pinnata, a rosy-flowered plant, and *æsculifolia*, pinkish-white flowers, both with leaves resembling those of the Horse Chestnut. 2–4 ft. All bloom in July and August.

ROELLA (rō-el′-a. Campanulaceæ). S. African Harebell. Greenhouse shrubs, mostly from S. Africa. Pot in March in a soil composed of equal parts of peat and loam, with a quantity of sand. Stand in a dry part of the greenhouse where plenty of light is obtainable and also plenty of air. Give little water, taking care not to wet the foliage. It is essential that the atmosphere be quite dry in autumn and winter. All flowers should be removed as soon as they fade, and those that form during autumn and winter should also be removed. Take cuttings of the points of strong shoots in spring and insert in sandy soil, shading them from direct sunshine.

SPECIES.

R. ciliator. White and purple in summer. Height, 1 ft.

R. decurrens. Blue, August. Height, 1 ft. An annual, raised from seed sown in a hot-bed in spring, planted out in early summer.

R. fruticulosa. Yellow. July.

R. muscosa. Blue. August. 3 in. This is increased by division of the root.

R. squarrosa. White. July. 6 in.

R. spicata. White. August.

RŒMERIA (ro-me-re-a. Papaveraceæ). S. Europe. A pretty poppy-like plant, with violet-purple flowers. *R. refracta* (syn. *hybrida*), hardy annual, is the only species grown. Sow in spring where to flower, ordinary soil. 2 ft.

ROLLING. This is necessary to keep lawns and gravel paths in good condition. It should not be done when the ground is wet or the gravel and grass will stick to the roller. Many mowers also act as rollers, thus saving time and energy.

ROMAN HYACINTH. *See* HYACINTHUS.

ROMANZOFFIA (ro-man-zof-fi-a. Hydrophyllaceæ). Sitcha Water Leaf. Hardy perennials like Saxifrages that are

well suited to the rockery. Plant in crevices between stones or rock in the sun. *Propagate* by division.

R. sitchensis. White. April. 3–4 in.

ROMNEYA (rom-ne-ya. Papaveraceæ). The Tree Poppy of California, 4–8 ft., according to position and climate. In Cornwall, grown against the wall of a mansion, it has reached the roof.

**ROMNEYA COULTERI
(CALIFORNIAN TREE POPPY)**

Although it prefers a sheltered spot, the Tree Poppy is worth growing for its satin-like flowers.

Culture.—Plant pot plants about March in open loamy soil, in sunny position, or against a south or west wall. It likes plenty of moisture at the root during the growing season.

Propagate by root cuttings. They should be cut up into 2 in. lengths, and placed in pots of sandy soil, and just covered therewith. The pots should then be placed in a gentle heat. The young plants should be kept in pots until ready to be put out in their permanent positions in the garden. Established plants send up young shoots, and these may be carefully removed and potted up and treated as the root cuttings. It may also be raised from seed. The great point of culture is to bear in mind its extreme sensitiveness to injury at the root.

SPECIES.

R. Coulteri. Flowers satiny-white, poppy-like, about 5–6 in. across, with a large central mass of golden stamens. Leaves glaucous, from 3–5 in. long.

R. trichocalyx. Distinguished from the preceding by the bristly hairs on the calyx. It is an easier plant to cul-

ROOM PLANTS. Many plants will thrive successfully in rooms if given intelligent care. They should never be allowed to stand in draughts. A good soaking of water weekly is better than the "little and often" method. The leaves of foliage plants need sponging with tepid water weekly, and the plants benefit by being stood out of doors in mild, showery weather. Turn the plants

Room Culture, Useful Plants For.

	Common Name.
Asplenium bulbiferum.	New Zealand Spleenwort.
Pteris cretica.	Ribbon Fern.
Platycerium alcicorne.	Elk's Horn Fern.
*Aspidistra.**	Aspidistra (also variegated kind).
Aralia japonica (or *Fatsia japonica*).*	Fig-leaved Palm, often called Castor-oil Plant by hawkers.
Araucaria excelsa.	Norfolk Island Pine.
Ficus elastica.†	India Rubber Plant.
Kentia Belmoreana or *Howea Belmoreana.*	Kentia Palm.
*Scolopendrium vulgare.**	Hart's Tongue Fern.
Cereus (various).†	Cactus (repot once in three years).
Saxifraga sarmentosa.†	Pedlar's Basket and Mother of Thousands.
Vallota purpurea.†	Scarborough Lily (repot every three or four years only).
Sauromatum guttatum.	Monarch of the East.
Pelargonium, Zonal (various).	Geranium.
Pelargonium crispum.†	Lemon-scented Pelargonium.
Fuchsia.†	Fuchsia (sometimes called Ear-Drops).
Anthericum variegatum.	St. Bernard's Lily.
Phœnix.	Phœnix Palm (should be syringed twice weekly with warm water).
Lippia citriodora.	Lemon-scented Verbena.

Those marked * are specially suitable for a dark room. Those marked † should be kept in the window or where they get sunshine.

tivate, being of a hardier constitution. Flowers and foliage are the same as *R. Coulteri.*

ROMULEA (rom-u-le-a. Irideæ). Hardy and greenhouse bulbous plants. Grow in light rich soil in either pots or borders. Plant the tubers 2 in. apart and 4 in. deep and lift annually.

Increase by offsets.

SPECIES.

R. bulbocodium. Hardy yellow and violet flowers in early summer. 6 in.

R. Columnæ. Hardy. Lilac. May. 6 in.

R. ramiflora. Yellow and lilac. May. 6 in. Hardy.

R. rosea. Carmine. Spring.

daily so that they do not become drawn on one side towards the light. The yellowing of leaves of plants such as the aspidistra is due to spasmodic watering and sudden changes of temperature. Where possible, plants benefit by being transferred to the greenhouse for a few weeks, others taking their places.

When the room is heated or lighted by gas, aspidistras and ficus are the best plants to grow, also palms, ferns, crotons, dracænas, etc. Other plants which thrive in rooms lit by other means are chrysanthemums, cinerarias, clivias, cyclamens, cytisus fragrans, francoa ramosa, fuchsias, geraniums, and bulbs in variety.

ROOT PRUNING. A laborious garden operation which is now superseded by the much simpler process known as ringing (which *see*).

ROOTS. It is important to see that roots of plants are strong and healthy, or well-grown plants are impossible. The main tap root of a tree or shrub is useful for keeping the tree firmly in the soil, and the small fibrous roots for obtaining the food supplies. The cultivator should aim at keeping the fibrous roots near the fertile top soil. This is done by top dressing with manure. There are also other types of roots such as aerial—seen in some orchids; adventitious—the climbing roots of ivy, etc.

ROSCOŒA (ros-ko-ea. Scitamineæ). Charming dwarf hardy and half-hardy perennials with flowers in terminal heads.

Propagate by division in spring and plant at the foot of a south wall in sandy loam. Cover with litter during very cold weather.

SPECIES.

R. purpurea. Purple. Summer and early autumn. 1 ft.

ROSE (Rosaceæ). Rosa. The Rose, in one form or another, is found in almost all countries of the world, and its cultivation goes back through the ages to remote periods of history.

Homer alludes to the rose in his "Iliad" and the "Odyssey." Sappho, the Greek poetess, in her writings about 600 B.C. chooses the rose as The Queen of Flowers.

The wild rose is distributed very widely, but it seems evident that blooms of much fuller substance and in considerable variety were cultivated during the time of Nero, who is credited by Suetonius, the Latin writer, with spending large sums upon roses to adorn his sumptuous feasts. During the reign of the Roman Emperor Domitian, roses were apparently forced into flower during the winter months. Pliny hints at artificial production, though not in detail. What quality these roses possessed one can only conjecture; it is hardly likely they would be the simple wild rose indigenous to the country.

Horace, who wrote at considerable length on horticulture, mentions the growing of roses in beds, but nothing has come down to us respecting their form, colour and variety.

The Cabbage or Provence rose seems to be the earliest recorded in Britain—1560—and comprises red, white and striped varieties, bearing full flowers with very sweet scent; these are still obtainable from rose nurseries that stock a representative collection. The Austrian Briar roses are recorded much about the same time; these, too, still survive and are very attractive with their copper and yellow single flowers in masses, quite early in the season.

TYPES OF ROSES

HYBRID TEA

POLYANTHA

SINGLE

HIPS OR FRUITS OF ROSE SPECIES

A Rose garden should find space for all the best types of roses and species.

HYBRID PERPETUAL ROSES.—This class dates back from about 1830; the origin is a little uncertain, but is probably a result of cross fertilisation between the old Chinese and the Damask roses.

Most of the varieties of this class came from the French raisers, and for a good many years they were the backbone of the rose garden, providing magnificent blooms for exhibition when grown on rich heavy soil.

The Hybrid Tea class and the still newer Pernetiana roses have completely ousted the Hybrid Perpetual, and comparatively few sorts of it are now grown.

To give of their best they need rich heavy soil, and hard pruning each spring.

TEA ROSES.—This class was in a very great favour during the time Hybrid Perpetual roses were largely grown.

The Tea roses provided the only real yellow, cream and white roses that were to be had to enliven the reds and deep crimsons of the H.P.'s.

Now, there is such an abundance of choice from among the hardier race of Hybrid Teas and the Pernetiana roses, ranging from delicate cream to the deepest orange and bronzy-yellow, that the old Tea class has gone very much out of favour. This can be attributed in a great measure to the tender constitution of the Tea rose as a class, and to the habit of hanging its head, owing to a thin weak neck. The Hybrid Tea and the Pernetiana roses mostly produce their blooms on firm upright stems. However, many of the Tea roses are very lovely, and if grown on Standard or Half-Standard English briars are worthy of a position in the garden.

They need hard pruning each spring and liberal treatment with manure.

HYBRID TEA ROSES are a cross between the Hybrid Perpetual and the Tea rose, and undoubtedly are the backbone of the Rose garden.

As a class they are more continuous flowering than the H.P. and hardier than the Tea. They have given, and are still giving a range of colours which neither of the parents possessed. It is now possible to have roses in bloom well into the autumn, in fact till frosts finally put a check to their activity and they obtain a much-needed rest.

The Hybrid Tea will give two crops of flowers, and if the late autumn continues genial, it is no uncommon event for a third crop of very highly-coloured blooms to open freely, though these, naturally, are not so large or full as the earlier flowers. This class does not need the heavy rich soil that was considered essential to the Hybrid Perpetual. A moderately retentive soil of a loamy nature is quite strong enough for Hybrid Tea roses; far better than strong clay. In pruning, the shoots can be cut back to about four eyes, leaving the stronger shoots the longest, but, as with all roses, any shoots damaged by frost must

be cut back to sound wood, even if it means shortening them to within an inch or two of the base.

PERNETIANA ROSES.—This comparatively new class obtained its name from the raiser, who introduced it in 1900, Mons. Pernet Ducher, of Lyons. It is the result of hybridising the Austrian Briar with the Hybrid Tea, and their progeny have added enormously to the popularity of the rose generally.

The brilliant coppery-yellow and vivid orange colours which we now have in plenty were unknown before the advent of the Pernetiana roses.

One of the charms connected with this class is the fine, firm, and glossy foliage it produces, which in most instances is mildew-proof, an incalculable advantage.

Pernetiana roses require much the same treatment as Hybrid Teas in respect to pruning, manuring, and so forth. They are exceedingly free flowering throughout the summer and autumn.

CHINA ROSES (*Rosa Indica*).—Introduced from China about 1789.

The Common Pink (or "Monthly Rose" as it is frequently termed) being the forbear of all varieties of this class since introduced.

The Common Pink is of semi-climbing habit; out in the open it will form a very large bush, flowering continuously till winter.

There are many beautiful varieties now, which have sprung from it, that are of short bush or dwarf habit of growth, most useful for bedding in masses.

China roses do not need such close pruning as the Hybrid Teas, but they appreciate generous treatment.

POLYANTHA ROSES (*Rosa Multiflora*).— The dwarf-growing varieties of this class are termed Pompons by the National Rose Society to distinguish them from the climbing Polyantha roses of such type as Crimson Rambler, Blush Rambler, etc.

The dwarf-growing group has a delightful range of colours, much increased of late years.

Exceedingly free flowering in large clusters of small rosette-shaped flowers, they make very attractive beds and borders.

Little pruning is necessary other than to cut out the centre shoots where overcrowded and trim the ends of the remainder.

WICHURAIANA ROSES (*Rosa Wichuraiana*).—This very distinct rose was discovered in Japan by Dr. Wichura, who introduced it into Europe about 1873.

The original variety, crossed with some of the Tea, Noisette, and Polyantha roses, has resulted in the wonderful group of climbing roses beginning with Alberic Barbier, and continuing with Dorothy Perkins, Hiawatha, and all the rest of these well-known climbing roses so attractive on arches and pergolas.

PROVENCE ROSES (*Rosa Centifolia*).—The Common Provence or "Cabbage" is about the earliest recorded rose in this country; it is a native of Asia Minor. The flowers are globular, sweetly scented, and the leaves are light green.

Provence roses need moderate pruning and generous cultivation.

MOSS ROSES (*Rosa Centifolia*).—The Moss Rose was introduced into England about 1596 and is really a sub-variety of the Provence rose, which it resembles in many ways except that the sepals and stems of the flowers are mossed. This class requires moderate pruning and good cultivation.

DAMASK ROSES (*Rosa Damascena*).—It is believed that this was the rose largely grown in Italy and referred to by Virgil in his Georgics.

The class includes such old and well-known varieties as York and Lancaster, *Rosa Mundi;* very sweetly scented and of hardy constitution. They need moderate pruning and good cultivation.

MUSK ROSES (*Rosa Moschata*).—This is a very old rose, and believed to have been introduced from Madeira about 1600.

The class comprised very few varieties until quite recently. During the last decade the late Rev. J. Pemberton raised many beautiful seedlings which have proved great acquisitions. Though not strongly scented, all possess a faint musk odour. Fairly strong and robust in growth, they need only slight pruning, but will respond to generous treatment.

THE SCOTS BRIAR (*Rosa Spinosissima*).—This is found growing wild in many parts of Scotland. Very short and bushy in growth, with abundance of tiny thorns, like needle points. There are several varieties; lemon, pink, white, red and yellow.

The flowers are small and semi-double; planted close together, the little bushes make admirable miniature hedges or borders to rose beds. They need no pruning.

SWEET BRIAR ROSES (*Rosa Rubiginosa*).—The sweet briar of the hedge and common is well known to all. After a shower

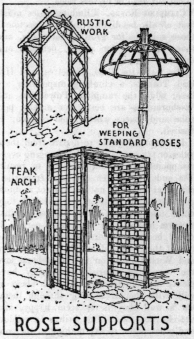

ROSE SUPPORTS

Climbing Roses can be supported by arches or trellis against house walls.

of rain the sweet scent from its foliage is delightful.

Equally sweet are the Penzance Hybrid sweet briars, raised by Lord Penzance and named after himself, Lady Penzance, and many of Sir Walter Scott's heroines.

They are exceedingly hardy, form very large bushes and require practically no attention when once planted and given a start.

JAPANESE ROSES (*Rosa Rugosa*).—This very hardy, strong-growing class is mostly useful for planting in borders and shrubberies to fill gaps.

It has delightful cool green foliage, and after flowering in the early summer it produces fine scarlet seed pods in the autumn, much beloved by pheasants, consequently it is considerably used in covert planting.

The two principal varieties are Alba, pure white, and Rubra, a rather dull red, both single flowers; the seed pods and the foliage are, however, the chief attractions. They do not need any pruning other than to cut out dead or useless wood.

CLIMBING ROSES.—Climbing roses must, first of all, be divided into two sections; those suitable for growing on walls, and those adaptable for arches, pergolas and screens.

For walls the Teas, Noisettes, and Hybrid Teas of a climbing disposition are best; while the ramblers, Polyanthas and Wichuraianas are better for arches, pergolas and spaces where rapid climbing is desired.

It is not advisable to depart from these rules or try experiments by changing over; disappointment would be sure to result. Tea and Hybrid Tea climbers, from their perpetual-flowering nature, are not so quick growing as the ramblers, etc., though they make fair progress when planted against a warm or sheltered wall; on a pergola it would be years before they met over the top, if they ever did at all. The ramblers and Wichuraianas on the other hand love the open and flourish when they have plenty of room to run and climb about at will, with the air blowing through them. On a wall they never seem happy, and the closeness of it often brings on mildew and other pests, to say nothing of the constant attention they would need nailing up the long trailing shoots, which grow very rapidly.

All climbing roses should be planted in the autumn; November is the best month for planting roses generally, and particularly so for climbers.

Many varieties of bush roses will plant quite successfully even in the early spring. Climbers, if they are to succeed, must be put in during the autumn.

When the pruning time arrives in March, those on walls can be cut back about half way for the first year, to induce young growth from the base. Prune only moderately in after years.

The climbers on pergolas, etc., can have their weaker shoots cut back fairly hard and the long rods left about two-thirds their length. This has reference to the first year's pruning only; in succeeding years they will need very little pruning other than cutting out weak and surplus wood and shortening the tip ends of the long rods. When they get older still, a serious overhauling is needed and can be done in the winter.

Untie the whole plant and let the shoots fall to the ground and lay them out so that it is possible to get among them and cut out all weak and stunted little shoots, and any that show a tendency to die back. Thin out the plant thoroughly, leaving the young rods, especially those thrown up from the base.

When completed, the plant can be trained anew, and will not require similar treatment for about another three years.

It must be remembered these ramblers are, for the most part, summer flowering only, and do not give another crop in the autumn, but they last a long time when they are in bloom.

STANDARD ROSES.—The Standard rose was introduced by the late Mr. Thos. Rivers, of Sawbridgeworth, about 1840, and created some considerable stir. It proved to be a great acquisition to the garden by breaking the flatness of bush rose beds. It soon became very popular in suburban gardens, where their heads are well out of attention from cats and dogs. Compared with the countless number of varieties grown as bushes, only a few sorts are budded on the briar stems to form Standard plants, but those offered are sorts that have proved suitable; in fact there are some kinds which are preferable on standard stems, especially those where the blooms have a tendency to drop their heads.

Standard roses are long lived when on the English briar stem. The Rugosa stock has been largely tried as a substitute, but it is hardly as reliable and certainly not so long lived.

It is imperative that every standard plant should be firmly staked. When pruning, treat it much the same as a bush plant, cutting the shoots back to within 4–6 in. of the base.

Lowis (Seeds) Ltd., Spalding, Lincs.

We have pleasure in supplying the enclosed items, and we should be obliged if you would check the contents as soon as you can. If you do not intend to plant the bulbs immediately, open up each bag and keep them in a cool, dry, airy place. Should any query arise, kindly notify us immediately, and enclose this slip with your letter.

THANK YOU.

IF YOU HAVE ORDERED ROSES, SHRUBS OR PLANTS (FROM CATALOGUE PAGES 1. AND 20-24). THESE WILL BE SENT IN NOVEMBER/DECEMBER AT THE APPRO-RIATE PLANTING TIME.

N⁰. ⁻34845⁻

A67

PRIMULAS

1. Primula obconica has a long flowering period.
2, 3, and 5. Sinensis varieties.
4. Primula malecoides, the daintiest variety for the amateur's greenhouse.

1, 2 and 5. Calceolaria, Pelargonium and Carnation cuttings ready for potting on.
3 and 6. Erica cuttings started under a bell-glass form healthy plants.
4. Cuttings showing stages of growth.

STANDARD WEEPING ROSES.—A Standard weeping rose on a 6 ft. stem is a most attractive object in any garden and makes a commanding specimen plant. The varieties suitable for growing in this form are mostly only summer flowering, but Scarlet Climber, American Pillar, Reine Andre, Alberic Barbier and, of course, Dorothy Perkins, with its various sports, last a long time while they are in flower and make beautiful weeping plants.

Although the growth of these varieties has a natural tendency to fall over, proper wire frames can be bought for training their shoots.

When planted in good time during the autumn, these weeping roses do not need hard pruning; shorten the tip ends of the long shoots and cut back any stumpy growth.

Pruning.—One of the most important operations connected with rose culture is pruning.

In normal seasons this should be done about the end of March, or may be delayed until early April if the spring is very late. In the case of newly-planted roses pruning is of vital consequence; if the trees are insufficiently or incorrectly pruned their first spring, it is a difficult matter to correct things afterwards.

With the young it is indeed a case of: "Spare the knife and spoil the plant."

Roses obtained from a nursery are always of one season's growth—"maiden plants" is the usual term applied to them —and they mostly have two to four well-ripened shoots. Taking the general run of bush Hybrid Teas, Teas and Pernetiana roses, their shoots should be pruned back the first year to within 3–6 in. of the ground, cutting to an eye pointing outwards as far as possible. This may sound drastic, but it is very necessary for the well-being of the plants.

They will now start growth from the base of the shoots (which, by the way, is always the soundest part of a plant, especially after a hard winter) and thus make a shapely bush for future years.

If they are left long in the shoot, the top eyes start first, as they always will, and continue to make growth at the expense of the lower eyes; eventually the plants will have that leggy appearance which is so unsightly in a rose garden. In all instances weaker shoots must be cut the hardest.

The following year, when new plants have had a season's growth, it will be observed how they vary in habit, some varieties growing more robustly than others; it is as well then to vary the pruning according to the strength of the shoots; again always cutting the weaker

ROSE MILDEW

Rose mildew on roses is caused by a spell of moist warm weather. Liver of sulphur solution is the best remedy.

shoots the hardest. Strong growers can be left longer. To point an exceptional case, Hugh Dickson and Snow Queen are much stronger than the general run of bush roses.

To cut these, and similar varieties, too hard will only result in their trying to make up the balance of growth at the expense of flowering.

For preference use secateurs when pruning, more especially in the case of newly-planted trees.

If a knife is used (let it be never so sharp) there is a certain drag on the plant in the process of cutting which may disturb

U

the root. In course of years it will be found necessary to trim out the centres of the plants to prevent shoots crossing and crowding.

A certain amount of what is termed "summer pruning" can be done to the roses after their first crop of flowers is over. All faded and old flowers can be cut off, not just broken off at the neck of the bloom, but cut with stem down to the lower eye of the shoot that is in, or has just started into growth. This will strengthen the secondary growth that is to produce the next crop, and will give the plants a trim and tidy appearance which they would never have if the old flowers were left to fall off. The pruning of standard roses has already been mentioned under its heading. They need treatment on the same lines as the bush roses.

The pruning of climbing roses is also dealt with under its separate heading.

Soils and their Preparation.—Opinions have changed vastly through the past 40 years as to the exact nature of soil required for successful cultivation of the rose. Even now one occasionally hears the old saying: "You *must* have clay to get good roses."

This has become quite a fallacy since the advent of the Hybrid Tea and allied classes; these do *not* need a stiff clay soil to do well; in fact it is far too cold for their active nature.

Soils in general can be classified in three degrees—light, loamy, and heavy.

If the soil is very light and poor it will be an advantage to obtain a few loads (according to the number and size of the beds) of good fibrous loam; the top spit from an old meadow for choice.

This, well broken up, with the addition of farmyard manure will do all that is required, if incorporated with the existing soil. A little of the natural soil can be removed to make room for the new if necessary, but as most rose beds are best slightly raised, there will be no need to take much away. The ground should be broken up to the depth of 2 ft., mixing the new soil well in, and then left for a week or so to settle down before planting is attempted.

If the soil of the garden is a natural loam of slightly greasy nature, that is

all that is required, except perhaps a little manure to enrich it, and not too much of that the first year.

Although the rose is a gross feeder and can put up with a liberal supply of manure, it is not advisable to overdo it with newly-planted roses.

They have their new young roots to make after transplanting, and if the soil is too hot with manure it will retard rather than help the formation of the new young roots.

One of the best preparations for heavy soils is burnt earth, and it is equal to any form of manure one can use. Finely-sifted cinders are also an excellent help to clay or very heavy soil, and help it to work much easier. In digging or forking after an application of ashes or burnt earth it is possible to tell to an inch where they have been distributed and where not. In preparing large beds or borders for roses, trenching is the best method, and if properly done it ensures keeping the top spit of soil on the top, where it should be. The bottom spit can be well broken up, but the surface soil must come on top of it, thus: commence at one end of the bed or border and dig out a trench of soil the width of a spade; barrow this top spit to the other end of the bed ready to fill in the final trench.

Sprinkle in the trench a coat of manure or burnt earth, whichever you are using, and break up the bottom with a fork. Then fill in the trench by turning the next top spit with the spade, continuing the operation till you reach the other end of the bed, where the carted soil lies ready for filling in the final trench.

The surface can be left rough when the trenching is finished—it will let the air into the soil—and can be fined down when planting operations are started.

In some instances where gardens are very flat and the soil likely to become waterlogged, the whole soil of the bed to the depth of about 3 ft. is removed and a layer of brick rubble placed at the bottom before putting back the soil. This is indeed an expensive preparation and only needed in exceptional cases where the soil needs draining.

One great point in preparing ground for rose beds is to get it done in fine weather

It is hopeless to do anything with soil in wet weather; poaching about on sticky land does infinitely more harm than good, whatever work it may be.

Planting.—If a garden is sufficiently large to enable a position for the rose bed to be carefully selected, it is always as well to choose an open space away from trees, certainly away from overhanging branches. The drip from the boughs, whether rain or heavy dew, is very detrimental to success of the plants, as it tends to sour the ground.

If the rose bed catches most of the morning sun, and is shaded during the afternoon, so much the better.

Where the ground has already been properly manured and dug as suggested in the chapter on SOILS, AND THEIR PREPARATION, the planting can be proceeded with any time in the autumn while the weather is open and the soil not too wet. The surface can be fined down by rustling it over with a fork or coarse rake.

It is best that roses should have a bed entirely to themselves.

Before starting to plant, stake out the positions for the trees; in the case of bush plants 21–24 in. (not more) is the best distance to allow between each, leaving a margin of 12 in. at all sides.

Inspect all the plants carefully, trimming any roots that may have unavoidably been bruised in the lifting.

Dig out a hole about 12 in. square and of sufficient depth to take the plant so that when filled in, the crown, or junction of the head with the root, will be just covered when planting is completed.

Spread out the root upon the bottom soil, avoid any criss-crossing as far as possible.

It is best to have help with this operation, one to hold the plant in position while the soil is being thrown in, a little at a time.

Lift the plant up and down slightly to insure that the soil will shingle in among the roots.

A little more soil, then firm it down well with the foot before putting in any more.

Firm planting is most essential; loose planting is more often the cause of failure than any other delinquency. Fill in the remainder of the soil, firm it well and finish off with a loose surface around the plant.

Staking is not necessary with bush roses; should any of them have an extra long shoot it can be shortened a little to prevent blowing about in the wind, and so avoid any movement at the root.

STANDARD ROSES can be planted in the same manner, but the holes must be dug out deeper than for bushes. A very good

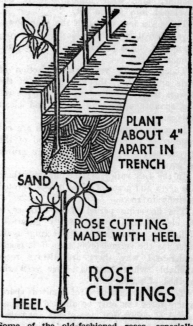

PLANT ABOUT 4" APART IN TRENCH

SAND

ROSE CUTTING MADE WITH HEEL

HEEL

ROSE CUTTINGS

Some of the old-fashioned roses, especially climbers, can be propagated by means of cuttings.

guide is to notice the ground-level mark on the stem of a standard, indicating the depth it was in the ground originally, and plant accordingly.

Standard roses must be staked; the top, when driven in, should be just below the junction of the head with the stem; a piece of matting between the stake and the stem to prevent chafing, and tie firmly.

CLIMBING ROSES, whether on walls or on arches, should have good large holes dug out and prepared for them by breaking up the subsoil with a fork and mixing in a liberal supply of manure. The holes must be big enough to take the roots without crowding; in other respects the planting and firming will be the same as with other roses. Tie the shoots together to a stake and leave them so till pruning time.

It is labour lost to spread them out and train methodically in position until after they have been pruned.

Roses under Glass.

The forcing of roses under glass to produce early spring flowers has become very popular, and with nurserymen it has developed into a fine art.

There are few weeks in the year nowadays when it is not possible to obtain rose blooms, if one is prepared to pay the price demanded.

Though not a very wide selection of sorts and colours, the fine quality of the flowers is beyond dispute, and all possess the advantage of long stems and clean foliage.

In many instances these blooms are cut from roses planted out in the soil of the greenhouse. In addition some are grown in pots.

In the Lea valley of Hertfordshire there are acres and acres of glass houses devoted entirely to roses.

The flowering period of each house is so cleverly and systematically governed, following in rotation and starting again later for the second crop, that it is easily understood why there are always roses available when one has once seen the method of production.

To suit greenhouses of limited space, where roses can only be allowed a certain period of occupation, pot plants are naturally the best means for producing early flowers.

Early Spring Flowering.—To save time it is best to obtain plants that are one year established in 6 or 7 in. pots.

They will need top-dressing with fresh soil and manure in the autumn, and should remain plunged outdoors till winter is almost upon them.

They can then be brought under glass, keeping the temperature of the house as cool as possible, using heat only to banish frost. Little or no water need be given during this period; it will thoroughly harden the wood ready for pruning. About a fortnight after bringing in the plants, prune hard back to three or four eyes from

the base all the general run of Hybrid Tea, Tea and Pernetiana roses. Cut out entirely all weak and useless wood, leaving the centre of the plants open.

The pots should stand on a thin layer of cinder ashes to help drainage.

In bright weather syringe the heads daily and maintain a moist atmosphere in the house.

Water the pots occasionally, as required, in all cases using water at the same temperature as the house.

By tapping the pot with the knuckles it is easily determined whether the plant is dry or not. If it gives a dull soft sound it is moist enough, if a sharp high sound it is dry.

When it is noticed that a pot retains water on the surface for a considerable time, it indicates that the soil is waterlogged. A small piece of stick thrust into the drainage hole will quickly remove the blockage.

On the other hand, if a plant looks sad, with drooping foliage, it has evidently been overlooked in the watering and become very dry. Immerse the whole pot and plant in a pail of water for half an hour and it will soon revive. Top ventilation when possible, is always best, but not given on a cold or windy day.

Draught is liable to cause mildew. If this trouble should appear, a little "flowers of sulphur" dusted on the affected foliage will check it; or syringe the plants with Jeyes' horticultural wash in the evening. This is also a preventative for greenfly. If the latter become very troublesome, smoke the house with fumigating shreds in the evening, syringing the plants with clean chilled water first thing in the morning.

Maggots and caterpillars can only be destroyed by hand picking.

A weak solution of liquid manure (such as cow droppings and soot) can be added occasionally when watering the plants. A very light dressing of Rose Fertiliser on the surface of the pots and watered in, will give added size and colour to the blooms.

When the roses begin to show colour and develop, syringing must be carefully done and only on bright days, otherwise the flowers will get spotty.

As the flowering period advances and

the foliage begins to get harder, more air can be given on quiet days.

If the sun becomes too powerful and causes the flowers to flag, light blinds for shade will be needed; as an alternative, syringe the roof and sides of the house with whiting to which has been added a little skim milk.

After flowering, the plants should be plunged outdoors and watered regularly to keep them in a healthy condition, decreasing the supply gradually to harden them off.

Forcing for Winter Flowering necessitates starting the pot plants under glass in the early autumn and using considerable heat from then onwards.

If ordinary ground-grown plants are potted up in the early autumn with the object of forcing under glass later, they must remain outdoors for a considerable time, placing them in cool frames when frost comes, and not attempting to force them the first season; they will flower a little about May or early June.

Next year, when their roots have become established, they can be forced for early flowering in the usual way.

Climbing roses planted out in a greenhouse need pruning each season. Cut the weakest shoots hard back each year to induce new growth from the base and shorten the long shoots by about one third their length.

Specimen rambler roses require little pruning, other than to take out all small snubby growth and tip the ends of the longer shoots. When in flower they require constant watering.

ROSE MANURES.

The rose is a gross feeder, and when once established will revel in good fare. One of the best fertilisers after ordinary farmyard manure is *Burnt earth. See also* FERTILISERS.

Rose Cuttings.

Propagating roses from cuttings is not a very sure or satisfactory method.

Practically all the newer high-coloured varieties now so much admired absolutely refuse to grow as cuttings.

A few of the old-fashioned roses and several of the old climbing varieties will strike from cuttings, but their progress is so slow and uncertain it would be far

wiser and save much time to bud them on a reliable parent stock:

Good hard wood, cut in lengths of about 9 in. from such varieties as Hugh Dickson, Caroline Testout, Gloire de Dijon and kindred sorts, will strike in good gritty soil. If the ground is strong and heavy, a little sand in the bottom of the trench will help matters.

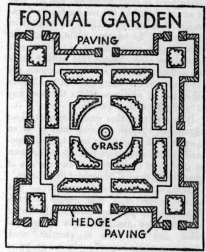

FORMAL GARDEN
PAVING
GRASS
HEDGE
PAVING

An effective design suitable for Roses, annuals or bulbs. The scale is 32 ft. to 1 in.

The cut at the bottom of the shoot must be close to an eye, and the shoot planted firmly almost full depth, only about an inch, or a little more, with an eye showing above ground.

Climbing roses such as Crimson Rambler, Blush Rambler, and most of the Wichuriana climbers will strike as cuttings, but experience has often shown that even these are seldom satisfactory in the long run; they make root, throw plenty of shoots which will grow to about 4–5 ft. high, then suddenly stop, and refuse to grow any taller.

The old Ayrshire roses are about the most satisfactory of the climbing classes to raise from cuttings, and good hard wood of the Common Pink China rose may make fair bushes in course of time.

Rose Gardens.

The principles which underlie the construction of a rose garden ought to be studied by every rose grower, whether he plants just a dozen roses or several hundreds.

Roses like an open sunny position, with plenty of air circulating through the branches, but not cold draughts. A site that is too windswept must be sheltered in some way or the losses, specially among newly-planted roses, will be considerable. Roses need regular attention, and for ease of access should be not too far from a pathway. They do not like to be hustled or crowded by herbaceous plants, but will tolerate the presence of a few dwarf annuals or carpet plants that neither shade nor suffocate them. All these factors make the conventional rose garden of small beds separated by numerous paths the best way of planning a rose garden.

It is also true that roses display to best advantage against a background of green lawn, and this accounts both for the popularity of the small rose bed cut in the lawn of the mixed-flower garden, and the use of grass walks through the larger rose garden.

GRASS AND PAVING COMBINED. — The actual design of a rose garden depends rather on the personal taste of the owner and the area available than on general rules, and beds can be circular, oval, square, rectangular, or any other shape as preferred. But the construction of the walks between the beds should be related to the size of the garden. In a large rosery where manure has to be wheeled from a distance, the combination of grass and paving for paths, i.e., brick, paving stones or tiles in the middle of the main walks, with grass verges, will effectually prevent unsightly wheel marks on the grass. It also means a cleaner pathway for visitors.

EVERY ROSE WELCOME.—Since the rose garden is primarily a place in which to grow roses, provision ought to be made for every type of rose, not limiting the choice to the hybrid teas and similar exhibition types. Pergolas on which the climbing roses can be trained, rose hedges in which full use can be made of the Austrian Briars, Scotch roses, and other interesting species, and a picturesque arrangement of standards among the bush and dwarf polyantha roses make the rose garden worthy of its name.

Makers of new rose gardens often fail to achieve good results because they are in too much of a hurry to get plants into the ground. When the rose-garden beds have been marked out by pegs, and the paths laid, the soil of the beds needs real hard spade work before it is ready to receive the plants. It must be broken to a depth of 2 ft., manure added below the top spit, and a liberal dressing of lime given— 2–8 oz. per sq. yd. according to the condition. Bonemeal, which is exceptionally beneficial to roses, can be dug into the top spit of soil at the same time as digging is done. The beds should be on the ground level, not banked high above the paths, or the roots of the plants will be over-dry, and the whole should be allowed a week or two to settle before planting begins.

Rose Exhibiting.

Apart from the joy of battle which animates all competitive flower exhibitions, there is a particular feeling of enjoyment in staging a collection of roses for the benefit of the general public. The blooms are staged, as the National Rose Society puts it, in the most "perfect phase of their possible beauty," and a fine display is worth all the trouble it entails, for the sheer joy it gives to visitors.

Exhibitions undoubtedly make the rose more popular, and there is no doubt that the shows held each year by the N.R.S. have placed the queen of flowers in the supreme position among garden favourites.

In days gone by, a rose show consisted of bench after bench of blooms all arranged in flat boxes. Only a few of these classes now survive. The amateur gardener still enjoys competing against his neighbours in a class for a limited number of individual blooms, but by far the most effective exhibits at rose shows are the larger displays of roses staged in vases, in which the beauty of stem and foliage is added to the beauty of the blooms.

The necessary staging needed for large groups of roses is often beyond the capacity of the amateur gardener and his limited means of transport, but a few amateurs do vie with the trade in staging large displays.

The remarkable groups now to be seen at big shows were only made possible when the hybrid tea rose established itself, augmented by the arrival of pernetiana roses. These types, in addition to providing the many exhibition varieties, comprise numerous others of great decorative beauty in the garden. These decorative garden roses form the foundation of large exhibition groups extending perhaps 40 ft. in length, 4 ft. deep and 8 ft. high. The amount of flowers needed to fill such a space is enormous.

Many exhibitors cut their roses with long stalks and slice the bottoms in order to help the flowers to last longer; then putting them into tall vases or buckets, so that the water nearly touches the petals, standing these overnight in a cool dark place, such as a cellar or shed. On no account should the roses stand in a draught.

When it is time to pack the roses for

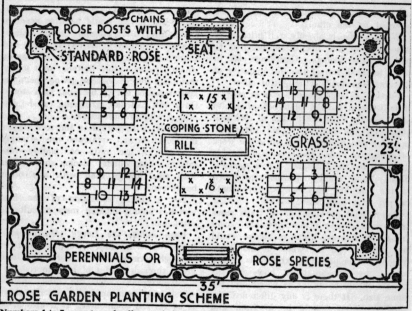

ROSE GARDEN PLANTING SCHEME

Numbers 1 to 7, orange and yellow varieties. Numbers 8 to 14, pink and red varieties. Polyantha roses in beds numbers 15 and 16.

Each bloom cut must be perfect in shape with petals smooth and clean. Some of the very full varieties may need support by wiring their necks, but the majority are now stout in the stem and hold their heads upright. In competitive classes it is always advisable to see that roses have adequately stout stems.

The flowers should be cut the day before the show and, in cutting, care should be taken to select blooms that will be just right when they are staged the following day. The best time to cut them is in the evening. They should then be placed straight into water and will keep much fresher in the vases after a good drink.

transport to the show, they should still remain in water. Large exhibitors therefore arrange for a number of crates with canvas sides and top in which tubes are fixed to hold the flowers in water.

For a large commercial exhibit of roses, a van-load of staging in sections, various size vases, and artistic baskets, tubes, etc., will be required. For the exhibition of individual blooms, special boxes are made in various sizes with tubes and special wires to hold the roses firmly in position. The boxes mostly hold either six, nine, twelve or twenty-four blooms. There are regulation boxes approved by the National Rose Society and these are used all over the country at shows which are affiliated with that society.

When a large exhibit is to be staged, the points at which to aim are quality (that is, perfection of shape and colour in the flowers themselves), lightness of arrangement, and variety. It is wise to take more blooms of each kind to a show than will be actually required, and the best blooms should be picked out first and arranged in the vases and baskets, allowing each to stand out by itself and not to be crowded by the others.

When a vase is already well filled, it is wise to stop and not to be tempted to put in more blooms. Crowding just in order to make use of the full quantity of flowers often spoils a delightful effect.

Further, if large groups are to be staged, it is wise to have a plan beforehand to show exactly where each kind of rose will stand on the staging. This saves the need for moving the vases while the work is going on and prevents considerable damage to the blooms. In a general display, and where not otherwise stated in the schedule, only one variety should be put into each vase.

Commercial growers like to stage roses in various stages of development, except full-blown flowers, which of course would not last through the whole of the show. When a competitive exhibit is being staged by an amateur, however, the flowers should be as far as possible of the same size. If there is any difference, the smaller flowers should be in front and the larger ones behind.

Each variety should be clearly labelled with its correct name—in Indian ink so that it does not run—before being placed in position. The arrangement of colours is largely a matter of taste; but the roses look much better if a rich yellow, for instance, is placed between two crimsons, instead of putting two vases of nearly-alike roses together.

"Dressing" roses—which, incidentally, is quite a different thing from "faking"— merely means cleaning them and sometimes partly opening them, so that they show to the best advantage. Large exhibition blooms are sometimes wrapped with cotton-wool and tied loosely with raffia over-night in order to prevent them from opening too wide, and when these are staged in the boxes at the show odd scraps of cotton-wool may cling to the petals, which is best removed with a camel-hair brush. At the same time any damaged petals are removed so that the flower appears perfect. Should any bloom be insufficiently opened, the brush is very gently inserted between the petals so that they are levered apart.

The question of syringeing when the stand is completed is a matter for experience. The novice would be wise *never to spray roses after staging*. Some exhibitors always spray if the day is warm and sunny, but they use a *very fine spray* which freshens the flowers and makes them last longer without giving them the appearance of having been out in a storm. On a dull cool day syringeing can be dispensed with in most cases.

Finally, with regard to the rose classes in local shows, amateurs are strongly advised to use only—or mainly—rose foliage. Fine quality blooms show better with rose foliage than with any other background.

For a brief description of the best varieties among modern roses consult the catalogues.

Rose Aphis, the Large (*Macrosiphum rosæ*). DESCRIPTION. *Adults.* — Subject to much variation in colour, ranging from green through shades of pink to red.

LIFE-HISTORY. Of the nine aphides which may occur upon the rose the above is by far the commonest. It is also to be found upon teasel and scabious, and as migrants from the former have definitely been traced to roses, there seems every reason to believe that colonies on roses are supplemented by fresh arrivals from scabious. The winter may be passed in two stages; namely, small black ova on the rose, or else by wingless females if the rose happens to be growing in a warm and sheltered corner. In June winged forms appear which fly from bush to bush, smothering the shoots in a very short time. About now a migration from the teasel occurs, and this accounts for the sudden appearance of the so-called "blight." A return migration may take place back to the teasels in September.

METHODS OF CONTROL.—Any spraying

must be done with care, for roses will not stand strong sprays. A soft soap, quassia, or one of the newer powders of vegetable origin will kill the greenfly. Owing to the great susceptibility of the rose to damage it is perhaps safer to use a dust rather than a wash.

Rose Leaf Cutter Bee (*Megachile centuncularis*). DESCRIPTION.—The adult bee, slightly more than ½ in. long, is blackish-brown in colour with a woolly thorax, white wings and a ⅞ in. expanse of the fore-wings.

LIFE-HISTORY.—It is most common during the summer months and especially in the early morning, when it attacks the leaves of roses. It cuts large pieces with its strong mandible and carries them off to use in building its nest, which is made of living vegetable matter and is usually underground. Its frequent return to the same plant renders it most destructive. The cuts made by this bee are distinguishable from those of caterpillars through being more circular and evenly cut, with no jagged edges.

METHODS OF CONTROL.—Spray the leaves with an insecticide or endeavour to catch the bee in a net when it is returning laden. It is liable to sting badly.

Another way is to trace it to its nest, which is then destroyed, but this is more difficult as it is skilful in hiding its whereabouts.

Rose Mildew (*Sphaerotheca pannosa*). This well-known disease is usually overlooked during its early stage, when it appears on the leaves soon after they have expanded. As this attack is generally slight it is therefore neglected. However, it is this stage which will give rise to the more serious form later on, which attacks not only the foliage but also the new wood and fruit. These when left on the tree set up a fresh attack in the following spring.

METHODS OF CONTROL. — Spray with liver of sulphur as soon as the leaf bud expands, or spraying with 1 oz. bicarbonate of soda to every 10 gal. of water has given good results abroad. A third wash which, however, should be used with care—but one which has given good results—is sulphuric acid, 1 part to 1,500 parts of water. Although some roses are more susceptible

than others, all varieties can be made more resistant by the application of suitable manures to induce vigorous growth.

ROSE ACACIA. *See* ROBINIA.

ROSE MALLOW. *See* HIBISCUS.

ROSEMARY. *See* ROSMARINUS.

ROSE OF HEAVEN. *See* LYCHNIS.

ROSE OF JERICHO. *See* ANASTATICA.

ROSE OF SHARON. *See* HYPERICUM.

ROSMARINUS (rŏz-ma-rī'-nus. Labiatæ). Rosemary. Europe and Asia. The well-known Rosemary has been cultivated from time immemorial. It is an evergreen shrub up to 6 ft. high, with aromatic glossy-green foliage, white-felted beneath. Flowers pale violet, blue and white, produced during May and June, and occasionally a second time in the autumn. From the leaves the fragrant essential oil so largely used in perfumery—and in some hairwashes—is produced.

Culture.—Plant in well-drained light loamy soil, in a sunny position.

Propagate by seeds, layers and cuttings. The plant bears clipping well and makes a good fragrant hedge.

R. officinalis (Europe and Asia Minor). The only species. *R. o. albus.* White.

R. o. prostratus. A distinct trailing form from Capri, but rather tender. A gem for the rock garden.

R. o. pyramidalis. An erect-growing form. The most useful variety for forming hedges.

The Rosemary is not a member of the Rose family (Rosaceæ), but takes its name from the Latin *ros-marinum*, or sea-dew, owing to its fondness for water. There is considerable romance and folk-lore in connection with rosemary. In olden times it was believed to possess a stimulating influence on the memory, and became known as "herb of memory." "There, Rosemary, that for remembrance."—*Ophelia.* It was also used at Christmas to deck the banqueting hall, and the boar's head, etc. There is a legend that the Virgin Mary spread the linen of the Holy Child on a bush of rosemary, and in memorial the rosemary flowers on the day of His passion. With the Romans it occupied an interesting place in their decorations and ceremonies. Guests at banquets were crowned with its foliage, as their famous heroes were crowned with "laurel" (*Laurus nobilis*). They planted it near tombs as they supposed its odour helped to preserve the bodies of their dead. A relic of the custom used to be observed in the North of England, when sprays of rosemary were carried in funeral processions, and cast on the coffin in the grave. Rosemary is a favourite with bees, and

The golden flowers of the tall Rudbeckia are a distinctive feature in the herbaceous border.

honey taken by them from its flowers is highly prized.

See also under HERBS, CULINARY.

ROTATION OF CROPS. *See* ALLOTMENTS.

ROUPALA (rō'-pa-la. Proteaceæ). Greenhouse evergreen flowering shrubs, with feather-shaped leaves covered with brown "fluff." Mostly from Guiana. Pot in early spring in a compost of fibrous loam, peat, leaf-mould and a little sand. Give plenty of water in the summer, but less after. In warm weather the plants may be stood in the open during the day. Winter temperature 45°–50°. Take cuttings of ripened shoots in summer, and insert in sand under a bell-glass, in a

dry atmosphere. After a few weeks the seedlings may be placed in bottom heat.

SPECIES.

R. boissieriana. Yellow.

R. elegans. Height, 6–10 ft.

R. nitida. Pale yellow.

R. Pohlii. Height, 6–15 ft. Orange-red.

ROWAN-TREE. *See* PYRUS.

RUBUS (rū'-bus. Rosaceæ). Raspberries and Brambles. A large genus of about 300 species, of wide geographical distribution throughout the tropical and temperate parts of the world. Many are hardy or half-hardy in this country; some species require the protection of a greenhouse. The hardy Rubi are highly esteemed for their fruit, and in some species, such as *R. deliciosus,* for their attractive flowers, foliage, and white stem.

Culture.—Plant in ordinary garden soil.

Propagation is by layering. The tips of many Brambles will root quite naturally when they come in contact with the soil. They may be pegged down. Also by cuttings, and to obtain new varieties, by seed. The older stems may be cut out if the plants are losing their vigour, as some species do after a few years, to make room for the new ones. The two-year-old stems of the biennial-stemmed species should be cut right out after fruiting.

SPECIES.

R. australis. The "Lawyer Vine" or "Tataramoa" of New Zealand. An evergreen rambling shrub, with slender stems covered with small spines. Flowers yellow, fragrant, followed by small reddish-orange fruits. Rather tender.

R. fruticosus. "Blackberry."

R. Giraldianus (China), 8–10 ft. Deciduous species with remarkable white stems and very elegant foliage. Fine for winter effect.

See BLACKBERRY, LOGANBERRY, ETC.

RUDBECKIA (rŭd-beck-ia. Compositæ). Cone Flower. A fine genus of hardy annuals and perennials, with flowers that are invaluable for cutting in late summer and autumn, usually with raised centres and drooping ray florets. They are suitable for the mixed sunny border.

Culture.—They do well in any good garden soil with copious supplies of water in spring and summer. *Propagate by* seeds sown in a frame in spring or early summer, the seedlings being pricked off when large enough into boxes or pans and later planted out in their flowering position, or by division of the roots at any times from March to October.

SPECIES.

R. Californica, golden yellow-ray florets, brown cone-shaped centres to the flowers, rather difficult to grow where there are many slugs, 4–6 ft.

R. laciniata, with very divided leaves and greenish-yellow disc in the yellow flowers and its beautiful variety.

R. l. flore pleno, Golden Glow, with masses of golden flowers on branching stems, in autumn, 2–8 ft.

R. maxima, a desirable species with clear yellow flowers having black centres and large leaves, 4–8 ft.

R. purpurea (syn. *Echinacea purpurea*), very showy purple flowers.

R. speciosa (syn. *Newmannii*), a profusion of bright yellow flowers with brownish-black centres, excellent for cutting. 2–3 ft. These are all perennial plants blooming in August and September.

R. bicolor, yellow and brown and *R. amplexicaulis*, yellow, are annuals, 2–3 ft. July and August.

RUE. *See* RUTA.

RUELLIA (ru-ell'-ea. Acanthaceæ). Christmas Pride. Stove perennial shrubs. Pot in early spring in a compost of fibrous loam, leaf-mould, peat and silver sand and stand in a shady part of the stove. Water freely in summer, and syringe twice daily. After that period, water moderately, and syringe only once a day. When the plants are in flower, weak stimulants may be given. Sow seeds in early spring in a sandy soil. Take cuttings in spring or summer and insert in a similar compost to that used for general cultivation. Place under a bell-glass or in the propagating frame in a temperature of 70°–75°.

SPECIES.

R. acutangula, scarlet with yellow throat, May.

R. amoena, 2–3 ft., scarlet.

R. biflora, 2 ft., July.

R. ciliosa, blue, 1 ft.

R. longiflora, purplish-lilac, October.

R. longifolia, scarlet, July, 2 ft.

R. macrantha, rosy-purple, winter. Height, 6 ft., shrubby.

R. portellæ, rose-pink, winter. Height, 1 ft.

RUMEX (ru-mex. Polygonaceæ). Sorrel. Hardy perennial herbs. Sow seeds 1 in. deep in March in ordinary moist soil in the open borders. The seedlings should be thinned to 1 ft. apart in April. Flower stems should be removed immediately they appear and the leaves gathered frequently.

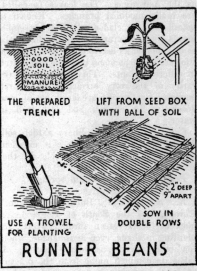

THE PREPARED TRENCH

LIFT FROM SEED BOX WITH BALL OF SOIL

USE A TROWEL FOR PLANTING

SOW IN DOUBLE ROWS

RUNNER BEANS

Runner Beans, in fact all vegetables which are planted out as seedlings, should be planted with a trowel.

Give plenty of water in dry weather. Increase by division of roots in March. These plants can also be grown as aquatics, when they should be planted in spring in ordinary soil on the margins of water. Divide the roots in spring.

SPECIES.

R. acetosa (Garden Sorrel), green, summer, 18 in. Edible leaves.

R. hydrolapathum (Water Dock). 4–6 ft.

R. Patientia (Herb Patience), leaves used as substitute for spinach. Height, 4 ft.

R. scutatus (French Sorrel), edible leaves. Height, 1–2 ft.

RUNNER. Some plants, such as the strawberry, send out prostrate shoots which form roots at intervals. It is possible to propagate the plant by means of these runners.

RUNNER BEANS. *See* BEANS, SCARLET RUNNER.

RUSCUS (rus'-kus. Liliaceæ). Butcher's Broom. A remarkable and very interesting genus of evergreen shrub-like plants, consisting of three species. It belongs to the Asparagus section of the Lily family, and renews itself by stems from the base of the plant in the same way as the Asparagus The leaves (so-called) are really modified branches. Known to botanists as "cladodes," they resemble leaves in appearance, and perform the same function as leaves do for other plants. Flowers inconspicuous, with the sexes often in different plants. This accounts for the rarity of the very attractive bright red berries. Cut sprays are most useful, and decorative in winter, and last well in water.

Culture.—Plant in ordinary garden soil. A shady or semi-shady place is excellent for this plant, and is valuable on that account.

Propagate by division in spring.

SPECIES.

R. aculeatus. "Butcher's Broom." Europe, and the South of England. A most useful evergreen shrub, 1½–3 ft., for planting in shade, even dense shade, where few other evergreens would flourish. It takes its common name from the practice of butchers using its branches to clean their blocks. In the south of Europe it is used as a garden besom.

R. a. hermaphroditus. A rarity with flowers of both sexes.

R. Hypoglossum (Europe), 8–16 in. high. Unsurpassed for growing under the shade of trees, etc.

R. racemosus. See DANÆA.

RUSTIC WORK. The term applied to any construction which is made of rough, unplaned branches. The wood most generally used is large; this is peeled to prevent the hibernation of insects. Trellis, arches, arbours, gateways and many other garden features may be constructed in this way, but the same theme should be carried out throughout the garden. If the house is of the modern, severe type, rustic work is completely out of harmony in the garden unless it is some distance removed from the formal lines of the house, or can be quickly covered with growth. It is recommended for its cheapness, but is not very lasting unless well made. The cross bars in trellis work of this type should be notched as well as nailed, the ends of the posts should be creosoted before being placed in the ground, and care should be taken to see that the structure is sufficiently strong to bear the weight of growth which is expected on it. Rustic work should be examined periodically to see if it is in need of repair.

RUTA (rū-ta. Rutaceæ). Rue. "Herb of grace."

R. graveolens. An evergreen shrub, 3 ft. high, with glaucous leaves, and dull yellow flowers. Forms a very good partition hedge in the kitchen garden, etc. Plant in ordinary garden soil on the light side. If heavy add sand or grit and mortar rubbish.

See also under HERBS, CULINARY.

S

SABAL (sa-bal. Parmaceæ). Fan Palm. Greenhouse palms, leaves fan-shaped. Florida, 1810.

Culture.—See KENTIA.

SPECIES.

S. adamsoni, 6 ft.; *S. Blackburniana*, 10–20 ft.; *S. palmetto*, Cabbage Palm. 20–30 ft.

Claytoni, Courtii, Sarracenia, Stevensii and *Williamsii* are good hybrids.

SABBATIA (sab-bat-i-a. Gentianeæ). American Centaury. Rose Pink. Annual and biennial hardy erect herbs of con-siderable value for moist places and for the bog garden.

Propagate by seed sown in light soil in pots which are placed in water. Soil, moist peat.

SPECIES.

S. calycosa. White, summer. 5–18 in.
S. campestris. Rose, summer. 6–15 in.

SACCHARUM (sak-kar-rum. Grami-neæ). Sugar Cane. Stove perennial grass, with silky inflorescence in pyramidal panicles something like Pampas Grass, appearing in July, and with ribbon-like green leaves covered with silvery hairs. Pot in early spring in two parts rich loam, one part leaf-mould or rotten manure, and a little sand. Water plentifully in summer, but after this only moderately, and syringe twice a day during spring and summer. The plants must be shaded from the midday sun.

Propagate by cuttings of stems in spring, or by suckers removed at the same time and inserted in light soil in a tempera-ture of 70°–80°.

SPECIES.

S. officinarum (Sugar Cane), white, in summer. 10–15 ft.

S. officinarum violaceum, stems violet tinted.

SAGE. *See* SALVIA.

SAGINA (sa-gi-na. Caryophyllaceæ). Pearl Weed. Hardy perennials that are chiefly weeds. Some are used for car-peting.

Propagate by seed sown out of doors in spring in sandy soil in a sunny position.

SPECIES.

S. glabra. White flowers in summer, is often used as a substitute for grass in forming lawns.

S. procumbens. White. Used for carpeting. 2 in.

S. subulata. White. Its golden leaved variety is also used for bedding.

SAGITTARIA (sag-it-tar-ia. Alisma-ceæ). Arrow Head. Hardy, perennial aquatic herbs. Can be planted in ponds in the same way as advised for Nymphæas. *See* WATER PLANTS.

SPECIES.

S. latifolia, white and purple, summer. Some species are a little tender and more suitable for cultivation under glass.

SAINT BERNARD'S LILY. *See* ANTHERICUM.

SAINT BRUNO'S LILY. *See* PARA-DISEA.

SAINT JOHN'S WORT. *See* HYPERI-CUM.

SAINTPAULIA (Gesneraceæ). A very interesting, warm greenhouse plant, with flowers somewhat resembling a violet.

Cultivation.—Seeds should be sown in early spring in good heat and pricked out when large enough. Pot up into 60's when large enough in a compost of good loam, peat and sand. They flower well in 60-size pots and, from seed, slight variations may be expected.

Species.—S. ionantha, violet; and *S. kewensis*, violet. Also varieties of *S. ionantha*.

SALADS. *See* CUCUMBER, LETTUCE, BEETROOT, TOMATO, SPRING ONIONS, etc.

SALIX (sal'-ix. Salicineæ). Willow. Hardy evergreen and deciduous shrubs and trees, quick growing, and very useful for planting in damp situations. They make quite a good substitute for bamboos in exposed positions. The bark of some of the varieties is very beautiful and most effective in autumn and winter, with brilliant orange, yellow, and crimson markings. Certain species are consider-ably valued as timber trees. *S. cærulea* is highly prized by cricket-bat manufacturers.

Culture.—Plant in moist loamy soils.

Propagate by seed sown as soon as ripe. Cutting root with care insert in damp soil, at almost any time of year. The pendulous or weeping forms should be grafted or budded on 6–8 ft. standards. The catkins in male plants are more showy than those of the opposite sex.

SPECIES.

S. alba. The "White Willow" of Europe, N. Asia, and Britain. 70 ft. Used by makers of cricket bats, but the wood is inferior to that of *S. cærulea* for that purpose.

Salads to be tender should be grown quickly, which means plenty of moisture and rich soil and warmth.

S. babylonica. The "Weeping Willow" of China. 30–50 ft. Seen at its best by the riverside.

S. caprea. The "Goat Willow," "Common Sallow," "Palm Willow." This is the species which provides "palm" for use on the Sunday before Easter, i.e., Palm Sunday. Good on chalky soils.

S. cærulea. The "Cricket Bat Willow." The wood of this willow produces the finest cricket bats. Of uncertain origin, and is found growing wild in the Eastern Counties, where it sometimes attains to a height of about 100 ft. It may be a natural hybrid between *S. alba* + *S. fragilis.*

S. daphnoides. The "Violet Willow." Europe to the Himalayas. 40 ft. The shoots are covered with a beautiful violet-coloured waxy bloom.

S. viminalis. The "Common Osier." Native of Britain, extending through Europe to the Himalayas. 20 ft. Much used for basket-making.

S. vitellina. The "Golden Willow," of doubtful origin. Used in basket-making. Its golden-yellow branches are very ornamental during autumn and winter, and sometimes up to April. For this purpose several plants should be grouped together, and pruned hard back every spring.

S. v. britzensis. An exceptionally fine rarity, with branches of a brilliant orange-scarlet, and yellow catkins in May.

SALLOW. *See* SALIX CAPREA.

SALPIGLOSSIS (sal-pi-glossis. Solanaceæ). Chile. Half-hardy annuals. The range of colours and markings in modern varieties of salpiglossis is truly remarkable. The flowers are large, funnel-shaped, and many are beautifully veined. They are not difficult to grow in a fairly light soil. Sow in March, plant out June, or sow in August–September, grow on during winter in cool greenhouse, repotting as required for flowering under glass. April–May. Good as pot plants, for bedding, or cut flowers.

For conservatory decoration seeds should be sown in August to produce flowering plants the following spring. Prick out when large enough and pot into size 60 pots towards autumn. The plants move very little during winter, and watering should be done with care. With the lengthening days of spring they begin to grow rapidly and should be potted on into larger pots as they require it, using a good compost of loam, leaf-mould and a little rotted manure, opened with crushed mortar, rubble and sand. They respond readily to feeding with dilute liquid manure in the latter stages of growth.

Varieties.—Purple and gold, violet, scarlet, rose and white with gold stripe. The *S. gloxiniæflora* varieties are chamois rose, light blue, violet, velvety red and yellow-edged white.

SALSIFY (*Tragopogon porrifolius*). Compositæ. This plant is actually a biennial, native in Northern Europe, and is often referred to as "The Vegetable Oyster."

It is an excellent vegetable but rarely found in any but the largest establishments, possibly because its preparation for the table is not properly understood.

Culture.—A deep rich soil of a light nature is ideal for this crop, and if the soil be at all heavy and retentive and good roots are desired it is advisable to "bore" as advised for exhibition parsnips, filling in the holes with some specially-prepared soil. If this crop follows celery the preparation and treatment of the soil for the latter leaves it in an excellent condition for salsify.

The seed should be sown in the spring in drills 1 ft. apart in the bed where they are to remain and mature.

When a few inches high the seedlings should be thinned to 4 in. apart, after which occasional hoeing and copious watering during drought are all that is required. About October the roots may be lifted, cleaned of earth and tops, and stored like carrots for winter use.

VARIETIES.

Mammoth. Sandwich Island.

Uses.—The roots are used as a boiled vegetable, and the youngest and tenderest leaves are used as a salad.

SALT-MARSH. Salt-marshes are being formed at various parts of the British coast. These are due either to the action of sea currents heaping up material in certain places, or by accumulations of river silt, largely at the mouths of estuaries. The material deposited may be clay, sand or gravel. As it is highly charged with sea salt, only specialised vegetation will grow in such a locality. Here we may find Sea-Marram-grass, Sea-campion, Sea-pink, Sea-blite, Sea-lavender, Sea-starwort, etc. As the rain washes out the excess salt, so the land becomes gradually good. England is gaining more land in this way than she is losing by sea-erosion.

SALT-TREE. *See* HALIMODENDRON.

SALVIA (săl-via. Labiatæ). Sage. This large genus includes annual, biennial and perennial herbs and sub-shrubs, some of which are very ornamental in the greenhouse while others are good border plants.

Culture.—The annuals are propagated by seed sown in the open in April or under glass in February and planted out in April 9 in. apart; the biennials by seed sown from May to June in the open or in a frame; the perennials by seed sown in the open in May by division in October or by cuttings taken in August and struck in sandy soil in a cold frame or taken in February and rooted in heat. For pot culture sow seed in gentle heat in February, prick off and pot on until the flowering size, which may be anything from 6–10 in., is reached, care being taken that the plants do not become pot-bound. Use a compost of 2 parts of loam to 1 of coarse sand, leaf-mould and manure. Water well with liquid manure and pinch back the plants during the first few months. They may be put out of doors in the summer and taken into the cool greenhouse in October. Near London they are often affected by fogs, and in foggy weather they should be kept fairly cool and dry. The pot plants may also be increased by cuttings of young wood in April, kept in heat for quick rooting.

SPECIES.

The perennial border salvias include *S. argentea*, with silvery rosettes of leaves and rosy-white flowers, 3 ft., *S. glutinosa* (Jupiter's Distaff) pale yellow, *S. grandiflora*, an evergreen of somewhat shrubby habit with large pale blue and white flowers, *S. hians*, with branching stems bearing spikes of blue flowers, a rather rare species; *S. pratensis*, a profusely flowering variety with bright violet-blue flowers, and its varieties, *alba*, white, *rosea*, red, and *Tenori*, violet, 2 ft. and *S. virgata*, a handsome species with deep blue flower and reddish stems, 2 ft.

S. Sclarea (Clary) naturalises well in the wild garden and has bluish-white flowers.

S. officinalis is the common Sage that is more useful in the kitchen garden than in the mixed border. *See* HERBS, CULINARY.

GREENHOUSE.

Height 1–2½ ft. according to variety.

Cultivation (under glass).—Sow the seed in boxes of well-drained soil, composed of leaf-mould, loam and sand; cover with ¼ in. of sand, after pressing the seeds into the surface of the soil and water in with tepid water. Place in a propagating pit to germinate and prick out after the seedlings have made enough root. Pot on into 60-size pots when about 2 or 3 in. high in a compost of leaf-mould, loam and sand, to which has been added a sprinkling of complete fertiliser. Grow on in good heat and, when well rooted in the 60's, pot on into 32-size pots, using a similar compost, but rather coarser in texture and somewhat richer.

S. splendens, is a beautiful green-house plant. Can be grown as a half-hardy annual for summer bedding, for which it is invaluable owing to its brilliant scarlet colouring, or in pots in the green-house, where it will bloom through the winter. Its varieties *Bruantii*, very fine, *compacta*, dwarf, *grandiflora*, large, and "Silver Spot" with silver-spotted leaves are equally useful.

S. patens, is a lovely blue-flowered evergreen that may be used for summer bedding or in pots, and should be treated in the same way as Dahlias, the roots being lifted in autumn, stored during the winter and started in heat in March prior to planting out in May.

SALVINIA (sal-vin-i-a. Salviniaceæ). A pretty little aquatic for stove or green-house that floats on the water like Azolla and increases very rapidly in summer. The plants have tiny fern leaves with no roots but the under sides of the leaves perform the functions of the roots.

Propagate by division or by spores that fall to the bottom of the tank and if there is a little loam at the bottom will germinate.

SPECIES.

S. auriculata (syn. *natans*), has pea-green foliage.

SAMBUCUS (sam-bū-kus. Capri-foliaceæ). Elder. Deciduous flowering shrubs, or small trees, with pithy wood and bold foliage. Flowers always some shade of white.

Culture.—Plant in moist loamy soil, in sun or shade. They are very partial to soils containing chalk.

Propagation by cuttings of half-ripened wood with a "heel" in frames.

SPECIES.

S. canadensis (Canada to Florida). "The American Elder." 12 ft. Fruit purple-black.

S. c. maxima. An exceptionally fine form, of robust habit of growth, with leaves up to 18 in. long. Flowers white in huge clusters from 10–18 in. across,

freely produced during late summer and autumn.

S. nigra. The "Common Native Elder," of this country and Europe. 15–20 ft. Berries shining black.

S. n. flore pleno. Double flowers.

S. n. foliis aureis. The "Golden Elder," useful for producing a broad patch of colour. The golden tone of the leaves intensifies as the season advances. Cut back in spring.

S. n. laciniata. The "Parsley-leaved Elder," with handsome cut leaves.

S. racemosa. The "Red-berried Elder" of Europe and Asia. A striking orna-mental bush up to 13 ft. high, in a soil and district which suit it. Its scarlet berries are produced more freely on the Continent than they are in this country.

SAMOLUS (sam-o-lus. Primulaceæ). Tasmanian Water Pimpernel. Hardy herbaceous perennials that grow in any garden soil and are increased by division in spring.

SPECIES.

S. repens. White. August. 6 in.

SANCHEZIA (san-ke-zi-a. Acantha-ceæ). Stove flowering and ornamental shrub that is grown in a compost of peat and loam, decayed manure and sand, potted in March and stood in a light part of the stove in winter, and in the shade in summer. It needs syringing once a day in summer, but only once a week after. Give plenty of water in summer, but only moderate quantities at other times. Weak stimulants may also be given during the growing season. In-crease by cuttings of young shoots in summer, inserted in fine soil under a bell-glass.

S. nobilis, yellow and red, March to October. Height 3–4 ft., and its variety *S. n. variegata*, leaves striped with yellow.

SAND AND SANDSTONE. Sand makes a poor soil, both chemically and physically. Chemically, it is not suffi-ciently varied. Physically, it lets the water run through too easily. Sand is largely broken-up quartz. Probably its origin was in ancient hills of granite, a rock containing about sixty-six per cent. of quartz material. Sandstones are merely hardened sands. The more impure and loamy the sand is, the better the plants will like it. If your garden is sandy mix in as much clay as you can. In Nature the loamy element is generally there, if only in patches. As we have already said, under the heading of GRAVEL, such chemically poor soils attract the order Leguminosæ. Here they can revel without too much fear of competition. Gorse loves the sunny side of a sandy hill, and when in full bloom makes a grand show. Pine and birch are hardy and for reasons of their own flourish on sandy heaths.

On sandstone hills, heather and bilberry will make a brave show. They are tough and can withstand the hardships of such a locality. When the heather is in bloom the pageant is grand. If a clayey patch retains moisture in a saucer-like hollow, there will be delicate-looking sphagnum moss and dainty white cotton-grass, Here we may also find that exquisite gem, the Bog Asphodel. And in the drier places again, perhaps Harebells and Eyebright, and the wonderful little blue Scabious. The variety may be limited, but the display is a rich one all the same. The plants that have conquered the hardships show the shining faces of those who have fought and won.

SAND MYRTLE. *See* LEIOPHYLLUM.

SAND VERBENA. *See* ABRONIA.

SANDWORT. *See* ARENARIA.

SANGUINARIA (san-guin-ā-ria. Papaveraceæ). Bloodroot. The only grown species of this genus is *S. canadensis*, a hardy perennial plant that likes a sunny position in the rock garden or border in moist sandy peat. It bears solitary white flowers in April and May before the leaves expand, and is propagated by division, or by seeds sown in a cold frame in spring.

SANSEVIERA (san-se-vi-e-ra. Liliaceæ). Bow-string Hemp. Stove herbaceous perennials, with ornamental foliage. Pot during spring in a compost of loam, leaf-mould and sand, and stand in a shady part of the stove. Water freely in summer, but moderately afterwards, also syringe during the summer. Increase by division of plants during spring.

SPECIES.

S. cylindrica, white in August. Height 2½-5 ft., leaves banded with dark green.

S. thyrsiflora (syn. *S. guineensis*). Greenish-white in September. Height to 1½ ft. Leaves banded pale green.

S. trifasciata Laurentii, greenish-white. Height 2 ft., leaves striped golden-yellow.

S. zeylanica, greenish-white. Height 2-2½ ft., leaves banded light-green. (Syn. *S. stenophylla*.

SANTOLINA (san-tŏ-lī´-na. Compositæ). Lavender Cotton. Evergreen hardy or half-hardy fragrant shrubs with small yellow-flowers.

Culture.—Plant in light, dry soil.

Propagate by cuttings and seeds.

SPECIES.

S. Chamæcyparissus (incana). The "Lavender Cotton" of the Mediterranean region. Valuable on account of its silvery-white foliage, and masses of yellow flower-heads. A very old plant of English gardens, having been grown in this country since the 16th century.

S. C. nana. Of dwarf habit.

SANVITALIA (san-vit-a-lea. Compositæ). Trailing. Mexico. *S. procumbens* and *S. p. flore pleno*, useful annuals for sunny rockery or edging. Flower yellow, black disk. Sow in April, ordinary soil. 6 in.

SAPINDUS (să-pin´-dus. Sapindaceæ). Soapberries. Interesting trees with elegant foliage and showy fruits. Hardy.

SPECIES.

S. Drummondii. The "Soapberry" of U.S.A. with foliage like the Robinia.

S. Mukorosii. A new species from Japan, similar to the preceding.

SAPIUM (săp´-i-um. Euphorbiaceæ). *S. sebiferum* (China). A small tree with brilliant autumn foliage. Of economic importance, yielding a black dye, and tallow.

SAPONARIA (săp-on-ā-ria. Caryophyllaceæ). Soapwort. A genus of hardy and half-hardy annuals and perennial herbs of which only a few are useful for the border or rock garden. The name Soapwort is derived from the fact that the leaves of *S. officinalis*, the common native plant, when bruised form a lather in water.

Propagate the annuals by seeds, the perennials by seeds, by cuttings taken after flowering, and by division in autumn or spring. Plant from October to April in ordinary light garden soil in a sunny or semi-shaded position for those used in the border and peaty loam for the rocky plants.

S. calabrica, a dwarf hardy annual with pink flowers and its white variety, *alba*, are the most useful for beds.

S. ocymoides, a summer blooming hardy perennial with rosy-pink flowers and its varieties *splendens*, deep rose, and *splendissimus*, which like partial shade, are good rock plants.

S. officinalis, with pink flowers is quite attractive, but the usefulness of its double form is marred by the spreading habit of the roots, which are apt to choke those of other plants. All bloom in July and August, 6–12 in.

S. vaccaria (pink) and *S. v. alba*, 2½ ft., are useful annuals for borders or cutting, and will grow almost anywhere in ordinary garden soil.

SARCOCOCCA (sar-kŏ-kok'-ka. Euphorbiaceæ). Evergreen, low-growing shrubs from Asia and the Himalayas with fragrant white flowers, followed by blue-black fruits.

Culture.—Plant in ordinary garden soil, on moist side for choice. They will thrive in shade or semi-shade; also under trees.

Propagate by cuttings taken in summer.

S. hookeriana (Himalayas), 3 ft. Leaves narrow. Flowers very fragrant in March, followed by egg-shaped blue-black fruits.

S. h. humilis (China). 1½ ft. A neat, narrow-leaved variety, with very fragrant white flowers, during February and March. Fruit blue-black.

S. ruscifolia (China), 1½–2 ft. Leaves dark lustrous green, paler beneath. Flowers milk white, very sweetly scented. A very pleasing little shrub that is quite happy under trees and in shady places. Fruit deep scarlet.

SARMIENTA (sar-mi-en-ta. Gesneraceæ). Chilian Pitcher Flower. Greenhouse evergreen creeper.

Plant in March in teak hanging baskets, or in pots placed where the plants can climb. Grow in a compost of soft peat, charcoal, and chopped sphagnum moss. Water copiously in summer, but after this period only moderate watering is necessary. Syringe daily in summer and shade from direct sunshine. Divide the plants in March, or increase by cuttings inserted in sand, or by seeds.

S. repens. Scarlet in summer. (Syn. *S. scandens*).

SARRACENIA (sarra-cē-nia. Sarraceniaceæ.) Side-Saddle Flower. Huntsman's Horn. Pitcher Plant. An interesting genus of half-hardy insectivorous perennials that originated in N. America. There are only a few species, but from these many handsome hybrids have been raised. The leaves are long, hairy, and shaped like pitchers or a huntsman's horn (the popular name), and serve as a trap for insects. The flowers are curious in that the umbrella-shaped style consists of five distinct pieces that are petaloid in appearance.

Culture.—Propagate by division in early spring before growth commences and plant in a compost of moist fibrous peat and sphagnum in an open sunny spot. For obtaining new types use seeds sown in a similar compost.

All the plants, whether grown in pots or outside, must have free drainage, ample supplies of water during the summer, less when resting and a close but not warm greenhouse with a winter temperature of 45° and as cool as possible in summer.

The hardiest of the genus is *purpurea*, which may in sheltered districts, remain out of doors during the winter if a little protection is given to the roots. The horn formed by the leaves is blood-red in colour and about 10 in. long, while the purple flowers are fairly small and inconspicuous.

SARSAPARILLA PLANT. *See* SMILAX.

SASSAFRAS (Lauraceæ). Hardy deciduous trees, 70–90 ft. high, with leaves of variable shape, of a glossy dark green colour, slightly glaucous beneath. Flowers of no account.

Culture.—Plant in well-drained lime-free soil in sheltered position.

Propagate by seed, which usually has to be obtained from American nurserymen. The young plants should be grown on in pots until ready for their permanent positions.

S. officinale (U.S.A.). A very handsome tree, of fine pyramidal habit. In Surrey it has reached to a height of 50–60 ft. Foliage very richly coloured in autumn.

Leaves and young bark very aromatic.

S. Tzumu (China). Represented at Kew, but not in general cultivation.

SATINFLOWER. *See* SISYRINCHIUM.

SATUREIA (sat-u-ri-a. Labiatæ). Aromatic herbs and shrubs; for cultivation, *see* SAVORY under HERBS, CULINARY.

SAUROMATUM (sau-rom-a-tum. Aroideæ). Monarch of the East. Half-hardy and stove perennials with tuberous roots and flower spathes like those of the arum.

Propagate by removing the offsets in spring and plant in loam and peat in equal parts with sand. Give plenty of water. The plants can also be grown without water by keeping them in a saucer in a warm room for a few weeks when the flowers will appear. After flowering the tubers should be planted outdoors in a moist place to make their leaf growth in order to form tubers for the following year, when the process is repeated.

SPECIES.

S. guttatum. Purple yellow and green.

SAURURUS (sau-ru-rus. Piperaceæ). Lizard's Tail. Aquatic perennials that do well by the margins of ponds.

Propagate by division at planting time in spring or by seed. Grow in moist sandy loam near a stream or near water.

SPECIES.

S. cernuus. American Swamp Lily. White flowers. Spikes 4–5 in. long.

SAVOY. *See* CABBAGE.

SAWS. *See under* PRUNERS.

SAXEGOTHÆA (sax-e-go'-thæa. Coniferæ). A monotypic genus from Chile with Yew-like foliage.

S. conspicua. "Prince Albert's Yew." Fairly hardy.

SAXIFRAGA (sax-e-fra-ga. Saxifragaceæ). From *saxum*, a stone, *frango*, I break, from their supposed power over gall-stones.

In Saxifrages we have the great stand-by of the rock garden. The number of varieties is very large, and since they hybridise freely, the number of hybrids of greater or less worth is even more numerous. The genus can be divided into several distinct types requiring some differences in cultivation. Accordingly they will be treated here under their sectional sub-headings, general notes on the cultivation proper for each class being included.

Kabschia Section. This group forms compact cushions of grey or green, usually lime-encrusted foliage. The flowers are proportionately large, white or yellow, the pink and red-flowered varieties being chiefly due to hybridisation with members of the *Engleria* section, which is closely akin and dealt with under this group for convenience. The Kabschias are not quite so

SAXIFRAGA BURSERIANA GLORIA

The cushion Saxifrages thrive best in a rock garden pocket of gritty soil.

easily grown as other groups, but in a gritty soil of good loam, leaf-mould and limestone chips, made firm when planting, or in a moraine, they should present little difficulty. They revel in full sun but must not be allowed to get dry at the root, otherwise they will scorch. As pot plants in a cold alpine house they are very effective. All flower early in spring.

S. apiculata is a garden hybrid between *S. sancta* and *S. marginata* and is one of the oldest in cultivation. It forms spring green cushions from which rise loose heads of primrose yellow on 3 in. stems. It is of the easiest culture. *S. a. alba* is a good white form. February.

S. Borisii is a hybrid between *S. Ferdinandi Coburgi* and *S. marginata*. Blue-grey rosettes and sulphur-yellow flowers on pinkish stems.

S. burseriana, with its superb offshoot *S. b. Gloria*, is the queen of the Kabshias if not the queen of the whole race of Saxifraga. It has enormous pure white flowers set singly or at most in pairs on red stems thrown up in February and March from grey-rosetted cushions, which almost disappear under the profusion of bloom. If this is happy in its situation it will increase mightily, but even if growth is slow it will never fail to bloom. 2 in. Dolomites.

S. Elisabethæ. A hybrid of *S. burseriana* and *S. sancta ;* has deep green foliage and sulphur-yellow flowers on glandular pink stems. The flowers are a better colour and larger than those of its parent, *S. sancta.*

S. Cherry Trees has neat yellow-green spiny rosettes and yellow flowers. It is a *burseriana* hybrid but, unlike its parent, difficult to flower. Hot sun and poor soil may bring these out, but those who acquire it will need optimism.

S. Faldonside is a hybrid of the blood of *S. burseriana*, to which it makes a fit consort. The flowers on their grey cushions are almost as large and quite as freely produced, but instead of being white are a clear citron yellow. February and March.

S. Ferdinandi-Coburgi, after the Balkan king of that name, whose hobbies consisted of the somewhat unexpected combination of botany and political intrigue, in both of which he attained eminence, has golden yellow flowers on neat silver-spined clumps. Bulgaria.

S. Irvingi, a hybrid between *S. burseriana* and *S. Frederici Augusti*, is one of the neatest and most compact, forming a tight, rounded little wad on which close against the leaves are numerous little flowers of lilac-pink.

S. marginata is on rather a larger scale. It has short, strap-shaped green foliage with a conspicuous band of lime round the margin of each leaflet. The flowers are carried in loose heads of pure white. 2 in. Central Italy.

S. Salomoni is a hybrid between *S. burseriana* and *S. marginata*. The blue-grey

tufts are somewhat loose and spiny, the flowers are white, in bunches of 3 or 4 on reddish stems. Of easy cultivation.

S. sancta. Spiny. Green tufts and yellow flowers. Spreads quickly. 2 in. Eastern Europe and Asia Minor.

Encrusted Section. The features of this group are the rosettes of grey strap-shaped lime-encrusted leaves, larger in every way than the Kabschias. These will grow in any good soil that is not waterlogged. They flower later than the Kabschias, generally in May or June.

S. aizoon has silvered rosettes and white flowers. It has given rise to a great number of varieties. Two of the best are *S. a. punctatissima*, with large, white, red-speckled flowers, and *S. a. rosea*, from Bulgaria, a good clear pink. 9 in.

S. cochlearis has close tufts of small, recurved grey leaves and four or five milk-white flowers on reddish stems, 4–8 in. S. Europe. *S. c. minor* is smaller and still neater, the flowers white.

C. Cotyledon has long panicles of white flowers rising from rosettes of strap-shaped silvery-encrusted leaves. The rosette dies after flowering but has previously produced others, so that this plant survives. There are a number of beautiful varieties, the best being *S. c. caterhamensis* and *S. c. pyramidalis.*

S. Dr. Ramsay. Spikes of large white flowers heavily spotted with crimson, on red stems.

S. incrustata has handsome spread-out foliage of blue-green with a white beading along the edge. The flowers are a dull white, and not attractive. Eastern Alps.

S. lingulata forms mats of curled leaves, long and narrow, with flowers in arching white sprays. This species has many forms, one of the best being *S. l. lantoscana*. This prefers shade.

S. longifolia is the star of this group. Huge rosettes of silvery, strap-shaped leaves beaded with white ; best seen when pressed flat against the rocks in whose crevices it should be planted. The flower head is a huge plume of crowded white blossoms. The plant dies after flowering, but is raised easily from seed sown in gritty soil. The garden variety, Tumbling Waters, is even finer than the type. From Spain, where it is called Crown Royal.

Mossy Section. Large green mounds and cushions of very rapid growth. The flowers are produced in great profusion in May. They grow well in any soil, though if it be very dry they are apt to turn brown in patches. There are many varieties and fresh ones are brought out very frequently. They are best selected from catalogues. Some leading sorts are *S. ceratophylla*, a strong-growing white, and a true species, but the name is applied in catalogues to many of similar appearance.

S. bathoniensis, brilliant crimson, the flowers, however, fade to a dingy pink with age. *Wenlock Peach*, pink; *Mrs. Stormouth*, red; *atro-purpurea*, a small-flowered, dark purple.

Oppositifolia Section. Prostrate, trailing shoots with carmine flowers set along them in May. They appreciate a cool open soil or moraine.

S. oppositifolia, a native of the Yorkshire Fells as well as of all the mountain chains of northern Europe, is the type. Improved developments of it are two varieties, *S. o. splendens* and *Wetterhorn*.

Umbrosa Section. This includes the London Prides. They have rounded scalloped-edged leaves and delicate sprays of pinkish flowers. They do best in shade and for that reason are useful in combination with ferns.

S. Bucklandi is very small and neat, *S. Geum* is larger, and *S. umbrosa*, London Pride, is largest of all. Except for these distinctions of size the appearance of all these is very similar.

Megasea Section. The Elephant's Ears used to be dignified with a genus to themselves, but are now united with Saxifraga. They have large, glossy, leathery leaves, which turn a red colour in autumn. The flowers are usually pink to purple-red. They like half-shaded positions, but do well in full sun. The best are *S. cordifolia*, pink; *S. c. purpurea*, *S. Smithii*, red.

SCABIOSA (ska-bi-o-sa. Dipsaceæ). Scabious, Sweet. S. Europe. *S. atropurpurea*, the original species, has purple-black flowers, while the garden varieties to which it has given rise range in colours from pale to dark blue, pink to deep red, and white, and although biennials, are best in most districts if treated as half-hardy annuals. They will thrive almost anywhere and sown in March under glass, planted out in June, or sown where to flower in April, give a wealth of flowers for cutting from July to autumn. 3 ft.

Scabiosa caucasica is a perennial species the flowers of which are so useful for cutting. They resemble the Sweet Scabious except that the outer florets are enlarged, making the flowers more decorative, though the colour range is not so great as in the case of the Sweet Scabious. Plant in spring. Ordinary treatment for hardy perennials is suitable, but care must be taken to see that the plants do not suffer from lack of moisture at any period and particularly in June and July. Some of the best modern varieties are:—

Clive Greaves, a mauve flower and particularly large.

Innocence, white.

Isaac House, violet-blue.

Elsie, pale blue.

Kenneth Ball, iris-blue.

SCALE. *See* MUSSEL SCALE.

SCALE, ASH (*Chionaspis salicis*). Ash and Willows are often covered with a whitish scale-like encrustation. This is the protecting cover of the insect known as the Ash Scale. If in the winter or early spring one of these scales is raised it will be found to contain countless small pink eggs. In May these eggs hatch out and the minute larvæ wander over the tree until they find a suitable position to rest. Having found such a place they dig their proboscis into the bark, suck the sap and grow rapidly. At this period a process of degeneration is gone through, the antennæ and legs being shed. The skin is now cast and it is at this period the sex is determined. If the resulting adult is to be a female she again casts her skin under which she lives till she is ready to repeat the process. Having cast her skin for the third time, she begins to cover herself with a scale which is whitish-grey in colour and more or less flask-shaped. The female is now merely a bag of eggs under the scale, but in the early autumn, when egg-laying commences, she gradually diminishes in size. Should the larva be destined to be a male, only change of skin takes place and the scale formed is smaller and more linear in shape. The male, which hatches out in July, has two wings, a pair of antennæ and six legs, and during its short life of from three to seven days it lives actively on the tree.

METHOD OF CONTROL.—Spray during the dormant season, but preferably after Christmas, with a caustic wash such as 3 lb. of caustic soda dissolved in 10 gal. of water. The eyes and skin should be protected, goggles and gloves being worn, and vaseline being applied to the face.

SCALE FERN. *See* ASPLENIUM CETERACH.

SCARBOROUGH LILY. *See* VALLOTA.

SCARLET AVENS. *See* GEUM.

SCHINUS (shi-nus. Anacardiaceæ). Evergreen aromatic shrubs or trees, only half-hardy. Plant in ordinary garden soil, on the poor side.

Propagate by cuttings in August and placed in gentle heat.

SPECIES.

S. dependens (Chile), 15 ft. Flowers greenish-yellow, followed by clusters of deep purple berries.

S. molle (*S. America*). Leaves finely divided, berries red in large clusters.

S. terebinthifolius (Brazil). Attractive foliage and clusters of red berries.

SCHIZANDRA (skïz-an′-dra. Magnoliaceæ). A genus of climbing shrubs, from Asia and N. America, allied to the Magnolias.

Culture.—Plant in rich loamy soil, on north or east walls. They dislike scorching sun.

Propagate by cuttings of half-ripened wood in mild bottom heat.

SPECIES.

S. chinensis (China and Japan). A beautiful, deciduous, climbing shrub, up to 20–30 ft. The fragrant, pale rose-coloured flowers are produced in April and May, followed by pendulous spikes of scarlet berry-like fruits.

S. grandiflora rubriflora (Himalayas). Flowers deep red during April and May. Fruit scarlet.

S. propinqua sinensis (China). Evergreen. Flowers orange-yellow in July; fruit scarlet.

S. sphenanthera (China). Vigorous-growing species with large leaves and orange-coloured flowers. 3 in. long spikes of red fruit.

SCHIZANTHUS (skiz-an-thus. Scrophulariaceæ). Butterfly Flower. A decorative and showy half-hardy annual, very popular for the greenhouse in spring. The flowers are very varied in colour, and often handsomely spotted with gold and black or with a deeper tone of the same colour as the flower. Purple, mauve, pink, rich red, crimson, orange, salmon, white and cherry-red are some of the shades included in a good strain, and the flowers are very numerous. The foliage is fresh green and beautifully cut, rather resembling a fern. Height, 1–3 ft., according to strain and cultivation.

Cultivation.—For flowering at the normal time (May) seeds should be sown in a cold frame during September in a box containing an open compost of loam, leaf mould, and sand. Sow thinly to avoid overcrowding in the early stages of growth. Prick out when large enough, and continue to grow in the frame to keep them short-jointed and sturdy. When about 2½ in. high they may be potted up singly into size 60 pots, using a similar compost, and the same cool treatment may continue, only excluding frosts. When thoroughly rooted in the pots they may be potted on into larger pots, using a richer and rather coarser compost, composed of fibrous loam (3 parts), sifted rotten manure (⅓ of a part), leaf-mould (⅓ of a part), mortar rubble and sand to open with a sprinkling of a complete fertiliser. Use rough leaf-mould as drainage over the crocks.

The size pot used depends largely on the strain being grown or the size the plants are required. Compact-growing strains should be flowered in 48's or 32's (5 or 6 in. pots), but larger-growing strains, if required, may be potted again from the 48's or the 32's, and flowered in 24's, or even 10–12 in. pots.

Schizanthuses have very brittle foliage, and great care should be taken not to break the leaves.

The plants should be grown as cool as possible, only supplying enough artificial heat to exclude frosts and to maintain an atmosphere free from stagnant moisture. It is an advantage to stop the plants when they are 6 or 8 in. high by pinching out the heads, and some of the plants may benefit by stopping all the laterals in the later stages of growth. This later stopping of some of the plants is sometimes a help in obtaining a mixed strain of hybrids in flower together.

Staking should be done neatly with very thin, green bamboos, and watering should always be done with care, only watering when necessary, but watering well when they require it. They respond readily to feeding when well rooted in the final pots. Use dilute liquid manure, about 1 pint to 2 gallons, with an occasional variation of soft water.

SPECIES.

Chiefly *S. wisetonensis* and its hybrids. Some of the finest modern varieties are:

Compact.—Roseus Compactus, Dwarf Hybrids, Excelsior Strain, Snowflake.

Large-growing but of compact habit.— Grandiflora Hybrids, Dr. Badger's Hybrids, Pansy-flowered strains (which are self-colours without spots).

Large-growing.—Butterfly-flowered.

Schizanthus retusus.—Pink Beauty is also useful, and *Schizanthus pinnatus* is sometimes grown. The latter is hardier, and may be sown out of doors in March or April in rich light soil for summer flowering. Choose a sheltered spot, and support with "twiggy" sticks. 1½ ft.

SCHIZOCODON (skiz-o-ko-don. Diapensiaceæ). A relative of Shortia, *which see* for culture.

SPECIES.

S. soldanelloides. A little dwarf gem for woodland conditions. Flowers deep rose, petals fringed, produced in March.

SCHIZOPETALON (sky-zo-pet-a-lon. Cruciferæ). Chile. Flowers white, nightscented. Rather a straggling grower, and curiously fringed rather than beautiful flowers. Requires a moist, sandy soil, and semi-shade. Sow under glass, March, or outside in April.

SCHIZOPHRAGMA (skiz-ō-frag′-ma. Saxifragaceæ). Deciduous climbing shrubs thriving in moist soil in shady positions.

SPECIES.

S. hydrangeoides (Japan). A handsome climber for a south-west or sheltered east wall. Flowers cream-coloured, small and very freely produced in July.

S. integrifolium (China). Vigorous-growing, large-leaved climbers for south-west or east wall, to which it clings like ivy. The large 12 in. inflorescences of white bracts are not always produced very freely in this country.

SCHIZOSTYLIS (schiz-o-sti-lis. Iridaceæ). From *schezo*, I cut, and *stulos,* style. The style is deeply divided.

These are very suitable for the cool greenhouse, making ideal pot plants and blooming in the early winter when flowers are scarce. The foliage and flowers closely resemble gladiolus, but are much smaller. S. Africa, 1864.

Culture.—Compost: 2 parts loam, 1 part leaf-mould and sand. Repot annually September and stand in cool house; after flowering stand outside in cold frame. Never allow roots to become dry. It is best to plunge pots up to the rims in ashes.

Propagate by division when repotting.

ONLY SPECIES.

S. coccinea. The Kaffir Lily. Crimsonscarlet, cup-shaped flowers set along slender 2 ft. stems. Narrow iris leaves. It has the advantage of flowering in October and November. Although from The Cape it seems perfectly hardy in a sunny rock garden. Mrs. Hegarty, a pink colour break from *S. coccinea*, and Viscountess Byng (rose) are good varieties for greenhouse culture.

SCIADOPITYS (sī-a-dop′-i-tis. Coniferæ). Monotypic genus from Japan.

S. verticillata (Umbrella Pine). 100 ft. and over in nature. Like Ginkgo, this is a tree of the very remote past. It takes its name from the leaves (so called) resembling as they do the ribs of an umbrella. Very striking as an isolated specimen. It likes a non-calcareous loam enriched with humus. Perfectly hardy, but slow-growing. Best in a semi-shady position.

SCILLA (Squill, Bluebell). Liliaceæ. Greenhouse and hardy bulbous plants.

These include the common bluebell of the British woods as well as other species which are more suitable for cultivation in pockets of the rock garden. Deep sandy loam is an ideal soil for the cultivation of Scillas, and any sunny position is suitable. They should be planted from August to November in lines, for edging borders, or in masses. Small bulbs should be planted 2 in. deep and 2 in. apart, larger bulbs being planted rather deeper and farther apart. Scillas look well naturalised in the turf of the Alpine garden.

For pot culture a compost of sandy loam, leaf-mould, well-decayed manure and river sand should be prepared. From 3 to 6 bulbs in a 5 in. pot could be used, setting the bulbs 1 in. deep. Keep them under a layer of ashes until growth commences, and then gradually bring them into more light and heat. They should never, however, reach the heated greenhouse and should always be grown cool throughout.

If good-sized bulbs are obtained, they will grow well in water, as well as the large bedding hyacinths. A good way to grow them effectively is to fill a shallow bowl or saucer with stones and water, and set the scilla bulbs on the stones so that the base almost touches the water.

They need no further attention beyond keeping up the water supply as the plants grow, and will form a delightful decoration. Do not stand the saucers in a heated room until the flowers are actually opening.

The species most commonly cultivated are: *S. sibirica*, beautiful bright blue; *S. bifolia*, this is an early variety of brilliant blue; *S. nutans major*, bluebells which are suitable for the wild garden.

SCIONS. The shoots taken from a tree to be used for grafting on to another tree or stock. *See also* PROPAGATING PLANTS.

SCIRPUS (scir-pus. Cyperacæ). Club Rush. A large genus of hardy and greenhouse perennials of which only a few are of any value in gardens. They are propagated by division, seeds and suckers, and like a position in the water garden or near it in boggy peat.

S. lacustris is the common bulrush of which there are several forms that are chiefly weeds in ponds and rivers. This bears reddish-brown spikelets and provides the bast used by gardeners and for mats, chair seats, etc. The genus Isolepis is now allied to Scirpus.

S. nodosus is largely used for greenhouse decoration, 4 in.

SCOLYMUS (skol-i-mus. Compositæ). Spanish Oyster Plant. Golden Thistle. Hardy biennial and perennial herbs. Plant the perennial species from October to April in ordinary soil, and the biennial species in March or April. Increase by seeds sown $\frac{1}{4}$ in. deep, in the position where they are to grow. When the seedlings are 2 in. high, they should be transplanted to 8–12 in. apart. Increase perennial species by division of roots in spring.

SPECIES.

S. hispanicus (Spanish Oyster, or Golden Thistle). Biennial. Yellow, August. 2–3 ft. Edible roots.

S. grandiflorus, yellow. May. Height, 3 ft. Perennial.

SCORZONERA (*Scorzonera hispanica*). Compositæ. This is a little-known vegetable, yet it was first introduced to this country about 1576. As its specific name implies, it is a native plant of Spain.

For those who like to vary their vegetable diet it makes a welcome change and is certainly very wholesome. In shape and size scorzonera resembles salsafy, but differs in the black colour of the skin.

Culture.—Its culture is practically identical with that of salsafy, except that only a single sowing is necessary, and this should not be made before May. Earlier sowings are apt to be checked and run to seed.

The roots should be ready for lifting in September, but unlike salsafy they are best left in the ground until they are required for use, covering some with dried bracken or evergreen boughs in winter to enable lifting to be done in frosty weather.

VARIETIES.

Only the one type.

Uses.—The roots are scraped or peeled, cut into sections and boiled like those of salsafy. The young leaves are also used in salads.

SCOTCH PINE. *See* PINUS.

SCREENS. The well-known expanding trellis or lattice work of diamond pattern has its uses, and its abuses too. Twenty years ago wherever a rose screen or high division fence was needed, the garden owner erected diamond trellis. Its very monotony, often combined with instability when this trellis was erected by the amateur gardener, brought it into disrepute.

The first point about any garden screen must be its rigidity in the face of buffeting winds. Side by side with this comes the question of artistic effect, for it must readily be recognised that a screen which leans out of the vertical, or which sways uneasily in the winds, cannot hope to look in any way artistic.

beaten as a material for these supports, though any other hard wood will do if it is protected by a coat of creosote or similar preservative. Soft wood is undesirable, because durability is next in importance to stability. It is only when the climbing plants with which it is ornamented are well grown that treillage reaches the height of its beauty, and a

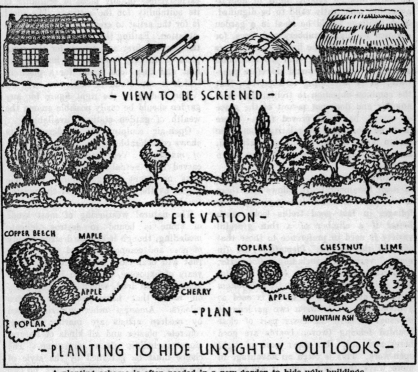

- VIEW TO BE SCREENED -

- ELEVATION -

COPPER BEECH   MAPLE   POPLARS   CHESTNUT   LIME

APPLE   CHERRY   APPLE

POPLAR   MOUNTAIN ASH

-PLAN-

-PLANTING TO HIDE UNSIGHTLY OUTLOOKS-

A planting scheme is often needed in a new garden to hide ugly buildings.

The large-squared type of trellis is nearly always preferable to the expanding diamond pattern It lends itself to the creation of good effects, both in screens and also in the design of arbours, pergolas, and gateways, and in fact any place where woodwork of a light and firm character is wanted.

The Framework Counts.—In the erection of all treillage, the framework counts most. Stout uprights, well driven into the soil, say 2 ft. under the ground surface, are essential. British oak cannot be

structure that does not last must therefore lose much of its value.

It is as important to have the thin crossbars which form the squares, of hard enduring wood, as to have the supports satisfactory, because soft wood breaks very easily with the weight of roses and other climbers, and if one piece gives way the rest follows with disastrous results.

The best types of treillage are of oak or of teak throughout, and both these woods can be used for permanent effects with every confidence.

Sunlight and treillage.—A solidly built structure of wood and stone, whether it be a pergola or gardenhouse, arbour or dividing fence, is attractive when used in a large garden of ample sunshine, and wide open spaces. In a smaller area, or where sunshine is lacking, heavy dark structures cannot be tolerated. This is where light trellis-work is specially effective. It can be built into an arbour, light in appearance, but sufficiently solid to be dignified. Such treillage would be ideal in a garden enclosed by high shrubbery and trees, for it would need only the lightest of climbers to complete its beauty, and the maximum amount of sunshine would therefore penetrate. It is interesting to note, too, that the common objection to trellis, that it is angular and does not permit of the grace of curves, has been proved false. There need be no undue angularity about the design and, in the hands of craftsmen, curved arches made of trellis are often produced.

Clothing the trellis.—Squared trellis is of itself ornamental. It follows that there is no need to cover it completely with foliage, in fact good trellis looks much better if a climber of a thin graceful variety is used in preference to those that smother the screens. *Clematis*, *Vitis* (in many varieties, including *Coignetiœ*, *purpurea*, etc.), *Wistaria*, *Akebia quinata*, and, if it is kept well thinned, *Polygonum Aubertii*, are useful. If trellis is used as a dividing fence between two gardens, it is usual to have the lower part of close boarded fencing (woven boards are good here) and only the upper part of light open-work. This is often an advantage in more ways than one, since it allows the gardener to plant climbers of rather more tender variety than could be used in a very open situation. While the plants are young, they have the protection of the close-boarded background, and later, even in a severe winter, they are not likely to die back below this level. On the south side of such a fence, therefore, climbers such as *Eccremocarpus scaber*, *Solanum jasminoides*, *Jasminum primulinum* and others of doubtful hardiness can be used, and these, together with the beauty of well-designed treillage, raise a garden to a position of distinction.

SCULPTURE FOR THE GARDEN.

There are two view-points regarding garden statuary. The exclusive model is the only way for some. Others claim that a good design loses nothing by repetition, and that there is ample room for a hundred copies of a fine model in the thousands of gardens scattered over the country. What seems rather more important than the exclusiveness of any piece of sculpture is its suitability for the setting. The ideal is for the artist to create a model for each situation. Failing that it is best to choose the position first and search for the right piece of statuary to fill it. To buy a figure first and then look round for a place in which it can stand is fatal.

The finding of the right figure for any garden should be easily possible among the wealth of garden statuary available.

Open-air sculpture by modern artists shows considerable originality in the *choice of materials*. Very striking figures are carved from actual tree trunks, the subjects no doubt being inspired to some extent by the natural forms of the twisted trunks.

The natural weathering of most kinds of stone is bound to destroy delicate modelling, though it cannot destroy beauty of pose and composition, and for a figure that will bear close inspection, even after years of exposure, there can be no better material than lead, which gradually takes on tones that harmonise with garden colours. Amongst other materials used by modern artists are marble, bronze, concrete, plaster and all kinds of natural stone including green serpentine. The choice must be governed by the style of the garden, cost, and other factors, no two gardens being exactly comparable. In choosing subjects, first consider the size of the garden. In a small garden, every piece of sculpture should have a use. Sundials, bird baths, fountain figures, and carved benches are acceptable, but purely ornamental statuary is best avoided.

In a larger garden the figures may be merely decorative; but even here figures that are linked with garden lore by their natural association are to be preferred. For instance, a water carrier as a fountain figure, symbolic figures of the seasons for various parts of the garden and shrubbery, characters from the Greek legends such as "Pan" for the semi-wild garden, or "Narcissus" for the waterside garden are all suitable subjects. Quaint little toads, rabbits and squirrels, though cheap, need not be despised. They have a natural home in the children's corner, or in some shady woodland retreat. As a rule sculpture should be kept out of the rock garden. Grass and evergreen shrubs are a better background for stone figures.

The centre of the garden is not always the best place. A large statue may catch the eye at the end of a long vista, but a small one should be hidden treasure, to be sought in some obscure corner of the garden.

SCUTELLARIA (sku-tell-a-ria. Labia-tæ). *Scutella*, a little saucer, from the form of the calyx. Skullcap. All propagate by seeds or cuttings.

SPECIES.

S. alpina. Handsome, helmet-shaped flowers in whorled heads; blue with a white lip. The stems are weak and somewhat straggling. August. Mont Cenis and Central Europe.

S. Brittoni, has blue and white flowers. 6 in. Late summer.

S. Novæ Libansticæ. A dainty, lilac-coloured thing from Lebanon. 4 in. July.

SCUTICARIA (sku-ti-kar-i-a. Orchidaceæ). Stove epiphytal orchids. Grow in sphagnum moss on teak blocks suspended from the warm greenhouse roof. When growth commences change to new blocks. Water freely in spring and summer, but very little in autumn and winter. Syringe freely during the growing period (February to March), and ventilate freely during the summer months. Increase by division of pseudo-bulbs after flowering.

SPECIES.

S. Hadwenii. Greenish-yellow, white and rose. May to September. Height, 1 ft.

S. Steelii. Yellow, chocolate, creamy-white and purple. August to September.

SEA BUCKTHORN. *See* HIPPOPHÆ.

SEA HOLLY. *See* ERYNGIUM.

SEAKALE (*Crambe maritima*). Cruciferæ. This is a perennial plant which can be found in the wild state around the sea coasts of the British Isles, and of certain European countries, but it is only in this country that it is extensively cultivated for culinary use.

It comes under the heading of white or blanched vegetables, and is extremely useful for winter and early spring use.

Culture.—Raising from seed. A stock of seakale crowns may be grown from seed sown in the open ground in good light soil

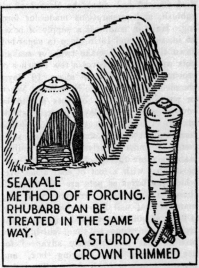

SEAKALE METHOD OF FORCING. RHUBARB CAN BE TREATED IN THE SAME WAY. A STURDY CROWN TRIMMED

Seakale is increased by root cuttings. It is a useful winter vegetable.

in March or April. Sow the seeds at 6 in. apart in rows 1 ft. apart. The seedlings should be allowed to stand where sown for two seasons, then planted in permanent beds or to produce crowns for forcing.

It is an easy and accommodating plant, and perhaps for this reason is so often neglected during the summer months, with consequent poor returns in winter and spring. A well-managed seakale bed should be almost as permanent as a bed of asparagus. Any ordinary garden soil will grow seakale well without any special preparation beyond trenching and heavy manuring, and as the position will be occupied for some years this should be done thoroughly, 2–2½ ft. deep during the winter months, so as to be ready for planting during March. One-year-old sets are best for planting; these should be put in triangular groups, giving a distance of

9 in. between the sets in each group, 3 ft. between the groups, and the same between the rows. Plant with a dibber, burying the crown just beneath the surface, afterwards placing an inch or so of coal ashes over each group to ward off slugs. No further attention beyond keeping the land well hoed will be required till growth is finished in the autumn, when, after the foliage has died off, the bed should be cleared of all rubbish, and preparations made for forcing. Have in readiness a supply of boxes 15 in. square and 18 in. deep (a sugar-box sawn through will make two), or seakale pots with which to cover a few bunches of crowns at intervals of about 10 days, commencing early in the New Year. When in position the boxes or pots are to be covered with a foot layer of fresh stable manure, the gentle heat generated by the fermentation of this material being sufficient to induce early growth. Failing stable manure the bunches of crowns may be covered with a foot of coal ashes over which the boxes or pots are to be placed, these in turn being covered with any material that will help to keep out frost, if early supplies are wanted. Examine the crowns from time to time, cutting any produce that is sufficiently advanced for use, removing the covering box, and placing it over a fresh group. The ashes should be removed as soon as cutting is completed, and not allowed to remain with the idea of giving protection, as this is not required. All crowns not covered for cutting should be cut off when growth is advancing, and it is apparent that when a flower spike is being produced, these must on no account be allowed to develop.

When cutting for the season has finished, remove all boxes and litter, fork over between the rows, and spread evenly over the whole bed the ashes used for covering, and if any further supply is available the bed may receive a 2–3 in. coating. This will help to keep down weeds and provide an efficient mulch during the summer months. During July, August and September, give thorough drenchings with liquid manure, or at fortnightly intervals during July and August apply nitrate of soda at the rate of $\frac{1}{2}$ oz. per clump in showery weather, or watered in if the weather is dry.

To provide crowns for lifting and forcing, plant one-year-old sets in rows at 1 ft. between the crowns, and 2 ft. in the rows, on heavily-manured land. Keep free from weeds, and feed liberally during the growing season. In November or December lift the roots carefully, trim off all stumps of leaves and the side shoots, storing the prepared crowns in moist sand till wanted. The smaller roots or "thongs" should be cut into pieces 6–8 in. long for making sets. Cut the top square and the bottom obliquely. They may then be stored in sand or buried in a sheltered border until planting time.

To force, place 5 or 6 crowns in an 8 in. flower-pot, fill in between them with any fine soil, water well in, and place under greenhouse stage, or in any other place having a temperature of 55°–60°, and cover with another flower-pot of the same size, blocking up the drainage hole in the covering pot to exclude light. The soil must never be allowed to become dry or the seakale will be strong flavoured.

Forced under conditions as above, the growths will be sufficiently far advanced for cutting in from 14 to 21 days, according to temperature, and constant supplies during February and March may be obtained by putting in weekly successional batches.

VARIETIES.

Lily-white.
Feltham white.

Uses.—The blanched shoots are boiled in almost the same way as asparagus. Well-grown seakale should have a slightly tart flavour, but poorly-grown produce is very acrid.

SEAKALE BEET. *See* SPINACH.

SEA LAVENDER. *See* STATICE.

SEA PINK. *See* ARMERIA.

SEAWEED. Seaweed is often used as manure, being very valuable. In Ayrshire it is used extensively with good results. The wet weed is applied at the rate of 25–30 tons per acre. In Jersey, 40–50 tons per acre are used. Trials have shown that fresh seaweed is little inferior to dung, and when dried it is a good substitute for concentrated manures.

SECATEURS. *See under* PRUNERS.

SEDUM (se-dum. Crassulaceæ). Stonecrop. This large genus of hardy perennials and sub-shrubs provides plants invaluable for dry borders in the case of the taller plants, and for dry places in the rockery or on walls in the case of the dwarf kinds, because of the fleshy leaves, that can withstand drought.

They are of easy culture as any pieces of branch will, if inserted in sandy soil, take root. They may also be increased

S. asiaticum, greenish-yellow flowers with orange anthers, 9 in.

S. glaucum, dense carpeting species with rosy-white flowers.

S. ibericum, trailing, purple, 6 in.

S. kamtschaticum, evergreen, bright foliage, rich yellow flowers, 6 in.

S. lydium, evergreen, small pink flowers, 3 in.

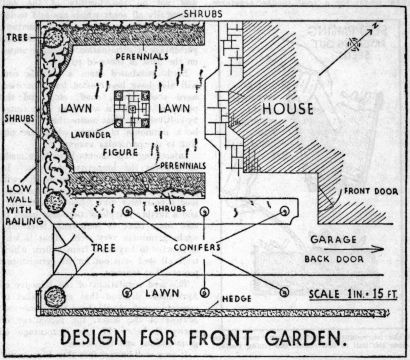

DESIGN FOR FRONT GARDEN.

Simplicity, privacy and convenience are the keynotes of this front garden.

by division in spring or summer, and by seeds sown under glass in spring. Ordinary garden soil with some lime for most of the species is suitable.

SPECIES.

There are numerous species including *S. acre*, summer-blooming, yellow flowers, 3 in., the common Stonecrop and its varieties, *aurem*, shoot-tips yellow, *elegans*, tips silvery, and *majus*, larger than the type.

S. album has large turves covered with white flowers, 6 in.

S. arboreum, woody stems bearing masses of white flowers, 9 in.

S. monstrosum, yellow, curious stems, 9 in.

S. pulchellum, rosy-purple flowers, 6 in.

S. roseum, yellow or purplish, 6–12 in.

S. rotundifolium, rosy-edged evergreen leaves and rosy-purple flowers, 6 in.

S. spathulifolium, rosettes of leaves and pinkish stems with yellow flowers.

S. s. purpureum is a remarkably good form of the latter variety.

All the plants bloom all the summer. The species not named here, for lack of space, differ from those given mainly in small constructional points.

Hardy annual and biennial species such as *S. cœruleum*, 6–9 in., blue, and *S. pilosum*, 3 in., pink, are well worth growing on sunny rockeries.

SEEDS. In ages long past, of which we have just a glimpse in geological records, there were no true seeds, merely spores similar to those found on ferns to-day. Spores are more simple in structure than seeds, for a seed in the vegetable

SEED RAISING
PRICKING OUT
SEEDS

USE A
WOODEN
LABEL
OR FORK
FOR
PRICKING
OFF

When transplanting seedlings take care not to lose the ball of soil round the young roots.

kingdom is similar to the egg of the animal world. It is a complete plant in embryo.

If one cuts open the seed of a broad bean which has been soaked, the plant can be distinctly seen, lying between the two cotyledons. When the seed is sown, it does not immediately begin to absorb plant food from the soil. What happens first, is that moisture is absorbed, and in this the action is purely mechanical, that is to say, the water soaks into the seed as it would into a sponge or a piece of cloth. In addition to water, a certain amount of warmth is necessary before any activity is

roused in the seed. The amount of warmth needed may vary from 41°–108° F.

When the necessary moisture and heat are present the seed begins the process of germination. This process consists of the digestion of the food stores which are contained in the cotyledon. It will therefore be seen that the process of germination depends on the vitality of the seed itself, and not on the fertility of the soil. Practically all seeds which are sold to-day are subjected to tests (*see* SEED TESTING), and in the case of vegetable seed the percentage of germination is usually stated on the back of the seed packet.

Seeds purchased from a reliable firm will also have been tested for impurities, weed seeds, dust, chaff, etc., and the purity of the strain will have been tested by cultivation. That means that there will be a minimum of plants which are not true to the particular variety.

Interesting experiments have been made to discover the longevity of seeds. In some cases seed sown as soon as ripe will germinate quickly. A sample of the same seed a year later may refuse to germinate, and a further sample of the same batch of seed sown three or four years later may again germinate very well. That is why it is wise to buy seed from a firm which tests all seed sent out for its germinating powers *that season*.

The seed regulations of the Ministry of Agriculture demand that each packet of vegetable seed should bear the name and address of the seller, the percentage of purity if below 97, the percentage of germination, and the season.

It is a well-known fact that home-saved seeds give every satisfaction in the matter of germination; but, unfortunately, they frequently do not come true to type. This is, of course, because cross-fertilisation has taken place, and though the resulting seedlings may be perfectly healthy, they may also be of very inferior type to the parent plant. However, in some cases, the seedlings are quite as good as the parent plant in colour and form, and amateur gardeners should be encouraged to collect a certain amount of seed from their own gardens.

Generally speaking, it is best to sow immediately the seed is ripe, which is

Nature's method, but most gardeners like to sow half at once, and save half the seed until the following spring, so that they have a double chance of success. In the very small garden the use of home-saved seed is scarcely advisable; but where the garden is large enough for a portion to be set aside as a nursery, the seed of both perennials and annuals can with advantage be collected for the raising of new plants.

When seed is collected from the amateur's garden, care should be taken to see that it is not gathered until almost fully ripe. It should then be exposed to sun for a time before storing. As a rule, it is most satisfactory to remove the seed from pods and capsules, and when it is thoroughly dry to store it in glass bottles which can be kept tightly corked. It must not be allowed to get damp or it may begin to germinate.

The Production of Seed. The production of seed is one of the marvels of Nature. If the flower of a plant is dissected it is generally possible to discover the following parts. The outer calyx, usually green, the corolla or petals, generally highly coloured, stamens and pistil. The stamens and the pistil form the sexual parts of the flower (actually the only essential parts), the stamens usually being referred to as the male organs and the pistil as the female organ. The stamens carry the pollen sacs, the pollen being usually a fine dust of yellow, green, brown, purple or black colour. The pistil is composed of an ovary or ovaries, style and stigma. When the pollen reaches the stigma of the pistil we say that pollination has taken place. It does not follow, however, that fertilisation has taken place. Before this can happen the pollen must actually reach the ovules in the ovary of the pistil. For this to happen the pollen grains grow after they adhere to the surface of the stigma, sending out tubes which go down through the tissues until they reach the embryo sac, when fertilisation is completed.

Most people understand that insects carry the pollen from one flower to another. This is Nature's method of cross-fertilisation. There are some cases in which pollen from the same flower will fertilise the ovules of that flower. For instance, in the case of the violet and one

or two similar flowers. the stamens will ripen and distribute their pollen while still entirely enclosed within the flower, so that fertilisation only takes place from the same flower.

In a number of cases, however, it is found that the pollen from the same flower, even if placed directly on the stigma, will not fertilise the flower. In these cases, we say that the flowers are self-sterile.

Seed-sowing in boxes calls for careful preparation. Here is an idea for sowing very small seeds economically.

A good deal of research work has been done lately in connection with the fertilising of fruit and certain varieties of fruit are now known to be practically self-sterile, that is to say, they will not set any fruits unless fertilised by some other variety of the same fruit.

For many centuries gardeners have practised hybridisation, but it was not until Darwin and Mendel between them set out to discover the underlying rules of this practice that hybridising reached its present position in the horticultural world. (*See also* FRUIT POLLINATION, MENDELISM, HYBRIDISATION, ETC.)

Soil for Seed Growing. To germinate seeds the mechanical condition of the soil is of even greater importance than its fertility. The food needed for the earliest stages of plant life is contained in the seed itself and what is needed is warmth, moisture and air, and in some cases, light. Soil for seed raising should contain little or no leaf-mould or manure, never more than sufficient to hold moisture, so as to

RAKE THE SOIL UNTIL THERE IS A FINE TILTH

DRILL SHOULD BE MADE WITH A LINE AND HOE

FOR SHALLOW DRILLS A WOODEN LABEL CAN BE USED

SEED-SOWING

Outdoor seed-sowing, showing the best method.

prevent the seed pans from becoming too dry. Excessive humus is a frequent cause of "damping-off" amongst seedlings, and a liberal quantity of sand in the compost will keep the soil open so that air can penetrate, and also make it friable so that the surface can easily be made fine and free from lumps.

In the case of seed beds in the open air sandy soil has a big advantage over stiff clay, because it keeps the seeds at a higher temperature while they are germinating.

Seeds in the Open Garden. Seeds sown outdoors are covered with fine soil for two reasons: First that they remain moist, even though the air is dry; and secondly

because the soil protects them from extremes of temperature.

Seeds sown early in the year need less soil over them than those sown later when water is scarce. In the case of exceptionally small seeds, the amount of covering given by lightly raking the surface after sowing is sufficient. It is advisable to firm the surface with the back of the spade to ensure that the seeds come into actual contact with soil moisture.

Seeds under Glass. Many of the plants in our gardens have come to us from warmer climates than our own, so that it will be readily understood that some seeds need more shelter and heat for their germination than they would receive in the open garden. In addition to seeds of such tender plants, the amateur gardener finds it desirable in many cases to raise expensive new varieties of seeds under glass, in order to protect them from pests and other troubles that might attack them in the open garden.

The principles of seed raising are very much the same in nearly every case. The soil must be light and open, well drained and well ventilated; sufficient but not too much moisture must be given; and the seedlings when they appear must not be allowed to grow too quickly.

For the simple seed raising of half-hardy annuals and border perennials, boxes 3–4 in. deep are mostly used, and filled to within an inch of the top with light sandy soil. The soil is made firm by pressing with a flat piece of board. Shallow drills can be made across the boxes by pressing one edge of the board into the levelled soil surface. Seeds are then sown thinly along the drills and covered with fine soil or sand. Water is needed immediately, and it is often best to partially immerse the boxes, and let the moisture soak up from below, so that there is no danger of washing out the fine seeds.

Alpine Plants from Seeds. Most of the Alpines are seed bearers, and usually raised from seed. In most cases the seed is very fine and on this account the soil needs special preparation. They can often be raised outdoors in the same way as other plants so long as the soil is fine and sandy, but the rare Alpines are more usually raised in shallow earthenware pans in a cool greenhouse. Extra care must be taken with the seeds of Alpine plants to ensure that they are not washed out of the soil when watering is done, and for this reason it is becoming the practice to sow Alpines in double pans; that is, one pan or flower-pot of small size put inside a larger one.

Prepared soil is put into both pots and the seeds are sown in the inner pot while water is always given to the outer pot of soil. (The seeds can just as well be sown in the outer rim and watering done in the inner pot.) Where a greenhouse is not available, seeds in boxes and pots can be covered with small sheets of glass. If moisture collects on it, the glass should be raised daily and wiped clean.

Shrubs and Trees from Seed. Most of our ornamental trees and shrubs can be quite easily raised from seed, which is sown in precisely the same manner as for ordinary seeds. Naturally, the depth depends on the type of seed. For instance, a Walnut needs to be buried 1 in. deep, while very fine seeds need not be covered at all. The best time for sowing seeds of trees and shrubs is generally about mid-February.

In the case of berries, such as holly berries, the outer covering of the berry must be allowed to rot before the seeds are ready for sowing. The usual practice in nurseries is to mix the berries with sand or fine earth in a heap, leaving it exposed to all weathers—in the case of hollies, for twelve months. When the dry covering of the berries has rotted and the seeds have separated, the heap is turned over, and soil and seeds together are sown in drills. They can be sown under glass or in the open as preferred.

Seed Troubles. The chief trouble among seedlings—whether flowers or vegetable—is the disease known as "damping-off." This is caused by a fungus known as *Pythium de Baryanum*. Zinnias and Asters are very commonly attacked by this disease, but almost any seedling is liable to an attack if the conditions of cultivation are not healthy. Where damping-off is very common, it is worth while to sterilise the soil used for seed sowing. This can be done by watering it before use with a solution of four ounces of formaldehyde to a gallon of water. Apart from this it is necessary to give the seedlings as much light and air as possible while the are growing, and in particular to prepare a soil compost which will not allow water to collect round the neck of the seedling. That is why many gardeners never use anything but pure sand as a covering for their seeds. Clean cultivation, timely thinning and weeding also help to keep down the damping-off disease.

Soil Pests are troublous at times among seedlings. Under glass, they can be prevented by sterilising the soil before use. Boiling water poured over the boxes until the soil is quite hot is a simple method of destroying pests before the seeds are sown. The soil must, of course, be allowed to cool before being used.

Slugs are often troublesome among seedlings. In the open the use of one of the patent slug killers will be effective (*see also* SLUGS). In the cold frame or the greenhouse it will be found that seedlings in boxes of sterilised soil, if stood on a bed of cinders, ashes, or other sharp material, will not be attacked by slugs, who object to dragging their soft bodies over these substances.

Seed Testing.

The method of seed testing adopted by large commercial firms may be briefly described as follows:

The seed, on arrival, is first of all thoroughly cleaned. That is to say, dust and chaff are removed by machinery. In addition to the removal of dust and chaff it is necessary in a good many cases to take special measures to eliminate weed seeds, and elaborate machinery of many kinds has been evolved for this purpose. For instance, some smooth-surfaced seeds are passed over a series of revolving velvet rollers; the rollers turning in the opposite direction to the way the seed falls. The seed, being smooth and shiny, does not cling to the velvet, but a number of weed seeds which are covered with minute hairs, do cling to the velvet and are carried away by the rollers.

Samples of the seed are subjected to microscopic tests both before and after cleaning, in order to ascertain whether the machinery has done its work effectively.

X

Further samples are taken into the laboratory and tested for germination. To do this, several trials are made. As a rule, 100 seeds are counted out into each receptacle, where they are allowed to germinate on damp blotting paper or some similar material.

Seeds have their definite peculiarities in the matter of germination. For instance, grass seed germinates more quickly in the

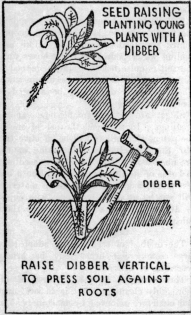

SEED RAISING PLANTING YOUNG PLANTS WITH A DIBBER

DIBBER

RAISE DIBBER VERTICAL TO PRESS SOIL AGAINST ROOTS

When planting out seedlings, see that the dibber does not come in contact with the tender roots.

light, and the seed-testing pans are therefore covered with miniature cloches while germination is proceeding. Turnip seeds germinate more readily in the dark, and light is therefore excluded from the seed pans. Some of the incubators in which the seed tests are carried out are allowed to vary considerably in temperature from time to time, as it has been found that the seeds germinate more readily when they are subjected to variable temperatures than when the temperature remains quite constant.

When the seed pans are inspected, and the number of germinated seeds counted

off, great care has to be taken that the seed has produced both leaf and root shoots. If it fails to do this, the germination is not satisfactory.

Tests for Purity. Nearly all the larger seeds firms in this country now devote a large area of ground to outdoor seed tests. Here samples of the seeds are sown under ordinary normal outdoor conditions, and when they reach the flowering stage the beds are inspected in order to ascertain the purity of the seed sample. Note is also made at the same time of the general habit of the plants under observation, and certain plants are selected for hybridising, etc.

Vitality of Seeds.

The following table shows the number of years during which various seeds retain their germinating powers. These valuable statistics are the result of experiments extending over twenty years or more:

Plant				Period
Artichoke	...	...	...	5–10 years
Asparagus	...	...	...	3–8 ,,
Beans, Broad	...	...	...	2–4 ,,
,, Dwarf	...	...	...	3 ,,
,, Kidney	...	...	...	3–8 ,,
,, Runner	...	...	...	3 ,,
Beet	...	...	...	5–10 ,,
Borage	...	...	...	7–8 ,,
Borecole	...	...	...	5–10 ,,
Broccoli	...	...	...	5–10 ,,
Cabbage, Savoys, Sprouts, etc.		...	...	4–8 ,,
Chicory	...	...	...	7 ,,
Cardoon	...	...	...	6–9 ,,
Carrots	...	...	...	5–10 ,,
Cauliflower	...	...	...	5–10 ,,
Celery	...	...	...	8–10 ,,
Cress	...	...	...	3–8 ,,
Cucumber	...	...	...	5–10 ,,
Endive	...	...	...	7–10 ,,
Fennel	...	...	...	3 ,,
Gourds	...	...	...	6–10 ,,
Khol-rabi	...	...	...	5–10 ,,
Lavender	...	...	...	4–6 ,,
Leek	...	...	...	3–9 ,,
Lettuce	...	...	...	5–9 ,,
Maize	...	...	...	2–4 ,,
Marjoram	...	...	...	3 ,,
Melon	...	...	...	6–10 ,,
Mustard	...	...	...	3–9 ,,

Plant				Period
Onion ...	...	...	...	2–7 years
Parsley ...	...	...	...	2–9 ,,
Parsnip ...	...	...	...	2–4 ,,
Pea, Garden	...	...	...	2–8 ,,
Pumpkin ...	...	...	...	5–9 ,,
Radish ...	...	...	...	3–10 ,,
Rhubarb ...	...	...	...	3–8 ,,
Rosemary	...	...	...	4–7 ,,
Rue ...	...	...	...	2–5 ,,
Sage ...	...	...	...	2–7 ,,
Salsify ...	...	...	...	2–8 ,,
Scorzonera	...	...	...	2–7 ,,
Seakale ...	...	...	...	1–7 ,,
Spinach ...	...	...	...	4–7 ,,
Strawberry	...	...	...	3–6 ,,
Thyme ...	...	...	...	3–7 ,,
Tomato ...	...	...	...	4–9 ,,
Turnip ...	...	...	...	3–10 ,,
Vegetable Marrow	...	...	5 ,,
Water Melon ...	...	...	6–10 ,,
Wormwood ...	...	...	4–6 ,,

Period of Germination.

Seeds vary considerably in the amount of time they take to germinate, as will be seen from the following table, which gives the time taken for the various seeds to germinate in a temperature varying from 60°–70° F.

Plant			No. of days germ.
Flower Seeds.			
African Marigold	...	...	5
,, ,,	...	...	21*
Antirrhinum ...	...	...	10
,, ...	...	...	6
Aquilegia cœrulea	...	...	21
,, glandulosa	...	...	25
,, hybrids	...	...	20
Auricula, Alpine	...	...	15
Calendula Meteor	...	...	6
Callistephus hortensis ...	...	...	14*
Candytuft ...	...	...	4
Centranthus macrosiphon	...	...	14*
Chrysanthemum tricolor	...	...	10
,, ,,	...	...	14*
Clarkia pulchella ...	...	...	14*
Dahlia double ...	...	...	5
Eccremocarpus scaber ...	...	...	11
French Marigold	...	...	7
Gaillardia aristata	...	...	7
,, grandiflora	...	...	7

Plant			No. of days germ.
Flower Seeds.			
Galega officinalis	...	...	4
Gilia tricolor ...	...	...	14*
Godetia ...	...	...	4
,, ...	...	...	14*
Hibiscus africanus	...	...	14
Hollyock, double	...	...	7
,, single	...	...	8
Ipomæa purpurea	...	...	10
Lavatera arborea	...	...	5
Nicotiana affinis	...	...	10
,, sylvestris	...	...	21
Papaver nudicaule	...	...	8
,, ,, double	...	...	4
Pea, Everlasting	...	...	11
Petunia grandiflora	...	...	9
Pyrethrum aureum	...	...	6
Solanum giganteum	...	...	19
,, pyracanthum	...	...	22
,, robustum	...	...	22
,, Warscewiczi	...	...	22
Stock, Ten Weeks	...	...	6
Sweet Sultan ...	...	...	5
Whitlavia grandiflora ...	...	...	5
Zinnia elegans ...	...	...	4
,, Haageana	...	...	6
Vegetables.			
Beet, Blood Red	...	...	30
,, Dell's Black	...	...	27
Broad Bean, Long Pod	...	...	28
Carrot, Early Nantes	...	...	17
,, Long Surrey Red	...	...	34
French Bean, Canadian Wonder	...	11
Lettuce, All the Year Round	...	16
,, Commodore Nutt	...	39
,, Paris White Cos	...	16
Onion, White Spanish	...	...	28
Parsnip, The Student	...	...	40
,, ,,	...	...	26
Pea, Perfection	...	...	9
Spinach, Victoria	...	...	16
Turnip, Early Snowball	...	...	18
,, ,, ,,	...	...	17

The kinds of flower seeds marked * were sown in the open ground, while the others were sown in the temperature stated.

SELF-HEAL. *See* PRUNELLA.

SEMPERVIVUM (semper-vi-vum. Grassulaceæ). Houseleek. A genus of fleshy, succulent-leaved perennials that are nearly all hardy, except in the case of those species which have a cobwebby tomentum on the rosettes of leaves and which in very wet districts should be covered with glass in winter. Houseleeks look well in chinks in walls or on the rockery as well as in edgings for beds and borders. They will grow in sandy, dry places where other plants fail for lack of moisture, and flower more freely if there is some lime in the soil. They are raised from seed sown in spring or by offsets taken in spring or summer.

SPECIES.

The various kinds are very much alike, with rosettes of leaves from the centre of which rise flower stalks bearing one or more flowers of red or yellow. Of the numerous species the best known are: *S. tectorum*, the Common Houseleek found on roofs and walls; *arachnoideum*, Cobweb Houseleek, red flowers in June; *Braunii*, yellow leaves tipped with purple, and *glaucum*, yellow, leaves hairy and tipped with purple. All bloom in summer. 4–12 in.

SENECIO (sen-ē-cio. Compositæ). Groundsel. Ragwort. Cineraria Jacobea.

A vast genus (possibly the most comprehensive of all flowering plants) of more than 1,000 species of evergreen, hardy, and tender plants, and shrubs, with daisy-like flowers and the last named with thick leathery foliage like that of the Olearias, to which genus they are closely related.

Those for outdoor culture like a moist, fairly light soil in a sunny position. For pot culture use a compost of two parts of fibrous loam, to one of sand, with some leaf-mould, and a little manure.

Propagate the greenhouse plants by seeds and by cuttings struck in spring in a frame heated at the bottom, the hardy annuals by seeds sown out of doors in April, the perennials by seeds, division, or cuttings. The shrubs may be increased by cuttings taken in summer and struck under a hand-light or in a frame in sandy soil. *S. Greyii*, 3–4 ft. Leaves green above, silvery beneath. Flowers bright yellow from June to August. This is the most familiar variety.

N.B.—All the Senecios make excellent seaside shrubs.

SENSITIVE PLANT. *See* MIMOSA.

SEPTEMBER WORK IN THE GARDEN.

THE FLOWER GARDEN.

Remove all seed pods and dead flowers.

This is the best month for planting peonies. They should be planted in soil that is deeply dug, and contains plenty of manure as well as some lime. If lime is absent or insufficient, the soil should be dressed six weeks before planting and well mixed as digging is done. The manure should be well rotted, and should not be allowed to come into direct contact with the roots.

Take viola cuttings and insert in boxes of sandy soil. Heavy sticky soil is fatal to the cuttings.

Pansies and Violas for spring bedding should be planted now in their permanent quarters.

Hollyhocks, Lupins, Coreopsis, Chrysanthemum maximum and other perennials raised from seed should now be ready for transplanting to the borders.

New herbaceous borders should be prepared this month by digging deeply incorporating manure at the same time. Bonemeal should be used on shaded borders instead of animal manure.

Attend to Roses. During the month examine the ties of buds, and loosen where necessary.

Stocks that were budded early in the season should have the ligatures loosened, shoots from the stock being shortened back to about ten leaves if the bud is still dormant.

Trench and prepare new rose beds for planting in November.

Dahlias should be tied up, disbudded, and the shoots thinned. Earwigs should be trapped and choice blooms protected against the sun's rays.

Divide and replant strong roots of primroses, polyanthus and border auriculas.

Plant out biennial and perennial seedlings that were sown in early summer into their winter or flowering quarters. They can be transplanted again in spring if necessary.

Plant out Wallflowers, Primroses, Auriculas and Polyanthus for spring decoration of the beds and borders.

Divide and replant bulbs of Lilium candidum without delay.

Plant English and Spanish Irises in beds.

Rooted cuttings of Pinks may be planted in their permanent position, preferably as an edging beside a long path.

Keep beds and borders tidy by removing exhausted annuals and cutting down withered perennials.

Lift Gladioli that have done flowering, tie in bunches and hang up in a shed to dry.

Thin out weak shoots of bush Roses, trim back old shoots and tie in new shoots of climbing Roses.

Plant out double Daisies, Honesty, Forget-me-nots, and Silene pendula compacta.

Plant Anemones, Crocuses, Montbretia, Narcissi, Snowdrops, Chionodoxas, Scillas, etc., but not Tulips. Take cuttings of Ageratums, Antirrhinums, blue Marguerites, Centaureas, Fuchsias, Gazanias, Lobelias, Zonal Pelargoniums, Heliotropes, Pentstemons, Petunias, Roses and most bedding plants. Many alpine plants can now be struck. Rooted layers and seedlings of carnations may now be planted out. Make new lawns from seed.

THE ROCK GARDEN.

Now is a good time to make a new rock garden. First decide on its shape, whether a mound, a ravine, a sloping bank, or any other design. Build a solid, but well-drained foundation. Use gritty soil, well mixed with decayed leaves or turf.

Dwarf evergreens can be planted now, and these are a distinct advantage to the rock garden. (*See* DWARF SHRUBS).

Spring-flowering bulbs can also be planted in the rock garden, and these will make a very attractive show, if planted with care.

Lift and divide alpines. Where complete renovation of the rockery is undesirable, the soil of the pockets can be lightly forked and an additional top dressing of gritty material given round established plants. For rock gardens that lack colour, plant either pink, red and white drifts, using Dianthus Cæsius (the Cheddar pink), Dianthus alpinus, Helianthemum "Sudbury Gem," Lychnis alpina and Phlox amœna for red and pink, and double Arabis (white), or plant drifts of yellow, blue and purple, using "Gold

Dust" Alyssum, Cheiranthus "Harpur Crewe," Viola gracilis, "Golden Wave," yellow and orange shades, with Aubreitia "Dr. Mules," Gentian Lagodechiana, Veronica spicata "Royal Blue," Lithospermum "Heavenly Blue," and Campanula pusilla for blue and purple shades.

PLANT ROCKERY BULBS.

The following bulbs are specially suited for cultivation on rock gardens, and

FLOWER AND FRUIT BASKET

WOOD TRUG BASKET

Garden baskets are always useful for weeding and collecting flowers and fruit. There is a village in Sussex where this useful wooden basket is made in large quantities.

should be planted in small groups in any available pockets. Once planted they should be left to come up year after year. Carpet plants can be grown in the pockets with these bulbs, to flower after the bulbs have faded.

Anemone, Crocus, Chionodoxa sardensis, Erythronium denscanis, Fritillaria meleagris, Muscari, Heavenly Blue, Scilla bifolia, Winter Aconites, Narcissus bulbocodium citrinus, Narcissus cyclamineus, Narcissus minimus, Narcissus triandrus albus, Tulipa clusiana, Tulipa Greigii, Tulipa Kaufmanniana.

The Shrubbery.

Trim all hedges.

Evergreen shrubs should be planted this month. Plant firmly, using the previous soil mark as a guide to depth of planting. Stake immediately the shrubs are planted, tying a label to the stake so that the variety may not be forgotten.

Deciduous shrubs are best planted when

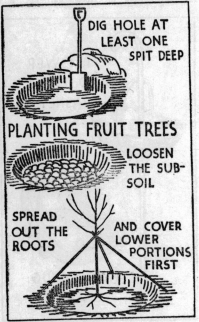

Prepare the site well for Fruit Trees by deep digging.

the leaves begin to fall, and this will in some cases be this month, but mostly in October. If the weather is dry after planting, syringe overhead each evening until showers arrive.

Select shrubs according to the soil.

Vegetables.

Use the hoe very frequently in the kitchen garden to keep down the weeds.

Clear off crops as they finish, burning rubbish or digging it immediately into the soil to decay.

Onions should have their necks bent down. Those which are ripe should be harvested. To assist bulbs to ripen the leaves may be twisted.

Potatoes should be lifted when the haulms decay, except those required for seed sets. Store the tubers away carefully in clamps or in boxes in a shed.

Dust Brussels sprouts with soot.

The soil between broccoli plants may receive a light dressing of nitrate of soda or sulphate of ammonia, preparatory to being stirred with the hoe.

The main batch of spring cabbages may be planted on land previously occupied by onions.

Corn salad can still be sown in warm places.

Lettuce may be sown on a warm border during this month to plant out in spring. Tie up heads fit for blanching and plant out seedlings.

The tops of old mint may be cut down, and a light dressing of old manure may be given.

Mustard and cress seeds may be sown about twice a week in a shady spot.

Make another sowing of radishes if necessary.

Tie up cardoons for blanching when ready.

Keep leeks well watered.

Lift and store beet and carrots, and store in sand for winter use.

Protect the heads of cauliflowers by covering them with their own leaves. Where young heads are forming draw their own leaves together above them and tie them loosely with raffia.

Keep runner beans well picked. If seed is allowed to mature, further growth and the production of beans will be checked.

Earth up celery and onions.

Two or three sowings of turnips should be made during the month.

Make a final sowing of spinach. Keep the earlier rows free from weeds by constant use of the hoe.

Fruit.

Most of the fruit is gathered this month and a new year of operations commences in the orchard. Do not, however, gather the fruit unless it parts readily from the tree when lifted in the palm of the hand.

Clean up the orchard, and fork or hoe the soil between the young fruit trees, and soft fruit bushes.

Prepare grease-bands and put them in position round the tree trunks.

Root-prune fruit trees where needed.

Plant trees if weather permits. Deep trenching is essential.

If the crops are heavy they should be thinned.

Early varieties of apples and pears which do not keep must be gathered, and all young shoots on pear trees should be stopped.

Apricots, peaches and nectarines should have their future bearing shoots nailed in closely. A final thinning should be made; any leaves that shade fruits should be removed.

Cherries require very little shortening back, but cut away cross and inferior shoots on standard trees and spur back those shoots which are too close together.

Currants should have all side sprays pruned away. Shoots of gooseberries should be stopped and thinned. Raspberry canes that have fruited should be cut down and the young growths thinned out to three or four. These should be stopped when sufficiently high. All superfluous strawberry runners should be removed. These may be replanted if new plants are wanted.

Order fertilisers for winter use. These include basic slag, superphosphate of lime, kainit, sulphate of potash, bonemeal, lime.

If obtainable, animal manure from farmyards, stables, poultry farms, etc., should be purchased now for use during winter.

SEQUOIA (sē-quōī′-a. Coniferæ). Bigeneric genus from western N. America, consisting of the two tallest-growing trees in the world.

S. gigantea. "Big Wood" of California, or "Wellingtonia." A huge tree of pyramidal outline, attaining to about 320 ft. and sometimes over that, with a trunk of 90 ft. in diameter. Leaves bluegreen, cones pale brown. Some of these specimens are supposed by competent authorities to be about 4,000 years old. Perfectly hardy but likes a fairly-sheltered position, and a good deep soil.

S. sempervirens (Taxodium sempervirens). The "Red Wood" of California. 200–300 ft. A worthy and beautiful rival to the preceding. A very valuable timber tree, of pyramidal form. Leaves dark lustrous green. Bark a rich brown-red.

Will succeed in chalky districts provided there is a good depth of soil.

SERAPIAS (se-rap-i-as. Orchidaceæ). Tongue-flowered orchid. Hardy terrestrial orchid. First introduced in 1786.

This orchid should be grown in a compost of calcareous loam, or clay mixed with pieces of limestone, and also leafmould, in sunny, deep, well-drained

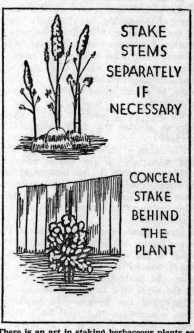

There is an art in staking herbaceous plants so that their blooms may be seen to their best advantage.

borders. When planting the tubers, which can be done any time from August to November, they should be placed 2 in. below the surface. Like most other orchids, the tongue-flowered orchid should be watered freely during the growing period. A mulch of decayed manure should be applied annually in March or April. These plants should be left undisturbed except when they appear to be unhealthy, when they may be lifted and replanted. Increase by division of the tubers any time from August to November.

SERVICE TREE. *See* PYRUS SORBUS

SHADDOCK TREE. *See* CITRUS.

SHADE. Shade is an important feature in a garden, but one frequently overlooked when laying out a new garden. It is desirable by way of contrast, and to provide shelter and protection from the sun's rays during the hot days of summer, not only for the owners of the garden, but also for its permanent inmates.

SHADY BORDERS. Colour and fragrance are always present in the sunny parts of the garden, but the shady border is not so easy to bring into the picture. Darkened by house walls, or soured by the constant drip from overhanging trees, it becomes a problem which many gardeners find extremely difficult to solve. It is possible, by a wise choice of plants and suitable treatment of the soil, to bring as much light and colour into the shady borders as into the other parts of the garden.

The secret of success is soil preparation and manuring. If the soil is naturally rather heavy clay, it must be brought into healthier condition by the addition of sand and bonfire ashes, bonemeal and lime. This treatment renders the soil lighter and warmer.

Many plants generally grown in the sunny border will do nearly as well in the shade if the soil is healthy. Too often shady borders are damp, inclined to be sour, and badly drained. Plants growing in the shade tend to develop an excess of foliage and few flowers. To counteract this, organic manures must be avoided, and phosphatic food, such as bonemeal and superphosphate of lime, employed instead. Plenty of lime, deep digging, and adequate drainage are other aids to success.

Many factors must enter into the selection and cultivation of plants in the shade. Possibly the most difficult arrangement to solve is the choice of flowers for a shady border that faces a sunny one in a garden of formal design, and must therefore match the sunny one in colour values. This problem is most acute in a town garden. Flowers of light tone, white, pale **mauve**, lemon-yellow and cream are best for such a border, as they reflect subdued light more than reds or oranges. Succession is needed here just as in the sunny border,

and a few showy border flowers that will give this succession are as follow:

Spring Flowering. Bulbs, Forget-me-not, Primulas, Doronicums, Columbines.

Summer Flowering. Turk's Cap Lilies, Meconopsis baileyi, Campanula persicifolia, Telham Beauty, Evening primrose, Calceolarias, Phlox, Violas, Nicotiana, Balsam.

Autumn Flowering. Heleniums, Solidago, Michaelmas daisies, Anemone japonica.

Corners of the garden which are *quite sunless* must be treated in a special manner. Shade and moisture together make an ideal spot for ferns, and these graceful plants are at home in that most difficult of all places, under the drip of trees. Here, too, the Rose of Sharon (Hypericum calycinum) can be freely used, for its bright yellow flowers will open in golden splendour with no direct sunshine on them. The coloured butterflies of Cyclamen coum and tiny stars of Arenaria balearica will also flourish under trees.

Two good shrubs for the shady part of the garden are the Daisy bush (Olearia haastii) and the fragrant Sarcococca ruscifolia. Both these are quite at home in smoky town districts.

All gardens reflect the personality of their owners, and in no sense is this more true than in the treatment of such odd corners. The real garden lover does not neglect them, but spends time and trouble without limit over the cultivation of these more difficult places.

SHALLOT or ESCHALOT (*Allium ascalonicum*). Liliaceæ. A native of Palestine, the shallot, or as it is sometimes called in the North and in Ireland, Eschalot or Scalion, was introduced to this country about 1546.

It may be classed as a valuable vegetable and deserves to be more widely grown, for its cultivation is of the simplest. It may be grown for several successive seasons on the same site, and give a heavy crop of usable produce from a comparatively small area. It is especially useful in those gardens where for one reason or another it is impossible to grow good onions.

Culture.—Whilst this is very simple and shallots will grow almost anywhere, they do pay for generous treatment in the way of deep digging and liberal feeding. Firm and fair-sized but not over-large bulbs should be selected for planting, and these should be set by pushing them into the soil to half their depth at distances of 9 in. apart in rows 1 ft. asunder. Planting should be done as early in February or March as soil and weather conditions will allow.

Frequent hoeings and dressings of old

SHEARS. It is just as important for shears to be of good quality steel as it is for pruners. It is on the quality and weight of steel that the class of workmanship usually depends.

As with pruners the grinding must be good, the fit of the bolt must be exact and should be spring-washered and burred over at the end to prevent it working loose. The handles and ferrules should be fast riveted.

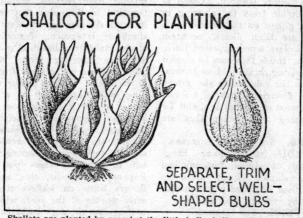

SHALLOTS FOR PLANTING

SEPARATE, TRIM AND SELECT WELL-SHAPED BULBS

Shallots are planted by pressing the little bulbs half-way into the soil.

soot during the growing season are of great assistance in promoting healthy growth, and weak doses of liquid manure applied after rain in May and June are also beneficial.

By July the bulbs should be fully developed and as soon as the tops commence to wither away, the clump should be lifted, thoroughly dried off in the sun or in an airy shed, after which they may be parted and stored in the same manner as onions.

VARIETIES.

Giant French Red.

Giant Golden Skinned.

Uses.—The bulbs are used for seasoning, being rather milder than onions. They may also be cooked and used as a substitute for the latter, and also pickled. The leaves, which are cut when green, are used in salads.

SHAMROCK. *See* TRIFOLIUM.

SHAMROCK PEA. *See* PAROCHETUS.

SHASTA DAISY. *See* CHRYSANTHEMUMS.

In the short hand shears the sizes range from 4½ in. to 11 in. blades. The most convenient sizes are 6 in. for ladies and 8 in. for men. They can be obtained with a notch let into the blades for the purpose of pruning thicker branches than are ordinarily met with in the usual hedge.

Long-handled shears are made for two purposes:

(*a*) Lawn shears for cutting the surface of the lawn where the mower cannot reach, i.e., in the case of the side-wheel machine they are used on the verge.

(*b*) Edging shears for trimming the edge of the lawn.

Both can be obtained with or without wheels. The latter are particularly useful on edging shears as they help to keep the blades of the shears up to the level of the top of the lawn. The 9 in. size of blade is the most useful for the long-handled shears.

The latest device for edging shears is an ingenious box, which is bolted on to the shears on the outside from the verge to be cut, and acts in the same way as does a grass box to a mower, thus saving a lot of work, wasted time and grass growing on the beds and paths.

SHEEP LAUREL. *See* KALMIA.

SHELTER BELTS. The value of a belt of trees and shrubs for protecting the garden has long been recognised. Since the introduction of the many new varieties of shrubs it is now possible, however, to make such a feature beautiful as well as useful. Suitable trees for planting in bold lines or groups on the exterior of a shelter belt are larch, limes, mountain ash, planes, poplars, scotch fir, silver birch, sycamore, etc. Inside these can be planted evergreen flowering shrubs such as Laurustinus, and on the side facing the garden a selection of flowering shrubs of a dwarf nature. A screen of wattles is useful for protecting young trees before they are established.

SHELTERS. *See* GARDEN SHELTERS.

SHEPHERDIA (shĕp-herd-i-a. Elæagnaceæ). Hardy, deciduous, flowering and berry-bearing shrubs, closely allied to Elæagnus. Plant in ordinary garden soil. *Propagate* by cuttings and seed.

SHIELD FERN. *See* ASPIDIUM.

SHIRLEY POPPY. *See* PAPAVER.

SHODDY is the waste from the mills, and is in different grades. High, or first, contains from 12 to 14 per cent. nitrogen; second 5–8 per cent.; and third 3 per cent. approximately. This is useful where stable manure is not obtainable, and its effect persists for two or three years.

SHORTIA (short-ia. Diapensiaceæ). Crimson Leaf. Beautiful dwarf hardy perennials with lovely flowers of white that fade to rose as they open. Pretty oval-shaped leaves of deep green that in autumn change and become almost crimson and thus form an attractive bit of colour in winter.

They are useful in the rockery in a sunny or partially shaded position in peat or sandy loam.

SPECIES.

Species.—Of the three known species only two are grown: *galacifolia*, 6 in., and *uniflora*, 4 in., both with tufts of leaves and flowering in May and June.

Galacifolia is equally successful in a pot,

where it makes a decorative plant. *Propagate* by the offsets taken from the plants in spring.

SHRUBS are definitely plants for all gardens, for there are varieties to solve every garden problem. Label shrub borders when planting, so that no mistake is made in any pruning which be required.

SHRUB BORDERS. The old idea of a shrubbery is at last gradually disappearing. We no longer think of a few laurels, inferior rhododendrons, hollies, etc., all beautiful in themselves but terribly dull in a small garden, whenever the word shrubbery is spoken. Instead we think of the hundreds of beautiful evergreen and deciduous flowering shrubs which have come to grace our gardens from all parts of the world. A shrub border needs planning in the same way as a herbaceous border to give a succession of bloom and a proper arrangement of heights. Allow for a good number of evergreens, especially towards the back of the border, to give stability to the garden during the winter, but in front of them put Forsythia, Daphne, Hamamelis, etc., and the gay flowers borne on leafless stems in the early months of the year, which contrast well against the dark background, besides appreciating the protection which they afford. For good effect a shrub border should not be less than 8 ft. wide, and can well be 20 ft., if a few trees are introduced to give height. Plant the shrubs in groups of not less than three. An average guide in planting is to space the shrubs as far apart as they will ultimately grow. Particulars of growth can be found in most nurserymen's catalogues. If a quick screen is desired, plant more closely but thin out some of the shrubs in three or five years time or they will choke one another and none will show to their best advantage.

SIBERIAN WALLFLOWER. *See* CHEIRANTHUS.

SIBTHORPIA (sib-thŏrp-ia. Scrophulariaceæ). Moneywort. Of this genus of greenhouse and hardy perennial herbs only one species and its varieties are grown, *europæa*, the Cornish Moneywort, Pennyleaf or Pennywort. This has small kidneyshaped leaves and pink flowers in summer. The variety *variegata*, with variegated leaves, is best grown in pots or in the greenhouse. Both make pretty subjects for hanging baskets where they will do well all the year round in a dwelling-room.

Use loam, leaf-mould and sand and plant out, if for outdoor culture, on moist shady banks or in the bog garden. *Propagate* by cuttings struck in sandy soil at any time by division of the roots in April.

SIDALCEA (sī-dal-cea. Malvaceæ). Greek Mallow. Hardy perennials of great beauty for the herbaceous border.

Propagate by seeds or divisions in spring cuttings struck in sandy soil at any time, or by division of the roots in April.

SPECIES.

S. candida with leafy stems and terminal spikes of white flowers, 2–3 ft., *malvæflora*, 1½–3 ft. (syn. *oregana*), lilac-blue, and its variety *atropurpurea* with deep purple flowers in summer, are the best of the species.

SIEBOLDII ARALIA. *See* FATSIA JAPONICA.

SILENE (si-lē-ne. Caryophyllaceæ). Catchfly.

Hardy and greenhouse annual, biennial and perennial herbs of which a certain number are useful for beds and borders while the dwarf plants are hardy little alpines for the rockery. All are easily cultivated and are of effective colours. The annuals and biennials are propagated by seeds, sown under glass in spring or in the open in summer, the perennials by division in spring and autumn. The border plants like light loamy soil and for the alpines some sand and grit added to the same type of soil.

Species.—Pendula with pink flowers and its white (*alba*), and various coloured varieties, are useful hardy annuals which may be sown in August for spring blooming, or outside in spring. *Pendula compacta* and *P. rupestris* are useful biennials also spring flowering. A few of the perennial species useful for the rockery are *acaulis*, Moss Campion or Cushion Pink, that forms hillocks of pale green foliage and has rosy pink flowers, and its double variety, which is an improvement on the type, *alpestris*, with numerous dainty white flowers, that likes to trail over stones, *Elisabethæ*, a rare species that forms tufts of leaves from which rise several

stems bearing red flowers, *Hookeri*, a prostrate species with rosy fringed flowers 2 in. across, and *Schafta*, purple flowers in summer, that forms prostrate mats covered with flowers. Amongst the best of the border plants are *altaica*, yellow flowers in August, 12 in., *asterias*, globular heads of deep red flowers, 12 in., *maritima*, popularly known as Witches' Thimble, with white or reddish flowers in July and August, and its improved variety *S. m. flore pleno*, double, with spreading leaves, *pennsylvanica*, red flowers in June, 12 in., and *virginica*, Fire Pink, with crimson flowers, 1–2 ft.

SILK-VINE. *See* PERIPLOCA.

SILPHIUM (sil-fi-um. Compositæ). Compass Plant; Cup Plant. Hardy perennials. Plant in ordinary soil from October to April in the open, sunny border. Once in three years the plants should be lifted, divided, and replanted. This should be done in spring or autumn.

SPECIES.

S. laciniatum (Compass Plant), yellow August–September, 6–8 ft.

S. perfoliatum (Cup Plant), yellow. August-September, 6–8 ft.

SILVERBELL-TREE. *See* HALESIA.

SILVER BIRCH. *See* BETULA.

SILVER FERN. *See* GYMNOGRAMME.

SILVER LEAF (*Stereum purpureum*). The usual symptom of this disease—a silvering of the foliage—is well known, but the fact that not only stone fruit, both wild and cultivated, but also apples, hawthorne and laurel are liable to attacks of silver leaf, is not appreciated, but it is of the greatest importance. The typical silvering of the foliage is caused possibly indirectly by a fungus on the wood. This wood form shows itself in two ways, either by a flat, film-like, purplish fungus on the branches and trunk, or else by brownish bracket-shaped growths on the wood. These growths appear usually in the autumn and if not cut out are liable to cause a fresh infestation the following year. It should also be borne in mind that stumps and posts can also harbour this disease. The spores are spread by wind, but they must gain entry to the wood through a wound which may have been caused by the pruning-knife or damage to trunk and branches by gales and other causes. One interesting feature of silver leaf is that the tree may recover completely, but it will not be immune from future attack.

METHODS OF CONTROL.—No amount of spraying, injection, manuring or other so-called "cures" which crop up from time to time are of any use, therefore, all branches showing silver leaf should be cut out and burned. In the autumn and winter, all dead wood should be cut away and any branches lying about collected and burned. An eye should also be kept on sloes and other host plants in the hedges and any showing a sign of disease should be grubbed and burned. By these means, and these only, is it possible to keep silver leaf down.

SILYBUM (sil-i-bum. Compositæ). Milk Thistle. Hardy annual or biennial herb, with ornamental foliage, the leaves being large, variegated, with broad white veins. These plants will thrive in any ordinary soil in the sunny open border. Sow the seeds in March, ⅛ in. deep where the plants are to grow. When the seedlings are large enough to handle they should be transplanted to 2 ft. apart.

S. maricinum (Milk Thistle), rose-purple, summer. Height, 1–4 ft.

SINK GARDENING. In recent years it has become more and more fashionable to use any odd kinds of containers for miniature gardens. Quite a number of really attractive gardens have been made in such things as pig troughs, old sinks, etc. This method of gardening can be overdone, and is open to abuse where it is practised by those who have no imagination; but there are many cases in which sink gardens are not only permissible, but are an added attraction to a garden or house. For instance, an oblong sink has been found to be an effective cover for one of the unsightly manhole lids which are sometimes put by the builders in prominent positions in front gardens. We have seen one such lid effectively camouflaged by a small alpine garden made in a stone sink, and surrounded by low banks of creeping plants.

It is also possible to grow alpines in this kind of container, in a garden which would otherwise be entirely unsuitable,

e.g., in a paved courtyard where no ordinary garden can be made.

A well-known collector of alpine plants who has been experimenting for many years in the construction of rock gardens in sinks, gives the following description of the best methods to employ in making a sink garden.

First the sink, pig trough, etc., must be found, and here the one important thing is that it must be of stone. The shape does not so much matter, nor its size. The best place to hunt for old sinks is in builders' yards. Old stone pig troughs may often be picked up around farms and cottages. Stone pig troughs are of all shapes, sizes and weights, and the best of them are delightfully rugged. Glazed earthenware sinks are not good. They are ugly, and they lack the porosity which makes stone so congenial to the roots of the plants. Concrete troughs should also be avoided.

In almost every case the sink should be raised off the ground. Sometimes a good resting-place is to be found on the coping of a low terrace wall. But failing any such ready-made position, make for each sink a couple of rough, stout piers of stone or old bricks about 9–12 in. square and 18–24 in. high, and stand it on these.

Needless to say, an outlet hole must be provided in the bottom of each trough for drainage. Pig troughs do not naturally possess them. Sinks, on the other hand, have drainage holes already. Having placed the sink in position, make sure that it is at such a tilt that it will completely empty itself of water. This is an important matter. Pour water in it while it is empty, and if all is not as it should be it is easy to pack up the low end to the right level.

Apart from this, drainage is a simple matter. A big crock or two arranged over the outlet hole and an inch or so of smaller crocks spread over the bottom of the sink and over these again a layer of rough turf fibre.

It only remains now to put in the soil, arrange your rocks and choose and place the plants. For soil make a gritty fibrous mixture. Good loam, silver sand, leaf-mould, a suspicion of peat, and plenty of broken stone chips or smashed-up flower pots. These last are excellent. They are sharp and porous. Use them from the size of split peas down to such dust as occurs in breaking. Broken charcoal is another luxury you may add; not essential, but good. It keeps the mixture open and sweet.

Build the rocks together, aiming to make them look like one rock which has been split into seven or eight pieces by a series of irregular cracks. This rock outcrop will now be sitting on a floor of soil, its base an inch or two below the edges of the sink. Now fill up the sink to the brim with soil and pour and pack the soil into the cracks between the rocks. This filling up of cracks and hiding the bases of the rocks pulls the whole composition together and does more than anything else to make the arrangement appear one coherent whole. And now the planting can begin.

If a tree or two are desired they must be chosen with care and placed with tact. The best tree of all is undoubtedly the tiny *Juniperus hibernica compressa*, dainty, compact, bolt upright, blue-green, and full of character. The first unthinking temptation is to plant this juniper on the summit of the hill, but this is not the best place. Find rather, a comfortable spot for it somewhere about two-thirds down the slope of the hill. Another splendid tree is the dwarf variety of the Scots pine called *Pinus sylvestris beauvronensis*. It is rare, and a little difficult to obtain, but a small specimen should be secured if possible and planted so as to lean out sideways from some cliff on your outcrop. It is difficult to place it thus without making it look stiff, but a season's growth will correct this and soon the leaves and branches will grow to their position and look natural.

Other good conifers are some of the dwarf Retinisporas, especially *R. obtusa nana* and *pygmæa*, also *R. pisifera nana*. Then there is the dwarf form of ivy, *Hedera conglomerata prostata*. It grows in an odd huddled way and is good for a carefully-chosen corner at the foot of a rock.

Before planting, the level of the ground between the base of the rock and the edge of the sink should be considered. Supposing that in some places the rocks come to within an inch or even less of the sink side, while elsewhere there are irregular spaces of from 6–18 in. across, the best plan will be to plant the more open level spaces with carpeting, mat-forming plants, to make a sort of grassless alpine flower lawn, and in the narrower crevices, between rock and sink, some close growers, with here and there a trailer to hang and partially clothe the sink side.

For lawn effects, *Gentiana verna* and *Thymus serpyllum minus*, a minute creeping thyme, are suitable plants. *Erigeron leiomerus* gives the effect of a lilac daisy an inch or so high. *Bellium minutum* (Little Mary) which is a white daisy less than an inch high; *Primula minima*, a fine turf maker, with big rosy flowers, erect and almost stemless; *P. farinosa*, rather taller with heads of lilac-pink flowers; *Androsace carnea*, pink; *Viola Bertolini*, lavender blue; *Polygala calcarea*, mat-forming and brilliant blue; and *Anemone vernalis*, are all useful.

Among these turf plants some of the smallest of the bulbs may be included. Crocus species, such as *C. Sieberi*, *C. reticulatus*, etc., *Iris Histrio* and *I. histrioides*, *Narcissus bulbocodium*, *N. cyclamineus*, *N. minimum*, *N. triandrus*. Also the lovely Oriental Allium, *A. cyaneum* with heads of lavender-blue flowers like fairy Agapanthus on 4 in. stems, and many others, will form a flowered lawn on the lowest levels. As plants to trail down the sides of the sink, the following are recommended: *Saxifraga apiculata*, *S. a. alba*, primrose-yellow and pure white respectively, and *S. Haagii*, golden yellow, all flowering in earliest spring. *Dryas octopetala*, with its lovely flowers in late summer; *Polygonum vaccinifolium* again for late summer and autumn, with slender rosy flower spikes and crimson autumn leaves. *Achillea Lewisii* will make a mat to bulge out over the sink side, and this good plant will go on producing its pretty sulphur-yellow flowers from early till late summer, and often after that. *Arenaria purpurascens* will trail forward if pushed from behind by a rock, and it covers its mossy cushion with charming lilac star flowers. If a mat of violet is desired, try *Calamintha alpina*. The old Cheddar pink, *Dianthus cæsius*, is first rate, and will give a mat of blue-grey with rose-pink fragrant blossoms. *Hypericum reptans* is excellent and spills from the sink in a thin stream of fresh green, with big stemless flowers nearly 1 in. across, citron-yellow and stained behind with a reddish flush.

On the north side of the mountain, in the cool, a primula or two would give good effect, especially *P. pubescens*, Mrs. Wilson, a small neat auricula, very free flowering and lilac in colour. Also *P. Ruby*, with intense ruby-red flowers and the old *nivalis* of gardens with snow-white flower-heads, cowslip scented.

Now a few flowers to grow on the sides, wedged in narrow crevices. For this, small compact-growing species to form tufts among the cliffs will be wanted. A family that first comes to mind is Saxifraga, and of these the kabschia section is especially good. *S. burseriana*, with its white flowers, on smooth red stems in earliest spring, is lovely. Of all the yellow kabschias, *S. Faldonside* is the best with its citron-yellow blossoms, perfectly rounded. *S. Irvingii*, tiny and neat, with hard cushions of close blue-grey foliage and countless little shell-pink flowers, and *S. Myra*, larger flowered but compact and dwarf and rich cherry-red will be useful. *Saxifraga oppositifolia* one must have, the best variety being *splendens*. *S. Aizoon baldensis* is appropriate to the sink garden with its minute rosettes of encrusted silver and white flowers on stems only a couple of inches high. Lastly, *S. Cochlearis minor*, with purest white flowers in sprays on red stems should be included. Other plants for the sink garden are: Androsaces, Campanulas (Zoysii), Pinks, dwarf Forget-me-nots (*Myosotis rupicola*), and Wahlenbergias.

SISYRINCHIUM (sĭsy-rĭn-chium. Irideæ). Satin Flower. Pretty hardy and half-hardy perennials, some of which are of considerable beauty in the border, rock garden or greenhouse.

They are propagated by seeds sown when ripe or by offsets and thrive in sandy loam with leaf-mould.

Species. — *Grandiflorum*, with purple flowers and grass-like leaves, is one of the first flowers to bloom in spring and is the best of the genus. 12 in.

S. album, a white variety.

S. bermudianum, violet flowers all the summer. 9 in.

S. angustifolum, 12 in., with terminal clusters of blue flowers.

SIUM (si-um. Umbelliferæ). Skirret. Hardy perennial with edible roots, very sweet-flavoured. These plants thrive well in any ordinary rich, deeply-dug soil which is fairly free from stones, in an open sunny spot. Sow in April in drills ½ in. deep and 18 in. apart or in clumps of three or four, setting them 12 in. apart. When the seedlings are 3 in. high they should be thinned. Immediately the flower heads appear they should be removed. Lift in October, twist the leaves as for beetroot, and store in a cool-dry place in layers, with sand or soil between each layer. Artificial manure is of great assistance if applied before sowing in spring.

SKIMMIA (skim'-mi-a. Rutaceæ). Low evergreen shrubs with lustrous laurel-like leaves and very attractive red berries. Plants of both sexes must be grown together, say one male to six females, to ensure a good crop of berries, which constitute the chief charm of the plant. A little time spent in artificial fertilisation is well repaid by a sure crop. With the aid of a camel-hair brush, or rabbit's tail, transfer the pollen from the male flower to the stigmas of the female flowers.

Culture.—Plant in moist loamy soil, in sun or semi-shade. Peat in the soil is appreciated.

Propagate by seeds sown when ripe, and by cuttings under a bell-glass or frame.

SPECIES.

S. Fortunei (*Reevesiana; japonica*). China. Leaves dark green, fragrant white flowers, followed by a profusion of small dull crimson berries. Height about 2 ft. Not a success on chalky soil. This is an hermaphroditic species, i.e., the flowers contain both male and female organs.

S. japonica (*oblata*). Japan, 3–5 ft. Leaves pale green, aromatic when crushed. Flowers white, fragrant, in April, followed by bright red berries. Prospers in most town gardens and in semi-shade, or shady places.

S. j. Foremanii. A very fine hybrid between *S. japonica* + *S. Fortunei*, with large leaves, and both pear-shaped, and round, scarlet berries on the same cluster. Very free berrying.

S. Laureola (Himalayas), 2–3 ft. Leaves larger than in the other species, up to 6 in. long, and aromatic when crushed. Indeed, the whole plant is aromatic (but to some people unpleasantly so), including the leaves, flowers and young wood. Berries red. This Skimmia does not always flower and berry very freely.

SKIRRET. *See* SIUM.

SKULL-CAP. *See* SCUTELLARIA.

SLIPPER FLOWER. *See* CALCEOLARIA.

SLOE. *See* PRUNUS SPINOSA.

SLUGS pass through a partial hibernation in particularly cold weather in winter, but if damp and muggy they are quite as active as in the spring and summer, though the damage they do is less noticeable. Being nocturnal in habit they live just below the surface of the ground by day or under stones, decaying leaves, etc. Only on dull, wet days are they in evidence during daylight; in the evening they leave their hiding quarters and then attack any suitable plant which may be handy. Eggs are laid in little clusters in the soil in the summer and the weather conditions then prevailing regulate to a great extent the number of slugs which will appear the following year. Should the weather be wet and dull when the young slugs hatch, they will grow away well before the winter. If, on the other hand, a long dry spell follows their hatching, the majority will not survive many days, with the result that there will be a scarcity the spring following.

METHODS OF CONTROL.—Of all the suggested remedies treatment with copper sulphate is by far the best. This consists of either applying the sulphate to the ground in the ordinary crystalline form or else spraying in the evening, when the slugs are out, with a solution of 1 in 100. If the first method be adopted the crystals should be applied at the rate of 1 cwt. per acre, and before a crop is put in. In the second case the liquid should be applied to the ground rather than to the crop which is being attacked. It should be remembered that slugs are able to exude a slime on first coming in contact with an irritant, but they are unable to repel in this way

for long, so two applications at an interval of from 15 to 20 minutes should be made. Poison baits as used for leather-jackets have controlled slugs, but apparently the bran loses its attraction if the weather is at all muggy. Freshly-powdered lime and soot sprinkled round choice plants will act as a deterrent.

SMILACINA (smi-la-si-na. Liliaceæ). False Spikenard. Hardy perennials. Plant in autumn or spring in ordinary light, deep rich soil in shrubberies, banks or borders. They prefer to be partially shaded, and like plenty of moisture. Increase by division of the roots at planting time.

SPECIES.

S. racemosa (False Spikenard), white, May. Height, 3 ft.

S. stellata (Star-flowered Lily of the Valley), white, May. Height, 2 ft.

SMILAX (smī'-lax. Liliaceæ). Sarsaparilla Plant. Rapid growing, climbing and shrubby plants with beautiful foliage. They are seen to best advantage when rambling over an old tree-stump, or some other support.

Culture.—Plant in any ordinary loamy soil.

Propagation is best by division of the plants in spring.

SPECIES.

S. aspera (Rough Bindweed). Mediterranean region. Evergreen, with graceful fragrant greenish flowers. Fairly hardy, but is more successful in warm districts.

S. a. maculata. Leaves blotched white.

S. Bona-nox hastata. "Stretchberry" of the eastern U.S.A. Semi-evergreen climbers, with pear-shaped leaves, deep green flowers and black berries.

S. rotundifolia. The "Horse Brier" of eastern N. America. The hardiest and most vigorous species, with stems up to 30 ft. long. Leaves variable from ovate to heart shaped. Flowers, greenish-yellow, followed by black berries with a glaucous bloom.

SMOKE-TREE. *See* RHUS COTINUS.

SMOTHER. *See* BONFIRE.

SNAILS. The appearance of these garden pests is so familiar to all that no special description is called for. The large garden snail (*Helix aspersa*) and other species of Helix are not uncommonly troublesome.

Treatment.—Various powder dressings, e.g., lime and soot, fine-sifted ashes, etc., have been tried from time to time as a preventive against snail attack. Recent investigations have shown that sulphate of copper (bluestone) is highly efficient for the destruction of slugs and snails and a mixture of 1 part by weight of finely-

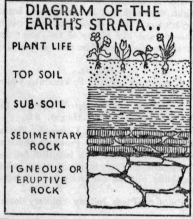

DIAGRAM OF THE EARTH'S STRATA..

PLANT LIFE

TOP SOIL

SUB·SOIL

SEDIMENTARY ROCK

IGNEOUS OR ERUPTIVE ROCK

The top layer of the earth is usually the most fertile, but additional plant food can be released by breaking up the subsoil.

powdered sulphate of copper and 18 parts of Kainit is a very effective agent. Kainit is a mineral substance containing potassium and magnesium sulphates, used as an ingredient in artificial fertilisers and obtainable from any fertiliser and seed merchant. This dressing should be sprinkled lightly on the surface of the soil surrounding individual plants or along the drills of seedlings, care being taken to avoid sprinkling the material on the plants. The dressings should be applied after sunset or very early in the morning and where severe infestations are found it is desirable to apply two or three dressings at intervals of half an hour or so.

SNAKE-ROOT. *See* CIMICIFUGA.

SNAKE'S BEARD. *See* OPHIOPOGON.

SNAPDRAGON. *See* ANTIRRHINUM.

SNEEZEWEED. *See* HELENIUM.

SNOW-BALL. *See* VIBURNUM OPULUS STERILE.

SNOW-BERRY. *See* SYMPHORICARPUS.

SNOWDROP. *See* GALANTHUS.

SNOWDROP TREE. *See* HALESIA.

SNOWFLAKES. *See* LEUCOJUM.

SNOWY MESPILUS. *See* AMELANCHIER.

SOAPWORT. *See* SAPONARIA.

SOBRALIA (so-bra-li-a. Orchidaceæ). Named after F. M. Sobral, a Spanish botanist. Greenhouse terrestrial orchids. Flowers much resemble Cattleyas, but without the same lasting quality. Guatemala, 1836.

Culture. — Compost: equal parts loam and peat, with the addition of coarse sand and charcoal. Repot when new growth commences, nearly half-filling pots with broken crocks. Water freely spring and summer, moderately at other times. Do not require a moist atmosphere like the majority of other orchids. Winter temperature, 50°; summer, 70°.

Propagate by division when repotting.

SOIL, as understood by those connected with the land, is that part of the earth's surface (usually from 4–18 in. deep) which is capable of supporting all forms of vegetation. It is formed chiefly from the weathering of underlying rocks by wind and rain, and breaking down of particles by expansion and contraction due to climatic conditions, and decay of vegetable matter and the action of earthworms.

The difference in soils between garden and garden becomes clear when · it is realised that, as is the underlying rock, so, within limits, will be the soil above it. Thus, in red sandstone country like Devon, red soils predominate and on chalk downs the greyish-white appearance of many garden soils will be familiar to summer visitors.

The analysis of a soil to find out what it is made of is not, as many appear to think, a guide to its fertiliser requirements. Because a soil contains nitrogen, phosphates and potash it does not follow that these are "available." Usually they are not. The chief guide to any requirements of plant food is provided by the appearance of herbage or weeds. Thus, a sickly yellowish appearance is a sure sign of nitrogen starvation and stunted growth means a lack of either lime or all three plant foods. Often it means both.

Lime deficiency is shown by the

presence of weeds like spurry, docks and the like, and a bare, miserable-looking garden, always full of weeds, will be improved by an application of phosphates.

Generally speaking, nitrogen is always lacking, phosphates frequently, and potash in about fifty per cent. of cases. With a little practice and as a result of observing carefully gardens where various fertiliser treatments are known, it is possible to say with great accuracy exactly what plant foods are required and even the quantity of fertiliser needed to bring any garden into a state of high productivity.

See also under CLAY, SAND, GRAVEL, CHALK, LIMESTONE, PEAT, GRANITE, ROCK, VOLCANIC ROCK, GLACIAL DEPOSITS, SALT-MARSH, COMPOST and HYDROPONICS.

SOIL FUMIGATION. A method of ridding the soil of insect pests and also of sterilising soil in large quantities.

The soil fumigant should be sprayed on to the soil by means of watering can or lumps of the material dibbled into the soil, which should then be covered with mats or sacking to prevent the escape of the fumes. The materials to use will be found under the various pests which are controlled by soil fumigants.

In the open air it is generally easier to fumigate soil than to attempt sterilisation. Fumigation is generally done in order to rid the soil of pests, and is particularly useful on newly-broken grass land, where wire-worms, leather-jackets, and other pests that are difficult to destroy, are often present in great numbers. The best way to fumigate the soil is to use naphthalene in some form. Crude naphthalene and lime, equal quantities, mixed and dressed over the soil in winter, allowing 8–12 oz. to the sq. yard., will effectively dispose of most soil pests. Other soil fumigants are obtainable commercially, most of them being best used in the winter months when the soil is vacant. There are also some specially prepared fumigants which can be used between growing crops without danger.

SOIL MOISTURE. Hoeing and harrowing of the soil act in several ways, but chiefly add to the health of the plants by keeping available both air and moisture. Loosening the caked surface lets more air into the soil. Tests have been made that

show that these operations also cause more moisture to be retained, as the following readings show:

Unhoed Ground.—Soil temperature, 35°. Moisture, 14.7 per cent.

Hoed Ground.—Soil temperature, 31.5°. Moisture, 16 per cent.

Mulching conserves the moisture in the soil, but does not so effectively aerate the soil as hoeing.

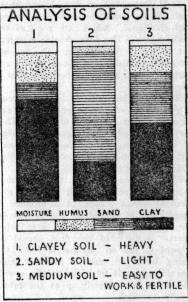

ANALYSIS OF SOILS

1. CLAYEY SOIL — HEAVY
2. SANDY SOIL — LIGHT
3. MEDIUM SOIL — EASY TO WORK & FERTILE

MOISTURE   HUMUS   SAND   CLAY

Medium soils are best for cultivation. Soils can be improved by adding the missing elements.

SOIL PESTS. *Moles.* The mole's food consists of mice, frogs, insects, etc., so that if it were not an underground dweller, given to navvying and throwing up unsightly mounds on lawns and borders alike, it would not trouble the gardener.

If steel traps are used, gloves should be worn when setting them, for moles have a keen sense of smell. The traps should be set in the main runs, not in the hillocks.

If a hole can be found where the mole enters the garden it can be plugged with rags soaked in carbolic acid, tar or creosote.

Pledgelets of cotton wool, soaked in carbon bisulphide can be placed in various parts of the runs and the holes covered with soil. The poisonous vapours will kill all animal life they come in contact with.

Pieces of calcium carbide dropped into various parts of the tunnels will drive the moles away, at least, for a time.

Great care should be taken in the use of poisonous preparations.

Mice. These sometimes do damage to seeds, especially peas. To protect the seeds, take a tin with a tight-fitting lid. Fill it about one-third full with peas, add a little linseed oil or varnish and shake until all the peas are thoroughly covered with the liquid. Add a little red lead and shake again. The peas should be spread out to dry before sowing. Do not use too much varnish. Fox, stoat, weasel and barn owl, etc., are the natural enemies of mice.

Rabbits.—These rodents harm the roots of plants, eat off tender green shoots and seriously harm the bark of trees. They may be excluded from the garden by means of wire netting sunk below the ground and turned outwards in the direction from which they approach.

Sticks placed upright in the ground round a tree or shrub will protect it if a piece of string soaked in a mixture of equal parts of animal oil and paraffin or creosote is wound round about three inches apart. A little of the fluid should be allowed to fall on the ground below the string which the rabbits will not pass. An alternative is to smear the trees with Stockholm tar as high up as the rabbit is able to reach.

Other means of being rid of them are of course, shooting, trapping, smoking out with sulphur or catching with ferrets.

Rats.—These animals which ravage stored crops can become a serious menace unless kept in check. There are several proprietary viruses on the market which can be used without harming human beings or pets. These are sufficient to keep rats at bay, but if wholesale extermination is desired poisons, such as calcium cyanide, should be used. This material is highly poisonous and should be used with extreme care.

See also LEATHER-JACKETS *and* WIRE-WORMS.

SOIL, SOUR. A sour or lime-free condition of the soil can usually be determined

by the type of weeds which are found growing. The following weeds only flourish under sour conditions, and if they are found on the soil of a new garden, a maximum dressing of lime should be given after digging: Spurry; Stinking Mayweed; Corn Chrysanthemum; Sour Dock; and Sheep Sorrel.

SOIL STERILISATION. The sterilisation of the soil is a practice which has now passed the experimental stage. It is practised extensively by commercial tomato growers and others, but it is seldom done by amateurs, except in the case of soil to be used for seed raising. There are three methods of soil sterilisation: baking, steaming and scalding. The soil to be used for seeds can be placed in a shovel over an open fire and heated until the soil is too hot to hold in the hand. Moisture will evaporate, but the soil should be removed from the fire before it actually begins to smoke. Do this at least two days before using the soil for planting or seed sowing. in greenhouse work, soil is sometimes sterilised by having red-hot bricks pushed into it, the bricks being heated again and again, and replaced, until the whole of the soil has been sterilised. *Steaming* is not often done by the amateur gardener, as it necessitates special apparatus, using pipes riddled with holes across the bottom of the box of soil through which steam is forced. *Scalding* is a favourite method. The pots, ready filled for planting or seed sowing, are thoroughly soaked with boiling water until they are thoroughly hot right through. They must of course be well drained and allowed to become quite cool before planting or sowing. (*See also* SOIL FUMIGATION.)

SOIL TESTING FOR LIME. Soil analysis is not a matter the amateur gardener should undertake, and as a rule the condition of the soil can be judged sufficiently by its appearance and the ease with which it can be worked. Should it be desirable to ascertain whether the soil is sufficiently charged with lime, the following simple test can be applied. Take about ½ lb. of soil and mix it into a thin paste with water. To this add a weak solution of hydrochloric acid. If the mixture fizzes audibly, lime is present in sufficient quantity for ordinary garden purposes. If not, then more lime is needed. This is only a simple test and to some extent based on probability. It is as well for the amateur gardener to remember that lime has a tendency to be washed out of the top layer of soil even where the garden is over a subsoil of chalk, and the ground will therefore need fresh dressings of life from time to time to keep it in a fertile condition.

SOLANDRA (so-lan-dra. Solanaceæ). Stove evergreen shrubs. Jamaica, 1781.

Culture.—Compost: 2 parts loam, 1 part peat, ½ part sand. Repot early spring. Water freely during summer months, but little in the winter. Remove all weak growths and slightly prune strong ones end of January or beginning of February. Winter temperature, 55°; summer, 75°–80°.

Propagate by cuttings of young shoots in sandy peat in the propagator, temperature, 70°. Spring.

SOLANUM. An important and extensive genus of shrubs and climbers, hardy and half-hardy, effective in bloom or foliage.

Cultivation.—Culturally, this plant is treated as an annual, sowing the seeds in gentle heat in early January for a display in early winter or up to the middle of April for later flowering. The seedlings should be pricked out when large enough into boxes containing a compost of loam, leaf-mould and sand, growing them on in gentle heat. As they progress they may be potted into 60-size pots in a similar compost and subsequently transferred to 48's or 32's, using a compost of good loam, leaf-mould and sand to which has been added a little sifted and well-decayed manure. During the summer months the plants should be stood in a cold frame in a sunny position, sinking the pots to their rims in ashes to keep them evenly moist. This exposure to sun aids growth and exposes the tiny white flowers for the attention of insects; thus a good setting of fruit is assured. Towards autumn, when the berries have set, they may again be taken into the greenhouse or conservatory.

Propagate by cuttings under glass and by seeds.

Variety.—The variety *Nanum* is compact in habit, making a useful pot plant. Much used by florists' shops.

Solanum pseudo-capsicum and hybrids of these two species are all cultivated in the same way.

SPECIES.

S. crispum (Chile). A quick-growing, semi-evergreen, flowering climbing shrub, up to 18 ft. covered with delicate bluish-purple fragrant flowers from June–August. In the warm southern maritime counties it is hardy, but inland it needs wall protection. In Hampshire it has withstood nearly 30° of frost.

S. c. autumnalis. A variety with a more prolonged flowering season.

S. jasminoides (Brazil). A beautiful, elegant-habited climber, for warm walls. On a sheltered south wall it is practically hardy. The true plant has grey-blue flowers, produced from July onwards.

S. j. alba. The white-flowering form, which is usually sent out for the type.

S. capsicastrum, has bright ornamental red berries in winter, about the size of cherries. Much used at Christmas-time for decoration in the conservatory or house.

See also AUBERGINE. POTATO, etc.

SOLDANELLA (soldan-ell-a. Primulaceæ). Moonwort. Charming little hardy perennials with rounded heart-shaped leaves and pretty drooping flowers that are suitable for the rockery.

They require to be grown in sandy loam, peat and leaf-mould with a top dressing of leaf soil and sand in autumn. A low position on the rockery with plenty of water in summer or by the side of a bog is best.

Propagate by seeds sown when ripe, or in spring. Use sandy peat or fine soil in pots or in a frame, or increase by division after flowering.

Species.—*Alpina* (Blue Moonwort), which has dainty stems bearing blue-fringed flowers in April, and its rarer white form (3 in.) are the best of the genus although *alpina Wheeleri*, a larger form, is thought by some to be better. *Minima*, lilac-blue and its white variety dwarfer than *alpina* are used with great success for carpeting. 2 in. *Montana* with bluer flowers than *alpina* and larger leaves and *Clusii*, blue, are quite good species.

SOLIDAGO (sŏl-i-dā-go. Compositæ).

Golden Rod. These rather coarse hardy perennials are most ornamental for shrubberies and large borders but on account of their weedy growth are not to be recommented for the small herbaceous border.

They thrive in sun or shade in any soil and should be staked in the first stages of growth to prevent them from becoming an unsightly mass of twisted stems.

Plant in spring or autumn.

Increase by seeds sown outdoors in April

SOLDANELLA

Soldanella. These are dainty little Alpines that bloom as soon as the snow has melted.

or by division in spring and autumn.

SPECIES.

S. canadensis has dense panicles of golden flowers in late summer and continuing into autumn.

S. Buckleyi, small flowers, grey foliage.

S. ulmifolia (Golden Wings), tall branching spikes.

S. serotina, masses of flowers in October.

S. Virgaurea, the common Golden Rod.

SOLLYA (sol′-li-a. Pittosporaceæ). Tender climbing plants with beautiful bell-shaped blue flowers, from Australia. Unfortunately they are not hardy, and can only be successfully grown out of doors in warm districts. In Cornwall they climb up the walls of houses and are most ornamental.

Culture.—Plant in well-drained loam and peat.

Propagate by cuttings in sand under bell-glass, also by seeds.

SOLOMON'S SEAL. *See* POLYGONATUM.

SOOT. There are three reasons why soot is valuable to the gardener: It contains a little nitrogen; it is a good insecticide; it darkens the soil surface, and therefore makes the soil warmer by retaining solar heat. Soot should always be stored dry, and can be used in making liquid manure, or as a surface dressing along the rows of growing crops, either alone, or mixed with lime. If mixed with lime it makes the best insecticide, as the fumes are objectionable to insects of all kinds.

SOPHORA (sŏf′-or-a. Leguminosæ). A genus of very decorative trees and shrubs, with elegant foliage and pea-shaped flowers. All are deciduous.

Culture.—Plant in ordinary loamy soil in sunny positions.

Propagate by seed sown under glass. Those of a shrubby nature may be increased by cuttings, the named varieties by grafting on the type.

SPECIES.

S. tetraptera (*Edwardsia grandiflora*). Native of Chile and of New Zealand, where it is known as "Kowhai." An extremely decorative and graceful tree from 15–30 ft high, with beautiful feathery or fern-like foliage, with each leaf composed of as many as 80 leaflets in matured specimens which have attained to the flowering stage. The golden-yellow flowers, 1–2 in. long, are freely produced in pendulous clusters during May and June. Only hardy in the warm counties, when it may be semi-evergreen, the persistence of its foliage depending on the climatic conditions.

S. t. microphylla. Not so tender as the preceding, it having survived successfully 27° of frost in the open border. The flowers are a little smaller than the *tetraptera*, otherwise the plant is equally beautiful.

SOPHRO - CATTLEYA (sof-ro-kat-le-ya. Orchidaceæ). A race of hybrid orchids from Sophronitis + Cattleya. A brilliant little group, for which the little red *Sophronitis grandiflora* is primarily responsible.

Their cultural requirements are similar to Cattleya (*which see*).

SOPHRO-LÆLIO-CATTLEYA (sof-ro-le-li-o-kat-le-ya). Trigeneric hybrids, combining Sophronitis, Lælia and Cattleya. This is becoming a very popular race of orchids, and their beautiful variation in colouring, and free-flowering habit, make them indispensible in every choice collection. The varieties are numerous, and only two or three of the best can be given.

Adonis, sepals and petals rich crimson, lips rose-purple with yellow throat.

Dora, sepals and petals rose-carmine, buff-colour at base, lips reddish-purple with orange-yellow throat.

Joseph Charlesworth, sepals and petals rose-mauve tipped with crimson, lips rich purple with golden lines extending into the throat.

Senator-Titian, sepals and petals Titian-red slightly flushed with mauve, lips reddish-purple with rose-mauve margin and buff-coloured throat.

SORBARIA. *See under* SPIRÆA.

SORBUS. *See* PYRUS.

SORREL. *See* RUMEX.

SOUTH AFRICAN HAREBELL. *See* ROELLA.

SOUTH AFRICAN THISTLE. *See* BERKHEYA.

SOUTHERNWOOD. *See* ARTEMISIA.

SOWBREAD. *See* CYCLAMEN.

SPADE. This tool should be made of forged steel and the handle of selected ash. The weight and size of the spade must necessarily depend on individual strength and capabilities.

One point to notice is that some spades are "treaded," i.e., the part of the spade on which you tread when digging is flat and not sharp and so does not make the arch of your foot sore or wear out your shoe leather so much.

For clay soil there is on the market a special patent digger which, instead of having a solid straight blade, has a pointed cut-away blade—making it lighter to use and easier to dig. Failing this, it is better to use a narrower curved blade

for digging trenches or such work in heavy soil. If, and when, the blade of the spade becomes blunt in use, a file should be used to resharpen.

SPANISH BROOM. *See* SPARTIUM.

SPANISH GARDENS. The Spanish Garden has grown out of the patio, and has not diverged far from it. The patio, which is particularly Arabic, although common all along the Mediterranean, is a square open to the sky and enclosed by

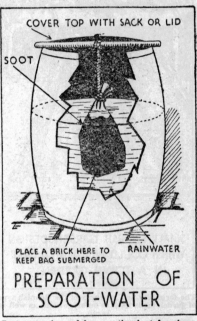

COVER TOP WITH SACK OR LID

SOOT

PLACE A BRICK HERE TO KEEP BAG SUBMERGED

RAINWATER

PREPARATION OF SOOT-WATER

Soot-water is useful as a stimulant for chrysanthemums and other pot plants.

the house walls. It is used as a room. In the poorer patios the housewives wash, prepare the food, and do other domestic duties. The patio is a paradise for the workers during the noonday heat; it is fragrant and cool, while retaining its privacy. It has few flowers and no grass, because it will not grow. The ground is bare or paved with tiles. From the walls cooling fountains gush forth, while the ground is traversed by shallow irrigation canals, fed often by a rippling fountain.

The beds, which are usually lower than

the pathways and enclosed by hedges, for shelter, are filled with palms, cypresses, oranges, apricots, pomegranates, roses, and a few sweet-smelling flowers such as verbenas and mignonettes. The hedges enclosing them are frequently of myrtle. Trees of sycamore, locust, apple, plum and cherry provide a restful shade.

As the patio is essentially a room, there

SMALL SPANISH GARDEN DESIGN WHICH COULD BE CARRIED OUT IN A TOWN GARDEN.

The formality and neatness of the Spanish type of garden lends itself to small gardens as well as large.

are always one or more seats to be found in it. These are usually made of tile or brick, beautifully patterned and coloured. The walls, covered with vines, oranges, lemons, jasmine, heliotrope and white musk rose, make the whole patio a haven of delight and restfulness.

Potted plants, too, find their place in Spanish gardens, and some of them are seen bordering a path or a wall, or hung upon the walls by hoops of wire.

Although the patio garden is the product of a hot climate, it is easily reproduced in other countries such as our own, being particularly suited for roofs and restaurants. It should not be slavishly

copied, but adapted. For tiled walks grass and paving stones can be substituted. Remember, too, that the Spanish Garden is not always so symmetrical and well-balanced as imagined, its charm is often the result of a kind of haphazard carelessness, typical of an easy-going, sun-nurtured people. This kind of garden is typical of Andalusia. To make it more Arabic in style, light it at night, cover the walls with ceramics, provide wooden doors and shutters, iron window grilles, and balconies, and the result will be a delight for all time.

SPANISH ONION. *See* ONION.

SPARAXIS (spar-ax-is. Iridaceæ). Half-hardy bulbous plants. Plant from September to January in light sandy soil in a sunny, well-drained border. Set the bulbs 4 in. deep and 2 in. apart. Mulch the surface in March with cow manure, and during the winter months cover the crown with litter. These plants may also be grown in pots. Grow in coconut fibre and allow 5 bulbs 3 in. deep in each pot. Water till the flowers fade and then gradually cease. Increase by offsets treated as bulbs.

SPARMANNIA (spar-man-ni-a. Tiliaceæ). African Hemp. Greenhouse evergreen flowering shrubs. Pot in early spring in a compost of two parts loam, one part peat with a little sand added. Place in a light, airy greenhouse from September to June. From June to September they may be stood in a sunny position outdoors. Water plentifully during the summer, but after this only moderate quantities should be given. Stimulants may also be given during the summer period. Prune back moderately in November or December. Take cuttings in spring or summer and insert in sandy soil under a bell-glass.

SPARTIUM (spar'-ti-um. Leguminosæ). Spanish Broom. A tall-growing (8–12 ft.) broom-like shrub with rush-like branches often without leaves. Flowers pea-shaped, rich yellow, fragrant, borne in racemes up to 18 in. long. It blooms from June until September, and is at its best during July. A very useful shrub for planting in hot dry banks. Very effective in a group, making a fine mass of colour when but few other shrubs are in bloom. It should be raised from seed, and the resultant seedlings grown in pots until they are ready to be placed in their permanent positions. The plants bear clipping well, and they may be gone over with the shears in early spring, if dwarf or formal specimens are desired. It is a very old plant in English gardens, having been introduced from Spain about the middle of the 16th century.

S. junceum. The only species. Award of Garden Merit, R.H.S., 1923.

SPATHOGLOTTIS (spath-o-glot-tis. Orchidaceæ). Stove terrestrial orchids. Pot in spring and grow in a compost of equal parts leaf-mould and fibrous loam. They like to be grown in partial shade and should be given plenty of water in summer, but little at other times. The flowers appear at the top of the last made bulb. Increase by division in spring.

SPEAR GRASS. *See* ACIPHYLLA.

SPECULARIA (spek-u-larea. Campanulaceæ). Venus's Looking Glass. *Specularia-speculum,* a hardy annual, 1 ft., is the common species, and is a good border plant. Blue. Sow in spring in fairly light soil where to flower.

SPENT HOPS. Spent hops form valuable humus in the soil. As a general rule it is cheaper to buy the spent hops direct from the brewer, and to add artificial fertilisers to the soil as required, rather than to buy patent hop manures; but the patent manures are easy to handle in small quantities. Spent hops are more useful if they can be mixed with a quantity of shoddy and stored for six months before use. Turn the heap over two or three times while it is maturing.

SPHÆRALCEA (sfe-ral-se-a. Malvaceæ). Half-hardy perennial and greenhouse shrubs. Plant perennial species in autumn or spring in any ordinary soil, in sunny dry position on sheltered banks or rock gardens. The shrubby species, however, require to be grown in a compost of loam, leaf-mould and sand in the cool greenhouse. Give plenty of water during the growing period. Increase perennial species by division at planting time and the shrubby species by cuttings of young shoots inserted in sandy soil in gentle bottom heat.

SPHAGNUM. A moss which grows in swampy places and is used by orchid

growers as it has the power of retaining moisture. It can also be used for packing cut flowers and roots.

SPHENOGYNE. *See* URSINIA.

SPICE-BUSH. *See* LINDERA.

SPIDERWORT. *See* TRADESCANTIA.

SPIGELIA (spi-ge-li-a. Loganiaceæ). Maryland Pink-root. Hardy herbaceous perennials. Plant in spring in the partially

SPARAXIS

Sparaxis is an unusual bulb with bright coloured flowers, suitable for decoration.

shaded border, and grow in a compost of loam, leaf-mould, peat and sand. Give plenty of water during the summer. Increase by division of roots at planting time.

SPECIES.

S. marilandica, red and yellow, summer. Height 1 ft.

SPINACH (*Spinacia oleracea*). Chenopodiaceæ. Spinach is a most wholesome vegetable, and it is undoubtably becoming popular now that market gardeners are cultivating for the market, and its preparation in the kitchen is becoming better known. One or other of its forms can be produced with ease at almost any season of the year if small successional sowings are made.

Culture.—This most useful green vegetable requires a fairly rich soil, as on poor land, especially from spring sowings, the plants soon run to seed. Spinach is perfectly hardy, and the earlier sowings can be made as soon as the land on a sheltered border can be had in sowing condition in February; and where continuous supplies are required, sow a few rows at fortnightly intervals from the end of March up to the beginning of October. At this date a good breadth should be sown for winter supplies. It is a fact not generally known that on heavy soils the round-seeded summer spinach will stand the winter better than the prickly-seeded or winter types. In all instances the plants should be thinned out to 6 in. apart in order that the foliage may develop to its full size and texture.

Perpetual Spinach is a species of beet—*Beta Cicla*—which develops large succulent leaves.

Silver Beet, also called Swiss Chard and Seakale Beet, is a variety of *Beta Cicla*, which has broad white stems and ribs. The stems and ribs are served as seakale, and the green leaf as spinach.

These are grown in similar manner to ordinary beetroot, but allowed to remain through the winter and following summer.

SPINACIA. *See* SPINACH.

SPINDLE-TREE. *See* EUONYMUS EUROPÆUS.

SPINOVITIS. *See under* VITIS.

SPIRÆA (spī-rē′-a. Rosaceæ). A genus of flowering shrubs and herbs of the most diverse habit of growth from the diminutive *S. pectinata*, with its resemblance to some mossy Saxifraga, to those of tree-like dimensions up to 30 ft. high. Many of the Spiræas are of great beauty and value for the garden, being very graceful in appearance, and flowering freely.

Culture.—Plant in moist loamy soil in full sun.

Propagation by cuttings taken 'in July and August, and placed in gentle bottom heat. Or by cuttings of more matured wood in September and placed under a bell-glass in a shady spot. Those species which throw up sucker-like growths from their base may be increased by division. The Spiræas can also be increased by seed, but they cross-breed with such ease

that unless the plants are isolated, they cannot be depended on to come true. Pruning is of the utmost importance in the cultivation of Spiræas if the best results are looked for. Those that flower in the current year's wood should be pruned during winter or early spring. Old shoots are entirely removed, and the young ones cut back to within about 1 ft. of the ground, and thinned out to 6 in. or so apart. They include such species as *japonica, Douglasii, Lindleyana, Salicifolia*, etc. Those that produce their flowers early in the season on the shoots formed the previous year should have the wood removed that has borne the flowers, *as soon as the flowers have faded.* The object is to allow of the utmost period of growth previous to the next season's blooming. Under this heading may be m e n t i o n e d: *Arguta, hypericifolia, Thunbergii. Van Houttei, Veitchii*, etc.

SHRUBS.

(All are deciduous except *S. pectinata*.)

S. Aitchisonii (Sorbaria augustifolia). Afghanistan, etc. A spreading-habited shrub up to 10 ft. high with flowers of the purest white, during July and August, Allied to *S. lindleyana*, but superior to that species in its more elegant foliage, and finer flowers.

S. arguta. A hybrid of graceful branching habit, wreathed with small white flowers in April and May. This may be regarded as the most beautiful of the early or spring-flowering Spiræas. Easily increased by layering. Award of Garden Merit, R.H.S.

S. bullata (crispifolia). Japan. A dwarf shrub about 1 ft. high, which is almost hidden by its deep rosy-crimson flowers towards the end of July. Cut back in spring.

S. canescens (flagelliformis). Himalayas, 6-10 ft. A strikingly beautiful shrub with graceful arching branches crowned with clusters of creamy-white flowers during June and July. The dull green leaves, with their greyish down beneath, impart to the plant a pleasing greyish appearance.

S. discolor (ariæfolia, Holodiscus discolor). N. W. America, 8-12 ft. A very fine species with extremely graceful arching branches, and pendulous plumes of creamy-white flowers during July, produced in the greatest profusion. Quite easily one of the best six Spiræas. It will reach to a height of 20 ft. and 40 ft. when favourably placed. Thrives best near water.

S. Douglasii (N. America), 4–6 ft. Flowers rose-purple in erect panicles from end of June to end of July. In February or March the flowering shoots of the year before should be cut back, and every 3 or 4 years the plants should be divided, and some manure or fresh soil added to the site before replanting. Not a success on chalky soils.

S. japonica (*calosa. Fortunei*). China and Japan. A dwarf species, 3–5 ft. high, with numerous corymbs of rosy-pink flowers during July and August. This species and its varieties should be pruned in spring by thinning out some of the old wood, and shortening back the shoots that are left.

S. j. Anthony Waterer. A fine hybrid, 2–3 ft. high. Flowers bright crimson, very continuously produced from July to October. Very effective in a mass.

S. lindleyana (Himalayas), 20 ft. A graceful shrub of spreading habit, and very large pyramidal panicles of white flowers. A very striking plant by the side of water. The branches should be pruned back in early spring.

S. Menziesii (Western N. America), 3–5 ft. Flowers purplish-rose in July and August.

S. m. triumphans. The finest variety.

S. opulifolia. See under NEILLIA.

S. prunifolia flore pleno (China), 4–6 ft. Although introduced so far back as 1847, this is still one of the finest Spiræas. Its slender shoots, up to 2 ft. long, are smothered from end to end with double white flowers during April and May. Foliage richly coloured in autumn. Easily increased by removing the side suckers, and either potting them up, or planting them in the open ground. The type plant is of no value, owing to its persistent sterility.

S. Thunbergii (China), 3–5 ft. A graceful-habited plant with arching, slender branches, almost hidden by a profusion of pure white flowers, during March and April. It needs a hot sunny season to

ripen its wood. Not a success in chalky soils.

S. Van Houttei (*Confusa*). A hybrid, probably between *S. trilobata* + *S. cantoniensis*, with elegant, arching stems, the upper side of which are covered with a wonderful profusion of white flowers during June. With the possible exception of *S. arguta*, this may be considered the finest white-flowered Spiræa. It is

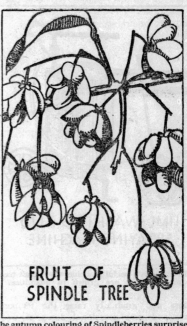

FRUIT OF SPINDLE TREE

The autumn colouring of Spindleberries surprises artists by the association of orange and red.

much grown in pots under glass, and bears forcing well. Immediately after flowering the older wood should be thinned out, to help in the development of the younger shoots.

HARDY HERBACEOUS SPECIES.

These thrive in rich, moist, light soil, for preference by the waterside in a partially shaded position.

Propagate perennials by division and seeds, and the shrubby species by cuttings of young wood struck in a frame or by rooted suckers. Thin out the old wood after flowering in the case of the spring-flowering shrubs.

Those that flower in summer on the current season's growth should be well thinned in spring and the shoots cut back to encourage strong growth on which to bear the inflorescence. For pot culture, use 8–10 in. pots with a compost of two parts of sandy loam to one of leaf-mould and a little manure. Pot up in autumn and keep nearly dry in a frost-proof frame until growth commences, then take in-

LIME - WASHING AND SPRAYING MACHINE

The above is a useful machine where fruit trees and potatoes are grown in quantities.

doors and gradually raise the temperature and give occasional doses of weak liquid manure. Sink the pots in a bed of ashes and leave out of doors during the summer.

Among the best of hardy perennials are :

S. aruncus, Goat's Beard, with pinnate leaves and creamy-white plumes; *S. a. Kneifii*, more elegant foliage. 4–6 ft.

S. astilboides, resembles *aruncus* and is useful for cutting.

S. filipendula, with prostrate fern-like leaves and creamy flowers, 2 ft., and its double form—*flore pleno*.

S. kamschatica, with palmate leaves and large feathery plumes of white flowers, and its variety *rosea* with masses of pink flowers. 7 ft.

S. palmata, handsome leaves and feathery plumes of rosy flowers. 3–5 ft.

S. ulmaria flore pleno, a lovely form of the native plant Meadow Sweet, 2–4 ft. and

S. venusta, with rosy flowers, and its more advanced form *rosea*, than which there are scarcely any plants more suitable for peaty soil in a bog garden.

All these plants bloom in July and August.

Good greenhouse plants are *japonica*, a hardy evergreen shrub with rosy flowers and its white (*alba*), crimson (Anthony Waterer) and red varieties. The garden plant *S. japonica* is usually known as *Astilbe japonica* (see ASTILBE).

POT PLANTS.

Culture of *S. astilboides* as a pot plant. Compost : 2 parts fibrous loam, equal parts leaf-mould and silver sand with a little charcoal. Pot in the autumn and stand in cold frame until required, i.e., January or February. If required for forcing, remove to temperature 55°, but for ordinary greenhouse flowering temperature 40° or 45° is sufficient. Water freely when growth commences and occasionally apply a little weak liquid manure. After flowering plant outside in moist sunny position. Plants do not flower successfully two years in succession, but may be lifted after the second year and again used for pot work. To obtain the best results it is better to buy new roots annually from a good nurseryman.

Propagate by division of roots.

Good species for pots are *S. astilboides* and its varieties *floribunda* and *Lemoinei*. Also several fine hybrids, such as Peach Blossom, Queen Alexandra, Granat, Ceres and Gladstone.

SPIRE LILY. *See* GALTONIA.

SPIT. A layer of soil as deep as can be conveniently turned on a spade. Thus in double digging the soil is broken up for a depth of two spits.

SPLEENWORT. *See* ASPLENIUM.

SPONDIAS (spon-di-as. Anacardiaceæ). Warm greenhouse trees with edible fruits. Grow in well-drained borders of the heated greenhouse, in a soil of fibrous loam and sand. Give plenty of water during the growing period. Take cuttings of half-ripened shoots and insert in sandy soil in a temperature of 75°.

SPECIES.

S. dulcis (syn. *S. cytherea*). Otaheite Apple. Fruits golden-yellow. Height to 60 ft.

S. lutea (syn. *S. Mombin*). Hog Plum. Fruits yellow. Height to 60 ft.

SPORT. A natural break from the usual characteristics of a plant. A change in colour or form is welcomed by nurserymen as the sport may be of value commercially.

SPRAYERS. It is an unfortunate necessity that in growing flowers, fruit or vegetables an insecticide, or some other form of poison for the pests that attack them must be used periodically. There are many ways of doing this according to the size of your garden. In all cases it must be remembered that it is most important to spray under as well as over the leaves so attacked and also that the spraying must be done regularly to be successful. Starting with the needs of the small garden and working larger, there are sprayers on the market as follows:

The Bottle Sprayer. There are many different kinds of bottle sprayer, but the chief difference is between the rubber bellows type and the type that is itself moved up and down. The disadvantage of the latter is that the spray cannot be directed accurately. In the bellows type of sprayers there is one in particular which, by turning the nozzle right or left, combines a variation of sprays from a fine mist spray to a jet. This can also be screwed into a copper container as a form of pneumatic sprayer.

Atomiser. This is a self-contained syringe, having a container for the fluid at the end. You just fill the container with the insecticide, etc., and go on spraying until the container, usually holding 1 or 2 pints, is emptied. The atomiser is made in either galvanised tin or brass, the latter being the stronger and less liable to damage from the liquid.

Syringe. The syringe is comprised of a metal tube, which has a fine nozzle at the end, and through which the liquid is forced by a cup leather washer on the end of a handled rod, which sprays the liquid out under pressure. The very cheap ones are made of galvanised iron, but generally speaking brass is used.

Points to look for when buying a syringe.

The more you pay for a syringe the more refinements you get on it.

On cheap ones there is just one nozzle; at more expense you get an elbow which facilitates spraying under the leaves, and also a ball-valve quick-filling device.

More expensive still, you get a rose as well as jet and probably a stuffing-box to prevent the liquid squirting up your sleeve

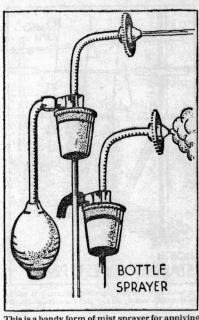

BOTTLE SPRAYER

This is a handy form of mist sprayer for applying insecticides in the greenhouse and can be fixed to any sized bottle.

when filling, and a drip preventer to do likewise when the nozzle is up in the air.

Still more costly makes have fine, medium and coarse jets with all the other refinements already mentioned, and also a large diameter and longer barrel.

In fact the whole question revolves on the size of your garden and the price it is worth while to pay. Good care and attention, especially to the leather washers, will ensure long life. A syringe should be washed in clean water after use.

Pneumatic Sprayers.

When there is a great deal of spraying to be done a pneumatic sprayer is most useful. This is a form of sprayer, either carried in the hand, on the back, or, when used for tall trees, on the end of a stick, which, when once filled with air, goes on spraying until it has all vaporised. Thus, after pumping it full of air, it will spray 10 or 20 trees according to its capacity.

Spraying Outfit.

This is in all ways similar to a syringe, except that the necessity for continually

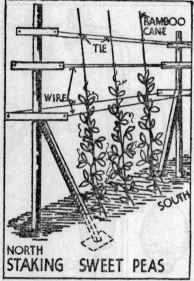

STAKING SWEET PEAS

For ordinary garden purposes where pea sticks are not obtainable, string and cane supports are useful.

filling the syringe from the bucket is obviated by the use of a length of hose fitted with a strainer which is dropped into the bucket and connected with the syringe. Thus, with a single-action syringe outfit, by pulling out the handle you charge the barrel and by pushing down you discharge, and so on without stopping. This outfit is invariably supplied with a lime-washing nozzle.

Bucket Pumps.

These are fixed to the bucket and are used to spray direct from the bucket in which the lime or insecticide has been mixed.

SPREKELIA (sprek-e-li-a. Amaryllidaceæ). Jacobean Lily. Warm green-

house bulbs. Grow in a compost of turfy loam, river sand and a little bonemeal. Pot in February, placing the bulbs two-thirds of their depth in the soil, and stand in a light part of the greenhouse. Good drainage is essential. Give plenty of water from time of growth until September. After this period the bulbs must be kept quite dry. Doses of liquid manure may be given when the flower spikes appear. Top dress the large bulbs annually. Repot every three or four years.

Increase by seeds sown in March in pots of sandy loam. Keep the seedlings moist for about three years. The flowers will not appear until after six or seven years. Also by offsets treated as bulbs.

SPRING BEAUTY. *See* CLAYTONIA.

SPRING MEADOW SAFFRON. *See* BULBOCODIUM.

SPRUCE. *See* PICEA.

SPRUCE, BLUE. *See* PICEA PUNGENS KOSTERIANA.

SPRUCE, HEMLOCK. *See* TSUGA.

SPRUCE, NORWAY. *See* PICEA EXCELSA.

SPURGE. *See* EUPHORBIA.

SPURGE LAUREL. *See* DAPHNE.

SQUILL. *See* SCILLA.

SQUILL, STRIPED. *See* PUSCHKINIA.

SQUIRREL TAIL GRASS. *See* HORDEUM.

STACHYS (stak-iss. Labiatæ). Many of the Hedge Nettles are rather coarse and weedy, but those mentioned below are well worthy of a place in the rock garden.

S. coccinea is a really beautiful variety from Texas, with flowers of a vivid and unusual old-rose shade. It will not as a rule survive a severe winter, but is easily raised annually from seed sown early under glass, or cuttings may be rooted in the autumn and kept through the winter under shelter. 1 ft. June.

S. corsica. This little plant forms a dense carpet of bright emerald-green, decked with large flowers of creamy-white or palest pink. It needs a sunny, well-drained soil of light loam. It can be propagated by division, or, since it roots as it runs, the outlying pieces can be dug up and replanted at any time. It flowers the whole summer. Corsica.

S. lanata. Lamb's Ear. The English

name is descriptive of leaves clothed with thin, long white wool. The flowers are crimson on 1 ft. spikes. A strong grower, it should be kept away from the smaller plants. A useful subject for some sunny, unconsidered spot in the rock garden. June. Caucasus.

See also ARTICHOKE, CHINESE.

STACHYURUS (stak-i-u-rus. Ternstrœmiaceæ). Deciduous, hardy flowering shrubs of considerable garden value due to their flowering as early as February, and continuing until April.

Culture.—Plant in a mixture of loam, peat, and leaf-mould; unless the soil is very light, then less humus need be added.

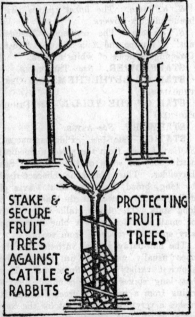

STAKE & SECURE FRUIT TREES AGAINST CATTLE & RABBITS

PROTECTING FRUIT TREES

Standard fruit trees need support for a few years after planting.

Propagation is by cuttings taken of fairly hard wood, in July, with a "heel," or piece of the old wood attached, and placed in gentle heat.

SPECIES.

S. chinensis (China). About 10 ft. Racemes of pale yellow flowers, produced about the middle of February. A very attractive shrub when in flower.

S. praecox (Japan). About 10 ft. Very similar to the preceding species, but distinct therefrom with its red branches. It flowers about a fortnight earlier than *S. chinensis*.

STAG'S HORN FERN. *See* PLATYCERIUM.

STAINLESS STEEL. This is a comparatively recent development in the garden tool range of metals and it is very

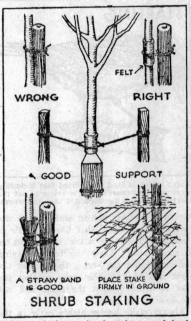

WRONG **RIGHT**

FELT

GOOD **SUPPORT**

A STRAW BAND IS GOOD **PLACE STAKE FIRMLY IN GROUND**

SHRUB STAKING

Staking and tying newly-planted trees and shrubs is a necessity where high winds occur.

useful. The metal itself, if manufactured correctly, is everlasting and the work to be done is easier with stainless steel tools.

A stainless steel tool to be really worth the price—for it is more expensive—should be forged and finished by being burnished. Without this the expensive metal is wasted by cheap manufacture and its advantages partly lost. Through its being burnished it has a very polished surface to which mud and heavy soil will not cling.

Amongst the tools made in stainless steel are solid socket and strapped spades —both ladies' and men's—small handforks, trowels, shears and edging irons.

STAKING. Use stakes sufficiently

strong, but not taller than the flower head, or the bottom of the flower spike. Bamboo canes or thin wooden stakes are best for most border flowers. Inch-square posts are needed for heavy plants, such as tall dahlias. Endeavour to hide the stake behind foliage as much as possible. Allow room for stem growth, but tie securely enough to make the plant really firm.

STARLING

A bird which is fond of a varied diet including wireworm and cherries. It is better to net the cherries and let the bird get the wireworm.

Spread the stems out in staking; do not gather a number together like a bundle of sticks. If necessary allow several stakes to each plant. Loop the bass or tying material round the stake, then round the plant and back to the stake so that the knot is made against the stake and not the stem of the plant.

Always stake border plants early in the summer before the stems become broken and bent by winds and rain. Look over the ties during the growing season and loosen them as required.

STANLEYA (stan-le-ya. Cruciferæ). Hardy perennial herbs. Plant in spring or autumn in any ordinary soil. They will thrive well in the open sunny border. Sow seeds in spring in a gentle heat. The seedlings should be planted out in May or June. Increase by division of roots in spring or autumn.

SPECIES.

S. pinnatifida, yellow, summer. 4 ft.

STAPHYLEA (staf-i-lē′-a. Staphyleaceæ). Bladder-nuts. Deciduous, May-flowering shrubs or small trees, with striking foliage and bladder-like fruits.

All the species are hardy, except perhaps *S. Bumalda*, which is liable to be injured in severe winters. They are quite easily grown in ordinary garden soil.

Propagate by cutting of half-ripe shoots, by suckers and by seeds.

SPECIES.

S. Bumalda (China and Japan), 3 ft. Flowers greenish-white.

S. colchica (Caucasus), 5–8 ft. Of erect habit, and white flowers.

S. Coulombieri. Thought to be a chance hybrid raised in France. Flowers white.

S. C. grandiflora. A distinct and fine variety, with larger flowers.

S. holocarpa (China), 20–30 ft. Flowers white or pink.

S. h. rosea. The finest species, with beautiful pink flowers.

S. pinnata. The common "Bladder-nut" of Europe and Asia Minor. 12–15 ft. Drooping panicles of white flowers.

STARFLOWER. See TRIENTALIS.

STAR OF BETHLEHEM. See ORNITHOGALUM.

STAR OF THE VELDT. See DIMORPHOTHECA.

STARWORT. See ASTER.

STATICE (stat-ĭ-se. Plumbaginaceæ). *Statizo*, I stop, from the powerful medical astringency of some of the species. Sea Lavender. This family is characterised by long, broad, leathery radial leaves of dull green, narrowed at the base with a long stalk. The flower stalks bear clouds of small lavender or dark blue flowers in airy sprays. *Propagate* from seeds.

The half-hardy annual varieties are the ones usually cultivated in pots. The showiest variety is *S. Suworowii*. This has long spikes of rose-coloured flowers rising from a rosette of green leaves. It makes a very decorative plant for the conservatory in July. Seeds should be sown in gentle heat during the early spring; the seedlings, after being pricked out, should be grown on in gentle heat. Pot up into 60's when large enough, then into 48's, using a compost of loam, leaf-mould and sand, to which has been added a little complete fertiliser.

The ordinary perennial Statice of the mixed borders can be planted in spring and succeeds admirably in any light sandy soil. Annual species also succeed outdoors in sandy soil in sunny positions. It is best to sow the seeds in small pots in a temperature of 55° in early spring. Transplant as soon as possible, and in May harden-off and plant them outdoors.

SPECIES.

S. bonduelli. Yellow (annual). 1 ft.

S. Gmelini has blue-grey leaves and dark purple flowers. 1 ft. June. Caucasus. (Perennial.)

S. incana. Pink and white (perennial). 6–9 in.

S. latifolia. Great Sea Lavender, is perhaps the one most commonly seen in gardens. It has handsome evergreen foliage and, at its best, flower stems 2–3 ft. high. July. Caucasus.

S. Limonium (syn. himonium vulgare) is a native of Britain, fairly common on the sea coasts. It also frequents the Mediterranean coasts, and is probably identified with a species found on Californian and S. American shores. Leaves are 2–6 in. long. Flowers a dull purple.

S. minuta. This is the gem of the family. It makes compact little tufts of tiny spoon-shaped leaves, with lavender flowers on little stems 3 in. high. July. Mediterranean.

S. sinuata. The large-flowered Sea Lavender grown for the cut-flower market (Royal Blue). 1–2 ft.

S. spicata. White or puce (annual). 6 in.

S. suworowii. Bright rose colour, the best for pots. 18 in.

S. vulgare. Common Sea Lavender, purple. 1 ft.

STATUARY. Statuary was first common in British gardens during the Stuart dynasty. Although it is not now used so extensively as by the French during the eighteenth and nineteenth centuries, life-size and larger figures still play an important part in garden design. Its architectural value lies in giving height and relief to a garden scheme. A flat garden gains interest and beauty by the addition of a suitable figure of the correct height. Statuary is particularly useful for "finishing" a vista. It is a mistake to place an elaborate figure in a small simple garden; such figures rarely look well in gardens other than those architectural in conception, for instead of emphasising the beauty of the garden,

they merely distract. The material of which statutary is made should be suitable, and should blend with its surroundings. Stone, lead, bronze, earthenware, cement and artificial stone are the chief materials used in the making of figures. The metals, especially, weather to delightful hues. Artificial stone and cement look very glaring at first, but they sometimes weather quite well, although they tend to crack.

Figures of every conceivable form are now obtainable—some beautiful, some quaint and eccentric, and often inappropriate in a garden setting. Figures in the form of frogs, animals and elves are much liked by children, and have a definite place in certain types of garden.

In placing statuary, keep to one *motif*. Do not, in the same garden or section of garden, place a figure portraying some thought or feeling with one quite incongruous in nature.

STAUNTONIA (stăun-tō′-ni-a. Berberidaceæ). Hardy or half-hardy evergreen climbing shrubs, closely related to Holbœllia, and needing the same cultivation.

STENOTAPHRUM (sten-o-taf-rum. Gramineæ). Variegated Grass. Greenhouse grass with ornamental leaves. Pot in March in a compost of peat, loam, leafmould and sand, and stand in a warm, moist part of the greenhouse. Give plenty of water in the summer, but less after this period. Take cuttings of shoots in spring. The roots can also be divided at this time.

STEPHANANDRA (stef-an-an-dra. Rosaceæ). Deciduous shrubs, allied to Spiræa, with pretty autumn foliage and inconspicuous flowers.

Culture.—Plant in moist loamy soil.

Propagate by cuttings or by division.

SPECIES.

S. flexuosa (*incisa*). Japan and Korea. 4–8 ft. high and more in diameter. A graceful shrub with greenish-white flowers in June, but no merit; handsome fern-like foliage. In some seasons the foliage is beautifully coloured in autumn.

S. Tanakæ (Japan). Up to 6 ft. or more. Much resembles *S. flexuosa*, with larger leaves, more deeply cut, turning rich orange in autumn.

STEPHANOTIS (stef-a-no-tis. Asclepiadaceæ). Clustered Waxflower. Stove evergreen twiner. White flowers, fragrant. Madagascar, 1839.

Culture.—Compost: 2 parts turfy loam and 1 part each peat and silver sand. It is best planted out into the bed and trained up wires to the roof of the house, although it does well in a pot or tub. Pot or plant early spring. Shade from strong sun. Water freely during growing and flowering period. Prune in early spring,

STEPS WITH ROCK PLANTS IN CREVICES

An informal treatment of garden steps with rock plants used to relieve the hard appearance.

removing all weak growths and cutting strong ones well back to their base. Winter temperature, 60°; summer, 80°.

Propagate by cuttings of well-ripened shoots in sandy peat, placed in propagator, temperature, 70°. Early spring.

STEPS. These are a very important consideration in garden design, especially if the garden is on a slope. As an average guide the tread of a step should not be less than 12 in. in depth and the rise about 6 in. A flight of ten steps is ample in a garden, but if more are required, a landing should be introduced. Steps may be constructed of solid blocks of stone, in which case the piers and blocks are usually chamfered. If the steps are of paving stone, the walls and piers may be coped with stone about 2 in. thick, or they may be left for planting down the

centre. Steps and treads should have a 2 in. nosing or overlapping under the risers to give security, and the best effect is obtained by allowing the coping stone a 2 in. nosing over the walls or piers. From this proportion it will be seen that a 3 ft. drop will require six steps, and so on. Paving steps may be cemented or left open for planting. Wood steps are quite in keeping with the wild garden, but rough stone slab steps are better in the bog and swamp garden to avoid rotting.

STERCULIA (ster-kū´-li-a. Sterculiaceæ). Evergreen and deciduous trees and shrubs, with panicles of showy petalless flowers. Plant in loam and peat.

Propagate by cuttings of well-ripened growths, in very sandy soil, or pure sand, under a bell-glass or hand-light.

STEVIA (ste-vi-a. Compositæ). Half-hardy herbaceous perennials. Plant in autumn or spring and grow in a sandy loam in a sheltered, well-drained border. During the winter they will need protection from excessive cold.

Propagate by division of plants in spring.

S. trifida. White. 1½ ft.

All species bloom in August.

STEWARTIA. *See* Stuartia.

STIGMAPHYLLON (stig-ma-fil-lon. Malpighiaceæ). Golden Vine. Stove evergreen climbing shrubs, bearing yellow blooms. Pot in early spring in peat and loam, and allow the shoots to trail up the trellis, or rafters of the greenhouse. Give plenty of water in the summer, but less afterwards, also syringe daily in the summer period. Prune in January, taking away the weak growths, and shortening the stronger ones.

Take cuttings of ripened shoots in spring or summer, insert in sand under a glass with slight bottom heat. Winter temperature, 48°–65°; summer temperature, 60°–85°.

STIPA (sti-pa. Gramineæ). Feather Grass. Hardy herbaceous perennial grass, with feathery inflorescence appearing in summer. Planted in spring, this grass will grow in any common soil in a sunny border. The grasses may be gathered in July and dried for winter decoration, for which they are excellent. Seeds may also be grown in pots in the cold greenhouse. Sow the seeds in February or March in a light soil, setting the seeds ½ in. deep. Harden-off and plant out in April. Increase by division of roots in March or April.

SPECIES.

S. capillata. July. 2 ft.
S. elegantissima. 2–3 ft.
S. gigantea. July. 3 ft.
S. humilis. July. 6 in.
S. juncea. July. 3 ft.

Cultivation.—For winter flowering, seeds should be sown in July or early August in boxes of good soil in a cold frame. The seed, if fresh, germinates readily; sowing should be done thinly to avoid over-crowding. Watering in the early stages of growth should be done with care as they are apt to damp off if allowed to become saturated in dull weather.

After pricking out the seedlings into

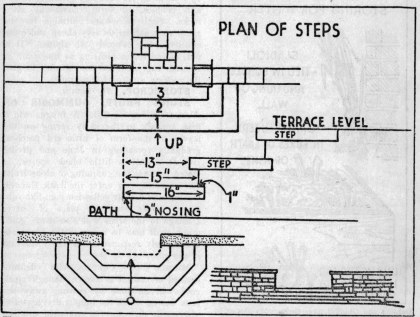

PLAN OF STEPS

The use of steps between portions of the garden on different levels calls for careful design. Above are two useful plans with constructional details.

S. pennata. July. 2 ft. (Feather Grass.)
S. spartea. (Porcupine Grass.)
S. tenacissima. (Esparto Grass.)

STOCK (Matthiola). Cruciferæ. Half-hardy annuals and biennials grown from seed chiefly in the open garden, but certain of the annual varieties are also very useful for growing in pots for winter decoration in the greenhouse. A good strain of seed throws as many as 65 to 70 per cent. plants with double flowers. The usual colours are purple, white, mauve, red, violet, old rose, pink, chamois and flesh colour. They are very sweetly scented. Height, 12–18 in.

fresh boxes of soil they may be potted into 60–size pots, when large enough, using an open compost of good loam, leaf-mould and sand. Stocks "draw up" very easily, and should be given full exposure to sun; when transferred to the greenhouse, they should be stood close to the glass. When the roots have formed a network round the ball of soil, they may be potted on into 48's and, since Stocks require plenty of nourishment, the potting compost should be fairly rich, being composed of mellow fibrous loam opened with leaf soil, old decayed manure which crumbles freely and some sand. To this may be added a sprinkling of some complete fertiliser and a little crushed mortar rubble.

When the plants are well rooted and the buds are showing, it is possible to enhance the flowers by feeding. They respond to dilute liquid manure or a very dilute solution of nitrate of soda. By taking away the lateral shoots in their early stages of growth, the central spike may be much

STORING FOR WINTER

GLADIOLI -TIED IN BUNDLES AND HUNG ON WALL

DAHLIA TUBERS IN BOXES OF EARTH OR ASHES

DAHLIAS TIED AND LABELLED READY FOR STORING

Dahlias and Gladioli have their roots placed in store during the winter to keep them from frosts.

enhanced, producing blooms fit for exhibition.

VARIETIES.

The varieties usually grown under glass are the Beauty or Nice Mammoth Stocks. (Prince Bismarck Stocks and Giant Perfection Stocks are very similar). Some of the best are Old Rose; Summer night (purple); Beauty of Nice (flesh pink); Parma Violet; Snowdrift; Chamois; Apple Blossom; Queen of the Belgians (lilac); and Antique Copper. Christmas Pink is a good Rose Pink variety. *See also* MATTHIOLA.

STOCK, VIRGINIAN. *See* MALCOMIA.

STOKESIA (stoke-sia. Compositæ). Stoke's Aster. Only one species of this genus of hardy perennials is grown, *cyanea*, which has alternate lanceolate leaves and numerous blue flowers (in August) in heads like asters. *Propagate* by division in March. It likes a loamy soil and in cold districts it should be protected in winter. Its varieties, *præcox*, blue, and *alba*, white, are larger and bloom earlier. 18 in.

STONE, ARTIFICIAL, can be made by cementing together odd pieces of stones and pebbles, to form convenient sized rocks. Such stonework, suitable for the small rock garden, is very cheap and quite effective when covered with alpines. It is not, of course, so pleasing as limestone or Kentish rag, as it has no "grain" to give the rockery a natural appearance.

STONECROP. *See* SEDUM.

STONE FRUIT, GUMMOSIS OF (*Coryneum beyerinckii*). A fungus which first appears in the early spring on the leaves in the form of little red patches, gradually spreading in June and giving rise to countless little black spores, is stated to cause the gumming of stone fruit. These spores may enter the bark through wounds and a clear yellowish gum-like substance forms over the place of entry. Damage to the trees will also cause gumming, so it may be assumed the fungus is not entirely responsible for the formation of the gum.

METHOD OF CONTROL.—No definite method of control is known, though much good will be done by cutting away the branches on which the fungus first appears, afterwards dressing the cut with pruning paint. It is as well to cut off all gum formed on the trees, painting over the area with pruning paint.

STOPPING. *See* PINCHING.

STORING CROPS. Before the soil is frostbound all the tender vegetables must be harvested and stored. To neglect this part of the home gardener's task is to waste many months of labour, for such crops as potatoes will be useless if they are allowed to become frosted.

Roots of all kinds keep best if they are covered with sand or with sacking or with some material that will prevent loss of moisture as well as keep out the frost.

Beetroots are best stored in boxes of sand or sifted ashes. Potatoes are generally too numerous to treat in this way, and for them an outdoor "pie" can be made.

To do this, clear a space on the soil. Clean and dry the potatoes in the sun, and pick them over to make sure there are no decayed specimens. Then pile them on the bare soil, making a heap about 3 ft. high. Round the edge of the heap dig a narrow trench so that the rain does not make the bed of the pie wet. Put a thick layer of straw over the potatoes and cover this with soil sufficient to prevent the frost reaching the tubers. A handful of straw should protrude through the soil at the top, as this will allow ventilation between the pie and the outer air. The potatoes are taken from the clamp or pie as desired.

Both carrots and white garden turnips are tender, and should be lifted and stored in sand like the beetroot, but the Swede turnips can be left, as they are said to gain in flavour from frost.

Jerusalem artichokes and parsnips can also be left to use from the ground as needed; but it worth while to remember that lifting the roots in severe weather is a hard job, and mild spells should be chosen for such work. There are some tender crops that cannot very well be lifted and stored. Celery, for instance, must remain in the trenches, though it can be protected by a layer of straw along the ridge during hard weather.

Another rather tender vegetable is the cauliflower, and to protect young ones just in promising condition, a leaf should be bent over the head, slightly cracking the midrib of the leaf so that it remains over the white flower. The supply will last many more weeks if this is done.

Storing Fruit. The last of the pears and apples should be removed from the trees and stored towards the middle of September. The best storage place for fruit is a cool shed free from frost, well ventilated and fitted with trays of perforated wood on which the fruits are laid.

Special trays in tiers are manufactured for this purpose and are worth their cost in the fruit they save from decay.

The greatest care should be taken in handling fruit, as the slightest dent will set up decay, and if one injured specimen is allowed to come in contact with other sound fruits all will become affected. For this reason all fruits, also vegetables, flower tubers, bulbs, and other stored produce should always be examined periodically and any bad specimens removed and burnt.

This is an important point to remember when the fruit is being packed away. It should be done so as to facilitate this periodical examination.

STOVE HOUSE. *See* MANAGEMENT OF THE GREENHOUSE.

STRAINING POST. *See* FENCES. A post with side struts used at even distances along a fence and at corners to strengthen the structure.

STRAMONIUM. *See* DATURA.

STRANVÆSIA (stran-vē'-zi-a. Rosaceæ). Evergreen shrubs from the East, with hawthorn-like flowers, followed by attractive fruits in autumn. They succeed in light or sandy loam.

Propagate by cuttings of half-ripened shoots, placed in gentle heat.

STRATIOTES (strat-i-ō-tes. Hydrocharideæ). Crab's Claw. Water Soldier.

The only species of this genus is a hardy native aquatic perennial, *aloides*, with long sword-like leaves that grow beneath the surface of the water, and white flowers in June. *Propagate* by division of the roots in March and plant in ordinary soil with several inches of water above the crowns. Once planted it needs no further care and increases so rapidly that it is apt to become a nuisance in ornamental waters.

STRAWBERRY. May be grown well in any good soil which does not dry out. From flowering time onwards a great deal of moisture is necessary, and if plants become dried out the crop is not successful. Very heavy soils require lightening with sand and leaf-mould or garden rubbish well decayed. All soils should be worked to a depth of 2 ft. and should be thoroughly manured.

Situation.—Any situation answers, providing it is not exposed to drying winds. Sheds must also be avoided.

Planting.—There are three times of the year during which it is usual to plant strawberries.

(1) August. The best time to plant is in early August as soon as well-rooted layers are available. Such a plantation may be expected to become well established during

the current season, and may be expected to bear fruit the following year.

(2) October. Where it is impossible to plant during August owing to lack of space or difficulty in watering, planting is best done in early October.

(3) March. New plantations may be put down during March providing the ground is in a fit condition to enable secure planting to be done. Plants put in at this

STRAWBERRIES

Fibrous loam in pots or cut turves are best for rooting Strawberry layers.

season should not be allowed to fruit the same summer.

Planting must be carefully done. The crown of the young plant must not be buried, nor yet placed too high out of the ground. Roots must be carefully spread out, and not tucked close together. These points are most important. Plants put in during summer require constant watering, if the weather is hot, until they become established.

Distances Apart.—18 in. apart in rows 2 ft. 6 in. apart.

Manuring.—An annual mulching of good manure put on as soon as the flowers

have set, is recommended. Many growers use very strawy manure, thus obviating the necessity of putting down straw or other material for the safe ripening of the fruit.

Renewal of Beds.—Strawberry beds are not of much service after their fourth fruiting season. Much can be done to lengthen the useful life of a plant. On older beds the old leaves should be cut off with a sharp knife, leaving the young ones to take their place. This also helps by letting the sun get to the crowns. An annual top dressing is also of great assistance. This should consist of leaf-mould and loam, and should be drawn up to the crowns without covering them. Fresh roots will then break from under the crowns.

Watering.—Watering is necessary during time of drought after flowering time. Sufficient must be given to reach the deepest roots. Once the plants have flagged, the resultant fruit is bound to be of poor quality.

Damage by Frost.—In cold districts it is wise to leave the straw, placed around the plants at fruiting time, through the winter.

Gathering.—Fruit should be gathered when dry, and not during the hottest part of the day.

Forcing.—In order to secure plants fit for forcing, it is necessary to obtain rooted layers at the earliest opportunity. These should be rooted direct into 3 in. pots at the end of July. When well rooted, transfer to a 6 in. pot, using a good potting compost of loam, cow-dung and bonemeal. Place in a shady spot until established, and then stand out in a sunny position on some ashes. Never allow the plants to want for water. Move the pots from time to time to prevent rooting through into the ashes. During December go over the plants, removing dead leaves, and place in a cold frame. They may be brought in in batches after the beginning of January and placed in a temperature of 45°–50°. Plenty of air must be given. The temperature may be increased to 65° or more when the fruit is set. Give plenty of water whilst the fruit is swelling, and one or two applications of liquid manure; but as soon as colouring starts be more sparing with water. Royal Sovereign is the best variety for forcing.

Propagation.—Strawberries are propagated by layering. Runners are produced in great quantities in July. It is wisest to select the few strongest of these. Secure them to the ground with small wooden pegs or hair-pins, and when the runner is rooted, pinch out any secondary runners which it may endeavour to produce. Be careful to select runners only from plants which have fruited well. Runners from "blind" parents are themselves unfruitful. Planting into permanent beds is then done as previously recommended.

VARIETIES.

Oberschleisen.—One of the most vigorous and heavy-cropping varieties. The flavour is not of the best and the texture a trifle mealy.

Royal Sovereign.—The best variety to select where only one is grown. It is very early, hardy, and has a splendid constitution. The fruit is large and of excellent flavour.

Sir Joseph Paxton.—A good mid-season variety. Very hardy and prolific. Deep crimson in colour when ripe. Good for heavy soil.

Alpine Strawberries.—These are late-fruiting varieties, not much grown but very useful for extending the season. Belle de Meaux, and Common White are the best. Cultivation is the same as for the ordinary crop.

STRAWBERRY TREE. *See* ARBUTUS.

STRELITZIA (stre-litz-i-a. Scitamineæ). Bird's Tongue Flower. Stove herbaceous perennials, with yellow blooms in spring and early summer.

Pot in early spring in fibrous loam, with a little peat, and grow in the warm beds of the greenhouse. Water should be given very freely during the summer, and the plants kept almost dry after this. They also need plenty of light. Sow seeds in spring in moist heat. Also increase by suckers, and division of plants in February or March. The latter methods are more common than seed sowing.

STREPTOCARPUS (strep-to-kar-pus. Gesneraceæ). Greenhouse perennials of many beautiful shades of colour. The flowers, which are carried two or three on a stem, are open and showy at the mouth and the tubular inner portion is often handsomely striped. Modern strains are of hybrid origin from three African species (*Dunnii, Rexii, Wandlandii*). They are among the most popular plants for greenhouse decoration, and are to be found in nearly every garden where pot plants are grown. The leaves at the base of the plant are rather long and often crinkled. Height 12 in.

Cultivation.—Although perennials, they are usually treated as biennials. Seed

The Streptocarpus are a race of colourful greenhouse perennials.

sown in the early spring and grown steadily produces flowers the following August and throughout the winter. During the following season the plants are larger and carry more flowers, making extremely handsome plants. The seeds should be sown in gentle heat and pricked out into fresh boxes of soil when large enough. 60–size pots should be the first pots used and the flowering size should be 48's. They like a rich open compost for the final pots, composed of fibrous loam opened with a little peat, old well-rotted manure and a little sand.

Pests to avoid are Begonia mite and Mealy bug.

STREPTOSOLEN (strep-to-so-len.

Solanaceæ). Evergreen greenhouse shrub, used for summer bedding. Pot in spring in a compost of fibrous loam, peat, leaf-mould and sand, and grow in well-drained pots stood near to the greenhouse glass. Prune back moderately after flowering. Water well in the summer, but less afterwards, and apply weak stimulants during the summer period. Shade from direct sunshine. Take cuttings in spring or summer and insert in sand under a bell-glass. Sow seeds in early spring in a little heat.

STUARTIA (stū-art′-i-a. Ternstrœmiaceæ). Deciduous shrubs or small trees, of great beauty. They flower in July and August, when few other shrubs are in blossom. They should be planted in sandy loam, with leaf-mould and peat added. The latter is not essential but helpful.

Propagation is by seed sown as soon as ripe. Also by cuttings and layers. The cuttings may be put in very sandy soil under a bell-glass, during late summer.

SPECIES.

S. monadelpha (China and Japan). Up to 30 ft. in nature, probably not more than half that height under cultivation in this country. Flowers white, fragrant.

S. pentagyna (Southern U.S.A.), 15 ft. Flowers 4–5 in. across, creamy-white, during July and August.

S. pseudo-camellia (Japan). Grows up to 50 ft. in nature, but in this country it is only a small tree or large shrub, of pyramidal outline. Flowers, cup shaped, creamy-white, about 2½ in. across, during July and August. In favourable seasons the foliage is yellow and red in autumn.

P. sinensis (China), 15 ft. Flowers cup shaped, white and fragrant during June and July. The foliage turns crimson-scarlet in autumn, and is very beautiful.

STYLOPHORUM (sti-lof-o-rum. Papaveraceæ). Celandine Poppy. Hardy perennial herbs. Plant in spring in any common garden soil in a moist, partly shaded bed or border. Sow seeds in spring ⅛ in. deep in ordinary soil in the position where they are to grow. The plants can be increased by division of roots in March. Good drainage is essential.

SPECIES.

S. diphyllum (Celandine Poppy). Yellow, June. Height 1 ft.

S. japonicum. Yellow, June. Height 1–1½ ft.

STYRAX (stī′-rax. Styracaceæ). Storax. Deciduous flowering shrubs of great beauty and distinction. Near to Halesia. They like a sandy loam and leaf-mould, or peat, to start them, in a sheltered spot.

Propagation is best by seed.

SPECIES.

S. americana. "American Storax." 3–8 ft. Flowers white, in slender racemes during July. At its best in warm counties.

S. dasyantha (China). A dense bush of lustrous green leaves, and racemes of white flowers in June.

S. *Hemsleyana* (China), 15 ft. high and as much through in Cornwall. Racemes of bell-shaped, snow-white, fragrant flowers during June. The foliage turns bright yellow in autumn. An extremely beautiful tree when in blossom.

S. japonica (Korea and Japan). Japanese "Snowdrop Tree." A very fine flowering shrub up to 15–20 ft. with graceful pendulous white flowers during June. Perfectly hardy, but likes a sheltered spot shaded from the morning sun if possible.

P. obassia (Japan). Grows to 30 ft. in nature, but only about half that height in this country. Leaves up to 8 in. long, deep green above, with an under-surface of velvety down. The fragrant pure white flowers are produced on terminal racemes 6–8 in. long, during June. A most beautiful and striking tree when in full flower, and may safely be regarded as one of the finest of all flowering trees introduced from Japan. Moisture at the roots is an important cultural item.

S. officinalis (Greece and Asia Minor). A small tree up to 20 ft. with clusters of white fragrant blossoms. Only suitable for Cornwall, and other mild parts.

S. Wilsonii (China), 5–10 ft. Flowers white. Quite young plants bloom freely. It should be sheltered from cold winds.

SUCKERS. Growths arising from the base of the plant. In the case of Roses and similar shrubs and trees these should be cut away as near their source as possible, otherwise they will reappear and take nourishment from the shrub. In the case of raspberries these suckers are removed and used for propagating purposes.

SUGAR CANE. *See* SACCHARUM.

SUGAR PEA. *Pisum japonicum. See* PEAS and FRENCH BEAN for culture and use.

SULPHATE OF AMMONIA. Sulphate of ammonia is the oldest and cheapest form of nitrogenous fertiliser on the market. No mixture is complete without it. It is easy to store and easy to use.

Sulphate of ammonia is not washed away by rain but is held in the soil whilst the plant, as it grows, draws steadily on the nitrates into which the ammonia is gradually converted. This change into nitrates is brought about by the two things which help plants to grow—warmth and moisture. It follows, therefore, that as the plant grows and needs more food, more and more nitrate is available to feed it.

SULPHATE OF COPPER. Used in the preparation of Bordeaux and Burgundy mixtures; also as a solution in water for *winter spraying* of fruit trees. The strength of the solution may range from ½-1 lb. to 10 gallons of water. The solution must never be used for spraying fruit trees after the buds have opened.

SULPHATE OF POTASH. *See* POTASH. Manufactured from muriate of potash by treatment with sulphate of magnesia. An excellent form of potash for application to potatoes.

SULPHUR. Of some value as a fungicide, particularly for the treatment of the powdery mildews. Sulphur for dry-spraying or dusting should be in the form of the finest powder that can be obtained.

SUMACH (Stag's Horn). *See* RHUS.

SUNDEW. *See* DROSERA.

SUNDIAL. A sundial is one of the most attractive and interesting ornaments to have in the garden. It dates from the days of Chaldea and survived the ravages of the first "landscape" gardeners headed by Capability Brown, because of its interest and use. The sundial may be placed on a wall or upon a pedestal. A sundial indicates the time by the daytime shadow of a metal pointer or gnomon generally set at an angle of 45°, the shadow being projected upon a circular or angular numbered dial. Sundials may be set to tell the time fairly accurately, i. e., within a few minutes, anywhere in the British Isles, or can be adjusted for greater accuracy to suit any particular degree of longitude.

Probably the best position for a pedestal sundial is at the junction of two or more paths, where it can be seen from several points, or at the centre of a flat, formal garden, to which it adds height. The latter quality is very important, for an otherwise flat garden can be given welcome relief by the inclusion of a sundial.

A sundial must, of course, be in the full sunshine, and is best placed in a quiet and restful part of the garden. A very attractive form of pedestal sundial is the Dutch or spherical. In this, gradated and numbered metal strips form a hollow sphere, while the gnomon is a metal rod passing through the centre. No more fitting place can be found for this than a Dutch Garden.

As with all ornaments, the great thing to remember in placing a sundial is harmony. A very attractive sundial pedestal can easily be made at home with a few bricks and some mortar. There are many designs to which a pedestal of this nature may be built, but do not strive after a complicated and elaborate appearance. A simple, straightforward design will almost always be the most satisfactory. In order to strengthen the pedestal it is best to place a piece of gas piping up the middle. This can be inserted into the ground at the start and the brickwork can then be built round it. If dwarf flowers and creeping plants are required between the brickwork it is best to plant them as the structure is made. For quickly spreading plants leave out a whole or half brick and place the plant in the aperture.

SUNFLOWER. *See* HELIANTHUS.

SUNK GARDENS. The design and layout of this now popular garden feature is nearly always formal. *See* FORMAL GARDENING. It is useful in a windswept or seaside garden for providing a degree of shelter for plants. As it is natural to look down on water, a pool invariably makes a pleasing centre piece. Dry walls are usually employed to retain the excavated soil and, sparingly planted with suitable alpines, they are very pleasing. It is often possible to use the excavated soil to form a rock garden.

SUN ROSE. *See* HELIANTHEMUM.

SUPERPHOSPHATE. The oldest form of phosphatic fertiliser with the exception of organic guanos. Usually made nowadays by treating good rock phosphate with sulphuric acid. Contrary to general belief, superphosphate is not an acid manure but is actually slightly alkaline. The whole of the sulphuric acid is absorbed to form phosphate of lime and gypsum.

SUTHERLANDIA (suth - er - lan - di - a. Leguminosæ). Cape Bladder Senna. Half-hardy evergreens, bearing scarlet flowers. Plant in autumn or spring in a

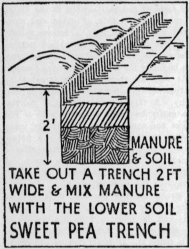

2'

MANURE & SOIL

TAKE OUT A TRENCH 2 FT WIDE & MIX MANURE WITH THE LOWER SOIL SWEET PEA TRENCH

For good results Sweet Pea trenches should be deeply dug and well manured in autumn.

compost of loam, peat and silver sand. They may be grown in a sheltered position in the open in the southern counties, but in the colder parts they should be grown in a cool greenhouse. Those grown in the open will need some protection during the winter months.

Take cuttings of young shoots in May and insert under a bell-glass. Seeds may be sown in spring in a compost similar to that for older plants. They need only be lightly covered with soil and placed under glass.

SWAINSONIA (swan-so-ni-a. Leguminosæ). Darling River Pea. Greenhouse evergreen shrubs. Pot in early spring in a compost of fibrous loam, peat and a little silver sand, and stand in the sunny greenhouse. Give plenty of water in the summer, but less after this period. Weak stimulants may also be given occasionally in the

summer period. These plants may also be grown in the open ground in a sheltered position, though they will need lifting to a cold frame in winter. After soaking the seeds, they may be sown in a hotbed in April, or if preferred they can be sown as soon as ripe.

Take cuttings of young shoots in summer and insert in sandy soil and keep in a cool frame or pit.

SWAMP GARDENS. *See* Bog Garden, Waterplants, etc.

SWAN RIVER DAISY. *See* Brachycome.

SWEET ALYSSUM. *See* Alyssum.

SWEET BRIAR. *See under* Rose, Rosa Rubiginosa.

SWEET CHESTNUT. *See* Chestnut, Sweet, and Castanea.

SWEET CICELY. *See* Myrrhis.

SWEET FERN. *See* Comptonia.

SWEET FLAG. *See* Acorus.

SWEET GALE. *See* Myrica.

SWEET GUM. *See* Liquidambur.

SWEET PEA (*Lathyrus odoratus*). Leguminosæ. Hardy annuals.

Cultivation.—The methods of cultivating Sweet Peas can be divided into different sections according to the aim of the cultivator. There is a considerable difference between the cultivation of Sweet Peas for exhibition and the cultivation of a few plants for decoration of the garden and to supply the home with cut flowers. Let us deal with the simplest method first.

For Garden Decoration.—Sweet Peas are of course, climbing plants, and wherever they are grown they need to be provided with some form of support. In using them for garden decoration, the support chosen should be as decorative as possible by itself, since the plants will take some time before they smother their supports. At the back of the herbaceous border or on each side of a pathway clumps of Sweet Peas are very effective, and in this case the supports can take the form of a few tall pea-sticks to each clump. One effective method is to put a stout stake in the middle of the clump. Plant the peas round this stake and at the same time push in the pea-sticks. One or two pieces of raffia tied round the sticks and stake will keep the whole firm even in high winds. The twiggy sticks are not in themselves unsightly, and when they are smothered with climbing plants they form a really striking feature either in the border or in separate small beds cut from the lawn. If it is preferred to grow the peas in a row along the back of a border, twiggy pea-sticks secured to the fence or wall or wire netting or straight wires stretched from end to end of the fence can be used. Should pea-sticks be unavailable, wire netting can be bent round into cylindrical shape to support individual clumps.

Soil Preparation.—Any kind of garden soil will produce Sweet Peas, but good flowers can only be expected if the soil is well prepared. It should be deeply dug—the deeper the better in all cases—and some decomposed farmyard manure or old garden refuse should be dug in at the same time. The lighter the soil the more need there is for animal manure, because it makes it more retentive of moisture and therefore holds the food supplies in the soil instead of allowing them to be washed through quickly by the rains. If the soil is heavy loam or clay, it will need plenty of stable manure, but this should preferably be of a light strawy nature supplemented by a fair amount of dried leaves collected in the autumn and dug into the soil during the winter. A dressing of lime will be needed in all cases.

Seeds of Sweet Peas grown for garden decoration can be sown in the place where they are to grow, in March or April, pushing each seed 1 in. into the ground. Better results are usually obtained by raising the young plants in pots or boxes under glass. The seeds can be sown in the autumn about the first week in September in the north, and the last week of September in the south; or they may be sown in January or February, according to which is more convenient. If the garden is fairly sheltered and the soil not too cold, the autumn sowing can be made in the open; but where it is thought undesirable to leave the plants in the open ground for the winter months, they can be sown in pots or boxes and left in the cold frame until March. Seeds that are sown very early in the year should always be sown in boxes or pots of soil in the greenhouse or frame.

Generally speaking it is much better to use an ordinary cold frame to raise the seedlings and not to use heat, because the plants grow more sturdily and are shorter jointed and this type of plant will give better results than tall, thin seedlings. When the young seedlings show their second or third pair of leaves in spring, pinch out the centre tip. The seedlings can, however, be left in the boxes where they are until the side shoots have begun to grow. Then it is advisable to pot them up singly into small pots in a mixture of old loam and leaf-mould with a little sand.

These pots can stand in the frame for a week or two in rather a close atmosphere until they recover from the shock of transplanting, but after that it is advisable to admit air at all times, except when the nights are likely to be very frosty. During favourable weather the lights can be removed entirely during the day-time. The seedlings should grow very quickly and make strong plants which, if hardened-off sufficiently, should be ready for planting out in April.

Assuming that the soil was deeply dug and manured during the winter months, it will need no further preparation at planting time except for forking over; but if there is any doubt about the fertility of the soil, a few handfuls of bone-meal can be added as the soil is forked.

Where clumps of Sweet Peas are planted, a hole 2 ft. in diameter and 18 in. deep should be dug. At the bottom of this scatter a handful of bonemeal, which should be roughly forked in. Three inches of well-decayed manure over this, and the ordinary soil returned to fill in the hole, will complete the preparation of the soil for each clump. This can be done a fortnight before the Sweet Peas are planted out so that the soil settles before planting time.

Turn about a dozen plants out of their pots and plant them in a circle. Six plants would be sufficient if well grown, but most amateurs will prefer the results if they use larger clumps. As soon after planting as possible put in a few small feathery twigs. These break the force of the wind and prevent the plants from being blown about too much. It may be necessary to train each plant to the twigs, but almost immediately they will begin to cling and climb naturally. Just at this stage slugs and birds are very troublesome amongst Sweet Pea seedlings. A ring of lime and soot round each cluster of plants will prevent attacks from slugs—or any of the other remedies for slugs may be used. The use of twigs is in itself a measure of defence against birds, but if they appear troublesome, a few strands of black cotton above the seedlings will be an effective scare.

Apart from the use of the supports already mentioned, very decorative clumps of Sweet Peas can be grown on supports made from young spruce trees. These should be about 10 ft. long and 4–5 in. thick at the bottom. Cut off all the branches about 1 ft. from the stem. Trim all brushwood from the branches, and cut away completely all the branches from the lowest 2 ft. of stem. This bottom 2 ft. will go down into the ground to make a firm support, and it is just as well to char this part before it is used to prevent it from rotting. If this is done the support will last for several years. These supports must of course be put in position before the plants are set out.

Sweet Peas for Cutting.—When Sweet Peas are grown purely for cutting to use in vases in the home, the general method of cultivation is the same as for garden decoration. It is not necessary, however, to use ornamental supports. Ordinary hazel or beech sticks can be used, or wires strained to posts, and the peas should be sown or planted in rows so that it is easy to reach the plants when the flowers are ready for cutting. In this case it is usually preferred to sow the seeds where the plants are to flower, and the easiest way is to draw drills 5 in. apart and 2 in. deep, to scatter a little seed along each drill, and drop the seeds 2 in. apart all along the drill. Afterwards cover and tread the soil firmly over them. Then lightly rake the row, and dust soot over the surface. If one colour is sown in each row, choosing colours that contrast well instead of colours that are nearly alike, the effect in the garden will be better, and flowers of distinctive colouring will be found more useful when cut. Mixed Sweet Peas are not usually so satisfactory as named varieties. The beginner in Sweet Pea culture is recommended to start with a collec-

tion of distinct colours such as the following:

Charm, red-cerise.
Constance Hinton, white.
Flamingo, scarlet.
Magnet, salmon-pink.
Mrs. A. Searles, rich pink.
Picture, deep cream pink.
Pinkie, rose-pink.
Powerscourt, lavender.
Reflection, pale amethyst-blue.
Royal Sovereign, orange.
What Joy, deep cream.
Youth, white, edged rose.
Other suitable varieties **for** outdoor cultivation are:
All Bright, scarlet-cerise.
Beatall, pink salmon rose.
Chieftain, mauve.
Dainty Maid, blush pink.
Elizabeth, lilac-pink on cream.
Idyl, salmon-pink.
Lilac Queen, pink suffused lilac.
Olympia, purple.
Sunkist, cream, edged carmine.
Sybil Henshaw, crimson.
The Flag Lieutenant, violet-blue.
Warrior, maroon.

Exhibition Culture.—When the amateur gardener visits any of the large shows and sees the magnificent displays of Sweet Peas grown by professional gardeners or by expert amateurs, he often asks why it is that his own garden Sweet Peas are smaller, shorter in the stalk, and with fewer blooms on each stem. The answer may be given in one word, "manure." It is only by deep digging and adequate manuring that fine Sweet Pea flowers can be grown, and it is quite impossible to achieve good results without.

Where it is intended to grow flowers for exhibition, the cultivation of the soil should be begun in October, or at any rate the first preparation of the soil should be done before Christmas. Many growers recommend trenching the soil to a depth of 3–4 ft., but it is doubtful whether any better results are obtained from such deep digging than from soil dug only to a depth of 2 ft. This top 2 ft. of soil must, however, be thoroughly worked if good results are to be achieved.

Generally speaking, exhibition Sweet Peas are grown in rows, and the first step to take is to open out a trench 3 ft. wide and 2 ft. deep. This should preferably run north and south. As the digging is done, place the top foot of soil on one side of the trench and the next foot of soil on the other side.

At the bottom of the open trench scatter crushed bones or rough bonemeal at the rate of 4 oz. to each yard of trench. Fork this roughly into the bottom. Next put a layer of manure 3 or 4 in. thick. Light stable manure is best on heavy soil, and cow or pig manure on light soil. Then put back the top spit of soil from one side of the trench, mixing it with the manure as it is put in. Spread another layer of manure over this and mix with it the soil of the bottom spit from the other side of the trench. Leave the surface as rough as possible, so that the full benefit of rain, frost and wind will be derived. By the time the weather breaks in the spring this top soil will have broken down to a fine texture.

In choosing seed, several points should be remembered. It is very unwise to buy cheap seed for exhibition culture, as only plants that are true to name are worth cultivating in this manner. The seeds should be perfectly ripened, and fresh enough to germinate almost 100 per cent. Chipping the seeds is a practice which some growers have adopted in dealing with those varieties of Sweet Peas which have hard outer seed cases and are therefore slow in germination. It is really quite unnecessary, as the seeds sown will germinate quite satisfactorily if no chipping is done. The cream, lavender and orange varieties need very careful watering, and the frames in which the seeds are sown should on the whole be kept rather close to encourage speedy germination.

If they are allowed to lie too long in cold, damp soil without germinating, they may possibly rot, and it is therefore wise to put a large proportion of sand in the compost used for the seeds.

Time to Sow.—To obtain flowers for exhibition in June and July, sow in autumn; that is, at the end of September or early October, in a cold frame or green-house. Seeds sown in February under glass will produce flowers for exhibition at the end of July, in August and September.

The soil used for the seeds can be a mixture of good loam, leaf-mould and sand. Probably the best compost for seed-sowing would be the soil from an old cucumber or marrow bed.

When the seeds are sown, stand the boxes or pots in cold frames and keep the lights on day and night until the seeds appear through the surface soil. Then take off the lights and leave them off except in very wet weather. Even when it is necessary to keep the lights on, admit plenty of air at all times. If the seedlings are coddled at this stage they will not make sturdy plants and the flowers will not be fit for exhibition.

In districts where birds are troublesome it may be necessary to put wire netting over the frame when the lights are moved, to avoid damage to the tender young plants. Mice are also troublesome in some districts. These can be prevented from eating the seeds as they are sown by dusting with red lead before sowing.

As the seedlings begin to grow, and show a third pair of leaves, pinch out the tips but leave the plants in the open frames until the side growths are about ½ in. long. Limit the number of side growths according to the variety of Sweet Pea. Some should only be grown as single stems, while others can be allowed two stems to each plant for exhibition work.

If the seeds were sown in boxes, they must now be potted singly in small pots, using a good rich compost, but no artificial manure. Stand the pots in the cold frame again, admitting air constantly during the day, but closing the frame at night for a few days until the plants are well established. Sweet Peas are quite hardy, and if grown without coddling, they will stand anything up to 8° of frost, so long as the sun does not reach the frame while the frost is still on the foliage. Should they be severely frosted, they should be sprinkled with cold water before the sun reaches them.

In the case of autumn-sown plants, it is wise to plunge the pots in 2 in. deep sand or ashes and to give only a minimum of water during the winter months. Some growers prefer to sow the seeds singly in 3 in. pots filled with good compost to within ½ in. of the rim. Three seeds can be sown in each pot if desired without any danger of overcrowding. The special seed-raising boxes now sold which make transplanting easy without any danger or damage to roots, are used by many amateurs, and are particularly valuable in gardens where space is limited and a large number of pots cannot be accommodated in a cold frame, as these con-

SWEET PEAS TRAINED AS CORDONS

Exhibition Sweet Peas are obtained by training single plants up bamboo canes.

tainers are square in shape and pack closely together in a small space.

Planting Out.—During the second week of March the planting out of Sweet Pea seedlings can begin. It may be desirable in some cases to delay this for a week or two, according to the district and the condition of the seedlings. Planting out also depends somewhat on the condition of the soil in the trenches. If it is in a wet, sodden condition, it is wiser to delay planting. A good dressing of wood ashes or soot forked lightly into the top of the trench will be very beneficial. At the same time the surface soil should be well broken

up, if there are any lumps left after the winter frosts.

Sweet Peas for exhibition are best grown on bamboo canes. The method adopted by one of the largest commercial growers is given here in his own words:

"Erect poles about 8 ft. high, and 15 ft. apart, in the centre of the trench, with cross-pieces of wood about 1 ft. long, nailed firmly across at the top, middle and bottom. The lowest cross-piece must be 3 in. from the surface of the ground. Strain three wires tightly on each side of the trench from end to end, fixed to the wood-cross-pieces with small staples. Tie canes 6 in. apart along the wires with the lower ends just resting on, not forced into, the ground. If the points are in the earth, the portion below the surface will decay and have to be removed every year, whereas if they are resting on the top—securely attached to the bottom strand of wire to keep them in position—they will last for years."

Set the plants out 6 in. apart all along the centre of the trench, making the holes with a trowel or a handfork and disturbing the soil round the roots as little as possible. The top of the soil from the pots should be 2 in. below the level of the ground. Be sure to keep each variety separate and to label them carefully as they are planted out. In the case of those plants which have two stems left, plant them between two canes so that each of the leaders can be trained to a separate cane. Where there is only one stem, put the plant as near the cane as possible. Make the soil very firm round the plants, but leave the surface loose and friable so that rain penetrates and the top soil does not crack. As a rule, it is not necessary to water the plants, because showers are frequent in the spring; but should dry spells occur, they may need water when they are newly planted.

It will be some weeks before there is much growth made at this season, but immediately the plants begin to climb, they must be carefully tied to the canes, and from that time onwards they will need attention, perhaps two or three times a week. All side growths and tendrils will be pinched off and the main stem tied from time to time to the cane.

Hoe the ground surface near the plants frequently during the dry weather, but always be sure not to use the hoe too near to the plants, as it may easily damage the roots. After May, hoeing can be dispensed with, but a mulch of spent hops or well-decayed manure should be put along the surface of the soil between the rows. Any weeds that appear after this will have to be removed by hand.

As soon as the crowns of the plants begin to develop flower buds, artificial feeding may commence. A weak solution of soot water once a week, and then an alternate supply of liquid manure diluted to the colour of weak tea, will be sufficient feeding for a few weeks. The plants should not be allowed to bloom until they are at least 3 ft. high, but after this they can be allowed to produce flowers freely through the summer. They will need occasional doses of fertiliser to maintain the supply, and at all times the dead flowers should be kept cut from the plants. If any are allowed to go to seed they immediately cease to flower, or the flowers become small and useless for exhibition.

Exhibition Culture under Glass.—The amateur who decides to cultivate Sweet Peas under glass will probably also want to use the same glass structure for other purposes. One of the best methods of utilising a single structure for two or three purposes, is to grow late tomatoes to follow the Sweet Pea crop, and, after the tomatoes, to fill the houses again with winter-flowering chrysanthemums. Early Sweet Peas are obtained, and the greenhouse is not idle when the outdoor flowers are ready and those under glass have finished blooming. The seeds can be sown in boxes about the last week in September. The boxes are stood in cold frames and given exactly the same treatment as plants intended for open-air culture.

The soil for potting should consist of good turfy loam, well-decayed old manure, and a little sharp sand. It should all be put through a sieve. The seedlings will first be potted into 60's. In the case of strong varieties, two stems will be allowed to develop, and these varieties can be put

two in each pot so that ultimately there will be four stems. The weaker varieties will be limited to one stem to each seedling, and of these, four can be put into each pot.

When the roots are filling the smaller pots, the plants will be moved into 5 in. pots, using the same mixture of soil. Be sure to see that these pots are well drained, and press the compost firmly down round the sides of the pot, at the same time giving it a good watering before the pots are moved to the cold greenhouse or frame. Plenty of ventilation must be allowed at this stage. The plants should be allowed to grow freely and should be carefully watered. They will be ready for their final pots (that is 10–12 in. pots) as soon as the roots are beginning to run round the 5 in. pot. This can be discovered by tipping out one of the pots to investigate. For the final potting use a soil composed of three barrow-loads of loam to one of decayed manure, with a 7 in. potful of bonemeal, the same quantity of dry soot, and some finely-crushed lime-rubble or sand. Before potting, the size of the hole in the bottom of each pot should be increased to 3–4 in. in diameter. To do this without breaking the pot, invert it over a solid block of wood and use a small hammer to chip away pieces from round the hole.

Scrub each pot clean, and dry it before use. Cover the drainage holes with broken crocks placed concave side downwards. Put about 3 in. deep of the roughest of the soil into the bottom of the pot, making it quite firm. Now tip the plants out of the 5 in. pot, remove the crocks from the bottom of the ball of soil, and place it carefully in the centre of the 10 in. pot, adding more soil to make the whole quite firm. The soil should be about 1½ in. from the rim of the pot.

Soak the soil with water after planting, and stand the pots in the cold greenhouse for about three weeks. Then give them all the light and air possible. They should be ready about the second week in February to plunge in the trenches where they are to flower. The trenches in the greenhouse are prepared in advance by digging out an 18 in. wide trench, 18 in. deep, and putting a layer of old manure mixed with crushed bones and soot at the bottom. Two inches of good soil over the manure will form a level base over which to stand the pots. These should be slightly apart from each other, and soil should be packed well round and between them. It is important to see that there are no hollows between the pots.

If the pots are set so that the rims are about 1½ in. below the normal of the ground in the trench, they are less likely to suffer from shortage of water. The trench itself will not require water until some weeks later, though the pots will need occasional watering, and when this is done the soil in the pots should be thoroughly soaked. Surplus water will drain down to the bottom of the trench, and it will be particularly useful here, as the object of the grower should be to encourage the roots to make their way to the bottom of the pots. The canes supporting the plants under glass will not be driven into the pots, but will be tied to a wire stretched along the trench in the same manner as recommended for plants growing outdoors. A row of canes will be on each side of the trench, and the four stems from each pot will be trained, two to each side, to four separate canes.

Plenty of ventilation must be given, but all draughts must be avoided. Ventilate early in the day, increasing the ventilation gradually until all the windows and doors are open. If a strong wind should be blowing, the ventilation on that side of the house must be lessened. Sudden changes in temperature encourage mildew and also cause buds to drop. Side growths will be rubbed out and tendrils cut off, and plants tied carefully as they grow.

When the plants have reached to within about 12 in. of the glass they are taken down and retied. When they are put back on the canes they are bent in the form of a circle, bringing the top of each plant back to a lower point on its original cane. This gives it more room to grow without undue crowding at the top of the plants where the flowers are developing. The stems of the first flowers may be a little bent after this treatment, but the recovery of the flowers will be very speedy, and the quality will be as good.

During the flowering period doses of soot water given occasionally improve the colour, and at all times the plants should be kept well supplied with water and other food. Should the weather be very sunny, the orange and salmon flowers may need a little shading if they are to keep their colour.

Trenches under Glass.—Sweet Peas can equally well be grown planted actually in the soil of the trenches under glass. The seeds are sown early, but are subjected to hardy treatment in order to make the seedlings strong and vigorous. At planting time the seedlings should have a mass of white, healthy roots. They are taken from the cold frames to the house where they are to grow about the second week in January and stood as near the glass as possible for about three weeks. The temperature of this house should be about 50°, and as far as possible kept to this temperature. Prepare the trenches 18 in. deep and 18 in. wide with crushed bones and soot at the bottom, then a layer of well-rotted manure, and, finally, good loam. The manure and the under-layer of soil should be well mixed as the trenches are filled. Soak the trenches with water about three days before the planting out is done. After planting, they are treated in exactly the same manner as plants in pots.

Pots without Trenches.—If Sweet Peas are wanted for decoration only, and a greenhouse is available, they can be grown quite easily in 10 in. pots. They are sown in boxes and potted into small pots and otherwise treated in the early stages as already described for exhibition Peas.

Instead of the trenches and the rows of canes on wire, the large pots will be stood on the ordinary greenhouse shelf and four 5 ft. canes will be pushed into each pot. Do not push the canes down the sides of pots or the roots will in most cases be severely injured. Put them about 1 in. from the rim parallel with the sides of the pots, that is, sloping outwards slightly. As the plants grow, tie a ring of raffia round the four canes to provide support. Water is required, but not to excess.

When the pots become full of roots give a little liquid manure once a week. Instead of top dressing with manure over the surface soil, stand each pot in a larger pan filled with the old well-decayed manure. Never allow dead flowers to remain on the plants, and if the flower stalks begin to shorten and the quality is deteriorating, give a little stimulant in the form of nitrate of soda dissolved at the rate of 1 oz. to 4 gal. of water.

Exhibition Hints.—Cut Sweet Peas for exhibition in the cool of the evening and when they are dry.

Put them in water in a cool shed or cellar for about six hours, or overnight.

Choose blooms on the young side, with as long stems as possible. The two top blooms on a stem should not be fully open.

While they are in water, let the flowers be loose in the jars so that air circulates between them.

Dry them a little before packing in boxes, rolling about 24 sprays into a bunch wrapped in tissue paper.

They can, if convenient, be taken to the show in water, but do not allow the water to be splashed on the blooms or they will be damaged so that they fall quickly.

Unpack the blooms as quickly as possible, shake the bunches gently to loosen them and to let air between the blooms, and put the stalks in water for a time before beginning to stage them.

Use only Sweet Pea foliage to accompany the blooms, except in decorative classes where the schedule clearly states that other foliage is allowed.

In most cases, it is best to stage only one variety in each vase, and the name of the variety should always be clearly indicated.

The varieties of Sweet Peas are legion, and the beginner, or even the experienced gardener, is a little bewildered at the complexities of varieties. The trouble arises from the fact that many of the varieties are so much alike. To help the beginner in this respect, the National Sweet Pea Society have bracketed the following together:

Too-much alike varieties:

Blue.—Gleneagles; Porcelain; Silver Sheen; Wembley.

Carmine.—Brilliant Rose; Marjorie Stevenson; Mascotts Ingman; Renown.

Cream.—Daffodil; Majestic Cream; Matchless; What Joy.

Pink (deep).—Hebe; Pinkie.

Crimson.—Charity; Crimson King; Honour; Marjorie Ryder; Sunproof Crimson; Sybil Henshaw.

White.—Constance Hinton; Model; Purity.

Twenty-four varieties of Sweet Peas for Garden Decoration recommended by the

SUMMER PRUNING

PRUNE BACK TO WITHIN 6 or 8 LEAVES FROM THE BASE

Trees which make unbalanced growth in the summer are cut back to more symmetrical shape.

Floral Committee of the National Sweet Pea Society are:

Ascot, pale pink; Avalanche, white; Charming, deep cerise; Corona, rose; Elegance, blush-lilac; Flamingo, scarlet-cerise; Huntsman, scarlet; International, rosy mauve; Ivory Picture, ivory; Magnet, deep cream-pink; Mrs. Arnold Hitchcock, pale cream-pink; Mrs. H. J. Wright, flushed, white ground; Olympia, purple; Picture, cream-pink; Pink Delight, pink; Pinkie, deep pink; Powerscourt, lilac-lavender; Reflection, blue; Sunkist, picotee-edged; Sybil Henshaw, crimson; Tom Webster, medium blue; Warrior, maroon; Wembley, pale lavender; Youth, picotee-edged.

See also LATHYRUS.

SWEET PEA MILDEW (*Erysiphe polygoni*). After a prolonged dry spell the foliage and stems of sweet peas often become covered with a white mildew. The resting stage is in the form of small black spores which get carried to the plants. The resulting mycelium which establishes itself in the plant tissues gives rise to the mildew which appears in the summer.

METHODS OF CONTROL.—Burn all haulm which has shown the disease and if, in the following spring there is the least sign of a recurrence, dust the plants with three parts of sulphur to one of slaked lime. This dusting should be done two or three times and preferably when the dew is on the plants.

SWEET POTATO. *See* MORNING GLORY.

SWEET ROCKET. *See* ROCKET, SWEET.

SWEET SCABIOUS. *See* SCABIOSA.

SWEET SULTAN. *See* CENTAUREA.

SWEET WILLIAM. *See* DIANTHUS.

SWEET WIVELSFIELD. *See* DIANTHUS.

SWEET WOODRUFF. *See* ASPERULA.

SWISS CHARD. *See* SPINACH.

SYCAMORE. *See* ACER PSEUDOPLATANUS.

SYCOPSIS (si-kop-sis. Hamamelidaceæ). Evergreen shrub or small tree about 20 ft. high, from China, allied to the Hamamelis (Witch Hazels). Flowers red and yellow produced in February and March, of little floral beauty. It is both handsome and ornamental as an evergreen, and is a suitable subject for a north wall. Plant in ordinary garden soil.

Propagate by cuttings of half-ripened wood, and placed in heat.

SYMPHORICARPUS (sim-fŏr-i-kar'-pus. Caprifoliaceæ). Deciduous shrubs, mostly from America and known there as "Snowberry" and "St. Peter's Wort," etc. They possess no floral charm to recommend them, their principal attraction being their snow-white or pink berries during the winter season. Thrives in moist soil, in sun or shade, and even under trees.

Propagate by cuttings and division.

SYMPHYTUM (sim-fit-um. Boragenaceæ). *Sumphuo*, I cause to unite; from its supposed healing qualities. Comfrey. Hardy herbaceous and tuberous-rooted perennials, which will grow in good common soil where it is difficult to grow other plants. They like a rather shady spot, and plenty of moisture. Plant in autumn or spring, and replant every third year, dividing if necessary.

SPECIES.
(Tuberous-rooted.)

S. officinale, white, June. Height, 4 ft.

S. o. bohemicum, red, May. Height, 3 ft.

S. o. luteomarginatum, leaves edged with yellow.

S. o. patens, purple, June. Height, 4 ft.

S. o. variegatum.

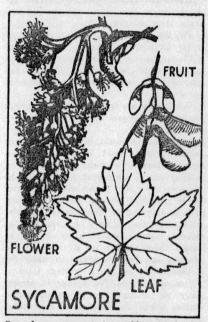

SYCAMORE

One of our commonest wayside trees is the Sycamore, of which the fruits are known as "Spinning Jennies." There are many garden Maples grown especially for their foliage.

S. tuberosum, yellow, July. Height, 4 ft.
(Herbaceous.)

S. asperrimum, red blue, July. Height, 6 ft.

S. a. aureovariegatum, leaves margined with yellow.

S. caucasicum, blue, June. Height, 4 ft.

S. cordatum, cream, June. Height, 2 ft.

S. Donii, azure blue, June. Height, 2 ft.

SYMPLOCOS (sim'-plo-kos. Styracaceæ). Deciduous shrubs or small trees of elegant habit. Plant in ordinary loamy soil.

Propagate by seed, which may take the best part of a year to germinate.

SYRINGA (si-ring'ga. Oleaceæ). Lilac

(for "Mock Orange" *see under* PHILADEL-PHUS). Well-known and very beautiful deciduous flowering shrubs and trees, natives of the north-east parts of Asia. The "Common Lilac" is a native of E. Europe.

Culture.—While growing moderately well in any ordinary garden soil, they really need fairly rich ground and full sun to provide the finest panicles or spikes of bloom. They all thrive in chalky soils.

The flower trusses should be removed immediately they fade, as the ripening of the seed impairs the energies of the plant, which must be directed to the production of new growth, and the succeeding crops of bloom. No regular pruning is needed, but to get the finest results, the weaker shoots should be cut out at the time the old flower spikes are removed. The named varieties of the common lilac make attractive ornaments for a lawn, and when grown for this purpose they are most effective when trained to a single stem. This is accomplished by removing all the lower buds and lower branches. The plants should always be obtained on their own roots, in preference to those grafted on the common lilac, or privet, as own-root plants grow better and are longer lived. Lilacs grafted on the privet will, unless persistently watched, soon become a thicket of suckers.

Propagation is best by layering. Cuttings may also be made of mature shoots in August and placed under hand-lights, or of immature shoots, taken earlier and placed in gentle heat.

SPECIES AND VARIETIES.

S. chinensis. A French-raised hybrid between the Persian and common lilacs. As this lilac has been known in China for well over 100 years, it is presumed to have had two distinct origins. Flowers similar to the common lilac, in arching panicles of about 6 in. long.

S. japonica (Japan). A large-growing shrub or tree up to about 30 ft. Flowers white, inodorous, produced in broad panicles up to 12 in. long, and 6–8 in. through, during June. Needs a warm position.

S. vulgaris. The Common Lilac, so well known and universally appreciated in English gardens, was introduced to this country over 300 years ago. It is found growing wild in the mountainous regions of eastern Europe. For years past some of the well-known French nurserymen have devoted much skill and patience to the improvement of this species, the result being a number of very beautiful varieties, both double and single flowered, the colours ranging from white, and pale lilac to pink, crimson and vinous purple, the best and most distinct of which are described hereunder.

VARIETIES WITH DOUBLE FLOWERS.

Belle de Nancy, satiny pink.

Charles Joly, dark red.

Madame Abel Chatenay, white, large spikes; late flowering.

Madame Lemoine, the most popular white.

Michael Buchner, pale lilac.

Miss Ellen Willmott, pure white, very fine flowers and trusses.

President Grevy, bluish-lilac, very large flowers and trusses.

Virginite, pale pink.

VARIETIES WITH SINGLE FLOWERS.

Charles X. Deep purple-lilac. Excellent for forcing.

Congo. Very large trusses of red-purple flowers.

Hugo Koster. Purple-crimson; very floriferous.

J. C. von Tol. Pure white.

Lavanensis. Pale pink.

Marie Legray. Pure white. Excellent for forcing.

Reaumur. Dark crimson.

Souvenir de L. Spath. Deep rich wine-purple. A very fine and popular variety.

SYRINGES. *See* SPRAYERS.

Table [690] Tangerine Orange

T

TABLE. *See* FURNITURE.

TACCA (tak-ka. Taccaceæ). Stove perennial, tuberous-rooted herbs. Pot in spring in sandy loam and a little fibrous peat and stand in the warm greenhouse. Give plenty of water in the summer, but less afterwards. *Propagate* by division of roots in spring. Summer temperature, 60°–85°; winter, 60°–65°.

TACSONIA (tak-sō'-ni-a. Passifloraceæ). Very showy climbers similar to the Passion Flower. Only suitable for sheltered walls in mild districts.

Culture.—Compost: equal parts loam, dried cow manure, leaf-mould and sand. They should be planted into tubs and then sunk into the bed of the house; if planted direct into the bed, as is so often advised, they produce a mass of luxuriant foliage that results in loss of bloom. Plant early spring. Prune back shoots that have flowered to the old wood in the winter. Thin out new shoots during growing period as needed. Syringe twice daily to keep in check mealy-bug and red spider to which it is very subject, and fumigate when necessary. Winter temperature, 40°; summer, 65°–70°.

Propagate by cuttings of young shoots in propagator in the spring; temperature, 65°–70°.

TAGETES (ta-ge-tees. Compositæ). French Marigold, African Marigold. Central America. An important family of half-hardy annuals, and although to some the odour of the foliage and the flowers are rather offensive, yet there are many positions where their rich orange-yellow and bronze shades may be effectively used. *T. signata pumila*, 6–9 in., double flowers, orange and bronze, and *T. patula* (Legion of Honour), 6 in., single flowers, yellow with dark centre, are both good for edgings. *T. patula*, or French Marigold, grows 1–2 ft. There are single and double-flowered varieties in many orange and bronzy shades. The African Marigold, *T. erecta*, is the boldest of the family, and produces huge double flowers of almost globular shape, and orange or lemon in colour. The type known as *fistulosa* is best. All should be sown under glass in March–April, and planted out into good soil end of May.

TAIWANIA (Coniferæ). Monotypic genus, resembling, and related to, Cunninghamia.

T. cryptomerioides (Formosa). A beautiful tree of a tender fresh-green hue.

TAMARINDUS (tam-ar-in-dus. Leguminosæ). Tamarind Tree. Stove evergreen tree, bearing yellow flowers. Pot or plant in February in sandy loam and leaf-mould and stand in the high part of the stove. Give plenty of water in the summer, but give only moderate quantities afterwards; also syringe daily during the summer, and shade from direct sunshine. When sowing seeds, they should be soaked for a few hours in warm water. Sow in a hotbed in spring. Also increase by cuttings inserted in sand and heat. Summer temperature, 60°–85°; winter temperature, 50°–70°.

TAMARISK. *See* TAMARIX.

TAMARIX (tam'-a-rix. Tamaricaceæ). Deciduous trees or shrubs, with "feathery" foliage, and plumes of pink or crimson flowers during summer and autumn. They are of easy cultivation, in light sandy loam, or ordinary garden soil if well drained, and flourish amazingly in seaside districts. Cuttings of the previous year's wood, about 8 in. long, and about the thickness of an ordinary lead pencil, inserted to about two-thirds of their length in the open ground during the late autumn will root with ease.

SPECIES.

T. gallica (France), 10–12 ft. and upwards, according to locality. Flowers pink, in plume-like panicles, from July to September.

T. pentandra (*hispida æstivalis; Pallasii*). Asia Minor and parts of Europe, 12–15 ft. Perhaps the most beautiful Tamarisk for gardens, with many rosy-pink plumes during August and September. It should be cut back to the old wood in winter.

T. tetrandra purpurea. Mediterranean region, etc., 10–15 ft. Flowers bright pink, very freely produced in May. A beautiful and effective shrub in a mass.

TANGERINE ORANGE. *See* CITRUS.

TARAXACUM (ta-rax-a-cum. Compositæ). Dandelion. Hardy perennial herbs, grown for salads, wine making, etc. Sow seeds in ordinary soil, April, setting them 1 in. deep in drills 12 in. apart. Thin to 6 in. apart in May. If the plants are to be used for salads, the flower stems should be removed as soon as they appear, but if it is desired to make wine, the flowers should be allowed to grow. The roots of *T. officinale* are sometimes lifted, ground, and used in coffee as chicory. For salad use, lift the roots in November, and plant them close together in pots in sand in the warm greenhouse, covering the pots to exclude light. These plants are best treated as annuals, and fresh seed should be sown each year.

TARRAGON. *See* HERBS, CULINARY.

TASSEL FLOWER. *See* CACALIA.

TAXODIUM (tax-ō'di-um. Coniferæ). Deciduous or Swamp Cypress. There are few more beautiful trees than the Swamp Cypress with their exquisite tender-green feathery foliage in spring, and rich brown tones in autumn.

Culture.—Plant from October to November in moist or swampy ground in full sun. *Propagate* by seed sown in a frame. Cuttings may be struck in water.

T. distichum. The "Deciduous Cypress" of the southern U.S.A. A very beautiful and elegant tree up to 150 ft. in swampy ground. It thrives, too, in ordinary soil.

T. d. pendulum. Smaller growing than the type; of a weeping or pendulous habit.

TAXUS (Coniferæ). Yew. A very widely-distributed genus of very hardy evergreen trees and shrubs, thriving in sun or shade, and in almost any soil, especially that of a chalky nature. The one great disadvantage is the poisonous quality of the foliage to animals. So far as is known the Canadian and Himalayan Yew is not poisonous. The Yew bears clipping remarkably well, and is much used for hedges and topiary work.

Propagation is best from seed, which should be kept in sand for a year before sowing. The named varieties are raised from cuttings of small shoots in July or August under a bell-glass or close frame.

SPECIES.

T. baccata. The "Common Yew," too well known to need any description.

T. b. adpressa (*brevifolia*). Of wide spreading habit and short broad leaves.

T. b. a. aurea. Young leaves golden.

T. b. Dovastonii (*pendula*). A distinct and handsome pendulous variety.

T. b. elegantissima (*aurea elegantissima*). A beautiful golden variety for hedges, etc.

T. b. erecta. Distinct, pyramidal habit.

T. b. fastigiata (*hibernica*). "Irish Yew," of columnar habit.

T. b. f. aurea. "Golden Irish Yew."

TAZZA. *See* VASE.

TEA. *See* CAMELLIA THEA.

TEA ROSE. *See* ROSE.

TECOMA (tĕ-kō'-ma. Bignoniaceæ). Trumpet Flower. Stove, greenhouse and hardy climbing shrubs with showy tubular flowers. N. America, 1640. Best grown against a warm sunny wall, in good loam. Prune by cutting back to within a few buds of the old wood. But this is only necessary when the plant fills its allotted space.

Culture.—Compost: 2 parts fibrous loam, 1 part peat, ½ part sand. Repot early spring. Prune lightly in February. Water freely during growing period, but very little afterwards. Stove temperature, winter, 60°; summer, 80°. Greenhouse temperature, winter, 45°; summer, 65°.

Propagate by cuttings of young shoots in sandy soil, or by root cuttings, the former in the summer in the greenhouse, the latter in the propagator in the spring; temperature, 60°.

SPECIES.

T. grandiflora (*Bignonia grandiflora*). China and Japan, 20–30 ft. Flowers deep orange and scarlet, trumpet shaped, in pendulous panicles.

T. hybridi (*Princei*). A hybrid between *T. grandiflora* + *T. radicans*, with orange-scarlet flowers.

T. radicans (N. America). Clusters of rich scarlet and orange flowers, 2–3 in. long, during August and September. Cultivated in English gardens since 1640.

STOVE SPECIES.

T. amboinensis, orange-red.

GREENHOUSE SPECIES.

T. australis, orange.

T. jasminoides, white and red.

T. Smithii, orange (hybrid).

TECOPHILÆA (te-kof-i-le-a. Hæmodoraceæ). Chilean Crocus. Half-hardy bulbous plants. Pot in autumn in a compost of loam, leaf-mould, and plenty of sand, setting the bulbs 3 in. deep and 6 in. apart, allowing three bulbs in a 5 in. pot. Plunge the pots into ashes until growth commences. Give water moderately, but keep dry when the foliage dies down, and allow a resting period until fresh growth commences. Allow plenty of air to reach the plants at all times, except in very severe weather. Increase

bronze. It is a quaint-looking plant which could grow under shade, but it is the reverse of showy. 18 in. June. N.W. America.

T. parviflora, white. Height, 1 ft.

TELOPEA (tel-op-ea. Proteaceæ). Greenhouse evergreen shrubs which bear conspicuous flowers. Grow in sandy loam in well-drained pots in the warm greenhouse. Allow plenty of water in the

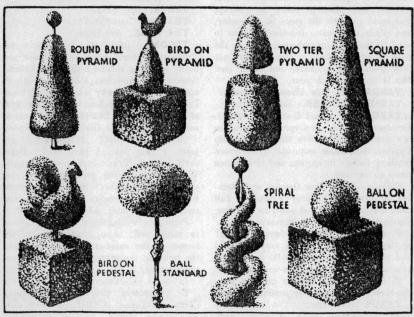

Topiary. Clipped Box or Yew in a variety of shapes give emphasis to the design of the formal garden.

by offsets removed at potting time and treated as bulbs.

TELLIMA (tel-im-a. Saxifragaceæ). The name is an anagram on Mitella, from which genus it was separated in botanical classification. Hardy herbaceous perennials. Planted in autumn or spring, these plants will grow in any ordinary soil, in the open or partially-shaded border, or in the wild garden. Increase by division of the roots in spring.

SPECIES.

T. affinis, white (half-hardy species).

T. grandiflora. Greenish spires of small flowers. The leaves are tinted greeny

summer, but less after this period and shade from direct sunshine. Take cuttings of ripened shoots and insert in sand under glass. Keep in a cool place until the base swells, when a little heat may be given. Also increase by layering the suckers which rise from the roots.

TEN WEEK STOCK. *See* MATTHIOLA.

TESTUDINARIA (tes-tu-din-ar-ia. Discoreaceæ). Hottentot's Bread. Elephant's Foot. Greenhouse deciduous climbers bearing yellow flowers. Pot in early spring and grow in a compost of sandy, fibrous loam and turfy peat. They should be planted in pots with ample drainage and may be stood in the sunny green-house. Give a moderate amount of water in the summer, but after this period the plants should be kept nearly dry.

Take cuttings of firm side-shoots in spring, and insert in sandy loam under a bell-glass. With care, cuttings of roots may also be taken. As the cuttings are very susceptible to "damping off" disease, care should be taken with them from the first place to prevent this.

TETRACENTRON (tet-ra-sen-tron. Trochodendraceæ). A monotypic genus from China. Deciduous tree, 50-90 ft. high, allied to the Magnolias, but in appearance similar to *Cercidiphyllum japonicum.* Flowers yellowish.

T. sinense, the only species.

TETRAGONIA (tet-ra-go-ni-a. Ficoidaceæ). New Zealand Spinach. Half-hardy trailing annuals with large, thick, succulent leaves, grown in gardens as a substitute for summer spinach. They thrive best in light dry soil in a sunny position. Sow the seeds at the end of March, in pots, and place in the warm frame. While the seedlings are quite small they should be pricked out singly into pots, and kept in the frame without heat until the end of May, when they may be planted out in rows 3-4 ft. apart each way. This crop will last a long time enduring a few degrees of frost.

For culinary use, the leaves only are gathered.

TEUCRIUM (tēu-crĭ-um. Labiatæ), *Germander.* Hardy and greenhouse ever-green shrubs and perennials, the latter useful for borders and rockeries and the former for greenhouse decoration.

Propagate the herbaceous species by division and the shrubs by cuttings. Both sections thrive in full sun in rather gritty ordinary soil.

SPECIES.

Half-hardy shrubs are *T. bicolor* (syn. *orchideum*), with purple or blue flowers; *T. flavum*, yellow; and *T. fruticans* (*latifolia*, lavender-blue. The "Shrubby Germander." South Europe. Of spreading habit up to 7 ft. high. Flowers pale lavender from June to October. Leaves silvery.

T. chamaedrys, with freely produced whorls of rosy-purple flowers, is the wild Germander.

T. marum, with rosy-lilac flowers is beloved of cats, but a sprinkling of tobacco powder will keep them away.

T. polium, a woolly-leaved species from the Mediterranean, bearing yellow flowers, is perhaps the best of the genus. The last-named species are hardy perennials. All bloom throughout the summer. 6-12 in.

THALIA (tha-lia. Marantaceæ). Half-hardy aquatic perennials. Plant in March

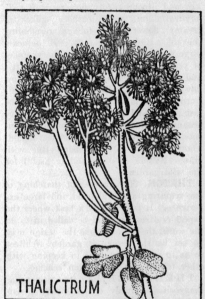

THALICTRUM

The dainty fern-like foliage of the Meadow Rue is very useful for cutting.

in tubs submerged in shallow water, in a peaty loam. These plants like a warm, sheltered spot and may be in the open from May to September, but after this they should be removed to the cold green-house. Increase by division in spring.

THALICTRUM (thal-ic-trum. Ranunculaceæ). Meadow Rue. Hardy herbaceous perennials that are as much valued for their pretty fern-like foliage as for their equally attractive flowers. They thrive in sunny well-drained borders, in moist sandy loam or by the side of a lake. The dwarf forms are useful for the rockery. *Propagate* by division in spring or autumn at which seasons they may be planted.

SPECIES.

The best of the species are *T. anemonoides*, a lovely plant with delicate foliage and numerous anemone-like flowers of pure white, 4 in.; *T. adiantifolium*, with elegant divided foliage and white flowers, useful for cutting, 6–12 in.; *T. dipterocarpum*, graceful flowers of rosy-purple with yellow anthers, and its rose and white varieties, 5 ft.; *T. Delavayi*, handsome glaucous foliage and drooping rosy flowers, 2 ft.; *T. aquilegifolium*, with feathery spikes of creamy flowers and foliage resembling that of a Columbine, 3 ft.; *T. glaucum* large glaucous leaves and feathery spikes of yellow flowers useful for cutting, 4 ft.; and *T. minus adiantifolium*, with yellow flowers and foliage like that of Maidenhair Fern. These all bloom in summer. The last named and *T. dipterocarpum* are very ornamental in the cold greenhouse in 6 in. pots in a compost of loam and leaf-mould. *Flavum* is the native Meadow Rue with orange flowers in June and is useful for the wild garden.

THATCH. The process of thatching is one requiring a skilful hand and large experience. It is definitely a task where the expert craftsman should be called in to do the work, though of course the design may be set by the owner or garden architect so as to ensure that it is in keeping with other features in the garden scheme.

THELESPERMA (the-les-per-ma. Compositæ). Hardy or half-hardy perennial herbs, which bear flowers very suitable for cutting. Sow the seeds as for annuals in the open, in April, in the place where they are intended to flower. They will grow in any ordinary soil in the sunny border. Increase also by division of plants.

THERMOPSIS (ther-mŏp-sis. Leguminosæ). False Lupin. Hardy herbaceous perennials that are useful for the border, and resemble lupins in the shape of the flower, but the leaves are quite dissimilar, as they are trifoliate.

Propagate by seeds sown in a frame in spring or in the open in summer. The roots do not divide successfully. Plant in light rich loam in a sheltered position.

SPECIES.

T. montana is very useful for nooks in the rockery, as well as the border, and has racemes of yellow flowers, 18 in. to 2 ft.

T. caroliniana is a very showy species with yellow flowers, from June to August. 5 ft.

See also PIPTANTHUS.

THORN. *See* CRATÆGUS.

THORN, COCKSPUR. *See* C. CRUSGALLI.

THORN, WASHINGTON. *See* C. CORDATA.

THRIFT. *See* ARMERIA.

THRIPS (*Thysanoptera*). Minute insects with four long, narrow fringed wings. They are dark in colour in the adult stage, but pale when young. There are many species of thrips, several of which damage plant life in various ways. The most common damage perhaps is a bleaching of the leaf, caused by the sucking of the sap. Peas are often attacked, the pods being stunted, curled and showing "silvery" areas. The life-history is somewhat complicated, several stages being passed in the ground.

METHODS OF CONTROL.—Spray with a nicotine wash, but it may be necessary to apply this wash again after about a week.

THUJA, THUJOPSIS. *See* THUYA.

THUJOPSIS BOREALIS. *See* CUPRESSUS NOOTKATENSIS.

THUNBERGIA (tun-ber-gi-a. Acanthaceæ). Beautiful evergreen greenhouse climbers. Perennials best treated as annuals. E. Ind., 1796.

Culture.—Compost: 2 parts loam, equal parts leaf-mould and sand. All except *T. alata* should be trained up pillars of house. *Alata* should be allowed to hang from pots over the side of the staging or from hanging baskets.

Propagate by seed sown in light sandy soil in the early spring; temperature, 60°; or by cuttings in sandy soil in the summer in the propagator; temperature, 70°. It is best to destroy the old plants after flowering as they rarely succeed the second year and are very subject to red spider.

SPECIES.

T. alata (yellow) and its varieties *alba* (white) and *aurantiaca* (orange) are the most popular; *T. erecta* (syn. *Meyenia erecta* (orange and blue), *T. fragrans* (white) and *T. grandiflora* (blue) are also good.

THUYA (*Thuja. Biota* and *Thujopsis*). The Arbor Vitæs, evergreen trees or shrubs of handsome pyramidal outline, very similar to Cupressus. They are often used instead of Cupressus macrocarpa and Yew for making hedges.

Culture.—Plant in September or May in a sunny position in moist garden soil. *Propagate* by seed sown in frame, or by cuttings taken in September.

T. dolabrata (Thujopsis dolabrata). Japan. 50 ft. Leaves dark green, glaucous beneath. Has been cultivated in English gardens since the 16th century. Succeeds in shade.

T. Lobbii. See T. PLICATA.

T. occidentalis. The "Arbor Vitæ" of eastern N. America. 50–60 ft. Leaves dull yellowish-green. Useful for shelter hedges, but inferior to *T. plicata* or Cupressus Lawsoniana for such purposes.

T. o. Ellwangeriana. A somewhat lanky pyramidal bush.

T. o. Vervaeneana. A faster-growing "Rheingold," and leaves darker bronze.

T. o. Wareana. Of dense habit, leaves bright green. Young branches sometimes vertical.

T. orientalis (Biota orientalis). The "Chinese Arbor Vitæ." 30–40 ft. A distinct species with branches curving upward.

T. o. elegantissima. Foliage golden tinted.

T. plicata (T. gigantea, T. Lobbii). "Giant Thuya" or "Lobb's Arbor Vitæ." A giant pyramidal tree up to 200 ft. in nature, and over half that height in this country. It bears cutting or clipping well and makes a beautiful hedge. The bright glossy green foliage remains attractive throughout the year.

THYME. *See* THYMUS.

THYMUS (ti-mus. Labitæ). From *thuo*, I perfume. The thymus are small intensely aromatic little plants with small lavender, pink or mauve flowers in summer. A suitable soil is sandy loam, though soil question presents no difficulty. They propagate easily from cuttings or seed.

SPECIES.

T. azoricus. The plant has a sparkling effect owing to the golden tips of the tiny leaves. 4 in. Azores.

T. citriodorus has a lemon scent.

T. citriodorus argenteus has pretty pale green and white variegated leaves. The variety *Silver Queen* is an improved form with larger leaves. These quickly form low bushes several feet across. 6–8 in.

T. Chamædrys is really a distinct form of our native *T. Serpyllum.* It is semi-erect with flowers of bright pink.

T. fragrantissimus. A small-leaved bush Thyme with the usual pale lilac-mauve flowers. In spite of its name, it does not appear to be any more fragrant than the rest, which in any case would be difficult. 9 in.

T. Herba-barona. The Seed-cake Thyme. A small prostrate plant with a smell so exactly like seed-cake as to be positively frightening (or enchanting, just according to one's reaction to this terror of the tea-table). It gets its specific name from having in former days been used to flavour the baron of beef, or so it is said. Corsica.

T. micans. Neat, small, bright green tufts; purple flowers. Azores.

T. montanus. A wiry bushling with pink flowers.

T. nitidus. Neat, compact little bushes bearing pink flowers over a long period. 4 in. Sicily.

T. Serpyllum. Our native Thyme. It makes purple-flowered tufts and mats of dark green foliage. *T. S. coccineus* is a deep-red coloured variety, and there is also a white form, *T. S. albus.*

T. villosus resembles *T. Serpyllum* but has wide downy leaves. Portugal.

T. vulgaris is the kitchen garden variety.

T. Zygis. A neat and narrow bush Thyme with pink flowers. Spain, Portugal. *See* HERBS.

TIARELLA (ti-ar-ella. Saxifrageæ). Foam Flower. Only one species of this genus of hardy perennials is grown; *T. cordifolia,* with white flowers in feathery racemes and prostrate heart-shaped leaves veined with red. It is a pretty subject for the rockery or the border in spring when the flowers are present.

Propagate by division and plant in moist peat if possible, but ordinary garden soil will do. 6–12 in.

TICKSEED. *See* COREOPSIS.

TIDY TIPS. *See* LAYIA.

TIGER LILY. *See* LILIES.

TIGRIDIA (ti-grid-i-a. Iridaceæ). Tiger

Iris. Half-hardy and hardy bulbs. Plant the bulbs 3 in. deep and 5–6 in. apart, in April, in a compost of rich loam and leaf-mould with an addition of sand, and grow in a well-drained, sunny border. Mulch with decayed manure and coconut fibre refuse when the plants are about 3 in. high.

Give plenty of water in dry weather, and protect from severe frosts and wet

These late summer bulbs of rich colouring—Tigridias—thrive best in sandy soil in a sunny spot.

weather in winter. The bulbs may be lifted in autumn and stored in a dry, cool place, and covered with a layer of earth until planting time. Seeds may be sown in spring in a fairly light soil. Increase by offsets removed and treated as old bulbs during planting time. These bulbs may also be grown as greenhouse plants.

SPECIES.

T. atrata, deep purple, August. 2 ft.

T. buccifera, greenish yellow and purple.

T. curvata, purple, April.

T. houttei, yellow-lilac, spring. 1 ft.

T. lutea, yellow, June. 1 ft.

T. pavonia, orange-red, June. 1 ft.

T. Pringlei, scarlet-red, blotched crimson. 1 ft.

T. violaceæ, purple, May. 1 ft.

TILIA (til'-i-a. Tiliaceæ). Lime or Linden. Deciduous trees of stately, spreading habit. Especially valuable as forest trees, and for parks, avenues, and large gardens. The white flowers are fragrant, and are surrounded by large bracts, several inches in length. They are followed by nut-like fruit about the size of a pea.

Culture.—Plant in October or November. They like moist rich soil, and open sunny positions.

Propagation is best by seed, sown in the open. The only pruning needed is to thin out the branches when overcrowded.

SPECIES.

T. americana. American Lime from eastern and central N. America. 60–70 ft. A handsome species with large leaves about 6 in. long and nearly as wide. Apt to die back unless in a sunny climate.

T. euchlora (*dasystyla*), 40 ft. Hybrid of doubtful origin. A very valuable Lime, not only on account of its large lustrous green leaves, but also owing to its re-markable freedom from insect pests of all kinds. An excellent avenue or street tree.

T. platyphyllos (Europe). A shapely tree up to 100 ft. high. Leaves downy.

T. tomentosa (*argentea; alba*). The White Lime of Europe. The silvery-white undersides of the leaves are very attractive when disturbed by a breeze.

T. vulgaris. The Common Lime, 100 ft. and over. Although this is the Lime used so extensively as a street tree, it is much inferior in several respects to some of the above-mentioned species and hybrids. Its inner bark is used in the manufacture of "bast" mats.

TINUS. *See* VIBURNUM TINUS.

TITHONIA (ti-tho-ni-a. Compositæ). Mexican Sunflower. Evergreen flowering shrubs, usually grown as half-hardy annuals. They grow in ordinary soil in the sunny border.

Sow seeds in March in sandy soil in a temperature of 60°. Prick out the seedlings when large enough to handle and harden off gradually for May planting

TOAD FLAX. *See* LINARIA.

TOBACCO PLANT. *See* NICOTIANA.

TOBAGO CANE. *See* BACTRIS.

TODEA (to-de-a. Filices). Crape Fern. Greenhouse evergreen ferns. Plant in March in a compost of peat, loam, leaf-mould, charcoal, sandstone and silver sand. These may be grown in moist, shady pockets of the rockery under bell-glasses. Give plenty of water in summer, but less afterwards. *Propagate* by means of spores.

TOLMIEA. Saxifragaceæ. Hardy perennial suitable for shady borders, interesting on account of the habit of the leaf growth—small leaves and stems appearing from the leaf surface where the leaf joins the stem. Flowers green with purple nerved calyx.

Plant in spring, lift and divide also in spring.

TOLPIS (tol-pis. Compositeæ). Hardy annuals, bearing yellow flowers. Sow seeds in April in any ordinary soil in the sunny beds or borders. Sow in the position where they are to grow, and cover thinly with fine soil. Thin out the seedlings when they are 3 in. high to 6 in. apart. Take cuttings of shrubby species in summer in sandy soil under a bell-glass.

TOMATO (*Lycopersicum esculentum.* Solanaceæ). Love Apple. Introduced into Europe in the 16th century.

INDOOR CULTURE.

The best type of house is the span-roof (see GLASSHOUSES) of plain glass, with, if heating is required, hot water pipes.

Seed sowing.—Since tomatoes can be relied upon to reproduce from seed, this is the usual method of propagation. Seed of a reliable strain should be obtained. For fruit in May this can be sown in January, but since the plants will require a good deal of heat and thus prove expensive to rear, it is better to sow in February and the fruit will be ready in June. Sow in a temperature of 50°-60° in well-prepared seed pans. Cover the bottom of the pan with crocks and cinders over which a layer of decayed leaves is placed. Then fill the pan with a compost of leaf-mould, sand and loam in equal proportions. For greater success sterilise the soil by pouring over it boiling water. Place the seeds on the surface of the soil about 1 in. apart and cover with finely sifted soil.

Once the seedlings have appeared keep them near the glass and allow a little air. Water carefully with water that is of the same temperature as the greenhouse and avoid killing the seedlings by " damping off." When they have two or more leaves transplant into pots or boxes, preferably the former of the kind known to gardeners as " Long Toms " which allow of deeper planting. For the first shift into pots the

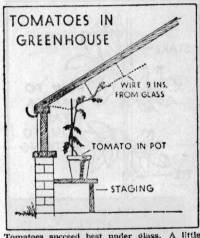

TOMATOES IN GREENHOUSE

WIRE 9 INS. FROM GLASS

TOMATO IN POT

STAGING

Tomatoes succeed best under glass. A little shade by means of whitewash may be required during bright sunny weather.

soil recommended for the seeds will be suitable. By the middle of March they will be ready for repotting using a compost of fibrous loam with manure or leaf-mould and a good dash of burnt garden refuse or wood ash and fine bonemeal. Pot firmly and water daily as growth increases rapidly. Use rain water if possible and stand the butt in the sun or in the greenhouse for several hours to take the chill off the water. When the flower trusses show, stake carefully.

The permanent quarters of the plants must now be decided upon.

Plants that are bought ready grown need a certain amount of care before they are ready for their final planting. When they arrive from the nursery trim off any damaged leaves and spray to refresh the foliage. If very small, pot singly and keep close for a week or so. Use for the first potting equal parts of leaf-mould and gritty sand with some old potting soil and make sure that good drainage is given by using potsherds or broken crocks.

Later the plants may be put out in prepared beds or potted up in a compost of good loam ("maiden" if possible), well rotted manure and burnt refuse from the garden.

When set out in beds allow plenty of room for each plant, about 18 in. at least

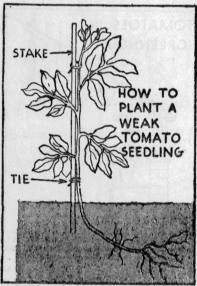

STAKE→

HOW TO PLANT A WEAK TOMATO SEEDLING

TIE→

Bad gardeners sometimes allow their Tomatoes to grow leggy, a state which can be remedied somewhat by laying the same into the soil at planting time.

and restrict the root run by making the bed so solid that a strong trowel is necessary for making the holes for the plants. By doing this, growth will be slow for a few weeks but it will be of the right kind for producing a record crop.

For pot culture use 10 in. pots with ample drainage, and water well *before* repotting. For the first few days spray the plants overhead but do not water until they are acclimatised.

When grown in the unheated greenhouse keep the plants drier than when they are in the greater heat of the warm house until the warm weather when they will need plenty of water. As soon as the

flowers form give air and begin to feed with fertilisers. When the flowers are mature shake gently so that fertilisation can take place.

Certain rules apply to all the methods of growing the plants.

Water carefully and avoid over doing it as a plant that has flagged from lack of moisture is much more likely to recover than one that is waterlogged. If the pots are tapped with a stick and give out a hollow sound the soil is dry enough to water, but if a dull thud is given there is sufficient water in the pot. Keep the temperature as even as possible (about 60°–65°), and when the sun is strong ventilate freely to counteract the heat.

All side shoots that form in the axils of the leaves must be removed. They are distinguishable from the flower buds as the latter do not grow in the same position and hang downwards. Tie up loosely so as not to cut the rapidly-growing stems.

Setting the Fruit.—Artificial aids, such as a rabbit's tail, are rarely necessary provided that the plants are shaken at midday when the sun is strong.

Leaves that touch those of other plants should be taken off and also those that turn yellow after the first bunches of fruit have formed.

Outdoor Culture.—For this purpose special varieties must be chosen. Seed should be sown about the middle of March in well-drained pans or boxes in a light compost similar to that for the indoor plants. Pot up for the first time in a compost of four parts of loam, one each of leaf-mould and manure and some wood ash or burnt garden refuse. Water daily after the first few days and when the roots fill the pots transfer to larger pots using the same compost. By the second week in May they should have formed a fruit truss and may be safely placed in cold frames or put out in the open with whatever protection is at the disposal of the grower.

Planting out.—Whether they are to be trained to a wall or grown in the open the sunniest and most protected spot in the garden should be chosen. When there is no protection this can be afforded by a temporary structure made of wattle hurdles or boarding. Before planting prepare the soil by digging to a depth of two feet and fill the excavation with a compost of 3 parts of loam, 1 of leaf soil or old manure and 1 of burnt garden refuse with a little bonemeal. Make the soil very firm before planting which should be done with a distance of at least 15 in. between each plant. Water well before turning the plants out of the pots and again after they are inserted in the soil. When the plants are bought ready grown they may be planted straightway into a prepared position on a south wall.

The best system of training is the cordon or single stem. Those varieties sold as " bush tomatoes " are, however, grown with four side stems, the main stem being stopped after the first flower truss forms. It is wise to protect them on cold nights.

Plants in the open without wall protection.—Where there is absolutely no protection available for the plants good crops are often raised. The soil should be well dug and manured some time before required for use. If too heavy, wood-ash, burnt refuse or road scrapings should be worked in but the soil may be richer than for indoor plants as the roots have a greater run.

During the winter previous to tomato planting, dress the soil with manure and about 3 lb. of superphosphate of lime to each rod. In May prior to use rake over and tread the soil firm. Plant in June and water well. As soon as the plants are established they will need constant care. Laterals must be removed and weeds kept down with the hoe. If the leader is pinched out when a few bunches of fruit have formed the lower fruits will benefit. When the weather is hot the soil should be mulched with leaves to a depth of 2 in.

Outdoor plants can have more food than is usually given and at least once a week can be watered with liquid manure. The type of stimulant should be changed so that one week they have stable manure and the next, soot water.

Defoliation will help the sun to reach the plants that are ripening fruits and by September the latter should be ready for the table.

Pests and Diseases.—Amongst the pests that attack tomatoes are Aphides, Green Fly (which *see*); Snowy Fly, which is a white four-winged fly that sucks the flesh

and damages foliage. This can be destroyed by fumigating with a special insecticide.

Red Spider which in spite of its name is sometimes of a greenish hue. It lives in colonies on the leaves from which it sucks the sap and its presence is revealed by the pallor of the leaves. Since it is encouraged by a hot dry atmosphere the best remedy is to ventilate more freely, or the greenhouse can be fumigated. A good

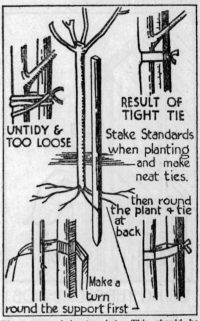

RESULT OF TIGHT TIE

UNTIDY & TOO LOOSE

Stake Standards when planting and make neat ties.

then round the plant & tie at back

Make a turn round the support first

Plants expand in growing. This should be allowed for in tying them to stakes.

scheme is to mix flowers of sulphur with milk and paint the hot water pipes with this. When heated the pipes give off fumes which will kill the pests.

Wireworms.—If the soil is sterilised these will be kept down (*see* WIREWORMS).

Hadena Moth.—The caterpillar of this moth has of recent years attacked the tomato. It works at night, usually in June and must be hand picked.

Bacterial Tomato Wilt.—When stricken by this disease the leaves and stem wither. All infected plants must be burnt.

Bacterial Tomato Rot. Soft Rot.—The fruits become a watery mass of bacteria.

Brown Rot. — Characterised by brown hard circular spots on the fruit. Burn diseased fruits.

Damping-off (*q.v.*).

Potato Blight (*see* APHIDES).

Tomato Leaf-mould. Leaf-rust.—When first detected apply flowers of sulphur to the leaves.

Sleepy Disease.—Yellow blotches which result in the wilting and withering of the leaves. Burn infected plants.

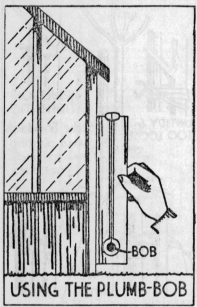

USING THE PLUMB-BOB

The Plumb-bob is an instrument used in the construction of garden buildings to test their erectness.

Manures.—Once the fruit has set several kinds of manures or "feeds" can be used with advantage. The chief thing to remember is the golden rule of successful growers, "little and often." Where the compost used fulfils ideal requirements manure may be unnecessary, but since tomatoes are gross feeders they will not be harmed by suitable manures, amongst which rank, superphosphate of lime in liquid form or sprinkled among the plants; bone meal mixed with the soil especially after the fruits have set and a top dressing is being applied; fowl manure, soot either diluted with water or sprinkled over the soil; and stable manures diluted with six times their own quantity of water (*see also* MANURES).

Exhibition.—The tomatoes for this purpose must be well grown, of a good colour, and firm flesh. Part of the crop must be sacrificed to allow the perfect development of the remaining bunches and leave two or three tomatoes only in each bunch. To store until the exhibition, pick before they are quite ripe and wrap in tissue. Keep in a cool shed and lay them on sawdust or bran. When staging keep those of one size together, and if this is impossible, graduate them so that differences in size are not noticeable. Where weight is aimed at it is best to leave one bunch only.

Winter Crops.—This is difficult where a constant temperature of 60°–65° cannot be maintained. The treatment is the same as that for the summer crop grown in the greenhouse, seed being sown in August and the seedlings potted up at the beginning of September. Grow outside in a cold frame or a bed of ashes during this month and change to winter quarters when one bunch is set, which is usually when frost is commencing.

VARIETIES.

Indoor.—Red Fruited; Best of All; Cropper; Jewel; Market King; Kondine Red; Perfection.

Outdoor.—Red Fruited; Essex Wonder; Evesham Wonder; Open Air; Sunrise; Supreme.

Yellow Fruited.—Golden Sunrise; Red Currant; Garland; Sovereign; Sunbeam.

Ornamental.—Garland; Red Currant; Red Cherry; Peach; Yellow Pear.

TOOLS. Tools should always be put away *clean* and smeared over with a very little oil.

TOOTH-WORT. *See* DENTARIA.

TOPIARY. Trees trained and regularly cut back to keep them to fancy shapes such as those shown on page 692.

TORCH-LILY. *See* KNIPHOFIA.

TORENIA (Scrophulariaceæ). A greenhouse annual with beautiful violet-blue and yellow flowers, making decorative pot plants in July and August. Grows 12 in. high.

Cultivation.—Seeds should be sown in a

warm greenhouse in early spring. Prick off when large enough and grind in a gentle heat. They may be flowered in 48-size pots, using a compost of loam, peat and silver sand for the final pots.

TORREYA (tŏr-rē'-a. Taxaceæ). Evergreen trees allied to Taxus (yew) with stiff, rigid, pointed leaves. They succeed in ordinary garden soil, including chalky, in sun or partial shade. *Propagation* by seed, and by cuttings under hand-light in August.

TOWN GARDENS. Even a tiny back yard or small fore-court can be made a thing of beauty by those who are keen and energetic, and the following is a brief and simple survey of the methods to be adopted in cultivating a tiny space in the heart of a great city.

The plan of the garden should be made first on paper. If the space is large enough for a path, use wooden pegs to mark it out before digging is commenced. The following points should be noted by those who have gardens to plan:

1. Study the aspect of the garden and, whenever possible, make paths run north and south. Make straight wide paths where washing has to be dried.

2. Retain any well-grown tree or shapely bush if possible. Cover all unsightly walls or fences with creepers.

3. A lawn is specially desirable, and should be as secluded as possible, also a little shaded. In fact, it should be an "outdoor room" where it is possible to rest, or to work, or to receive visitors.

4. For the same reason, special features in a small garden should include a shaded seat, or arbour, where this can be arranged.

5. Study the views from the house windows and also from the street, and see that there is something of exceptional interest to catch the eye—a well-grown plant or bush, sundial or archway.

6. Consider the position of the flower borders, whether sunny or shaded, and select plants accordingly.

Manures.—These depend naturally on the condition of the soil. *Slaked Lime* is the best manure to use on a neglected garden, and can be applied during digging operations at the rate of four ounces to a square yard. Lime acts as a key, it liberates potash in the soil, and this is

specially useful for flowering plants. It corrects over-acidity, it destroys injurious insects and assists the action of the weather in breaking up heavy soils.

Soot is valuable as a fertiliser, and also as an insecticide. For the former purpose it can be applied to the surface alone, but for use as an insecticide it should be mixed with lime and sprinkled near the stems of plants which are attacked. Soot also darkens the soil, and so gives it added

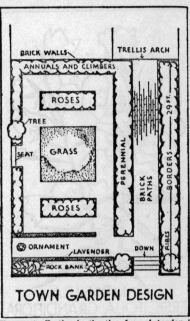

TOWN GARDEN DESIGN

The most effective in the tiny formal garden is the use of formal beds.

warmth. It is good for lawns, producing a rich, velvety green grass.

Wood ashes from bonfires are good fertilisers. These also should be applied to the surface, as the rain will wash them into the soil. Never use coal ashes, except as a dressing on lawns (*see* LAWNS) as they will do more harm than good.

Organic Manure. The stable, is of course, a good source of supply, but if you are fortunate enough to get stable manure, be sure it is not mixed with sawdust. Such manure would be liable to make the soil sour, and would be a breeding-ground for all kinds of insect pests. Most town gardeners will, however, have to look to other sources for organic manure, and for this purpose we advise the use of a compost pit. This can be constructed in a corner of the garden and screened from view by tall-growing plants, such as sunflowers. A small pit should be dug and all refuse—weeds, dead leaves, sweepings from the lawn, old rags well torn up, household refuse, peelings, etc., thrown into the pit and covered now and again with a layer of soil

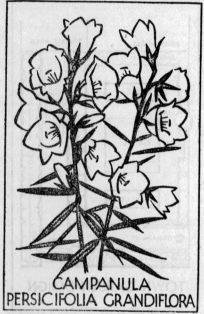

CAMPANULA PERSICIFOLIA GRANDIFLORA

Campanulas like lime in the soil. They will grow in a half-shady position.

and a handful of lime. When the time comes for digging, a compost pit of this kind will provide sufficient manure for the borders. Where it is desired to supplement this, supplies of fish manure, hop manure, etc., can be bought, and will be an effective addition. Refuse from fowls, rabbits, etc., is useful, but should be allowed to decay for two months before using.

It should always be remembered by those who own small gardens overshadowed by trees or other houses that the supply of humus in the soil is best kept as low as possible in the shady border. It is preferable to use bonemeal to add to the sunless border rather than to use either stable manure or the contents of the compost pit.

Artificial Manures. During the growing season, quick-acting manures such as nitrate of soda, or ammonium sulphate, and superphosphate may be applied at the rate of ½ oz. per square yard. A "little and often" should be the rule if artificial manures are to be used. For convenience in use, there are several ready-compounded manures on the market and, provided these are purchased from a reliable source, they will be found very handy and useful by town gardeners, to whom the storing of quantities of separate chemicals would present difficulties. A good home-made manure for most purposes can be made from one part sulphate of ammonia, three parts superphosphate of lime and one part sulphate of potash, mixed well together and applied at the rate of 1 oz. per square yard two or three times during the growing season; substituting basic slag for the superphosphate on very heavy soils.

The Hardy Flower Border. *Annuals, Biennials, Perennials.* All flowers group themselves under one of the three headings given above, according as to whether they live one, two or more years. For town gardens, we would lay particular stress on the effects which can be achieved by a wise selection of *Annuals*. These are particularly easy to grow and give early results. The seeds are usually sown in the spring, and the plants will flower from May to October. Some may be sown in autumn, and the flowers will then be a little earlier, and the plants a little stronger. After digging and manuring the ground, the surface soil should be raked to a fine tilth. The seeds may then be sown broadcast and raked in (care should be taken not to allow the rake teeth to sink more than ¼ in. in the soil), or sown in shallow drills. The ground should afterwards be pressed down lightly with the back of the spade to make it firm.

For a succession of flowers, three rows sown at intervals of a fortnight, can be grown, of the same kind of seed, allowing about 6 in. between each row, the rows being parallel with the border edge. In towns it is advisable to protect seeds from cats and birds by stretching thread over the seed bed from small sticks. Above all, do not forget that it pays to buy good seed.

Do not sow annuals in isolated ones or twos. Mass them in clumps for colour effects. Thin out the seedlings ruthlessly as soon as they are big enough, for if they are overcrowded you will only get thin, weedy-looking specimens instead of strong bushy plants. Blend your colours harmoniously. Study the height of the plants. Make edgings of Sweet Alyssum, Dwarf Candytuft, or Virginian Stock, and your backgrounds of the taller plants. Finally, put a finishing touch by growing at least a few sweet-smelling flowers, such as Mignonette, Stocks, and Sweet Peas. Sparrows like the Sweet Peas, but only attack them when young.

Lists of Flowers which have been found suitable for Town Gardens.

ANNUALS TO BE GROWN FROM SEED.

Botanical Name	Common Name	Height	Colour
Alyssum maritimum*	Sweet Alyssum	4–6 in.	White
Calendula officinalis	Marigold	12–18 in.	Orange
Campanula Loreyi	Lorey's Bellflower	1 ft.	Lilac
Centaurea cyanus	Cornflower	6–36 in.	Various
Centaurea suaveolens	Sweet Sultan	2 ft.	Various
Chrysanthemum tricolor	Chrysanthemum	18 in.	Various
Chrysanthemum segetum	Corn Marigold	2 ft.	Yellow
Clarkia (double)	Clarkia	2 ft.	Various
Collinsia	Collinsia	1 ft.	Various
Convolvulus minor	Lesser Bindweed	1 ft.	Various
Coreopsis	Tickseed	2–4 ft.	Yellow and Brown
Delphinium	Larkspur	1–2 ft.	Various
Erysimum peroffskianum*	Alpine Wallflower	12–18 in.	Yellow and Orange
Eschscholtzia	Californian Poppy	1–2 ft.	Various
Gaillardia	Blanket Flower	1–3 ft.	Red and Yellow
Gilia		6–12 in.	Various
Godetia	Godetia	6–24 in.	Various
Gypsophila	Chalk Plant	18 in.	White and Pink
Helianthus	Sunflower	6–10 ft.	Yellow
Humulus	Hop	6–10 ft.	Various
Iberis*	Candytuft	1–2 ft.	Various
Impatiens	Great Balsam	3–6 ft.	Various
Lathyrus*	Sweet Pea	6–10 ft.	Various
Lavatera splendens rosea	Rose Mallow	3–6 ft.	Rose
Linaria	Toadflax	1 ft.	Various
Linum grandiflorum	Flax	1–2 ft.	Red
Lupinus	Lupin	1–2 ft.	Various
Malcomia	Virginian Stock	6 in.	Pink and White
Malope	Mallow Wort	1–3 ft.	Various
Matthiola bicornis*	Night-scented Stock	18 in.	Pink
Nemophila	Californian Bluebell	3–9 in.	Blue, etc.
Nigella	Love-in-a-Mist	18 in.	Blue and White
Oxalis corniculata	Wood Sorrel	3–6 in.	Yellow
Papaver	Poppy (many)	1–4 ft.	Various
Reseda*	Mignonette	6–12 in.	Various
Saponaria calabrica	Soapwort	6 in.	Rosy Red
Silene	Catchfly	6–18 in.	Pink or Red
Tropæolum	Common Nasturtium & Canary Creeper	1–10 ft.	Red and Yellow

* Fragrant.

ANNUALS TO BE GROWN FROM SEED (*continued*).

Botanical Name	Common Name	Height	Colour
HALF-HARDY ANNUALS.			
Ageratum	Floss Flower	6–18 in.	Blue or White
Amaranthus	Love-lies-bleeding	2–3 ft.	Red or Purple
Brachycome	Swan River Daisy	8 in.	Blue, Red, White
Callistephus	China Aster	½–¾ ft.	Various
Datura	Angel's Trumpets	1½–3 ft.	Various
Dimorphotheca	Star of the Veldt	1–2 ft.	Orange
Helichrysum	Everlasting Flower	1½–3 ft.	Various
Helipterum	Immortelle	1–2 ft.	Various
Kochia	Burning Bush or Summer Cypress	2–3 ft.	Autumnal foliage, Crimson
Lobelia erinus	Lobelia	5 in.	Blue and White
Matthiola*	Ten-week Stock	½–2 ft.	Various
Nicotiana*	Tobacco Plant	2–3 ft.	White and Red
Nemesia	Nemesia	9–12 in.	Various
Petunia	Petunia	1 ft.	Various
Phlox Drummondii	Annual Phlox	6–12 in.	Various
Salpiglossis		1–2 ft.	Various
Salvia	Clary	18 in.	Various
Verbena	Verbena	1 ft.	Various
BIENNIALS.			
Althæa ficifolia	Fig-leaved Hollyhock	6–10 ft.	Red and Yellow
Antirrhinum	Snapdragon	1–4 ft.	Various
Campanula	Canterbury Bells	1–4 ft.	Blue, White and Rose
Cheiranthus*	Wallflower	1–2 ft.	Various
Dianthus barbatus*	Sweet William	1–2 ft.	Various
Dianthus chinensis*	Indian Pink	6–12 in.	Various
Digitalis purpurea	Foxglove	1–5 ft.	Pink and White
Glaucium tricolor	Horned Poppy	1–2 ft.	Orange
Lunaria biennis*	Honesty	2–3 ft.	Purple, Lilac or White
Matthiola*	Stocks	1–2 ft.	Various
Myosotis	Forget-me-not	6 in.	Blue
Œnothera*	Evening Primrose	1–3 ft.	Yellow, White tinted Rose
Œnothera acaulis	Stalkless Sundrop	Trailing	White, tinted Rose
Scabiosa*	Sweet Scabious	1–3 ft.	Various
Viola*	Viola, Pansy	6 in.	Various
PERENNIALS.			
Achillea	Pearl Flower	2 ft.	White
Aconitum	Monkshood	1–6 ft.	Various
Adenophora	Gland Bellflower	1–3 ft.	Blue
Ajuga	Bugle	½–1½ ft.	Blue, Rose and White
Althæa	Hollyhocks	6–10 ft.	Various
Alyssum	Madwort	2–18 in.	Yellow and White
Anchusa	Alkanet	2 ft.	Blue and White
Anemone japonica	Japanese Windflower	1–4 ft.	Various
Antennaria	Cat's Ear	1–3 in.	White and Pink
Aquilegia	Columbine	1–3 ft.	Various
Arabis	Rock Cress	4–9 in.	Various
Arenaria	Sandwort	2–6 in.	White

* Fragrant.

1. Polyanthus in riotous colours brighten the garden in spring.
2. Balsam—an old garden favourite for shady places
3. Hardy Cyclamen shown in an ideal setting.

1. Tamarix massed in a lawn bed.
2. Grouped Rhododendrons give interest to the informal garden.
3. The use of light and dark foliage in grouping trees and shrubs.

PERENNIALS *(continued)*.

Botanical Name	Common Name	Height	Colour
Armeria	Thrift	2–18 in.	Rose or Crimson
Artemisia*	Old Man	1–5 ft.	Yellow
Asperula	Woodruff	3–9 in.	White and Pink
Aster	Michaelmas Daisy .	1–6 ft.	Various
Astrantia	Masterwort	1–2 ft.	White or Pink
Aubretia	Purple Rock-cress .	2–4 in.	Various
Bellis	Daisy	6–12 in.	Red and White
Buphthalmum	Ox-eye	18 in.	Yellow
Calamintha*	Calamint	1 ft.	Purple
Calystegia	Bindweed	6 ft.	Various
Campanula	Bellflower	1–6 ft.	Blue and White
Centaurea	Perennial Cornflower	2–8 ft.	Various
Centranthus	Valerian	2–3 ft.	Red or White
Cephalaria	Scabious	5 ft.	Yellow
Cerastium	Snow-in-summer ...	3–6 in.	White
Chrysanthemum	Shasta Daisy ...	3 ft.	White
Chrysanthemum	Chrysanthemum ...	2–4 ft.	Various
Chrysanthemum maxi- mum	Ox-eye Daisy ...	3 ft.	White
Convallaria*	Lily of the Valley...	6 in.	White
Coreopsis	Tickseed	2–4 ft.	Yellow or Yellow and Purple
Corydalis	Fumitory	½–1 ft.	Purple or Yellow
Crocus	Crocus	3–4 in.	Various
Dahlia	Dahlia	2–6 ft.	Various
Delphinium	Larkspur	1–6 ft.	Various
Dianthus*	Carnations and Pinks	½–2 ft.	Various
Dicentra	Lyre Flower	2 ft.	Rosy-crimson
Dictamnus	Burning Bush ...	3 ft.	Purple
Doronicum	Leopard's Bane ...	2–3 ft.	Yellow
Echinops	Globe Thistle ...	3–6 ft.	Blue
Epilobium angustifolium	Rose Willow Herb .	2–5 ft.	Rose
Erigeron	Fleabane	6–30 in.	Various
Eryngium	Sea Holly	1–18 in.	Various
Erysimum*	Fairy Wallflower ...	1 ft.	Sulphur-yellow
Fuchsia	Ear Drops	3–6 ft.	Red and Purple
Funkia	Plantain Lily ...	9–24 in.	Blue, Lilac, White
Gaillardia	Blanket Flower ...	18 in.	Yellow
Galega	Goat's Rue	3–5 ft.	Various
Geum	Avens	1–2 ft.	Red
Gypsophila	Chalk Plant	½–2 ft.	White, Pink
Helenium	Helen-flower or Sneezeweed ...	2–5 ft.	Yellow, Brown and Red
Helianthus	Sunflower	4–6 ft.	Yellow
Helleborus niger	Christmas Rose ...	6–15 in.	White, Red. etc.
Hemerocallis	Japanese Day Lily	1–3 ft.	Yellow and Orange
Hesperis*	Sweet Rocket ...	1–3 ft.	Various
Heuchera	Alum Root.	1–2 ft.	Red
Humulus	Hop	10–15 ft.	Green

*Fragrant.

Z

PERENNIALS (*continued*).

Botanical Name	Common Name	Height	Colour
Iberis*	Candytuft	1–2 ft.	White or Pink
Iris germanica* ...	Flag	2–3 ft.	Blue
Iris siberica	Siberian Iris	2–3 ft.	Various
Kniphofia	Red Hot Poker ...	3–5 ft.	Yellow or Red
Lathyrus	Everlasting Pea ...	6–10 ft.	Pink and White
Linaria Hendersonii	Toadflax	3 ft.	Rich Purple
Linum	Flax	½–2 ft.	Blue and Golden
Lobelia cardinalis ...	Cardinal Flower ...	2–3 ft.	Scarlet
Lupinus arboreus* ...	Lupins	2–5 ft.	Various
Lupinus	Tree Lupin	3–4 ft.	Yellow or White
Lychnis chalcedonica ...	Cross or Scarlet		
	Campion	3 ft.	Scarlet and White
Lysimachia nummularia			
aurea	Creeping Jenny ...	—	Creeping Yellow
Lythrum	Purple Loosestrife .	3–4 ft.	Red-purple
Meconopsis Wallichii	Satin Poppy	4–6 ft.	Pale Blue
Mentha*	Mint	1–2 ft.	Purple
Mimulus cardinalis ...	Cardinal Flower ...	1–2 ft.	Scarlet
Monarda didyma* ...	Bergamot	3 ft.	Scarlet
Oxalis corniculata rubra	Purple-leaved Wood		
	Sorrel	6 in.	Yellow
Paeonia	Peony	2–3 ft.	Various
Papaver orientale ...	Oriental Poppy ...	3–4 ft.	Orange-scarlet
Pelargonium, Zonal	Bedding Geranium .	1 ft.	Various
Pentstemon	Beard Tongue ...	1–2 ft.	Various
Phlox*	Phlox	1–4 ft.	Various
Polygonatum	Solomon's Seal ...	1–3 ft.	White
Polygonum multiflorum	Climbing Knotweed	10–15 ft.	White
Polygonum sachalinense	Tall Knotweed ...	4–10 ft.	White
Primula auricula* ...	Auricula	6 in.	Various
Rudbeckia	Cone-flower	3–6 ft.	Various
Salvia patens	Blue salvia	1 ft.	Blue
Saxifraga umbrosa ...	London Pride	6–10 in.	Pink, White
Scabiosa caucasica .	Scabious	1–3 ft.	Blue and White
Sedum acre	Stonecrop or Wall		
	pepper	3 in.	Yellow
Sempervivum	Houseleek	4–12 in.	Various
Solidago	Golden Rod	4–8 ft.	Golden
Spiraea ulmaria ...	Meadow Sweet ...	2–3 ft.	White
Statice	Sea Lavender ...	6–24 in.	Various
Thalictrum	Meadow Rue	1–4 ft.	Various
Thyme*	Thyme	3–12 in.	Various
Tolmiea	Tolmiea	1 ft.	Various
Tradescantia virginiana	Virginian Spiderwort	1–2 ft.	Blue, Red
Veronica	Speedwell	6–18 in.	Blue
Vinca major	Great Periwinkle ...	2 ft.	Purple-blue
Vinca minor	Periwinkle	9 in.	Purple-blue
Viola*	Violas and Pansies .	6 in.	Various

* Fragrant.

In addition to the above herbaceous perennials, almost all bulbous plants will succeed in the town garden for one season and in some cases will last longer.

LAWNS, HEDGES AND TREES IN TOWN GARDENS.

It is astonishing what a difference a small patch of grass will make to a town garden. It is at once inviting and restful and is most desirable in towns where one's eyes and nerves grow weary from the ceaseless hurrying to and fro of the traffic. It also shows off the flower borders to the best advantage. A few instructions for the guidance of those who are confronted with the problem of changing the stony rubbish heap, which the former tenant called his garden, into a fine green lawn, may be given.

If you are fortunate enough to have a supply of good turves available by all means make use of them, of course making sure that the ground is properly levelled before the turves are laid. However, in towns this method will nearly always be impracticable, but a lawn can be grown from seed in a comparatively short space of time. Dig over the whole of the ground to be used, at the same time burying all the rubbish and large stones. Leave the rough soil for a time to weather, and when it is fairly dry go over it with a roller, or use the back of a spade, to break up the large lumps. Choose a dry day for sowing, and rake over the surface of the soil to make sure there are no large stones left; then sow your seed broadcast. Where ground is particularly stony, a part of the soil may be sifted and spread over the surface, but most ordinary soils will do very well if prepared as already recommended. The best time to make your lawn is in April, but it may be done in early summer if required. If it is possible a net spread over the newly-sown patch will prevent the birds taking their meal at the expense of your seed, or the seed can be dusted with carbolic powder before sowing.

To keep the town lawn in really good condition it should be soaked with water occasionally on summer evenings, especially after a hot dry day, and in spring a dressing of guano or other fertiliser may be given. Any bare patches that appear should be raked over, sown with fresh seed and covered with twigs until the grass has begun to grow, when they are removed.

Hedges.—There are *hedges and hedges*.

Those solid masses of mutilated privet— sometimes more than a yard wide—which collect the dust and soot from the atmosphere and draw the nourishment from the soil should no longer be tolerated. They at best present a sorry exchange for the wealth of flower and foliage which might have been in their place.

Where a hedge is merely required as a screen, to hide a back entrance or keep prying eyes from a corner of the lawn, it is infinitely preferable that it should be ornamental, say a light trellis covered with Polygonum, Clematis or Winter Jasmine, or even with Scarlet Runner Beans. We have seen Loganberries used as screens in London gardens, providing not only an ornamental background to the flower border but also a very profitable source of supply to the housekeeper. Where shrubs are used preference should be given to such treasures as Lilac, Bladder Senna and Flowering Currant, all of which will flourish well in towns, as numbers of them flowering freely on smutty railway embankments will demonstrate. A simple way of forming a light hedge between two sections of a garden is just by planting a row of tall Sunflowers or Jerusalem Artichokes. The latter will form a fine screen all the summer and in winter will help to swell the family larder.

Trees.—Generally speaking, trees have to be excluded from the town garden owing to poverty of space, and even when some may be possible, only those can be chosen which can attain their full growth and beauty without being subjected to the unsightly mutilations of the pruner. Fruit trees are seldom successful except in suburban areas, and even then much trouble must be taken to protect the fruit from the birds. We should therefore advise that in the heart of towns, where it is important that everything planted shall thrive, such trees as Laburnum, Bird Cherry, or Mountain Ash should be selected. Mulberries do well in towns but their growth is very slow. Figs too will grow—we have seen a fig tree growing from a deep area in an East-End street and bearing fruit on the ground level!

Lists of trees and shrubs suitable for town gardens are given below. We do not suggest that no other trees and shrubs will grow, but those here given have proved their adaptability to town conditions. They may therefore be planted with a reasonable hope of success, provided that every possible means within the reach of the town gardener is contributed by providing a depth of soil for the plants to grow

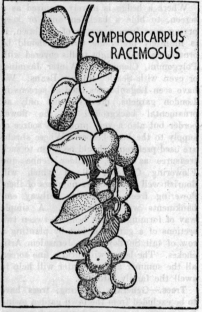

SYMPHORICARPUS RACEMOSUS

The white glistening fruits of the Snowberry add interest to the winter garden.

in and, if necessary, making this more fertile by the addition of some form of decayed vegetable matter. This in some cases may have to be brought from a distance but this should not and will not, we hope, deter the town dweller from attempting to achieve success in the cultivation of these beautiful trees and shrubs.

Shrubs Useful in Town Gardens.

	Common Name.
Aesculus Hippocastanum	Horse Chestnut
Catalpa bignonioides	Indian Bean
Colutea arborescens	Bladder Senna
Cornus sanguinea	Dogwood
Forsythia	Japanese Golden Bell Tree
Ilex	Holly (green & variegated)
Laburnum vulgare	Laburnum
Morus nigra and Morus alba	Mulberry
Philadelphus	Mock Orange (Syringa)
Prunus amygdalus	Almond
Prunus cerasifera atropurpurea	Purple - leaved Plum
Prunus padus	Double Bird Cherry
Pyrus aria	White Beam
Pyrus aucuparia	Mountain Ash
Rhus cotinus	Venetian Sumach
Ribes aureum } Ribes sanguinum }	Flowering Currants
Robinia pseudacacia	Acacia
Symphoricarpus	Snowberry
Syringa	Lilac (sunny positions)
Veronica traversii	Veronica (sheltered position)
Viburnum	Snowball Tree or Guelder Rose

Trees for Beauty of Foliage.

Acer platanoides	Norway Maple
Aileanthus glandulosus	Tree of Heaven
Ginkgo biloba	Maidenhair Tree
Prunus lusitanica	Portugal Laurel

Climbing Plants for Towns.

Restricted as town gardens are by the limitations of architecture and design, it is difficult to preserve or create an atmosphere of naturalness. It is in this direction that the town gardener finds ample opportunity for improving the garden by introducing features, each of which may be at the same time an object of special interest and a natural specimen.

For example, an archway covered with Clematis Jackmanii makes a unique feature in any small garden, and also displays its natural climbing habit.

A green trellis placed against a wall may likewise be covered with climbing plants such as Clematis, Climbing Knotweed, Winter Jasmine, etc. Not only does this enable the gardener to grow more plants in a restricted area, but it provides a picturesque covering for an otherwise ugly object, for nothing is more depressing than a sooty town wall. The making of an archway presents no special difficulty, but if galvanised wire is used it should be coated with green paint, and any wooden supports which have to go into the ground should be either charred or coated with tar to prevent decay. Neatness and naturalness should always be the keynotes for designing any special feature. Rustic archways can be purchased ready for erection, or the home carpenter can make one from loose pieces obtained from a local wood-yard.

These form admirable supports for the different plants recommended at the end of this section. It is also useful to remember when erecting a new archway that there are a number of annuals which will cover an archway in one season, notably Hops, Cobœa scandens, and Scarlet Runner Beans. By planting these for the first year one can avoid the barren appearance so common to newly-established arches. Roses, Clematis, or other perennials may be planted near and these will make growth for another year. Care must be taken however to see that the leaves of the annuals do not choke or shade the perennials. It may be desirable to put a large stake near the archway and to tie the perennial shoots to it until the autumn when they can be taken on to the archway ready for the next year.

While we are dealing with climbing plants we must make mention of the beautiful creeper Ampelopsis Veitchii which is most admirable for covering house walls. This creeper should not be planted if the walls are in need of pointing as it has to be cut down while the builder is at work. The Virginian Creeper is an excellent plant for training over arbours, but only those of the self-clinging kind should be used for walls, as nailing damages the pointing.

Pillars, made from a tall piece of rustic wood (preferably a tree top with the forked branches cut off six inches or so from the main stem), will be very ornamental when covered with Hops, Honeysuckle, or what is considered best of all town climbing plants, Polygonum Baldschuanicum (Climbing Knotweed). The

following list contains a wide selection of climbing plants suitable for town gardens:

Climbing Plants for Town Gardens.

Clematis (montana and Jackmanii).
Climbing Knotweed.
Everlasting Peas.
Firethorn (Cratægus pyracantha).
Grape Vines
Ivy.

A few plants of Aubrietia will quickly smother a rockery bank with a carpet of violet and mauve flowers.

Jasmine (summer and winter).
Loganberries.
Morello Cherry.
Roses such as "Excelsa" "American Pillar" and "Alberic Barbier."
Virginian Creeper.

Annual Climbers.

Canary Creeper.
Cobaea scandens.
Convolvulus.
Eccremocarpus scaber (Chilian Glory Flower).
Hops.
Nasturtiums.
Runner Beans.

Of the above, Morello Cherry, Ivy and Climbing Knotweed are specially recommended for gardeners where no sunshine is received.

The Town Rock Garden.

One of the most suitable features of a miniature garden is a rockery. On this many kinds of dwarf plants can be grown, and if the designer aims at a natural effect, an ugly corner can often be converted into an object of beauty. At the outset we would warn readers that many Alpine plants are simply useless for town conditions, they usually die in the winter, but the following plants may be safely recommended:

Alyssum (annual). Mad-Wort.
Arabis. Rock Grass.
Aubrietia.
Auricula.
Campanula pusilla.
Cerastium. Snow in Summer.
Creeping Jenny.
Crocus.
Festuca (Fescue Grass).
Heuchera. Alum Root.
Oxalis alba. Sorrel.
Saxifraga umbrosa. London Pride.
Stonecrop.
Thrift.
Veronica (dwarf).
Virginian Stock.

Making the Rockery.

If you have no natural stone in your garden, you can use any old bricks or clinkers for this purpose. Good soil is necessary to place in between the stones. The stones or bricks should be so built as to leave pockets for different plants. A rockery has many advantages as part of a small garden scheme. Its shady side may be used to grow ferns of different sorts and also early flowering bulbs such as Crocuses and Snowdrops, while the sunny side may be made into a perpetual floral carpet from early spring to late autumn.

Again, Auriculas with their tough evergreen leaves may always be relied on to thrive under extreme difficulties, and no less hardy is the London Pride (Saxifraga umbrosa). When once planted, a rockery gives very little trouble and is an ever changing scene.

Plant the taller growing plants at the back and keep the dead leaves cleared away as they appear. One more word of warning. Do *not* build up your rockery against the house so that the soil comes above the damp-proof course, otherwise the walls will become damp and endless trouble will ensue. London rockeries are usually best if re-made every few years, as the surface soil is apt to become over-acid owing to the presence of chemicals in the air.

Other features the town gardener may introduce are arbours and seats. No garden should be without its seat, which may or may not be hidden from prying eyes, as the gardener wishes. Within an arbour is a good place to put one, but we prefer a movable seat which can be placed in shade or sun as desired.

Here the artist has plenty of scope. Endless are the designs for this feature of the garden, and the only advice we offer lies in the word simplicity. Let the garden furniture always be in harmony with the general scheme. The natural colour of the wood is preferable when rustic timber is used, and a coat of ordinary varnish or solignum stain will prevent decay. When planed wood is employed, green paint may be safely used at all times.

Much as we should like, it is inadvisable to use specimen plants of Pampas Grass in town, for its plumes get so dirty.

A few grasses may be grown but, on the whole, it is unwise to attempt to make a special feature of tall grasses, as the feathery inflorescence invariably gets sooty and dirty. Some of the following specimen plants can be grown with better results:

Bocconia cordata—Plume Poppy.
Eremurus robustus—Fox Tail Lily.
Funkia—Plantain Lily.
Lilium auratum (Golden-rayed lily of Japan).
Spiræa gigantea.
Tritomas, in variety (Red-hot poker).
Yuccas, of sorts (Adam's needle).

Vases, bird-baths, and sundials may be used with effect. These can be purchased ready made, but we have seen very pretty plant vases made from worn-out enamel bowls, covered with cement and clinker, and planted with Creeping Jenny and Nasturtiums—a vase for a few pence that would have cost a guinea from a florist! The devotion of a little time to small contrivances of this sort makes a garden far more interesting both to its owner and also to his visitors.

Some special difficulties of the Town Gardener. It must be borne in mind that though the actual manual labour involved in the making of a garden is very much the same everywhere, the successful town gardener will need to give far more thought and preparation to the matter than will the gardener in the country districts. There are a number of special difficulties which he has to face, and a few suggestions for dealing with some of these are given here.

Cats.—These are by no means the least difficult problem to solve, town cats being perhaps the "hardiest of all hardy perennials."

It is very distressing to find one stretched very comfortably out on a bed of once flourishing seedlings or gnawing the tops of the young shoots. A useful method of warning off these intruders is by means of an ammonia bottle. Choose a bottle with rather a small neck (to prevent too rapid evaporation) and fill it with ammonia. Then sink it, uncorked, into the soil where the cats are most troublesome, so that the neck of the bottle only just reaches the surface level. The smell of the ammonia will be very objectionable to the cats, who will soon learn to leave that corner of your garden severely alone. The same result is achieved by a liberal sprinkling of cayenne pepper put over the surface of the soil. Soot is also a deterrent. Cats—even town cats—generally like to keep their paws clean.

Seedlings can, of course, be protected from cats by inserting a few stakes and stretching across either a network of thread or a piece of wire netting. It is possible to protect isolated plants by placing a barrier of small stakes around them.

Sparrows.—To prevent sparrows from attacking seedlings it is best to cover them over with wire netting, or threads or twigs, until they are well grown. Even then it is difficult to keep such plants as Sweet Peas free from attack. Do not avoid growing these plants altogether, but sow more seeds than you think will be

required, to allow for some loss, and also place a shallow dish or two of water in the garden. In dry weather, the sparrows frequently peck off the young shoots just to obtain moisture. Many people scare off the birds by scraps of paper tied to a string after the manner of a kite tail and hung immediately above the tempting seedlings.

Slugs and Snails.—These are, indeed, devastating creatures, and the havoc they work is most disheartening. Hand-picking either in the early morning or on a damp evening (pieces of potato or carrot will act as traps) is probably the most efficacious way of tackling them, or a quantity of soot sprinkled round the plants is useful. Roots often get attacked by slugs, and when this happens the plant may be lifted, and its roots cleaned, and replanted in soil into which a liberal allowance of soot and lime have been dug. A simple insecticide to use against slugs can be made by boiling half a pound of quassia chips and about two tablespoonsful of soft soap with a gallon of water for ten or fifteen minutes.

Strain the liquid and dilute for use with about ten times the amount of water. This mixture can be sprayed into the crowns of such plants as Delphiniums, which are frequently attacked by slugs just below the ground surface.

Greenfly (Aphides).—For this and, indeed for all insect pests, the most effective method is to spray the plants with a solution of reliable insecticide. Isolated shoots affected can be washed in a solution of strong soapsuds, care being taken not to break off the tip during the operation. A good insecticide, which can be made at home, is paraffin emulsion. Put a double handful of soft soap into half a gallon of water and bring to the boil. Remove from the fire and pour in a gill of paraffin. Stir well until a thick emulsion has been formed. Surplus paraffin will float on the surface and should be either skimmed off or more soap added until no free paraffin remains. A pint of this emulsion in a gallon and a half of water will make a valuable insecticide for general use.

Dirty Atmosphere. — Plants are even more particular than human beings with regard to cleanliness, and many of them simply refuse to grow where the atmosphere is sooty and dirty. As a general rule it is wise to select smooth-leaved plants for towns as these are less liable to be affected by dust and they are more readily washed clean in the rain.

A good syringing may be given over the leaves occasionally in the evening time. Carnations, and most plants with glaucous green leaves, are not much affected by

PENDANT RUSTIC BIRD TABLE

BATH

FOOD BOWL

(H. M. B. Patent)
Birds can be encouraged to visit your garden by providing a table to hold scraps of suet and crumbs, etc., from the house.

dust, and for that reason will thrive well in towns. Chemical impurities in the atmosphere caused by factory chimneys are most troublesome, and render it impossible for us to draw a hard and fast line between what will and will not grow in town. We can only suggest that the novice takes careful note of any flowers he may see thriving in neighbouring gardens, and selects the bulk of his plants accordingly.

Neighbours' Trees have been known to present a difficulty to more than one would-be gardener in town. It is, of course, possible to insist on the cutting back of all branches which overhang your ground, but even this will not prevent a tree from giving an unwelcome shade to your borders. We fear that this is a situation where the limitations imposed have to be faced. But there are such a number of beautiful plants suitable for shady places that the trees need not trouble the gardener over much. (*See* Shady Borders).

Children.—We suggest that there is no other remedy for the mischief done by the youngsters in their own and other people's gardens than education. Children taught to appreciate and love flowers, and to understand something of the pleasures and the toils of gardening, will not wantonly destroy.

The gardener who is troubled by them should certainly bring all his influence to bear on the local educational authorities, with a view to incalculating in the children a knowledge and understanding of the art of gardening. Garden Societies should always be urged to provide special competitions for children, in order that an appreciation of flower-culture should be developed amongst them.

Soil Pests.—Wireworms and other soil pests can be destroyed when digging. If the soil is well-drained, and dug during the frosty weather, lime being applied at this time, pests will not be found to be troublesome. Constant soil working especially with the hoe, is the secret of clean soils.

To sum up main differences between gardening in towns and gardening in the country districts are as follows :

1. The air in towns is polluted with soot and often with chemical impurities. Unless counteracted, this tends to choke the leaves of the plants. Plants will keep much healthier if they are syringed daily with clear water overhead. This should be done in the evenings. In addition to this, care should be taken not to allow the plants to crowd each other unduly.

2. The air of towns is usually drier than the air of the country districts. Syringing overhead will also help in this matter, but it may also be essential to give more water at the roots of the plants.

3. The soil tends to be sour, due to sulphurous acid which is washed down by

the rains from the sooty atmosphere. Lime applied annually, rather more generously than it would be in the country districts, will counteract this.

4. The absence of direct sunshine in the town garden makes it specially desirable to select the right type of plants, and also to treat the soil a little differently from that in country districts. Phosphatic fertilisers should be employed, and plenty of lime, while organic manures should be reduced to a minimum.

5. House walls, overhanging eaves, fences, etc., often prevent rain from reaching the roots of certain of the plants, and in this case occasional soaking with a few pailfuls of water is necessary to keep the soil in good condition.

6. Town garden pests are different but not necessarily more troublesome than those of country gardens. For instance, in country districts rabbits gnaw the barks of trees, and pheasants root up bulbs. In towns, cats, children and sparrows are the chief nuisances.

TRACHELIUM (Campanulaceæ). A handsome hardy perennial which, while hardy in dry soils and in sheltered places, is usually used as a greenhouse annual or biennial. The small lilac flowers are carried in large corymbs, making handsome and decorative heads. Height 1½–3 ft., according to cultivation.

Cultivation.—The seeds are very small, and should be sown with care. To ensure an even distribution over the pot or pan, mix the seeds with some dry silver sand and afterwards sow the mixture as though it were all seed. Water by dipping the pan in tepid water until moisture rises to the surface. Seeds should be sown during the latter part of the season for the following year, or quite good plants may be obtained from seed sown in January or February. Prick out when large enough and pot on as they require it. The final pots may be 32's or 24's, according to the size plants required, and for the larger pots the soil compost should be rich and open. Use mellow loam for the chief ingredient and open with sifted, well-decayed manure, leaf-mould, sand and a little old mortar rubble. Use rough leaf-mould as drainage over the crocks. The plants respond to feeding with dilute liquid

manure when well rooted in the final pots.

TRACHELOSPERMUM (trā-ki-los-per-mum. Apocynaceæ). Twining evergreen shrubs, with leathery leaves and flowers reminiscent of white jessamine.

Culture.—Plant in light loamy soil, against a warm wall. A little peat and sand added when planting is very helpful to give the young plants a start.

Propagate by cuttings taken in July and August.

TRACHYCARPUS (tra - ki - kar′ - pus. Palmaceæ). Fan Palms, one of which is hardy in all parts of the British Isles. The most suitable soil is fibrous loam, and about a third of peat, and some sand.

SPECIES.

T. Fortunei (Chamaerops excelsa). Chusan Palm. Leaves, fan-shaped, 2½ ft. long, and about 4 ft. wide. This species grows to 12–15 ft., except in the warm parts of the country, where it may reach to 30 ft. It is a valuable plant for imparting a tropical appearance to the garden.

TRACHYMENE (tra-ki-me-ne Umbelliferæ). Syn. *Didiscus.* 1¼–2 ft. Western Australia. *T. cœrulea* is the only species worth growing. It has pretty pale blue flowers in clusters, or umbels on thin stalks, but is rather straggling in growth. Loosely staked, it makes a pretty pot plant for cool greenhouse. Sow in mild heat in spring. Its American name is Blue Lace Flower,

TRADESCANTIA (trăd - es - căn - tia. Commelinaceæ), Spiderwort. Handsome stove, greenhouse and hardy perennial herbs, the latter being useful for borders and all of considerable value.

Propagate the stove and greenhouse species by cuttings rooted in light soil, and the hardy species by division in spring, or by seeds. Plant in ordinary soil in sun or shade. Add gravelly lime for the hardy plants.

SPECIES.

T. zebrina pendula has purple flowers and prettily-striped foliage, and is a great favourite for hanging baskets on account of its pendulous habit. If well watered it is of luxuriant growth, and propagates readily by cuttings as new shoots form at the broken tips.

T. virginiana (virginica), the common hardy Spiderwort with blue flowers, has several varieties with blue-violet, rose and white single or double flowers.

T. crassifolia (half-hardy), with purplish rose or blue flowers.

T. elongata (stove plant), with pink flowers and green leaves lined with white. 2 ft.

T. Warszewicziana (stove), purple or lilac flowers. 6–15 in.

TRAGOPOGON. *See* SALSIFY.

TRADESCANTIA

Called after the great Botanist, Tradescant, two types are shown above. The variegated one is used in the greenhouse and the mauve flowered form in the herbaceous border. Botanical students place its stamens under the microscope to see the circulation of protoplasm.

TRANSPIRATION. A process by which the plant gives off surplus moisture. For the plant to absorb sufficient mineral food, more water is absorbed by the root-hairs than the plant requires. This surplus water is given off through the leaves, and helps to keep the plant in an even temperature. It is unwise to pick flowers in full sunshine, when transpiration is rapid, for there is no supply of water in the stems to keep the plant from flagging.

TRAPA (tra-pa. Onograceæ). Water Caltrops. Hardy or tender aquatics.

Plant in late spring in rich loamy soil in shallow ponds or tubs in a sunny position in the cool greenhouse. Sow seeds in spring in loamy soil and water in a temperature of 65°–75°.

TRAVELLER'S JOY. *See* CLEMATIS VITALBA.

TREADS. *See* STEPS.

TREASURE FLOWER. *See* GAZANIA.

TREE OF HEAVEN. *See* AILANTHUS.

TREE MALLOW. *See* LAVATERA.

TREE POPPY. *See* ROMNEYA.

TREE STUMPS. To remove tree stumps bore several holes 1½ in. in diameter, and from 12–20 in. deep, in the stump and fill with copper sulphate, crystalline, or strong sulphuric acid, and plug up the holes with bungs or clay. A solution of nitrate or chlorate of potash, 2 lb. to a gallon of water, used in the same way, except that the solution requires renewing when the first lot is absorbed, will also cause the stump to decay.

If the stumps are dry and away from houses, pour petroleum into the holes and round the tree and ignite. The stump will gradually smoulder away.

Before removing stumps by means of explosives, liquid air, etc., obtain full particulars of how to proceed from the makers of the chemicals.

TREES IN GARDEN DESIGN. Trees in a garden are no longer the monopoly of a few. For large gardens there are the beautiful trees, such as pines, oaks, etc., but for small gardens there are wonderful flowering cherries, laburnums, almonds, etc., which are a valuable addition to any garden. One or two trees placed in the flower border or as a specimen on the lawn make all the difference between a beautiful and a mediocre garden. In the small garden, fruit trees can be grown amongst the flowers, thus combining utility with beauty and saving space. Trees which bear berries or have autumn-tinted foliage should not be forgotten. A selection of various flowering trees is charming in the small front garden and it takes very little imagination to see what a transformation would be affected in suburban streets if all garden owners realised the beauty and value of the modern flowering trees. *See* SHELTER BELTS.

TREFOIL. *See* TRIFOLIUM.

TRELLIS. *See* SCREENS.

TREVESIA (tre-ve-si-a. Araliaceæ). Stove shrubs, with ornamental leaves. Pot in early spring in loam, leaf-mould, and sand, and stand in the warm greenhouse. Water plentifully during the season of growth, but after this, less should be given. A moist atmosphere is essential during the summer. Take cuttings of half-ripened shoots and insert in sand in a frame with mild bottom heat.

SPECIES.

T. eminens.

T. palmata, whitish in March. Height 10–15 ft.

T. sundaica, greenish white. Height 10 ft.

TRICHOLÆNA (trik-o-li-na. Gramineæ). Ruby Grass. Half-hardy annual grass. Sow seeds in early spring in any ordinary soil, ¼ in. deep and 1 in. apart. When the seedlings are 2 in. high, put them singly into 2 in. pots, and later into 4½ in. pots, when they should be hardened off for planting out in June. They need plenty of water.

SPECIES.

T. rosea. Height 3–4 ft.

TRICHOMANES (tri-ko-man-ez. Filices). Killarney Fern. Greenhouse ferns. Plant in March in a compost of peat, loam, leaf-mould, charcoal, sandstone and silver sand, in the greenhouse, or in a moist shady pocket of the rockery under a bell-glass. A damp atmosphere and shade are essential. These plants can also be grown in pots in the house, where they should be placed in a shady window. Increase by spores.

TRICHOPILIA (trich-o-pil-i-a. Orchidaceæ). From *trichos*, a hair, and *pilcon* a cap; the anther is concealed below a cap, surmounted by three tufts of hair. Greenhouse orchids. An easily-cultivated genus, some of the species being delightfully fragrant.

Culture.—Compost: equal parts fibrous peat and sphagnum moss. Best grown in baskets or pans suspended from the roof. Replant into baskets or pans when new growth commences. Shady position. Water freely during growing period, but only enough to keep roots moist during rest period. Winter temperature, 45°; summer, 65°.

Propagate by division when new growth commences.

TRICUSPIDARIA (tri-kus-pi-dar-ia. Tiliaceæ). Very striking and handsome evergreen shrubs from Chile, with bell-shaped flowers on pendulous stalks. In the home counties they need the protection of other shrubs, or small trees; but in the milder parts of the country they thrive admirably in the open and rank

TRICYRTIS HIRTA

An autumn-blooming hardy perennial which grows 2 ft. high and bears white flowers, spotted with purple.

among the most attractive of all flowering shrubs.

Culture.—Plant in cool, moist, lime-free soil, in semi-shade.

Propagate by cuttings of half-ripened wood in a close frame.

TRICYRTIS (tri-ser-tis. Liliaceæ). Toad Lily. Hardy or half-hardy bulbs, which need protection in severe weather. Plant the rhizomes in autumn or spring in well-drained garden soil with a little peat and sand added, setting them 2 in. below the surface. Increase by offsets treated as bulbs at potting time. These plants may also be grown in pots in the greenhouse, where they will flower earlier than those grown in the open, autumn being the period of outdoor blooms.

T. hirta, white, spotted purple, October. 2 ft.

T. macropoda, yellow, spotted purple.

T. striata, leaves lined with creamy-white.

T. pilosa, green, marked red, October. 1½ ft.

TRIENTALIS (trī-en-tā-lis. Primulaceæ). Wintergreen. Starflower. These

TRILLIUM GRANDIFLORUM

Wood Lily, or Trillium, has its parts in three—petals, calyx and leaves. It thrives in the woodland.

pretty hardy perennial herbs are useful in the rock garden or border and have small whorls of leaves, from which rise slender stalks bearing white flowers.

Propagate by seeds under a hand-light in spring, or in the open in summer, or by division of the creeping root stocks in spring. Plant in rich loamy soil in a shady site.

SPECIES.

Only two species are grown, *T. americana*, the Starflower that blooms in May; and *T. europæa*, Wintergreen, a native of Britain and arctic Europe, 6–9 in.

TRIFOLIUM (trī-fō-lium. Legumi-

nosæ). Trefoil, Clover, Shamrock. A genus of annual and perennial herbs, of which the majority are of more use in the kitchen or farm garden than amongst flowers. There are, however, a few species worth growing in the rockery. All grow readily from seeds and are suited to any soil.

SPECIES.

A great number of the native species are weeds, but *T. alpestre*, the Owl-headed Clover with spikes of rosy flowers; *T. alpinum* with pink flowers, June, 6 in. and *T. repens*, white and its bronzy-purple-leaved variety *purpurea* are all grown in the rockery and bloom in the early summer.

T. pannonicum, white and yellow; and *T. hybridium* (*Alsike*), white or rose are also grown.

T. minus and *repens* bear about equal honours in the claim to being the true Shamrock used by St. Patrick, to demonstrate the doctrine of the Trinity, although *Oxalis acetosella*, a native British plant, is also in the running.

TRILLIUM (trill-i-um. Liliaceæ). American Wood Lily. Trinity Flower. Hardy tuberous-rooted perennials.

They are excellent subjects for the wild garden or for the moist shady border. They prefer sandy peat, but will also grow in any other soil. Tubers can be planted any time from August to November, or, if preferred, the plants can be raised from seed sown in shallow pans on sandy peat, placed in a cold frame, and shaded from direct sunshine.

Species.—*T. grandiflorum* (Wake Robin), white; *T. grandiflorum roseum*, rose; *T. incarnatum*, rose.

TRINITY FLOWER. *See* TRILLIUM.

TRITOMA. Syn. KNIPHOFIA, *which see.*

TRITONIA. *See* MONTBRETIA.

TROLLIUS (troll-ius. Ranunculaceæ). Globe Flowers. These are useful hardy herbaceous perennials with orange or bright yellow flowers like large Buttercups, that are at their best in damp shady places in the bog garden or border, where they yield quantities of flowers.

Propagate by seeds or by autumnal division and plant in moist heavy loam enriched with manure, for best results, but in practice they grow anywhere in any soil.

T. asiaticus, with its single-flowered stems bearing flowers of dark yellow in May, and its varieties *aurantiacus* and *Fortunei*, with glowing orange flowers, 18 in.; and *T. europæus*, with pale yellow flowers in May and June, with its several varieties, having both single and double forms, are the most popular.

TRONCHUDA, COUVE, or Portugal Cabbage (*Brassica olearacea costata*). Cruciferæ. This is a continental vegetable, the cultivation of which is steadily increasing in this country.

Like all other Brassicas it requires good treatment, and the land should be liberally manured, and deeply dug during the winter.

Seed should be sown outside on a warm border in March or April, and afterwards transplanted to a reserve bed, until finally planted out in May or June at 2 ft. apart each way.

Frequent hoeing during the summer is all that is usually necessary.

Uses.—Used in winter as a boiled vegetable, the outer leaves are gathered first, and of these only the thick fleshy mid-rib is used; finally the hearts are cut and cooked.

TROPÆOLUM (tro-pe-o-lum. Geraniaceæ). Canary Creeper. Nasturtium (Indian Cress). Peru. Probably the most popular of all hardy annuals as they will thrive almost anywhere in even the poorest soils; in fact a rich soil is detrimental, as the plants make rank growth and do not flower satisfactorily. The tall, or *T. majus*, section grow many feet in length, and are invaluable for quickly covering rough fences, or unsightly sheds, etc., and flower most freely from July to late autumn There are many colours. The *T. nanum* or dwarf varieties are really good for edgings or for small beds. They can be had in separate colours, and come quite true from seed. Some of the varieties, such as King of Tom Thumb, have dark foliage and scarlet flowers, while those of the Queen of Tom Thumb section have the foliage beautifully variegated with silver. *T. peregrinum* is the well-known Canary Creeper. The newest addition to the family is *T. Golden Gleam*. It has beautiful rich yellow flowers, with several rows of petals, which give a semi-double effect, and is rather sweetly-scented. On poor soils it grows about 1½ ft., with branching trails, and flowers most freely, but on rich soils it grows coarse and out of character. Seeds of all species should be sown out of doors where to flower in March or April, in poor soil, which should be made very firm as soon as the seedlings are through. Or if more convenient, seed may be sown

Globe Flowers, or Trollius, make a bright splash of orange and gold in the spring flower border. They prefer a moist soil.

in boxes in cold frame, and planted out in April to May.

TRUMPET-CREEPER. *See* TECOMA.

TRUMPET FLOWER. *See* TECOMA *and* BIGNONIA.

TROWEL. This is a necessary tool in the garden and is generally used for planting and transplanting. It has a small curved blade and can be obtained with a different length of handle from 6–17 in. The cheap ones are made of stamped steel and are rather liable to bend or break at the socket. The better ones are forged steel and in the majority of cases are tanged right through the handle and capped (*see* FORKS).

TSUGA (tsū´-ga. Coniferæ). Hemlock Firs. In districts where they thrive, no evergreen trees surpass the Hemlock Firs or Hemlock Spruces in beauty and elegance of form. They prosper in well-drained deep loamy soil, and where the rainfall is abundant. In shallow chalky soil they do not thrive, except *T. Canadensis* and *T. Brunoniana*. *Propagation* is best by seed.

TROPAEOLUM or CANARY CREEPER

The Tropæolum is a gay annual climber. It needs twigs or string for support.

SPECIES.

T. Albertiana (*heterophylla; Mertensiana*). The "Western Hemlock" of W.N. America. Of rapid growth, up to 200 ft. in nature, and well over half that height in Britain. Of a graceful tapering habit of growth, reddish-brown trunk, and glossy dark green foliage. One of the most beautiful of the genus, its pendulous extremities adding greatly to its attractiveness.

T. Canadensis. The "Canadian Hemlock" or "Common Hemlock" of eastern N. America. 70–100 ft. A vigorous and very hardy species and the best to plant in calcareous soil.

T. C. pendula (*Sargentiana pendula*).

A very attractive variety for a large rock garden, with weeping branches completely hiding the interior of the tree.

TUB. Stone and lead ones can of course be bought, but very charming wooden ones can easily be made at home. Perhaps the most attractive of these are those made from an ordinary barrel by sawing it in half. By selecting barrels of different sizes, tubs for different positions may be made. These, although varying in size, will be in perfect harmony with each other, and, according to their surroundings, may be creosoted, or painted a suitable colour, such as dark green, with the hoops black, or left as they are. Others, of different shapes, square, hexagonal, etc., can be constructed of other wood such as oak or teak, or even from sugar boxes.

The flowers in the tub may be changed from time to time as the seasons alter. Those which look particularly well are King of Denmark Geraniums, Verbenas, Tulips, Fuchsias, Calceolarias, Hydrangeas, and Agapanthus. Palms and standard trees are widely grown in tubs. So also are specimens of topiary. One advantage of a tub is that plants which are not quite hardy can be grown in it, as it can be taken to sheltered quarters during cold weather.

Flowers in tubs should always be kept well watered — all tubs should have a drainage hole in the bottom — and the soil should be changed periodically.

TULIP (*Tulipa*). Liliaceæ. Hardy bulbs, not British, although there are a few varieties now growing almost wild here. The tulip first reached Europe as a garden flower from Turkey, and is probably of Persian origin.

Modern garden tulips are almost hybrids, their exact origin is somewhat doubtful.

The chief classifications are as follows:

Single Early Tulips.—These are the first to flower and are the ones most used for formal bedding schemes. These tulips are also the best for forcing into early flowers for decoration at Christmas-time and in early January. One of the best-known varieties is *Keizerskroon*, the common scarlet and yellow tulip.

Double Early Tulips.—There is also a double tulip which flowers early, and which, because of its double habit is even more lasting as a bedding flower than the single variety. But, though the flowers last longer, they are actually not so beautiful, and the majority of them are not so brilliant in colour, as the singles. The best-known variety of this type is *Murillo*, a pinkish-white double tulip.

Cottage Tulips, sometimes called *May Flowering Tulips.*—These are more showy

Breeder Tulips are similar to Darwins, being also tall and substantial and mostly self-coloured. They are generally sweetly scented, and for the most part are of bronze, purple or buff colouring. The *Bizarres* and *Bybloemens* are the "broken" forms of Breeder tulips, with "feathered" or "flamed" petals.

Parrot Tulips have the rather curious

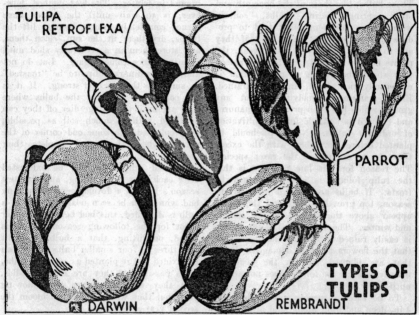

TULIPA RETROFLEXA

PARROT

DARWIN

TYPES OF TULIPS

REMBRANDT

The modern Tulips are now obtainable in various types, quite distinct in character. They also flower at different times, the last to bloom being the Darwins.

than the early singles on account of their tall stems. These again can be obtained in double or single varieties.

The Darwin Tulips are the most popular of all. The stems are from 24–30 in. high and the flowers are globe-shaped, with rounded petals, and rather substantial in appearance. Amongst them are found tulips of almost every colour, except a clear yellow.

The Rembrandt Tulips are exactly similar to Darwins except that the colours have "broken," that is to say, instead of being of one colour the flowers are sometimes "feathered" or "flamed." (For distinction between feathered and flamed *see* diagram.)

and fantastic flowers with large untidy petals broken or fringed at the edge. Until recently, they have been inclined to be dwarf, and to have rather weak stems, but this fault is being overcome by modern hybridists. As the flowers are particularly showy and brilliant, there is probably a big future of popularity in front of this race.

Lily-flowered Tulips are the result of a cross between the Tulip *retroflexa* and the Darwin tulip. The shape of the flower is particularly charming, being, as its name suggests, somewhat like the shape of a trumpet lily.

Bunch-flowered Tulips are also appearing in catalogues. Some of the wild species of tulips habitually have two or three flowers on a stem instead of the single flower head which is most common, and the new bunch-flowered varieties have been obtained by crossing with these species.

The cultivation of most of the garden tulips is similar. The novice first receives a tulip in the form of a bulb, which is almost similar to the bulb of the onion. These bulbs, like those of the hyacinth and other spring-flowering bulbs, contain within them sufficient plant food to produce flowers for one season, but if they are to flower again year after year, the plants need extra food, and for this reason they should be grown in ground that is moderately rich, light, and well drained. Fresh manure is inadvisable, but any ground which has been previously manured and cropped is suitable for the cultivation of ordinary tulips. No tulip should be planted before November, with the exception of one or two of the rarer species. The reason for this late planting is that the tulip foliage is easily damaged by frosts. If bulbs are planted early in the season, top growth begins and the leaves appear above the surface of the soil in mid-winter. The appearance of the foliage is easily ruined by frosts, and it may be that the flowers are also damaged. Bulbs that are planted late in the year are usually safe, as the foliage does not appear until early spring.

To be sure of success, plant the bulbs 4 in. deep and 6 in. apart, and after planting them put a mulch of well-decayed manure or coconut fibre all over the surface of the bed. This will protect any shoots which venture to come above the soil in winter time. If the soil is inclined to be heavy, a little sand at the base of the bulb at planting time will be of assistance, and the easiest way to provide this is to cover the surface of the flower-bed with an inch depth of sand before planting is begun.

As the holes are made, either with the dibber or trowel, a little of the sand will trickle into each hole and the bulb will rest on this, and thus perfect drainage immediately under the bulbs will be ensured. Tulips do not need any support as the stems should hold the flowers erect without any artificial aid.

Tulips should always be lifted annually (except in the case of certain species), as if they are left in the ground, they tend to begin a new season's growth too early, and may be damaged by frost. At the same time certain of the bulbs, for instance, the Darwin and late-flowering tulips, do not harm if left for three years, so long as care is taken to keep them away from frosts if their leaves come above the ground in winter. The best method, however, is to wait until the leaves have turned completely brown, then to lift the tulips, dry them in the sun, clean them, and store them in a cool, airy shed until planting times comes again. But do not allow the ordinary tulips to be "roasted" in sunshine that is over-strong. If it is not convenient to leave the bulbs where they are until the foliage dies off they can be lifted with as much soil as possible, and replanted into some odd corner of the garden where they can complete their growth.

The old tulip bulb will be exhausted after each year of flowering, and the new season's bulb is a development of the tiny bud which can be seen near the base if a bulb is dissected, this bud being the flower shoot for the following season. If it is found, on lifting, that a bulb has split into three or four smaller bulbs, these can be divided and re-planted as separate bulbs. It is possible, if they are much smaller, that they will not flower the following year, but they will probably all bloom the second year afterwards.

TULIPA. *See* TULIP.

TULIP TREE. *See* LIRIODENDRON.

TUNBRIDGE FILMY FERN. *See* HYMENOPHYLLUM.

TUNICA (tu-ni-ca. Caryophylleæ). The only grown species of this genus of hardy annual and perennial herbs, is *T. saxifraga*, a desirable dwarf perennial, with numerous pale rose flowers. Suitable for edgings to beds and borders, and for crevices in walls and rockeries.

Propagate by seeds sown in the desired flowering position in April, or by division, in spring. Plant in ordinary soil.

TURF. *See* LAWNS.

TURKEY'S BEARD. *See* XEROPHYLLUM.

TURNIP. *Brassica campestris Rapa.* Although not regarded as a necessity, turnips are very much used to vary the menu. There is a fairly constant demand especially for the early crops.

Culture.—The chief point to aim at in the culture of the turnip is a succession of crops, as it soon becomes stringy and uneatable.

For the first crop sow in January under glass on a specially prepared bed. Gentle heat only is necessary as over-forcing is not successful.

Prepare a bed for the seeds from one that has previously been used for radishes or from the compost advised for turnips. The seed may be broadcast or sown in groups of two or three in holes, 1 in. deep and 4 in. apart. When the seedlings appear they are thinned out to one in each hole. If a frame is not available a hot-bed is prepared by throwing out half a spit of soil and replacing it with hot manure which is trodden down firm to a depth of 1 ft. The soil which was thrown out is replaced and the seed sown 5 in. apart, rolled in and the bed well watered. The bed is covered with mats until the seed has germinated when the mats can be left off and are only used to screen the beds when the weather is cold. For the first crops sown out of doors choose a warm sheltered position. Sow at intervals of 3 to 5 weeks to obtain a succession of crops.

For the later sowings a north or east border is better, as, if exposed to too much heat the plants are dried up. Sow in rows about 1 ft. apart and later thin out the plants to 6 in. apart.

VARIETIES.

Early Red Milan, Early White Milan. For later crops, Early Snowball, Early Six Weeks, Red Globe.

For winter, Chirk Castle Blackstone, Golden Ball.

For "Tops," Green Globe.

Soil. — Turnips thrive best on moist friable sandy loam but they will grow on any soil. For early crops the lighter soil is better, while for the others a cool stable will be found suitable.

For the winter crop sow in July and continue until September and seed may be broadcast after potatoes have been lifted.

The soil must always be kept moist, and where it is possible to water in dry weather, this should be done. For "tops"

which are sold as greens in spring when other green vegetables are scarce, sow in September in rows 2 ft. apart and leave the plants unthinned.

Storing.—This is rarely practised but may be done by cutting off the tops and placing the roots in small heaps and covering them with straw and earth in the same way as is done with potatoes in a clamp.

Manures.—Lime should be present in

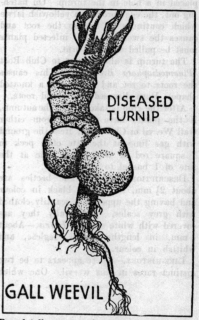

DISEASED TURNIP

GALL WEEVIL

Round galls are sometimes seen on the roots of turnips. This is due to a little insect which sets up irritation and causes swelling.

the soil and a supply of phosphates must be provided. When grown as catch crops the plants benefit by the preparation of the soil for the main crop. When the soil is very poor natural manure at the rate of 10 tons to an acre must be added.

Pests.—The worst pest is the Turnip Fly or Beetle (*Halticanemorum*) which feeds upon the leaves of the plants. They are small, black, and lay white eggs which mature in a week and then pupate in the soil. The best controls are to keep the land clean by clearing out weeds and rubbish, to dig deeply in winter to bury the pupæ and to dust with soot or lime when the seedlings are damp with dew. If a nitrogenous manure is applied, the leaves will grow so quickly that the beetles will not have time to injure them, as once turnip plants are beyond the seedling stage they will not attack them.

TURNIP GALL WEEVIL (*Ceutor-hynchus pleurostigma*). This produces swellings on cabbages and turnips. The beetle is black and lays eggs which are placed in a hole in the turnip. On hatching out, the eggs produce a yellowish larvæ which continues to live in the root and causes the swelling. All infected plants must be pulled up and burnt.

The turnip is also subject to Club Root (*Plasmodiophora Brassicæ*). This causes the roots to rot and swell into a knotted shape. Burn diseased stems and roots.

After the crop is taken up in the autumn, if the plants have suffered from either Gall Weevil or Club Root, dress the ground with gas lime at the rate of 1 peck to 1 square rod or with quick lime at the rate of 1 bushel to a rod.

DESCRIPTION. *Adult.*—The beetles are about 2½ mm. in length, black in colour and having the upper side scantily clothed with grey scales. Ventrally they are covered with white scales. *Larvæ.*—About 4 mm. in length, curved, legless, and whitish in colour.

LIFE-HISTORY.—There appears to be two distinct races in this weevil. One which appears in the spring lives solely upon charlock and does not attack cabbage or turnip, while the summer form causes the well-known marble-like growths on the roots of most cruciferæ but more especially turnips and cabbage. The life-history of this race is as follows. The beetles may be found first of all on any cruciferous flowers there may be. When these are finished they migrate to the young cabbage and turnip and there lay their eggs in incisions made by the female on the root. On hatching out, the larvæ feed upon the plant tissue, thus upsetting the flow of sap which causes the well-known swellings to appear. It is within this swelling or gall that the larvæ continue to live till late winter, when they eat their way out, pupate in the soil and hatch into a fresh generation of beetles in April.

METHODS OF CONTROL. — Destroy by burning all roots showing the typical gall-like growths. All attempts to kill the larva or repel the beetle have failed, though a partial control in the seed bed may be obtained by dusting with a mixture of one part soot and two of lime.

TURKEY OAK. *See* QUERCUS.

TURK'S CAP LILY (Lilium Martagon). *See* LILIES.

TURTLE HEAD. *See* CHELONE.

TWINFLOWER. *See* LINNÆA.

TWIN-LEAVED LILY OF THE VALLEY. *See* MAIANTHEMUM.

U

ULEX (ū-lex. Leguminosæ). Very spiny shrubs related to the brooms, and known as "Furze," "Gorse," or "Whin." They are found growing in poor dry soil in heather districts, or down land. Very valuable for covering dry banks, and for planting in stony ground. They are not satisfactory in rich soils, or in shady positions.

Propagate by seed sown singly in small pots, and the young plants put out in their permanent positions without repotting, as they are impatient of root disturbance.

SPECIES.

U. europæus. Europe, including Britain, where it abounds, 2–4 ft., occasionally higher. Flowers brilliant gold. At their best in April and May. It commences to bloom about February, and flowers appear intermittently for the greater part of the year.

U. e. flore pleno (plenus). Double-flowered Gorse. It is of interest to note that in this variety petals take the place of stamens. No seed is produced. The plant is increased by cuttings of current season's wood taken during August. They may be about 3 in. long, and placed in very sandy soil in a frame. When well rooted the young plants should be potted in small pots, and planted in their permanent positions during the winter. Award of Merit, R.H.S.

ULMUS (ŭl-mus. Urticaceæ). Elm. Deciduous trees of noble proportions, thriving in almost any kind of soil, and in the most exposed positions. They make good seaside trees and, with the exception of our native elm, are useful for street planting. Some of the variegated varieties are very handsome. The flowers are of no beauty.

Propagate by seed, which should be sown as soon as ripe. The named varieties are increased by grafting.

SPECIES.

U. americana. The White Elm of N. America is both handsome and rare, with large glossy green leaves. Up to 120 ft.

U. campestris. The English Elm. A most noble and beautiful tree in stature

and in richness of foliage. Attains a height of 120–150 ft. Probably the finest specimens are to be found in the rich moist soil of river valleys. It is generally regarded as a native of the southern parts of England, in spite of the fact that its seed is nearly always sterile. Some authorities are of opinion that it may be a hybrid from other native elms. The

URSINIA

The Ursinia is a new annual from The Cape, where it is known as "Jewel of the Veldt."

usual means of increase are by root-suckers and by layering.

U. montana (glabra). The "Wych" or "Scotch Elm," 100 ft. A very handsome tree with hazel-like leaves. Plentiful in Ireland and Scotland.

U. pendula. Very suitable for a lawn specimen.

U. stricta (cornubiensis). Cornish Elm, 80–100 ft. A slender, columnar, or pyramidal tree, admirably suited for street or avenue planting.

UMBELLULARIA (um-bel-u-lar'-ia. Lauraceæ). *Oreodaphne californica.* Californian Laurel, or Spice Bush. California and Oregon. An attractive evergreen shrub or small tree reaching to a height of 80 ft. in favoured parts of its native country. Handsome laurel-like leaves, 2–5 in. long, very aromatic when crushed. The flowers are yellowish, produced during April, and followed by pear-shaped, purplish fruits. Thrives in good garden soil with a little peat or leaf-mould added to give the plant a start.

Propagate by seed, layers and cuttings. It is best grown against a wall.

UMBRELLA FERN. *See* GLEICHENIA.

UMBRELLA LEAF. *See* DIPHYLLEIA.

UMBRELLA PINE. *See* SCIADOPITYS.

UMBRELLA PLANT. *See* CYPERUS.

UNIOLA (u-ni-o-la. Gramineæ). See Oat. Spike Grass. Hardy perennial grasses with flowers borne in large loose panicles in July and August.

Propagate by seeds or division and plant in any soil. Gather the flowers when almost open and dry for winter decoration.

SPECIES.

U. latifolia. U. paniculata.

UPRIGHTS. *See* PERGOLAS.

URCEOLINA (ur-se-o-li-na. Amaryllideæ). Golden Urn Flower. Drooping Urn Flower. Bulbous-rooted greenhouse plants. Pot up in February in a compost of 2 parts of loam to 1 of sand and a little bone meal. Increase by seeds sown in heat in March in well-drained pots of sandy loam or by offsets. Water freely during growth and keep the plants almost dry in winter. Give liquid manure when the flower spike is in evidence. Top dress and repot every three or four years.

SPECIES.

U. pendula (syn. *aurea*). Umbels of pendent green flowers. June.

URGINEA (ur-gin-e-a. Liliaceæ). Greenhouse bulbous plants. Plant in pots of well-drained loam and leaf-mould, and keep in the cool greenhouse.

Propagate by offsets.

SPECIES.

U. altissima. White. May. 3 ft.

U. maritima. White and purplish. Sea Onion.

URN. *See* VASE.

URSINIA (Compositæ). Half-hardy annual. Daisy-shaped flowers of rich orange-yellow with a beautiful ring of deep purple-black, carried on long, wiry stems. This plant, which comes from The Cape, has been re-introduced quite recently, and is much in vogue. The leaves are finely cut and decorative. Height, 12–15 in.

Cultivation.—Sow the seeds in January in gentle heat and, after germination, prick out into fresh boxes of soil when large enough. Pot on into 60-size pots in a compost of leaf-mould, loam and sand; flower in 48-size pots, using for the final pots a similar soil compost which is rather coarser and enriched with a sprinkling of some complete fertiliser. The plants require cool treatment as the season advances and plenty of sun, and can be transplanted to the open as bedding plants if desired. They flower during June and July.

Species.—*Ursinia anethoides* is the most common and easily obtainable.

UTRICULARIA (u-trick-u-lar-i-a. Lentibulariaceæ). Bladder Wort. This is an interesting genus of insectivorous aquatic, terrestrial or epiphytal plants. The leaves have tiny pitcher-like formations, which have valve-like lids that open inwards to admit insects but cannot open outwards to eject them, so that the insects are assimilated by juices into the food of the plant.

Propagate by division, by winter buds when these are formed, and by separation of the tubercles. Grow the aquatics in ponds, and the terrestrial species in baskets of sphagnum and fibrous peat, in the stove or greenhouse.

SPECIES.

U. montana. White flowers with yellow disk. Stove.

U. vulgaris. Yellow. Floating.

UVULARIA (u-vu-lar-i-a. Liliaceæ). Bell Wort. Hardy herbaceous perennials that are propagated by division in spring or October, and grow in moist peat or sandy loam.

SPECIES.

U. grandiflora. Yellow May. 1 ft.

U. sessilifolia. Greenish-yellow. May. 1 ft.

V

VACCINIUM (vak-sin'-i-um. Vaccini-aceæ). A genus of hardy evergreen and deciduous shrubs, valuable on account of their rich autumn foliage and berries of varied colours. Flowers bell-shaped, white to rosy red.

Culture.—Plant in sun or shade, in a moist peaty soil, or a sandy loam with peat or leaf-mould added, moisture is important. No lime.

Propagate by seed which may be treated like Rhododendron seed. Cuttings of half-ripened wood in July, in sandy peat and placed in bottom heat.

SPECIES, ALL OF WHICH ARE DECIDUOUS UNLESS OTHERWISE STATED.

V. Arctostaphylos. Caucasian Whortle-berry. A vigorous shrub up to 10 ft. Leaves 2½–4 in. long, turning to a rich red in autumn. Flowers bell-shaped, white, tinted crimson.

V. bracteatum (Andromeda chinensis). Japan and China, 3–5 ft. Flowers white, freely produced, even on quite small plants. Leaves red, ageing to dark green.

V. canadense. The Canadian Blueberry. A dense, dwarf shrub about 1 ft. Flowers white, tinged pink. Berries dark blue.

V. corymbosum. The Swamp Blueberry of eastern N. America. An exceptionally fine Vaccinium, if not the finest. It is a deciduous shrub from 4–12 ft. high, with oval leaves, turning to a brilliant vivid red in autumn. Flowers white, lily-of-the-valley-like, produced in great profusion during May.

V. glauco-album (Himalayas). An ever-green species 2–4 ft. high. Flowers pinkish-white during May and June, followed by black edible berries. The under-surface of the leaves and the berries are covered with a vivid blue-white bloom. Rather tender.

V. Myrtillus. Our native Whortleberry or Bilberry.

V. ovatum (N. America), 10–12 ft. Ever-green. Flowers white, lily-of-the-valley-like in September. In spring the young growth is very attractive. Berries black, which very seldom ripen in this country owing to the plant flowering so late in the season.

VALERIAN, RED. *See* CENTRANTHUS.

VALERIANA (va-le-ri-a-na. Vale-rianeæ), Valerian. A large genus of hardy and half-hardy perennials, shrubs and sub-shrubs quite distinct from the Greek Valerian (Polemonium). Very few of the species are worth cultivating.

The Erica family are moorland plants. They like sandy soil with peat or leaf-mould. By selecting suitable varieties they can be obtained in bloom throughout the year. (See Erica).

Propagate the perennials by seeds, or division, and the others by cuttings placed under glass. Plant in ordinary soil in a warm dry sunny position.

The plant commonly known as Red Valerian is really *Centranthus Ruber.* See CENTRANTHUS.

SPECIES.

V. officinalis is the common Valerian (All Heal), largely used medicinally for nervous complaints. Cats are very fond of chewing the roots and leaves. With its panicles of white flowers it makes a fine wild garden plant. 3 ft.

V. Phu aurea, the Golden Cretan Spike-nard, has golden leaves that are its chief attraction, and white flowers. 3 ft. This and *montana,* a dwarf species suitable for the rockery, with shiny leaves and rosy pink flowers in spikes, are the best of the garden plants.

VALERIANELLA. *See* CORN SALAD.

VALLOTA (val-lo-ta. Amaryllidaceæ). Scarborough Lily. Greenhouse bulbous plants that are useful for the cool house. S. Africa, 1774.

Culture.—Compost: equal parts loam, leaf-mould and sand. Repot June, but

VALERIAN

A plant for chalky soils is the Valerian in its pink, white or scarlet forms. It occurs on tops of walls in the West country.

this should only be done when necessary. To top-dress annually with above compost is much better, as plants like to become well pot-bound. New bulbs should be potted in spring Water freely during growing period, copiously during the hot days of summer, very little in the winter, only just enough to keep plant going until new growth commences. Winter temperature, 40°.

Propagate by offsets when repotting. It is a good plan to buy one or two new bulbs annually.

SPECIES.

V. purpurea (red); its varieties, *magni-*

fica (red), and *major* (red) are larger than the species; its variety, *minor* (red), is dwarf.

VANCOUVERIA. (van-kou-ver-i-a. Berberideæ). A genus of only two hardy perennials that are propagated by division and grow in moist sandy peat.

V. hexandra. Lilac or white flowers in May. The prettier of the species.

VANILLA (van-nil-la. Orchidaceæ). Stove orchids that climb by means of their clinging roots and twining stems.

Propagate by divisions or cuttings of the stems in 2 or 3 in. lengths embedded in sphagnum and peat, which make the

VALLOTA

The Scarborough Lily or Vallota is a useful plant for the sunny window.

best rooting medium, and allow the stems to twine on large poles. Water plentifully from March to October, but moderately during the winter.

SPECIES.

V. aromatica. White. Summer. 12 ft.

V. planifolia. Greenish-white. Summer. 20 ft.

VASES. The meaningless introduction

of vases is to be avoided in a garden, but rightly used they may be a source of interest. Architecturally they can be important features, and when filled with flowers such as geraniums they make delightful pictures. The chief positions for them are upon pillars (or pedestals), walls, terraces, and at the edge of pools. They are often used as terminals to piers or as ornaments in the small garden. The materials most often used to make them are lead, stone, or earthenware. Care should be taken in selecting vases to choose a non-porous material that will not dry out the soil, and ample space should be allowed for plant growth. Lead vases, although more expensive than stone or earthenware ones, are worth the extra money, as after a short time they take on a delightful greeny-grey hue. Plain earthenware vases look very well where the house is of red brick, whereas Portland stone blends well with roughcast or light-coloured houses. Flatter, saucer-shaped vases are often called tayzæ (*sing.* tayza).

Fill the vases with good soil and keep them well watered. Change the soil each year if possible and apply a general fertiliser to the plants in the growing season.

A series of vases in a pale shade planted with spring-blooming bulbs is very pleasing, and makes an interesting feature. Very profusely ornamented vases should only be used in rare cases.

VEGETABLE MARROW (*Cucurbita Pepo ovifera*). Although not an essential crop, the marrow is a useful additional vegetable and does yeoman service in covering the unsightly patches in the garden, since it can be trained to trail over fences, up the sides of houses and over rubbish heaps.

Culture.—The chief cultural requirements of the marrow are rich well-drained soil with plenty of moisture and sunshine. The main crop can be grown on ground from which an earlier crop has been lifted, and which was generously manured. If the ground has had no previous crop in the same season, prepare for the marrow about two months before planting-time as although a gross feeder, the roots should not come into direct contact with manure.

Dig out holes about a yard square and a foot in depth, or make furrows a foot wide and of the same depth. Put in hot half-decayed manure to a depth of from 6–9 in. and cover with the soil that was excavated. This will form a ridge on which the plants can be set. On very light soils the furrows should be deeper, so that when filled in, the level of the prepared ground is below the level of the surround, so that in dry weather any moisture is conserved near the plants.

Seed Sowing.—For planting out at the end of May, the correct time, sow seed in heat in April. Choose plump seeds and insert them, broad end downwards, in pots containing good turfy loam with some manure and sand. Plunge the pots up to the rim in a hot bed, or keep them in the greenhouse or in a cold frame. If these are not available keep the pots in a corner by a window, but growth will be slightly retarded if germinated in a hot bed, place in a cold frame at the beginning of May to harden-off. The seedlings will be ready to plant in their permanent position by the third week in May. Water the plants the day before they are to be transplanted. Set them about a yard apart and keep the ball of soil intact round each plant. Cover this ball of soil with about an inch of new soil. For a week or so after planting out, each plant should be protected at night with a hand-light, cloche, or even a basket. For the next two or three weeks some kind of covering material should be kept nearby, so that if the weather becomes cold the plants can be covered, as a degree or two of frost would prove fatal to unprotected plants.

For a later crop the seed can be sown in the open. The method of preparing the soil is the same, and the seeds are sown in the middle of May, two or three close together at intervals of 3 ft. Cover the patches of seeds with flower pots inverted. Once the first leaves appear remove the flower-pots by day, but replace them at night for a week or two. When the strength of the seedlings can be determined, thin out to one in each patch.

While the plants are growing, the soil should be kept free of weeds and moist by a mulch of manure. Pinch the end of each leader when the plants are growing freely, to encourage side shoots. When grown on a refuse heap this must be well matured and turned over before use. It should consist of the sweepings of the garden, from lawns, or weeds and other decayed vegetable matter. The seedlings

VENIDIUM

Venidium, an annual with yellow and black flowers, recently introduced from The Cape. It is best treated as a half-hardy annual.

can be planted out in this in the same way as in the beds, and the shoots allowed to trail over it.

Setting the Fruit.—Artificial pollination is not necessary, but if it is found that the fruits are reluctant to set, copious supplies of water will usually help to remedy the defect.

Fertilisers.—Soot water is of course invaluable, while nitrate of soda at the rate of ½ oz. to a square yard and a little guano dissolved in water, are excellent.

If needed for seed allow one marrow to develop to its full size but cut off the rest before they are fully grown, as by this means the crop can be doubled, and the

plant is not exhausted by producing seed.

Pests.—The plants are sometimes attacked by mildew in autumn but seem to suffer little from its depredations. Black fly appear occasionally, when the plants are in the young stages, and should be dusted with tobacco powder and washed off after a few hours.

VARIETIES.

Custard, Feltham, Prolific, Long Green, Long White, Moore's Cream, Pen-y-Byd.

VELLA (vel-la. Cruciferæ). Cress Rocket. Evergreen or deciduous hardy and half-hardy flowering shrubs.

Propagate by cuttings of immature wood inserted in sandy soil under a bell-glass with gentle bottom heat. Plant at any time from October to November in ordinary light garden soil.

SPECIES.

V. pseudo-cytisus. Purple with yellow spur. April to May. Choose a sheltered position in a fairly dry border for this species. 1–2 ft.

V. spinosa with yellow and brown flowers in May and June will do well on the rockery. 1 ft.

VELTHEIMIA (vel-tim-i-a. Liliaceæ). Greenhouse bulbous plants. Soil: two parts of sandy with one of well-decayed manure and a little sand. Increase by offsets or by leaves taken off close to the bulb and inserted in sandy soil. They make quite good window plants during the summer and can be kept in a cold frame for the rest of the year. Water well in the flowering season but little when the leaves have died down. Winter temperature, 40°–50°; summer, 55°–65°.

SPECIES.

V. glauca. Flesh-pink flowers in March. 2 ft.

V. viridifolia. Yellowish-red. August. 2 ft.

VENIDIUM (ven-id-e-um. Compositæ). South Africa. *V. calendulaceum,* a half-hardy annual, is the best for general purposes, as it is so easy to grow and flowers over a long period, the orange-yellow flowers are freely produced, and last well in water. The newer *V. fastuosum* is much coarser growing, and the flowers are much larger, orange-yellow in colour, and with a jet black disk. They need staking to prevent them being bent by winds, as the stems are hollow and easily kinked. Sow in April under glass, plant out in June, in a fairly light sandy soil in a sunny position.

VENUS' FLY TRAP. *See* DIONÆA.

VERATRUM (ver-a-trum. Liliaceæ). False Hellebore. Hardy herbaceous perennials that are valued in spring for their decorative foliage, and for rather less attractive flowers in summer. The plants are poisonous, and should not be grown where children or animals are likely to come in contact with them. They are most beautiful when grown in as rich a soil as possible in a shady position, and are propagated by summer-sown seed or by division in autumn or spring.

SPECIES.

V. album, the White Hellebore, blooms from July onwards and provides the powder used for destroying caterpillars. It has dense spikes of flowers and large handsome plaited leaves. 3–4 ft.

V. nigrum has narrower foliage and blackish-purple flowers in racemes 2–3 ft. long. 4 ft.

V. viride resembles *album*, but has greenish flowers.

VERBASCUM (ver-bas-cum. Scrophularineæ). Mullein. Herbaceous plants of stately growth that are useful for borders or the wild garden. Mostly biennials with a few perennials. Once planted they care for themselves and spring up year after year like Foxgloves. Freely planted in bold groups they make a good display. The showy spikes of flowers last for a long time on the plants. All the species may be propagated by seeds, the perennials by division also, and the sub-shrubs by cuttings. Any common soil suits them.

The best of the perennial border species are: *V. Chaixii*, with branching spikes of yellow, purple-centred flowers, 6–10 in.; *V. cupreum*, a beautiful hybrid from *V. phœniceum* and *V. ovalifolium*, with coppery-coloured flowers, 3 ft.; *V. nigrum*, yellow; and *V. phœniceum*, with red, white, violet and lilac varieties, 3 in.; *V. Blattaria*, a large-flowered species; *V. gnaphaloides*, with woolly white leaves and yellow flowers; *V. olympicum*, as its name suggests, a stately plant smothered with golden flowers; and *V. phlomoides*, "Woolly Mullein" with very woolly

leaves and stem covered with large yellow flowers, are the best of the biennials.

Good new hybrids are Caledonia, sulphur-coloured flowers; Cotswold Beauty, pale bronze with lilac anthers; Cotswold Queen, reddish-fawn; Miss Wilmott, huge spikes of white flowers, 6 ft.; and Gainsborough, with soft yellow flowers.

V. thapsus is the familiar Aaron's Rod, a

VERBASCUM

Mullein or Verbascum are plants that thrive in chalky soils.

yellow-flowered plant with downy leaves, 6 ft.

Verbascum Phœniceum is often used as a pot plant for the greenhouse. The flowers are carried in long graceful spikes and are of soft pastel shades of white, pink, salmon and violet.

Cultivation.—Seeds sown in July will produce flowering plants the following season. Sowing may be made in boxes of open soil in a cold frame and the seedlings may be pricked out when large enough. They may be potted into 60–size pots when a rosette of 4 leaves has been made and they may be flowered in 48's or 32's to make useful plants. The compost should be open and well drained, being composed of loam, leaf-mould, old manure and sand.

VERBENA (ver-be-na. Verbenaceæ). Vervain. Half-hardy annuals, biennials and perennials that are excellent border or bedding plants. Formerly cultivated chiefly for florists and in pots, but now recognised as of great garden value on account of the lengthy period of blooming.

Culture.—Propagate by seeds sown in

VERBENA

The annual Verbena has bright colours and produces more flowers if pegged down during growth.

March or April in a warm frame or a hot bed and plant out the seedlings towards the end of May. The plants will then flower in the same year. For named varieties cuttings should be struck preferably in spring after the plants have been wintered in the greenhouse. Take off the young shoots and peg them down in a frame. Plant out in mid-June 10 in. apart. If struck in autumn they are best left in the cutting pots until February. Only the hardiest species may be increased by division. For pot-culture use a compost of sandy loam and leaf-

mould with a little manure. Pot up in March in 5 in. pots and stop back the shoots to make bushy growth. A packet of mixed seed will usually give a great variety of colours and really provides the most satisfactory method of growing these plants, as the flowers are beautiful the first year and are spared the risks of disease and pests during the winter. The beds must be well drained and the soil light and rich. In a sunny position the plants will cover the ground with deep green foliage and produce a profusion of lovely fragrant flowers for three months. The colours blend well and a mixed bed is most effective.

Species.—Few species are grown as the named varieties have superseded them in favour; however, *V. aubletia*, Rose Vervain, a hardy biennial with loose heads of rosy-crimson flowers, 12 in., and *V. chamædrifolia*, a creeping sub-shrub with scarlet heads of flowers which requires a warm corner, are still grown. These with *phlogiflora* and *teucrioides* (species not now grown) are the parents of the hybrids used for bedding.

V. venosa is hardier than the hybrids and comes readily from seed. It has lilac or purplish flowers and makes a pretty edging.

Miss Willmott is the best known of the named varieties, with pink flowers, but blue, white, scarlet and rose kinds are all offered by seedsmen.

VERBENA, LEMON SCENTED. *See* LIPPIA CITRIODORA.

VERONICA (ver-on-i-ka. Scrophulariaceæ). Speedwell. After Saint Veronica. A vast family of ornamental evergreen flowering shrubs, some members small to the point of invisibility, and trees forming bushes 20 ft. high, and many intermediate sizes. With the exception of *V. elliptica*, which is found also in S. America, all are natives of New Zealand, where they are known as "Koromiko."

Culture.—Plant in April or September in well-drained garden soil in a somewhat sheltered sunny position. Under such conditions many species will stand uninjured through ordinary winters. The only pruning necessary is to cut hard back every few years, and trim to shape annually. Soil appears to be a matter of indifference in that any ordinary ground will grow them without difficulty.

Propagation is by cuttings of matured wood taken in August, and placed in a close frame. The young plants should be pinched occasionally, but not after June.

SPECIES AND HYBRIDS.

V. Andersonii. A hybrid between *V. salicifolia* + *V. speciosa.* Vigorous, flowers violet-blue, paleing to white. Rather tender.

V. anomala, 3–5 ft. Flowers white to pink, during June and July.

V. Autumn Glory. A low-growing, shrubby hybrid with leathery, dark green leaves and deep purple flowers. A hard winter will sometimes kill it. It is easily grown from cuttings of which a supply should be rooted under glass yearly. It flowers from autumn till winter. 1 ft.

V. buxifolia. The leaves are like magnified box-tree leaves, the habit semi-prostrate, the flowers white and unexciting. The decorative value of the plant is in the foliage. 6 in. New Zealand.

V. cupressoides. Resembles a miniature cupressus. The plant is sweetly scented; the flowers inconspicuous. Grows to 2 ft. eventually. New Zealand.

V. Hulkeana. A favourite species, and a plant of great merit. 3–4 ft. high. Leaves an attractive shade of green. Flowers of a delicate lavender shade, very freely borne in panicles up to 18 in. long. They should be removed immediately after flowering. This very beautiful and distinct Veronica is, unfortunately, very tender, and is only suitable for mild districts. It is a magnificent wall shrub.

V. Traversi. 4–5 ft. A very hardy species, with white flowers, and purple-brown anthers. It is a shapely shrub, and excellent as a lawn specimen. Blooms very freely in late summer.

VERVAIN. *See* VERBENA.

VESICARIA (ve-si-ka-ri-a. Cruciferæ). Bladder Pod. Hardy perennial and annual herbs that are suitable for the border or the rockery, and have peculiar bladder-like seed pods. Increase by seeds and the perennials by division, and grow in ordinary soil.

SPECIES.

V. gracilis. Yellow, June. 6 in. Annual.

V. utriculata. Yellow. April–June. 1 ft.

VIBURNUM (vi-bur'-num. Caprifoliaceæ). Deciduous and evergreen hardy shrubs or small trees (rarely), with single leaves, and white and pinkish flowers borne in clusters.

Culture.—They thrive in deep, well-drained loamy soil, in sunny positions. The deciduous species should be planted in October, November, or March. The evergreen section is best planted in May or

VERONICA

There are mauve, blue, purple, pink and white varieties of Veronica. All will grow by the seaside.

September. They should be trimmed into shape annually, the old wood of the deciduous species cut out in July, and in May the evergreen species should be treated similarly.

Propagate by cuttings of ripe wood in July or August, and if possible, placed in bottom heat. Also by layering in October.

SPECIES.

V. Carlesii (Korea), 3–4 ft. Deciduous. A very beautiful shrub bearing clusters of white fragrant flowers in April. Quite hardy when established, but needs a little nursing while young. Thrives remarkably well in seaside districts. Cuttings taken in June and placed in heat root readily. It may also be rooted from leaf cuttings taken in June and put in sand, and kept close. But grafted plants are found to give the best results. Award of Garden Merit, R.H.S.

V. Henryi. Evergreen. China, 10 ft. and over. Berries bright red, turning to black, very freely produced.

One of the best of recent shrubs is Viburnum Carlesii. It is sweetly scented.

V. Opulus. Deciduous. Native "Guelder Rose" of the British Isles and Europe, 10–15 ft. Exceedingly beautiful when laden with its numerous bright red berries and showy crimson foliage in autumn.

V. O. sterile. The well-known "Guelder Rose" or "Snowball Tree." One of the most beautiful of all hardy flowering shrubs, but owing to the flowers being sterile, it lacks berry beauty.

V. Tinus. Evergreen. Mediterranean region. Generally known as "Laurustinus," and deservedly popular. It produces many clusters of rosy buds and flowers, which age to white during the dull months of the year. The buds usually begin to

unfold about November, and the plants continue in bloom up to April.

V. t. plicatum. Sterile. The Japanese Snowball Tree. Quite hardy when established. Young plants may need protection during the first winter. Its globose inflorescences 3 or 4 in. across, composed of pure white flowers, are very attractive during June and help to place this fine Viburnum in the first rank of deciduous flowering shrubs. It should always be included in the first dozen.

VICTORIA (vik-tor-ia. Nymphæaceæ). Royal Water Lily. *V. regia* is a handsome stove aquatic with bronzy-green leaves

Viburnum Opulus—the common Guelder Rose— has white snowball-like flowers in spring.

that float on the surface of the water, and are from 4–6 ft. across, and fine purplish or rose flowers that are about 1 ft. across.

Propagate by seeds in a pot of loam in a tank, in a temperature of not less than 85°. Sow in January and prick out seedlings in May in a temperature of 80°. The variety *Trickeri* is hardier and will do quite well in a greenhouse.

VINCA (vin-ka. Apocynaceæ). *Vinculum*, a chain or bond, from the tough long shoots. Periwinkle. Evergreen trailing shrub, thriving in ordinary garden soil in sun or shade. Easily increased by dividing the old plants, or by cuttings.

SPECIES.

V. major. Larger Periwinkle. Central and S. Europe. Although found growing wild in this country it is not a native. Flowers bright blue from May to September. Thrives in half-shady positions, and makes a good ground cover; but it flowers more freely in sunny positions.

V. m. elegantissima. Leaves margined golden yellow.

V. minor. Lesser Periwinkle. Europe. Flowers small, bright blue, produced from April until autumn.

VINE. *See* VITIS.

VINE MILDEW (*Uncinula spiralis*). In the early summer a greyish mildew may appear on the leaves of vines; this quckly spreads if not checked and covers the shoots and even young fruit. In the autumn small black pustules are formed; these contain the wintering spores. In the spring the pustules break up, liberating the spores which, falling on the foliage, give rise to fresh mildew.

METHODS OF CONTROL.—Either dust with flowers of sulphur as soon as the leaves are full grown, again when the fruit is beginning to set and later when the fruit is swelling, or spray with a solution of potassium sulphide at the periods suggested for dusting.

VIOLA (Violaceæ). Violet, Tufted Pansy, Pansy, Heart's Ease. Hardy perennial herbs, useful in borders and in rock gardens. The genus viola includes the garden pansies, and violets, as well as the plants more commonly known as violas.

Cultivation of violas and pansies.—One of the most common questions with regard to violas and pansies is, what is the difference between a pansy and a viola. The true pansy has a pansy "face." It belongs to the free-growing and free-flowering species. The show pansies should have circular blooms, flat, smooth without any wave in the edges, with thick velvety petals overlapping each other. A dark circular blotch appears in the centre of the blooms and there is usually an orange eye. There is also a dark narrow belt to the three lower petals which should be the same colour as the upper petals. The diameter of the blooms should be at least 1½ in. The fancy pansies are somewhat similar, but have wavy or crinkled edges. The tufted pansies are the class commonly called violas, and are really hybrids between the ordinary pansy and the viola cornuta. The blooms are similar and more numerous than those of the ordinary pansy and the colours are very varied. In habit the plants are dwarf, but not so spreading and straggly as the pansy proper.

Violas are very accommodating perennial plants. They are in bloom from early spring until September or October, and are suitable for both exhibition and garden decoration.

In cultivating for exhibition, the soil should be deeply dug in the autumn, at least two spits deep, and at the same time some well-rotted manure should be worked into the bottom spit. Bone meal is also useful, especially where stable manure is difficult to obtain, and this should be incorporated also when digging is done. The ground should be left rough until the spring, when it can be given a further dressing of artificial fertiliser, and the beds raked over ready for planting.

Over-feeding should be avoided, particularly in the case of violas which are being grown partly for garden decoration and which are to be cultivated for several years, but small doses of artificial fertiliser during the growing season may be used with advantage. Begin planting in March as soon as the weather is favourable.

Exhibition violas as a rule are too straggly in growth to make good border plants, and those who are growing for exhibition usually grow their show violas in beds by themselves, making each bed about 3 ft. wide, and setting the plants 10–12 in. apart each way.

The plants are also staked to prevent them being broken by the wind, and to keep the blooms clean. The number of growths to each plant should be restricted to three, side shoots being removed as they appear.

About three weeks before a show, the

plants should be stripped of all blooms and buds, and if green fly or other insects are present, no matter in how small a number, the plants should be sprayed with a good insecticide. The next blooms to appear will be on the small side; the following batch will give the blooms required for exhibition.

The following is a suitable method for staging. In a class calling for six blooms of one variety to be staged in a vase, a small tin receptacle, such as a child's sand pail painted green, is very suitable. This is filled with damp sand, the blooms are then secured by a piece of foliage, and inserted in glass tubes which have previously been filled with water. These tubes should be set into the sand, say three 7 in. tubes in the back row, two 5 in. tubes in the middle row and one 3 in. tube in the front row.

The foliage used need not be of the variety staged. It is generally advisable to grow a few old plants from which to pick foliage for use at the shows.

The correct angle at which these tubes should be set in the sand is at a slanting angle, as it must always be remembered that the judge requires to see the blooms looking up at him, as it were. The novice will gain from experience in this matter.

Among the chief points in a standard to be aimed at are:

Colour.—The colour should be clear and bright, without any semblance of a blotch.

Size.—No bloom should be considered fit for award under 2½ in. in diameter.

Substance.—The petals should be thick and fleshy.

Shape and quality.—The contour of the bloom should be as near circular as possible round a centre at a point where the eyebrows meet. It should be free from any serrature, notch or unevenness; the petals lying close and evenly on each other. The bottom petal should be large and full, occupying nearly half the bloom and well covering the side petals, which should be well rounded and meet at the shoulders above the eye. The top petals should be full and evenly proportioned.

Eye.—This should be of bright gold or orange colour and be situated almost in the centre of the flower. It should be small, round and clearly defined, without running into the ground colour.

To secure the best results, cuttings of exhibition violas must be taken each year for the following year's plants. This may be done from the end of July to November, and the less coddling they receive, the better.

The most suitable type of cuttings are basal shoots, about 3 in. in length; they should be cut cleanly just below the joint and inserted in soil of a sandy nature. Cuttings taken in July, August, and September may be inserted in the open ground, but if taken later than this, put them into shallow frames until well rooted, and then give as much air as possible to them.

It must be remembered that the lights must be entirely removed for at least a month before the plants are bedded out.

VARIETIES.

A good reliable collection would comprise:

White—Helen W. Cochrane.

Primrose—*Princess Elizabeth.

Yellows—John Adamson, Harry Merrifield.

Dark Selfs—Milton Jumbo and Mary Hatton.

Fancies—*Chriss Littlejohn, Mrs. M. B. Wallace and Wallace Sport.

White ground banded—Mrs. H. J. Milner and Woodsmoor.

Yellow ground banded—Mrs. Andrew Stevenson, Mosley Ideal and Mrs. John H. Little.

Striped—Andrew Jamieson.

The above varieties, generally speaking, are quite easy to grow with the exception perhaps of those starred, which are a little more difficult to bring to perfection, but nevertheless well worth their place in the keen exhibitor's collection.

A good half a dozen having a more or less "bedding" habit would be Mosley Ideal, John Adamson, Rosie Bell, Helen W. Cochrane, Sue Stevenson and Rowan Hood.

VIOLET (SWEET), *Viola odorata.* Hardy perennials, found all over Europe and in Northern Asia.

They have underground stems emitting rooting stolons.

Propagation.—By detaching the rooted crowns, or by seed. Some varieties seed very freely, but many of the large ones produce seed only from their cleistogamous flowers, and then usually only one fertile seed to a flower. The seeds are uncertain in germination; some lie dormant for a year or two. Parma varieties practically never make seed. Their origin is unknown. Some think that they are referred to when Robert de Dodome, writing in 1564, says: "To this genus belongs the double violet of multiple petals, which is found in gardens only."

Height.—*V. odorata* comprises varieties whose flowering stems vary from 2–10 in.

Colour.—The colours range from deep purple to blue, pale blue, wine-red, rose-pink, and white.

Season of Flowering.—Usually October to April. A few varieties flower for ten months in the year.

Culture.—A medium loam is best, but

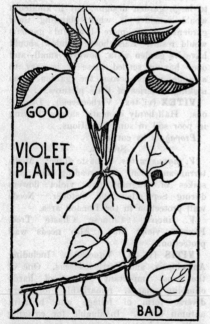

Violets may be increased by division. They like semi-shade and moisture until established.

they will also grow well in clay or chalk. The position should be open and sunny. Of fertilisers, farmyard manure is best, the amount being determined by the nature

of the soil. There should be plenty of lime in the soil. The chief pests are red spiders and surface grubs. The principal diseases are Crown rot, and American Spot (*Altunaria Violæ*).

Packing for Post.—Pick early while it is cool, leaving the blooms in water at least for an hour or two before posting. Violets are essentially simple flowers, and should be arranged as naturally as possible with

The clear colours and free-flowering habit of the Viscarias makes this annual useful for the flower border.

just their own green. Proximity to any brilliant colour tends to deaden them.

Varieties.—There are a large number of names, but many of the varieties are to all intents the same. The following is a small selection of the most distinctive:

SINGLES.

Princess of Wales—large dark blue, very long stems. Good for either glass or outdoors.

Admiral Avellan — claret-red, small flower, but very prolific in spring.

Souvenir de Jean Josse—red, with large white eye, not free, late spring.

Princess Mary—large blue violet flowers with pink-streaked rosette in centre. Very sweet, also free.

Askania — large deep purple, wing-shaped petals, delicate stems.

Semperflorens—compact plant, bearing many small, deep purple flowers. Very sweet; flowers for ten months.

Cœur d'Alsace—much like *Semperflorens* in size and habit, but rose pink. Very sweet; good in rockeries.

PARMAS.

Marie Louise—with touch of red.

Lady Hume Campbell—pale mauve, long stems, compact plant.

PROPAGATING THE VINE

A VINE "EYE" CUT FROM SHOOT WHEN PRUNING

PLANT "EYE" IN SMALL POT

Vines are increased by inserting cuttings of the "eye" in the soil. Moisture is essential.

Mrs. J. J. Astor—heliotrope-pink.

Comte de Brazza (or *Swanley White*)—fine white blooms, dark foliage, and many other varieties. These are all better grown under glass.

VIPER'S BUGLOSS. *See* ECHIUM.

VIRGILIA. *See* CLADRASTIS TINCTORIA.

VIRGINIAN COWSLIP. *See* MERTENSIA.

VIRGINIAN CREEPER. *See* VITIS QUINQUEFOLIA.

VIRGINIAN POKE. *See* PHYTOLACCA.

VIRGINIAN STOCK. *See* MALCOMIA.

VISCARIA (vis-kar-i-a. Caryophylleæ). German Catchfly. Rock Lychnis. This genus is now linked with Lychnis, but one or two of the old species still classified as Viscarias are sold by nurserymen. Charming, easily grown annuals for borders, beds or pots in cold greenhouse. For bedding, etc., sow in April where to flower in ordinary garden soil; for pots sow in autumn, winter under glass.

V. cardinalis, *V. cærulea* and *V. oculata* are pretty annuals much used for bedding. For culture *see* LYCHNIS.

VISCUM (vis'-kum. Loranthaceæ). Mistletoe. The well-known parasitic shrub, with pearly-white translucent berries. Apple trees are its usual host plant, and it is desirable to get both sexes on the same plant, if ordering from the nurseryman. It is, however, easily propagated by pressing the seed into the bark of the host plant. It will also grow on oak trees, but is rarely seen there, and more rarely still on *Pinus sylvestris*, the Scotch Pine.

V. album, the only species.

VISTAS. This word is usually applied to large garden designs, but if amateurs would consider it when planning their gardens, much more beautiful gardens would result. Each house window should have its garden vista, however small, and once having settled these it is easy to arrange vistas across the garden, thus making a series of little pictures.

VITEX (vī'-tex. Verbenaceæ). Deciduous. Half-hardy aromatic shrubs thriving in poor soil in sunny positions.

Propagate by cuttings.

SPECIES.

V. agnus-castus. Chaste Tree. Mediterranean region. Of spreading habit, and spikes of fragrant pale violet flowers during September and October. Needs wall protection in the London area.

V. incisa. Chinese Chaste Tree. Flowers violet blue. Also needs wall protection.

VITIS (vī'-tis. Vitaceæ). Including Ampelopsis, and Parthenocissus. One of the most important genera of hardy climbing plants, remarkable for very diverse form of foliage and brilliant autumn colour. Invaluable for covering walls, out-houses, pergolas, tree-stumps, posts, etc. They are all deciduous except *V. striata.* Their flowers are of no floral beauty. Fruit is in the form of a berry, and may be black, blue, red, or yellow. The cultivation is quite simple, subject to the climate being sunny and warm enough.

1. Viburnum—Guelder Rose covered with snowball flowers in spring.
2. Robinia—Locust tree. Rosy pea-like flowers in spring.
3. Pittosporum—evergreen shrub for sheltered walls. White scented flowers in summer.

1. Sweet Peas transform a wooden fence.
2. The ideal bloom for flower vases.
3. Sweet Pea—Tip Top—nearly true blue in colour.

They like a good loamy soil, and an unrestricted root run.

Propagation is by seeds and layers. The true vines can also be increased by cuttings, and better still by "eyes." This is fully described under GRAPES. The Ampelopsis group is easily increased by cuttings taken in August.

SPECIES.

V. Coignetiæ. Japan. A very vigorous grower, and with regard to magnificence of autumn colour, and size of leaf, which may be 1 ft. across, and in favoured districts even exceeding that, this may be regarded as the finest of all vines. Sargent tells us that "it climbs into the tops of the largest trees in the forest of Yezo, filling them with its enormous leaves, which in autumn assume the most brilliant hues of scarlet." Its glorious riot of colour persists for several weeks.

V. Henryana. China. A very beautiful, self-clinging species, allied to the Virginian Creeper. The leaves are deep velvety green, with white and pink mid-ribs and veins, which become more prominent as the leaves turn to a beautiful red colour in the autumn. Best on a north, north-west, or east wall, where its fine coloured variegation is better defined, than in a more sunny aspect.

V. quinquefolia (muralis). This is the true "Virginian Creeper" of N. America. Foliage beautifully coloured in autumn, in shades of orange, scarlet and crimson.

V. vinifera. The Common Grape Vine.

V. v. Brandt. A variety with beautifully coloured autumn foliage, assuming shades of orange, pink, crimson and scarlet. Perfectly hardy. The fruit is very edible.

V. v. purpurea. The "Claret-leaved Vine," so called for its beautiful translucent claret-coloured leaves, becoming a deep vinous purple before they fall.

VOLCANIC ROCK. This exists in plenty in the English Lake District, in Wales and in Scotland. It is hard, resistant, bold and splintery, making sternly grand scenery. It is very rich in all the chemicals needed by plants, and so makes excellent soil once it has had time to break up sufficiently. Foxgloves, Yellow Poppies, Canterbury Bells and Mulleins make a brave show in such scenery. On the higher levels are to be found such quaint things as Stag's-horn Moss (Lycopodium) and Cloud-berry.

W

WACHENDORFIA (va-ken-dorf-i-a. Hæmodoraceæ). Half-hardy tuberous-rooted perennial herbs.

Propagation is by seeds and offsets. Soil, sandy loam and a little peat. Plant out in well-drained beds of light soil for the summer. Give no water when the plants are resting.

Golden, orange and red wallflowers add colour to the spring garden They are best grown as biennials.

SPECIES.

W. paniculata. Yellow. April. 3 ft.
W. thyrsiflora. Yellow. May.

WAHLENBERGIA (vah-len-berg-ia. Campanulaceæ). After Dr. Wahlenberg author of "Flora Lapponica." Dwarf plants very close to Campanula and Edraianthus.

W. serpyllifolia has huge purple flowers on small prostrate foliage. The variety *W. s. major* has even larger blooms. A satisfactory plant in gritty soil.

Propagate by seed or cuttings. 3 in. June. Balkans.

WAKE ROBIN. See TRILLIUM.

WALDSTEINIA (vald-sti-ni-a. Rosaceæ). Barren Strawberry. Hardy perennial herbs like creeping Fragarias. They are easily cultivated and grow in any soil.

Propagate by division in spring or by seed sown almost on the surface of pots of light soil or out of doors.

SPECIES.

W. fragarioides. Yellow. June. 6 in.
W. trifolia. Yellow. April and May. 4–6 in.

WALKS (*See* PATHWAYS, for construction). Garden walks should be as few as possible and should only be introduced for a definite purpose, such as giving access to a seat, or point of interest. If possible, arrange for a walk to lead round the garden, for it is unsatisfactory to have to turn and come back the same way. In very small gardens where width cannot be spared for solid pathways, stepping-stones set just below the level of the grass will give dryness underfoot without introducing unnecessarily hard lines into the design. The mower can easily be run over them if they are carefully set. An alternative is to have a narrow 2 ft. pathway running the length of the garden against one of the boundary fences. This need only be a soil or ash pathway, but will provide means of reaching the vegetable plot or compost pit which is usually at the far end of the garden, and yet be out of sight from the main flower garden.

Straight walks are usually greatly to be preferred to those which wind.

Quite a large amount of space is required to introduce a really graceful curve, but where space will permit, the curved walk can be used to add variety to the design by leading to some interesting feature round the bend. As a general rule sloping garden paths should not rise more than one foot in fourteen, to give ease of walking. Steeper paths are of course permissible in places such as the rock, and wild garden.

WALLFLOWER (Cheiranthus Kewensis). Winter flowering. A hybrid product of *C. Cheiri* and *C. mutabilis* which forms a bush about 2 ft. high. The flowers, which are very fragrant, are borne continuously from November to March. The blackish-brown buds upon opening show sulphur-yellow flowers which change with age to orange-yellow or purple-violet. Seed sown in July provides flowers in autumn, or cuttings of established plants can be taken. *See also* CHEIRANTHUS.

WALL FOUNTAIN. A garden feature which originated in Italy, where it was used on a large scale. Smaller types, however, are very pleasing, and can be used as an interesting feature in gardens where space will not allow for the introduction of water to any great extent.

A small semi-circular basin of an ornamental kind should be provided, to catch the jet of water which is projected through some feature fastened to the wall, such as a lion's mouth. Water-lilies should only be grown in the basin if they can be planted out of reach of the continual spray of water. In a large garden a wall fountain may be used to add interest to a blank wall, but in the small garden it may be used as a terminal feature to the whole garden design. In this case the basin could be coloured either blue or green, the area surrounding it paved and stone or wooden flower-tubs placed in the vicinity. The blue agapanthus or heliotrope would be ideal plants for tubs in this position.

WALLICHIA (wal-lik-i-a. Palmaceæ). Dwarf stove palms with feather-shaped leaves.

Propagate by suckers or by seeds sown in brisk heat. Soil: two parts of rich loam with one of leaf-mould and a little sand. Water copiously and syringe daily in summer.

Winter temperature, 55°–65°; summer, 75°–85°.

SPECIES.

W. caryotoides. 6–9 ft.

W. densiflora. Stemless. Leaves white on under side.

WALLS. Not only is the wall garden fascinating, but it is an artistic method of treating excavated parts of the garden where soil banks must be supported. A few things must be borne in mind in constructing a wall intended to retain a soil bank. A little ballast and concrete, say 6 in. in depth and 1 ft. or so wide, according to the site and weight of the wall, is desirable at the base, to prevent move-

ment. This stone will have to be trimmed with a straight face, or stone of similar thickness selected for coursing.

No soil is placed between the stones in building, it is simply left to be washed in by rains from the soil bank behind. An inclination from the vertical of 1 in. to each foot height of wall, is also desirable to prevent thrust in wet weather. This is known as the batter. At the corners, and

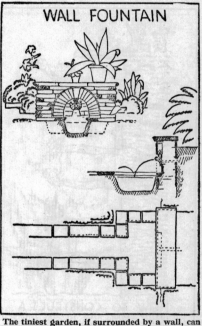

WALL FOUNTAIN

The tiniest garden, if surrounded by a wall, can be made beautiful by means of a wall fountain.

at other important points of the wall, cement may be necessary to prevent movement. "Weep" or "tear" holes should be allowed for in the construction, to assist drainage.

Dry Walls.—This is usually the name applied to a wall which is built with the joints uncemented. It may be used to take the place of a grass bank, in a change of garden levels. Take out a trench the required length and width, and make a firm foundation with rubble well rammed down. Use fairly large flat stones for the first course, building up the succeeding courses with the stones dipping slightly towards the back, so that moisture drains back to the plant roots. Allow also for a slight batter, i.e., the wall front sloping slightly backwards. Set each course on a bedding of good loamy soil, and allow for some stones to set right back into the bank for stability. Holes may be left as desired, to take special shrubs or strong growing plants. A coping stone is not always necessary, especially if a wall is built up double-faced with a central filling of soil.

drought. Division walls of this kind, properly constructed and planted, are very delightful.

The kinds of stone used depend on the district. Sandstone, since it can easily be split into small pieces, is usually preferred, but there are various forms of ironstone and limestone which can be used with good effect if they can be faced sufficiently. A very even surface is not essential. A protruding knob of stone here and there,

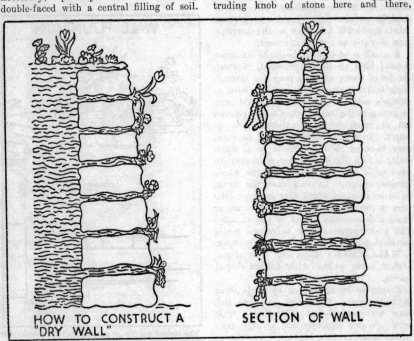

HOW TO CONSTRUCT A "DRY WALL"   **SECTION OF WALL**

Dry walls are useful to support steep banks or as a combination between two parts of the garden. Various rock plants may be inserted between the stones as the building progresses.

This method should be adopted when a soil bank is not available as a backing.

Another method of dry walling, where it is used between one garden and another, is a double-sided wall, wider at the base than at the top. The cavity between the two wall faces is filled with soil, and planting proceeds on both sides as the building is done. The soil in the cavity should be of a character to suit rock plants, and capable of holding moisture during dry weather. The top of such a wall can be planted with various dwarf shrubs which do not object to spells of

serving as a ledge on which rock plants can rest, is not out of keeping with a country garden. Landscape nurserymen usually have a competent man for this particular work, and even if stone is available on an estate, the employment of a skilled worker for wall making is well worth the expense. It is not a job which every professional gardener is able to do.

In the West country one meets with many delightful wall gardens, most of which have simply been planted by Nature. One that lingers in the memory is moss grown, with ferns here and there

in the crannies. At the top, between
rounded stones, are clumps of pink
valerian. The weatherworn appearance of
the stone, and many-coloured lichens and
mosses, make it a veritable fairyland. By
a little planning, and a little thought,
similar effects can be created in the garden
in any district where the air is clean and
pure. A wall takes a few years before it
becomes moss grown, but it is surprising
how soon Nature adds her touch to ours.
Within a year a dry stone wall, happily
planted, will take on a century-old
appearance.

Old walls may also be planted with rock
plants, without actually rebuilding. This
is done by removing stones here and there,
and substituting quantities of soil. Each
hole is then planted, and a little cement
used where necessary to hold the plants in
position. An unsightly wall becomes an
object of real beauty after treatment in
such a manner.

Brick Walls.—These are not so suitable
for building as dry walls, as those made of
rough stone slabs. If it is desired to plant
on an existing brick wall, a long chisel
should be driven with a downward slope
into the joints and mortar, so that parts of
the wall are chipped away without
rendering it unstable. Fill these holes
with good turfy loam to help retain
moisture.

Planting.—Walls are best planted as
building proceeds, so that the plant can
be well spread out. In the case of sowing
seed, roll two or three seeds into a ball
of soil and press them well down into the
hole. Care should be taken to select
plants which will thrive in their prepared
position. Thus, a wall facing south will
dry out more quickly than one facing east,
and should not be planted with moisture-
loving plants. Some wall plants will not
thrive so well in the shade as others and
should be selected with care.

Wall Nails. Climbers which are not
self-clinging need fastening into position
against house walls. If the new type of
wall nail which bends over and holds the
stem is not used, pieces of felt will be
required for use with ordinary nails. Do
not stretch the felt across the branch, and
nail it flat to the wall either side. This
method does not allow freedom of growth.

If the felt is looped round the branch and
one nail put through both ends and
fastened to the wall the plant is less
restricted.

WALNUT (*Juglans regia.*) The Walnut
is a native of Eastern Europe and Asia
Minor. It makes a large tree up to 100 ft.
in height. It has probably been grown in
this country for five generations.

Soil.—A warm position should be
selected, and the soil should be well
drained and not wet.

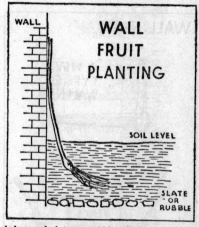

WALL FRUIT PLANTING

A layer of slate or rubble will keep the roots
of wall plants reaching out for good soil, away
from the base of the wall.

Planting.—Walnuts require careful
transplanting owing to their straggling
root system. The best time to move is in
October, just after the last leaves have
fallen. March is an alternative time.
Trees should always be moved with a ball
of soil.

Pruning.—No pruning is necessary
other than assisting the tree in forming a
well-balanced specimen.

VARIETIES.

Most specimens offered by nurserymen
are seedlings raised from parents of noted
qualities. At the present moment the
Royal Horticultural Society is endeavour-
ing to assist in standardising the numerous
seedlings under general cultivation. These
will eventually be named, and propagated
true to type by means of budding and
grafting. This nut grows so well in this
country that the classification of seedlings

may lead to the laying down of commercial plantations. Trees for such purposes would have to be placed about 75 ft. apart.

Storing.—It is not generally appreciated that walnuts are best stored in sand until required for use. Those with shrivelled kernels can easily be renewed by means of steeping in milk and water for several hours.

General.—The walnut is a very valuable tree, as quite apart from its fruit, the timber is in great demand. It is used

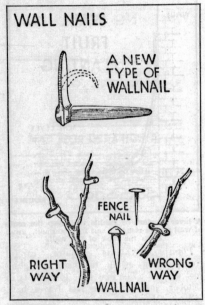

WALL NAILS

A NEW TYPE OF WALLNAIL

FENCE NAIL

RIGHT WAY

WRONG WAY

WALLNAIL

Certain climbers must be nailed to their support when grown on walls. The leaded wall nail is one of the best for convenience.

extensively for veneering, and is the best wood for the manufacture of gunstocks.

The time-honoured practice of beating a walnut tree has nothing to commend it. This was a barbarous method of "ringing" the bark, thereby preventing sap from flowing down the trunk to the roots. *See* Ringing. This method of bringing a tree into bearing is more simple than root-pruning, and is probably to be preferred.

WANDFLOWER. *See* Dierama.
WAND PLANT. *See* Galax.

WASHINGTONIA (wash-ing-ton-ia. Palmaceæ). Tall palms with almost round leaves fringed with fine thread-like filaments and white flowers followed by black berries. Increase by seed sown in heat (85°) in spring. Compost: loam, leaf-mould and sand. Water moderately in winter and plentifully in summer. Winter temperature, 55°–65°; summer, 65°–75°.

Species.

W. filifera (syn. *robusta*). Leaves green. 20–40 ft.

WASPS. The common wasp *Vespa vulgaris* is the chief culprit in damaging fruit, for it will attack not only apples, especially those with thin skins, but also pears, plums, late-hanging gooseberries and grapes in hot-houses. Should these latter be discovered to be infected, there is great difficulty in preventing the total destruction of the crop. In the spring the "queen" may be seen flying about banks in search of a suitable nesting-place. Having found a hole, she enters and begins to clean it out. If suitable, a kind of stalk is suspended from the ceiling and around this cells are made, in each of which an egg is placed. As soon as the young have hatched, the queen gives up building operations and concentrates on feeding her offspring. When full grown these larvæ pupate, eventually hatching out into the first brood which are "workers." The queen is now relieved of all duties except egg-laying, and as the workers construct and finish fresh cells she lays her eggs in them. As the layers of "comb" increase, the sides of the hole are lined with so-called "wasp paper" (vegetable matter chewed up and spread out), thus forming a large wall. In the autumn queens and males are born and after fertilisation the queens scatter and the males die. The workers devour any larvæ or pupæ left and then dismantle the nest, eventually being killed off by the cold. The queens who have scattered feed for a short period but soon seek out a suitable place in which to hibernate.

Methods of Control. Several methods of taking wasps' nests are recommended, but possibly the two most successful are to either place rags steeped in a solution of potassium cyanide down the hole by

means of a stick or else to place a proprietary vegetable dust in the hole. This
dust is carried in by the wasps and it
destroys all the inmates. In either case
it is advisable to dig out the nest and break
up the layers of cells.

WATER-CANS. A water-can must be
chosen according to the job it has to do.
If it is for rough watering or killing weeds
on paths a cheap galvanised one with
a rough copper rose will do. If, however,
it is for delicate watering, such as seedlings
or greenhouse work, then the essential is a
very fine rose which has to be hand-made
and is fitted only to the better quality
cans. From your own personal point of
view, see that it is nicely balanced, thus
taking a lot of weight off your hands.

WATER CHESTNUT. *See* TRAPA.

WATER-GARDEN. *Fountains.*—This
garden feature is best in a sunny, sheltered
corner of the garden where the atmosphere
would be oppressive on a hot day without
the freshness imparted by the falling
water. A pool with a jet fountain should
not be placed in an exposed windy part of
the garden, or the water will be blown on
to the surrounding grass or pathway,
rendering it permanently damp. In
estimating the height of a jet, allow for the
pool being slightly wider in diameter than
the height of the fountain jet.

The design of a fountain and its basin
should always err on the side of simplicity.
Pools with four corner jets are a pleasing
variation from the usual central type.
The pool may be set flush with the ground
level or raised slightly by means of a coping. The former is recommended. The
fountain shaft should be simple in design
and in proportion with its basin and the
garden.

Fountains may be used as focus points
for formal gardens, or as a lawn feature. In
any case it should be away from the shade
of trees and where sunlight can have full
play upon the sparkling water.

The basin should be finished off
smoothly to allow for thorough cleaning,
and the gradual battering of the sides
will allow for the expansion of ice in
winter, without bursting the rim (*see also*
PONDS).

WATER HAWTHORN. See APONO-
GETON *under* WATER PLANTS.

WATERING. Where a garden hose, or
sprinkler is to be used for the garden, the
tenant must notify the water company,
as the water supplied by them to his house
is not intended for use in his garden and is
not covered in his water rate. The water
rate will then be altered to include the
water used for the garden. It is more
satisfactory and incidentally less expensive to keep a large butt for rain-water
and use this for the garden.

The Watering of Outdoor Plants.—All

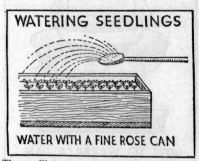

WATERING SEEDLINGS

WATER WITH A FINE ROSE CAN

Tiny seedlings are easily washed out of the soil,
and should either be treated as shown above, or
partly immersed in a pail of water.

shrubs, trees, perennials, etc., benefit by
a soaking of water during dry summer
spells. In this connection a heavy soaking
twice a week is much more satisfactory
than driblets of water each day. The
latter method causes the soil to become
caked and draws the tender roots to the
soil surface in search of water, thus leaving them more exposed to the heat. Evening
is the best time to water, but in any case
never water plants while the sun is on
them. Watering before picking or transplanting will be of benefit. Climbing
plants growing against house walls need
frequent soakings of water as the soil in
this position rarely gets the full benefit of
rain.

Seedlings.—These when in boxes should
be watered lightly through the fine rose of
a can, thus ensuring that the seedlings are
not washed out of the soil. A slight
pressure with the fingers on the soil round
the seedlings will raise them to the vertical
again, if watering has been too heavy.
Water from a tub should be used in preference to tap water, or if tap water only

is available it should be stood in a can out of doors for a few hours before use. This raises it more nearly to the temperature of the atmosphere, and so avoids shock to tender seedlings or plants.

Pot plants.—If a plant has been potted up well, the soil will reach to within half an inch of the rim of the pot, thus allowing ample room for watering. Pot plants can be watered by standing them in a pail of

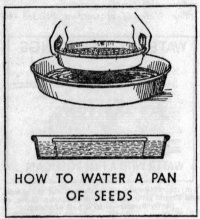

HOW TO WATER A PAN OF SEEDS

Very delicate seeds, like those of Begonias, should be watered by allowing the water to soak up through the soil.

water for half an hour or so, thus ensuring that the soil is thoroughly damp. A pot plant needs watering if a hollow sound is heard when the pot is rapped with the knuckles.

WATER LETTUCE. *See* PISTIA.

WATER LILY. *See under* WATER PLANTS.

WATER MELON. *See* CITRULLUS.

WATER PLANTAIN. *See* ALISMA.

WATER PLANTS. True aquatic plants are those which have their roots totally submerged, with submerged, floating or aerial leaves. There are, however, many plants which adapt themselves to aquatic surroundings.

Aquatics may be grouped as Oxygenating (aerating), Decorative and Marginal. So far as fish-keeping is concerned, the former group are most important in a garden pond, and their necessity and function are described under PONDS (PLANTING).

Oxygenating Plants (Aerators). All oxygenating plants are essentially aquatic in that their rootstock and leaves are totally submerged. These plants, when established, are prolific growers and can be cultivated easily in tubs and small garden ponds where there is adequate light. A good growing medium is composed of a bed of heavy meadow loam or inverted turf about 2–3 in. deep covered with 1–2 in. of coarse white sand, the latter being for cleanliness, and to prevent the loam being disturbed by fish. Most of the aquatic plants will grow from any young plant stem imbedded in the sand, and will rapidly form a good root system, reaching into the loam.

The following are the principal oxygenating plants, and some or all should find a place in every garden pond. Further details are given under plant names.

SUITABLE OXYGENATING PLANTS.

Anacharis Alsinastrum. *See* ELODEA CANADENSIS.

Callitriche (Water Starworts).
Ceratophyllum (Hornworts).
Elodea Canadensis.
Elodea Crispa.
Elodea Densa.
Fontinalis Antipyretica (Willow Moss).
Myriophyllum (Milfoils).
Potamogetons (Pondweeds).
Ranunculus (Lodeworts or Water Buttercups).

All the aforementioned plants are suitable for outdoor growing and easy to cultivate, giving the maximum amount of oxygen. There are many other native plants, but as these are indifferent in aerating qualities and not always easy to grow, they have been omitted. With the exception of the Ranunculus, which has a profusion of attractive white flowers, the flowers of oxygenators are insignificant. The foliage, on the other hand, apart from its direct utility, is always pretty and attractive.

Decorative Plants. The decorative aquatic plants include those with fully submerged roots, floating or aerial leaves, and also the true floating plants. Waterlilies are of course typical of this group, and of particular interest to the gardener. The details given as to the cultivation of Water-lilies are generally applicable to other decorative aquatics, which are chiefly:

Nymphæas (Water-lilies).

Nelumbiums (Sacred Lotus).

Nuphar (Allied to Water-lilies).

Aponogeton Dystachion (Water Hawthorn or Cape Lily).

Limnanthemum (Villarsia) Nymphæoides (Villarsia).

Sagittaria (Arrowheads).

Saggitaria (Arrowheads). *See also* AERATORS.

The Cultivation of Water-lilies. The best way to cultivate water-lilies is to plant them in the muddy bed of a natural lake or pool. Planting in such a situation is quite simple. The roots of the water-lilies can either be enclosed in a loosely-woven basket, together with suitable soil, and then dropped into their permanent position, or alternatively, the roots can be tied between two pieces of turf before they are lowered into the water. Where the water is deeper than 2 ft. it is sometimes advisable to raise the lilies from the bed of the pond by lowering into it old barrels filled with stones and soil.

Where the pond is artificially constructed and is rather shallow, from about 5–6 in. of soil should be placed all over the bottom, in which the water-lilies can grow. Heavy loam and shingle are used for this bottom covering. Alternatively, the water-lily can be planted in a good large basket of suitable soil and dropped to the bottom of the pond, but this is not generally quite as satisfactory.

The larger water-lilies must not be closer together than 6 ft. but the smaller varieties can be planted 2–3 ft. apart.

These dwarf varieties of water-lilies are all easily cultivated in 18 in. of water, and this method is particularly suitable for the very small garden where the ordinary lily pool cannot be included.

Planting dormant Roots. It is not safe to plant still dormant roots of water-lilies in their permanent position in deep water. They should first be started in growth under a covering of 2–3 in. of water, adding more water from time to time as the plants grow. If you are going to plant in a natural pool, where the water supply cannot be controlled, the roots can be put into boxes until they have made their first few floating leaves, and moved

into deeper water as they grow. Or the basket and water-lily can be kept in a barrel or other receptacle to which water can be added from time to time until the plant is in suitable condition for permanent planting.

Kind of Soil. The ideal soil for water-lilies is heavy muddy loam enriched with well-decayed manure. If cow manure is unobtainable, use coarse bonemeal. Ram

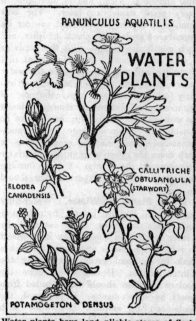

RANUNCULUS AQUATILIS

WATER PLANTS

ELODEA CANADENSIS

CALLITRICHE OBTUSANGULA (STARWORT)

POTAMOGETON DENSUS

Water plants have long pliable stems of fleshy rather than woody tissue. This means they are able to stand the strain of moving water.

the soil very firm and plant the lilies before admitting water. If you are planting in an artificial pool, do not use soil from other ponds or swamps, but use fresh soil. The best time to plant water-lilies in Britain is about the first week in May, but they can usually be planted from any time after the third week in April up to the last week in June.

Pests. Water plants are just as much subject to attacks by pests as are the plants in the open garden. Blackfly is the most common. Where goldfish are kept there is no need to use insecticide; in fact, it is undesirable. A strong syringe with clear cold water will wash the pests from the leaves to be devoured by the fish. If fish are not kept, spray with a weak solution of nicotine to get rid of the fly.

Green Slime. This is a common trouble in water gardens, and is invariably associated with a spell of hot sunny weather. The "green slime" is actually a mass of filaments of a primitive type of plant life, known as Algæ, and is inevitable in every pond sooner or later. The best remedy is to keep a watchful eye for its appearance around the plants or lilies, and then gently disentangle with the hands or a stick and remove. It is significant that the Algæ will not appear where the water is not good, and for this reason, particularly where fish are kept, the use of chemical preventatives or remedies should be avoided. If animal life has not to be considered, copper sulphate and permanganate of potash may be used, but as in both cases the effective quantity is variable according to the species of Algæ forming the "green slime," expert advice should be sought.

Water Plants in Winter. Water-lilies growing in shallow basins, fountains or rock pools are very often damaged by winter frosts. In some cases it is wisest to remove the plants and house them in a tank in the cool greenhouse during the winter months. If this is not done, the pool or fountain should be protected from frosts by some means. If preferred, the pools can be emptied and filled with leaves or moss, to hold sufficient moisture during the winter months, but if this method is adopted, some measure must be taken to keep rats or mice from gaining admission. They are very fond of the roots of water-lilies, which they eat readily during the winter when food is scarce.

FLOATING PLANTS.

Azolla caroliniana.
Hydrocharis morsus ranae (Frogbit).
Lemna (Duckweeds).
Limnobium spongia (American Frogbit).
Riccia fluitans (Crystalwort).
Stratiotes aloides (Water Soldier).
Trapa natans (Water Chestnut).

Marginal Plants.—The Marginal is a large and diversified group of plants, which includes all those which may be associated with damp surroundings. True marginals, however, are those which are natives of bog and marshland and which will grow with their rootstock fully submerged. They are useful in water-gardens as a relief to the pond outline, and can be grown in shelves or pots just below the level of the water, in heavy meadow loam. The root system of most of them is extensive and they require plenty of room to reach perfection in stature. The following is a list of the most prominent marginal plants for growing in the ordinary garden pond:

(Generic names only given in most cases.)

Acorus (Sweet Flag).
Alisma (Water Plantains).
Butomus (Flowing Rush).
Calthas (Marsh Marigolds).
Carex (Sedges).
Iris (Water Flags).
Juncus (Rushes).
Menthas (Water Mints).
Menyanthes trifoliata (Bog Bean).
Mimulus (Musks).
Myosotis palustris (Water Forget-me-not).
Phragmites communis (Arundo phragmites). Reeds.
Scirpus (Bullrushes—for large ponds).
Sparganium (Burr-reeds).
Typhads (Bullrushes).
Veronicas (Water Bird's-eye).
See PONDS and TUB WATER-GARDENS.

WATER SHIELD. See BRASENIA.
WATER SOLDIER. See STRATIOTES.
WATER SUPPLY. See PUMPS.
WATER VIOLET. See HOTTONIA.
WATER WAGTAIL or DISHWASHER is often seen following horses or cattle to catch the small insects disturbed by their hoofs.

WATSONIA (wat-son-ia. Irideæ). Bugle Lily. Handsome bulbous plants that need a greenhouse temperature.

Propagate by offsets planted out of doors in April or by seed sown in heat in pans of light rich soil in February. Soil, sandy loam and peat for pot culture, or any deep, rich, well-manured soil when planted out in the open. When planted in borders the flowers are very much stronger. Plant out in spring in drifts with a little sand under each bulb and protect in winter with a little manure, or lift the bulbs and store. When grown in pots plant five bulbs in a 6 in. pot and keep in a cold frame until the tops of the bulbs show. Then transfer to a greenhouse or window.

WATTLEHURDLES. Woven wattles made up into hurdles of varying lengths and heights have many uses in the garden. Hazel hurdles are rough in appearance but are cheap, and very useful for protecting peas and early potatoes. They may be left in natural colour, or creosoted. Willow woven hurdles are neater in appearance and make useful fences in the new garden, giving instant protection and privacy. For enclosing the children's garden, surrounding the base of tennis-court netting, and giving shelter for seaside gardens, hurdles are useful.

When erecting hurdles, a hazel, ash or chestnut stake should be driven into the ground between each two hurdles, to which the hurdles may be wired.

There is one point to be considered before using wattle hurdles as permanent garden features, that is, that this type of work does not suit every type of garden. The rural appearance of wattle is not in harmony with very formal houses or gardens, and should be reserved for informal parts of the garden, unless it is being used immediately as a screen for rambler roses and climbers. *See* ACACIA.

WAX FLOWER. *See* HOYA.

WEATHER-VANES. The charm of the weather-vane is in its antiquity, coupled with the fact that it is of some practical use in a garden. The modern designs are so pleasing that they have an instant appeal, and would grace any summer house or similar garden erection.

A vane should be made of wrought iron and not cut from thin sheet-metal, and the design of the vane should be proportioned so that it will bend, but not be brittle or break easily. The spindle should be set true to vertical and revolve on ball bearings, so that it will be influenced by the slightest wind and so be really useful and accurate. The vane should be treated with paint so that it will not rust. If the weather-vane is lifted down once a year and the ball bearings

greased, the vane will give efficient service for many years.

WEDDING FLOWER. *See* MORÆA.

WEEDS. By law a garden owner is required to destroy such weeds as thistles, docks, etc., which will seed and cause trouble on neighbouring land. A notice may be sent to the owner requesting him to destroy such weeds within a specified time. Failure to do this may result in a fine.

A good definition of a weed is, a plant growing out of its place, that is, a plant growing to the detriment of crops which the gardener has sown. Weeds are definitely harmful in several ways. They take the space which should rightly belong to the cultivated crop and rob the crop of food, light, air and moisture. Many weeds harbour insects and fungi which spread to the crop; they prevent thorough cultivation of the soil. In the case of bindweed, it twines round the cultivated crop and stops its proper growth. They cause waste of time and money in connexion with pathways, ponds, etc., by breaking through the foundations.

Weeds, however, have some uses, chief amongst these being that their presence makes it imperative to keep the hoe going. This aerates the soil and makes it friable, which is all to the benefit of the crops. Annual weeds, if dug into the soil before they seed, or even hoed up and left on the surface, act as a green manure and add humus to the soil. Weeds free from seed may be gathered up for adding to the compost pit. It should be remembered that our most beautiful garden flowers came originally from the wild plants, and some of the weeds which are common in our gardens to-day may be treasured garden flowers in years to come. Annual weeds usually have a long flowering period and so produce many seeds, thus allowing for waste. For this reason annual weeds should be destroyed before they seed.

Perennial weeds, or those which reproduce by means of underground stems, such as creeping buttercup, twitch, grass, etc., can only be eradicated by constantly keeping the weeds cut down and removing the roots by hand while digging in the autumn. Weeds are spread by the sowing of impure commercial seed—it pays to deal with reliable seedsmen—and by manuring with farmyard manure which contains weed seeds.

Bracken.—The plants can be reduced in quantity by cutting them down each year in May, and again in September. A dressing of lime also helps by encouraging a better herbage at the expense of the bracken. A quicker method is to spray the plants in July with a 5 per cent. solution of sulphuric acid. Spraying should be repeated in August.

Bindweed.—A trailing plant which creeps over garden crops, strangling and starving them. The leaves are arrow-shaped, and the large white flowers open from June to October.

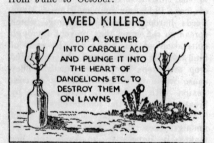

An easy method of removing deep-rooted weeds from the lawn where only a few occur.

This weed has very strong-growing root-stocks, every piece of which, if broken by digging, and the removal by hand of every piece of root seen, will gradually eradicate the pest. Ground infested with weeds of this nature can be improved by growing a crop of potatoes on the site. These will loosen the soil and simplify the work of picking out the weed roots in the autumn.

Black Nightshade.—An annual weed which is often troublesome in neglected gardens. It appears in shady places and between rows of peas, beans and potatoes. It blooms in July and seeds in August. Constant hoeing from spring right through the summer will keep the weeds in check and stop them from seeding.

Charlock (Wild Mustard or Yellow Weed). Tall branching plant which infests cultivated land. It has large, toothed leaves, yellow flowers, and quickly discolours the hand when pulled. It increases by seed which is produced in

great abundance. A weak solution of copper sulphate (1 lb. to 10 gal. of water) should be sprayed over the tops of the plants just when they are coming into flower. This solution will not harm peas, beans, etc.

Coltsfoot.—Yellow daisy-like flowers in February or March. The thick flower stems are covered with scaly bracts. After flowering the leaves develop rapidly, often growing nearly a foot broad, and thus manufacture food which is stored in the rootstock for next year's flowers. Coltsfoot thrives on poorly-drained soil, and its presence shows that the soil needs a dressing of farmyard manure. Cut the flower stalks before seeding occurs, keep the leaves cut back and the weed will gradually be weakened.

Dock.—Strong-growing weeds with long tapering roots which can only be eradicated by digging up each plant. The plants should be burnt when pulled out, especially if full grown, or they will seed whilst lying on the ground.

Garlic.—All the species are difficult to eradicate. Cutting down the leaves at the time of flowering will prevent new bulbs from forming. In June the bulbs come near the surface and should be pulled up and burnt. Spraying with a 5 per cent. solution of carbolic acid will reduce the weed.

Nettle.—Small patches may be dug up and burnt. Cut down the shoots when they are six inches high and dress the ground with salt. Spray the young shoots, which will form again, with a solution of Kainit.

Thistles.—All the thistles are trouble-some in gardens, and should never be allowed to reach the flowering stage. Constant cutting back through the summer will effect this. Digging out individual roots is the only satisfactory method of eradication.

Shepherd's Purse produces many seeds in curious, flat, heart-shaped pods. It flowers in March and has a flat rosette of leaves. It often appears amongst freshly sown seed and thrives on a light soil. It is easily pulled up by hand and this is the only satisfactory remedy. Hoeing will keep down young plants. It often harbours insect pests.

Groundsel.—An annual weed which produces several crops of small yellow flowers during a season. Its white plumed seeds are quickly scattered to all parts of the garden. Hoeing should begin early and be thoroughly continued throughout the summer.

Red dead nettle.—Bears purple flowers in crowded whorls from April to October. The stems are square and purplish in colour, being 6–18 in. high. Constant hoeing and hand pulling are the best remedies.

Persicaria.—An annual weed which is controlled by preventing seeding. Hoeing and hand pulling will effect this. The stems are reddish and have swollen nodules. The leaves are lens-shaped and almost stalkless. The flowers which appear from July to October are reddish-white and borne in spikes.

Knotweed.—Thrives on light sandy soil and seeds rapidly. It is a prostrate annual with greenish-pink flowers from May to October, which are borne clustered in the axils of the leaves. Hand pulling and hoeing will keep the weed under control.

Twitch or Couch grass.—A perennial weed which is one of the worst of weeds, yet best known, in British gardens. To deal with a new garden which is frequently infested with this coarse grass, trench the ground thoroughly, burning the couch at the bottom of the trench. Alternatively the weed roots should be collected and burnt. When digging remove every piece of white rootstock which is seen, for if left the tiniest piece will grow and form a strong plant. A crop of potatoes on the ground the first year will loosen the soil and simplify eradication of the weed. (*See* Lawns for lawn weeds).

Weeds on Pathways. These can be eradicated by applying a weed-killer in spring after a showery day. Give a good soaking, which should be effective if rain does not fall for a day or two. Do not hoe up the paths as this renders the garden unsightly and is not a permanent method of dealing with the trouble. Good weed-killer solutions are: 1 lb. of copper sulphate in 6 gal. of water, 1 lb. of salt in 1 gal. of hot water, 1 lb. of caustic soda in 8 gal. of water. Spray the solution through a fine rose of a galvanised watering can, keeping it well stirred while in use. As some of these are poisonous all the solution should be used and dogs, etc., kept away from the paths for three days. Be careful not to spray the edges of grass verges or edging plants or they will be killed, and do not let the poisons touch the hands or clothes.

Non-poisonous weed killers are obtainable

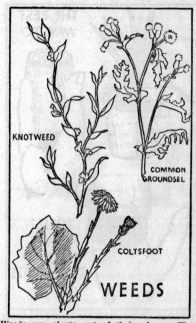

KNOTWEED

COMMON GROUNDSEL

COLTSFOOT

WEEDS

Weeds are plants out of their places. They should be removed as soon as they appear, to prevent seeding.

from reliable firms, and these are recommended rather than poisonous preparations.

WEEDS, OBNOXIOUS. Thistles, Dock, and Ragworts. The Ministry of Agriculture and Fisheries reserve the right, under the Corn Production Acts (Repeal), 1921, to serve on the occupier of any land infested with the above-named weeds, a notice requiring him to destroy or cut down these weeds. Should the occupier unreasonably fail to do so he is liable to a fine not exceeding £20 on summary conviction, and a further fine not exceeding £1 per day so long as he fail to remove the weeds after conviction.

The term "Occupier" means, in the case of any public road, the authority by whom the road is being maintained and, in the case of unoccupied land, the person entitled to the occupation.

All communication on the subject of putting the Act into operation regarding any particular piece of land should be

THE BEST WAY TO

TURN PLANTS OUT OF THEIR POTS

There is an art in turning out pot plants without damaging the roots. A sharp tap on the pot will bring the ball of soil out intact.

addressed to the Clerk of the County Agricultural Committee at the County Council offices in which the land is situated.

Where there is no Agricultural Committee for the County Borough in which the land is situated, communications should be sent to the Ministry of Agriculture and Fisheries, 10, Whitehall Place, S.W.1.

The above Act applies to the following weeds:

Spear Thistle (*Carduus Lanceolatus L.*).
Creeping or Field Thistle (*Carduus arvensis Curt*).
Curled Dock (*Rumex Crispus L.*).

Broad-leaved Dock (*Rumex Obtrusifolius L.*).
Ragwort (*Senecio Jacoboea L.*).

The Board of Agriculture for Scotland has similar powers to compel the destruction of these weeds.

WEIGELA. *See* DIERVILLA.

WEINMANNIA (vin-man-i-a. Saxifrageæ). Stove and evergreen trees and shrubs that are of little cultural value.

Propagate by cuttings rooted in sandy soil in a close propagating case over bottom heat. Pot up in light rich soil.

SPECIES.

W. hirta. White, May. Stove. 6–8 ft.
W. ovata. White, tree. Greenhouse, 6 ft.

WELL-HEAD. If there is an old well in a garden, it can easily and successfully be made the central feature of the design if an attractive well-head is placed over it. Especially in the case of an old cottage garden is this suitable, but in any garden site where there is a well, a well-head can be made a commanding feature. The whole depends upon the design of the well-head. This can be either formal or very rustic in character. One near the house, unless the latter is thatched or of a similar nature, should be formal or strictly architectural, while farther away, in an informal part of the garden, may be of rustic appearance. Old brick edging, with roughly-sawn boards for a roof cover, make a very charming informal well-head.

Where there are children, the well should always be covered over. This is best done by placing a heavy wooden lid over the mouth of the well. This is almost unnoticeable, and in no way detracts from the beauty of the well-head.

WELLINGTONIA. *See* SEQUOIA.

WESTRINGIA (west-ring-i-a. Labiatæ). *W. rosmariniformis* with pale blue flowers in summer is a pretty half-hardy shrub from Australia. It grows well in shady shrubberies or in a cool greenhouse. Plant in spring or autumn in light rich loam. The indoor plants must be watered freely during the summer.

WHEELBARROWS. *See* BARROWS.
WHORL FLOWER. *See* MORINA.
WHORTLEBERRY. *See* VACCINIUM MYRTILLUS.
WIDDRINGTONIA (wid'-ring-to'-

ni-a. Coniferæ). African Cypress. Half-hardy evergreen trees for the mildest districts only, resembling the Cupressus in appearance with glaucous foliage. They like a light sandy soil and leaf-mould. *Propagate* by seeds sown under glass.

SPECIES.

W. cupressoides. The "Sapree Wood" of South Africa. 10–15 ft.

W. juniperoides. The "Clanwilliam Cedar" of the Cedarburg Mountains, South Africa. 10–30 ft. Cones in threes and fours, smaller than preceding.

W. Schwarzii. A tall-growing small-leaved species.

WILD GARDEN. A feature which needs a fair amount of space to be carried out successfully, but the term, strictly speaking, covers all informal types of garden such as rock, water, and bog gardens.

In the large garden a portion devoted to shrubs, with interlacing paths, gives an opportunity to grow many plants which are unsuited for formal borders. It also forms a pleasing link between the formal garden near the house, and the surrounding countryside.

In the small garden a few shrubs planted near the boundaries will give a much more pleasing effect than the straight lines of fences. Paths in the wild garden may be of grass or soil, or stepping-stones set at intervals in a soil path. A seat should be included in the design. In addition to shrubs and trees there are many strong-growing plants which are suitable for planting to grow on undisturbed.

Suitable Plants. Excess plants from the herbaceous border, such as Kniphofia, Day Lily, Michaelmas Daisy, Solidago, Galaga, Helenium, Polyanthus.

For Shady Corners. Allium, Anemone appenina, Aquilegia, Arenaria, Artemisia, Balsam, Crown Imperial, Foxgloves, Gunnera, Golden Rod, Lilium gigantum, Lily of the Valley, Martagon, Periwinkles, Primrose, Snowdrop, Solomon's Seal, hardy Cyclamen, would be suitable.

If open stretches of grass are arranged for in the design, bulbs such as Daffodils, Narcissus, Snowdrops, Crocus, Chionodoxa, Scillas, Leucojums, small Irises, Bluebells, etc., may be allowed to naturalise.

For Informal planting, a standard pink

Japanese flowering Cherry, with blue Grape Hyacinths naturalised in grass round its base, is a charming combination. Bold clumps of Daffodils and Narcissi under fruit trees in grass, are a simple form of informal planting suited to quite a small garden. Rooted ivy cuttings, planted so that the ivy will ramble over tree-stumps or other rough material, also add a touch of informality to this part of the garden.

WILLOW. *See* SALIX

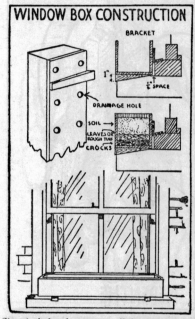

WINDOW BOX CONSTRUCTION

Strong window-boxes can easily be made at home by following these instructions.

WILLOW, CRICKET-BAT. *See* SALIX CŒRULEA.

WILLOW HERB. *See* EPILOBIUM.

WILLOW, WEEPING. *See* SALIX.

WIND FLOWER. *See* ANEMONE.

WINDOW GARDENING. Thousands of would-be gardeners live in flats and rooms without any scope for ordinary gardening, but flowers can nevertheless be grown very successfully even in rooms and tenements. Here are a few simple directions for making a garden on the window-sill.

Window-boxes should be used to achieve

the best results. To stand pots on the sill is unsatisfactory and not a little dangerous to passers-by! Ornamental tile boxes are often used and are quite satisfactory, especially the porous types, but they are expensive and likely to be broken. Wooden boxes, if well made, last many years

How to make a window-box.—First take measurements as to the size required. In length the box will be limited to the size of

NEPENTHE

The Pitcher Plant (Nepenthe) belongs to the insectivorous group. It catches flies in its curious cup-shaped leaves.

the window ledge, but in depth it should be about six inches, and in width about the same, or more if there is room. Well-seasoned three-quarter-inch timber is best, but of course, a box can be made from packing cases, egg boxes, etc., though it will not then be so strong and durable. Paint outside, and char the inside. This can be done very simply by brushing over the inside with paraffin, and then putting a match to it. Do this in the open, and as soon as the surface oil has burnt off, turn the box upside down to extinguish the flames. Bore half-inch holes about five

inches apart in the bottom to ensure drainage and aeration. Fasten small pieces of wood on the underside to lift the box from the sill. Secure with a small bracket screwed to the window-frame, leaving half an inch space.

Planting.—Place crocks, concave side downwards, over the holes and surround these by other broken pieces. Then put a layer of leaves, manure, or fibre over the bottom, one or two inches thick. Fill within an inch of the top with good loamy soil, to be had from any seedsman—or, in some places, from the local Council's depots. Plant firmly; water as soon as planted, and repeat when the soil dries. Water in the evenings. Window-boxes, especially in sunny positions, require watering almost daily during the growing and flowering seasons. Drainage holes can be made in the side instead of the bottom to save watering, but if so it is advisable to add a few pieces of charcoal to the crocks placed at the bottom of the box.

Suitable plants.—These depend on varying circumstances. Where the cultivator has also a garden, and the boxes are an added ornament to the home, it is quite effective to plant twice or three times a year, using only one or two kinds of plants at a time. For example, Auriculus and Wallflowers for early spring; Geraniums and White Alyssum for summer; and dwarf shrubs and Crocus for winter. But where there is no garden, more variety in the choice of plants will add to the interest of window-box cultivation, and by a careful study of the height and habit of the plants given in our lists, a selection of plants suitable for sunny or shady windows can be made.

Bulbs are especially good for window-boxes, and climbing plants such as Canary Creeper (annual) or Virginian Creeper (perennial) can be used very effectively to train over the wall and up the window sides. Some plants may need staking to prevent damage by winds, but generally those which are self-supporting, or which can be allowed to trail over the front, are best to grow.

Fertilisers.—In addition to the manure which is included in the under-layer when the box is filled, liquid fertilisers given during the growing season will assist plants in boxes, but care should be taken in applying these. Water first, if the soil is dry, and apply the fertiliser in small but frequent doses, rather than in large quantities at one time. Bone-meal mixed with the soil at the time of planting is excellent but slow acting. (*See also* YOUR PROBLEM ANSWERED.).

Boxes for Balcony and Roof Gardens are made on the same principles as window-boxes. Choose deep and narrow boxes to stand on balconies, raise them on pieces of wood or other supports, and remember to allow for drainage. All kinds of flowers can be grown, according to aspect, but for roofs it is advisable to choose those which can stand sun and dry weather—Carnations, Antirrhinums, Tomatoes, etc. In all of these box-gardens it is well to remember that it is the initial trouble of properly preparing the box, soil and drainage that counts, and great care over these matters will be well repaid.

Window-Box Problems Solved. Many objections are raised in regard to window-boxes. The most common are the following:

(1) *The rain splashes the soil on to the windows.* This will not occur if the soil surface is covered with coarse coconut fibre.

(2) *Flower boxes will block the windows so that the light does not enter the rooms.* Flowers should not be crowded in the centre of the box. The ideal is to create a floral framework round the window, with flowers over-hanging the sill, not blocking the window itself.

(3) *Watering often makes trouble with the people "downstairs."* A tray to catch surplus water would solve this difficulty, but careful and regular watering reduces the trouble to a minimum. Do not let the box get really dry, as this makes the soil break away from the box sides, leaving a cavity through which water runs very quickly.

(4) *Landlords refuse permission to install a box for fear of damage to property.* By raising the box an inch or two from the sill, a free circulation of air on all sides is allowed. This prevents the rotting of the sill, and the landlord's objection can thus usually be overcome.

(5) *There is a difficulty in filling the*

boxes, where no garden is available. The best materials are as follows:

1st. layer. Pieces of broken crocks, concave side down, to cover the drainage holes, which should be eight or nine in number, and ¾ in. in diameter. (They can be burnt out with a hot poker if desired.) Failing a supply of broken crocks, use large stones, or *oyster-shells*. The shells will be supplied gladly by any

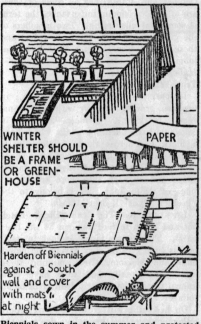

Biennials sown in the summer and protected from frosts during the winter form strong plants for the following summer.

fishmonger. This layer will keep the drainage holes clear.

2nd layer. Leaves, or decayed turf upside down, or spent hops, or straw. Wine merchants will oblige with one or two bottle covers if no other supply is available. This layer holds moisture and plant food, and also prevents fine soil from sifting through to the bottom of the box and blocking the drainage holes.

3rd layer. Good loam. *Buy* this if you cannot get good soil from your parks or open spaces. If you use poor soil, you need to add bonemeal and other fertilisers, and do not save money in the end. A bushel of soil will fill a good-sized window box.

WINTER ACONITE. *See* ERANTHIS.

WINTER CHERRY. *See* PHYSALIS.

WINTER GREEN. *See* PYROLA.

WINTER HELIOTROPE. *See* PETASITES.

WINTER MOTHS. "Winter Moth" is a term now loosely applied to all moths which appear between the months of October and March, but as some of these are of little economic importance, the term is somewhat misleading. Two members of the group are of importance, however, and these are the True Winter Moth—*Chiematobia brumata*—and the Mottled Umber—*Hybernia defolaria.*

True Winter Moth.

DESCRIPTION. *Male*—Nearly 1 in. in expanse, greyish in colour with faint transverse marking. *Female*—Greyish in colour with rudimentary wings which have a black bar across them. *Caterpillar.*—Varies in colour, but always of some shade of green. Down the back there is a darker stripe and on each side there are indications of white lines. They belong to the "geometer" or "looper" class.

LIFE-HISTORY.—The caterpillars hatch out and begin to feed as soon as the buds burst. This causes much damage in itself but as time goes on they devour the flower buds and blossom, often spinning these up. When really bad they have been known to completely strip fruit trees of all foliage.

On becoming full grown the caterpillars either crawl or let themselves down to the ground by a web, where they pupate just under the surface of the soil. The moths begin to hatch out at the end of October, the males being the first to appear. The females, which are unable to fly, crawl up the trees to lay their eggs, the place selected being on the twigs around the buds.

Mottled Umber.

DESCRIPTION. *Male.*—About 1½ in. in expanse and varying in colour from pale buff only to buff with rich brown markings across the upper wings. *Female.*—Nearly ½ in. in length, grey in colour with rows of black spots. *Caterpillar.*—Rich chestnut brown on the dorsal surface, sides and ventral surface yellow.

LIFE-HISTORY.—The life-history is very similar to the Winter Moth, the moths, however, appear a week or so later, also the caterpillars are somewhat later in appearing in the spring. The damage done is very similar, but as the fruit is formed before they pupate they often do considerable damage by biting holes in the small apples or pears.

METHODS OF CONTROL.—Owing to the inability of the female to fly, she has to gain access to the tree for egg-laying by crawling up the trunk, therefore a band of some sticky substance known as a "greaseband" placed round the tree will prevent this. If a grease-band has not been applied, a wash of vegetable origin such as nicotine or derris should be used as soon as the buds burst.

WINTER SWEET. *See* CHIMONANTHUS.

WIRE FENCING. *See* FENCES.

WIREWORMS. The larvæ of click beetles or skip-jacks (*Agriotes*, various species). Troublesome destructive pests attacking most field and garden crops. Wireworms attack all kinds of culinary vegetables, particularly lettuce and seedlings of the cabbage tribe. In the flower-garden, pansies, carnations, dahlias, lobelia and many annuals are often completely destroyed. Light soils appear to be more favourable to wireworms than heavy clay soils and severe wireworm attack is liable to occur in gardens newly made on the site of old pasture land.

Treatment. Regular cultivation to expose the wireworms to insect-eating birds. Soil insecticides, especially those containing naphthalene as the active ingredient, are obtainable from firms who market horticultural insecticides, these supply full instructions as to method of application.

WISTARIA (wis-tar'-i-a. Leguminosæ). These comprise a small genus of exceedingly beautiful climbing plants, with many pendent racemes of lavender, purple, or white flowers. They are almost too well known to need any description. Wistarias are of easy cultivation, and hardy in most parts of the country. They like a good rich loam, although flourishing in very ordinary garden soil. A sunny position is necessary. *Propagate* by layering, grafting and cuttings.

SPECIES.

W. chinensis. See SINENSIS.

W. floribunda (brachybotrys) (polystachya). The Japanese Wistaria. Flowers in 3–5 in. long racemes.

W. f. alba (multijuga alba). Flowers white in racemes up to 1½ ft. long.

W. f. macrobotrys (multijuga). Flowers light purple, in drooping racemes up to 3 ft. in length, during May and June. The "Noda Fuji" of Japan.

WOOD ASH. Ashes from the bonfire which are left after burning wood from the shrubbery contain about half as much potash as ordinary kainit (i.e., about 6 per cent.) in addition to calcium, magnesium, aluminium, iron, etc. They can therefore be used at twice the rate of kainit. Always keep them dry until used, as the potash is soluble.

WOODBINE. *See* LONICERA PERICLYMENUM.

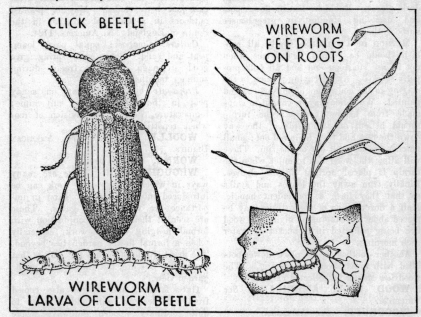

CLICK BEETLE

WIREWORM FEEDING ON ROOTS

WIREWORM LARVA OF CLICK BEETLE

Wireworm is common in any newly-dug soils. In the sketch it is enlarged slightly. It is straw-coloured and feeds on the roots of grass, carnations, etc., causing the leaves to turn yellow.

W. multijuga. See W. FLORIBUNDA MACROBOTRYS.

W. sinensis (chinensis). China. Perhaps the most popular of the Wistarias. A very rapid climber bearing a great wealth of fragrant lilac or lavender-coloured flowers, in dense racemes 8–12 in. long, towards end of May. During August a second smaller crop of flowers is produced. Possibly seen at its best climbing up the branches of an old Laburnum. By pruning hard annually this Wistaria can be grown as a shrub from 5–8 ft. high.

WITCH HAZEL. *See* HAMAMELIS.

WOLFSBANE. *See* ACONITUM.

WOOD LICE. The three common species likely to do damage are:

The COMMON WOOD LOUSE (*Oniscus asellus*).

The GRANULATED WOOD LOUSE (*Poscellio scaber*).

The PILL WOOD LOUSE (*Armadillidium vulgaris*).

The Common Wood Louse varies in colour considerably in different localities and even in the same district forms may be found ranging from pale yellow through brown to dark grey. It is somewhat convex and smooth.

The Granulated Wood Louse, on the

other hand, is flatter and usually grey in colour with a rough upper surface.

The Pill Wood Louse is quite distinct. It is very convex, shining, and is capable of rolling itself up into a tight ball when disturbed.

Wood Lice attack all kinds of plants, both young and old, and they have also been known to damage such fruits as peaches when grown on a wall. They are nocturnal in habit, living by day in damp, dark places. Rubbish, boxes, flower-pots and decaying staging in greenhouses harbour them.

METHOD OF CONTROL.—Firstly all rubbish should be burned, and boxes when not in use stood on end and all pots properly stacked. Any decaying portion in the staging in the house should be repaired and painted. Wood lice may be caught in traps made from hollow turnips; the turnip should be cut off two-thirds of the way down the root and then hollowed out; small notches are now cut out of the rim. These will allow the wood lice to enter when the turnip is placed upright on the shelves. Finally trim away the leaves and stalks so that they form a convenient handle. Half a dozen or so of these traps may be placed about the staging at night, the wood lice being collected in a bucket of water each morning.

Another method is to place flower-pots filled with moss about the staging. The wood lice should be collected each day.

WOOD LILY, AMERICAN. *See* TRILLIUM.

WOODRUFF. *See* ASPERULA.

WOODSIA (wood-si-a. Filices). Hardy and greenhouse ferns. The hardy species do well in shady positions on banks or in borders and like a compost of equal parts of peat and loam. Plant in April, water freely.

The greenhouse plants should be grown in a similar compost with the addition of charcoal and sand. Pot or plant in borders

in the greenhouse in February and water well during the spring and summer. Winter temperature, 45°–50°; summer, 50°–60°.

Propagate by spores sown on the surface of well-drained pans of peat in a temperature of 75° or divide the plants in March or April.

WOOD SORREL. *See* OXALIS.

WOODWARDIA (wood-war-di-a Filices). Greenhouse evergreen ferns. Suitable for the cold house, where frost can just be excluded. May be planted outdoors in a sheltered position in the South of England. N. America, 1724.

Culture.—Compost: equal parts loam, peat and sand. Repot early spring, give good drainage. Water freely during summer months.

Propagate by spores sown on sandy peat in the propagator at any time; temperature, 70°; or by division of root when repotting.

WOOLLY APHIS. *See* AMERICAN BLIGHT.

WORMS. *See* LAWNS.

WROUGHT IRON. There are many ways in which wrought-iron work can be introduced into the garden. First in importance are wrought-iron gates. These are seen at their best in conjunction with formal hedging or stonework, especially when a formal flower garden lies beyond. The great charm of such a gateway is that it does not obscure, but rather adds to the garden view.

Gate latches, and hinges also copied from old designs, will add interest to quite ordinary wooden gateways where the expense of wrought-iron gateways is not warranted.

WULFENIA (wul-fe-nia. Scrophulariaceæ). Hardy herbaceous perennials that like a moist, well-drained shady corner of the border or the rock garden. *Propagate* by division of the roots in spring or autumn.

X

XANTHISMA (zan-this-ma. Compositæ). Hardy annuals with yellow flowers that are raised from seed sown in the open in April and grown in any garden soil.

SPECIES.

X. texanum. 2–3 ft. Texas.

XANTHOCERAS (zan-thŏs'-ĕr-as. Sapindaceæ). Monotypic genus from China. A very beautiful deciduous small tree or shrub, growing to about 15 ft. high. Leaves pinnate, 5–8 in. long. Flowers white, each of the five petals being stained carmine at the base, in spikes 8 in. long, resembling the inflorescence of the horse chestnut. It likes a moist position or woodland conditions. When happy, there are few more beautiful flowering small trees than this.

Propagate by seeds sown out of doors in light soil in spring or autumn or by root cuttings inserted in sandy soil in a greenhouse in early spring. Plant at any time from October to February in a sunny position in a border or shrubbery. The species has white flowers blotched red at the base in May. 5–15 ft.

X. sorbifolia. The only species.

XANTHOSOMA (zan-thos-o-ma. Aroideæ). Stove perennials that are allied to Caladium and have ornamental leaves.

Propagate by division of the tubers in February or March. Grow in a compost of equal parts of loam, leaf-mould, manure, peat and silver sand. Pot up in February in small pots and transfer to larger pots in April or May. Water copiously from April to September, but keep the plants fairly dry during the winter. Winter temperature, 65°–75°; summer, 70°–80°.

SPECIES.

X. atrovirens. Leaves, greyish on under side and dark green above.

X. Lindenii. Leaves bright green with white midrib.

X. violaceum. Leaves green with purplish veins.

XANTHORRHIZA (zan-thor-rhï'-za. Ranunculaceæ). Monotypic genus. *X. apiifolia.* The "Yellow Root" of N. America. Deciduous, 2 ft. Leaves pinnate. Flowers brownish-purple in pendulous racemes. Best in a semi-shady position.

XANTHOXYLUM. *See* ZANTHOXYLUM.

XERANTHEMUM (zer-an-the-mum. Compositæ). S. Europe. *X. annuum,* 1 ft., is a very pretty everlasting flower, in many colours, and in single and double forms. May be sown in March in boxes under glass for transplanting, or out of doors in April to May. Ordinary garden soil.

XANTHOCERAS

A beautiful deciduous tree which is not quite hardy. The flowers are white, streaked red, and the foliage is dainty and feathery.

XEROPHYLLUM (zer-o-phyl-lum, Liliaceæ). Turkey's Beard. Hardy perennials that are useful for the border, the wild garden, or the marsh garden. They bear tall graceful spikes of ivory-white flowers in May. *Propagate* by seeds sown in the open in June or by division of the roots in March and plant out in permanent position in moist, gritty loam in a shady place.

Species.—X. asphodeloides, 2 ft.

XIPHION. English and Spanish Irises. *See* IRIS.

XIPHION

Xiphion or Spanish Iris belong to the bulbous section of Irises. They are sweetly scented and delightful for cutting.

XYLOBIUM (zī-lo-bi-um. Orchidaceæ). A small genus of epiphytal orchids allied to Maxillaria and deriving their name from *xylon*, wood, and *bios*, life, referring to the substance on which they grow.

Propagate by division of the pseudobulbs after flowering. Grow in a compost of equal parts of peat and chopped sphagnum with a little sand and charcoal. Pot when new growth is commencing in pots or baskets hung in the greenhouse. Water freely during growth and syringe occasionally. Winter temperature, 45°–50°; summer, 55°–65°. When in flower the plants are useful for indoor decoration.

SPECIES.

X. *leontoglossum*. Yellow and red flowers in spring.

XYLOSMA (zī-los-ma. Bixaceæ). The Tung-Ching Tree of Japan, China, and Korea. Evergreen trees up to 80 ft. in nature.

SPECIES.

X. *racemosa*. Not in cultivation.

X. *r. pubescens*. A sturdy shrub of bushy habit. Branches well armed with stout spines. Leaves dark green, very glossy. Flowers yellow, fragrant.

Y

YARROW. *See* ACHILLEA.

YEW. *See* TAXUS.

YOUR PROBLEM ANSWERED.
Over a number of years, the editor of this book has received and answered several thousands of inquiries from amateur gardeners concerning various common and uncommon problems. It is thought that the publication of a selection of these problems and answers may be more helpful to some amateurs than the more orthodox information given elsewhere.

In most cases, question and answer are given. But in some cases, the ideas are those which have been sent to the author by amateur gardeners who are anxious to broadcast to others the methods which they have tested by practical experience in their own gardens.

How can I prevent rabbits from nibbling plants?—Mix a little creosote with sand and make a trail of this all round the edge of the garden or round the individual beds. The rabbits dislike the smell and will not cross over it.

I sowed a handful of orange seeds in a pot of soil. The "trees" are now about 3 in. high and thickly crowded together in a pot. Are they any use and should I transplant them?—If you were intending to grow orange trees for fruit you would not grow them from seeds in this way, and it is presumed that the only desire is to grow something ornamental. If the seedlings are allowed to crowd each other, and kept in a warm, sunny position, they will very rapidly begin to flower, since it is Nature's method for a plant to try to reproduce itself before it dies. As a result, you will have a small potful of dwarf orange blossom which is quite pretty.

Why should potatoes be earthed up? What will happen if they are not?—The chief reason for earthing up potatoes is that the tubers which we eat are really stems, swollen to hold plant food. If the potatoes are not earthed up there is a tendency for these stems to creep *above* the ground, in which case they become green instead of white. Green potatoes are both unpalatable and slightly poisonous. Apart from this the process of earthing up aerates the soil and destroys weeds, so that the potato plants are healthier.

What can I grow on the north wall that will flower?—The most favourable plant is the Morello cherry. Others which are almost as suitable are Cotoneaster horizontalis, Clematis Jackmanii, The Seven Sisters Rose (Félicité et Perpétue), Honeysuckle, Hops (annual) and Cobœa scandens (annual).

YEW TREE

FRUIT OF YEW

In addition to forming a fine evergreen tree, varieties of Yew (Taxus) can be obtained for hedge making and for conical specimens in the formal garden.

I have tried several times to take cuttings of lemon-scented verbena, but they always fail. Is there some witchcraft about the process?—A good many people find it difficult to raise cuttings of this plant. Where this is so, it is found best to propagate by means of layers. Do this in the autumn. Take a half-ripened side-shoot and bend it down towards the soil, cut a notch, leaving a small tongue, which will be open when this part of the stem is pegged down under the soil. Make it firm with more soil (leaf-mould and sand for preference) after pegging. Leave the layer in this condition until the following spring, when it can be severed from the parent plant as soon as it shows signs of new growth.

What fertiliser should I use for heavy clay soil and what fruit will grow on this soil?—4 oz. to the sq. yd. of basic slag should be used in autumn and 2–3 oz. of kainit in January or February. Sulphate of ammonia when growth begins in early summer will also help. Apples, black currants and loganberries would be the best fruit to grow. Gooseberries would also thrive on heavy soil. Strawy manure and leaf-mould as obtainable should be dug into the soil to lighten it.

Can you give me a remedy for killing ants that will not kill the flowers?—The best method is to find the nest, and make a hole in the centre about 1 ft. deep, into which should be poured 1 oz. of carbon bisulphide. Then stop up the hole again. The fumes will rise and destroy the ants, but as the eggs, or pupæ are not destroyed, a second dose is necessary a fortnight later, when they will have hatched.

Why should my carnations fail just as they are about to flower? They have rotted off round the surface.—The trouble was caused by wireworm, and a potato or carrot should be placed as a bait to catch the grubs, which can then be destroyed. Alternatively, a naphthalene ball between each carnation plant will scare the grubs away.

How can I save my raspberries from birds?—The best method is to protect them by means of fish netting. Prepare a cage of light wooden laths, and stretch the net over this. The cage should be raised above the plant tops in order to prevent the birds from pecking through the net.

How can I cure club root in cabbages grown on heavy clay soil?—As club root disease is unknown on soil containing much lime, slaked lime at the rate of 10 oz. to the sq. yd. should be applied, and a non-cruciferous crop, such as potatoes, should be planted on the affected area for one season. Seedlings raised in well-salted soil are said to be free from the disease.

What is the best method of fighting black fly on broad beans?—At the first sign of this trouble pinch off the tops of the plants and burn them, then spray with a non-poisonous insecticide (e.g., paraffin emulsion).

Can you tell me the names of eight shrubs of a flowering nature suitable for a climbing trellis, and practically evergreen; two for a South aspect, two for West and two for North and two for East?—For South aspect: *Abelia grandiflora*, delicate pink-tinted flowers; *Escallonia Langleyensis*, rosy-carmine flowers; evergreen. For North aspect: *Cotoneaster Franchetti*, orange-scarlet fruit in autumn; evergreen; *Berberis Darwinii* evergreen, free flowering. For East aspect: *Polygonum aubertii*, white clusters of flowers; *Pyracantha coccinea Lelandeir*, evergreen; white flowers. For West aspect: *Myrtus tarantina*, evergreen; fragrant; *Lonicera aurea reticulata*, evergreen; leaves netted with golden yellow.

Can you tell me what perennial flowers I can grow suitable for cutting in early spring?—Spring-flowering perennials suitable for cutting are Doronicum, Peonies, Lily-of-the-Valley, Iris sibirica, Alyssum saxatile, Solomon's seal, double white Arabis. Apart from these there are the spring bulbs. If you want flowers on long stems to display well, the early-flowering shrubs are best, such as Forsythia, Broom, Philadelphus, Lilac, Japanese Quince.

What could I plant between laurels that would grow in shady surroundings?—This depends on how far apart the laurels are spaced. If there is room, Foxgloves would look well. Solomon's Seal, Phlox, bulbs and tobacco flowers are other suggestions, according to the amount of space available.

Can you tell me a few standard flowering trees which I could grow as a screen between the front garden and the roadway? —Any of the following can be grown as standards. Almond, Purple-leaved plum, Laburnum, Mock orange, Lilacs, Ornamental crabs, *Acer negundo variegatum*, *Cornus mas*.

I have a bed of violets which seems very overcrowded. Can I divide them or should I cut off all the runners now (summer)?— Lift the plants from the soil and divide them into single crowns, cutting off all the runners and the dead foliage. Replant the best outside crowns from 10–15 in. apart each way. Do not bury the crowns, but press the soil very firmly about the roots. Pinch off any further runners that appear.

When is the best time to apply fertilisers in liquid form?—It depends entirely on the type of plant and what growth it is making, but the golden rule is *never feed a sickly plant.* As a rule liquid fertilisers are given with the idea of taking immediate effect, and in the case of border flowers it is often wisest to wait until the flower buds are just showing before any feeding is done.

I am constructing a rockery made in the angle of a house. It faces N.E. and consequently only has the morning sun, and practically has no rain as our prevailing winds are W. and S.W. At the top there is a planting surface about 18 in. square, but it is difficult to know what to grow there. Can you make any suggestions?— The difficulty is due to dryness and scarcity of sunshine, but plants able to stand these conditions are Sedums, Sempervivum, Periwinkle, with bulbs such as Snowdrops and Cyclamen coum. The Ramondias, and various Primulas, would succeed if you could keep them well watered.

My "Mrs. Sinkins" pinks give splendid promise of bloom each year, but after a few flowers have bloomed the rest of the many buds go brown and soft and do not develop. Is this due to the soil, which is light and sandy?—Apparently, as the pinks thrive in the early summer when the soil is naturally more moist than later in the year, the trouble is due to their drying out too much during June and July. It may also be due to lack of lime in the soil. Try using more rotted leaf-mould or spent manure from old hotbeds, or failing either of these, some spent hops in the soil; in February dress some slaked lime round the plants.

Can you tell me whether the small miniature prepared hyacinths that have just finished flowering in bowls of fibre are of any further use? I usually plant out the ordinary hyacinths after growing one season indoors and find them quite valuable in the

garden.—The prepared hyacinths are not likely to be of much use as bedding plants, but it would be advisable to plant them in a wild corner of your garden where you may possibly be rewarded with a few flowers in subsequent seasons.

Can you tell me how to keep geraniums through the winter? I have no greenhouse or cold frame.—The secret of keeping geraniums through the winter is to keep

Two edible members of the family, Compositæ, Chicory, a winter salad, and Globe Artichoke, a tasty vegetable.

them moderately dry, or entirely dry, and away from frost. By bringing the plants indoors (in pots) and watering them occasionally, you can keep them safe. If inconvenient to keep the pots indoors, you may find the following method successful. Let the geraniums be taken from their pots, or from the borders, and tied in bunches with no soil round the roots. Hang them in a dark cupboard or cellar from which frost is entirely excluded. In spring replant them in pots, cut back the tops, and give a little water to start them into growth. This method is not always a success but may be found useful where the plants cannot possibly be stored in soil.

My tulips failed owing to disease this season. Some never came up and others turned a horrible purple and died without flowering. On digging them I found the old bulbs covered with black sclerotia of some fungus. As the tulip makes a completely new bulb each year, will it be safe to use the bulbs which appear healthy another season?—The tulips are affected by tulip mould (*Sclerotiana parasitica*), for which no cure has yet been discovered. It would be advisable to destroy all the tulips in the places where the disease was prevalent, and to obtain new bulbs next autumn and to plant them in a fresh position. Dress the soil well with lime before planting.

My irises seem to be diseased. Some of the rhizomes have gone soft.—This is due to "rhizome rot," which is very infectious. The plants affected should all be lifted and the soft parts cut away. Dip the roots into a weak solution of permanganate of potash before replanting. Use fresh soil, dressed with superphosphate of lime. The soil for irises should be well limed from time to time.

Can you tell me how to nail roses on to a wall which is stuccoed?—Use "vine eyes" driven in with rawl plugs, and stretch galvanised wire between them. The vine eyes are obtainable from any ironmonger.

I am changing houses, and I should very much like to take my rose trees with me. Do you think this would be possible at this season (July)?

Although it is not usual to move roses at this time, there is no reason why you should not make an attempt if you think it worth while. You should water the plants thoroughly before lifting them, and remove all flower spikes and blooms. They should be packed immediately in layers of wet moss. Move them as quickly as possible. On arrival they should be planted immediately and thoroughly watered. In dry weather this watering should be continued at frequent intervals until autumn.

Can you tell me how to rid a lawn, 25 ft. × 50 ft., of clover?

Your lawn should be dressed two or three times, at intervals of a month, with sulphate of ammonia, at the rate of ½ oz.

to the square yard. Clover dislikes nitrogen, and the use of this nitrogenous compound discourages the clover while the grass is encouraged to grow.

Will you kindly tell me when is the right time to take cuttings of flowering berberis?

Berberis roots very freely from cuttings inserted in sandy soil early in the autumn. Although this is a slow method of propagation, it is quicker than raising from seeds, which can be done in spring.

Will you kindly tell me how, and when, I ought to prune Penzance Briar Roses?

Thin out the unwanted growths and old ones, replacing these by young ones, and clip back the long shoots to the part where the wood is ripened. In some cases, pruning must be fairly severe to keep the briars within bounds, but if there is plenty of room, they may be allowed to ramble. Pruning should be done in September.

I have a greengage tree that has blossomed but it bears no fruit. I planted it six years ago and it has now grown to be a very large tree.

This is probably due to the fact that greengage trees are self-sterile, that is to say, the flowers are incapable of pollination without the aid of neighbouring plum trees blooming at the same time. The remedy, therefore, if this is the case, is to plant a tree of a Victoria or other early-flowering plum in close proximity.

What can I plant in a border 12 ft. long, facing north, with sandy soil?

If the sun reaches the border for an hour or two in morning or evening you should be able to grow most of the half-hardy and hardy annuals and also biennials, quite successfully, unless trees overhang the plot. Solomon's Seal, Lilies of the valley, Meconopsis Baileyi, and Galtonia candicans are pretty sure to succeed.

Can you tell me if ampelopsis Veitchii injures the walls of a house in the same way as ivy is said to do, or do you think wistaria would grow on a wall of north aspect instead?

Ampelopsis does not injure the walls of a house. The roots of ivy are very strong and in time work their way through the bricks, but in the case of ampelopsis this is not possible. I do not think that wistaria would be likely to succeed, owing to the lack of sun.

I have grown tomatoes in boxes in the greenhouse for several years now, and when they get to the size of a walnut they stop swelling. Can you explain this?

There is no reason why the tomatoes should stop swelling if their simple requirements have been given. They like plenty of root room, and ventilation. Otherwise the ordinary cultivation of tomatoes will be sufficient. (*See* TOMATOES.)

Can you tell me the cheapest seeds to sow on vacant ground to make green manure?

White mustard is an excellent crop for green manuring. In showery weather it should reach a height of about eighteen inches in six weeks, when it should be cut or rolled down and dug into the land before it seeds.

Failing this, you might try rye. This can be sown from August to November, but in this case it should be allowed to remain until spring before being dug into the land. In both cases the seed should be scattered broadcast thickly over clean, cultivated soil.

Should my hydrangeas be repotted every year?

The hydrangeas will do better by being repotted every spring before leaf growth begins. In the case of large established plants, however, liquid manure may be given and repotting will not be necessary.

I have a red camellia in my garden which I find it necessary to remove. Can you tell me the best time to do this, as I do not want to spoil its beauty?

Your camellia may be transplanted either in spring or mid-October, but of the two, March is the better time.

I have a passion flower in my garden, and although it makes tremendous growth it will not flower. Can you tell me what to do to encourage it to bloom?

This plant likes sandy soil, and if it is too richly fed it will not bloom. The best way to make such a plant turn its attention to flowers would be to restrict the roots by pushing a few slates into the soil.

Can you tell me why my cannas will not bloom, although they seem to make good growth?

This is because they are overfed with nitrogenous manure, or else not receiving enough sunshine. Cannas will sometimes fail to flower for one of these reasons.

When they are repotted in March a compost of equal parts of loam, leaf-mould well-decayed manure and pure sand should be prepared.

They need a warm, sunny position and a soil that has been deeply dug and dressed with lime during the winter. The cannas should then flower freely most of the summer.

My pansies grow tall and straggly. Can anything be done to keep them a normal height?

Pansies should not be allowed to grow tall, and should be pinched back if they send out long straggly stems. Old plants are frequently troublesome in this way, and it is therefore best to raise pansies fresh from seed each year.

I have grown some dahlias from seed and one or two are specially fine. Can I keep them for another year?

As soon as the winter frosts approach, the tops should be cut down and the tubers lifted like older tubers and stored in boxes of dry sand. If preferred the tubers can be hung in bunches in a frost-proof shed or cellar. They will keep quite well through the winter so long as no frost touches them, unless they are already diseased.

Next spring they will be started into growth by being placed in moist soil.

I have grown an apple tree from a pip. How long will it take before it bears fruit?

It is impossible to state accurately when an apple tree will begin to fruit. It may take twenty years, and even then the fruit may be worthless, as the chances of cross-fertilisation make it impossible to say what variety of fruit will be produced.

How can I get rid of greenfly on the plants in my sitting-room?

A very simple method of exterminating these pests is to mix a large basin full of soapsuds prepared in the ordinary way. Hold the plant and soil firmly in the pot, and immerse the affected leaves for two or three minutes. Afterwards rinse in clear water.

One corner of my garden seems to attract all the cats of the neighbourhood. What can I do to keep them away?

Sink a few small uncorked bottles, each containing about a teaspoonful of liquid ammonia, into the part of the garden frequented by the cats. Renew the ammonia occasionally. This will be an effective method of keeping them away.

Is there any cure for Madonna lilies which seem to have developed disease, and will not flower?

A method which has proved successful is to lift the bulbs at resting time, and thoroughly cleanse them of the surrounding soil. They should be well dusted with

Adam's Needle or Yucca has sharp points to its leaves, hence its name. The flowers are creamy-white in colour.

flowers of sulphur and then replanted some distance away, in different soil. The lilies may not flower the following year, but after this they will probably bloom freely.

Can you tell me how to cut an oval bed that will be accurate in outline?

Knock two sticks firmly in the ground 4 ft. apart. Take a piece of twine 9 ft. long and tie the ends together. Place the loop of the string over the sticks. Next take a sharpened stake and place the point within the loop of string and press outwards. Then move this round to the radius allowed by the taut string,

marking the surface of the ground. A perfect oval 5 ft. by 3 ft. will be formed.

Each year I buy some new plants of "Catmint" and every spring they die off. Can I do anything to prevent this? Should they be lifted for the winter?

No, do not lift the plants, but leave the dying tops to protect the crowns during the winter season. If you have already removed the dead tops, cover the plants with a layer of coconut fibre refuse, removing this in spring.

Can I keep beech leaves in autumn, other than by pressing them?

Yes, stand the stems in a mixture of glycerine and water in equal quantities for a short time, and the leaves will keep well and be natural in appearance.

The top of one of my conifers has broken off. Can I do anything to restore the symmetry of the trees?

The best plan is to cut the main stem across cleanly below the break. Then cut off the tips of the surrounding branches. This generally causes one or more strong shoots to grow straight up. Leave only one of these to develop. In a short time this lead will grow stronger than the branches and make a new top, which will bring back the shape of the tree.

YUCCA (yŭk-ka. Liliaceæ). A genus of stately evergreen shrubs from N. and C. America, with rush-like leaves, and erect spikes of drooping lily-like flowers. Of great value in imparting a sub-tropical effect to gardens. Very successful as town plants. They thrive in hot, dry, sunny positions, and are indifferent as to the soil, although preferring a sandy loam.

Propagation is by cutting off the underground stems as they appear and potting them up. And in the case of the dwarf species, by division. The tops of the plants will root if half the leaves are removed, and the stem placed in a pot of sandy soil, kept in a greenhouse until well rooted. They may then be planted out in the garden.

SPECIES.

Y. angustifolia (glauca). Leaves pale sea-green, 1–2½ ft. long, with white margins. Flowers greenish-yellow, borne in erect racemes 3–4 ft. high, during July and August. It requires a very sunny position on sloping ground. The smallest species.

Y. filamentosa. A beautiful species, with leaves up to 2½ ft. long, and 1–2 in. wide. The pendulous, yellowish-white flowers, are produced in erect panicles, 3–6 ft. high, during July and August. It flowers in a young state. A group or mass of this striking plant, against a dark evergreen background, is very effective.

Y. f. flaccida. Very similar to the preceding.

Y. gloriosa. "Adams Needle," 6–8 ft. A handsome species; leaves up to 3 ft. long. Flowers pendulous, creamy-white, occasionally tinged purple outside, borne in conical panicles, 3–4 ft. high; July to September.

Y. recurvifolia. 6–8 ft. A beautiful species with glaucous leaves, all but the upper ones recurving gracefully. Flowers creamy white, 2–3 in. across, in erect panicles up to 3 ft. high. Very free flowering.

Y. r. variegata. A variety with a yellow line down the centre of the leaves.

Y. Whipplei. Perhaps the most beautiful species capable of being grown outside in this country. It used to be considered a very tender plant, but has withstood nearly 30° of frost without injury. It requires a hot sunny position, and is best on slightly sloping ground. The narrow dark green leaves, 1–1½ ft. long, arch very attractively at the ends. Flowers greenish-white, in an inflorescence about 12 ft. high. It suckers freely from the base, and soon grows into a good bushy specimen.

YULAN. *See* MAGNOLIA CONSPICUA.

Z

ZAMIA (za-mi-a. Cycadaceæ). Jamaica Sago Tree. A rather peculiar genus of plants intermediate between Palms and Ferns. Mostly from South Africa. The leaves, for which they are grown, are feather-shaped.

Propagate by seed sown in light soil in spring at a temperature of 75°, or by offsets placed singly in small pots in a propagator in spring. Also by suckers or division of the plant in early spring as growth is commencing. Grow in equal parts of loam and peat with a little silver sand. Pot in February or March and keep in a shady part of the stove. They require a moist atmosphere at all times and plenty of water in summer as well as a daily syringing.

Winter temperature, 55°-60°; summer, 70°-75°.

SPECIES.

Z. amplifolia.

Z. furfuracea. Jamaica Sago Tree, 3 ft., West Indies.

Z. integrifolia. 3 ft.

Z. Wallisii.

ZANTHORHIZA (zan-thor-i-za. Ranunculaceæ). Yellow Root. *Z. apiifolia* is a hardy deciduous flowering shrub from eastern U.S.A. It does well in moist soil in a partially shaded shrubbery and should be planted at some time between November and February.

Propagate by division in early spring. It bears purple flowers from March to April. 1-2 ft.

ZANTHOXYLUM (zan-thox-il-um. Rutaceæ). Toothache Tree. Stove evergreen shrubs and hardy deciduous trees and shrubs that grow in deep loamy soil in shrubberies or as specimens on lawns.

Propagation.—Increase the hardy species by seeds sown in February in a cool greenhouse, or by cuttings of ripened shoots under a hand-light in sand; the stove plants by cuttings in sand in heat.

SPECIES.

Z. alatum. Yellowish flowers in spring. 10-15 ft.

Z. americanum. Prickly Ash or Toothache Tree. Greenish-yellow in spring. 10-25 ft.

Z. aromaticum. Stove evergreen.

Z. Bungei. China. 10 ft. Leaves up to 9 in. long. Fruit red.

Z. piperitum (China and Japan. A compact, neat-growing shrub, with graceful foliage.

ZAUSCHNERIA (zawsh-neer-ia. Onagraceæ). After M. Zauschner, a German.

Z. californica. The California Fuchsia has brilliant vermilion-red hanging tubes with grey woolly stems and leaves. It requires a hot sunny place, and flowers from June onwards, when it does flower; for there appear to be two strains in cultivation, one of which blooms freely whatever the weather, while the other requires the hottest of summers to induce it to bud. When purchasing it is advisable either to see the plant in bloom or to stipulate that it must be a free-flowering strain. 1 ft.

Propagate from the young shoots which push up round the main plant. It will endure most South of England winters, but is less certain in the North and Midlands.

ZEA (zea. Gramineæ). Maize (Indian Corn). *Z. gracillima variegata* (striped), 3 ft., *Z. Japonica variegata* (green and white), 4 ft., and *Z. gigantea quadricolor* (striped white, rose and yellow), 5 ft., are half-hardy annuals, usually grown for bedding. Their handsome graceful foliage is an admirable foil, or relief, to beds of such subjects as Begonias, etc. Sow in warm house in April, plant out in June: ordinary soil.

ZEBRA STRIPED GRASS. *See* EULALIA.

ZEBRINA (ze-bri-na. Commelinaceæ). *Z. pendula* is a greenhouse herbaceous trailing perennial with ornamental leaves. It should be grown in baskets or pans hanging from the roof containing equal parts of leaf-mould, loam nd sand. Pot in spring and water freely during the summer but moderately in winter. Keep in a shady position and if desired grow as a window plant but protect from frost. Winter temperature, 40°-50°; summer, 55°-65°.

Z. pendula (syn. *Tradescantia zebrina*)

has leaves striped white, purple on under side, while its variety *quadricolor* has its leaves striped red and white.

ZELKOVA (zel-ko′-va. Urticaceæ). A genus of hardy, handsome trees, near allies of the Elms and very like Beech trees in general appearance. They need a deep moist soil and a fairly sheltered position. *Propagate* by seed.

SPECIES.

Z. acuminata. The "Keaki" of Japan. Grows to a height of 100 ft. or more in Japan. In this country it is an elegant shrub from 20–30 ft. high. Its ovate-lanceolate leaves become yellowish in autumn. A valuable timber tree in Japan, producing durable, tough, and elastic wood.

Z. crenata. Caucasus. A very beautiful and distinct tree, growing to a height of 100 ft. in nature, and in this country. It is a slow-growing and long-lived tree, and very suitable for commemorative purposes. It has no distinct trunk as in the ordinary way of trees, but a cluster or group of stems, of which there may be a dozen or more.

Z. sinica (China). A new species of somewhat pendulous habit.

ZENOBIA (ze-nŏ′-bi-a. Ericaceæ). Sub-evergreen shrubs bearing very beautiful bell-shaped white flowers from June to July. They like a peaty soil, or a loamy soil with peat or leaf-mould added, in semi-shade.

Propagation is by seed, treated as recommended for Rhododendrons. Also by cuttings of half-ripened shoots taken about July, and placed in bottom heat. If seed is not required, the flowering parts of the branches should be cut off immediately after the flowers have faded.

SPECIES.

Z. speciosa (*Andromeda speciosa*). Eastern U.S.A. 3–5 ft. Leaves dark shining green. The pure white, pendent, Lily-of-the-Valley flowers are freely produced during June and July. A very beautiful shrub.

Z. s. pulverulenta. Even more lovely than the preceding. It is distinguished by its glaucous, blue leaves, and larger flowers, ½ in. or more across. An extremely beautiful and attractive shrub, which should find a place in every garden with a lime-free soil.

ZEPHYRANTHES (zef - i - ran - thes. Amaryllidaceæ). From *zephyr*, the west wind, and *anthos*, a flower.

Culture.—Compost: 2 parts fibrous loam, 1 part each leaf-mould and sand. Repot autumn, give good drainage. Water freely during growing period. After flowering allow plants to dry off gradually. Keep dry until repotting time. *Propagate* by offsets when repotting.

ZEPHYRANTHES CARINATA

Summer-flowering greenhouse bulbs with pink flowers.

SPECIES.

Z. Andersoni, yellow.

Z. atamasco, pink.

Z. candida. The Peruvian Swamp Lily, is a small bulbous plant with dark shining grass-like foliage and white glistening wide-open crocus flowers with stamens of yellow gold. Despite its name it does not need a swamp in England; quite the reverse. A dry light soil seems best for it. It is hardy in most places and is a most attractive plant, multiplying freely from offsets if left to itself. There are many beautiful coloured varieties of Zephyranthes, but these are strictly for greenhouse culture. They might survive outside but of a certainty would not flower.

ZINGIBER (zin-gi-ber. Zingiberaceæ). Ginger. Tuberous-rooted stove perennials.

Propagate by division in February and keep the pieces in a close propagating case until they have formed roots. Grow in rich loam, peat and sand.

ZINNIAS

Zinnias bring all the bright colours of Mexico to the garden. They like a rich soil and full sun.

SPECIES.

Z. officinale. Flowers purplish blue with yellow lip. July. Furnishes the ginger of commerce.

Z. Cassumunar. Bengal Root. Pale yellow flowers with red bracts. July. 5 ft.

ZINNIA (zin-e-a. Compositæ). Mexico. Half-hardy annuals. In sunny districts and rich soil Zinnias succeed remarkably well, but in less favoured places they are seldom seen at their best. The new Dahlia-flowered types are of immense size—fully double—and in delightful colours; the flowers last particularly well

in water, and if cut when half expanded will develop fully; in fact the flowers may be cut when of the required size to suit any particular decorative purpose. There is a dwarf or Lilliput section which grows 1 ft. to make compact little bushes suitable for bedding, and also a group with single flowers. To grow Zinnias well they should be grown without a check. Sow in April under glass, pot off singly as soon as large enough, and plant into rich soil in sunny position end of May.

ZIZANIA (zi-za-ni-a. Gramineæ). Water Rice. Water Oats. Canadian Rice. Indian Rice. Tall growing, hardy aquatic grasses that are most effective when grown in shallow water.

Propagate by seeds which must be kept in water from the time of ripening until they are sown. Sow in gentle heat in spring, and harden-off the seedlings in May prior to planting out. Any ordinary soil will suit them. The young plants need protection from frost.

SPECIES.

Z. aquatica. Green and brown flowers in summer. 6–10 ft.

ZONAL PELARGONIUMS. *See* PELARGONIUM.

ZYGADENUS (zig-a-de-nus. Liliaceæ). Hardy North American perennials with bulbous roots.

Propagate by seed sown in sandy loam in a cold frame in spring, or by removing the offsets in autumn. Grow in peat, leaf-mould and sand in a moist position, in a fairly shady border or bed. Lift and replant every two or three years.

SPECIES.

Z. angustifolius. With white and purple flowers in May. 18 in.

Z. elegans. White and green flowers in July. 2–3 ft.

Z. muscitoxicus. Green flowers in July. 2 ft.

ZYGOCOLAX (zi-go-ko-lax. Orchidaceæ). A genus of bigeneric orchids obtained from crossings of Zygopetalum species with Colax species. They have the same cultural requirements as Zygopetalums, while their habit is intermediate between the two.